CONTEMPORARY
WOMEN POETS

Contemporary Writers Series

Contemporary Dramatists
Contemporary Literary Critics
Contemporary Novelists
    (including short story writers)
Contemporary Poets
Contemporary Popular Writers
Contemporary Women Poets
Contemporary World Writers

CONTEMPORARY WOMEN POETS

INTRODUCTORY FORWARDS BY
ELIZABETH M. MILLS
DIANE WAKOSKI

EDITOR
PAMELA L. SHELTON

St. James Press
AN IMPRINT OF GALE

DETROIT • NEW YORK • TORONTO • LONDON

Pamela L. Shelton, *Editor*
Ashley A. Shelton, *Associate Editor*

Kristin Hart, *Project Coordinator*

Laura Standley Berger, Joann Cerrito, Dave Collins, Miranda Ferrara,
Margaret Mazurkiewicz, Michael J. Tyrkus,
St. James Press Staff

Peter M. Gareffa, *Managing Editor, St. James Press*

Mary Beth Trimper, *Production Director*
Shanna Heilveil, *Production Assistant*

Cynthia Baldwin, *Product Design Manager*
Christi Fuson, *MacIntosh Artist*

The paper used in this publication meets the minimum
requirements of American National Standard for Information Sciences—
Permanence Paper for Printed Library Materials, ANSI Z39.48-1984.

Printed in the United States of America
Published simultaneously in the United Kingdom

St. James Press is an imprint of Gale

10 9 8 7 6 5 4 3 2 1

CONTENTS

FOREWORD

"A word after a word / after a word": The Power of Contemporary Women Poets

by Elizabeth M. Mills

Imagine a space large enough for all poets to gather. Call it earth. Imagine yourself an astronaut, moving in from a great distance, homing from a defamiliarized perspective toward that swirl of white and blue and green. Listen for the sounds you would hear were all but the women silent: first a great hum, the music from a sphere; then a multiplicity of sounds, the full International Phonetic Alphabet at play; then, closer, the drifting sounds from continents and countries; the peculiar ideolects of regions, states, cities, towns. Let yourself hear, more clearly the closer you move in, the variety of sounds: the quiet, the loud; the joyful, the distressed; the blue with sorrow, the red in anger; the coo, the cry, the boast, the threat, the laugh, the snarl. All of them, as Margaret Atwood claims, "Mothertongue Mothertongue Mothertongue," yet none exactly the same, for like other combined sounds—the gospel choir, the women's chorus—these flow out upon the air from separate individuals.

Up close, then, an intimate audience, we encounter distinct voices, who, as Muriel Rukeyser writes in "Poem Out of Childhood," "breathe in experience, breathe out poetry." They are each "one woman [telling] the truth of her life," as Rukeyser describes in "Kathe Kollwitz," and because they risk that choice, "the world [has] split open." Much that has been hidden, suppressed and repressed, now flows into language, and as Atwood asserts in "Spelling," "A word after a word / after a word is power." The lesson the poet passes, the casting of spells, the making of words, goes down the generations, but it always begins with personal identity:

> your own name first,
> your first naming, your first name,
> your first word.

What we in the last years of the 20th century are privileged to hear, clearer and stronger than ever before, through contemporary women poets' faithful and daring revelations, Carolyn Kizer claims has been "the world's best-kept secret, / Merely the private lives of one-half of humanity." As these poets reveal themselves as subjects, however, they also faithfully and daringly expose what Virginia Woolf in *A Room of One's Own* calls "that spot the size of a shilling at the back of the head" which the other—father, husband, son, doctor, teacher, preacher, policeman, politician, or anyone in a position of power over another—cannot see. Three examples will suffice.

We hear first a speaker's flat report in Carolyn Forché's "The Colonel," as she describes events she witnessed in Salvador, May 1978:

> . . . The colonel returned with a sack used to
> bring groceries
> home. He spilled many human ears on the table. They were like
> dried peach halves. There is no other way to say this. He took one
> of them in his hands, shook it in our faces, dropped it into a water
> glass. It came alive there. I am tired of fooling around he said. As
> for the rights of anyone, tell your people they can go fuck them-
> selves. He swept the ears to the floor with his arm and held the last
> of his wine in the air. Something for your poetry, no? he said. . . .

The speaker's words bear the colonel's; the dissonance between them bares the colonel's inhumanity, exposes the vicious emptiness that lies beneath his posturing power.

In a completely different form and tone, British poet Wendy Cope in her pastiche "A Policeman's Lot" uses W.S. Gilbert's rhythmic patterns in the comic satire she creates when taking a statement from England's poet laureate Ted Hughes into her own fantasy. Following the thread of Hughes's words describing "his own inner police system," she imagines the testimony of the policeman who is "patrolling the unconscious of Ted Hughes." Her license with both men's verbal creations, especially her cloaking Hughes's most private inner forces in Gilbert's royally humorous rhythms, shows them to the world in new ways. The fact that Hughes is the former husband of Sylvia Plath and is frequently condemned for his decision to reorder Plath's final book of poems after her death, as well as the designated laureate of her profession, has not escaped Cope's vision. Her wrapping the riposte in humor may make it a more dangerous exposure.

In lines of six words or less, Lucille Clifton's poem "at the cemetery, / walnut grove plantation, south carolina, 1989" shows what lies beneath the beautifully restored plantation's facade. The poet maintains lowercase letters throughout the poem, although she includes five stanza divisions and end punctuation such as the comma and period. The repetition of the line "tell me your names" five times with two variations, speaks the urgent request of a descendant who sees the unmentioned "honored work" the "honored dead" have done and "will testify." The poem concludes,

> tell me your dishonored names.
> here lies
> here lies
> here lies
> here lies
> hear

The poem ends with no mark of punctuation. Carried in the repetition, buried in the homophone's deceptive sameness (here / hear), and left for the audience to say for themselves the final word on this plantation life—"lies"; endless lies.

Such revelations of their own lives, of their perceptions of the people and powers outside themselves, though a common practice of today's women poets, did not seem so safe at first. In 1928 Woolf asked her audience to imagine Shakespeare's sister Judith, the poet born this time in woman's body, and further, to consider how her body, with its sexual power and provocations, aroused Nick Green to such "pity" that he left her "with child." Woolf then asks, "Who shall measure the heat and violence of the poet's heart when caught and tangled in a woman's body?" The 20th century looking back at the Renaissance could imagine the inner distress, and perhaps dismiss it as "way back then." Fifty-eight years after Woolf, however, Adrienne Rich describes a similar internal strain. In "Blood, Bread, and Poetry," she relates that, during the 1950s and early 1960s, "to write directly and overtly as a woman, out of a woman's body and experience, to take women's existence seriously as theme and source for art . . . placed [her] nakedly face to face with both terror and anger." The "heat and violence" in the poet's heart continued, often, as with many women, turned in on the poet herself as much as out on the world. As Carolyn Kizer reveals in a 1988 interview, "Not Their History but Our Myth":

> I think the most painful think about poets when I started writing was "the poet he."
> According to Eliot and everybody else talking about the poet, only men were poets, men
> addressing men—and the painful exclusion that one felt! And it was very painful. I don't
> know if it's possible for men to understand how damaging and wounding it was to sense
> that they "drew a circle and shut me out." It's very hard because there were so many
> people like that.

In the 1997 issue of *Green Mountains Review* Maxine Kumin recalls a conversation with John Ciardi, poetry editor of the *Saturday Review of Literature,* who once told her, "I'd love to publish one of the poems in this batch, but I published a woman last month, and my editor-in-chief would never accept another one so soon." The poems were acceptable, that the author was a woman was not and silence seemed the inevitable result. Kumin wryly remarks that at the time his statement "struck [her] as entirely reasonable."

Although the earliest identified author in world literature is Enhaduanna, daughter of the Sumerian King Sargon, who ruled in Ur around 2300 BCE; in the 1950s and the early 1960s, "woman poet" was an oxymoron, a freakish combination. That is true no longer; just look at the numbers of poets who are women. Consider the many whose work is recognized in traditional arenas once solely male: Wislawa Szymborska earned the Nobel Prize in 1996; Gwendolyn Brooks, Maxine Kumin, Mary Oliver, Carolyn Kizer, Rita Dove, Mona Van Duyn, Louise Glück, Jori Graham, and Lisel Mueller have all won the Pulitzer Prize in American Poetry, an honor that Adrienne Rich declined. Although a woman has not yet become Poet Laureate of England, Mona Van Duyn and Rita Dove have served that role in the United States. Kizer, Kumin, and Van Duyn also currently make up one-fourth of the Academy of American Poets Board of Chancellors. In 1997 Eavan Boland received the first Lawrence O'Shaughnessy Award for Poetry presented to an Irish poet. Certainly, it is through the combination of courage, discipline, and genuine nurture given by Kizer, Rich, Kumin, and others who battled restrictive visions of themselves (their own and others) and lived to tell about it, that so many different women's voices speak their truths through poetry today.

As the entries in this collection of *Contemporary Women Poets* demonstrate, the women speak from many places around the world and represent many nationalities. They are Italian, Lebanese, Chilean, Nigerian, Russian, French, Indian, Irish, Romanian, Welsh, Canadian, Jamaican, Dutch, Australian, Maori, Scottish, Caribbean, Guyanese, Polish, and Danish, as well as being British and U.S. citizens—including Native Americans, Hispanics, African Americans, and Amerasians. They inhabit such different space; their language is so varied; their experiences spring from unique circumstances of time and space, class and race; and all of these differences affect their poetry.

The difference that place makes in the work of the poet is the subject of Canadian Elizabeth Brewster in her poem "Where I Come From" which begins with the statement, "People are made of places." What they incorporate are "hints," "graces," a certain way of seeing, "atmosphere[s]," and "smell[s]." The way that "spring and winter" appear in the landscape, the poet says, intimately affects their minds. Where she comes from "Spring and winter / are the mind's chief seasons: ice and the breaking of ice."

Guyanese poet Grace Nichols describes the desire of "the fat black woman" in her poem "Tropical Death." She does not want "a cold sojourn / in some North Europe far / forlorn"; what she wants connects her being with her landscape:

> The fat black woman want
> some heat/hibiscus at her feet
> blue sea dress
> to wrap her neat

Only one thing will satisfy her, "a brilliant tropical death yes." The diction and speech pattern that Nichols uses in her poem reflects a Caribbean dialect and gives the woman in the poem a distinct voice.

Quite different, but equally distinct, is the voice from the Dorset landscape that serves as the setting for U.A. Fanthorpe's poem "'Soothing and Awful'"; in fact, the poet draws some of her words, the ones that speak in other voices, from the Visitors' Book at Montacute church. From the "land of the perpetually-flowering cliché, / The rigid lip" come the visitors' unself-conscious comments, ones that emphasize through their very blandness the empty and chilling horror of the Church of England, which has become, finally, "Very Cosy."

Experiences common to many women, but not to men, such as menstruation and childbirth, also appear as unique in the poems that describe them. Sharon Olds's poem "That Year," with its straight-forward associations of personal shame, female destruction, and genocide with starting "to bleed, / crossing over that border in the night," relays an opposing interpretation to Lucille Clifton's humorously pointed menstruation poems in *Quilting*. Clifton, in fact, shows the varieties of perspectives the same poet can have. From "poem in praise of menstruation," to "poem to my uterus" and "to my last period," she even extends her expositions to include "wishes for sons," who, in her fantasy, must suffer each particular indignity of the female, from "cramps" to "gynecologists / not unlike themselves."

Childbirth becomes as unsentimentalized as "great war" labor in Elaine Feinstein's "Calliope in the Labour Ward," where the muse of epic poetry finds herself. The sailing women have as little "self" and "will" as the goddess herself, who aids in songs of destruction and death. For Anne Stevenson, on the other hand, "The Victory" of childbirth is ambiguous. The speaker claims her "victory " after surviving her birth-pain, "you cut me like a knife"; only to realize that the "blind thing," the "Snail! Scary knot of desires!" is also her "small son," who has won her love despite her suffering. "The Mother" by Gwendolyn Brooks presents another view, this one from the perspective of the mother who hears her aborted babies, and tries to explain to them that, though they "never giggled or planned or cried," they were loved, "Believe me, I loved you all." The love Louise Erdrich conveys in her unfolding poem "Birth," goes back before birth as well, but not in excuses, rather with enticements of "milk" and language to "lure them" into a life of careful nurture. Sharon Olds's well-known poem "The Language of the Brag" takes the private, personal birth beyond its importance to parents and family out to the realm of public heroism. Her speaker challenges Whitman and Ginsberg, emblems of creative American poetic achievement, by declaring her own linguistic feat,

> I have done this thing,
> I and the other women this exceptional
> act with the exceptional heroic body,
> this giving birth, this glistening verb,
> and I am putting my proud American boast
> right here with the others.

As Diane Wakoski's essay in this volume demonstrates, the same variety of perspective, voice, thought and form can be found in women poets' treatment of myth. Not only the American versions of the American dream, but the myths of Eve, in poets such as Judith Wright, or the revisions of Yeats's Leda, by Mona Van Duyn and Luci Tapahonso and June Jordan, each of whom takes the mythic figure and places her in a new context, gives her a new future, a different life, for better or worse. The playful assurance that they too have the power to interpret mystery motivates these poets to imagine and to create through word, image, sound, and form a vision of their own. One of the most daring and successful attempts at sustained incorporation of ancient story in contemporary life is Louise Glück's collection *Meadowlands*. The poems, which form a continuous narrative, combine Odysseus, Penelope, and Telemachus with three people in a disintegrating marriage, their neighbors the Lights, who play klezmer music, and the New York Giants, who play games in the Meadowlands stadium. Maria Callas's performance in *Norma* sets the tragic tone, but Otis Redding also sings his part. Imaginative union of such disparate elements, levels of emotion and of art conveys the ironic absurdity of the life the poems portray. Personal life bleeds into community; Homer's order is a myth in *Meadowlands*.

A conviction of the plenitude within contemporary women poets' writing may leave one wondering if anything other than the female body unites these writers. What they share is the ability to take the world—nature, people, society, the known and the desired—and through an imaginative process both intuitive and sensual, bring it into themselves and hold it until images and words move out to the page. That, and what Elizabeth Jennings terms a "vocation," that provides "a flash, a moment's peace." Their words are their power, their calling to name. As Wislawa Szymborska writes,

> Not a thing will ever happen unless I say so.
> Without my blessing, not a leaf will fall,
> not a blade of grass will bend beneath that little
> hoof's full stop.
>
> . . . .
>
> The joy of writing.
> The power of preserving.
> Revenge of a mortal hand.

FOREWORD

American Myth And The Way American Women Poets Use It

by Diane Wakoski

Perhaps the most prevailing myth of American culture is that of the American Dream. It is a story of entitlement, how we all have the opportunity to make ourselves happy and successful by working hard. Another of the great American myths is that we are pioneers, innovators, inventors, explorers, extenders of frontiers with unusual toughness and vigor. We also inherit a version of the Garden of Eden myth, portraying Americans as being innocent in a huge natural Paradise from which the American Adam and Eve will never fall or be ejected. And of course, as an extension of our American Dream, we embrace an American version of the myths of the Holy Family and the Divine Child as our birthright—i.e., each American is part of an ideally happy father-mother-child constellation, where the mother is pure and loving, the father is a strong provider and friendly mentor, while the child is adored for its divine innocence and the idea of childhood as a time for carefree love, play and growth is sanctified. Myths obviously represent the possible, the expectation of a culture whereas much of a culture's literature is devoted to portraying both the success of the mythic story or the ways in which it goes wrong or is denied.

Adrienne Rich, who began her career as a very conventional writer and intellectual, lived the American Dream of a successful and prosperous career in a mythic happy Holy Family. But on becoming involved in the early 1960s with the immense problems of the urban culture of poverty, working in the Upward Bound programs of New York City for the educationally disenfranchised, she moved away from her own version of living the American Dream. One of the first poems in which she opens the door to a different vision of her life is "Diving into the Wreck," which begins a whole new body of work, encompassing her Feminist and later lesbian journey to rewrite the "book of myths." In this poem, which is a descent to the undersea world of a shipwreck, she wears the androgynous clothing of a rubber skin-diving suit, calls herself both "mermaid" and "merman" and portrays herself as a mythic figure, exploring and reinventing the possibilities of the culture.

Another poet who has worked extensively with the implications of the American Dream is Gwendolyn Brooks. In her case, there is always the search for ways in which the American Dream could also apply to Afro-Americans. In her famous poem "The Life of Lincoln West," Brooks portrays a little boy—"ugliest little boy / that everyone ever saw"—who is very dark and with archetypal Negroid features, whom even his light-skinned mother finds repulsive. After a long series of rejections described vividly and dramatically in the poem, "little Linc," as he is called, hears some white men in a movie theater discussing his appearance: "There! That's the kind I've been wanting / to show you! One of the best / examples of the species. Not like / those diluted Negros you see so much of on / the streets these days, but the / real thing." The ironic ending of the poem, a pun on "missing link" shows Lincoln West having a revelation about how his ugliness is actually a sign of his authenticity, the mark of being "the real thing," ironically alluding to the American faith in the beauty of the natural world. The poem is a powerful reclaiming of the myth of the Garden of Eden for Brooks's little Lincoln West, and is typical of many of her poems in which she portrays being black as the natural state of innocence and grace, the source of the evolution of the human race. For Brooks, the American Dream is not despoiled, impossible, or a fiction, but she is required to reinvent ways to achieve it, being a black American.

In Joy Harjo's poems, the world of Native Americans is a despoiled Garden of Eden, though largely despoiled by white Americans and their ravages on Indian landscape. In many of her poems, the speaker or the people being described by the speaker live in urban environments which deprive them of their natural connection with the earth, the land. "I hear a deer outside; her glass voice of the invisible / calls my heart to stand up and weep in this fragile city" she tells us in "Deer Ghost" from *In Mad Love and War,* her William Carlos Williams Prize-winning volume. And in "A Song for the Deer and Myself to Return On," from the same collection, she laments, "and I am certainly hunting something as magic as deer / in this city far from the hammock of my mother's belly." Adding, "now the deer and I are trying to figure out a song / to get them back." She also writes often about longing for a Native version of the American Dream and the ways in which such a myth is in conflict with the despoiled American Garden of Eden, often by drugs or alcohol which seem to be products of urban life: "This is the bar of broken survivors / ...How do I say it? In this language there are no words for how the real world / collapses / ...She was the myth / ...I imagined her / like this, not a strained red dress with tape on her heels but the deer who / entered our dream in white dawn, breathed mist into pine trees, her fawn a / blessing of meat, the ancestors who never left" (from "Deer Dance").

Mary Oliver, who writes poetry depicting the natural world of plants, animals, water and earth, largely in the Cape Cod area, uses American Garden of Eden imagery constantly in her poems. The single speaker, observer, in most of her poems is someone who is innocently in harmony with her natural setting. In "August," from her Pulitzer Prize-winning book, *American Primitive,* she declares "the blackberries hang / swollen in the woods, in the brambles / nobody owns" and declares "all day my body / accepts what it is... / this thick paw of my life darting among / the black bells." But her subtext in many of the poems underlines the fact that this innocence, the natural world that "nobody owns," is not always undisturbed or unviolated. In her poem "Tecumshu" she says, "Where are the Shawnee now?" and "Anyway, / this much I'm sure of: if we ever meet him, we'll know it, / he will still be / so angry." In this book, and even more pervasively in subsequent books, Oliver's imagery, while always situated in an American Garden of Eden setting, introduces chthonic deity figures in many forms, including blue herons or owls, and a lonely wanderer on the rose-covered sand dunes. These figures—often the speaker—take communication with the earth, and usually know they must be sacrificed for some greater good.

The mythic garden of our continent which is so prevalent in the poetry of American writers appears in the poems of women often as a grounding or means to portray some version of a Goddess myth, including variations on the role of Eve or Lilith, but more often as images of magical connection with the earth than as sexual temptresses. In poems by Pulitzer Prize-winning poet Maxine Kumin we have the obvious and frequent working out of an American version of the Dionysian myth of Demeter, earth mother, who loves her daughter so much she will descend to the underworld to rescue her from death, as in "Seeing the Bones," from *The Retrieval System,* where a mother who misses her grown-up daughter, who now lives in Europe, becomes a kind of witch or enchantress, making a spell meant to recreate the daughter, in the model of the return of the seasons. ("Working backward, I reconstruct / you," she says.)

Sharon Olds transforms the traditional virgin-mother Christian myth into an interesting version of the American Garden myth. Her poems often are explicitly sexual and erotic. The seduction of the body and an Eve-like woman in the garden of sensual pleasures are characteristics of her poems, but this is combined most uniquely with her constant subject-matter of parent and child bonding. In fact, Olds's poems do portray an almost idealized Holy Family of loving parents and wonderfully responding children. But this idealization is in the spirit of Whitman's "I Sing The Body Electric," a celebration of the pleasures of the body, maintaining their Eden-like innocence. "My daughter's pajamas lie on the floor / inside out, thin and wrinkled as / peeled skins of peaches when you ease the whole skin off at one. / ... Her shed / skin shines at my feet, and in the air there is a / sharp fragrance like peach brandy— / the birth-room pungence of her released life."

However, many of the garden myths portray a deprivation or loss of the American Dream, a descent or fall from the perfect earthly garden, to some darker, less perfect place. Ruth Stone, who as a young wife and mother of three suffered through the suicide of her husband, works out the myth of descent from the American Dream, the fall from the garden of family delights, into that darker, less perfect place. Her vision of women is one of being ignored, out of hearing range: "You can talk to yourself all you want to. / After all, you were the only one who ever heard / What you were saying" ("Being a Woman," from *Second Hand Coat*). Marge Piercy's famous poem "The Moon Is Always Female" vividly portrays the practice of clitoridectomy and other abuses of women in a watery (birth-like) landscape, "I am all the time / climbing slippery rocks in a mist while / far below the waves crash in the sea caves; / I am descending the stairway under the groaning / sea while the black waters buffet me / like rockweed to and fro." And June Jordan, in "Poem about My Rights," argues eloquently about her woman's body as a source of problems, rather than joy or beauty, "I have been wrong the wrong sex the wrong age / the wrong skin the wrong nose the wrong hair the / wrong need the wrong dream the wrong geographic / the wrong sartorial I / have been the meaning of rape / I have been the problem everyone seeks to / eliminate".

Also working with American Garden mythology in much of her work, but particularly in the collection *Life in the Forest,* Denise Levertov portrays women who want to be in natural harmony with the earth but who frequently can do so only by artificially controlling or taming the garden. In "Death in Mexico" she portrays her mother retired to Mexico from England, after the death of her husband, where she plants and maintains an English country garden for twenty years until she falls into a terminal illness. Yet, within weeks of her illness, the garden begins to return to its native jungle: "Gardens vanish. She was an alien here, / as I am. Her death / was not Mexico's business. The garden though / was a hostage. Old gods / took back their own." Levertov's poems are full of the fall from the garden, and often offer an image of herself as a helpless Eve, drawn to the beauty of trees, or identifying with the natural world enough to mingle with it, as she does in this later poem from *A Door in the Hive,* "August Houseplant": "As if you knew / fall is coming, you seem to desire / everything that surrounds you, / all of air, / all of light, / all of shade."

Like their male counterparts in this second half of the century, American women poets have been writing out of the myths of the American Dream, the Holy Family and the American Garden. These same poets and many others are still making a claim on our mythic roles as pioneers, innovators, and explorers of new territory, often in the context of portraying our failures in other aspects of American myth: Gwendolyn Brooks, Joy Harjo and June Jordan, like Allen Ginsberg chronicling and describing the loss of the American Dream; Mary Oliver and Maxine Kumin, like Gary Snyder investigating our ecological place in, and perhaps fall from, this American Garden of Eden; and Adrienne Rich and Ruth Stone vividly portraying the ways in which our actual families are dysfunctional, unholy, and far from divine, while other poets like Sharon Olds and Denise Levertov are redefining what is holy for a new culture and a new millennium.

EDITOR'S NOTE

Intended primarily for use in academic and public libraries to meet the needs of students and the general public, *Contemporary Women Poets* provides biographical/bibliographical/critical entries on nearly 250 of the most prominent women poets currently writing and/or publishing in the English language today. While the preponderance of writers featured are English-language poets, significant foreign-language authors whose works are of current academic interest have also been included. In addition, efforts have been made to include several important new women poets just gaining widespread critical attention. The entries are organized into the following sections:

Biographical Data: Listing, if known, the entrant's nationality, date and place of birth, education, family members, career, awards, agent, and address information.

Bibliography: Listing the title, location, publisher, and publication date of original editions of the entrant's separately published works, including books of verse, novels, works for children, collections of short stories or plays, nonfiction, and works edited or translated by the entrant. Some entries provide information on media adaptations, manuscript collections, and theatrical activities, as well as a list of critical studies.

Personal Statement by the Entrant: When provided to us, discussing such things as early influences, approaches to writing, or general views on poetry.

Critical Essay on the Poet's Work: Written by an established critic, poet, or editor. The views discussed in the essays are wholly the authors' and should not be seen as those of St. James Press or the editor of this book. Each essay ends with the author's byline.

Indexes: A **Title Index** listing literary works by title; and a **Nationality Index** listing authors by country of origin.

Contemporary Women Poets owes its existence to the work of many people, some of whom are listed on the staff page. We would like to thank the volume's many contributors, not only for composing the essays but also for their enthusiasm for the work at hand. We would also like to thank our advisors, Marjorie Perloff, Diane Wakoski, Rita Dove, Anthony Thwaite, and Judith Rodriguez, who provided invaluable help in determining the entrants and contributors from a pool of so many talented individuals.

Finally, special thanks must be given to the poets themselves, who took the time from their busy schedules to provide biographical and bibliographical information for their respective entries. Without their poetry and the enthusiasm their work has sparked in their readers, *Contemporary Women Poets* would not exist.

The staff of St. James Press hopes that *Contemporary Women Poets* is found to be a useful reference work. Comments or suggestions regarding this volume are welcome; please address them to: The Editor, *Contemporary Women Poets,* St. James Press, 835 Penobscot Bldg., Detroit, MI 48226-4094.

—Pamela Shelton
Editor

ADVISERS

Rita Dove
Marjorie Perloff
Judith Rodriguez

Anthony Thwaite
Diane Wakoski

CONTRIBUTORS

Dannie Abse
Duane Ackerson
Kathleen Aguero
Nan Bowman Albinski
Michael Andre
Robert Archambeau
Jane Augustine
Fred Beake
Jennifer Birkett
B.J. Bolden
Anne Born
Will Broaddus
Joseph Bruchac
Hugh Buckingham
Rose Marie Burwell
George F. Butterick
Katie Campbell
Rivers Carew
James Caton
Ann Charters
Paul Christensen
John Robert Colombo
William Cookson
John Cotton
Tony Curtis
Cynthia Davidson
Michel Delville
R.H.W. Dillard
Max Dorsinville
David Dowling
Jim Elledge
Carrie Etter
Jennifer Fink
Graham Foust
Kathleen Fraser
Edward B. Germain
Reid Gilbert
Edvige Giunta
Michael Glover
Lorrie Goldensohn
Lois Gordon
Jenny Gough

Anne-Elizabeth Green
Lavinia Greenlaw
Naomi Guttman
Cathy Halley
Anne Herzog
John Hinchey
Philip Dennis Hobsbaum
Allen Hoey
Janis Butler Holm
Theodore R. Hudson
Ramona Huk
Charles L. James
Devindra Kohli
Estella Lauter
Rose Lucas
Lynne MacGregor
Wes Magee
Ashok Mathur
William Matthews
Glyn Maxwell
Thomas McCarthy
Robert McDowell
David Meltzer
Bruce Meyer
Julie Miller
Tyrus Miller
John Montague
Edwin Morgan
Colin Nicholoson
Maril Nowak
Sean O'Brien
Michael O'Neil
William Oxley
Christine Pagnoulle
Angelina Paul
Jay S. Paul
Marjorie Perloff
Kristen Holst Petersen
Rena Potok
Glyn Pursglove
David Ray
Liam Rector

Julia M. Reibetanz
Gary Roberts
James K. Robinson
John Roche
Alan Roddick
Judith Rodriguez
Michael Rodriguez
Geoff Sadler
Susan Schenk
Susan M. Schultz
Fred Sedgwick
Thomas W. Shapcott
John Shoptaw
Jon Silkin
Minnie Singh
A.J.M. Smith
Anna Smith
Laurel Smith
Stan Smith
Kendrick Smithyman
Eugenia Sojka
Aruna Srivastava
Carol Simpson Stern

Anne Stevenson
Anthony G. Stocks
Jennifer Strauss
Fraser Sutherland
William Sylvester
Henry Taylor
Carol Thomas
Saundra Towns
Michael True
Linda W. Wagner-Martin
Diane Wakoski
Priscilla L. Walton
R.J.C. Watt
Theresa Werner
Patience Wheately
Margaret Willy
Denise Wiloch
Janet Wilson
George Woodcock
Jon Woodson
David Young
Zhou Xiaojing

CONTEMPORARY
WOMEN POETS

LIST OF ENTRANTS

Diane Ackerman
Fleur Adcock
Etel Adnan
Marjorie Agosín
Ai
Ama Ata Aidoo
Bella Akhmadulina
Anne-Marie Albiach
Meena Alexander
Paula Gunn Allen
Moniza Alvi
Maya Angelou
Gloria Anzaldúa
Rae Armantrout
Margaret Atwood

Elizabeth Bartlett
Robin Becker
Patricia Beer
Anne Beresford
Caroline Bergvall
Sara Berkeley
Sujata Bhatt
Chana Bloch
Eavan Boland
Jenny Bornholdt
Roo Borson
Marilyn Bowering
Alison Brackenbury
Dionne Brand
Di Brandt
Elizabeth Brewster
Lucie Brock-Broido
Gwendolyn Brooks
Nicole Brossard
Olga Broumas
Heather Buck

Caroline Caddy
Nina Cassian
Ana Castillo
Lee Cataldi
Lorna Dee Cervantes
Diane Chang
Maxine Chernoff
Marilyn Chin
Sandra Cisneros
Kate Clanchy
Gillian Clarke
Lucille Clifton
Anne Cluysenaar
Norma Cole
Jane Cooper
Wendy Cope
Julia Copus

Lucha Corpi
Jayne Cortez
Jeni Couzyn
Lorna Crozier

Beverly Dahlen
Tina Darragh
Kamala Das
Toi Derricotte
Eunice de Souza
Imtiaz Dharker
Mary di Michele
Diane di Prima
Rosemary Dobson
Sharon Doubiago
Rita Dove
Barbara Drake
Carol Ann Duffy
Maureen Duffy
Helen Dunmore
Rachel Blau DuPlessis
Jane Duran

Lauris Edmond
Louise Erdrich

Ruth Fainlight
U. A. Fanthorpe
Vicki Feaver
Elaine Feinstein
Alison Fell
Joan Finnigan
Carolyn Forché
Janet Frame
Kathleen Fraser
Anne French
Alice Fulton
Erica Funkhouser

Tess Gallagher
Elizabeth Garrett
Sandra M. Gilbert
Nikki Giovanni
Louise Glück
Patricia Goedicke
Lorna Goodison
Jorie Graham
Judy Grahn
Lavinia Greenlaw
Susan Griffin
Barbara Guest
Kristjana Gunnars

Marilyn Hacker
Rachel Hadas

Jessica T. Hagedorn
Sophie Hannah
Joy Harjo
Claire Harris
J. S. Harry
Anne Hebert
Lyn Hejinian
Judith Herzberg
Dorothy Hewett
Selima Hill
Jane Hirshfield
Linda Hogan
Fanny Howe
Susan Howe
Keri Hulme

Kathleen Jamie
Lisa Jarnot
Elizabeth Jennings
Paulette Jiles
Amryl Johnson
Jenny Johnson
Judith Johnson
Patricia Spears Jones
June Jordan
Jenny Joseph

Sylvia Kantaris
Shirley Kaufman
Jackie Kay
Judith Kazantzis
Antigone Kefalá
Jan Kemp
Jane Kenyon
Faye Kicknosway
Siew-Yue Killingley
Carolyn Kizer
Irena Klepfisz
Joy Kogawa
Lotte Kramer
Maxine Kumin
Joanne Kyger

Anne Lauterbach
Michele Leggott
Denise Levertov
Gwyneth Lewis
Lyn Lifshin
Shirley Geok-lin Lim
Liz Lochhead

Jay Macpherson
Naomi Long Madgett
Sarah Maguire
Jennifer Maiden
Daphne Marlatt
Bernadette Mayer
Gerda Mayer
Rachel McAlpine
Medbh McGuckian
Heather McHugh

Rhyll McMaster
Florence McNeil
Sandra McPherson
Cilla McQueen
Paula Meehan
Judith Minty
Elma Mitchell
Susan Mitchell
Honor Moore
Thylias Moss
Erin Mouré
Wendy Mulford
Rona Murray
Susan Musgrave
Carol Muske

Suniti Namjoshi
Grace Nichols
Eiléan Ní Chuilleanáin
Nuala Ní Dhomhnaill
Alice Notley
Naomi Shihab Nye

Joyce Carol Oates
Sharon Olds
Mary Oliver
Alicia Ostriker
Maggie O'Sullivan
Alice Oswald
Jan Owen
Rochelle Owens

Linda Pastan
Molly Peacock
Marlene Nourbese Philip
Marge Piercy
Fiona Pitt-Kethley
Minnie Bruce Pratt
Sheenagh Pugh

Naomi Replansky
Joan Retallack
Adrienne Rich
Elizabeth Riddell
Denise Riley
Carolyn M. Rodgers
Judith Rodriguez
Wendy Rose
Amelia Rosselli
Carol Rumens
Gig Ryan

Mary Jo Salter
Sonia Sanchez
Carole Satyamurti
Leslie Scalapino
Gjertrud Schnackenberg
Mabel Segun
Olive Senior
Ntozake Shange
Jo Shapcott

Penelope Shuttle
Leslie Marmon Silko
Elizabeth Smither
Mary Ellen Solt
Cathy Song
Elizabeth Spires
Pauline Stainer
Anne Stevenson
Susan Stewart
Jennifer Strauss
Anne Szumigalski
Wisława Szymborska

Pia Tafdrup
Fiona Templeton
Sharon Thesen
Chase Twichell

Constance Urdang

Jean Valentine
Mona Van Duyn
Ellen Bryant Voigt

Diane Wakoski
Anne Waldman
Rosmarie Waldrop
Ania Walwicz
Phyllis Webb
Susan Wicks
Nancy Willard
C. D. Wright
Judith Wright

Fay Zwicky

A

ACKERMAN, Diane

Nationality: American. **Born:** Waukegan, Illinois, 7 October 1948. **Education:** Boston University, 1966-67; Pennsylvania State University, University Park, 1967-70, B.A. in English 1970; Cornell University, Ithaca, New York (Academy of American Poets prize, Corson French prize, Heermans-McCalmon playwriting prize, Corson Bishop prize, Rockefeller fellow), M.F.A. in creative writing 1973, M.A. in English 1976, Ph.D. in English 1978. **Career:** Social worker, New York, 1967; government researcher, University Park, Pennsylvania, 1968; editorial assistant, *Library Journal,* New York, 1970; lecturer, Cornell University, 1971-78; assistant professor, University of Pittsburgh, 1980-83; staff writer, *The New Yorker,* New York, 1988—. Writer-in-residence, College of William and Mary, 1982-83, Ohio University, fall 1983, spring 1983, and director of Writers Program, Washington University, St. Louis, 1984-86; visiting writer, New York University, fall 1986, Columbia University, fall 1986, Cornell University, spring 1987; master artist-in-residence, Atlantic Center for the Arts, 1988. Associate editor, *Epoch,* Ithaca, New York, 1971-77; contributing editor, *Parade,* New York, and *Travel-Holiday,* New York. **Awards:** Abbie Copps Poetry prize, 1974; National Endowment for the Arts fellowship, 1976, 1986; Creative Artists Public Service fellowship, 1980; Black Warrior Review Poetry prize, 1981; Pushcart Prize VIII, 1984; Peter I. B. Lavan award, 1985; Lowell Thomas award, Society of American Travel Writers, 1990; Wordsmith award, 1992; New and Noteworthy Book of the Year, *New York Times Book Review,* 1992, for *The Moon by Whale Light,* 1993, for *Jaguar of Sweet Laughter: New and Selected Poems;* "Literary Lion," New York Public Library, 1994. Also the recipient of numerous other awards and honors, including Board of Directors, Associated Writing Programs, 1982-85 and Poetry Panel, National Endowment for the Arts, 1991. **Agent:** Morton Janklow, Janklow & Nesbit, 598 Madison Avenue, New York, New York 10022, U.S.A.

PUBLICATIONS

Poetry

The Planets: A Cosmic Pastoral. New York, Morrow, 1976.
Wife of Light. New York, Morrow, 1978.
Lady Faustus. New York, Morrow, 1983.
Jaguar of Sweet Laughter: New and Selected Poems. New York, Random House, and London, Chapman's, 1991.
I Praise My Destroyer. New York, Random House, 1998.

Plays

All Seasons Are Weather, in *Texas Arts Journal* (Dallas), Fall 1979.
Reverse Thunder: A Dramatic Poem (produced New Brunswick, New Jersey, 1982). Sections published in *American Poetry Review* (Philadelphia), July-August 1980, and *Denver Quarterly,* Winter 1984; published complete, New York, Lumen, 1988.

Television Documentaries: *Ideas—Flying,* 1990; *Mystery of the Senses,* 1995.

Other

Twilight of the Tenderfoot: A Western Memoir. New York, Morrow, 1980.
On Extended Wings. New York, Atheneum, 1985.
A Natural History of the Senses. New York, Random House, 1990.
The Moon by Whale Light, and Other Adventures among Bats, Crocodilians, Penguins and Whales. New York, Random House, 1991.
A Natural History of Love. New York, Random House, 1994.
Monk Seal Hideaway (for children). New York, Crown, 1995.
Bats: Shadows in the Night (for children). New York, Crown, 1997.
A Slender Thread. New York, Random House, 1997.

Recordings: *The Naturalists,* Gang of Seven, 1992; *A Natural History of Love,* 1994.

*

Manuscript Collection: Boston University.

Critical Sources: "Horsehair Sofas of the Antarctic: Diane Ackerman's Natural Histories" by Mark Doty, in *Parnassus,* Fall 1995.

Diane Ackerman comments:

People sometimes ask me about all of the science in my work, thinking it odd that I should wish to combine science and art, and assuming that I must have some inner pledge or outer maxim I follow. But the hardest job for me is trying to keep science out of my writing. We live in a world where amino acids, viruses, airfoils, and such are common ingredients in our daily sense of Nature. Not to write about Nature in its widest sense, because quasars or corpuscles are not "the proper realm of poetry," as a critic once said to me, is not only irresponsible and philistine, it bankrupts the experience of living, it ignores much of life's fascination and variety. I'm a great fan of the Universe, which I take literally: as one. All of it interests me, and it interests me in detail.

Writing is my form of celebration and prayer, but it is also the way in which I inquire about the world. I seem to be driven by an intense, nomadic curiosity; my feeling of ignorance is often overwhelming. As a result, prompted by unconscious obbligatos, I frequently find myself in a state of complete rapture about a discipline or field, and rapidly coming down with a poem or a book. For as little as six months, perhaps, or as long as three years, I will be obsessed with flying, whales, love, the senses, or the oceans, and eagerly learn everything I can about the field. Any raw facts I might acquire about the workings of Nature fuel my creative work and are secondary to my rage to learn about the human condition, which I don't think we can see whole from any one vantage point. If I hadn't spent a year as a soccer journalist many years ago, to get atmosphere for a novel set in the soccer world, I would never have learned as much as I did about the history of play, and certainly never written the four soccer poems at the end of *Lady Faustus,* which have little to do with soccer, but are really about the rhythm of the mind and what it means to know something.

I try to give myself passionately, totally, to whatever I'm observing, with as much affectionate curiosity as I can muster, as a means to understanding a little better what being human is, and what it was like to have once been alive on the planet, how it felt in one's senses, passions and contemplations. I appear to have a lot of science in my work, I suppose, but I think of myself as a nature writer, if what we mean by nature is the full sum of Creation.

Poets tend to be bothered by disturbing questions. Only two questions bother me, but they bother me a lot: 1) How do you start with hydrogen and end up with us? Or, if you like, How did we get from the Big Bang to the whole shebang? and 2) What was it like to have lived? Everything I've written thus far, in poetry or prose, has been an attempt to elaborate or find answers to those two questions. Deep-down, I know they should take from birth to death to answer and include all consciousness. And I suppose some would find that rather overwhelming and fraught with built-in failure. I don't think of it in that way—in terms of goal, success, or self-esteem—but rather as a simple mystery trip. The world revealing itself, human nature revealing itself, is seductive and startling, and that's fascinating enough to send words down my spine.

*   *   *

The work of Diane Ackerman in poetry and prose is a history of her extraordinary enthusiasms. Her memoirs recount her experiences on a cattle ranch (*Twilight of the Tenderfoot*) and in learning to fly (*On Extended Wings*), and, like her later books (*A Natural History of the Senses, The Moon by Whale Light,* and *A Natural History of Love*), they explore in depth and with intensity the full extent of the subject—its history, its detailed ins and outs, its poetry, and ultimately its meaning. She is a prodigious explorer of the world, if by "world" we mean, as she puts it, "the full sum of Creation." Her poetry is distinctive in finding its source in that same enthusiastic energy; she explores the world, inner and outer, with a scientist's poetic eye, recognizing, as the chaos scientist Mitchell Feigenbaum put it, that "art is a theory about the way the world looks to human beings."

Ackerman's two book-length poems, *The Planets: A Cosmic Pastoral* and *Reverse Thunder: A Dramatic Poem,* are perhaps the two most impressive results of her effort to draw scientific and poetic curiosity (and understanding) together into a unified field of electric language. The first is a long meditation on the planets in our solar system, and the second is a verse play about Sor Juana Inés de la Cruz, a late-seventeenth-century Mexican woman who actually lived Ackerman's ideal life as poet, scientist, and genuinely independent and creative thinker.

The Planets: A Cosmic Pastoral is a set of poetic explorations and meditations on the planets, Cape Canaveral, the asteroids, and even the blurry disappointment of Comet Kohoutek. In form and content it ranges widely and well—its science is up-to-date and accurate and its poetry a display of dazzling wit. It roused astronomer Carl Sagan to say that it demonstrates "how closely compatible planetary exploration and poetry, science and art really are." It bridges the "two cultures" with a vigor and success not witnessed in English and American poetry since the 18th century, when Newton's *Opticks* and its implications excited poets and roused their imaginative, poetic responses.

At the end of *The Planets,* Ackerman returns to Earth "like a woman who, / waking too early each day, / finds it dark yet / and all the world asleep." This situation also sums up her dilemma as a poet, having pressed poetry to a service far beyond that of most of the poems of her contemporaries and now being faced by a choice of whether to join that sleeping world or to return to planetary exploration. In the poem she concludes, "But how could my clamorous heart / lie abed, knowing all of Creation / has been up for hours?"

Sor Juana Inés de la Cruz, the heroine of *Reverse Thunder,* faces that same dilemma and answers it in much the same way. She is tragically out of step with her place and time, but she triumphs in the work that she passes down to our time when she finally can be (or almost can be) fully understood in all her complexity. This fascinating woman, as Ackerman pictures her, draws together in her life as a nun in 17th-century Mexico almost all of the conflicting and contradictory strands of life in that time; she is a nun who loves a man passionately, a believing Christian who explores the scientific view of the world, a spiritual and spirited poet who draws her inspiration from both the life of the body and of the mind, a materialist who comes to understand that matter is so very much more than it appears to be:

If ever there was a good person in this world,
one just or pure or altruistic or visionary,
no matter who, or how many, or if only one,
then purity, or justice or mercy or vision,
is something of which matter is capable.
That paradox of the apparent indifference
of matter to such things as Good and Evil,
and, yet, at the same time, the reality
of its complete involvement:
that's why beauty stuns and touches us.

In her collections of short poems, *Wife of Light* and *Lady Faustus,* and in the 52 new poems in *Jaguar of Sweet Laughter: New and Selected Poems* Ackerman apparently strives to write as Sister Juana would if she were writing today, recognizing no limits to the range of her interests or her voice. Whether she is being earthy, playing a bluesy "Menstrual Rag" or singing the true joy of sex with a metaphysical force, or diving under the sea, flying an airplane, brooding over rivers and bridges, confessing the depth of her love, or speculating about the very nature of thought, her wit runs a full range, exhibiting mind, memory, sense, the senses, sensuality, sanity, ingenuity, acumen, real thought, witty banter, and productive persiflage.

In his essay in *Parnassus,* Mark Doty compared Ackerman's work to that of another, more "metaphysical" nature poet, Mary Oliver, whose poetic quest remains a search for *meaning* in what she finds in the natural world. In contrast, Doty maintained, Ackerman "does not look for an overarching metaphysic, a coherence, because she fundamentally doesn't believe there is such a thing.... Where Darwin amassed a lifetimes's worth of observed detail in order to generalize and arrive at evolutionary patterns, Ackerman prefers the sensuous, puzzling, intractable particular." Conscious of science, she is also conscious of the chaos of nature. Her enthusiasm, thus unbounded, carries her forward but never beyond the bounds of genuine feeling and serious understanding. As she put it in the title poem of her collection *Lady Faustus:*

I itch all over. I rage to know
what beings like me, stymied by death
and leached by wonder, hug those campfires
night allows,
aching to know the fate of us all,
wallflowers in a waltz of stars.

—R.H.W. Dillard

ADCOCK, Fleur

Nationality: British. **Born:** Papakura, New Zealand, 10 February 1934; immigrated to the United Kingdom in 1963. **Education:** Studied in England, 1939-47; Wellington Girls' College and Victoria University of Wellington, New Zealand, M.A. (honors) in classics, 1956. **Family:** Married the poet Alistair Campbell in 1952 (divorced 1958); two sons. **Career:** Temporary assistant lecturer in classics, University of Otago, Dunedin, 1958. Held library posts at the University of Otago, 1959-61, and at Turnbull Library, Wellington, 1962; assistant librarian, Foreign and Commonwealth Office Library, London, 1963-79. Arts Council Creative Writing Fellow, Charlotte Mason College of Education, Ambleside, Cumbria, 1977-78; Northern Arts Fellow, universities of Newcastle upon Tyne and Durham, 1979-81; Eastern Arts Fellow, University of East Anglia, Norwich, 1984. **Awards:** Festival of Wellington prize, 1961; New Zealand State Literary Fund award, 1964; Buckland award, 1967, 1979; Jessie MacKay award, 1968, 1972; Cholmondeley award, 1976; New Zealand Book award, 1984; Arts Council award, 1988. **Address:** 14 Lincoln Road, London N2 9DL, England.

PUBLICATIONS

Poetry

The Eye of the Hurricane. Wellington, Reed, 1964.
Tigers. London, Oxford University Press, 1967.
High Tide in the Garden. London, Oxford University Press, 1971.
The Scenic Route. London, Oxford University Press, 1974.
The Inner Harbour. Oxford, Oxford University Press, 1979.
Below Loughrigg. Newcastle upon Tyne, Bloodaxe, 1979.
Selected Poems. Oxford, Oxford University Press, 1983.
Hotspur: A Ballad for Music. Newcastle upon Tyne, Bloodaxe, 1986.
4-Pack 1: Four from Northern Women, with Maura Dooley, S. J. Litherland, and Jill Maugham. Newcastle upon Tyne, Bloodaxe, 1986.
The Incident Book. Oxford, Oxford University Press, 1986.
Meeting the Comet. Newcastle upon Tyne, Bloodaxe, 1989.
Time-Zones. Oxford, Oxford University Press, 1991.
Looking Back. Oxford, Oxford University Press, 1997.

Other

Editor, with Anthony Thwaite, *New Poetry 4.* London, Hutchinson, 1978.
Editor, *The Oxford Book of Contemporary New Zealand Poetry.* Auckland and Oxford, Oxford University Press, 1982.

Editor, *The Faber Book of Twentieth-Century Women's Poetry.* London, Faber, 1987.
Editor and translator, *Hugh Primas and the Archpoet.* Cambridge, Cambridge University Press, 1994.
Editor, with Jacqueline Simms, *The Oxford Book of Creatures.* Oxford, Oxford University Press, 1995.

Translator, *The Virgin and the Nightingale: Medieval Latin Poems.* Newcastle upon Tyne, Bloodaxe, 1983.
Translator, *Orient Express,* by Grete Tartler. Oxford, Oxford University Press, 1989.
Translator, *Letters from Darkness,* by Daniela Crasnaru. Oxford, Oxford University Press, 1991.

*

Critical Studies: Introduction by Dannie Abse to *Corgi Modern Poets in Focus,* no. 5, 1973; Julian Stannard, *Fleur Adcock in Context: From Movement to Martians,* Lampeter, Wales, Edwin Mellon Press, 1996.

Fleur Adcock comments:

I can't give a code of my poetic practice or a set of rules by which I have operated; I can only point to certain tendencies and outline an attitude. Poetry is a search for ways of communication; it must be conducted with openness, flexibility, and a constant readiness to listen. The content of my poems derives largely from those parts of my life which are directly experienced: relationships with people or places; images and insights which have presented themselves sharply from whatever source, conscious or subconscious; ideas triggered off by language itself. In recent years I have tended increasingly to use poetry as a method of writing fiction: the narratives of my poems (seldom ever merely autobiographical) often now tell invented stories.

My verse forms are relatively traditional (traditions alter). In general they have moved away from strict classical patterns in the direction of greater freedom—as is usual with most artists learning a trade. It takes courage, however, to leave all props behind, to cast oneself, like Matisse, upon pure space. I still await that confidence. In the meantime I continue to learn; and sometimes find it fruitful to return to a rigid metrical form as a discipline and for a different kind of exploration.

I write primarily for the printed page, not for performance (regarding poetry readings as the trailer, not the movie). But because the sound of words is central to the experiencing of a poem I read my work aloud as it develops and try to remove anything which is clumsy or unacceptable to the ear. As for the eye, the patterns of lines in type don't particularly interest me; words, not their shape on the page, are what matter. If one is fortunate their destination, like their origin, will be as voices speaking in the mind.

*   *   *

Fleur Adcock is one of the most popular poets in Britain. Though New Zealand born, she spent much of her childhood in wartime England. Her work shows a strong attachment to place, whether it be the English countryside, the beaches of New Zealand, or the dirt tracks of Nepal. Coupled with this is an acute awareness of the barriers between people. Adcock is, by her own admission, a solitary person—a true expatriate, with her cool, dispassionate eye and her reluctant nostalgia.

After the war Adcock's family returned to New Zealand, and it was there that she produced the prizewinning elegy "Flight, with Mountains." The poem is characteristic of her later work in its clear, conversational tone and in its preoccupation with friendship, death, and landscape:

> ... Another one for the mountains. Another one
> Who, climbing to stain the high snow
> With his shadow, fell, and briefly caught between
> Sudden earth and sun, projected below
> A flicker of darkness ...

The poems ends:

> ... neither
> Rope, nor crumbling ice, nor your unbelieving
> Uncommitted hands could hold you to living.
> Wheels turn; the dissolving air rolls over
> An arc of thunder. Gone is gone forever.

In 1963 Adcock moved back to England. In her first British publication, *Tigers,* she abandoned the romanticism of her earlier works. Influenced by the informality of the 1960s, she experimented with syllabics, discarding conventional meter and rhyme to embrace a more prosy, colloquial style. Although she tends to extrapolate from her own life, Adcock is too reticent to be classed among the "confessional" poets. Preferring understatement to exaggeration, she tends to suggest, rather than plummet. A poem like "Incident" hints at disconcerting truths as the speaker wakes from a nap on the beach to find her lover "Waiting for the lapping tide to take me / Watching, and lighting a cigarette." In "Miss Hamilton in London" a spinster goes through her daily rituals, "Then went to bed; where for the hours of darkness, / She lay pierced by thirty black spears...." Again, the calm, oblique style gives a shocking punch to the poem.

The love poems in this volume are, to say the least, astringent; "Advice to a Discarded Lover" begins by describing a bird's corpse and then goes on to warn the lover that "... In you / I see maggots close to the surface. You are eaten up by self-pity, / Crawling with unloveable pathos ... Do not ask me for charity now: / Go away until your bones are clean." Relationships get equally short shrift in Adcock's next volume, *High Tide in the Garden,* where "Against Coupling" begins

> I write in praise of the solitary act:
> of not feeling a trespassing tongue
> forced into one's mouth ...
> Pyramus and Thisbe are dead, but
> the hole in the wall can still be troublesome.
> I advise you, then, to embrace it without encumbrance ...

Adcock also draws on the imagery of dreams and mythology; "Afterwards" begins "We weave haunted circles about each other, / advance and retreat in turn, like witchdoctors / before a fetish...," and the long fantasy "Gas" tackles the theme of the doppelganger.

In *The Scenic Route* Adcock explores the Ireland of her ancestors. Death creeps into the volume with "In Memoriam: James K. Baxter," but any fear of sentimentality is undercut by the poet's characteristic candor:

> I'd write with more conviction about death
> if it were clutching at my every breath.
> And now we've come to it. The subject's out:
> the ineluctable, the all-pervasive...
> and if so far I've seemed a bit evasive
> it's not from cowardice or phoney tact—
> it's simply that I can't believe the fact ...

In "Kilpeck" the poet and a lover, "dried out and brittle this morning / fragile with continence," examine the grotesques of a Norman church. Although the poem is laced with erotic imagery, the poet affirms her commitment to poetry above all else, including, presumably, the relationship in question.

Adcock's next volume, *The Inner Harbour,* concentrates on the beginnings and ends of relationships. It also contains some short, Imagistic pieces, as in the title poem, a sequence of lyrical observations such as

> Under the sand at low tide
> are whispers, hisses, long slithers,
> bubbles, the suck of ingestion, a soft
> snap: mysteries and exclusions ...

This volume contains one of Adcock's most poignant poems, "The Soho Hospital for Women," which describes a women's cancer ward: "...Doctor, I am not afraid of a word. / But neither do I wish to embrace that visitor...."

The Incident Book is more outward looking than Adcock's previous collections. A section called "Thatcherland" explores contemporary Britain. There are ironical reflections on language and art; "Leaving the Tate" concludes with "Art's whatever you choose to frame." In this volume Adcock experiments with voices other than the autobiographical: "On the Land" is written as by a World War I land girl; in "Drowning" a woman condemned to drown for the murder of her husband ruminates,

> Then let the fishes feast on us
> and slurp our blood after we're finished:
> they'll find no souls to suck from us.
> Yours, perhaps, has a safe-conduct:
> you're a bishop, and subtle, and Greek.
> Well, sir, pray and ponder. But our language has no word
>   for dilemma.
> Drowning's the strongest word for death.

As this poem suggests, Adcock's work reveals a subtle feminist streak. Increasingly over the years her poems have turned toward the politics of relationships.

In 1987 Adcock edited *The Faber Book of Twentieth-Century Women's Poetry.* In her introduction to that anthology she explained that what she values in a poem is "the odd or the unexpected ... the kind of detail which throws new and startling light ... related to another quality I admire: wit." Certainly her work both startles and amuses. Without sacrificing any of its delightful, acerbic humor, Adcock's poetry has also become more compassionate with time.

—Katie Campbell

ADNAN, Etel

Nationality: Lebanese. **Born:** Beirut, 24 February 1925; resident of the United States since 1955; naturalized U.S. citizen, 1986. **Education:** French convent schools in Beirut; L'Ecole Supérieure des Lettres de Beyrouth; Sorbonne, Diplôme d'Etudes Supérieures de Philosophie 1950; postgraduate studies in philosophy at the University of California, Berkeley, 1955-57, and Harvard University, Cambridge, Massachusetts, 1957-58. **Career:** Worked for the Bureau de la Presse, Beirut, 1941-45; high school teacher of French literature, Al-Ahliya School for girls, Beirut, 1947-49; professor of philosophy, Dominican College, San Rafael, California, 1958-72; literary editor for Lebanese French-language newspapers *al-SAFA,* then *L'Orient-Le Jour,* Beirut, 1972-75; author of two television documentaries on the war in Lebanon, 1976; commissioned to write French part of *Civil warS* (multi-language opera) by American stage creator Robert Wilson, 1984. Internationally recognized painter, with works in museums including Tunis Modern Art Museum, Royal Jordanian Museum, British Museum, Musée de l'Institut du Monde Arabe, Paris, and National Museum of Women in the Arts, Washington, D.C.; tapestry designs on file in contemporary crafts museums, New York and Los Angeles. Participated in over 20 one-person shows and over 50 group shows in Belgium, England, France, Italy, Germany, Japan, Kuwait, Lebanon, Morocco, Saudi Arabia, Tunisia, the United States, and West Germany. **Addresses:** 35 Marie Street, Sausalito, California 94965, U.S.A.; 29 Rue Madame, Paris, 75006 France.

PUBLICATIONS

Poetry

Moonshots. Beirut, Reveil, 1966.
Poems. Bienne, Reactions, 1966.
Five Senses for One Death. New York, The Smith, 1971.
Jebu [and] *L'express Beyrouth-Enfer.* Paris, P. J. Oswald, 1973.
L'Apocalypse Arabe (illuminated verse, in French). Paris, Editions Papyrus, 1980.
From A to Z. Sausalito, California, Post-Apollo Press, 1982.
Pablo Neruda Is a Banana Tree. Lisbon, Da Almeida, 1982.
The Indian Never Had a Horse & Other Poems. Sausalito, California, Post-Apollo Press, 1985.
The Arab Apocalypse (illuminated verse, translated from the French by the author). Sausalito, California, Post-Apollo Press, 1989.
The Spring Flowers Own & The Manifestations of the Voyage. Sausalito, California, Post-Apollo Press, 1990.
Kitab Al Bahr [The Book of the Sea] (translated into Arabic from unpublished French manuscript). Beirut, n.p., 1994.
There (prose poem). Sausalito, California, Post-Apollo Press, 1996.
There: In the Light of the Darkness of the Self and of the Other. California, Post-Apollo Press, 1997.

Fiction

Sitt Marie Rose (novel). Paris, Editions des Femmes, 1978; translated by Georgina Kleege, Sausalito, California, Post-Apollo Press, 1982.

Al Confini Della Luna (short stories; translated into Italian). Rome, n.p., 1995.

Other

Khams hawass li-mawt wahid. Beirut, hamaska'in, 1973.
L'artisanat createur au Maroc (study of Moroccan crafts). Paris, Casablanca, Dessain-et-Tolra, 1983.
Journey to Mt. Tamalpais (illuminated essay). Sausalito, California, Post-Apollo Press, 1986.
Paris, When It's Naked (essay). Sausalito, California, Post-Apollo Press, 1993.
Of Cities and Women (Letters to Fawwaz). Sausalito, California, Post-Apollo Press, 1993.

*

Media Adaptations: Poem set to music by Tania Leon, produced New York, 1990; *The Adnan Songbook* (eight poems set to music by Gavin Bryars), broadcast on BBC-Radio, 1995.

Theatrical Activities:
Narrator, *A funeral march for the first cosmonaut,* music by Eugene Stewart, produced Dominican College, 1968.

Critical Studies: *Women of the Fertile Crescent,* edited by Kamal Boullata, Washington, D.C., Three Continents Press, 1978; interview with Hilary Kilpatrick in *Unheard Words,* edited by Mineke Schipper, London and New York, Allison & Busby, 1985; "Life after Lebanon (October, 1984)" by June Jordan, in *On Call: Political Essays,* Boston, South End, 1985; review of *The Indian Never Had a Horse & Other Poems* by Barbara Lesch McCaffry, in *NWSA Perspectives,* vol. 4, no. 1, Winter 1986; "Toward the Heights with Etel Adnan" by David Volpendesta, in *Poetry Flash,* November 1987; *Opening the Gates,* edited by Margot Badran and Miriam Cooke, Bloomington and Indianapolis, Indiana University Press, 1990; "Our Memory Has No Future" by Ammeil Alcalay, in *The Nation,* 7 March 1994; "Cities of Oppression, Circles of Repression: Etel Adnan's *Sitt Marie Rose*" by Thomas Foster, in *PMLA,* vol. LX, no. 1, January 1995.

*   *   *

Etel Adnan has said that "poetry is the purpose of life." She is a poet, novelist, essayist, painter, tapestry designer and teacher of philosophy. She is an internationally acclaimed writer, and a bilingual poet who writes in English and in French. Adnan's poetry, like her fiction and nonfiction, is at once personal and political, and describes philosophical explorations, historical tragedies and the construct of cities. Images of birds, the sun and the sea populate Adnan's work; hers is a sophisticated imagination absorbed with poetic imagery, and with the rhythms and textures of poetic language. "Words became my landscape," Adnan writes in *The Manifestations of the Voyage.*

While she does not classify herself as a political poet, Adnan writes often on political subjects. She was an outspoken opponent of the Vietnam War and the Lebanese Civil War, and images from these wars weave in and out of her verse. Her first published political poem, a long piece titled *Jebu,* refers to the Jebusites—the Canaanite tribe that founded the city of Jerusalem, later captured by King David—and is something of a metaphor for the condition of Palestinians today. Adnan's first novel, *Sitt Marie Rose*, was written during the civil war in Lebanon, and is a harsh critique of the Lebanese Christian militia and their activities during that war.

The Arab Apocalypse is an experimental book of political poetry in which ink-drawings signs and images are interspersed with the words and lines of poetry. The book is at once a chaos of language and a penetrating outcry against the suffering both endured and produced by Palestinians, Lebanese, and Syrians in Lebanon. The primary symbol of the book is the sun, which appears—whether by image or by work—in nearly every poem; it is at times a nurturing symbol, but more often a cruel, scorching, apocalyptic presence: "the sun cut their toes and told the Palestinians: this is your dinner." Numerous references to Native American Indians, Mexican Indians, Che Guevara, and the poetry of Rimbaud establish an identification across cultural lines between disenfranchised peoples and political revolutions, and point to the magical capacity of poetry to transcend, or at least express and process traumatic, even apocalyptic experiences.

In addition to writing of political matters, Adnan is concerned with the irony of nature, and with the ongoing existential challenges confronting her poetic imagination. *The Spring Flowers Own* (published with *The Manifestations of the Voyage*) describes the ironic conflation of nature's ongoing life-cycle with the cycle of death brought on by war. In describing flowers—and, indeed, many aspects of nature—Adnan muses on their dual nature:

> I know flowers to be funeral companions
>   they make poisons and venoms
>   and eat abandoned stone walls
>
> I know flowers shine stronger
>   than the sun
> their eclipse means the end of
>   times

There is perhaps Adnan's most philosophical poetic work. It is a series of prose poems on a range of existential, historical and personal issues arranged in one or two page sections, each of which bears the title, "There." These poems, most of which are posed as questions, deal with the problem of where the individual—or, in this case, the poet—can place herself in the increasing chaos and the ongoing betrayals of the modern world:

> Where are we? Out of History, of his or her story, and back into it..., who are we?... Where is where, where the terror, the love, the pain? Where the hatred? Where your life, and mine?

Adnan is a master of poetic innovation. Her work is replete with unusual combinations of images and ideas, alternating lilting lyrics with enigmatic verse—as in these lines from *The Indian Never Had a Horse*:

> A bee fell in love with a peach
> blossom. Shakespeare wrote a
> story about it.
> ...
> He had his mother's bones made
> into a necklace because horses
> came from Spain. He moved about
> the country like a sword.

Adnan is not only an innovator in her own poetry; she often acknowledges her literary heritage, making frequent references in her own writing to some of the great poets of the Arab literary tradition. She has clearly taken her place among them.

—Rena Potok

AGOSÍN, Marjorie

Nationality: Chilean. **Born:** Bethesda, Maryland, 15 June 1955. **Education:** University of Georgia, B.A. in philosophy, 1976; Indiana State University, M.A. in Spanish literature, 1977, Ph.D., 1982. **Family:** Married John Wiggins in 1977; one son. **Career:** Wellesley College, Wellesley, Massachusetts, associate professor of Spanish, beginning 1982. Visiting lecturer, University of Los Andes, Bogotá, Colombia, 1986; visiting professor, Babson College, 1990-93; Hilliard Professor in the Humanities, University of Nevada at Reno, 1991; visiting writer, Guadalupe Cultural Center, San Antonio, Texas, 1993, 1995, and Illinois Weselyan University, 1995. Member of advisory board, *Cintas, Multicultural Review, Ms.,* and WGBH, Boston. **Awards:** Fulbright summer scholarship, 1985, research grant, 1990; Massachusetts Artist Foundation translation grant, 1987; National Endowment for the Arts grants, 1987; National Association of Christians and Jews Good Neighbor award, 1988; New England Foundation for the Arts grant, 1988; Jeanetta Rankin award, 1990; Peabody award, 1992; National Endowment for the Humanities grant, 1994; Mexican Cultural Institute Prize, 1995; *Letras de Oro* First Prize for Poetry, 1995; Latino Literature Prize, 1995. **Address:** Spanish Department, Wellesley College, Wellesley, Massachusetts 02181, U.S.A. **Online address:** magosin@wellesley.edu.

PUBLICATIONS

Poetry

Gemidos y cantares. Chile, Editorial el Observador, 1977.
Conchalí, illustrations by Della Collins Cook. New York, Senda Nueva, 1980.
Silencio que se deja oír, with Emma Nolan. Bloomington, Indiana, Third Woman Press, 1982.
Brujas y algo mas=/Witches and Other Things, translated by Cola Franzen. Pittsburgh, Latin American Literary Review Press, 1984.
Hogueras. Santiago, Editorial Universitaria, 1986; translation by Naomi Lindstrom published as *Hogueras=Bonfires,* Tempe, Arizona, Bilingual Review Press, 1990.
Mujeres de humo. Madrid, Editiones Torremozas, 1987, translated by Naomi Lindstrom as *Women of Smoke,* Pittsburgh, Latin American Literary Review Press, 1987.
Zones of Pain / Las zonas del dolor, translated by Cola Franzen. Fredonia, New York, White Pine Press, 1988.
Sargaxo. Buenos Aires, Editorial Carlos Lohlé, 1991; translated by Naomi Lindstrom as *Sargasso,* Pittsburgh, Latin American Literary Review Press, 1993.
Circles of Madness: Mothers of the Plaza de Mayo=Circulos de locura: madres de la Plaza de Mayo, translated by Celeste Kostopulos-Cooperman. Fredonia, New York, White Pine Press, 1992.

Dear Anne Frank. Washington, D.C., Azul Edition, 1994.

Toward the Splendid City, translated by Richard Schaaf. Tempe, Arizona, Bilingual Press, 1994.

Noche estrellada. Santiago, Lom Ediciones, 1996; translated as *Starry Night,* Fredonia, New York, White Pine Press, 1996.

The Council of the Fairies. Washington, D.C., Azul Editions, 1997.

Melodious Women. Pittsburgh, Latin American Literary Review Press, 1998.

Fiction

La Felicidad. Santiago, Cuarto Propio, 1992.

Happiness: Stories, translated by Elizabeth Horan. Fredonia, New York, White Pine Press, 1993.

Las Alfareras. Santiago, Cuarto Propio, 1994.

Furniture Dreams. Reno, University of Nevada Press, 1995.

Women in Disguise. Washington, D.C., Azul Editions, 1996.

Other

Las desterradas del paraíso: protagonistas en la narrativa de María Luisa Bombal. New York, Senda Nueva, 1983.

Pablo Neruda, translated by Lorraine Roses. Boston, Twayne, 1986.

Silencio e imaginación: Metáforas de la escritura femenina. Mexico, Katún, 1986.

Scraps of Life: The Chilean Arpilleras: Chilean Women and the Pinochet Dictatorship, translated by Cola Franzen. Trenton, New Jersey, Red Sea Press, 1987.

Violeta Parra, santa de pura greda: Un estudio de su obra poetica, with Inés Doz Blackburn. Santiago, Planeta, 1988.

A Cross and a Star: Memoirs of a Jewish Girl in Chile, translated by Celeste Kostopulos-Cooperman. Albuquerque, University of New Mexico Press, 1995.

Hay Otra Voz: Essays on Hispanic Women Poets, with Emma Sepulveda. Puerto Rico, Maerena, 1995.

Tapestries of Hope, Threads of Love: The Arpillera Movement in Chile, 1974-1994, translated by Celeste Kostopulos-Cooperman. Albuquerque, University of New Mexico Press, 1996.

Ashes of Revolt: Essays on Human Rights. Fredonia, New York, White Pine Press, 1996.

Always from Somewhere Else: My Jewish Father. New York, Feminist Press, 1998.

Editor, with Elena Gascon-Vera and Joy Renjilian-Burgy, *Maria Luisa Bombal: Apreciacios criticas.* Bilingue, 1987.

Editor, *Landscapes of a New Land: Fiction by Latin American Women.* Fredonia, New York, White Pine Press, 1989.

Editor, *Chilean Folk Tales Retold,* translated by Celeste Kostopulos-Cooperman. Stratford, Ontario, Williams-Wallace, 1992.

Editor, *A Gabriela Mistral Reader,* translated by Maria Giachetti. Fredonia, New York, White Pine Press, 1993.

Editor, *Surviving beyond Fear: Women, Children, and Human Rights in Latin America.* Fredonia, New York, White Pine Press, 1993.

Editor, *These Are Not Sweet Girls: Latin American Women Poets.* Fredonia, New York, White Pine Press, 1994.

Editor, *What Is Secret: Stories by Chilean Women.* Fredonia, New York, White Pine Press, 1995.

Editor, *A Dream of Light and Shadow: Portraits of Latin American Women Writers.* Albuquerque, University of New Mexico Press, 1995.

*

Critical Studies: "Marjorie Agosín as Latina Writer" by Nina Scott in *Breaking Boundaries: Latina Writings and Critical Readings,* Amherst, University of Massachusetts Press, 1989; "Books and Quilts" in *Bloomsbury Review,* July / August 1995; "Marjorie Agosín: Judaism and Latin American Literature" by Illan Stavans in *Bloomsbury Review,* Fall 1995.

*   *   *

Marjorie Agosín was born in Maryland, raised in Chile, and has lived in the United States since the age of 16. Her life in two widely disparate cultures and her resulting sense of alienation are constant themes in her poetry, as are Agosín's strong feminist sensibility and pride in her Jewish heritage.

Agosín's first poetry collection published in the United States, *Conchalí,* is an exploration of her place in the world, focusing on her dilemma as the product of two cultures but a member of neither. Specifically, Agosín attempts to gauge the influence upon her own poetic expression of such fellow Chilean poets as Pablo Neruda, María Luisa Bombal, and Nicanor Parra. Confronting the achievements and international reputations of these earlier poets, Agosín works to define her own place in the tradition. Not only does Agosín examine the poetics of Neruda and Bombal but also the patriarchal tradition she believes these poets represent. Thus, her own poems occupy a distinctly female perspective. Agosín also writes of the dispossessed, the poor, and the oppressed of her native land, especially the women of her culture. Her best poems, however, are those where Agosín allows the surreal, haunting quality of her poetic voice full rein. Agosín's concern for Latin American women and the injustices they endure is also found in the poems she wrote for *Silencio que se deja oír* to accompany the photographs of Emma Nolan.

Agosín brings the strengths of her writing to bear on social issues with greater effect in the collection *Brujas y algo mas.* Here, she writes of Anne Frank in feminist terms, criticizing Anne for her inability to denounce the holocaust she and her people faced and for her naive belief in the ultimate goodness of humanity, a fallacy Agosín attributes to the influence of the patriarchy on Anne's thinking. The poem "The Billiard Table: New Bedford, Mass." is based on the actual gang rape of a young woman in a working-class, Portuguese-American bar. Agosín transforms the violent event by reversing the usual sexual metaphors, attempting to rewrite the patriarchal category-system into a new kind of sexual imagery.

In *Zones of Pain* Agosín speaks of the "disappeared women," that is, those women who were arrested, jailed, and killed in Chile during the dictatorial repression of the 1970s. As Agosín explains in her prologue to the book, "The zones of pain represent the wandering of buried women and the wandering of searching mothers. The zones of pain are ours, are dark, and at times too easily slip the mind. For those reasons I wrote them down, because I wish to accompany my dead sisters." In a series of six "Disappeared Woman" poems, Agosín directly commemorates victims of the Chilean government in richly symbolic language. As she explains her work in one of these poems, "Don't conspire with /

oblivion, / tear down the silence."

Agosín tells Illan Stavans in the *Bloomsbury Review*: "I always wrote to denounce, to give voice to the oppressed, to pay respect to those who died, to rescue memory from oblivion." Her own experience of political persecution in Chile inspired Agosín's determination to champion those in need and to provide a voice for those who have none. Her father, a university professor in Chile, came under suspicion by the Chilean government both for his leftist politics and his Jewish heritage. At the same time, Communist Party officials viewed him as a tool of capitalists for his acceptance of grant money from U.S. foundations. The threats from both sides escalated until Agosín's father finally moved the family to the United States.

Agosín addresses her Jewish heritage in her nonfiction work *A Cross and a Star: Memories of a Jewish Girl in Chile*. After relating her family's history in the town of Osorno, where Agosín explains that many ex-Nazis have made their home, she tells of a 1993 trip back to her homeland in hope that she could recapture the country of her childhood. The attempt failed, however, when she realized that her hometown still had Hitler portraits for sale in the local shops.

Agosín's strong commitment to providing a voice for the powerless, the victimized and the oppressed shapes all of her poetry. Because her beliefs are rooted in her own experiences, her work displays an honesty sometimes missing in the work of other poets who write on similar themes.

—Denise Wiloch

AI

Nationality: American. **Born:** Albany, Texas, 21 October 1947. **Education:** University of Arizona, Tucson, 1965-69, B.A. 1969; University of California, Irvine, 1969-71, M.F.A. 1971. **Career:** Visiting poet, Wayne State University, 1977-78, George Mason University, 1986, 1987; writer-in-residence, Arizona State University, 1988-89; visiting associate professor, University of Colorado at Boulder, 1996-97. **Awards:** Guggenheim fellowship, 1975; Bunting fellowship, 1975; American Academy of Poets Lamont Poetry Selection, 1978; Pushcart Prize (with others), 1978; National Endowment for the Arts fellowship, 1978, 1985; Ingram Merrill fellowship, 1983; St. Botolph Foundation grant, 1986; Before Columbus Foundation American Book Award, 1987, for *Sin*. **Address:** c/o Jill Bialosky, Editor, W.W. Norton, 500 Fifth Avenue, New York, New York 10110-0017, U.S.A.

PUBLICATIONS

Poetry

Cruelty. Boston, Houghton Mifflin, 1973.
Killing Floor. Boston, Houghton Mifflin, 1979.
Sin. Boston, Houghton Mifflin, 1986.
Fate. Boston, Houghton Mifflin, 1991.
Greed. New York, Norton, 1993.

Novel

Black Blood. New York, Norton, 1997.

*

Manuscript Collection: New York Public Library, New York.

Ai comments:

Ai is the only name by which I wish, and indeed, should be known. Since I am the child of a scandalous affair my mother had with a Japanese man she met at a streetcar stop, and I was forced to live a lie for so many years, while my mother concealed my natural father's identity from me, I feel that I should not have to be identified with a man, who was only my stepfather, for all eternity.

My writing of dramatic monologues was a happy accident, because I took so much to heart the opinion of my first poetry teacher, Richard Shelton, the fact that the first person voice was always the stronger voice to use when writing. What began as an experiment in that voice became the only voice in which I wrote for about twenty years. Lately, though, I've been writing poems and short stories using the second person, without, it seems to me, any diminution in the power of my work. Still, I feel that the dramatic monologue was the form in which I was born to write and I love it as passionately, or perhaps more passionately, than I have ever loved a man.

*   *   *

Ai is a dangerous writer and means to be. Hers is a poetry that aims to be disturbing, and less sophisticated readers may take the violence and sometimes brutal sex that propel her writing at face value. There is considerably more at work, however.

This is poetry about people seeking transformation, a rough sort of salvation, through violent acts. The poems sometimes lift up stones and hurl them at the reader. At other times, especially in her later collections, the poet steps back with her burden so that we can see bits of the national psyche, wriggling and squirming in a new, raw light.

Ai's poems are almost all dramatic monologues. In earlier books like *Cruelty* and *Killing Floor* the voices we hear are often those of the anonymous poor. "Why I Can't Leave You," an early poem from *Cruelty*, Ai's first collection, demonstrates the author's power to suggest erotic entrapment in relationships devoid of tenderness:

> I know that we can't give each other any more
> or any less than what we have.
> There is safety in that, so much
> that I can never get past the packing,
> the begging you to please, if I can't make you happy,
> come close between my thighs
> and let me laugh for you from my second mouth.

Killing Floor is in some ways a transitional book, mixing the anonymous voices from the first collection with those of the famous, including Yukio Mishima as he commits hara-kiri and Marilyn Monroe reflecting on her mother's death. In the latter book the acts of violence that fill *Cruelty* and *Killing Floor* become emblems for psychic violence, as in "Guadalajara Cemetery," where the speaker apparently contemplates sex with a widowed man:

It's time to cross the border
and cut your throat with two knives:
you wife, your son...
You, me, these withered flowers,
so many hearts tied in a knot,
given and taken away.

In *Fate* and *Greed* speakers often bear the names of real people, many famous to the point of being cultural icons. Ai reinvents each persona, taking real or perceived traits to an even more archetypal extreme. What each says, returning after death, expresses more about the American psyche than about the real figures, and Ai intends it this way. Her speakers include Mary Jo Kopechne, J. Edgar Hoover, Jack Ruby, Jimmy Hoffa, James Dean, Elvis Presley, and Alfred Hitchcock. Characters include both the anointed famous and recipients of Andy Warhol's fifteen minutes of fame, like the possible rape victim and certain victim of media penetration in "Evidence from a Reporter's Notebook," from *Fate*:

Six straight days, she's front-page news
She makes guest appearances by the dozen
Everybody's cousin wants their piece
of tender meat...

By the end of the poem the reporter realizes that she has violated the victim whether an actual rapist has done so or not.

In other poems in the later collections the speakers return to perform other acts of violation, often visited on themselves as much as on real or imagined victims. Sometimes the poems pick up, as does one on Jack Ruby, on scurrilous material published about the notorious, and Ai proceeds to discover the deeper truth lurking even in lies. In "Oswald Incognito & Astral Travels," from *Greed,* Oswald sees himself vanishing into his own act:

I write my name on the wall
beside the Coke machine. OSWALD
in capital letters.
I erase it with spit and my shirttail,
but it keeps reappearing,
each time the letters get larger,
until the "O" is a hole
I can walk through
and when I finally do, it closes around me
like a mouth around the mouth of a rifle.

In "Miracle in Manila" (*Greed*) a posthumous Ferdinand Marcos reflects on his wife Imelda, who perhaps as much as any contemporary figure has come to personify greed. Here she stages a mock crucifixion, displays phony stigmata on her palms, and then

After a transfusion, a facial,
and a manicure,
she's campaigning again, although it's useless
and I'm back to tap-dancing at her side,
while she proclaims herself
the only candidate
who can rise from the dead.

This is poetry that hardly lays claim to being poetry. It is addressed to ordinary people, not to politicians or academics. Ai

faces essential questions and lies about racial and sexual politics with great assurance.

—Duane Ackerson

AIDOO, Ama Ata

Nationality: Ghanaian. **Born:** Abeadzi Kyiakor, 23 March 1942. **Education:** University of Ghana, Legon, B.A. in English 1964. **Family:** Married; one daughter. **Career:** Lecturer in English, University of Cape Coast, Ghana, 1970-83; consulting professor, Phelps-Stokes Fund Ethnic Studies program, 1974-75; Minister for Education, Ghana, 1982-83; currently distinguished professor of English, Oberlin College, Oberlin, Ohio. **Member:** Zimbabwe Women Writers Group (chair). **Address:** Department of English, Oberlin College, Oberlin, Ohio 44074, U.S.A.

PUBLICATIONS

Poetry

Someone Talking to Sometime. Harare, Zimbabwe, College Press, 1985.
Birds and Other Poems. Harare, Zimbabwe, College Press, 1987.
An Angry Letter in January and Other Poems. Sidney, Dangaroo Press, 1992.

Fiction

Our Sister Killjoy; or, Reflections from a Black-eyed Squint (novel). Harlow, Longmans, 1970; New York, NOK, 1979.
No Sweetness Here (short stories). Harlow, Longmans, 1970; Garden City, New York, Doubleday, 1971.
The Eagle and the Chickens and Other Stories (juvenile). Enugu, Nigeria, Tana, 1986.
Changes: A Love Story (novel). London, Women's Press, 1991.

Plays

The Dilemma of a Ghost (produced Legon, Ghana, 1964). Harlow and Accra, Longmans, 1965; New York, Collier, 1971.
Anowa (produced England, 1991). Harlow, Longmans, 1970; Washington, D.C., Three Continents Press, 1980.

*

Critical Studies: "Women in African Literature" by G.C.M. Mutiso, in *East African Journal,* vol. 8, no. 3, 1971; "Ama Ata Aidoo: The Art of the Short Story and Sexual Roles in Africa" by Lloyd Brown, in *World Literature Written in English,* no. 13, November 1974; "Womanism: The Dynamics of the Contemporary Black Female Novel in English" by Chikwenye O. Ogunyemi, in *Signs,* no. 11, Autumn 1985; "The Feminist Impulse and Social Realism in Ama Ata Aidoo's *No Sweetness Here* and *Our Sister Killjoy*" by Chimalum Nwankwo, in *Ngambika: Studies of Women in African Literature,* edited by Carole Boyce Davies and Anne Adams Graves, Trenton, New Jersey, African World, 1986; "The Afro-American-West African Marriage Question: Its Literary and Historical Contexts" by Brenda Berrian, in *African Literature Today,* no. 15, 1987; "Canons under

Siege: Blackness, Femaleness and Ama Ata Aidoo's *Our Sister Killjoy*" by Kofi Owusu, in *Callaloo,* no. 13, Spring 1990; "'A New Tail to an Old Tale': An Interview with Ama Ata Aidoo" by Rosemary Marangoly George and Helen Scott, in *Novel: A Forum on Fiction,* Spring 1993; interview with Mary McKay, in *Belles Lettres,* Fall 1993; *The Art of Ama Ata Aidoo: Polylectics and Reading against Neocolonialism* by Vincent O. Odamtten, Gainsville, University of Florida Press, 1994; interview with Anuradha Dingwaney Needham, in *Massachusetts Review,* Spring 1995.

*   *   *

Ama Ata Aidoo's identity as an African woman is as much a compelling force in her poetry as it is in her highly acclaimed plays, novels, and short stories. Well known for her feminist concern with the oppression of women, Aidoo interlaces her focus on the lives of women with the themes of nationalism, neo-colonialism, and Africans in the diaspora. In an interview with Anuradha Dingwaney Needham in *Massachusetts Review,* Aidoo states: "the decay of Africa's social, political, and economic systems is directly related to the complete marginalization of women from developmental discourses."

Though Aidoo wrote the initial poem for her first of three poetry collections, *Someone Talking to Sometime* (1985), in the 1960s, the volume was not published until nearly 20 years later in Zimbabwe. She has also published a poetry collection for children, *Birds and Other Poems* (1987), and *An Angry Letter in January* (1992). Aidoo's profound love for her country, a staunch sense of cultural allegiance, and an abiding respect for the richness of the African continent are evident in *Someone Talking to Sometime.* Poems like "1977" mirror her clarifying perspective on the destruction being waged in and against her homeland in the "bloody time" of war.

The two-parts of the volume—"Of Love and Commitment" and "Someone Talking to Sometime"—piercingly scrutinize how neo-colonialism negatively impacts the continent, yet delicately interlace Aidoo's sensitivity for the well-being and survival of family and friends in poems like "Carolyn," where the speaker says, "I wish / lots of / blessings upon your house / plenty of / laughter within its walls." In a continuing symmetry, poems of death and disaster, like "Ghana Funerals," "Wondering about Him Who Said No to the Glare of the Open Day," and "Heavy Traffic" are balanced by the landscape of affirmation in poems like "Of Love and Commitment—for Omafumi," "For a Zulu in the Bayous," "Lorisnrudi," and a poem addressed to her daughter, titled "Kinna II."

Aidoo is ever mindful of the reality of revolution in Africa, and in "Kinna I," the speaker likens the decay of nature, visible in a seedless cocoa pod, to the guns of revolution:

> And now,
> not remembering
> what mouth or
> how
> likened hollow pod to a
> gun
>
> Gun?
> To fight the revolution.

Likewise, in "For Steve Hymer—A propos 1966," the speaker acknowledges betrayal of those "who came good-intentioned":

> fanged doomcasters and
>
> their agents who lick
> bloody lips
>
> savoring
>   —in advance—the
> sweetness of the fall
> for which they had
> toiled?

Even as Aidoo sketches a portrait of Africa as a land beset by the heat of revolutionary turmoil and its devastating ravages on the individual's sense of home, her international orientation as a member of the world community is clear in poems like "Greetings from London," and in the section "New Orleans Mid-1970's." In the opening lines of "Mardi Gras," the poet positions herself as an astute commentator who juxtaposes America's legacy of lynching Black people with the brutality foisted against her own Black countrymen in Africa.

> Here in the South
>
> where
> trees used to grow
> such
> strange and
> sudden fruits,
>
> people have learned
> not
> to see
> the Africa
> that is
> everywhere
> in things
> in their own words
> in their own deeds.

In an ironic twist, the poet clarifies the unquestioned racial reversals that illuminate America's legacy of miscegenation:

> Since in
> this land of
> sharp descriptions, and
> determined name-calling,
> no one seems to have a
> name for either the
> kinky-haired
> thick-lipped
> honkies,
>   or
>
> the straight-nosed
> blue-eyed
> spooks...

In the final poem of the volume, "Wanted Urgently for Immediate Employment," the poet offers a tempered optimism for the survival of her country: "We have to / nurse our flickering hopes / through this damp night."

An Angry Letter in January (1992) is a powerful poetic testament to Aidoo's anger at the neo-colonial world order. In the title poem, a female loan applicant perceives the loan criteria to be "white, male, and a 'commercial' farmer," and is outraged at the bank's rejection letter; she asks: "whose land is this anyway?" The two-part volume—"Images of Africa at Century's End" and "Women's Conferences and Other Wonders"—is gripping; the poet laments the loss of ownership of her native land in "In Memoriam: The Ghana Drama Studio," where the speaker mentions her "sacred duty" to "love every little bit of this / battered and bartered continent which / I still, perhaps naively, / call my own."

Aidoo also addresses the social ramifications of Africa's political storms and the overwhelming sense of alienation felt by those who are forced into exile. In "Speaking of Hurricanes," the poet recognizes the havoc wreaked by Africa's "years of economic and political tornadoes," and in "June 7, 1989 on Tiananmen Square," she admonishes her fellow countrymen for sleeping while vandals stripped the land of its vast resources. The speaker asks: "after a millennia in a coma, / when do we wake up?" And in "A Modern African Story," the poet declares, "I got deported this morning from my home, my village, my country and the land which / my forefathers and foremothers bled for."

But, characteristically, Aidoo tempers her wrath with a lighter touch, as in the imitate statement of self-actualization in the opening poem "As Always, a Painful Declaration of Independence / —For Me"; a poem for the deceased South African writer "Bessie Head"; "Three Poems for Chinua Achebe," and several dedicatory poems "for Kinna," where she offers tributes to friends, literary colleagues, and family.

Aidoo's poetry exemplifies the wide ranging subject matter for which her fiction has been noted, as well as her ambitious use of language. In *Anger,* her growth as a poet is visible in the heightened use of rhetorical strategies, especially alliteration, and in her distinctive storytelling technique, which combine to produce a forceful and direct style of writing that turns on a lyrical irony.

In speaking with Needham, Aidoo addresses what she views as the need for a collective effort to solve the problems of Africa, not just a "Third World leadership." She states: "To solve our problems you need all of us. And I genuinely think that's how I see my work. If somebody says you have put your finger on the problem I feel so good because that, I think, is part of the responsibility of being writers and artists—that we point out some of these things."

— B. J. Bolden

AKHMADULINA, Bella

Nationality: Russian. **Born:** Moscow, 10 April 1937. **Education:** A.M. Gorky Institute of World Literature, Moscow, expelled. **Family:** Married 1) the poet Yevgeny Yevtushenko in 1954 (divorced); 2) writer Yury Navigin (divorced); 3) writer Gennadi Mamlin. **Career:** Poet and translator of Georgian and Central Asian poetry. Member, Union of Soviet Writers; delegate to the Second All-Russian Congress of Writers, 1965.

PUBLICATIONS

Poetry

Struna ("String"). Moscow, Sovetskii Pisatel, 1962.
Oznob: izbrannye proizvedenija. Frankfurt am Main, Posev, 1968; translated by Geoffrey Dutton and Igor Mzhakoff-Koriakin as *Fever and Other Poems,* New York, Morrow, 1969; London, P. Owen, 1970.
Uroki muzyki ("Music Lessons"). Moscow, Sovetskii Pisatel, 1969.
Metel: stixi. Moscow, Sovetskii Pisatel, 1977.
Sny o Gruzii. Toblinsk, Merani, 1979.
Three Russian Poets, with Margarita Aliger and Yunna Moritz, compiled and translated by Elaine Feinstein. Manchester, Carcanet, 1979.
Taina: novye stikhi. Moscow, Sovetskii Pisatel, 1983.
Three Russian Poets, with Anna Akhmatova and Marina Tsvetayeva, edited and translated by Mary Maddock. Trumansburg, New York, Crossing Press, 1983.
Stikhotvoreniia. Moscow, Khudozh, 1988.
The Garden: New and Selected Poetry and Prose, translated and introduced by F.D. Reeve. New York, Holt, 1990.
Griada kamnei: 1957-1992. Moscow, Pan, 1995.
Zvuk ukazuiuschii. Saint Petersburg, Lenizdat, 1995.
Stikhotvoreniia. Moscow, Slovo, 1995.

Play

Screenplay: *Clear Ponds* (based a story by Yury Nagibin), 1965.

Other

Odnazhdy v dekabre ("Once upon a Time in December"; stories, essays, and memoirs). Saint Petersburg, Pushkinskii fond, 1996.

Recordings: *Stikhotvorenii,* 1970; *Romeo i Dzhuletta* (excerpts from Hector Berlioz's symphony, "Romeo and Juliet"), 1980; *Potom ia vspomniu,* 1980.

*

Bibliography: "A Bibliography of Works by and about Bella Akhmadulina," by Christine Rydel, in *Russian Literature Triquarterly* (Ann Arbor), vol. 1, no. 1, 1971.

Critical Studies: "The Metapoetical World of Bella Akhmadulina" by Christine Rydel, in *Russian Literature Triquarterly* (Ann Arbor), vol. 1, no. 1, 1971; "The Metapoetry of Evtusesnko, Axmadulina, and Vosnesenskij, Analyzed in the Context of Soviet Aesthetic Theory" by Nancy P. Condee (Ph.D. dissertation), Yale University, 1978; "Axmadulina's POEMY: Poems of Transformations and Origins" by Nancy P. Condee, in *Slavic and East European Journal* (Tucson), vol. 29, no. 2, Summer 1985; "Poetry and Conscience: Russian Women Poets of the 20th Century" by Elaine Feinstein, in *Women Writing and Writing about Women,* New York, Barnes & Noble, 1979; "Poetic Creation in Bella Axmadulina" by Sonia Ketchian, in *Slavic and East European Journal,* vol. 28, no. 1, Spring 1984; "The Wonder of Nature and Art: Bella Axmadulina's Secret" by Sonia Ketchian, in *New Studies in Rus-*

sian Language and Literature, edited by Anna Lisa Crone and others, Columbus, Ohio, Slavica, 1986; "The Journal 'Iunost' in Soviet Russian Literature, 1955-1965" by Timothy Pogacar (Ph.D. dissertation), University of Kansas, 1985; "Have the Poets Yielded Their Former Positions? (A Talk with Bella Akhmadulina)" in Soviet Literature (Moscow), no. 6, 1988; interview with Valentina Polukhina, in Brodsky's Poetics and Aesthetics, edited by Lev Loseff, New York, St. Martin's, 1990; interview in The Beat Generation and the Russian New Wave, edited by Inger Thorup Lauridsen and Per Dalgard, Ann Arbor, Ardis, 1990; The Poetic Craft of Bella Akhmadulina, by Sonia Ketchian, University Park, Pennsylvania State University Press, 1993.

*   *   *

Now recognized as one of Russia's premier poets and translators, Bella Akhmadulina had to fight her way out of her husband Yevgeny Yevtushenko's shadow to gain deserved recognition. Expelled from the prestigious A.M. Gorky Institute of Literature, it took her nearly a decade to publish a first book of poems, Struna ("String"), in 1962. The book was not well received by government critics, and it would be six years before her next book could be published. Travelling to the Central Asian republics of the U.S.S.R., Akhmadulina began to translate the works of Armenian, Kazakhstani, Chuvash, Tatar, and, especially, Georgian poets. Her growing reputation as a translator eventually overcame official disapproval, and she was invited into the Union of Soviet Writers. Yet she has continued to maintain a rebellious stance, writing poems critical of her homeland's materialistic and unimaginative elites. Not restricted to Russia, her barbs often find their mark abroad.

Akhmadulina is primarily a personal poet, however, and her social satires usually occur within more-or-less autobiographical poems that are concerned with the creative process, the poet's emotional life, and obstacles to both. The arrogance that privilege conveys and the claustrophobia of a life of creature comforts are no less damaging to the poet than overt acts of censorship. It is the imagination, she believes, that is continually threatened by a thousand-and-one temptations, as in the long poem "Oznob," where the narrator is plied with cognacs, a warm hearth, and social niceties, in hopes that she will conform. In Akhmadulina's case, the act of writing does not come easily. Her own struggle with "muteness," or writer's block, is perhaps most fully developed in one of her most popular long poems, "A Fairytale about the Rain" ("Skazka o dozhe"). In this poem, rain is a metaphor for Inspiration, a divine force connected to the natural world. Necessary to the poet's creative health, as to the growth of crops, rain can nevertheless be destructive. In fact, Akhmadulina's narrator insists on the destructive element, which disrupts the routine of normality and frees the poet from the stifling world of bourgeois life, symbolized by an overheated house.

In numerous poems, Akhmadulina deals with the painful blessing that is, for her, artistic creation. Metaphors of child-birth, fever, flood, and torture abound, representing, in Nancy Condee's phrase, "acquiescence to physical mutilation." Like a Russian mystic or Siberian shaman, Akhmadulina cannot enter her poetic mediumship without enduring a loss of selfhood expressed as physical pain. "I bear my exultant punishment," she says in "Music Lessons," as a condition far preferable to extended periods of blockage. And the onset of inspiration elicits playful, almost surrealistic passages about children playing in puddles or "cycling

into white shafts of light" ("Autumn"), airplanes with "eyes of sad dachshunds" ("Small Aircraft"), and rain washing her lips "with the scent of a puppy" ("A Fairytale").

Never one to take the easy route, Akhmadulina has long crisscrossed the divergent paths of tradition and experimentation. She honors forbearers like Pushkin, Lermontov, Mandelstamm, and Pasternak, while freely acknowledging her debt to early-twentieth-century women poets Anna Akhmatova and Marina Tsvetayeva. Her habit of writing by candlelight becomes a metaphor for her love of greatness past, what Sonia Ketchian calls "the native tongue which is distinct from artificial stiltedness": "All you need is a candle, / a simple wax candle, / and venerable old-fashionedness / will become so fresh in your memory."

Yet her devotion to the creative imagination is too great to allow her ever to accept the role of imitator. Muteness is, for her, not so much the absence of words as the absence of living words. The pressures placed upon Soviet poets to conform also made her aware of the importance of resisting the usual and expected. It was only fitting, thus, that in the 1960s Akhmadulina became associated with an avant-garde journal whose title was Yunost ("Youth"). Even earlier, along with then-husband Yevtushenko, she drew the attention of American writers of the Beat Generation, who shared the Russian couple's uncompromising honesty. Indeed, Yevtushenko's description of his wife sounds remarkably like a Beat manifesto: "Bella Akhmadulina wants to tear away the garments of decorum from everything, to tear away everything from her own soul and place it, fearlessly naked and contemptuous, right before the slippery gaze of other people."

Not a radical in formalistic terms, Akhmadulina has, according to Christine Rydel, given freshness and variety to traditional forms through complex rhyme patterns, diverse rhythmic "scud patterns," and "the juxtaposition of archaisms and colloquial diction." In later work, she moved increasingly towards metrical and stanzaic experimentation. But the characterization by Aliki and Willis Barnstone remains apt: "A formal poet, she has all the freshness of daring free verse."

—John Roche

ALBIACH, Anne-Marie

Nationality: French. Born: 1937. Career: Founding editor, with Claude Royet-Journoud and Michel Courtier, of the journal Siécle à mains.

PUBLICATIONS

Poetry

Flammigère. Paris, Siècle à mains, 1967.
Etat. Paris, Mercure de France, 1971; translated by Keith Waldrop, n.p., Awede, 1988.
"H II" linéaires. N.p., Le Collet de Buffle, 1974.
CÉSURE: le corps, avec des collages originaux de Raquel. Paris, Orange Export, 1975.
Objet. Paris, Orange Export, 1976.

Mezza Voce. Paris, Flammarion, 1984; translated by Joseph Simas
and others, Sausalito, California, Post-Apollo Press, 1988.
Anawratha. Le Revest-les-Eaux, France, Spectres familiers,
1984.
"Figure vocative." N.p., Lettres de casse, 1985; translated by
Anthony Barnett and Joseph Simas as *"Vocative Figure,"* n.p.,
Moving Letters Press, 1986.
"Le chemin de l'ermitage." N.p., Premiere Saline, 1986.

Other

Translator, *"A,"* by Louis Zukofsky, in *Vingt poètes américains.*
Paris, Gallimard, 1980.
Translator, *Poéme de mémoire,* by Keith Waldrop. Paris, Orange
Export, 1982.

*   *   *

With the publication of *État,* her second collection of poetry,
Anne-Marie Albiach established herself as one of the most re-
spected and influential figures of the French literary avant-garde.
Since then, her work has won the attention and respect of leading
American writers as diverse as Michael Palmer, Rosmarie Waldrop,
and Paul Auster. Much of Albiach's work deviates from tradi-
tional syntax and semantics. Experimenting with punctuation, spac-
ing and typography, many of her poems also abandon stanzaic
divisions, isolating and dispersing words and phrases in what
Michael Palmer has described as a "theater of the page." This pro-
cess of semantic and syntactic dislocation does not merely create
a multiplicity of referential orientations. Its purpose is also to
convey the full complexity of the subject's attempts at self-ex-
pression. Instead of privileging the sense of emotional intimacy
associated with the traditional lyric, Albiach indeed opts for what
she terms, in *État,* a "(lyricism) of precision" in which subjectiv-
ity is the measure of the gap between the perceiving subject and
her object:

"I have perpetrated on you
by my incompetence
this lapsus"

                    that in the space
of a memory

he I'm afraid
falls with the earth

trajectory of the object
                where the trajectory
would recover the subject

Albiach's use of the page as an "open field" unencumbered
by formal constraints sketches out a network of linguistic rela-
tionships whose logic is to be unveiled by the reader's own
intellectual and associative competence. Conveying gaps,
caesurae, hesitations, relationships, and silences that are inevi-
tably repressed by the linear nature of conventional modes of
writing and reading, Albiach's poem tangents to different alter-

native patterns by which to understand "the splendor of syntax
and of rhythm." The opening "quotation"—which points to the
unreliability and treacherousness of language—is also typical of
Albiach's desire to create a polyphonic space around which ral-
lies a movement for change suggesting different manners of facing
oneself and each other. One could also compare the syncopated
structure of Albiach's poems with that of a music score weaving
a wide range of intonations and cadences into a contrapuntal tex-
ture whose meaning resides above all in the distances and rela-
tionships between its various components. The opening sequence
from *Sketch: "the cold,"* the seventh section of *Mezza Voce,* reads
like a manifesto of Albiach's differential poetics:

"The red facade of this 20th century
building reflects in the water of its
windows how and where breath has
been transferred . . ."

                        "the ground opens—the music
            reveals the order of renewal
            —the deviation—
                        this violent dissociation
operates the cut:
                                reflexiveness
                    of the statement undoing itself—"

retreat's stave
runs through speech
            "and its resonances"

the gap amplifies the Discourse

        "tension   takes on
                    graphic figure"

    in the impossible   from one body
                                        to the Other

This passage is emblematic of Albiach's ability to engage in a theo-
retical reflection on the materiality of the visual and aural repre-
sentation of language. The initial quotation, which parodies the
expository rhetoric of guidebooks, is a good example of Albiach's
capacity to subvert the language of logic or, rather, to create logi-
cal statements that are liable to "undo themselves." The reference
to the "transfer" of breath reminds us that Albiach's writing strat-
egies, despite their commitment to abstraction, are not strictly
scriptural and still preserve the vocal (or sub-vocal) quality of
the lyric.

As suggested by the closing fragments of the above-quoted pas-
sage, poetic language, in Albiach's *Mezza Voce,* is also the site of
an impossible but nevertheless highly productive dialogue between
a disembodied mouth and an inarticulate body whose contours
and gestures are awaiting definition. Also typical of Albiach's po-
etry is her translation of physical and psychological tensions into
graphic, and primarily geometrical, terms. In the opening section
of *Mezza Voce,* Albiach's interest in the intersecting trajectories
of language and the body is articulated through the more conven-
tionally discursive cadences of prose poetry (a medium to which
Albiach returned to in a more recent work titled *"Le chemin de
l'ermitage"*):

In the power of his geometric statements, he had perhaps
established it at right angles to the irreversible. An ocular
    BLUE
would be his result, transmitted by retinal and memory
    impressions.

Here as elsewhere in Albiach's poetry, the focus remains on the
conjugated geometries of self and world, as well as on the effect
of linguistic structures on the individual consciousness. The re-
sult is an alternate mode of the lyric alternating between corpo-
real and linguistic realities, creating a juncture between mind and
body, subject and object—a principle of linguistic and phenom-
enological uncertainty that becomes a tribute to what Albiach calls
the "imponderables of desire."

—Michel Delville

ALEXANDER, Meena

Nationality: Indian. **Born:** Allahabad, 17 February 1951. **Edu-
cation:** Unity High School, Khartoum, Sudan, graduated 1964;
University of Khartoum, B.A. (honors) 1969; University of
Nottingham, Ph.D. in English 1973. **Family:** Married David
Lelyveld in 1979; one son and one daughter. **Career:** Tutor in
English, University of Khartoum, 1969; lecturer in English, Uni-
versity of Delhi, 1974, and Central Institute of English and For-
eign Languages, Hyderabad, 1975-77; CSIR Fellow, Jawaharlal
Nehru University, New Delhi, 1975; lecturer, 1977-79, and reader,
1979, University of Hyderabad; visiting fellow, Sorbonne, Paris,
1979; assistant professor of English, Fordham University, Bronx,
New York, 1980-87; assistant professor, 1987-89, associate pro-
fessor, 1989-91, and professor 1992—, Hunter College and the
Graduate Centre, City University of New York. Visiting assistant
professor, University of Minnesota, Minneapolis, 1981; lecturer
in writing, Columbia University, 1991—; visiting university grants
commission fellow, English Institute, University of Kerala,
Trivandrum, 1987; writer-in-residence, Centre for American Cul-
ture Studies, Columbia University, New York, 1988; MacDowell
Colony fellow, 1993; poet-in-residence, American College,
Madurai, India, 1994; Arts Council of England international writer-
in-residence, 1995. **Awards:** National Endowment for the Humani-
ties travel grant, 1985; New York State Council for the Arts grant,
1988. **Agent:** Louise Quayle, Ellen Levine Agency, 15 East 26th
Street, Suite 1801, New York, New York 10010. **Address:** En-
glish Department, Hunter College, City University of New York,
695 Park Avenue, New York, New York 10021, U.S.A.

PUBLICATIONS

Poetry

The Bird's Bright Ring. Calcutta, Writers Workshop, 1976.
I Root My Name. Calcutta, United Writers, 1977.
Without Place. Calcutta, Writers Workshop, 1978.
Stone Roots. New Delhi, Arnold Heinemann, 1980.
House of a Thousand Doors. Washington, D.C., Three Continents
    Press, 1988.
The Storm. New York, Red Dust, 1989.

Night-Scene, the Garden. New York, Red Dust, 1992.
River and Bridge. New Delhi, Rupa, 1995.
The Shock of Arrival: Reflections on Postcolonial Experience. Bos-
    ton, South End Press, 1996.

Novels

Nampally Road. San Francisco, Mercury House, 1991.
Manhattan Music. San Francisco, Mercury House, 1997.

Play

In the Middle Earth. New Delhi, Enact, 1977.
Other

The Poetic Self: Towards a Phenomenology of Romanticism. New
    Delhi, Arnold Heinemann, 1979; Atlantic Highlands, New Jer-
    sey, Humanities Press, 1980.
*Women in Romanticism: Mary Wollstonecraft, Dorothy
    Wordsworth, and Mary Shelley.* London, Macmillan, 1989.
Fault Lines (memoir). New York, Feminist Press, 1993.

*

Critical Studies: "Exiled by a Woman's Body: Substantial Phe-
nomena in the Poetry of Meena Alexander," by John Oliver Perry
in *Journal of South Asian Literature* (East Lansing, Michigan), vol.
21, no. 1, Winter / Spring 1986; "The Inward Body: Meena
Alexander's Feminist Strategies of Poetry," by John Oliver Perry
in *Feminism and Literature,* edited by K. Radha, Trivandrum, Uni-
versity of Kerala, 1987; "Poetry, Language and Feminism: The
Writings of Meena Alexander" by K. Raveendran, in *Kala Gomati*
(Kerala), October 1987; "Meena Alexander's Poetry" by
Konnakuzhy Ittira, in *Mathrubhumi* (Kerala), 1989. "Meena
Alexander" by Denise Knight, in *Reworlding: Writers of the In-
dian Diaspora,* Westport, Connecticut, Greenwood Press, 1993;
"Towards the Creation of a Vital Aesthetics: A Survey of Con-
temporary Indian English Poetry and Criticism with Special Ref-
erence to Meena Alexander" by Sumitra Mukerji, in *Journal of
the School of Languages,* no. 3, 1993; "The Poetry of Multiple
Migrations" by Hema Nair, in *Ms.,* January / February 1994.

Meena Alexander comments:

Sometimes people one has just met will say, "What sort of po-
ems do you write?" It seems fair enough as a question but I am
always hard put to reply. Poems about childbirth, poems about
my grandparents' small town in Kerala, on the southwest coast
of India, poems about coming to America, short poems, irregular
sonnets, long poems, poems of sexual desire, all of that would be
true. But even to say that seems such a bits-and-pieces answer—
after all what can one do except move in memory to the dense
particularity of each poem? But perhaps I can try now to sketch
out a rough map, an internal geography, as it were, formed by the
poems.

The volume of poetry *House of a Thousand Doors* I think of
as a beginning. The grandmother figure in it is drawn from
memory and dream, she stands as a power permitting me to
speak in an alien landscape. The sense of newness, of the per-
sistent difficulty of another landscape, another life, becomes
in those poems part of a search for a precarious truth. My
two long poems *The Storm* and *Night-Scene, The Garden,* both

published in 1989, were composed side by side in roughly a year and a half, starting in 1986. Together they form part of a poetic autobiography. The first moves from a vivid childhood memory, my father's father tearing down the ancestral house in Kozencheri to build a modern one. It moves then to the repeated passages away from that first home, taking in airports, dislocations, war. It ends with a "bitten self / cast back into its intimate wreckage." *Night-Scene* I think of as female, dealing with the molten stuff that lies between a mother and a daughter, between a daughter and her maternal home. This poem, which was performed Off-Off-Broadway in 1988, is set in my mother's ancestral house in Tiruvella, in contemporary India. The language takes in the roughness, the crudity of speech. Unlike *The Storm* which contemplates, frames, this poem swallows chaosses. I think of it, foolishly perhaps, as "unformed," though readers have seen a persistent patterning in it. In my own mind it is related to the poem "Passion" composed in 1986 about the aftermath of childbirth. Now I am working on a series of short poems, 14 to 20 lines in length, which bring together the two landscapes of my life, that of rural Kerala and that of Manhattan, city of subways and dark underground passages.

*   *   *

In the 1980 essay "Exiled by a Dead Script," Meena Alexander articulates the dilemma of the Indian poet writing in English. Calling Indian English "a nowhere language," Alexander suggests that the poet "necessarily grasps himself as exiled ... estranged from the place around him, whose body cannot appropriate its given landscape." In words strikingly similar to those of Canadian poet Dennis Lee, whose "Cadence, Country, Silence: Writing in Colonial Space" was taken by a generation of Canadian poets to articulate their postcolonial condition of silence, Alexander writes that Indian English poets must "resolutely refuse exile, the language itself must transform. It must contort itself to become mimetic of *muteness—their muteness* which is appropriated as the poet's own." She suggests that her and others' writing in India is marked by two sorts of "terror"—"babble" and "non-sense," because of the imperial history of English in India, which "will always remain a colonizing power till those whom it oppresses steal it for themselves, rupture its syntax till it is capable of naming the very structures of oppression."

Alexander's own poetry is marked by a tension, then, between different traditions of poetry, history, myth, and language. A highly Imagistic poetry, her work attempts, at times somewhat romantically (Alexander's academic expertise in English Romantic poetry often resonates in her own creative work), to make sense of and create a place in the various worlds the poet finds herself inhabiting:

I learn song is being:

That song might be being as Rilke dreamt
I sing for all who work head bent
close against the great red sun
who labour tooth nail sinew bone
against glass metalpaper stone
through sting of sand and lash of snow
they carve this rock to make a sky to breathe in

They forge that land
where Song has second place
and Being thrives alone.

Images, syntax, and structures reminiscent, then, of Coleridge and especially Eliot, of Rilke and Neruda, for the reader trained in a European tradition, are also inflected by Indian rhythms, syntax, structures, and stories. Some of Alexander's best early poetry also uncovers the contested space between individual memory, national history, and the poet's attempt to recreate being and identity through writing. In the long poem *The Bird's Bright Ring,* for example, her typical use of (among others) recurring images of blood, flowers, salt, birds, and animals finds effective and powerful juxtaposition with the consequences of British rule in India:

The writhing subsides
but the dark space
still cuts the air
my sight
        you said

"It was here the shadow fell
the shadow of the British soldiers
here
    here
        they dragged their guns
over the slope to the cleft of the Ridge
1857 a cold bad winter and they broke our backs."...

"Not only shadows fell that cold hard winter
But bruises like down from hidden veins of porphyry
as the belly of the mother
was torn open
wrought metal
cold cannon
sharp cleft
of bayonet and sword..."

Later in this poem, as in other verse, contemporary politics also interrupt, often violently; poem XIV in *The Bird's Bright Ring* consists only of documents: a calendar advertisement, a call for protest, and a newspaper article describing police violence in 1974. Such disjunctures between a poetry rich in imagery and the poet's / speaker's explicit concerns mark the skepticism and hybridization of much postcolonial poetry. Ben Downing writes in a review of her work, "Attracted to both the 'hierarchical unity' of Indian tradition and a modern, Western poetics of rupture, Alexander is faced with the difficult necessity of mediating between them."

This process of poetic mediation and meditation becomes more marked with Alexander's double exile: her immigration to the United States. Alexander herself suggests that the poems "Hotel Alexandria," "Broadway Poem"—"my first 'American' poem"—and "Waiting for Rain" are attempts to bridge internal cultural displacement and the fragmentation of identity that comes with it; these early "American" poems "permitted an erasure of difference," momentary consolation, even though they simultaneously write of "the gulf of not-knowing, a pit, a placelessness" that has doubled and redoubled upon the existing placelessness of being a postcolonial Indian English poet. Although exploring the "discrepant nature of what I found myself to be in America," Alexander's poetry has continued to be predominantly Indian in image, content, and use of myth and history.

15

Alexander's speakers, always female, attempt to articulate these discrepancies by recalling and rewriting specifically female experience. Alexander is considered to be a feminist poet; her populism, her return to the political and historical moment, is often addressed to and for women: "Women of Delhi / You do not see how centuries of dream are flowing from your land / And so I sing knowing poetry to be like bread." The collection *I Root My Name,* containing more intimate poetry, reflects the pain of a woman's experience, as, for instance, in "After the Wedding": "I did not think I would try to die / when yesterday they hennaed my hands / in the patterns of stars and moons / and flowers, for joy."

A longer poem, "A Mirror's Grace" in *Without Place,* rewrites the story of Cleopatra, linking the position of the female speaker / poet to that of Cleopatra who, like the postcolonial poet, finds herself rendered inauthentic in a patriarchal language:

> This is a poem about Cleopatra
> she did not tell her brilliance
> to its mirrors, so broke his wings...
>
> A poem by a woman, wiping
> her voice dry of fire
> and flood, reining it
>
> to speech which is not hers
> though its syllables
> cut her dusty footsoles.

The poet's remembering through poetry takes the shape of childhood reminiscences in which women—sisters, mothers, especially grandmothers—figure prominently in the creation of self. Alexander explains that her "House of a Thousand Doors" is about a poeticized grandmother, citing the poem "Her Garden" to "explain the haunting inexistence of my grandmother": "She died so long / before my birth / that we are one, entirely / as a sky disowned by sun and star: / a bleakness beneath my dreams." For Alexander, the recovering or uncovering of personal and cultural history through poetry is archaeological, and the mother or grandmother is a figuration of that unearthing: "Why do I turn to her?... Answering my own question backwards. There seems to be no-one else. No-one else, that is, from whom I can draw both the lines of ancestry and poetry. And she both is and is not real." Mother / grandmother / sister also symbolize for the poet her "mother tongue, which is pure speech"; for Alexander this is Malayalam, a language in which she is illiterate and upon whose oral patterns, childhood patterns, she overwrites English, "the colonial language which I must melt down to my purposes."

Alexander's 1989 work *The Storm* continues in this project of rescuing and re-creating memory. Perhaps more clearly autobiographical than some of her other poetry, the poem is narrated in fragments, echoing in title, in structure, and in the opening metaphoric scene of burial the modernist dream of "shoring fragments against one's ruin," the feminist dream of creating a sense of self and identity through the fragments of a life remembered, and the ongoing poetic project of celebrating and decrying the postcolonial fragmentation of self / culture / nation, of (re)writing in order to create new, hybrid, and fluid political and personal identities. Thus, Alexander manages to provide another temporary appearance of closure and resolution, attempting in her poetry to translate, "in the old sense of transporting, of ferrying across," "the gap, the cleft there between wordless intimacy and functioning script [which] is so co-equal in intensity with the fissures, the sudden cracks in my daily life." *The Storm* thus provides the poetic illusion of mediating between "pure" experience and the act of poetic re-creation:

> With the bleached mesh of root
> exposed after rainfall
> my bitten self cast back
> into its intimate wreckage
> each jot poised, apart, particular
> lovely and rare.
> The end of life delved back
> into the heart of it all.

Autobiography continues to thread its way through Alexander's work, which has broadened into fiction—the novels *Nampally Road* and *Manhattan Music* that straddle each side of her geographical experience—and her 1993 memoir *Fault Lines,* where she begins:

> Multiple birth dates ripple, sing inside me, as if a long stretch of silk were passing through my fingers. I think of the lives I have known for forty years, the lives unknown, the shining geographies that feed into the substance of any possible story I might have.

—Aruna Srivastava

ALLEN, Paula Gunn

Nationality: American. **Born:** Cubero, New Mexico, in 1939. **Education:** Holder of B.A., M.F.A., degrees; University of New Mexico, Ph.D. in American studies. **Career:** Lecturer, San Francisco State University, University of New Mexico, Albuquerque, and Fort Lewis College, Durango, California; professor of ethnic and Native American studies, then professor of English, University of California, Berkeley; currently professor of English, University of California, Los Angeles. **Awards:** National Endowment for the Arts award; Ford Foundation grant; American Book Award, 1990, for *Spider Woman's Granddaughters.* **Address:** Department of English, University of California—Los Angeles, 405 Hilgard Ave., Los Angeles, California 90024-1301, U.S.A.

PUBLICATIONS

Poetry

The Blind Lion. Berkeley, California, Thorp Springs Press, 1974.
Coyote's Daylight Trip. Albuquerque, La Confluencia, 1978.
A Cannon between My Knees. New York, Strawberry Hill Press, 1981.
Star Child. Marvin, South Dakota, Blue Cloud Quarterly, 1981.
Shadow Country. Los Angeles, University of California Indian Studies Center, 1982.

Wyrds. San Francisco, Taurean Horn, 1987.
Skins and Bones. Albuquerque, West End, 1988.
Life Is a Fatal Disease. Albuquerque, West End, 1996.

Novel

The Woman Who Owned the Shadows. San Francisco, Spinsters /
   Aunt Lute Books, 1983.

Other

Sipapu: A Cultural Perspective. Albuquerque, University of New
   Mexico Press, 1975.
*The Sacred Hoop: Recovering the Feminine in American Indian
   Traditions.* Boston, Beacon Press, 1986; portion published as
   "Lesbians in American Indian Cultures," in *Hidden from His-
   tory: Reclaiming the Gay and Lesbian Past,* edited by Martin
   Bauml Duberman, Martha Vicinus, and George Chauncey Jr.,
   New York, New American Library, 1989.
Grandmothers of the Light: A Medicine Woman's Sourcebook. Bos-
   ton, Beacon Press, 1991.
Indian Perspectives. Southwest Parks and Monuments Associa-
   tion, 1992.
As Long as the Rivers Flow: The Stories of 9 Native Americans,
   with Patricia Clark Smith. New York, Scholastic Press, 1996.

Editor, *From the Center: A Folio: Native American Art and Po-
   etry.* New York, Strawberry Hill Press, 1981.
Editor, *Studies in American Indian Literature: Critical Essays and
   Course Design.* New York, Modern Language Association, 1983.
Editor, *Spider Woman's Granddaughters: Traditional Tales and
   Contemporary Writing by Native American Women.* New York,
   Fawcett, 1990.
Editor, *Voice of the Turtle: American Indian Literature, 1900-1970.*
   New York, Ballantine, 1994.
Editor, *Song of the Turtle: American Indian Literature, 1974-1995.*
   New York, Ballantine, 1996.

*

Critical Studies: "Paula Gunn Allen (Laguna-Sioux-Lebanese)"
by John R. Milton, in *Four Indian Poets,* Vermillion, South Da-
kota, n.p., 1974; "A Laddered, Rain-bearing Rug: Paula Gunn
Allen's Poetry" by Elaine Jahner, in *Women and Western Litera-
ture,* edited by Helen Winter Stauffer and Susan Rosowski, Troy,
New York, Whitston, 1982; "A MELUS Interview: Paula Gunn
Allen" by Franchot Ballinger and Brian Swann, in *MELUS,* vol.
10, no. 2, Summer 1983; "Paula Gunn Allen and Joy Harjo: Clos-
ing the Distance between Personal and Mythic Space" by James
Ruppert, in *American Indian Quarterly,* vol. 7, no. 1, 1983; "I
Climb the Mesas in My Dreams: An Interview with Paula Gunn
Allen" in *Survival This Way: Interviews with American Indian Po-
ets* by Joseph Bruchac, Tucson, Sun Tracks / University of Ari-
zona Press, 1987; "Paula Gunn Allen, 'The Autobiography of a
Confluence'" in *I Tell You Now: Autobiographical Essays by Na-
tive American Writers,* edited by Brian Swann and Arnold Krupat,
Lincoln, University of Nebraska Press, 1987; "Native American
Literature" by Patricia Holt, in *San Francisco Chronicle,* 2 July
1989; *Paula Gunn Allen* by Elizabeth I. Hanson, Boise State Uni-
versity Press, 1990; "The Journey Back to Female Roots: A La-
guna Pueblo Model" by Annette Van Dyke, in *Lesbian Texts and*

Contexts: Radical Revisions, edited by Karla Jay and Joanne
Glasgow, New York University Press, 1990; *Winged Words: Ameri-
can Indian Writers Speak* by Laura Coltelli, Lincoln, University
of Nebraska Press, 1990; *Women Reading Women Writing: Self-
Invention in Paula Gunn Allen, Gloria Anzaldua, and Audre Lorde*
by AnnaLouise Keating, Philadelphia, Temple University Press,
1996; "Desire's Revision: Feminist Appropriation of Native
American Traditional Sources" by Victoria Bynton, in *Modern
Language Studies,* vol. 26, no. 2-3, Spring / Summer 1996.

*   *   *

Of Laguana, Sioux, Lebanese, and Scottish descent, lesbian Paula
Gunn Allen has written successfully in a variety of genres. Her *Stud-
ies in American Indian Literature* (1983), for example, was a ground-
breaking volume of essays, and her *The Sacred Hoop: Recovering
the Feminine in American Indian Tradition* (1986), which investigates
woman's place in Native American culture, is the penultimate word
on the topic. She has also written a novel, *The Woman Who Owned
the Shadows* (1983), and edited a number of anthologies. Yet, the pub-
lication of her most recent book, *Life Is a Fatal Disease: Collected
Poems, 1962-1995* (1997), has crowned Allen's career as a writer,
firmly establishing her place not only in women's poetry, in Native
American women's poetry, and in lesbian poetry but, more impor-
tant, in 20th-century American poetry as a whole.

While mostly written as free verse, Allen's poetry tends to-
ward the narrative and, to a lesser extent, the lyric, with an occa-
sional prose poem. Her principal focus is Native American top-
ics, individuals, and events regardless of the gender or sexual ori-
entation of the individuals who appear or are referred to in the
poems. In her most often anthologized poem, "Pocahontas to Her
English Husband, John Rolfe," which is also her most famous one,
Allen assumes the persona of the historical Native American
woman and corrects the record that has been handed down to us
by tradition. The help Pocahontas actually gave Rolfe—and, by
extension, the help that, historically, many natives gave whites
exploring or settling the North American continent—is succinctly
enumerated and clarified, as is what Pocahontas earned for her
troubles: tuberculosis, "a wasting / putrefying Christian death."

Allen has written other persona-based narratives (one each
from the point of view of the Mayan Malinal, the Iroquois
Molly Brant, and the Shoshone Sacagawea) that also investi-
gate native-white relationships in an historical setting, but her
interest in native-white relationships isn't limited to the past.
Whether she's investigating her uncles's life ("Never Cry
Uncle"), the forced sterilization of native women ("Laguna La-
dies Luncheon"), children ("Teaching Poetry at Votech High,
Santa Fe, the Week John Lennon Was Shot"), or love ("The
Blind Lion"), Allen welds the personal and the political together
into a seamless representation of Native-American life in the
last moments of the twentieth century.

In the lovely lyric "Moonshot: 1969," for example, she inves-
tigates technology's influence on contemporary life and, perhaps
more important, on one of the most important emblems of our
time, the moon as a symbol of romance:

   But I love you.
   How equate the moonlight falling
   soft across your shoulders with ash and stone
   so deceptively light, impossibly cohesive?
   Where They are is not where we have been.

In "Some like Indians Endure," she draws a parallel between the lives and fate of Native Americans and of lesbians:

> they were massacred
> lots of times
> they always came back
> like the grass
> like the clouds
> they got massacred again.

That both Native Americans and lesbians "always came back" is a concept that lies at the core of Allen's poetry and is the foundation of her poetic vision. Her collections of poetry remind us over and over again that, regardless of how harmful contemporary life may be to the "tribe" or to the individual, there is in each human being an indomitable spirit that will continue despite what happens in the physical world, offering all peoples hope.

—Jim Elledge

ALVI, Moniza

Nationality: British. **Born:** Lahore, Pakistan, 2 February 1954. **Education:** University of York, 1973-76, B.A. in English (honors) 1976; Whitelands College, London, 1976-77, postgraduate certificate in education 1977; London University Institute of Education, 1982-85, M.A. in education 1985. **Family:** Married Robert Coe in 1995. **Career:** Teacher, Scott Lidgett School, London, 1978-80. Since 1980 teacher, and since 1989, head of English department, Aylwin School, London. **Awards:** Poetry Business prize (co-winner with Peter Daniels), 1992. **Address:** c/o Oxford University Press, Walton St., Oxford OX2 6DP, England.

PUBLICATIONS

Poetry

Peacock Luggage, with Peter Daniels. London, Smith Doorstop Books, 1992.
The Country at My Shoulder. Oxford and New York, Oxford University Press, 1993.
A Bowl of Warm Air. Oxford and New York, Oxford University Press, 1996.

*

Moniza Alvi comments:

With *The Country at My Shoulder,* I found myself recreating a past, as if to introduce the possibility of returning in my actual life to my birthplace, Pakistan, which I left when a few months old. Now having made the return visit, I am working on a group of poems centered in my impressions of family and country. The points where East and West converge are crucial. The poems which do not concern my Asian background are equally important to me. I am attracted to the strange-seeming and to fantasy, and find there some essence of experience. I have written about Pakistan partly because it was, in the first instance, a fantasy. It is difficult to say who has influenced

me. Edward Thomas, Jacques Prévert, and Stevie Smith are amongst those poets who have made a strong impression. When I started writing seriously, I was reading Angela Carter's work and J. G. Ballard's science fiction. I have probably been as much influenced by prose writers as by poets.

*   *   *

Moniza Alvi writes in a beautifully controlled conversational style lit by flashes of fantasy. The titles of some of her poems indicate this: "I Was Raised in a Glove Compartment," "I Would Like to Be a Dot in a Painting by Miro," and "The Great Pudding." In "A Map of India" she tells us that, when she looks at a map,

> If I stare at the country long enough
> I can prise it off the paper,
> lift it like a flap of skin.

Alvi's idiosyncratic vision can be seen as a way of coming to terms with worlds not only distant geographically but also disparate in cultures and ethos. Her poetry is an exploration toward the reconciliation of these worlds and the discovery of her place in them. Her worlds are also those of inner landscapes, as in the poem "Houdini":

> It is not clear how he entered me
> or why he always has to escape.

More importantly, they are worlds to which the only joint key is the imagination, as in "Afternoon at the Cinema":

> The film—you've seen it before—
> it was a mystery then, and now you've missed
> the sheet with the interpretations on it.

For years Pakistan, where Alvi was born, was an imaginary world to her, for she left it for England when she was only a few months old. It was not until much later that she returned to Pakistan to visit and meet relatives there. Before that time the exploration of the world of her cultural origins had to be via the images in her mind. It is no wonder that she writes

> There's a country at my shoulder,
> growing larger—soon it will burst,
> rivers will spill out, run down my chest.

These are the first lines of the title poem of her collection *The Country at My Shoulder,* and they set the theme for much of the book.

The poem "Presents from My Aunt in Pakistan" touches on the feeding of the vision of Alvi's imagined world and the sense of contrast and ironies the presents conveyed. While the aunt sent gifts of exotic garments—a salwar kameez peacock-blue, embossed slippers, saris, and candy-striped glass bangles, "alien in the sitting room"—these were accompanied by requests for cardigans from Marks & Spencers. These were the clues to the Pakistan that Alvi had to embrace via her imagination and language ("The Country at My Shoulder"):

> I water the country with English rain,
> cover it with English words.
> Soon it will burst, or fall like a meteor.

Alvi is aware of the complexity of her intentions ("Hindi Urdu Bol Chaal"):

> I introduce myself to two languages,
> but there are so many—of costume,
> of conduct and courtesy.

Her intentions are to discover where her twin cultures converge. It is an exploration that is clearly related to the discovery of her own identity vis-à-vis the cultures. In "You Are Turning Me into a Novel" she says,

> In the great silent hour
> you are giving me a title
> fashioning me, coaxing me.

It is Alvi's ability to explore and come to terms with her world imaginatively that is the special quality of the poetry. The clarity of her direct and transparently honest approach is what illuminates it.

—John Cotton

ANGELOU, Maya

Nationality: American. **Born:** Marguerita Johnson, St. Louis, Missouri, 4 April 1928. **Education:** Attended schools in Arkansas and California; studied music privately, dance with Martha Graham, Pearl Primus, and Ann Halprin, and drama with Frank Silvera and Gene Frankel. **Family:** Married 1) Tosh Angelou (divorced); 2) Paul de Feu in 1973 (divorced); one son. **Career:** Actress and singer; associate editor, *Arab Observer*, Cairo, 1961-62; assistant administrator, School of Music and Drama, University of Ghana Institute of African Studies, Legon and Accra, 1963-66; freelance writer for *Ghanaian Times* and Ghanaian Broadcasting Corporation, both Accra, 1963-65; feature editor, *African Review*, Accra, 1964-66; lecturer, University of California, Los Angeles, 1966; writer-in-residence or visiting professor, University of Kansas, Lawrence, 1970, Wake Forest University, Winston-Salem, North Carolina, 1974, Wichita State University, Kansas, 1974, and California State University, Sacramento, 1974. Reynolds Professor, Wake Forest University, 1981—. Northern coordinator, Southern Christian Leadership Conference, 1959-60. Also composer, television host and interviewer, and writer for Oprah Winfrey television series *Brewster Place*. **Awards:** Yale University fellowship, 1970; Rockefeller grant, 1975; *Ladies Home Journal* award, 1976. Also the recipient of numerous other awards and honors, including the North Carolina Award in Literature, 1987; Langston Hughes award, City College of New York, 1991; Innaugural poet for President Bill Clinton, 1993; Grammy, for Best Spoken Word Album, 1994; NAACP Spingarn Award, 1994. Honorary degrees: Smith College, Northampton, Massachusetts, 1975; Mills College, Oakland, California, 1975; Lawrence University, Appleton, Wisconsin, 1976. **Member:** American Revolution Bicentennial Council, 1975-76; board of trustees, American Film Institute, 1975; advisory board, Women's Prison Association; Harlem Writers Guild; National Commission on the Observance of International Women's Year. **Agent:** Lordly & Dame Inc., 51 Church Street, Boston, Massachusetts 02116-5493, U.S.A.

PUBLICATIONS

Poetry

Just Give Me a Cool Drink of Water 'fore I Diiie. New York, Random House, 1971; London, Virago Press, 1988.
Oh Pray My Wings Are Gonna Fit Me Well. New York, Random House, 1975.
And Still I Rise. New York, Random House, 1978; London, Virago Press, 1986.
Poems. New York, Bantam, 1981.
Shaker, Why Don't You Sing? New York, Random House, 1983.
Now Sheba Sings the Song. New York, Dial Press, and London, Virago Press, 1987.
I Shall Not Be Moved. New York, Bantam Books, 1991.
The Complete Collected Poems. New York, Random House, 1994.
Phenomenal Woman: Four Poems for Women. New York, Random House, 1996.

Recordings: *Miss Calypso,* Liberty, 1957; *The Poetry of Maya Angelou,* GWP, 1969; *Women in Business,* University of Wisconsin, 1981.

Plays

Cabaret for Freedom (revue), with Godfrey Cambridge (produced New York, 1960).
The Least of These (produced Los Angeles, 1966).
Ajax, from the play by Sophocles (produced Los Angeles, 1974).
And Still I Rise (also director: produced Oakland, California, 1976).
King (lyrics only, with Alistair Beaton), book by Lonne Elder III, music by Richard Blackford (produced London, 1990).
Moon on a Rainbow Shawl (produced London, 1988).

Screenplays: *Georgia, Georgia,* 1972; *All Day Long,* 1974.

Television Plays: *Sisters, Sisters,* with John Berry, 1982; *Brewster Place* (series).

Television Documentaries: *Black, Blues, Black,* 1968; *Assignment America,* 1975; *The Legacy,* 1976; *The Inheritors,* 1976; *Trying to Make It Home (Byline* series), 1988; *Maya Angelou's America: A Journey of the Heart* (also host); *Who Cares about Kids, Kindred Spirits, Maya Angelou: Rainbow in the Clouds,* and *To the Contrary* (all Public Broadcasting Service productions).

Other

I Know Why the Caged Bird Sings. New York, Random House, 1970; London, Virago Press, 1984.
Gather Together in My Name. New York, Random House, 1974; London, Virago Press, 1985.
Singin' and Swingin' and Gettin' Merry Like Christmas. New York, Random House, 1976; London, Virago Press, 1985.
The Heart of a Woman. New York, Random House, 1981; London, Virago Press, 1986.
All God's Children Need Traveling Shoes. New York, Random House, 1986; London, Virago Press, 1987.

Mrs. Flowers: A Moment of Friendship (for children). Minneapolis, Redpath Press, 1986.
Conversations with Maya Angelou, edited by Jeffrey M. Elliot. University of Mississippi, and London, Virago Press, 1989.
Wouldn't Take Nothing for My Journey Now. New York, Random House, 1993.

*

Manuscript Collection: Wake Forest University, Winston-Salem, North Carolina.

Theatrical Activities:
Director: **Plays**—*And Still I Rise,*Oakland, California, 1976; *Moon on a Rainbow Shawl* by Errol John, London, 1988; **Film**—*All Day Long,* 1974. Actress: **Plays**—in *Porgy and Bess* by George Gershwin, tour, 1954-55; *Calypso Heatwave,* New York, 1957; *The Blacks* by Jean Genet, New York, 1960; *Cabaret for Freedom,* New York, 1960; *Mother Courage* by Berthold Brecht, Accra, Ghana, 1964; *Medea,* Hollywood, 1966; *Look Away,* New York, 1973; **Film**—*Roots,* 1977; *How to Make an American Quilt,* 1996.

*   *   *

While Maya Angelou's autobiographical novels have consistently sold in the millions, her poetry received little serious critical attention for several decades. Then her poem for President Clinton's first inauguration was republished in her *Collected Poems* (1995), causing an increase of comment, critical studies, and scholarship about her life and accomplishments. Harold Bloom, the distinguished professor at Yale University, has included Angelou in his series of study guides, an accolade that places her in a significant cannon of literature.

Despite such academic interest, Angelou's poetry is not serious; rather, it is, as she herself puts it in the title poem of her volume *And Still I Rise,* "sassy." "Sassy" implies—we should assume from her own words—that "the impudent child was detested by God, and a shame to its parents and could bring destruction to its house..." This use of litotes is congenial with a peculiar sort of "coding," as with kenning. Thus, "God's candle bright" is more of a token for the sun than a metaphor. So, too, the title of her autobiography, *I Know Why the Caged Bird Sings,* is not a sentimental metaphor, but a litotes for humiliation. In her poetry understatement is a style for presenting a shared experience, in its inconsistency and its energy, and the coding can reinforce the anger implied by the humor, as in "Sepia Fashion Show":

Their hair, pomaded, faces jaded
bones protruding, hip-wise,
The models strutted, backed and butted,
Then stuck their mouths out, lip-wise.

They'd nasty manners, held like banners,
while they looked down their nose-wise,
I'd see 'em in hell, before they'd sell
me one thing they're wearing, clothes-wise.

The Black Bourgeois, who all say "yah"
When yeah is what they're meaning
Should look around, both up and down
before they set out preening.

"Indeed" they swear, "that's what I'll wear
When I go country-clubbing,"
I'd remind them please, look at those knees
you got a Miss Ann's scrubbing.

The last line strikes the ear as comic, and we share that sense of it, but then we react as we remember that black women literally had to show their knees to prove how hard they had cleaned. That change—the hearing, and then the reaction—is central to her poetry.

The best starting place for a background to Angelou's poetry is her own best-selling autobiography, *I Know Why the Caged Birds Sings,* which has received a comprehensive and probing study. As a child, Angelou was caged in by abuse, prejudices, and poverty, from which she escaped by her character and also by the crucial discovery that a voice can deepen the "shades of meaning" and serve as a way to form connections with other people.

She has intense social interests, as in her response to the Ebonics controversy during the mid-1990s, or earlier, her coming to the defense of Washington, D.C., mayor Marion Barry. She was a member of the Commission for the International Women's Year during the presidency of Jimmy Carter, and she was the Northern Coordinator for the Southern Leadership Conference for Dr. Martin Luther King. There is a Maya Angelou Community Project in Portland, Oregon, and she appears frequently at conferences. She is a professor at Wake Forest University in North Carolina.

Angelou has been a cook, a dancer, a singer, an actress. She has collaborated with musicians Branford Marsalis, Roberta Flack, and Quincy Jones. She had a leading role in the 1996 film *How to Make an American Quilt.* She has done segments for *Sesame Street* and has written books for children.

In all of these activities she has been aware of the phenomenal power of the rhythm of words. She has the ability to capture a voice on the printed page, as in the title of her verse collection *Just Give Me a Cool Drink of Water 'fore I Diiie,* but the strange phenomenon is that expressing the particulars of one experience can also open up a range of sensibilities. She has the rhythms from black experience, yet William Shakespeare was her first "white love." She has adapted Sophocles' *Ajax* for the stage, TV, and film.

In a BBC broadcast, she sang—unaccompanied and impromptu—the opening bars of two versions of "When the Saints Come Marching In" (this was after the 1987 publication of *Now Sheba Sings the Song*). First she sang "the way whites" do, with bright, cheerful surface, waggling her palms back and forth. And then, in a deep, slow contralto, she sang "from the soul" the way blacks do, drawing upon a strange pulsing phenomenon that everybody can respond to.

She is indeed, as in the title poem for one of her books, "A Phenomenal Woman," not easily categorized:

Men themselves have wondered
What they see in me.

—William Sylvester

ANZALDÚA, Gloria

Nationality: American. **Born:** Jesus Maria of the Valley, Texas, 26 September 1942. **Education:** Pan-American University, Edinburg,

Texas, B.A. 1969; University of Texas at Austin, M.A. 1973; studied at University of California at Santa Cruz. **Career:** Has taught high school English and in migrant, adult, and bilingual programs in Texas; teacher of creative writing, women's studies, and Chicano studies at University of Texas at Austin, Vermont College of Norwich University, and San Francisco State University. Writer-in-residence, the Loft, Minneapolis; artist-in-residence, Pomona College. Contributing editor, *Sinister Wisdom.* Poetry and essays published in numerous journals and periodicals, including *Conditions: Six, Ikon: Creativity and Change,* and *Tejidos,* as well as anthologies. Has given lectures, panels, and workshops throughout the United States, Canada, and Mexico. **Awards:** MacDowell Colony fellowship, 1982; National Endowment of the Arts award for fiction, 1991; Astraea National Lesbian Action Foundation Lesbian Writers Fund Sappho Award, 1992. **Address:** c/o Literature Board, University of Santa Cruz, Santa Cruz, California 95064, U.S.A.

PUBLICATIONS

Poetry

This Way Daybreak Comes, with Annie Cheatham and Mary Clare Powell. N.p., 1986.
Borderlands / La Frontera: The New Mestiza. San Francisco, Spinsters / Aunt Lute, 1987.

For Children

Prietita Has a Friend—Prietita tiene un Amigo. San Francisco, Children's Book Press, 1991.
Friends from the Other Side—Amigos del otra lado. San Francisco, Children's Book Press, 1993.
Prietita and the Ghost Woman—Prietita y La Llorona. San Francisco, Children's Book Press, 1996.

Other

Lloronas, Women Who Howl: Autohistorias-Torias and the Production of Writing, Knowledge, and Identity. San Francisco, Aunt Lute, 1996.
La Prieta (novel). San Francisco, Aunt Lute, 1997.

Editor, with Cherrie Moraga, *This Bridge Called My Back: Writings by Radical Women of Color.* Watertown, Massachusetts, Persephone Press, 1981.
Editor and contributor, *Making Face, Making Soul / Haciendo Caras: Creative and Critical Perspectives by Women of Color.* San Francisco, Aunt Lute, 1990.

*

Critical Studies: "Dare to Write: Virginia Woolf, Tillie Olsen, Gloria Anzaldúa" by Carolyn Woodward, in *Changing Our Power: An Introduction to Women's Studies,* Dubuque, Kendall / Hunt, 1988; interview with Elizabeth Baldwin in *Matrix,* May 1988; "Living on the Borderland: The Poetic Prose of Gloria Anzaldúa and Susan Griffin" by Diane P. Freedman, in *Women and Language* (Urbana, Illinois), Spring 1989; "Experience, Writing, Theory: The Dialects of *Mestizaje* in Gloria Anzaldúa's *Borderlands / La Frontera"* by Hector A. Torres, in *Cultural and Cross-Cultural Studies and the Teaching of Literature,* 1991; "On *Borderlands / La Frontera:* An Interpretive Essay" by Maria Lugones, in *Hypatia,* Fall 1992.

Media Adaptations: *This Bridge Called My Back: Writings by Women of Color* (sound recording), 1983.

*   *   *

A versatile author who has published poetry, stories and children's books—and edited two collections of works by women of color— Gloria Anzaldúa expresses a Chicana / lesbian politics in all of her writing. She has also postulated a new type of literature for Third World women which would tear down distinctions of all kinds and foster the emergence of multiple-voiced spokespersons.

Anzaldúa's first published work, the anthology *This Bridge Called My Back: Writings by Radical Women of Color,* appeared in 1981. Edited by Anzaldúa and Cherrie Moraga, *This Bridge* features writings by a variety of women, including several essays written by Anzaldúa herself which help to clarify her own stance as a writer and activist. In the essay "Speaking in Tongues: A Letter to 3rd World Women Writers," Anzaldúa argues for a new theory of writing that mixes fact and theory in a more individual way to counter the abstract and distanced writing of academia. In practice, this approach is highly subjective. As Hector A. Torres writes in the *Dictionary of Literary Biography,* "for Anzaldua, in the construction of a theoretical framework that would articulate the experience of the minority writer, anything is allowed."

In her poetry collection *Borderlands / La Frontera: The New Mestiza,* Anzaldúa mixes genres in an idiosyncratic manner meant to open new literary terrain and allow a multitudinous voice to express itself. Combining poetry and prose, English and Spanish, and the real with the imaginary, *Borderlands* speaks in a myriad of voices to create a kind of creative autobiography. The collection begins with an extended essay, "Atravesando Fronteras / Crossing Borders," in which Anzaldúa explores various aspects of living on a border, particularly the movement of people over the Texas / Mexico border. She references historical instances of migration in the region, suggests similar borders existing between scholarly writing and the writing of immigrants, and finally proposes that humanity is on the verge of a disintegration of borders of all kinds, resulting in a "radical, ideological, cultural and biological cross-polinization" which will break down all existing formations and lead to a new and hybridized humankind.

The collection's second section is a gathering of Anzaldúa's poems dealing with lesbian feminism, religion, migrant workers, and her own personal history. The character of the undocumented woman appears in several pieces; this character straddles such borders as those between rich and poor, between people with different religious and political beliefs, and between those with differing sexual preferences. "This is her home / this thin edge of / barbwire," Anzaldúa explains in one poem.

Anzaldúa has more recently turned to writing children's fiction. *Prietita and the Ghost Woman* is based on a traditional Mexican folktale about a young girl seeking aid for her sick mother from a ghost woman with strange powers. In *Friends from the Other Side,* Anzaldúa spins another tale of Prietita, a Mexican-American girl who befriends a Mexican boy.

—Denise Wiloch

ARMANTROUT, (Mary) Rae

Nationality: American. **Born:** Vallejo, California, 13 April 1947. **Education:** California State University, San Diego, 1965-68; University of California, Berkeley, 1969-70, B.A. 1970; California State University, San Francisco, 1972-75, M.A. 1975. **Family:** Married Charles Korkegian in 1971; one son. **Career:** Teaching assistant, California State University, San Francisco, 1972-74; lecturer, California State University, San Diego, 1980-82. Lecturer, University of California, San Diego, La Jolla, 1980—. **Awards:** California Arts Council fellowship, 1989; Fund for Poetry award, 1993. **Address:** 4774 East Mountain View Drive, San Diego, California 92116, U.S.A.

PUBLICATIONS

Poetry

Extremities. Great Barrington, Massachusetts, The Figures, 1978.
The Invention of Hunger. Berkeley, California, Tuumba, 1979.
Precedence. Providence, Rhode Island, Burning Deck, 1985.
Necromance. Los Angeles, Sun & Moon Press, 1991.
Made to Seem. Los Angeles, Sun & Moon Press, 1995.

*

Critical Studies: *A Suite of Poetic Voices: Interviews with Contemporary American Poets* by Manuel Brito, Kadle Books, 1992; "The Siren Song of the Singular" by Jeffrey Peterson, in *Sagetrieb* (Orono, Maine), vol. 12, no. 3, Winter 1993; article by Michael Lally in *Contemporary Literature,* vol. 35, no. 4, Winter 1994; *The Marginalization of Poetry: Language Poetry and Literary History* by Bob Perleman, Princeton University Press, 1996.

Rae Armantrout comments:

I began reading poetry seriously in high school. The first poets I responded to were William Carlos Williams and Robinson Jeffers. A little bit later I encountered the work of Robert Creeley, Denise Levertov, and Charles Olson. I studied with Levertov when I was a student at Berkeley. It was there, too, that I met people such as Ron Silliman and Barrett Watten. We formed one nexus of the group later known as "language poets."

I am interested in the psychology of perception, especially in the way the mind distinguishes discrete objects. What is a thing; what is a self? I think I deal with this problem mimetically by producing the dubious unity of the poem.

*   *   *

Throughout her career as a poet Rae Armantrout has aligned herself with the movement generally known as language poetry—or sometimes, after the title of an important theoretical journal published by this group of writers, L=A=N=G=U=A=G=E poetry. In the years around 1970 a group of poets that included Ron Silliman, Lyn Hejinian, and Charles Bernstein, among others, sought to move beyond the search for a unique personal voice that had set the tone of the poetry of the 1960s, both the confessional poetry of Amy Lowell, Sylvia Plath, and Anne Sexton and the projectivism of Charles Olson and his followers. The leaders of this new avant-garde argued instead that poetry should engage in a critical interrogation of language itself as the mechanism that creates the illusion of an "authentic" subjectivity and thereby trammels us in socially constructed ways of perceiving and acting. The language poets found precedents for their own practices in the syntactic dislocations of William Carlos Williams and Louis Zukofsky and in Gertrude Stein's attempts to probe the limits of referentiality in such works as *Tender Buttons.*

By the mid-1970s language poetry had established itself as a coherent and well-organized movement with its own journals and publishers, and Armantrout had emerged as a poet within the movement. *In the American Tree,* the 1986 anthology that first brought language poetry to a larger public, includes a substantial selection of her work, and two of her later books were issued by Sun & Moon, a principal publisher of language poetry. In an essay appended to *In the American Tree,* moreover, Armantrout explicitly aligns herself with this movement. She praises Susan Howe for "call[ing] our attention to the effect of linguistic structure on belief," and she salutes Carla Harryman for putting "content at odds with syntactical (or sometimes narrative) structures in order to make these structures stand out, enter our consciousness." "The writers I like," Armantrout declares, "bring the underlying structures of language / thought into consciousness. They spurn the facile. Though they generally don't believe in Truth, they are scrupulously honest about the way word relates to word, sentence to sentence."

Armantrout's own poetry seeks and often achieves many of the qualities that she admires in Howe and Harryman. Armantrout writes lean, almost minimalist poems, and she publishes them in equally lean volumes. While other language poets have experimented with extended prose poems (Hejinian, Harryman) or with poetic sequences (both Susan and Fanny Howe), Armantrout has remained faithful to the short poem, usually written in a clipped Creeleyesque line—although her books generally also include occasional forays into the prose poem. Her publisher places her within the tradition of Emily Dickinson, and the comparison is apt. Like Dickinson, Armantrout compresses linguistic structures until they implode. Dickinson saw poetry as a "gift of screws" which wring out the "essential oils," and Armantrout agrees. The work of both poets takes fire from the friction of disparate, even clashing words rubbing up against each other. In part, the impulse behind these verbal juxtapositions is simply a spirit of play: Armantrout shares Dickinson's sometimes murderous wit. But both poets want to look at—and thus perhaps to see beyond—the linguistic and social structures that hem us in.

As compared even to the most enigmatic of Dickinson's poems, Armantrout's may seem willfully opaque. Yet if we pay careful attention to her words as they have been placed on the page, without demanding some immediately recognizable human feeling, new possibilities of interconnection begin to come together in our minds. Only by looking in some detail at a specific Armantrout poem can we see how this process takes place. "Family Resemblances" is a relatively simple example:

> Old broom,
> is it straw-yellow?
> stitched with parallel
> lightning bolts
> like the skirt of a square-dancer
>
> who seems familiar
> though she won't notice you,
> displaying her do-si-dos
> in the flicker
> from Lawrence Welk's studio.

The title locates us in a comfortably domestic sphere, and the first phrase of the poem seems to invite a mild nostalgia. Remember when your mother swept the kitchen with a "real" broom made of straw, not a plastic imitation? But the next line reminds us that we live in a realm of commodities. This broom, however old it might be, is perhaps not made of real straw. Rather it is, or it might be, "straw-yellow"—and why, after all, *do* the manufacturers of plastic brooms almost always make them yellow? The question mark also suggests that we're not sure what color the broom is. Perhaps we are seeing not the broom itself but a picture of it—perhaps, as the last line of the poem suggests, on a television screen. In any case, the fibers of the broom are bound together by two rows of lightning bolt stitches, and the poet notices a similar pattern on the whirling skirt of a square dancer. Hence the title—there is a family resemblance between the broom and the dancer. Both seem familiar. Both speak to our hunger for tradition.

Both broom and dancer, however, are in fact commodities, "ideologically overdetermined" as critical theory might say. The dancer on the screen looks into our eyes, smiles reassuringly, but doesn't really see or know us. The illusion of familiarity, the affirmation of "traditional family values," is a trap. The flicker of the television screen defines our distance from the world of the dancer. As we recognize the dancer as a commodity, her willingness to display her "do-si-dos" for us becomes obscene, a kind of prostitution. The nominalization of the caller's command to the dancers also enacts a process we may observe throughout the poem. Grammatically, the syntax here never quite resolves itself into a sentence, although it seems constantly on the verge of doing so. The failure of the nouns to find a main verb shifts the focus back to the nouns: "broom," "bolts," "skirt," "square-dancer," "do-si-dos," "flicker," "studio." "A noun," Armantrout suggests in another poem, "is a kind of scab." "Family Resemblances" wants not to pull away the scab but to remind us that these nouns *are* scabs and that there are real wounds under them.

—Burton Hatlen

ATWOOD, Margaret

Nationality: Canadian. **Born:** Ottawa, Ontario, 18 November 1939. **Education:** Victoria College, University of Toronto, 1957-61; B.A. 1961; Radcliffe College, Cambridge, Massachusetts, A.M. 1962; Harvard University, Cambridge, Massachusetts 1962-63, 1965-67. **Family:** Married Graeme Gibson (divorced); one daughter. **Career:** Lecturer in English, University of British Columbia, Vancouver, 1964-65; instructor in English, Sir George Williams University, Montreal, 1967-68; teacher of creative writing, University of Alberta, Edmonton, 1969-70; assistant professor of English, York University, Toronto, 1971-72. Writer-in-residence, University of Toronto, 1972-73, University of Alabama, Tuscaloosa, 1985, Macquarie University, North Ryde, New South Wales, 1987, and Trinity University, San Antonio, Texas, 1989; Berg Visiting Professor of English, New York University, 1986; writer-in-residence, Macquarie University, North Ryde, Australia, 1987. Editor and member of the board of directors, House of Anansi Press, Toronto, 1971-73. **Awards:** E.J. Pratt Medal, 1961; President's Medal,

University of Western Ontario, 1965; Governor-General's award, 1966, 1986; Centennial Commission prize, 1967; Union League Civic and Arts Foundation prize, 1969, and Bess Hokin prize, 1974 (*Poetry,* Chicago); City of Toronto Book award, 1976; St. Lawrence award, 1978; Radcliffe Medal, 1980; Molson award, 1981; Guggenheim fellowship, 1981; Welsh Arts Council International Writers prize, 1982; Ida Nudel Humanitarian award, 1986; Los Angeles *Times* Book award, 1986; Arthur C. Clarke Science-Fiction award, for novel, 1987; Commonwealth Writer's prize (regional), 1987, 1994; Humanist of the Year award, 1987; City of Toronto Book award, 1989; Canadian Bookseller's Association Author of the Year award, 1988; Centennial Medal, Harvard University, 1990; Trillium award, 1992, 1994; Candian Authors Association Novel of the Year award, 1993; Chevalier dans l'Ordre des Arts et des Lettres, 1994; Swedish Humor Association International Humorous Writer Award, 1995, for *The Robber Bride;* D.Litt.: Trent University, Peterborough, Ontario, 1973; Concordia University, Montreal, 1980; Smith College, Northampton, Massachusetts, 1982; University of Toronto, 1983; Mount Holyoke College, South Hadley, Massachusetts, 1985; University of Waterloo, Ontario, 1985; University of Guelph, Ontario, 1985; Victoria College, 1987; L.L.D.: Queen's University, Kingston, Ontario, 1974, University of Leeds, Ontario, 1994. Companion, Order of Canada, 1981. Fellow, Royal Society of Canada, 1987. **Member:** American Academy of Arts and Sciences (honorary member), 1988. **Agent:** Phoebe Larmore, 228 Main Street, Venice, California 90291, U.S.A. **Address:** c/o Oxford University Press, 70 Wynford Drive, Don Mills, Ontario M3C 1J9, Canada.

PUBLICATIONS

Poetry

Double Persephone. Toronto, Hawkshead Press, 1961.
The Circle Game (single poem). Bloomfield Hills, Michigan, Cranbrook Academy of Art, 1964.
Talismans for Children. Bloomfield Hills, Michigan, Cranbrook Academy of Art, 1965.
Kaleidoscopes: Baroque. Bloomfield Hills, Michigan, Cranbrook Academy of Art, 1965.
Speeches for Doctor Frankenstein. Bloomfield Hills, Michigan, Cranbrook Academy of Art, 1966.
The Circle Game (collection). Toronto, Contact Press, 1966.
Expeditions. Bloomfield Hills, Michigan, Cranbrook Academy of Art, 1966.
The Animals in That County. Toronto, Oxford University Press, 1968; Boston, Little Brown, 1969.
Who Was in the Garden. Santa Barbara, California, Unicorn, 1969.
Five Modern Canadian Poets, with others, edited by Eli Mandel. Toronto, Holt Rinehart, 1970.
The Journals of Susanna Moodie. Toronto, Oxford University Press, 1970.
Oratorio for Sasquatch, Man and Two Androids: Poems for Voices. Toronto, Canadian Broadcasting Corporation, 1970.
Procedures for Underground. Toronto, Oxford University Press, and Boston, Little Brown, 1970.
Power Politics. Toronto, Anansi, 1971; New York, Harper, 1973.

You Are Happy. Toronto, Oxford University Press, and New York, Harper, 1974.

Selected Poems. Toronto, Oxford University Press, 1976; New York, Simon & Schuster, 1978.

Marsh, Hawk. Toronto, Dreadnaught, 1977.

Two-Headed Poems. Toronto, Oxford University Press, 1978; New York, Simon & Schuster, 1981.

True Stories. Toronto, Oxford University Press, 1981; New York, Simon & Schuster, and London, Cape, 1982.

Notes towards a Poem That Can Never Be Written. Toronto, Salamander Press, 1981.

Snake Poems. Toronto, Salamander Press, 1983.

Interlunar. Toronto, Oxford University Press, 1984; London,s Cape, 1988.

Selected Poems II: Poems Selected and New, 1976-1986. Toronto, Oxford University Press, 1986; Boston, Houghton, 1987.

Morning in the Burned House. Toronto, McClelland & Stewart, and Boston, Houghton, 1995.

Recordings: *The Poetry and Voice of Margaret Atwood,* Caedmon, 1977; *Margaret Atwood Reads from The Handmaid's Tale,* Caedmon.

Plays

Radio Play: *The Trumpets of Summer,* 1964.

Television Plays: *The Servant Girl,* 1974; *Snowbird,* 1981; *Heaven on Earth,* with Peter Pearson, 1986.

Novels

The Edible Woman. Toronto, McClelland & Stewart, and London, Deutsch, 1969; Boston, Little Brown, 1970.

Surfacing. Toronto, McClelland & Stewart, 1972; London, Deutsch, and New York, Simon & Schuster, 1973.

Lady Oracle. Toronto, McClelland & Stewart, and New York, Simon & Schuster, 1976; London, Deutsch, 1977.

Life before Man. Toronto, McClelland & Stewart, 1979; New York, Simon & Schuster, and London, Cape, 1980.

Bodily Harm. Toronto, McClelland & Stewart, 1981; New York, Simon & Schuster, and London, Cape, 1982.

The Handmaid's Tale. Toronto, McClelland & Stewart, 1985; Boston, Houghton, and London, Cape, 1986.

Cat's Eye. Toronto, McClelland & Stewart, 1988; New York, Doubleday, and London, Bloomsbury, 1989.

The Robber Bride. Toronto, McClelland & Stewart, 1993; New York, Doubleday, 1993.

Alias Grace. New York, Doubleday, 1996.

Short Stories

Dancing Girls and Other Stories. Toronto, McClelland & Stewart, 1977; New York, Simon & Schuster, and London, Cape, 1982.

Encounters with the Element Man. Concord, New Hampshire, Ewert, 1982.

Murder in the Dark: Short Fictions and Prose Poems. Toronto, Coach House Press, 1983; London, Cape, 1984.

Bluebeard's Egg and Other Stories. Toronto, McClelland & Stewart, 1983; Boston, Houghton, 1986; London, Cape, 1987.

Unearthing Suite. Toronto, Grand Union Press, 1983.

Wilderness Tips. Toronto, McClelland & Stewart, 1991; New York, Doubleday, 1991.

Good Bones. Toronto, Coach House Press, 1992; as *Good Bones and Simple Murders,* New York, Doubleday, 1994.

Other

Survival: A Thematic Guide to Canadian Literature. Toronto, Anansi, 1972.

Days of the Rebels 1815-1840. Toronto, Natural Science of Canada, 1977.

Up in the Tree (for children). Toronto, McClelland & Stewart, 1978.

Anna's Pet (for children), with Joyce Barkhouse. Toronto, Lorimer, 1980.

Second Words: Selected Critical Prose. Toronto, Anansi, 1982; Boston, Beacon Press, 1984.

Margaret Atwood: Conversations, edited by E. Ingersoll. Princeton, New Jersey, Ontario Review Press, 1990.

For the Birds (for children). Toronto, Firefly Books, 1991.

Princess Prunella and the Purple Peanut (for children). New York, Workman, 1995.

Strange Things: The Malevolent North in Canadian Literature (lectures). Toronto and Oxford, Oxford University Press, 1996.

Editor, *The New Oxford Book of Canadian Verse in English.* Toronto, New York, and Oxford, Oxford University Press, 1982.

Editor, with Robert Weaver, *The Oxford Book of Canadian Short Stories in English.* Toronto, Oxford, and New York, Oxford University Press, 1986.

Editor, *The Canlit Food Book.* Toronto, Totem, 1987.

Editor, with Shannon Ravenel, *The Best American Short Stories 1989.* Boston, Houghton, 1989.

Editor, with Barry Callaghan, *The Poetry of Gwendolyn MacEwan.* Toronto, Exile Editions, 2 vols., 1993-94.

*

Bibliography: "Margaret Atwood: An Annotated Bibliography" by Alan J. Horne, in *The Annotated Bibliography of Canada's Major Authors 1-2* edited by Robert Lecker and Jack David, Downsview, Ontario, ECW Press, 2 vols., 1979-80.

Manuscript Collection: Fisher Library, University of Toronto.

Media Adaptations: *The Handmaid's Tale* was filmed by Cinecom Entertainment Group, 1990.

Critical Studies: *Margaret Atwood: A Symposium* edited by Linda Sandler, Victoria, British Columbia, University of Victoria, 1977; *A Violent Duality* by Sherrill Grace, Montreal, Véhicule Press, 1979; *Margaret Atwood: Language, Text, and System* edited by Grace and Lorraine Weir, Vancouver, University of British Columbia Press, 1983; *The Art of Margaret Atwood: Essays in Criticism* edited by Arnold E. and Cathy N. Davidson, Toronto, Anansi, 1981; *Margaret Atwood* by Jerome

H. Rosenberg, Boston, Twayne, 1984; *Margaret Atwood: A Feminist Poetics* by Frank Davey, Vancouver, Talonbooks, 1984; *Margaret Atwood* by Barbara Hill Rigney, London, Macmillan, 1987; *Critical Essays on Margaret Atwood* edited by Judith McCombs, Boston, Hall, 1988; *Margaret Atwood: Vision and Forms* edited by Kathryn van Spanckeren and Jan Garden Castro, Carbondale, Southern Illinois University Press, 1988; *Margaret Atwood's Power: Mirrors, Reflections, and Images in Select Fiction and Poetry* by Shannon Hengen, Toronto, Second Story Press, 1993; interview in *San Francisco Review of Books,* February / March 1994; *The Influence of Painting on Five Canadian Authors* by John Cooke, Lewiston, New York, Edwin Mellen, 1996.

Margaret Atwood comments:

I feel that the task of criticizing my poetry is best left to others (i.e., critics) and would much rather have it take place after I am dead. If at all.

*   *   *

In "This Is a Photograph of Me," the opening poem of Margaret Atwood's *The Circle Game,* the speaker proffers the reader a grainy snapshot. After momentary confusion, the photo resolves itself into a recognizable scene:

as you scan
it, you see in the left-hand corner
a thing that is like a branch: part of a tree
(balsam or spruce) emerging
and, to the right, halfway up
what ought to be a gentle
slope, a small frame house.

The picture is banal enough, a familiar evocation of middle-class security, a haven of domesticity nestled in a benevolent nature. Little in the photo, however, is what it initially seems. A sudden parenthesis informs us that the speaker lies drowned, Ophelia-like, in the lake:

I am in the lake, in the center
of the picture, just under the surface.

It is difficult to say where
precisely, or to say
how large or small I am:
the effect of water
on light is a distortion

but if you look long enough
eventually
you will be able to see me.

With a single twist, the poem foregrounds our received, perhaps unconscious, habits of reading the world, insisting that a close effort of attention will reveal the idyllic image of home and hearth as a smothering trap for its female victim.

The poem, with its short, free-verse lines, its precise, austere diction, and its glancing allusion to myth, is stylistically typical of Atwood's work. But in its insistence on critically

examining the images which structure our understanding of the world, it also voices a theme present, in one way or another, in all her poetry. Like other female poets who came of age in the 1960s, and like other Canadian writers who have long been aware of the political and cultural domination of their country by outside forces, Atwood is extraordinarily sensitive to the ways in which power relations between humanity and nature, between men and women, and between nations shape the modes of representation, the methods of reading and writing, through which we make sense of our lives. Her poetry insists on looking closely enough to identify the marginalized, the hidden, the other: that which has been suppressed or passed over by our inherited maps and legends. Such recognitions compel a search for new modes of representation, new ways of writing which aim to give voice to that which has been silenced. Atwood's poetry thus seeks to move from the old languages of dominance, mastery, and victimization to a new language of tolerance, understanding, and illumination.

This overarching project has played itself out in various registers during the course of Atwood's career. In her early poems, dating from the late 1960s, it often takes the form of a confrontation with the Canadian wilderness, a landscape at once bleak and alien, even hostile, and yet eliciting a strong feeling of identification in the poet. The challenge, broached in many of Atwood's early poems, is to map one's surroundings, find one's place in the world, without denying the otherness and sovereignty of nature, without imposing a false, anthropomorphic pattern on a nonhuman wilderness. It is a difficult project at best, and the characteristically bleak tone of the early poems often proceeds from the failure of Atwood's protagonists to avoid a disastrous ecological imperialism:

He dug the soil in rows,
imposed himself with shovels
He asserted
into the furrows, I
am not random.

The ground
replied with aphorisms:

a tree-sprout
weed, words
he couldn't understand.

The hapless settler described in these lines from "Progressive Insanities of a Pioneer" fails to come to terms with the "ordered absence" that is nature and finds himself overwhelmed by "the green vision, / the unnamed / whale" of the wilderness.

In poems published in the early 1970s Atwood shifted her focus to relations between men and women, relations which, as the title of her book-length cycle *Power Politics* implies, she perceives as equally fraught with the potential for domination and exploitation. The cycle acidly chronicles a stultifying love affair to reveal the pain which lies just behind the traditional tropes of romantic love: "you fit into me / like a hook into an eye / / a fish hook / an open eye." But Atwood is less concerned with documenting male aggression than with delineating the oscillating cycle of victimization practiced by both partners in a relationship dominated by competition, selfish-

ness, and fear, and with finding, if possible, some space be-
yond the old oppressive structures of gender relations where
love might separate itself from power. Such a utopian space
seems unimaginable in the world of *Power Politics:* its couple
dissolves, exhausted by each other. But a happier alternative is
at least glimpsed in Atwood's next collection, *You Are Happy,*
whose final poem rewrites the archetypal image of the sacrifi-
cial victim as a vulnerable but trusting lover, unafraid of hon-
est emotional exchange:

> On the floor your body curves
> like that: the ancient pose, neck slackened, arms
> thrown above the head, vital
> throat and belly lying
> undefended. light slides over you,
> this is not an altar, they are not
> acting or watching
>
> You are intact, you turn
> towards me, your eyes opening, the eyes
> intricate and easily bruised, you open
>
> yourself to me gently, what
> they tried, we
> tried but could never do
> before. without blood, the killed
> heart. to take
> that risk, to offer life and remain
>
> alive, open yourself like this and become whole

You Are Happy can be seen to mark a turning point in
Atwood's poetry in other ways as well. Its brilliant cycle,
"Circe / Mud Poems," a feminist recasting of the Circe myth,
provides the model for later, politically charged reinterpreta-
tions of such figures as Orpheus and Eurydice, Giselle, and the
Robber Bridegroom. The book's "Songs of the Transformed,"
a series narrated by creatures half-human and half-animal, in-
augurates a slightly less guarded view of the natural world and
opens the way for the reverent, almost mystical encounters
with nature appearing in *Interlunar* (1984).

Yet, if Atwood managed to attain a guarded confidence, a tenta-
tive transcendence in her love and nature poetry, her optimism re-
mained tempered by a keen awareness of the strife and oppression
which continues to saturate the modern world. Since *Two-Headed
Poems* (1978), Atwood's poetry has increasingly addressed political
issues on a national and international level, balancing these with the
more meditative poems of *Morning in the Burning House* ("Half-
Hanged Mary," "In the Secular Night") and *Selected Poems II.* The
title sequence of *Two-Headed Poems* explores the possibility of a
common language that could provide dialogue between English- and
French-speaking Canada, concluding, despairingly, that "this is not a
debate / but a duet / with two deaf singers." The poet's involvement
with Amnesty International has produced a searing sequence of po-
ems, most notably "Notes towards a Poem That Can Never Be Writ-
ten," which graphically addresses the continuing practice of torture
and political violence. As this poem's title suggests, the works dis-
play a strong continuity with Atwood's earlier efforts in that they
question the possibility of accurately representing the reality of tor-
ture, especially when one writes in the language of a first-world ob-
server who is, if only indirectly, implicated in that violence:

> In this country you can say what you like
> because no one will listen to you anyway,
> it's safe enough, in this country you can try to write
> the poem that can never be written,
> the poem that invents
> nothing and excuses nothing,
> because you invent and excuse yourself each day.

Even while acknowledging the limitations of her language, Atwood
refuses the option of silence, grimly offering witness to horrors
her words can at best suggest. It is this consistently double con-
sciousness of the limits of language and the necessity of speech
that has given all of Atwood's work, no matter what her subject,
its complex blend of caution and commitment, irony and pas-
sion. It is her unflinching perception of both the impossibility
and necessity of writing that has made her one of our most can-
did and inspiring poets.

—Anthony G. Stocks

BARTLETT, Elizabeth

Nationality: British. **Born:** Deal, Kent, 28 April 1924. **Education:** Dover County School for Girls, 1935-39. **Family:** Married Denis Perkins in 1943; one son. **Career:** Clerk, Bells Ltd., 1940-41, Caffyns Ltd., 1941-42, and Barclays Bank, 1942-43, all Lewes, Sussex; lecturer, Workers Education Association, Burgess Hill, Sussex, 1960-63; receptionist and secretary, West Sussex Health Authority, and home help, West Sussex Country Council, both Burgess Hill, 1966-86. **Awards:** Cheltenham Poetry Competition prize, 1982; Arts Council bursar, 1985; British Society of Authors Cholmondeley Award, 1996. **Address:** 17 St. John's Avenue, Burgess Hill, West Sussex RH15 8HJ, England.

PUBLICATIONS

Poetry

A Lifetime of Dying. Calstock, Peterloo, 1979.
Strange Territory. Calstock, Peterloo, 1983.
The Czar Is Dead. London, Rivelin Grapheme, 1986.
Instead of a Mass. Liverpool, Headland, 1991.
Look, No Face. Bradford, Redbeck Press, 1991.
Two Women Dancing. Newcastle upon Tyne, Bloodaxe, 1991.

Recording: *William Scammell and Elizabeth Bartlett,* Peterloo, 1984.

*

Elizabeth Bartlett comments:

The poems are linked by one obsession, which is a curiosity about people and their emotions, stimulated originally by a five-year stint of psychoanalysis with its freedoms and disciplines, and its exploration of self. I am drawn to people with maimed personalities because I know I am one myself. I write about what I know, but I also write about imaginary events and people, using whatever the poems needs for its own purpose. I trade in fear and delight, strength and weakness, hate and love, and I'm inclined to agree with Geoffrey Grigson that "the right place for writers of poems, in relation to themselves as poem-writers, is in their poems."

I cannot explain a lifelong passion for this private art, and I have no academic background or qualifications of any kind. The poetry world has been reasonably kind to a rank outsider. I cannot think of anything that has pleased me more than being included in *The Faber Book of Twentieth-Century Women's Poetry.*

*   *   *

The strength of Elizabeth Bartlett's poetry lies in its concerns and compassions. It is not poetry of verbal or stylistic innovation. It has a controlled speaking voice whose narratives tend to seize the reader by the lapel after the manner of the Ancient Mariner. This often happens at the outset, as in "Salad Dreams," which begins,

I am like the lady who dreamed
she prepared a salad for her guests
and grated her own skin over it,

or "Voyeur," which begins,

Watching from the bed, with a bleeding cunt
and gin-painted nipples, she saw at last
what he meant about having had a certain
nobility in his youth.

The world of Bartlett's poetry is not always a comfortable one, stemming from a world some of us would rather pretend wasn't there but which in her work in a doctor's office and in social services she has encountered and refused to look away from. It is an intensely and uncompromisingly physical world of blood, bowels, sickness, vomit, menses, and semen, in which people are often deranged. In this world the day of the death of the czar of all Russia is remembered as that when

Menarche and murder link with fear
in my mind.

It is a world sometimes on the edge of the precipice of insanity, where the "indefinable odour he carried round with him" was "the smell of loneliness."

What makes the poems acceptable is the compassionate and humane concern that underlies them. The poem "A Plea for Mercy" does not ask God to remake the world or anything so fundamentally unreasonable. All it asks is that some respect be shown and some peace allowed:

From dormitories
to geriatric homes and all the institutions in between,

a fair fantasy, a brief respite, and a dreamless sleep,
before the matrons, doctors, screws and curates muscle in.

It is a plea for a world in which we are allowed the fantasies and illusions that make it bearable and a *cri de coeur* against the dreaded tendency to institutionalize. As with Willy Loman in Arthur Miller's *Death of a Salesman,* attention should be paid.

It is not, it must be quickly said, a poetry that celebrates the bloody awful but one that demands compassionate attention be paid. It reveals a world of natural and common human concerns and sensibilities beneath that from which we tend to avert our eyes. Bartlett's poetry is not designed to shock or dismay. Rather, it arouses understanding and recognition and from these compassion. To misquote what is now almost a poetic commonplace, "The poetry is in the compassion."

—John Cotton

BECKER, Robin

Nationality: American. **Born:** Philadelphia, Pennsylvania, 7 March 1951. **Education:** Boston University, B.A. in creative writing 1973,

M.A. 1976. **Career:** Lecturer in creative writing and humanistic studies, Massachusetts Institute of Technology, Cambridge, 1977-93; associate professor of English and Women's Studies, Pennsylvania State University, University Park, 1994—. Visiting professor, Kent State University, 1992. Writer-in-residence, Wyoming Council on the Arts, Sheridan, and The Writers' Place, Madison, Wisconsin, both 1991; *American Poetry Review* scholar-in-residence, Central High School, Philadelphia, May 1994. Member of board of trustees of Cummington School of the Arts, 1976-83; member, board of directors, Associated Writing Programs, 1992-95. Co-coordinator of reading series at New Words bookstore, 1981-83. Contributing editor, Alice James Books, beginning 1976; contributing editor and poetry editor, *Women's Review of Books,* 1984—; poetry editor, *Bay Windows,* 1983-85. Contributor of poetry and short fiction to numerous periodicals. **Awards:** Massachusetts Artists Foundation fellowship, 1985; Cambridge River Festival Poetry prize, 1986; *Prairie Schooner* Readers' Choice Award, 1989; National Endowment for the Arts grant, 1989; Anna Davidson Rosenberg award, 1990; National Writers' Union Poetry Competition prize, 1992; Radcliffe College Mary Ingraham Bunting fellowship, 1995-96; Pushcart Prize nomination, 1995-96. **Address:** Department of English, Pennsylvania State University, 103 Burrowes Bldg., University Park, Pennsylvania 16802-6200, U.S.A.

PUBLICATIONS

Poetry

Personal Effects. Cambridge, Massachusetts, Alice James Poetry Cooperative, 1977.
Backtalk. Cambridge, Massachusetts, Alice James Books, 1982.
Giacometti's Dog. Pittsburgh, University of Pittsburgh Press, 1990.
All-American Girl. Pittsburgh, University of Pittsburgh Press, 1996.

*

Critical Studies: In *Village Voice Literary Supplement,* June 1982.

Robin Becker comments:

The resurgence of the feminist movement in the 1970s had a deep and abiding influence on my work. Feminist scholarship and art allowed me to investigate the social, political, and familial aspects of my life. As a Jewish lesbian, I have been influenced by the work of other marginalized writers and thinkers—in the United States and in other countries. In my writing, I seek to merge the personal and the political, illuminating me with the other and showing, finally, that they cannot be separated.

I work in free verse and in received forms such as the villanelle and the sestina. To me, form is not a "container" but an essential aspect of the poem's meaning.

*   *   *

Robin Becker's poetry is as engaging and immediate as the best conversation. One is drawn in by the energy with which she addresses her subjects. Her poems manage to be both ironic and compassionate, to be deeply involved with the things of the world while maintaining the distance necessary to see them clearly. Her strongest work moves toward reconciling apparent contradictions enabling a sense of life's possibilities to coexist with an awareness of human frailty.

She uses vivid detail to root large concerns in the specifics of our lives. Richly populated by friends, lovers, family, Becker's poems chronicle a search for community. The speaker manages to be intensely involved in such relationships while maintaining an outsider's stance: "Like a diligent agent / stationed in a foreign country. / I'm waiting for a signal / to come home" ("In Conversation"). "Bicycle Days" returns to memories of a love affair "guarded, / with my old fear that events / and the people inside them / will ask more of me / than I'm prepared to give." In "The New Year," however, we find a woman wise enough to know the cost of true relationship and brave enough, perhaps, to risk it:

> Now you surrender
> the pleasure of description, the known
> subject, the religion of closure,
> a soldier who disarms in fear
> straining to catch the rumors
> of new borders and the undefended life.

Becker's poems have a wide emotional range. She charms us with humor to make a devastating point. In "Shopping," for example, the speaker mocks herself for seeking consolation for the end of a love affair in the purchase of a belt, a Navajo blanket, an Anasazi pot, only to confront us with the starkness of grief: "I'll do what my mother did / after she buried my sister: / outfitted herself in an elegant suit / for the rest of her life." She knows that "love is really / the subject of our lives" ("The Subject of Our Lives") and that to love we must see ourselves clearly. "The Taj Express" puts the disdainful traveler in her place, pointing out that the homeless "want nothing—not the air you breathe, not the space you claim, / not your guidebook to their country, / not your second-class passage through this life."

Her lesbian subject matter becomes more overt in her later books and her erotic poems are playful and sensual. "We Thought of Each Other as Food" evokes the erotic in images ranging from "taut skin / of the apple burnished with stars" to "coral reefs where sea horses glittered." In her love poems, Becker is both vulnerable— "When you ask me to touch you / I kneel by the water like a blind woman / guided into the river by a friend" ("The Bath")— and knowing—"In time she will open her shirt, / she will show me her neck, she will close her eyes" ("Hold Back"). She describes the spiritual with great delicacy. She understands we must learn "the patience to live / alongside the dead who will not speak / and will not go away" ("Birch Trees"). Her encounter in "Meeting the Gaze of the Great Horned Owl" becomes a lesson in "how fear and longing sometimes go together, / how one small percussive surprise / in the trees can turn you / from one self to another, this one with wings."

Inclusive in their concerns, her poems move easily from one subject to another, synthesizing them into an organic whole. Becker conflates time and place to pretend an innocence she knows she cannot keep in "Dreaming at the Rexall Drug," while the remarkable, "A History of Sexual Preference" shifts seamlessly between eighteenth-century Philadelphia and a contemporary 17-year-old's first love affair with another woman.

She employs a direct tone—colloquial, conversational—and striking visual imagery. The possible menace of a hoard of curious children is captured in the phrase "Like shiny bullets, one hundred toes / pointed at my tent" ("The Children of Siran Darda"); fog wraps "the fir trees and rotting wharves / like a gauze bandage" ("On Vashon"). But her strategies also include the skillful use of form. The terza rima of "Contradancing in Nelson, N.H." mirrors the pattern of its subject matter. The word play invited by the sestina propels the witty "Peter Pan in North America," and the music of the villanelle reinforces the tenderness of "Villanelle for a Lesbian Mom." "From Taos to Santa Fe" makes good use of syllabics to structure a long descriptive poem.

Each new volume of Becker's poetry gives us a writer whose craft grows to keep pace with a deepening vision.

—Kathleen Aguero

BEER, Patricia

Nationality: British. **Born:** Exmouth, Devon, 4 November 1924. **Education:** University of Exeter; University of London, B.A. (honors) in English; St. Hugh's College, Oxford, B.Litt. **Family:** Married John Damien Parsons in 1964. **Career:** Lecturer in English, University of Padua, 1946-48, British Institute, Rome, 1948, and Ministero Aeronautica, Rome, 1950-53; senior lecturer in English, Goldsmiths' College, London, 1962-68. **Address:** 1 Oak Hill Park, London NW3, England; Tiphayes, Up Ottery, near Honiton, Devon, England.

PUBLICATIONS

Poetry

Loss of the Magyar and Other Poems. London, Longmans, 1959.
The Survivors. London, Longmans, 1963.
Just like the Resurrection. London, Macmillan, 1967; Chester Springs, Pennsylvania, Dufour, 1968.
The Postillion Has Been Struck by Lightning. London, Macmillan, 1967.
The Estuary. London, Macmillan, 1971.
Spanish Balcony. London, Poem-of-the-Month Club, 1973.
Driving West. London, Gollancz, 1975.
Selected Poems. London, Hutchinson, 1980.
The Lie of the Land. London, Hutchinson, 1983.
Collected Poems. Manchester, Carcanet, 1988.
Friend of Heraclitus. Manchester, Carcanet, 1993.

Plays

The Enterprise of England (produced Up Ottery, Devon, 1979).

Radio Play: *Pride, Prejudice, and the Woman Question,* 1975.

Novels

Moon's Ottery. London, Hutchinson, 1978.
The Star Cross Ferry. London, Hutchinson, 1991.

Other

Mrs. Beer's House (autobiography). London, Macmillan, 1968.
An Introduction to the Metaphysical Poets. London, Macmillan, and Totowa, New Jersey, Rowman & Littlefield, 1972.

Reader: I Married Him. London, Macmillan, and New York, Barnes & Noble, 1974.
Patricia Beer's Devon. London, Hutchinson, 1984.
Wessex, photographs by Fay Godwin. London, Hamish Hamilton, 1985.

Editor, with Ted Hughes and Vernon Scannel, *New Poems 1962.* London, Hutchinson, 1962.
Editor, *New Poems 1975.* London, Hutchinson, 1975.
Editor, with Kevin Crossley-Holland, *New Poetry 2.* London, Arts Council, 1976.
Editor, *Poetry Supplement.* London, Poetry Book Society, 1978.

*

Critical Studies: In *Kenyon Review,* no. 5, 1968; *British Poetry 1964 to 1984: Driving through the Barricades* by Martin Booth, London, Routledge, 1985; essay by Caroline L. Cherry in *Dictionary of Literary Biography,* vol. 40: *Poets of Great Britain and Ireland since 1960,* Detroit, Gale Research, 1986.

Patricia Beer comments:

(1970) In my opinion my verse has changed radically since the publication of *Loss of the Magyar* in 1959. I do not repudiate my early work but I am now aiming at something quite different. I am trying to break away from the limitations imposed by traditional meters and have been turning increasingly to free verse and syllabics. I am also aiming at using less obvious metaphor.

The writing of my autobiography has influenced my work in two ways: the intensive use of prose has made me try for greater precision in my poetry; and since the publication of the autobiography I have felt able to deal poetically with subjects of a more overtly personal nature. I am not speaking in terms of confessional poetry because that is a mode which, though I respect it, is not for me. But I find I have less need to present my themes objectively by the use of, for example, legend.

The poets whom, currently, I most admire are Yeats, Robert Lowell, Ted Hughes.

*   *   *

Patricia Beer's work has a solid, dependable feel that many readers find reassuring. She uses various means—the layout of the poem on the page, an unforced and straightforward method of narrative, and a recognizable and comprehensible subject matter—to make well-wrought poems whose place is thoroughly mainstream. And always, working away underneath, is a wry, chuckling sense of West Country humor. Yet beyond the everyday nature of the poems' subjects (a postcard, a branch railway line, a scratch) there are intimations of darker possibilities, real threats. With a nudge here and a wink there the reader is led by the hand to a grimmer awareness, as in "Concert at Long Melford Church":

> They spread all over the churchyard. They scan
> The crowd, recognise, smile and shake hands.
> By each tombstone a well-dressed person stands.
> It looks just like the Resurrection.

In many respects—its economy, its social observations, that oblique glance—this quotation is typical work from Beer. Even though she moved in her later collections to a freer line and developed an interest in syllabics, the style remains. The input of a sense of semisurprise gives her work an element of charm.

The poems strike an independent note, not noticeably feminist or strident but singularly determined to stand their ground. A toughness inhabits a number of pieces, but any tendency to overstatement is usually put down by that unfailing ability to control the material, as in "Christmas Eve":

> As it gets dark a drunk
> Comes tacking up the road
> In a white macintosh
> Charming as a yacht

While the vast majority of the poems fit comfortably on a single page, "The Loss of the Magyar" is a sequence comprising eight sections. Generally, though, the narratives and anecdotes run their course and are confined to the single page with economy and a highly readable flow. The casual look of the stanzas is not easy to catch, and therein lies the poet's skill. She handles her material without strain.

Death makes its presence felt in many of Beer's pieces, not gloomily or in a mordant vein but with a measure of respect. That wry humor also alleviates what could be painful, as in "Head of a Snowdrop":

> Anti-vivisectionists show men
> Keeping dogs' heads alive, yapping even.
> Schoolboys studying the Stuarts laugh
> About Charles talking with his head off.

and "Arms":

> ... He put his arms
> Round his son and there he stood,
> Protector, up to his knees
> In death, and that was the last
> That anyone saw of him.

Beer often makes mention of family and her childhood experiences. She sets her roots firmly and so offers the reader something to latch on to; her other life—one of academic pursuits—also pops up now and then. This isn't cloistered, windbag, posing poetry but more an ordered and considered communication with people. Beer's poems do not offer many answers or profundities, but they are a consolation in their humanity and elegance and for that reason deserve the widest possible readership.

—Wes Magee

BERESFORD, Anne (Ellen)

Nationality: British. **Born:** Redhill, Surrey, 10 September 1929. **Education:** Privately schooled; attended Central School of Speech Training and Dramatic Art, London, 1944-46. **Family:** Married Michael Hamburger in 1951 (divorced 1970, remarried 1974); one son and two daughters. **Career:** Stage actress, 1948-70, and broadcaster, BBC, 1960-70; drama teacher, Wimbledon High School, 1969-73, and Arts Educational School, London, 1973-76; teacher

at the Poetry Workshop, Cockpit Theatre, London, 1971-73. Former committee member, Aldeburgh Poetry Festival; member of editorial board, *Agenda* magazine. **Member:** Poetry Society (general council, 1976-79). **Address:** Marsh Acres, Middleton, Saxmundham, Suffolk IP17 3NH, England.

PUBLICATIONS

Poetry

Walking without Moving. London, Turret, 1967.
The Lair. London, Rapp & Whiting, 1968.
Footsteps on Snow. London, Agenda, 1972.
Modern Fairy Tale. Rushden, Northhamptonshire, Sceptre Press, 1972.
The Courtship. Brighton, Unicorn Bookshop, 1972.
The Curving Shore. London, Agenda, 1975.
Words, with Michael Hamburger. East Bramley, Surrey, Words Press, 1977.
Unholy Giving. Knotting, Bedfordshire, Sceptre Press, 1978.
The Songs of Almut from God's Country. Oxford, Suffolk, Oxford Publications, 1980.
Songs a Thracian Taught Me. London, Boyars, 1980.
The Sele of the Morning. London, Agenda, 1988.
Snapshots from an Album 1884-1895. London, Katabasis, 1992.
Charm with Stones. Germany, Verlag Claudia Gehrke, 1993.
Landscape with Figures. London, Agenda, 1994.
Duet for Three Voices and Coda. London, Dedalus Press, 1997.
Selected Poems. London, Agenda & Belue Press, 1997.

Plays

Radio Plays: *Struck by Apollo,* with Michael Hamburger, 1965; *The Villa,* 1968.

Television Play: *Duet for Three Voices,* 1983.

Other

Translator, *Alexandros: Selected Poems,* by Vera Lungu, London, Agenda, 1974.

*

Manuscript Collection: Humanities Research Center, University of Texas, Austin.

Anne Beresford comments:
I don't like to comment on my own work or, for that matter, on other poets—I like to read other poets and hope that they might like to read my work.

* * *

Ezra Pound wrote that "Our life is, in so far as it is worth living, made up in great part of things indefinite, impalpable; and it is precisely because the arts present us these things that we—humanity—cannot get on without the arts." Much of the subtlety of Anne Beresford's poetry stems from her attempts to define moments and states of mind of this nature—those aspects of consciousness and daily life which are most impatient of words. Beresford's "Heimweh" is short enough to give in its entirety:

a thrush sings
every evening
in the ash tree

it has been singing
for as long
as I can remember
only then
the tree was probably
an oak

the song
aches and aches
in the green light
if I knew
where it was
I would go
home

Beresford seldom overstates but is reticent and elliptical. This gives her work an impersonal quality which is rare. At its best her writing expresses an imagination (not fancy) unlike that of any other contemporary poet. This is connected with humor and satire in a strange way. Her irony succeeds because it is not obvious.

A fault present in some poems is a tenuousness of rhythm, where the emotions do not seem strong enough to generate sufficient rhythmic energy. But this is sometimes offset by a clarity and simplicity of imagery which evoke much, particularly if these poems are lived with rather than read quickly: "outside, high on the mountains / is the great plain with wild flowers / wild flowers and air so fresh / one's head goes light" ("Eurydice"). At times the imagery is menacing: "You have come to a tower of slate / crumbling into grey sky. / Don't climb, not there..." ("Half-Way"). This is not poetry which strives for immediate effect; hence, a first reading often misses how much meaning Beresford's usually very simple words contain.

Beresford uses dream and myth to express states of mind which are real and never as ornament or literary device. Her later work makes use of dramatic monologue and shows a historical consciousness which raises her poetry above that of contemporary writers of the short poem, who seem to be incapable of embodying subjects other than the personal and the incidentals of everyday life. "Nicodemus" can serve as an example:

Keeping a sense of proportion
lip service to what is considered correct
I have brought what is needed to bury the dead.
Once again I come to you by night.
This time to take away all visible proof of my understanding.
In secret I have applied myself
to seek out wisdom
to know what is before my face—
the inside and the outside are reversed
that which is
has become that which is not—
displaced, troubled
I live naked in a house that is not my own
and the five trees of Paradise evade me.

Beresford's later books, *The Sele of the Morning* and *Landscape with Figures,* show a new depth in exploring human relationships, both love and friendship, by using a hard-earned simplicity of language. As the Scottish poet W.S. Milne has written, "Rarely today does one find such calmness and sanity, such an understanding of life's gifts, in art."

Despair stands aside
prayer is the answer
in this house
where a baby is soon to be born
in the upstairs room.

Landscape with Figures closes with a particularly fine sequence, "Fragments of a Torn Tapestry," and although the poems concern the past, it is their "nowness," to use a word of David Jones, that will make them live. "London" is short enough to quote entire:

In the great city
is much noise and stench
of business here
I can say little
for in these hard days
no man is to be trusted.

Our masters tell us:
"Make yourselves friends of Mammon"
therefore many are betrayed
Alas! it is true that
Judas does not sleep

The novelist David Storey has written of Beresford, "The finest of mystic poets, her work is pitched on the very edge of perception: celebratory, frightening, elusive—meditative and unique."

—William Cookson

BERGVALL, Caroline

Nationality: French-Norwegian. **Born:** 1963. **Education:** Universite de la Sorbonne, Paris, Licence-es-Lettres, 1984; University of Warwick, Coventry, M.Phil. in English 1993. **Career:** Guest tutor, Time-Based Media, Cardiff Institute of Fine Arts, 1991-93; freelance writer, journalist, and performance artist in Oslo and England, 1993—; lecturer, 1995—, then director of performance writing, Dartington College of Arts, Tontes, England. Co-editor of video magazine, Cardiff, Wales, 1994-95. Guest lecturer, Jesus College, Cambridge, and poet-in-residence, U.N.H. summer Program, Cambridge, both 1997. Contributor to numerous periodicals, including *Critical Quarterly, Trois, Angel Exhaust, Raddle Moon, Tongue to Boot, Big Allis, Performance Research, Words Worth, CHAIN,* and *PAJ.* **Address:** Dartington College, Tontes, England.

PUBLICATIONS

Poetry

An Oblique View of a Room in Movement. Oslo, Monolith, 1989.
Strange Passage—A Choral Poem. Cambridge, Equipage, 1994.

A Queer Dresser (tale for the dashing). London, Diva 3, 1994.
Eclat—Sites 1-10. Lowestoft, England, Sound & Language, 1996.

Other

Translator, *Typhon Dru* by Nicole Brossard. London, Reality Street, 1997.

*

Caroline Bergvall comments:

Brought up bilingual [in Norway]. Adopted English for writing ten years ago. Now trilingual. Which is much more complicated than being here and here and here at once and the same time. Geographical grounding escapes me. Portable geography finds its fields in the body—my own, others' architecture—and in language.

*   *   *

Caroline Bergvall has, in a very brief space of time (since 1989), made an important name for herself as one of Europe's leading young innovators in the arts of performance writing and "experimental" poetry. The latter term, when used in the British context out of which she is presently working, refers to writing that responds to recent philosophies concerning the social construction of space and self through the medium of language. As a performance writer of such poetry, Bergvall investigates the inscribed locations that "make us visible" by moving actively, "flicker and mass," across culture's built-in spaces and pages in the effort to intersect and interfere with conventional lines in their blueprints. One reason that her work has been quickly and readily received in other contexts and on other continents is that like her it has, from the outset, depended on the crossing of boundaries for its life.

Bergvall's location of the body's "portable geography" through language evidences her avoidance of mystifying the non-verbal, though the tension between it and the verbal sets the (st)(p)age for her work. The notorious eroticism of her texts is generated, in part, by the productiveness of this tension, though nothing in Bergvall's work becomes a metaphor for anything else. Sex, writing, and walking through a house (as we do in several of her works) all happen in overwritten spaces, and though no one of these performances becomes a vehicle for figuring any more deeply interior process, they all illuminate the mental steps we make to go inside the containers we build to house experience. "If to belongs (is to erase) is to appear," as she puts it in *Strange Passage—A Choral Poem*, the non-verbal exists as a space that remains latent within or adjacent to the current historical framework and its limiting textual architecture that all words / selves must enter into in order to effect communication, become visible, "[i]f to be recorded is to be seen." The flagging of such seeming contradictions which are actually intersections—belonging = erasing = appearing—brings spaces of greater and lesser accessibility into proximity with one another; "strange passage" happens when the excessive or non-belonging, which sometimes takes the form of punctuation run spatially amok, or (often lesbian) sexual / discursive movements gone "over the top," opens up a space by surprise.

One of her most recent works, *Eclat* (1996), French for such surprising events as a burst of noise or laughter, or a flash of light, makes this project / process into a walk-through experience for the reader.

> 1. **This is not a doorframe and that is T H A T**
> (doorframe that) divider: lines up intersections between
> room: and room: and corridor: to join & split at each such:
> :::::**HEREand**:::::
> : Pull in & widen up & widen up & pull in. And not there:
> and nor here: and nor there. Conflict exchange. Amassed
> pressure stimuli.

Every "here" become a "HEREand" in the sequence—an intersection; a possible doorframe too, to another way of looking at things, despite the also possibly authoritative disavowal in the first line's emboldened announcement that it is not "and that is THAT." "Prolonged station" at any such potential impasse threatens, as the next verse paragraph tells up, everything from "aphasia" to "nationalism"; the drawing of artificial architectural lines which, with forgetfulness of their construction, become "natural" boundaries expands with such implications for other spaces at every one of the ten "sites" in the sequence.

Eclat is a good example of Bergvall's earlier works as well in that is has had several incarnations—first as a site-specific installation, recorded for walkman as a guided tour (of a house); next as "visual and textual documentation" for the "Artist's pages" of the London journal *Performance Research;* and publication in book form for the innovative British press, Sound & Language—all of which spatialize the texts in turn, and in endless dialectic, inform our creation of spaces and ways of moving. "It is the distribution of the textual across such a range of environments which I'm interested in," she writes in an essay delivered to an international gathering of experimentalist published in *Assembling Alternatives* (1996); rather than deciding which of the texts is the original, she prefers to "think through how each siting affects the next one, highlighting or disabling certain aspects of the previous texts in the process... Here Borges' allegory of the book of sand which one can never read back, must always read on, describes quite accurately the mixture of excitement and horror this kind of practice generates from the point [of view] of what we call literary practice." Bergvall's dedication to such continuous movement—both in the envisioning of epistemological boundaries and in the enscripting of her own texts—says much about her innovative form of feminist thinking as well, and the dynamism with which she realigns all potential identifications for herself and for her work.

—Romana Huk

BERKELEY, Sara

Nationality: Irish. **Born:** Dublin, Ireland, 7 March 1967. **Education:** Trinity College, Dublin, B.A. 1989; University of California, Berkeley, and South Bank Polytechnic, London, 1991. **Career:** Digital Equipment Corporation, Reading, England, technical writer, 1991-92; Autodesk, Inc., San Rafael, California, technical writer, 1992—. **Awards:** Irish Book Awards shortlist, and *Sunday Tribune* Arts award shortlist, both 1986, both for *Penn*.

PUBLICATIONS

Poetry

Penn. Ireland, Raven Arts Press, and Saskatoon, Thistledown Press, 1986.
Home Movie Nights. Ireland, Raven Arts Press, and Saskatoon, Thistledown Press, 1989.
Facts about Water. Newcastle upon Tyne, Bloodaxe Books, and Saskatoon, Thistledown Press, 1994.

Short Stories

The Swimmer in the Deep Blue Dream. Ireland, Raven Arts Press, 1991.

*   *   *

Sara Berkeley writes a poetry that shimmers with lyrical energy. Frequently ringing changes on an elemental imagery of fire and water, she tends less to describe than to evoke. Unlike many male Irish poets she focuses her gaze on an interior rather than exterior domain; a misty absence of recognizable landmarks is the occasional risk she takes in so doing. "The Road to the Interior" challenges comparison with poems by, say, Seamus Heaney about venturing into a lonely landscape; in contrast with Heaney's "The Peninsula," Berkeley's poem is an explicitly dreamed encounter with inner bleakness.

Berkeley is a poet of opposed feelings, often blurring into one another within the same poem. For all her directness she is also a poet of reserve and repression. In "Pole-bound" she veers between asserting "I am the jubilant one, / highflown" and conceding "everything's under lock and key / in my heart," both statements depending for their impact on a canny use of line-breaks. She has a gift for the unnerving perception, as in "A Time of Drought" where she seems scared that the poem's "you" will (metaphorically) sink, but then writes: "I saw it suited you to drown."

Berkeley's precocious first collection *Penn* contains poems that refer obliquely to the process of creating poetry. "Out in the Storm" deploys its central image—of riding the storm—to sketch the poet's need to stay in control of exhilarating but dangerous forces; the poem concludes, "Driving storms is fun until they crash." A poet's early poems often map out her future (one thinks of Adrienne Rich's comparable "Storm Warnings"), and it's not improbable that still-to-be-written poems by Berkeley will explore what happens when storms crash. "Brainburst" indicates the poet's stance towards experience in these early poems. It opens with a Janus-faced image of light standing "shyly before intrepid shadow." Despite Berkeley's pronouncement "I am too bright," the reader may feel that the poet finds something of her inner being embodied by "intrepid shadow."

Berkeley's poems don't, as a rule, give up their secrets easily. The close of "Brainburst" suggests her awareness of the way that I becomes another in a poem: "soon it is no longer I who am bright, / who cries out." But the poems continually invite us to explore their stealthy yet staccato explorations. Often written in short lines yet occasionally flowering into lyrical pentameters, rhymes, and refrains, they seem at once attracted by and wary of a full-throated poetic music. The result is a fascinating mix of surrender and control, restraint and feeling. "The Figures in the Rain" from Berkeley's second collection, *Home Movie Nights,* is a beautiful lyric about promise and disappointment, and the dubious compensations of imagining what might have been.

"Maker of Rain," in the same volume, uses a ballad-like refrain as a cord to tie together a bundle of memories, and illustrates Berkeley's ability to write an affectingly bittersweet love poetry. In the title-poem of *Facts about Water,* water and fire are redeemed from the suggestions of danger with which they are invested by warning voices. Rather, the poet uses her images to imply the sustaining value of relationship, even through the relationship appears now to be over: "He left me sleeping, / I woke without fear." The collection shows a fine willingness to trust in its images to suggest emotional states and their changes and development; in the punningly titled "Sea-borne" Berkeley quietly allegorizes the ripening of intimacy (and her slight reluctance to succumb to it) through a series of metaphors drawn from the sea. There is also a greater confidence in her own poetic mode of knowing, obliquely celebrated in lines at the end of "Sung through Fire," lines which might stand as an epigraph to the work of this talented poet:

> Most of knowing
> is not knowing but a guess,
> rage at the signs of nothingness,
> fury and fear,
> disappointment, disillusionment
>
> and in the end
> among the ashes
> love.

—Michael O'Neill

BHATT, Sujata

Nationality: American. **Born:** Ahmedabad, India, 6 May 1956; immigrated to the United States, 1968. **Education:** Goucher College, Baltimore, Maryland, B.A. in philosophy and English 1980; University of Iowa Writers' Workshop, Iowa City, M.F.A. 1986. **Family:** Married Michael Augustin in 1988; one daughter. **Career:** Freelance writer and translator; Lansdowne Visiting Writer/Professor, University of Victoria, British Columbia, spring 1992. Freelance writer and translator. Contributor to periodicals, including *Calyx, The Painted Bride Quarterly, Yellow Silk, PN Review, New Statesman & Society, Poetry Review,* and *Iowa Journal of Literary Studies.* **Awards:** Alice Hunt Bartlett award, 1988; Dillons Commonwealth Poetry prize, 1989; Poetry Society Book Recommendation, 1991, for *Monkey Shadows;* Cholmondeley award, 1991. **Address:** c/o Carcanet Press, 4th Floor, Conavon Court, 12-16 Blackfriars St., Manchester M3 5BQ, England.

PUBLICATIONS

Poetry

Brunizem. Manchester, Carcanet, 1988; New Delhi, Penguin India, 1993.
Monkey Shadows. Manchester, Carcanet, 1991; New Delhi, Penguin India, 1993.

Freak Waves (chapbook). Victoria, British Columbia, Reference West, 1992.
The Stinking Rose. Manchester, Carcanet, 1995.
Point No Point. Manchester, Carcanet, 1997.
Angatora. Manchester, Carcanet, 1998.

*

Critical Study: "Sujata Bhatt in Conversation with Eleanor Wilner," in *PN Review* (Manchester), vol. 19, no. 4, March / April 1993.

*   *   *

Sujata Bhatt's is unabashedly a poetry of confession. Born in India, educated in the United States, and now residing in Germany, Bhatt has found her most compelling subject in the vast disparities of these worlds. Yet she never exploits difference simply to point a neat or ironic juxtaposition, nor is she content with an easy nostalgia. Instead, her best poems wonderingly, and often poignantly, attempt to form an authentically hybrid imaginative whole from experiences that of necessity resist coherence.

Bhatt's poetry insistently returns to a ground note of exile, as when a Bremen flower stall is filtered through the mature speaker's memory of a childhood garden in Poona, India, and simultaneously registered through the eyes of the speaker's newborn, half-German daughter ("At the Flower Market"). In the earlier "Go to Ahmedabad," "home" is formulated by an eloquent mnemonic: "for this is the place / I always loved / this is the place / I always hated / for this is the place / I can never be at home in / this is the place / I will always be at home in." In "Devibhen Pathak," one of many poems about Bhatt's ancestors, the poet-speaker meditates (in Germany in the 1980s, we are to assume) on the gold necklace, adorned with a swastika (for Hindus a potent religious symbol), that she has inherited from her grandmother: "Oh didn't I love the Hindu Swastika? / And later, one day didn't I start wishing / I could rescue that shape from history?" The interrogative mode permits Bhatt to assume a persona that is simultaneously sincere and wry, and her habitual sensitivity to place is amplified here by the translator's attuned ear for cultural idiom.

An important set of Bhatt's poems anticipates, and answers, the criticism frequently leveled against Indian poets in English, that genuine poetry cannot be written in a foreign language. The word "brunizem," referring to a prairie soil common to Asia, Europe, and North America, and from which her award-winning first collection takes its name, signals Bhatt's powerfully organic concern with language. Thus, we read in the title poem of the volume,

> The other night
> I dreamt English
> was my middle name.
> And I cried, telling my mother
> "I don't want English
> to be my middle name.
> Can't you change it to something else?"
> "Go read the dictionary." She said.

Bhatt's method in these poems moves swiftly from the discursive to the imagistic, as in "A Different History":

> Which language
> has not been the oppressor's tongue?
> Which language
> truly meant to murder someone?
> And how does it happen
> that after the torture,
> after the soul has been cropped
> with a long scythe sweeping out
> of the conqueror's face—
> the unborn grandchildren
> grow to love that strange language.

The long poem "Search for My Tongue" bravely struggles with similar problems:

> You ask me what I mean
> by saying I have lost my tongue.
> I ask you, what would you do
> if you had two tongues in your mouth,
> and lost the first one, the mother tongue,
> and could not really know the other,
> the foreign tongue.

In this ambitious experiment in bilingual poetry English and a remembered Gujarati (the "mother tongue") are pitted against each other in urgently escalating typographic and dialogic conflict. Resolution comes only when the conversational cadences of Bhatt's English freeze into the staccato, extralinguistic rhythms of an accompanying tabla: "I can't (dha) / I can't (dha) / I can't forget I can't forget / (dha dhin dhin dha)" [with the Gujarati script omitted and typographic exactitude sacrificed].

In the title poem of her second volume, *Monkey Shadows,* Bhatt finds in the monkey—at once bestial and human, inarticulate and expressive, a dissected object in a laboratory and a living denizen of a childhood garden—a versatile emblem of liminality. Her method is cross-mythologizing, informed by two distinct literary traditions: Eurydice and Demeter coexist in her work with Hanuman and Ganesh. Other significant poems sketch the emotional localities of a specifically female experience ("Marie Curie to Her Husband," "Clara Westhoff to Rainer Maria Rilke," "Written after Hearing about the Soviet Invasion of Afghanistan," "White Asparagus"). Less successful, I think, are her later poems after paintings—"Rooms by the Sea," "Sunlight in a Cafeteria," "Portrait of a Double Portrait"—which seem arch and mannered in a self-conscious writing workshop style.

Bhatt's unrelenting confessional self-examination, with a passionate and fluid free-verse line as its unit, announces a new direction in Indian poetry in English—a movement away from the rhythmic control and ironic detachment of a Nissim Ezekiel or an R. Parthasarathy. Finally, no one poem does justice to the complexity of Bhatt's talent, which makes itself known from the accretion of sensory detail sifted through an engaged and vigilant consciousness. She has mastered, and possibly exhausted, her chosen form, the memorializing of intensely lived experience.

—Minnie Singh

BLOCH, Chana

Nationality: American. **Born:** New York City, 15 March 1940. **Education:** Cornell University, B.A. 1961; Brandeis University, M.A. in Near Eastern and Judaic studies 1963, M.A. in English literature 1964; University of California, Berkeley, Ph.D., 1975. **Family:** Married Ariel A. Bloch in 1969 (divorced 1996); two sons. **Career:** Instructor in English literature, Hebrew University of Jerusalem, Jerusalem, Israel, 1964-67; associate, department of Near Eastern Studies, University of California, Berkeley, 1967-69; instructor, 1973-75, assistant professor, 1975-81, associate professor, 1981-87, chair, 1986-89; professor of English literature, 1987—, W.M. Keck Professor, 1996—, and director, creative writing program, 1993—, Mills College, Oakland, California. **Awards:** Discovery Award for poetry, 1974; Pomona College Graves award, 1976-77; Columbia University Translation Center award, 1978, for *A Dress of Fire;* National Endowment for the Humanities fellowship, 1980; Conference on Christianity and Literature Book of the Year award, 1986, for *Spelling the Word: George Herbert and the Bible;* Exchange Writers award (*Poets and Writers*), 1988; National Endowment for the Arts fellowship, 1989-90. **Agent:** Georges Borchardt, 136 East 57th St., New York, NY 10022. **Address:** 12 Menlo Place, Berkeley, California 94707, U.S.A.

PUBLICATIONS

Poetry

The Secrets of the Tribe. New York, Sheep Meadow Press, 1980.
The Past Keeps Changing. New York, Sheep Meadow Press, 1992.

Other

Spelling the Word: George Herbert and the Bible (criticism). Berkeley, University of California Press, 1985.

Translator, *A Dress of Fire: Selected Poetry of Dahlia Ravikovitch.* London, Menard, 1976.
Translator, with Ariel Bloch, *The Window: New and Selected Poems,* by Dahlia Ravikovitch. New York, Sheep Meadow Press, 1989.
Translator, with Stephen Mitchell, *Selected Poetry,* by Yehuda Amichai. New York, Harper, 1986; revised and expanded, Berkeley, University of California Press, 1996.
Translator, with Ariel Bloch, *The Song of Songs.* New York, Random House, 1995.

*

Critical Studies: "A Place to Put the Pain: Three Cancer Stories" by Marilyn Chandler McEntyre, in *Literature and Medicine,* Spring 1995, and her "Letters from Exile: Poetry and Pain, in *Santa Barbara Review,* Spring 1996.

Chana Bloch comments:

My primary subject, as one critic put it, is "the mixed pain and joy of intimate connections." In my first book, *The Secrets of the Tribe,* I wrote about my roles as daughter, new wife, and member of the tribe, and about the conflicts of family life as they are illuminated by the tales in Genesis. *The Past Keeps Changing,* my second book, is about my struggle against cancer and my husband's against an acute depression; the ways in which we (often unwittingly) shape the lives of our children; and the strains of a long marriage, particularly in the face of crisis. My third collection of poems (in progress), *The Caterer's Knife,* is about the dis-

solution of that marriage of 25 years as a result of my husband's increasingly severe manic-depressive illnesses. The poems in this book are not simply documentary or elegiac. What interests me, now as before, is the inner life: how we are formed by our losses and those of our parents, how we learn what we know, how we wrestle with our confusions and intuitions, how we deny and distort and finally discover who we are.

My skills as a poet have been sharpened by my work as a translator from Yiddish and Hebrew—work which has taught me a great deal about tone, register, and rhythm. Translation has engaged me since my 20s, when Robert Lowell suggested to me in a poetry workshop that I could learn the craft of poetry from my own translations. I have translated Yiddish poetry by Jacob Glatstein and Abraham Sutzkever, Yiddish fiction by Isaac Bashevis Singer, Hebrew poetry by Yehuda Amichai and Dahlia Ravikovitch, and the biblical Song of Songs. Finally, my scholarly study of George Herbert has shaped my poetry as well: Herbert's clarity, artistic control, and unsparing self-analysis remain a model and a guide.

*   *   *

"To be the object of so much weather!" declares Chana Blotch in "Alone on the Mountain," and many of her poems could be the object of this exclamation: small in focus, tough in element, stripped of all baroque tendencies, yet tried by passions. Dave Smith has observed, "Her wisdom is fully mature and her portraits as strikingly unadorned as the great Appalachian photographs of Doris Ullman. This is not street poetry but it has the grit and wind and changelessness of streets because it has the durable face of people striding forward, bent on living."

Her first book of poems, *The Secrets of the Tribe,* intersperses personal memories with Biblical storyscape, creating a world where the mythological enters unobtrusively into the suburbs. Myth and the great histories shrink like aging parents into the panel of the present, indelible yet barely visible, as in "Exile":

What happened to the ten lost tribes
is no great mystery:
they found work, married, grew smaller,
started to look like the natives
in a landscape nobody chose.
Soon you couldn't have picked them out of a crowd.

So often Bloch writes of this situation, the loss of a pre-lapsarian paradise which is ultimately unbelievable—yet traces of it cannot help but be seen in the mundane present:

We salvage
a pewter dish cross-hatched as a bubba's face,
a bent spoon. But the naked

dance of the mouth and the eyes before
we knew were smiling,
promises
of that land ...

Nothing is exempt from the stain and strain of the day-to-day life: angels "bicker and agree," "spiteful as children who won't be told" ("The Angels"); "Adam is clay, the dumb / stuff of kids' / games" ("Paradise"); after killing Abel, "Cain blunders down the alleyways of / barren towns, the suburbs / of memory" ("Brothers"). Judaism is a reliable frame of reference, but offers no transcendence of banality; in "The Converts," these faithful seem to believe in the paradise that Bloch's speaker finds a chimera: "and I covet / what they think we've got."

The Past Keeps Changing, Bloch's second book of poetry, is a celebration of relationships with persons both dead and living—not a romanticization but a recognition and a distillation in the poem. Through these poems, Bloch also raises the issue of poetic tropes: are they truly essence of the subject, or are they simply an escape from hard truths as the poet makes an image stand in for an entire history? Bloch seems to imply that these tropes are the most "accurate" manner to portray complex relationships, which embrace and evade pain as well as pleasure, and sometimes simply slip off into (again) the banality of routine:

> Whatever you gave me, I made it serve,
> I couldn't save it
> for later. That's why only your handprints
> are left, faintly visible
> pressed into the clay.
> ("The Valley of the Dead")

The book ends with a statement on the veracity of dreams, or what creates them: "All day you grope in a web of invisible stars / ...They must be out there in all that dazzle" ("Day-Blind"). Bloch's poetry shows a movement away from mythological and historical backgrounds, including those of her own past, to freer constructs of her own immediate reckoning, many of which have to do with maternity and other particular experiences of a woman's rich and varied life—the "dazzle" which belongs to this particular speaker's present and future, out of which she must weave her web of stars.

—Cynthia Davidson

BOLAND, Eavan

Nationality: Irish. **Born:** Dublin, 24 September 1944. **Education:** Trinity College, Dublin, B.A. in English (first-class honors), 1967. **Family:** Married Ken Casey in 1969; two daughters. **Career:** Junior lecturer, Trinity College, Dublin, 1967-68; lecturer, School of Irish Studies, Dublin, 1968—. **Awards:** Macaulay fellowship in poetry, 1968; Jacobs award for broadcasting, 1977; Irish American Cultural award, 1983; American Ireland Fund Literary award, 1994. **Member:** Irish Academy of Letters. **Address:** c/o *Irish Times,* 13 D'Olier Street, Dublin 2, Ireland.

PUBLICATIONS

Poetry

23 Poems. Dublin, Gallagher, 1962.
Autumn Essay. Dublin, Gallagher, 1963.
Poetry. Dublin, Gallagher, 1963.
New Territory. Dublin, Alan Figgis, 1967.
The War Horse. London, Gollancz, 1975.
In Her Own Image, illustrations by Constance Short. Dublin, Arlen House, 1980.

Introducing Eavan Boland. Princeton, New Jersey, Ontario Review Press, 1981.
Night Feed. Dublin, Arlen House, and London and Boston, Marion Boyars, 1982.
The Journey. Deerfield Press, 1983.
The Journey and Other Poems. Manchester, Carcanet, 1987.
Selected Poems. Manchester, Carcanet, 1989.
Outside History: Selected Poems, 1980-90. Manchester, Carcanet, and New York, Norton, 1990.
In a Time of Violence. Manchester, Carcanet, 1994.
Collected Poems. Manchester, Carcanet, 1995.
An Origin like Water: Collected Poems, 1967-1987. New York, Norton, 1996.

Other

A Kind of Scar: The Woman Poet in a National Tradition. Dublin, Attic Press, 1989.
Object Lessons: The Life of the Woman and the Poet in Our Time. Manchester, Carcanet, and New York, Norton, 1995.

*

Critical Studies: "A Material Fascination" by Lachlan Mackinnon, in *Times Literary Supplement* (London), no. 4403, 21 August 1987; "Toward Her Own Image" by Amy Klauke, in *Northwest Review* (Eugene, Oregon), vol. 25, no. 1, 1987; "'What You Have Seen Is beyond Speech': Female Journeys in the Poetry of Eavan Boland and Eilean Ni Chuilleanain" by Sheila C. Conboy, in *Canadian Journal of Irish Studies* (Saskatoon), vol. 16, no. 1, July 1990; "Improvising the Blackbird" by David Walker, in *Field* (Oberlin, Ohio), no. 44, Spring 1991; "Ecriture Feminine and the Authorship of Self in Eavan Boland's 'In Her Own Image'" by Jody Allen-Randolph, in *Colby Quarterly* (Waterville, Maine), vol. 27, no. 1, March 1991; "Contemporary Irish Women Poets: The Privatisation of Myth" by Clair Wills in *Diverse Voices,* edited by Harriet Devine Jump, New York, St. Martin's Press, 1991; "'We Were Never on the Scene of the Crime': Eavan Boland's Repossession of History" by Patricia L. Hagen, in *Twentieth-Century Literature,* no. 37, Winter 1991; "Eavan Boland's Journey with the Muse" by Ellen M. Mahon, in *Learning the Trade: Essays on W.B. Yeats and Contemporary Poetry,* edited by Deborah Fleming, West Cornwall, Connecticut, Locust Hill, 1993; "'Out of Myth into History': The Poetry of Eavan Boland and Eilean Ni Chuilleanain" by Deborah Sarbin, in *Canadian Journal of Irish Studies* (Saskatoon), vol. 19, no. 1, July 1993; "Finding a Voice Where She Found a Vision" by Jody Allen-Randolph, in *PN Review* (Manchester), vol. 21, no. 1, September-October 1994; "Anxiety, Influence, Tradition and Subversion in the Poetry of Eavan Boland" by Kerry E. Robertson, in *Colby Quarterly* (Waterville, Maine), vol. 30, no. 4, December 1994; "'An Origin like Water': The Poetry of Eavan Boland and Modernist Critiques of Irish Literature" by Ann Owens Weekes, in *Bucknell Review* (Cranbury, New Jersey), vol. 38, no. 1, 1994; *Women Creating Women: Contemporary Irish Women Poets* by Patricia Boyle Haberstroh, Syracuse, New York, Syracuse University Press, 1995.

*   *   *

Eavan Boland is very self-consciously an Irish woman poet. As she said in the 1994 Ronald Duncan lecture, "I am an Irish poet. A woman poet. In the first category I enter the tradition of the English language at an angle. In the second, I enter my own tradition at an even more steep angle." Many of her poetry's strengths, and some of its weaknesses (principally, a tendency to go for flat declarations), derive from the difficult relation to poetic tradition which is articulated here. In the midst of, and often propelling, her changes of style there is a steady yearning to draw inspiration from a figure addressed in a poem from *Night Feed* (1982) as "The Muse Mother." Here the poet looks at a woman with a child and writes in weighted short lines (a reaction against the careful rhyming of her early work) of her desire "to be a sibyl / able to sing the past / in pure syllables / ... / able to speak at last / my mother tongue."

For all the craving for "pure syllables," the great virtue of Boland's work, like that of Adrienne Rich, is the way it at once contests and negotiates with the impurities of the quotidian. One of her many fine meditations on paintings, "Self-Portrait on a Summer Evening," concludes with "I am Chardin's woman / edged in reflected light, / hardened by / the need to be ordinary." "Hardened" implies a strengthening or clarifying that is perilously close to a certain obduracy, and much of Boland's work counts the cost of self-definition. In "The New Pastoral" she sees herself, a shade cumbersomely, as a "displaced person / in a pastoral chaos." But the cumbersome is laid aside at the end, where she describes what she sees as "amnesias / of a rite / I danced once on a frieze." Even in this graceful recapturing there is irony, as Boland is compelled to use a traditional pastoral image for her antitraditional sense of a lost self.

Boland's concern with self is, for the most part, unsolipsistic, and her career has been a long struggle to remain true to her own experience yet to find a way of speaking in more universal terms about "herstory." "Ode to Suburbia" is a witty example from her earlier work, where Boland's command of a long sentence spun across a tightly rhymed stanza helps to give the feel of one experience "multiplied":

> How long ago did the glass in your windows subtly
> Silver into mirrors which again
> And again show the same woman
> Shriek at a child, which multiply
> A dish, a brush, ash...

In subsequent poems Boland experiments with a Plath-like voice of controlled ferocity. These poems can, as in "Woman in Kitchen," take on a little too well the blanched hues of the very restrictedness against which they protest. That said, a poem such as "Anorexic" is a superb tour de force, partly because of the conceit it employs of the anorexic speaker seeking to "slip / back into him again / as if I had never been away." More complexly satisfying are Boland's poems of motherhood, found mainly in *Night Feed*. As is the case in Plath's poems about her children, Boland is able to suggest a range of feelings; a credible love is shadowed and intensified by awareness of a range of differences— between experience and innocence, between the celebrated moment and the future. "Night Feed" lets the silences between its short assertions do most of the poem's work: "Poplars stilt for dawn / And we begin / The long fall from grace. / I tuck you in." Here the final gesture and rhyme hold at bay the saddened onset of a "fall from grace."

Boland's best work, however, is written in the longer, fluent line of poems such as "The Journey." The staccato syntax of *Night Feed* yields to a more dreamlike eddying progression as the poet (possibly influenced by Seamus Heaney's example in *Station Island*) is led in reverie by Sappho into an underworld of "women and children." Boland's characteristic desire to "'let me at least be their witness'" is delicately rebuked by Sappho, who replies that "what you have seen is beyond speech, / beyond song, only not beyond love." The moment has a Dantescan ring, yet it also shows how Boland is able to adapt Dante to her own concerns. The poem's movement and atmosphere of dream vision are impressively sustained.

In a Time of Violence (1994) builds on the achievement of *The Journey,* revealing a new appetite for detail and a corresponding ability to weave detail into finely cadenced meditations. This is not to suggest that Boland's poetry has lost its edge, quietly apparent in the sequence "Writing in a Time of Violence." But it is to claim for the volume an authority which, in her Duncan lecture, Boland speaks of as hard for her as an Irish woman poet to attain. There is in the collection a hard-won awareness that art can serve not only to express problems but also to provide solutions, however provisional. In "Time and Violence" Boland is visited by a (female) voice she ventriloquizes as saying "Write us out of the poem. Make us human / in cadences of change and mortal pain / and words we can grow old and die in." At this stage in her career Boland is able to span the vast gap between the ruthless imperatives of art and the claims of the "human" and to span it in such a way that art begins to seem a qualified source of consolation. Thus, in the final poem, "The Art of Grief," she ends with an implied question that is also a calmly "unflinching" statement, the poet wondering "whether she flinched as the chisel found / that region her tears inferred, / where grief and its emblems are inseparable."

—Michael O'Neill

BORNHOLDT, Jenny

Nationality: New Zealander. **Born:** Jennifer Mary Bornholdt, Lower Hutt, 1 November 1960. **Education:** Victoria University, Wellington, 1981-84, B.A. in English literature 1984. **Family:** Married Gregory O'Brien in 1994; one son. **Career:** Bookseller, Unity Books, Wellington, 1989-92; copywriter, Haines Recruitment Advertising, Wellington, 1992-97; currently public programs coordinator, City Gallery, Wellington. **Address:** c/o Victoria University Press, Private Bag, Wellington, New Zealand.

PUBLICATIONS

Poetry

This Big Face. Wellington, Victoria University Press, 1988.
Moving House. Wellington, Victoria University Press, 1989.
Waiting Shelter. Wellington, Victoria University Press, 1991.
How We Met. Wellington, Victoria University Press, 1995.

Editor, with Gregory O'Brien, *My Heart Goes Swimming: New Zealand Love Poems.* Auckland, Godwit, 1996.
Editor, with Gregory O'Brien and Mark Williams, *An Anthology of New Zealand Poetry in English.* Melbourne, Oxford University Press, 1997.

*   *   *

Since the late 1980s Jenny Bornholdt has begun to accumulate a body of work that is recognizably her own. Her first book, *This Big Face,* shows her experimenting with two kinds of writing: sensitive, intimate lyrics, and more outgoing dramatic dialogues, prose poems, and playlets—almost multimedia performance pieces. Both types, however, are informed by sharp observation and precise description of feeling and event.

Here are the first lines from "Breath":

Your warm breath
mists up my skin
like glass...

The conceit conveys the intimacy of the moment and also delicately hints at a coolness on the part of the speaker. There is a sense of fragility and risk in the third line, which leads on to

quick, finger in the message
write me a note of
your intentions
I have forgotten already
what we are doing here,
why we lie this close
breathing each other's
breath this way

The medium (misted glass) requires there to be "the message" that might help her recover the passion that is "forgotten already." Although this is a slight poem and the tension perhaps dissipates towards the end, it illustrates where Bornholdt's strengths lie.

It is with some assurance that Bornholdt tackles the challenge of the longer sequence in the title poem of *Waiting Shelter* and in "We will, we do," an exploration of family and origins and of the tension between New Zealand, where she was born, and her European heritage. In the shorter lyrics she continues to pursue her own individual vision: "You approach the world / with open arms and hope / it wants you. Hope to be / asked in to sit amongst the / fine furniture... / Here it is. / Here's the world on a good / day, turned slightly / away, but this is no / offence, merely the sun was / in its eyes..." ("The Visit").

Bornholdt's collection *How We Met* opens with a set of 18 poems whose titles are those of Estonian folk songs: for example, "My sister, my little cricket"; "Urging her into the boat"; "My mouth was singing / My heart was worrying." In the last the poem is merely a gloss on the title: "O deceptive mouth / covering up / for the heart like that." In several of these poems the folk element combines with a surrealism that touched some earlier works; in others she establishes a nicely judged balance of the passionate and the dispassionate, as in "Praising the cook":

They say the sexual impulse
is like a fiery horse.

When you break an egg
          one-handed
into the frying pan
it sounds like distant hooves
crossing a dusty plain.

With four uneven but interesting collections to her credit, it is clear that Jenny Bornholdt enjoys her writing and wants her reader to experience and enjoy the world she creates. Not all of her poems work, but as a collection they show us a young writer with a feel for words, the patterns they make, and the resonances they strike.

—Alan Roddick

BORSON, Roo

Nationality: American and Canadian. **Born:** Ruth Elizabeth Borson, Berkeley, California, 20 January 1952. **Education:** University of California, Santa Barbara, 1969-71; Goddard College, Plainfield, Vermont, 1971-73, B.A. 1973; University of British Columbia, Vancouver, 1975-77, M.F.A. 1977. **Career:** Teacher of writing workshops and writer-in-residence, University of Western Ontario, London, 1987-88, and Concordia University, Montreal, 1993. **Awards:** University of British Columbia Macmillan prize, 1977; Canada Council grant, 1982, 1984, 1988, 1991, and 1994; Canadian Broadcasting Corporation Literary award, 1984, 1989, and 1991; National Endowment for the Arts fellowship, 1986. **Address:** c/o Writers' Union of Canada, 54 Ryerson Avenue, Toronto, Ontario M5T 2P3, Canada.

PUBLICATIONS

Poetry

Landfall. Fredericton, New Brunswick, Fiddlehead, 1977.
In the Smoky Light of the Fields. Toronto, Three Trees Press, 1980.
Rain. Moonbeam, Ontario, Penumbra Press, 1980.
A Sad Device. Dunvegan, Ontario, Quadrant, 1981.
Night Walk. Toronto, Missing Link Press, 1981.
The Whole Night, Coming Home. Toronto, McClelland & Stewart, 1984.
The Transparence of November Snow, with Kim Maltman. Kingston, Ontario, Quarry Press, 1985.
Intent, or, The Weight of the World. Toronto, McClelland & Stewart, 1989.
Night Walk, Selected Poems. Toronto, Oxford University Press, 1994.
Water Memory. Toronto, McClelland & Stewart, 1996.

*

Roo Borson comments:

(1995) In recent years I've been interested in the interplay of physical sensation and memory; in how the fine distinctions of emotional nuance are encoded or enacted in speech; how rhetoric is made up of rhythm, pitch, tonality, atonality; how consciousness wanders musically.

*   *   *

Roo Borson is one of the young Americans who went north to Canada in the 1970s to take a higher degree. She settled first in

Vancouver, where the panorama of islands and snowcapped mountains are as spectacular and beautiful as the scenery of her native California. Later, she lived in Toronto. A third-generation poet, she was in her middle 20s when her first book of poems appeared. Five other collections followed quickly. At age 32 she won first prize in the Canadian Broadcasting Corporation's literary competition with "Folklore," which later appeared as a section of her 1984 collection *The Whole Night, Coming Home.* The book is an evocation of Borson's childhood in Berkeley. The sensual, almost mystical appreciation of the scents and the lush gardens and hillsides and the consciousness of another, working life going on in San Francisco, lit up across the Bay, and Oakland, the industrial port to the east, invoke a world both beautiful and tough.

Memories of her parents, their love for each other and their children, the solidarity of her family, are luminously symbolized by her mother's beautiful garden, an exotic paradise inhabited by snakes, dogs, spiders, snails, lizards, goldfish, frogs, and, particularly, cats. Occasionally the cumulative effect is powerful. The sweep of memory carries the reader along until, in the last lines of the title poem of the last section, "Folklore," it is summed up:

> And that which now comes alight, the house you grew
> up in: sometimes it is a lantern small enough to carry be-
> fore in one hand.

The Whole Night, Coming Home is also a chronicle of coming-of-age in the California of the reckless 1960s—the world seen from a speeding car full of flower children. These poems describe the comradeship of the adolescent gang, deeper friendships, sexual and spiritual awakening, as in the poem "Sixteen":

> She's seen it.
> How the tomcat bites the scruff
> of the female's neck so she can't get away:
> you can hear it hurting her and still she wants it.
> The girl doesn't want it though. It's not that
> she wants. She wants the part he keeps to himself,
> what's back of those eyes.

As Borson matured, her form moved from free verse to prose poems. Density of meaning and concentration of emotion make these poems as effective, if not more so, than those arranged with varying line lengths and rhythms. Here is a consciousness that observes and contemplates, a calm voice presenting the details we need for the same flash of understanding.

Borson is an avowed but gentle feminist who has said in an interview in the Montreal literary magazine *Rubicon* that she feels women have been conditioned to find their sense of worth by pleasing others and acquiring men to look after them; boys, on the other hand, have been conditioned to build and do things. She is against women-only anthologies, but feels that women need better access to publication; as it is women must be unusually accomplished to be recognized and appropriately rewarded. She has admitted that she unconsciously and inadvertently used patriarchal language in her 1981 collection *A Sad Device.* Now she is more careful. But she does not, like Erin Mouré and others among her contemporaries, feel the necessity for a new language to express women's concerns; nor does she believe that the language of the patriarchy, in existing before the poem does, shapes it, and must therefore be reformed.

If one has a criticism of Borson's poetry it might be that it is too beautiful, too cloying, perfect, and unreal. Perhaps this is why she has turned to the more stringent form of the prose poem, which she handles with such skill. For example, from *The Whole Night, Coming Home:*

> Purple, papery, wisteria wreathed the house, and each May a white box would arrive, its lid lifting to release not music but the smell of gardenias, their number compounded by one. What defines the union this gift symbolized, my father to my mother, if one who came of it may speak for it? But I can't. In the end we carry forward only a little of each story.

> In the evenings white ginger stood exalted in its leaves, anticipating stars, each point of origin, each needle in a nerve. Always the freedom, always the need, unresolved. Whatever came or is yet to come is of this middle realm, for which the human eye is the inevitable instrument. Awe and disappointment, unique and to scale. Out of bounds the unin-habitable regions, both larger and smaller, in which all of this lies innocently hidden. Just as here among us go unnoticed those merry-go-rounds whose horses appear or reappear, ghostwise, in the fuschia leaves.

In her collection *Intent, or, The Weight of the World* Borson would continue to explore the beauty and flexibility of the prose poem.

—Patience Wheatley

BOWERING, Marilyn (Ruthe)

Nationality: Canadian. **Born:** Winnipeg, Manitoba, 13 April 1949. **Education:** University of Victoria, British Columbia, 1966-68, 1969-71, B.A. 1971, M.A. 1973; University of British Columbia, Vancouver, 1968-69; University of New Brunswick, Fredericton, 1975-76. **Family:** Married Michael S. Elcock in 1982; one daughter. **Career:** Radio control room operator, CKDA, Victoria, 1972-73; writer-in-residence, Aegean School of Fine Arts, Paros, Greece, 1973-74; secondary teacher, G.M. Dawson, Masset, British Columbia, 1974-75; instructor in continuing education, University of British Columbia, 1977; lecturer in creative writing, University of Victoria, 1978-80, 1982-86, 1989; editor and writer, Gregson Graham Marketing, Victoria, 1978-80; editor, Noel Collins and Blackwells, Edinburgh, 1980-82. **Awards:** Canada Council Award, 1972, 1981, 1984, 1986, 1988, 1989, 1991; National Magazine award, 1978, 1989; Ontario Arts Council award, 1980, 1986; *Malahat Review* long poem prize, 1994. **Address:** 3007 Manzer Rd., Sooke, British Columbia V0S 1N0, Canada.

PUBLICATIONS

Poetry

The Liberation of Newfoundland. Fredericton, New Brunswick, Fiddlehead, 1973.
One Who Became Lost. Fredericton, New Brunswick, Fiddlehead, 1976.

The Killing Room. Victoria, British Columbia, Sono Nis Press, 1977; Victoria, British Columbia, Porcépic, 1991.

Third Child; Zian. Knotting, Bedfordshire, Sceptre Press, 1978.

The Book of Glass. Knotting, Bedfordshire, Sceptre Press, 1978.

Sleeping with Lambs. Victoria, British Columbia, Press Porcépic, 1980.

Giving Back Diamonds. Victoria, British Columbia, Press Porcépic, 1982.

The Sunday before Winter: New and Selected Poetry. Toronto, General, 1984.

Anyone Can See I Love You. Erin, Ontario, Porcupine's Quill, 1987.

Grandfather Was a Soldier. Victoria, British Columbia, Press Porcépic, 1987.

Calling All the World. Victoria, British Columbia, Press Porcépic, 1989.

Interior Castle. Victoria, British Columbia, Reference West, 1994.

Love As It Is. Victoria, British Columbia, Beach Holme, 1993.

Autobiography. Victoria, British Columbia, Beach Holme, 1996.

Plays

Anyone Can See I Love You (broadcast 1986; produced Victoria, British Columbia, 1988).

Hajimari-No-Hajimari (produced Japan, 1987).

Temple of the Stars (produced Victoria, British Columbia, 1996).

Radio Plays: *Grandfather Was a Soldier,* 1983; *Marilyn Monroe: Anyone Can See I Love You,* 1986; *Laika and Folchakov,* 1987; *A Cold Departure,* 1989.

Novels

The Visitors All Returned. Erin, Ontario, Press Porcépic, 1979.

To All Appearance a Lady. Mississauga, Ontario, Random House Canada, 1989; New York, Viking, and London, Hamish Hamilton, 1990.

Visible Worlds. New York, HarperCollins, 1997.

Other

Editor, with David, *Many Voices: An Anthology of Contemporary Canadian Poetry.* Vancouver, Douglas, 1977.

*

Critical Studies: "The Hidden Dreamer's Cry: Natural Force as Point of View" by M. Travis Lane, in *Fiddlehead* (Fredericton, New Brunswick), Winter 1977; "Verse into Poetry" by George Woodcock, in *Canadian Literature* (Vancouver), Autumn 1983.

Marilyn Bowering comments:

My poems, I'm told, are full surprises: the juxtaposition of the metaphysical with the sensuous and the everyday. Not that I'm after surprise, but that in speculating about the large things I can only use what I know. Serious in intent, certainly, but also with some irony, especially when considering men and women, and relatives.

Death remains a favorite topic.

Poetry is always an attempt to make sense and order and is a conjunction of the emotional and physical life with something that "cannot be said." In that sense it attempts to go beyond words, yet keeps the pleasure and shock of words as reward and impe-

tus for the journey. My early work was (as is so often the case) much concerned with the natural world and the past: the links of history and mythology that give the illusion of substance (and order) to the process of being alive. Later I became much more interested in exploring consciousnesses other (if that's possible) than my own. In the two verse radio works, *Grandfather Was a Soldier* and *Marilyn Monroe: Anyone Can See I Love You,* especially.

I admire poems that suggest story and this has led me to write more fiction. Most of all I like the dissatisfaction that the best poems encourage, as if there is something just out of reach beyond the edge of perception and with right risks taken it can be held in the hands.

* * *

A prolific writer, Marilyn Bowering remains best known as a poet even though she has also turned her energies to prose. A line in her first book, *The Liberation of Newfoundland,* sums up her poetic predilections: "all things are full of gods." In addition, the aqueous imagery found in this book recurs in much of her later work, as does an obsession with islands, caves, cliffs, dreams, bones, and killing. The early poem "Thera," in *One Who Became Lost,* sets forth this skeletal vision:

> The island hills
> arch grey spines
> from the sea.
> Facing them—
> white jagged ribs of the land,
>
> Bonemakers

Although in other poems she frequently derives her diction from the surrealists, Bowering does not cast their wide net of content. Indeed, her preoccupations appear private, even in their projection into natural forms of sea and land centered on personal agonies. As if to exorcise the latter, she is attracted to fairy tales and often resorts to charms, incantations, spells, and curses as mediums of expression. In her early work, such as *One Who Became Lost,* a certain monotonousness of perception tends to make one poem blur into another; later books like *Sleeping with Lambs* evidence greater variety and grasp of shape. She adroitly weaves these lines into the title poem of *Giving Back Diamonds:*

> I love you forever
> there's no one like you
> I'd do anything for you
> I want you just as you are
> goodbye forever, goodbye

The repetitive emphasis of this ironic refrain is given extra point by the book's epigraph from Zsa Zsa Gabor: "I never hated a man enough to give diamonds back." Perhaps a title in the "Giving Back Diamonds" section of *The Sunday before Winter* best describes Bowering's attitude to her materials: "Well, it ain't no sin to take off your skin and dance around in your bones."

Anyone Can See I Love You is a cycle of poems as told by Marilyn Monroe about her life. The book has been broadcast and staged—a measure of Bowering's success at re-creating the star's tough but vulnerable voice.

Bowering's later works build on earlier preoccupations. Inspired by the "fearful wonder" she felt as a child seeing Sputnik II in the sky, *Calling All the World* imaginatively and charmingly reconstructs the epochal journey of Laika, the Soviets' canine cosmonaut, and the terrestrial travels of Folchakhov, the dog's trainer. A larger collection, *Love As It Is,* is dominated by a series of dramatic monologues based on the correspondence of George Sand and Frédéric Chopin. Love, Bowering implies, has a dangerous fragility, and the broken pieces of it can cut.

—Fraser Sutherland

BRACKENBURY, Alison

Nationality: British. **Born:** Gainsborough, Lincolnshire, 20 May 1953. **Education:** Brigg High School for Girls, Lincolnshire, 1964-71; St. Hugh's College, Oxford, 1972-75, B.A. (honors) in English 1975. **Family:** Married Guy Sheppard in 1975; one daughter. **Career:** Librarian, Gloucestershire College of Arts and Technology, Cheltenham, 1976-83; clerical assistant, Polytechnics Central Admissions System, Cheltenham, 1985-90; electroplater in family business, 1990—. **Awards:** Eric Gregory award, 1982. **Address:** c/o Carcanet Press, 4th Floor, Conavon Court, 12-16 Blackfriars St., Manchester M3 5BQ, England.

PUBLICATIONS

Poetry

Journey to a Cornish Wedding. Walton-on-Thames, Surrey, Outposts, 1977.
Two Poems. London, Many Press, 1979.
Dreams of Power and Other Poems. Manchester, Carcanet, 1981.
Breaking Ground and Other Poems. Manchester, Carcanet, 1984.
Christmas Roses and Other Poems. Manchester, Carcanet, 1988.
Selected Poems. Manchester, Carcanet, 1991.
1829 and Other Poems. Manchester, Carcanet, 1995.

Play

Radio Play: *The Country of Afternoon, 1985.*

*

Alison Brackenbury comments:
    My poetry is a bad habit, of talking to someone who may not be there. It is hard to know what this listener likes. I prefer my very long narrative, and very short poems, but expect I will end up represented in anthologies by a single, medium-length piece about toads.
    I write a good deal about animals—especially unruly horses—gardens, and the past. This sounds comfortable. It is not meant to be. Do you—listener—take your poetry as Ovaltine? Or do you like space: wild grass at the end of the garden; sky, seen suddenly between houses?
    I like poetry that is rhythmically supple and pleases by rhyme. I find it very hard to try to write like this. But I think a poem

stands a better chance of moving its listener if it stops talking for a moment to sing.

*   *   *

    Alison Brackenbury's first collections were dominated by two eponymous long poems (or poem sequences). *Dreams of Power* takes its title from a sequence of eight poems spoken by the Elizabethan court lady Arbella Stuart (though perhaps the poems might best be regarded as letters and the sequence seen as a modern continuation of the Ovidian tradition stemming from the *Heroides*), who is trapped in the suspicions of others. There is much psychological acuteness in the poems, a developing sense of a convincing personality whose sufferings are forcefully presented through sensuously exact imagery. Only occasionally does one feel the obtrusive presence of the researcher's notebook, and for the most part the language achieves a plausible idiom, by no means pastiche Elizabethan, but not anachronistically modern either:

> This fugitive and winter love
> silvers the lips to frost. I wake, and shine,
> The lean trees have no sap to write of us
> —nor any rag of leaf, that we may hide...
> I dare not write. One frozen afternoon—
>
> cold birds—we huddled on the draughty floor.
> You kissed my throat in firelight. The logs flowered.
> Jasmine, clear yellow for the winter sun
> burned on the sills. In darkness, half unsure,
> the wind's dogs scratch the thick transparent door.

    The title poem of *Breaking Ground* operates more by dialogue than monologue, recounting an imagined visit to John Clare in the asylum. It displays a similar control of iambic pentameter and the same sensitivity to natural detail. Again, the sense of isolation and imprisonment is powerfully evoked. In both sequences, however, there is a certain diffuseness, an occasional loss of focus, which makes the reader long for greater concision. When the sequences turn toward the concentration of lyricism, they are at their most compelling—they become more than simply interesting. Nowhere is this more true than in the remarkable lyric "On the Boards," included in *Breaking Ground,* which has the intensity of Clare's own poems of madness, without ever being merely imitative:

> But He with eyes remote as stars
> Reared up to twice my size
> With one great blow, He split my head
>   and so I sank and died.
>
> [The children] ... filled the church and stood in rows
> to watch the coffin pass
> and on the bare and boarded box,
> cast every flower there was,
>
> marigolds of sun and flame
> light stocks as sweet as women's love
> briar roses, frail as wrists of girls,
> with every thorn plucked off—
>
> because I faced the sun for them
> and cast the dark shapes down
> still they will sing me, warm and free,
> though I am locked in ground.

The shorter poems of these first two volumes betray an uncertainty of idiom; a few drop into somewhat prosaic anecdote, while others are rather archly poetic. There are, though, some very definite successes, especially those poems which enact a kind of memorial invocation, summoning up family ghosts, for example, in "Robert Brackenbury" or renewing mental contact with figures remembered from childhood in "Two Gardeners." The opening lines of this last poem declare that

Too far: I cannot reach them: only gardens.
And stories of the roughness of their lives.

The poet proceeds to retell these stories, and, the stories told, the poem can end thus:

Dazzled by dry streets I touch their hands,
Parted by the sunlight, no man's flowers.

Family themes are often at the heart of some of Brackenbury's best poems, such as "My Old," with its almost refrainlike repetition of the poignant phrase "my old are gone," or the attractive poems on her daughter's childhood, such as "Constellations" and "At Night." Equally in evidence is her responsiveness to the natural world, as well as her capacity to find language in which to articulate that response. *Breaking Ground* contains a whole section of poems on horses, and there is much vivid writing in poems such as "Hare" or "Tracking" from Brackenbury's third volume, *Christmas Roses*.

Christmas Roses contains no long poem; it is marked, though, by some very fine lyrics which have a formal tightness greater than had been consistently present in the earlier collections. There is a genuine and attractive magic to the best of these lyrics, reminiscent of the best of that underrated poet Walter de la Mare or of Edward Thomas. Poems such as "Tower" or "Stopping" have a simplicity not readily found in Brackenbury's earlier work—a simplicity which is the product of considerable sophistication—and they are resonant with unspoken significance. "Owl" is one such poem which belongs in a long tradition of English song and which is not disgraced by comparison with its forebears:

Love: I heard an owl call:
but none of you were with me,
dearest body or my child,
to hear the owl call.

Deep in the stranger's garden,
where ferns blew, and the wild
blue of tall flowers has gone to dark,
the bird drew near: then called.

The air sinks quietly. Now I shake,
drained, by clean, white walls.
Next day's broad sun will not bring you.
Listen. The owl calls.

Brackenbury's work has been uneven in achievement. Certainly her first two collections contain more than a few poems which, one suspects, would not appear in a later volume of selected poems. The best of her work, however, testifies to the sharpness of her eye and her intelligence, and she has produced a number of wholly successful poems with a distinctive beauty and power.

—Glyn Pursglove

BRAND, Dionne

Nationality: West Indian-Canadian. **Born:** Guayguayare, Trinidad, 7 January 1953. **Education:** University of Toronto, B.A. 1975; Ontario Institute for Studies in Education. **Career:** Associated with Black Education Project, Toronto; Caribbean women's health counselor, Immigrant Women's Centre, Toronto; information and communications officer, Agency for Rural Transformation, Grenada, 1983. **Awards:** Ontario Arts Council publisher's grant and Artist in the Schools award, both 1978; Canada Council Arts grant, 1980; Ontario Arts Council grant, 1982. **Address:** c/o Women's Educational Press, 517 College St., Suite 233, Toronto, Ontario, Canada M6G 4A2.

PUBLICATIONS

Poetry

'Fore Day Morning. Khoisan Artists, 1978.
Earth Magic, illustrated by Roy Crosse. Toronto, Kids Can Press, 1980.
Primitive Offensive. Toronto, Williams-Wallace, 1982.
Winter Epigrams and Epigrams to Ernesto Cardenal in Defense of Claudia. Toronto, Williams-Wallace, 1983.
Chronicles of the Hostile Sun. Toronto, Williams-Wallace, 1984.
No Language Is Neutral. Toronto, Coach House Press, 1990.

Short Stories

Sans Souci, and Other Stories. Ithaca, New York, Firebrand Books, 1989.

Other

Rivers Have Sources, Trees Have Roots: Speaking of Racism, with Krisantha Sri Bhaggiyadatta. Toronto, Cross Cultural Communications Centre, 1986.
Sight Specific: Lesbians and Representation. Toronto, A Space, 1988.
No Burden to Carry: Narratives of Black Working Women in Ontario, 1920s-1950s, with Louis De Shield. Toronto, Women's Press, 1991.
Bread out of Stone: Recollections, Sex, Recognitions, Race, Dreaming, Politics. Toronto, Coach House Press, 1994.
In Another Place, Not Here. New York, Grove Press, 1997.

*

Critical Studies: "After Modernism: Alternative Voices in the Writings of Dionne Brand, Claire Harris, and Marlene Philip" by Lynette Hunter, in *University of Toronto Quarterly,* vol. 62, no. 2, 1992 / 1993.

*   *   *

Dionne Brand, a native of the Caribbean nation of Trinidad who immigrated to Canada as a teenager, is a poet whose work reflects her political, racial and gender concerns. Brand's poetry explores the thoughts and feelings of a black female coming to realize her place in history. Rooted in her own immigrant experience, and her work with the Immigrant Women's Centre in Toronto, Brand's poems speak from the perspective of the outsider—the narrator who, because of race, gender, sexual preference and ethnic background, finds herself at odds with the surrounding society. In *No Language Is Neutral,* a 1990 collection of Brand's poems, she writes of the "blood-stained blind of race and sex" which black women must struggle against. This struggle Brand wages in all of her writing.

Brand's *Earth Magic* is a collection of poems recalling the poet's childhood in Trinidad. The poverty of that time and the hard work in the fields are a constant in these bitter, realistic evocations of a difficult period. In *Primitive Offensive,* Brand turned from her own personal history to a contemplation of the situation of black females worldwide to compose a long poem in 14 cantos which addresses the need for a common history and identity for blacks throughout the world. In addressing this issue, the poem becomes a mythic embodiment of the racial dream of unity. Brand uses rhythmic repetition to drive the poem forward in a manner similar to a musical chant. At times she employs a dialogue between the narrator and an elderly black African woman who represents an ancestral spirit speaking to the present age. Moving from the long poem, *Offensive to Winter Epigrams* shows Brand's talent for the short poem, here inspired by the Nicaraguan poet Ernesto Cardenal. Bitingly political, the poems in *Offensive to Winter Epigrams* are short, wry blasts of resentment and anger which distill in a few words powerful emotions.

The political struggles which inspire so much of her poetry are also found in Brand's fiction and nonfiction as well. The stories gathered in *Sans Souci, and Other Stories* draw upon the incidents of Brand's own childhood in Trinidad, her immigration to Canada, and her strongly feminist and politically leftist take on the nature of both her homeland and her adopted country. Although they have political intentions, female sexuality is particularly celebrated in the stories in this collection. "Madame Alaird's Breasts," one story from *Sans Souci,* is described by Rhonda Cobham in *Women's Review of Books* as "a perfect vignette of adolescent female eroticism." The poet's concerns have also motivated Brand to write nonfiction books such as *Rivers Have Sources, Trees Have Roots: Speaking of Racism, Sight Specific: Lesbians and Representation* and *No Burden to Carry: Narratives of Black Working Women in Ontario, 1920s-1950s.* Because of her ability to effectively present her beliefs in several different genres, Brand is fast becoming a powerful spokesperson on the Canadian literary left.

—Denise Wiloch

BRANDT, Di(onne)

Nationality: Canadian. **Born:** Winkler, Manitoba, 1952. **Education:** University of Manitoba, B.A.; University of Toronto, M.A.; University of Manitoba, Ph.D. in English. **Career:** University of Winnipeg, currently teacher of creative writing and English. Formerly poetry editor, *Prairie Fire, Contemporary Verse 2,* and *HERizons.* **Awards:** Governor General's award finalist, 1987; Commonwealth Poetry Prize shortlist, 1987; Gerald H. Lampert award, 1987, for *questions i asked my mother;* McNally Robinson Book of the Year award, 1991, for *Agnes in the sky,* shortlist, 1993. **Member:** Manitoba Artists-in-the-Schools Program.

PUBLICATIONS

Poetry

questions i asked my mother. Winnipeg, Manitoba, Turnstone Press, 1987.
Agnes in the sky. Winnipeg, Manitoba, Turnstone Press, 1990.
mother, not mother. Stratford, Ontario, Mercury Press, 1992.
Jerusalem, beloved. Winnipeg, Manitoba, Turnstone Press, 1995.

Other

Wild Mother Dancing: Maternal Narratives in Canadian Literature. Manitoba, University of Manitoba Press, 1993.
Dancing Naked: Narrative Strategies for Writing across Centuries. Stratford, Ontario, Mercury Press, 1996.

*   *   *

Di Brandt's work has, from the first, received a warm reception in Canada, and won her a number of literary prizes quite early in her career. Due largely to the difficulty in distributing Canadian small press editions abroad, however, her work has yet to receive the international attention it deserves. Her poetry, which at its best manages to be both lyrical and somewhat formally innovative at the same time, addresses two great themes of broad importance: the struggle between rootedness in a particular cultural past and the lure of cosmopolitanism; and the recovery of maternal experience within a cultural tradition that has repressed the expression of such experience.

While Brandt's two main themes have remained constant throughout career as a poet and writer of prose, her poetic practice has undergone a slow formal evolution. Her earliest collection, *questions i asked my mother,* is the least conventional of her volumes, eschewing punctuation and capitalization in pursuit of a line that can capture what Brandt has spoken of as the "breathless, hurried, scared" voice of the "unlistened-to childhood self" that is the subject of her early poems and prose-poems. While Brandt's second volume, *Agnes in the sky,* retains elements of this early, run-on line, its shorter lines also show the influence of H.D. (whose *Trilogy* has been an important touchstone for Brandt) and the Canadian poet Phyllis Webb. The short, free verse couplets of *mother, not mother* represent the culmination of this direction of development in Brandt's work.

Brandt's concern with the tug-of-war between her specific cultural roots, on the one hand, and her attachment to modern, secular, pluralistic society, on the other, comes out of her strict Ukrainian Mennonite upbringing. Raised in the tiny rural Mennonite community of Rhineland, Manitoba, Brandt spent her youth in a culture that, in her own words, "retained much of its pre-industrial, pre-Renaissance character" and was "marked by an extremely repressive, patriarchal Christianity that enforced strict obedience to the Church, fathers and the Bible" (*Wild Mother Dancing*). While Brandt chose to leave this closed community for mainstream Canadian society, many of her best poems dramatize her struggles with the hold of her childhood religion. One of the best early examples of this theme in Brandt's early work is the short lyric "i wish the sky was still pasted on" from *questions i asked my mother,* which concludes with the following lines:

i want the old jesus with his
tin lantern and his sheep knocking
knocking on my wooden door i want
crashing alone into this black river
someone beside me the old old clutch
still at my soul

The second great theme of Brandt's work, that of the recovery of maternal experience from the silence in which it has been enshrouded in the Western literary tradition, receives its fullest expression in the prose study *Wild Mother Dancing: Maternal Narrative in Canadian Literature*, which examines the experience of motherhood in Canadian writing and oral history, and in *mother, not mother*, a sequence of linked lyrics in which Brandt explores the absence of the mother in literature, examines the roles of daughters and mothers, and treats the theme of the failed, or "not" mother. Although *mother, not mother* is ultimately a celebration of maternity, it is not a sentimentalizing of maternal experience. Indeed, Brandt insists upon the violence inherent in maternity, violence manifested in the act of giving birth, in the struggle between mother and daughter, and even in the mother's protectiveness of her children, as we see in the following passage from one of the books untitled sections:

the color mothers see most often
is red
remembering, fiercely, in the
night, tiger's eyes

Perhaps Brandt's greatest strength as a poet, regardless of the theme she treats, lies in a habit of quietly transgressing the boundaries of that which she is expected to say or believe. This habit of transgression can manifest itself in a child's misreading of the moralizing Bible stories read to her on Sundays (as in "Diana"), or in a committed feminist announcing that she catches herself dreaming of "the hero still to carry me away" and "all the ironies swept away Cinderalla rising / from the ashes glassy eyed," ("& what do i want in this my contradictory"), but wherever we find it, it is this transgressiveness that shows Brandt at her most sensitive to the vagaries of an ever-divided consciousness.

—Robert Archambeau

BREWSTER, Elizabeth (Winifred)

Nationality: Canadian. **Born:** Chipman, New Brunswick, 26 August 1922. **Education:** Sussex High School, New Brunswick, graduated 1942; University of New Brunswick, Fredericton, B.A. 1946; Radcliffe College, Cambridge, Massachusetts, A.M. 1947; King's College, London, 1949-50; University of Toronto, B.L.S. 1953; Indiana University, Bloomington, Ph.D. 1962. **Career:** Cataloguer, Carleton University Library, Ottawa, 1953-57, and Indiana University Library, 1957-58; member of English Department, Victoria University, British Columbia, 1960-61; reference librarian, Mount Allison University Library, Sackville, New Brunswick, 1961-65; cataloguer, New Brunswick Legislative Library, Fredericton, 1965-68, and University of Alberta Library, Edmonton, 1968-70; visiting assistant professor of English, University of Alberta, 1970-

71; assistant professor, 1972-75, associate professor, 1975-80, professor of English, 1980-90, professor emeritus, 1990—, University of Saskatchewan, Saskatoon. **Awards:** Pratt Gold Medal and prize, University of Toronto, 1953; Canada Council award, 1971, 1976, 1978, 1985; President's Medal, University of Western Ontario, 1980; Saskatchewan Arts Board Lifetime Achievement Award, and Governor General's Award shortlist, both 1996. Litt.D.: University of New Brunswick, 1982. **Address:** Department of English, University of Saskatchewan, Saskatoon, Saskatchewan S7N 0W0, Canada.

PUBLICATIONS

Poetry

East Coast. Toronto, Ryerson Press, 1951.
Lillooet. Toronto, Ryerson Press, 1954.
Roads and Other Poems. Toronto, Ryerson Press, 1957.
Five New Brunswick Poets, with others, edited by Fred Cogswell. Fredericton, New Brunswick, Fiddlehead, 1962.
Passage of Summer: Selected Poems. Toronto, Ryerson Press, 1969.
Sunrise North. Toronto, Clarke Irwin, 1972.
In Search of Eros. Toronto, Clarke Irwin, 1974.
Sometimes I Think of Moving. Ottawa, Oberon Press, 1977.
The Way Home. Ottawa, Oberon Press, 1982.
Digging In. Ottawa, Oberon Press, 1982.
Selected Poems of Elizabeth Brewster, 1944-1984. Ottawa, Oberon Press, 2 vols., 1985.
Entertaining Angels. Ottawa, Oberon Press, 1988.
Spring Again. Ottawa, Oberon Press, 1990.
Wheel of Change. Ottawa, Oberon Press, 1993.
Footnotes to the Book of Job. Ottawa, Oberon Press, 1995.

Novels

The Sisters. Ottawa, Oberon Press, 1974.
Junction. Windsor, Ontario, Black Moss Press, 1982.

Short Stories

It's Easy to Fall on the Ice. Ottawa, Oberon Press, 1977.
A House Full of Women. Ottawa, Oberon Press, 1983.
Visitations. Ottawa, Oberon Press, 1987.

Other

The Invention of Truth (Stories and Essays). Ottawa, Oberon Press, 1991.
Away from Home (Stories and Essays). Ottawa, Oberon Press, 1995.

*

Critical Studies: "The Poetry of Elizabeth Brewster" by Desmond Pacey, in *Ariel* (Calgary, Alberta), July 1973; "Next Time from a Different Country" by Robert Gibbs, in *Canadian Literature* (Vancouver), Autumn 1974; "Speeding towards Strange Destinations: A Conversation with Elizabeth Brewster" by Paul Denham, in *Essays on Canadian Writing* (Downsview, Ontario), Summer / Fall 1980.

* * *

"I have written poems principally to come to a better understanding of myself, my world, and other people," explained Elizabeth Brewster. Her work dramatizes (again in her own words) "the struggle to lead a human rational life in a world which is increasingly inhuman and irrational."

This credo applies particularly to Brewster's *Passage of Summer: Selected Poems,* which brings together the best work of the writer's earlier collections. Her poems are seen to be sometimes slight, often sentimental, yet ever honest and celebratory, especially of the small things and the little moments and meanings of life. Brewster has been described as a quiet poet, and it is true that she prefers the gentle shade to the fierce sun, ironic reflections to strong statements. Often her poems are moving without being at all memorable. Her imagination is more fanciful than imaginative. Yet her work is like a wine which improves with age; its taste mellows in memory.

The critic Morris Wolfe wrote, "One has to read a fair bit of Elizabeth Brewster's poetry to realize just how good she is." The opportunity to do so was finally offered with the publication of her *Selected Poems, 1944-1984,* which showcases her finest work. Over the years, it has become apparent, she has found a way to turn fancies and musings into meaningful subjects for poems. At the same time she has mastered the art of the casual aside: "Why do I feel guilty / that I am sometimes bored?" and "Love is never deserved, / is mostly imagination anyway." She has nourished a genius for understatement, and a pleasant wit has taken flower in her garden.

Entertaining Angels offers further evidence of the strength and individuality of Brewster's achievement. This is a likable collection with many strong moments. Indeed, she writes about this fact in the poem "Cloud Formations":

> Some time, I think,
> the perfect arrangement
> of words will come
> (though, even as I write the word,
> I doubt if I would like perfection)
> some time there will be
> the moment of illumination
> (but aren't all moments
> moments of illumination?)

The poem discusses her own background in poetry: the eight-year-old in the attic, writing like Shelley; the ten-year-old copying poems in the scribbler; the 12-year-old composing "my little poems / as letters to myself ... written conversations." In the poem "Blue Chair" Brewster finds a homey approach to refer to the wear and tear of the years:

> I like my blue chair, though I can see
> spots which will soon be,
> though they aren't yet,
> shabby.

Throughout the collection there are references to aunts as great storytellers and also to the ghost stories of the Maritimes, the region where Brewster was born and raised, the region she left behind when she moved west to the prairie provinces. Perhaps she did not really leave the region behind, for its ghosts flit through a number of her poems written on the prairie. In "The Ungrateful Dead Man," for instance, she describes ghosts as "slipping out of the room / to haunt elsewhere." Ghosts haunt people more than they do places, and the poet herself is among the people they haunt.

It is fair to say that Brewster has succeeded in her resolve to understand herself, as well as to write poems that remain in the mind and mellow in the memory.

—John Robert Colombo

BROCK-BROIDO, Lucie

Nationality: American. **Born:** Pittsburgh, Pennsylvania, 22 May 1956. **Education:** Johns Hopkins University, 1976-79, The Writing Seminars, B.A. 1978, The Writing Seminars, M.A. 1979; Columbia University, 1979-82, M.F.A. 1982. **Career:** Briggs-Copeland Assistant Professor in Poetry, 1988-93, and director, creative writing program, 1992-93, Harvard University, Cambridge, Massachusetts; associate professor in poetry, Bennington Writing Seminars, 1993-95; visiting professor of poetry, Princeton University, Princeton, New Jersey, 1995; associate professor and director of poetry, Columbia University, New York, 1993—. **Awards:** Grolier Poetry prize, Cambridge, 1983; poetry fellowship, Fine Arts Work Center, Provincetown, 1983; Hoyns fellowship in poetry, University of Virginia, 1984; National Endowment for the Arts poetry fellowship, 1985; *New Letters* Literary award, 1987; *New England Review* Narrative Poetry award, 1987; Massachusetts Artist fellowship in poetry, 1988, 1996; Harvard-Danforth award for distinction in teaching, 1989, 1990; *American Poetry Review* Jerome Shestack Prize for poetry, 1991; Harvard University Phi Beta Kappa Teaching award, 1991; Guggenheim fellowship in poetry, 1996; Witter-Byner Prize, 1996. **Address:** c/o Dodge Hall, Writing Division, School of the Arts, Columbia University, New York, New York 10027, U.S.A.

PUBLICATIONS

Poetry

A Hunger. New York, Knopf, 1988.
The Master Letters. New York, Knopf, 1995.

*

Critical Studies: Interview in *Harvard Review,* Fall 1995; interview in *Bomb,* Fall 1995.

* * *

A Hunger, Lucie Brock-Broido's first book of poems, was published in 1988 by the major trade house Knopf. One of the more notable debuts of the period, the book had three reprintings between then and the autumn of 1994. This is extraordinary given the proliferation of poetry volumes, the generally acknowledged (though much debated) shrinking audience for poetry, and the usual conduct of major trade houses toward poetry (publish a very small number of volumes, then remainder or pulp all but one or two high-octane sellers after 12 months).

The commercial performance of Brock-Broido's first book is all the more astonishing when one considers that the poetry clearly evolves from the difficult model of Wallace Stevens. Intense, brooding, and complex, Brock-Broido's poems incessantly probe the terms and terrain of love, depression, friendship, popular culture, and art itself. Such qualities can be seen in these lines from "Domestic Mysticism":

> When I come home, the dwarves will be long
> In their shadows & promiscuous. The alley cats will sneak
> Inside, curl about the legs of furniture, close the skins
> Inside their eyelids, sleep. Orchids will be intercrossed and
>   sturdy.
> The sun will go down as I sit, thin armed, small breasted
> In my cotton dress, poked with eyelet stitches, a little lace,
> In the queer light left when a room snuffs out.

The speaker in this poetry, casting an almost too highly developed eye on detail, brings a merciless honesty to the task of painful witnessing. That the orchids will be "intercrossed and sturdy" is an unusual observation, and so is the speaker's attention to the cats' inner eyelids as they sleep. But most accomplished, and perhaps most revealing, is the narrator's description of herself as a small, vulnerable doll both threatened by and part of "the queer light left when a room snuffs out." Though aware of the consequences, the narrator will not avert her glance from the brightness of the sun. Rather, she stares, driven by a belief that the revealing calm resides always at the heart of chaos. She stares, but she does so with full awareness of the inherent danger. Thus, she shares a more than passing sympathy with the intriguing poet Thomas James, who published one volume of verse in 1972 before committing suicide. Brock-Broido acknowledges the bond by quoting one of James's most revealing lines—"I am afraid of what the world will do"— in her poem "The Beginning of the Beginning."

Brock-Broido is afraid perhaps, but her vulnerability is not the kind that herds its host into silence and passivity. Her weapon, the tool that separates the chaff from the kernel of truth, is poetry, a language that, though introspective, may lead to accessibility, understanding, and kinship with a larger audience. If we compare Brock-Broido's poems to those of her contemporary Jorie Graham (whose notes, wordplay, and obfuscation finally make us wonder what if anything such poems have to say), we find in the former a much more productive and meaningful use of the Stevens legacy. Like Sylvia Plath before her, Brock-Broido confronts urgent issues and does so in inventive ways that help her readers confront—and survive—them, too.

—Robert McDowell

BROOKS, Gwendolyn

Nationality: American. **Born:** Topeka, Kansas, 7 June 1917. **Education:** Hyde Park High School, Wendell Phillips High School, and Englewood High School, all Chicago, until 1934; Wilson Junior College, Chicago, graduated 1936. **Family:** Married Henry L. Blakely in 1938; one son and one daughter. **Career:** Publicity director, NAACP Youth Council, Chicago, 1930s. Teacher, Northeastern Illinois State College, Chicago, Columbia College, Chicago, and Elmhurst College, Illinois; Rennebohm Professor of English, University of Wisconsin, Madison; Distinguished Professor of the Arts, City College, City University of New York, 1971. Editor, *Black Position* magazine. Consultant in poetry, Library of Congress, Washington, D.C., 1985-86. **Awards:** Guggenheim fellowship, 1946; American Academy grant, 1946; Pulitzer Prize, 1950; Thormod Monsen award, 1964; Ferguson memorial award, 1964; Anisfield-Wolf award, 1968; Black Academy award, 1971; Shelley memorial award, 1976; Frost Medal, 1988; New York Public Library award, 1988; National Endowment for the Arts award, 1989. Has received 51 honorary degrees from American universities. Poet Laureate of Illinois, 1968. **Address:** c/o Contemporary Forum, 2529A Jerome Street, Chicago, Illinois 60645-1507, U.S.A.

PUBLICATIONS

Poetry

A Street in Bronzeville. New York, Harper, 1945.
Annie Allen. New York, Harper, 1949.
Bronzeville Boys and Girls (for children). New York, Harper, 1956.
The Bean Eaters. New York, Harper, 1960.
Selected Poems. New York, Harper, 1963.
We Real Cool. Detroit, Broadside Press, 1966.
The Wall. Detroit, Broadside Press, 1967.
In the Mecca. New York, Harper, 1968.
Riot. Detroit, Broadside Press, 1969.
Family Pictures. Detroit, Broadside Press, 1970.
Black Steel: Joe Frazier and Muhammad Ali. Detroit, Broadside Press, 1971.
Aloneness. Detroit, Broadside Press, 1971.
Aurora. Detroit, Broadside Press, 1972.
Beckonings. Detroit, Broadside Press, 1975.
To Disembark. Chicago, Third World Press, 1981.
Black Love. Chicago, Brooks Press, 1982.
Mayor Harold Washington; and Chicago, The I Will City. Chicago, Brooks Press, 1983.
The Near-Johannesburg Boy and Other Poems. Chicago, David Company, 1986.
Blacks. Chicago, Third World Press, 1987.
Winnie. Chicago, Third World Press, 1988.
Gottschalk and the Grande Tarantelle. Chicago, David Company, 1988.
Children Coming Home. Chicago, David Company, 1991.

Recordings: *The 1987 Consultants' Reunion: Two Evenings of Readings Celebrating the 50th Anniversary of the Consultanship in Poetry,* Gertrude Clarke Whittall Poetry and Literature Fund, 1987; *Poets in Person,* Modern Poetry Association, 1991.

Novel

Maud Martha. New York, Harper, 1953.

Other

A Portion of That Field, with others. Urbana, University of Illinois Press, 1967.

The World of Gwendolyn Brooks (miscellany). New York, Harper, 1971.

Report from Part One: An Autobiography. Detroit, Broadside Press, 1972.

The Tiger Who Wore White Gloves; or, What You Are You Are (for children). Chicago, Third World Press, 1974.

A Capsule Course in Black Poetry Writing, with Don L. Lee, Keorapetse Kgositsile, and Dudley Randall. Detroit, Broadside Press, 1975.

Primer for Blacks. Black Position Press, 1980.

Young Poets' Primer. Chicago, Brooks Press, 1981.

Very Young Poets. Chicago, Brooks Press, 1983.

Editor, *A Broadside Treasury.* Detroit, Broadside Press, 1971.

Editor, *Jump Bad: A New Chicago Anthology.* Detroit, Broadside Press, 1971.

*

Bibliography: *Langston Hughes and Gwendolyn Brooks: A Reference Guide* by R. Baxter Miller, Boston, Hall, and London, Prior, 1978.

Critical Studies: *Gwendolyn Brooks* by Harry B. Shaw, Boston, Twayne, 1980; *Gwendolyn Brooks; Poetry and the Heroic Voice* by D.H. Melhem, Louisville, University Press of Kentucky, 1987; *A Life Distilled: Gwendolyn Brooks, Her Poetry and Fiction* edited by Maria K. Mootry and Gary Smith, Urbana, University of Illinois Press, 1987; *A Life of Gwendolyn Brooks* by George E. Kent, Louisville, University Press of Kentucky, 1990; *Gwendolyn Brooks,* Mankato, Minnesota, Creative Education, 1993.

*   *   *

In what has since become a well-known episode, Gwendolyn Brooks describes an auspicious turning point in her career, a turning point that came in 1967 when she attended the Second Black Writers' Conference at Fisk University in Nashville. The Pulitzer Prize-winning poet was stunned and intrigued by the energy and electricity generated by LeRoi Jones (Amiri Baraka) and Ron Milner, among others, on that predominantly black campus. The excitement was at once surprising, stirring, and contagious, and Brooks admits that from that moment she entered a "new consciousness." She had discovered a "new" audience: young people full of a fresh spirit and ready, as she characterized them, to take on the challenges. The sturdy ideas that she earlier held were no longer valid in this "new world," and several years later she would untendentiously remark: "I am trying to weave the coat that I shall wear."

The older coat that Brooks doffed is made of the material for which she is best known: such vignettes of ghetto people in Chicago as "The Anniad," "The Sundays of Satin-Legs Smith," "The Bean Eaters," or "We Real Cool," for example. They are works of a poet who brings a patrician mind to a plebeian language; a poet always searching for the stirring, unusual coloration of words; the poet in whom Addison Gayle Jr., has noted what he calls "a tendency toward obscurity and abstraction" and "a child-like fascination for words." But, like Emily Dickinson, Brooks searched for fresh sounds and imagery produced by word clusters that startle rather than obscure:

Let it be stairways, and a splintery box
Where you have thrown me, scraped me with your kiss,
Have honed me, have released me after this
Cavern Kindness, smiled away our shocks.

Most of her poems written before 1967—before the Fisk conferences—are her "front yard songs," poems that reflect the self-consciousness of a poet whose audience seeks lessons in a lyric that ostensibly transcends race. They are solid, highly imaginative poems, and if they suggest comparisons with Wallace Stevens, as several critics have noted, they also recall Emily Dickinson's ingenuity with language, her ironic ambiguities:

A light and diplomatic bird
Is lenient in my window tree.
A quick dilemma of the leaves
Discloses twist and tact to me.

They recall as well the "grotesques" who habituate the fictional world of Sherwood Anderson's Winesburg, Ohio:

True, there is silver under
The veils of the darkness,
But few care to dig in the night
For the possible treasure of stars.

But above all, there is the unmistakable rhythmic shifting—"My hand is stuffed with mode, design, device. / But I lack access to my proper stone"— and the haunting incongruity—"Believe that even in my deliberateness I was not deliberate."

The startling Fisk conference may be viewed metaphorically as Brooks's peek at "the back yard" ("Where it's rough and untended and hungry weed grows")—the escape, as George Kent says, from the highly ordered and somewhat devitalized life of her "front yard training." The backyard offers a new vitality, a new consciousness. Brooks, around 50 years old at the time of the conference, strikes up a dialogue in free verse with the subjects of her earlier poetry. The distances narrow and the angles flatten: "we are each other's / harvest: / we are each other's business: / we are each other's magnitude and bond."

The angles of vision have changed to suit what Brooks describes as "my newish voice": "[It] will not be an imitation of the contemporary young black voice, which I so admire, but an extending adaptation of today's G.B. [sic] voice." So there is something of a near elegiac tone in Brooks's "transcendence" of her poetic past; but it is elegy without regrets, for she has moved from a place of "knowledgeable unknowing" to a place of "Know-now" preachments:

I tell you
I love You
and I trust You.
Take my Faith.
Make of my Faith an engine.
Make of my Faith
a Black Star. I am Beckoning.

Still, as Barbara Christian reminds us, there are moments when we need to be admonished to recollect that the "poet has always been a synthesizer and a thermometer, whether she is aware of it or not." By this observation, Christian means to suggest that

Brooks—attentive poet as she is—intuitively synthesizes her tradition as she goes about taking the measure of the current time.

—Charles L. James

BROSSARD, Nicole

Nationality: Canadian. **Born:** Montreal, 27 November 1943. **Education:** University of Montreal, Licence ès Lettres 1968, B.A. 1971; Scolarité de Maîtrise 1972. **Career:** Founder and editor, *La Barre du Jour* (then *La Nouvelle Barre du Jour*), 1965—; performance coordinator, Pavillon de la Jeunesse, Expo '67, Montreal, 1967; member, Cultural Congress, Havana, Cuba, 1968; imprisoned under War Measures Act, 1970; cofounder, *Les Têtes de pioche* magazine; co-producer, *Some American Feminists* (film), 1976; president, Third International Feminist Book Fair, Montreal, 1988. Visiting professor at Queens University, Kingston, Ontario, 1982, 1984, and Westword School of Writing for Women, Vancouver, 1987; scholar-in-residence, Bucknell University, 1990, Princeton University, 1991. Speaker at feminist writers conferences and poetry festivals in Canada, Argentina, Australia, England, France, Holland, Italy, Norway, Spain, the United States, and Yugoslavia. Contributor to periodicals, including *La Barre du Jour, Revue de l'Université Laurentienne,* and *Etudes Françaises.* **Awards:** Governor General award, 1974, for *Mécanique jongleuse,* and 1984, for *Double Impression;* Therafields Foundation Chapbook award, 1987, for *Sous la langue/Under Tongue;* Fondation Les Forges Grand Prize for poetry, 1989, for *Installations;* Prix Athanase-David du Québec, 1991. **Member:** Union des Ecrivains Québécois (executive board).

PUBLICATIONS

Poetry

"Aube à la saison" (Dawn in Season), in *Trois,* with Michel Beaulieu and Micheline de Jordy. Montreal, A.G.E.U.M., 1965.
Mordre en sa chair (To Bite the Flesh). Montreal, Esterel, 1966.
L'Echo bouge beau. Montreal, Esterel, 1968.
Suite logique. Montreal, L'Hexagone, 1970.
Le Centre blanc. Montreal, Orphée, 1970; translated as *The White Centre,* Toronto, n.p., 1980.
Mécanique jongleuse. Colombes, France, Génération, 1973; with her *Masculin grammaticale,* Montreal, L'Hexagone, 1974; translated as *Daydream Mechanics,* Toronto, Coach House Press, 1980.
La Partie pour le tout. Montreal, L'aurore, 1975.
Le Centre blanc: poèmes 1965-1975. Montreal, L'Hexagone, 1978.
D'Arc de cycle la derive, illustrated by Francine Simonin. Saint-Jacques-le-Mineur, La Maison, 1979.
Amantes. Montreal, Quinze, 1980; translated by Barbara Godard as *Lovhers,* Montreal, Guernica Press, 1986.
Double Impression. Montreal, L'Hexagone, 1984.
L'Aviva. Montreal, Nouvelle Barre du Jour, 1985.
Domaine d'écriture. Montreal, Nouvelle Barre du Jour, 1985.
Mauve, with Daphne Marlatt. NBJ / Kootenay School of Writing, 1985.
Character / Jeu de lettres, with Daphne Marlatt. NBJ / Kootenay School of Writing, 1986.

Sous la langue / Under Tongue, English translation by Susanne de Lotbinière-Harwood. Montreal, Ragweed Press, 1987.
Installations. Paris, Les Ecrits des Forges, 1989.
A tout regard. Montreal, NBJ / BQ, 1989.
Typhon gru. Paris, Générations, 1990.
Langues obscures (Obscure Tongues). Montreal, L'Hexagone, 1992.

Novels

Un Livre. Montreal, Éditions du Jour, 1970; translated as *A Book,* Toronto, Coach House Press, 1976.
Sold-Out (étreinte / illustration). Montreal, Éditions du Jour, 1973; translated as *Turn of a Pang,* Toronto, Coach House Press, 1976; translated as *A Pang's Progress,* N.p., 1986.
French Kiss (étreinte-exploration). Montreal, Éditions du Jour, 1974; translated, Toronto, Coach House Press, 1986.
L'Amèr; ou, Le Chapitre effrité (fiction théorique). Montreal, Quinze, 1977; translated by Barbara Godard as *These Our Mothers; or, The Disintegrating Chapter,* Toronto, Coach House Press, 1983.
Le Sens apparent. Paris, Flammarion, 1980; translated as *Surface of Sense,* Toronto, Coach House Press, 1989.
Picture Theory. Montreal, Nouvelle Optique, 1982; translated by Barbara Godard, Montreal, Guernica Press, and New York, Roof Press, 1990.
Journal intime; ou, Voilà donc un manuscrit. Montreal, Les Herbes rouges, 1984.
Le Désert Mauve. Montreal, L'Hexagone, 1987; translated as *Mauve Desert,* Toronto, Coach House Press, 1990.
Baroque d'aube (Baroque Dawn). Montreal, L'Hexagone, 1995.

Plays

"L'Ecrivain," in *La Nef des sorcières,* with Marie-Claire Blais, Marthe Blackburn, Luce Guilbeault, France Théoret, Odette Gagnon, and Pol Pelletier (produced Montreal, 1976). Montreal, Quinze, 1976; translated as *A Clash of Symbols,* Toronto, Coach House Press, 1979.

Radio Plays: *Narratuer et Personnages,* 1971; *Une Impression de fiction dans le retrovisur,* 1978; *La falaise,* 1985; *Souvenirs d'enfance et de jeunesse,* 1986; *Correspondance,* with Michèle Causse, 1987.

Other

La Lettre aérienne. Montreal, Remu-Ménage, 1985; translated as *The Aerial Letter,* Toronto, Women's Press, 1988.

Editor, *Les Stratégies du réel / The Story So Far 6.* Toronto, Coach House Press, 1979.

*

Critical Studies: "The Novels of Nicole Brossard: An Active Voice" by Louise Forsyth, in *Room of One's Own,* vol. 4, no. 1-2, 1978, her "L'Ecriture au féminine," in *Journal of Canadian Fiction,* nos. 25 / 26, 1979, and her *Traditionalism, Nationalism and Feminism: Women Writers of Québec,* n.p.; "The Avant-Garde in Canada: *Open Letter* and *La Barre du Jour*" by Barbara Godard, in *Ellipse,* vol. 4, no. 23, 1979.

*   *   *

Nicole Brossard enjoys a dual reputation as an experimental poet and novelist and as a feminist theorist. Her work is also colored by her longtime involvement in the Quebec nationalist movement.

Brossard's first poetry collection, "Aube a la saison," was published in 1965. Influenced by surrealist poetics and by the Quebec nationalist movement of the time, Brossard addressed the tendency of Quebec nationalists to speak of their homeland as a female body. At the time, Quebec nationalist writers spoke of "mapping" their homeland to define its distinctive characteristics and, thus, to locate the true nature of the Quebecois people. Brossard consciously set out to subvert this metaphor and invent a new poetics of the female body. Using blood, muscles, hair, and veins as metaphoric terms in her poems, she turned the idea of mapping into a means of redefining the symbolic body of Woman. Taking a decidedly avant-garde stance in regards to other Quebecois writers, she turned her attention to language as a tool for exploring new dimensions of freedom.

Drawing on the ideas of Michel Foucault and Roland Barthes, Brossard soon postulated poetry as a system of symbols beyond the fixed meanings imposed upon words by ideology and patriarchy. Exploring further her idea of a poetry of the body, she sought to create a poetry which in its very structure was as erotically playful as was the human body. By overthrowing accepted syntax, grammar and spelling—and by using odd spacing, underlines, hyphens, parentheses, and similar typographical symbols and devices—Brossard fought against what she saw as a phallocentric language system which forced words into particular meanings and for a poetry created as much by the reader as by the poet. This language / body parallel, and the joint creation of poetry by both reader and poet in an almost erotic act, combined for Brossard the literary avant-garde with the revolutionary movement. As her ideas of poetry developed further, Brossard began to call for a feminine grammar in juxtaposition to the phallic authoritarianism of traditional grammar. Increasingly her poetry has become more openly lesbian in its concerns, a perhaps unique stance among the poetic avant-garde.

Common characteristics in Brossard's work are an emphasis on the language of the poems as words-on-the-page rather than as symbols for something else; an assumption that the creative process of a poem is shared and / or completed by the reader in the act of reading the text; and the conscious and overt use of poetry primarily as a means to make political and social statements. Because her literary works—her novels as well as her poems—fight against traditional grammar to such a radical extent, her writings are often labeled difficult and, according to more severe critics, even unreadable and senseless. But "sense," if by that term is meant a rational meaning according to the traditional rules of what Brossard argues is a phallocentric grammar system, is precisely what she is working to overcome.

—Denise Wiloch

BROUMAS, Olga

Nationality: Greek. **Born:** Hermoupolis, Greece, 6 May 1949. Moved to the United States in 1967. **Education:** University of Pennsylvania, Philadelphia, B.A. 1970; University of Oregon, Eugene, M.F.A. 1973. **Family:** Married Stephen Edward Bangs in 1973 (divorced 1979). **Career:** Instructor in English and women's studies, University of Oregon, 1972-76; visiting associate professor, University of Idaho, Moscow, 1978; poet-in-residence, Goddard College, Plainfield, Vermont, 1979-81, and Women Writers Center, Cazenovia, New York, 1981-82; founder and associate faculty member, Freehand women writers and photographers community, Provincetown, Massachusetts, 1982-87; visiting associate professor, Boston University, 1988-90; Fanny Hurst poet-in-residence, 1990-92, poet-in-residence and director of creative writing, beginning 1992, Brandeis University, Waltham, Massachusetts. Since 1983 licensed bodywork therapist, Cape Cod, Massachusetts. **Awards:** Yale Younger Poets award, 1977; National Endowment for the Arts grant, 1978; Guggenheim fellowship, 1981-82; Witter Bynner translation grant (with T. Begley), 1991. **Address:** 162 Mill Pond Drive, Brewster, Massachusetts 02631, U.S.A.

PUBLICATIONS

Poetry

Restlessness (in Greek). Athens, Greece, Alvin Redman Hellas, 1967.
Caritas. Eugene, Oregon, Jackrabbit Press, 1976.
Beginning with O. New Haven, Connecticut, Yale University Press, 1977.
Soie Sauvage. Port Townsend, Washington, Copper Canyon Press, 1980.
Pastoral Jazz. Port Townsend, Washington, Copper Canyon Press, 1983.
Black Holes, Black Stockings, with Jane Miller. Middletown, Connecticut, Wesleyan University Press, 1985.
Perpetua. Port Townsend, Washington, Copper Canyon Press, 1989.
Sappho's Gymnasium, with T. Begley. Port Townsend, Washington, Copper Canyon Press, 1994.
Ithaca: Little Summer in Winter, with T. Begley. Radiolarian Press, 1996.

Recording: *If I Yes,* Watershed, 1980.

Other

Translator, *What I Love: Selected Translations of Odysseas Elytis.* Port Townsend, Washington, Copper Canyon Press, 1986.
Translator, *The Little Mariner,* by Odysseas Elytis. Port Townsend, Washington, Copper Canyon Press, 1988.
Translator, *Open Papers: Selected Essays of Odysseas Elytis,* with T. Begley. Port Townsend, Washington, Copper Canyon Press, 1995.
Translator, *Eros, Eros, Eros: Poems, Selected and Last, of Odysseas Elytis.* Port Townsend, Washington, Copper Canyon Press, 1997.

*   *   *

Olga Broumas's collection *Beginning with O* sets sail with "Marine / eyes, marine / odors" behind the first letter of her given name. Flicking aside patriarchal constraint along with the patronymic, the book takes on as subject the naming and shaping body, "a curviform alphabet ... beginning with O, the O- / mega, horse-shoe, the cave of sound." In the omen letter the Greek-born Broumas wills a concentration on beginnings and plots reference points for her voluntary exit from the Greek language and her arrival in English. Her *O* is an open mouth, as the alphabet of the body begins to assemble a language outside the customary configurations of gender, family, and nation.

In her first publications in English Broumas tests a variety of rubrics. A long sequence of poems establishes "Twelve Aspects of God," retrofitting a pantheon of Greek goddesses within feminist and lesbian experience. In homage to Anne Sexton fresh, quirky, and memorable poems replay fairy tales, reweaving contemporary and mythic events with a keen sense of the painful and radical adjustments of relations to mother, father, sister, and husband that such revision requires. Her Cinderella emerges as a woman

> strung on a windy clothesline a
> mile long. A woman co-opted by promises: the lure
> of a job, the ruse of a choice, a woman forced
> to bear witness, falsely
> against my kind, as each
> other sister was judged inadequate, bitchy, incompetent,
> jealous, too thin, too fat. I know what I know.

Other poems contain dedications to specific women. Everywhere Broumas situates herself within communities of women, the instruments of knowing born of women's pleasure, the earth itself richly female. The following is from "Dactyls":

> Up the long hill, the earth rut steamed in the strange sun.
> We, walking between its labia, loverlike, palm to palm.

Beginning with O invokes Broumas's seaside childhood self. In the birth metaphors that dominate much of her work, she emerges from the Greek sea "clean caesarean":

> Something immaculate, a chance
>
> crucial junction: time, light, water
> had occurred, you could feel your bones
> glisten
> translucent as spinal fins.

Within the body the bones melt into light burning out time. Again and again the body's transformations are the self's road to understanding; when self joins other in erotic conjunction, lovers derive their chief knowledge of the sacred. In *Perpetua* this belief becomes

> The text
> of sex, word for word and by heart
>
> divined, enacted
> in the antechamber of the soul so kindly
> also provided me, is my guide and prayer.

Drawn to narrative in the 1980s, Broumas wrote terse, pungent stories in which couples turn into trios and quartets and then, split and scattered, reassemble into other couples, trios, quartets. Families and conventional marriage then and now are largely seen as sources of misery. The speaker of "Landscape with Driver," from

Soie Sauvage, has her tubes tied; "For Every Heart," from *Perpetua,* says that "I like it when my friend has lovers, their happy moans, / unrestrained, fill the house with the glee of her prowess." Here and elsewhere awareness lights up the salty microrub of parts against and within parts, while Broumas also acknowledges as part of the lyric's subject a glancing penetration of both the metaphysics and the sociology of the erotic. Both early and late the political invades the personal possibility, and all of her books bear witness to the fierce agonies of modern Greek history.

Later poems continue the thematic preoccupations of the early work, even as Broumas varies her formal interests. In sensitive translations of the poems and essays of Odysseas Elytis she indicates the duality of her life in Greece and America, reaching across gender and time to an older Greek poet in a culturally stabilizing act. In *Black Holes, Black Stockings,* in collaboration with U.S. poet Jane Miller she affirms her sense of poetry as emanating from a community of working female artists. Both projects lead to different successes; in earlier work many beautiful poems are simply autobiographical, but later there is a broader range of portraiture and often a quietly savage observance of the current historical moment.

Early Broumas poems are occasionally rhythmically awkward and unconvincing, and in their phrasing some poems show their debt too baldly to Adrienne Rich's later declarative style. Broumas's poetry from *Pastoral Jazz* onward experiments more effectively with the timing and pacing of rhythmic units, working with a deliberately varied line length. Developing their own tightly coiled syntax, later poems unroll their sentences down the page in serene flotillas unimpeded by internal punctuation. Broumas has become increasingly interested in close association with other poets, and the following is a sentence from the prose poetry of Broumas and Miller, its sinuous quick-change virtuosities typical of their work together:

> But in the summer she fell back onto the bed where we
> came over and over to tangle ourselves without mercy,
> she in my plans for leaving the following autumn, and I
> in her long legs, white body of summer; and in winter—
> where having to be clandestine was more difficult—
> whiter, less floral, except at her lips which were always
> rose-fair, rose-large, cavernous like the couch she first
> sat on at the party where we met, in aparlor under the
> fair shade of her hair.

The aphoristic style of Odysseas Elytis shows the way to other affinities, other angles of influence, as in this passage from Broumas's translation of Elytis's *The Little Mariner:* "Few know the emotional superlative is formed of light, not force. That a caress is needed where a knife is laid. That a dormitory with the secret agreement of bodies follows us everywhere referring us to the holy without condescension." The same knowing hand, in a 1994 coauthorship with the classical scholar T. Begley, shapes the brief lyrics which comprise *Sappho's Gymnasium.* This nugget suggests the sharp turns and pleasures of that fusion:

> Blueprint I have hearing over knife
> prime workshop these forests verbed by breezes
>
> Horizon helicoptera
> Lesbian your cups
> Hermaphrodite phototaxis

—Lorrie Goldensohn

BUCK, Heather

Nationality: British. **Born:** Heather Entwistle, Kent, England, 6 April 1926. **Education:** Left secondary education at age 16 due to World War II; self educated through reading and attending evening classes and study courses. **Family:** Married Hadley Buck in 1952; one son, one daughter. **Career:** Cartographer for the War Department, London, 1942-45; town planner for Ministry of Town and Country Planning, London, 1945-47, Essex County Planning Department, Chelmsford, 1947-49, and London City Council, 1949-52. **Address:** 14 High Street, Lavenham, Suffolk CO10 9PT, England.

PUBLICATIONS

Poetry

The Opposite Direction. London, Outposts Publications, 1971.
At the Window. London, Anvil Press, 1982.
The Sign of the Water Bearer. London, and Wolfeboro, New Hampshire, Anvil Press, 1987.
Psyche Unbound. London, Anvil Press, 1995.

Other

T.S. Eliot's Four Quartets (essay). London, Agenda Editions, 1996.

*

Heather Buck comments:

I began writing in my early forties, as a result of Jungian analysis. My major formative influence was T.S. Eliot, followed by Wallace Stevens and Rilke.

My writing reflects my involvement in the spiritual, i.e., the unseen presences which deepen our understanding of everyday life, coupled with the insights of psychoanalytical theory and practice, particularly that of Jung.

My first books charted a journey inwards and back to the world towards rebirth and a quickening of love and spirit. As an explorer beyond the frontiers of ordinary consciousness, one is constantly aware of the need to find words for the inarticulate, hence the need to use imagery firmly rooted in the world of the senses.

In an age of clamour and disintegration I seek to point a way towards personal integration.

*   *   *

In today's world of rapid and constant communication—the "infoculture", as it has been dubbed—it is particularly interesting to encounter poetry as consistently mediative, private and inward as Heather Buck's. That her work exhibits these qualities in such distinct measure may be connected with the fact that she came to writing relatively late and after Jungian analysis. She was born in 1926, but her first full-length collection, *At the Window*, only appeared in 1982, although she had been contributing to magazines for ten years or so before that. Whatever the precise cause, Buck's attention is pre-eminently focused on the interior world and the process of self-discovery—something which, as she writes in "Self-knowledge" in her second volume, *The Sign of the Water Bearer*, can "cost so dear." There are, as another poem in the same collection remarks, "no easy exits from ourselves."

If the sources of Buck's inspiration allow the label "traditionalist" to be applied to her, so does her choice of poetic tools. Formally, her poems are unambitious. While she does not employ conventional verse forms, iambic meter is seldom far away and there is an occasional—and not always successful—use of rhyme. Sometimes a sharply defined image does spring off the page: thus a trickle of water down a cliff is seen as a "snail's smear." But generally her diction is at once conservative and resonant—aimed at capturing the half-tones and shadows that dominate her imaginative landscape, in which "the day for a few short hours" can retrieve "a little light" ("The Deserted Fen"). It is seldom that she attempts the big effect, although the three-poem Biblical sequence with which *At the Window* concludes demonstrates that the dramatic is by no means out of her reach.

T.S. Eliot wrote famously in *The Waste Land*: "These fragments I have shored against my ruins." Buck is another poet for whom the past has an unusually active role in the present. As she declares in "The Heritage" in *Psyche Unbound,* "we inherit more than we know / from the dust and bones / of those lying under the churchyard's stones." Biblical and historical references abound, and there are many echoes from poets of the past. "The Return" (in *The Sign of the Water Bearer*) reflects the mood and the message of Eliot's "Little Gidding" while "The Gold Threads in the Pattern" (the last poem of *Psyche Unbound*) owes a debt to Tennyson's "Mariana," although Buck's poem finally avoids the Tennysonian inanition. Other echoes come from Coleridge, Wordworth, and Yeats. But this is not to argue that Buck is derivative. In her case, tradition is not a dead hand but a source of renewal and strength—like contact with the earth for the mythical giant Antaeus. In the face of "footsteps that swell ... abysses of terror," she has found "that sanity is rigged / upon the underpinning / of habitual things" ("Prisoners").

Psyche Unbound, Buck's third volume, marks a clear advance on her earlier collections. The presentation of the material is more confident, sure-footed, and deft, with a tighter control over structure. The persona of the poet is also more firmly delineated, although still portrayed with discretion and decorum. What is perhaps most notable about Buck's achievement is her success in connecting with and articulating currents of feeling which in most people remain sunk under the weight of routine and habit. In *The Sign of the Water Bearer* there is a poem describing a visit she made to Dodona in Greece, the site of an ancient oracle dedicated to Zeus. There

> bare-footed priests used to reap
> words from whispering oak-leaves, binding
> and braining them into fragile responses
> solid enough for pilgrims petitioning gods.

It is in such a spirit that Buck holds up "the lamp of interrogation."

—Rivers Carew

C

CADDY, Caroline

Nationality: Australian. **Born:** Caroline Mavis Rumple, Perth, Western Australia, 20 January 1944. **Education:** Received high school diploma of dental nursing. **Family:** Married Daniel C. Caddy in 1965 (died 1972); one son and one daughter. **Career:** Dental nurse, Perth, 1960-65. Since 1965 self-employed in farming, teaching writing workshops, and working at clerical jobs. **Awards:** Western Australian Literary Week award, 1991, for *Beach Plastic;* National Book Council Banjo Patterson award, and Phillips Fox Turnbull award, 1992, for *Conquistadors.* **Address:** 709/34 Wentworth St., Glebe, New South Wales 2037, Australia.

PUBLICATIONS

Poetry

Singing at Night. Perth, Fremantle Arts Centre Press, 1981.
Letters from the North. Perth, Fremantle Arts Centre Press, 1984.
Beach Plastic. Perth, Fremantle Arts Centre Press, 1990.
Conquistadors. Melbourne, Penguin Australia, 1991.
Antarctica. Perth, Fremantle Arts Centre Press, 1996.
The Working Temple. Perth, Fremantle Arts Centre, 1997.

*

Caroline Caddy comments:

My need to be able to read my work aloud to my own satisfaction was a big impetus to my development as a poet. Although I knew I had achieved the poem on the page, I felt it was not complete unless I could read to an audience and have my voice come off the page, the script to translate truly into sound. It was not till I had begun to work in the form and pacing of my later books, *Beach Plastic* being transitional, that I felt able to "voice" my poetry.

Some of my later poems, especially in *Conquistadors,* have been seen by critics as obscure or difficult. I believe that the imagery used should not be private to the poet and aim in my work for the universal or the universal embedded in the idiosyncratic. No, no, I hear you say, not the dreaded word "symbol." Sometimes I feel I am trying to steer my poetry around the "dreaded word" and come up with a silhouette of sight, smell, and touch like those popular 3-D pictures that you have to go into a "brown study" to see.

My latest books, drawn from time spent in Antarctica and China, are more easily accessed with many of the poems close to what I would call lyric essays.

*   *   *

The Western Australian poet Caroline Caddy has had a slow rise to national visibility. This is perhaps partly owing to a childhood spent in the United States and to country jobs and a country address in Australia since then.

Singing at Night announces Caddy's interest in different traditions (Japanese, Chinese, Tarzan after the jungle) and her tendency to look for a structure, a larger grouping (the title sequence of eight poems). Although "The Lions of Ghir" is perhaps the best early poem, the short poem "Rain," with its flexible phrasing and scattered layout between the two margins of the column of print, points the way to her later work.

Caddy finds voices in *Letters from the North.* The title sequence, about the rough life of mining workers and the isolation of their families in corporation towns of the northwestern Australian desert, consists of the abrupt, sometimes banal remarks—verbal jottings—of a colloquial voice. Another sequence, "A Member of the Tribe," sketches seven deprived lives as monologue "Testaments" in the mode of Edgar Lee Masters's *Spoon River Anthology.* The distance between the dialect of the North Americans of Masters's work and the Australian voices of Caddy's sequence is an impressive measure of her skill.

Beach Plastic, like all of Caddy's books spanning a wide range of interests, is nonetheless keyed to her knowledge of bushland and of the coast of southwestern Australia. In this book she definitively claims the constraints and liberties of the columnar poem: both margins are justified, and both long and short lines are placed within the column, with some free at either end and others stayed at the margin. In her early work Caddy insisted on the exact placing of the lines and letters to conform with her typescript—to the point of demanding a typewriter font, for its equal letter spaces, in her fourth book.

Not just the form she has developed but also a restless ingenuity with language guarantee the energy of Caddy's voice, as in "Fire 3":

> Down one side of the house
> piston backs hoe a wall of flame
> while I
> filling buckets and can't helping it
> make aghast in my own head
> lines of poetry
> Now I've had it!
> Three trees fall at my presumption.
> Away from the house! Who's got who licked.
> Negative negative We have lift-off
> and the whole hill erupts
> phlogists our backs our necks -
> shoulders imp with ash-sting
> and the sun
> IS GONE...
> Oh Wiz Oh Witcher hear me cry
> with everybody
> bring back the light!
> no! no! not this that...
> - the Heavenly Disc - (whispered).

Doctrine, desire, and the powers in one's life occupy Caddy in several of the poems of *Conquistadors,* winner of the Phillips Fox Turnbull national award for poetry. Her travels to China and Antarctica, where she accompanied the Australian Antarctic Research Expedition team, have provided the inspiration for *Antarctica* and

The Working Temple, which particularly impresses with its vivid evocation of living and working in China.

Despite the verbal and vocal virtuosity of Caddy's work and despite her effectiveness as a reader, she is rarely scheduled to perform. Her writing, too, may seem arcane if the reader opens it with the idea of merely being entertained. She is a poet with ambitious projects whose time is perhaps yet to come; quite apart from the riches of what Caddy observes and has to say, her stubborn labor to control her own responsive form will not go out of fashion and has remained a defining point in her work.

—Judith Rodriguez

CASSIAN, Nina

Pseudonym: Maria Veniamin. **Nationality:** Romanian. **Born:** Galati, Romania, 27 November 1924. **Education:** Pompilian Institute, Bucharest, University of Bucharest, and Bucharest Conservatory of Music. **Family:** Married Vladimir Jany Colin in 1943 (divorced); 2)Al.I. Stefalnescue in 1948. **Career:** Worked as a journalist, film critic, and translator; New York University, teacher of creative writing, 1985—. **Awards:** Romanian State Prize, 1952; Writers' Union award, 1969, 1983; Bucharest Writers' Association award, 1982; Fulbright fellowship, 1985.

Publications

Poetry

La Scara 1/1 ("On a Scale of One to One"). Bucharest, n.p., 1947.
Sufletul mostru ("Our Soul"). Bucharest, n.p., 1949.
A vin, noua sute si sapteprezece ("1917—A Living Year"). Bucharest, n.p., 1949.
Cintece pentru republica ("Songs for the Republic"). Bucharest, n.p., 1950.
Horea nu mai este singur ("Horea Is Alive No More"). Bucharest, n.p., 1952.
Tinerete ("Youth"). Bucharest, n.p., 1953.
Versuri alese ("Selected Verse"). Bucharest, Stat Pentru Literatura si Arta, 1955.
Vîrstele annului ("Measures of the Year"). Bucharest, n.p., 1957.
Dialogul vîntului cu marea ("Dialogue of Wind and Sea"). Bucharest, n.p., 1958.
Sarbatiru zukbuce ("Daily Holidays"). Bucharest, n.p., 1961.
Spectacol in aer liber ("Spectacle in the Open Air"). Bucharest, n.p., 1961.
Sane facem daruri ("Let's Give Gifts to One Another"). Bucharest, n.p., 1963.
Cele mai frumoase pezii ("The Most Beautiful Poems"). Bucharest, n.p., 1963.
Disciplina harfei. ("The Discipline of the Harp"). Bucharest, Editura pentru literatura, 1965.
Sîngele ("Blood"). Bucharest, n.p., 1967.
Destnele paralele ("Parallel Destinies"). Bucharest, n.p., 1968.
Ambitus ("Ambit"). Bucharest, n.p., 1969.
Chronofagie ("Time Devouring"). Bucharest, n.p., 1970.

Marea conjugare ("Grand Conjugation"). Bucharest, n.p., 1971.
Recviem. Bucharest, n.p., 1971.
Lotopoeme ("Lottery Poems"). Bucharest, n.p., 1972.
Soave. Bucharest, Cartea Româneasca, 1977.
Spectacol in aer liber II. Bucharest, Albatros, 1974.
O suta e poeme ("100 Poems"). Bucharest, n.p., 1975.
Viraje ("Orbits"). Bucharest, n.p., 1978.
Virages: 50 Poemes, translated into French by Cassian, Eugene Guillevic and Lily Dennis. Bucharest, Editura Eminescu, 1978.
De îndurare ("Mercy"). Bucharest, Editura Eminescu, 1983.
Blue Apple, translated by Eva Feiler. Merrick, New York, Cross-Cultural Communications, 1981.
Lady of Miracles, translated by Laura Schiff. Berkeley, Cloud Marauder Press, 1982.
Numaraoarea inversa ("Countdown"). Bucharest, Editura Eminescu, 1983.
Call Yourself Alive?, translated by Andrea Deltant and Brenda Walker, introduction by Fleur Adcock. London and Boston, Forest Books, 1988.
Life Sentence, edited by William Jay Smith. London, Anvil, and New York, Norton, 1990.
Cheerleader for a Funeral, translated by Cassian and Brenda Walker. London and Boston, Forest Books, 1992.

Fiction

Nica fara frica ("Fearless Niki"; for children). Bucharest, n.p., 1950; revised, Bucharest, Editura Ion Creanga, 1976.
Ce-a vazul Oana ("What Oana Saw"; for children). Bucharest, n.p., 1952.
Florile patriel ("Flowers of the Fatherland"; for children). Bucharest, n.p., 1954.
Pintul Miorlau ("Prince Miaow"; for children). Bucharest, n.p., 1957.
Bot-gros, catel fricos ("Big Muzzle, Puppy Fearful"; for children). Bucharest, n.p., 1957.
Chipuri hazlii, pnetru copii ("Funny Faces for Kids"; for children). Bucharest, n.p., 1958.
Adventurile lui Trompisor ("Adventures of Trucky the Elephant"; for children). Bucharest, n.p., 1959.
Povestea cu doi pui detigru numiti Ninigram si Aligru (for children). Bucharest, n.p., 1969; translated as "Tigrino and Tigrene: A Narrative Poem for Children," in *Lion and the Unicorn,* Berkeley, n.p., 1987.
Atit de grozava si alte proze ("You're Terrific—I'm Leaving You, and Other Prose"). Bucharest, Cartea Româneasca, 1971; enlarged edition, 1976.
Jocuri de vacanta: versuri si proza ("Parlor Games: Verse and Prose"). Bucharest, Cartea Româneasca, 1983.

Other

Recording: *Nina Cassian and Sandra Cisneros Reading Their Poems,* 1995.

*

Critical Studies: By Marguerite Dorian, in *World Literature Today,* no. 64, 1990; by Fleur Adcock, in *Poetry Review,* vol. 80, no. 2, 1990; by Constance Hunting in *Parnassus,* no. 16, 1990; by

Sandra Golopentia, in *Modern Women Writers,* edited by Lillian S. Robinson, New York, Continuum, 1996.

*   *   *

Brenda Walker, translator and editor of 1992's *Cheerleader for a Funeral,* says Nina Cassian has "a linguistic versatility that makes a translator virtually redundant." Cassian has been her own translator in many instances, reveling in the fluidity of the medium she has mastered and seeing translation as at least an essential an act as creation itself; the title of her first collection, *La Scara 1 / 1 (On the Scale of One to One),* states her ultimate aspiration and perhaps unachievable goal. Despite her astonishing flexibility of mind and tongue, her work is rooted firmly in her native Romanian with a relentless physicality that, if restrained, threatens to explode in pleasure or violence or perhaps prayer:

Please God take pity
on the roof of my mouth,
on my tongue,
on my glottis,
on the clitoris in my throat
vibrating, sensitive, pulsating,
exploding in the orgasm of Romanian ("Licentiousness").

For Cassian, Romanian is a natural vernacular much as Italian was for Dante, rooted in a unity of primary experience and mystical knowing.

A victim of political persecution in her own country, Cassian and her work have found a new home in the United States; distinguished poets seem to be clamoring to translate her poems (in *Life Sentence,* a total of 20, including the author). Howard Moss has said she "strikes him as one of the best poets alive," while Stanley Kunitz calls her "a world-class poet, high-spirited, fierce, intelligent, uncompromising and wonderfully nervy." *Life Sentence* editor William Jay Smith finds in her poetry the "clear line and the strikingly simple texture" of the sculptor Brancusi and the comic spirit of the dramatist Ionesco, both her countrymen. Both these attributes have made her a successful writer for children, even during those years when communist party policy forbade her from exercising them as a writer for adults; *Fearless Niki* alone has been through three revisions, a republishing, and an incarnation as a puppet play. Cassian herself cites Romanian poets as her influences: Mihai Eminescu, Tudor Arghezi, Lucien Blaga, and especially Ion Barbu, a hermeticist with a surrealistic bent in the tradition of Mallarme but equally formed by Romanian folklore.

One of Cassian's favorite subjects is love, which includes not only the conventions of romance, but any pain and joy-wracked connection between living beings. A stood-up protagonist muses upon her betrayal as a failed sacrament in "Bread and Wine;" another hopes for an ideal coupling, "ancient couples of kings and queens," but settles for a brilliant self-sufficiency: "I took snow and drank / that white place you never crossed" ("Stained-Glass Window"). She sees "Everywhere absence— like a new and total winter;" the defeat of love—of conventional connection—is the triumph of this poetry of consummated solitude. "Intimacy"—whose title may be ironic or not— speaks not of human bonds but of the alchemical sympathy between the solitary poet and her writing environment. Touches of surreality and House-of-Usher drama pervades "The First and Last Night of Love," a narrative about a couple who find love in a framework which they carefully devise but cannot maintain:

This time no-one had followed them—
except themselves—abandoned and annexed to themselves—
and so, numerous in body and soul, they rested
in a motionless dance.

In "Face to Face," connection is accidental ("the train jerks us into each other's arms") and occurs only after "alienating ourselves with our whole capacity of misunderstanding, / in a true species' adversity;" its resolution is "the revelation of death / as probably the mammoths had / when they leapt into the next era."

As a participant in the convention of love—like water, a key Cassian image, love is forever in flux and seduces lovers into a false security—the poetic persona is vulnerable to disappointment; but as observer she finds her niche, the translator between conventions: "I dilate myself—to fill up the conventional space between people" ("Cold"). In doing so, she creates a warming friction between others, often destroying the comfortable (or at least familiar) distances of habit:

...willy-nilly they notice themselves and their similarities
and that happens at the surface of the massacre, in the open,
or higher still at the level of conscience
—who could name the place where something begins to change?

Even as observer, the poet is not detached but a catalyst, a lighting rod for the sometimes dangerous but often rewarding—"at the level of conscience"—emotive world in which she is rooted.

—Cynthia Davidson

CASTILLO, Ana

Nationality: American. **Born:** Chicago, Illinois, 15 June 1953. **Education:** Northern Illinois University, B.A. 1975; University of Chicago, M.A. in Latin-American and Caribbean studies 1979; University of Bremen, Ph.D. in American studies, 1991. **Family:** One son. **Career:** Has taught and lectured at numerous colleges and universities, including Northwestern Illinois University, San Francisco State University, Sonoma State University, Mill College, and Mount Holyoke College; dissertation fellow, University of California, Santa Barbara, 1989-90. German Association of Americanist reading tour of Europe, 1987; writer-in-residence, Illinois Arts Council. Contributor to periodicals, including *Essence, Frontiers, Heresies, Letras Femininas, Los Angeles Times, Nation, Prairie Schooner, Revista Chicano-Riqueña, San Francisco Chronicle, Spoon River Quarterly,* and *Washington Post.* **Awards:** Before Columbus Foundation American Book Award, 1987, for *The Mixquiahuala Letters;* Women's Foundation of San Francisco award, 1988; California Arts fellowship for fiction, 1989; National Endowment for the Arts fellowship, 1990, 1995; New Mexico Arts Commission grant, 1991; Carl Sandburg Literary Award, 1993, for *So Far from God;* Gustaves Myers Award, 1995, for *Massa-*

cre of the Dreamers. **Agent:** Susan Bergholz, 17 West 10th St., #5, New York, New York 10011, U.S.A. **Address:** 701 Southwest 62nd Blvd., # J-67, Gainesville, Florida 32607-6012, U.S.A.

PUBLICATIONS

Poetry

Otro Canto. Chicago, Alternative Publication, 1977.
The Invitation. Chicago, n.p., 1979; rev., San Francisco, La Raza, 1986.
Pajaros enganosos. Cross Cultural Communications, 1983.
Women Are Not Roses. Houston, Arte Público, 1984.
My Father Was a Toltec. New York, West End, 1988; enlarged as *My Father Was a Toltec and Selected Poems,* New York, Norton, 1995.

Novels

The Mixquiahuala Letters. Tempe, Arizona, Bilingual Press, 1986.
Sapogonia (An Anti-Romance in 3 / 4 Meter). Tempe, Arizona, Bilingual Press, 1990.
So Far from God. New York, Norton, 1993.

Short Stories

Loverboys. New York, Norton, 1996.

Play

Clark Street Counts (produced 1983).

Other

Massacre of the Dreamers: Essays on Xicanisma. Albuquerque, University of New Mexico Press, 1994.

Editor and translator, with others, *Esta Puente, Mi Espalda.* San Francisco, ISM Press, 1988.
Editor, with Heiner Bus, *Chicago Poetry.* University of Bamberg, 1994.
Editor, *Goddess of the Americas.* New York, Putnam, 1996.

Translator, with Daniel Fogel and Cathy Mahoney, *On the Edge of a Countryless Weariness / Al filo de un cansancio apatricia,* by Victoria Miranda and Camilo Feñini. San Francisco, ISM Press, 1986.

*

Media Adaptations: *The Invitation* (musical score), 1982.

Manuscript Collection: University of California, Santa Barbara.

Critical Studies: Interview in *Contemporary Chicano Poetry II / Partial Autobiographies,* edited by Wolfganger Binder, West Germany, Palm & Enke Erlander, 1985; "The Sardonic Powers of the Erotic in the Work of Ana Castillo" by Norma Alarcón, in *Breaking Boundaries: Latina Writings and Critical Readings,* edited by

Asuncion Horno-Delgado, Eliana Ortega, Nini M. Scott, and Nancy Saporta-Sternbach, Amherst, University of Massachusetts Press, 1989; "Entrevista a Ana Castillo" (interview) by Jacqueline Mitchell, Silvia Pellarolo, Javier Rangel, Xochitl Shuru, and Leticia Torres, in *Mester,* vol. 20, no. 2, Fall 1991; "The Multiple Subject in the Writing of Ana Castillo" by Yvonne Yarbro-Bejarano, in *The Americas Review,* vol. 20, no. 1, 1992; "Debunking Myths: The Hero's Role in Ana Castillo's *Sapogonia*" by Ibis Gómez-Vega, in *The Americas Review,* Spring / Summer 1994; "Claiming the Present: Ana Castillo" by Rafael Pérez-Torres in *Movements in Chicano Poetry,* Cambridge and New York, Cambridge University Press, 1995.

* * *

Poet, novelist, essayist, Ana Castillo is one of the most original voices in Chicana and contemporary American feminist literatures. In her work, she has created a complex and multifaceted world in which she explores issues relating to multiculturalism and feminism from the position of a Chicana feminist and, even more specifically, as she points out in an interview published in *Mester,* a Chicana from Chicago with a history quite different from that of Chicanas in Texas and California. For Castillo, it is essential to bring to the forefront of literary debates questions relating to the condition of women of color in the United States; to examine the relationship between Latin American and Chicana women; and to call attention to the fact that Chicana women face a form of racism comparable to, if historically different from, that suffered by African American women. Castillo always includes in her work, fictional and theoretical, a consideration of how gender and sexuality intersect with racism and cultural marginalization, generating "multiple oppression," as Castillo argues in *Mester.* This author's work, however, cannot be described solely in terms of her political commitment. Castillo's political ideals inform and are informed by the exquisite craftsmanship that characterizes her opus.

In response to a culture that is largely unwilling to legitimize difference, Castillo forges a language that enacts her cultural specificity. In her book of poems *My Father Was a Toltec,* biculturalism is articulated through a different kind of bilingualism, juxtaposing poems in English and Spanish without translation. The four sections into which the book is divided touch upon issues of female and lesbian identity and outline the journey towards self-creation that women must undertake in order to understand their place in culture and re-invent a world free of prejudice and racism. Castillo's early poetry, published in chapbooks (*Otro Canto* and *The Invitation*), exhibits a greater concern with rooting her identity in Mexican traditions and mythologies than her later poetry, in which she broadens and complicates her political vision. In "The Toltec," the opening poem of *My Father Was a Toltec,* the word "Toltec" serves, as Rafael Pérez-Torres explains, as "an ultimately diminished evocation of the lost world of Meso-American indigenous populations." In "In My Country," the last poem in *Toltec,* Castillo claims the need not only for social changes but aesthetic changes as well: "so these are not poems / i readily admit, / as i grapple with non-existence, / making scratches with stolen pen ... / Rape is not a poem. / Incest does not rhyme." Castillo wants to extricate her art from the trappings of a Western tradition that has historically ignored or misrepresented people of color, especially women.

While Castillo believes that a certain kind of nationalism was necessary in the beginnings of the Chicano movement in the 1970s and still argues for the recognition of one's own ethnic / racial roots, she dismisses facile nostalgia for traditions and customs that oppress women as well as exclusionary forms of nationalism. Thus in her 1991 interview in *Mester* she claimed: "I'm looking for a broader vision for us as a humanity and part of that means breaking down nationalism and understanding what nationalism means.... I don't go for nationalism.... I'm a poet and a visionary, so I'm not always very practical. And in my dream of what I would like to see would be that we could move on as a humanity. And it's not about assimilation, it's really about looking for ways for us to survive as people." In the ten essays of her *Massacre of the Dreamers: Essays on Xicanisma,* Castillo provocatively outlines the situation of women of color in the United States and claims that as a Chicana she has "much more in common with an Algerian woman" than with a Mexican man. Coining the term "Xicanisma" (which replaces Chicana feminism), Castillo argues for the need for political *conscientización* as well for a poetics of *conscientización* for the self-empowerment of Mexic Amerindian women. Dreamers, like the dreamers massacred by Moteuczoma, are at risk in a society that fears their visionary powers. In the concluding essay, "The Resurrection of the Dreamers," Castillo prophetically announces the awakening of the dreamers and encourages the awakening of all Xicanas: "Let us be alchemists for our culture and our lives and use this conditioning as our raw material to convert it into a driving force pure as gold." *Massacre of the Dreamers* is a text to be added to the list of key-texts of Chicana theoretical and political feminist thought, which includes Gloria Anzaldúa's *Borderlands / La Frontera: The New Mestiza,* Cherríe Moraga's *Loving in the War Years: Lo que nunca pasó por sus labios,* and *This Bridge Called My Back: Writings by Radical Women of Color,* edited by Moraga and Anzaldúa and translated into Spanish by Castillo and Norma Alarcón.

—Edvige Giunta

CATALDI, Lee

Also published under the name Lee Sonnino. **Nationality:** Australian. **Born:** Lee Sonnino, in Sydney, New South Wales, 15 July 1942. **Education:** Friends School, Hobart, Tasmania, 1948-58; University of Sydney, B.A. (with honors) 1962; Oxford University, B.Litt., 1967. **Family:** Married Gianni Cataldi in 1966 (divorced, 1992), one son. **Career:** Lecturer in English, University of Bristol, 1967-73; teacher, Tempe High School, Sydney, 1975-81; teacher and linguist, Lajamanu School, Lajamanu, Northern Territory, 1983-91; lecturer in linguistics, Batchelor College, Batchelor, Northern Territory, 1991-94; linguist, Kimberly Language Resource Centre, Hills Creek, Western Australia, 1994-95; lecturer in sociology, Macquarie University, Sydney, 1996. **Awards:** Anne Elder Memorial Prize, 1978, for *Invitation to a Marxist Lesbian Party;* Red Earth Poetry Prize, 1985, for "The Honey Tree"; Human Rights Commission Prize for Poetry and New South Wales State Literary Award shortlist, 1990, for *The Women Who Live on the Ground.* **Address:** P.O. Box 226, Aldinga Beach, South Australia 5173.

PUBLICATIONS

Poetry

Invitation to a Marxist Lesbian Party. Glebe, New South Wales, and Eugene Oregon, Wild & Woolley, 1978.
The Women Who Live on the Ground: Poems 1978-1988. Ringwood, Victoria, and New York, Penguin, 1990.
Race against Time. Ringwood, Victoria, Penguin, 1997.

Other

A Handbook to 16th-Century Rhetoric (as Lee Sonnino). London, Routledge, 1967.

Translator and collector, with Peggy Rockman Napaljarri, *Yimikirli-Warlpiri Dreamings and Histories.* San Francisco, HarperCollins, 1994.

* * *

Aged 38 when her first book was published, Cataldi is yet one more example of late development of women writers as compared with men. She is typical too of many Australian women poets, in having been brought before readers in International Women's Year (1975) in Kate Jennings' Outback Press anthology *Mother I'm Rooted. Invitations to a Marxist Lesbian Party,* easily the most provocative title of the decade, is a first book in its literary echoes, parodic notes ("Art Nouveau Muse," "Pool"), and essays in genres (fable, "four elements" sequence, etc.). However, both in short-lined, skillfully unpunctuated verse and in prose poems, Cataldi's mature manner is forming, apparently off-hand until you encounter the directness and ballad-like concision of her emotions: "I am the poet you do not remember / you are the song" (*Riddle*). Sexual and political positioning are declared with pioneering clarity ("northshoredirector'sdaughterweds/easternsuburbsdirector'sdaughter" and "Fairy tales"; "The poem in the classroom" and "Tourist").

Much of her 1990 book *The Women Who Live on the Ground* is written out of Cataldi's experience as a linguist at Lajamanu, near the Tanami Desert, with Warlpiri Aborigine women. This book invited comparison with *Singing the Snake* by Billy Marshall-Stoneking, and American poet writing of Papunya Aborigines. The reviews carry a discussion of principle and taste. The *Sydney Morning Herald*'s Heather Cam wrote of *Singing the Snake,* "What is so refreshing about this collection, and what I sadly miss in [Cataldi's book] is the sound of Aboriginal voices.... Cataldi's Warlpiri never speak directly to us; the voice is a white's, albeit that of a Marxist dedicated to the people of the 'Third World.'" Carol Treloar countered in the *Adelaide Advertiser,* "Her book is steadfastly centred in her own consciousness and experience—she has not appropriated theirs ... her refusal to indulge either herself or white cultural voyeurism ... highlights the 'otherness,' the essential dignity, and difference of Aboriginal life." Calling the book "one of the real finds of 1990," Marie Tulip in *Refractory Girl* agreed: "Cataldi's writing comes out of close involvement with Aboriginal women and the way that has changed not only her own relation with herself and the land, but even the rhythms of her words. 'If you stay too long in the third world,' Cataldi says, 'it will fill the space in your psyche / with a different discourse.'"

A year later, quoting the same poem, Lyn McCredden of *Editions* found "a strong and idealistic project" but was "on guard at first in the face of the political acceptability of such a voice and the often bland, conversational tone. Potential for political human knowledge does hover around the edges of this poetry.... But the language of the poetry only rarely prompts or stings or moves me to guess at the significance of this 'understanding.'" Her preference goes to Kevin Hart's "poised, shaped, educated poetry." "The spiritual individualising is so pointed—and peculiarly different to Cataldi's earthy, political, material images."

Cataldi's third book, *Race against Time,* is due out at the 1997 Adelaide Festival. She has also a body of unpublished work, some of it ornate, almost medievalizing writing sidelined in earlier years.

Despite her small output, Cataldi carries the standard for honesty to the role of white people in contact with Aborigines. Her other political poetry, on the environment and social pretensions, goes rather in the shade as a result. She has written much fine love-poetry which is insufficiently remarked upon; several of the quoted reviewers simply fail to mention it.

Philip Mead's remarks on Cataldi's "subtly angled shots into relationship" and "deftness with lineation" call attention to neglected aspects of her craftsmanship. Cataldi continues to work on educational and research compilations of Warlpiri language and lore. Close to this site of interracial cooperation and understanding, she might be regarded as taking up an aspect of Judith Wright's work. She would undoubtedly value Mead's remarks on "Lee Cataldi's skillful work with words" being paired with the comment: "poetry can make a political difference."

—Judith Rodriguez

CERVANTES, Lorna Dee

Nationality: American. **Born:** San Francisco, California, 6 August 1954. **Education:** California State University, San Jose, B.A. 1984; University of California, Santa Cruz, 1985-88. **Career:** Editor, *Mango* literary review; founder, Mango Publications, c. 1976; editor, *Red Dirt* magazine. Currently instructor in creative writing, University of Colorado, Boulder. **Awards:** National Endowment for the Arts grant, 1978, 1989; American Book Award, 1982, for *Emplumada.* **Address:** Department of English, University of Colorado, Box 226, Boulder, Colorado 80309-0226, U.S.A.

PUBLICATIONS

Poetry

Emplumada. Pittsburgh, University of Pittsburgh Press, 1981.
From the Cables of Genocide: Poems on Love and Hunger. Houston, Arte Público Press, 1991.

Recording: *An Evening of Chicano Poetry,* 1986.

*

Critical Studies: "*Emplumada:* Chicana Rites-of-Passages" by Lynette Seator, in *MELUS,* no. 11, Summer 1984; interview with Bernadette Monda, in *Third Woman,* vol. 2, no. 1, 1984; "The Chicana as Scribe: Harmonizing Gender and Culture in Lorna Dee Cervantes' 'Beneath the Shadow of the Freeway'" by Marta Ester Sánchez, in *Contemporary Chicana Poetry,* University of Cali-

fornia Press, 1985; by Roberta Fernandez, in *Dictionary of Literary Biography,* vol. 82: *Chicano Writers, First Series,* Detroit, Gale Research, 1989; by Agueda Pizarro Rayo, in *Latin American Literature and Arts,* no. 45, July / December 1991.

*   *   *

Of Mexican and Native American ancestry, Lorna Dee Cervantes came to poetry through her working class upbringing; as a child she spent her days reading books in the upper-class San Francisco homes where her mother worked as a cleaning lady. Beginning to write verse at age eight, Cervantes had, by age 20, begun to pursue her poetry with a dedication that has not faltered since. Poetry has allowed her to synthesize her cultural roots, and provided a means for expressing her feelings of alienation from both Mexican and U.S. culture: "a captive / aboard the refugee ship. / The ship that will never dock. / El barco que nunca atraca." ("Barco de refugiados"). As both founder of Mango Publications, a small press dedicated to publishing the works of Chicano writers, and editor of the related literary journal *Mango* during the mid-1970s, Cervantes can be credited for raising the cultural profile of the growing Chicano movement, as well as for establishing a strong Chicana-feminist presence.

Emplumada (1981) is a collection of bilingual free verse in simple diction—a glossary of Spanish terms is included—that paints strong visual images and diverse moods. The poems in this volume trace Cervantes' emerging identity as a woman, as a Chicana, and as a poet. The title combines the Spanish words for "feathered"—*emplumado*—and "pen flourish"—*plumado*—that marks the poet's attempts to link language with images of such feathered creatures as the mythic Quetzalcóatl, the Aztec god of wind. The first section of *Emplumada* focuses on how women's ways of relating to each other, as well as to men, are patterned by their social and cultural environment, as in Cervantes' most well-known work, "Beneath the Shadow of the Freeway." The poet also confronts the violence often directed toward working-class women of color; in "Uncle's First Rabbit," the scream of a dying rabbit draws the narrator into his childhood, to memories of witnessing his mother's loss of her unborn child as a result of being beaten by his father: "... She had a voice / like that, growing faint / at its end; his mother rocking, / softly keening."

In the second section of *Emplumada,* the natural world provides a wealth of metaphors for racial harmony—"Poem for the Young White Man Who Asked Me How I, an Intelligent Well-Read Person, Could Believe in the War between Races"—and economic deprivation—"An Interpretation of Dinner by the Uninvited Guest." "Starfish" reflects upon the loss of one's native tongue and cultural traditions, considering language as both a problem and a solution to the resulting discontinuity. The two parts of "Visions of Mexico While at a Writing Symposium in Port Townsend, Washington" suggest that, while cultural conflicts arising from dislocation and economic inequality may be resolved through the act of writing, the poet must not devalue her traditional oral culture:

I don't want to pretend I know more
and can speak all the names. I can't.
My sense of this land can only ripple through my veins
like the chant of an epic corrido.
I come from a long line of eloquent illiterates
whose history reveals what words don't say.

The last section, also titled *Emplumada,* contains exaltations of love, bird imagery, and reflections on the passage of the seasons, on rebirth. The poet is regenerated, phoenix-like, and her verses here resolve the conflicts and discontinuities established in the first two sections. As Roberta Fernandez noted in *Dictionary of Literary Biography,* "Cervantes has found what is good in her life.... She accepts the dimensions of her life, immerses herself in her various realities, and comes of age as a woman, as a Chicana, and as a poet."

Like Cervantes' first book, *From the Cables of Genocide: Poems on Love and Hunger* combines concrete imagery with theoretical abstraction. Here the poet's style is more complex, a result, perhaps, of coping with the violent death of her mother several years before, from which the poet had only lately recovered. Stream-of-consciousness passages abound, interwoven with almost surreal imagery. Spanish words now stand on their own, unbuoyed by translation. The poetic voice is stronger, more self-assured, more confident. Love and hunger, genocide, injustice, and intercommunication are the cables binding together the poet's reflections upon women's roles, Native American history, and minority culture. Again the volume ends optimistically: Section three is composed of clear, more concise, more structured lyrics that express the ways love is grounded—cabled—to the destructive tendencies, as well as to those inexhaustible forces that affirm life.

—Lynn MacGregor

CHANG, Diane

Nationality: American. **Born:** New York City, 1934. **Education:** Barnard College, New York, B.A. in English. **Career:** Worked as an editor for New York publishers; Barnard College, New York, teacher of creative writing until 1989. Painter, exhibiting in New York City. **Awards:** John Hay Whitney Foundation fellowship. **Address:** New York, New York.

PUBLICATIONS

Poetry

The Horizon Is Definitely Speaking. Port Jefferson, New York, Backstreet Editions, 1982.
What Matisse Is After. N.p., 1984.
Earth Water Light. N.p., 1991.

Novels

The Frontiers of Love. New York, Random House, 1956; with a new introduction by Shirley Geok-lin Lim, Seattle, University of Washington Press, 1994.
A Woman of 30. New York, Random House, 1959.
A Passion for Life. New York, Random House, and London, W. Allen, 1961.
The Only Game in Town. New York, New American Library, 1963.
Eye to Eye. New York, Harper, 1964.
A Perfect Love. Boston, Harcourt, 1978.

Play

Radio Play: *Falling Free,* n.d.

*

Critical Studies: "Writers in the Hyphenated Condition: Diana Chang" by Amy Lng, *MELUS,* vol. 7, no. 4, 1980; interview with Leo Hamalian in *MELUS,* vol. 20, no. 4, 1995; in *Asian American Literature* edited by Shawn Wong, Berkeley, University of California Press, 1996.

*   *   *

Diane Chang is most often noted for her six novels, especially *Frontiers of Love* (1956), the first novel to offer an in-depth examination of the internal psychological conflicts of being Eurasian. However, Chang is also a painter and frequent contributor to poetry anthologies. In *Breaking Silence: An Anthology of Contemporary Asian American Poets,* Chang discusses her focus in creative writing:

> While my main concerns in my novels seem to be in character, emotion and being, in my poetry I often write of the land, the ocean, the moon. Is it because they are less mortal than I, and keep me in touch with the eternal? Of course, I have other themes too: the word itself; love or love manque; creativity and art.

Chang infuses the poem "The Horizon Is Definitely Speaking," with compact imagery that suggests "the great chain of being" hierarchical system. The poet addresses the powerful mystique of nature—how it surrounds us and beckons us to mimic its harmony, from the lofty clouds to the earth where "the water is too still / and we are on edge." The final lines hint that the freedom of movement symbolized by the clouds is actually attainable: "the sky is in pieces at our feet."

> When clouds inch
> and the hill stays
>
> what are we to know?
>
> Geese overhead
> chew the fat all the way
> Trees like wishbones
> are nested with knowledge
>
> I stare into a bush
> until I become secrets, too
>
> All around, suggestions
> that the sky is in pieces at our feet
>
> the water is too deep
> and we are on edge

In addition to observations on nature, Chang's poems often address the tensions woven into her dual heritage. In a *MELUS* interview with Leo Hamalin, Chang responds to a question about being Chinese American, what she terms her "lopsided identity":

Being a Chinese-American woman is an elusive identity and a confusing one, even to myself. I feel that I am a minority person, but as a writer I know that sometimes I don't write 'ethnic' work, that often my imagination takes me to other situations, themes and voices. My imagination frequently doesn't seem to belong to me. Rather, I belong to it and wherever it takes me I go.

In Chang's poem "Second Nature," the speaker's struggle with a dual heritage is clear in the opening stanza: "How do I feel / Fine Wrists to small feet? / I cough Chinese." In a continuing sense of contrasting identities, the poet announces: "The old China muses through me.... My hair is America.... I shuttle passportless within myself."

What is enticing about Chang's poetry is the way she creates tight little phrases, lines, and stanzas of elegant complexity that nudge meaning to new heights. Her probing imagination and acute creative spirit are evident throughout her poetry, and often she merges her painterly eye with her lyrical voice to create new portraits. In "What Matisse Is After," the poet speaker opens with an oxymoronic image: "the straight is a curve / is what Matisse is after" and closes by announcing "He exhales paint we need / to / breath." And in the poem "Still Life," the act of lovemaking becomes an artistic excursion:

> Particles of you,
> Straining to become
>
> Before they are born,
> Stampede my womb.

In her interview with Hamalian, Chang discusses her extensive reading and acknowledges her familiarity with the works of writers like Toni Morrison, Ralph Ellison, John Williams, and Wesley Brown. She states: "African Americans are Americans who seem to me have contributed so much to this culture, politically and artistically, in every sphere. They've exercised the Constitution for all of us. In fighting for their own rights, they have fought for everyone else's, including mine." In poetry, Change identifies the influences of Emily Dickinson, whose imagery she finds thrilling and Theodore Roethke for his affinity to nature and his lyricism.

Ultimately, Chang's experiences as artist-novelist, painter, and poet-inform her identity as an Asian American woman. She shapes the images of her artistic identity into a palpable form that signifies what Shirley Geok-lin Lim has termed the "plural singularity" of Asian American women writers. Though Chang celebrates her American identity, poems like "Once and Future" explore the associative memories of her Chinese heritage:

> In China they have ghost chairs
> Time sits in them
> and on its lap rocks the vanished
> forever gathering up the worn

As Chang states in Dexter Fisher's anthology *The Third Woman,* "I feel I'm an American writer whose background is Chinese."

—B.J. Bolden

CHERNOFF, Maxine

Nationality: American. **Born:** Maxine Hahn, Chicago, Illinois, 24 February 1952. **Education:** University of Illinois, Chicago, 1968-74, B.A. 1972; M.A. 1974. **Family:** Married 1) Arnold Chernoff in 1971 (divorced 1972); 2) Paul Hoover in 1974; one daughter and two sons. **Career:** Lecturer, University of Illinois, Chicago, 1977-80; instructor, Columbia College, Chicago, 1977-85; assistant professor, 1980-87, and associate professor, 1987-94, Chicago City Colleges; adjunct associate professor, Art Institute of Chicago, 1990-94; since 1994 professor of creative writing and department chair, San Francisco State University. **Awards:** Carl Sandburg Award, 1985, for *New Faces of 1952;* Friends of American Writers award, 1987; PEN Syndicated Fiction award, 1988; *Southern Review*/Louisiana State University short story award, 1988; *Sun-Times* Friends of Literature award, 1993; five Illinois Arts Council fellowships. Since 1989 honorary fellow, Simon's Rock of Bard College, North Barrington, Massachusetts. **Address:** 369 Molino Avenue, Mill Valley, California 94941, U.S.A.

PUBLICATIONS

Poetry

A Vegetable Emergency. Venice, California, Beyond Baroque Foundation, 1976.
Utopia TV Store. Chicago, Yellow Press, 1979.
New Faces of 1952. Ithaca, New York, Ithaca House, 1985.
Japan. Bolinas, California, Avenue B Press, 1988.
Leap Year Day: New and Selected Poems. Chicago, ACM, 1991.

Novel

Plain Grief. New York, Simon & Schuster, 1991.
American Heaven. Minneapolis, Coffee House Press, 1996.

Short Stories

Bop. Minneapolis, Coffee House Press, 1986.
Signs of Devotion. New York, Simon & Schuster, 1993.

Other

In the News, with Ethel Tiersky. Chicago, National Textbook Company, 1991.
Attractions, with Ethel Tiersky. Chicago, Contemporary Books, 1993.

*

Critical Studies: "Fiction as Language Game: The Hermeneutic Fables of Lydia Davis and Maxine Chernoff" by Marjorie Perloff, in *Breaking the Sequence: Experimental Women Fiction Writers,* Princeton, New Jersey, Princeton University Press, 1989; *Writing Illinois* by James Hurt, Urbana, University of Illinois Press, 1992; *Interviews with American Women Writers* by Aruna Sitesh, New Delhi, East-West Press, 1994.

*   *   *

Maxine Chernoff's poems skate and glide from aperçu to insight to witticism and on to surreal conclusion. They are usually leavened by ingratiating perkiness. She starts spinning words that, in her best poems, turn into stories and finally myths. But her work is uneven and has evolved choppily. She has been influenced by the New York school of O'Hara via Berrigan, as well as by the Coolidge-like language school, but she seems truly inspired only by the prose of Russell Edson.

It is useful to begin with Chernoff's weakest work, *Japan,* published in 1988. Its final poem is "Zones":

> Sun
> > shut Wednesday
> swank of
> > missing
> ball-point
> > dodger
> radiant mud
> > moving
> poor
> > a quiet
> lapse
> > austerely
> yours
> > endured colossal
> sleep
> > to reckon
> bliss by
> > curtained
> hearty
> > thinness
> child's word
> > wavers
> thinking world
> > to open
> languor's
> > naked
> door

Within this book are 26 aleatory, language-oriented poems arranged alphabetically by title, one per letter. They run a weary gamut, utterly unlike, for example, her witty "Abridged Bestiary":

> The aardvark and the zebra were the only animals that
> the concise Noah allowed to join him. "Bears to yaks be
> damned," he shouted....

The work recalls David Rosenberg's much earlier *39 Excellent Articles of Japan,* which is simply found poems from a Japanese catalog written in pidgin English. While that work is wacky and camp, however, *Japan* seems to be an aesthete's abecedarium. If the poems of *Japan* have themes, they are generated, as Chomsky would say, by the tendency language has to mean. Abandon all hope ye who interpret here.

In contrast, her poem "For My Father" is forceful and strong, beginning, "He was my face on a necessary white." Chernoff's local allusions to Chicago, her home for many years, also glow, as in "April Fool," for a certain dean at the University of Chicago:

> The Early Warning System buzzed
> the TV screen while I made
> coffee: Oh good, the end of
> the world. Then I told my mother
> we'd have lunch at two.
> Happy April Fools',
> Professor Wayne C. Booth
> who claims our use of irony
> shows our fear of God
> the Father not liking
> his smirking children.

Chernoff can also write excellent prose. Her shortest prose she calls prose poetry, the kind of work of which Edson is the pre-eminent contemporary master. Her best pieces, such as "The Last Auroch," twist a tall tale into a myth. In "The Apology Store," for example, she tries to buy an all-purpose apology, but the store won't accept her currency and then claims to be sold out until spring or until the strike's over or until whenever. She then asks the store to phone when they can help; "I'm sorry," the clerk says, "we don't have a phone."

Chernoff's first book of short stories, *Bop,* was published in 1986. Although she has since been making a mark with her fiction, there is always something buoyant and exceptional in her best poetry, such as "Leap Year Day," the title poem from her 1991 book of new and selected poems:

> The paleolithic heart might burst
> with news of slowness, news of feathers.
> All the softness listed in the register
> you keep: day of finite crashing.
> Who's to say the deafness that you wore
> was needed by the Greeks? Depression
> sounded like a whole note sewn with
> lilac thread. I wanted to assure you
> that the small biology of kissing
> would not last until the pebble dried
> and a flag wobbled and a list faded and a map
> was drawn and a green planet drifted
> under your lens. The elbowed dawn lifted,
> and you said nothing of the storm that flashed
> off-shore, as if to mean, forgotten winter
> without signs. You will not fade.
> I believe your wholeness as it rests its future
> on our lengthening half-lit letters.

—Michael Andre

CHIN, Marilyn

Nationality: American. **Born:** Hong Kong, 14 January 1955; naturalized U.S. citizen, 1967. **Education:** University of Massachusetts, Amherst, B.A. (cum laude) 1977; University of Iowa, M.F.A. 1981. **Family:** Married to Charles Moore in 1993. **Career:** Translator and editor in International Writing Program, University of Iowa, Iowa City, 1978-82; assistant professor, 1989-92, associate professor, 1982-85, then professor of English and Asian American studies, beginning 1996, and director, Living Writers Series, beginning 1989, San Diego State University, San Diego.

Visiting assistant professor, University of California—Los Angeles, 1990, and University of California—San Diego, 1993. Panelist, National Endowment for the Arts translation prize, and National Book Award for poetry. **Awards:** National Book Council award, 1982; Mary Roberts Rinehart Award, 1983; Virginia Center for the Creative Arts fellowship, 1983; Stamford University Stegner fellow, 1984-85; National Endowment for the Arts grant, 1984-85, 1991; Centrum fellowship, 1987; Macdowell Colony fellowship, 1987; Gjerassi Foundation fellowship, 1989; P.E.N. Josephine Miles Award, 1994, 1995; Pushcart Prize, 1994, 1995, 1997; Yaddo fellowship, 1990-94. **Address:** Department of English and Comparative Literature, San Diego State University, San Diego, California 92182-8140, U.S.A.

PUBLICATIONS

Poetry

Dwarf Bamboo. Greenfield Center, New York, Greenfield Review Press, 1987.
The Phoenix Gone, the Terrace Empty. Minneapolis, Milkweed Editions, 1994.

Recordings: *Marilyn Chin and Andrew Hudgins Reading Their Poems,* 1994; *Marilyn Chin Reading from Her Poetry,* 1994.

Other

Editor, *Writing from the World* (originally published in *Iowa Review,* 1984). Iowa City, University of Iowa Press, 1985.
Editor, *Dissident Song: A Contemporary Asian American Anthology.* Santa Cruz, University of California Press, 1991.

Translator, *Devil's Wind: A Thousand Steps or More* by Gozo Yoshimasu. Oakland, California, Oakland University Press, 1980.
Translator, with others, *Selected Poems of Ai Quing.* Bloomington, Indiana University Press, 1982.

*

Bibiographies: In *Poetry for the People* by June Jordan, New York, Routledge, 1995.

Critical Studies: Interview with Maxine Hong Kingston, *MELUS* (Amherst, Massachusetts), 16(4), winter 1989-90; *Reading the Literatures of Asian America* by Shirley Geok-lin Lim, Philadelphia, Temple University Press, 1992.

Marilyn Chin comments:

I am interested in cultivating the consummate political poem. I believe that my work is daring, both technically and thematically. I am working on material which is very ambitious in thematic scope and form and is both a delicate and apocalyptic melding of East and West.

Sometimes this may mean breeding hybrid forms. Once I blended the epigrams of Horace with the haiku of Basho and came up with a strange brew of didacticism and pure image that made a powerful political statement.

Also, I have been working on love poems with a strong postcolonial subtext. In the Chinese American context—love always means assimilation. For, in love, one must completely destroy one's identity to merge with "the other" in a culpable, beautiful way. This is true on the surface level, perhaps. However, in a terrifying subtext—to assimilate into America means to annihilate one's culture, language, religion, and to be usurped by a culture that is monolingual, monotheistic, and whose world view is tied to the vicissitudes of commerce. My work is steeped with the themes and travails of exile, loss, and assimilation. What is the loss of country if it were not the loss of self?

*   *   *

Born in Hong Kong in 1955, Marilyn (Mei Ling) Chin immigrated with her family to Portland, Oregon, when she was just a young girl. The pains of cultural assimilation infuse her two collection of poems: *Dwarf Bamboo* (1987), and *Phoenix Gone, the Terrace Empty* (1994). In these collections, Chin struggles passionately and eloquently in the pull between the country left behind and America—the troubled landscape that is now home.

Chin has been praised for the intensity and clarity of her voice, as well as for an often bold and unshrinking articulation of her view from the boundaries of two cultures. She does not shy away from expressing anger. In "How I Got That Name (an essay on assimilation)" from her second collection, Chin takes on the American myth of the Asian "model minority:" "Oh, how trustworthy our daughters, / how thrifty our sons! / How we've managed to fool the experts / in education, statistics and demography—."

Earlier in the same poem, Chin speaks of how she was renamed "Marilyn" by her father: "obsessed with a bombshell blonde / transliterated 'Mei Ling' to 'Marilyn'." Chin, returning to that past moment, witnessed herself as the "wayward pink baby, / named after some tragic white woman / swollen with gin and Nembutal." Her name itself represents both the sudden shock and long-term process of assimilation—a name is violently transformed, and yet retains its connections to the prior name by that transliteration. In the new name lies always the echo of the old.

One of Chin's most distinctive marks as a poet is her skilled play with language. She is not afraid of mixing tones and styles within the same poem, evoking radically variant moods and creating strange juxtapositions with differing literary voices. These juxtapositions may be playful, or may shock in the sudden aggressiveness of her shift in tone. In "I Confess" (*Dwarf Bamboo*), Chin writes an imagined letter to her literary mentors in a tone both serious and deliberately absurd: "Dear mentors: / one day I am filial / monkey, practicing reading / and writing. Next day / I wear ink eyeliner, open up / Mandarin frock for the boys."

In "Barbarian Suite" (*The Phoenix Gone*), dedicated to Asian-American writer David Wong Louie, Chin speaks of loss and a doubled consciousness in the poem's first section: "My loss is your loss, a dialect here, a memory there— / if my left hand is dying will my right hand cut it off?" Chin sustains this reflective tone, until the sudden shock of the third section. There is then an explosion in language: "What did ya think? Life's that hunky-dory? / What did ya expect, old peasant, old fool..." Chin might be speaking of herself in a line that follows: "Orchids doth not bloom, baby, they cry, they explode." And in her deft manipulation of tone and language, Chin is able to express the *seductions* as well as the griefs of cultural assimilation, as the title of the poem "I'm

Ten, Have Lots of Friends, and Don't Care" implies (*Dwarf Bamboo*).

Chin does indeed carry a doubled consciousness. She is able in her poetry to articulate skillfully that interplay of, and tension between, cultures which constitutes her experience of the world. A critical part of this process of articulation includes establishing links and continuities between an ancestral past and cultural history, and an American present. She reaches back over time to makes these continuities clear, as in "The End of a Beginning" (*Dwarf Bamboo*), where she writes to her "Grandfather, / on your one-hundredth birthday":

> The beginning is always difficult
> The immigrant worked his knuckles to the bone
> only to die under the wheels of the railroad.
> One thousand years before him, his ancestor fell
> building yet annex to the Great Wall—
> and was entombed within his work. And I
> the beginning of an end, the end of a beginning,
> sit here, drink unfermented green tea,
> scrawl these paltry lines for you...

In these few phrases, Chin unites more than a thousand years in this moment that she sits to compose her lines of poetry.

Throughout her imaginative journeys across the spaces of time and place, and between cultural paradigms, Chin retains an awareness of her inability to regain completely what has been left behind. On a trip to Hong Kong, she writes to a friend in the poem "Repulse Bay" (*Dwarf Bamboo*): "The rain over Hong Kong falls / Over all of us, Li Ching, through / This postcard will tell you nothing / About the country I have lost." In moments such as these, the still and powerful core that lies within the anger, the jazz and the player of her language is unmistakable.

—Anne-Elizabeth Green

CISNEROS, Sandra

Nationality: American. **Born:** Chicago, Illinois, 1954. **Career:** Writer. Guest lecturer, California State University, Chico. Contributor to periodicals, including *Imagine, Contact II,* and *Revista Chicano-Riqueña.* **Awards:** Before Columbus Foundation American Book Award, 1985, for *The House on Mango Street;* Library Journal Best Book designation, 1992, for *Woman Hollering Creek.* **Address:** c/o Susan Bergholz Literary Services, 340 West 72nd Street, 4-B, New York, New York 10023, U.S.A.

PUBLICATIONS

Poetry

Bad Boys. Mango Publications, 1980.
The Rodrigo Poems. Bloomington, Indiana, Third Woman Press, 1985.
My Wicked, Wicked Ways. Bloomington, Indiana, Third Woman Press, 1987.
Loose Woman. New York, Knopf, 1994.

Short Stories

Woman Hollering Creek and Other Stories. New York, Random House, 1991; London, Bloomsbury, 1993.

For Children

The House on Mango Street. Houston, Arte Público, 1983; London, Bloomsbury, 1992.
Hairs = Pelitos. New York, Knopf, 1994.

Other

Recordings: *Woman Hollering Creek* [and] *The House on Mango Street* (cassette), 1992; *Nina Cassian and Sandra Cisneros Reading Their Poems,* 1995.

*

Critical Studies: "On the Solidarity of Being Mexican, Female, Wicked, and 33" (interview) by Pilar E. Rodriguez Aranda, in *American Review,* Spring 1990; "Claiming the Bittersweet Matrix: Alice Walker, Sandra Cisneros, and Adrienne Rich" by Nancy Corson Carter, in *Critique,* vol. 35, no. 4, Summer 1994; "What Is Called Heaven: Identity in Cisneros' *Woman Hollering Creek*" by Jeff Thomson, in *Studies in Short Fiction,* Summer 1994; "A Silence between Us like a Language: The Untranslatability of Experience in Sandra Cisneros' *Woman Hollering Creek*" by Harryette Mullen, in *MELUS,* Summer 1996.

* * *

For Sandra Cisneros, "our familia is our culture." Her stories and poems explore ethnicity, gender, language, and place where intimate and communal women-centered space provides ways of knowing the world of meaning and identity. Women's relationships, magic, myth, religion, and politics figure prominently in Cisneros' work, providing a rich matrix for her attempt to balance love and artistic work. In contrast to traditional representations of women, Cisneros foregrounds women characters who are often engaged to escape from the confinements of patriarchal determined roles common to two cultures, to interpret their own experience and redefine their lives. Her characters and situations are diverse and complex, reflecting realities that transcend stereotypes and categories. Once she found her own voice, Cisneros says, "I could speak up and celebrate my otherness as a woman, as a working-class person, as an American of Mexican descent" (*Mango*).

Cisneros' narrative style rejects traditional short story forms in favor of collage, often a mosaic of interrelated pieces, blending the sounds of poetry with oral story telling techniques. Her ingenious use of language includes the rhythm, sound, and syntax of Spanish, its sensibilities, emotional relationships to the natural world and inanimate objects, and its use of tender diminutives. She also uses the poetry of urban street slang, children's rhymes, and song creating her own innovative literary style at once musical, spontaneous, primal, and direct.

In her introduction to the 1994 edition of *Mango Street* she notes:

The language of *Mango Street* is based on speech. It's very much an anti-academic voice—a child's voice, a girl's voice, a spoken voice, the voice of an American-Mexican. It's in this rebellious realm of antipoetics that I tried to create a poetic text with the most unofficial language I could find. I did it neither ingenuously nor naturally. It was as clear to me as if I were tossing a Molotov.

In the series of 44 brief, poetically charged vignettes which compose *Mango Street*, the voice of Esperanza Codero observes and documents the lives around her, women who look out the window and "sit their sadness on an elbow" ("My Name"). In this coming of age story, Esperanza writes about women who are alienated, confined, restricted, trapped by poverty, and often deserted by lovers and husbands. There is Rose Vargas, with too many kids and a husband who "left without even leaving a dollar for bologna or a note explaining how come" ("There Was an Old Woman She Had So Many Children She Didn't Know What to Do"), and Esperanza's own mother, "a smart cookie" who says, "I could've been somebody, you know?" She speaks two languages and can sing an opera but can't get down on the subway ("A Smart Cookie"). Esperanza's environment is characterized by both poverty and racism as well as the warmth, intimacy, and humor of her culture. She is nurtured and empowered by women who share stories and poems with her, who encourage her to keep writing because it will keep her free, who remind her never to forget who she is, that she "will always be Mango Street." As Esperanza's voice gains strength, she provides a powerful, carnal, poetic, and "unofficial text" which critiques traditional western discourse. Unlike the women around her, Esperanza escapes confinement and isolation, refusing to accept socioeconomic and gender-determined limitations. Instead, she discovers her inner poetic self and moves away from feelings of shame, away from silence towards artistic freedom and a fullness of identity. In the last story she says, "One day I will pack my bags of books and paper." But she leaves to return "for the ones I left behind. For the ones who cannot out" ("Mango Says Goodbye Sometimes").

In *My Wicked Wicked Ways*, published in 1987, the voice of the youthful Esperanza merges with that of the grown woman / poet. "Tell me," she asks, "how does a woman who / a woman like me. / Daughter of / a daddy with no birthright in the matter. / What does a woman inherit / that tells her how / to go?" Her first felony she tells us is to have taken up with poetry, chucking the "life of the rolling pin or factory" (Preface). She says, "I've learned two things. / To let go / clean as kite string. / And never to wash a man's clothes. / These are my rules" ("For a Southern Man"). Her feminist Mexican American voice is playful, street smart, vigorous, and original continuing to transgress the dominant discourse of canonical standards, linguistically and ideologically.

In *Woman Hollering Creek*, published in 1991, in contrast to those living on Mango Street, women struggle to take control of their lives in a place where love sours, men leave, and becoming a female artist is an arduous struggle. Against a background of *telenovelas*, religion, magic, and art, women find ways to escape and transform their lives. Clemencia, an artist rejected by her white married lover, paints and repaints his portrait, engaging in an imaginary conversation: "You think I went hobbling along with my life, whining like some twangy country-and-western when you went back for her. But I've been waiting. Making the world look at you from my eyes. And if that's not power, what is?" ("Never Marry a Mexican"). In "The Eyes of Zapata," the general's long time lover patiently waits for him, turning herself "into the soul of a *tecolote*" (owl), keeping "vigil in the branches of a purple jacaranda outside your door to make sure no one would do my Miliano harm while he slept." Invoking magic, offering a prayer in "*mexicano* to the old gods," and a plea to La Virgen, Ines endures. In the final story, Cisneros contrasts a highly educated Chicana artist with a young man whose poetic sensibilities challenge her values and perspectives. Lupe asks Flavio to make love to her in "*That* language. That sweep of palm leaves and fringed shawls. That startled fluttering like the heart of a goldfinch or a fan," not in English "with its starched r's and g's. English with its crisp linen syllables. English crunchy as apples, resilient and stiff as sailcloth. But Spanish whirred like silk, rolled and puckered and hissed" ("*Bien* Pretty").

In *Loose Woman*, her most recent book of poetry, Cisneros' lyricism is characterized by sassy deftness and precision of language. She's a woman who talks back. Addressing her lover she says: "You bring out the Mexican in me. / The hunkered thick dark spiral. / The core of a hear howl. / The bitter bile. / The tequila *lagrimas* on Saturday all / through next weekend Sunday." In the title poem Cisneros warns she is a woman-on-the-loose, both bitch and beast: "I'm an aim-well / shoot-sharp / sharp-tongued / sharp-thinking, / fast-speaking, / foot-loose, / loose-tongued, / let-loose, / woman-on-the-loose, / loose woman. / Beware, honey." In these poems Cisneros is concerned with women's erotic power, the joy of the female "Sinew / and twist of flesh, / helix of desire and vanity" (*Well, If You Insist*). She deftly explores and celebrates the wonder, possibilities, and consequences of being Mexican American and a woman—tough, independent, free-spirited, revolutionary and loose.

"I have always believed that, when a man writes a record of a series of events, he should begin by giving certain information about himself: his age, where he was born, whether he be short or tall or fat or thin," Ann Petry wrote in her 1947 novel, *Country Place*. "This information offers a clue as to how much of what a man writes is to be accepted as truth, and how much should be discarded as being the result of personable bias. For fat men do not write the same kind of books that thin men write; the point of view of tall men is unlike that of short men." In each of her works Ciseros throws the literary equivalent of a Molotov cocktail into Western discourse aimed at revolutionizing its monocultural representational system. Within her Chicana feminist alternative discourse, she privileges the wondrous and particular lives of those often defined as other, the *different*, those perceived as marginalized, as less than. She than illuminates these untold lives. When asked if she is Esperanza, she replies, "Yes, and no. And then again, perhaps maybe. One thing I know for certain, you, the reader, are Esperanza." And she asks a reader, will you learn to be "the human being you are not ashamed of?" Sandra Cisneros' work is not only original, unrelenting, and eloquent, it is essential.

—Carol Thomas

CLANCHY, Kate

Nationality: British. **Born:** 1965.

PUBLICATIONS

Poetry

Slattern. London, Chatto & Windus, 1995.

*   *   *

The themes of Kate Clanchy's poems are adult themes. Although young herself, she leaves to youngsters the lyric raptures of heady first love. Hers are the detached observations of children she teaches, meditations upon the laundry basket, ironic contemplation of a relationship in terminal decline. This does not mean that she is a gloomy poet. On the contrary, hers is one of the most sharp and enlivening wits to have emerged in verse since the heyday of Stevie Smith, or even that of Dorothy Parker.

Her characteristic vein is playful. Many readers will go for pieces such as "Men," "Foreign," "Cambridge" ("This softened, cheesy, gracious place"), "Pathetic Fallacy" ("You can't get drenched, however much you wish it"), and "Poem for a Man with No Sense of Smell." In this last, the author ends, saying of the delicate hairs on the nape of her neck that they "hold a scent frail and precise as a fleet / of tiny origami ships, just setting out to sea." She is, however, capable of effects that are more exploratory.

Take her poem "For a Wedding." Most writers attempting an epithalamium aim for poise; they try to trace the dignity of marital union. Indeed, Clanchy's poem begins like that: "Cousin, I think the shape of a marriage...." But the nobility of tone suffers an ironic decline. The shape of a marriage "turns out to be like that of furniture, and not ceremonial furniture at that. It is, rather, tatty, utilitarian, battered by children—"marriage has lumps like / their button-backed sofa, constantly, / shortly, about to be stuffed." She has turned the poem, back from the impending marriage of her cousin, to that of her parents living through three houses and the raising of a family. But after that she turns the poem forward—past the high romance of a wedding and on to a likely marriage. This is foreseen in terms of a suburban garden, where ease is hard-won and relationships have to be worked at; as, on a Sunday pond, "the waterboatmen / skate with ease across the surface tension." The inference is that this will not be a situation she herself would choose. "For a Wedding" may be a marriage song, but it implies some unusual overtones.

The image of the skating insect is the end of the poem. Not only does it sum up all that goes before it but it also brings the verse structure to a climax. Often the hardest thing to do with a poem is to end it. Kate Clanchy has no such problem. On the whole, her endings prove to be the most remarkable feature of her work.

"Overnight" depicts a lover sleeping, and it is all done in terms of a particular cast of weather. As the lover drifts into a deeper sleep, his breathing thickens "like the first / inquisitive gust of a storm on the roof." A dream flickers across his eyelids "swift as the twitch of dry leaves in the wind." Even deeper slumber, slumber beyond dreams, is characterized in terms of snow. Indeed, the poem turns into sleep seen in terms of snow gathering and snow settling until, at length, the two people awake to see that something has changed during the night. That change is characterized by "the levelled white we saw / in the morning, the lawn expectant as an empty page." What was a running metaphor has condensed into reality.

This sense of a conclusion, to a relationship as well as to a poem, is brought out with characteristic wit in "Towards the End." Here the central image is that of a wrecked street cat. The couple tend the stricken animal, spray her, inject her, stroke her body, frail and trembling as it is; but to no avail. The imagery of her dying—"just greasy bones in a bag"—is poignant enough, but the real power of the poem is released at the end, when it is made clear what the cat symbolizes;

> you turned away I think,
> I know I cried.
> There was not enough between us
> to keep the cat alive.

It is later poems in Clanchy's first collection, *Slattern,* that carry this kind of emotional charge. Her wit is unfailing: any apparent cliché turns out to have a double meaning and to imply, beneath the suave statement, a perilous undertow. The volume ends with a strange poem, "Patagonia." This begins in mid-statement—"I said *perhaps Patagonia*"—and there follows the development of a fantasy land. The waves bore themselves to sleep—"bore" being a pun on a secondary meaning of that word—influx, eagre—as in the Severn Bore. Then the last clinging barnacles paddle off in tiny coracles; an odd metaphysical image. But it is the last lines that, as ever, bring out the full meaning, until then withheld. The fantasy land is a fantasy relationship:

> When I spoke of Patagonia, I meant
>
> skies all empty aching blue. I meant
> years. I meant all of them with you.

This is an adult poem, facing grief, treating it with wit and detachment. The tone is controlled, but in Clanchy's work there is real passion to be kept under control. Distance often is the poet's response to emotion, but she makes a mythology out of it.

In a recent and as yet uncollected poem, she turns a lover into Stylites on a monument and herself, ironically, into an acolyte. Indeed, "The Acolyte" is the title of the poem. It contrives to mock the man "nearer to God by a clear sixty feet," and also herself, portrayed as a foolish worshiper. It is a turning on the dead of Milton's chauvinistic line, "He for God only, she for God, in him." In the detached, witty and essentially adult writing of Clanchy, this comes out as:

> a woman prostrate
> at the foot of a glaring
> white pillar, pursuing,
> through noon and siesta,
> to rotating shadow
> of a foreshortened, athletic,
> odd form at the peak.

—Philip Hobsbaum

CLARKE, Gillian

Nationality: Welsh. **Born:** Gillian Williams, Cardiff, Glamorgan, 8 June 1937. **Education:** St. Clare's Convent, Porthcawl, Glamorgan; University College, Cardiff, B.A. in English 1958. **Career:** News researcher, 1958-60, occasional broadcaster, 1960—, BBC, London; freelance writer, 1985—.

Lecturer in art history, Gwent College of Art and Design, Newport, 1975-84; writing fellow, St. David's University College, Lampeter, Dyfed, 1984-85; editor, *Anglo-Welsh Review,* 1976-84; chair, 1988-93, Welsh Academy, and since 1989, Taliesin Trust; tutor, M.A. in creative writing, University of Glamorgan. President, Writer's Centre, Ty Newydd. **Awards:** Cardiff University fellow; University of Wales, Swansea, fellow. **Address:** c/o Carcanet Press, Conavon Court, 12-16 Blackfriars St., Manchester M3 5BQ, England.

PUBLICATIONS

Poetry

Snow on the Mountain. Swansea, Christopher Davies, 1971.
The Sundial. Llandysul, Dyfed, Gomer, 1978.
Letter from a Far Country. Manchester, Carcanet, 1982.
Selected Poems. Manchester, Carcanet, 1985.
Letting in the Rumour. Manchester, Carcanet, 1989.
The King of Britain's Daughter. Manchester, Carcanet, 1993.
Collected Poems. Manchester, Carcanet, 1994.

Plays

The King of Britain's Daughter (libretto for cantata), 1993.
The Time of the Wolf (produced in Powys, Wales, 1996).

Radio Plays: *Talking in the Dark* (poem), 1975; *Letter from a Far Country* (poem), 1979; *Talking to Wordsworth,* 1997.

Other

Editor, *The Poetry Book Society Anthology 1987-1988.* London, Hutchinson, 1987.
Editor, *The Whispering Room: An Anthology of Haunted Poems for Children.* London, Kingfisher, 1996.
Editor, *I Can Move the Sea: 100 Poems by Children.* Wales, omu Press, 1996.

Translator, *One Moonlit Night* (Welsh children's stories). Wales, omu Press, 1991.
Translator, *One Bright Morning,* by Kate Roberts, forthcoming.

*   *   *

Gillian Clarke writes of her native Wales, of the elements that form and shape it: "It is not easy. / There are no brochure blues or boiled sweet / Reds. All is ochre and earth and cloud-green / Nettles tasting sour and the smells of moist earth and sheep's wool...." ("Blaen Cwrt"). Rain, unyielding stone, the "uncountable miles of mountains," and the "big, unpredictable sky" underlie her work. Beneath her apparently artless syntax is a complex system of assonance; repeated vowels and consonants keep the poems both tight and resonant. Many of Clarke's syntactical experiments are based on the metrical devices of traditional Welsh poetry.

Her collection *The Sundial* deals with death, abandonment, time passing; there is a constant sense of people pushing back the wilderness, keeping primordial forces at bay. But these huge themes

are carefully concealed in domestic disguises; in the title poem a young son's sundial gives rise to the final stanza:

All day we felt and watched the sun
Caged in its white diurnal heat,
Pointing at us with its black stick.

Though rural life looms large, this is the province of primitive archetypes rather than country idylls. In "Storm Awst":

...This then is the big weather
They said was coming. All the signs
Were bad, the gulls coming in white,
Lapwings gathering, the sheep too
Calling all night. The gypsies
Were making their fires in the woods
Down there in the east...always
A warning...

There is no comfort in this world; even in the secure setting of "Baby-Sitting" the speaker fears the waking of her charge:

...To her I will represent absolute
Abandonment. For her it will be worse
Than for the lover cold in lonely
Sheets; worse than for the woman who waits
A moment to collect her dignity
Beside the bleached bone in the terminal ward.
As she rises sobbing from the monstrous land
Stretching for milk-familiar comforting,
She will find me and between us two
It will not come. It will not come.

Clarke's second major collection, *Letter from a Far Country,* exhibits the same preoccupations, though the tone is less intense, more refined. Here the rhythms of rural life prevail in poems like "Scything," "Buzzard," and "Friesian Bull." Death is always close, but there is an acceptance, as in "The Ram," which begins, "He died privately. / His disintegration is quiet. / Grass grows among the stems of his ribs...."

The title poem of the collection is a wonderful, rambling meditation written originally for radio. Centered around a real parish in Wales, it explores "the far country" of the past and the imagined lives of its women inhabitants. Here Clarke reveals a remarkable eye for detail: "sea-caves, cellars; the back stairs / behind the chenille curtain; the landing when the lights are out; / nightmares in hot feather beds..." or "A stony track turns between ancient hedges, narrowing, / like a lane in a child's book. Its perspective makes the heart restless / ...The minstrel boy to the war has gone. / But the girl stays. To mind things. / She must keep. And wait. And pass time. / There's always been time on our hands." In such discreet phrases Clarke voices women's discontent: "The gulls grieve at our contentment. / It is a masculine question. / 'Where' they call 'are your great works?' / They slip their fetters and fly up / to laugh at land-locked women. / Their cries are cruel as greedy babies."

In its solemn, reticent way this poem celebrates the lives of women: "It has always been a matter / of lists. We have been counting, / folding, measuring, making, / tenderly laundering cloth / ever since we have been women." The poem concludes with an easy rhythmical verse which, for all its lightness of touch, expresses a profound confusion about the choices facing contemporary women: "If we launch the boat and sail away ... Who'll catch the nightmares and ride them away ... Will the men grow tender and the children strong? ... Who will do the loving while we're away?"

The poetry in *Selected Poems* is more lyrical than her previous works. There is a maturity about these poems; in "October" the poet proclaims, "I must write like the wind, year after year / passing my death day, winning ground"; "Climbing Cader Idris" begins, "You know the mountain with your body, / I with my mind, I suppose. / Each, in our own way, describes / the steepening angle of rock." Here nature is no longer the vengeful adversary, but more an accomplice. Other poems, like "Epithalamium," reveal unbridled, joyful celebration and even the stark, sad "The Hare," written in memory of the poet Frances Horovitz, ends on a note of calm acceptance:

... When they hand me insults or little hurts
and I'm on fire with my arguments

at your great distance you can calm me still.
Your dream, my sleeplessness, the cattle
asleep under a full moon,

and out there
the dumb and stiffening body of the hare.

—Katie Campbell

CLIFTON, (Thelma) Lucille

Nationality: American. **Born:** Thelma Lucille Sayles, Depew, New York, 27 June 1936. **Education:** Howard University, Washington, D.C. 1953-55; Fredonia State Teachers College, New York, 1955. **Family:** Married Fred J. Clifton in 1958 (died 1984); four daughters and two sons. **Career:** Claims clerk, New York State Division of Employment, Buffalo, 1958-60; literature assistant, U.S. Office of Education, Washington, D.C., 1969-71; professor of literature and creative writing, University of California, Santa Cruz, 1985—. Visiting writer, Columbia University School of the Arts; poet-in-residence, Coppin State College, Baltimore, 1972-76; visiting writer, George Washington University, Washington, D.C. 1982-83; Poet Laureate for the State of Maryland, 1976-85; Distinguished Professor of Humanities, St. Mary's College of Maryland, 1989—. **Awards:** YM-YWHA Poetry Center Discovery award, 1969; National Endowment for the Arts grant, 1970, 1972; Juniper Prize, 1980; American Library Association Coretta Scott King Award, 1984; National Book Award and *Los Angeles Times* Book Award finalist, both 1996; Lannan Award, 1996. **Agent:** Marilyn Marlow, Curtis Brown, 10 Astor Place, New York, New York 10003, U.S.A.

PUBLICATIONS

Poetry

Good Times. New York, Random House, 1969.
Good News about the Earth. New York, Random House, 1972.

An Ordinary Woman. New York, Random House, 1974.
Two-Headed Woman. Amherst, University of Massachusetts Press, 1980.
Good Woman: Poems and a Memoir, 1969-1980. Brockport, New York, BOA, 1987.
Next. Brockport, New York, BOA, 1987.
Ten Oxherding Pictures. Santa Cruz, California, Moving Parts Press, 1989.
Quilting: Poems, 1987-1990. Brockport, New York, BOA, 1991.
The Book of Light. Port Townsend, Washington, Copper Canyon Press, 1993.
The Terrible Stories. Brockport, New York, BOA, 1996.

Recordings: *The Place for Keeping* (audiocassette), Watershed, 1977; *Lucille Clifton* (video), reading and interview with Lewis MacAdams, the Lannan Foundation in association with Metro Pictures and EZTV, 1989; "Where the Soul Lives" (video), from *The Power of the Word* with Bill Moyers, Public Affairs TV and David Grubin, 1989; *The Language of Life,* with Bill Moyers, Public Affairs TV, 1994.

Other

Generations. New York, Random House, 1976.

Other (for children)

The Black BC's. New York, Dutton, 1970.
Some of the Days of Everett Anderson. New York, Holt Rinehart, 1970.
Everett Anderson's Christmas Coming [Year, Friend, 1-2-3, Nine Month Long, Goodbye]. New York, Holt Rinehart, 6 vols., 1971-83.
Good, Says Jerome. New York, Dutton, 1973.
All Us Come Cross the Water. New York, Holt Rinehart, 1973.
Don't You Remember. New York, Dutton, 1973.
The Boy Who Didn't Believe in Spring. New York, Dutton, 1973.
The Times They Used to Be. New York, Holt Rinehart, 1974.
My Brother Fine with Me. New York, Holt Rinehart, 1975.
Three Wishes. New York, Viking Press, 1976.
Amifika. New York, Dutton, 1977.
The Lucky Stone. New York, Delacorte Press, 1979.
My Friend Jacob. New York, Dutton, 1980.
Sonora Beautiful. New York, Dutton, 1981.

*

Lucille Clifton comments:
I am a black woman poet, and I sound like one.

*   *   *

Lucille Clifton creates a poetry of ideas in which the ordinary is revealed to be extraordinary, in which the indigenously commonplace yields universal truth. Two realities influence the mode and substance of her poetry: she is African-American, and she is a woman. "I write," she asserts, "what I know."

Early in her career, in "after Kent State," Clifton wrote, "white ways are / the ways of death / come into the / Black / and live." In a later volume, in a poem addressed "To Ms. Ann" (a historically ubiquitous title and name applied derisively to white "ladies"), she wrote, "you have never called me sister / and it has only been forever and / i will have to forget your face." Thus, she turned from whiteness to affirm and celebrate blackness.

The optimism that pervades Clifton's poetry is rooted in her ethnic heritage and milieu. She teaches that black life is, indeed, fraught with danger and adversity: "i went into my mother as / some souls go into a church / ... listen, eavesdroppers, there is no such thing / as a bed without affliction; / the bodies all may open wide but / you enter at your own risk." Still, one must take the risks: "i'm trying for the lone one mama, / running like hell and if i fall / i fall / i fall." The result is that

> i survive
> survive
> survive.

One must see the beauties and lessons in the lives of forerunners, and, Clifton teaches, one must see the beauties and possibilities in one's own life. In "Last Note to My Girls" she says, "i command you to be / good runners / to go with grace."

In the autobiographical prose work *Generations* Clifton asserts, "Things don't fall apart. Things hold. Lines connect in thin ways that last and last and lines become generations made out of pictures and words just kept." This heritage-inspired, almost mystical, faith and motivation are common in her poetry, as in the lines "someone calling itself Light / has opened my inside, / i am flooded with brilliance / mother, / someone of it is answering to / your name."

Clifton's sense of extended black family is especially strong in poems written from a female writer's or persona's point of view. Her feminism manifests itself neither in a strident voice of protest nor in concepts of fragile daintiness, shielded vision, protective seclusion, or cloying sentimentality. Hers is a dignified, active, poised, self-assured, insightful, and sensitive womanness. Poems such as "the lost baby poem," about an abortion, and "Conversation with My Grandson, Waiting to Be Conceived" obviously were written by such a woman. She sees her woman's strength, resolve, and independence in generations to come:

> sing the names of the women sing
> the power full names of the women sing
> White Buffalo Woman who brought the pipe
> Black Buffalo Woman and Black Shawl
> sing the names of the women sing
> the power of name in the women sing
> the name i have saved for my daughter sing...
> the name of my daughter sing she is
> They Are Afraid of Her.

The settings and situations that inform Clifton's poetry are those in which "little" people endure and function admirably, even heroically. The heroes that inspire or populate her poetry are public African-American heroes such as Angela Davis, Little Richard, and, more important, unexpected and unsung heroes such as "Miss Rosie," a "wet brown bag of a woman."

That religion is a source of Clifton's optimism is evident in her poems. A number of them are built upon metaphorical constructs derived from the Bible. In one poem, immediately after confessing that "i am not equal to the faith required," the speaker reports that, although "i try to run from such surprising presence; / the angels stream before me / like a torch." Clifton's God, it might be said, can be perceived by black people. In one poem the biblical Mary speaks with syntax and grammar identified with African-Americans, and in "Palm Sunday" the people lay "turnips / for the mule to walk / on waving beets / and collards in the air." In keeping with African-American religious traditions, it is a beatific faith.

Consistent with the prevailing theme of survival in her work, Clifton's essay "A Letter to Fred" reflects poignant memories of the life she shared with her deceased husband and responds to the persistent question, posed by family and friends, of whether or not she will remarry:

> Why shouldn't I? Why do they think that I wouldn't? Or shouldn't? After more than 30 years I know how to mate almost better than anything. Why would anyone learn something well, then promptly decide not to do it?

Poetically, Clifton shows resolution and insight as she clarifies death as new life. The male speaker in "the death of fred clifton" states that

> i seemed to be drawn
> to the center of myself
> leaving the edges of me
> in the hands of my wife
> and i saw with the most amazing
> clarity
> so that i had not eyes but
> sight,
> and, rising and turning
> through my skin,
> there was all around not the
> shapes of things
> but oh, at last, the things
> themselves.

The themes of womanness, history, and religion create a symmetry of survival in Clifton's *Quilting: Poems 1987-1990,* where the shared and intertwined histories of women are replicated in sections named for traditional quilt designs: "log cabin," "catalpa flower," "eight-point star," and "tree of life." The opening poem, "quilting," is suggestive of that history:

> in the unknown world
> the woman threading together her need
> and her needle
> nods toward the smiling girl
> *remember*
> *this will keep us warm.*

In "at the cemetery, / walnut grove plantation, south carolina, 1989," Clifton celebrates the histories of unnamed slave women: "some of these dark / were slaves / some of these slaves / were women ... / tell me your names." She acknowledges the dichotomies of women's unique gifts in poems such as "poem in praise of menstruation," "poem to my uterus," and "to my last period."

The poet's wry humor is evident in "wishes for sons," where the speaker announces that "i wish them hot flashes / and clots like you / wouldn't believe."

In several poems Clifton's religious optimism is tinged with ambivalence. In "wild blessings" she weaves her lyrical voice with biblical imagery to create an analogy of the dubious virtues of knowledge. The speaker is clearly discomfited with the gift of insight: "i am grateful for many blessings / but the gift of understanding, / the wild one, maybe not." In the section "tree of life" the speaker frets over the loss of innocence created by Lucifer's fall from grace and the resulting "perpetual evening" of carnal knowledge that has had an impact on the world:

> i the only lucifer
> light-bringer
> created out of fire
> illuminate i could
> and so
> illuminate i did.

Ultimately, Clifton's rocklike faith is clear. In "still there is mercy, there is grace" the speaker states, "how otherwise / could i ... curl one day safe and still / beside You / at Your feet, perhaps, / but amen, Yours." The final section of the work, "Prayer," injects a note of quiet religious faith as the speaker suggests, "and may you in your innocence / sail through this to that."

In her work *The Book of Light* Clifton creates an extended metaphor of survival by suggesting that the light is the path to personal survival: "woman, i am lucille, which stands for light." In short signature poems she acknowledges heroes and antiheroes, but in the poem "final note to clark" there is a clear disclaimer of superheroes: "why did i think you could fix it?" Finally, in "she lived" the speaker accepts personal responsibility: "she walked away / from the hole in the ground / deciding to live. and she lived."

Clifton's poems are short, graceful, incisive. They continue to open as the reader contemplates or reexperiences them. Their understated yet insistent, and occasionally wryly humorous, endings often surprise. The best generic term to characterize their form and technique is free verse. Her lines are sinewy, lithe, rather matter-of-fact, and her diction is clear, precise, often in the idioms of black Americans.

—Theodore R. Hudson and B.J. Bolden

CLUYSENAAR, Anne (Alice Andrée)

Nationality: Irish. **Born:** Brussels, Belgium, 15 March 1936. **Education:** Trinity College, Dublin (Vice Chancellor's prize, 1956), B.A. (honors) in English and French 1957; University of Edinburgh, diploma in general linguistics 1963. **Family:** Married Walter Freeman Jackson in 1976; three stepchildren. **Career:** Reader to writer Percy Lubbock for one year; assistant lecturer, Manchester University, 1957-58, and King's College, Aberdeen University, 1963-65; lecturer in general linguistics, Lancaster University, 1965-71; senior lecturer in language and literature, Huddersfield Polytechnic, Yorkshire, 1972-73; lecturer in linguistics, Birmingham University, 1973-76; senior lecturer, then principal lecturer in English

Studies, Sheffield City Polytechnic, 1976-87. Chair, Verbal Arts Association, 1983-86; active in National Poetry Society Poets-in-Schools workshops. Formerly general editor, *Sheaf,* and regular poetry reviewer, *Stand,* Newcastle upon Tyne. Tutor in creative writing, University of Wales, Cardiff, and freelance song writer and librettist. **Address:** Little Wentwood Farm, Llantrisant, Usk, Gwent NP5 1ND, Wales.

PUBLICATIONS

Poetry

A Fan of Shadows. Manchester, David Findley Press, 1967.
Nodes. Dublin, Dolmen Press, 1969.
Double Helix, with Sybil Hewat. Manchester, Carcanet, 1982.
Time-Slips. Carcanet, Manchester, England, forthcoming.

Other

Introduction to Literary Stylistics: A Discussion of Dominant Structures in Verse and Prose. London, Batsford, 1976; as *Aspects of Literary Stylistics,* New York, St. Martin's Press, 1976.
Verbal Arts: The Missing Subject. London, Methuen, 1985.

Editor, *Selected Poems,* by Burns Singer. Manchester, Carcanet, 1977.

*

Anne Cluysenaar comments:

(1985) I consider *Double Helix* the best I have done so far. In a review of *Double Helix* in *Writing Women* Linda Anderson caught exactly what I had hoped would be the effect of the book. In particular, she sees my mother's memoirs, together with other family documents, letters and photographs, as providing "an eloquent record of family history reaching back over three generations." My poems seek to interpret this in terms of "the boundaries of self and others." They are "meditations...on precisely those gaps and silences where lives meet and separate, where writing begins and ends." In writing the book, I was attempting to set down only what appeared to me to be literally true and to find poetry in such reality. Without, of course, believing that this is the only way in which poetry can be written, I felt the need to assure myself that "poetry" is not so much a sophisticated fiction as a simple, everyday experience shared by everyone if not always recognized for what it is. I hoped *Double Helix* would be receivable as this reviewer received it: "What the reader experiences is the repeated sense of overlapping subjectivities—not just what can be created and told of another life but also where that understanding ends. The gaps, absences, differences between the various texts create space for the reader and necessitate a kind of collaborative reading experience, the meeting of our own subjectivity with that evidenced by the text"; so that the reader's realities come to enrich those whose traces survive on the written page.

(1995) Certain dimensions of family history which I explored in *Double Helix* were to lead me into human prehistory and geology. Again, I was concerned with crossing the boundaries of self and others, but in wider terms: by this time I was living in the Border Country of Wales, where landscape and ways of living inevitably take on political and linguistic implications, and are especially moving to someone like myself who in the last World War lost both her original language and her original country. My forthcoming *Time Slips* will contain a sequence of poems exploring personal experience in the context of a reading of the 17th-century poet Henry Vaughan, who lived nearby and suffered during the British Civil War. In particular, "Vaughan Variations" attempts to relate the pressures of personal and social coincidence to those "quick vibrations" (Henry's phrase) which may seem to connect us less haphazardly to our natural surroundings.

*   *   *

Anne Cluysenaar's earlier poetry belongs to the school of Valéry and Beckett. Her poems evoke formally what it is to be human—the perceiving center, constantly changing, of a universe itself in a constant state of flux. *A Fan of Shadows* is a collection of models of the human condition, explained in appended notes as figures of "continuous creation" or "radiations from an occasionally moving centre." In "Figures" the image of Derwentwater is "love's point of balance" between opposites—stillness and movement, presence and absence, love and solitude, liquid and solid:

> The variant self awakes
> To hills, fields, open water
> Newly aware of their stillness.
>
> Between a kiss and the stillness
> Of lonely thought, water
> Off balance on a stony shore.

In "Sea" the stillness of midocean is complemented by the moving tides; in "Petrarch" the "still pool" is speechless and only knows itself in its overflow, "river-song." The sameness of experiences is underlined by the accumulation of archetypes of desire—Orpheus, Laura, Balder—and by a repetition of words, phrases, and whole verses which in several poems dictates the entire structure. The love lyric "Sea" falls into two near-mirror halves; "Epithalamium" opens as "The rings of the sun rise" to close on an echo: "The rings of the winter sunrise." The details of the differences are what make the present moment, which Cluysenaar seeks to flesh out, charting, in the words of "La Belle Otero," what she calls "The strangely similar gaze in two chance moments."

The changes in the quality of Cluysenaar's perceptions of the present are what distinguish her development—and progress—as a poet. In her earlier work she doesn't always successfully cross the divide between eternal verity and dead cliché. Her landscapes remain abstract, shot through by mind rather than sensuous matter. A poem like "Figures" can in its separate moment pinpoint an interesting and self-defining interpretation of thinker and perceived world:

> A slim wave's shadow
> Sinks into the hammered gold
> Of dry stone creased with water.
>
> Fish become concentrations
> Of light, on which waves wind
> Tongue-rolls of clear water.

But the vein it works is limited, and the strain of avoiding the twin evils of banality and preciosity constantly shows through. In later works there is more warmth, and a personal voice finally makes itself heard. "Maker" recognizes the poet's problem—the distance between the vivid color of the real world and the abstractly arid version on the dead paper before him. "The May Fox" solves it; a surprise confrontation with death (the narrow escape of a fox, caught in the car's headlights) turns into love, a moment of shared human and animal warmth which dramatically reenacts the exchange of meaning between man, nature, and the ideas and objects of man's creation.

Double Helix is a blend of letters, photographs, family documents, and poems which raises all human experience to the level of lyric. The voice of "the unnecessary poet" ("In Time-lapse") blends with others, past and present, in a celebration of human community where "I" is no more or less than the individual inflection of the "universal experiences," the "natural signs," of all daily life. To be human is to re-create from the abstract flow the sensuous detail of reality: "the stream / whose tiny, illegal trout / come to fingers patient with memories" ("Resting the Ladder"). "The Line on the Map," in the poem of that title, "has become hills, trees / A place not a direction." This place is not circumscribed; its expanding ripples reach out to include whole literary traditions (Milosz, Housman), cross the frontiers of class, nation, and politics, and abolish all limits, even those of death. Where private possession is abolished by community, there is no loss ("Resting the Ladder"):

> Watching, this first year, the swallow
> change to a silent icicle
> over the stable door,
> and knowing this will be the view
> of my old age, I warn myself
> we shall never own this place outright.

Cluysenaar's poetry reserves its anger for the merchants of loss and destruction, the authors of the concentration camps, the atom bomb, unemployment, repression. Against these her closing pages rise to a dignified rage that twists syntax but not sense, linking indissolubly poetic, personal, and political value ("7 September—Ready to Leave"):

> What duty can we meantime fulfil
> other than that which has always been ours?
> To grow with such persistent angry will
> that what is to be killed is worth dying for?

Whereas *Double Helix* draws on the strength of past lives, Cluysenaar's later poems, experiments in sonnet form, look to the future. The mirror of a new "Double," the child, reveals the real terrors concealed by the familiar language and rituals of everyday life. "In the Midst," its mirror-pattern schemes constraining writhing, broken rhythms, points the destructive nature of abstract and abstracted adult language, "the lip nice / on shattering syllables," for which the sole remedy is the baby's primitive scream: "It cries, and their mimed fear / Is as nothing to the real, modern horror. / It cries, we laugh. We catch our breath."

—Jennifer Birkett

COLE, Norma

Nationality: Canadian. **Born:** Toronto, Canada, in 1945. **Education:** University of Toronto, B.A. in modern languages and literature 1967, M.A. in French 1969. **Family:** One son. **Career:** Poet, translator, and painter; visiting poet and lecturer at schools in the United States and Canada, including Pasadena Arts Center, San Francisco State University, Brown University, Barnard College, and University of California, Berkeley; resident, Naropa Institute, Boulder, 1995. **Awards:** Gerbode Foundation Award for poetry, 1992; Ministry of French Culture Translation grant, 1992; Gertrude Stein awards, 1993-94, 1994-95; Fund for Poetry award, 1994. **Address:** San Francisco, California, U.S.A.

PUBLICATIONS

Poetry

Mace Hill Remap. Paris, Moving Letters Press, 1988.
Metamorphopsia. Elmwood, Connecticut, Potes & Poets Press, 1988.
My Bird Book. Los Angeles, Littoral Books, 1991.
MARS. Berkeley, California, Listening Chamber, 1994.
MOIRA. Oakland, California, O Books, 1995.
Contrafact. Elmwood, Connecticut, Potes & Poets Press, 1996.

Other

Translator, *It Then* by Danielle Collobert. Oakland, California, O Books, 1989.
Translator, with Michael Palmer, *The Surrealists Look at Art.* Venice, California, Lapis Press, 1990.
Translator, *Nude* by Anne Portugal. Los Angeles, Sun & Moon Press, forthcoming.

*

Critical Studies: "Visual Parole, Norma Cole's MARS" by Leslie Scalapino, in *Talisman* (Hoboken, New Jersey), no. 12, Spring 1994.

*   *   *

Warning: When reading this poet's work, you may be cracking heretofore unnoticed codes of North American expression. In Norma Cole's poems, one overhears language warming up like an orchestra, the word-universe expanding and contracting like a heart. You can see the headline coming: "all the years of work have resulted in a complete dismantling." "This" is what it's "all" about.

The eighth section of her sequence "Letters of Discipline" (from *Metamorphopsia*) is a response to Donald Kuspit's interrogation of the reason behind representing objects. Cole replies: "one paints because of the impulse to paint, one grows / To love what is paintable, true or false." There is more talk of growth and what is "paintable" in "Poetic Economy," from her 1996 volume *Contrafact,* where she says that "naming ma[kes] the words grow stranger," as if to tell us that making strange is part of any (r)evolution, any exchange. To distance is to make foreign, but it also gives us ground to be covered. It gives without taking anything as a given. What's close is far; a way is inevitable. Writing,

then, is work: words and wishes "wrought, forged." They are beaten and false, but also beautiful and made. Such is Cole's method: "to make full."

"Shadows," she says, "give lessons," and so the shapes of television, literature, and textbook hoodoo get thrown on the wall for inspection's sake. All of our phone calls are tapped, cut, and pasted. Our letters are read and rearranged. In the great traditions of William Carlos Williams, George Oppen, Mina Loy, and Ted Berrigan, we find idiom amuck and the world once again. Witness section "s" of *Metamorphopsia*'s "Paper House":

> writing burnt my tongue
> reading a book
> or feeding the fire
> developing old pictures
> released the image
> you really ought to see
> Ste Refrigerator
> cries real tears

"Personally," "arming," "other," "imported." These are words we might see and say every day. But in Cole's *MARS,* they take on different meanings, and indeed they "take on" meaning itself. Like the Gulf War they resonate with and react to; the sequences in Cole's fourth book seem a technology made primitive, fact gone fairy tale and back again. Shards of drama, prose, and verse work to create a dazzling, haunting portrait of the voices at our throats. From the "Mercury" sequence of *MARS:*

> To read
> hearts' ease
>
> faking presence
> a statement of beloved power
>
> no messenger
>
> that there could be no
> messenger

We risk shooting that messenger (there or not) if we are too at ease or inattentive with this work, a work which helps language to examine itself, and in this process, ourselves. On any one page, we see brutality, mockery, tenderness, joy. We see some of the old, false safety come crumbling away, and in turn we are given new possibilities for action, for utterance. Although her words themselves are not unfamiliar, the way she puts and pulls them might startle or upset. Warning: This is okay. The worst thing you can do in the space of Cole's poems is to stand still. As Leslie Scalapino comments, Cole's "language is not falsified by interpretation." Her's are poems to be, as Paul Celan says of reality, "sought after and won."

—Graham Foust

COOPER, Jane (Marvel)

Nationality: American. **Born:** Atlantic City, New Jersey, 9 October 1924. **Education:** Vassar College, Poughkeepsie, New

York, 1942-44; University of Wisconsin, Madison, B.A. (Phi Beta Kappa) 1946; University of Iowa, Iowa City, M.A. 1954. **Career:** Instructor, then professor of writing and literature and poet-in-residence, Sarah Lawrence College, Bronxville, New York, 1950-87. **Awards:** Guggenheim fellowship, 1960; Lamont Poetry Selection award, 1968; Ingram Merrill Foundation grant, 1971; Creative Artists Public Service grant 1974; Shelley memorial award, 1978; National Endowment for the Arts grant, 1982; Maurice English award, 1985; Bunting fellowship (Radcliffe College), 1988-89; American Academy of Arts and Letters Award, 1995; New York State Poet, 1996-97. **Address:** 545 West 111th Street, Apt. 8K, New York, New York 10025, U.S.A.

PUBLICATIONS

Poetry

The Weather of Six Mornings. New York, Macmillan, 1969.
Maps and Windows. New York, Macmillan, 1974.
Threads: Rosa Luxemburg from Prison. New York, Flamingo Press, 1979.
Scaffolding: New and Selected Poems. London, Anvil Press Poetry, 1984; as *Scaffolding: Selected Poems,* Gardiner, Maine, Tilbury House, 1993.
Green Notebook, Winter Road. Gardiner, Maine, Tilbury House, 1994.

Other

"Meeting-Places," foreword to *The Life of Poetry,* by Muriel Rukeyser. Ashfield, Massachusetts, Paris Press, 1996.

Editor, with others, *Extended Outlooks: The "Iowa Review" Collection of Contemporary Women Writers.* New York, Macmillan, 1982.
Editor, with others, *The Sanity of Earth and Grass: Complete Poems of Robert Winner.* Gardiner, Maine, Tilbury House, 1994.

*

Critical Studies: "An Ecstasy of Space" by Rachel Hadas, in *Parnassus: Poetry in Review* (New York), vol. 15, no. 1, 1989; "An Interview with Jane Cooper" by Eric Guetas, *Iowa Review* (Iowa City, Iowa), vol. 25, no. 1, 1995.

Jane Cooper comments:

Green Notebook, Winter Road, my most recent collection, deals with friendship, aging, the lives of girls and women, the humor and "complex shame" of a white Southern heritage, illness, and the enduring mysteries of art. It is a book that is meant to be very fluid, as the private and public worlds intersect, the present is opened out by glimpses of the past (and not just the personal past but the inherited or hearsay past as well), and song exists side by side with speech (long lines, prose lines). The book has an epigraph from Emily Dickinson's *Letters,* "My friends are my 'estate,'" but I suppose the real quest is to find out who the self is—to delve deep into the wisdom of the body, intuition, and dreams, and at the same time to record accurately, with loving if sometimes skeptical attention, details of social life, history, fam-

ily, race, class. Someone complained that there is too much death in the poems. Not at all, I am over 70, and I celebrate "ongoingness."

*   *   *

Jane Cooper's *Maps and Windows* of 1974 pulled a group of 12 poems from the decades-old oblivion of an unpublished manuscript, just as in 1984 *Scaffolding* reached back to acknowledge yet other early work, reclaiming a group of five poems written between 1954 and 1969. The rescued poems became part of Cooper's drive to make her own chronologies match a constantly changing but governing preoccupation with historical patterning. Never quite synchronous, the author's life and her awareness of its shaping forces have moved in charged interchange, and within each successive book an older self of the writer is confronted by the current self, soberly and self-consciously rearranging its canon to reflect different urgencies, newly promising directions. In 1994, against time's mounting losses, *Green Notebook, Winter Road* continues and triumphantly intensifies that prodding and testing of Cooper's relations to persons, places, and traditions, as the poet reorders the psyche's props for survival, altering the earlier confrontation of self against self to reflect instead a greater concern for the fit of the writing self within a tradition of women artists. Packed densely with reference to works and lives, Cooper's short, clustered, jewell-like lyrics dedicated to Georgia O'Keeffe ("The Winter Road") and Willa Cather ("Vocation: A Life") speak about the inevitable sexual and psychosocial crises and conflicts that existed so painfully for these women who were primary makers.

Scaffolding put Cooper's need to contextualize in place. Within a sequence entitled "Dispossessions" Cooper quotes from Rilke's *Malte Laurids Brigge:* "it is not enough / to have memories, they / must turn to blood inside you." While people die, houses remain husks, and things speak mutely only as things, poetry remains the constant; yet, the troubled search for vocation, for its life blood, becomes the fluid scaffolding of Cooper's poetry.

Scaffolding includes an essay, rather formidably titled "Nothing Has Been Used in the Manufacture of This Poetry That Could Have Been Used in the Manufacture of Bread," in which the Cooper of 1974 traces the growth of her poetry away from its initial focus on war and heroic themes to what she calls "the poetry of development." The impulse of both the essay and the collecting process is recursive and meditative; the whole of *Scaffolding* insists stubbornly but without vanity on tracing the particular figure of a career shaped by the facts of gender, culture, and history, refusing to fracture the tender sinuosities of the life it records.

As Cooper draws the connecting links in both prose and poetry, her early work and its intentions bear witness for a generation of American women growing up directly in the aftermath of World War II. It is a generation of women writers for whom, she comments, "The men's lives seemed more central than ours, almost more truthful. They had been shot down, or squirmed up the beaches. We had waited for their letters." Sojourning as a student of 22 in Oxford in the summer of 1947, Cooper marked these years as the opening of a struggle to sustain herself as a poet, a struggle sharply linked to the cultural circumscription of women's lives: "'Didn't anyone ever tell you it was all right to write?' asked the psychiatrist who came along much later. 'Yes, but not to be a writer,'" she says. In "The Knowledge That Comes Through Experience" she asked sardonically,

When shall I rest, when shall I find myself
The way I'll be, iced in a shop window?

Failing to find herself reflected as the edible woman desired by her time, she concluded:

Meanwhile I use myself. I am useful
Rather foolishly, like a fish who yearns
Dimly toward daylight. There is much to learn
And curiosity empties our rewards.
It seems to me I may be capable,
Once I'm a skeleton, of love and wars.

The poet remains a woman who, strip as she might, can never divest herself of a problematic feminine creativity bound to collide with cultural convention. "Obligations" blends sensuousness and watchful sobriety as it tracks "The dark home of our polarities / And our defense, which we cannot evade."

While a number of early poems dealing with gender relations have their own quietly wicked bite, others have the glassy good manners of the 1950s. All of the poems are solid affairs, with skillful construction and impeccable diction, and if they are occasionally too elliptical and understated, the personal and domestic themes are always perceptively treated.

Once past the more tentative 1950s an appealing rawness and fresh innocence dominate Cooper's middle and later work. In both prose and poetry there is a plain, stripped, almost severe speech whose truthfulness is always enhanced by delicacy of feeling; the poems press meaning through pauses and silences, through the white spaces of short lines and brief stanzas. Cooper's poems continue to represent the conflicts between our needs as separate people and the claims that we necessarily allow others to make on us as friends, lovers, family members, and citizens. There are scalding poems about childlessness. Several of the best, like "My Young Mother" and "Hunger Moon," practice a curious detachment in which a disembodied poet-speaker moves back before her own birth or observes a stage set with past selves; this characteristic gesture, used with an eerie flash, concludes the 1985 poem "Estrangement": "You watch your own back growing smaller up the beach."

Scaffolding closes with "Threads: Rosa Luxemburg from Prison," a dramatic monologue written as a sequence. "Threads" stretches the poet's early absorption with war, recovering the heroic for a perspective now both emphatically female and pacifist. It is Luxemburg's voice speaking persuasively from beginning to end, yet it is Cooper's achievement that from within poems both restrained and passionate continuities of style and vision weld the sequence to the rest of her own writing life.

Cooper's most recent meditations on the trajectory of female lives have touched on colleagues and writing friends, most notably Muriel Rukeyser. The spine of *Green Notebook, Winter Road* is elegy. The same empathy, insight, and imaginative historical intelligence that joined with lyricism in "Threads" now freely and authoritatively move back and forth between prose and poetry, and a new comic deftness leavens the pieces about Cooper's Jacksonville family. Cooper's probes into the ongoing trauma of her troubled health also expand the emotional compass of her work, and both the internal and external perspective increasingly enlarge and brighten for a poetry more compelling and interesting with each subsequent book.

—Lorrie Goldensohn

COPE, Wendy

Nationality: British. **Born:** Erith, Kent, 21 July 1945. **Education:** Farringtons School, Chislehurst, Kent, 1957-62; St. Hilda's College Oxford, B.A. in history 1966, M.A. 1970; Westminster College of Education, Oxford, Dip. Ed. 1967. **Career:** Teacher, Portway Junior School, London, 1967-69, Keyworth Junior School, London 1969-73, Cobourg Primary School, 1973-81, and Brindishe Primary School, 1984-86; arts editor, *ILEA Contact* (teachers' newspaper), 1982-84. Since 1986 freelance writer. **Awards:** Cholmondeley Award, 1987; Royal Society of Literature fellow, 1992; American Academy of Arts and Letters Michael Braude Award, 1995. **Agent:** Pat Kavanagh, Peters Fraser & Dunlop, 5th Floor, The Chambers, Chelsea Harbour, Lots Road, London SW10 OXF, England.

Publications

Poetry

Across the City. Berkhamsted, Hertfordshire, Priapus, 1980.
Hope and the 42. Leamington Spa, Warwickshire, Other Branch Readings, 1984.
Making Cocoa for Kingsley Amis. London and Boston, Faber, 1986.
Poem from a Colour Chart of Housepaints. Berkhamsted, Hertfordshire, Priapus, 1986.
Men and Their Boring Arguments. Winchester, Hampshire, Wykeham Press, 1988.
Does She Like Word-Games? London, Anvil Press Poetry, 1988.
Twiddling Your Thumbs (for children). London, Faber, 1988.
The River Girl. London and Boston, Faber, 1990.
Serious Concerns. London and Boston, Faber, 1992.

Other

Editor, *Is That the New Moon?: Poems by Women Poets.* London, Collins, 1989.
Editor, *The Orchard Book of Funny Poems.* London, Orchard, 1993.

*

Wendy Cope comments:

(1990) I began writing poems in the early 1970s when I was 27. My earliest poems were short, lyrical, and intense. Many of them were in free verse, some were haiku. None of them rhymed. There were no jokes in them. After about six years, I began to allow my sense of humor into my poems. I invented an unpleasant South London poet called Jason Strugnell, who wrote Shakespearean sonnets about the trials and tribulations of a middle-aged man of letters. He was also influenced by some of his contemporaries and a series of parodies of living poets was published under his name.

At around the same time I became interested in using rhyme and traditional rhyming forms. At first the subject-matter of these poems was mostly literary. Then I began to use rhyming forms to write more personal poems, many of them about love affairs.

(1995) My second full-length collection, *Serious Concerns*, is a bleaker book than my first (*Making Cocoa for Kingsley Amis*).

Although it includes quite a few humorous poems, those who perceive it as a volume of comic verse are overlooking a fair proportion of the contents.

*   *   *

Wendy Cope's *Making Cocoa for Kingsley Amis* was greeted with acclaim, and, skillfully marketed, it became a best-seller. "The most accomplished parodist since Beerbohm," wrote an enthusiastic blurb writer. This is not without truth, for Cope is a brilliant parodist. There are, for example, the splendidly Shakespearean sonnets:

> Not only marble, but the plastic toys
> From cornflake packets will outlive this rhyme ...

With "Budgie His Voice" (Hughes), the "Wasteland Limericks" (Eliot), and "The Strugnell Rubaiyat," *Making Cocoa for Kingsley Amis* is replete with parodies.

I would maintain, however, that Cope is more than a parodist. She is an original, needle-sharp satirist. Jason Strugnell, the "author" of so many of the parodies and an honorable member of a long line of fictional poets, together with Enoch Soames and Sebastian Arrurruz, is a brilliant invention. He epitomizes a particular type of suburbanite with certain attitudes toward poetry and art. He is a cousin of Ann Whickham's "Croydon Man" and Matthew Arnold's philistine writ large. He is delightfully funny as he reveals a whole vista of the British spiritual malaise. We can sense which way he would vote, the newspaper he reads, his attitude to life in general, all linked to the enterprise culture as expressed in

> I need a woman, honest and sincere,
> Who'll come across on half a pint of beer.

Cope's Strugnell is a razorlike dissection of certain British attitudes, and through him she sends up beautifully the convention of British anti-intellectualism. It is good to see such subversive stuff attracting such acclaim.

After *Making Cocoa for Kingsley Amis*, Cope published two booklets of verse, besides one for children, *Twiddling Your Thumbs*. One booklet, *Does She Like Word-Games?*, was nicely produced by Anvil Press; the other, *Men and Their Boring Arguments*, was rather badly designed and printed by Wykenham Press (Cope's work deserves better). Both contain acidly sharp and neatly crafted verses. Those concerned with the attitudes of men are specially keen edged and perceptive:

> Bloody men are like bloody buses—
> You wait for about a year
> And as one approaches your stop
> Two or three others appear

or

> If you want to be one who's irresistibly appealing,
> Don't change the subject when she tells you how she's feeling.

Good as they are of their kind, however, there is a worrying aspect. Is Cope in danger of being typecast by publishers' marketing departments as a witty squib writer, as a sort of comedienne, an intellectual Pam Ayres? I hope not, for long before the publication of *Making Cocoa for Kingsley Amis* Cope published a small Priapus Press booklet, *Across the City*, in which she explored her own feelings and concerns. They were the tentative poems of a new writer feeling her way, but they expressed a truth of feeling which I hope does not get lost or neglected. For instance, consider these lines from "From Your High Window":

> Alone in your room
> I have abandoned
> this day's plans, attempts
> to regulate the
> tide, it carries me.
>
> And you are warm stones
> on a shore, my palms
> remember every
> curve of bone, I taste
> traces of sea spray.

Not that there are no hints of such feelings in *Making Cocoa for Kingsley Amis*. "Tich Miller," for example, in spite of its jaunty-jokey style and seemingly offhand ending, is a poem deep with concern and feeling. Further, the title of Cope's second major collection, *Serious Concerns*, suggests a shift in emphasis. This book contains a fair proportion of squibs and jokes, even while it rebuts the criticism that she "writes to amuse":

> Write to amuse? What an appalling suggestion!
> I write to make people anxious and miserable and to
>   worsen their indigestion.

In the fourth section of *Serious Concerns* there are several deeply felt if sometimes not quite achieved love poems and poems of even more profound feelings, as seen in "Leaving":

> Next summer? The summer after?
> With luck we've a few more years
> Of sunshine and drinking and laughter
> And airports and goodbyes and tears.

We look for the development of this side of Cope's poetry with interest.

—John Cotton

COPUS, Julia

Nationality: English. **Born:** London, England, 16 July 1969. **Education:** St. Mary's College, Durham, 1987-90, B.A. in Latin, 1990. **Family:** Married David Morley in 1996. **Career:** Copywriter, Tim Aston Designs, London, 1990; editorial assistant, Pearson Young Ltd., Kent, England, 1992; teacher, Dilco School of English, Istanbul, 1994; writer-in-residence, Southampton Institute, Southampton, England, 1996. **Awards:** South East Arts Writers Bursary award, 1993; Society of Authors Eric Gregory Award, 1994; Hawthornden fellowship, 1996; first prize in Lincolnshire and Tabla poetry competitions. **Address:** 5 Thomas Road, North Baddesley, Southampton, Hants, S052 9EW, England.

PUBLICATIONS

Poetry

Walking in the Shadows (pamphlet). Huddersfield, Smith / Door-step, 1994.
The Shuttered Eye. Newcastle upon Tyne, Bloodaxe Books, 1995.

* * *

As other critics have found, it is difficult to write about Julia Copus's work without citing Sylvia Plath. The first poem in *The Shuttered Eye* is almost embarrassingly rich in Plathisms, and flags a significant debt: the lines "Is it / my destiny to wander this dark / forever, getting lost on the way?" send us to Plath's poignant line "I simply cannot see where there is to get to." "The Moon and the Yew Tree" is echoed again in the next stanza: "I cannot see / where they end...." The final stanza of the Copus poem has a typically Plathian construction: the proud simplicity of "I am a woman" lulls the reader before modulating into a disturbing and complex mixture of sounds, meanings, and nuances (Gretel? menstruation?): "the forest ... / ... feels my absence like a wound." One could fill a dozen essays like this with resemblances to the American genius, dead by her own hand at 31.

But Copus, who, like Plath, deals disturbingly and often distressingly with her relations with her father in terms of the Electra Complex, has her own music and her own games to play. For example, she uses colour as though she is a Venusian who has just discovered it: the "blue, blue skies / of Malta, your red eyes enacting a smile"; the priest in his purple robes (the red had been sent for cleaning, regardless of the needs of the church's year); the "earth-reds, ochres and umbers" of "The Botanical Artist"; the "fierce red / glare of the sand" that greets Jonah emerging from the whale's belly.

Frequently—too frequently, perhaps—the colour is an ominous and disgusting orange. A deserted husband "flings wide the doors on their / hinges like the orange jaws / of lions" and gets drunk (revolting thought) on orange home-brew, reflecting on, among other things, "that orange-haired bitch," until he lies on the carpet, "the black / phone hang[ing] silent like the / shell of a foetus in its coiled / umbilicus." One is back with Plath again, "the black telephone" in "Daddy" that is "off at the root." Often Copus's colours threaten, even more ominously, to fade into the whiteness of Plath's bedclothes in hospital.

In all this colour, all this darkness, all this paleness, there is a grim wit, as there is in Plath's work. Copus plays a brilliant, entertaining game with proverbs. She displays (this is an all too appropriate word) a virtuoso gift with chiasmus in two poems, where she reverses the order of the first stanza's lines in the second to dramatic effect. The music of her assonance, as in her little Creation Myth "The Making of Eve," the sureness of her technique with line-endings and, above all, her daring (a poem about a mastectomy ends with "a calm hand resting / flat against a bandaged chest") promise much from this fine poet.

Copus has absorbed so much of what matters to her—Eliot as well as Plath, and Wordsworth, and the experiences of other women beside herself. She has built up a store of reference and technique

that will make her a significant poet once she has lived through the heady influence of her mentor.

—Fred Sedgwick

CORPI, Lucha

Nationality: Mexican-American. **Born:** Jáltipan, Veracruz, Mexico, 13 April 1945; immigrated to the United States. **Education:** University of California, Berkeley, B.A.; San Francisco State University, M.A. **Family:** Married. **Career:** Vice-chair of Chicano Studies executive committee, 1970-71, coordinator of Chicano Studies Library, 1970-72, University of California, Berkeley; teacher of English as a second language, Oakland Public Neighborhood centers, Oakland, California, 1973—. Founding member, Aztlán Cultural, 1971, and Centro Chicano de Escritores, 1980. Poetry has been published in periodicals including *Prisma, Semana de Bella Artes, Imagine, Poetry San Francisco, Boston Review,* and others, as well as in anthologies. **Awards:** National Endowment of the Arts fellowship, 1979-80; *Palabra Nueva* prize, 1983, for short story "Los cristos del alma." **Member:** Oakland Museum and Latin American Commission.

PUBLICATIONS

Poetry

Fireflight: Three Latin American Poets, with Elsie Alvarado de Ricord and Chocha Michel. Kensington, California, Oyez, 1976.
Palabras de mediodía: Noon Words, translation from Spanish by Catherine Rodríguez-Nieto. Oakland, El Fuego de Aztlán, 1980.
Variaciones sobre una Tempestad / Variations on a Storm. Third Women Press, 1990.

Novels

Delia's Song. Houston, Arte Público, 1988.
Eulogy for a Brown Angel. Houston, Arte Público, 1992.
Cactus Blood. Houston, Arte Público, 1995.

Other

Mascaras. Third Woman Press, 1997.

*

Critical Studies: "Poets on Poetry: Dialogue with Lucha Corpi" by Barbara Brinson-Pineda, in *Prisma,* vol. 1, no. 1, 1979; in *Contemporary Chicana Poetry: A Critical Approach to an Emerging Literature* by Marta Ester Sánchez, University of California Press, 1985.

* * *

Lucha Corpi's poetry is imagistic and rooted in the reality of her own life, the short lines of clear and simple language building as they express the poet's emotions and concerns. Isolation, loneliness, love, and the role of women in the family and in the larger society are recurring themes in Corpi's work. Her bilingual collection *Palabras de mediodia / Noon Words* gathers together for English readers many of her early poems, while the much-anthologized four-poem series "The Marina Poems" draws on historical events at the time of the Spanish conquest of Mexico.

The poems in *Palabras de mediodia / Noon Words* are divided into three sections, each section concerned with a particular geographical location in Corpi's life. The first section focuses on Jáltipan, the Mexican coastal town where she was born. Corpi has described the lush and sunny location as being "full of the smell of mango blossoms." The second section concerns San Luis Potosi, a town in central Mexico where Corpi's family moved when she was nine years old. The final section is set in the United States, where she has lived for some 30 years.

The poems in each section of *Palabras de mediodia / Noon Words* reflect the place in which they are set, expressing some of Corpi's thoughts and emotions associated with her time there. Speaking of coastal Jáltipan, for example, Corpi writes: "Something of the sea / stayed in my veins: / The salty freedom / of restless water." In a poem from the section on San Luis Potosi, where Corpi grew up, she notes that "It was there / I first discovered / the terrible sin / of silence." The poems set in the United States focus on domestic themes, particularly housework, which Corpi uses as a metaphor for larger concerns. While ironing clothes in the poem "Patchwork," the narrator hears a voice within telling her "The soul has need / of wrinkles, / need of pleats, / tucks and other / signs of age."

Corpi has also received critical attention for "The Marina Poems," first published in English in the anthology *The Other Voice: 20th-Century Women's Poetry in Translation* and reprinted in many other anthologies since that time. This series of four poems tells of the historical character Dona Marina, a woman in Aztec Mexico who, because of having been traded between many tribes as a girl, knew many of the native languages. She served as one of Hernan Cortes's translators when the Spaniard conquered Mexico; she also had a child with him. Because of her role in the Spanish conquest, Marina is usually seen as a traitor to her people. But Corpi presents her as a victim of the clash between the Old and New Worlds, a victim of both cultures' maltreatment of women. In "Marina virgen," the second poem of the series, Corpi writes of Marina's conversion to Christianity and her personal identification with the sufferings of Christ. Marina becomes, in Corpi's version of her life, the mother of Mexico and its long history of victimization. At poem's end, she plants her soul in the soil like a seed to give birth to the Mexican people. The final poem in the series ends with Marina described as both a "mourning shadow of an ancestral memory" and with her hands "full of earth and sun." With this final image of sadness and hope, Corpi bestows a dignity upon a woman who has long been scorned by her own people.

—Denise Wiloch

CORTEZ, Jayne

Nationality: American. **Born:** Arizona, 10 May 1936. **Education:** Compton Junior College, Los Angeles; studied drama at Ebony Showcase, Los Angeles. **Family:** Married 1) jazz musician Ornette Coleman in 1954 (divorced, 1964); one son; 2) sculptor and illustrator Melvin Edwards in 1975. **Career:** Poet and performance artist; took part in voter registration drives in Mississippi, 1963-64; co-founder, Watts Repertory Theater Company, Los Angeles, 1964; founded Bola Press, New York, 1972; lecturer at Dartmouth College, Howard University, Queens College, Wesleyan University, and University of Ibadan; writer-in-residence, Livingston College of Rutgers University, 1977-83; co-founder, Organization of Women Writers of Africa; has toured with jazz musicians and had poetry readings worldwide. Member of board, Poetry Society of America, Coordinating Council of Literary Magazines, and Poet's House. **Awards:** New York State Council on the Arts Poetry award, 1973, 1981; National Endowment for the Arts fellowship, 1979-86; Before Columbus Foundation award, 1987; Afrikan Poetry Theatre tribute and award, 1994; Fannie Lou Hamer Award, 1994, for "outstanding contribution through her poetry to the struggle for justice, equality, and the freedom of the human spirit." **Address:** c/o Bola Press, P.O. Box 96, Village Station, New York, New York 10014, U.S.A.

PUBLICATIONS

Poetry

Pisstained Stairs and the Monkey Man's Wares, illustrated by Mel Edwards. New York, Phrase Text, 1969.
Festivals and Funerals, illustrated by Mel Edwards. New York, Bola Press, 1971.
Scarifications, illustrated by Mel Edwards. New York, Bola Press, 1973.
Mouth on Paper, illustrated by Mel Edwards. New York, Bola Press, 1977.
Firespitter, illustrated by Mel Edwards. New York, Bola Press, 1982.
Merveilleux Coup de Foudre: Poetry of Jayne Cortez and Ted Joans. France, Handshake Editions, 1982.
Coagulations: New and Selected Poems, illustrations by Mel Edwards. New York, Thunder's Mouth Press, 1984.
Poetic Magnetic. New York, Bola Press, 1991.
Fragments: Sculpture and Drawing from the "Lynch Fragment" Series by Melvin Edwards, with the Poetry of Jayne Cortez. New York, Bola Press, 1994.
Somewhere in Advance of Nowhere. New York, Serpents Tail / High Risk Books, 1996.

Recordings: *Celebrations and Solitudes,* Strata East, 1975; *Unsubmissive Blues,* Bola, 1980; *Poets Read Their Contemporary Poetry,* with others, Folkways, 1980; *There It Is,* Bola, 1982; *Maintain Control,* Bola, 1986; *Everywhere Drums,* Bola, 1990; *Cheerful and Optimistic,* Bola, 1994; *Taking the Blues Back Home,* Polygram, 1996.

Plays

Screenplays: *War on War,* 1982; *Poetry in Motion,* 1983.

*

Critical Studies: In *Yardbird Reader* (Berkeley), no. 5, 1976; interview with D.H. Melhem, in *Greenfield Review,* no. 11, Summer / Fall 1983, and *Heroism in the New Black Poetry,* Lexington, University Press of Kentucky, 1990; "There It Is: The Poetry of Jayne Cortez" by Barbara T. Christian, in *Callaloo* (Baton Rouge), no. 9, Winter 1986; interview with Melhem in *Melus* (Los Angeles), vol. 21, no. 1, Spring 1996.

*　　*　　*

Over four decades, Jayne Cortez has perfected her personal expression of an exuberant poetry steeped in African-American traditions of jazz, blues, dance, drama, and painting, and connected to the needs of the communities that continue to shape her voice. In Cortez's work, the personal is always intensely political, both in topical poems that address specific issues of war and injustice, and in her recurring vision of a community of strong, resourceful, and free women and men. The poet's role is to record wrongs, to chastise wrongdoers, and to give heart to the individuals whose struggles create the community. Her poetic personae, thus, include the griot, the jeremiah, and the shaman. Critically praised as one of the most forthright voices raised in opposition to racism and sexism, Cortez, herself, says in an interview with D.H. Melhem, "I think that poets have the responsibility to be aware of the meaning of human rights, to be familiar with history, to point out distortions, and to bring their thinking and their writing to higher levels of illumination." Her poem, "It's Nothing," embodies these concerns:

> It's nothing
> this tragedy in our arms
> we can invent new bones
> new flesh
> new flowers against madness
> another red dress
> another applejack
> another mug from
> the neck bend of our conflict
> yes
> we can tolerate a still heart
> against our ears and
> relax with the crusted
> confessions of a blood cake
> it's nothing

Her poetic mentors include Amiri Baraka (LeRoi Jones), with whom she has toured, Langston Hughes, Aime Cesaire, Leon Damas, Gwendolyn Brooks, Margaret Walker, and Pablo Neruda. Her free verse characteristically builds to an impassioned crescendo, utilizing anaphora, repetition, alliterative effects, startling juxtapositions, and modulations in diction. She often combines African iconology, American colloquialisms, and leftist political themes with surrealist body imagery, as in poems like "If the Drum Is a Woman," "Rape," "Give Me the Red on the Black of the Bullet," and "For the Brave Young Students in Soweto." Employing unexpected phrases and exploring emotional complexities, Cortez usually goes well beyond the doctrinaire political poem. Her recent works have tended towards patterning on the page, sometimes approaching concrete poetry. This emphasis on the visual dimension, complemented by the striking illustrations of her husband Mel Edwards, is an extension of her full attention to the production of her books.

Not belying their strength on the printed page, Cortez's poems gain tremendous energy when one hears them recited or sung, and their polyrhythmic potential is released by hearing them accompanied by a percussion-driven ensemble. This is nowhere so apparent than in collaborative treatments of her tribute to Dizzy Gillespie's Cuban-born drummer, "I see Chano Pozo":

> A very fine conga of sweat
> a very fine stomp of the right foot
> a very fine platform of sticks
> a very fine tube of frictional groans
> a very fine can of belligerent growls
> a very fine hoop of cubano yells
> very fine very fine

Cortez, therefore, is perhaps best known as a "jazz poet," adept at live performance of her poems, often with instrumental accompaniment. Poetry and jazz have long been partnered, from Harlem Renaissance collaborations, to the 1950s explosions that included Langston Hughes' "Montage of a Dream Deferred" and Jack Kerouac's "October in the Railroad Earth," to contemporary explorations like Amiri Baraka's tours with jazz great David Murray, Steve Swallow's settings of Robert Creeley's poetry, and jazz-rap fusions by Digable Planets or the Nuyorican Cafe poets. Cortez's connections to the jazz world are unique: her first marriage was to a legendary musical iconoclast, Ornette Coleman, and she frequently tours with their son Denardo Coleman, himself an accomplished musician. In the 1970s and 1980s, mother and son were joined on stage by members of Ornette's Prime Time Band, including Dewey Redman, and Jamaaladeen Tacuma. In the 1990s, Denardo formed his own band, "The Firespitters," that include three Prime Time veterans (Denard on drums, Bern Nix on guitar, and Al MacDowell on bass).

"Firespitter" (a type of African mask) would be an apt adjective to describe Cortez as performer, as would the title of one of her poems, "The Red Pepper Poet." A playwright and founder of the Watts Repertory Theater, her own dramatic background is in evidence. As D.H. Melhem recalls a 1981 appearance in his *Heroism in the New Black Poetry,* "The performance was distinguished by her voice, ranging from shimmering silk to steel; her bearing, majestic in African robe; the stunning imagery of the poems; the democratic ambience and group sense that allowed each performer alternately to star; and the enthusiasm of the audience." Cortez has appeared on several continents, including the Berlin Jazz Festival, UNESCO events in Europe, a tour of Brazil, and the Fourth World Conference on Women in Beijing. She has also appeared in such formats as the Canadian film "Poetry in Motion" and the Globalvision music video "Nelson Mandela Is Coming." Her poem "I Am New York City" appeared in one episode of the Fox television series *Tribeca.*

—John F. Roche

COUZYN, Jeni

Nationality: Canadian. **Born:** South Africa, 26 July 1942; became Canadian citizen, 1975. **Education:** University of Natal, B.A. 1962, B.A. (honors) 1963. **Career:** Drama teacher, Rhodesia, 1964; producer, African Music and Drama Association, Johannesburg,

1965; teacher, Special School, London, 1966; poetry organizer and gallery attendant, Camden Arts Centre, London, 1967. Freelance poet, lecturer, broadcaster, 1968—. Writer-in-residence, University of Victoria, British Columbia, 1976. Practicing psychotherapist, 1968—. **Awards:** Arts Council grant, 1971, 1974; Canada Council grant, 1977, 1984; Fondation Espace Enfants Mention d'honneur (Geneva), 1989. **Member:** Guild of Psychotherapists (Canada). **Address:** c/o Bloodaxe Books, P.O. Box 1SN, Newcastle upon Tyne NE99 1SN, England.

PUBLICATIONS

Poetry

Flying. London, Workshop Press, 1970.
Monkeys' Wedding. London, Cape, 1972; revised edition, Vancouver, Douglas & McIntyre, and London, Heinemann, 1978.
Christmas in Africa. London, Heinemann, and Vancouver, Douglas & McIntyre, 1975.
House of Changes. London, Heinemann, and Vancouver, Douglas & McIntyre, 1978.
The Happiness Bird. Victoria, British Columbia, Sono Nis Press, 1978.
Life by Drowning: Selected Poems. Toronto, Anansi, 1983; revised edition, Newcastle upon Tyne, Bloodaxe, 1985.
In the Skin House. Newcastle upon Tyne, Bloodaxe, 1993.

Other

Tom-Cat-Lion (for children). London, Gollancz, 1987.
Bad Day (for children). London, Gollancz, 1988.

Editor, *Twelve to 12: Poems Commissioned for Poetry D-Day, Camden Arts Festival 1970.* London, Poets' Trust, 1970.
Editor, *The Bloodaxe Book of Contemporary Women Poets.* Newcastle upon Tyne, Bloodaxe, 1985.
Editor, *Singing down the Bones: A Poetry Collection.* London, Women's Press, 1989.

*

Jeni Couzyn comments:

I am interested in using symbol rather than image, and tend to write with as much clarity as I can. I am at times monosyllabic, and look for the shortest and simplest words I can find. I believe poetry should be "true" at the deepest possible level, and dislike the kind of poetry that appears to be complex on the surface, crammed with learned references and tricky images, but which finally has little to say.

I write in free verse, using rhythm and stress to underline meaning and to counterpoint the sense whenever I can. Similarly I use rhyme for surprise and emphasis rather than in any metrical pattern. I am particularly fond of imperfect rhymes, especially where the rhyming syllable falls on the unstressed part of the word.

I believe that poetry should be spoken, and read on the page only as a kind of specialized reference—as music is written to be played and listened to. Reviewers at this time in the history of poetry use the words "poetry circuit" as a dirty word, as though it were some kind of big roundabout that only the common and the simple people climbed aboard. The simply expressed but pro-

found truth of a poem like Robert Frost's "Nothing Gold Can Stay" is what I most admire in poetry and most seek for. The criteria I use to judge my own work are: is it interesting; is it relevant to other people's lives; is it music; is it true in the deepest sense—in a lasting way. To the extent that these criteria are approached, I am pleased or displeased with a poem.

In sound I have been most influenced by Dylan Thomas—not so much in his technique as in his courage in defying the dry tradition of poetry he was born into.

That I am a poet in an age where the "unintellectual" (i.e., almost everybody) think of poetry as something they didn't like when they were at school, and the intellectual think it something the masses should be excluded from, is sad for me. This age has too much reverence for poetry, and too little respect—for by the same token it is very difficult indeed to earn a living from poetry. Nor are poets considered valid members of the community—you will never see a panel set up to discuss drug usage, for example, or terrorism in Ireland, with a poet among the psychiatrists, students, businessmen, clergy, and housewives being asked to give their view.

For me being a poet is a job rather than an activity. I feel I have a function in society, neither more nor less meaningful than any other simple job. I feel it is part of my work to make poetry more accessible to people who have had their rights withdrawn from them. Standing in the way of this are the poetry watchdogs who bark in the Sunday reviews, trying to preserve their sterile territory. Also it is necessary to overcome the apathy and ignorance of a whole society with a totally untrained ear and a profoundly sluggish imagination.

*   *   *

Jeni Couzyn's first book, *Flying,* came as a surprise even to readers who thought themselves sophisticated. Few of the poems contained in it had reached the usual magazines and anthologies, though Couzyn was known for her appearances on the recital circuits. *Flying* consisted, among other things, of reflections upon her South African background, descriptions of London's gray suburbia, dramatizations of love relationships, and revelations of mental stress. These last were at their best when the author expressed her internal conflicts by way of her flow of exotic imagery. For example, "The Farm" deals with what looks like a depressive illness, but it does so in terms almost of a child's holiday.

> On the farm there are two
> cows.
> And there are a lot of
> trees. They change their leaves
> whenever they like. When they change their leaves you know
> that it is autumn. The two cows have a calf and then you know
> that it is spring.
> You can take your cat with you to the farm or whatever you like. You can take your
> bicycle
> or your
> typewriter
> or all your books
> you can take whatever you like with you to the farm ...

These patient monosyllables ratify a childish acceptance of what becomes more abnormal the further the poem proceeds. The resultant conflict, between the innocent and the sinister, sets up an uneasy tension, too, in the reader. Couzyn, when she projects a parable of the mind's cliffs of fall, is a distinguished poet.

But her second book, *Monkeys' Wedding,* suffers from overexplicitness. The collection contains some powerful work, perhaps most notably "The Babies," a painful poem about contraception and abortion: "On the table the baby lay / pulped like a water-melon, a few / soft bits of skull protruding from the mush..." One may feel here, however, that the skin of fiction is stretched too thin over the agony. We are more conscious of outcry than of experience. Emotion of this sort demands an objective correlative if it is not to seem shrill.

Such a correlative is sought for in *Christmas in Africa.* Couzyn makes considerable use of science fiction, notably the work of Brian Aldiss: "I am your priest and your prophet. / May the long journey end / may the ship come home." But this would be obscure to a reader who did not know *Non-Stop.* And the reader who does know that remarkable book may wonder why he or she has need of Couzyn's poem. More striking are what seem to be reminiscences of Couzyn's childhood in South Africa, e.g., "In the House of the Father":

> The snakes were the price. In their hundreds they inhabited
> our world at Christmas. They were the hazard
> in the garden. And they were everywhere
> tangled in undergrowth, slithering over your feet in the
>   pathway
> stretched across doorways in the sun
> lurking under the banana plant and nesting in the luckybean
>   tree...

But, sharp though these details are, they don't have the pressure of implication that we find in the African imagery of *Flying.* Nor are they contained within a sufficiently decisive form: the verse is discursive.

In *House of Changes* we are, for the most part, deprived even of sharp details. Imagery gives way to incantation: "Leprechaun take back thy curse / Leprechaun take back thy curse..." This seems to be wrenched from a context, but no adequate context is given to us in the book. There are more science fiction poems, but they are even more dependent upon Philip K. Dick than the earlier ones were upon Aldiss. Only occasionally do the two interrelate—

> Insatiable one, I'm exhausted with eating
> I'm a bag of stones, I am all stomach. Bloated
> I lie here unable to move in my sea of flesh.
> My thighs and breasts flow without shape
> my head sags in a heap of chins
> I lie here defiled in a mound of
> self-disgust, in a pool of half digested fluids
> yet you hunger and hunger in me.
> I was a woman once...

This is from a poem called "I and Wolverine" which I take to be a dialogue between an exhausted woman and the unappeasable sexuality that devours her. It suggests that Couzyn is by no means at the end of her poetic range. Yet one is conscious, in all her books, of a gap between potentiality and achievement. Though she has touched notes beyond the set register of her early work, Couzyn cannot really be said to have improved her tessitura. No fiction has quite replaced her early formalism as a correlative for incipient violence and hysteria. The science fiction analogues and the incantations alike show that she is still in search of a form that will also be a plot. Her many admirers will follow her future explorations in the hope of sharing in a fresh sense of discovery.

—Philip Hobsbaum

CROZIER, Lorna

Pseudonym: Lorna Uher. **Nationality:** Canadian. **Born:** Swift Current, Saskatchewan, 24 May 1948. **Education:** University of Saskatchewan, Saskatoon, B.A. 1969; University of Alberta, Edmonton, M.A. 1980. **Family:** Lives with the poet Patrick Lane. **Career:** High school English teacher, Glaslyn, Saskatchewan, 1970-72, and Swift Current, 1972-77; creative writing teacher, Saskatchewan Summer School of the Arts, Fort San, 1977-81; writer-in-residence, Cypress Hills Community College, Swift Current, 1980-81, Regina Public Library, Saskatchewan, 1984-85, and University of Toronto, 1989-90; director of communications, Saskatchewan Department of Parks, Culture, and Recreation, Regina, 1981-83; broadcaster and writer, Canadian Broadcasting Corporation (CBC) Radio, 1986; guest instructor, Banff School of Fine Arts, Alberta, 1986, 1987; special lecturer, University of Saskatchewan, 1986-91; associate professor, University of Victoria, 1991—. Vice president, Saskatchewan Writers' Guild, 1977-79; committee president, Saskatchewan Artists' Colony, 1982-84. **Awards:** CBC prize, 1987; Governor General's award for poetry, 1992; Canadian Authors award for poetry, 1992; League of Canadian Poets' Pat Lowther Award, 1992, 1996; National Magazine Gold Medal award, 1996; Mothertongue Chapbook winner, 1996. **Address:** c/o McClelland & Stewart Inc., 481 University Avenue, Suite 900, Toronto, Ontario M5G 2E9, Canada.

PUBLICATIONS

Poetry

Inside Is the Sky (as Lorna Uher). Saskatoon, Saskatchewan, Thistledown Press, 1976.
Crow's Black Joy (as Lorna Uher). Edmonton, Alberta, NeWest Press, 1978.
No Longer Two People (as Lorna Uher), with Patrick Lane. Winnipeg, Manitoba, Turnstone Press, 1979.
Animals of Fall (as Lorna Uher). Vancouver, Very Stone House, 1979.
Humans and Other Beasts (as Lorna Uher). Winnipeg, Manitoba, Turnstone Press, 1980.
The Weather. Moose Jaw, Saskatchewan, Coteau, 1983.
The Garden Going On without Us. Toronto, McClelland & Stewart, 1985.
Angels of Flesh, Angels of Silence. Toronto, McClelland & Stewart, 1988.

Inventing the Hawk. Toronto, McClelland & Stewart, 1992.
Everything Arrives at the Light. Toronto, McClelland & Stewart, 1995.
A Saving Grace: The Collected Poems of Mrs. Bentley. Toronto, McClelland & Stewart, 1996.
The Transparency of Grief. Ganges, Mothertongue Press, 1996.

Play

If We Call This the Girlie Show, Will You Find It Offensive, with Rex Deverel, Denise Ball, and David Miller (produced Regina, 1984).

Other

Editor, with Gary Hyland, *A Sudden Radiance: Saskatchewan Poetry.* Regina, Saskatchewan, Coteau, 1987.
Editor, with Patrick Lane, *Breathing Fire: The New Generation of Canadian Poets.* Pender Harbour, British Columbia, Harbour Publishers, 1995.
Editor, with Patrick Lane, *The Selected Poems of Alden Nowlan.* Toronto, Anansi, 1995.

*   *   *

Since her emergence from the so-called Moose Jaw Movement in the mid-1970s, Lorna Crozier has earned a significant place in Canadian poetry, not only for the penetrating wit of her poetry and impressive command of satirical skills but also for the depth of perception and feeling she infuses into her work. In such works as *The Weather, The Garden Going On without Us, Angels of Flesh, Angels of Silence,* and *Everything Arrives in the Light,* Crozier has become a spokesperson for the feminist heterosexual woman, a keen observer not only of the consequences of relationships but also of their dynamics and an apologist for desire, love, and caring.

Crozier is not the typical prairie poet. Her terrain, aside from the use of her native Saskatchewan landscape as a backdrop for poems such as "The Photograph I Keep of Them" in *The Garden Going On without Us,* is the realm of metaphysics and the metaphysical complexities of time, place, history, thought, and emotions:

Behind them the prairies
tells its spare story of drought.

They tell no stories.
Not how they feel
about one another
or the strange landscape
that makes them small.

I can write down only this
for sure:
they have left the farm
they are going somewhere.

Poems such as "The Women Who Survive" and "My Aunt's Ghost" are written in the voice of a small-town Saskatchewan woman—an effort on Crozier's part which reflects a growing movement in Canadian poetry away from a purely physical depiction of external landscape to a more intimate, psychological, and internalized re-creation of the voices that inhabit both the inner and outer worlds. As she once noted in an interview, her poems arise out of an "emotional response to what is going on in the world ... filtered through my way of seeing things."

Crozier examines her subjects with the intricacy of a "freeze-frame philosopher" who has forsaken pure reason for the cul-de-sacs of possibility, political points, and the verity of truth through feeling, as in "A Poem about Nothing" (*The Garden Going On without Us*):

When the Cree chiefs
signed the treaties on the plains
they wrote X
beside their names.

In English, X equals zero.

While still political in its tone and preoccupation (whether in the sense of sexual politics or, as in the case of "A Poem about Nothing," in the traditional sense) Crozier's work has become more playful. In her later books she has shown a marked movement away from the dark overtones of her earlier books, when she shared many of the solemn concerns and motivations found in Margaret Atwood's verse. The change, in retrospect, seems to have taken place with publication of her pivotal *No Longer Two People,* a volume of poem dialogues between a male and a female poetic anima that she coauthored with Patrick Lane. The book, the result of a reconciliation after a disagreement, took its title from a quote by Picasso: "They are no longer two people, you see, but forms and colours; forms and colours that have taken on, meanwhile, the idea of two people and preserve the vibration of life." *No Longer Two People,* which was unjustly maligned by critics when it appeared, has taken on an important role in Crozier's canon for two reasons: it shifted the focus of her work onto the details of the male / female relationship and allowed her to redefine her own femininity and her partner's masculinity within that context; and it brought to her work an idea of "metamorphosis," which has become a key element in her late collections.

"The Penis Poems" in *Angels of Flesh, Angels of Silence,* for example, or "The Sex Lives of Vegetables" in *The Garden Going On without Us* are sequences of poems which approach human sexuality with a partially satirical, partially magical sense of wit and metamorphosis. In "The Penis Poems" the male phallus is subjected to a range of speculative possibilities, some historical, some sensual, some mythical—and all humorous. To accomplish this, Crozier has taken up the poetic sequence as a forte, and, as in "The Foetus Dreams" in *The Garden Going On without Us,* she explores her subjects by "taking more than one look at something." In this sense Crozier is a refreshingly cinematic poet who offers different angles and variations on the same subject, the same theme, without cumbersome repetition. For her, poetry is not a linear experience but a range of experiences, just as her perception of the prairie, the landscape of her psychological orientation, is not linear or even infinitely horizontal but rather multidimensional, metaphysical, and playfully pliable.

Mythology, both as a literary source and a model for metamorphosis, has become increasingly important to Crozier's work as it represents the impossible within the realm of the possible. Whether she is writing about Icarus or penises, classical mythology or personal biography, the sheer delight that comes from a playful transformation is one of the readers' several rewards. The need to transform, in essence the need to mythologize, to identify and re-create wonder, is at the core of her work, so that her poems ultimately are retellings of known stories, accepted facts, and plotable landscapes. In "Icarus in the Sea" in *Angels of Flesh, Angels of Silence,* she concludes,

> He is what moves under
> green shadows in prairie sloughs,
> what nests in blue
> reflections in mountain lakes...
>
> Icarus of sky and water,
> you who know the paths of birds
> and spawning fish,
> we will think of you
> as the one we cannot catch,
> the one that keeps us
> dreaming, the broken
> line, the
> Ah!

That same sense of wonder, of making old things new, is extended in Crozier's work to the realm of the domestic, where small everyday objects and tasks are scrutinized with a warmth and sensitivity that lifts them above the level of the merely mundane. In the found poem "Dreaming Domestic" in *Angels of Flesh, Angels of Silence,* commonplace dreams are elevated by the sense of possibilities they foretell for the women who dream them.

> A young woman dreaming of eating pickles
> foretells an unambitious career.
> If she dreams of basting meats
> she will determine her expectations
> by folly and selfishness.

Crozier's images are those of the concrete rather than the abstract world, the temporal rather than the extemporal. When she allows herself excursions into the biography of others, as in such Russian-influenced poems as "Pavlova" and "Nijinsky" in *The Garden Going On without Us,* it is to explore the details of the everyday lives of her subjects; this in turn humanizes them. It is that sense of humanizing the subject, of making the real more real by making it magical and believable, that gives Crozier's work its life.

—Bruce Meyer

D

DAHLEN, Beverly

Nationality: American. **Born:** Portland, Oregon, in 1934. **Address:** 15 Mirabel Avenue, San Francisco, California 94110.

PUBLICATIONS

Poetry

Out of the Third. San Francisco, Momo's Press, 1974.
A Letter at Easter: To George Stanley. Emeryville, California, Effie's Press, 1976.
The Egyptian Poems. Berkeley, California, Hipparchia Press, 1983.
A Reading (1-7). San Francisco, Momo's Press, 1985.
A Reading (11-17). Elmwood, Connecticut, Potes & Poets Press, 1989.
A Reading (8-10). Tucson, Arizona, Chax Press, 1992.

*   *   *

Though often included in that large and varied body referred to as "language poetry," the poetry of Beverly Dahlen has consistently distinguished itself by its technical resourcefulness, its vigorous intimacy, and the coherence and development of its ambitious project. Dahlen's talents as a poet are considerable; the menace and lyricism of these lines from *A Reading (1-7)* are exemplary: "in the myth of the unicorn the lady collaborates. she, lovely, is working for / the enemy, a spy, a trap, a snare. a man's lady. / she comes on the scene. of / course the unicorn is innocent, the child's body, slain. for her sake." The very seduction of such lyricism, however, and indeed the capacity of language itself to impose a meaning upon an experience, to reduce the subject to a voice, and to persuade form from the formless evoke an apprehension in Dahlen through which all her work is refracted ("this is talk. talk is cheap"). Concurrent with this apprehension of language, though, is the recognition that the power of speech to create meaning has been an exclusively male possession.

Throughout Dahlen's work we find women choked, gagged, bruised about the throat, with mouths bloody or dry and empty of words. "Gesture," the first poem in her first book, *Out of the Third,* presents us with a mannerism the speaker has acquired from her mother:

> I am trying to remember
> what she
> was afraid to say
> all those
>
> years, fingers folded
> against her mouth,
> head turned away.

Out of the Third is a book concerned with origins. There is the migration of the poet's family to the West Coast, which left behind "The Great Plains a burial mound. / The ditched bodies of women / and Indians." There is also a migration in language, a searching and a leaving behind. Dahlen asserts, almost haltingly,

> I am trying
> to learn
> to speak
> the American language

Though she acknowledges, "this is my mother tongue / this is my mother's tongue," the poet cannot accept it the way it has been prepared, "...roasted / sliced fan-shaped / she calls it flank steak." It is a pathetic figure, a tongue that misrepresents itself, and Dahlen concludes, "I know it's heart / I won't eat it." "The Occupation," a powerful poem that tells of the death of the poet's grandmother, also confronts this numbing speech: "My father at home naming all the vegetables / growing in his garden," and "No one says the word *dying.*" Language is itself an occupying force, keeping "Everything in order. / Eating and dying."

> How they talk. She passed away.
> Gone in the rainy air.

To engage this language, both as everyday speech and as a poetic tradition, to counter the language that trivializes experience and attempts to silence women, is perceived as a political imperative: "I will make a voice. / It will be alone. You will hear it all night long falling away / towards the west. It will carry you." The making of this voice, however, the identification of its source and the choice of its texture, provides the problem that energizes much of Dahlen's work, and indeed this very question has become a touchstone for critics concerned to differentiate among language poets as a group. For Dahlen, language is a thing that endlessly recedes. *A Reading (1-7)* commences with the words "before that and before that. everything in a line." Yet she does not conclude from this that language is the limit of consciousness. Along with Julia Kristeva, Dahlen understands language to signify an absence. The following is from *Out of the Third:*

> Beginning at the skin
> I work my way inward along the branches
> looking for the one that leads to the ground.
> I have been out here a long time now.

Dahlen's poetry, then, is most compelling as an intensely personal search for this "ground." In *A Letter at Easter: To George Stanley,* Dahlen finds the terms for such a search in an intimate correspondence, which is liberating in the imaginative scope it affords but frustrating in its exclusion from the "real world": "This old mothering split. The crack of doom in which / we speak to each other." In *The Egyptian Poems* this split becomes wider, but to luminous effect. Here the poetry is compact, calm with a sense of its own power, the rhythm of its stanzas giving a sense of incantation. The gods have been invoked, and through poetry their attributes may be incorporated.

> Eat the heart, the leg, the thigh,
> all the parts. Take into the darkness of your mouth
> this eye. It will be enough light.

It seems that the ground has been achieved, or at least the means to speak it and to see it (now the same thing, the eye in the mouth). In her three later books, each entitled *A Reading,* Dahlen explores experience with a language that generates possibilities, that invites rather than establishes meaning. As Rachel Blau DuPlessis has noted in her excellent essay on Dahlen, the poetry of *A Reading* works metonymically to frustrate closure and encourage multiple readings. It resists participation in the reflex repressions that normally accompany all acts of language: "that's where the wind comes, for wind read calm, and the darkness, and for / darkness read light. that's where she is one or another so must be both. / the murdered or murderer."

The three volumes of *A Reading* are impressive, perhaps essential, works of postmodern poetry. Written in a form that combines the journal with the long poem, released from the constraints of stanza and line, given instead to a constantly rearranging lyricism, and cast with a truly multivocal feminist subject, this poetry is Dahlen's invitation to the reader to join her in learning to speak the American language.

—James Caton

DARRAGH, Tina

Nationality: American. **Born:** Mary Martina Darragh in Pittsburgh, 21 November 1950. **Education:** Trinity College, Washington, D.C., B.A. 1972; University of Maryland, College Park, M.L.S. 1985. **Family:** Married Peter Inman in 1976; one son. **Career:** Librarian, currently at National Reference Center for Bioethics Literature, Kennedy Institute of Ethics, Georgetown University. **Awards:** Watson fellowship to Ireland and the United Kingdom, 1972-73; National Endowment for the Arts fellowship, 1979-80. **Address:** 56-J Crescent Road, Greenbelt, Maryland 20770, U.S.A. **Online address:** darraghm@medlib.georgetown.edu.

PUBLICATIONS

Poetry

My First Play, bound with *Malenkov Takes Over* by Michael Lally. Washington, D.C., Dry Imager, 1974.
my hands to myself. Washington, D.C., Dry Imager, 1975.
on the corner to off the corner. College Park, Maryland, Sun & Moon Press, 1981.
Striking Resemblance: Work, 1980-1986. Providence, Rhode Island, Burning Deck Press, 1989.
a(gain)²st the odds. Elmwood, Connecticut, Potes and Poets Press, 1989.
adv.fans—the 1968 series. Buffalo, New York, Leave Books, 1993.

Other

"Procedure," in *The L=A=N=G=U=A=G=E Book,* edited by Bruce Edwards and Charles Bernstein. Carbondale, Southern Illinois University Press, 1984.

*

Critical Studies: By Marjorie Perloff in *American Poetry Review,* May/June, 1984; by Joan Retallack, in *Parnassus,* Fall 1984; "Contemporary Poetry, Alternate Routes" by Jerome J. McGann, in his *Social Values and Poetic Arts: A Historical Judgement of Literary Work,* Cambridge, Harvard University Press, 1988.

*   *   *

Tina Darragh, writes Joan Retallack, "sees the act of writing a poem as a form of research." Operating from the assumptions of Language poetry, which sees words, syntax, and grammar as having inherent meanings apart and beyond those imposed upon them by the poet, Darragh creates (one hesitates to say writes) poems that resemble an arbitrary game or a form of scientific experiment. For Darragh, the poet's role is to uncover language's hidden operations by means of procedures similar to scientific theorems.

In the collection *on the corner to off the corner,* Darragh takes pages from a common dictionary as the basis for her poems. For each poem, she uses the key words found on a random dictionary page, building a pattern or story from one key word to the next to form a kind of found narrative that examines the fluid nature of words and their meanings. The relationships between the random words are drawn from the multiple definitions given for each word, the essentially ambivalent and arbitrary nature of language thus being exposed. The poet's role in the proceeding is that of a detective or scientist on the scent of some pre-existing principle regulating the raw material of the text. As Marjorie Perloff says of these poems, "How curious, the text suggests, the vagaries of *words* that can, with the shift of a single phoneme or two, mean such different things.... The signifier, it seems, is never merely transparent—a replica of the signified." Jerome McGann, in his *Social Values and Poetic Acts: A Historical Judgment of Literary Work,* finds that in these poems "the page of a dictionary is suddenly exposed as a field of strange and unrecognized deposits—odd bits and pieces scattered across a surface."

Darragh herself explains her approach in the book: "What interests me is the coincidence and juxtaposition of the words on the page in their natural formation (alphabetical order). In reference to each other, they have a story of their own." Her approach as explained here (note the use of the term "natural formation") and in other of her nonfiction writings echoes that of the scientist. She has spoken of the procedures behind the creation of certain poems, giving step-by-step details as to how particular works were assembled as if they were language formulas or the results of a particular chemical process. In an article for *Moving Borders: Three Decades of Innovative Writing by Women,* Darragh has also speculated as to "whether we can experience ourselves as being 'statistically irregular'" and has told of how she has drawn inspiration from Benoit Mandelbrot's *The Fractal Geometry of Nature.*

In borrowing elements from the scientific method in order to examine language, Darragh writes poetry radically different from much other contemporary work in its refusal to see the poem as a handcrafted object of art or as a tool for personal expression. Perhaps more interesting as a means of uncovering new territory for poetic exploration than as poems in their own right, Darragh's works are nonetheless an uncompromising example of a poet defiantly following her own path of creation.

—Denise Wiloch

DAS, Kamala

Pseudonym: Madhavi Kutty. **Nationality:** Indian. **Born:** Kamala Nair in Malabar, South India, 31 March 1934. **Education:** Studied privately. **Family:** Married K. Madhava Das in 1949; three sons. **Career:** Poetry editor, *Illustrated Weekly of India,* Bombay, 1971-72, 1978-79; former editor, *Pamparam,* Trivandrum, Kerala; former director, Book Point, Bombay; former president, Jyotsha Art and Education Academy, Bombay; former member governing council, Indian National Trust for Cultural Heritage, New Delhi, and State Planning Board Committee on Art, Literature, and Mass Communications. Independent candidate for Parliament, 1984. Chair, Forestry Board, Kerala; founder and president, Bahutantrika Group; vice president, State Council for Child Welfare, Trivandrum. **Awards:** P.E.N. Asian Poetry prize, 1964; Kerala Sahitya Academy awards, 1969, 1970; Chairman Lau Award for journalism, 1971; Asian World Prize for literature, 1985; Indira Priyadarsini Vrikshamitra Award, 1988. D.Litt.: World Academy of Arts and Culture (Taiwan), 1984. **Address:** Sthanuvilas Bungalow, Sathamangalam, Trivandrum 10, Kerala India.

PUBLICATIONS

Poetry

Summer in Calcutta: 50 Poems. Delhi, Everest Press, 1965.
The Descendants. Calcutta, Writers Workshop, 1967; East Glastonbury, Connecticut, Ind-US, 1975.
The Old Playhouse and Other Poems. Madras, Orient Longman, 1973.
Tonight This Savage Rite: The Love Poetry of Kamala Das and Pritish Nandy. New Delhi, Arnold-Heinemann, 1979.
Collected Poems. Privately printed, 1984.
The Best of Kamala Das. Kozhikode, Bodhi Publishing House, 1991.

Novels

Alphabet of Lust. New Delhi, Orient, 1977.
Madhavikkuttiyute munnu Novalukal (three novels; for children; as Madhavi Kutty). Trivandrum, Navadhara, 1977.
Manomi. Trichur, Current Books, 1987.
Chandana Marangal (The Sandalwood Tree). Kottayam, D.C. Books, 1988.
Katalmayuram: Munnu Ceru Novalukal. Kottayam, Current Books, 1991.

Short Stories

Pathu Kathakal (Ten Stories), *Tharisunilam* (Fallow Fields), *Narachirukal Parakkumbol* (When the Bats Fly), *Ente Snehita Aruna* (My Friend Aruna), *Chuvanna Pavada* (The Red Skirt), *Thanuppu* (Cold), *Rajavinte Premabajanam* (The King's Beloved), *Premathinte Vilapa Kavyam* (Requiem for a Love), *Mathilukal* (Walls). Trichur, Kerala, Current Books, 1953-72.
A Doll for the Child Prostitute. New Delhi, India Paperbacks, 1977.
Ente Kathakal. Calcutta, Mathrubhumi, 2 vols., 1985.
Palayanam: Kathakal. Trichur, Current Books, 1990.
Padmavati, the Harlot and Other Stories. New Delhi and New York, Sterling Books, 1992.

Other

Driksakshi Panna (Eyewitness) (for children). Madras, Longman, 1973.
My Story. New Delhi, Sterling, 1976; London, Quartet 1978.
Bhayam Ente Nisavastram (Fear Is My Nightgown). Calcutta, Mathrubhumi, 1986.
Balyakala Smaranakal (Childhood Reminiscences). Kottayam, D.C. Books, 1987.
Varshangalku Mumbu (Years Ago). Trichrur, Kerala, Current Books. 1989.
Nirmatalam Puttakalam. Kattayam, D.C. Books, 1993.

*

Critical Studies: *Kamala Das* by Devindra Kohli, New Delhi, Arnold-Heinemann, 1975; *Expressive Form in the Poetry of Kamala Das* by Anisur Rahman, New Delhi, Abhinav, 1981; *Kamala Das and Her Poetry* by A.N. Dwivedi, New Delhi, Doaba, 1983; *Kamala Das,* Bedford Park, South Australia, Flinders University, 1987; *Untying and Retying the Text: An Analysis of Kamala Das's "My Story,"* by Kaura Ikabala, New Delhi, Bahri Publications, 1990; *Feminist Revolution and Kamala Das's "My Story,"* by Kaura Ikabala, Patiala, Century 21 Publications, 1992; *Contemporary Indian Poetry in English: With Special Reference to the Poetry of Nissim Ezekiel, Kamala Das, A.K. Ramanujan, and R. Parthasarathy* by P. K. J. Kurup, New Delhi, Atlantic, 1991; *The Poetry of Kamala Das* by K.R. Ramachandran Nair, New Delhi, Reliance Publishing, 1993; *The Endless Female Hungers: A Study of Kamala Das* by Vrinda Nabar, New Delhi, Sterling Publishers, 1994.

Kamala Das comments:

(1970) I began to write poetry with the ignoble aim of wooing a man. There is therefore a lot of love in my poems. I feel forced to be honest in my poetry. I have read very little poetry. I do not think that I have been influenced by any poet. I have liked to read Kalidasa. When I compose poetry, whispering the words to myself, my ear helps to discipline the verse. Afterwards, I count the syllables. I like poetry to be tidy and disciplined.

(1974) My grand-uncle is Nalapat Narayana Menon, the well-known poet-philosopher of Malabar. My mother is the well-known poetess Nalapat Balamani Amma. I belong to the matriarchal community of Nayars. Our ancestral house (Nalapat House) is more than 400 years old and contains valuable palm-leaf manuscripts like the *Varahasamhita, Susrutha Samhita,* and books of mantras.

As I have no degree to add to my name, my readers considered me in the beginning like a cripple. My writing was like the paintings done by "foot and mouth" painters or like the baskets made by the blind. I received some admiration, but the critics, well-known academicians, tore my writing to shreds. This only made my readers love me more. All I have wanted to do is to be real and honest to my readers.

* * *

Kamala Das is a bilingual who writes poetry in English and fiction and autobiography in Malayalam and English. Her first book of poems, *Summer in Calcutta,* with its spontaneous speech rhythms and individual tone of voice, established her as a distinctly contemporary and refreshingly original poet. As an expression of a married Indian woman's search for "an identity that was loveable," her poetry has opened up new possibilities for other Indian women writers.

At the age of 15, Das was forced into a traumatic, arranged marriage—one devoid of love and companianship. This experience brought the rebel in her to the surface. Chapter 25, "The Blood-Stained Moonlight," of *My Story,* her autobiography, reveals the powerful link between her marriage and her need to write poetry. Thus "confessing / By peeling off my layers" or by "letting my mind striptease," she wrote with an uncompromising honesty poems that "flaunt a grand, flamboyant lust." To see this aspect of her poetry as mere sensational self-dramatization is to overlook its underlying sensitivity; she suggests this herself when she declares: "I'm too emotional to be pornographic." Her frequently quoted poem "An Introduction" is doubtless confessional to a degree, but it is also an assertion of a writer's freedom. It transforms an Indo-English woman writer's alienation from "critics, friends, visiting cousins"—who, as spokesmen of the patriarchal culture, tell her not to write in English and advise her to conform—into a larger and more universal alienation—sexual, social, and artistic—that is perhaps at the heart of any attempt at self-exploration and self-integration:

> ...I met a man, loved him. Call
> Him not by any name, he is every man
> Who wants a woman, just as I am every
> Woman who seeks love. In him ... the hungry haste
> Of rivers, in me ... the ocean's tireless
> Waiting. Who are you, I ask each and everyone,
> The answer is, it is I. Anywhere and
> Everywhere, I see the one who calls himself
> I; in this world, he is tightly packed like the
> Sword in its sheath.

Das has often been criticized, ironically by her own countrywomen, for not conforming to the norms of traditional grammar and for not being technique-conscious. Indeed, she lacks an academic background, and she rarely revises her poems; one would look in vain for literary echoes in her work. On the positive side, her style derives its authenticity precisely from the linguistic "distortions" and "queernesses" and her innate rhythms, which are part of the process of the Indianization of English that Raja Rao prophesied in his preface to *Kanthapura* (1938) as both desirable and inevitable.

Das's favorite theme has always been the shadowy borderline between fulfillment and unfulfillment in love, between where lust ends and spiritual love begins, as experienced by a married Indian woman. Poems such as "In Love," "Summer in Calcutta," "The Freaks," "The Fear of the Year," "A Relationship," "An Apology to Goutama," "Winter," "Spoiling the Name," "With Its Quiet Tongue," "The Sea Shore"—all from *Summer in Calcutta*—demonstrate this amply. In these poems Das synthesizes the changing reality of her private passion and the apparently unchanging reality of the Indian sun and landscape.

Her concern with disease, illness, aging, fragmentation, and death—dominant themes in her second volume, *The Descendants*—recurs in many of her later poems, including "Life's Obscure Parallel," "Death Is So Mediocre," "The Sensuous Woman, III," "Woman without Her Shadow," "Words Are Birds," and "I Shall Not Forget." In the latter, memories of happiness and the sense of imminent death are interwoven to produce a more focused and mellow acceptance of life as it is.

In the 1973 volume *The Old Playhouse and Other Poems,* however, Das deals with how a broken marriage makes a woman conscious of the need to create a space of her own. In "The Stone Age," for example, the husband, an "old fat spider weaving webs of bewilderment" around the woman-persona, turns her into "a bird of stone, a granite dove." He becomes an unwelcome intruder into the privacy of her mind: "With loud talk you bruise my premorning sleep, / You stick a finger into my dreaming eye." Other men who haunt her mind "sink / like white suns in the swell of my Dravidian blood." She drives along the sea and climbs "the forty steps to knock at another's door." At this point, the act of defiance having taken place and the dull cocoon of domesticity assaulted, the poem becomes alive with energetic questioning, and the theme of winning and losing asserts itself.

Under Das's deceptively simple surfaces lies a complexity that is imperfectly controlled; she defies categorizations that are not heavily qualified. While she empathizes with the rebel, she can also celebrate her rootedness in her tradition; outspoken about her womanhood, she does not, however, typecast genders. When she speaks of love outside of marriage, she is not recommending adultery but merely searching for a relationship that gives both love and security and preserves her individuality. Her focus is not on the sexual act. In "I Shall Some Day" she visualizes her taking refuge in the cocoon the husband builds around her with morning tea, "in your nest of familiar scorn," after her world has become "just a skeletal thing." Some of Das's better poems deal with the memories of her childhood, of her grandmother's house, of "the warmth that she [her great grandmother] took away" in contrast to "the great brown thieving hands [that] groped beneath my / Clothes, their fire was that of an arsonist's, / Warmth was not their aim..."

Das is capable of intense detachment and can empathize with the larger world of ordinary people, the victims in one way or another of the same system. Her rebellion is evident in such early poems as "The Child in the Factory," "The Flag," "Someone Else's Song," "The Sunshine Cat," "Forest Fire," "A Hot Noon at Malabar," and "Visitors to the City." The social awareness of some of her later poems, including "The House Builders," "The Lunatic Asylum," and poems provoked by the politically charged ethnic situation in Sri Lanka, all from *Collected Poems,* is evidence of the same quality of detachment.

—Devindra Kohli

DERRICOTTE, Toi

Nationality: American. **Born:** Toinette Derricotte, in Hamtramck, Michigan, 12 April 1941. **Education:** Wayne State University, B.A. in special education 1965; New York University, M.A. in creative writing and English literature, 1984. **Family:** Married 1) Clarence Reese in 1960 (divorced); 2) Clarence Bruce Derricotte in 1967; one son. **Career:** Teacher, Manpower Program, Detroit, 1964-66; teacher of mentally impaired, Farand School, Detroit, 1966-68; remedial reading teacher, Jefferson School, Teaneck, New Jersey, 1969-70; master teacher and poet-in-residence, poet-in-the-schools program, New Jersey State Council on the Arts, 1974—; associate professor of creative writing, Old Dominion University, Norfolk, Virginia, 1988-90; Commonwealth Professor of English,

George Mason University, 1990-91; associate professor of English, University of Pittsburgh, 1991—. Panelist for Massachusetts Artists Foundation fellowship program, 1983; educational consultant, Columbia University, 1979-82; founder of African-American poet retreat, 1996—; implementer of workshop, "Freeing the Voice in a Racist Society," Goddard College, summer 1997. **Awards:** New School for Social Research Pen and Brush award, 1973; Academy of American Poets prize, 1974, for "Unburying the Dead", 1978, for *Natural Birth;* MacDowell Colony fellowship, 1982; New Jersey State Council on the Arts fellowship, 1983; National Endowment for the Arts fellowship, 1985, 1990; Poetry Society of America Lucille Medwick Memorial Award, 1985; Maryland Arts Council fellowship, 1987; Pushcart Prize, 1989, nomination, 1996; Folger Shakespeare Library Poetry Committee Book award, 1990; United Black Artists Distinguished Pioneering in the Arts award, 1993. **Address:** 166 North Dithridge St., Apt. 3E, Pittsburgh, Pennsylvania 15213, U.S.A.

PUBLICATIONS

Poetry

The Empress of the Death House. Detroit, Lotus Press, 1978.
Natural Birth. Trumansburg, New York, Crossing Press, 1983.
Captivity. Pittsburgh, University of Pittsburgh Press, 1989.
Tender. Pittsburgh, University of Pittsburgh Press, 1997.

Recording: *Toi Derricotte and Marie Howe Reading Their Poems,* 1993.

Other

Creative Writing: A Manual for Teachers, with Madeline Bass. New Jersey State Council on the Arts, 1985.
The Black Notebooks. New York, Norton, 1997.

*

Critical Studies: Interview with Charles H. Rowell in *Callaloo,* vol. 14, no. 3, 1991.

*   *   *

Toi Derricotte's poetry is remarkable for its unrelenting inquiry into the repressed contents of the self, society, and history; these attentions have not escaped critical approval, for she has been widely praised for her unwavering appraisals of the painful path towards postmodern personhood that she delineates in her passage through the universal stages of life—child, woman, mother, artist. Derricotte's poetry springs from the unique social conditions with which she has engaged in a life-long psychic and artistic struggle: as an African American woman who looks white, her very being interrogates the construction of American social reality and situates her as a poet whose every expression generates controversy. It is Derricotte's willingness to confront the taboos that inhabit ordinary reality in clear and compelling language that have caused Sharon Olds to speak of the beauty and necessity of her voice.

Derricotte has characterized the course of her development as that of a poet whose practice is centered on language that is expressive of social transgressions; in an interview with Charles H.

Rowell she stated that "For me speaking is a very political act. I think in every book I have tried to claim some part of myself that has been stifled. In the first book, *The Empress of the Death House,* it was anger. In *Natural Birth,* shame was the emotion that I wanted to be able to express. In the third book, *Captivity,* I wanted to talk more directly about race, class, and color, and about the complex ways the violence of racism crosses over the threshold of our homes." Her poems begin in ordinary experiences but she dissects the routine definitions supplied by society as a way towards making discoveries about what unsuspected resources the self actually contains. Thus her vocabulary is geared to the quest for new awakenings offering such words as "consciousness," "mind," "ignorant," and "dream."

In *The Empress of the Death House* her appropriation of transgressive language was related to issues that remained from an upbringing in which anger was ruled out. Inspired by the personal anger of poet Sylvia Plath and the atmosphere of militant social protest that issued from nationalist African Americans and feminists during the 1970s, Derricotte forged a voice that was charged with a determination to explore new freedoms through the disclosure of "private" experiences, sexual frankness, nightmarish imagery, black vernacular, the demotion of patriarchal poets, blasphemy, scatology, and a feminist revaluation of values. In "Nun" the attack on religion is accomplished through shockingly tangible innovations such as "the womb of used laundry." Even more radical displacements are managed in the poems on her grandmother in which the pains inflicted by members of a family are confronted without the evasions "until you recognize who you are" ("the naming"). Equally, the style of these poems—with their use of lower case letters, ampersands, sardonic puns (e.g. "apse" for ass in "Nun")—are gestures that are departures from what is conventionally to be looked for in poetry.

Natural Birth is a tour de force, at once a book-length experimental poem, an exploration of the extremes of human experience, and an examination of the social construction of identity; with arresting particularity she tells the story of giving birth out of wedlock at the age of 17. Derricote's stylistic experiment was to force a narrative dimension into the lyric mode that has come to dominate the practice of contemporary poetry. The flexible forms of the poem adjust to the subject matter, which ranges from the meandering, diaristic prose poetry of "November" when she finds herself a stranger in the home of a white family, to the hallucinatory moments of expanded consciousness in "Transition." The reader is forced to witness an experience bracketed from the world by shame (who / is this / child / / who / is his father" ("Delivery"), to inhabit the mystery of a child "without / credentials / credit cards without / employee / reference or / high school grades or / anything / to make him / human...."

The first poem of *Captivity* uses the word "underlife" to describe the skin beneath the pelt of a harvested mink, and it is the scrutiny of that general underlife that is the organizing theme for the collection. The methodical violence and calculated appropriation of mink farming is horrifically rejoined in the penultimate poem in the collection, "On the Turning Up of Unidentified Black Female Corpses"; characteristically, the poet chooses not to turn away from the reality of the slaughtered women: "Part of me wants to disappear...." Nevertheless, the poet turns to poetry to face the truth about her society as the part of her that demands that fears be met "turns my sad black face to the light."

—Jon Woodson

de SOUZA, Eunice

Nationality: Indian. **Born:** Poona, 1 August 1940. **Education:** University of Bombay, B.A. (honors) 1960, Ph.D. 1988; Marquette University, Milwaukee, Wisconsin, M.A. 1963. **Career:** Since 1969 lecturer in English, and since 1990 head of the Department of English, St. Xavier's College, Bombay. Arts columnist, *Economic Times,* Bombay, 1973-84; literary editor, *Indian Post,* Bombay, 1987. **Address:** Department of English, St. Xavier's College, Bombay 400 001, India.

PUBLICATIONS

Poetry

Fix. Bombay, Newground, 1979.
Women in Dutch Painting. Bombay, Praxis, 1988.
Ways of Belonging: Selected Poems. Edinburgh, Polygon, 1990.
Selected and New Poems. Bombay, St. Xavier's College, 1994.

Other (for children)

All about Birbal. Bombay, India Book House, 1969.
Himalayan Tales. Bombay, India Book House, 1973.
More about Birbal. Bombay, India Book House, n.d.
Tales of Birbal. Bombay, India Book House, n.d.

Other

Editor, with Adil Jussawalla, *Statements: An Anthology of Indian Prose in English.* Bombay, Orient Longman, 1976.
Editor, *Nine Indian Woman Poets.* New Delhi, Oxford University Press, 1997.

*

Critical Studies: "Three Poets Come of Age" by Kersey Katrak, in *Sunday Observer* (Bombay), 12 December 1982; in *Modern Indian Poetry in English* by Bruce King, Oxford, Oxford University Press, 1987; by Elizabeth Reuben, in *Indian PEN,* April-June 1989.

Eunice de Souza comments:

The first poems I wrote were about what it was like to grow up in Poona, in a conservative Goan Roman Catholic milieu. Most of these poems are in the form of dramatic monologues. I generally like to use the speaking voice when I write, and many poems are in the form of conversations—about relationships, about critics who tell me how to write, and so forth. I like poems to be spare and economical. There are a number of poets whose work I feel close to, particularly the medieval saint poets in India, and Emily Dickinson.

*   *   *

In her first collection, *Fix,* Eunice de Souza established herself as a writer of short poems in which a surface structure of controlled irony masks an often painful and violent subject matter. The title is instructive, suggesting both a problem and the repair work that is needed. As a satirist of Roman Catholic, middle-class

hypocrisy in the Goa of her birth and upbringing, de Souza favors a conversational idiom, urbane and seemingly matter-of-fact, with very English cadences, that at first conceals and then reveals an often extreme distress. Beneath a fluent and knowing utterance there stir feelings of anger, confusion, and desolation. The opening poem, "Catholic Mother," focuses initially upon the father of a large Catholic family but then turns from apparent celebration of the male to the mother whose silence speaks volumes:

> Pillar of the Church
> says the parish priest
> Lovely Catholic Family
> says Mother Superior
>
> the pillar's wife
> says nothing.

Such understatement is typical as de Souza, taught by Irish nuns in a convent school in Poona in Maharashtra state, brings an astringent wit to bear upon tensions and stresses which are, in part, a legacy of Portuguese colonialism. "Marriages are Made" explores the peculiar mingling of Indian and Christian practices as the life of a young woman is arranged for her in ways that reduce her to the status of an animal being examined for possible faults in pedigree, while "Feeding the Poor at Christmas" exposes the self-serving and unfeeling elements in supposedly Christian charity. In similarly dry, laconic tones, "Sweet Sixteen" presents the fear and ignorance of sexuality promoted by a Catholic upbringing as it affects young girls:

> At sixteen, Phoebe asked me:
> Can it happen when you're in a dance hall
> I mean, you know what,
> getting *preggers* and all that, when
> you're dancing?
> I, sixteen, assured her
> you could.

In different ways, de Souza examines problems and uncertainties associated with color and with ethnic divergences. The aging Anglo-Indian "Miss Louise" lives in a world of fantasy, where she retains the sexually desirable attractiveness she had dreamed of all her life. The light-skinned "Mrs. Hermione Gonsalvez" reveals other aspects of nostalgia and of male oppression:

> In the good old days
> I had looks *and* colour
> now I've only got colour
> just look at my parents
> how they married me to a dark man
> on my own I wouldn't even have
> looked at him.

As she dramatizes these voices, de Souza's ear for the trick of speech in Anglicized middle-class Indians lends conviction to her portrayals. "Conversation Piece," which generated considerable hostility in the Indian press from Hindus angry at what they took to be an insult to their religion, quietly registers cross-cultural divisions and misunderstandings when a Portuguese-bred aunt picks up a clay lingam, a phallic representation of Siva, and asks,

Is this an ashtray?
No, said the salesman,
This is our God.

It is clear that de Souza's brief inscriptions, often seemingly casual in their mode of delivery, are taut with repressed levels of deep anxiety. Her father died when she was a young child, and difficulties related to this can surface in a traumatizing imagery of cutting, slashing, and sometimes self-laceration. "Forgive me, Mother" is one such poem, tracing complications in the developing and sustaining of a relationship: "I was never young. / Now I'm old, alone. / In dreams / I hack you." The poem "Autobiographical," which affects a cavalier, distancing stance at the beginning—"Right now, here it comes. / I killed my father when I was three"—goes on to chart deeper senses of failure and self-recrimination, including suicidal urges, and "One Man's Poetry" encodes an imagery of disintegration: "My limbs begin to scatter / my face dissolve."

De Souza's second volume, *Women in Dutch Painting,* much of it written during a six-month visit to England in 1983-84, presents a somewhat more relaxed countenance to the world, as she broadens her horizons and produces poems of more measured self-interrogation. "The Hills Heal" draws strength from a natural environment and acknowledges therapeutic value in the writing of a poetry which can contain destructive impulses by giving them form:

Yet the world will maul again, I know,
and I'll go gladly for the usual price,

Emerge to flay myself in poems,
The sluiced vein just a formal close.

In a similar gesture, which nonetheless retains discomfiting elements, "She and I" returns to a maternal relationship where, after a lifetime's silence between them on the subject of the father's / husband's death, the mother begins to speak about him. The release seems to portend her own death, thereby creating a further complication between mother and daughter, as the poem acknowledges: "I am afraid / for her, for myself, / but can say nothing."

If *Women in Dutch Painting* is generally more composed in its attitudes, it is still a record of troubled feelings. Although "Another Way to Die" ends on a restorative note, its imagery of dissolution picks up a thread of concern from *Fix,* and while "The Road" can contemplate a Catholic childhood with greater equanimity, it also recognizes continuing uncertainties. "Songs of Innocence" traverses the enclosing securities of a catechized childhood only to register the gap of difference between then and now. Its fourth section tells of a return to Goa "searching for roots," but finding instead a crumbling place of origination that no longer sustains a sense of self. But in the fourth poem of the sequence, "Return," de Souza discovers different ways of relating to a domestic community. Referring to a newspaper account of an attempt by Bombay prostitutes to break with their past and improve their life prospects, the poem wryly concludes, "I know something / of how you feel." It seems, too, in the poem "Notations" that de Souza can find in ballads a way of locating her own very different writing in a tradition that may offer sustenance. At least she discerns in ballad writing qualities to which her own poetry can respond: "No cut to abstractions. / It happened: that is all they say. / It happened."

—Colin Nicholson

DHARKER, Imtiaz

Nationality: Pakistani; "British by documentation, Indian by adoption." **Born:** 31 January 1954, in Pakistan. **Family:** Married; one daughter. **Career:** Poet and artist; has had six solo exhibitions of drawings; author of scripts and director of audio-visuals. **Address:** B-2, Purshottam Bhavan, Little Gibbs Road, Malabar Hill, Bombay-400 006, India.

PUBLICATIONS

Poetry

Purdah: And Other Poems. New Delhi and Oxford, Oxford University Press, 1988.
Postcards from god. New Delhi and New York, Viking, 1994; Newcastle upon Tyne, Bloodaxe, 1997.

*   *   *

Imtiaz Dharker's maturation as a poet is an impressive phenomenon in contemporary Indian writing in English. She has moved from the frankly polemical diatribes that made up her first collection, *Purdah: And Other Poems,* to a highly condensed, prophetic utterance able to combine directness with obliquity. Her indignation at oppressive social structures has by no means lost its force, but the outrage has found a new fluency and a medium that can fully bear its weight.

Even Dharker's early writing sometimes shows an adroit handling of form. Thus, in "Grace" the doorkeeper of a mosque decries the defiling presence of a menstruating woman:

He rolls his reason on his tongue
and spits it out.
You know again the drought
the blazing eye of faith
can bring about.

Another example is seen in these lines from "Purdah I":

She half-remembers things
from someone else's life,
perhaps from yours, or mine—
carefully carrying what we do not own:
between the thighs, a sense of sin.

The controlled intimacy of tone (achieved by casual and partial rhymes, a line adapted to speech, and a sly manipulation of the reader's complicity) persists in Dharker's second, breakthrough collection, *Postcards from god.* The eponymous series of 28 poems that makes up the first part of the book is organized by what might have been little more than a witty conceit: a carefully lowercase god addresses his / her human constituents as a fellow traveler. It is remarkable that Dharker pulls off this risky device, for it is no mean feat to play god in a manner neither Olympian nor coy. Some of the poems are illustrated by Dharker's own Kathe Kollwitz-like drawings, mostly of the human face in agony. But their power comes from the vivid colloquialism of Dharker's images. In "Question I" god has "the biggest remote control / of all."

In "Taking the Count" god is a *dhobi,* a washerman "bow-legged from carrying a bundle / that has always been too big for me":

> Every day, I take the count,
> I separate the dusters from the sheets,
> I beat and rinse and squeeze and pound
>
> till each one is ready to be thrown free,
> laid across the ground
> under the white-hot critical eye.
>
> Rows of souls washed clean,
> all accounted for,
> spread out to dry.

Dharker's vision is mystical, but at its most sharply realized her poetry approaches the jeremiad, its political criticism raised by moral fervor to an intense rhetorical pitch. "6 December 1992," which allusively commemorates the outbreak of communal violence in Bombay, visualizes "the whole world / changed to glass":

> Glass leaders laugh
> and the whole world can see
> right through their faces
> into their black tongues.
>
> And through the crystal night
> the bodies begin to burn.

Dharker's poetic grasp is occasionally less sure, however, as in "Adam from New Zealand," where the speaker refuses to collaborate in a visiting journalist's quest for information about the Bombay poor:

> How can I serve up Zarina
> or her brother Adam
> to their random cameras?
> They will smile shyly.
> The aperture will open
> to swallow up their souls.

The self-righteous "I" is problematical, permitting the poetry of protest to slip into an anecdotal sensationalism.

Dharker's writing always recognizes the centrality of the image. A filmmaker as well as a visual artist and poet, she is painfully aware of the proliferation of the image through the mass media, particularly in Bombay, the established center of the Indian film industry. As god remarks in "Aperture," one of his postcards,

> I placed eyes everywhere.
> Men added more.
> The pupil, dilated,
> the open aperture, the watching lens.
>
> The wound in the forehead,
> flashing fire.
>
> These are the organs
> of a predatory power.

"Question II" gnomically asks, "Did I create you / in my image / or did you create me / in yours?" Against the manifold images propagated by neofundamentalist religion and corrupt politics, in "Living Space" Dharker shores up the timely and uncompromising integrity of her art:

> Into this rough frame,
> someone has squeezed
> a living space
>
> and even dared to place
> these eggs in a wire basket,
> fragile curves of white
> hung out over the dark edge
> of a slanted universe, gathering the light
> into themselves,
> as if they were
> the bright, thin walls of faith.

—Minnie Singh

di MICHELE, Mary

Nationality: Canadian. **Born:** Lanciano, Italy, 6 August 1949. **Education:** University of Toronto, B.A. in English language and literature 1972; University of Windsor, M.A. in English and creative writing 1974. **Career:** Writer-in-residence, University of Toronto, 1985-86, Metro Reference Library, Toronto, 1987, Regina Public Library, 1987, University of Rome, Italy, May 1991; lecturer at Banff Center for the Arts, summer 1983, Upper Canada Writers' Workshop, 1989, University of Toronto Writers' Summer Workshop, 1990. Reynolds Creative Atelier, McGill University, Montreal, spring 1997; currently associate professor, creative writing program, Concordia University, Montreal. Poetry editor, *Toronto Life* and *Poetry Toronto.* Awards: Canadian Broadcasting Corp. First Prize for Poetry, 1980; DuMaurier Silver Medal, 1982; Air Canada Award, 1984; Toronto Arts Award, 1990, for *Under My Skin;* Trillium Book Award finalist, 1990, for *Luminous Emergencies;* ARC Confederation Poets award, 1996. **Address:** 5180 Beaconsfield, Montreal, Quebec H3X 3R8, Canada. **Online address:** mdm@alcor. concordia.ca.

PUBLICATIONS

Poetry

Trees of August. Toronto, Three Trees Press, 1978.
Bread and Chocolate. Ottawa, Oberon Press, 1980.
Mimosa and Other Poems. Brampton, Canada, Mosaic Press, 1981.
There's Sky above My Sky (chapbook). League of Canadian Poets, n.d.
Necessary Sugar. Ottawa, Oberon Press, 1983.
Immune to Gravity. Toronto, McLelland & Stewart, 1986.
Luminous Emergencies. Toronto, McLelland & Stewart, 1990.
Stranger in You: Selected Poems and New. Toronto, Oxford University Press, 1995.

Novel

Under My Skin. Quarry Press, 1994.

Other

Editor, *Anything Is Possible.* Toronto, Oberon Press, 1984.

*

Critical Studies: "Discovering the Sizes of the Heart: The Poems of Mary di Michele" by Robert Billings, in *Essays in Canadian Writing,* no. 27, Winter 1983 / 84; "The Dynamics of Mary di Michele's Moral Vision" by Corrado Federici, in *Italian Canadiana,* no. 4, 1988; "Mary di Michele: On the Integrity of Speech and Silence" by Nathalie Cooke, in *Canadian Poetry Journal,* June 1990; *Mary di Michele and Her Work: Canadian Writers and Their Work Poetry Series,* no. 11, edited by M. Morgan Holmes, ECW Press, 1995.

Mary di Michele comments:

When the angel moves among us, s / he does not distinguish the living from the dead; I believe Rilke and that the act of writing is moving, is searching, in this way. Writing is a conversation among the living and the dead. Its mystery is in the moment of sudden hush in a crowded room that we call the angel of silence. This is the figure of trance, this is the moment of entrance, this is the sphere where the poetry begins for me.

I write with a keen awareness of the word as archeological site. Current usage may be our home, but beneath lie buried cities, resonate with suppressed meanings with echoes, with the speaking of stones, old bones, the dead, the silenced. This study is devotional; its bible is the dictionary. Descent is derivation.

*   *   *

Mary di Michele is a prolific poet who has produced a distinctive range of poetry over the past 20 years. Beginning with *Tree in August* (1978) and extending through some six volumes to her new work in *Stranger in You* (1995), she writes with sensitivity concerning her passage through the world and through words. Her lyric poems are rich in texture, layered with the observations and feelings of a woman whose senses are awake to experience and whose mind maintains, at the same time, a critical and sometimes ironic distance. Di Michele is always aware of difficulties women writers face. Yet she bravely celebrates a vision that transcends those limitations and creates its own values through its generous verbal response to the world.

In *Anything Is Possible,* her 1984 collection of the works of 11 women poets, di Michele argues that women writers have few role models and that women need to slough off the old ideas of greatness and imitation of the canonical poets of the past. As editor of this volume, she collects representative work of eleven women who have tried to do just that, who have explored "the limits of the notion of perfectibility of people, honing, devising an acute and passionate language" in the process. Her description of this "new generation of women writers" is an apt introduction to the driving motive of her own work:

> Because they are women to whom the world of feeling has been abandoned by many men and because they are incisively intelligent, their work has a special integrity and a facility to illuminate some vital areas of experience which have been ignored by our literature to date.

Di Michele calls on women poets on choose their own visions, to decide for themselves "how we are *determined* to live," and to avoid hero worship of any kind; and in this volume, she surrounds herself with her peers, in whom she finds "a kind of collective courage," a "vital energy," which is heroic in its own right. Many of these poets find their place in this volume on *Contemporary Women Poets* and together they enunciate a community of values which is crucial to women writers of all kinds.

An early poem, "Born in August," gives us an indication of what those values are. This poem is one of many that chronicle the poet's roots, her early life, her family, and her growth into womanhood. In defining itself in opposition to many of the destructive acts of male supremacy—Hiroshima, Austerlitz, Aushchwitz—the poem suggests something of that different space inhabited by this woman poet: "my mother lost her teeth / while I grew miniature bones / like pearls in an oyster mouth." The rich Mediterranean archetypes, the immigrant experience, the details of domestic life, the overpowering strangeness of the world to the growing child, the seductiveness of North American materialism, and above all, the life of the body and the power of the emotions—these are di Michele's recurring centers. "The Disgrace," a poem from her second volume, takes its title in ironic reference to William Arrowsmith's statement "But there's one disgrace we've never known: / we've never been women, we've never been nobodies." Her response is recorded throughout her work and here especially, in her life writing: "I am marking the day of my first bleeding / in red pencil in my work book" (*Bread and Chocolate*). While the old women are in the kitchen, "eating / the unwritten stories of their lives," this new woman is writing; she is "the spilling cup," and nothing can keep her from shaping her nature in words. Blood and ink merge and flow into a powerful testimony of the poet's perceptions.

In her next volume, *Mimosa and Other Poems,* a short piece titled "So It Begins" offers a syntactical tight statement grounded in the rhetorical strategy of anaphora, "Whatever passes through my head / whatever sits on my tongue," concluding with the essential and now familiar imagery of the body: "whatever the water gives me, I gives me, I give back / with my open and singing mouth." The poet's motive is to transform her experience into song, however others may perceive it. In "Necessary Sugar," she celebrates the birth of her daughter, and the poem underlines the essential difference once again, between male and female experience: "Giving birth I realized that men / build cathedrals in an attempt / to sculpt light." By contrast, "You are the firefly / I collected between my legs."

Is the poet to achieve a state that is *Immune to Gravity,* as the title of her next volume suggests? Di Michele strives to achieve this state of balance, to write "a love scene / from a female point of view" without the "blind drive," the consuming energy that is characteristic of male expression ("Gravity"). Yet in a different mood, she speaks of male and female metaphors as "False Analogies," even as she explores them. But most importantly, she responds deeply to these oppositions, voicing both aspects of the whole—always inclusive, always stretching her vision and the poetic medium to its limits. We also see her responding to the work of other poets and painters as well, reaching out to comment on the experience of diverse artists—Rilke, Hart Crane, Patrick Lane, Bronwen Wallace, Gwendolyn MacEwen, Edvard Munch, Diego Rivera, to name only a few. In *Stranger in You* (1995), she revises some of the earlier poems which she includes in the volume, and she ends with new work, ever true to the epigraph she quotes from Hélène Cixous: "We write, we paint, throughout our entire lives as if we were going to a foreign country." In "Self-Portrait 1994," she speaks of her art as an "Asymmetry," an "Ambiguity in shades of blue or green," for there is always in her poetry an element of astonishment and wonder. She leaves us with the thought that her intention is ultimately to be a poet who "turns away from the page" and "opens the door / for the reader / who is her true lover." Perhaps the most valuable lesson Mary di Michele offers her readers is how to be surprised, how to remain open.

—J.M. Reibentanz

di PRIMA, Diane

Nationality: American. **Born:** New York City, 6 August 1934. **Education:** Swarthmore College, Pennsylvania, 1951-53. **Family:** Married 1) Alan S. Marlowe in 1962 (divorced 1969) 2) Grant Fisher in 1972 (divorced 1975); three daughters and two sons. **Career:** Contributing editor, *Kulchur* magazine, New York, 1960-61; co-editor, with LeRoi Jones, 1961-63, and editor, 1963-69, *Floating Bear* magazine, New York; also associated with *Yugen, Signal, Guerilla,* San Francisco *Sunday Paper,* and *Rallying Point.* Publisher, Poets Press, 1964-69, and Eidolon Editions, San Francisco, 1974—. Founder, with Alan Marlowe and others, New York Poets Theater, 1961-65. Teacher in the Poetry-in-the-Schools program, 1971-77; visiting faculty member, Naropa Institute, Boulder, Colorado, 1974—; artist-in-residence, Napa State Hospital, 1976-77. Member of the Core Faculty, New College of California, San Francisco, 1980-87. Working privately as a psychic and healer, 1981—. Founded in 1983, with Janet Carter, Carl Grundberg, and Sheppard Powell, and worked as writer and teacher, 1983-91, San Francisco Institute of Magical and Healing Arts. Senior lecturer, California College of Arts and Crafts, Oakland, 1990-92; visiting faculty, San Francisco Art Institute, 1992; adjunct faculty, California Institute of Integral Studies, 1994-95. Columnist, *Mama Bear's News and Notes,* 1987-93, and *Harbin Quarterly,* 1992-93. Artist: individual shows—Museum of Modern Art, San Francisco, 1974; Point Reyes Dance Palace, 1977; San Francisco Dharmadhatu, 1985; Naropa Institute, 1989. **Awards:** National Endowment for the Arts grant, 1966, 1973; Coordinating Council of Little Magazines grant, 1967, 1970; Lapis Foundation, 1978, 1979; Institute for Aesthetic Development, 1986; National Poetry Association Lifetime Service award, 1993; Aniello Lauri Award for Creative Writing, 1994. **Address:** 584 Castro Street, Suite 346, San Francisco, California 94114, U.S.A.

PUBLICATIONS

Poetry

This Kind of Bird Flies Backward. New York, Totem Press, 1958.
The Monster (broadside). New Haven, Connecticut, Penny Poems, 1961.
The New Handbook of Heaven. San Francisco, Auerhahn Press, 1963.
Combination Theatre Poem and Birthday Poem for 10 People. New York, Brownstone Press, 1965.
Haiku. Topanga, California, Love Press, 1967.
Earthsong: Poems 1957-59, edited by Alan S. Marlowe. New York, Poets Press, 1968.
Hotel Albert. New York, Poets Press, 1968.
New Mexico Poem, June-July 1967. New York, Roodenko, 1968.
The Star, The Child, The Light (broadside). Privately printed, 1968.

L.A. Odyssey. New York, Poets Press, 1969.
New As.... (broadside). Privately printed, 1969.
The Book of Hours. San Francisco, Brownstone Press, 1970.
Kerhonkson Journal 1966. Berkeley, California, Oyez, 1971.
Prayer to the Mothers (broadside). Privately printed, 1971.
So Fine (broadside). Santa Barbara, California, Yes Press, 1971.
XV Dedications (broadside). Santa Barbara, California, Unicorn Press, 1971.
Revolutionary Letters. San Francisco, City Lights, 1971.
The Calculus of Variations. Privately printed, 1972.
Loba, Part 1. Santa Barbara, California, Capra Press, 1973.
Freddie Poems. Point Reyes, California, Eidolon, 1974.
Brass Furnace Going Out: Song, after an Abortion. Syracuse, New York, Pulpartforms-Intrepid Press, 1975.
Selected Poems 1956-1975. Plainfield, Vermont, North Atlantic, 1975; revised edition, 1977.
Loba as Eve. New York, Phoenix Book Shop, 1975.
Loba, Part 2. Point Reyes, California, Eidolon, 1976.
Loba, Parts 1-8. Berkeley, California, Wingbow Press, 1978; expanded edition, New York, Viking Penguin, 1988.
Wyoming Series. San Francisco, Eidolon Editions, 1988.
Pieces of a Song: Selected Poems. San Francisco, City Lights, 1990.
Seminary Poems. Point Reyes, California, Floating Island, 1991.
The Mask Is the Path of the Star. Louisville, Kentucky, Thinker Review International, 1993.

Plays

Paideuma (produced New York, 1960).
The Discontentment of the Russian Prince (produced New York, 1961).
Murder Cake (produced New York, 1963).
Like (produced New York, 1964).
Poets' Vaudeville, music by John Herbert McDowell (produced New York, 1964). New York, Feed Folly Press, 1964.
Monuments (produced New York, 1968).
The Discovery of America (produced New York, 1972).
Whale Honey (produced San Francisco, 1975; New York, 1976).

Novels

The Calculus of Variation. New York, Poets Press, 1966.
Spring and Autumn Annals. San Francisco, Frontier Press, 1966.
Memoirs of a Beatnik. New York, Olympia Press, 1969; revised, San Francisco, Last Gasp, 1988.

Short Stories

Dinners and Nightmares. New York, Corinth, 1961; revised edition, 1974.

Other

Notes on the Summer Solstice. Privately printed, 1969.
The Mysteries of Vision (criticism). Santa Barbara, California, Am Here Books, 1988.
Recollections of My Life as a Woman. New York, Viking Penguin, 1998.

Editor, *Various Fables from Various Places.* New York, Putnam, 1960.

Editor, *War Poems.* New York, Poets Press, 1968.

Editor, with LeRoi Jones, *The Floating Bear: A Newsletter, Numbers 1-37.* La Jolla, California, Laurence McGilvery, 1973.

Translator, with others, *The Man Condemned to Death,* by Jean Genet. New York, Poets Press, 1963.

Translator, *Seven Love Poems from the Middle Latin.* New York, Poets Press, 1965.

*

Manuscript Collection: Southern Illinois University, Carbondale.

*   *   *

Diane di Prima is, sadly, the only major female poet to emerge out of the Beat generation's upheaval in American poetry. Her work lucidly reflects as well as transcends Beat assumptions, however; radical spirits permeate her writing, including emancipatory romanticism, anarchism, feminism, and chthonic esotericism. A resilient web of assertive traditions and practices informs her work, revealing a powerful and uncompromising history of herself as woman, artist, citizen, and sage. Early Beat collections like *This Kind of Bird Flies Backward* retain their clarity and unity of purpose. The magical poems in *The New Handbook of Heaven* do not cancel out the polemics of *Revolutionary Letters,* and the exacting lyric particulars of *Kerhonkson Journal 1966* complement the transgressive charm of *Memoirs of a Beatnik.*

Loba is a major serial poem that synthesizes much of di Prima's earlier work and enters more deeply into ritual realms and the hermetic. Through meta-actual female myths and symbols expressed and embodied in Loba, Lilith, Eve, Iseult, and Persephone, the poet restores disallowed literary and mythic examples of female power and history into a grand narrative. The dialectic of wildness and civilization as feminine spheres of action and re-creation is compellingly sustained.

Within her 32 volumes of poetry and prose, Di Prima has participated in and contributed to many critical schisms in U.S. culture—the 1950s Beat movement, the 1960s countercultural carnivals of self and collective politics, the redefining of feminine consciousness during the 1970s, and the teaching of esoteric praxis and healing arts in the 1980s. Her 1998 autobiography, titled *Recollections of My Life as a Woman,* should provide a broader experiential knowledge of these epochs, just as her poetic work has offered a richly emblematic unfolding of significant visible and invisible histories. Works in progress continue to reflect the poet's versatility: the collections *Death Poems for All Seasons* and *Not Quite Buffalo Stew;* a surrealistic fictional portrayal of life in California; a collection of essays on H.D.; and a critical study of traditional Western magic in the verses of Shelley.

— David Meltzer

DOBSON, Rosemary (de Brissac)

Nationality: Australian. **Born:** Sydney, 18 June 1920. **Education:** Frensham, Mittagong, New South Wales. **Family:** Married A.T. Bolton in 1951; one daughter and two sons. **Awards:** *Sydney Morning Herald* prize, 1946; Myer award, 1966; Robert Frost award, 1979; Australia Council fellowship, 1980; Patrick White award, 1984; Grace Leven award, 1984; Victorian Premier's literary award, 1984; officer, Order of Australia, 1987; Australia Council Emeritus fellowship, 1996; Honorary D.Litt., University of Sydney, 1996. **Agent:** Curtis Brown (Australia) Pty. Ltd., P.O. Box 19, Paddington, New South Wales 2021. **Address:** 61 Stonehaven Crescent, Deakin, Canberra, ACT 2600, Australia.

PUBLICATIONS

Poetry

In a Convex Mirror. Sydney, Dymock's Book Arcade, 1944.

The Ship of Ice and Other Poems. Sydney, Angus & Robertson, 1948.

Child with a Cockatoo and Other Poems. Sydney, Angus & Robertson, 1955.

(Poems), selected and introduced by the author. Sydney, Angus & Robertson, 1963.

Cock Crow. Sydney, Angus & Robertson, 1965.

Selected Poems. Sydney, Angus & Robertson, 1973; revised edition, 1980.

Greek Coins: A Sequence of Poems. Canberra, Brindabella Press, 1977.

Over the Frontier. Sydney, Angus & Robertson, 1978.

The Continuance of Poetry. Canberra, Brindabella Press, 1981.

Journeys, with others, edited by Fay Zwicky. Melbourne, Sisters, 1982.

The Three Fates and Other Poems. Sydney, Hale & Iremonger, 1984.

Collected Poems. Sydney, Angus & Robertson, 1991.

Untold Lives. Canberra, Brindabella Press, 1992.

Other

Focus on Ray Crooke. St. Lucia, University of Queensland Press, 1971.

A World of Difference: Australian Poetry and Painting in the 1940s (lecture). Sydney, Wentworth Press, 1973.

Summer Press (for children). St. Lucia, University of Queensland Press, 1987.

Editor, *Australian Poetry 1949-1950.* Sydney, Angus & Robertson, 1950.

Editor, *Songs for All Seasons: 100 Poems for Young People.* Sydney, Angus & Robertson, 1967.

Editor, *Australian Voices: Poetry and Prose of the 1970s.* Canberra, Australian National University Press, 1975.

Editor, *Sisters Poets One.* Carlton, Victoria, Sisters, 1979.

Translator, with David Campbell, *Moscow Trefoil.* Canberra, Australian National University Press, 1975.

Translator, with David Campbell, *Seven Russian Poets.* St. Lucia, University of Queensland Press, 1979.

Recording:*Rosemary Dobson Reads from Her Own Work.*

*

Manuscript Collections: National Library of Australia, Canberra; Fryer Memorial Library, University of Queensland, Brisbane.

Critical Studies: "The Poetry of Rosemary Dobson" by James McAuley, in *The Grammar of the Real,* London, Oxford University Press, 1975; "A Frame of Reference: Rosemary Dobson's Grace Notes for Humanity" by Adrian Mitchell, in *Australian Literary Studies* (St. Lucia, Queensland), May 1981; "Reclusive Grace: The Poetry of Rosemary Dobson," in *The Lyre in the Pawnshop: Essays on Literature and Survival 1974-1984,* by Fay Zwicky, Nedlands, University of Western Australia Press, 1986; "Rosemary Dobson's Modernist Elegies: A Reading of *The Three Fates*" by James Tulip, in *Southerly* (Sydney), 1985.

Rosemary Dobson comments:

At various times I have been asked for statements about the writing of poetry. The following are extracts from these.

I have always regarded the writing of poetry as a vocation, believing that in writing poetry one enters a world of privilege. This is perhaps not a widely accepted attitude but I stand by it.

Poetry is an act of communication between writer and reader to which both contribute.

Of all those who value freedom of expression poets are the best equipped to assert and defend it.

I early determined to write with clarity, and an edge of wit, or as close as I could come to it. That wish for clarity has developed into an appreciation of, and an aim towards, the austere—perhaps desirable in many other areas besides literature in our time.

*   *   *

Rosemary Dobson wrote, designed, and printed her first collection of poems in 1937 while she was still in school. They were juvenilia, but a sense of purpose and a quiet elegance were already apparent. 1944's *In a Convex Mirror* is to a large extent made up of poems originally published in the Sydney *Bulletin;* they attracted considerable interest by their vivacity and concern with an immediately experienced world without loss of lyric poise. The title poem, which takes as its starting point a famous Vermeer interior, is significant also for its preoccupation with time, a subject that became of overriding concern for a number of poets in this period of dramatic upheaval.

For Dobson time was most fully explored in the long title poem of her next collection, *The Ship of Ice and Other Poems,* which begins with "Time is a thief at the end of a road, is a river" and which maintains a fine balance between wit and tension. The book also contains the vivacious sequence "The Devil and the Angel," which broke new ground in Australian writing of the period with its joyful irony and alert conversational tone. But it was in her next volume, *Child with a Cockatoo and Other Poems,* that Dobson fully explored what has become her most admired achievement, the "Poems from Paintings." Art has always played an important part in her concerns, and its particular capacity to exist, as it were, outside time provides the essential *frisson* behind these witty and perceptive poems. The underlying sensibility remains elegant and alert, though perhaps the poems in monologue form most sharply retain that particular freshness which made their first appearance so notable.

It was to be ten years before Dobson's next publication, *Cock Crow.* There is a considerable deepening of feeling in the opening poems, "Child of Our Time" and "Out of Winter," poems of personal apprehension reminiscent perhaps of the work of Judith Wright. Dobson has always been careful about intruding the naked personality into her poems, and the first section of *Cock Crow* represents, through its very attempts at overcoming a natural reticence, a moving testament to the poet's inner agony. The second section of the book is more playful, especially in the poems that translate figures from classical mythology into thoroughly Australian settings.

Another long period of silence intervened before the publication of *Selected Poems.* This volume contained 26 new poems, some written in England and some in Greece and Crete. Their firm lyrical tone and occasional moments of witty observation place them securely in the characteristic Dobson style. *Over the Frontier* was published in 1978. Its most engaging quality is still that carefully modified informality, as in "Callers at the House" or "Oracles for a Childhood Journey," as well as the more overtly lyrical "Canberra Morning" or poems that explore classical, literary, and even scientific themes. Her translation, with David Campbell, of contemporary Russian poets, *Moscow Trefoil,* has added a subtle flavor and tension to the best of her work (and most notably in the title poem of this collection), though the centerpiece is the sequence "Poems from Pausanias." Attracted by the immediate vividness of Pausanias's *Guide to Greece,* she has used her own response to renegotiate its immediacy; thus the theme of time, always essential to her vision, becomes a subtly recurring third theme explored here. The reader becomes part of an ongoing chain of recognition and discovery.

The Three Fates and Other Poems, which received a Victorian Premier's literary award in 1984, is widely regarded as Dobson's most important volume since *Cock Crow* in 1965. In it she shows a subtle attunement to contemporary practices without in any way impairing her long-defined sense of precision and tautness. It is a book in which an implicit elegiac tone is balanced with a mature and warm, often playful, sensibility. *The Three Fates and Other Poems,* though it deals with subjects and responses firmly within her established framework of reference, shows the poet once more as one of the leaders of her generation in Australian literature.

—Thomas W. Shapcott

DOUBIAGO, Sharon

Nationality: American. **Born:** Long Beach, California, 26 April 1941. **Education:** California State University, Los Angeles, B.A. and M.A. in English. **Family:** Married George Doubiago in 1959 (divorced, 1969); one son and one daughter. **Career:** Artist-in-residence and teacher at numerous schools and colleges, including University of Denver, University of Minnesota, and the Naropa Institute. Has lived in her van and travelled the western United States since 1980. **Awards:** Oregon Book award for poetry, 1991, for *Psyche Drives the Coast, Poems 1975-1987.* **Address:** c/o University of Pittsburgh Press, 127 North Bellefield Ave., Pittsburgh, Pennsylvania 15260, U.S.A.

PUBLICATIONS

Poetry

Visions of a Daughter of Albion. Ten Mile River Press, 1979.
Hard Country. Minneapolis, West End Press, 1982.

Oedipus Drowned. Pygmy Forest Press, 1988.
Psyche Drives the Coast, Poems 1975-1987. Empty Bowl Press, 1990.
South America Mi Hija. Pittsburgh, University of Pittsburgh Press, 1992.

Short Stories

The Book of Seeing with One+s Own Eyes. St. Paul, Minnesota, Graywolf Press, 1988.
El Niño. Providence, Rhode Island, Lost Roads, 1989.

*

Critical Studies: By Lynn Keller in *American Literary History,* Cary, North Carolina, 1992; "An Interview with Sharon Doubiago" by Jenny Goodman, in *Contemporary Literature* (Madison, Wisconsin), 1997.

*   *   *

While she can be classified as a feminist autobiographical writer, Sharon Doubiago transcends the cultural categories that would circumscribe her and critiques their limits in her writing. For example, growing up blonde in southern California, she found others expected her to be the "dumb blonde," a Marilyn Monroe figure. Rather than simply reject this position, Doubiago acknowledges its role in our culture and speaks from it, giving a voice to the unheard. Simultaneously, the intelligence of this voice undermines the dumb blonde stereotype.

The title of Doubiago's 1985 talk at the Napa Valley Poetry Conference, "The Evolution of an Epic Poet, or I Was Destined to Be a Language Poet but Story and the 'I' Got in My Way," identifies the influence on her work by the Black Mountain poets as well as her divergence from them to pursue her own autobiographical narrative(s). Despite her speaking from a self-identified I and exclusive use of free verse, this is not to call Doubiago a confessional poet. Her lyric focus on her personal life leads her to consider historical and cultural dynamics, and those larger dynamics in turn inform her life. In "Forests," from *Hard Country,* she compares the fate of the redwoods to her fate in a relationship: "my famous awesome beauty gone / my enormous roots still snarled / everywhere beneath the ground." Doubiago's emphasis on relation asserts her belief in an undergirding complementarity; yet this complementarity has been frustrated if not entirely upset by patriarchal hierarchization and can only be restored by subverting (though, ideally, ending) such power relations.

In her epic, *Hard Country,* Doubiago interrogates the patriarchal legacy of the United States. She imagines the lives of her ancestors amid the changing cultural and historical conditions in juxtaposition with her own experiences; thus, she contemplates her ancestry to develop an understanding of both her own heritage and the nation's. Concurrently, she details her quest for a balanced heterosexual relationship, acknowledging the difficulty of its existence given that men and women have become accustomed to patriarchal power relations. Seeing male and female as essentially complementary rather than antagonistic, Doubiago explores the qualities of male and female in the land, in herself, and in others in an effort to find that complementarity and, hopefully, create it in her own life.

Doubiago does not restrict her investigation of gender dynamics to romantic relationships; she also scrutinizes how gender af-

fects her relationships with her son and daughter. In 1979 Doubiago took her daughter, Shawn, to Colombia, Ecuador, and Peru; out of this trip came *South America Mi Hija,* an intricate tapestry of local stories, travel journal entries, history, and reflections on mother-daughter and male-female relations. Throughout, Doubiago strives to share with her daughter an intimacy of personal truth which her mother did not share with her. This evinces Doubiago's autobiographical impulse: the drive to communicate one's own story, one's own truth. Currently she is at work on *Son* with her son Danny, a former professional football player; she calls it both "a feminist narrative of raising a male athlete" and "a look at the mother-son relationship," which she maintains is "the greatest taboo of our culture and the source and seed of our great problems, gender problems and war problems."

Ultimately, Doubiago's poetry emphasizes the potential within individuals to remake myths and mores. In one of the last sections of *South America Mi Hija,* a "new Eve" prophesizes: "I touch the stone and see / all men / as their mothers' sons." When men reclaim their identity as their mothers' sons, "the world break[s] open" as male and female achieve their natural balance. Doubiago's poetry demands we scrutinize our assumptions with her and consider the possibility of a world united rather than divided by its awareness of gender dynamics and of patriarchy's ruinous legacy.

—Carrie Etter

DOVE, Rita (Frances)

Nationality: American. **Born:** Akron, Ohio, 28 August 1952. **Education:** Miami University, Oxford, Ohio, B.A. (summa cum laude) 1973; University of Tubingen, West Germany, 1974-75; University of Iowa, Iowa City, M.F.A. 1977. **Family:** Married Fred Viebahn in 1979; one daughter. **Career:** Research assistant, 1975, and teaching assistant, 1976-77, University of Iowa; assistant professor of creative writing, 1981-84, associate professor, 1984-87, professor of English, Arizona State University, Tempe, 1987-89. Since 1989 professor of English, and since 1993 Commonwealth Professor of English, University of Virginia, Charlottesville. Writer-in-residence, Tuskegee Institute, Alabama, 1982; Rockefeller Foundation residency, Bellagio, Italy, 1988. Member of editorial board, *National Forum,* 1984-89; associate editor, *Callaloo,* 1986—; advisory editor, *Gettysburg Review,* 1987—, *Triquarterly,* 1988—, *Ploughshares,* 1990—, *The Georgia Review,* 1994—, and *Bellingham Review,* 1996—; member of advisory board, *Iris,* 1989—, and *Civilization,* 1994—. Commissioner, Schomburg Center for Research in Black Culture, New York Public Library, 1987—. Member of board of directors, Associated Writing Programs, 1985-88 (president 1986-87); member of advisory board, North Carolina Writers' Network, 1991—, and U.S. Civil War Center, 1995—; since 1994, member, Council of Scholars, Library of Congress, and Awards Council, American Academy of Achievement. Final judge, Walt Whitman award, 1990, and Brittingham & Pollak prizes, 1997; juror, Ruth Lilly prize, National Book award (poetry), and Pulitzer prize in poetry, 1991, Anisfield-Wolf Book awards, 1992—, Newman's Own/First Amendment award, PEN American Center, 1994, and Shelley

Memorial award, Amy Lowell travelling fellowship, 1997; chair, poetry jury, Pulitzer Prize, 1997. **Awards:** Fulbright fellowship, 1974-75; National Endowment for the Arts grant, 1978, fellowship, 1982, 1989; Ohio Arts Council grant, 1979; Guggenheim fellowship, 1983; Lavan Younger Poets award, 1986; Pulitzer prize, 1987, for *Thomas and Beulah;* Mellon fellowship, 1988-89; Ohioana awards for *Grace Notes,* 1990, for *Selected Poems,* 1994; named New York Public Library "Literary Lion," 1991; Harvard University Phi Beta Kappa poet, 1993; Virginia College Stores Association Book award, 1993, for *Through the Ivory Gate; Glamour* magazine Women of the Year award, 1993; NAACP Great American Artist award, 1993; Folger Shakespeare Library Renaissance Forum award for leadership in the literary arts, 1994; American Academy of Achievement Golden Plate award, 1994; International Platform Association Carl Sandburg award, 1994; W. Alton Jones Foundation grant, 1994; Kennedy Center Fund for New American Plays award, 1995, for *The Darker Face of the Earth;* Heinz Award in the Arts and Humanities, 1996; The White House/National Endowment for the Humanities Charles Frankel Prize, 1996. U.S. Poet Laureate/Consultant in Poetry, Library of Congress, 1993-95. H.D.L.: Miami University, 1988; Knox College, 1989; Tuskegee University, University of Miami, Florida, Washington University, St. Louis, Missouri, Case Western Reserve University, and University of Akron, all 1994; Arizona State University, Boston College, and Dartmouth College, all 1995; Spelman College, and University of Pennsylvania, both 1996; University of North Carolina at Chapel Hill, and University of Notre Dame, both 1997. **Address:** Department of English, 219 Bryan Hall, University of Virginia, Charlottesville, Virginia 22903, U.S.A.

PUBLICATIONS

Poetry

Ten Poems. Lisbon, Iowa, Penumbra Press, 1977.
The Only Dark Spot in the Sky. Tempe, Arizona, Inland Porch, 1980.
The Yellow House on the Corner. Pittsburgh, Carnegie-Mellon University Press, 1980.
Mandolin. Athens, Ohio Review, 1982.
Museum. Pittsburgh, Carnegie-Mellon University Press, and London, Feffer & Simons, 1983.
Thomas and Beulah. Pittsburgh, Carnegie-Mellon University Press, 1986.
The Other Side of the House. Tempe, Arizona, Pyracantha Press, 1988.
Grace Notes. New York, Norton, 1989.
Selected Poems. New York, Pantheon, 1993.
Lady Freedom among Us. West Burke, Vermont, Janus Press, 1994.
Mother Love. New York, Norton, 1995.

Plays

The Siberian Village. In *Callaloo* (Charlottesville, Virginia), vol. 14, no. 2, 1991.
The Darker Face of the Earth (verse drama; produced Oregon Shakespeare Festival, 1996). Brownsville, Oregon, Story Line Press, 1994; completely revised second edition, 1996.

Short Stories

Fifth Sunday. Lexington, University of Kentucky Press, 1985.

Novel

Through the Ivory Gate. New York, Pantheon, 1992.

Other

The Poet's World. Washington, D.C., Library of Congress, 1995.

Musical Collaborations: *Between Sisters,* with composer Alvin Singleton, 1990; *Rita Dove Tryptich,* with composer Sabin Pautza, 1994; *Sing'n Sepia,* with composer Tania Leon, 1996; *Umoja—Each One of Us Counts,* with composer Alvin Singleton, 1996; *Grace Notes,* with composer Bruce Adolphe, 1997; *Seven for Luck,* with composer John Williams, 1997.

*

Critical Studies: "A Conversation with Rita Dove" by Stan Rubin and Earl Ingersoll, in *Black American Literature Forum* (Terre Haute, Indiana), vol. 20, no.6, Fall 1986; "The Assembling Vision of Rita Dove" by Robert McDowell, in *Callaloo* (Charlottesville, Virginia), vol. 9, no. 1, 1986; "The Poems of Rita Dove" by Arnold Rampersand, in *Callaloo,* vol. 9, no. 1, 1986; "Scars and Wings: Rita Dove's *Grace Notes*" by Bonnie Costello, in *Callaloo,* vol. 14, no. 2, 1991; "Rita Dove: Crossing Boundaries" by Ekaterini Gorgoudaki, in *Callaloo,* vol. 14, no. 2, 1991.

*   *   *

Rita Dove's poetry is concerned with history. Skimming the titles of her poems reveals such figures as Catherine of Alexandria, Nestor, Boccaccio, Shakespeare, and Schumann, as well as Dove's grandparents, Thomas and Beulah. Yet historical fact plays a smaller role in Dove's poetry than does lyrical truth. She seeks the untold moments of life which, once discovered, reveal and illuminate more than a historical narrative could. In "Robert Schumann, Or: Musical Genius Begins with Affliction," the moment is a tormented encounter with a prostitute during which the music in the composer's head becomes an alarm and "pulls higher and higher, and still / each phrase returns to *A* / no chord is safe from *A*." In "Boccaccio: The Plague Years," the moment which reveals Boccaccio's passion for Fiammetta originates in the collection of corpses:

> ...He closed his eyes
> to hear the slap
> of flesh onto flesh, a
> liquid crack like a grape
> as it breaks on the tongue.

This sensual image, because of its grisly contrast, embodies the need to live fully in the senses, to love most passionately when surrounded by death.

Dove's poetry also explores the history of the African-American experience. The poems in the third section of *The Yellow House on the Corner* are written from the point of view of American slaves. The Pulitzer prize-winning *Thomas and Beulah* recounts the story of Dove's grandparents from courtship to death. Just as "[t]hese poems tell two sides of a story," this selection from the Dove family history tells a second story of the American experience: Thomas "[h]eading North, straw hat / cocked on the back of his head" ("Jiving") and Beulah waiting in Akron, Ohio, "Papa's girl, / black though she was" ("Taking in Wash"). Their lives become a part of our collective history. *In Grace Notes* Dove discovers a metaphor for the African-American experience in the buckeye, "its fruit / so useless, so ugly":

> We piled them up
> for ammunition.
> We lay down
>
> with them
> among the bruised leaves
> so that we could
>
> rise, shining.

In the poem "Crab-boil," the speaker remembers being on a "whites only" beach for a crab boil, but she refuses to be like the crabs scratching uselessly in the bucket:

> I decide to believe this: I'm hungry.
> Dismantled, they're merely exotic,
> a blushing meat...If
> we're kicked out now, I'm ready.

The discovery of the buckeye or the crabs is more than the *means* of articulating the speaker's experience, but it becomes the experience itself. The poems reenact discovery.

Just as Dove's poetry explores history through the individual, it also explores time through the moment. Within the moment lies possibility. In "The Fish in the Stone," for example, the fossil is no longer trapped in stone but is permitted for a moment to come alive:

> In the ocean the silence
> moves and moves
>
> and so much is unnecessary!
> Patient, he drifts
> until the moment comes
> to cast his
> skeletal blossom.

For the fish, analysis discovers "the small predictable truths"; the real mystery of life is found only by living. In "Canary" Dove writes, "If you can't be free, be a mystery," because mystery, an essential quality of human life, *is* liberating. Dove's poems enter the mysterious by opening themselves to the moment of discovery. Usually, that discovery is not rational but rather emotional or physical. In "Pastoral" the speaker describes breast-feeding, her daughter "[l]ike an otter, but warm, / ... eyes / unfocused and large: milk-drunk." She discovers

> what a young man must feel
> with his first love asleep on his breast:
> desire, and the freedom to imagine it.

What allows the poetry "desire, and the freedom to imagine it" is Dove's ability to sublimate her own will to the will of the poem, to surrender historical fact to greater truth. In doing so, Dove gives up the security of what she "knows" through logic to the greater assurance of what she discovers through prosody and the integrity of the line. The poem "Silos," for example, is not satisfied with silos in their prosaic function as warehouses for grain; they become "martial swans in spring paraded against the city sky's / shabby blue." In the end they become "the ribs of the modern world." In "Ars Poetica" Dove writes,

> What I want is this poem to be small,
> a ghost town
> on the larger map of wills.
> Then you can pencil me in as a hawk:
> a traveling x-marks-the-spot.

As the hawk's eyes detect movement even in a ghost town, so Dove's poems, though sharply focused in the subjective moment, see our history far and wide.

—Julie Miller

DRAKE, Barbara

Nationality: American. **Born:** Kansas, in 1939. **Education:** University of Oregon, B.A. 1961; M.F.A. 1966. **Family:** Married; eight children. **Career:** Teacher, Department of American Thought and Language, Michigan State University, 1974-83; visiting writer, Whitman College, 1982, and Lewis & Clark College, 1979-80 and 1982-83; guest lecturer at Willamette University and Southern Oregon Community College; full professor of English, 1983—, Edith Green Distinguished Professor, 1993, Linfield College, McMinnville, Oregon. **Awards:** National Endowment for the Arts award, 1966, and fellowship, 1986; Northwest Arts Foundation study grant, 1985. **Address:** 6104 Northwest Lilac Hill Road, Yamhill, Oregon 97148, U.S.A.

PUBLICATIONS

Poetry

Narcissa Notebook. Okemos, Michigan, Stone Press, 1973.
Field Poems. Okemos, Michigan, Stone Press, 1975.
Love at the Egyptian Theatre. East Lansing, Red Cedar Press/ Michigan State University, 1978
Life in a Gothic Novel. Baltimore, Maryland, White Ewe Press, 1981.
What We Say to Strangers. Portland, Oregon, Breitenbush, 1986.
Bees in Wet Weather. Traverse City, Michigan, Canoe Press, 1992.
Space before A:. Portland, Oregon, 26 Books Publishing, 1996.

Other

Writing Poetry (textbook). Boston, Harcourt, 1983; 2nd rev. ed., 1994.

*   *   *

Barbara Drake's poetry is in some ways reminiscent of the work of Cornelia Otis Skinner. Ms. Skinner, best remembered now as the co-author of the co-autobiography *Our Hearts Were Young and Gay,* was also famed, in her lifetime, as a dramatic monologist who commented with wry humor on life's vicissitudes. (A more contemporary example, employing the essay form to somewhat similar effect, might be the late Erma Bombeck.)

A typical example of poetry of Drake's displaying this sort of rueful humor and first-person immediacy is "What a Relief" from the 1978 collection, *Love at the Egyptian Theatre*:

> How wonderful.
> My throat is really sore.
> Listen to my voice. It's going.
> All week I thought I might be getting
> psychosomatic premature senility,
> I thought it was my liver
> or something the government
> was putting in the water.
> Congratulations.
> It's a cold.

Though we feel we're being approached in this poem on a one-on-one, homely basis, this is still poetry, seeing the familiar in new light, artful and often image-driven beneath the guise of artlessness, as in "Imperfect Prisms," where the poet / speaker tells of buying a collection of prisms the salesman has called imperfect.

> They looked fine to me.
> I'm not perfect.
> So I bought seven
> and took them home in a box,
> like hamsters ...
>
> Next morning
> it was like when your dog
> has puppies.
> The white ceiling
> wavered with young rainbows.

As with much good humor, there's a great deal of wisdom beneath the wit, as in poems from the same collection such a "Garbage," which cautions us to

> Watch out for the ones who insist
> everything counts for something
> and won't throw anything away.

The author admits that "garbage, like grief, is real" and that she has also been guilty of collecting ultimately useless stuff, but resolves that

> I won't, I won't, I won't
> go looking
> for old tires
> or empty mayonnaise jars
> or suffering.

In the later, also book-length, collection, *What We Say to Strangers* (1986), the voice we hear is once more conversational, reflective, ready and able to take us into its confidence. Though the humor is there, darker undercurrents show at times. Some of the best poems in this collection, like "The Bed," "Driveaway," "What We Say to Strangers," and "Plums," are almost garrulous. However, this rambling does not try the reader's patience; we know there is something at work here, a payoff at hand. In "The Bed"

and "Driveaway," the speaker reflects on her first marriage, objectified in the first poem in an old bed she and her estranged husband have shared, and, in the second poem, by a new car they haven't. "Plums" addresses the oblique ways in which people establish new relationships. A new friend has promised to bring some plums by: "new friends, I suppose / are not to arrive empty-handed." The author embarks on a lengthy rumination on her encounters, over the years, with plums, and on the varieties of plums, and concludes: "I will be pleased if you come to see me, / even if your hands are empty." In "What We Say to Strangers," the poet makes a rare disappearance, though her wit is still much in evidence. We are standing in a long line at the supermarket, overhearing a young woman who loves buying herself flowers talking to another woman in the line. Her conversation is like a loop that repeats itself, with slight variations, as other women join the line and admire the flowers. And there's a loop within this loop; the woman, talking, persuades herself she needs more flowers, and asks these people to hold her place in line while she returns for flowers, first on the pretext of getting more for a friend, then some for her mother, the $3.98 bouquet growing into an $11.94 arrangement. What starts as the most casual of exchanges, and a harmless bit of self-indulgence, grows into something scarier, a glimpse of a loopy person's compulsive behavior.

Drake finds these strange kinks and quirks, not only in this extreme form or in others, but in herself as well. In the latter collection, there's the poem "Shoelaces," in which she upbraids herself over some ragged shoelaces, finally replaced, and her failure to keep the neat, orderly home, the iron always close at hand, that her mother did. But, like many of these fine poems, this one arrives at hard-won wisdom:

> I have nothing to regret,
> my shoes look fine,
> and we can survive
> even the best upbringing.

—Duane Ackerson

DUFFY, Carol Ann

Nationality: British. **Born:** Glasgow, 23 December 1955. **Education:** St. Joseph's Convent, Stafford, Staffordshire; Stafford Girls' High School; University of Liverpool, 1974-77, B.A. (honors) in philosophy 1977. **Career:** Poetry editor, *Ambit* magazine, London, 1983—. Visiting fellow, North Riding College, Scarborough, 1985; writer-in-residence, Southern Arts, Thamesdown, 1987-88. **Awards:** C. Day Lewis fellowship, 1982-84; National Poetry Competition award, 1983; Gregory award, 1984; Scottish Arts Council award, 1986; Somerset Maugham award, 1988; Dylan Thomas award, 1989. **Agent:** Tessa Sayle Ltd., 11 Jubilee Place, London SW3 3TE, England.

PUBLICATIONS

Poetry

Fleshweathercock and Other Poems. Walton-on-Thames, Surrey, Outposts, 1973.
Fifth Last Song. Wirral, Merseyside, Headland, 1982.

Standing Female Nude. London, Anvil Press Poetry, 1985.
Thrown Voices. London, Turret, 1986.
Selling Manhattan. London and Wolfeboro, New Hampshire, Anvil Press Poetry, 1987.
The Other Country. London, Anvil Press Poetry, 1990.
William and the Ex-Prime Minister. London, Anvil Press Poetry, 1992.
Mean Time. London, Anvil Press Poetry, 1993.
Selected Poems. London, Penguin, 1994.

Plays

Take My Husband (produced Liverpool, 1982).
Cavern of Dreams (produced Liverpool, 1984).
Little Women, Big Boys (produced London, 1986).

Radio Play: *Loss,* 1986.

Other

Editor, *Home and Away.* Thamesdown, Southern Arts, 1988.
Editor, *I Wouldn't Thank You for a Valentine: Poems for Young Feminists.* London, Viking, 1992; New York, Holt, 1993.
Editor, *Stopping for Death: Poems of Death and Loss.* New York, Holt, 1996.

*

Critical Study: "The Poetry of Carol Ann Duffy" by Jane E. Thomas, in *Bête Noire* (Hull) no. 6, 1989.

*   *   *

The poet's "eye" and "ear" are familiar commonplaces of contemporary criticism. These terms readily suggest the sister arts of poetry and painting and the obvious relationship of poetry to the formal measures of music. But all too often as poets and critics we neglect the equally important analogy of poetry and drama. One of Britain's most popular and highly regarded poets, Carol Ann Duffy, launched her career with two plays staged at the Liverpool Playhouse, and her best verse evinces the most valuable skills of the playwright—dramatic timing and characterization.

Duffy has covered an impressive range of styles throughout her three collections, from love lyrics (the critic Robert Nye remarked that she writes love poems "as if she were the first to do so") to razor-sharp political satire. But the hallmark of her work remains the dramatic monologue. Most poets who attempt this genre fail because they cannot resist imposing clever metaphors and well-wrought similes—in effect their own voices—on the character's diction. The trick of the successful dramatic monologue, however, consists of elevating speech to poetry without leaving the closed set of the character's vocabulary. Duffy handles this easily, coaxing pathos and a rarefied music from the sentence fragments of maniacs or, as in "Words of Absolution," the neologisms of the senile: "Blessed art thou among women even if / we put you in a home. Only the silent motion / of lips and the fingering of decades. / How do we show that we love God? / Never a slack shilling but good broth / always on the table. Which are the fasting days? / Mary Wallace, what are the days of abstinence?"

Duffy's first collection, *Standing Female Nude,* is heavily weighted with such "points of view." There are war photogra-

phers, immigrant schoolchildren, and Franz Schubert, and there is even a poem from the point of view of a pair of dolphins confined in an aquarium. But the most intriguing and formally engaging of these poems are spoken by morally ambiguous personalities. (It is safe to say that the most successful dramatic monologues from Browning on deal with speakers who are in some way reprehensible.) The fact that a poem is a monologue helps to determine our sympathy for the speaker—since we must adopt his viewpoint as our entry into the poem—and Duffy exploits the effect created by this tension between sympathy and moral judgment in poems spoken by murderers and crypto-Nazis.

In a poem like "Education for Leisure," for example, we can trace the character's progressive degeneration from alienation ("Once a fortnight, I walk the two miles into town / for signing on. They don't appreciate my autograph") to dangerous psychosis ("The pavements glitter suddenly. I touch your arm"), but there is something unmistakably attractive in his grim humor. We are drawn to him even as we are repelled: "Today I am going to kill something. Anything ... / I squash a fly against the window with my thumb. / We did that at school. Shakespeare. It was in / Another language and now the fly is in another language. / I breathe out talent on the glass to write my name." This last image recurs in a number of poems; "My breath wipes me from the looking glass," says the fairground "Psychopath" of that poem. It is almost an emblem of dramatic irony; we know more than the character because he is kept from self-knowledge by his own words.

Duffy frequently collects a chorus of voices in a single poem to produce a kind of dramatic collage. In "Dies Natalis" (from *Selling Manhattan*), for example, she adopts a series of markedly different dictions as one personality undergoes a succession of reincarnations as an Egyptian queen's cat, an albatross, a man, and a baby. She returns to this form throughout her three collections; "Comprehensive," "A Clear Note," and "Model Village" are further examples.

The menacing ventriloquist's prop of "The Dummy" in *Selling Manhattan* recalls the film *Dead of Night,* and its presence in the collection redirects our attention to Duffy's whole voice-throwing enterprise. It is a brilliantly conceived poem in which a persona has finally turned on the poet herself:

> Balancing me with your hand up my back, listening
> to the voice you gave me croaking for truth, you keep
> me at it. Your lips don't move, but your eyes look
> desperate as hell. Ask me something difficult.

Duffy's collection *The Other Country* contains fewer dramatic monologues, but "The Way My Mother Speaks" offers another insight into her uncanny facility with this genre: "I say her phrases to myself in my head / or under the shallows of my breath, / restful shapes moving." No other poet writing in Britain listens so carefully.

—Michael Donaghy

DUFFY, Maureen

Pseudonym: D.M. Cayer. **Nationality:** British. **Born:** Worthing, Sussex, 21 October 1933. **Education:** Trowbridge High School for Girls, Wiltshire; Sarah Bonnell High School for Girls; King's Col-

lege, London, 1953-56, B.A. (honors) in English 1956. **Career:** School teacher for five years. Co-founder, Writers Action Group, 1972; joint chair, 1977-78, and president, 1985-89, Writers Guild of Great Britain; chair, Greater London Arts Literature Panel, 1979-81; vice-chair, 1981-86, and chair, 1989—, British Copyright Council; chair, Authors Lending and Copyright Society, 1982-94; chair, Copyright Licensing Agency, 1986—; vice president, Beauty without Cruelty; fiction editor, *Critical Quarterly,* Manchester, 1987. **Awards:** City of London Festival Playwright's prize, 1962; Arts Council bursary, 1963, 1966, 1975; Society of Authors traveling scholarship, 1976. Fellow, Royal Society of Literature, 1985. **Agent:** Jonathan Clowes Ltd., Ironbridge House, Bridge Approach, London NW1 8BD. **Address:** 18 Fabian Road, London SW6 7TZ, England.

PUBLICATIONS

Poetry

Lyrics for the Dog Hour. London, Hutchinson, 1968.
The Venus Touch. London, Weidenfeld & Nicolson, 1971.
Actaeon. Rushden, Northamptonshire, Sceptre Press, 1973.
Evesong. London, Sappho, 1975.
Memorials of the Quick and the Dead. London, Hamish Hamilton, 1979.
Collected Poems. London, Hamish Hamilton, 1985.

Plays

The Lay-Off (produced London, 1962).
The Silk Room (produced Watford, Hertfordshire, 1966).
Rites (produced London, 1969). Published in *New Short Plays 2,* London, Methuen, 1969.
Solo, Olde Tyme (produced Cambridge, 1970).
A Nightingale in Bloomsbury Square (produced London, 1973). Published in *Factions,* edited by Giles Gordon and Alex Hamilton, London, Joseph, 1974.
The Masque of Henry Purcell (produced London, 1995).

Radio Play: *Only Goodnight,* 1981.

Television Play: *Josie,* 1961.

Novels

That's How It Was. London, Hutchinson, 1962; New York, Dial Press, 1984.
The Single Eye. London, Hutchinson, 1964.
The Microcosm. London, Hutchinson, and New York, Simon & Schuster, 1966.
The Paradox Players. London, Hutchinson, 1967; New York, Simon & Schuster, 1968.
Wounds. London, Hutchinson, and New York, Knopf, 1969.
Love Child. London, Weidenfeld & Nicolson, and New York, Knopf, 1971.
I Want to Go to Moscow: A Lay. London, Hodder & Stoughton, 1973; as *All Heaven in a Rage,* New York, Knopf, 1973.
Capital. London, Cape, 1975; New York, Braziller, 1976.
Housespy. London, Hamish Hamilton, 1978.
Gor Saga. London, Eyre Methuen, 1981; New York, Viking Press, 1982.

Scarborough Fear (as D.M. Cayer). London, Macdonald, 1982.
Londoners: An Elegy. London, Methuen, 1983.
Change. London, Methuen, 1987.
Illuminations. London, Flamingo, 1992.
Occam's Razor. London, Sinclair-Stevenson, 1993.

Other

The Erotic World of Faery. London, Hodder & Stoughton, 1972.
The Passionate Shepherdess: Aphra Behn 1640-1689. London, Cape, 1977; New York, Avon, 1979.
Inherit the Earth: A Social History. London, Hamish Hamilton, 1980.
Men and Beasts: An Animal Rights Handbook. London, Paladin, 1984.
A Thousand Capricious Chances: A History of the Methuen List 1889-1989. London, Methuen, 1989.
Henry Purcell. London, Fourth Estate, 1994.

Editor, with Alan Brownjohn, *New Poetry 3.* London, Arts Council, 1977.
Editor, *Oroonoko and Other Stories,* by Aphra Behn. London, Methuen, 1986.
Editor, *Love Letters between a Nobleman and His Sister,* by Aphra Behn. London, Virago Press, 1987.
Editor, *Five Plays by Aphra Behn.* London, Methuen Drama, 1990.

Translator, *A Blush of Shame,* by Domenico Rea. London, Barrie and Rockliff, 1968.

*

Manuscript Collection: King's College, University of London.

Critical Studies: By Dulan Barber, in *Transatlantic Review 45* (London), Spring 1973; *Guide to Modern World Literature* by Martin Seymour-Smith, London, Wolfe, 1973, as *Funk & Wagnalls Guide to Modern World Literature,* New York, Funk & Wagnalls, 1973; *Lesbian Images* by Jane Rule, London, Peter Davies, 1976; *Maureen Duffy,* London, Book Trust / British Council, 1989.

*　　*　　*

Famous for her novels and her championing of social causes, Maureen Duffy has also written poems that echo her humane and libertarian views. Whether speaking out forcefully on women's rights, animal rights, or the horrors of famine, homelessness, and poverty, the voice is recognizable from the earliest of her published work to the mature expression of her later collections. Above all, her writings celebrate the liberating power of physical love, in particular the love between women. Such themes are hinted at in her early poems, where tributes to political and literary giants are mingled with keener insights into the nature of various types of women and the growth of sexual awareness. Duffy's first efforts include a sobering study, "My Sisters the Whores," which is counterbalanced by her vision of the drab, imprisoned existence of young housewives in "A Woman's World": "Their lives, a mesh / / Of tiny incident, entrap and bind / Them." Elsewhere, in her "Women" sequence of poems, Duffy explores the burgeoning sexuality of girls dancing together and the repressed longings of love-starved spinster schoolteachers, where "Love is an outcast, beauty hides away / Behind a gymslip or a manly tie." The same early writings include other significant thematic devices, the poet using fairy-tale conventions and Greek legends to express personal and contemporary concerns. "Rapunzel" and "Ulysses" are notable examples of a method that Duffy uses more subtly in later collections to describe the overwhelming joys and pangs of love.

Love in its physical and spiritual forms is central to Duffy's writing and provides her with the core of her finest work. Its passion imbues the bulk of her poetry—collections like *Lyrics for the Dog Hour, The Venus Touch,* and *Evesong* almost totally given over to an expression of its strength, its violence, and its ultimate fulfillment. Duffy presents herself as one caught helplessly in the grip of an awesome cataclysmic act, compared directly at times to a nuclear attack or to some kind of trench warfare: "And we renew our love / Under the whine of the guns." Liberated by forbidden pleasure to a paradisal state beyond the reach of others, she remains fearfully aware of her own vulnerability in the face of loss and separation, the pain rendered more bitter after the joys that have been shared: "I hoard now against our winter, / Pack in the black hole of my heart / And stamp down hard, / Words, looks to nourish / When I stir in the long sleep / Troubled by dreams / And all is bitter outside."

Classical allusions abound—to legends, musical and artistic masterpieces. Duffy and her beloved are hymned as Orpheus and Eurydice, Minotaur and labyrinth, while through their acts of passion the love-goddess Venus is continually invoked, the liberated female of the Olympian age who serves as their spiritual ancestress. Yet however ecstatic the transports, the poet retains a sense of proportion throughout, finding time to explore the old myths with a less than flattering eye, especially in her cynical commentary on *The Iliad* in "Helen and the Historians": "The whole affair was just a trick of trade / Paris not prince of course / but merchant chief. / Achilles, Patroclus two / banking firms; his rage / takeover bid; his death a crash." In other poems Duffy gives vent to self-mockery, deriding her mannish walk and big backside, claiming that: "I have been / a bull in a porcelain shop trampling china roses." Imagining herself as "beast" to the beloved's "beauty," she prepares once more for the bruising but desired encounter: "Waiting on love I flex / thews, thighs like a dancer / or boxer knowing / I will get as good as I give.

Other concerns intrude in *Memorials of the Quick and the Dead,* where Duffy looks outward to the world and its wrongs. In a series of hard, clear-cut verses she traces her origins in an Irish graveyard and attacks her own government for its neglect of writers and homeless children. The rule of the Greek colonels is condemned in "Antigone," while in "Lemonchic" the author mourns the death in space of the dog Laika. Duffy comments on the environmental problems of drought and Dutch elm disease and admits a sad kinship with Nigerian rebels whose execution she witnesses on her television screen: "Three thousand miles away / by satellite I mourn / the rest of their lives unborn / those islands of flesh and bone / mine / whatever they had done." Tributes to Benjamin Britten and Gracie Fields are offset by "Bestialry," with its fierce impassioned outcry against humans' cruelty to other creatures, the author detailing the atrocities inflicted on rabbits and battery hens. Yet in the end, it is to love and its healing power that Duffy returns, affirming in the latter part of *Memorials* and subsequently in "The Garland" section of *Collected Poems* her allegiance to the goddess: "But you brought me up in your worship / though I'm old and ridiculous too / to be panting after your favours / what else am I to do." The range of her poetry—from neat, poised clas-

sical verse to a loose, conversational style—the variety of subjects covered, and the pure, intense clarity of her vision lift her work above the ordinary, giving to it the quality of a personal testament.

—Geoff Sadler

DUNMORE, Helen

Nationality: British. **Born:** Yorkshire, 1952. **Education:** York University, B.A. in English 1973. **Family:** Married; one son and one stepson. **Career:** Writer. **Awards:** Poetry Book Society Choice; Poetry Book Society Recommendation, 1991, for *Short Days, Long Nights;* Alice Hunt Bartlett award, 1987; McKitterick Prize, 1994, for *Zennor in Darkness;* Signal Poetry award, 1995, for *Secrets;* Orange Prize for fiction, 1996, for *A Spell of Winter.* **Address:** c/o Caradoc King, A.P. Watt Ltd., 20 John St., London WC1N 2DR, England.

PUBLICATIONS

Poetry

The Apple Fall. Newcastle upon Tyne, Bloodaxe, 1983.
The Sea Skater. Newcastle upon Tyne, Bloodaxe, 1986.
The Raw Garden. Newcastle upon Tyne, Bloodaxe, 1988.
Short Days, Long Nights: New & Selected Poems. Newcastle upon Tyne, Bloodaxe, 1991.
Secrets (for children). London, Bodley Head, 1994.
Recovering A Body. Newcastle upon Tyne, Bloodaxe, 1994.
Bestiary. Newcastle upon Tyne, Bloodaxe, 1997.

Novels

Zennor in Darkness. London, Penguin, 1993.
In the Money (for children). London, Red Fox, 1993.
Going to Egypt (for children). London, Julia MacRae, 1994.
Burning Bright. London, Penguin, 1994.
A Spell of Winter. London, Viking, 1995.
Talking to the Dead. London, Viking, 1996; Boston, Little Brown, 1997.

Other

Amina's Blanket (juvenile). London, Reed Books, 1996.
Go Fox (juvenile). London, Corgi, 1996.
Love of Fat Men (short stories). London, Viking, 1997.
Allie's Apples (juvenile). London, Reed Books, forthcoming.

*   *   *

Since her first collection of poems, *The Apple Fall,* appeared in 1983, Helen Dunmore has proved herself a prolific and versatile writer, publishing novels and children's verse as well as further volumes of poetry. *The Apple Fall* introduced a poet who, at 31, was already clearly in possession of her own intense, humane, and individual voice. Dunmore's sensitivities respond acutely to a broad spectrum of concerns which runs from the political to the domestic, from the abstract to the anecdotal. Themes as diverse as recollections of Proust, Berlin in the last days of the Wall, the development of a baby within her own body, or a man waiting for a heart operation all engage her creativity. More than most, perhaps, Dunmore's is a world in which sensation plays a central role:

> It's not that I'm afraid,
> but that I'm still gathering
> the echoes of my five senses—
>
> how far they've come with me, how far
> they want to go on.

Dunmore frequently writes from a perspective which reverses the stereotypical viewpoint. A poem about a child escaping from bed to interrupt the adults watching television presents the writing of poetry as a mundane activity when contrasted with the child's exploration of its dream world:

> ... the nightly row of the typewriter
> and piles of discontented paper by the table.
> I make poetry common as floor washing
>
> but still you wade in, thigh-deep in dreams
> at nine-thirty, while we are doped
> on one sofa, numb to excellent acting.

In *The Raw Garden* Dunmore aimed at producing an elaborately structured, thematically linked work. The poems discuss perceived ideas of natural and unnatural in the context of landscape and, in her own words, are "intended to speak to, through, and even over each other." Wide, occasionally surreal leaps of the imagination come to Dunmore with sometimes disconcerting ease. There can be an almost cinematic abruptness to her changes of focus, though the technique often produces images of startling power. In "Permafrost" a close-up of "frozen things / snowdrops and Christmas roses" pulls back to "nuclear snowsuits bouncing on dust" and then

> ... moon-men lost on the moon
> watching the earth's green flush
>
> tremble and perish.

Recovering a Body is built around another community of concerns, this time those related directly to the body: "Sexuality, aging, death, reproduction." The title poem fantasizes about a woman waking in the morning to find her body gone and then recounts the various stratagems she employs to retrieve it. This poem and many of its companion pieces are a striking demonstration of Dunmore's sensitivity to nuance and her insight into these vital areas of human feeling. The shorter poems in particular convey intense emotion in language which eschews rhetoric in favor of economy and precision:

> meet me where the fire
> lights the bayou
>
> watch my sweat shine
> as I play for you.

> It is for you I play
> my voice leaping the flames,
>
> if you don't come
> I am nothing.

Dunmore is generally at her best when working on a relatively miniature scale. The creative territory she occupies is one of markedly fluid boundaries, and it may be because of this that her longer poems, with their sometimes unwieldy structures, can seem too improvisatory and discursive for their own good.

—Rivers Carrew

DuPLESSIS, Rachel Blau

Nationality: American. **Born:** Brooklyn, New York, 14 December 1941. **Education:** Barnard College, B.A. 1963; Columbia University, M.A. 1964, Ph.D. 1970. **Career:** Assistant professor, Trenton State College, Trenton, New Jersey, 1972-73; lecturer, Douglass College, Rutgers University, New Brunswick, New Jersey, 1973-74; assistant professor, 1974-83, associate professor, 1983-87, and professor of English, 1987—, Temple University, Philadelphia. **Awards:** Fulbright professorship, 1985; National Endowment for the Humanities grants, 1986, 1988; Pennsylvania Council on the Arts Poetry fellowship, 1990. **Member:** Editorial boards of numerous publications. **Address:** English Department, Anderson Hall, Temple University, Philadelphia, Pennsylvania 19122, U.S.A. **Online address:** rdupless@vm.temple.edu.

PUBLICATIONS

Poetry

Wells. New York, Montemora, 1980.
Gypsy / Moth. Oakland, California, Coincidence Press, 1984.
Tabula Rosa. Elmwood, Connecticut, Potes & Poets Press, 1987.
Draft X: Letters. Philadelphia, Singing Horse Press, 1991.
Drafts 3-14. Elmwood, Connecticut, Potes & Poets Press, 1991.
Drafts 15-xxx, The Fold. Elmwood, Connecticut, Potes & Poets Press, 1997.

Other

Writing beyond the Ending: Narrative Strategies of 20th-Century Women Writers. Bloomington, Indiana University Press, 1985.
H.D.: The Career of That Struggle. Bloomington, Indiana University Press, and London, Harvester, 1986.
The Pink Guitar: Writing as Feminist Practice. New York, Routledge, 1990.

Editor, *The Selected Letters of George Oppen.* Durham, North Carolina, Duke University Press, 1990.
Editor, with Susan Stanford Friedman, *Signets: Reading H.D.* Madison, University of Wisconsin Press, 1990.

*

Bibliography: In *Contemporary Canadian and U.S. Women of Letters: An Annotated Bibliography* by Thomas M.F. Gerry, New York, Garland, 1993.

Critical Studies: "'The Parchment of Negative Spaces': Rachel Blau DuPlessis" by Bruce Campbell, in *Temblor,* no. 9, 1989; "The Essay on Recent Anthologies of Literary Criticism" by James Bennett, in *Substance,* no. 60, 1989; "No Margins to This Page: Female Experimental Poets and the Legacy of Modernism" by Caroline Bergvall, in *Fragmente,* no. 5, 1993; by Martha Nell Smith, in *Tulsa Studies in Women's Literature,* no. 13, Fall 1994; "Poetry in Our Political Lives" by Jeanne Heuving, in *Contemporary Literature,* vol. 37, no. 2, 1996; *Forms of Expansion: Recent Women's Long Poems* by Lynn Keller, Chicago, University of Chicago Press, 1997.

Rachel Blau DuPlessis comments:

Since 1986 I have been writing a series of interdependent, related canto-like poems called *Drafts.* My practice of essay writing, since the late 1970s with "For the Etruscans," and with essays published in *The Pink Guitar,* has strong bearing on my poetry.

In an objectivist mode, technique is the test (and text) of a person's sincerity. This makes an ethics of writing emerge simultaneously with the making of language. The basic "rule" of technique is that every single mark, especially the merest jot and tittle, the blankest gap and space, all have meaning. The problem of memory is the largest motivation for my poetry. However, the sheer memorializing function attributed to poetry, especially as that singles out female figures to be surrounded by "the male gaze," has been an ethical and intellectual issue for me since the early 1970s. This stance, which also involves the desire to criticize and undermine the lyric, to wring its ideology out, and to envelop it in the largeness of another practice, has been consistent as a motivation for 25 years. It does not necessarily lead to feminist declarations in my poetry, but to questions, the research of cultural materials, in short, a feminism of critique. This commitment to analysis within the poetic act and text creates a powerful force field for me. This impulse to critique has long been joined with a tonal and structural interest in something like midrash—doubled and redoubled commentary, poetry with its own gloss built in.

I consider myself a writer of a post-Holocaust era. The relation of this fact to my poetics is straightforward: I try to write so that if a single shard were rescued in the aftermath of some historical disaster, that one shard would be so touching and lucid as to give the future an idea of who we were. This is, of course, an impossible standard, but not the less compelling for that reason.

*　　　*　　　*

Extremely prolific in her poetry, in her critically "positional letters ladies," as she calls some of her speculative writings, and in her literary theory and philology as praxis in style and stances, Rachel Blau DuPlessis is a deeply intellectual and socially engaged poet whose career as a feminist writer has been a career of great clarity of conception and method. Her poetry is a translation, ethic and moray, and foray into the social history of writers and what they have written.

DuPlessis' work addresses itself directly and self-consciously to poetry itself, puncturing it as a social practice, and nurturing it through critical readings of paradigmatic theoretical writings of many kinds: feminist, Marxist, psychoanalytic, aesthetic, and stylistic. For DuPlessis, the edifice on which poetry and its conditions for meaning have been built is a complex layering of racial, class, gender, and sexual ideologies that throw into relief the question of what contemporary poetry, situated in this edifice, is for. This is a question which, when asked by a practicing poet, creates an epistemological crisis about the why and how of acknowledgement and ethical response to hegemonic traditions of poetry, traditions that conform a standardizing constellation of energies, values and cultural practices.

DuPlessis has written a great deal on the manner of meditation and manifesto on her own work as well as that of others, remarkable because it is a relatively unusual practice for contemporary American poets. Major tenets of her poetic project are explored and defended in her groundbreaking and influential book, *The Pink Guitar: Writing as Feminist Practice,* titled as a revision of Wallace Stevens' poem, "The Man with the Blue Guitar," wherein Stevens wrote "things as they are / Are changed upon the blue guitar." In this book, the "pink guitar" is a metaphor for feminist poetic practice, in particular the practice and possibility of representing and responding to specific modernist poetic and artistic conventions. "For the Etruscans," published in 1990, is the introductory essay of the book and is now widely used by scholars as a "classic" feminist text. The Etruscans were an ancient civilization that was overshadowed by the Greeks and conquered by the Romans. History is written by the victorious; that of the Etruscans was said to be "written in a script with the dominant culture's (Roman) alphabet," and such writings yield no information about the culture because they are "written in an unknown language with no known parallel." For DuPlessis, the Etruscans function as a symbol for the losers to poetry's dominant "civilizing" practices, those whose authority and mastery over language have been destroyed, erased, limited, (mis)appropriated or otherwise rendered as lost.

In "For the Etruscans" DuPlessis theorizes "female aesthetic, but not a female aesthetic, not one single constellation of strategies." The struggle, DuPlessis has written, is "to translate ourselves from our disguises" (those foisted on us by poetic tradition and those women take up ourselves in assuming poetic authority) and to theorize the recovery and consciousness and agency of the woman writer. Still, as she is at pains to point out, "female aesthetic" is not an essentialist or even uniquely female stance. It could stand as a term of convenience for the resistant aesthetic practices of any socially marked and subjugated national, gender, racial, class, sexual, or other group. What DuPlessis calls for her own purposes a "female aesthetic" is available to "all social practices which wish to criticize, to differentiate from, to overturn the dominant forms of knowing and understanding." It is an aesthetic of rupture, purposeful (mis)appropriation and challenges to codified manipulations of understanding and a reputed mass consciousness.

DuPlessis' poetry has been an ongoing investigation of the labor, existence, position, and praxis of the woman writer who is inevitably compromised in the act of writing, since the history of the act in which she is engaged is a history that over and again has as "an artifact in the traditions meaning on which she draws." The female figure in poetry is often a charming and charmed muse figure, a "riddle" whose own sexual difference is excessive and "overdetermined" by masculine writers' "reassertion of the polarized sexes," and an intransigent embedding of a male / female dichotomy in the mythopoetics of ancient and modern lore and authority, most specifically in the institutionalization of Oedipal and religious narratives as codes for cultural work perpetuated by dominant social formations. In her analyses by examples of the thorough assimilation of this lore into Western culture, DuPlessis asserts her belief that there is a female "relationship to language" where language is a dominant form of knowing and understanding" and in which Woman and women are "saturated" with predictable knowledge about their "social position[s]." This knowledge is especially volatile in the conceits or Petrarchan "deceits" as she call them, of poetry. Importantly, what DuPlessis observes as the "marked" relationship of the female to language is challenged in her poems with great accuracy and generous disclosure of her thought processes and practices. While she writes of "those invertebrate muses" of poetry, with "armes long and small" in her 1996 essay "Manifests," her poem "Crowbar" in *Tabula Rosa*, her first major book of poetry published nine years before "Manifests," proves the continuity of her struggle to both reconcile and contradict her position as a female writer with relation to female muse figures. In the poem "Crowbar" she writes: "Rush from those arms / rush to those arms / there "I" am is is certain / I am there?"

There is an additional critique of the lyric poem enveloped within other concerns throughout DuPlessis' poetic oeuvre. The lyric mode that many people think of as synonymous with poetry itself is ordinarily characterized by characteristics that include: brevity; a privileging of the personal; a universalizing tendency and claims to transcendent meaning; an incorporation of and equation with song or harmony; an obsession with beauty, sound, and unity; an avoidance of the polemic; a lack of the overtly explanatory; and the implicit advertisement of itself as occasional, complete, and finished. One other less widely observed characteristic of the lyric, DuPlessis notes, drawing on Adorno in her 1996 essay "Manifests," is the lyric poem's denial of its own material and social bases from textuality to production." Most evidently DuPlessis' work assays the conditions imposed by gender as a central material condition of poetry while it refutes the finality and proportedly original status of those conditions. She writes in her poem "writing on Writing" in *Tabula Rosa* of "Writing from the center of, the centers of, otherness. Making otherness central.... Genres that create themselves as imperfect.... Poetry too pretty; creating "beauty"? Creating chora. Beginning-middle-end, ha."

Thus the importance of the thematic of "Drafts" in her poetry. Starting in the second half of *Tabula Rosa*, DuPlessis' "Drafts" now comprise three books of poetry that have the word "draft" in their titles, *Draft X: Letters, Drafts 3-14*, and most recently, *Drafts 15-xxx, The Fold*. The poems in these books are, among other things, revisions of the finished lyric. In *Drafts 3-14*, DuPlessis writes in the poem "In" of being **inside the ruminant middle** of that which is conceived as "other" to poetry. At the same time, her "Drafts" are "in" "the world / The sorde serif I call myself. Because I am inside / am a mite in the letter / a traveler thru **are the senses of** dark holes tunneling grainy paper / Gathering all because of being in it, / yet / I am getting the force of it, **in**." Few details or sub-textual facets of the work of poetry, "micro and macro things" in the poem "Of," go unremarked here. Articles, prepositions, conjunctions typography, paper, rough drafts, letters, notes, the desires of the poet, the "grubbed marginal plots" of "Page," the abandoned—none of this goes unremarked. Furthermore, in her "Manifest" she writes, "Drafts evoke and override binary systems of limit. These are restless urges on both sides of a number of things; Male / female; speech / silence; Jew / non-Jew; dead / living; lyric finish / encyclopedic inclusion; memory / amnesia."

DuPlessis' poetry is a long discursive project about the exposure of her choices of response to entrenched poetic traditions and to the aftermath of massive historical devastations of humans and of cultures. In "Conjunctions" she writes, "Call this poetics "posthumous." / The articulation of previous silences / the invention of memory, *and, and, but*." They are about the incomplete, the provisional, the temporary and the lost—of memory, of access to institutional information, of marginalia, of poetry, of mastery, and of the world without the poem.

—Jenny Gough

DURAN, Jane

Nationality: British. **Born:** Havana, Cuba, 2 October 1944. **Education:** Cornell University, B.A. 1966; University of Sussex, certificate in education 1967. **Family:** Married 1) Barkat Hussain Chida in 1969 (divorced 1977); 2) Redha Benhadj-Djilali in 1985. **Career:** Teacher of English in British secondary schools, 1967-72; assistant in fellowship department, 1974-76, media production assistant, 1976-81, media officer, 1982-85; regional officer for Latin America and Pacific department, 1985-87, education officer, 1987-92, British Council, London; freelance writer and tutor 1993—. **Awards:** Cheltenham Festival of Literature Poetry Competition prize, 1987; Blue Nose Poets-of-the-Year Competition (joint recipient), 1994. **Address:** c/o Enitharmon Press, 36 St. George's Avenue, London N7 OHD, England.

PUBLICATIONS

Poetry

Boogie Woogie (pamphlet). London, Hearing Eye, 1991.
Breathe Now, Breathe. London, Enitharmon Press, 1995.

*   *   *

We live in an age of things zany, oddball, whimsical, slightly queer: all of which characteristics have been released in poetry by the general engrafting of the ideas of surrealism on the tree of imagery. Before this century it is extremely doubtful that a poem like Jane Duran's "The Wonderful Belly Dance of Rabah Saïd" could have been written. But now that so many poets have absorbed the imaginative irresponsibility of Gallic surrealism, such pieces abound. What is much less common is the coupling of such playfulness—so ludic a sensibility and strategy—with an, at times, haunting and, at times, beautifully subtle use of imagery. Compare this stanza from Duran's "Braided Rug":

In the middle of London
I am elsewhere. To the long gone,
to the dead in me
I cry breathe now, breathe...

with the subtlety of this description of a coat:

The small red and white checks
of your collar stick out
over your grey wool coat

like the slightest mention
of candlelight in a village
before morning...

All of which is to say that, in many poems in Duran's first full-length collection to date (though one that has won plaudits and awards in many quarters) there is the flair of the gifted poet for breath-taking lines and, from time to time, also "a tenderness / that overcomes the senses all at once, / a riverboat bearing down on the morning." ("The Horses in the Gaucho's Head," from *Breathe Now, Breathe*).

There are several poems, too, in this fine first collection that concern themselves with the difficulties, the tragedies centered around pregnancy and birth. Poems like "Stillborn" or "Miscarriage," which are written obliquely and with great feminine tact. They might have been written by Sylvia Plath, only they are less clotted with imagery, less "raw," and somehow more civilizedly urbane. The pain is there, but a sanitizing clarity too.

Duran was born in Cuba to a Spanish father and an American mother. There is a quiet cosmopolitanism in her poetic voice. As she puts it, "I speak all the riverland tongues / of my mother tongue. / My accent fathers me." There is a fine poem "The Orange Tree in Córdoba" which has a touch of Moorish richness about it, yet which speaks of "the cry of the childless." There is another that tells of a great grandfather "as if all the forests of Lancashire / had been used to build him." (An odd comparison that, though, for there are precious few forests in Lancashire now: but it all adds to the sense of Duran's geneological "range"). Elsewhere, there are some poems that give hint of Classical Chinese poetry read; or of a small-town child whose whole world, whose universe existed "just a few miles off the highway." And, on top of this, the poet has lived for the last 30 years in London—yet giving no especial sense of having become a Londoner.

So what is the persona that comes from her poems—these poems which fellow American expatriate Michael Donaghy has described as being "richly textured with a quiet authority"? I would say that they are a bit American but a great deal internationalist; rather like those of Elizabeth Bishop who lived much out of the U.S. too. There is the same calm interior to the poems which one finds in Bishop's; only to my taste Duran's are much more spare and consciously crafted and less meandering. If there is a problem with Jane Duran's work—and it is rather soon to speak of such with only one full collection available—there is not that fecundity of idea and theme which would give strong promise for the future. But we shall see.

—William Oxley

EDMOND, Lauris (Dorothy)

Nationality: New Zealander. **Born:** 2 April 1924. **Education:** Napier Girls High School, 1937-41; University of Waikato, Hamilton, B.A. 1968; Victoria University, Wellington, M.A. 1972. **Family:** Married Trevor Edmond in 1945; five daughters and one son. **Career:** Teacher, Huntly College, 1968-69, and Heretaunga College, Wellington, 1970-72; editor, Post-Primary Teachers Association, Wellington, 1973-80; off-campus tutor and lecturer, Massey University, Palmerston North, 1980—. Writer-in-residence, Deakin University, Melbourne, 1985. **Awards:** New Zealand P.E.N. award, 1975; Katherine Mansfield-Menton fellowship, 1981; Commonwealth poetry prize, 1985; Lilian Ida Smith award, 1987; New Zealand Arts Council scholarship, 1990; New Zealand Book Awards shortlist, 1992, for *Bonfires in the Rain.* D.Litt.: Massey University, 1988. O.B.E. (Officer, Order of the British Empire), 1986. **Address:** 22 Grass Street, Oriental Bay, Wellington, New Zealand.

PUBLICATIONS

Poetry

In Middle Air. Christchurch, Pegasus Press, 1975.
The Pear Tree and Other Poems. Christchurch, Pegasus Press, 1977.
Salt from the North. Wellington, Oxford University Press, 1980.
Seven. Wellington, Wayzgoose Press, 1980.
Wellington Letter. Wellington, Mallinson Rendel, 1980.
Catching It. Auckland, Oxford University Press, 1983.
Selected Poems. Auckland, Oxford University Press, 1984.
Seasons and Creatures. Auckland, Oxford University Press, and Newcastle upon Tyne, Bloodaxe, 1986.
Summer near the Arctic Circle. Auckland, Oxford University Press 1988.
New and Selected Poems. Auckland, Oxford University Press, and Newcastle upon Tyne, Bloodaxe, 1991.
Five Villanelles. Peppercorn Press, 1992.
Scenes from a Small City. Daphne Brasell Association, 1994.
Selected Poems 1975-1994. Bridget Williams Books, 1994.
A Matter of Timing. Auckland, Auckland University Press, 1994.
In Position. Newcastle upon Tyne, Bloodaxe, 1996.

Play

Between Night and Morning (produced Wellington, 1980).

Radio Play: *The Mountain* (cycle of 4 plays), 1980-81.

Novel

High Country Weather. Sydney, Allen & Unwin, and Wellington, Port Nicholson Press, 1984.

Other

Hot October: An Autobiographical Story. Sydney, Allen & Unwin, 1989.

Bonfires in the Rain. Bridget Williams Books, 1991.
The Quick World. Bridget Williams Books, 1992.

Editor, *Dancing to My Tune: Verse and Prose,* by Denis Glover. Wellington, Catspaw Press, 1974.
Editor, *Young Writing.* Wellington, P.E.N. New Zealand Centre, 1979.
Editor, *A Remedial Persiflage,* by Chris Ward. Wellington, Post Primary Teachers Association, 1980.
Editor, *Selected Letters of A.R.D. Fairburn.* Wellington, Oxford University Press, 1981.
Editor, with Carolyn Milward, *Women in Wartime: New Zealand Women Tell Their Story.* Wellington, Government Printing Office, 1986.

*

Manuscript Collection: Alexander Turnbull Library, Wellington.

Critical Studies: In *New Zealand Listener* (Wellington), no. 11 June 1983; *Landfall* (Christchurch), September 1983.

Lauris Edmond comments:

(1984) I came to poetry publishing late—though I had always written some, even during the busiest years when I lived in country towns and brought up my six children. In 1974 I first sent poems to an editor (of *Islands,* a N.Z. literary journal); they were accepted, and I began seriously to work on half-finished drafts and notes. By 1975 I had a manuscript ready for publication, and I have published five further volumes since then, with a *Selected Poems* this year.

The chief effect of this pattern of living my life first, as it were, and becoming a committed writer second, is that all my work is filled with a sense of relationship. This is sometimes with people, but also with events, experiences, the natural world; I don't think I write anything without this sense of being a part of a larger experience, and in relationship with it, being expressed in some way.

This quality is reflected in the process of writing by my awareness that the creation of a poem is as much a matter of listening as speaking; the experience which lies at the center of the poem has from the moment of inception its own life, to which I as poet respond. Since I have an abiding sense of the living quality in the natural environment, and the psychological environment in which I live, it seems natural to me to find this relationship again and again, even in the smallest details of existence, each of which has its own uniqueness.

I wrote my first novel because I was awarded the writer's fellowship which sends a New Zealand writer to the south of France for a year, to live in Menton. I do not believe that poetry can be written according to any kind of organized program, so I wrote a novel, and having done so I intend to write others. I found an immediate parallel between the vitality of the "world of the poem" and that of the fictional world of my novel, though many of the details of the writing process were different.

Beginning late has some obvious advantages (though I didn't do it by conscious choice). The main one is that the maturity that one hopes has been learned in 30 years of adult life forms the basic outlook or point of view in everything I write. Some kinds of apprenticeship, it seems, do not have to be passed through. There is also a considerable sense of urgency, which I think may give pace and energy to my writing. The volume of *Selected Poems* shows rather less variation between early and later poems than a poet who began writing in youth would display. And I could never regret my children!

(1995) During the last six years I have been working on a three-volume autobiography, recently reissued as a single volume. I have found the process extraordinarily revealing as a way of understanding why my writing began so late. It has aroused a major response, and has been seen as a central story of women of my generation. Now that the work is finished my concern has been to discover if—and in what ways—this has affected my poetry writing. Certainly the internal reverberations have taken a long time to settle and only in the last few months have I been able to go back—or move on—to a new departure in poetry. I find that writing poems is still my first choice of occupation, rather than the fiction I thought I would return to. I am working at present on a long sequence of poems that documents in various ways the moral, intellectual, and spiritual journeys of my later life.

*   *   *

Lauris Edmond's outpouring of poetry, including a volume of selected poems that won the 1985 Commonwealth poetry prize, comes comparatively late in a life devoted initially to a large family in a small New Zealand town. While recognizing in her *Landfall* interview that she has "the powerful enthusiasm of the late starter," Edmond is pleased to have been able to experience a "personal life" and then a career.

Her first volume, *In Middle Air,* sounds recurrent themes: the brutality of rural living (of a sensitive boy it is sneered, "He'll roughen up"), the cold alienness of the physical environment, the ravages of time, the necessity for love ("We starve alone") and for putting observation into words. There is, however, a strain of high romantic lyricism, which is at odds with the more supple, intimate dramatic sense that was slowly to emerge as the poet's distinctive voice, along with an uncertainty of line. In *The Pear Tree* the line fits more naturally a more forthright voice, often addressing friends (male or female) as "you" and arguing for philosophical positions such as the importance of the here and now. A series of portraits of older women forms a minor theme in Edmond's writing, as in "At Mary's House," which typically draws analogies between body, spirit, and the natural landscape ("nobody / has weeded here for a long time").

In *Wellington Letter* the poet criticizes her people—"we cultivate mind's middle distances." Instead, Edmond tries to move up close to experience, or to stand back and make a crisp generalization, for instance, that the great poets had "unshakeable courage." The dangers of bald poetic philosophizing are obvious, and Edmond has since wisely moved toward the quotidian—"it was not anything achieved; / the art was just to let it happen." Thus, the first half of *Salt from the North* shows a surer focus and sense of line and an unforced completeness in each poem. Unfortunately, in the second half of that volume and of *Catching It* the moralizing does creep in, effective only when proceeding from a vivid personal setting, e.g., in "Latter Day Lysistrata," an antiwar poem where the poet in her garden protests male folly:

> Let us show them the vulnerable
> earth, the transparent light that slips
> through slender birches falling over
> small birds that sense in the minuscule
> threads of their veins...

Many of Edmond's poems are about trees, their rootedness and memories. The Mansfield fellowship in Menton in 1981 gave her roots and a perspective elsewhere to revitalize her poetry. In *Catching It* the lines are often shorter and surer, the moment or performance brought off more often. Whether she is gazing back home ("I am the child of exiles who dreamt / of the lost garden") or at Frenchmen sitting in a town square, she "catches it." Her dominant sense of transience and death finds strong dramatic form in the poem "At Delphi," where she imagines the sacrifice of an older woman.

Although Edmond's work in poetry slowed while she wrote her multi-volume autobiography, she has consolidated her reputation as one of New Zealand's foremost poets with several further volumes, including *Seasons and Creatures* and *Summer near the Arctic Circle.* While *Seasons* continues to use as subject matter the things of daily life—flowers, cats, cows, family, neighbors—*Summer,* as its title suggests, often goes further afield, indicating a widening scope and audience. In "Commonwealth Poetry Tour" Edmond acknowledges this movement out: "So it grew, tiny convincing universe / feeling its frailty, marvelling at its passion..."

Less varied in her tone and subject matter than her countrywoman Fleur Adcock, less philosophically inclined than Judith Wright, Edmond also sometimes lacks the metrical variety of each of these poets, but this is the distinguished company in which she now belongs. She has built up a commanding body of work, and her voice has always been crisp, clear, and articulate. If her writing seems addressed primarily for her own pleasure—as is evidenced by "Cows":

> They do not suppose this matters,
> nor that anything else does—indeed,
> they do not suppose. Their time is entirely
> taken up with the delicious excruciating
> digestion of existence
> and if they please me on the by-pass road
> in the ripening sun this morning
> that is wholly my affair.

—then we are privileged to be party to it.

—David Dowling and Theresa Werner

ERDRICH, (Karen) Louise

Nationality: American (Native American: Turtle Mountain Band of Ojibwa). **Born:** Little Falls, Minnesota, 7 June 1954. **Education:** Dartmouth College, Hanover, New Hampshire, B.A. 1976; Johns Hopkins University, Baltimore, Maryland, M.A. 1977. **Family:** Married Michael Dorris in 1981; three sons and three daughters. **Career:** Visiting poetry teacher, North Dakota State Arts Council, 1977-78; creative writing teacher, Johns Hopkins University, 1978-79; communications director and editor of *Circle,*

Boston Indian Council, Massachusetts, 1979-80; text book writer, Charles-Merrill Company, 1980; visiting fellow, Dartmouth College, 1981. Also has worked as a beet weeder in Wahpeton, North Dakota; waitress in Wahpeton, Boston, and Syracuse, New York; psychiatric aide in a Vermont hospital, poetry teacher in prisons; lifeguard; and construction flag signaler. **Awards:** MacDowell fellowship, 1980; Yaddo fellowship, 1981; Nelson Algren award, 1982; National Book Critics Circle award, 1984; Virginia Sully prize, 1984; Sue Kaufman award, 1984; *Los Angeles Times* Book award, 1985; Guggenheim fellowship, 1985. **Address:** c/o HarperCollins, 10 East 53rd Street, New York, New York 10022, U.S.A.

PUBLICATIONS

Poetry

Jacklight. New York, Holt, 1984.
Baptism of Desire. New York, HarperCollins, 1989.

Recordings: *Louise Erdrich and Michael Dorris with Paul Bailey* (videotape), Roland Collection of Films on Art, 1980; *Conversations with Louise Erdrich and Michael Dorris,* Jackson, University Press of Mississippi, 1994.

Novels

Love Medicine. New York, Holt, 1984; London, Deutsch, 1985; expanded edition, Holt, 1993.
The Beet Queen. New York, Holt, 1986; London, Hamish Hamilton, 1987.
Tracks. New York, Holt, and London, Hamish Hamilton, 1988.
The Crown of Columbus, with Michael Dorris. New York and London, HarperCollins, 1991.

Short Stories

The Bingo Palace. London, Flamingo, and New York, HarperCollins, 1994.
Tales of Burning Love. New York, HarperCollins, 1996.

Other

Route 2, with Michael Dorris. Northridge, California, Lord John Press, 1990.
The Bluejay's Dance: A Birth Year. New York, HarperCollins, 1995.

Editor, with David Solheim, *Plainsong: Writings from North Dakota's Poets-in-the-Schools Program, 1975-1977.* Fargo, North Dakota, North Dakota Council on the Arts, 1978.

*   *   *

Louise Erdrich's standing as a poet rests with the two volumes of poetry that she published in the 1980s, *Jacklight* (1984) and *Baptism of Desire* (1989). Even if she were to continue to concentrate on writing prose fiction, as she has done since then, and never publish another collection of her poems, her reputation as a poet would be solid. She has already established herself with the truthful intensity of her poetic expression, her fearlessness in the use of myth to express the realities of the human heart, and the imaginative exactness of her language.

Of Ojibwa (Chippewa) and German heritage (she is a member of the Turtle Mountain band of Ojibwa), Erdrich was raised in Wahpeton, North Dakota, and she uses all of these elements of ancestry and place in her poetry. The *Jacklight* poems tend to fall into five overlapping thematic categories: poems of Indian heritage in conflict with the dominant white culture; poems of sisterhood and family; love poems; poems peopled with the shadows of figures from her past; and mythic poems, which draw upon Native American myths and the habit of mythmaking.

Among the poems of tension between the Indian and white worlds are some of Erdrich's best and most frequently anthologized poems, including "Indian Boarding School: The Runaways," which recounts the habitual running away of children from an Indian boarding school to the Indian place of their dreams "just under Turtle Mountains." They know that the sheriff will be "waiting at midrun / to take us back," but "Home's the place we head for in our sleep." Like the tracks on the land of the railroad they ride, "The worn-down welts / of ancient punishments lead back and forth." "Dear John Wayne" presents the reaction of young Indians to a John Wayne Western at a drive-in movie. When it is over, they continue to hear his voice speaking its real message: *"Come on, boys, we got them / where we want them, drunk, running. / They'll give us what we want, what we need."*

"A Love Medicine" represents Erdrich's sisterhood-family poems. When "This dragonfly, my sister" feels the boot of her man planting "its grin / among the arches of her face," the speaker responds with her whole feminine being: *"Sister, there is nothing / I would not do."*

Erdrich's love poems tend to have a poignantly sad note that is echoed in "Train": "Here is the light I was born with, love. / Here is the bleak radiance that levels the world." Mary Kröger is the most powerful figure in the character poems of "The Butcher's Wife" section of *Jacklight.* Futilely pursued by Rudy J.V. Jacklitch, the sheriff, until he crashed his truck and died cursing her, Mary hears her name destroyed by the townspeople until she "feared to have it whispered in their mouths!"

Among the best poems in the fine "Myths" section of *Jacklight* is "Whooping Cranes," a haunting poem about a foundling boy, "strange and secret among the others, / killing crows with his bare hands / and kissing his own face in the mirror," who ends up flying into the mystical formation of whooping cranes that "sailed over / trumpeting the boy's name." Noteworthy, too, is the Potchikoo mythical prose poem cycle about a man born as a "potato boy" after "a very pretty Chippewa girl" is raped by the sun in a potato field. Archetypically, Potchikoo dies when his three lovely daughters visit him in his old age, sit on his lap, and block the sun from him: "He hardly knew it when all three daughters laid their heads dreamily against his chest. They were cold, and so heavy that his ribs snapped apart like little dry twigs."

Baptism of Desire projects very much the same range and depth as the earlier volume. Indeed, some of the very same characters—Rudy J.V. Jacklitch, Mary Kröger, the mythic Potchikoo—do encore appearances, for which readers of *Jacklight* must be grateful. The main change is that *Baptism* is, paradoxically, even more spiritual in its earthiness. In "The Sacraments," for example, a richly portrayed rain dance merges with the Christian sacraments. In "Mary Magdalene," after she washes "your ankles / with my tears," Mary sardonically resolves to "drive boys / to smash empty bottles on their brows. / I will pull them right off of their skins."

She concludes with an observation that is at once earthy and spiritually rebellious: "It is the old way that girls / get even with their fathers— / by wrecking their bodies on other men."

The poet and critic Simon Ortiz has summed up the strength of Erdrich's poetry succinctly: "by knowing a bit of truthful fear we may know courage, love, faith, life. That is the way I experience Erdrich's poems of revelation. She is a remarkable, remarkable writer."

—Alan Shucard

FAINLIGHT, Ruth

Nationality: American. **Born:** New York City, 2 May 1931. **Education:** Attended schools in the United States and England; studied at Birmingham and Brighton Colleges of Art. **Family:** Married Alan Sillitoe in 1959; one son and one adopted daughter. **Career:** Poet-in-residence, Vanderbilt University, Nashville, Tennessee, 1985, 1990. **Award:** Cholmondeley award, 1994. **Address:** 14 Ladbroke Terrace, London W11 3PG, England.

PUBLICATIONS

Poetry

A Forecast, A Fable. London, Outposts, 1958.
Cages. London, Macmillan, 1966; Chester Springs, Pennsylvania, Dufour, 1967.
18 Poems from 1966. London, Turret, 1967.
To See the Matter Clearly and Other Poems. London, Macmillan, 1968; Chester Springs, Pennsylvania, Dufour, 1969.
Poems, with Alan Sillitoe and Ted Hughes. London, Rainbow Press, 1971.
The Region's Violence. London, Hutchinson, 1973.
21 Poems. London, Turret, 1973.
Another Full Moon. London, Hutchinson, 1976.
Two Fire Poems. Knotting, Bedfordshire, Sceptre Press, 1977.
The Function of Tears. Knotting, Bedfordshire, Sceptre Press, 1979.
Sibyls and Others. London, Hutchinson, 1980.
Two Wind Poems. Knotting, Bedfordshire, Martin Booth, 1980.
Climates. Newcastle upon Tyne, Bloodaxe, 1983.
15 to Infinity. London, Hutchinson, 1983.
Selected Poems. London, Century Hutchinson, 1987.
Three Poems. Child Okeford, Dorset, Words Press, 1988.
The Knot. London, Century Hutchinson, 1990.
Sibyls. Searsmont, Maine, Gehenna Press, 1991.
This Time of Year. London, Sinclair-Stevenson, 1994.
Selected Poems. London, Sinclair-Stevenson, 1995.
Sugar-Paper Blue. Newcastle upon Tyne, Bloodaxe, 1997.
Pomegranate, illustrated by Judith Rothchild. Ceret, France, Editions de l'Eau, 1997.

Plays

All Citizens Are Soldiers, with Alan Sillitoe, adaptation of a play by Lope de Vega (produced London, 1967). London, Macmillan, and Chester Springs. Pennsylvania, Dufour, 1969.

The Dancer Hotoke (opera libretto), music by Erika Fox (produced London, 1991).
The European Story (opera libretto), music by G. Alvarez (produced London, 1993).

Television Play: *Bedlam Britannica* (opera liberetto), music by Robert Jan Stips, 1995.

Short Stories

Penguin Modern Stories 9, with others. London, Penguin, 1971.
Daylife and Nightlife. London, Deutsch, 1971.
Dr. Clock's Last Case. London, Virago Press, 1994.

Other

Editor, *Selected Poems,* by Harry Fainlight. London, Turret, 1987.
Editor, *Journeys,* by Harry Fainlight. London, Turret, 1992.

Translator, *Navigacions,* by Sophia de Mello Breyner Andresen. Lisbon, Casa da Moeda, 1983.
Translator, *Marine Rose,* by Sophia de Mello Breyner. Redding Ridge, Connecticut, Black Swan, 1988.

*

Critical Studies: By Mark Jarman, *Hudson Review,* vol. 15, no. 2, Summer 1987; by Michèle Duclos, in *La Traductiere 10* (Bordeaux, France), June 1992; by Barbara Hardy, in *New European Review* (London), August / September 1992.

Ruth Fainlight comments:

I try to keep the words of a poem close to the feelings and sensations that inspired it, in the hope that it will inspire the same feelings, recognitions, and memories in its reader. In this way, he or she becomes involved in its reality, even a participant in its creation—because reading is an active relationship between reader and writer.

But writing is a relationship between writer and language. A poem develops organically from the first inspiring phrase. That phrase, or cluster of words, includes every essential element, and my work is to allow all its potential of sound and meaning to realize themselves. And like every other living organism, its development is a unique combination of unassailable laws and the entirely unexpected.

(1995) Though I appreciate the arguments of those who believe that a poem should be left in its first published state, I feel that the relationship between poet and poem, like a living marriage, is continually changing, and so have taken the opportunity to revise some of the work. As in any relationship, it is very hard to know if one's actions will have good or bad results.

*   *   *

The poetry of Ruth Fainlight reflects a systematic mining of personal experience. Central to her work are the interwoven themes of the poet's role in "normal" life and that of a woman in a world whose standards are still defined by men. Both of these concerns are explored directly, the woman-poet giving evidence of their effect upon her. As a writer, Fainlight is conscious of herself as being in possession of a gift that to some extent distances her from the ordinary world. It is a mixed blessing, for the compulsive urge for expression devours her own existence as its raw material. The force of this need within her and the paralyzing frustration in those arid periods when she is unable to write are keenly observed in a number of poems, not least in the hospital convalescence of "Late Afternoon." Warring with the poetic urge is the harder, more practical side of Fainlight's nature, what she refers to as "My Stone-Age Self," its earth-bound cynicism denying all spiritual values, insisting that "nothing / but the body's pleasure, / use, and comfort, matters." Such works as "Passenger" indicate that on more than one occasion the poet has found herself wondering if creativity is worth the trouble, if it would not in fact be better were she a nonpoetic person, unravaged by the debilitating forces that cannibalize the self.

The roles of woman and poet interlock once more in Fainlight's relationship with her mother, which is presented in several of her poems. The relationship is seen as ambivalent, varying somewhere between love and resentment, and in some ways it equates with her attitude toward poetry itself; it is significant that Fainlight regards the muse as a mother figure whose status she is not always willing to acknowledge. Similarly, in the case of love, while responding to the compulsive urge, she is aware of the threat it poses, the gradual absorption of the self into family life. "Here" presents domesticity as at once a prison and a dangerous lure, the attractions of which compel her to accept it against her better judgment. The male-female confrontation, its conflict and resolution, is tracked by Fainlight back into the looming shadow of myth and fairy tale, imaged in Adam's Fall or in "Beauty and the Beast." At once a wife and mother and an individual, she balances the warring opposites with a clear, unjaundiced vision, setting them down in measured polarities in her verse.

More than second-class citizenship or lack of inspiration, death is the final restriction, the limit placed on all created things. Robbed of her loved brother, a fellow poet who died young, Fainlight is aware of death as a constantly lurking threat, reminders of its presence appearing when least expected, in a chance sighting of the moon in the night sky, for example, or in the coming of another spring. In her account of her brother's funeral, the sudden breaking of a storm matches her grief, his death the crucial event that convinces her of the fearful end to everything: "I shall not meet my dead again / as I remember them / alive, except in dreams or poems. / Your death was the final proof / I needed to accept that knowledge."

This Time of Year reexamines the familiar themes with a growing depth and intensity of expression. In the sequence of poems "Twelve Sibyls," Fainlight evokes a range of archetypal female figures who are gifted with the power of utterance and self-creation yet who are still denied, frozen, and curbed by the controlling strength of the male "god." "This Time of Year" blends the fallen leaves of autumn with recollections of her dead parents, the images subtly and indissolubly woven together in a few words, while "Tosca" depicts the memory of other relatives and their everyday talismans. Fainlight subjects herself to ironic self-analysis in "The Author" and "Reflection," humorously visualizing her mirror image in the latter poem as "all contrary." Her ambiguous view of domesticity surfaces once more in "Romance," where she warns of the enslaving properties of fairy tales; the contrasting vision is shown in "Art," where her musings on the preparation of food recall the earlier "Box and Sampler," with its message of shared ritual as a liberating influence. As with all of Fainlight's collections, the poems of *This Time of Year* mirror their author's com-

plex personality, and the more immediate the experience, the stronger the message. Her vision is faithfully conveyed to the reader, and her voice remains unmistakably her own.

—Geoff Sadler

FANTHORPE, U(rsula) A(skham)

Nationality: British. **Born:** Lee Green, London, 29 July 1929. **Education:** St. Anne's College, Oxford, 1949-53, B.A. 1953, M.A. 1958; University of London Institute of Education, 1953-54, Dip.Ed. 1954; University College, Swansea, diploma in school counseling 1971. **Career:** Assistant English teacher, 1954-62, and Head of English, 1962-70, Cheltenham Ladies' College, Gloucestershire; clerk in various businesses in Bristol, 1972-74: hospital clerk and receptionist, Bristol, 1974-83. Arts Council creative writing fellow, St. Martin's College, Lancaster, 1983-85. **Awards:** Society of Authors traveling scholarship, 1984; Royal Society of Literature fellow, 1987; Arts Council Award, 1995; Hawthornden fellowship, 1997. D.Litt.: University of West England, 1996. **Address:** Culverhay House, Wotton under Edge, Gloucestershire, England.

PUBLICATIONS

Poetry

Side Effects. Liskeard, Cornwall, Harry Chambers / Peterloo Poets, 1978.
Four Dogs. Liskeard, Cornwall, Treovis Press, 1980.
Standing To. Liskeard, Cornwall, Harry Chambers / Peterloo Poets, 1982.
Voices Off. Liskeard, Cornwall, Harry Chambers / Peterloo Poets, 1984.
The Crystal Zoo (for children), with John Cotton and L.J. Anderson. Oxford, Oxford University Press, 1985.
Selected Poems. Calstock, Cornwall, Peterloo Poets, 1986.
A Watching Brief. Calstock, Cornwall, Peterloo Poets, 1987.
Neck Verse. Calstock, Cornwall, Peterloo Poets, 1992.
Safe as Houses. Calstock, Cornwall, Peterloo Poets, 1995.
Penguin Modern Poets 6, with Elma Mitchell and Charles Causely. London, Penguin, 1996.

*

Critical Study: *Taking Stock: A First Study of U.A. Fanthorpe,* by Eddie Wainwright, Calstock, Cornwall, Peterloo Poets, 1994.

*   *   *

U. A. Fanthorpe had an Oxford education and went on to teach at a prestigious school. She gave this up to become, after various temporary jobs, a clerical worker at a hospital. Such a biography may sound like that of an English eccentric, but there is nothing eccentric about Fanthorpe's verse. It is true that she gives more than a passing nod to Betjeman and is clearly aware of the more comedic aspects of Auden. These affinities, however, are as much a matter of rivalry as of imitation. Her most obvious literary relationship seems to be with a phase of poetry, colloquial and not infrequently acidulous, which began in Great Britain soon after World War II. By that time Fanthorpe was already a young adult, but she had many years to go before she would publish a book of her own. Further, behind any of the more palpable analogues are the poets preserved for Fanthorpe's generation in the attractively bound Oxford Editions of Standard Authors.

Fanthorpe's verse is not related to the classics in every respect. This is a result of her subject matter, which, socially speaking, is rather down the hill. Wordsworth had some odd encounters and so did Coleridge, but they never met Julie the encephalitic or Alison with the damaged brain. Tennyson wrote of sick beds, it is true, but not quite like Fanthorpe—"The smashed voice roars inside the ruined throat / Behind the mangled face..." Yet we have not lost the Standard Authors entirely. Further on, the poem, ironically entitled "Linguist," modulates into a style that Tennyson would have recognized—"A silent clock that speaks / The solemn language of the sun..." All this goes to show how genuinely inclusive the English tradition is.

Even Fanthorpe's subject matter, that which would seem to set her apart, is not quite what it seems. There is always a positive note somewhere, though occasionally it is deceptive: "rain falls in every life, / But rainbows, bluebirds, spring, babies or God / Lift up our hearts..." This is, of course, a special effect. For purposes of parody Fanthorpe has donned the singing robes of Patience Strong and wears them with a flourish that even the bard of *Woman's Own* never knew. Such nonce-style is, moreover, a clue as to how much of this poetry works. Fanthorpe tends to infiltrate her quarry, using the quarry's own tactics to bring him down. In her poem "Sir John," "dear distractions" and "dreary inner eye," phrases which Betjeman himself might have coined, serve to indicate a sense of the void beneath the somewhat chintzy cheeriness of the great man.

Though fraught with wit, Fanthorpe's world is not a cozy one. The functionaries in her poems deal with sickness and death at close quarters. The hospital secretary requires a sense of order in typing out her fatal lists, and the clerk needs a strong back to tote her files. Moreover, all of this takes place in a busily social atmosphere. Perhaps the best of these poems is "Lament for the Patients." Here, a startling use is made of interpolated statement:

> To me came the news of their dying:
> From the police (*Was this individual*
> *A patient of yours?*); from ambulance
> Control (*Our team report this patient*
> *You sent us to fetch is deceased already*);
> From tight-lipped telephoning widowers
> (*My wife died in her sleep last night...*)

The interpolations are not so prosaic as they might seem out of context. An ironic effect is gained through the way in which natural language is displaced by official language, causing odd ambiguities. The word necessarily used by the police, "individual," fortuitously drains its referent of identity. The "deceased" is no longer a patient but has, precipitately, become a corpse. All this, moreover, is contrasted with the central persona who has to cope with these incoming calls, succinctly and with a degree of alliterative skill. That, in its turn, produces a rhythmic momentum which may remind us of the breakthrough in the early 1950s when James Kirkup inaugurated a new mood in poetry with "A Correct Compassion" and D.J. Enright sent back his wry dispatches from Egypt and Japan.

Much of that about which Fanthorpe writes seems as drab and basic as the topics chosen by Kirkup and Enright. Characteristically, however, each subject is irradiated by an enlivening gleam. What Fanthorpe says of the winter adventurers in her poem "Hanggliders in January" also is true of her own verse: "Like all miracles, it has a rational / Explanation..." Here, as elsewhere, it is the naturalistic detail that seems to carry the romantic charge—"We saw the aground flyers, their casques and belts / And defenceless legs..." The detail gives the immediately preceding statement, "It was all quite simple, really," an ironic turn, and we are tempted to follow the poem beyond its literal meaning. Fanthorpe's skill and perception make her appear, among the gyrations of so many latter-day Imagists, "Like a bird at home in the sky."

The later verse does not so much develop the earlier technique as add to it. There is no diminution of skill, but there is no sense, either, of fresh territory. This is not so much a restriction of subject matter, though it does remain essentially the same, as a limitation of sensibility. Although there was a faint promise of lyricism in the early work, it was never fulfilled. Instead, in *Neck Verse,* for instance, we have the overworked doctor, the superannuated psychiatrist, and patients past and present. All are observed by the accomplished satirist, mapping the "land... / Of the early Ovaltine nightcap" and chronicling "the man on the stretcher, the woman who cannot walk." The prowess of Fanthorpe, and it is considerable, is in displaying powers of evocation concurrently with the crucial trait of being utterly unsentimental.

—Philip Hobsbaum

FEAVER, Vicki

Nationality: British. **Born:** Nottingham, England, 14 November 1943. **Education:** University of Durham, B.A. (with honors) 1962; University of London, M.A. 1982. **Family:** Married William Andrew Feaver in 1960; three daughters and one son. **Career:** Creative writing teacher, and subtitle composer for British television.

PUBLICATIONS

Poetry

Close Relatives. London, Secker & Warburg, 1981.
The Handless Maiden. London, Cape Poetry, 1994.

*   *   *

Despite the 13 years that lie between the publication of Vicki Feaver's two collections, the books are firmly connected through subject, imagery and voice. *The Handless Maiden* (1994) is a powerful and ambitious extension of the themes of *Close Relatives* (1981). While these themes are traditional—the female experience of love, domesticity and parenthood—they are made remarkable in Feaver's hands. Her emotional range encompasses the finest and lowest of feelings; she argues both for and against the feminine, and explores power and helplessness in both sexes. She draws on myth, folklore, and art to reflect the differences between expectation and outcome, ideal and reality. She is emphatic about the value of passionate experience, but does not shy away from the risk and damage it can bring.

The world of Feaver's poetry is confined by physical and social constructs. She understands the resistance of a child who is slow to read: words will pin him down. A man builds a wall while his wife is dying; marriage begins as a dream of flight and becomes a desperate balancing act; the seven deadly sins are replaced by nine specifically female ones. Customs are observed: her mother making crab-apple jelly each year disgusts and entrances her as does menstruation, something she wants, quite literally, to hoard.

The bonds of parenthood and love are inescapable. Feaver is unflinching in her observation of how we invest our hopes in our children and the burden that is thus inherited: "We feed them with our dreams / then wait and watch / like gardeners for flowers." Feaver knows, too, the risks of love but does not want to be without it, an insistence celebrated in "Swimming in January," in which lovers are "gulping half air, / half salt-water, drifting almost to the edge / where there's no returning." The risk of losing oneself is a way to feel alive.

Close Relatives articulates the moment when failure and loss have been recognized but have not quite given way to despair. Hope lies in clean sheets, a white page, a second honeymoon. It is an honest but modest collection, looking no further than domestic possibility and quietly voiced. *The Handless Maiden* is a far more ambitious work: raw, dark and violent, it is enriched with consonantal music and measured into gulping phrases or long exhalations of intense emotion, often rage. The physical effort of emotion adds texture to Feaver's linguistic simplicity and gives her lyricism material strength. In these poems, technical and aural effects can make the subject resound as Feaver employs sibilant hiss, emphatic monosyllabics, and percussive alliteration.

Feaver's motif of flowers, before used as a conventional symbol of ephemeral beauty, has become something more interesting: "Not the flowers men give women / / ... but flowers / that wilt as soon as their steams / are cut, leaves blackening / as if blighted by the enzymes / in our breath..." Feaver takes a fierce joy in this decay and these flowers "remind us / we are killers, can tear the heads / off men's shoulders." They are as potent and sensual, a source of threat. A lily pond becomes a place in which she might drown someone; tulips are where a wasp might hide in order to sting.

Female archetypes, Cince and Judith, give wonderfully fluent accounts of their passionate acts in poems which reveal Feaver's talent for dramatic monologue. Her retelling of *Beauty and the Beast* shows the effects of desire to be truly bestial. There is a persistent wish to release the animus; an empathy with the wild, unwanted and troublesome. Artists such as Lucien Freud and Andrew Wyeth are confronted through their power to create images and realize fantasies. Typically, she confronts their models as well, not least about the uneasy desire to be desired. "The Handless Maiden" of the title is trapped by her own legend in the way that Feaver describes women as controlled by convention and expectation and above all, by men:

I let myself cry. I cried for my hands
my father cut off; for the lumpy, itching scars
of my stumps; for the silver hands—
my husband gave me—that spun and wove
but had no feeling; and for my handless arms
that let my baby drop...

—Lavinia Greenlaw

FEINSTEIN, Elaine

Nationality: British. **Born:** Bootle, Lancashire, 24 October 1930. **Education:** Wyggeston Grammar School, Leicester; Newnham College, Cambridge, B.A. in English 1952, M.A. 1955. **Family:** Married Arnold Feinstein in 1956; three sons. **Career:** Editorial staff member, Cambridge University Press, 1960-62; lecturer in English, Bishop's Stortford Training College, Hertfordshire, 1963-66; assistant lecturer in literature, University of Essex, Wivenhoe, 1967-70. Writer in residence for the British Council in Singapore, 1993; writer-in-residence, British Council, Tromsø, Norway. **Awards:** Arts Council grant, 1970, 1979, 1981; Daisy Miller prize, 1971, for fiction; Kelus prize, 1978; Cholmondeley award, 1990. D.Litt: University of Leicester, 1990. Fellow, Royal Society of Literature, 1980. **Agent:** Gill Coleridge, Rodgers, Coleridge & White, 20 Powis Mews, London W11, England; (plays and films) Lemon Unna & Durbridge, 24-32 Pottery Lane, London W11 4LZ, England.

PUBLICATIONS

Poetry

In a Green Eye. London, Goliard Press, 1966.
The Magic Apple Tree. London, Hutchinson, 1971.
At the Edge. Rushden, Northamptonshire, Sceptre Press, 1972.
The Celebrants and Other Poems. London, Hutchinson, 1973.
Some Unease and Angels: Selected Poems. London, Hutchinson, and University Center, Michigan, Green River Press, 1977.
The Feast of Euridice. London, Faber, 1980.
Badlands. London, Hutchinson, 1986.
City Music. London, Hutchinson, 1990.
Selected Poems. Manchester, Carcanet, 1994.
Daylight. Manchester, Carcanet, 1997.

Plays

Lear's Daughters (produced London, 1987).

Radio Plays: *Echoes,* 1980; *A Late Spring,* 1982; *A Captive Lion,* 1984; *Marina Tsvetayeva: A Life,* 1985; *A Day Off,* from the novel by Storm Jameson, 1986; *If I Ever Get on My Feet Again,* 1987; *The Man in Her Life,* 1990; *Foreign Girls,* 1993; *Winter Meeting,* 1994; *Women in Love,* from the novel by D.H. Lawrence; *Lady Chatterly's Confession,* from Feinstein's novel, 1996.

Television Plays: *Breath,* 1975; *Lunch,* 1982; *Country Diary of an Edwardian Lady* series, from work by Edith Holden, 1984; *A Brave Face,* 1985; *The Chase,* 1988; *A Passionate Woman* series, 1989.

Novels

The Circle. London, Hutchinson, 1970.
The Amberstone Exit. London, Hutchinson, 1972.
The Glass Alembic. London, Hutchinson, 1973; as *The Crystal Garden,* New York, Dutton, 1974.
Children of the Rose. London, Hutchinson, 1975.

The Ecstasy of Dr. Miriam Garner. London, Hutchinson, 1976.
The Shadow Master. London, Hutchinson, 1978; New York, Simon
    & Schuster, 1979.
The Survivors. London, Hutchinson, 1982.
The Border. London, Hutchinson, 1984.
Mother's Girl. London, Century Hutchinson, 1988.
All You Need. London, Century Hutchinson, 1989.
Loving Brecht. London, Hutchinson, 1992.
Dreamers. London, Hutchinson, 1994.
Lady Chatterly's Confession. London, Macmillan, 1995.

Short Stories

Matters of Chance. London, Covent Garden Press, 1972.
The Silent Areas. London, Hutchinson, 1980.

Other

Bessie Smith. London, Penguin, 1985.
A Captive Lion: The Life of Marina Tsvetayeva. London, Century
    Hutchinson, and New York, Dutton, 1987.
Marina Tsvetayeva. London, Penguin, 1989.
Lawrence's Women. New York and London, HarperCollins, 1993.

Editor, *Selected Poems of John Clare.* London, University Tuto-
    rial Press, 1968.
Editor, with Fay Weldon, *New Stories 4.* London, Hutchinson,
    1979.
Editor, *PEN New Poetry.* London, Quartet, 1988.

Translator, *The Selected Poems of Marina Tsvetayeva.* London,
    Oxford University Press, 1971; rev. ed., Oxford and New York,
    Oxford University Press, 1981; rev. ed., Oxford and New York,
    Oxford University Press, 1993.
Translator, *Three Russian Poets: Margarita Aliger, Yunna Moritz,*
    Bella Akhmadulina. Manchester, Carcanet, 1979.
Translator, with Antonia W. Bouis, *First Draft: Poems,* by Nika
    Turbina. London, Boyars, 1988.

*

Manuscript Collection: Cambridge University.

Critical Studies: "Modes of Realism: Roy Fisher and Elaine
Feinstein" by Deborah Mitchell, in *British Poetry since 1970* ed-
ited by Michael Schmidt and Peter Jones, Manchester, Carcanet,
and New York, Persea, 1980; Peter Conradi, in *British Novelists
since 1960* edited by Jay L. Halio, Detroit, Gale Research, 1983;
interview with Michele Roberts, in *Poetry Nation Review,* no. 101,
1994.

Elaine Feinstein comments:

When I began writing in the early 1960s I felt the influence of
the Americans (Stevens and perhaps even Emily Dickinson as
much as W.C. Williams); and I suppose the turning point in find-
ing a voice of my own arose, paradoxically, from working on the
translations of Marina Tsvetayeva and other modern Russian po-
ets. And perhaps also from writing prose, which began at first as
an extension of the poetic impulse, but (after several novels) works
as a channel for the exploration of my humanist concerns, and
leaves me freer now to take greater risks with language when I

choose to write lyric poetry. Perhaps both experiences have en-
couraged me to write longer poems (such as the title poem of *The
Celebrants* and more recently "New Poems for Dido and Aeneas"),
and to find longer lines and new rhythms, as well as richer subject
matter.

(1995) I find my poems get bonier and more bare as I get older,
and usually spring from some experience in my own life, as if the
impulse to make poems now has to connect with a need to puzzle
out personal thoughts and feelings. And I want the verse to be clear
and quiet, even though lyric poetry rises most powerfully from in-
tense emotion, and it is the lyric I love. I have no ambition to write a
long poem. If I'm going to tell stories, I'd rather write novels.

The poets I most read are still, above all, lyric poets: Herbert's
simplicity, Pound's marvelous ear for syllables, Lawrence's sharp-
ness of response, and Charles Reznikoff's humanity remain my
models. My one-time Black Mountain mentors had some of these
virtues too, but neither their passion for geography and local his-
tory nor their insistence on uncorrected spontaneity were ever
truly mine. And they were often obscure even on a close reading.

These days I work most of all for directness and lucidity. I
don't want the music of the lyric to drown what has to be said.
There is always a tug between speech and music in poetry; what
I'm looking for is a music which has the natural force of spoken
feeling, the Wordsworthian "language really used by men;" though
I confess I enjoyed the street language of slang rather more in the
days when it was not so smart to make use of it

It was from Tsvetayeva I first learned to use personae, finding
mythical figures particularly useful as vehicles for the passions.
Like characters in fiction, personae allow poets to go outside au-
tobiography, without forfeiting their own patterns of feeling. It's
rather like writing drama. I don't know whether I will do more.

Tsvetayeva thought a poet had to let "the hand race, (and when
it doesn't race to stop)"; and I may well write fewer poems of
any kind. It's hard to predict. I shall probably not do many more
translations. The pressure is elsewhere: in the work of understand-
ing, assessing, and confronting the passage of time.

I'm not conscious at the moment of being part of any particu-
lar grouping, nor have I been, since the English Intelligencer poets
who followed Jeremy Prynne came and sat on my Trumpington
floor in the sixties; and even then I'm not sure how much I shared
with them. Over the last 20 years or so my closest literary friend-
ships have been with novelists. But I'm very much aware of the
good women poets who are writing now. When I began writing
there were so few of us, and now some of the best young poets
are women. And I haven't written many overtly political poems;
I continue to feel a poet should serve poetry rather than putting
his art at the service of any politics.

*   *   *

"Anniversary," which opens the collection *The Magic Apple
Tree,* expresses the act of faith in humanity on which all Elaine
Feinstein's poetry is posited:

    Listen, I shall have to whisper it
    into your heart directly: we are all
    supernatural / every day
    we rise new creatures / cannot be predicted.

Confronting the banal, flat surfaces of modern existence, symbol-
ized by the mud, mists, and rain of the East Anglian fens, "our

brackish waters" ("The Magic Apple Tree"), she acknowledges the limitations set for humans by "the tyranny of landscape" ("Moon") and by our rooting in a particular and all-pervasive present: "How do you change the weather in the blood?" ("I Have Seen Worse Days Turn"). The techniques of poetry are the "alembic," the alchemist's vessel which effects a transformation which is not the transcendence but a sharpening of the real, the celebration of "what in the landscape of cities / has to be prized" ("Some Thoughts on Where"). Feinstein shares with the reader the liberating power of new perceptions: "We have broken some magic barrier" to become "open to the surprises of the season" ("Renaissance February 7"). She delights in the surprises of imagery, color, syntax, tone, and rhythms which set "your own East Anglian children / ...dancing. To an alien drum" ("Moon"). "Our Vegetable Love Shall Grow" develops the surrealist quality of Marvell's image, in the mock horror of a vampire crocus, grotesquely yoking the energies of nature and the city to drain away the lesser vitality of the human. Black humor is the vehicle for modern man—and woman—to reassert dominance of a reality that threatens to overwhelm. The invocation of Buster Keaton ("Out") is no accident, nor is the marvelous punning cynicism of "West," whose hesitating and stabbing rhythms embrace exactly the bitterly revealing twists of Mae West's comedy.

Feinstein moves incessantly between creative turmoil and a sense of peace, carrying the poet's burden of personal responsibility for the remaking of harmony and unity out of a torn, disjointed world. The broken utterances of "Marriage" catch the pain of human separateness on an intensely personal note:

tender whenever we touch   what
else we share   this flesh   we
bring together   it hurts to
think of dying as we lie close

In the realm of private loves Feinstein can convey the kind of rare emotion she found in Marina Tsvetayeva, whom she praised in the introduction to her translations for the "wholeness of her self-exposure." She also, however, goes beyond the purely personal. *At the Edge* evokes a new understanding reached through the "lyric daze" of carnal passion but makes it clear that the knowledge gained at these frontiers can only be kept through the interpretative but distancing medium of poetic language: "We were washed in salt on the same pillow together / and we watched the walls change level gently as water."

The title poem of her 1973 collection *The Celebrants* recounts the perpetual struggle for meaning through love, science, art, and religion, seeking to evade the limits of death and corruption bounding the world of the body, waiting for the gratuitous moment of poetic surprise "to free us from the / black drama / of the magician." The other poems in this volume have a darker tone than earlier work, a deeper and richer seriousness, and a more biting and bitter humor. *Some Unease and Angels,* essentially a well-chosen retrospect with some new poems, confirms Feinstein's determination to create through language a new balance of man, woman, and their world with nature and its warring elements, as in "Watersmeet":

everywhere plant flesh
and rich ores had eaten into each other, so that
peat, rain, green leaves and August fused
even the two of us together; we took

a new balance from the two defenceless
kingdoms bonded in hidden warfare underfoot.

In Feinstein's work published in the 1980s—*The Feast of Euridice* and the "Nine Songs for Dido and Aeneas"—the perspective of myth and legend throws that balance back into question. Virgil's epic celebration of empire is brilliantly turned into a denunciation of the devouring lust for power and possession that drives the imperialist hero. Dido's ancient, orderly kingdom, freely offering its nurturing affections to exorcise Aeneas's ghosts, is laid waste by his ambitions. But at the end, it is Dido who wins immortality, not by any witch's magic but by natural powers of endurance and love.

Badlands collects together, across time and space, landscapes of exile, suffering, and loss. Present-day California is given over to "entrepreneurs and bandits"; in England "the old gods are leaving"; in Carthage and Ithaca, or deep in the volcanic passage to Hades, Dido, Penelope, and Eurydice yearn toward hopelessly lost loves; in dream and in reality childhood homes or empty lodging house rooms enshrine the absences of dead parents or of poet friends. Again, the volume pays tribute to the necessary pain of poetry. Mute matter must be forced to speak: to release the dead soul in "England," the poet must "crack the / tarmac of the language." The poet too must constantly "fight for breath" ("Park Parade, Cambridge"). Turn and turn about, Feinstein's poetry demonstrates its double face: the cool Apollonian "weaving and waiting," practiced by the waking Penelope, and the frenzied onslaught on language in Penelope's dream, presided over by Dionysus or by "Hermes, the twister, the pivoter" ("Three Songs for Ithaca"). The god-magician enters Penelope's sleep with language that embodies the cruel mystery of poetic creation, "to remind me of strangers, returning, who speak in the language / of timberwolves, feeding on human flesh, sorcerer's prey." The loose, twisting syntax and the savage, melodramatic vocabulary generate a radical disturbance that evokes the sacred terror of the poetic experience: "I blench at his voice."

Landscapes of exile, suffering, and loss also enter Feinstein's work through her Jewish heritage, as well as through her role as one of the pioneers of woman-centered poetry in the 1960s and 1970s, during the start of the feminist movement. While not an explicitly "Jewish" poet, she acknowledged the influence of her heritage in an interview with Michele Roberts:

As a poet, you mustn't have a very hard outside wall to protect you, and so you receive a great deal of damage. Yet you have to move on and continue. Perhaps that is similar to the way in which the Jewish sensibility has survived.

—Jennifer Birkett

FELL, Alison

Nationality: Scottish. **Born:** Dumfries, Scotland, 4 June 1944. **Education:** Edinburgh College of Art, diploma in sculpture, 1967; Institute of Education, University of London, education certificate, 1980. **Family:** Married Roger Coleman in 1964 (divorced 1965); one son. **Career:** Wrote for *Scotland Magazine,* 1962; co-founder, Welfare State (radical theatre group), Leeds, England, 1969, and Women's Street Theatre Group, London, 1971; worked as a journalist in London; member of editorial board, *Spare Rib*, 1975—; active in women's rights movement; runs writer's workshops. Writer-in-residence, New South Wales Institute of Technology, 1986; member, Greater London Arts Literature Panel, 1984-86. **Awards:** Alice Hunt Bartlett Award for poetry, 1984, for *Kisses for Mayakovsky;* Boardman Tasker Award for Mountain Literature, 1991, for *Mer de Glace*. **Agent:** Tony Peake, Peake Associates, 14 Grafton Crescent, London NW1 8SL, Engand.

PUBLICATIONS

Poetry

Kisses for Mayakovsky. London, Virago, 1984.
The Crystal Owl. London, Methuen, 1988.
Dreams, like Heretics. London, Serpent's Tail, 1997.

Novels

The Grey Dancer (juvenile). London, Collins, 1981.
Every Move You Make (autobiographical). London, Virago, 1984.
The Bad Box. London, Virago, 1987.
Mer de Glace. London, Methuen, 1991.
The Pillow Boy of the Lady Onogoro. London, Serpent's Tail, 1994.

Plays

Radio Play: *The Shining Mountain*, 1989; *Whispers in the Dark*, 1995.

Other

Editor, *Hard Feelings: Fiction and Poetry from Spare Rib*. London, Women's Press, 1979.
Editor, *The Seven Deadly Sins*. London, Serpent's Tail, 1988.

*   *   *

Poet, novelist, children's author, and passionate campaigner for feminist causes—Alison Fell has directed her talents into a number of channels with remarkable energy and commitment. She had contributed more than a dozen poems to each of two feminist anthologies published during the 1970s before her first collection, *Kisses for Mayakovsky*, appeared. At this time she was working in London in the Women's Street Theater Group and for various left-wing and feminist publications including the magazine *Spare Rib*. Fell's poems, in both subject matter and mode of expression, reflected the concerns voiced in the preamble to the first of the anthologies, *Licking the Bed Clean*. She and her four fellow contributors declared: "we agreed that it is vital as feminists and writers to express what we *are*, even if it isn't what we would like to be, and to try and honestly grasp the tension of that contradiction." Fell's first priority as a poet, then, was to achieve self-expression as a woman aware both "of feminist struggle and change" and of how "female subject matter has generally been ignored or trivialised within the predominantly male literary tradition." What matters, in this view, is not so much the achievement of literary merit as the accurate depiction of what was being felt and thought at the moment reported on.

In line with this agenda, *Kisses for Mayakovsky* contains many poems which consciously "attempt to spread new politics" both in feminist and a wider sense. The volume's penultimate poem, "The Hallowe'en Witch" celebrates women who cut the wires of the perimeter fence around a U.S. airbase (Greenham Common) as part of a persistent campaign against the facility. Another ("The Victors") blazes with indignation about the deaths in 1977 of three hijackers at Mogadishu airport in Somalia, and of three members of the (West) German Baader-Meinhof urban guerrilla group who committed suicide in prison:

Six more silences
for the State,
the wrong voices
stilled
and the grey-faced liars
whirr out murder

However, Fell's complex personality mixes vulnerable elements with the volcanic, and other poems develop more private and intimate themes. There is poignancy in "The Wish," which describes a dream that touches on the problem of communication:

And on the shelf of the shore,
slanting like a long wish,
a mailbox stood askew
in the warp of weathers;
a tarpaulin lid banging loose
a blue letter
a promise of return

Tenderness surfaces in "Girl's gifts", about a little girl making a flower basket for her grandmother: "I will carry it cupped like a jewel or a robin's egg / It will lie, perfect, in her wrinkled palm / I will cross the grass and give it." And "Stripping Blackcurrants" offers humor besides sensuality in its account of the mounting desire which a woman picked blackcurrants feels for her friend lying on a garden rug. To no avail

I flaunt my golden back,
It glows from within, a raging aura.
Unbelievable, how you resist me.
You read.
The bush catches fire.

A similar range of public and private themes is tackled with characteristic confidence and muscular imagination in *A Crystal Owl*. Poems on friendship and family contact include the title poem, which mulls over a meeting with the author's sister in Tasmania. Images reflecting coldness and death suggest the underlying unease:

An ancient fridge
hums at the heart
of my sister's house
Dead
hydrangea heads
bludgeon the high window.

Concerns of a public kind are examined in poems on issues such as the siege of a Palestinian refugee camp outside Beirut, and the trial in South Africa of two Afrikaners sentenced to death for the murder of a black girl. Whether Fell's wholehearted espousal of the roles of polemicist and propagandist ultimately makes or mars her work, it cannot be disputed that this angry sense of mission results in poems of considerable—at times disconcerting—force. Some readers might even find themselves shocked by a poem like "Atlanta Streets" which describes a vicious encounter in that city. Or they could feel uneasy at the way in which for Fell the knife often seems to emblematize communication between the sexes: "like me do you like my gash" ("Knife"). But it seems unlikely that Fell would be disturbed by such reactions. On the contrary, she would probably argue that a campaign to redirect the moral aspirations of a complacent society could not operate without the high octane fuel of a capacity to shock.

—Rivers Carew

FINNIGAN, Joan

Nationality: Canadian. **Born:** Ottawa, Ontario, 23 November 1925. **Education:** Lisgar Collegiate, graduated 1945; Carleton University, Ottawa; Queen's University, Kingston, Ontario, B.A. in English, history, and economics, 1967. **Family:** Married Charles Grant MacKenzie in 1949 (died 1965); two sons and one daughter. **Career:** Teacher in Beechgrove, Quebec, 1945-46; reporter, Ottawa *Journal,* and freelance journalist, 1949-67; public relations, promotion, and special events director, Kingston and District United Way, 1969-74. Freelance writer for the National Film Board of Canada, 1966-71, and the Canadian Broadcasting Corporation, Toronto. Writer-in-residence, Ottawa Public Library, 1987. Also photographer: individual shows—Upstairs Gallery, Renfrew, Ontario, 1982; Gallery Cafe, Pembroke, Ontario, 1982; Octogan Gallery Show, Calabogie, Ontario, 1986; Ottawa Public Library, 1988. **Awards:** Borestone Mountain poetry prize, 1959, 1961, 1963; Canada Council grant, 1965, 1967, 1968, 1969, 1973, 1977; Centennial prize, 1967; President's Medal, University of Western Ontario, 1969; Genie award, for screenplay, 1969; Ottawa-Carleton literary award, 1986; Pat Lowther award, 1988; Trillium Award shortlist, 1992. **Address:** Moore Farm, Hambly Lake, Hartington, Ontario K0H 1W0, Canada.

PUBLICATIONS

Poetry

Through the Glass, Darkly. Toronto, Ryerson Press, 1963.
A Dream of Lilies. Fredericton, New Brunswick, Fiddlehead, 1965.
Entrance to the Green-house. Toronto, Ryerson Press, 1968.
It Was Warm and Sunny When We Set Out. Toronto, Ryerson Press, 1970.
In the Brown Cottage on Loughborough Lake. Toronto, CBC Learning Systems, 1970.
Living Together. Fredericton, New Brunswick, Fiddlehead, 1976.
A Reminder of Familiar Faces. Toronto, NC Press, 1978.
This Series Has Been Discontinued. Fredericton, New Brunswick, Fiddlehead, 1981.

The Watershed Collection, edited by Robert Weaver. Kingston, Ontario, Quarry Press, 1988.
Wintering Over. Kingston, Ontario, Quarry Press, 1992.

Plays

Up the Vallee! (produced Toronto, 1978).
Songs from Both Sides of the River (produced Ottawa, 1987-1992).

Screenplay: *The Best Damn Fiddler from Calabogie to Kaladar,* 1969.

Radio Plays: *Songs for the Bible Belt; May Day Rounds: Renfrew County; In the Brown Cottage on Loughborough Lake; Children of the Shadows; There's No Good Times Left—None at All; Coming over a Country of No Lights,* 1976; *The Lakers,* 1977; *Valley of the Outaouais,* 1979; *Poems from Pontiac County,* 1984.

Other

Canada in Bed (as Michelle Bedard). Toronto, Pagurian Press, 1967.
Kingston: Celebrate This City. Toronto, McClelland & Stewart, 1976.
I Come from the Valley. Toronto, NC Press, 1976.
Canadian Colonial Cooking. Toronto, NC Press, 1976.
Canada, Country of the Giants. Burnstown, Ontario, General Store, 1981.
Giants of Canada's Ottawa Valley. Burnstown, Ontario, General Store, 1981.
Some of the Stories I Told You Were True. Ottawa, Deneau, 1981.
Look! The Land Is Growing Giants: A Very Canadian Legend (for children). Montreal, Tundra, 1983.
Laughing All the Way Home. Ottawa, Deneau, 1984.
Legacies, Legends, and Lies. Toronto, Deneau, 1985; revised edition, Kingston, Ontario, Quarry Press, 1987.
Finnigan's Guide to the Ottawa Valley. Kingston, Ontario, Quarry Press, 1988.
Tell Me Another Story. Toronto, McGraw Hill-Ryerson, 1988.
The Dog Who Wouldn't Be Left Behind (for children). Toronto, Groundwood 1989.
Old Scores, New Goals. Kingston, Ontario, Quarry Press, 1992.
Lisgar Collegiate, 1843-1993. Ottawa, Ontario, Lisgar Alumni Association, 1993.
Witches, Ghosts and Loups-Garous. Kingston, Ontario, Quarry Press, 1994.

*

Manuscript Collections: Queen's University, Kingston, Ontario; National Library, Ottawa.

Joan Finnigan comments:

Since the age of seven I have been writing poetry. At 40 I came to creative film-scripts and so began to write long poems. My poetry had always veered towards the dramatic and my film-scripts are strongly poetic: done with intensity, a boiling down to the quintessence, a search for ultimate essence. At 40 I had matured enough to move from the short form—the poem—to the one requiring greater sustaining power—the screenplay. At 60 *The*

Watershed Collection, a collection of the best of all my long poems edited and with an introduction by Robert Weaver of CBC Anthology, was a milestone in my movement in the poetic direction; *Songs from Both Sides of the River,* my 1987 play at the National Art Centre, Ottawa, was a high-water mark in the dramatic course of my work. I am working seriously on fiction now but I know that, when I grow older and wiser, I will be able to return to my poetry.

*   *   *

That "poetry is not a turning loose of emotion but an escape from emotion" has become axiomatic in the criticism and the writing of modern poetry. In Canada, this consciousness is central to the work of E.J. Pratt and the poets of the McGill Movement, and it is emblematized in the wilderness-garden mythos of the Frye school of poets from D.G. Jones to Margaret Atwood. The rejection of facile Romanticism at the core of Eliot's pronouncement was germane to the poetics initiated in the 1920s in Canada as a reaction against nineteenth-century Confederation Poets. At any rate, it is a commonplace now that the eternal verities can be improved upon by being expressed in a diction and vision attuned to the age.

Thus, it is no small surprise to encounter the poetry of Joan Finnigan celebrating a domestic world revolving around family life: the family cottage, family friends, love, and nature rendered in language free from sophistication. An openness toward self and others characterizes an outlook whose subjective correlative is the operations of benevolent nature. Finnigan's world is Edenic and pristine, dominated by radiant colors and cheerful sounds controlled by the key symbol of the sun shining at the height of summer. There exudes a feeling of oneness with the elements that culminates in transcendental intimations of immortality, no doubt sincerely felt by the poet. Eve-like, but unlike Eve since her boundless innocence cannot precipitate any Fall of Man, she celebrates a garden whose paradisiacal emoluments she has no reason to suspect. To be sure, a few queries are raised ("Oh, who in all of heathendom, / Is half so sad as I?"), but they pose no threat of disruption to this Arcadia, where no vital concerns are entertained.

Finnigan's two favorite themes—love and nature—recur in her books. The related feelings of nostalgia, flight of time, and urbanophobia conveying an undercurrent of sweet melancholy are accentuated with the intrusion of death. In *It Was Warm and Sunny When We Set Out,* the theme is, at first, embarrassingly stated— "And I think perpetually now of your dead HEART (for no one could get directions to that place, not even yourself)..."—in the not surprising, ingenuous confessional style—"Who, who could ever believe our private murders or the possibility of this revenge?"—which Finnigan delights in. It finds a more felicitous expression, however, in the contrasting use of symbols. The sun that hitherto glowed on a bountiful world presently reflects the destruction of the Covenant: it is blinding, bleeding, mocking, scorching. Though the diction falters—"If people really love one another, / snow, why do they die?"—one finds interesting, nonetheless, the substitution of the symbolic winter grip for the vision of warmth generated by summer.

The intensity of personal suffering finally yields a sober consciousness in *In the Brown Cottage on Loughborough Lake.* In a book markedly contrasting with Finnigan's earlier work, the weaving of alternating polarities (light and dark, summer and autumn, outer life and inner life, life and death, happiness and sorrow) ger-

minates in the mature expression of pain endured, challenged, and possibly conquered. Her beloved nature is still there, as anthropomorphic as ever, the language is still mined with clichés, the world as restricted as usual. But this elegy, which can all too easily be assigned to the Wordsworthian canon, is quite moving in its expression of emotions barely recovering from the trauma of exposure to the existence of pain and cruelty. Even fractionally, Finnigan has been able to master and contain pain and bear witness to this control over emotion by finding a structure of objective correlatives. Maybe Eliot was not wrong after all.

—Max Dorsinville

FORCHÉ, Carolyn (Louise)

Nationality: American. **Born:** Detroit, Michigan, 28 April 1950. **Education:** Michigan State University, East Lansing, B.A. in international relations and creative writing 1972; Bowling Green State University, Ohio, M.F.A. 1975. **Family:** Married Harry E. Mattison in 1984; one son. **Career:** Visiting lecturer, Michigan State University, 1974; visiting lecturer, 1975, and assistant professor, 1976-78, San Diego State University; visiting lecturer, University of Virginia, Charlottesville, 1979, 1982-83; assistant professor, 1980, and associate professor, 1981, University of Arkansas, Fayetteville; visiting lecturer, New York University, 1983, 1985, and Vassar College, Poughkeepsie, New York, 1984; adjunct associate professor, Columbia University, New York, 1984-85; writer-in-residence, State University of New York, Albany, 1985; visiting associate professor, University of Minnesota, Minneapolis, summer 1985. Poetry editor, *New Virginia Review,* Norfolk, 1981; editor, *Tendril,* Green Harbor, Massachusetts. Journalist for Amnesty International in El Salvador, 1978-80, and Beirut correspondent, "All Things Considered" radio program, 1983. **Awards:** Yale Series of Younger Poets award 1975; *Chicago Review* award, 1975; Devine Memorial prize, 1975, Bread Loaf Writers Conference Tennessee Williams fellowship, 1976; National Endowment for the Arts fellowship, 1977, 1984; Guggenheim fellowship, 1978; Emily Clark Balch prize, *Virginia Quarterly Review,* 1979; Lamont Poetry Selection award, 1981 Poetry Society of America Alice Fay di Castagnola award, 1981. H.D.L.: Russell Sage College, Troy, New York, 1985. **Agent:** Virginia Barber Literary Agency, 101 5th Avenue, 11th Floor, New York, New York 10003, U.S.A.

PUBLICATIONS

Poetry

Gathering the Tribes. New Haven, Connecticut, Yale University Press, 1976.
The Country between Us. Port Townsend, Washington, Copper Canyon Press, 1981; London, Cape, 1983.
The Angel of History. New York, HarperCollins, and Newcastle upon Tyne, Bloodaxe, 1994.

Recording: *Ourselves, or Nothing,* Watershed, 1982.

Other

Women in American Labor History 1825-1935: *An Annotated Bibliography,* with Martha Jane Soltow. East Lansing, Michigan State University School of Labor and Industrial Relations, 1972.

El Salvador: The Work of 30 Photographers, edited by Harry Mattison, Susan Meiselas, and Fae Rubenstein. New York and London, Writers and Readers, 1983.

Colors Come from God—Just like Me, illustrated by Charles Cox. Nashville, Abingdon, 1995.

Editor, *Women and War in El Salvador.* New York, Women's International Resource Exchange, 1980.

Editor, *Against Forgetting: Twentieth-Century Poetry of Witness.* New York, Norton, 1993.

Translator, *Flowers from the Volcano,* by Claribel Alegria. Pittsburgh, University of Pittsburgh Press, 1982.

*

Critical Study: By Terrence Diggory, in *Salmagundi* (Saratoga Springs, New York), Spring 1984.

*   *   *

Since the publication of Carolyn Forché's second collection of poems, *The Country between Us,* she has become visible as a political poet, as well as a poet of consummate craft. (The latter is attested to by the fact that her first book won the Yale Younger Poets award; the second, the Lamont.) But there are dangers in all such categorizations: to call Forché "political" is to deny the excellence of all her poems, not only those that deal with life in El Salvador or the political concerns of both America and the world. Forché is political in the broadest, healthiest possible sense, in that her poems grow from the genuine, intense concerns of the poet as living person. They bespeak her age, her craft, her education, her origins, her sex, and her intellectual persuasions. They also reflect the fact that she spent a number of years living in El Salvador, becoming a translator of several poets, a friend of many others, and a keen observer of life in that country. But her Salvadoran experience is no more important to her development as a poet than was her experience in the desert of the American Southwest or in the Midwest. Forché is a poet who uses whatever she has experienced, transmuting her material regardless of its source into sharply defined images that reach far past the personal or local.

Forché's roots are clearly in the Williams and Roethke schools of American poetry, but she has moved past their sometimes academic limitations to a free expression of all her concerns. She is an impassioned poet, whether she writes about a girlhood friend she has lost track of, a dying idealist, or a brutal military man. Whatever subject Forché chooses, the shape and movement of the poem evokes the appropriate mood.

Forché is a poet of great versatility. What unifies poems in her collections is not style, but rather the repetition of images. Images of loss, absence, muted or stilled voices, broken lives, the simple and often tawdry objects of poverty, and—in contrast—touch appear in poems that range from stark external description to implicit dramatic monologue to letter to confession.

When Forché writes in "The Visitor," a short, image-centered poem, "In Spanish he whispers there is no time left," she estab-

lishes the pattern of language forestalled, forbidden. That whisper is amplified in other of the Salvadoran poems. "The Memory of Elena" gives us apparent language ("We find a table, ask for *paella...*As she talks, the hollow / clopping of a horse, the sound / of bones touched together"), but the central image, of the dark tongues of bells, ends in perversion. "The Island" also re-creates language, a dialogue between the poet persona and the worn Salvadoran woman, who insistently demands, "Carolina, do you know how long it takes / any one voice to reach another?" "San Onofre, California" sets up another ironic dialogue between the living and the missing. Ironically, the only successful communication in *The Country between Us* occurs in "The Colonel," when the military figure pours a sackful of human ears on the dinner table where the poet has been dining. Speech has been realized, but instead of saving, it desecrates everything human. *The Country Between Us* becomes Forché's "epistemology of loss," just as *Gathering the Tribes* was her more positive statement of human endurance. As she writes in "Message," where voices are "sprayed over the walls / dry to the touch of morning" and patriots are sent off to be killed as the poet pledges,

> I will live
> and living cry out until my voice is gone
> to its hollow of earth, where with our
> hands and by the lives we have chosen
> we will dig deep into our deaths.

For all the variety of Forché's forms, for all the somber stain of her Salvadoran experience, for all the poignancy of her personal fabric of recollection, *The Country between Us* succeeds in creating a sense of joy. "Because One Is Always Forgotten," "Poem for Maya," "Ourselves or Nothing," "For the Stranger"—each poem embodies images and tones of hope: "all things human take time"; "We have, each of us, nothing. / We will give it to each other."

Forché's poems are meditative and lyrical, narrative and songlike. They draw from dream and myth, both directly and subtly. They escape categorization as they lace together images of terrain and language, touch and separation, brutality and love that are so closely related as to fuse through metaphor. The unity of Forché's collections is achieved through a singleness of vision, a finely expressed, various vision, delightful in its chameleon-like trappings despite the seriousness of its intention. She has become a major poet.

—Linda W. Wagner-Martin

FRAME, Janet (Paterson)

Nationality: New Zealander. **Born:** Dunedin, 28 August 1924. **Education:** Oamaru North School; Waitaki Girls' High School; University of Otago Teachers Training College, Dunedin. **Awards:** Hubert Church Prose award, 1952, 1964, 1974; New Zealand Literary Fund award, 1960; New Zealand Scholarship in Letters, 1964, and Award for Achievement, 1969; University of Otago Robert Burns fellowship, 1965; Buckland Literary award 1967; James Wattie award, 1983, 1985; Commonwealth Writers prize, 1989. D.Litt.: University of Otago, 1978. C.B.E. (Commander, Order of the British Empire), 1983. **Address:** P.O. Box 1118, Palmerston North, New Zealand.

PUBLICATIONS

Poetry

The Pocket Mirror. New York, Braziller, and London, W.H. Allen, 1967.

Novels

Owls Do Cry. Christchurch, Pegasus Press, 1957; New York, Braziller, 1960; London, W.H. Allen, 1961.
Faces in the Water. Christchurch, Pegasus Press, and New York, Braziller, 1961; London, W.H. Allen, 1962.
The Edge of the Alphabet. Christchurch, Pegasus Press, New York, Braziller, and London, W.H. Allen, 1962.
Scented Gardens for the Blind. Christchurch, Pegasus Press, and London, W.H. Allen, 1963; New York, Braziller, 1964.
The Adaptable Man. Christchurch, Pegasus Press, New York, Braziller, and London, W.H. Allen, 1965.
A State of Siege. New York, Braziller, 1966; London, W.H. Allen, 1967.
The Rainbirds. London, W.H. Allen, 1968; as *Yellow Flowers in the Antipodean Room,* New York, Braziller, 1969.
Intensive Care. New York, Braziller, 1970; London, W.H. Allen, 1971.
Daughter Buffalo. New York, Braziller, 1972; London, W.H. Allen, 1973.
Living in the Maniototo. New York, Braziller, 1979; London, Women's Press, 1981.
The Carpathians. London, Bloomsbury, and New York, Braziller, 1988.

Short Stories

The Lagoon: Stories. Christchurch, Caxton Press, 1952; revised edition, as *The Lagoon and Other Stories,* 1961; London, Bloomsbury, 1991.
The Reservoir: Stories and Sketches. New York, Braziller, 1963.
Snowman, Snowman: Fables and Fantasies. New York, Braziller, 1963.
The Reservoir and Other Stories. Christchurch, Pegasus Press, and London, W.H. Allen, 1966.
You Are Now Entering the Human Heart. Wellington, Victoria University Press, 1983; London, Women's Press, 1984.

Other

Mona Minim and the Smell of the Sun (for children). New York, Braziller, 1969.
An Autobiography. Auckland, Century Hutchinson, 1989; London, Women's Press, 1990; New York, Braziller, 1991.
  1. *To the Is-Land.* New York, Braziller, 1982; London, Women's Press, 1983.
  2. *An Angel at My Table.* Auckland, Hutchinson, New York, Braziller, and London, Women's Press, 1984.
  3. *The Envoy from Mirror City.* Auckland, Hutchinson, New York, Braziller, and London, Women's Press, 1985.
The Janet Frame Reader, edited by Carole Ferrier. London, Women's Press, 1995.

*

Media Adaptations: *Three Poems of Janet Frame* (musical composition by Malcolm Speirs), 1985; *An Angel at My Table,* 1991.

Bibliography: By John Beston, in *World Literature Written in English* (Arlington, Texas), November 1978.

Critical Studies: *An Inward Sun: The Novels of Janet Frame,* Wellington, New Zealand University Press, 1971, and *Janet Frame,* Boston, Twayne, 1977, both by Patrick Evans; *Bird, Hawk, Bogie: Essays on Janet Frame* edited by Jeanne Delbaere, Aarhus, Denmark, Dangaroo Press, 1978; *Janet Frame* by Margaret Dalziel, Wellington, Oxford University Press, 1981; *The Ring of Fire: Essays on Janet Frame* edited by Jeanne Delbaere, Sydney, Dangaroo Press, 1992; *I Have What I Gave: The Fiction of Janet Frame* by Judith Dell Panny, New York, Braziller, 1993.

*   *   *

Best known as a writer of short stories, novels, and autobiography, Janet Frame writes verse that grapples with concerns similar to those of her prose in more condensed form, unmistakeably questioning intellectual assumptions and challenging our constructions of reality. Poetry saturates all her novels for to her the boundaries between the genres are amorphous. She has also published, in the collection *The Pocket Mirror* (1967), many poems that date from the period surrounding her tenure as Burns Fellow at Otago University (1965). Despite a cerebral cast, their settings are local and specific: North East Valley, and other Dunedin suburbs, including landscapes of her early Otago childhood. In "Wyndham" the depopulated railway town's desolation evokes bitter-sweet loss:

> The big stick
> has given up stirring
> the Wyndham pool. Stones do not move here;
> people sleep while
> the cows make milk
> the sheep
> make wool
> and in the empty
> railway houses
> no Dad sits each morning
> on the
> satin-smooth dunny seat.

Frame's interest in exotic landscapes is minimal. Other locations are generalised, or non-existent, for as with the novels investigation of the construction of reality dominates over its representation. Language, the slippery vehicle by which we define reality, is also scrutinised. The title poem of the collection suggests that linguistic misconceptions stem from a basic distortion in perception, and to misread visual images is to engage in a form of self-deception. The pocket mirror reflects manufactured light, revealing an inconsistency (imaged as street lamp-lights going out) due to imperceptible bands of darkness. Light's imperfect appearance to the eye symbolises the human incapacity for "too much reality," and correlates to an imperfect way of speaking:

> To undeceive the sight a detached instrument like a mirror is necessary.
> The human sense never speak the truth if they can get away with it.

Frequently anthologised pieces like "Yet Another Poem about a Dying Child" and "The Clown" illustrate Frame's habitual deconstruction of binary oppositions: life and death, presence and absence; truth and fiction. These dislocations jolt familiar stereotypes into newly resonant meanings: the dying child hates adult compassion and waits for the "kind furred spider ... with the night lamp eyes" who will "carry him home / to a dark place and eat him." The Clown's tears inspire an address to sterotypical figures and their interchangeable opposites, because single meanings ("one truth") are never enough for a complex world:

> Dear crying clown death childlike old man
> dear kind murderer dear innocent guilty
> dear simplicity I hate you for making me pretend
> there are several worlds to one truth when
> I know, I know there are not.

Frame's ironic, satiric mode is omnipresent: in "Wet Morning" "cunningly contrived," bisexual earthworms, washed away by rain, are comemmorated as "the official precis of woman and man." Intertextual allusion and cliché are used with devastating effect: "I must go down to the seas again / to find where I / buried the hatchet with Yesterday"; and her epithets convey, lurchingly, her uniquely comic-serious vision. In "Her Thoughts": "Her thoughts like poppies go to sleep in their clothes / With no west wind to iron out the creases in the morning," and in "The Sun": "The sun / is a universal / shining / bank messenger / with a consuming inner life / and an Honours Degree in Perspective."

Like the verse in *The Pocket Mirror*, the poetry of the novels pays scant attention to the formal demands of rhyme scheme and stanza form. It ranges from familiar nursery rhymes, to brief, pithy, unrhymed verse, or to extended meditations often constituting a separate chapter. The prose-verse is always typographically distinct (lineated, indented, italicized), and it may either represent a character's thoughts, or in the narrator's voice allude to the story, or project authorial anxieties. Indeed Frame's use of verse interactively with prose seems to extend her fictional concerns, by inflecting different voices or introducing alternative discourses. She has published no verse formally since *The Pocket Mirror*, but her importance as a poet will only be recognised when her verse is studied in the widest sense of its generic possibilities: the innovative poetry of the novels in relation to the prose in which it is embedded, and also in relation to the poetry published independently in this volume.

—Janet Wilson

FRASER, Kathleen

Nationality: American. **Born:** Tulsa, Oklahoma, 22 March 1937.
Education: Occidental College, Los Angeles, B.A. in English 1959;
Columbia University and New School for Social Research, both
New York, 1960-61; San Francisco State University, 1976-77,
Doctoral Equivalency in creative writing. **Family:** Married Jack
Marshall in 1961 (divorced 1970); one son. **Career:** Visiting professor, Writers Workshop, University of Iowa, Iowa City, 1969-71; writer-in-residence. Reed College, Portland, Oregon, 1971-72.
Director of the Poetry Center, 1972-75, associate professor of
creative writing, 1975-78, and since 1978 professor, San Francisco
State University. Founding editor, *HOW(ever)*. **Awards:**
YMYWHA Discovery award, 1964; National Endowment for the
Arts grant, 1969, and fellowship, 1978. **Address:** 1936
Leavenworth Street, San Francisco, California 94133, U.S.A.

PUBLICATIONS

Poetry

Change of Address and Other Poems. San Francisco, Kayak, 1966.
In Defiance of the Rains. Santa Cruz, California, Kayak, 1969.
Little Notes to You from Lucas Street. Iowa City, Penumbra Press, 1972.
What I Want. New York, Harper, 1974.
Magritte Series. Willits, California, Tuumba Press, 1978.
New Shoes. New York, Harper, 1978.
Each Next. Great Barrington, Massachusetts, Figures, 1980.
Something (Even Human Voices) in the Foreground, A Lake. Berkeley, California, Kelsey State Press, 1984.
Notes Preceding Trust. Venice, California, Lapis Press, 1987.
Boundary. Santa Monica, California, Lapis Press, 1988.
Giotto, Arena. Elmwood, Connecticut, Abacus, 1991.
when new time folds up. Minneapolis, Chax Press, 1993.
il cuores: The Heart, Selected Poems 1970-1995. Middletown, Connecticut, Wesleyan University Press, 1997.

Recordings: *The Poetry of Kathleen Fraser*, McGraw Hill, n.d.; *Even Human Voices*, Watershed, 1986.

Other (for children)

Stilts, Somersaults, and Headstands: Game Poems Based on a Painting by Peter Breughel. New York, Atheneum, 1968.
Adam's World: San Francisco, with Miriam F. Levy. Chicago, Whitman. 1971.

Other

Editor, *Feminist Poetics: A Consideration of the Female Construction of Language.* San Francisco, San Francisco State University, 1984.

*

Critical Study: *Poetics of the Feminine: Authority and Literary Tradition in William Carlos Williams, Mina Loy, Denise Levertov, and Kathleen Fraser,* by Linda A. Kinnahan. Cambridge, Cambridge University Press, 1994.

Kathleen Fraser comments:
  My poetry has moved from girlish, Plath-fed lyrics, first published in the mid-1960s, towards a recognition—inside the poem—of life as a more undecided and precarious process. Language is, for me, exploratory—the fluid and changing record of daily risk-taking. I use my writing to locate myself in particulars, to catch the multiplicity, the layering of thoughts, feelings, visual impressions experienced simultaneously. Writing is, in a sense, taking a reading on what has thus far transpired and what my attitude to-

ward it is...there is, hopefully, a movement back and forth. I use my poetry as my most serious way of paying attention to the world outside of my own interior struggle. The poems begin as acts of attention and try to allow in whatever is there waiting to make itself heard. And seen. I regard the ability to write as a gift which must be honored with the utmost seriousness. My great permission-giver, in learning to use that gift, was Frank O'Hara. He still appears in my dreams as a guide and friend. I am also deeply indebted to Virginia Woolf and Gertrude Stein, for complexity. American jazz (particularly Eddie Jefferson's lyrics and Betty Carter's scat) has made a much greater range of tonalities and movements available to me. Painting has always been important and often provides paths to unconscious material which I bring into the poetry. Surely my father's early chanting of limericks and lyrics from *Alice through the Looking-Glass* will always be there as playful resonance in my work. And my mother's singing. To catch the exact angle of light as two planes shift. To catch the unbroken moment between two people and speak it.

*   *   *

Kathleen Fraser's early poetry bears the imprint of the New York school, especially of Kenneth Koch, with whom she studied in the 1960s. The tone is one of playful self-mockery, as in

> But over here, where it's dark out,
>   I'm just me
>   feeling uneasy in these nights
> cold and black.
>   I turn the heat up
>   higher
> thinking other people's lives
> are warmer

In "Because You Aren't Here to Be What I Can't Think Of," Fraser invents a dazzling inventory reminiscent of Koch's "Sleeping with Women" or Frank O'Hara's "Having a Coke with You." In this catalog poem the speaker blithely tries to convince herself that she is *not* going to care about her lover's involvement with someone else, all the while doing everything in her power to conjure up his presence. The distance between the lovers takes on fantastic proportions: "Because the moon's another streetlight and your lights are off, and on in someone else's," or "Because there's a saxophone playing between our telephones but you can't pick it up." Yet, injured party that she is, the speaker wryly and wisely concludes that, life being what it is, things could be worse: "because I'm not on a dancefloor with you, but here, / hanging out with my shadow over a city of windows, / lit-up, imagining another kind of life almost like this one." The lover's absence is irritating but not, finally, tragic. The same rueful comedy and witty analysis are found in "The Fault," in which the poet watches another woman make the wrong moves toward a man she herself has not hitherto paid much notice to but whom she now suddenly finds an attractive challenge:

> I felt myself in love with him watching his tongue run
> over his lips
>
> and remembered Fredericka
>
> always keeping the tube of vaseline in her purse

> always gliding it over her mouth should there be someone
> to kiss
>
> and thought how I liked space and long unending lines,
>   how my life
> was that way, without visible connections or obvious
> explanations
>   how I was glad
> I'd washed my hair

From this early, jaunty poetry Fraser has moved on to compose a much more serious and ambitious lyric. The confluence of the feminist movement, in which Fraser has been extremely active—she was the founding editor of *HOW(ever),* an important journal of women's avant-garde poetry and poetics—and the language school, together with a strong sense of the visual arts, already latent in her New York period, gave birth to the series of prose poems and complex phenomenological lyrics collected in *New Shoes, Each Next,* and *Notes Preceding Trust.* "L'Invention Collective / Collective Invention" (one of the *Magritte Series*), for example, is based on the painter's grotesque and haunting image of a sort of reverse mermaid: a fish with human legs, slender and feminine, and with pubic hair. In Magritte's painting the fish-woman is oddly erotic and repulsive; the single blank fish eye confronts the beholder, whose eye is drawn downward to her (its?) lower parts. She lies on the edge of the beach, the whitecaps of a picture-book blue ocean beating pointlessly behind her. Fraser invents a narrative that can incorporate this image: her story is of a tacky domestic heroine, part comic book, part fairy tale, whose role in life is to keep things "neat and tidy," so that she is quite unable to "see / her seducers in a line and shaking their fingers." Only in her dreams does she see herself lying "at the edge of the waters," the sand scratching her body, and watch herself turn into a fish— "a face cut deep with gills and the sad eyes panting / and the absolute quiet of something about to arrive." What this something is we don't know, but it is frightening in the poem as well as in Magritte's painting. The pose of the figure invites rape, but what would that mean in this context? Fraser is playing with notions of smugness and self-deception, exploring the fantasy life of the little woman who wanted life for herself and her boy to be "as fresh as Watermelon slice."

The prose poems in *Each Next* carry on the painterly motive of the *Magritte Series,* but Fraser now fragments her texts, shifting from one pronoun to another and collaging snatches of conversation (remarks by Grace [Paley] and Francie [Shaw]) with images of green and blue (the swimming pool setting) and memories of previous swims, so as to create a taut "field of action" where words become the actors. The poet's drive toward greater density and ellipsis reaches its height in *Notes Preceding Trust,* many of whose poems are dark dreamscapes like "Everything You Ever Wanted," which begins with

> I do not trust these glaring invitations to break into green.
> An apple, viewed as a journey: have a bite, another bite.
> A red and yellow street, all dashes and splashing. Or white
> teeth moving in, just under the skin. First comes the
> comma, then the period. Walking on water, then stepping
> into a long breath trying to catch up. I am having trouble
> finding where to take the first step.

The narrative begins in a fairy-tale vein but is broken by "commonsense" observations like "First comes the comma, then the period." The ensuing dream creates a curious doubling: the poet is aware of her legs, tucked up under her, but sees them "swinging up and out over the edge to the floor." She starts to eat, but "there is nothing to eat but a small dish of buttons." Even when she awakes and finds "a key in my wine glass," put there by a "person I desire," she cannot respond. Rather, she is recalled to routine, to "the list of necessary distractions," where "Each task has a check mark next to it, a little gesture on the map's white silence." "Everything you wanted," this delicate prose poem implies, is nevertheless not within "your" grasp, for women are conditioned to be practical, to take care of others, to put "check marks" where they belong. Hence the difficulty of "break[ing] into green," a difficulty subtly dramatized in this and related poems in *Each Next.*

In her book *when new time folds up* (1993) Fraser moves into more public spaces. The lead poem, "Etruscan Places," alternates meditative free verse, pictograms, and documentary prose (for example, the letters to a friend named Annalisa) so as to probe the marks and traces of Etruscan culture as it continues to animate our lives today. Fraser's *einfühlung* into the artifacts of ancient Rome, into the "narrow walkway wide enough for territorial smuggle," is masterly on all counts. The "remorse" of the city becomes hers in these spare and delicate poems, poems that "include history" in new and subtle ways.

—Marjorie Perloff

FRENCH, Anne

Nationality: New Zealander. **Born:** Wellington, New Zealand, 5 March 1956. **Education:** Victoria University of Wellington, 1973-79, B.A. 1976, B.A. (honors) 1977; M.A. 1980; Auckland Secondary Teachers' College, Diploma in Teaching 1977. **Family:** One son. **Career:** Teaching assistant, Victoria University of Wellington, 1979; editor, 1980-82, Oxford University Press, Wellington; managing editor, 1982-89, and publisher, 1990-93, Oxford University Press, Auckland; managing editor, then publisher, Museums of New Zealand, Wellington, 1995—; managing editor, *New Zealand Strategic Management,* Auckland, 1994—. Writer-in-residence, Massey University, 1993. **Awards:** New Zealand Book award for poetry, 1988; PEN Best First Book of Poetry, 1988 **Address:** P.O. Box 1799, Wellington, New Zealand.

PUBLICATIONS

Poetry

All Cretans Are Liars. Auckland University Press, 1987.
The Male as Evader. Auckland University Press, 1988.
Cabin Fever. Auckland University Press, 1990.
Seven Days on Mykonos. Auckland University Press, 1993.

Other

Editor, *Elsdon Best—Maori Religion and Mythology, Part II.* Wellington, Government Printing Office, 1980.

*   *   *

One of the feminist writers who emerged in the 1980s, Anne French won the 1988 New Zealand Book award for poetry with her collection *All Cretans Are Liars* (1987). Its three parts move from personal disclosures to relationships with a lover to a nationalistic emphasis. The poetic comprehends both a modernist emphasis on form and diction and an intertextuality that verges on the postmodern, as in the pivotal "Eucalypts Greenlane," with its references to James Baxter, Allen Curnow, Ian Wedde, and T.S. Eliot. The earlier poems tend to be occasional, building a sense of immediacy as the narrator records an incident and then reflects on it. "Cricket," for example, begins with glimpses of a wet, desolate weekend, but by the second verse it moves to something more abstract:

That was how it appeared. The difference
between inventing something, and not
is imperceptible...

French's second collection, *The Male as Evader* (1988), pursues this relatively simple poetic in a vigorous series of poems about men's relationships to women. Many of the poems' titles, as well as the titles of the first two of the book's three sections ("A catalogue of evaders," "The language and literature of evasion"), reflect the collection's interest in males' possession of language and the problem of women in achieving some kind of status in relation to it. "The Dangers of Literature" begins

So I ended up in your book? That's
Marvellous to see myself undressed
and systematically examined in the clear
unblinking light of your malice.

Most of the poems maintain this tone and directness, but they have difficulty in solving the problem of female subjugation by language, which is at the center of the collection, as well as in dealing with the more basic entrapment by language that is represented by the traditional paradox of the title of her first collection. Only the last of the forty-four poems, "Catullus's answer book," deals with the problem and gestures beyond itself at a possibility of seeing a face reflected back that is "Not, necessarily, a man."

The claustrophobic feel of the second collection provides the title of French's third, *Cabin Fever* (1990), and its theme of journeying by sea. "In a North Harbour" begins

There's no room
for attitudes of renunciation or despair—not here,
not today, while sky waits to be filled with spinnaker...,

and in general the collection proceeds away from the earlier aggression. In fact, the collection is informed by the imagery of a male writer, Stéphane Mallarmé. Like him, French identifies with the voyager and sailor in order to escape constriction by exploring possible identities. In "The Words" the narrator learns the masculine world of sailing terms ("The leading edge of a sail is called the luff"), and more generally in the collection the boat represents some kind of continuing entrapment in male constructions, as well, paradoxically, as offering a dexterous maneuverability. But her narrator, as a woman, must leave the boat and enter the traditionally female element around it: "I—who have always been / incautious— swim out into the deep water" ("Motaketekete").

Seven Days on Mykonos (1993) gives a sense that the journey is completed, that territories have been mapped and boundaries fixed. The first section, "Postcards from Hamilton," represents a journey in poetry throughout the world. But there is also a sense of uncertainty once the boundaries have been reached. The remaining sections, "Stories from the Blue Chair" and "The Anthropology of New Zealand Literature," hark back to the themes of the earlier collections rather than pushing forward. In some of these poems French's customarily ironic tone is revealed as limited, particularly in those referring to the world of New Zealand literature, in which the tone may become edgy or even paranoiac, as in "New Zealanders at Home":

> ...while above their heads the admonitory
> pohutukawa points its blood-red sta-
> mens at nobody in particular.

—Anna Smith

FULTON, Alice

Nationality: American. **Born:** Troy, New York, 25 January 1952. **Education:** Empire State College, Albany, New York, B.A. in creative writing 1978; Cornell University, Ithaca, New York, M.F.A. in creative writing 1982. **Family:** Married Hank De Leo in 1980. **Career:** Assistant professor, 1983-86, William Wilhartz Professor, 1986-89, associate professor, 1990-92, professor of English, 1992—, University of Michigan, Ann Arbor. Visiting professor of creative writing, Vermont College, Montpelier, 1987, University of California, Los Angeles, 1991, Ohio State University, Columbus, 1995, and University of North Carolina, Wilmington, 1997. **Awards**: MacDowell Colony fellowship, 1978, 1979; Millay Colony fellowship, 1980; Emily Dickinson award, 1980; Academy of American Poets prize, 1982; Associated Writing Programs of America award, 1982; Consuelo Ford award, 1984; Rainer Maria Rilke award, 1984; Michigan Council for the Arts grant, 1986, 1991; Yaddo Colony fellowship, 1987; Guggenheim fellowship, 1986-87; Bess Hokin prize (*Poetry,* Chicago), 1989; Ingram Merrill Foundation award, 1990; Elizabeth Matchett Stover award, *Southwest Review,* 1994; John D. and Catherine T. MacArthur Foundation fellow, 1991-96. D.Litt: State University of New York, 1994. **Address:** 2370 LeForge Road, R.R. 13, Ypsilanti, Michigan 48198, U.S.A.

PUBLICATIONS

Poetry

Anchors of Light. Oneonta, New York, Swamp Press, 1979.
Dance Script with Electric Ballerina. Philadelphia, University of Pennsylvania Press, 1983.
Palladium. Urbana, University of Illinois Press, 1986.
Powers of Congress. Boston, Godine, 1990.
Sensual Math. New York, Norton, 1995.

*

Critical Studies: By David Lehman, in *Epoch* (Ithaca, New York), vol. 36, no. 3, 1986-87; "Bright Sources" by Stephen Yenser, in *Yale Review* (New Haven, Connecticut), vol. 77, no. 1, Autumn 1987; "A Poet Who Ventures Where Others Are Reluctant to Tread" by Matthew Gilbert, in *Sunday Boston Herald,* 8 March 1987; "'The Erogenous Cusp' or Intersections of Science and Gender in Alice Fulton's Poetry" by Cristanne Miller, in *Feminist Measures: Soundings in Poetry and Theory,* edited by Lynn Keller and Cristanne Miller, Ann Arbor, University of Michigan Press, 1994.

Alice Fulton comments:

My first book, *Dance Script with Electric Ballerina,* was published when plain style was the prevailing poetic mode. I think the language of my poetry appeared dense and rather baroque in the context of the flat, unadorned expression that constituted the mainstream. Sincerity was equated with plainness of style, and any manipulations of language that deviated from spoken norms were accused of artificiality, even glibness. I have made a strong effort to incorporate contemporary American speech, culture, and ideas in my work, rather than write exclusively about nature or high culture. I mix varying registers of diction in order to create rich, perhaps subversive, subtexts. And my use of the line questions equilibrium and linguistic singleness by means of syntactic doubling on enjambed words.

My second book, *Palladium,* underscored my commitment to textured, energized language. Its formal strategies are more wide-ranging. The book includes dramatic monologues and meditative or narrative poems that tend to be longer, more digressive, and intellectually more ambitious than my earlier work. I continued to explore some of the subjects touched upon in *Dance Script.* These include the search for faith (by "faith" I mean the assumptions that allow us to live in the world); the struggle between engagement and estrangement; the balance of risk and convention; the meanings of popular culture; and familial legacies and loves. I also expanded my subjects in poems that perceive and value peripheral aspects of our culture; question the assumptions surrounding gender; and explore the wayward forms classicism and mythology take in America. The word "palladium" is capacious enough to include all of these meanings. Each of the six sections of the book relate to a denotation or connotation of the title.

My third book, *Powers of Congress,* is structurally very different from *Palladium.* There are no part openings, and the movement of the book is something of a cascade. One poem is intended to trigger the next, so that the book's large scheme has more in common with waterfalls than with compartmentalized plots. The title suggests merging and transformation through government, discourse, assemblage, and sexuality. It implies both hierarchy ("powers" indicating dominance) and a disintegration of hierarchy by means of "congress." The book's undivided structure enacts the enmeshed union and removal of boundaries implicit in the title. The poems in this book are sometimes in argument with various philosophical first principles: What, if anything, can be known with certainty? Is there any evidence to indicate that consciousness does or does not persist after death? What is the nature of God? How might I redefine God? Why do we feel that mind and body are separate entities despite all scientific evidence to the contrary? In the broadest sense, the poems question assumptions and emphasize the interconnectedness of seemingly disparate things.

My interest in American culture continues in poems that explore the rift between private and public domains, the objectifying of the self as product, and our national obsession with aerobics and body building. The latter theme leads to the human fascination with unattainable perfection, and the realization that one cannot be both conscious and durable. Other threads include the intrinsic pain of consciousness; the impermanence of memory; the cultural nihilism of greed; confining gender roles; the relativity of seemingly objective facts; and dual heroic spheres of war and childbirth.

*   *   *

Upon first reading, Alice Fulton's poetry has the neon appeal of an arcade. It is filled with Jacuzzis and Tilt-a-whirls, escalators and guitars. It is peopled with strippers, studs, steel plant owners, and nuns. While these figures of popular culture are attractive in their own right, they are not responsible for W.D. Snodgrass's introduction to Fulton's first book, *Dance Script with Electric Ballerina,* or for the selection of *Palladium,* published in 1986, for the National Poetry Series. As Fulton writes in "Semaphores and Hemispheres," "everything ... [is] / rich in metaphor," including the changes technology and science have brought to the world.

Fulton's poetry is concerned both with these changes and their metaphorical possibility. In *Palladium,* for example, palladium in all its forms, as metallic element, music hall, and talisman (among others), provides a structure for the book. In part 1, which is introduced by the definitions of palladium in its elemental form, Fulton places "Babies"—

born gorgeous with nerves, with brains
the pink of silver polish or
jellyfish wafting ornately
through the body below

—and "Nugget and Dust," a poem about her father's death. Birth and death are elemental subjects. Other sections of the book, introduced by palladium in its other forms, are concerned with subjects which, if less elemental, are equally complex in their embodiment of the human experience.

Faith is one of the themes central to Fulton's poetry. Religious faith, especially Roman Catholicism, plays a part in such poems as "The Great Aunts of My Childhood" in *Dance Script with Electric Ballerina* and "Sister Madeleine Pleads for Our Mary" in *Palladium.* "Orientation Day in Hades" even depicts hell as "a vat, / a barrel slatted with darkness / contained by hoops of energy" where sinners pick peppers all day, while Heaven looks like a salt mine in the distance, "all grayish hills and gooey lights, / as if seen through Vaseline." In "The Perpetual Light" the speaker suggests the dead "no longer wait with heavy patience / ...at some ever-open gate" but rather "hotfoot it through the universe / like supple disco stars."

Fulton's poems have less to do with a faith in the afterlife, however, than with the faith which enables humans to live with hope in a world which seems increasingly chaotic. The speaker in "603 West Liberty St.," when handed words like "faith," "sin," and "penance," questions "futures inlaid with *forever*" and instead believes in "the quantum world's array of random / without chaos, its multiplicity...alone seemed moral." In "Fables from the Random" the human impulse to create order from chaos attracts the speaker to her lover, despite his "insistent rejection / of what is / and shouldn't be" and her knowledge that he just "make[s] fables /

from the random." Science is one fable through which humans impose order on chaos; chemistry, for example, "locates elements in order / to control them." Fulton turns to science again and again in her poetry. Through the metaphorical possibility of science and technology, faith increases rather than diminishes. In "The Wreckage Entrepreneur" a woman, aided by wrecking balls and "Carborundum-bladed saws," sifts through junk. When she glimpses herself in the Art Deco mirrors of an abandoned warehouse, she looks dirty and small; ultimately, however, she is in the business of salvation:

It takes faith—this tripping through the mixed blessings
of debris with eyes peeled for the toxic
toothpaste green of copper keystones...
...[S]he wants
a shower and lather of pumice
to melt the gritty casing of her
nakedness. How small she looks
beside what she has saved.

While the usefulness of the goods she saves is dubious, the fact of her work, of activity, saves her from hopelessness.

Poetry itself is one means by which we can enter into faith. Fulton writes in "In the Beginning," the introductory poem of *Dance Script with Electric Ballerina,* that our lives carry "unknowable cargo":

The wild green groans
by which I lived before language
now gesture and have at me
only in dreams...

Yet the meaning of those "green groans," the dreamworld of memory, can begin to be named through poetry, as Fulton suggests in "Everyone Knows the World Is Ending":

...So long as we keep chanting the words
those worlds will live, but just
so long, so long, so long. Each instant waves
through our nature and is nothing.
But in the love, the grief, under and above
the mother tongue, a permanence
hums: the steady mysterious
the coherent starlight.

Thus poetry, a chant, a humming of grief and love "under and above / the mother tongue," allows permanence in a world where "[e]ach instant waves" through us and is gone. Fulton's poetry allows us to enter that mysterious permanence.

—Julie Miller

FUNKHOUSER, Erica

Nationality: American. **Born:** Cambridge, Massachusetts, 17 September 1949. **Education:** Vassar College, B.A. (with honors) 1971; Stanford University, M.A. in English 1973. **Family:** Married Thaddeus Beal in 1973 (divorced 1995); one son and one daughter. **Career:** Writer, Cambridge Historical Commission, Cambridge, Massachusetts, 1974-77; part-time teacher at colleges in Boston metropolitan area, 1976-87; scriptwriter, Revels, Inc., Cambridge, 1986—; adjunct lecturer in adult degree program, Lesely College, 1987—. Poetry editor, *Dark Horse,* 1975-79, and *Andover Review,* 1977-80. **Awards:** *Ploughshares/Boston Phoenix* Sylvia Plath Poetry prize, 1979; Artists Foundation of Massachusetts poetry fellow, 1982, poetry fellow finalist, 1989; Poetry Society of America's Consuelo Ford award, 1989, Gertrude B. Claytor award, 1990, and George Bogin Memorial award, 1995; MacDowell Colony fellowship, 1994. **Member:** Academy of American Poets, Poetry Society of America. **Address:** 179 Southern Avenue, Essex, Massachusetts 01929, U.S.A.

PUBLICATIONS

Poetry

Natural Affinities. Cambridge, Massachusetts, Alice James Books, 1983.
Sure Shot and Other Poems. Boston, Houghton, 1992.
The Actual World. Boston, Houghton, 1997.

Play

The Long Haul (produced Cambridge, Massachusetts, 1991).

Other

This Is Boston: A Walking Guide to Boston, edited by Dan Dimancescu. Boston, Houghton, 1974.

*   *   *

Erica Funkhouser has published only two collections of poetry. These collections, however, mark her as a poet of great range who can celebrate the domestic or fantasize mythological relationships between human beings and inanimate objects.

In her first collection, *Natural Affinities,* Funkhouser begins with poems celebrating such ordinary tools as the hammer, the pipe wrench, and the screwdriver. Each tool is the subject of a separate poem and its usefulness and its role in human life are examined. Using simple, declarative language, Funkhouser succeeds in creating a charming mythology for the neglected instruments of everyday life. In her poem about the hammer, for example, she writes: "The hand is not always extremity enough. / At times we must go farther, / and so the hammer comes to mind." The wood plane, the reader is told, dreams of a world made flat by its smoothing action. "Lie down and be the same as all the rest," it asks, while the saw "moves with the incessant logic of progress." Funkhouser ends the collection with a group of wry love poems. "Today, again, I need you, / but this is no plea to stay in place," she writes in the poem "Goodbye." Other poems in this section speak of family love. In "Night Vigil" Funkhouser writes of her grandmother, honoring the wisdom the older woman imparted to her. "Waiting" speaks of the child the pregnant narrator is carrying; she sees herself "Like a tree that has been chosen / for the owl's home, / I stand up differently today."

Nine years after the publication of *Natural Affinities,* Funkhouser published *Sure Shot and Other Poems.* This collection is divided into two parts. The first part is comprised of 26 short poems on such familiar poetic topics as love, friendship, and death. Each brief lyric encapsulates a story, leading to the book's second part which contains three long narrative poems about Sacajawea, Louisa May Alcott, and Annie Oakley. In these long poems Funkhouser allows the three historical figures to speak in their own voices. Funkhouser's storytelling is effective in both the short and long poems in this collection, especially when her voice takes over from the story it is relating.

—Denise Wiloch

G

GALLAGHER, Tess

Nationality: American. **Born:** Tess Bond, Port Angeles, Washington, 21 July 1943. **Education:** University of Washington, Seattle, B.A. 1963, M.A. 1970; University of Iowa, Iowa City, M.F.A. 1974. **Family:** Married 1) Lawrence Gallagher in 1963 (divorced 1968); 2) Michael Burkard in 1973 (divorced 1977); 3) writer Raymond Carver in 1988 (companion 1979-88; died 1988). **Career:** Instructor, St. Lawrence University, Canton, New York, 1974-75; assistant professor, Kirkland College, Clinton, New York, 1975-77; visiting lecturer, University of Montana, Missoula, 1977-78; assistant professor, University of Arizona, Tucson, 1978-80; professor of English, Syracuse University, New York, 1980-90; currently professor of English, Whitman College, Walla Walla, Washington. Visiting fellow, Willamette University, Salem, Oregon, 1981. Taught inner city high school and college students, Trinity College, Hartford, Connecticut, 1993; instructor of poetry aboard the *Crusader,* Seattle Resource Institute Seminars Afloat, 1992—. Participant, London International Poetry Festival and European Poetry Festival, Sibiu, Romania, 1992. **Awards:** Creative Artists Public Service grant, 1976; Elliston award, 1976; National Endowment for the Arts grant, 1977, 1981, 1987; Guggenheim fellowship, 1978; *American Poetry Review* award, 1981; Washington State Governor's award 1984, 1986, 1987, 1993; New York State Arts grant, 1988; Maxime Cushing Gray Foundation award, 1990; American Library Association's Most Notable Book List, 1993; Lyndhurst prize, 1993-95. **Address:** Department of English, Whitman College, 345 Boyer Ave., Walla Walla,Washington 99362, U.S.A.

PUBLICATIONS

Poetry

Stepping Outside. Lisbon, Iowa, Penumbra Press, 1974.
Instructions to the Double. Port Townsend, Washington, Graywolf Press, 1976.
Under Stars. Port Townsend, Washington, Graywolf Press, 1978.
Portable Kisses. Seattle, Sea Pen Press, 1978.
On Your Own. Port Townsend, Washington, Graywolf Press, 1978.
Willingly. Port Townsend, Washington, Graywolf Press, 1984.
Amplitude: New and Selected Poems. St. Paul, Minnesota, Graywolf Press. 1987.
Portable Kisses: Love Poems. Santa Barbara, California, Capra Press, 1992.
Moon Crossing Bridge. St. Paul, Minnesota, Graywolf Press, 1992.
The Valentine Elegies, drawings by Carl Dern. Fairfax, California, Jungle Garden Press, 1993.
Portable Kisses Expanded. Santa Barbara, California, Capra Press, 1994.
My Black Horse: New and Selected Poems. Newcastle upon Tyne, Bloodaxe Books, 1995.

Recording: *Some with Wings, Some with Manes,* Watershed, 1982.

Plays

Screenplay: *The Night Belongs to the Police,* 1982; *Dostoevsky,* with Raymond Carver, Santa Barbara, California, Capra Press, 1985.

Television Play: *The Wheel,* 1970.

Short Stories

The Lover of Horses and Other Stories. New York, Harper, 1986; London, Hamish Hamilton, 1989.
At the Owl Woman Saloon. New York, Scribner, 1997.

Other

A Concert of Tenses: Essays on Poetry. Ann Arbor, University of Michigan Press, 1986.

Editor, *A Guide to Forgetting,* by Jeffrey Skinner. St. Paul, Minnesota, Graywolf Press, 1988.

*

Critical Studies: Reviews by Hayden Carruth in *Harper's* (New York), April 1979, and Peter Davison, in *Atlantic Monthly* (New York), May 1979; interview in *Ironwood* (Tucson), October 1979; by Harold Schweizer, in *CEA Critic* (Lewisburg, Pennsylvania), 1987; by William Doreski, in *Harvard Review* (Cambridge, Massachusetts), November 1992; "To Speak Aloud at a Grave" by Jeanne Heuving, in *Northwest Review* (Eugene, Oregon), vol. 32, no. 1, 1994.

Tess Gallagher comments:

When I was a young girl salmon fishing with my father in the Strait of Juan de Fuca in Washington State I used to lean out over the water and try to look past my own face, past the reflection of the boat, past the sun and the darkness, down to where the fish were surely swimming. I made up charm songs and word-hopes to tempt the fish, to cause them to mean biting my hook. I believed they would do it, if I asked them well and patiently enough, and with the right hope. I am writing my poems like this. I have used the fabric and the people of my life as the bait. More and more I have learned how to speak for the others, the ones who do not speak in poetry, though their lives are of it. What do I write about? The murder of my uncle by thieves in the night, the psychic death of my husband in the Vietnam war, walking through Belfast in 1976, a horse with snow on its back circling a house where the dancers have fallen to the floor by daybreak. I have wanted the words to go deep. I have wanted music and passion and human tenderness in the poems. Intelligence and loss. Only in the language I have made for myself in the poems am I in touch with all the past, present, and future moments of my consciousness. The poem is the moment of all possibilities where I try to speak in a concert of tenses. I don't want to disappear into the present tense, the awful NOW. I want to survive it and take others with me. I am more concerned about the kind of writing that allows WITH than I was in the beginning. Not just TO or FOR or AT. The Irish have no word for "mine" or for "wife"...only "he or she who goes along with me." My poetry. I can't say that. Only "that which goes along with me."

I'm presently feeling American poetry suffers from too much light and am concentrating on a certain density which allows mystery without making the poem too obscure. For instruction I'm thinking a lot about Emily Dickinson and John Donne and Lorca, learning ghost songs from the Irish, oriental folktales, and reading books about our relationship through history to horses (a preoccupation).

*   *   *

Born in the Pacific Northwest, the oldest of five children of a logger turned longshoreman, Tess Gallagher was a member of the last class taught by Theodore Roethke at the University of Washington, and was also a student of David Wagoner. This is not to say that her work bears much resemblance to theirs beyond great vitality and an obsessive desire to make words count.

Instructions to the Double is full of doubles of two sorts: people with whom the speaker closely identifies—father, mother, uncle, husband—and likenesses—reflections in a mirror, water or eyes, resemblances, shadows, ghosts, photographs. Whichever the kind, the poems that disappoint are those whose subjects remain generalized, such as "When You Speak to Me," "The Perfect Sky," and "Instructions to the Double." The most successful are concrete, rooted in intimate and intimately felt family experience: "Two Stories," about an uncle murdered by thieves, "Coming Home," "The Woman Who Raised Goats," "Black Money," and "Time Lapse with Tulips." This last is one of Gallagher's best; it brilliantly considers and rejects illusion and fixes on reality. The wedding photograph that is the occasion for the poem is illusory in at least two senses: a photographic image is an illusion, and the particular image "preserves / a symmetry of doubt with us / at the center." The poem has its own symmetry of statement. The first stanza retrospectively denies the impact of a marital kiss and the prospects of living in connubial bliss into old age. The second stanza denies the assumption that tulips will be accepted by the bride, while the third voices the uncertainties of the wedding guests, the "symmetry of doubt." The turn suggested in stanza two ("But they are wrong") is declared at the beginning of stanza four: "Whatever the picture says, it is wrong." The real picture is something more certain. Instead of what the photograph portrayed—passion suppressed—is passion ready to be released, passion comprehending love and death:

> Inside, the rare bone of my hand and that harp
> seen through a window suddenly so tempting
>
> you must rush into that closed room, you must
> tear your fingers across it.

Symmetry and harmony are about to be achieved.

After *Instructions to the Double, Under Stars* is a letdown. The first half of the book, "The Ireland Poems," derives from Gallagher's travels in Ireland in 1976. A traveler's impressions, even those of a sensitive poet with ethnic affinities for the land visited, almost inevitably disappoint. After reading Seamus Heaney, say, with his profoundly apprehended vision of the Irelands, one

is tempted to characterize Gallagher's poems, especially "Disappearances in the Guarded Sector" and "The Ballad of Ballymote," with their eternal notes of sadness, as simply more news from that unhappy land. The second half of the book, "Start Again Somewhere," is not so much a second start as a return to subjects explored in *Instructions to the Double,* as in "My Mother Remembers That She Was Beautiful." Yet even these less successful poems indicate that Gallagher has a strong voice, passionate, elegant, passionate, painstaking.

Willingly, the next major book after *Under Stars,* is much better. Dedicated to Raymond Carver, with whom she lived from 1978 and whom she married six weeks before his death in 1988 from cancer, it is full of the passion of a highly successful love affair between artists. In the several poems to Carver, various in their subject matter, we get a clear picture of an admirable man, as in "I Save Your Coat, But You Lose It Later," "Skylights," "The Hug," and "Each Bird Walking." Other poems are to Gallagher's father—"Boat Ride," "Accomplishment," and "Candle, Lamp, Firefly." There are also four fine poems to horses—"From Dread in the Eyes of Horses," "Death of the Horses by Fire," "The Cloudy Shoulders of the Horses," and "Legacy"—which capture the mysteriousness of that noble beast, so much desired by her maternal Cherokee grandfather, who wanted more horses, as Gallagher tells us in "If Poetry Were Not a Morality," the first of the new poems in *Amplitude.* Another new poem from the varied collection *Amplitude,* "Bonfire," is about Carver and ends with the doctor's news, which "Flushed us through with dread." The poet is reminded of a violin when the dying Carver is thrown into her arms:

> It wasn't for music
>   you came to me, but
>   for daring—mine and yours.
> When they have to, they will write in the Book
>   of Welcome:
>   Two darings, two darlings.

The last two words may seem at first reading merely cutesy. On later readings—daring. Themes of Gallagher's post-mourning phase make up *Portable Kisses: Love Poems,* published in 1992; they would be further developed in *Portable Kisses Expanded,* wherein the poet imbues the "Kiss" with both wit and irony.

In Gallagher's *Moon Crossing Bridge,* the poet makes manifest the psychic and emotional pain of mourning and grief over lost love. As she herself describes it, "I have been engaged in writing the 'untenable text' which occurs in the silent space between what is actually said. The density of language and image have hopefully extended areas of thought and feeling, partly through transgressional means of taking on subject matter formerly forbidden, as in poems such as 'Red Poppy,' 'Wake,' and 'I Don't Know You,' among others, poems which attempt to renegotiate temporal and spiritual dimensions." In addition to working on a translation of works by the Romanian poet Liliana Ursu, in the early 1990s Gallagher began a period of short-story writing, a form that she began working in during the mid-1980s under the influence of Carver. As she explained the theme of *At the Owl Woman Saloon:* "I am writing towards the proverb 'If you contemplate revenge, dig two graves.'"

—James K. Robinson and Lynne MacGregor

GARRETT, Elizabeth

Nationality: British. **Address:** c/o Bloodaxe Books, P.O. Box 1SN, Newcastle upon Tyne NE99 1SN, England.

PUBLICATIONS

Poetry

The Mortal Light (pamphlet). Mandeville Press, 1990.
The Rule of Three. Newcastle upon Tyne, Bloodaxe Books, 1991.
A Two-Part Invention. Newcastle upon Tyne, Bloodaxe Books, 1998.

*   *   *

Elizabeth Garrett has more in common with John Donne or Emily Dickinson than with most of her contemporaries. Her poetry has rare, and unfashionable, qualities of expansion and conclusiveness. It succeeds through its tensions—between metaphysical scrutiny and lyrical sensation, intellectual engagement and emotional intensity, emphatic statement and playfulness.

Garrett is interested in "random treasures" that have "Gone, unnumbered and unmeasured / Into the slipstream of memory" ("Envoi"), objects or experiences that offer themselves up for quantification. Ephermerality pervades her work: things made palpable for a brief moment; a coalescence or conjunction that is inevitably shortlived. This combines interestingly with the sense of pleasure and excitement Garrett conveys when she has something in her grasp. Meaning itself is elusive, even illusory in "Fata Morgana":

> Focus your mind, my love,
> Upon the dark interstices of words,
> For there truth lies uncovered,
> Innocent of hands, lips, eyes,
> Like a sleeping lover,
> Nightly with whom death lies.

The themes that most commonly occur in Garrett's work are traditional ones—love, childhood, looking back. Equally conventional is her use of elemental imagery—the sun, sea, sky, moon and earth. Yet her poems are surprising for the energy of their language in which she combines formality with liveliness, and the romantic with the scientifically precise: "By heart, a journey of the blood, the slow / Footfall of diastole and systole through the night." ("Rumaucourt"). Garrett is as conscious of etymology, ambiguity and resonance as she is of aural effects. In "Nilak," a meditation on a shade of Persian blue, the title is quickly echoed in the half rhymes of "lilac" and "lalique," amplifying the colour and texture described.

Words are gauged for their meaning but also their music. Garrett uses sinewy alliteration, full and half rhyme, as well as traditional forms such as the villanelle. Her truncated sestina, "Wedding Breakfast," is reminiscent of Elizabeth Bishop's full blown version, "A Miracle for Breakfast." Garrett's use of formal devices is generally subtle but she can also intensify the mood of a poem through heightened effects. In "La Maddalena," relentless enjambment amplifies the argument between a real woman and her representation as each line catches us by surprise: "History has left her whole / As he painted her." In the sonnet "Andree." half-rhymes are locked in couples that undermine this woman's importance and aspirations: "wife / grief", "Mother' / neither," "possessing / guessing."

Female types are one of Garrett's subjects and, like Vicki Feaver, she often confronts them through their portrayal in art. "Two Floras" compares Botticelli's treatment of the subject with that of Titian; Degas' "Ecoliere" captures the moment that childhood is lost: "As she retreats, her posture alters: / Not her step, but the eye that falters." Garrett also uses folklore, the spinster, and the Russian doll to confront women's conventional role and fate. "Testament," about a girl's birth, warns "Not the dream that violates, / But the script—its cues and prompting."

Powerful poems of reminiscence such as the sequence "Rumaucourt" about her French relatives' home suggest that Garrett's most successful subjects are autobiographical. Such poems have an emotional charge and individuality missing from her more studied childhood acuity intact:

> Then the skilled hand spooning;
> In one long viscous drip
> That measures centuries
> A stalactite of golden-syrup drools
> And spills away.

Where the self is as present as the wider historical world, Elizabeth Garrett's subjects sing.

—Lavinia Greenlaw

GILBERT, Sandra M(ortola)

Nationality: American. **Born:** Brooklyn, New York, 27 December 1936. **Education:** Cornell University, B.A. (honors) 1957; New York University, M.A. in English 1961; Columbia University, Ph.D. 1968. **Family:** Married Elliot Gilbert in 1957 (died 1991); one son, two daughters. **Career:** Assistant professor of English, California State University, Hayward, 1968-71; associate professor, Indiana University, 1973-75; associate professor, 1975-85, then professor, 1989 –, University of California, Davis; associate professor, Princeton University, 1985-89. **Awards:** AWP Poetry Series Prize, 1979, for *In the Fourth World;* International Poetry Foundation Charity Randall award; *Poetry* (New York) Eunice Tietjens Memorial Prize; Guggenheim fellowship; Rockefeller Foundation Humanities fellowship. **Address:** Department of English, University of California, Davis, California 95616-8581, U.S.A.

PUBLICATIONS

Poetry

In the Fourth World. University of Alabama Press, 1979.
The Summer Kitchen. Woodside, California, Heyeck, 1983.
Emily's Bread. New York, Norton, 1984.
Blood Pressure (includes *The Summer Kitchen*). New York, Norton, 1988.
Ghost Volcano. New York, Norton, 1995.

Other

Acts of Attention: The Poems of D.H. Lawrence. Ithaca, New York, and London, Cornell University Press, 1972; revised, Carbondale, Southern Illinois University Press, 1990.

The Madwoman in the Attic: The Woman Writer and the 19th-Century Literary Imagination, with Susan Gubar. New Haven and London, Yale University Press, 1980.

No Man's Land: The Place of the Woman Writer in the 20th Century: The War of the Words [Sexchanges] [Letters from the Front], with Susan Gubar. New Haven, Yale University Press, 3 vols., 1988-94.

Wrongful Death: A Medical Tragedy. New York, Norton, 1995; as *Wrongful Death: A Memoir,* N.p., 1997.

Masterpiece Theatre: An Academic Melodrama, with Susan Gubar. New Brunswick, New Jersey, Rutgers University Press, 1995.

Editor, with Susan Gubar, *Shakespeare's Sisters: Feminist Essays on Woman Poets.* Bloomington and London, Indiana University Press, 1979.

Editor, *Kate Chopin's "The Awakening" and Selected Stories.* New York, Penguin, 1984.

Editor, with Susan Gubar, *The Female Imagination and the Modern Aesthetic.* New York, Gordon & Breach, 1986.

Editor, with Susan Gubar, *The Norton Anthology of Literature by Women: The Tradition in English.* New York, Norton, 1985; revised edition, 1996.

Editor, with Wendy Barker, *The House Is Made of Poetry: The Art of Ruth Stone.* Carbondale, Southern Illinois University Press, 1996.

Editor, with Susan Gubar and Diana O'Hehir, *Mothersongs: Poems for, by, and about Mothers.* New York, Norton, 1995.

*   *   *

Sandra M. Gilbert has produced an impressive body of work as a poet. Her five volumes, starting with *In the Fourth World,* manage to be both enjoyable and, at the same time, display an originality that challenges to the reader to see the world in new ways.

From the first poem ("Getting Fired, or 'Not Being Retained'") on, the first collection presents a world filled with fear and anxiety. However, the writer's wit and imagination help to hold these fears in check, at the same time we experience these emotions vividly through her imagery:

> But in the meantime, while I wasn't looking, the letter
> took possession of the house. The letter
> stretched out on the livingroom sofa and asked for a newspaper,
> which it scrutinized with eyes of steel.

The poems in this collection are full of visual surprises; many have the feeling of waking dreams, as in "The Cassandra Dream":

> I open my bureau drawer
> and there I find
> my beautiful cousin Cassandra.

At other times, the poems take off from mundane events as if the speaker is lapsing into a daydream, as in "The Dream of My Daughter," where Gilbert pictures herself brushing her daughter's hair till she's brushed it into non-existence. Also, in these dreams, she sometimes becomes others: a shoe minus its twin, a black cow, a "Grandmother," who, in the last poem, sees bits of herself departing with her relatives:

> Other faces, small and white and round as
> peeled apples
>
> fall from the long dark
> face I wear:
>
> my round grandchildren!
> One is taking my nose away,
>
> another my lips, a third my cheeks...
> In the morning
>
> I find they've moved to California
> with all my features intact

The third collection, *Emily's Bread,* reflects the feminism Gilbert was also exploring through critical prose works on women in literature with her collaborator Susan Gubar. The title's "Emily" refers to both Emily Brontë and Emily Dickinson, and the bread that both women provided—Brontë, to her village; Dickinson, to her household—becomes the spiritual sustenance they've shared, through their writing and lives, with other women. Again, as in the first collection, the visual appeal of the poems is strong, and becomes part of the organization of the work: the second part of this collection consists of "daguerreotypes," the stereotypical pictures of women we've inherited, and the fourth section gives us "still lives," studies that dig deeper into the lives of women. The poems often draw their images from activities like cooking and cleaning, and imagination and a playful sense of humor push against the limits of this world, as in "The Parable of the Clothes":

> In the cold wash of dawn
>
> one pale shirt
> sets off across cold fields,
> its elbows filling with mist,
> its collar undone.

Gilbert's more recent volumes, *Blood Pressure* and *Ghost Volcano,* show a continued growth in her work. *Blood Pressure* deals frequently with scenes from personal life and history; the "blood" in the title also suggests lineage. The imagery in many of these poems is intense and powerful, as in "Blood Pressure":

> Behind your eyes, something
> like a serpent moves, an acid tongue
> flicking at your cheekbones, something
>
> voracious, whipping your whole body
> hard...

In *Blood Pressure,* the author weaves her way through the lives of others to find her own self, as in "Low Tide":

I am the mother who taught you plus and minus,
the father who cried "It's never too late!"....

as you drift through through the tidepools in a pleated
     skirt
and knee socks, writing clumsy poems,

I'm groping my way toward you,
down the long pier,
in the sea fog,
among the screaming gulls.

1995's *Ghost Volcano,* centers around the 1991 death of the author's husband, Elliott Gilbert, in the course of what should have been routine surgery. Mount Rainier, one version of the "ghost volcano," is introduced in the first poem, "October 6, 1992: Seattle, Looking for Mount Rainier," as it

surges out of the clouds,
just opposite the spot
where she thought perhaps I'd find it

Similarly, the author's grief, and images of her husband, erupt unexpectedly throughout book. By the penultimate poem in this collection, "February 11, 1994: Berkeley, Anniversary Waltz Again," she has achieved a certain acceptance, still tinged with pain, of his death.

as if when I took my first three giant steps
into another somewhere,

you could never be the same,
you took had to go on becoming
and becoming other....

—Duane Ackerson

GIOVANNI, Nikki

Nationality: American. **Born:** Yolande Cornelia Giovanni, in Knoxville, Tennessee, 7 June 1943. **Education:** Fisk University, 1960-61, 1964-67, B.A. (magna cum laude) in history, 1967; University of Pennsylvania School of Social Work, Philadelphia, 1967; Columbia University, New York, 1968. **Family:** Has one son. **Career:** Assistant professor of Black Studies, Queens College, Flushing, New York, 1968; associate professor of English, Livingston College, Rutgers University, New Brunswick, New Jersey, 1968-72; visiting professor of English, Ohio State University, Columbus, 1984; professor of creative writing, Mt. St. Joseph on the Ohio, then Virginia Polytechnic Institute and State University, 1985—. Founder, Niktom Publishers, New York, 1970-74. Editorial consultant, *Encore* magazine, Albuquerque, New Mexico. **Awards:** Ford Foundation grant, 1968; National Endowment for the Arts grant, 1969. D.H.L.: Wilberforce University, Ohio, 1972; D.Litt.: University of Maryland, Princess Anne, 1974, Ripon University, Wisconsin, 1974, Smith College, Northampton, Massachusetts, 1975, Mt. St. Joseph on the Ohio, 1983. **Address:** Department of English, Virginia Polytechnic Institute and State University, P.O. Box 0112, Blacksburg, Virginia 24063-0001, U.S.A.

PUBLICATIONS

Poetry

Black Judgement. Detroit, Broadside Press, 1968.
Black Feeling, Black Talk. Privately printed, 1968.
Re:Creation. Detroit, Broadside Press, 1970.
Black Feeling, Black Talk / Black Judgment. New York, Morrow, 1970.
Poem of Angela Yvonne Davis. New York, Afro Arts, 1970.
My House. New York, Morrow, 1972.
The Women and the Men. New York, Morrow, 1975.
Cotton Candy on a Rainy Day. New York, Morrow, 1978.
Those Who Ride the Night Winds. New York, Morrow, 1983.
The Selected Poems of Nikki Giovanni. New York, Morrow, 1996.
Love Poems. New York, Morrow, 1997.

Recordings: *Truth Is on Its Way,* Right On, 1971; *Like a Ripple on a Pond,* Niktom, 1973; *The Way I Feel,* Niktom, 1975; *Legacies,* Folkways, 1976; *The Reason I Like Chocolate,* Folkways, 1976; *Cotton Candy on a Rainy Day,* Folkways, 1978.

Verse (for children)

Spin a Soft Black Song, illustrated by Charles Bible. New York, Hill & Wang, 1971; revised edition, illustrated by George Martins, 1985.
Ego Tripping and Other Poems for Young People. Westport, Connecticut, Lawrence Hill, 1973.
Vacation Time. New York, Morrow, 1980.
Knoxville, Tennessee, illustrated by Larry Johnson. New York, Scholastic, 1994.
The Sun Is So Quiet, illustrated by Ashley Bryan. New York, Holt, 1996.
The Genie in the Jar, illustrated by Chris Raschka. New York, Holt, 1996.

Other

Gemini: An Extended Autobiographical Statement on My First 25 Years of Being a Black Poet. Indianapolis, Bobbs Merrill, 1971; London, Penguin, 1976.
A Dialogue: James Baldwin and Nikki Giovanni. Philadelphia Lippincott, 1973.
A Poetic Equation: Conversations between Nikki Giovanni and Margaret Walker. Washington, D.C. Howard University Press, 1974.
Sacred Cows ... and Other Edibles (essays). New York, Morrow, 1988.
Conversations with Nikki Giovanni, edited by Virginia C. Fowler. Jackson, University Press of Mississippi, 1992.
Racism 101. New York, Quill, 1994.

Editor, *Night Comes Softly: An Anthology of Black Female Voices,* Newark, New Jersey, Medic Press, 1970.
Editor, with Cathee Dennison, *Appalachian Elders: A Warm Hearth Sampler.* Blacksburg, Virginia, Pocahantas Press, 1991.

Editor, *Grandmothers: Poems, Reminiscences, and Short Stories about the Keepers of Our Traditions.* New York, Holt, 1994.

Editor, *Shimmy Shimmy Shimmy like My Sister Kate: Looking at the Harlem Renaissance through Poems.* New York, Holt, 1996.

*

Manuscript Collection: Mugar Memorial Library, Boston University.

Critical Study: *Nikki Giovanni,* by Virginia C. Fowler. New York, Twayne, 1992.

*   *   *

Fame came early for Nikki Giovanni. Her first three books attested to "the possibility of / Blackness / and the inevitability of / Revolution," confirmed the force of colloquial talk, and used this power to deal with social change while whispering something "counterrevolutionary" like making love ("Seduction"). Comparing poems to photographs, she later said, "I was trying to capture the moment because we as a people did not have a voice." Poems like "Nikki-Rosa," "Beautiful Black Men," and "Ego Tripping," all celebrating blackness, made this voice with its humor and anger and compassion one that would be heard the rest of the century.

Throughout her career, speaking has been essential. From readings and recordings, people know her physical voice, and she writes with orality in mind. She focuses on people, writing and speaking with, of, for, and to them. She has come to seem a spokesperson, editing anthologies and offering her own essays. Her poem "The Genie in the Jar" became one of several books she has written for children. But unlike poets who regard themselves as gifted with superior insight and unaccountable to an audience, Giovanni takes the journey everyone takes, not as "the guide... nor technical assistance...I will be your fellow passenger...," she writes in "A Journey."

Since her first fame, multiple aspects of her voice have resounded. Plain as her diction usually is, her thinking can flash unpredictably. Instead of stating the obvious, "Poems for Aretha" evokes the difficult, sometimes fatal demands of fame. Because of the quickness of Giovanni's mind, she catches insights like, in "Walking down Park," "We can't be on / the stock exchange / we are the stock / exchanged." She doesn't mind telling stories on herself ("Alabama Poem") or allowing that being militant might not be the complete, definitive agenda and that dreaming "natural / dreams of being a natural / woman" might also be "a revolution" ("Revolutionary Dreams"). She speaks intimately of desires and warmly of strong relatives, especially women. They gain prominence as they "sit and wait" for love, resent one another, keep their integrity into old age, aspire to greatness, or assert themselves with their men. "The Women Gather" shows their effectuality in preparing for a funeral as well as having the mercy to make a generous accounting of the dreams and deeds of the dead.

A darker side of Giovanni appears in *Cotton Candy on a Rainy Day,* in which she sees "The sweet soft essence of possibility / Never quite maturing" and likens herself to "the unrealized dream of an idea unborn," deciding in "Being and Nothingness," "i don't want to exert anything."

She finds her way out of the blackness in *Those Who Ride the Night Winds.* Writing on personages like Lorraine Hansberry, John Lennon, and Billie Jean King, Giovanni emphasizes their attempts to realize their ideals, but allows her thoughts to range over politics, art, and history without losing the energy of her voice and character. Here is part of her celebration of Phillis Wheatley, the first published black American poet, in "Linkage": "Why couldn't she ... they want to know ... be more like ... more like ... more like... The record sticks ... Phillis was her own precedent...her own image ... her only ancestor..." Inventing this lineless form full of ellipses let Giovanni move freely among ideas without losing the rhythm of poetry.

Energy, not style, may be the secret of Nikki Giovanni's resiliency. Her sense of commitment has expanded since her politically revolutionary days. She remains committed to honest, individual thought and feeling; she speaks forthrightly, and often playfully, to the many people who listen to and buy her poems. Calling herself a "poet of information," she does not apologize for the topical nature of her work: "I do today's job today." Unlike writers for whom style or a certain diction may be foremost, Giovanni adapts to the topic and the mood of the times. "Poetry," she says in "This Is Not for John Lennon," "like photography ... functions best not only in the available light but in the timelessness of the subject."

—Jay S. Paul

GLÜCK, Louise (Elisabeth)

Nationality: American. **Born:** New York City, 22 April 1943. **Education:** Sarah Lawrence College, Bronxville, New York, 1962; Columbia University, New York, 1963-65. **Family:** Married 1) Charles Hertz Jr. in 1967 (divorced); 2) John Dranow in 1977 (divorced); one son. **Career:** Taught at Goddard College, Plainfield, Vermont, 1971-72, 1973-74, 1976-80, University of Virginia, Charlottesville, 1973, University of North Carolina, Greensboro, 1973, University of Iowa, Iowa City, University of Cincinnati, 1978, Columbia University, 1979, Warren Wilson College, Swannanoa, North Carolina, 1978-80, University of California at Berkeley, 1982, at Davis, 1983, and at Irvine, 1984, and Harvard University, 1995. Scott Professor of poetry, 1993, and member of the faculty, 1984—, Williams College, Williamstown, Massachusetts. Regents Professor, University of California, Los Angeles, 1985-87; Fanny Hurst Professor, Brandeis University, 1996. **Awards:** Academy of American Poets Prize, 1966; Rockefeller fellowship, 1967; National Endowment for the Arts grant, 1969, 1979, fellowship, 1988-89; Eunice Tietjens Memorial Prize (*Poetry,* Chicago), 1971; Guggenheim fellowship, 1975; 1987-88; American Academy award, 1981; National Book Critics Circle Prize, 1985; Melville Cane Award, 1986; Sara Teasdale Memorial Prize, 1986; Phi Beta Kappa Poet, Harvard University, 1990; Bobbitt National Prize (with Mark Strand), Library of Congress, 1992; Pulitzer Prize, 1993, for *The Wild Iris;* William Carlos Williams Award, 1993. Fellow, American Academy of Arts and Sciences, 1993. Honorary D.Litt.: Williams College, Williamstown, Massachusetts, Skidmore College, Middlebury College. **Member:** American Academy of Arts and Letters. **Address:** Creamery Road, Plainfield, Vermont 05667, U.S.A.

PUBLICATIONS

Poetry

Firstborn. New York, New American Library, 1968; London, Anvil Press Poetry, 1969.
The House on Marshland. New York, Ecco Press, 1975; London, Anvil Press Poetry, 1976.
The Garden. New York, Antaeus, 1976.
Descending Figure. New York, Ecco Press, 1980.
The Triumph of Achilles. New York, Ecco Press, 1985.
Ararat. New York, Ecco Press, 1990.
The Wild Iris. New York, Ecco Press, 1992.
The First Four Books of Poems. New York, Ecco Press, 1995.
Meadowlands. New York, Ecco Press, 1996.

Other

Proofs and Theories. New York, Ecco Press, 1994.

Editor, *The Best American Poetry 1993,* with David Lehman. New York, Collier, 1993.

*

Critical Studies: By Calvin Bedient, in *Sewanee Review* (Tennessee), Winter 1976, and in *Parnassus* (New York), Spring / Summer 1981; by Joan Hutton Landis, in *Salmagundi* (Saratoga Springs, New York), Winter 1977; by Helen Vendler in *New Republic* (Washington, D.C.), 17 June 1978; "The Poetry of Louise Glück" by Burton Raffel, in *Literary Review: An International Journal of Contemporary Writing* (Madison, New Jersey), vol. 31, no. 3, Spring 1988; "'Free / of Blossom and Subterfuge': Louise Glück and the Language of Renunciation" by Lynn Keller, in *World, Self, Poem: Essays on Contemporary Poetry from the "Jubilation of Poets,"* edited by Leonard M. Trawick, Kent, Ohio, Kent State University Press, 1990; "The 'harsher figure' of Descending Figure: Louise Glück's 'Dive into the Wreck'" by Laurie E. George, in *Women's Studies,* vol. 17, no. 3 / 4, 1990; *The Veiled Mirror and the Woman Poet: H.D., Louise Bogan, Elizabeth Bishop, and Louise Glück* by Elizabeth Caroline Dodd, Columbia, University of Missouri Press, 1992; "'It Meant I Loved': Louise Glück's Ararat" by Eric Selinger, in *Postmodern Culture: An Electronic Journal of Interdisciplinary Criticism* (Cary, North Carolina), vol. 3, no. 3, May 1993; "Without Relation: Family and Freedom in the Poetry of Louise Glück" by Suzanne Matson, in *Mid-American Review* (Bowling Green, Ohio), vol. 14, no. 2, 1994.

*   *   *

Louise Glück's first volume, *Firstborn,* does not lack for influences, as discerning critics have been quick to remark. Most obvious are the traces of Stanley Kunitz, with whom she studied at Columbia University, and of early Robert Lowell. There are also indications that she has looked to Plath and Sexton, Crane, Jarrell, and Dugan. "My Life before Dawn," with its emphasis on sexual violence and male mental cruelty, may well represent such influences. The poem begins

Sometimes at night I think of how we did
It, me nailed to her like steel, her
Over-eager on the striped contour
Sheet (I later burned it) and she makes me glad
I told her—in the kitchen cutting bread—
She always did too much—I told her Sorry baby you have had
Your share (I found her stain had dried into my hair).

Here, already, is a subtle command of a basically five-beat line, of slant rhyme, of a character sharply conceived and convincingly rendered.

One experiences a great leap, however, with the collection that comes six years later, for *The House on Marshland* is decisively Glück's own. Its pervasive theme is loss. The obsessive feeling is pain in relationships with men. The triumphant achievement is the balancing of an almost bitter attitude with an undeterred hopefulness. Most of the poems are in the confessional tradition, though there is no reason to assume that they are autobiographical. Paradoxically, Glück, like Tennyson and others, writes most powerfully when she turns away from presumably private or personally apprehended experience. The less personal the experience, the more intense is the feeling with which the expression is charged. "All Hallows" seems to derive from a landscape painting: a scene of "barrenness / of harvest or pestilence" points to a wife leaning out of a window; amid all this barrenness can she be fertile? "Brennende Liebe—1904" is a poetized love letter from an aristocratic woman in which the mood of longing is elegantly conveyed. If the supposed writer was an ancestor, one can understand why Glück has retained the umlaut in her name.

The most psychologically penetrating poem is "Abishag." The account in *I Kings* of the young woman brought to King David's bed is from David's perspective, as are treatments by Rilke, the Hebrew Fichman, the French Spire. Glück, however, offers Abishag's voice and perspective in a dreamlike recollection. Only a single mark of punctuation impedes the flow of the opening stanza, but the concluding stanza of the first section is firmly end-stopped, staccato, bitter:

They took me as I was.
Not one among the kinsmen touched me,
No one among the slaves.
No one will touch me now.

Abishag has a classical Electra fantasy. She rages at her father for letting her be taken by someone other than himself. The final section deserves quotation in full:

In the recurring dream my father
stands at the doorway in his black cassock
telling me to choose
among my suitors, each of whom
will speak my name once
until I lift my hand in signal.
On my father's arm I listen
for not three sounds: *Abishag.*
but two: *my love—*

I tell you if it is my own will
binding me I cannot be saved.
And yet in the dream, in the half-light

of the stone house, they looked
so much alike. Sometimes I think
the voices were themselves
identical, and that I raised my hand
chiefly in weariness. I hear my father saying
Choose, choose. But they were not alike
and to select death, O yes I can
believe that of my body.

Rage at her father has become hatred of self for feeling that she
has been used.

In *The Garden* Glück may be signaling her next phase. As she
has written, "The impulse to write is usually spent in a brief lyric."
(The 49 lines of "Abishag" make it by far the longest poem in
The House on Marshland.) Consisting of five almost independent
lyrics about fear, *The Garden* is a coherent, powerful whole, per-
haps Glück's highest achievement.

Descending Figure reminds one in its title of Duchamp's *Nude
Descending a Staircase,* for it, too, takes descents as a subject.
Beginning with the first section, "The Garden," it gives us the
conversationally triumphant "The Drowned Children" and then
proceeds to incorporate the previous book. "Descending Figure"
is a child's view, in three parts, of a dead sister—a figure descending,
a sick child in a painting in the Rijksmuseum, and the speaker's
dead sister. Collectively, the three lyrics deal vividly with the fear
of death. The second part of *Descending Figure,* "The Mirror,"
begins with "Epithalamium," a lyric ode to a bride and bridegroom
that suggests an end to descending—

the terrible charity of marriage
husband and wife
climbing the green hill in gold light

and then refutes the suggestion.

Descending Figure has as its final sequence "Lamentations,"
reminding us of the biblical book. The five chapters of the Old
Testament book are a lamentation for Jerusalem, like a widow
bitterly mourning loss. Glück's poem, however, has four parts:
"The Logos," "Nocturne," "The Covenant," and "The Clear-
ing." "The Logos" speaks of the Creation, God's withdrawal
from the universe, and man and woman alone. "Nocturne" de-
tails God's abandonment of the vegetable, animal, and human.
"The Covenant" describes parenthood. "The Clearing" presents
the evolution of beauty as "seen from the air," that is, dis-
tantly.

Biblical and other spiritual perspectives continue to illuminate
The Triumph of Achilles, Ararat, and *The Wild Iris,* in the latter
collection manifesting themselves in the contemplative "Violets":

Because in our world
something is always hidden
small and white,
small and what you call
pure, we do not grieve
as you grieve, dear
suffering master; you
are no more lost
than we are, under the hawthorn tree, the hawthorn
holding balanced trays of pearls: what
has brought you among us
who would teach you, though, you kneel and weep.

Glück's poetry is intimate, familial, and what Edwin Muir has
called the fable, the archetypal. She often goes to the source of
things—to the Old Testament, as in "Abishag" and in "Lamenta-
tions," or to Greek myth as in "Aphrodite" and the title poem in
The Triumph of Achilles, which moves from fable to story, for the
great hero becomes humanized in lamenting the death of his friend
Patroclus.

—James K. Robinson

GOEDICKE, Patricia

Nationality: American. **Born:** Patricia McKenna, Boston, Mas-
sachusetts, 21 June 1931. **Education:** Middlebury College, Ver-
mont, B.A. (cum laude) 1953 (Phi Beta Kappa, 1952); Ohio Uni-
versity, Athens, M.A. 1965. **Family:** Married 1) Victor Goedicke
in 1956 (divorced 1968); 2) Leonard Wallace Robinson in 1971.
Career: Editorial assistant, Harcourt Brace & World publishers,
New York, 1953-54, and T.Y. Crowell publishers, New York, 1955-
56. Instructor in English, Ohio University, 1963-68, and Hunter
College, New York, 1969-71; reader-writer, Book-of-the-Month
Club, 1968-69; associate professor of creative writing, Instituto
Allende, San Miguel de Allende, Guanajuato, Mexico, 1972-79;
writer-in-residence, Kalamazoo College, Michigan, 1977; guest fac-
ulty member of the writing program, Sarah Lawrence College,
Bronxville, New York, 1980-81. Poet-in-residence, 1981-83, as-
sociate professor, 1983-90, and professor, 1990—, of creative writ-
ing, University of Montana, Missoula. Co-editor, *Page,* 1961-66.
Awards: National Endowment for the Arts award, 1969, fellow-
ship, 1976-77; William Carlos Williams Award *(New Letters),* 1977;
Duncan Frazier Prize, *Loon,* 1976; *Quarterly West* prize, 1977;
Carolyn Kizer award, 1987; Prairie Schooner Strousse award, 1987;
Arvon International Poetry Competition special commendation,
1987; Memphis State Review Hohenberg award, 1988; Univer-
sity of Montana research grant, 1989; *New York Times* Notable
Book of the Year 1990, for *The Tongues We Speak: New and Se-
lected Poems;* University of Montana Distinguished Scholar award,
1991; Edward Stanley Award *(Prairie Schooner),* 1992; Rockefeller
Foundation residency at Villa Serbelloni on Lake Como, Bellagio,
Italy, 1992. **Address:** Department of English, University of Mon-
tana, Missoula, Montana 59812, U.S.A.

PUBLICATIONS

Poetry

Between Oceans. New York, Harcourt Brace, 1968.
For the Four Corners. Ithaca, New York, Ithaca House, 1976.
The Trail That Turns on Itself. Ithaca, New York, Ithaca House,
1978.
The Dog That Was Barking Yesterday. Amherst, Massachusetts,
Lynx House Press, 1979.
Crossing the Same River. Amherst, University of Massachusetts
Press, 1980.
The King of Childhood. Lewiston, Idaho, Confluence Press, 1984.
The Wind of Our Going. Port Townsend, Washington, Copper
Canyon Press, 1985.

Listen, Love. Muncie, Indiana, Barnwood Press, 1986.
The Tongues We Speak: New and Selected Poems. Minneapolis, Milkweed, 1989.
Paul Bunyan's Bearskin. Minneapolis, Milkweed, 1992.
Invisible Horses. Minneapolis, Milkweed, 1996.

*

Critical Studies: "The Fruit of Her Orchard" by Tom O'Grady and Shirley Bossert, in *New Letters* (Kansas City), Fall 1977; "The Desperate Tongue" by Ron Slate, in *Three Rivers Poetry Journal* (Pittsburgh), March 1979; *Virginia Quarterly Review* (Charlottesville), Summer 1980; Robert Phillips, in *New Letters* (Kansas City), Summer 1980; Donald M. Hassler, in *Tar River Poetry* (Greenville, North Carolina), Spring 1981; "Intellect, Grit, and a Chance to Sing in Our Chains" by Douglas Myers, in *Missoulian* (Missoula, Montana), 31 May 1985; "Poetry: Changes and Channels" by Robert McDowell, in *Hudson Review* (New York), Summer / Fall 1985; in *Virginia Review*, vol. 61, no. 4, Autumn 1985; Betty Thiebes, in *Cutbank,* 1985; "Lion" by Richard Simpson, in *Tar River Poetry Review,* Fall 1985; Hans Ostrum, in *Small Press Review,* November 1985; Lex Runciman, in *Western American Literature,* vol. 11, no. 3; Bette Tomlinson, in *Missoulian,* 12 December 1986; Floyd Skloot, in *Calapooya Collage,* (Manmouth, Oregon), no. 11, Summer 1987; "Poetry in Moments," in *Missoulian* (Missoula, Montana), 28 July-3 August 1989; "Wordsworth and Four Americans" by Richard Simpson, in *Tar River Poetry Review* (Greenville, North Carolina), Fall 1989; "Taking Nothing for Granted" by Bette Tomlinson, in *New Letters* (Kansas City), Spring 1990; Gennie Nord, in *Missoulian,* 29 March 1992, Carolyn Kuebler, in *Hot Dish,* March / April 1992; Janet Homer, in *Cutbank,* no. 38, Summer 1992; John Bradley, in *Calapooya Collage,* 16 August 1992; Alice Derry, in *Hubbub,* vol. 2, no. 1, Fall 1992; "Emblems of Authenticity" by Frank Allen, in *Poet Lore* (Bethesda, Maryland), Spring 1993; "Parody, Passion, and Communion" by Richard Simpson, in *Tar River Poetry Review* (Greenville, North Carolina), vol. 32, no. 2, Spring 1993; "American Latitudes" by Calvin Bedient, in *Southern Review* (Baton Rouge, Louisiana), vol. 29, no. 4, October 1993; by James Finn Cotter, in *Hudson Review* (New York), Summer 1994.

Patricia Goedicke comments:

I write to set myself and perhaps a few others free: free politically in the sense that the process of "sharing" the private views of reality each of us sees from the separate hotel room windows of our lives is part and parcel of the assertion—indeed even a validation—of the very idea of community; and free spiritually in the sense that the intensity of poetry's concentration on the already deeply metaphorical character of language is chiefly important for the way it enables the individual, apparently incorporeal psyche to move back and forth between the material world of exterior reality and the invisible, eternally isolated interior world of the self.

Also, trusting in poetry's fierce insistence on the—at least—double-edged, continually punning nature of language to keep me true to the many-folded complexities of "the real story" of whatever experience brings me, I write to keep myself honest. And finally I write for pleasure, not only for the sheer delight—familiar to everyone who has ever loved nursery rhymes—of rolling words around in my mouth, but also for rhythm's sake; in a prosy

world of walkers to evoke the joyously liberating power of the dance, of poetry's great, healing ability to *move* us, as we say, "beyond ourselves."

*   *   *

In her first volume, *Between Oceans,* Patricia Goedicke treated with spasmodic power the chief themes that have haunted her since—myth and dreams, childhood fantasies, the I-Thou relationship wherever it is found (be it in marriage, friendship, or the larger community), and the issue of paradise and hell in human experience. She has spoken powerfully of the experience of death. Her first book has a poem about a suicide ("Priscilla") and a loved one's death in a hospital ("The Gift"), and a sense of death pervades poems like "The World Draped in White Sheets," which treats the miracle of childhood, when the capacity for perceiving even tragedy and accident as beautiful has not yet been lost:

> No one ever remembers how it rained when we were children.
> There may have been bucketfuls more than now
> bigger
>   better
>   sluicing down over the hills
> Great wet gallons of it spilling down the streets
> but no, it is the snow, the snow we remember
>   the scabbed corpse covered up
>   the world draped in white sheets.

The poet moves with the eyes of the children who are inventing myth, learning to abstract the unacceptable into the acceptable, and continuing their survivors' duty to marvel:

> The couple that smothered in the car
> and the cold, the cold
> the turnip-white fingers and toes
> the old feet stumbling, stumbling

In her later books Goedicke copes as bravely as any poet of our time with her own mortality; her poems sometimes describe the fight against a life-threatening illness, and she uses all the resources of wit and metaphor to hold onto poetry's sustaining power and to the people whose love can be crucial. Yet, she acknowledges the loneliness and alienation of her struggles:

> Slipping out of the sleeping bag of our love
> Only for a little, to try it
> In the warm bedroom, in the city
>
> I am astonished, at first
> The air is empty, I am naked
> None of your arms enfold me
>
> Nevertheless I must walk
> Once in awhile by myself

At every turn she reminds the beloved addressed and the reader (sometimes the reader *is* her beloved addressed) that it is essential, even a duty, to grasp the beauty of every moment. Yet "the future is lying in wait / with sad eyes looking back / like a huge slaughtered mountain."

Goedicke is a romantic, and her love poems are always intense and willing to risk:

> I'm drinking nothing but rain these days
> Thinking how much I love you
>
> I still pour tears
> Even in brilliant sunshine,
> Even in snow

She is also alert to the need for change and social responsibility:

> Each day's a hot potato, let me see
> How to say it...
> Between the milk and the orange juice
> I think of the night before, the knife
> Edge of my own tongue—
> But the soldier never intended
> To murder the women and children—

Goedicke's poems often express a startled awareness of the I-Thou fellowship of those who have loved and suffered:

> What faces we hold out to each other! See
> We take off our glasses,
> At meetings our startled smiles
> Shine in the lamplight like such good children
> Nobody believes us, nobody
> Believes anybody

Her concern with what's wrong with the world pervades both personal grief and everyday mundanity:

> While we're out there standing beside a general doing noth-
>   ing,
> Standing beside the latest rocket doing nothing,
> While we're standing beside the cash registers doing noth-
>   ing.

Clearly Goedicke's search is for serenity: "For the shape of self pity is a real swamp, finally." There also is comfort in a relationship, even with the dead: "I put my arms around you / My last sight of you / For I am about to be killed, too." Goedicke has documented the familiar but unavoidable stages of grief and concluded, "In the courtyard of my ears / Everyone's death comes whispering." Yet she bravely, even wisely, asserts hope: "We must build more on less."

In her mature poetry, showcased in *Paul Bunyan's Bearskin,* Goedicke moves through themes already familiar to her readers to a grander vision—one more objective, as if she were observing earth from a spaceship. The title poem is itself a dazzler, reminding one of Ginsberg's discursive poems on a troubled America. The arrogance that has threatened the very existence of the nation, not only a betrayal of its ideals, seems to both poets a manifestation observable at every turn. Men meddle impiously with nature; their technology gives them "claws / to pull down Ursa Major." They wish, like the fools Shakespeare depicted in the days of Henry IV, to change the course of rivers, to make their impression on the heavens. As if from an airship, Goedicke inspects with a worrying compassion a nation that seems to have cancer—"the corpse pinned to coordinates...one-of-a-kind cells breathing / the

live rippling spirit of a bear taking up his bed / and walking, no one can predict how or when or where." That Native American bear is trying to survive, and the poet sings of her bond with him and the earth—not with those who have created the stone monuments of Washington, D.C., and Salt Lake City ("dazzling white bone"), showcases of death. A cancer survivor herself, Goedicke has made of her own odyssey through life-threatening illness a journey which has given her much to share with the world—especially a sense of the sacred and how precious the world was before men began their Faustian gambles, staking life on their new discoveries or the inventions of new weaponry, which are their toys.

In "Weight Bearing" an obese Native American seems to bear his caloric burden like the weight of his sufferings. A handsomer image of his isolation strikes the poet as she observes his landscape: "Out there on the mesa he is a lone cottonwood / Muttering to itself in the wind." Goedicke's poetry is almost entirely, in fact, the voicing of an equally painful isolation. Even at a cocktail party (depicted in "The Periscope of the Eye"), where others are numbing themselves, angst is intrusive and commands attention, the posing of questions—an obligation to acknowledge that "there's never enough time / to think about how trapped we are, how terrified / Of drowning, of losing ourselves in the ocean / Out there with all those others...My friend says to be able to bear it / We must put on our blinders." This is the dilemma, but for being concerned the speaker is merely further alienated, even punished, a payoff hardly to be desired.

Yet complacency and indifference seem as elusive to Goedicke's speakers as they are easy to the others who surround her at cocktail parties. "But now all we have is our own life jackets" seems a pathetic wail, a cry for help that is answered only by "steamy saunas of self help..." and some joy of the body—"Cruising along in the one body / That keeps me and my family safe." Her ramblings—philosophic and provocatively near theology with their questionings of life's ultimate meanings—never seem far from a nostalgia for Eden, a simpler world, a praise of poverty and simplicity, lost to intellectuals of every ilk: "My friend says Poetry blooms best / On bread and water, even slipped through the barred / Metal hatchways of prisons." Goedicke's work affirms the old truth that only the outsider sees through sham and pretense and can offer truth with which to confront the world's evil. "But here," she says of the unreal "real world" (this reader suspects that she includes the academic as well as the military-industrial and the political establishment, bureaucratic power structures of every description, not exempting religion), "Poetry is invisible: / As strange silos thrust themselves up...." The silos come not just from under the earth but also from those haunted caverns where the designs first formed themselves—the aggressive mind of man, "Out of the troughs of the unconscious." The poet survives by "Pretending I don't care, hurling myself into the statistics / In the land of instant gratification..." Yet that is no gratification at all, she confesses. Such complacency and metooism offers as temporary a fix as ice cream on the tongue.

Goedicke does not seem to think that technology has helped. In "Coin of the Realm" all money seems tainted by the weapons industry that endangers the lives of all—most poignantly, the children. The worst-case scenario that the Cold War's end promised to resolve—beneath the sham and false promises—is a continuing and terrible cause for anxiety. The doomsday scenario is kept active as a possibility and an option. Goedicke's poem seems to see purported progress as a tease and a torture. The threat is still present, and we still bankrupt ourselves to keep humanity terrified. The "missile silo near Great Falls / Montana" is still manned.

We share a planet, then, with those who are aware, terrified, and concerned—and also with the indifferent who prowl about them. Unfortunately, as Goedicke maintains in "Beyond the Mountains," our compassion is limited to what we can identify with, what we have ourselves suffered. "Pain has no shape" so long as it is known only through photographs. Only when we have walked in another's shoes can we get outside ourselves enough to care what he has been through. We are left, therefore, with a terrible vulnerability, an inadequate sense of what we need to protect ourselves and others from. In many poems Goedicke explores the ramifications of these dilemmas and paradoxes. Her people seem to be caught in a vise of suffering yet are too concerned for the world to beg for release, for that would make them the equals of those who do not care, whose indifference helps perpetuate suffering.

There is not space to praise adequately *Paul Bunyan's Bearskin*, a landmark book in a major poet's career. But one can safely assert that Goedicke's stature as a major contemporary poet will be acknowledged more and more, even by critics who have been diverted by chimerical wordplay elsewhere. In making this breakthrough she has benefited the art of poetry itself.

—David Ray

GOODISON, Lorna (Gaye)

Nationality: Jamaican. **Born:** Kingston, 1 August 1947. **Education:** St. Hugh's High School, Kingston, 1959-66; Jamaica School of Art, Kingston, 1967-68; School of the Art Students League, New York, 1968-69. **Family:** Divorced; one son. **Career:** Art teacher, Jamaica College, 1969-70; copy chief, McCann Erickson advertising, Jamaica, 1970-72; assistant creative director, LNCK Advertising, Jamaica, 1972-74; creative director, Don Miller Advertising, Jamaica, 1974-76; public relations officer, Jamaica Broadcasting Corporation, 1976; creative consultant, CARIFESTA '76 Jamaica, 1976. Freelance writer and painter, 1977—. Writer-in-residence, University of the West Indies, Kingston; 1973; fellow, Bunting Institute, Radcliffe College, Cambridge, Massachusetts, 1986-87; visiting professor, University of Michigan, Ann Arbor, 1992-97; visiting instructor at University of Toronto, Sitka Summer Institute, Alaska, and University of Miami Caribbean Summer Institute. Editor, CARIFESTA '76 magazine, 1976. **Awards:** Institute of Jamaica Centenary Medal, 1981, and Musgrave Medal, 1987; Commonwealth Poetry prize, 1986. **Agent:** New Beacon Books, 76 Stroud Green Road, London N4 3EN, England. **Address:** 8 Marley Close, Kingston 6, Jamaica.

Publications

Poetry

Poems. Privately printed, 1974.
Tamarind Season. Kingston, Institute of Jamaica Press, 1980.

I Am Becoming My Mother. London, New Beacon, 1986.
Heartease. London, New Beacon, 1988.
Lorna Goodison. New York, Research Institute for the Study of Man, 1989.
To Us All Flowers Are Roses. London. New Beacon, and Urbana, University of Illinois Press, 1990.
Selected Poems. Ann Arbor, University of Michigan Press, 1992.
To Us, All Flowers are Roses. Chicago, University of Illinois Press, 1995.

Play

Pepper, with Trevor Rhone and Sonia Mills (produced 1989).

Short Stories

Baby Mother and the King of Swords. London, Longman, 1990.

*

Critical Studies: "Wooing with Words: Some Comments on the Poetry of Lorna Goodison" by Pamela Mordecai, in *Jamaica Journal* (Kingston), 45, 1981; "Goodison on the Road to Heartease," by Edward Baugh, in *Journal of West Indian Literature*, vol. 1, no. 1, October 1986; "On Becoming One's Mother: Goodison in the Context of Feminist Criticism," by Edward Baugh, in *Journal of West Indian Literature,* vol. 4, no. 1, 1990; "Overlapping Systems: Language in the Poetry of Lorna Goodison" by Velma Pollard, in *Carib,* no. 5, 1989; *Three Caribbean Poets on Their Work* edited by Victor L. Chang, Mona, Jamaica, Institute of Caribbean Studies, 1993.

Lorna Goodison comments:

(1984) I have spent a great deal of time trying to avoid writing poetry because, really, I'd like to live a less difficult life. But it (poetry) keeps intruding on everything. It comes in dreams, in the middle of ordinary conversations; while trying to talk to God, when I'm cooking or going about woman's business. So I surrendered. It is more powerful than all the other less difficult things I'd rather be doing.

(1990) I now feel very blessed to be called poet.

*   *   *

Lorna Goodison is among the most vibrant and original poets to emerge from the Caribbean. While demonstrating tremendous sympathy for the oppressed, she neither patronizes nor sentimentalizes her subjects; she writes with an easy, colloquial style which wears its truths lightly.

Her first published collection, *Tamarind Season,* is her most overtly political. Though encompassing tributes to the writer Jean Rhys and the musician Miles Davis as well as poems about Toronto and New York, its major preoccupations are with race and class. "England Seen," written, as many of her poems are, in an effective combination of Creole patois and educated English, describes the disillusionment of the chief hair presser of Catherine Commonwealth Hairdressers:

> ...Icylyn's accents embrace all of Great Britain
> and she does not like England.
> "I tell them white people that England is
> nowhere, at least I can't starve at home
> if is even a breadfruit tree I can stone."

More subtle are the poems describing characters who deny their own heritage; in "My Late Friend" the poet explains, "...She's fled the tropics / because the sun darkens her / my friend wants to be one with the snow." "Ocho Rios" cleverly reveals layers of compromise as the poet modulates her language in a local market:

> "how much for the curry goat?"
> "Three dolla"
> "Fi wan curry goat"
> "A four dolla fi tourist sista."
> I beat her down to a dollar fifty,
> she says I am clearly roots.
> I tell her the curry goat irie...

The poem's message is neatly underlined in the final stanzas:

> The sign in the square says "Tourism, not socialism"
> · and though I eat this curry sitting on a feed bag from
> Florida...
> which Colonizer is winning in Ocho Rios?

Goodison writes with a strong sense of community. Indeed some of her most effective poems, like "Bridge Views," draw on her own family:

> ...My mother did not forget to tell us
> we did not really belong there.
> Her family gave their name to rivers
> her children should not play in gullies
> we were always on our way back to where
> she originally petite bourgeoisie came from...

Moving to "concrete suburbia / acquiring the first weapons for / committing class suicide," the boys slowly succumb to "the schizoid waters," becoming thieves, alcoholics, and hit men: "and what is now a curfew zone / was then just, Home."

Her second collection, *I Am Becoming My Mother,* moves increasingly from the political to the personal. The poems in this volume are wonderfully lyrical and assured. Many of them celebrate women's lives, as does the title poem—"Yellow / brown woman / fingers always smelling of onions"—or "For My Mother (May I Inherit Half Her Strength)," which begins,

> My mother loved my father
> I write this as an absolute
> in this my thirtieth year
> the year to discard absolutes...

Describing her mother's acceptance of her father's infidelity, the poem ends:

> When he died, she sewed dark dresses for the women
> among us
> and she summoned that walk, straight-backed, that she
> gave to us
> and buried him dry-eyed...

> and she fell down a note to the realization that she did
> not have to be brave, just this once
> and she cried.

> For her hands grown coarse with raising nine children

> for her body for twenty years permanently fat
> for the time she pawned her machine for my sister's
> Senior Cambridge fees
> and for the pain she bore with the eyes of a queen

> and she cried also because she loved him.

In this prizewinning volume Goodison writes mostly about relationships, though politics appears in "For Rosa Parks," written to the woman who unwittingly started America's civil rights movement by refusing to give up her bus seat to a white person: "And how was this soft-voiced woman to know / that this 'No' / in answer to the command to rise / would signal the beginning / of the time for walking?..." Another political poem is the delightful "Bedspread," based on a real incident in which the South African police raided Winnie Mandela's home and arrested a bedspread in the colors of the African National Congress: "It was woven by women with slender / capable hands / accustomed to binding wounds / hands that closed the eyes of / dead children, / that fought for the right to / speak in their own tongues...They wove the bedspread / and knotted notes of hope / in each strand / and selvedged the edges with / ancient blessings / older than any white man's coming..." As always in Goodison's work the potential anger is tempered by wisdom and hope.

Her third collection, *Heartease,* seems to be searching for a new direction. Though the rhythms of reggae are still found, hymns and incantations prevail. In many of these poems the vivid language, memorable personalities, and wry politics of her earlier work seem to have been sacrificed to a vague spirituality: "A Rosary of Your Names (II)" is merely an uninspiring catalog: "The Merciful / The Peace / The Source / The Hidden / The All Strivings Cease..." But in other poems like "Blue Peace Incantation" Goodison's lyricism and rich visual descriptions are still evident: "Within blue of peace, / the azure of calm, / beat soft now bright heart, / beat soft, sound calm..." This volume suggests a period of transition in the work of a poet whose enduring quality is optimism.

—Katie Campbell

GRAHAM, Jorie

Nationality: American. **Born:** New York City, 9 May 1951. **Education:** Sorbonne, Paris; New York University, B.A. 1973; University of Iowa, Iowa City, M.F.A. 1978. **Family:** Married James Galvin in 1983; one daughter. **Career:** Assistant professor of English, Murray State University, Kentucky, 1978-79, and California State University, Humboldt, 1979-81; workshop instructor, Columbia University, New York, 1981-83; staff member, University of Iowa, 1983—. **Awards:** Academy of American Poets prize, 1977; Ingram Merrill Foundation grant, 1981; Bunting fellowship, 1982; Guggenheim fellowship, 1983; National Endowment for the Arts grant; Whiting award, 1985. **Address:** 436 EPB, University of Iowa, Iowa City, Iowa 52242, U.S.A.

PUBLICATIONS

Poetry

Hybrids of Plants and Ghosts. Princeton, New Jersey, Princeton University Press, 1980.
Erosion. Princeton, New Jersey, Princeton University Press, 1983.

The End of Beauty. New York, Ecco Press, 1987.
Region of Unlikeness. Hopewell, New Jersey, Ecco Press, 1991.
Materialism: Poems. Hopewell, New Jersey, Ecco Press, 1993.
The Dream of the Unified Field: Poems, 1974-1994. Hopewell,
   New Jersey, Ecco Press, 1995.
The Errancy. Hopewell, New Jersey, Ecco Press, 1997.

Other

Editor, *Earth Took of Earth: A Golden Ecco Anthology.* Hopewell,
   New Jersey, Ecco Press, 1996.

*

Critical Studies: By Helen Vendler in *New York Times Book Re-
view,* 17 July 1983; Peter Stitt, in *Georgia Review* (Athens), Spring
1984.

*   *   *

American poet Jorie Graham's "Flooding," from *Hybrids of
Plants and Ghosts,* begins:

Just rain for days and everywhere it goes it fits,
like a desire become too accurate
to be of use, the water
a skirt the world
is lifting and
lifting

like a debt ceiling...

For Graham the world is like a vast text deserted by its author
late in the process of composition. One can almost read it fully.
"The clues are everywhere," says one poem, and in another star-
lings make "a regular syntax on wings." In yet another: "Indeed
the tulips / change tense / too quickly." She sees "small building
materials / awaiting an idea." Her characteristic *explication du
monde* is evident in "One in the Hand":

A bird re-entering a bush,
like an idea regaining
its intention, seeks
the missed discoveries
before attempting
flight again.

and "The Mind":

The leaves,
pressed against the dark
window of November
soil, remain unwelcome
till transformed, parts
of a puzzle unsolvable
till the edges give a bit
and soften. See how
then the picture becomes clear,
the mind entering the ground
more easily in pieces,
and all the richer for it.

Graham's work is sustained by continuous associative activity;
her poems seem almost to be woven, and into her raw material go
ideas, visual images, abstract and very concrete nouns, and, again
and again, figures for language itself. The play of perception over
the waters of the perceivable world make a kind of continual ref-
erence to Genesis and remind us what an important poet Wallace
Stevens is for Graham. Occasionally, as in "Flooding," her asso-
ciative urgency causes a skein to ravel, but her intellectual abili-
ties and ambitions give her work gravity and free her from anec-
dote and occasion.

For her 1983 volume, *Erosion,* Graham developed some new
formal strategies. One is a short-line stanza, usually of six lines,
with indentations, as in this one from "Love":

Here it's harvest. Dust
      coarsens
the light. In the heat
      in the distance
the men burn
      their fields

to heal them...

The stanzas swirl down the page in long, complex sentences, re-
sembling the other stanza form Graham uses frequently in *Ero-
sion,* a long, single-strophed poem with all the lines printed flush
left to the margin and the lines of carefully varied lengths. Thus
"Mother of Vinegar" begins like this:

Because contained damage makes for beauty, it shines
like a brain at the bottom of each vat, the sand
in the shell,
a simple animal.

Graham has spent a lot of time in Italy, much of it looking at
paintings. Pieces by Piero della Francesca, Luca Signorelli,
Masaccio, Goya, and Gustav Klimt are central to poems in *Ero-
sion;* one poem from that book is called "Still Life with Window
and Fish." By such means her poems refer not to a body of knowl-
edge—"art history"—but to a live tradition, a palpable continu-
ity in the present of the longer sense of history Italy gives in
comparison to the American landscape. Graham's sense that cul-
ture is an organism rather than an artifact distinguishes her work
and keeps it free from cultural tourism.

The closing lines of "San Sepolcro" suggest the reach and am-
plitude her best poems attain:

            ... It is this girl
      by Piero
della Francesca, unbuttoning
      her blue dress,
her mantle of weather,
      to go into

labor. Come, we can go in.
      It is before
the birth of god. No-one
      has risen yet
to the museums, to the assembly
      line—bodies

and wings—to the open air
       market. This is
what the living do: go in.
       It's a long way.
And the dress keeps opening
       from eternity

to privacy, quickening.
       Inside, at the heart,
is tragedy, the present moment
       forever stillborn,
but going in, each breath
       is a button
coming undone, something terribly
       nimble-fingered
finding all the stops.

—William Matthews

GRAHN, Judy

Pseudonym: Carol Silver. **Nationality:** American. **Born:** Judith Rae Grahn in Chicago, Illinois, 28 July 1940. **Education:** San Francisco State University, B.A. 1984; and at various other institutions. **Military Service:** Served in the U.S. armed forces; discharged in 1961. **Career:** Has held a variety of jobs, including waitress, short-order cook, clerk, barmaid, artist's model, typesetter, photographer's assistant, and nurse's aide, all prior to 1969; co-founder, publisher, editor, and printer, Women's Press Collective, Oakland, California, 1969-78; instructor of literature and lesbian cultural classes at New College of California, San Francisco, 1984—, and California Institute of Integral Studies, 1995; instructor of a course on Gertrude Stein at Stanford University, 1988; teacher in women's writing programs in Cazenovia, New York, Ithaca, New York, Berkeley, California, and San Francisco. **Awards:** American Poetry Review Poem of the Year award, 1979; National Endowment for the Arts grant, 1980; Before Columbus Foundation American Book Award, 1983; American Library Association Gay Book of the Year award, 1985; with Alice Walker, Tillie Olsen, Janice Mirikitani, and Alice Adams, Women's Foundation (San Francisco) Women of Words Award, 1985; Lambda Book Award for nonfiction, 1988; Outlook Foundation Pioneer Gay Writer Award, 1989; Publisher's Triangle Bill Whitehead Award, 1995; Thanks Be to Grandmother Winifred Foundation grant, 1996. **Address:** Box 11164, Oakland, California 94611, U.S.A.

PUBLICATIONS

Poetry

The Common Woman Poems. San Francisco, n.p., 1969.
Edward the Dyke, and Other Poems. Oakland, California, Women's Press Collective, 1971.
Elephant Poem Coloring Book. Oakland, California, Women's Press Collective, 1972.
A Woman Is Talking to Death. Oakland, California, Women's Press Collective, 1974.
She Who: A Graphic Book of Poems with 54 Images of Women. Oakland, California, Women's Press Collective, 1978.

The Work of a Common Woman: The Collected Poetry of Judy Grahn, 1964-1977, introduction by Adrienne Rich. Oakland, California, Diana Press, 1978.
The Queen of Wands. Freedom, California, Crossing Press, 1982.
Spider Webster's Declaration: He Is Singing the End of the World Again. San Francisco, Interval Press, 1983.
Descent to the Roses of the Family (chapbook). Iowa Women's Press, 1986.
The Queen of Swords. Boston, Beacon Press, 1987.

Plays

The Cell (produced Yellow Springs, Ohio, 1968).
She Who (produced San Francisco, 1973).
The Queen of Wands (produced Ithaca, New York, 1985; London and other European cities, 1986).
March to the Mother Sea (produced Ann Arbor, Michigan, 1989).
The Queen of Swords (produced Oakland, California, 1989).

Novel

Mundane's World. Freedom, California, Crossing Press, 1989.

Essays

Another Mother Tongue: Gay Words, Gay Worlds. Boston, Beacon Press, 1984; updated and expanded, Boston, Beacon Press, 1990.
The Highest Apple: Sappho and the Lesbian Poetic Tradition. San Francisco, Spinsters Ink, 1985.
"Drawing in Nets," in *Conversant Essays: Contemporary Poets on Poetry,* edited by James McCorkle. Detroit, Wayne State University Press, 1990.
"The Common Woman, A Map of Seven Poems," in *Inversions: Writing by Dykes, Queers, and Lesbians,* edited by Betsy Warland. Vancouver, Press Gang Publishers, 1991.
Blood, Bread and Roses: How Menstruation Created the World. Boston, Beacon Press, 1993.
Butch / Femme, with Nisa Donnelly, edited by M.G. Soares. New York, Crown, 1995.

Editor, *Lesbians Speak Out.* Trumansburg, New York, Diana Press, 1974.
Movement in Black, foreword by Audre Lorde. Trumansburg, New York, Diana Press, 1978.
Editor and author of introduction, *True to Life Adventure Stories.* Vol. 1, Trumansburg, New York, Diana Press, 1978; vol. 2, Freedom, California, Crossing Press, 1989.
Editor, *Really Reading Gertrude Stein: A Selected Anthology.* Freedom, California, Crossing Press, 1989.

Recordings: *Where Would I Be without You: The Poetry of Pat Parker and Judy Grahn,* 1975; *Lesbian Concentrate,* 1978; *March to Mother Sea: Healing Poems for Baby Girls Raped at Home,* 1990; *A Woman Is Talking to Death,* 1991.

*

Media Adaptations: *The Common Woman Poems* (one-woman stage play; performed in Australia); *Edward the Dyke* (stage play; performed off-Broadway); *A Woman Is Talking to Death* (interpretive dance; performed in Seattle); "Contemplating Chrystos" (interpretive dance; performed in San Francisco); "Funeral Plainsong" (musical presentation; performed in New York).

Critical Studies: "Judy Grahn" by Lisa Tipps, in *American Women Writers,* New York, Ungar, 1980; "Helen of Troy and Female Power" by Lynda Koolish, in *San Francisco Chronicle,* 20 February 1983; "The Re-Vision of the Muse: Adrienne Rich, Audre Lorde, Judy Grahn, Olga Broumas" by Mary J. Carruthers, in *Hudson Review* (New York), Summer 1983; *Women Writers of the West Coast: Speaking of Their Lives and Careers,* edited by Marilyn Yalom, Santa Barbara, California, Capra, 1983; *Stealing the Language: The Emergence of Women's Poetry in America* by Alicia Suskin Ostriker, Boston, Beacon Press, 1986; "The Politics of the Refrain in Judy Grahn's *A Woman Is Talking to Death*" by Amitai F. Aviram, in *Women and Language* (Fairfax, Virginia), Spring 1987; *Feminism and Poetry: Language Experience, Identity in Women's Writing* by Jan Montefiore, London and New York, Pandora Press, 1987; "Judy Grahn's Gynopoetics: The Queen of Swords" by Sue Ellen Case, in *Studies in the Literary Imagination* (Atlanta), Fall 1988; *The Safe Sea of Women: Lesbian Fiction, 1969-1989* by Bonnie Zimmerman, Boston, Beacon Press, 1990; *The Reflowering of the Goddess* by Gloria Orenstein, Elmsford, New Jersey, Pergamon Press, 1990; "A Mundane Utopia" by Ron Erickson," in *Trumpeter,* Winter 1992; "She Who is a Tree: Judy Grahn and the Work of a Common Woman" by Alicia Suskin Ostriker, in *Poetry East* (Ann Arbor, Michigan), 1993; "Blood, Bread, and Roses, Judy Grahn" by Judith Arcana, *Sojourner,* vol. 20, no. 7, March 1995; "A Conversation with Judy Grahn" by Nisa Donnelly, in *Harvard Gay & Lesbian Review,* vol. 2, no. 2, Spring 1995.

*   *   *

Although probably best known for her ground-breaking nonfiction, in particular *Another Mother Tongue* (1990) and *The Highest Apple: Sappho and the Lesbian Poetic Tradition* (1985), Judy Grahn has published a number of important collections of poetry. While individual books of her poems are relatively small—both because so few have been issued and those which have been are very short in terms of their page count—their influence and depth has been vast, equally influencing lesbian and heterosexual woman poets throughout the world. Hers is a "common woman" sensibility, creating a no-frills poetry focused on subject and emotion. The best introduction to Grahn's poetry is her *The Work of a Common Woman* (1978), which collects her books from *Edward the Dyke and Other Poems* (1971) though *A Woman Is Talking to Death* (1974) and concludes with an unfinished series of love lyrics, "Confrontations with the Devil in Form of Love."

The untitled opening poem of *Edward the Dyke and Other Poems* sets the stage for much of the type of poetry for which Grahn is known. In it, she expresses anger honestly and plainly:

I'm not a girl
I'm a hatchet
...
I'm not a good lay
I'm a straight razor
look at me as if you had never seen a woman before
I have red, red hands and much bitterness.

Yet the book's centerpiece is the sometimes humorous but always satiric and sarcastic prose poem "The Psychoanalysis of Edward the Dyke." Edward's therapist, one Dr. Merlin Knox, who ignores everything Edward tells him, means to "cure" her of her "deadly affliction," her lesbianism, despite the fact that he, other men, and all the other women in the poem misunderstand it. The same book includes the enigmatic "[I have come to claim / Marilyn Monroe's body]" and a large number of other lyrics both political (such as the poignant "Vietnamese Woman Speaking to an American Soldier") and erotic (such as the lovely "[in the place where / her breasts come together])."

Indeed, it is either politics or love which, in one way or another, in larger or lesser degrees, is the chief theme of most of the poetry which Grahn has published since "Edward the Dyke." Often the two themes coexist within one poem. In *The Common Woman Poems,* Grahn reveals the lives—the trials and the joys—of seven real women, those who, Grahn has called in her introduction to the series, are neither "superhuman or pathetic." In one of her best and best-known poems, the lengthy *A Woman Is Talking to Death,* which includes sections in free verse but also one section in prose, Grahn investigates violence on numerous levels unflinchingly. It is undoubtedly her tour de force. And the intricately structured "Confrontations with the Devil in the Form of Love" is a roller-coaster ride through emotions, leaving the reader breathless over Grahn's ability to mesh the political and love together into one expression of a single individual's life. Indeed, in it, a woman named Love appears, and it is her "identity" which imbues the poem with its powerful politics and romance.

—Jim Elledge

GREENLAW, Lavinia (Elaine)

Nationality: British. **Born:** London, 30 July 1962. **Education:** Kingston Polytechnic, Surrey, 1980-83, B.A. in English (honors) 1983; London College of Printing, 1984-85, diploma in publishing/production 1985. **Family:** One daughter. **Career:** Publications editor, Imperial College of Science and Technology, London, 1985-86; desk editor, Allison & Busby, London, 1986-87; managing editor, Earthscan, London, 1988-90; assistant literature officer, South Bank Centre, London, 1990-91; principal literature officer, London Arts Board, 1991-94. Freelance writer and reviewer, 1994—. Writer-in-residence, Science Museum in London, 1994-95, Wellington College, Berkshire, fall 1996, and Sevenoaks School, Kent, spring 1997; British Council Fellow in Writing, Amherst College, fall 1995. **Awards:** Eric Gregory award, 1990; Arts Council of England Writers' award. 1995. **Agent:** Derek Johns, A. P. Watt, 20 John Street, London WC1N 2DR, England. **Address:** c/o Faber & Faber, 3 Queen Square, London WC1N 3AU, England.

PUBLICATIONS

Poetry

The Cost of Getting Lost in Space. London, Turret Books, 1991.
Love from a Foreign City. London, Slowdancer Press, 1992.

Night Photograph. London, Faber, 1993.
A World Where News Travelled Slowly. London, Faber, 1997.

*

Critical Studies: By Ian Gregson, in *Jacaranda Review* (Los Angeles), 1994.

*   *   *

Lavinia Greenlaw is mistress of the declarative sentence. Her poems begin decisively, as these three examples show:

The monks on Caldey make perfume and chocolate...

Her features unfold as she lowers her head
back against the basin...

With a head full of Swiss clockmakers,
she took a job at a New Jersey factory...

The last comes from a poem called "The Innocence of Radium," which tells of a girl employed to paint figures on dials with a substance that proves to be radioactive. The chemist who invented the paint is proud of his product, but it has deleterious effects on those who use it:

Over the years he watched her grow dull.
The doctors gave up, removed half her jaw,
and blamed syphilis when her thighbone snapped
as she struggled up a flight of stairs.

A lot of the interest of Greenlaw's poetry is in the facts that she retails. One should not, however, underestimate the quality of the craftsmanship that clears the way for her various revelations. For example, she seeks to surmise the nature of the suspension bridge at Clifton:

I curl over the railings, unable to grasp
the push-and-pull dynamics of Brunel's success...

But a tithe of mental struggle gives her a clue, and her hint about the design is self-reflexive. It is, indeed, almost a description of her own poetic process:

...then I start to accept Brunel's equation,
the simplicity holding it all in place.

Simplicity in this instance is the result of a control of language and rhythm far from simple. For example, the medium through which Greenlaw's meditations come to us is an elegantly inflected free verse—the real thing, not chopped-up prose or loosened-up blank verse. In true free verse there is a pattern of relationships; there is the line that thrusts, so to speak, and the line or lines accepting that thrust. Greenlaw seems to comprehend the pattern thoroughly:

Now it looks too easy, I can't go on,
my sense of balance is suddenly lost
along with my ignorance, the framework of
the physics of what keeps us from falling.

The poem is not only about the physics of the suspension bridge but also about the art of writing verse. In effect, it reinterprets the dictum of Alexander Pope: "Those move easiest who have learned to dance."

Greenlaw's subjects look unusual at first sight. She is shown a fragment of a meteor. She notices the sunset's play of color in the smoke from a power station smokestack. She details the history of the River Thames. She tells of "The Man Whose Smile Made Medical History," a guinea pig in the pioneering stages of plastic surgery who nevertheless succumbed to viral pneumonia because of ignorance concerning antibiotics. Reviewers have commented upon the scientific basis of Greenlaw's poetry, and indeed she has been appointed poet-in-residence at the National Science Museum in South Kensington. What she shows, however, is that science is part of life, not an entity removed from it. Her poetry, so far from being cerebral, is touchingly human.

Night Traveller and *A World Where News Travelled Slowly,* as well as more recent uncollected verse, have built upon the distinction of Greenlaw's first book. These later poems are more colorful, more metaphorical, more fanciful than her earlier work, with a greater extent of play upon words and perhaps a more self-conscious dedication to style. In the poem "Akhmatova in Lambertville" the legendary Soviet poet is imagined contemplating the Delaware River in winter. (In fact she was confined to Russia for most of her life and certainly never visited the United States.) The verse sustains a kind of metaphysical yoking together of heterogeneous images:

The revelations of ice, exactly:
each leaf carries itself in glass,
each stem is a fuse in a transparent flex,

each blade, for once, truly metallic.
Trees on the hill explode like fireworks
for the minute the sun hits.

The poem would seem to have learned from its illustrious heroine, and its linguistic richness augurs well. There is no young poet whose work is more eagerly awaited.

—Philip Hobsbaum

GRIFFIN, Susan

Nationality: American. **Born:** Los Angeles, California, 26 January 1943. **Education:** University of California, Berkeley, 1960-63; San Francisco State College (now University), B.A. (cum laude) 1965; California State University, San Francisco (now San Francisco State University), M.A. 1973. **Family:** Married John Levy in 1966 (divorced 1970); one daughter. **Career:** Assistant editor, *Ramparts* magazine, San Francisco, 1966-68; instructor in English, San Francisco State College (now University), 1970-71; high school poetry instructor, Poetry-in-the-Schools program, Oakland, California, 1972-73; instructor in creative writing and women's studies, University of California, Berkeley, extension school, 1973-75; instructor, San Francisco State University, 1974-75. Visiting writer, Delta College of San Joaquin and Cazenovia College. Contributor to numerous periodicals, including *Aphra, Los Angeles Times, Ms., Ramparts, Shocks, Sundance,* and *Whole Earth Review.* **Awards:** Ina Coolbrith Prize for Poetry, 1963; Emmy Award, 1975, for *Voices;* National Endowment for the Arts grant, 1976; Malvina Reynolds Award for cultural achievement, 1982; Schumacher fellow, 1983; Ph.D., Graduate Theological Union, 1985; Kentucky Foundation for Women grant, 1987; Commonwealth Medal, 1987, for *Unremembered Country;* Women's Foundation Award for Women in the Arts, 1988; MacArthur Foundation grant, 1990. **Address:** 904 Keeler Ave., Berkeley, California 94708, U.S.A.

PUBLICATIONS

Poetry

Dear Sky. Berkeley, Shameless Hussy Press, 1971.
Like the Iris of an Eye. New York, Harper, 1976.
Unremembered Country: Poems. Port Townsend, Washington, Copper Canyon Press, 1987.

Short Story

The Sink. Berkeley, Shameless Hussy Press, 1973.

Plays

Voices (produced San Francisco, 1974). Old Westbury, New York, Feminist Press, 1975.
Thicket (produced San Francisco, 1992), in *Kenyon Review,* Spring 1994.

Radio Plays: *Enter the Circle,* National Public Radio, 1984.

Other

Le Viol. Montreal, L'Etincelle, 1972.
Let Them Be Said. Berkeley, Ma Ma Press, 1973.
Letters. Berkeley, Effie's Press, 1973.
Woman and Nature: The Roaring inside Her. New York, Harper, 1978; London, Harper Collins, 1985.
Rape: The Power of Consciousness. San Francisco, Harper, 1979.
Pornography and Silence: Culture's Revolt against Nature. New York, Harper, 1981.
Made from This Earth: Selections from Her Writing, 1967-82. London, Women's Press, 1982, published as *Made from This Earth: An Anthology of Writings,* New York, Harper, 1983.
A Chorus of Stones: The Private Life of War. Garden City, New York, Doubleday, 1992.
The Eros of Everyday Live: Essays on Ecology, Gender and Society. New York, Doubleday, 1995.

*

Media Adaptations: *Voices* (television film), 1974.

Critical Studies: Interview with Nannerl Koehane, in *Women Writers of the West Coast: Speaking of Their Lives and Careers,* edited by Marilyn Yalom, Santa Barbara, Capra Press, 1983; "In Defense of Separatism" by Susan Hawthorne, in *A Reader in Feminist Knowledge,* edited by Sneja Gunew, New York, Routledge, 1991; "Poetry and the Pity of War" by K.K. Roeder, in *Women's Review of Books,* vol. 17, no. 3, Winter 1992; *Skirting the Issue: Pursuing Language in the Works of Adrienne Rich, Susan Griffin, and Beverly Dahlen* by Alan Shima, Uppsala, Uppsala University Press, 1993.

*   *   *

From the earliest stage of her career, Susan Griffin has been political, perhaps because she is both female and lesbian. Indeed, politics informs her poetry and is the focus of much of her nonfiction. In her early collections of poetry—the chap-book *Dear Sky* or the omnibus "anthology" of her writings, *Made from This Earth* (which includes poems as well as essays and a play)—Griffin investigates the plight of women with an in-your-face honesty which is nevertheless tempered by her desire for truth, revelation, healing—not revenge. While she includes a large number of socially focused poems in such books, among them "I Like to Think of Harriet Tubman," her political agenda and her personal life are, more often than not, so tightly intertwined that they're indistinguishable from one another. In "Geraldine," for example, she movingly allows her mother to admit that "The movies... / ruined [her] life," then to explain her pronouncement: film gave young women of her generation a false view of the world and their place in it. Similarly in "Revolution," Griffin excludes the expected political rhetorical for an image-centered examination of a failed relationship:

> what else was there to do,
> struggle
> in a boat with a leak
> over cold water?

Unremembered Country, reveals Griffin at her most mature, uncompromising, and powerful. Its clipped lyrics strike the heart with their simplicity and honesty. Never has she been so utterly in charge of her talent. Many of the topics associated with Griffin since the beginnings of her career find their way into this book, yet its poems are more precise than ever and suggest a spiritual awakening. Its first part vaguely traces the development of the relationship between a mother and her child, from the earliest moment within that relationship to the child's realization that it is separate from its mother while simultaneously and forever linked to her. Part II, a series of closely interrelated poems, investigates with a depth rare in contemporary poetry what it may mean to be a mother, her practical and ideal "role." These are told from the child's point of view. The two sequences of Part III position the poet in the rich yet threatening landscape of contemporary American life. Her voice is as powerful as it is honest, merging the Nazi Holocaust with, first, the possibility of a nuclear holocaust then, second, with love. Yet, the most powerful poems of the book—the love poems, elegies, and the singular "Torture," which is about women tormented in Chile and Salvador—are those which comprise the concluding section (Part IV) of the collection.

Regardless of which of Griffin's collections one reads, her chief concern remains the interaction between individuals and their relationship to one another. For her, that interaction is in no way isolated from the relationship of the individual to the world which, more often than not, is urban, industrial, and politically propelled. In such a place, Griffin's poetry reminds us again and again, the individual—especially if the individual is female—is ignored, even abolished by those who control it.

—Jim Elledge

GUEST, Barbara

Nationality: American. **Born:** Wilmington, North Carolina, 6 September 1920. **Education:** University of California, Berkeley, A.B. 1943. **Family:** Married 1) Lord Stephen Haden-Guest in 1948 (divorced 1954), one daughter; 2) Trumbull Higgins in 1954, one son. **Career:** Editorial associate, *Art News,* New York, 1951-54. **Awards:** Yaddo fellowship, 1958; Longview Foundation award, 1968; Foundation for Poetry awards, 1970, 1996; National Endowment for the Arts grant, 1980; Laurence Lipton award for literature, 1989; Jerone J. Shestack Poetry Prize, 1992; San Francisco State award for poetry, 1994; San Francisco State College award, 1995; American Award for poetry, 1996, 1997; Columbia Book Award, 1996; P.E.N. Josephine Miles Award for poetry, 1996. **Address:** 1301 Milvia Street, Berkeley, California 94709, U.S.A.

PUBLICATIONS

Poetry

The Location of Things. New York, Tibor de Nagy, 1960.
Poems: The Location of Things, Archaics, The Open Skies. New York, Doubleday, 1962.
The Blue Stairs. New York, Corinth, 1968.
I Ching: Poems and Lithographs, with Sheila Isham. Paris, Mourlot, 1969.
Moscow Mansions. New York, Viking Press, 1973.
The Countess from Minneapolis. Providence, Rhode Island, Burning Deck, 1976.
The Türler Losses. Montreal, Mansfield, 1979.
Biography. Providence, Rhode Island, Burning Deck, 1980.
Quilts. New York, Vehicle Press, 1980.
The Nude, lithographs by Warren Brandt. New York, Art Editions, 1986.
Musicality. Berkeley, California, Kelsey Street Press, 1988.
Fair Realism. Los Angeles, Sun & Moon Press, 1989.
Defensive Rapture. Los Angeles, Sun & Moon Press, 1994.
Selected Poems. Los Angeles, Sun & Moon Press, 1995.
Stripped Tales, with art by Anne Dunn. Berkeley, California, Kelsey Street Press, 1995.
Quill Solitary APPARITION. Sausalito, California, Post-Apollo Press, 1996.

Recording: *The Location of Things,* Watershed, 1984.

Plays

The Ladies Choice (produced New York, 1953).
The Office (produced New York, 1963).
Port (produced New York, 1965).

Fiction

Seeking Air (novel). Santa Barbara, California, Black Sparrow Press, 1978.
The Confetti Trees (short stories). Los Angeles, Sun & Moon Press, 1997.

Other

Robert Goodnough, with B. H. Friedmann. Paris, G. Fall, 1962.
Herself Defined: The Poet H.D. and Her World. New York, Doubleday, 1984; London, Collins, 1985.
The Altos, with Richard Tuttle. San Francisco, Hawk Hine Editions, 1991.

*

Manuscript Collections: University of Kentucky, Lexington; Lockwood Memorial Library, State University of New York, Buffalo; New York University; Yale University Beinecke Library.

Critical Study: In *HOW(ever)* (San Francisco), vol. 1, no. 3.

Barbara Guest comments:
   The poem gathers itself (becomes embodied) the way a narrative diffuses and is sustained by movements, auditory and visual.

*   *   *

   Barbara Guest was originally associated with the so-called New York school of poets, which included Frank O'Hara, John Ashbery, Kenneth Koch, and James Schuyler. Throughout her career her work has retained contact with the visual arts and music, the tendency toward "painterly" abstraction, and the notable formal experimentation that characterized the writing of all of these poets. Guest's work, however, embodies a tension between two opposed impulses: a lyric, or purely musical, impulse; and a graphic, or painterly, impulse, which emphasizes the materiality and arrangement of words in the poem. Both elements vie for dominance in her individual poems, determining their character.
   A key aspect of Guest's work, in keeping with her interest in the arts in general, is its self-reflexiveness. She often considers the problem of artistic composition and consciousness itself, and it is within this context that the interartistic metaphor of poetry as painting or music functions in her work. In the poems "Roses" and "The Poetess," from *Moscow Mansions,* or "Dora Maar" and "The Screen of Distance," from *Fair Realism,* for example, Guest explores the tension between the black-and-white, depthless "sense" of words and the dimensional, coloristic sensuality of painting. "The Poetess" (after Miró) employs a Gertrude Stein-like literary Cubism to dramatize the difference and interaction between figure and discourse:

   A dollop is dolloping
   her a scoop is pursuing
   flee vain ingots   Ho
   coriander darks   thimble blues
   red okays adorn her
   buzz green circles in flight
   or submergence?   Giddy
   mishaps of blackness make
   stinging clouds what!

Analogously, Guest explores the sonorous qualities of poetic language and the expressive possibilities of form and variation in "Expectation" (*Defensive Rapture*), which makes reference to Arnold Schoenberg's atonal composition *Erwartung*:

masked throat—

      gradual broken ascent
      —means intensify

through an aperture—the tilt

      grave—
      ropings.

This dichotomy of coloristic effect and musicality is not only thematically considered, however; it is also formally enacted by the poems in Guest's handling of syntax and form. Her coloristic use of the line recalls, in its symbolistic luxuriance, the late work of Wallace Stevens. This can be seen in "The Rose Marble Table," from *Fair Realism*:

Sea whose translucence disturbs inferior atoms,
that passage from ice to shallow removes familiars
as glass changes to foam, the parallel lake diminished,
combs drop into fur.

But elsewhere Guest stresses the musical qualities of language, mobilizing its latent capacities for pulse, rhythm, volume, euphony, and notation. Here, as in "Musicality," from *Fair Realism,* her poetry takes on a performative quality:

Hanging apples half notes
in the rhythmic ceiling red flagged
rag clefs

      notational margins

      the unfinished

      cloudburst

For the early Wittgenstein the syntax of propositions, the hierarchy of their relations, and their order of succession gave a "logical picture" of the world. In an analogous way Guest explores the world-picturing or world-making—she leaves the question open—properties of the language of poetry. In her exploration of "what is the case," she is deeply concerned with syntax and with other modes of connection between words like spatial form, lineation, and typography. Two antipodal features of her poetry follow from this concern: Guest's use of parataxis and typographical fragmentation, illustrated by lines from "Ilex" (*Fair Realism*)—

      we lost him. he disappeared.

rinds of gold stitched to his aura—
at the entrance armed with blocks—
the stylus blunt—

      mood of helmeted star light

—and her use of a self-consuming, self-enfolding syntax, illustrated by "Prairie Houses" (*The Countess from Minneapolis*)—

Unreasonable lenses refract the
sensitive rabbit holes, mole dwellings and snake
climes where twist burrow and sneeze
a native species

into houses

corresponding to hemispheric requests
of flatness

euphemistically, sentimentally
termed prairie.

Guest conceives of poetry as open-ended, contingent, and risky. It remains suspended in a space between the world of perception and the world of imagination. Again, this is a Stevens-like view of poetry that is illustrated by lines from "Heavy Violets" (*Fair Realism*):

The world makes this division
copied by words each with a leaf
attached to images it makes of this
half in air and half out
like haloes or wrists

But Stevens's supreme fiction of a world "revolving in crystal," the utopia of imagination, may unexpectedly shatter, again reopening the question of reality in the ambiguous movement of liberation and pain ("'Look now forwards and let the backwards be,'" from *Fair Realism*):

A wrist for every watch
releasing doves

In the blown haze
a search for crystal

Broken glass

—Tyrus Miller

GUNNARS, Kristjana

Nationality: Canadian. **Born:** Reykjavik, Iceland, 19 March 1948. **Education:** Oregon State University, B.A. 1973; University of Regina, Saskatchewan, M.A. 1978. **Family:** One son. **Career:** High school teacher, Althyduskolinn, Eidum, Iceland, 1974-75; instructor of twentieth-century literature, University of Regina, Saskatchewan, 1979; editorial assistant, *Iceland Review,* Reykjavik, 1980-81. Currently professor of English and creative writing, University of Alberta, Canada. **Address:** Department of English, University of Alberta, Edmonton, Alberta, Canada.

PUBLICATIONS

Poetry

One-Eyed Moon Maps. Toronto, Press Porcepic, 1980.
Settlement Poems. Winnipeg, Turnstone Press, 2 vols., 1980.
Wake-Pick Poems. Toronto, Anansi, 1981.
The Night Workers of Ragnarok. Toronto, Press Porcepic, 1985.
Carnival of Longing. Winnipeg, Turnstone Press, 1989.
Exiles among You. Regina, Saskatchewan, Coleau Books, 1992.

Novels

The Prowler: A Novel. Red Deer, Alberta, Red Deer College Press, 1989.
The Substance of Forgetting. Red Deer, Alberta, Red Deer College Press, 1992.

Short Stories

The Axe's Edge. Toronto, Press Porcepic, 1983.
The Guest House, and Other Stories. Concord, Ontario, Anansi, 1992.

Other

Zero Hour. Red Deer, Alberta, Red Deer College Press, 1991.
The Rose Garden. Red Deer, Alberta, Red Deer College Press, 1996.

*

Critical Studies: "Icelandic Rhythms" by George Johnson, in *Canadian Literature* (Vancouver), no. 92, Spring 1982; "Troll Turning: Poetic Voice in the Poetry of Kristjana Gunnars," in *Canadian Literature* (Vancouver), no. 105, Summer 1985, and "Ground of Being," in *Canadian Literature* (Vancouver), no. 111, Winter 1986, both by M. Travis Lane; "Arctic Miracles, Dethroned Fables" by Patricia Keeney Smith, in *Canadian Forum,* vol. 67, no. 758, April 1986; "Transformation of the 'I': Self and Community in the Poetry of Kristjana Gunnars" by Paul Hjartarson, in *Canada and the Nordic Countries,* edited by Jorn Carlsen and Bengt Streijffert, Lund, Lund University Press, 1988; "The White Inuit Speaks: Contamination as Literary Strategy" by Diana Brydon, in *Past the Last Post: Theorizing Post-Colonialism and Post-Modernism,* edited by Ian Adam and Helen Tiffin, Calgary, University of Calgary Press, 1990.

Kristjana Gunnars comments:

Since we are living in a world wherein change takes place faster than our ability to absorb it, the writer's task is more urgent than ever. Writers are there to absorb new realities and examine how our lives are impacted by shifts in consciousness and understanding. A careful writer will allow the forms of literature to respond to changing needs of readers. Rather than adhering to centuries-old divisions between genres, new writers are better off interrelating prose and poetry, fiction and nonfiction, in ways that allow the reader's imagination to be open to new realities. It is worth remembering that the categories of "novel" and "poetry" and "nonfiction" are market-driven terms. It is up to the writer to make the market respond to the work, rather than the other way around.

*   *   *

If there is a key to Kristjana Gunnars's writing, both poetry and prose, it is the following sentence: "I am enamoured of ... the rediscovery of life" (from the chapbook *Water, Waiting,* issued in 1987). Many poets have expressed their love of life and some have lamented its loss, but few have given expression to their love of its rediscovery. For Gunnars the past is there to be brought back to life through the act of remembering those who went before. This is the act of turning one's predecessors into one's ancestors, and it is an important act for this poet because she has staked her poetry and prose on the act of remembering the lives of the hardy pioneers from Iceland who settled along the shores of the lakes of Manitoba in the second half of the nineteenth century. Gunnars herself is a latter-day immigrant from Iceland. Along with the story writer W. D. Valgardson, she has made it her mission to draw to the attention of Canadian readers this square in the country's multicultural patchwork quilt.

Her poetry seems to reverberate with the heavy stresses of Old Norse. The poet George Bowering has written that "Gunnars's poems sound and feel as if they have lasted a few thousand years, they are that careful." Her early work, found in the two volumes of *Settlement Poems* (1980), makes use of documentary technique and the so-called found manner to bring back to life the early pioneer settlers. Some of the poems reproduce lines from settlers' journals and other documents, as in the following:

> july 1, 1877: the first
> rain may 5, grass
> sprouts, leaves burst

Other poems are more expressive of the poet than they are of the lot of the settler. In "From Memory II" Gunnars wrote,

> You want to know the trick of fertility
> want to know the trick of infertility
> to know how to stay together
> know if the other is faithful
>
> i'm forgetting fast
> it's a long trip from glasgow to Quebec
> this is the last story i'll tell

At times Gunnars's poems recall the first-person narratives of Edgar Lee Masters's *Spoon River Anthology.* The 30 poems that comprise *One-Eyed Moon Maps* (1980) are "shaped by ancient Norse myth, the mystery of runes, and the magic of modern technology." Rather in the manner of a meditation on the tarot cards, Gunnars free-associates on rune stones. The results are enigmatic, inconclusive. Here are some lines from "Wall":

> the grave of rest
> the doors that open
> i don't want to look at earth
> but up, at moon
> ...
> in the north, up there
> you can't die

A grim and remorseless humor is expressed in *Wake-Pick Poems* (1981), where in "Changeling XV" Gunnars writes that

> it isn't easy to be troll
> trolls take everything you've got
> take your innocence
> throw it away

The poem "The Silent Hand" from *The Night Workers of Ragnarök* (1985) seems to imply a shift in the author's concern from the past and even the present to the future:

> we cannot be sure where
> we come from. all
> that matters is
>
> where we long to go
> the silent hand that draws us
> in

Later books offer more personal poems. One example is "Gullfoss" in *Carnival of Longing* (1989), with its contemporary sentiments about the danger that lurks in apparently harmless words:

> I have written words to you
> and I imagine they have become knives
> that my words injure

In the journal-like contents of *Zero Hour* (1991), there is a sense of looking ahead to a future fraught with the threat of global or even celestial conflagration:

> I have come to that place in life where
> there is nothing below. There are no
> lower numbers.

In her writing Gunnars has embraced the distant past, the difficult present, and the unforeseeable future. She has celebrated nearly forgotten heroes of the nineteenth century and contrasted their almost mythic lives with the ironic lives of denizens of the late twentieth century. She writes with an intensity that is surprising, given her spare, lean style. Her achievement lies in her willingness and ability to imbue Canadian poetry with a sense of the passing of generations.

—John Robert Colombo

H

HACKER, Marilyn

Nationality: American. **Born:** New York City, 27 November 1942. **Education:** Bronx High School of Science, New York; Washington Square College, New York University, B.A. 1964; Art Students League, New York. **Family:** Married the writer Samuel R. Delany in 1961 (divorced 1980); companion of Karyn J. London since 1986; one daughter. **Career:** Worked as a teacher, mail sorter, and editor of books, magazines, and trade journals; antiquarian bookseller, London, 1971-76; Jenny McKean Moore Chair in Writing, George Washington University, Washington, D.C., 1976. Editor, *City Magazine,* 1967-70, *Quark,* 1969-70, *Little Magazine,* 1977-80, *13th Moon,* 1982-86, all New York, and *Kenyon Review,* Gambier, Ohio; guest editor, *Ploughshares,* 1989, 1996. George Elliston poet-in-residence, University of Cincinnati, Ohio, 1988; distinguished writer-in-residence, American University, Washington, D.C., 1989; visiting professor, Barnard College, New York, fall 1995; Fannie Hurst visiting professor of poetry, Brandeis University, fall 1996; Fannie Hurst Writer-in-Residence, Washington University, St. Louis, spring 1997. **Awards:** YM-YWHA Discovery award, 1973; Lamont Poetry Selection award, 1973; National Endowment for the Arts grant, 1974, 1985. 1994; National Book award, 1975; Guggenheim fellowship, 1980; New York State Council on the Arts grant, 1980; Ingram Merrill Foundation fellowship, 1984; Coordinating Council of Little Magazines Editor's fellowship, 1984; Lambda Literary Award, 1991, 1995; Academy of American Poets' Lenore Marshall Prize, 1995; Poets' Prize, 1996. **Address:** 230 West 105 Street, #10A, New York, New York 10025, U.S.A.

PUBLICATIONS

Poetry

The Terrible Children. Privately printed, 1967.
Highway Sandwiches, with Thomas M. Disch and Charles Platt. Privately printed, 1970.
Presentation Piece. New York, Viking Press, 1974.
Separations. New York, Knopf, 1976.
Taking Notice. New York, Knopf, 1980.
Assumptions. New York, Knopf, 1985.
Love, Death, and the Changing of the Seasons. New York, Arbor House, 1986; London, Onlywomen Press, 1987.
Going Back to the River. New York, Random House, 1990.
The Hang-Glider's Daughter: Selected Poems. London, Onlywomen Press, 1990.
Selected Poems, 1965-1990. New York, Norton, 1994.
Winter Numbers: Poems. New York, Norton, 1994.

Recording: *The Poetry and Voice of Marilyn Hacker,* Caedmon, 1976.

Other

Editor, with Samuel R. Delany, *Quark 1-4.* New York, Paperback Library, 4 vols., 1970-71.

Editor, *Woman Poet: The East.* Reno, Nevada, Women in Literature. 1982.

Translator, *Edge,* by Claire Malroux. Chapel Hill, North Carolina, Wake Forest University Press, 1996.

*

Critical Studies: Interview with Karla Hammond in *Frontiers,* 5(3), 1981; with Annie Finch, in *American Poetry Review,* vol. 25, no. 3, May / June 1996.

* * *

Marilyn Hacker's poems from the beginning of her career have established a unique counterpoint between classical rhyming forms—sestina, sonnet, villanelle—and blunt declarative sentences to display the deranged obsessiveness of contemporary minds. Her hard-edged language in the 1970s is darkly jewel-encrusted, redolent of a devastated inner world of difficult loving, tangled sexuality, and convoluted relationships. Semiprecious gems—onyx, amethyst, alexandrite—express the hardness, mystery, and richness of experience. Lured by the foreign and strange, Hacker invents "imaginary translations," playing with exotic locales and overblown emotions. Almost tours de force, these poems lead into her central concern, the elucidation of her own intense passions, sexual, moral, and political.

Love is the premier passion which runs as a continuing strand from the earlier to the later work. Because the poem sequence "Separations," from the volume of that title, is written in sonnet form, it de-emphasizes obsession and becomes a graceful, almost Shakespearean delineation of the aspects of love, which always springs up lively and ubiquitous despite the poet's difficulties. But love always arouses thoughts of death, as in the opening poem of *Presentation Piece* (1974), in which she speaks to "the skull of the beloved" as a brooding nobleman in a Jacobean play addresses the skull of his dead mistress. "The Navigators" foreshadows the heartbroken elegy "Geographer" in *Separations* (1976), a poem which unites in formal sestinalike word repetition her continuing themes of death, cities, gems, language, and painful but persisting love.

"Persisting love" as a descriptive phrase grossly understates the obsession with a young lover that besieges Hacker for a year in *Love, Death, and the Changing of the Seasons* (1986). This "verse novel," as she calls it, is a book-length sonnet sequence emphasizing physical love almost exclusively as the poet waits, in various situations, to be united with Rachel, called Ray. The poems perform in explicit, masculinized language a *Kama Sutra* of fantasized ways of lovemaking. When Ray breaks off the affair, the poet plunges into the utter bleakness, without perspective, of the coda's final poems. But these clarify an underlying motif: her lust arose from the foredoomed but irresistible wish to be young again.

By 1990, in *Going Back to the River,* Hacker is on a more even keel, enjoying good food, drink, and the landscapes of two continents and appreciating quotidian objects. All is not pleasure, however; the unassimilable horrors of wartime experience and persecution of the Jews in France are evoked in "Days of 1944: Three Friends." Thus reminded of her Jewishness, Hacker meditates further on her ethnic background and her parents' lives in the title poem of this volume, as the rivers she goes back to—Thames, Hudson, Seine—are seen not as destinations but as reminders of the flux and uncertainties of experience.

Flux has, however, in a sense become a way of life—Hacker has homes in both New York and Paris—by the time she writes *Winter Numbers* (1994). Here the incorporation of French words renders her forms more supple and varied while also enriching the poems' sense of place. Her internationalism lessens the pain of change, making it a modus vivendi, a respite from narrow American prejudices. But her consciousness of painful change escalates as personal losses through AIDS and cancer assail her. Death is the ultimate change which everyone fears. The word "numbers" in the book's title has multiple associations: with the metrics of poetry, with mileage, with dates and time periods—the length of time, for instance, between diagnosis of illness and surgery or death. In the book's last section, "Cancer Winter," meditation on her own uncertain fate after breast cancer is enlarged to include history and the fates of those dead in the Holocaust.

The skilled use of form to serve candid observation, the ability to register ephemeral beauty, the strength to face oncoming death for herself, for everyone—these powers infuse Hacker's poems and serve as a mark of their profundity and accomplishment.

—Jane Augustine

HADAS, Rachel (Chamberlayne)

Nationality: American. **Born:** New York, New York, 8 November 1948. **Education:** Radcliffe College, Cambridge, Massachusetts, 1965-69, B.A. 1969; John Hopkins University, Baltimore, Maryland, 1976-77, M.A. 1977; Princeton University, New Jersey, 1977-82, Ph.D. 1982. **Family:** Married 1) Stavros Kondylis in 1970 (divorced 1978); 2) George Edwards in 1978; one son. **Career:** Assistant professor, 1981-87, associate professor, 1987-92, and professor, 1992—, Rutgers University, Newark, New Jersey; has taught at Columbia University, New York, New York, and Princeton University, Princeton, New Jersey. **Awards:** Isobel M. Briggs traveling fellowship, 1969-70; Vermont Council on the Arts Writers grant, 1975-76; Bread Loaf Writers Conference scholarship, 1976; Ingram Merrill Foundation fellowship, 1977, 1994; Guggenheim fellowship, 1988-89; Literature award, American Academy and Institute of Arts and Letters, 1990; McGinnis award (*Southwest Review*), 1990; Elizabeth Matchett Stover Poetry award (*Southwest Review*), 1991; *Hellas Magazine* award, 1993. **Member:** National Book Critics Circle (board member), 1994; American Academy of Arts and Sciences, 1995. **Address:** 838 West End Avenue, #3A, New York, New York 10025, U.S.A.

PUBLICATIONS

Poetry

Starting from Troy. Boston, Godine, 1975.
Slow Transparency. Middletown, Connecticut, Wesleyan University Press, 1983.

A Son from Sleep. Middletown, Connecticut, Wesleyan University Press, 1987.
Pass It On. Princeton, New Jersey, Princeton University Press, 1989.
Unending Dialogue: Voices from an AIDS Poetry Workshop. Boston, Faber, 1991.
Mirrors of Astonishment. New Brunswick, New Jersey, Rutgers University Press, 1993.
The Empty Bed. Middletown, Connecticut, Wesleyan University Press, 1995.

Other

Form, Cycle, Infinity. Cranbury, New Jersey, Associated University Presses, 1983.
Living in Time (essays and poem). New Brunswick, New Jersey, Rutgers University Press, 1990.
The Double Legacy. Boston, Faber, 1995.

Translator, *Other Worlds Than This: Translations from Latin, French, & Modern Greek Poetry.* New Brunswick, New Jersey, Rutgers University Press, 1994.

*

Manuscript Collection: Special Collections and Archives, Alexander Library, Rutgers University, New Brunswick, New Jersey.

Rachel Hadas comments:

My writing seems more various than it really is: I've translated Seneca and Tibullus, Karyotakis and Baudelaire; have written a scholarly study and personal essays, and poems about subjects ranging from motherhood to classical mythology to teaching to AIDS. Throughout my work, though, a personal approach tends to be balanced by a technically formal, decorous manner. The personal voice, withheld by formal technique, talks about education, books, love, teaching, death, elegy. To be a bit more logical about it, love is linked to loss, but loss is healed or redeemed by language, which expresses and fosters love, which is linked to loss. And so on.

My recent work in New York City with people with AIDS has received more journalistic attention than my previous poetry. I ran a poetry workshop at Gay Mens' Health Crisis for some six years, and my experiences there continue to nourish my imagination. But then so do my happy childhood, my classical education, my years in Greece or life in New York, my career as a teacher, my being wife and mother, or my rural summers.

The titles of some of my books attest to the sense of loving, losing, giving back, carrying on: *A Son from Sleep, The Empty Bed, Pass It On, Unending Dialogue, The Double Legacy.*

*   *   *

Rachel Hadas is a poet whose fine sense of technique matches her sensitivity to both the universal constants and the particular variables of human experience. She is also a poet whose work reflects a profound awareness of the goals and implications of her art. These concerns all coalesce in *Living in Time,* a work which consists of a long poem surrounded by prose essays. The volume's mixed form reflects Hadas's consciousness that she shares a commitment with such writers as Frost and Merrill "to mend the rift between fact and fiction, prose and poetry." Its contents point to three of the central concerns of her work over twenty years: her awareness of the past and of how it impinges on and merits attention from the present, her sense of the importance and the depth of what is often dismissed as "everyday" experience, and her keen effort to explore the workings of imagination as it simultaneously shapes and guides us through the webs of memory and immediate experience.

The title of her first collection, *Starting from Troy,* bears out Hadas's consistent belief that "the attempt to write as if writing were an unprecedented action is doomed to failure." Throughout her career her poems have acknowledged precedence in both their richly allusive texture (attempting to make connections with, and not merely allude to, such predecessors as Homer, Sappho, Keats, Beaudelaire, Karyotakis, Stevens) and their masterful handling and variation of traditional poetic forms. Thus, a fruitful dialogue between present circumstances and past forms (with their attendant values) unfolds through her use of the sestina for "The Colours of the Place" and terza rima for "The Lesson of the Elements" and through her "Pantoum on Pumpkin Hill" (all from *Slow Transparency*), and the dialogue continues through the different frameworks offered by the villanelle of "Fix It (Winter)" and the epistolary style of "Hortus Conclusus" (both from *Pass It On*).

Hadas has been overly critical of her early work. Characterizing its spirit as one of "distinct powerlessness" ignores too much of its wit and intellectual energy, yet her observations that these poems are "skimpy on connections, whether of narrative or argument," and that "they attempt to capture complex states of mind by excluding a great deal and disguising the rest" show typically sharp critical self-awareness. Poems such as "Village Triptych" (*Starting from Troy*) and "Alien Corn" (*Slow Transparency*) achieve a terseness that borders on obscurity by following Auden's early practice of dropping articles and connectives, and Hadas's observation in "Kaleidoscope" (*Slow Transparency*) that distinct parts "die / to form a pattern" is self-descriptive of the affective cost of such hard-edged poetry. Other early poems, however, also point toward the two means by which Hadas has overcome these limitations: the commitment to everyday experience, and the exploration of the dialogical workings of the imagination, both mentioned above as keystones in her work.

A commitment to everyday experience may be viewed simply as a broadening of the concern for provenance found in Hadas's respect for the past. It is a further way of "stationing oneself in time, at a particular moment," and so one is not surprised to find signs of it in the descriptive fullness of such early poems as "Landlady" (*Starting from Troy*) and "Siesta in the Summer House" (*Slow Transparency*). But this emphasis becomes central to the success of Hadas's later collections. The birth of her child, focused on in *A Son from Sleep,* fundamentally changed her sense of herself and her place in the world, and since her art is so vitally attuned to its maker, the event changed the nature of her art. The sense of connectedness between mother and newborn caught so fully and unsentimentally in "Amnesia, Changes" is embodied there and in such poems as "In Lieu of Lullaby" into a new wholeness, a directness achieved without any loss of lyric concision. Six short lines from "Up and Down" demonstrate both the solid detail and the metaphoric power of Hadas's later work, and their overlapping sounds also embody the interconnectedness of these areas: "Still night sweats / and bleeding still, / its bleachy smell. / Your bleat softly / shears the thick / fleece of dark."

This more broadly responsive style also has roots in the third central feature of Hadas's work, its preoccupation with the imagination's shaping power in the dialogue between inner and outer experience, past and present. Appropriately, this concern supplies the title for the long poem "The Dream Machine" at the center of *Living in Time.* As with Hadas's focus on everyday experience, one can find anticipations of this emphasis in her early work; "Two Sleepers" (*Starting from Troy*) and "Dry Season" (*Slow Transparency*), for example, both depict the rapid changes of inner and outer weather that proceed from the dream machine. Yet, it is in Hadas's later poetry that the subtle, shaping continuities (and the distortions and limitations) of the imagination receive their most probing and powerful treatment. Thus, "Generations" (*Pass It On*) turns into poetry a series of close observations on the acquisition and use of language by pursuing the threads of their implications through various times and places—what "the baby / points to," what "you / look at," what "we talk of"—with amazed awareness that "the link between imagination and event" can be at once "so weak" and so necessary. The troubling ambiguity of a world "that lasts / because it never was" ("Art") gives a double edge to the title of her volume *Mirrors of Astonishment,* and yet the heft and brilliance of the blade make the reader echo her response to the rainbow in "Cupfuls of Summer" and eagerly await more: "Look! the light!"

—Julia Reibetanz

HAGEDORN, Jessica T(arahata)

Nationality: American. **Born:** Philippines, in 1949. **Family:** One daughter. **Career:** Writer; performance artist and creator of *Airport Music* (performance art), late 1970s; commentator for *Crossroads* (radio program). Member, Gangster Choir. **Address:** New York, New York, U.S.A.

PUBLICATIONS

Poetry

Four Young Women: Poems, with others, introduction by Kenneth Rexroth. New York, McGraw-Hill, 1973.
Dangerous Music. San Francisco, Momo Press, 1975.
Pet Food & Tropical Apparitions. San Francisco, Momo Press, 1981.
Danger and Beauty. New York, Penguin, 1993.

Novels

Dogeaters. New York, Pantheon, 1990.
The Gangsters of Love. Boston, Houghton, 1996.

Plays

Where the Mississippi Meets the Amazon, with Thulani Nkabinda and Ntozake Shange (produced New York, 1977).
Screenplays: *Fresh Kill,* 1994.

Other

Editor, *Charlie Chan Is Dead.* New York, Penguin, 1995.

*   *   *

Jessica Hagedorn's poetry adapts the Beat style of Allen Ginsberg, Gregory Corso, and others from the 1960s to express the post-colonial consciousness of a Filipino woman. They are often monologues, spoken by such outcast figures from the mean streets as prostitutes and drag queens. These personae are literary surrogates for women alienated by a male-dominated society, and for Asians cut off from their original culture, now adrift in a society that demonizes them.

Hagedorn is a multi-media artist, having not only written poetry and novels, but also performed in a rock band, scripted performance art, and written screenplays. It is easy to imagine her poems being performed. The Beats also used mixed art forms, especially with jazz poetry, which was recited to the accompaniment of jazz music. While Hagedorn's work was written for the page, it possesses what Rexroth describes as a signature element of jazz poetry, "something of a public surface—meanings which can be grasped by ordinary people," as in the best Elizabethan drama, which had to satisfy both the crowd in the pit and those sitting in expensive seats. That directness also expresses a belief in poetry as "communication, statement from one person to another," and rejects the formalist idea of a poem as "an anonymous machine for providing aesthetic experiences."

Popular music, from jazz to rock and roll, are a recurrent theme and source of allusion in Hagedorn's poetry. To some degree, this simply acknowledges the truth of American culture, where the first art form teenagers respond to is rock and roll music. Her poem "Autobiography Part Two: Rock and Roll" presents a girl's emotional development as a series of preferences for different rock groups. Her attachment to their music, and her excitement at discovering new groups, is presented as a process of identity formation where real life offers only ugliness, "a gray dream / A gray meat market harbor." Rock music, especially in the late 1960s when Hagedorn wrote "Autobiography Part Two," was also strongly tied to the political activism of that era, and its emotional frankness is a fitting model of anger and, often, depression.

Hagedorn's first published poems were selected by Rexroth, and were collectively titled "The Death of Anna May Wong." This title refers to an Asian-American film actress whose career spanned the early, silent movie era of Hollywood to well after the end of World War II. Anna May Wong played stereotyped Asian women, exotic and mysterious villainesses who seem camp today in their excessive, stylized gestures, but who typified the image of an Asian woman for generations of Americans. For Hagedorn, moving to San Francisco from the Philippines, Wong represents the plight of all Asian-Americans who suffer from media representations conveying racist preconceptions rather than human life. Anna May Wong is an especially poignant figure for Hagedorn in that, as she grew up in the Philippines, American movies, like rock and roll, were a powerful, persuasive art form, more so even than the literature written in her native language. Through them, she came to believe in the American ideals of equality and fraternity, only to have her beliefs compromised by first-hand experience of reality in the States.

Her ambivalence about movies, her attraction to their powerful imagery and yet suspicion of their political message, whether implicit or explicit, is explored in the poem "Filipino Boogie." Hagedorn describes a Christmas when she was little and her parents gave her "a Dale Evans cowgirl skirt," which she cuts up with scissors because "I seen the Indian Fighter too many times."

She's also seen a movie where "Kirk Douglas rubs his chin / and slays Minehaha by the campfire." Even at this early age she knows that, living in America, her lot is cast with the Indians. The end of the poem rehearses the historical events of World War II that she has both lived, as a Filipino liberated from the Japanese by Americans, and seen in the movies. The final line presents the irony that, although the Japanese were referred to as "the yellow peril" in the racist propaganda of the war, it is now an image that she as an Asian is stamped with. "Filipino Boogie" was written in 1971, but Hagedorn's ambivalence about forms of art that can oppress while they educate and gratify, is at work in a poem from 1980's, "The Mummy." Here, she imagines a mummy coming to life in a museum, taking revenge on those who have torn her from her history, culture, and final resting place.

—Will Broadus

HANNAH, Sophie

Nationality: English. **Born:** Manchester, England, 28 June 1971. **Education:** University of Manchester, 1990-94, B.A. (with honors), 1993, M.A. 1994. **Family:** Companion of Dan Jones since 1989. **Career:** Writer-in-residence, Portico Library, Manchester, England, 1994-97; Fellow Commoner in the Creative Arts, Trinity College, Cambridge, 1997—. **Awards:** Eric Gregory award, 1995, for *The Hero and the Girl Next Door;* Northwest Arts Writer's award, 1995, for *Hotels Like Houses;* Arts Council Writer's award, 1996, for *Hotels Like Houses.* **Address:** c/o Carcanet Press, 4th Floor, Conavon Court, 12-16 Blackfriars St., Manchester M3 5BQ, England.

PUBLICATIONS

Poetry

Early Bird Blues (pamphlet). Huddersfield, Smith / Doorstop Books, 1993.
Second Helping of Your Heart (pamphlet). Kent, England, Frogmore Press, 1994.
The Hero and the Girl Next Door. Manchester, England, Carcanet Press, 1995.
Hotels Like Houses. Manchester, England, Carcanet Press, 1996.

Other

Carrot the Goldfish (for children). London, Hamish Hamilton, 1992.

*

Sophie Hannah comments:

I use rhyme and metre a lot because I like poems to have strong musical qualities. It's hard to describe my own writing; often I'm not fully aware of what I'm doing until I've done it. Thematically, my main interest is people and relationships. I often write in order to express a certain feeling (confessional poetry, I suppose) or resolve something problematic. My poems are usually quite personal and autobiographical, and my style tends to be fairly accessible. I like to think that people can understand what I'm saying and read my poems without getting a headache. Occasionally I write surreal poems which don't make sense in a conventional way because I find it refreshing to get out of my usual voice from time to time.

My favourite poets are W.B. Yeats, Percy Bysshe Shelley, John Dryden, Edna St. Vincent Millay, Robert Frost, e.e. cummings, and Wendy Cope.

*   *   *

The popular and immediate success of Sophie Hannah's first full length collection of poems, *The Hero and the Girl Next Door*, was probably due to its good-natured humor and its sharply brittle observations expressed in neatly turned verses in a recognizable contemporary language. Then there is the persona, embracing the perky, almost throw-away insouciance projected by the satirical poems.

The technique employed is often a simple but effective one: the construction of a list of paradoxically contrasting images or ideas, rounded off with a pleasantly surprising ending. A technique with a long and distinguished pedigree via the 17th-century's George Herbert, at its best it leads to a conclusion that will reverberate, however gently, in the reader's mind. Thus her poem "Difference" begins:

Not everyone who wears a hat
Is copying the Queen.
Not everything that's large and flat
Thinks it's a movie screen.

to end:

The world had better learn what's what
(If it remotely cares)—
A ladder is a ladder, not
A failed attempt at stairs.

Light verse, easily read and accessible, but not without some depth of meaning.

While some of Hannah's "lists" will be deliberately provocative, we find them collapsed in the following stanzas.

Ninety per cent of places are not worth going.
Ninety per cent of jobs are not worth doing.
Ninety per cent of men are not worth knowing.
Ninety per cent of women are not worth screwing.
An attitude like yours must take some practice.
Part apathetic, mostly condescending,

It is a formula ensuring popular success.

In other poems Hannah's "tough" stance is attractive. It projects a refreshingly no-nonsense character with which the reader can empathise. Her hilarious denunciation of external examiners in "Skipping Rhyme for Graduates" touches a universal chord of anti-authoritarianism that endears you to the poet.

I've got the motive.
I've got the stamina.
I'm going to kill
The external examiner.

She can also produce a cheeky vein of outrageousness, to which we again warm:

I am in favour of a law being passed,
forbidding, to everyone but you, the use
of the word *whirlwind.*

Nevertheless, every now and then there appears an element of self-deprecating sadness that tempers the edge of the persona presented.

You meet a man. You're looking for a hero,
Which you pretend he is.

And it is this element that impinges more in Hannah's second collection, *Hotels Like Houses*, where through the carapace of well-honed humor there emerges a voice of feeling that allows the reader to empathize with the poet. Love poems emerge that are movingly close to expressions of "Tristesse D'Amour." The same recognizably sharp analytical voice is there, but it is employed more wide-rangingly and self-probingly.

When his turned back makes one bed feel like two—
At that point you no longer have a clue.

And then there is the very moving "Preventative Elegy," with its touchingly repeated refrain:

Your death is not allowed.

While this offsets the chirpy insouciance of the earlier poems it also signals a welcome widening of Hannah's subject matter and technique that promises well for the future development of her work.

—John Cotton

HARJO, Joy

Nationality: American (Native American: Muscogee [Creek]). **Born:** Tulsa, Oklahoma, 9 May 1951. **Education:** University of New Mexico, Albuquerque, 1971-76, B.A. 1976; University of Iowa, Iowa City, 1976-78, M.F.A. 1978; Anthropology Film Center, Santa Fe, New Mexico, 1982. **Family:** One son and one daughter. **Career:** Instructor, Institute of American Indian Arts, Santa Fe, New Mexico, 1978-79, 1983-84; lecturer, Arizona State University, Tempe, 1980-81; assistant professor, University of Colorado, Boulder, 1985-88; associate professor, University of Arizona, Tucson, 1988-90; professor, University of New Mexico, Albuquerque, 1991-97. Editor, *Americans before Columbus,* 1979-80; contributing editor, *Contact II,* and *Tyuonyi,* 1984—; poetry editor, 1986-89, and poetry advisor, 1989—, *High Plains Literary Review.* Writer-in-residence, New Mexico Poetry in the Schools Program, 1974-76, 1979, 1980; Navajo Community College, 1978; Flaming Rainbow University, Tahlequah, Oklahoma, 1978; State Arts Council of Oklahoma, 1980-81; Sacaton Public Schools, Gila Indian Reservation, 1981; University of Alaska Prison Project, Anchorage, 1981; Arizona Commission on the Arts, Paradise Valley Public School, 1981; Institute of Alaska Native Arts, Nome, 1984; Richard Hugo Chair, University of Montana, 1985; State University of New York, Stonybrook, 1987. Also musician: plays saxophone and performs poetry with her band, Poetic Justice. **Awards:** William Carlos Williams award, Poetry Society of America, 1991; Before Columbus Foundation American Book award, 1991; Josephine Miles Poetry award, 1991; Witter Bynner Poetry fellowship, 1994; Native Writers' Circle of American Lifetime Achievement award, 1995; Oklahoma Book Arts award, 1995, for *The Woman Who Fell from the Sky;* Delmore Schwartz Memorial award, 1995, for *In Mad Love and War;* Mountains and Plains Booksellers award, 1995. D.Litt.: Benedictine College, 1992. **Agent:** Charlotte Sheedy, Sheedy Agency, New York, New York 10012, U.S.A. **Address:** P.O. Box 40726, Albuquerque, New Mexico 87196, U.S.A.

Publications

Poetry

The Last Song. Las Cruces, New Mexico, Puerto del Sol Press, 1975.
What Moon Drove Me to This. New York, I. Reed Books, 1979.
She Had Some Horses. New York, Thunder's Mouth Press, 1985.
Secrets from the Center of the World (with prose and photographs). Tucson, University of Arizona Press, 1989.
In Mad Love and War. Middletown, Connecticut, Wesleyan University Press, 1990.
Fishing. N.p., Oxhead Press, 1992.
The Woman Who Fell from the Sky. New York, Norton, 1994.

Recordings: *Power of the Word* series, with Bill Moyers (videotape), 1989; *Furious Light,* Watershed, 1986; *The Woman Who Fell from the Sky,* Norton, 1994; *Letter from the End of the Twentieth Century,* with band Joy Harjo & Poetic Justice, 1996.

Screenplays: *The Gaan Story,* with Henry Greenberg, 1984; *The Beginning,* with Henry Greenberg, 1984.

Television Plays: *We Are One, Umonho,* 1984; *Maiden of Deception Pass,* 1985; *I Am Different from My Brother,* 1986; *The Runaway,* 1986.

Other

Editor, with Laura Coltelli, *Spiral of Memory.* Ann Arbor, University of Michigan Press, 1995.
Editor, with Gloria Bird, *Reinventing the Enemy's Language: North American Native Women's Writing.* New York, Norton, 1997.

*   *   *

At midcareer Joy Harjo continues to develop as a writer, having moved from the competent, though occasionally predictable, language of the early poems ("I give you, my beautiful and terrible / fear") to work that resembles some of the best poetry in American English since Whitman. "Eagle Poem," a later work, for example, speaks of similarities between prayer and life in this way:

> We are truly blessed because we
> Were born, and die soon within a
> True circle of motion,
> Like eagle rounding out the morning
> Inside us.

In interviews Harjo has identified herself with currents in modern American writing, particularly with the regional depth of Meridel LeSueur and Flannery O'Connor and the strong voices of Audre Lorde and Alice Walker. As with LeSueur and O'Connor, Harjo exploits the genius of landscapes (the wide open spaces of her native Oklahoma and the deserts and mountains of the West) and cityscapes (Albuquerque, Cheyenne, Okemah, Gallup, Okmulgee) that are relatively unfamiliar to the national literature. She also makes valuable use of and builds upon oral traditions that allow room for suppressed memories, silences, dreams.

A Creek in background, Harjo often wonders aloud about her own survival and how it was accomplished, when most of her people have disappeared and continue to disappear. In "Night Out" she talks about people who, like herself, "fought to get out, fought to get in," fearful, even after paying "the cover charge thousands of times over with your lives" that they "can never get out." In such poems Harjo speaks of herself and the Native Americans who people her poems—Navajo, Shawnee, Cherokee, Kiowa—as survivors.

"Anchorage," from the same period, speaks about "the fantastic and terrible" stories of persistence among people whom many regard as "those who were never meant / to survive." There, as in "For Alva Benson, And For Those Who Have Learned To Speak," Harjo identifies herself with those who

> go on, keep giving birth and watch
> ourselves die, over and over.
> And the ground spinning beneath us
> goes on talking.

Although forces have chipped away at her world, as "white soldiers" chipped away at Native American culture from the beginning, Harjo remains determined "to turn the earth / around" in a cooperative effort to save memories, histories, dreams.

As her body of work unfolds, Harjo speaks with increasing confidence, more certain of the value of her own voice and the authority of the voices she makes room for in her poems. That voice has become, in fact,

> memory alive
> not just a name
> but an intricate part
> of this web of motion,
> meaning: earth, sky
> stars circling
> my heart
> centrifugal.

From the beginning Harjo not only has celebrated what was destroyed or lost but also has worked to reclaim it through prayer ("One Cedar Tree"), active resistance ("The Black Room"), and imagination ("Vision"). Beginning with *In Mad Love and War,* her work has suggested new strength, insight, and direction. Although it continues to reflect anger, regret, and anguish over what she and the people she identifies with have endured, it also carries a powerful sense—in "Transformations," for example—"that hatred can be turned into something else, if you have the right words, the right meanings, buried in the tender place in your heart where the most precious animals live."

—Michael True

HARRIS, Claire

Nationality: Canadian. **Born:** Born in Trinidad in 1937; immigrated to Canada in 1966. **Education:** St. Joseph's Convent, Port of Spain, Trinidad; University College, Dublin, B.A. in English; University of the West Indies, Jamaica, post-graduate diploma in education; University of Nigeria, Lagos, diploma in mass media and communications. **Career:** Teacher of English in Calgary in the Separate Schools; poetry editor, *Dandelion,* 1981-89; founding and managing editor, *Blue Buffalo,* 1984-87. **Awards:** Commonwealth Prize, 1985, for *Fables from the Women's Quarters;* Writer's Guild of Alberta Award for Poetry, 1987, and first Alberta Culture Poetry Prize, both for *Travelling to Find a Remedy;* Alberta Culture Special Award for Poetry, 1990, for *The Conception of Winter;* Governor General Award nomination, 1992, for *Drawing Down a Daughter.*

PUBLICATIONS

Poetry

Fables from the Women's Quarters. Toronto, Williams-Wallace, 1984.
Translation into Fiction. Fredericton, Goose Lane Editions, 1984.
Travelling to Find a Remedy. Fredericton, Goose Lane Editions, 1986.
The Conception of Winter. Toronto, Williams-Wallace, 1988.
The Drawing Down a Daughter. Fredericton, Goose Lane Editions, 1992.
Dipped in Shadow. Fredericton, Goose Lane Editions, 1996.

Other

Editor, with Edna Alford, *Kitchen Talk: Contemporary Women's Prose and Poetry.* N.p., Red Deer College Press, 1992.

*

Critical Studies: "Choosing Control: Interview with Claire Harris" by Monty Reid, in *Waves,* no. 1, 1984; *On the Edge of Genre: The Contemporary Canadian Long Poem* by Smaro Kamboureli, Toronto, University of Toronto Press, 1991; "A Writing of Resistance: Black Women's Writing in Canada" by Barbara Godard, in *Tessera,* no. 12, 1992; "After Modernism: Alternative Voices in the Writings of Dionne Brand, Claire Harris, and Marlene Philip" by Lynette Hunter, in *University of Toronto Quarterly,* vol. 62, no. 2, 1992-93; "'I dream of a new naming ...'"(interview) by Janice Williamson, in *Sounding Differences: Conversations with 17 Canadian Women Writers,* Toronto, University of Toronto Press, 1993; *Grammar of Dissent: Poetry and Prose by Claire Harris,*

M. Nourbese Philip, Dionne Brand, edited by Carol Morrell, Fredericton, Goose Lane Editions, 1994; "an autobiography. of sorts (reading Claire Harris, *Drawing Down a Daughter*)" by Ian Sowton, in *Open Letter,* no. 3, Summer 1995.

*   *   *

Being a Canadian writer of Afro-Caribbean descent, Claire Harris is caught between two cultures. Her writing examines the experience of multiple displacements caused by chosen or imposed migration. Although her texts are anti-colonial and anti-imperialist she does not claim to speak for all Africans; nevertheless, her writing reflects, as she states in "Poet in Limbo," her "race, gender and aspects of the culture [she] was born to."

Harris "survived" a Eurocentric education that indoctrinated her into Western European language, culture, and tradition but negated her experience as a black African woman. Since the beginning of her literary career she has been challenging thematic, stylistic and generic conventions of European literature and substituting them with writing that lets her "dream new dreams" and see through and beyond "screens of culture / gender / race" (*Dipped in Shadow*).

She acknowledges influences of writers that are known to question and interrogate accepted literary and cultural conventions: European surrealists, Fanon, Sartre, Césaire, bell hooks, Doris Lessing, Adrienne Rich, and such prose poem writers as Baudelarie, Rimbaud, Claudel, Lorca, Machado, and Ashberry. One of the crucial influences on her writing are the West Indian folk-tales, "the oral folklore [that] 'saved out imaginations'" ("Poets in Limbo").

Thematically Harris's writing, similar to that of Marlene Nourbese Philip and Dionne Brand—other Trinidadian writers who live in Canada—is engaged in a critique of sexism and racism in Canadian society. It also reveals her particular interest in the lives and position of women in a patriarchal world.

In *Fables from the Women Quarters* Harris writes about lives of displaced and traumatized women. "Nude on a Pale Staircase" looks into the life of an East Indian Woman living in Calgary as a wife of an Italian man; her sense of displacement is augmented by her anxiety caused by a news on "massacres in Assam." "Policeman Cleared in Jaywalking Case" is a denunciation of a society which uses double standards towards its citizens depending on the colour of their skin: "black girl child jaywalking to schools is stripped spread searched." "Where the Sky Is Pitiful Tent" examines the anguish of a woman whose husband is a Guatemalan guerilla fighter.

The long title poem in *Travelling to Find a Remedy,* a narrative of love relationship between an African man and a West Indian woman, "explores difficult issues of expatriation and loss of home and family. In *Translation into Fiction* there is an indictment of the patriarchal God who allows women's lives to be turned into fiction: "in Your silence / we were ravaged." "Burying the Hero" shows the tragedy of young men and women in a war-ravaged Argentina. Many poems in this book also critique a divided society "gouged by racism, cauterized by custom." They also reveal the barbarism of modern civilization: bomb testing, outrageous medical experiments, "the pure research / of mega death / the planet destroyed / if necessary / for the supremacy / of an economic / theory."

Most of Harris's writing sorts out her relationship with Africa; it is a re-visioning of history, myth, and the present culture; she questions the glory and greatness of the European civilization that colonized and enslaved her ancestors. In many of her texts Harris examines racial memory. In *The Conception of Winter*, for instance, a journey to Spain of three women friends becomes a basis for reflection on issues of women and slavery. *Drawing Down a Daughter* is an exemplary text focusing on racial and family history. The text is a story of a pregnant woman talking to her unborn daughter about problems of her race, class, and gender. Apart from expressing the woman's feminist longings, it examines West Indian history and mythology and it critiques the American institutions and media for perpetuating stereotypes and falsifying African history: "Here every cliché is underlined. It is in the advertisements, the newspapers, TV, film, radio, in the assumptions of moral superiority, in church, and more important, school." The book is also a celebration of black heritage. The unborn girl child listens to a poetic narrative not only about African history but also about African culinary secrets ("gospel on bakes"), and folklore (the story of Diablesse).

The importance of story and mythology and celebration of blackness and sisterhood is also affirmed in Harris's recent book of poetry *Dipped in Shadow*. In "O What Are You Thinking My Sisters" the beauty of blackness is stressed by a series of interesting metaphors relating to the colour of African skin: "cinnamon skin," "bright night skin," "milk and cream skin," "sun wheat skin," "bisque china skin" and "northern lights skin." Most of the long poems here deal not only with problems of verbally, sexually, and psychologically abused women, but they also affirm their sisterhood. "Woeman Womb Prisoned" is a long poem narrating the pain, suffering and the terror of a sexually abused school girl who is about to give birth to a child fathered by her father. "Dipped in Shadow" and "Nude in an Armchair" deal with sexually abused women and children. In "Sister (Y)our Manchild at the Close of the Twentieth Century" Harris expresses her concern for those who are dispossessed, colonized, and suffering—women of Iraq, Africans, native people, children of the Davis Inlet; she is against the exploitation of North America by Europe, and against the horrors of Iraq, Panama, Grenada, Somalia, and Bosnia. The poem condemns "mutilation of peoples planet skies" and it points to the dangers of civilization: cigarette's cancer, chemical abuse, nuclear waste. It critiques the American presence in Africa. Praise and celebration of Africa is juxtaposed with a statement that reveals the American attitude towards Africans: "I think that every marine came here with the idea that he might get / a chance for a confirmed kill." An interesting development of Harris's writing takes her to ponder the fate of victims of AIDS. In "The Fierce Body" she examines the lives of those who are torn between the desire of the body and personal religion and philosophy.

Harris's writing has been highly politicized. She hopes her writing will create an awareness that will help "change / the fictions before the fictions / play us out" (*Dipped in Shadow*). Linguistically and stylistically, it distinguishes itself from traditional texts. Language for Harris is not an instrument of expression only; it also has the power to transform. Harris is interested in experiments with language. She claims that the English language encodes the imperial and patriarchal law of dominance that is hostile not only to blacks but to women in general. Her writing raises the consciousness of language as a political and cultural authority. She accomplishes it through linguistic innovation and challenging of customary connotations and meanings. Similar to other language-focused writers, Harris does not invent a new language, but at times she works with an "*interlanguage*" which is a combination

of standard English and Trinidadian and Jamaican dialect. One of the most successful language experiments can be found in *Drawing Down a Daughter*, in the section titled "A Matter of Fact." It is a story of a man's encounter with La Diablesse. The choice of language marks Harris's distinct move towards the African oral tradition. She appropriates standard English and makes it "dance sing / to sunlight on the Caribbean." Through the use of dialect Harris makes effective political and artistic points.

In many of her texts Harris plays with phonic, syntactic, and semantic levels of language. In *Drawing Down a Daughter* in order to render the movement of the baby in amniotic fluid she chooses language that is not yet succumbed to the laws of grammar and reason ("a shu-a shua suck shu-a rush shu-a ashuash / shuash shu and ash / she is an ocean / waterbaby"). This is an example of synaesthetic writing where all senses seem to be activated within the domain of the print experience. Another interesting play with language is evident in *Dipped in Shadow* in such poems as "Nude in an Armchair," "Woeman Womb Prisoned" and "Sister (Y)our Manchild at the Close of the Twentieth Century." Here Harris makes her writing appeal both to the eye, ear and even to the sense of touch and smell. The disjointed and disintegrating language helps to translate the suffering of women. In general, Harris's writing strives towards a space or language where social codes, laws, and traditional concepts are exploded.

In addition to language experimentation Harris also questions the use of traditional genre. Her favourite genre is a long poem because its "law is 'lawlessness'" (Kamboureli). Moreover, it is important for her that she "can do anything with form ... anything to make meaning visible" ("I dream"). She mixes formal literature with folkloric tradition. In her texts there is a tension between a narrative and lyric impulse (In "Where the Sky Is a Pitiful Tent" lyrical voice is juxtaposed with passages from Rigoberta Manchu's account of the horrors of Guatemalan civil war). Long poems frequently appear in books which also feature short-lined haiku; in *The Conception of Winter* a series of postcards—poetical vignettes framed in squares reminding of real postcards—are contrasted with that Japanese verse form. There are many different voices in Harris's poetry. Moreover, her interesting use of space destroys linearity and multiplies the possibilities of interpretation.

—Eugenia Sojka

HARRY, J.S.

Nationality: Australian. **Born:** Adelaide, South Australia, in 1939. **Career:** Writer-in-residence, Australian National University, Canberra, 1989. **Awards:** Harri Jones memorial prize, 1971; P.E.N. International Lynne Phillips prize, 1987. **Address:** P.O. Box 184, Randwick, New South Wales 2031, Australia.

PUBLICATIONS

Poetry

The Deer under the Skin. St. Lucia, University of Queensland Press, 1970.

Hold, for a Little While, and Turn Gently. Sydney, Island Press, 1979.
A Dandelion for Van Gogh. Sydney, Island Press, 1985.
The Life on Water and the Life Beneath. Sydney, Angus & Robertson, 1995.
Selected Poems. Ringwood, Victoria, and New York, Penguin, 1995.

*

Critical Studies: By Martin Duwell, in *Overland Magazine* (Mt. Eliza, Victoria), no. 106, March 1987; Rose Lucas, in *Poetry and Gender,* edited by David Brooks and Brenda Walker, St. Lucia, University of Queensland Press, 1989.

*   *   *

The poetry of J.S. Harry encompasses a wide range of conflicting and competing impulses on both stylistic and thematic levels. Hers is a poetic that revels in this array of contradiction, allowing the shifting faces of incongruity, uncertainty, possibility, negation, stasis, and change to coexist in an ever-turning linguistic and imagistic prism. This refusal to reduce differences and contradictions to a synthesizing homogeneity is mirrored in the forms and structures of the poems themselves, in their oscillations between the metaphysical and the concrete, the delicately aesthetic or painterly, the deliberately abrasive and subversive. In this context, Harry's poetry challenges the boundaries and assumptions constructed about the interaction of life and art—the nature and role of poetry, what it means to be a poet (and, in particular, a woman poet), and how it might be possible, with the available tools of language and imagination, to weave together the threads of experience and impression to form a coherent and at least transiently "meaningful" poetic or life pattern.

Much of the poetry reveals itself to be caught on the horns of a metaphysical dilemma: on the one hand, Harry's work seems to yearn toward notions of a stable identity for the self and the speaking voice in the poems, which would concomitantly imply a point of ontological meaning or presence that might be clung to in the face of change and uncertainty; on the other hand, there is evident an equally strong impulse to expose the naiveté of positing such fixed or transcendent points of meaning, which leaves the poems free to engage in a philosophically destabilized jouissance. While there is an inevitable ricocheting movement between these diametrically opposed positions, I would argue that Harry's poetry seeks out a new and potentially deconstructive mode of understanding, and hence of expression, that is able to sustain generatively—albeit not to reconcile—such differences. In the imaginative spaces evoked between and beyond the formal structures of language, the poet evolves styles and strategies of perception designed to maintain the multiplicities of experience in such a way as to confront on a fundamental level the suffocating linearity and fixity of hegemonic ways of reading and seeing.

Harry most conspicuously seeks to disrupt prevailing assumptions about identity and meaning by a challenge to the codes and structures of punctuation, syntax, and the graphic presentation of the words on the page. She utilizes a range of devices to sever her poetic phraseology from the assumed formulations of logical thought progression—dashes, dots, additional colons, extra spacing between words, altered margins, typescript symbols and abbreviations, unconventional uses of upper and lower cases. All these function as strategies to disturb the surface of linear narrative, thereby creating "added space" or a means of levering open latent contradictions within the finitude of the text. Such strategies thus make a clearing for "other voices" within the poetic text, be they the voices of philosophical difference, the unconscious, the emotions, the imagination, or an emerging female-centered consciousness.

In the poem "Parts towards a Meaning" from *The Deer under the Skin* Harry juxtaposes a seemingly random and unlikely accumulation of impressions—the "sewers ... under victoria street," "the four thousand year old dead," "Soul Pattinson's baskets," "a two-foot boy in red sandals," etc.—in an apparent attempt to generate, by sheer accretion of detail, a cohering significance in what might be otherwise overwhelmingly anarchic. The poet also realizes that she herself may "grow four thousand years old / looking" for this probably mythic unifying significance, the "secret name" of the gods, or the ultimate "birthbook of myth and language." Perhaps, however, with the power and talisman of language, she can construct, if not discover, a dike wall of "meaning" to prevent a landslide into chaos and negation. Confronted with the looming depths and uncertainties which puncture the surface of the poem as "Eyes press against the edges of things" to reveal the "shadows [which] go back like pansies black black deep into the sun," Harry explicitly takes on the role or responsibility of the poet, asserting

I have to work to find nails ...
the purpose of grass is the purpose of nails is the purpose of words ...
I have to work to feel shaped sharpness grip like grass ...

In this poem, the desire to see "beyond" the suffocating weight of accumulated detail is imaged in the conventional terms of a descent, an underwater or chthonic exploration of what may be either knowledge or despair. This movement is echoed by the layout of the words on the page:

onto
    /
    downfrom
        /
        grass
            b
             l
              a
               d
                e
                 s
                    : the wrists the ankles know

It is at this point of juncture or gap—"the wrists the ankles"—that the knowledge the poem seeks can be found. Paradoxically, uncertainty, or the point of nonarrival, is the poem's "discovery" at these moments of support and transition, substance and hollowness. The only words and the only lives "To be believed" must come "shaped as a question," as it is only the question which prizes open the heart of the flower to uncover the risks and the promises of the shadows within and beyond.

Harry's use of her initials J.S. as a writing signature might be seen as a device to defuse or even deny her gender specificity. However, while some of her earlier poems, such as "How Old Pity Left the Poem" and "The Little Grenade," use neuter or even masculine pronouns, Harry's work does seem to gain an increasing awareness of the complex subject position of the woman who writes within an essentially patriarchal social and linguistic system. The poem "The Baby, with the Bath-Water, Thrown Out" from *Hold ...*, for instance, likens the struggle of the poet to find the language to allude to or to shape experiences to her biological capacity and choice to carry a child. Formulations which prove somehow ineffective, worn out, or clichéd are "Dropped ... by accident" by the poet in the same way as the lost fetus slides from her body and battles its doom-laden way "through the grid / at the bottom of the shower-alcove / ... resistant / to being broken up." Not only does Harry liken the poet's struggle to conceive meaning and form in language to the woman's ability to produce independent life, but she also aligns herself with this intensely private experience in direct opposition to an unspecified "them" who would understand neither the experience of the woman nor that of the poet. Perhaps it is "they" who would trivialize such intensely felt loss with the use of clichés such as the title. Harry's poem, however, emerges out of and away from the cliché; beginning with a colon, it suggests the unfinished or inadequate business which preceded it:

> : it will not seem
> a meaningful exercise, to them,
> to hunt new life

This hunt for new life takes on mythic proportions in the later poem "The Gulf of Bothnia" (in *A Dandelion for Van Gogh*), itself a distillation of some of the central issues within Harry's poetry. In this unique place "flounder and pike ... / ... seaweed and freshwater plants" live side by side, thus suggesting an environment or a philosophical framework which will nourish elements which are otherwise antithetical. However, the gulf has a shifting significance within the poem; "cows [who] drink the sea" can exist there, yet it is also subject to its own tides and to the subtlest pulsations of change in the land or continental shelves which underpin it. It may also be suggestive of the historical or psychological origin of human life as it gives birth to "our imaginary relatives" who "grow tails to rise" in the dimmest regions of collective memory. The possible rigidity of such an equation of the sea with the matrix of life is, however, disrupted by the matter-of-fact tone which reminds us that "we are unable to breathe / in the gulf of bothnia." If there is an anesthetizing nostalgia for this apparent place of origins, or "birthbook of myth and language," where opposites can be maintained without tension, it is undercut by the realization that such a region is no longer accessible or indeed supportive of generative life and thought. Within Harry's personal and poetic terms therefore, the recalcitrant prospect of life within such a place, with its mythic stasis and resolutions, must remain an impossibly utopian, if inevitably powerful and informing, dream.

—Rose Lucas

HEBERT, Anne

Nationality: Canadian. **Born:** Sainte-Catherine-de-Fossambault, Quebec, Canada, 1 August 1916. **Education:** Privately educated. **Career:** Worked for Radio Canada, 1950-53, and for National Film Board, 1953-60. **Awards:** Prix David (Quebec), 1943, 1978; Canadian government grant, 1954; France Canada prize, 1957; Duvernay prize,

1958; Province de Quebec prize, 1959; Canadian Council of Arts grant, 1961; Guggenheim Foundation grant, 1963; Province of Quebec grant, 1965; Molson prize, 1967; Governor General of Canada's award, 1975; Grand Prix de Monaco, 1975; award from the French Academy, 1975; Prix Femina, 1982, for *Les fous de Bassan;* honorary degrees from University of Toronto, 1969, Universite de Quebec a Montreal, 1970, and McGill University, 1980. **Member:** Royal Society of Canada, Union des ecrivains quebecois. **Address:** c/o Musson Book Co., 30 Lesmill Rd., Don Mills, Ontario, Canada M3B 2T6.

PUBLICATIONS

Poetry

Les songes en equilibre. Montreal, Les Editions de l'arbre, 1942.
Le tombeau des rois. Montreal, n.p., 1953; translated by Peter Miller as *The Tomb of the Kings,* Toronto, Contact Press, 1967.
Poemes. Montreal, Editions de seuil, 1960; translated by Alan Brown as *Poems,* Don Mills, Ontario, Musson, 1975.
Selected Poems, translated by A. Poulin, Jr. Brockport, New York, BOA Editions, 1987; Toronto, Stoddart, 1988.
Day Has No Equal but Night, translated by A. Poulin, Jr. Brockport, New York, BOA Editions, 1994.

Novels

Les chambres de bois. Montreal, Editions du seuil, 1958; translated by Kathy Mezei as *The Silent Rooms,* Don Mills, Ontario, Musson, 1974.
Kamouraska. Montreal, Edition du seuil, 1970; translated by Norman Shapiro, New York, Crown, 1973.
Les enfants du sabbat. Montreal, Editions du seuil, 1975; translated by Carol Dunlop-Hebert as *Children of the Black Sabbath,* Don Mills, Ontario, Musson, 1977.
Heloise. Montreal, Editions du seuil, 1980; translated by Sheila Fischman, Toronto, Stoddart, 1982.
Le premier jardin. Montreal, Editions du seuil, 1980.
Les fous de Bassan. Montreal, Editions du seuil, 1982; translated by Sheila Fischman as *In the Shadow of the Wind,* Toronto, Stoddart, 1983.
La cage. N.p., Boreal, 1990.

Short Stories

Le torrent. Montreal, Editions du seuil, 1963; new edition published as *Le torrent, suivi de deux nouvelles inedites,* Montreal, Editions HMH, 1963; translated by Gwendolyn Moore as *The Torrent: Novellas and Short Stories,* Montreal, Harvest House, 1973.

Other

Saint-Denys-Garneau and Anne Hebert: Translations (selected works). Vancouver, Klanak Press, 1962.
Seasons of the Mind: Photo-Poetic Essay, photography by Chick and Anne Hebert. Santa Barbara, Standard Print, 1974.

Plays

Le temps sauvage, La merciere assassinee, Les invites au proces: Theatre. Montreal, Editions HMH, 1967.

*   *   *

Anne Hebert was born in 1916 at her family's summer home, Sainte-Catherine-de-Fossambault, just north of Quebec City, Canada. Her father, Maurice-Lang Hebert, was a well-known critic and member of the Quebec City establishment and literary elite. Exposed to some of the best minds of Quebec amongst her father's friends, and educated at home because of childhood illness, Anne read widely in both English and French.

She started to write in her adolescence, encouraged by both her father and her cousin, the poet Hector de Saint-Denys-Garneau, who lived nearby. Hebert's poems and stories began to appear in literary magazines, and in 1942, her first book of poetry, *Les songes en equilibre* ("Dreams in Equilibrium") was published.

In 1948, along with Paul-Emile Borduas and others from the Ecole de Beaux Arts de Montreal, Hebert signed the Refus global. A simple mimeographed sheet, it was also the manifesto of a group of young intellectuals in which they repudiated the leadership of the clergy and the dominant group of provincial politicians whose eyes were on the past. The influence of the Refus global would be felt in both art and writing, and it contributed to the Quiet Revolution of 1959.

In 1950 *Le torrent,* a collection of short stories originally printed in a censored form, was published at Hebert's own expense. A classical expression of the spiritual drama of French Quebec and a stark depiction of the repressive effects of strict and puritan Jansenist Catholicism, the book received negative reviews.

Meanwhile, between 1945 and 1954, Hebert had become involved in theater, radio, and film, writing screenplays and joining the staff of the National Film Board of Canada in 1953. While her career as a writer was progressing, her personal life contained several tragedies.

Saint-Denys-Garneau had died in 1943, and in 1952 Hebert lost her younger sister. A year later, 27 poems collected as *Le tombeau des rois,* appeared.

In both Quebec and France, *Le tombeau des rois* received high praise. The economy of Hebert's language, the depth of poetic feeling, and the austere beauty of the imagery in this cycle of poems illuminate and press home an emotional confrontation with the idea of death. The poet transcends the personal and achieves meaning at a universal and mythical level. She depicts a world in which choice—whether of order or chaos—is not available. It is a final rejection of Jansenism. Here are the haunting opening stanzas of *Le tombeau des rois,* beautifully translated by Frank Scott, himself a leading Canadian poet:

I carry my heart on my fist
Like a blind falcon.

The taciturn bird gripping my fingers
A swollen lamp of wine and blood
I go down
Toward the tombs of the kings
Astonished
Scarcely born.

What Ariadne-thread leads me
Along the muted labyrinths?
The echo of my steps fades away as they fall.

(In what dream
was this child tied by her ankle
Like a fascinated slave?)

The maker of the dream
Presses on the cord

And my naked footsteps come
One by one
Like the first drops of rain
At the bottom of the well.

In 1954, as a result of an award from the Royal Society of Canada, Hebert went to live in Paris, France. Although continuing to be known principally as a poet she has written for the theater and has published several novels. The stirring and romantic *Kamouraska,* which appeared in 1970 and was subsequently made into a film, takes up the characteristic French Canadian theme of the inhibiting burden of the past. Hebert's poems, including 1960's *Poemes,* continue to appear in translation, the most recent collection being the tellingly titled *Day Has No Equal but Night,* published in 1994. Honored with numerous awards in both Canada and her adopted country of France, Hebert remains one of the most distinguished of our Canadian poets.

—Patience Wheatley

HEJINIAN, Lyn

Nationality: American. **Born:** San Francisco, California. **Career:** Editor, Tuumba Press, and *Poetics Journal,* both Berkeley, California. **Address:** Tuumba Press, 2639 Russell Street, Berkeley, California 94705, U.S.A.

PUBLICATIONS

Poetry

A Thought Is the Bride of What Thinking. Willits, California, Tuumba Press, 1976.
A Mask of Motion. Providence, Rhode Island, Burning Deck, 1977.
Writing Is an Aid to Memory. Berkeley, California, The Figures, 1978.
Gesualdo. Berkeley, California, Tuumba Press, 1978.
Redo. Grenada, Mississippi, Salt-Works Press, 1984.
The Guard. Berkeley, California, Tuumba Press, 1984.
Individuals, with Kit Robinson. Tucson, Arizona, Chax Press, 1988.
The Cell. Los Angeles, Sun & Moon Press, 1990.
The Hunt. La Laguna, Islas Canarias, Zasterle Press, 1991.
Leningrad, with Michael Davidson, Ron Silliman, and Barrett Watten. San Francisco, Mercury House, 1991.
The Cold of Poetry. Los Angeles, Sun & Moon Press, 1994.
Wicker, with Jack Collom. Boulder, Colorado, Rodent Press, 1996.
The Little Book of a Thousand Eyes. Boulder, Colorado, Smokeproof Press, 1996.
Guide, Grammar, Watch, and the 30 Nights. Perth, Australia, Folio Books, 1996.

Novels

My Life. Providence, Rhode Island, Burning Deck, 1980.
Oxota: A Short Russian Novel. Great Barrington, The Figures, 1991.

Other

Translator, with Elena Balashova, *Description,* by Arkadi Dragomoshchenko. Los Angeles. Sun & Moon Press, 1990.

Translator, with Elena Balashova, *Xenia,* by Arkadi Dragomoshchenko. Los Angeles, Sun & Moon Press, 1993.

*

Manuscript Collection: University of California-San Diego, La Jolla.

Critical Studies: "Too Clear" by Ross Feld, in *Parnassus: Poetry in Review* (New York), vol. 8, no. 1, 1978; "Mayer on Hejinian" by Bernadette Mayer, in *L=A=N=G=U=A=G=E* (New York), no. 13, December 1980; "Notes on Lyn Hejinian" by Carla Harryman, in *American Poetry Archive News,* no. 1, winter 1984; "Hejinian's Notes," in *Content's Dream: Essays 1975-1984,* by Charles Bernstein, Los Angeles, Sun & Moon Press, 1986; "Her Favorite Device Is the Echo" by Emily Leider, in San Francisco *Chronicle,* 18 October 1987; "Two Hejinian Talks" by Stephen Ratcliffe, in *Temblor,* no. 6, 1987; "What Then Is a Window?" by Marnie Parsons, in *Brick* (Toronto), no. 38, winter 1990.

*   *   *

American practicality has always been a goad to poets to find some loophole in its philosophical plainness or to puncture it with ribald humor in an attempt to dismiss its deep-rootedness in the American psyche. As long as practicality remains an essential norm of taste, it will make poems squirm to overcome it or to find humorous alternatives. Certainly New England's poets have troubled themselves deeply to unseat the prominence of this slightly disguised Puritan virtue. Robert Frost and Wallace Stevens both lavished much irony on the homely virtue; e.e. cummings mocked it tirelessly in childlike nonsense poems and love lyrics.

Lyn Hejinian, like Frost, was born in San Francisco and educated in New England. At age 27 she returned to the Bay area and began writing a hauntingly ungraspable mode of lyric in which a voice, disembodied but felt, unidentifiable and yet familiar, whispers to the reader of things that never converge to argument but that evaporate as softly as they came. She too has waged war on practicality, on the utilitarian notion of the poem as message or advice.

Also like Frost, Hejinian seems undecided between two orders of things in the mind or between two narratives or subjects, neither of which gains her attention long enough to become belief. Instead, like a double helix unwinding from a spool, two possibilities simply travel together loosely in parallel as she teases and frustrates her readers with seemingly ordered speech, but speech which defies resolution or interpretation.

Gesualdo, a prose meditation published by Hejinian's own Tuumba Press in 1978, offers this curious but typical observation on the doubleness of her poetry:

> The capacity of artists to manipulate for their own ends
> forms invented in a different spirit is one of the facts of
> life ... was dying by artists whose passion and sensuous-
> ness essentially distinguished them ... because they
> tremble, as it were, on the brink of one or the other com-
> mitment.

Gesualdo, Prince of Venosa, was a composer of late 16th-century Naples who took the madrigal form as far it would go musically and collaborated with the poet Tasso on numerous canzones and sonnets to create the equivalent of a pre-Baroque language poetry set to music. He whipped up complicated six-voice harmonies that even Stravinsky found overwrought, but which Hejinian interprets as the multivocality of consciousness. She duplicates the technique in her prose and dazzles the reader with its overlay of continuous tracts of thought.

Gesualdo offers more admonitions than advice—with a sinister undertone stemming from the composer's murder of his first wife and her lover, a celebrated scandal for half a century. But an admonitory voice is also present in one of Hejinian's previous prose pamphlets, *A Thought Is the Bride of What Thinking,* published by her Tuumba Press in 1976. More tentative than *Gesualdo,* it nonetheless reveals the intention of all her later work—experiments in tonality, in reordering syntax, in riddling her grammar with interjection and transposition. Her meditations draw heavily on older styles of eloquence, much of it coming from the Victorian and Edwardian eras, giving her poems a mood like that of old films and photographs.

The theme of these books is partly the irreality of language against the backdrop of the real world and the menacing forces that hamper human existence. Like other language poets Hejinian plumbs the sense of terror in the 20th century, of holocaust and sinister forms of government, of authority bearing down on one's freedom to think. Only by the eruptions of unsorted or uncontrolled language can one tear free of grammatical traps and the incarceration that all language poets suffer in their mental lives.

A Mask of Motion, Hejinian's first open-verse poems, was issued by Keith Waldrop's Burning Deck Press in 1977. The work is a further extension of the suspended style of the other two prose books: "I'm confusing two different stories, she said; I know I'm mixing them up. But somehow, strange as it seems, completely unrelated events can intertwine in my memory and then I see they had something in common." This is as good an explanation of Hejinian's own method as will be found in her work. It indicates the nervous doubling of her thought and speaks to her indeterminate movements.

In *Writing Is an Aid to Memory,* Hejinian's preface prepares the reader for what follows:

> I am always conscious of the disquieting runs of life
> slipping by, that the message remains undelivered,
> opposed to me. Memory cannot, though the future
> return, and proffer raw confusions. Knowledge is
> part of the whole, as hope is, from which love
> seeks to contrast knowledge with separation.

The book is a sequence of 42 passages, a relentlessly unpredictable discourse in monologue form that moves from one topic to another and from tone to tone without transition. But like a palimpsest the language reveals patterns and meanings buried in the flow of the text, submerged like the stones or fish forms in a swiftly flowing river. There are enough such glimpses of actual things in the discourse, as in the tour of the caves at Dordogne in *A Mask of Motion,* to make the reader grasp at them as the language moves along with its shimmering but intangible possibilities. Hejinian proves that language can do more than state explicit arguments; it can move a reader to different emotional states merely by the configurations of its words and tones, its subtle and un-yielding mysteries.

In the prose book *My Life* we find Hejinian working from another source of ideas on language poetry: Gertrude Stein's animistic prose in *Tender Buttons*. Here Hejinian works in small units of prose reminiscence and description to vitalize the ordinary, inert "things" in one's landscape. "Long time lines trail behind every idea, object, person, pet, vehicle, and event," she says of her epistemology. It is as apt a definition of her poetics as you will find in her small canon.

More recent work continues the dismantling of generic boundaries and identities. The diaristic mode of *The Cell* transforms prose only partly into poetry, leaving a stark, prosaic surface as the distancing, sometimes distracting foreground to what is essentially a poetic exploration of fragments, loose threads of experience within. Prose is also transformed into a quasi-poetic medium in *Oxota: A Short Russian Novel,* where novelistic conventions are maintained in the story of a hunt, if only to distort them into the more fluid world of poetic narration. Any assumption becomes for her a fence to dissolve away by fantasy, paradox, and mere repetition. In *The Cold of Poetry* and *The Little Book of a Thousand Eyes,* Hejinian is the ultimate jester with public knowledge, striking at basic assumptions so casually, one hardly notices the sky is falling. Her poems seem like epitaphs on the age of empiricism, and a way back into the alchemical imagination, where paradox is the threshold to wisdom.

—Paul Christensen

HERZBERG, Judith

Nationality: Dutch. **Born:** Amsterdam, The Netherlands, 4 November 1934. **Education:** Montessori Lyceum, graduated 1952. **Career:** Scriptwriter and poet; teacher at film schools in The Netherlands and Israel. **Address:** c/o De Harmonie, Postbus 3547, 1001 AH Amsterdam, Netherlands.

PUBLICATIONS

Poetry

Zeepost ("Slow Boat"). Amsterdam, Van Oorschot, 1963.
Beemdgras ("Meadow Grass"). Amsterdam, Van Oorschot, 1968.
Vliegen ("Flies"). Amsterdam, Rap, 1970.
27 Liedesliedjes ("27 Love Songs"). Amsterdam, Rap, 1971.
Strijklicht. Amsterdam, Van Oorschot, 1974.
Botshol. Amsterdam, Van Oorschot, 1980.
Dagrest. Amsterdam, Van Oorschot, 1984.
But What: Selected Poems, translated by Herzberg and Shirley Kaufman. Oberlin, Ohio, Oberlin College Press, 1988.
Zoals. Amsterdam, De Harmonie, 1992.

Recordings: *An Evening of Postwar Poetry of The Netherlands and Flanders: Hugo Claus, Judith, Herzberg, Gerrit Kouwenarar, and Cees Nooteboom Reading Their Poems,* 1984.

Plays

Screenplays: *Charlotte,* 1981; *Een goed hoofd,* 1991; *Rijgdraad,* 1995.

* * *

The poetry of Judith Herzberg is post-World War II in more than the historical sense of the word. It is a poetry of the forms left behind by the violence of those times, an aftershock, a postwar whisper. In his introduction to *But What: Selected Poems,* Henk Romijn Meijer writes that Herzberg "keeps a tight rein on feeling, understating what could become shrill or even disturbed. It is not a poetry of gaudiness or heroic stances." He also states that "the scrupulous attention to physical detail brings a toughness of form and language that is there, no matter how elusive the subject." This toughness of form allows the reader to view the poem-scene through the shrewd eyes of an innocent observer—a child, perhaps, or an animal, or simply an observer caught like a fish, wordless, in a net of natural beauty. Herzberg is fascinated, simultaneously, by the music of language and the language of music, especially as it is found in natural settings. In "Travelache," the speaker desires to hear "No radio first thing in the morning. / Just the local singing. / with words we don't understand." Half-understood language creates a world as real as that of the fully-known, and such worlds exist inevitably, perhaps of necessity. In "Yiddish," an earlier poem, the speaker "Sing[s] to my children / what I myself don't grasp ... / We had to throw the roses out. / We needed the water to drink." Full meaning, like the roses, may produce order and beauty, but there is something more key to survival in these songs, in the half-grasped vital connection the speaker feels to her father and children.

This half-grasped domain is the setting for Herzberg's more deliberate attempts to recreate the post-war period. She was a young child when her parents were relocated to a concentration camp and she was sequestered by a Dutch family. Both parents survived. "Reunion" relates the meeting between a "strange mother" at her homecoming and the "too grown-up, / too skinny and countrified daughter" as the daughter exchanges a pretended, in-absentia intimacy for a real, present-day distance. No mention is made of the missing historical reference, the parent's suffering or relief, that might turn the reunion into anything more than a difficult moment. In "1945," a child's intense presence again succeeds at obliterating a historical context, making some visiting war heroes as mute and shy as the animal protagonists to which Herzberg is particular: gulls, bears, reindeer, starlings, and many others.

While the child speaker of Herzberg's war-era poems deconstructs the possibility of ordinary adult discourse—only the half-grasped is of any significance to these poems since it makes up the child's perception—the adult speaker of her nature poems takes on the task of creating a discourse with the non-speaking world. Often, though, all the poet can achieve is a recognition of the private language of nature. The furry visitor of "Bear in Bed" can't respond to the speaker's questions, but hearkens immediately to the "message" of a hawk circling overhead. "1944," ostensibly a post-war memory, recalls birds flying "wherever and back again / wherever they wanted in their peace." "Starling" is a "frivolthroated imitator, / pearl spattered weasel, a flying, / analphabetic celebrator"; "Jackdaw II" is "alone, black, an alien / like the Greek, who, with his broken leg, / wants to get out into the air / where the girls are." The creatures have characteristics which remind one of the human, but simile is always implied if not made explicit; they remain impenetrable in their wildness.

This wildness is a part of individual humanity as well, and Herzberg seems to imply that it, and not society, is the place where "peace" occurs. In "A Late Encounter II," an older lover realizes that she and her partner see things differently because their lives are shaped by different stories, even the sunset— "the way he sees it / like a copper tray / she as a redhot / circular saw." Yet they find a bond outside of speech or stories:

> We don't have to understand
> the language of our feet.
> But at the waterfall
> where we were speechless
> our feet stood still
> lingered impressed
> then, together
> went on.

In all her poems, Herzberg reaches for this place where "higher and lower than I can think songs / notes more insisting than my presence" ("Quartz Mica Feldspar").

—Cynthia Davidson

HEWETT, Dorothy (Coade)

Nationality: Australian. **Born:** Perth, Western Australia, 21 May 1923. **Education:** Perth College; University of Western Australia, Perth, 1941-42, 1959-63, B.A. 1961. **Family:** Married Lloyd Davies in 1944 (marriage dissolved 1949), one son (deceased); lived with Les Flood, 1949-58, three sons; married Merv Lilley in 1960, two daughters. **Career:** Millworker, 1950-52; advertising copywriter, Sydney, 1956-58; senior tutor in English, University of Western Australia, 1964-73. Writer-in-residence, Monash University, Melbourne, 1975, University of Newcastle, New South Wales, 1977, Griffith University, Nathan, Queensland, 1980, La Trobe University, Bundoora, Victoria, 1981, Magpie Theatre Company, Adelaide, 1982, Rollins College, Florida, 1988, and Edith Cowan University, Western Australia, 1990. Member of editorial board, *Overland* magazine, Melbourne, 1970—, and *Westerly* magazine, Nedlands, Western Australia, 1972-73. **Awards:** Australian Broadcasting Commission prize, 1945, 1965; Australia Council grant, 1973, 1976, 1979, 1981, 1983, 1984, 1985; Australian Writers Guild award, 1974, 1982; International Women's Year grant, 1976; A.O. (Member, Order of Australia), 1986; Nettie Palmer award, 1991, for nonfiction; Australian Artists Creative fellowship, 1993-96; National Book Council Poetry award, 1994; Christopher Brennan Award, 1996; Western Australia Premier's Award for Poetry, 1996; Australia Council Lifetime Emeritus grant, 1997; D.Litt: University of Western Australia, 1995. **Member:** Communist Party, 1943-68. **Agent:** Hilary Linstead and Associates, Suite 302, "Easts Tower," 9-13 Bronte Road, Bondi Junction, New South Wales 2022, Australia. **Address:** 496 Great Western Highway, Faulconbridge, New South Wales 2776, Australia.

PUBLICATIONS

Poetry

What about the People, with Merv Lilley. Sydney, Realist Writers, 1962.
Windmill Country. Sydney, Edwards and Shaw, 1968.
The Hidden Journey. Newnham, Tasmania, Wattle Grove Press, 1969.
Late Night Bulletin. Newnham, Tasmania, Wattle Grove Press, 1970.
Rapunzel in Suburbia. Sydney, New Poetry, 1975.
Greenhouse. Sydney, Big Smoke, 1979.
Journeys, with others, edited by Fay Zwicky. Melbourne, Sisters, 1982.
Alice in Wormland. Paddington, New South Wales, Paper Bark Press, 1987; as *Alice in Wormland: Selected Poems.* Newcastle upon Tyne, Bloodaxe, 1990.
A Tremendous World in Her Head: Selected Poems. Sydney, Dangaroo Press, 1989.
Selected Poems. Newcastle upon Tyne, Bloodaxe, 1990; South Fremantle, Western Australia, Fremantle Arts Centre Press, 1991.
Peninsula. South Fremantle, Western Australia, Fremantle Arts Centre Press, 1994.
Collected Poems. South Fremantle, Western Australia, Fremantle Arts Centre Press, 1995.

Plays

Time Flits Away, Lady (produced 1941).
This Old Man Comes Rolling Home (produced Perth, 1966; revised version produced Sydney, 1968). Sydney, Currency Press, 1976.
Mrs. Porter and the Angel (produced Sydney, 1969).
The Chapel Perilous; or, The Perilous Adventures of Sally Banner, music by Frank Amdt and Michael Leyden (produced Perth, 1971). Sydney, Currency Press, 1972; London, Eyre Methuen, 1974.
Bon-Bons and Roses for Dolly (produced Perth, 1972). With *The Tatty Hollow Story,* Sydney, Currency Press, 1976.
Catspaw (produced Perth, 1974).
Miss Hewett's Shenanigans (produced Canberra, 1975).
Joan, music by Patrick Flynn (produced Canberra, 1975). Montmorency, Victoria, Yackandandah, 1984.
The Tatty Hollow Story (produced Sydney, 1976). With *Bon-Bons and Roses for Dolly,* Sydney, Currency Press, 1976.
The Beautiful Miss Portland. Published in *Theatre Australia* (Sydney), November / December and Christmas 1976.
The Golden Oldies (produced Melbourne, 1976; London, 1978). With *Susannah's Dreaming,* Sydney, Currency Press, 1981.
Pandora's Cross (produced Sydney, 1978). Published in *Theatre Australia* (Sydney), September / October 1978.
The Man from Mukinupin (produced Perth, 1979). Sydney, Currency Press, 1980.
Susannah's Dreaming (broadcast 1980). With *The Golden Oldies,* Sydney, Currency Press, 1981.
Golden Valley (for children; produced Adelaide, 1981). With *Song of the Seals,* Sydney, Currency Press, 1985.
The Fields of Heaven (produced Perth, 1982).

Song of the Seals (for children), music by Jim Cotter (produced
    Adelaide, 1983). With *Golden Valley,* Sydney, Currency Press,
    1985.
Christina's World (opera libretto; produced Sydney, 1983).
The Rising of Pete Marsh (produced Perth, 1988).
Collected Plays. Volume 1. Sydney, Currency Press, 1992.

Screenplays: *For the First Time,* with others, 1976; *Journey among
    Women,* with others, 1977; *The Planter of Malata,* with Cecil
    Holmes, 1983; *Song of the Seals,* 1984; *Catch the Wild Fish,*
    with Robert Adamson, 1985.

Radio Plays: *Frost at Midnight,* 1973; *He Used to Notice Such
    Things,* 1974; *Susannah's Dreaming,* 1980.

Novels

Bobbin Up. Sydney, Australasian Book Society, 1959; rev. ed.,
    London, Virago, 1985; rev. ed., New York, Penguin, 1987.
The Toucher. Ringwood, Victoria, McPhee Gribble, and New York,
    Penguin, 1993.

Short Stories

The Australians Have a Word for It. Berlin, Seven Seas, 1964.
Sisters. London, Angus & Roberston, 1993.

Other

Wild Card (autobiography). Melbourne, McPhee Gribble, and Lon-
    don, Virago Press, 1990.

Editor, *Sandgropers: A Western Australian Anthology.* Nedlands,
    University of Western Australia Press, 1973.

*

Bibliography: *Dorothy Hewett: A Bibliography* by Anne Casey,
Sydney, Australian Library and Information Association Press,
1989.

Manuscript Collections: Australian National Library, Canberra;
Fisher Library, University of Sydney; Flinders University,
Adelaide, South Australia; University of Queensland, St. Lucia;
University of Western Australia, Nedlands.

Critical Studies: "Confession and Beyond" by Bruce Williams,
in *Overland* (Melbourne), 1977; interview with Jim Davidson, in
Meanjin (Melbourne), 1979; "On a Lonely Beach" by Paul
Kavanagh, in *Southerly* (Sydney), 1984; "Dorothy Hewett as
Poet," in *Southerly* (Sydney), vol. 44, no. 4, 1984; *The Feminine
as Subversive: The Plays of Dorothy Hewett* by Margaret Will-
iams, Sydney, Currency Press, n.d; *Dorothy Hewett: Selected Criti-
cal Essays* edited by Bruce Bennett, South Fremantle, Western
Australia, Fremantle Arts Centre Press, 1995.

Dorothy Hewett comments:
    My first collection, *Windmill Country,* was long delayed and
therefore incorporated much that I had already outgrown. The lo-
cale of the book is firmly Western Australian, with consequent
emphasis on landscape and ancestor-worship. There is also a
strong strain of politicizing in the book, influenced by regionalism
and the Australian poets of my own generation, particularly Judith
Wright. The book is uneven, romantic, and didactic. *Rapunzel in
Suburbia,* my second collection, covers my time as an academic.
It is strongly confessional, obviously influenced by Lowell and
Plath, and romantic in style and subject. Fantasy is a central ele-
ment in the book; there is also an introverted imagination linked
with a sense of the dramatic. *Greenhouse* is an even more radical
departure. The book covers my last three years in Sydney and is
influenced by the city and by younger Australian city poets. There
are a wider range of experimentation, a firmer control, and more
substantial intellectual content. The lyrical, the fantastic, and the
analytical predominate.
    Alice in Wormland covers the last five years, and using a per-
sona and a clipped contemporary shorthand, is the poetic biogra-
phy of an Australian woman from childhood to death, and after
it.

                              *   *   *

Dorothy Hewett is a writer of extraordinary versatility whose
work as a dramatist and novelist is reflected in the theatricality
and strong narrative sense of her poetry. Combined with her sure
lyrical voice, these are the elements that extend her poetic range.
Each book sustains continuity with those before but gathers en-
during themes and symbols into fresh shapes.
    Although she continues to write in many genres, Hewett's first
publications were poems, and some of her most enduring work is
to be found in *Windmill Country.* The romantic lyric "Legend of
the Green Country," for example, engagingly captures her own
and her forebears' relationships with the wheat country of West-
ern Australia, beginning with a flourish reminiscent of Dylan Tho-
mas: "September is the spring month bringing tides, swilling green
in the harbor mouth, / Turnabout dolphins rolling-backed in the
rip and run, the king waves, / Swinging the coast." It then settles
into a more individual voice—"this was my country, here I go
back for nurture, / To the dry soaks, to the creeks running salt
through the timber"—and concludes, once parents, grandparents,
and landscape have been explored, with

> I will pay this debt, go back and find my place,
> Pick windfalls out of the grass like a mendicant.
> The little sour apples still grow in my heart's orchard,
> Bitter with grief, coming up out of the dead country.
> Here I will eat their salt and speak my truth.

Hewett's 1970s poetry is unrelentingly and flamboyantly the-
atrical, reflecting her intense dramatic output during this period.
The feminist-inspired *Rapunzel in Suburbia* and *Greenhouse* in-
clude poems of fantasy, erotically assertive, with a high level of
role playing, as in "Miss Hewett's Shenanigans"—"They call, 'The
Prince has come,' / & I swan down in astrakan & fur, / the lemon
curtains blown against the light"—or as in "Coming to You"—"I
ride across the flat land / like General Gabler's daughter." "Grave
Fairytale" retells the Rapunzel legend—"Three times I lent my
hair to the glowing prince"—but the object of the prince's lust is
the black witch, "the beasts unsatisfied / roll in their sweat, their
guttural cries / made the night thick with sound." "Each time I
saw the framed-faced bully boy / sick with his triumph. / The
third time I hid the shears ... / Three seasons he stank at the tower's
base."

In *Alice in Wormland* these roles are concentrated in the persona of Alice, and the autobiographical references take on a different form through the detachment that this affords as well as by having been worked out in earlier, shorter poems. The extent of change may be perceived by comparing the lines on Hewett's grandfather in "Legend of the Green Country" with the very dissimilar treatment of the same character in *Alice:*

> He mended the gates, once a month he drove into town
> to his
> "lodge,"
> A white carnation picked at dusk from my grandmother's
> garden,
> A dress suit with a gold watch, a chain looped over his
> belly,
> Magnificent! ("Legend of the Green Country")

> her grandfather was a window dresser
> at the Bon Marche
> he swaggered to Lodge to ride the goat
> naked a gold watch bounced on his belly (*Alice*)

The landscape is still recognizably Australian, but it is overlaid with mythic references that serve to unite the poem:

> The ocean of yellow wheat
> turns green in winter
> & waves like the sea ...
> This was Eden perfect circular
> the candid temples of her innocence
> the homestead in the clearing
> ringed with hills
> the paddocks pollened deep in dandelions
> the magic forest dark & beckoning ...
> Alice was driven howling from the garden.

The sexual energy of the poems finds its place in a voice unmistakably Hewett's, but there is a poignant restlessness running like a tracer throughout *Alice.* Nim, an elusive figure representative of male sexuality, appears after Alice is driven out of Eden into her "secret garden / under the hump of the hill," and his "changing face / laid waste her garden." Their final meeting is described in an intensely erotic sequence ("Japan"), but Nim's refusal to stay leads in "The Infernal Grove" to a second Fall and the destruction of this new, erotic Eden—"the garden's soft with fruit fly / the black snake coils / across the path to spring":

> But I would rather
> live in hell she said
> & forfeit heaven
> to have been with him.

"... she'd wait for him ... till hell froze over ... Hell froze over / the night came down / as Nim betrayed her." In the final section of the poem Alice and Nim, as owl and falcon, are reunited after her death: "it is the beast fable / it is the myth of ourselves / & only just beginning"; "that was the time / when they made friends with death."

Alice in Wormland is also a tale of political beliefs fought for and then lost ("Socialism with a human face was dead ... she reinstated Art as her religion") and of an artist's journey to her sources.

Alice's travels take her on a literary pilgrimage in which the most striking figure is Emily Brontë "coughing up blood and *Gondal,*" but there are echoes of Yeats, Lawrence, and Byron. In focusing on the myth of the Fall and the quest for love, *Alice in Wormland* states more poignantly and consistently than any of Hewett's earlier poetry the paradox of the unattainable Eden.

Hewett's 1994 collection *Peninsula* is set in a naturalistic garden lapped by the waves (ebb and flow are also important in her concurrent novel *The Toucher*). This is a "silent garden / furred with frost / remote and still / where no one comes / where time itself is lost" ("Return to the Peninsula"). The waiting silence is not resigned but characteristically vital and questioning, captured in a striking natural image in "Return to the Peninsula":

> the dry cough
> of the foxes on the cliff
> sitting together
> their sparkling eyes
> reflected off the sea

Interspersed with three peninsula poems—the first is "On the Peninsula" and the last is "The Last Peninsula"—are revisions of earlier images and childhood scenes. Australian landscape and Tennysonian myth are combined in "Lines to the Dark Tower":

> Across the water meadows
> on the grey sky
> the dark tower stood alone
> my father said
> *you can't live in a wheat silo*
> *stinking of mouldy straw*
> *and blood and bone*
> but he couldn't see
> the plumes nodding above the hedges

In "Lady's Choice" the Lady of Shalott refuses to take the three paces to her death, and the knight is "pontificating / on God and mercy and grace and faces"; instead, "tomorrow I'll get up early / work on my poems and thread my loom."

The world of *Windmill Country* returns in "Still Lives," poems of "Uncles and aunts and country cousins ... they sift the dark fields / of my mind." But *Peninsula* always returns to the growing shadows of the garden by the sea, asking "what is the distance / between / bone and infinity? / bliss pain solitude / a breath of air" ("The Last Peninsula"). Spare, direct, and honest, the dramatic gesture remains possible. *Peninsula* celebrates the mystery at the heart of the familiar:

> and shall I too
> eventually disappear
> in a garden hat and cloak
> possibly accompanied by
> a Platonic angel
> leaving a note

> *I have been called away*
> *from the dark cottage*
> *but on what errand*
> *and for what purpose?*

—Nan Bowman Albinski

HILL, Selima

Nationality: British. **Born:** Selima Wood in London, 13 October 1945. **Education:** New Hall College, Cambridge, special degree 1966. **Family:** Married Roderic Hill in 1968; one daughter and two sons. **Career:** Writing fellow, University of East Anglia, 1991; writer-in-residence, Royal Festival Hall Dance Festival, 1992. **Awards:** Cholmondeley prize, 1986; Arvon/*Observer* Poetry Competition prize, 1988. **Address:** c/o Bloodaxe Books, P.O. Box 1SN, Newcastle upon Tyne, NE99 1SN, England.

PUBLICATIONS

Poetry

Saying Hello at the Station. London, Chatto & Windus, 1984.
My Darling Camel. London, Chatto & Windus, 1988.
The Accumulation of Small Acts of Kindness. London, Chatto & Windus, 1989.
A Little Book of Meat. Newcastle upon Tyne, Bloodaxe, 1993.
Trembling Hearts in the Bodies of Dogs: New & Selected Poems. Newcastle upon Tyne, Bloodaxe, 1994.

*

Selima Hill comments:

"All that is personal soon rots: it must be packed in ice." I have this quotation from W.B. Yeats copied into my notebook—I don't know where I first came across it, but I often remind myself, and the people I work with, of it. I also like Bonnard's "It's what I live by." And he goes on: "I feed the picture as one feeds a large animal." So my work is a combination of rot, ice, and animal food, it sounds like.

*   *   *

Selima Hill's art is one of extreme sensitivity to the reverberation of memory (both personal and cultural) in the everyday, to speech (particularly the rhythms of suppressed anxiety), and to the subtleties of the craft itself. A deceptively relaxed iambic pace masks an intensity that can be both disturbing and disturbed; a poet who can recall Larkin at his most detached and Plath at her most stressed—sometimes in the same poem—can hardly be regarded as derivative of either. Hill can lure, lull, surprise, and scare; she has superb timing.

In Hill's first book, *Saying Hello at the Station,* moments are both spotlit by her observational skill and given shape and depth by the way she lets chinks of light (or shards of darkness) from the infant or distant past fall upon her subjects. The disquieting deities of ancient Egypt are often featured, haunting contemporary voices with their estranging names and the sheer potency of their myths. Not surprisingly, the most striking of these poems, "Inshallah—God Willing," sees a white man of the 20th century menaced by these forces in their very heartland, the Valley of the Kings. One world seems to slide into another as Howard Carter's assistant ("O Pecky Callendar ... you have disturbed / the King's long night") is addressed:

After the gold was discovered,
and you came back late
to the rest house, over the sound
of your donkey padding on the sand,
you heard someone call
for a light, and the door
of your room stood open.

These lines are beautifully subtle on two levels. Hill shows a storyteller's gift for the quiet mention ("came back late," "on the sand") that expands to fill the reader's inner screen, and she has a poet's unmistakable power to fill a single word—"stood"—with more significance than would be thought possible. The particular chill engendered by that word alone is beyond the scope of visual art.

Hill combines the common sense of knowing how much eye- or ear-catching detail one poem can hold with a true sense for single words, a sense existing somewhere between the true eye and the true ear and encompassing both. In a childhood memory, for example, a girl recalls the innate menace of sharing a swimming pool with an older boy: "His hands in the moving water / seemed to float between my legs." Here the subdued "moving" is another quietly perfect option.

Hill is a natural and flexible enough poet to employ images so fused with one another that they easily avoid the relentless hiccup of clever simile that lesser writers stick and are stuck with. The following image cannot be broken down but streams in several ways: "You imagine soldiers' blood / trickling down Europe's / ice-cream-coloured map / like syrup." Elsewhere, Hill relishes clusters of suggestive consonants. We hear Flaubert in the Koseir Desert imagining eating lemon sherbet; the fact that this recollection is being refracted through a writer's (thirsty) imagination gives Hill the perfect license to enjoy: "You dip the spoon into the frosted glass, / you crush the little mound and lift the splinters / gently to your lips, you swoon with snowy joy." The ability to describe the outlines as well as the daydreamed essences of painful wants serves the poet well as she begins to turn her attention to disintegrating states of mind.

The voices and characters of *My Darling Camel* are much troubled by limitations, surfaces, and barriers, and they often break to admit menacing figures, Plath-like disturbers of sleep or repose: the Umbrella Man, the Ptarmigan Hunter, or Father John, holding the hand of whom "was like holding a helping of trifle." They tend to be male, demonic, transfigurations of childhood memory either responsible for past distress or symbolizing it. Whatever the connection, these voices tug us through the nightmare fairground of schizophrenia, paranoia, dense memory loss: "Little feathers / journey past my cheeks / like boats. / I'm bubbling diamonds. / I'm just a head." Structurally, the poems often zigzag to a costly mental peace or at least to a balance.

Hill has the gift of stringing together apparently fragmented details so that they not only portray a state of mind but also create a tableau, a glimpsed scene. The tiny poem "Plums," for example, explodes outwards and is more than suggestive in its plot, scenery, costumes, and props:

The music rises like a party dress.
Nocturnal marriages are always best.
Parrot feathers. Ancient seas. Soft plums.
Shelter in my bedroom when she comes.

In "The Culmination of All Her Secret Longings" voices of Laura, a mental patient, visiting friends, and letters from home are mixed up with camels, set free after the Civil War, roaming the Arizona desert, copulating, out on the rim of Laura's sanity. Other voices intrude. These incongruous splinters and the fracturing of narrative into disembodied quotation, menacing italic, and lonely, disturbed self prefigure Hill's third book, *The Accumulation of Small Acts of Kindness,* which charts the mental illness and slow recovery of a girl in a psychiatric ward.

For much of this work Hill employs an incantatory iambic pentameter, though often splitting the five feet over two or three lines. This has the effect of accentuating the rhythm and jailing the girl in it, just as she is penned in with memories, fantasies, and outer and inner voices that are barely distinct. When rhythms knock so metronomically, the reader is conditioned to expect strong rhyme, half rhyme, or no rhyme at all, but by alternating strong rhyme with none Hill voices a disturbed, frustrated inner life where the tragedy takes trivial forms and the comedy is awful. Notice how disconcertingly close to each other "kindness" and "kind" are said in what is a blithe, distracted voice:

> "Afternoons of fruit and acts of kindness."
> "I treasure every word I think he said."
> "His hand is lying on my lap like liver.
> Wiping up the blood. He's very kind."

Few poets know as unflinchingly as Hill how to hit these right "wrong" notes. *The Accumulation of Small Acts of Kindness* is a risk that absolutely comes off because its poet, having long abandoned the appearance of narrative reasons for the rich and dangerous field of the troubled psyche, couples an exposing eye for the subterranean life of the mind with a magnificent gift for harnessing poetic form to depict it.

—Glyn Maxwell

HIRSHFIELD, Jane (B.)

Nationality: American. **Born:** New York, New York, 24 February 1953. **Education:** Princeton University, New Jersey, A.B. (magna cum laude) 1973. **Career:** Affiliated with California Poets in the Schools, 1980-85; master artist, Chevron Foundation Artist in the Schools Program, 1982-84; visiting poet, Wyoming Poets in the Schools, 1987, and University of Alaska, Fairbanks, 1993; adjunct professor, Northern Michigan University, 1994; associate faculty member, Bennington Writers Seminars, 1995; visiting associate professor, University of California, Berkeley, 1995. Member of faculty, Napa Valley Poetry Conference, 1984, 1985, 1993, 1994, 1996, 1997; Port Townsend Writers Conference, 1987, 1988, 1991, 1994; Foothills College Writers Conference, 1989—; Truckee Meadows Writers Conference, Reno, Nevada, 1991, 1994; Squaw Valley Art of the Wild Writers Conference, 1992, 1993, 1995, 1996, 1997; University of Minnesota Split Rock Summer Arts Seminars, 1995. Freelance editor and assistant to literary agent Michael Katz, 1983—. Lecturer, University of San Francisco, 1991—. **Awards:** Poetry Competition prize (later named Discovery award), *Nation,* 1973; Poetry prize, *Quarterly Review*

of Literature, 1982; Yaddo fellowship, 1983, 1985, 1987, 1989, 1992, 1996; Guggenheim fellowship, 1985; Joseph Henry Jackson award, San Francisco Foundation, 1986; Gordon Barber award, Poetry Society of America, 1987; Columbia University Translation Center award, 1987, for *The Ink Dark Moon;* Djerassi Foundation artist-in-residence, 1987, 1988, 1989, 1990; Commonwealth Club of California Poetry medal, 1988, for *Of Gravity & Angels,* and 1994, for *The October Palace;* Cecil Hemley award, Poetry Society of America, 1988; Pushcart prize, 1988; Dewar's Young Artist Recognition award in poetry, 1990; MacDowell Colony fellowship, 1994; Poetry Center Book Award, 1994, for *The October Palace;* Rockefeller Foundation fellowship, Bellagio Study Center, 1995; Bay Area Book Reviewers award in poetry, 1995, for *The October Palace.* **Address:** c/o HarperCollins, 10 East 53rd Street, New York, New York 10022, U.S.A.

Publications

Poetry

Alaya. Princeton, New Jersey, Quarterly Review of Literature, 1982.
Of Gravity & Angels. Middletown, Connecticut, Wesleyan University Press, 1988.
The October Palace. New York, HarperCollins, 1994.
The Lives of the Heart. New York, HarperCollins, 1997.

Other

Nine Gates: Essays on Poetry. New York, HarperCollins, 1997.

Editor and translator, *The Ink Dark Moon: Poems by Komachi & Shikibu, Women of the Ancient Court of Japan.* New York, Vintage Classics, 1990.
Editor and translator, *Women in Praise of the Sacred: 43 Centuries of Spiritual Poetry by Women.* New York, HarperCollins, 1994.

*

Jane Hirshfield comments:

My primary reason for writing has always been the attempt to understand and deepen experience by bringing it into words. Poetry, for me, is an instrument of investigation and a mode of perception, a way of knowing and feeling both self and world; and I believe that a good poem not only holds experience but creates it, by allowing reader or writer to step into that place at the center where all things rise newly into being. I write, then, as a way to attend with deeper accuracy to the difficult business of being a human being in the world. But poetry is also a mode of being in which subjective and objective can approach and become each other—outer description holds inner being, and the most seemingly subjective expression touches universal experiences of passion, grief, love, loss, and the subtler experiences of both daily life and what, for lack of any better term, I will call metaphysical inquiry.

The speaking voice of a poem during its composition is intensely private for me, but the finished work is nonetheless a way of bringing fruit of inner thinking to others. Technically, I am interested in making poems that find a clarity without simplicity; in a way of thinking and speaking that does not exclude complexity but also does not obscure; in poems that know the world in many ways at once—heart, mind, voice, and body. There are many kinds of poem-making that seem like valid roads to me, but all encompass both word and world.

My "lineage" as a poet includes both the Western and Eastern traditions. Greek and Roman lyrics, the English sonnet, those foundation stones of American poetry Whitman and Dickinson, "modern" poets from Eliot to Akhmatova to Cavafy to Neruda—all have added something to my knowledge of what is possible in poetry. But equally important to me have been the classical Chinese poets such as Tu Fu, Li Po, Wang Wei, and Han Shan, and the classical Japanese poets, particularly the two foremost women poets of the Heian era, Ono no Komachi and Izumi Shikibu, whom I translated in *The Ink Dark Moon.* I am also interested in the lesser known traditions—Eskimo poetry, Nahuatl poetry; I believe that full realizations of the lyric impulse can be found in every tradition and culture, and I have tried to draw on as wide a range as possible in the various essays and craft lectures I have written. The two books I have edited, *The Ink Dark Moon: Love Poems by Ono no Komachi and Izumi Shikibu* and *Women in Praise of the Sacred: 43 Centuries of Spiritual Poetry by Women,* were each undertaken in the effort to make more widely known the work of historical women poets whose words I found both memorable and moving, able to enlarge our understanding of what it is to be human, as well as to counteract the lingering myth that there were no historical women writers of significance.

*   *   *

In the afterword to *Alaya,* her first collection of poems, Jane Hirshfield notes that her intent is "to find the level of truth in a situation which is incontrovertible, as a dream is, by reason of its particularity." What emerges most clearly in this volume, which collects poems written between the poet's eighteenth and twenty-seventh years, is the first appearance of themes to be developed at greater length and with greater individual style and skill in later volumes. That she regards poetry as a kind of gift, of perception and sensibility distilled into language, is clear from the first poem, "How To Give," which suggests that ordinary moments can compensate for the loss of monuments of greater cultural or historical magnitude:

> The only life to be had starts here:
> without seams,
> this daily life a coming ordinariness,
> a mine to replace the chameleon history of power,
> a power to replace that other power—
> things shining, & things growing dark,
> loud with crickets,
> with bees,
> the patina of use,
> the habit of care.

James Wright's influence on Hirshfield can be detected in the opening poem of her second collection, the title of which, *Of Gravity & Angels,* aptly encapsulates the twin pulls in her work. "After Work" echoes the imagery and flow of Wright's "A Blessing"; like Wright, Hirshfield stops by a pasture at evening and, in this case, whistles the horses close to accept her gift of corncobs:

> They come, deepened and muscular movements
> conjured out of sleep: each small noise and scent
> heavy with earth, simple beyond communion ...
> ... and in the night, their mares' eyes shine, reflecting stars,
> the entire, outer light of the world here.

The second section of the book, however, presents a clear departure, gathering poems often explicit in their erotic imagery. The title poem begins with the speaker telling her lover that she "want[s] the long road of your thigh / under my hand, your well-traveled thigh, / your salt-slicked & come-slicked thigh...." Yet this sexual situation opens to a sense of erotic joining in a larger sense:

> ... all fontanel, all desire, the whole thing beginning
> for the first time again, the first,
> until I wonder then how is it
> we even know which part we are,
> even know the ground that lifts us, raucous,
> out of ourselves,
> as the rising sound of a summer dawn
> when all of it joins in.

If an erection signals a kind of rising counter to the ordinary heaviness of things, it also reflects the intrinsic impulse to rise against the tug of other forces.

In *The October Palace* Hirshfield widens her net to gather Zen monks, Cycladic figures, modernist painters, Praxilla, Grant's *Common Birds and How To Know Them,* and a car named Big Mama Tomato. Such references allow her, as she writes in "The Wedding," to "think of world / in which nothing is lost, its heaped paintings, / the studded statues keeping their jewels." Her knowledge never seems donned like a valedictory robe, however, but serves to illuminate recesses of thought; it does not rest on elegant surfaces, for, as she begins "Perceptibility Is a Kind of Attentiveness,"

> It is not enough
> to see only the beauty,
> this light
> that pools aluminum
> in the winter branches of apple—
> it is only a sign
> of the tree looking out
> from the tree,
> of the light looking
> back at the light,
> the long-called attention.

But the things of this world do not serve only to "distract / in their sweetness and rustling"; the body is also a "net," "The one / we willingly give ourselves to ... / each knot so carefully made, the curved / plate of the sternum tied to the shape of breath, / the perfect hinge of knee ..." ("Of the Body"). What Hirshfield hopes to help us see is a way, as she titles one poem, of "Meeting the Light Completely." The goal of Zen practice is to see the world as it is, just as it is, not other than an ideal world of enlightened experience, not quite the same. "Not one, not two," a Zen saying insists. But in the details, banal as "the chipped lip / of a blue-glazed cup," we see the beauty of "the found world," which surprises as profoundly as being able, in those odd moments when we are truly present, to recognize the former "unrecognized stranger" in "the long beloved," leading us to say with "all lovers," "What fools we were, not to have seen."

—Allen Hoey

HOGAN, Linda

Nationality: American (Native American: Chickasaw). **Born:** Born Linda Henderson, in Denver, Colorado, 16 July 1947. **Education:** University of Colorado, M.A. in English 1978. **Family:** Married Pat Hogan (divorced); two daughters. **Career:** Diverse jobs as nurse's aide, dental assistant, waitress, homemaker, secretary, administrator, teacher's aide, library clerk, freelance writer and researcher; poet-in-schools in Colorado and Oklahoma, 1980-84; workshop facilitator in creative writing and creativity, 1981-84; assistant professor in TRIBES program, Colorado College, 1982-84; associate professor of American Indian and American Studies, University of Minnesota—Twin Cities, Minneapolis, 1984-89; associate professor of English, University of Colorado, Boulder, 1989—. Active in volunteer worker for wildlife rehabilitation. Guest editor of *Frontiers*, 1982. **Awards:** Five Civilized Tribes Playwriting award, 1980; Colorado Independent Writers fellow, 1984, 1985; Before Columbus Foundation American Book award, 1986, for *Seeing through the Sun;* Colorado Writer's fellowship in fiction; Minnesota Arts Board grant in poetry; National Endowment for the Arts fellowship and award; Oklahoma Book award for fiction; Colorado Book Award, 1993, for *The Book of Medicines;* Mountain and Plains Booksellers award; Pulitzer Prize finalist, 1994, for *Mean Spirit;* National Book Critics' Circle award, 1994; Guggenheim award; Pushcart Prize; Lannan Foundation award, 1994. **Address:** BB 226, English Department, University of Colorado, Boulder, Colorado 80309, U.S.A.

PUBLICATIONS

Poetry

Calling Myself Home. Greenfield Center, New York, Greenfield Review, 1979.
Daughters, I Love You, introduction by Paula Gunn Allen. Loretto Heights, Women's Research Center, 1981.
Eclipse. Los Angeles, American Indian Studies Center, 1983.
Seeing through the Sun. Amherst, University of Massachusetts Press, 1985.
Savings. Minneapolis, Coffeehouse Press, 1988.
The Book of Medicines. Minneapolis, Coffeehouse Press, 1993.

Fiction

That Horse. N.p., Pueblo of Acoma Press, 1985.
The Big Woman. N.p., Firebrand Press, 1987.
Mean Spirit. New York, Atheneum, 1990.
Solar Storms. New York, Scribner, 1995.
Power. New York, Norton, 1998.

Play

A Piece of Moon (produced Stillwater, Oklahoma, 1981).

Other

Red Clay: Poems and Stories. New York, Greenfield Press, 1991.
Dwellings: A Spiritual History of the Living World (essays). New York, Norton, 1995.
From Women's Experience to Feminist Theology. Ithaca, New York, Almond, 1996.

Editor, with Carol Buechal and Judith McDaniel, *The Stories We Hold Secret: Tales of Women's Spiritual Development.* Greenfield Center, New York, Greenfield Review Press, 1986.
Editor, with others, *Intimate Nature: The Bond between Women and Animals.* New York Ballantine, 1997.

*

Critical Studies: *Survival This Way: Interviews with American Indian Poets* by Joseph Bruchac, Tucson, University of Arizona Press, 1987; "A Heart Made Out of Crickets: An Interview with Linda Hogan" by Bo Schöler, in *Journal of Ethnic Studies,* 1988; *This Is about Vision: Interviews with Southwestern Writers* by John Crawford, William Balassi, and Annie O. Eysturoy, Aubuquerque, University of New Mexico Press, 1990.

Linda Hogan comments:

I have considered my writing to come from close observation of the life around me, a spoken connection with the earth and with the histories of the earth. More and more I find that my writing comes from a sense of traditional indigenous relationship with the land and its peoples, from the animals and plants of tribal histories, stories, and knowledge. I am trying to speak this connection, stating its spirit, adding to it the old stories that have come to a new language. My influences are sometimes the language of ceremony and transformation, sometimes science. I research my work and think of how to translate a world view, a different way to live with this world. I try to keep up on contemporary poetry, not only American, but in translation and from other countries as well.

*   *   *

Linda Hogan is widely known as an American Indian writer. Her concern for nature as a spiritual imperative for human life reflects her Chickasaw heritage and her own theological explorations. Hogan combines lyrical and political elements in her poetry that prompt us to reconsider the ways we know our world and ourselves. Her technique is free verse, with concrete imagery and a dream-like quality to many narrative presentations in her poems. Critics acknowledge her graceful language and a spiritual consciousness that complements rather than opposes the activist ideals forming the foundation of her work.

Hogan's first collection, a chapbook entitled *Calling Myself Home* (1979), introduces ideas of identity and community that continue to be compelling elements in all of her writings. After her discovery of the poetry of Kenneth Rexroth, Hogan began writing poems to help bridge "a growing abyss" she felt between the different cultures in her life. Creating poetry helped restore order by allowing her to "call home" her connections to tribal life while living in the notoriously fragmented world of "mainstream" United States. "Calling myself home" suggests a conscious effort to reconsider one's identity as part of the meaning of "home." In a later poem, "Truth Is," the relentless conflict between Native and white cultures becomes a call for "amnesty."

While the spirit of place is a theme that we come to expect in Native American writing, Hogan has a particularly strong commitment to the notion of connectedness with nature. In an interview with Bo Schöler, she stated that "my heart is made of crickets"; insects are not only part of our natural family, but part of the self. For Hogan, such human bonding with nature depicts the highest truth that is found in myth. The intermingling of all life holds magic as well as healing beauty: "My daughter rises at water's edge. / Her face lies down on water / and the bird flies through her. / The world falls / into her skin" ("Morning: The World in the Lake"). Hogan uses vivid juxtapositions to re-invent our sense of the energy in our world. In "The Rainy Season" the earth expresses "unknown sorrows" in the melancholy of darkness and rain as do the humans for whom "a single thought of loneliness / is enough to bring collapse." Significantly, the season itself is neither indifferent nor independent of people: "Every day collapses / despite the women / walking to town with black umbrellas / holding up the sky."

Dissolving the false boundary between nature and humanity is one way for Hogan to restore connectedness in her poetry. Denouncing the symbols of division seems to be an important step toward restoring wholeness. In her award-winning collection *Seeing through the Sun* (1985), many boundaries are abolished. In "Folksong," the surviving songs of Latvia are connected to those of Native Americans, of any dispossessed people. Such songs carry the spirit of community more powerfully than the decisions of statesmen who "speak, yes or no / and change the living / to the dead." The songs and the singers share common cause in spite of different cultures. With the force of chanting verse, Hogan is further able to help us re-imagine the walls we impose on ourselves: "May all walls be like those of the jungle, / filled with animals / singing into the ears of night" so that by listening, we will know "again / that boundaries are all lies" ("Wall Songs"). Unexamined perceptions represent the most significant boundaries that must be broken. Hogan has consistently documented her concern for all life in a nuclear age, a time when death has and may again come in the form of an overpowering brightness. After centuries of celebrating the sun, we must recognize that in an atomic age, a blinding light is not god but nuclear holocaust, "this person left with only fingerprints" ("Seeing through the Sun"). Moreover, the light that we have associated with enlightenment, a philosophy that has justified manifest destiny, male privilege, and white dominance, has brought death and danger instead of universal goodness after all: "*Sun, we see through you / the flashing of rifles and scythes.*"

Hogan has stated that "poetry is a process of uncovering our real knowledge." This definition helps us to see the value of history and language through creative exploration. Past and present come together; they overlap in very simple details: an apartment that is new to the poet is not new at all but "holds the coughs of old men / and their canes tapping on the floor" ("The New Apartment: Minneapolis"). False barriers of houses and private property dissolve so that we see "people suspended in air." Finally, entering the apartment means coming home to time immemorial: "Hello aunt, hello brothers, hello trees / and deer walking quietly on the soft red earth." The surreal quality of time and space here suggests the detail of myth and dream.

Hogan is consistently anthologized in American Indian collections, but critics find much in her work that enhances our under-

standing of American culture in general. In addition to providing a more inclusive view of the American experience, Hogan's expressive language and images of connection and disconnection stretch beyond the conflicts of Native versus white culture or the need to restore nature. As an artist, Hogan reminds us that language / art is powerful: "This is the truth not just a poem" ("Neighbors"). And the opposite is true as well, "This is a poem and not just the truth." Art does have real power, and truth demands the expressions of poets. Hogan's expressions of transforming vision, like "Let the talkers grow silent. / The prison yard is flying" ("Changing Weather"), make her poems particularly rewarding.

—Laurel Smith

HOWE, Fanny (Quincy)

Nationality: American. **Born:** Buffalo, New York, 15 October 1940. **Education:** Stanford University, Stanford, California, 1958-61. **Family:** Married 1) Frederick Delafield in 1961 (divorced 1963); 2) Carl Senna in 1968 (divorced 1975); two daughters and one son. **Career:** Lecturer, Tufts University, Boston, 1968-71, Emerson College, Boston, 1974, Columbia University, New York, 1975-78, Yale University, New Haven, Connecticut, 1976, Harvard Extension, Cambridge, Massachusetts, 1977, Massachusetts Institute of Technology, Cambridge, 1978-87. Associate director, University of California Study Center, London, England, 1993-95; professor, University of California, San Diego, 1987—. **Awards:** National Endowment for the Arts fellowship, 1969, 1991; St. Botolph award for fiction, 1976; Writer's Choice award for fiction, 1984; *Village Voice* award for fiction, 1988. MacDowell Colony fellowship, 1965, 1990; Bunting Institute fellow, 1974; Fondation Royaumont Translations Center Guest Poet, France, 1990; Cambridge University Conference on Poetry Guest Poet, 1993; Southampton University Conference on Poetry Guest Poet, 1994. **Address:** 151 South Sycamore Avenue, Los Angeles, California 90036, U.S.A.

PUBLICATIONS

Poetry

Eggs. Boston, Houghton Mifflin, 1970.
The Amerindian Coastline Poem. New York, Telephone Books, 1976.
Alsace Lorraine. New York, Telephone Books, 1982.
For Erato. Berkeley, California, Tuumba Press, 1984.
Introduction to the World. New York, The Figures, 1985.
Robeson Street. Boston, Alice James Books, 1985.
The Vineyard. Providence, Lost Roads, 1988.
The End. Los Angeles, Littoral Books, 1992.
The Quietist. Oakland, California, O Books, 1992.
O'Clock. London, Reality Street Editions, 1995.

Novels

Forty Whacks. Boston, Houghton Mifflin, 1969.
First Marriage. New York, Avon Equinox, 1975.
Bronte Wilde. New York, Avon Equinox, 1976.
Holy Smoke. New York, Fiction Collective, 1979.

The White Slave. New York, Avon Books, 1980.
The Blue Hills (for children). New York, Avon Books, 1981.
Yeah, But (for children). New York, Avon Books, 1982.
Radio City (for children). New York, Avon Books, 1983.
In the Middle of Nowhere. New York, Fiction Collective, 1984.
The Race of the Radical (for children). New York, Viking, 1985.
Taking Care. New York, Avon Books, 1985.
The Lives of a Spirit. Los Angeles, Sun & Moon, 1986.
The Deep North. Los Angeles, Sun & Moon, 1988.
Famous Questions. New York, Ballantine, 1989.
Saving History. Los Angeles, Sun & Moon, 1992.

*

Manuscript Collection: Stanford University Libraries, Stanford, California.

Fanny Howe comments:

My whole effort as a novelist has been to study the imaginary, invisible, and utopian trend of each character alongside their active (political) social business. This terrible stress is expressed for me in fictional forms that separate thought from enterprise. That's what I do when I write a story: attempt to clarify the boundaries and turn them into escapes, as in the rubbery walls of an amoeba, there is the ingredient for fusion.

My poetry has continued to work as a response to the daily world and how strange it is in every aspect, and I think the Arabic poetic form—the ghazal—is closest to the paths my own poems take. Translating a line from one of Ghalib's ghazals, Adrienne Rich wrote: "The lightning-stroke of the vision was meant for us, not for Sinai."

*   *   *

Fanny Howe has established herself as a prolific and innovative craftsperson both in poetry and in fiction. Besides several collections of poetry she has also published a number of works of fiction. But such a distinction may be misleading, for in Howe's work the boundary between poetry and fiction is blurred. Howe began her career with two books published by the major commercial publisher Houghton Mifflin: a collection of relatively traditional short stories, *Forty Whacks* (1969), and a collection of shapely lyric poems, *Eggs* (1970). In the 1970s Avon Books, a mass-circulation paperback house, published three of Howe's novels. But the trajectory of Howe's career since then has carried her away from commercial publishers toward more avant-garde venues: the Fiction Collective, various small poetry presses, and Sun & Moon, an important publisher of experimental writing. As Howe has moved away from commercial presses, her work has increasingly been located on the shifting boundary between poetry and fiction.

Howe's later novels, such as *The Deep North* and *Saving History,* intermittently move from narrative into extended poetic riffs, in which the focus shifts from such traditional fictional concerns as character and action to the pleasures and the perils of verbal play. At the same time in her poetry Howe has moved away from self-contained lyrics to sequences that often include a distinct narrative dimension, and the most dazzling of these sequences, *The Lives of a Spirit,* is a long prose poem. In significant measure, then, Howe has invented her own forms, and any adequate survey of her work must take into account the interplay between her poetry and her fiction.

Howe has often been grouped with the so-called language poets, an avant-garde group that since the 1970s has dedicated itself to an analytic deconstruction of the semantic and syntactic texture of language. One of Howe's sequences, "Alsace-Lorraine," is included in the principal anthology of language poetry, Ron Silliman's *In the American Tree*, and her publisher, Sun & Moon, is best known as the publisher of such language poets as Charles Bernstein, Lyn Hejinian, and Clark Coolidge. Howe is also linked to this movement through her sister, Susan Howe, who is generally seen as one of the major figures among the language poets.

Like the work of other writers in this movement, Howe's poetry is assertively difficult. She eschews the fragmentary syntax of some language poets and instead normally writes in sentences. But the logical connections among her sentences are often radically attenuated, so that we are forced to puzzle out the linkages for ourselves. Her longer sequences in particular work with subtle and muted patterns of recurrence that emerge only with repeated rereadings. Despite these stylistic links to language poetry, however, Howe returns again and again to certain themes that make her work atypical of the movement. First, Howe's work presents itself under the sign of Eros. Both in her poetry and her fiction she gives voice to the longings that draw human beings together—woman and man, parent and child. Second, for Howe these fundamental human relationships always have both political and spiritual dimensions. In Howe's world human beings always hunger not only for love but also for justice and righteousness. Her fiction regularly has its climax in a moment of ethical choice in which her characters, even if they are not themselves believers, act as if G-d (to use her own spelling) were watching. Her poetry, too, is consistently haunted by the possibility of G-d's presence, often envisioned in explicitly Christian—indeed, Roman Catholic—terms.

Howe's most significant poetic achievement is *The Lives of a Spirit*, which locates itself within the tradition of Rilke's *Duino Elegies*. In this book-length sequence the openness of the text, the sometimes dizzying abysses between the sentences, invite the reader to embark on a spiritual pilgrimage parallel to the author's. Howe avoids Rilke's ostentatiously high rhetoric, emphasizing not the potentially transformative power of the angelic visitation but the everyday discipline of spiritual preparation, a stance underscored by the use of thickly textured prose rather than verse. Her sequence of nine elegies begins in a cemetery by the sea and with a baby who is insistently physical—"Her damp skin, soft as a rose petal, was sweet to the cheek"—but who also seems miraculous:

> They surmised that she had floated from the stars in the navy blue sky. Like rain at sea and no one to see, the coherence of these events and conjectures was never going to be accounted for. Now nested in sea heather, the baby will, later, learn her tens and alphabets on a pillow in bed. And will sometimes wonder: Little word, who said me? Am I owned or free?

In the elegies that follow, this spirit, sometimes "she" and sometimes "I," does indeed live multiple lives, as the title of the book suggests. The presence of the mother hovers over the second and third elegies as the child begins to explore her world; the third elegy ends "I would have said, Mother, stay at the window, but don't call me in." Later, the father-as-rule-maker and sister-as-companion move to center stage, and with her lover the spirit comes to know "every level of being ... from bone to bare skin; and why love is so close to G-d and d—th." But at the end of the ninth elegy the spirit is still—in the words of Simone Weil, Howe's alter ego in this book and throughout her career—"waiting for God":

> If I could just get my little cell in order, they would let me out again. I'm ready to go out. Through my open window, I can see the stone bank along the pond, its serpentine curve beside the path, and beyond the path, the trees. My bench is there, where I sit with folded hands.

Quietly but eloquently, *The Lives of a Spirit* invites us—with Mother watching from the window perhaps—to join her waiting on the bench in the park.

—Burton Hatlen

HOWE, Susan

Nationality: American. **Born:** 1937. **Education:** Museum of Fine Arts, Boston, B.F.A. in painting 1961. **Career:** Butler Fellow in English, 1988, and professor of English, 1989, State University of New York, Buffalo; visiting scholar and professor of English, Temple University, Philadelphia, Spring 1990, 1991; visiting poet and Leo Block Professor at University of Denver, 1993-94; Visiting Brittingham Scholar, University of Wisconsin, Madison, 1994; visiting poet, University of Arizona, 1994. **Awards:** Before Columbus Foundation award, 1980, for *Secret History of the Dividing Line,* and 1986, for *My Emily Dickinson*; New York State Council of the Arts residency, 1986; Pushcart prize, 1987; New York City Fund for Poetry grant, 1988. **Address:** 115 New Quarry Road, Guilford, Connecticut 06437, U.S.A.

<small>PUBLICATIONS</small>

Poetry

Hinge Picture. New York, Telephone, 1974.
The Western Borders. Berkeley, California, Tuumba Press, 1976.
Secret History of the Dividing Line. New York, Telephone, 1978.
Cabbage Gardens. Chicago, Fathom Press, 1979.
The Liberties. Guilford, Connecticut, Loon, 1980.
Pythagorean Silence. New York, Montemora, 1982.
Defenestration of Prague. New York, Kulchur, 1983.
Articulation of Sound Forms in Time. Windsor, Vermont, Awede, 1987.
A Bibliography of the King's Book or, Eikon Basilike. Providence, Rhode Island, Paradigm Press, 1989.
The Europe of Trusts: Selected Poems. Los Angeles, Sun & Moon Press, 1990.
Singularities. Middletown, Connecticut, Wesleyan University Press, 1990.
Silence Wager Stories. Providence, Rhode Island, Paradigm, 1992.

The Nonconformist's Memorial. New York, New Directions, 1993.
Frame Structures: Early Poems, 1974-1979. New York, New Directions, 1996.

Other

My Emily Dickinson. Berkeley, California, North Atlantic, 1985.
Incloser. Santa Fe, New Mexico, Weasel Sleeves Press, 1990.
The Birth-mark: unsettling the wilderness in American literary history. Middletown, Connecticut, Wesleyan University Press, 1993.

*

Critical Studies: Susan Howe issue of *Abacus* (Elmwood, Connecticut), no. 30, 15 November 1987, and *The Difficulties,* vol. 3, no. 2, 1989; "Howe's Hope: Impossible Crossings" by Linda Reinfeld, in *Tremblor,* no. 6, 1987; "The Mysterious Vision of Susan Howe" by George Butterick, in *North Dakota Quarterly* (Grand Forks), vol. 55, no. 4, Fall 1987; "Whowe: An Essay on Work by Susan Howe" by Rachel Blau Du Plessis, in *Sulfur* (Ypsilanti, Michigan), no. 20, Fall 1987; "Susan Howe: The Book of Cordelia" by Stephen-Paul Martin, in *Open Form and the Feminine Imagination, Postmodern Positions,* no. 2, Washington, D.C., Maisonneuve Press, 1988; essays by Kathleen Fraser, and Charles Bernstein and Bruce Andrews, in *Postmodern Line in Poetry,* edited by Robert Frank and Henry Sayre, Urbana, University of Illinois Press, 1988; "Collision or Collusion with History: The Lyric of Susan Howe" by Marjorie Perloff, in *Contemporary Literature* (Madison, Wisconsin), 1989; Susan Howe issue of *Talisman* (Hoboken, New Jersey), no. 4, Spring 1990; *The Pink Guitar: Writing as Feminist Practice* by Rachel Blau DuPlessis, New York and London, Routledge, 1990; *Language Poetry: Writing as Rescue* by Linda Reinfeld, Baton Rouge and London, Louisiana State University Press, 1992; *Disjunctive Poetics: From Gertrude Stein and Louis Zukovsky to Susan Howe* by Peter Quatermain, Cambridge and London, Cambridge University Press, 1992; "Articulating the Inarticulate: Singularities and the Counter-Method in Susan Howe" in *Contemporary Literature,* no. 36, 1995.

*   *   *

Susan Howe, one of America's covert triumphs of poetry, began as a visual artist whose canvases gradually became sites for the written. Her first books of poetry were published in the 1970s, unfolding into the singular and significant works *The Liberties, Pythagorean Silence,* and *Defenestration of Prague.* Her manifold brilliance is grounded in a deeply webbed sense of self in history and history in self, and her lyric and bold linguistic experimentation serve only to layer each line with a rich profusion of references both public and private. In her work, as she writes of Emily Dickinson's work, "Poetry is affirmation in negation, ammunition in the yellow eye of a gun that an allegorical pilgrim will shoot straight into the quiet of Night's frame." In the preface to *The Europe of Trusts: Selected Poems* she says, "I write to break out into perfect primeval Consent. I wish I could tenderly lift from the dark side of history, voices that are anonymous, slighted—inarticulate."

Howe's work with words begins in midlife. In Pythagorean Silence she reworks formative memories of World War II perceived as a child and addressed as an adult; formed in the newsreel fires of film, it is a perception and reception of war as ancient male praxis in a Jacob-wrestling tension (and torment) of female questioning. "For me there was no silence before armies," she writes in "There Are Not Leaves Enough to Crown to Cover to Crown to Cover": "Malice dominates the history of Power and Progress. History is the record of winners. Documents were written by the Masters. But fright is formed by what we see not by what they say. / From 1939 until 1946 in news photographs, day after I saw signs of culture exploding into murder. Shots of children being herded into trucks by hideous helmeted conquerors—shots of children who were orphaned and lost—shots of the emaciated bodies of Jews dumped into mass graves on top of more emaciated bodies—nameless numberless men women and children, uprooted world almost demented. God had abandoned them to history's sovereign Necessity."

Howe's interrogation of history (and subsequently its official and marginal languages) commingle with both experimental and high lyric richness in *Defenestration of Prague* and *The Liberties*. The latter awakens out of Swift's allegorical name, Stella, for Esther Johnson. Her voice completes that unheard other which *Journal to Stella* was addressed to. Howe interweaves rich Gaelic sensitivity with serious play entangling Shakespeare's *Lear* as seen through Cordelia's eyes.

A poet of original intelligence, Howe's critical revelations on Emily Dickinson—*My Emily Dickinson*—represent a landmark in creative scholarship, showing once again the possibility of poets being invariably the most potentially profound readers of poetry. The book is a marvel of feminist criticism which disrupts many normative feminist assumptions of Dickinson. Howe's grasp and use of historical texts enable her to fuse Calvinist and Indian captivity texts into influences, entering into the languages of early American rhetorics of spiritual and material ideologies. Howe writes that "Categories and hierarchies suggest property. My voice formed from my life belongs to no one else. What I put into words is no longer my possession. Possibility has opened. The future will forget, erase, or recollect and deconstruct every poem. There is a mystic separation between poetic vision and ordinary living. The conditions for poetry rest outside each life at a miraculous reach indifferent to worldly chronology."

—David Meltzer

HULME, Keri

Nationality: New Zealander. **Born:** Christchurch, New Zealand, 9 March 1947. **Education:** North Beach primary school; Aranui High School; Canterbury University, Christchurch, 1967-68. **Career:** Formerly, senior postwoman, Greymouth, and director for New Zealand television; writer-in-residence, Otago University, Dunedin, 1978, and Canterbury University, 1985. **Awards:** New Zealand Literary Fund grant, 1975, 1977, 1979, and scholarship in letters, 1990; Katherine Mansfield Memorial award, for short story, 1975; Maori Trust Fund prize, 1978; East-West Centre award, 1979; ICI bursary, 1982; New Zealand writing bursary, 1984; New Zealand Book Award, 1984; Mobil Pegasus prize, 1985; Booker McConnell prize, 1985; Chianti Ruffino Antico Fattor award, 1987. **Member:** New Zealand Literary Fund (mem-

ber, advisory committee), New Zealand Indecent Publications Tribunal. **Address:** Okarito Private Bag, Hokitika Post Office, Westland, New Zealand.

PUBLICATIONS

Poetry

The Silences Between (Moeraki Conversations). Auckland, Auckland University Press, 1982.
Strands. Auckland, Auckland University Press, 1991; Sydney, Hale & Iremonger, 1992.

Novels

the bone people. Wellington, Spiral, 1983; London, Hodder & Stoughton, and Baton Rouge, Louisiana State University Press, 1985.
Lost Possessions (novella). Wellington, Victoria University Press, 1985.

Short Stories

The Windeater / Te Kaihau. Wellington, Victoria University Press, 1986; London, Hodder & Stoughton, and New York, Braziller, 1987.

Other

Homeplaces: Three Coasts of the South Island of New Zealand, photographs by Robin Morrison. Auckland, Hodder & Stoughton, 1989; London, Hodder & Stoughton, 1990.

Recordings: *Keri Hulme and Les A. Murray Reading from Their Work*, 1985.

*

Media Adaptations: *Hooks and Feelers* (film; adaptation of her short story), 1983; *Hinekaro Goes on a Picnic and Blows Up an Obelisk* (film; adaptation of her short story), 1995.

Critical Studies: "Keri Hulme: Breaking Ground" by Shona Smith, in *Untold,* no. 2, spring 1984; "Sandi Hall and Keri Hulme Talk about 'the bone people' in *Broadsheet,* no. 121, July / August 1984; "In My Spiral Fashion" by Peter Simpson, in *Australian Book Review* (Kensington Park), August 1984; "Spiraling to Success" by Elizabeth Webby, in *Meanjin* (Melbourne), January 1985; "Keri Hulme's 'the bone people' and the Pegasus Award for Maori Literature" by C.K. Stead, in *Ariel* (Calgary, Alberta), no. 16, October 1985; "Rewriting Their Stories: Postcolonialism and Feminism in the Fictions of Keri Hulme and Audrey Thomas" by C. Prentice, in *Span,* no. 23, September 1986; interview with Harry Ricketts, in his *Talking about Ourselves: 12 New Zealand Poets in Conversation,* Wellington, Mallison Rendel, 1986; "Violence as lingua franca: Keri Hulme's *the bone people*" by M. Dever, in *World Literature Written in English,* vol. 29, no. 2, autumn 1989; *Leaving the Highway: Six Contemporary New Zealand Novelists* by Mark Williams, Auckland, Auckland University Press, 1990; interview with Elizabeth Alley in *In the Same Room:*

Conversations with New Zealand Writers, edited by Alley and Mark Williams, Auckland, Auckland University Press, 1992; "Hu(l)man Medi(t)ations: Inter-Cultural Explorations in Keri Hulme's 'The Windeater' / Te Kaihau" by Otto Heim and Anne Zimmerman, in *Australian and New Zealand Studies in Canada* (London, Ontario), 8 December 1992; "The Reawakening of the Gods: Realism and the Supernatural in Silko and Hulme" by Thomas E. Benediktson, in *Critique* (Atlanta, Georgia), no. 33, winter 1992.

Keri Hulme comments:

My mother comes from a line of covert matriarchs, women who run their households surely, but—and most importantly—also let their families run—

She has had six very different children. One way or another, we have all made our mark. I have, for example, two sisters who are midwives, inventive women-centered tautoko domiciliary midwives. They are partners in a business: they have different emphases in their individual practices: they are family-oriented people.

I am, by nature, a loner. I have been, since I was very young indeed. I was always trailing off up a beach, bemazed by the buzzing wondrous everything around, sand insects surf birdcries wind stink yearn—

I am also, in my depths / heights, family-oriented.

Our family comes from diverse people: Kai Tahu, Kati Mamoe (South Island Maori iwi); Orkney islanders; Lancashire folk; Faroese and / or Norwegian migrants. I have a mother—my father died when I, eldest of my siblings, was 11—and two maternal uncles; I have two paternal aunts; I have three sisters and two brothers, and a helluva lot of small fry (some of them now in their 20s) engendered thereby. I won't start on the cousin rings ...

I have always been pro-female, not least because I come from a line of matriarchs. Being female is a position of strength, like being Maori. Yes, it can be eroded. Yes, it is eroded by economic factors and historical factors and societal factors. But together, all of us, we survive. We not only survive, we laugh. We eat fatly, we drink well, and we weep when it is time to weep, and we laugh—from this base I live and move and have my being. From this base, I write—

* * *

Born in Christchurch, the New Zealand poet Keri Hulme has chosen to identify with her Maori heritage as a writer, and much of her work constructs Maori identity through explorations of the *tangata whenua* ("people of the land" or, more specifically, "people of the placenta"). The female quality of the land and of nature and themes of connectedness dominate much of her poetry, as in "Pa mai to reo aroha" ("Reach me your speech of love") in her first collection, *The Silences Between (Moeraki Conversations):*

Every morning the shags stretch their
necks and slip off Maukiekie. Every
evening they return in a wavering
line.
Sometimes we have seen the living
black wheels of caa'ing whales out in
the woman sea.

Once I found an earwig big as my
thumb in the cliffs, moulding her
body round her pale brood.

The moments of joy experienced at the fusion of inner and outer worlds can give way, however, to the opposite, experiences of loss and absence and the longing that results. The elegiac and plangent tone with which Hulme expresses such moments haunts her verse and often overwhelms the more celebratory passages. Clearly the emotional center of her writing, the passages of lamentation also give it a stronger sense of structure. The repeated questions of "E nga iwi o ngai tahu" ("By the bones [people] of the Ngai Tahu") give the poem force and direction, driving it to a typically powerful conclusion:

Mihi. Greeting. Weeping hello.
And to me, standing out as though
I'm the cripple in a company of runners;
to me, pale and bluegrey-eyed,
skin like a ghost, eyes like stones;
to me, always the manuhiri when away from home—
the weeping rings louder than the greeting.

Hulme's first collection expresses variety and amorphousness through variations of typeface and typographical arrangement It is given a dialogic form through the interactions of six "Conversations" and the five "Silences" that lie between them, the latter expressing experiences in which the narrator is far from her *turangawaewae* ("place to stand") and is forced to question her identity and the nature of her relationship to her home: "And on what shore does the wandering / fragment of seaweed finally ground?"

Many of the poems in Hulme's later collection, *Strands* (1991), verge on the arena that is ordinarily occupied by prose, pushing against the boundaries of both genres, with some loss of the evocative power of her more lyrical verse. The long opening poem, "Fishing the Olearia Tree," is spoken by a sardonic narrator who describes and maps a local terrain invested with the numinous:

o my love, there are lean hammer-headed clouds
menacing us from the horizon
and red-eyed moths beating on the doors

and the kettle, snoring away on the hob ...

This work appeals to an older oral tradition, both European (as in the medieval ballad) and Maori (as in the *waiata,* or "song"), and frequently involves the use of repetition, or anaphora, which in its better moments lends Hulme's writing a distinctive momentum. These influences and qualities persist in the occasional poems that make up the second section, "Against the Small Evil Voices," and the ten slight but delightful wine songs (some written considerably earlier than the rest of the collection) that make up the third. Here Hulme shows the full range of her poetic repertoire with the lightness and deftness of skill that turns the English medieval ballad form toward an expression of the vernacular.

—Anna Smith

J

JAMIE, Kathleen

Nationality: Scottish. **Born:** Johnston, Renfrewshire, 13 May 1962. **Education:** University of Edinburgh, M.A. (honors) in philosophy. **Career:** Writer-in-residence, Midlothian District Libraries, 1987-89, Dundee University, 1991-93, and University of Western Ontario, 1994-95. **Awards:** E.C. Gregory award, 1980; Scottish Arts Council Book Awards, 1983, 1988, 1994; K. Blundell Trust Fund grant, 1989; Hawthornden International Retreat for Writers fellow, 1989; Compton Fund grant, 1989; Somerset Maugham Award, 1995; Geoffrey Faber Memorial award, 1996. **Agent:** David Fletcher Associates, 58 John Street, Penicuik, Midlothian, Scotland. **Address:** 149 High Street, Newburgh, Fife KY14 6DY, Scotland.

PUBLICATIONS

Poetry

Black Spiders. Edinburgh, Salamander Press, 1982.
A Flame in Your Heart, with Andrew Greig. Newcastle upon Tyne, Bloodaxe, 1986.
The Way We Live. Newcastle upon Tyne, Bloodaxe, 1987.
The Autonomous Region: Poems & Photographs from Tibet. Newcastle upon Tyne, Bloodaxe, 1993.
The Queen of Sheba. Newcastle upon Tyne, Bloodaxe, 1994.

Other

The Golden Peak: Travels in Northern Pakistan. New Delhi, Penguin, and London, Virago, 1992.

*

Manuscript Collection: University College, University of New South Wales, Canberra, Australia.

Kathleen Jamie comments:

An introduction to my work—I don't write about things, but my work is full of them, and places, and voices. There's a strong awareness of the transcendent, too. Neither do I write *for* anyone, not readers, nor myself. My poetry is a product of the engagement between myself and my world. It's been called strong and rigorous; I try to channel the strength and music of the language; both English, and, recently, a personal form of Scots: because of the tones of Scots and as a response to the present threat to the culture. It's zestful work.

I'm a poet first (though I prefer the word "artist" as it's retained the life-force the word "poetry" seems to have lost), but my work is conditioned by my being female and Scottish; not caused by that. I travel; foreign places affect me; so do ideas.

*   *   *

Kathleen Jamie's first verse collection, *Black Spiders,* was published when she was only 20 years old. It shows an impressive confidence in the handling of both lyric and narrative pieces. The love poem "November" typifies the book's boldness, shifting focus from an unsettled lover longing to be abroad—"He can touch me with a look / As thoughtless as afternoon / And think as much of hindering me / As he would of sailing away"—to the statement "... I am left to tell him in a voice that / Seems as casual as his thought of travel: / I think as much of leaving as / Of forcing him to stay." The combination of clarity and ambiguity is a persistent strength in Jamie's work. So is the cryptic economy of the title poem, whose three brief sections imply both conflict and attraction between a man and a woman in an Aegean setting of sea, rocks, and a ruined convent, closing on a note at once erotic and sinister:

> She caught sight of him later, below, brushing salt from the hair of his nipples. She wanted them to tickle; black spiders on her lips.

The book is dominated by estrangement, whether in travel pieces such as "Women in Jerusalem," which tackles problems of identity through a meeting of cultures, or in the Big House narrative "The Barometer," or "Permanent Cabaret," where circus performers signal their identities via costumes. As a whole, *Black Spiders* marks a talent on the verge of discovering its purpose.

Jamie's second book, *A Flame in Your Heart,* was written in collaboration with fellow Scots poet Andrew Greig. Originally broadcast on the radio, it tells by means of monologues and linking passages the story of a love affair between Len, a Spitfire pilot, and Katie, a nurse, during the Battle of Britain in the spring and summer of 1940. While the subject seems ripe for mawkishness and ventriloquism, Jamie seizes the chance to create a character. Katie is by turns passionate, ironical, observant, and humorous—a young woman whose appetite for life is sharpened by the circumstances of war, only to be denied by Len's death in combat.

In "Karakoram Highway," the central section of her 1987 collection, *The Way We Live,* the author instructs herself: "Stop thinking now, and put on your shoes," as a plane prepares to land. "Karakoram Highway" is a sequence of the present tense, resisting the temptation to dwell on and interpret landscape and people. Fittingly, the poem breaks off halfway across a rope bridge. It clarifies a tension in Jamie's work between interpretation and experience, which is in fact more satisfyingly handled elsewhere in the book. "Peter the Rock" is a debate between a climber who insists that "There is nothing / but rock and the climbing of rock under the sun" and the authorial voice's equally forceful pursuit of meaning, while "Bosegran" finds that "'why?' is just salt blown in the mind's eye. / The sea delights. The sun climbs higher as the world goes about." Drawn to consider a resolution of the debate in religious experience, Jamie's response is "Julian of Norwich," a monologue at once wry and exultant by an anchoress longing for the restoration of mystical insight: "Everything I do I do for you. / Brute. You inform the dark / inside of stones, the winds draughting in / from this world and that to come, / but never touch me. / ... (And yet, and yet, I am suspended / in his joy, huge and helpless / as the harvest moon in a summer sky.)" The title poem ends the book on a note of determined celebration: "Pass the tambourine: let me bash out praises," whose subjects must include "misery and elation, mixed, / the sod and caprice of landlords / ... the way it fits, the way it is, the way it seems / to be...."

Jamie's work betrays only marginal influences, Sylvia Plath to begin with and, perhaps from time to time, Elizabeth Bishop. To an unusual degree her work seems made from the quick of experience: poetry seems almost more of a mode of inquiry than an end in itself. Yet her writings are the product of a sophisticated dramatic imagination and an increasing formal assurance. She is undoubtedly one of the most intriguing poets of her generation.

—Sean O'Brien

JARNOT, Lisa

Nationality: American. **Born:** Buffalo, New York, 26 November 1967. **Education:** State University of New York at Buffalo, B.A. 1992; Brown University, M.F.A. 1994. **Career:** Archivist, Poetry/Rare Books Collection, State University of New York at Buffalo, 1989-92; assistant professor, Long Island University, Brooklyn, beginning 1995. Instructor, creative writing workshops, Brown University, Providence, Rhode Island, 1993-94; reading coordinator, The Ear Inn, New York, beginning 1994; educational curriculum consultant, The Labor Institute, New York, beginning 1994. Editor, *Project Poetry Newsletter,* New York, beginning 1996. **Awards:** Fund for Poetry grant, 1996. **Address:** P.O. Box 185, New York, New York, 10009, U.S.A.

PUBLICATIONS

Poetry

Phonetic Instructions. London, Northern Lights Press, 1989.
The Fall of Orpheus. Buffalo, Shuffaloff Press, 1996.
Sea Lyrics. New York, Situations Press, 1996.
Some Other Kind of Mission. Providence, Rhode Island, Burning Deck, 1996.

Other

Editor, *An Anthology of New American Poets.* Jersey City, New Jersey, Talisman House, 1997.

*   *   *

Lisa Jarnot has characterized her poetry in several ways that would seem, at first, to be in conflict. She is intensely interested in extending traditions (note the plural use of the word) and, at the same time, identifies her working methods with those that would aim to deconstruct, declassify, detumesce the totem models that the word "tradition" usually tends to evoke. While recently moving into a highly collaged and visually innovative compositional method, she is clearly familiar with the pluralistic literary traditions upon which she has drawn, from Shakespeare to Dada to Bob Dylan's driving musical line.

Jarnot's first published poems modeled themselves on the discretionary line and syllabic foregrounding evident in the works of modernists H.D. and Ezra Pound and their descendants—Black Mountain poets Robert Creeley and Charles Olson; Objectivists Lorine Niedecker and George Oppen; and West Coast off-shoot Jack Spicer.

In the opening lines of "Previous Graces," *Phonetic Instructions,* Jarnot chooses simple diction, mostly monosyllabic stone steps leading the poem to its firm placement in the natural world—"eyes and sea / elements / the ice had left"—then breaking into a liquid fall of syllables unfolding their family resemblance:

> each
> fallow
> following
> fallen

allowing the reader to plummet through increments of sound, led through their progressions to immensity and sudden shifts of understanding. After such sound-tripping, she pulls the poem's familiar beauty up short, imbedding an unidentified quote (a modernist / Poundian gesture) and pairs that quote with her own warning response:

> "lack of doctrine is like care,"
> we must not do anything.

These gestures repeat themselves, seeming to land one in a place of solidity and emotional certainty, then interrogating that place by juxtaposing a quote that disturbs any conclusion:

> common our communal   hearing
> "enthralled in language"
>   in my faith not   forward
> for words in drift

She wants the reader *not* to be lulled, but to mine the echoes of further meaning that single words and phrases may suggest; her poetic quest involves song and linguistic skepticism.

In Jarnot's second chapbook, *The Fall of Orpheus,* we are in radically new territory, as signalled by its prefatory quote from *A Midsummer Night's Dream,* ending:

> ... imagination bodies forth
> ......
> and gives to airy nothing
> A local habitation and a name.

followed by her two lines, placed near the top of page one:

> i'm not in jail anymore,
> i'm on a greyhound to memphis.

The "I" speaks from split but related identities—Sheep, Seth and Orpheus—all of whom sign their letters / (poems) and attempt to describe their positions, warning the reader from various planes of isolation. Sheep says "I trusted not my brother. / And I tell you, stray from petty jealousy and / read not from what is hidden. In the dark...." Seth says: "I'm nothin but a thief. Aloof / in the middle." Sheep writes his Dad: "It's the tightupness that's haunting, / between the trees. A tress of tension / wire or the wind unstopping the day time." Orpheus writes to Jack: "He sent his representatives down here on earth / for us to feel Him. Mr Random is one of his / representatives." A great deal of private suffering comes through these voices, lost from their binding narrative. An earlier tradition might have tried to make "sense" of them, through the author's overview and final linking of their fates. Instead, Jarnot lets us *hear* them, their fears and peculiar dictions. She permits instability of meaning, proposes its validity.

In 1996 Jarnot published two stylistically polarized books. *Sea Lyrics* is a sequence of 31 highly compressed, lyrically re-cycled prose poems, the "I am" speaker like a 1990's, female version of Whitman hallucinating through the territory of northern California. Avocado, bridge, pit bull, albatross, hottub, and shiny truck are interchangeable parts, repeating with the build of Ravel's "Bolero." "I" merges with "All." Jarnot takes notes. *Some Other Kind of Mission* is a brilliant tour-de-force of collaged notebooks, handwritten letters, drawings, found / re-constructed texts blackenedout with magic markers, leaving tiny words or all "e"s and commas. It is word games, secrets, misnamings, fun-poking at academe ... and her version of on-the-road, NOW, in full, Living Black & White.

Any idea of poetry that could seem to support a final interpretation or picture of life—be it in the imagination or firmly earthbound—simply gives the lie to how Jarnot sees the world. She is a tight-rope walker and her reader must be willing to enter that precarious journey with her, able to tolerate the uncertain space that drops beneath her securely stretched and knotted rope.

—Kathleen Fraser

JENNINGS, Elizabeth (Joan)

Nationality: British. **Born:** Boston, Lincolnshire, 18 July 1926. **Education:** Oxford High School; St. Anne's College, Oxford, M.A. in English language and literature. **Career:** Assistant, Oxford City Library, 1950-58; reader, Chatto & Windus Ltd. (publishers), London, 1958-60. Freelance writer, 1961—. Guildersleeve Lecturer, Barnard College, New York, 1974. **Awards:** Arts Council award, 1953, bursary, 1965, 1968, 1981, grant, 1972; Maugham award, 1956; Richard Hillary memorial prize, 1966; W.H. Smith award, 1987. **Agent:** David Higham Associates Ltd., 5-8 Lower John Street, London W1R 4HA, England. **Address:** 11 Winchester Road, Oxford OX2 6NA, England.

PUBLICATIONS

Poetry

(Poems). Oxford, Fantasy Press, 1953.
A Way of Looking. London, Deutsch, 1955; New York, Rinehart, 1956.
The Child and the Seashell. San Francisco, Poems in Folio, 1957.
A Sense of the World. London, Deutsch, 1958; New York, Rinehart, 1959.
Song for a Birth or a Death and Other Poems. London, Deutsch, 1961; Philadelphia, Dufour, 1962.
Penguin Modern Poets 1, with Lawrence Durrell and R.S. Thomas. London, Penguin, 1962.

Recoveries. London, Deutsch, and Philadelphia, Dufour, 1964.
The Mind Has Mountains. London, Macmillan, and New York, St. Martin's Press, 1966.
The Secret Brother and Other Poems for Children. London, Macmillan, and New York, St. Martin's Press, 1966.
Collected Poems 1967. London, Macmillan, and Chester Springs, Pennsylvania, Dufour, 1967.
The Animals' Arrival. London, Macmillan, and Chester Springs, Pennsylvania, Dufour, 1969.
Lucidities. London, Macmillan, 1970.
Hurt. London, Poem-of-the-Month Club, 1970.
Folio, with others. Frensham, Surrey, Sceptre Press, 1971.
Relationships. London, Macmillan, 1972.
Growing-Points: New Poems. Manchester, Carcanet, 1975.
Consequently I Rejoice. Manchester, Carcanet, 1977.
After the Ark (for children). London, Oxford University Press, 1978.
Moments of Grace: New Poems. Manchester, Carcanet, 1979.
Selected Poems. Manchester, Carcanet, 1979.
Winter Wind. Sidcot, Somerset, Gruffyground Press, and Newark, Vermont, Janus Press, 1979.
A Dream of Spring. Stratford-upon-Avon, Celandine, 1980.
Celebrations and Elegies. Manchester, Carcanet, 1982.
Extending the Territory. Manchester, Carcanet, 1985.
In Shakespeare's Company. Shipston-on-Stour, Warwickshire, Celandine Press, 1985.
Collected Poems 1953-1985. Manchester, Carcanet, 1986.
Tributes. Manchester, Carcanet. 1989.
Times and Seasons. Manchester, Carcanet, 1992.
Familiar Spirits. Manchester, Carcanet, 1994.
In the Meantime. Manchester, Carcanet, 1996.

Other

Let's Have Some Poetry. London, Museum Press, 1960.
Every Changing Shape (religion and poetry). London, Deutsch, 1961.
Poetry Today 1957-60. London, Longman, 1961.
Frost. Edinburgh, Oliver & Boyd, 1964; New York, Barnes & Noble, 1966.
Christianity and Poetry. London, Burns Oates, 1965; as *Christian Poetry,* New York, Hawthorn, 1965.
Seven Men of Vision: An Appreciation. London, Vision Press, and New York, Barnes & Noble, 1976.

Editor, with Dannie Abse and Stephen Spender, *New Poems 1956.* London, Joseph, 1956.
Editor, *The Batsford Book of Children's Verse.* London, Batsford, 1958.
Editor, *An Anthology of Modern Verse 1940-1960.* London, Methuen, 1961.
Editor, *A Choice of Christina Rossetti's Verse.* London, Faber, 1970.
Editor, *The Batsford Book of Religious Verse.* London, Batsford, 1981.
Editor, *In Praise of Our Lady.* London, Batsford, 1982.

Translator, *The Sonnets of Michelangelo.* London, Folio Society, 1961; revised edition, London, Allison & Busby, 1969; New York, Doubleday, 1970.

*

Manuscript Collections: Oxford City Library; University of Washington, Seattle.

Critical Study: By Margaret Byers, in *British Poetry since 1960* edited by Michael Schmidt and Grevel Lindop, Oxford, Carcanet, 1972.

Elizabeth Jennings comments:

I do not much care for writing about my own poems. The main reason for this is, I believe, that it makes one too self-conscious. However, I would like to say that I am always interested in what I am writing at present and hope to write in the future. I like to experiment with different poetic forms, and, at this time, I am constantly seeking for more and more clarity. I am working on a series of prose poems about paintings (painting is my second favorite art), and a series of poems, in various forms and from several viewpoints, on religious themes. I have also been writing poems about craftsmen and various aspects of nature, particularly skyscapes. For me, poetry is always a search for order. I started writing at the age of 13 and wrote only one four-line poem I now wish to preserve from childhood. My Roman Catholic religion and my poems are the most important things in my life.

* * *

Elizabeth Jennings was the only woman to be included in Robert Conquest's anthology *New Lines.* In her lucid diction, her use of traditional meters, and the keen and subtle intelligence in her exploration of ideas, she shares with the other so-called "Movement" poets a "coolness which is worked for," to quote her own description of a Chinese painter.

Jennings's absorption in the processes of "art with its largesse and its own restraint" has led to many poems that attempt to enter the experience of fellow writers and artists in other media: the sculptor, the composer, the dancer, and painters ranging in time from Rembrandt to Rouault, Botticelli to Bonnard, Cézanne and—recurringly—Van Gogh. She is also especially interested in childhood and aging. Her portraits of children are based on personal recollections of a timeless peace and safety from adult ambiguities but still more on the distresses that ultimately "built a compassion that I need to share"; in addition, she writes about the feelings of the very old with a tender intuitive sympathy. The poet's insight into contemplative states of being resulted in intense imaginative projections into the lives of such personalities as St. John of the Cross, St. Teresa of Avila, St. Catherine, and St. Augustine. She pondered the nature of the Virgin in fine poems like "Annunciation" and "The Visitation" and even explored the loneliness and human conflicts of Christ. Jennings's prose poems and dramatic monologues, her translations of Michelangelo's sonnets, and an increasingly adventurous freedom and flexibility in her rhythms and verse patterns demonstrate the versatility of her gifts.

Italy, where she has traveled extensively, is the background for a number of poems that epitomize her great difference from the rest of the "Movement" group. A profound religious conviction colors her vision of life and permeates all her work. As a foreigner at confession, at a Roman mass, or at Assisi "where silence is so wide you hear it," she communicates the quietism most vividly realized in the magnificent "San Paolo Fuori le Mura," where the cool stillness of stone engenders an interior calm that functions as "a kind of coming home." In "Song for a Birth or a Death" the mystic's apprehensions of reality are as eloquently articulated as anywhere in contemporary poetry. "Notes for a Book of Hours" conjures the raptness of the visionary and his struggle for the elusive language capable of expressing the numinous. "A World of Light" recreates "A mood the senses cannot touch or damage, / A sense of peace beyond the breathing word," which grows in "a dazzling dark" as reminiscent of Vaughan as later poems like "Winter Night" and "Let there be dark for us to contemplate."

This poet is, however, equally and bitterly familiar with another kind of darkness, one of doubt, desolation, and despair—the abysses of Hopkins's "winter world" implied in her title "The Mind Has Mountains." Recurrent breakdowns led to spells in a mental hospital; the guilt, bewilderment, frustrations of unfulfilled love and "very absolute of fear," which culminated in a state "clothed in confusion," are conveyed with poignant directness in many poems of her middle period. Yet this agonized experience of "climates of terror" and compassionate vulnerability to the sufferings of her fellow patients led to a recognition that "Perhaps to know no desert is a lack"—an acceptance of the necessity of "The painful breaking / Which brings to birth."

The recovery chronicled in "Growing-Points" and "Consequently I Rejoice" shows a greater maturity of acceptance, a full repossession of her lost capacity for contemplative stillness, and a renewed receptivity to moments of mystical revelation. The notable broadening of range of her choice of subject, a more objective awareness of the contemporary world and of problems and predicaments other than her own, are matched by a new assurance and virtuosity in the handling of language. Jennings's words describing a disabled countryman apply with equal aptness to her own impressive testimony, courage, and spiritual resilience: "gentleness / Concealing toughness," which takes "pain as birds take buffets from / The wind, then gather strength and fly and fly."

—Margaret Willy

JILES, Paulette

Nationality: American and Canadian. **Born:** Salem, Missouri, 4 April 1943; immigrated to Canada, 1969. **Education:** University of Missouri, B.A. in Spanish literature 1968. **Career:** Freelance reporter, Canadian Broadcasting Corporation (CBC), Toronto, 1968-69; journalism consultant and trainer for Native communication groups in the Arctic and sub-Arctic, 1973-83; instructor, David Thompson University, Nelson, British Columbia, 1983-84; writer-in-residence, Phillips Academy, Andover, Massachusetts, 1987-88. **Awards:** President's Gold Medal, 1973; Pat Lowther Memorial award, 1984; Gerald Lampert award, 1984; Governor-General's Award, 1985, for *Celestial Navigation;* A.C.T.R.A. award for radio play, 1989. **Address:** c/o Oxford University Press, Toronto, Canada.

PUBLICATIONS

Poetry

Waterloo Express. Toronto, Anansi, 1973.
Celestial Navigation. Toronto, McClelland & Stewart, 1984.
The Jesse James Poems. British Columbia, Polestar Press, 1988.
Blackwater. New York, Knopf, 1988.
Song to the Rising Sun. Winlaw, British Columbia, Polestar Press, 1989.

Flying Lessons: Selected Poems. Toronto, Oxford University Press, 1995.

Novels

Sitting in the Club Car Drinking Rum and Karma-Kola: A Manual of Etiquette for Ladies Crossing Canada by Train (novella). Winlaw, British Columbia, Polestar Press, 1986.
The Late Great Human Road Show. Vancouver, Talonbooks, 1986.
Cousins. New York, Knopf, 1991.

Plays

Screenplays: *Rose's House,* 1976.

Radio Plays: *My Mother's Quilt,* 1987; *Money and Blankets,* 1988.

Other

North Spirit: Travels among the Cree and Ojibway Nations and Their Star Maps. Toronto, Doubleday Canada, 1995; as *North Spirit: Sojourns among the Cree and Ojibway,* St. Paul, Minnesota, Hungry Mind, 1995.

*

Critical Study: Special issue of *Malahat Review* edited by L. Sheier, S. Sheard, and E. Wachtel, no. 83, Summer 1988.

Paulette Jiles comments:

My use of language is strongly influenced by the area where I grew up, the rich oral tradition of Missouri's Ozark hills which were populated with lots of talkative, story-telling cousins.

*   *   *

The sensitivity and compassion of Canadian women poets in the 1940s and 1950s frequently led them into social work. With the 1960s, a new generation of women poets were more likely to choose a career in broadcasting. Verse plays, documentaries, and poetry readings were being heard in the Canadian Broadcasting Corporation's (CBC) Arts programs The Canada Council began to sponsor reading tours for poets. By the 1970s a new school of Performance Poetry led by the late Gwendolyn MacEwan, an accomplished performer, had appeared.

Paulette Jiles came to Canada from her native Missouri, in 1969, at the age of 26. She worked first with the CBC as a journalist and broadcaster, then went, in 1973, to the Arctic and the sub-Arctic to work with native communications groups. In 1984 Jiles took a position as a teacher of creative writing at the David Thompson University Centre in Nelson, British Columbia. The following year she made a sweep of Canadian prizes for poetry: *Celestial Navigation* (1984), won the Governor General's Award for 1985, then the Gerald Lampert Award, and the Pat Lowther Award for the best book of poetry by a woman, both conferred by the League of Canadian Poets.

Celestial Navigation, incorporating many of the poems from an earlier collection, *Waterloo Express* (Anansi 1973), is notable for an insistent voice, thrusting rhythms, and few poetic devices. The title poem, "Waterloo Express," rushes forward impetuously in-

voking all the North American mythology of mournful train whistles, lure of the frontier, and blues in the night. This momentum suits Jiles's dramatic delivery. Its effect read from the page is equally stirring:

> ... I bet you think I'm running away from home or
>
> a man who never done me wrong. I bet you think
> I'm twenty, with the fragile soul of a wild fawn.
>
> Well, I used to think so too, but the job didn't pay much
> and anyhow I never liked the taste of wages.
>
> I like it here in the middle element where this
> express is ripping up the dawn like an old ticket
>
> whose engine is blowing the towns away
> and even I am barely holding on.
>
> There they go—a toe, a finger, my coat—honey,
> you'd hardly recognize me, pared down to one white eye.
>
> It has the cynical glint of a dynamite salesman.

Although this poem is invigorating, the cumulative effect of the "Waterloo Express" section of *Celestial Navigation* is of concentrated pain. Compulsive travelling is to get away from a man, to find another man. In "The Looney Bin," from the section titled "Paper Matches," the poet fights depression:

> First they want you to come in for observation,
>   they want to know if you are
> crazy or depressed ...
>   If you are crazy you have to go in your bathrobe
> and talk to men who are in suits and ties.
> They want to know if you are hearing things
>   besides them.

In the section "Northern Radio," based on her experiences in the sub-Arctic, the poet comes to terms with herself, and, finally, in "Turning Forty," goes back to the Missouri of her childhood in prose poems which conclude, "This is a new time, and it too has come without warning."

The Jesse James Poems (1988) originated as an experimental radio script for the CBC's "State of the Arts." Jiles had already assumed the voice of historical characters in the "Griffon Poems" of *Celestial Navigation,* and, like Michael Ondaatje, was fascinated by the legends surrounding notorious outlaws. Jesse James came from Missouri, Jiles's native state. Research produced contemporary newspaper reports, photographs, and reproductions of posters, which are mixed in with poems written in the voices of the gang and their women. These people have been brutalized by their place in space and time. In "The Trial of Frank James: 1882," Frank James, Jesse's brother, speaks in conclusion:

> No one ever says I am your prisoner without
> believing somehow in clemency, in mercy
>   or in short memories, it is
> not something said
> by battered wives or people
>   held in unnumbered rooms or

children with cigarette burns. It is not said
by those who can no longer talk.

Song to the Rising Sun (1989), a collection of mixed poetry and
radio scripts, is about the people of the Ozark mountains. The
poet's voice sounds everywhere with a strong incantatory beat
and a marked use of repetition. In "Money and Blankets" a char-
acter says:

> "Tell about the time Daddy shot the refrigerator; tell about
> Bucky's dead squirrel dog; tell about Nannie Hanlin and
> the rose on her grave. Just run your mouth, Rita Jean,
> like you always do. It's just pouring out of you all the
> time; you might as well do something with it. Unless
> we're going to hook you to a generator."

Since *Song to the Rising Sun,* the only poetry Jiles has pub-
lished has been 1995's *Flying Lessons: Selected Poems.* She has,
however, published another novel, *Cousins* (1991), and the travel
/ sociological study, *North Spirit: Travels among the Cree and
Ojibway Nations.*

—Patience Wheatley

JOHNSON, Amryl

Nationality: Trinidadian, British. **Born:** Trinidad. **Education:**
University of Kent, Canterbury, B.A. (with honors) 1985. **Ca-
reer:** Poet and teacher of creative writing. **Address:** 61 Bridgeman
Road, Radford, Coventry CV6 1NS, England.

PUBLICATIONS

Poetry

Shackles. London, Sable, 1983.
Long Road to Nowhere. London, Virago Press, 1985.
Tread Carefully in Paradise (included *Shackles* and *Long Road to
    Nowhere.*) Coventry, Cofa Press, 1991.
Gorgons, Coventry, Cofa Press, 1992.
Rainbow Dragon Trilogy. London, London Arts Board News,
    1995.

Recording: *Blood and Wine,* Cofa Press, 1991.

Other

Sequins for a Ragged Hem. London, Virago Press, 1988.

*

Amryl Johnson comments:
   Early influences are Edward Camu Braithwaite's *The Arrivants*
and T.S. Elliot's "The Love Song of J. Alfred Prufrock."
   I teach creative writing at all educational levels and always be-
gin a session by reminding my students that all we have, in the
English alphabet, are 26 letters. It is how we group these letters

which will make what we are saying banal or interesting. They
are, therefore, to think along the lines of "painting with words."
As an artist, they'd make certain that they use the correct shade
of colour, depth, and tone. The nuances in language make it, then,
vital to recognize the sliver of difference between words such as
"maybe" and "perhaps." When they are experiencing difficulty in
understanding any poem, write it as prose ignoring the fact that
each line might begin with a capital. Read through the poem as
prose several times to get the sense of what is being said, then go
back to it, in its original poetic form. That's when they'll often
recognise the true artistry and texture of the poet's language. By
the same token, the first draft of a poem can be written as prose.
With the second draft, delete the "and," "but," "so," "if," "then,"
"because," "the," etc., which will not in the slightest alter what
they are trying to say before, in the final draft, shaping it into a
poetic form. This technique is one I still, sometimes, use.

*   *   *

   Amryl Johnson is a poet of the voice and a poet for the stage.
Her dedication to the spoken word in a dramatic setting is in-
creasingly manifest in her published poetry, from *Tread Carefully
in Paradise* (1991, reproducing poems from the early 1980s) to
the dramatic poem issued by the London Arts Board on the occa-
sion of the 1995 edition of the Notting Hill Carnival, *Rainbow
Dragon Trilogy.* Similarly, over the years her voice has become
more collective and less involved in autobiographical emotions and
memories.
   Though educated in England from the age of 11, she was born
in Trinidad, that is on the Caribbean island most passionately de-
voted to Carnival and to Calypso. This can be keenly felt. With
or without any acquaintance with Bakhtin we know that Carnival
is that "season of metamorphosis" when "all things are possible,"
the "time of year" when "the near impossible can leapfrog real-
ity," a "time in which / to mislay tradition / Leapfrog / the order
of things / Confuse / the laws of nature." The three "J'Ouvert"
poems in *Tread Carefully* describe the unfolding of revelry in
Trinidad from the early dawn promise on Monday to the exhaus-
tion of parading dancers at the next sunrise ("we / weary / war-
riors / footsore / defeated"). Traditionally Carnival takes place just
before Lent, that is to say, 40 days before Easter. Yet in Britain,
the date of Carnival rejoicings has been shifted to late August,
"the most quiet, tranquil time of the year." This loss of its reli-
gious moorings might be resented as a further uprooting, another
displacement. But in a neat (Carnival?) reversal the change releases
the celebration from the "shriving" it is supposed to prelude. As
a result, the Rainbow Dragon, dazzled by its own beauty, pro-
tests "Poet, stop now! / This is not Trinidad, today is not Shrove
Tuesday / You are not obliged to take me forward in time / back
to penance in drab grey (eternal Ash / Wednesday)." The magnifi-
cent Carnival recovery of voices to speak with and to give the old
world the lie can thus be said to be more fully achieved at Notting
Hill than in Port-of-Spain.
   On the other hand several of her poems stress the "swindle"
that lures immigrants to England. In the second part of *Rain-
bow Dragon* in particular ("Oil on Troubled Waters"), the
power of the Carnival Dragon is needed to turn "Rebuff—re-
sent—reject—refuse—repel" to "Rekindle—restore—recover—
rectify—retrieve." (This part consists of a dozen 12-line stan-
zas, the last lines of each consisting of five verbs beginning
with re-.)

Even without listening to the tape recording *Blood and Wine*, those exposed to Johnson's work immediately perceive with what expertise she weaves various Englishes, either lacing "standard English" with calypso syntax and repetitions, or fully embracing the island speech, as in the hilarious conflictual dialogues of "Granny in the Market Place":

> Yuh mango ripe?
> Gran'ma, stop feelin' and squeezin' up meh fruit!
> You ehn playin' in no band'. Meh mango ehn no concertina
>
> Ah tell yuh dis mango hard just like yuh face
> One bite an' ah sure tuh break both ah meh plate—;

in the macho rigmarole of the "Peanut Vendor"—

> darlin' ah love yuh as soon as ah see yuh
> Ah hah a car, meh own house an' a lotta property
> Leave yuh husban', ah sure ah go make yuh real happy
> Stop fer yuh nuts!
> Dohn be in a rush!
> Ah sellin' out fas'!
> Meh stock wohn las'!;

or in the bitter-sweet reproach of the old woman interviewed by some returning immigrant in "Learnin'":

> Whey me roots?
> Wha roots?
> Wha' yuh talkin' 'bout?
> Roots?!
>
> De only roots ah know 'bout is from
> meh dasheen cassava breadfruit an'
> yam ah does take tuh de market tuh sell
> All ah we hah tuh sell
> dey ehn teach yuh dat?
> We sell up we sell out
> We sell in we sell off
> Is all de same dam' ting

In fact most of Amryl's poetry can be read as an exercise in blending and bridging. She brings home to citizens of former colonizing nations the suffering and hypocrisy involved in the imposition of a colonial order—then and now—and she retrieves for herself and her fellow descendants of transported African slaves a history of cruelty and oppression that had long been suppressed. In this respect four poems stand out as particularly impressive in *Tread Carefully:* "Far Cry," with a title that echoes Derek Walcott's famous poem "A Far Cry from Africa" and an elaborate structure reminiscent of chaingangs that takes readers from one stanza to the next on the threefold repetition of "coming"; "The New Cargo Ship," in which the voyage of Caribbean immigrants back to their islands is fraught with memories of the Middle Passage; "How Do You Feed the Ghosts?" ("How do you fill the sound which echoes like / slow footsteps through the black / slime of a never- / ending tunnel?"); and "The Wheel," about enforced labour on a Tobago sugar mill, "revolving knowledge of how it was." In *Rainbow Dragon*, the first part of the trilogy indicates how the music of steel bands both resurrects and redeems the memory of enslavement. Its title "Marking the Beast" may be a reference to Saint Mark and the Beast in a church in Port-of-Spain, as Amryl explains; it also rings with branding irons. Connected with the double slavery of women, some of her poems tell of men walking away, leaving their women to cope ("The Unpaved Road," "The Last Goodbye"), and it is hardly surprising that the male figures in *Gorgons* (the hunter, "Driver") should be threatening.

The warning expressed in the poem which gives its title to the collection *Tread Carefully in Paradise* is addressed to white friends understandably tempted by the "sun-filled golden beaches." But paradise was "discovered" and colonized, and an undiscriminating resentment is still alive. The people addressed here mean well, for all their helplessness. This is not necessarily the case of the tourists in the opening poem, who enjoy "A fan screen blowing in a random breeze" while being blind and deaf to the hardships that beset the lives of most island inhabitants. The theme of conquest parading as discovery is sounded with bitter humour in a poem called "Spices and Guns—Grenada—March 1983," which juxtaposes Columbus' landing and the U.S. invasion with a naive visitor "stunned" by the "pungence of the nutmegs and / cloves" and hopeful for the future "of those gentle people with / their friendly ways."

Like Jackie Kay's *Adoption Papers*, *Gorgons* stages a number of different voices in dramatic interaction. Yet there are several major differences. In Kay's poem voices are clearly identified and speak up for themselves, in the first person. In *Gorgons* there are some nine or ten different voices, if we trust the indications provided by the author in the introduction: the voice of the writer who perceives, receives and records those "spheres of resistance" that "came from the margin" (at times, I find, indulging in rather cheap sound effects), the voice of the Gorgon herself, still trapped in her Greek myth, but appalled at the petrifying impact of her gaze and yearning for a life-giving vision, and the voices of her "daughters," who are listed as Lucille the drug-addict ("one more needle in the vein"), Dulcine the prophetess who is sometimes the fool (as in "Stone-breaker," where she wants people to stone her until some strong wicked boys do it in earnest), Inez the calypsonian / politician who learns how to trust her voice and ends up yielding enough power for the PM to beg that she write a song on how hard his job is, the Island Woman who has been driven away from her island by an irresistible urge, Cat the rebellious "wayward ballerina," the blind frustrated woman, and Mayo the freedom-fighter. Yet these figures are linked to attitudes rather than to social roles, and I do not think it matters if we do not identify them all as we read. Some of the best poems in the sequence are those relating to the submissive woman who has endured all: "Learnin'" and "She had followed him through." The latter ends with the husband whom she had apparently meekly followed through a life of deprivation finding himself at a loss when she dies, wondering "how he would find / courage without even / the echo of her footsteps / to guide him."

Johnson's technique is extremely versatile, like her use of Englishes and registers. Very often she will start from a powerful image, such as an "unpaved road" or "de boat ah we paddling," will use it first literally and then turn it into a metaphor. In "Long Road to Nowhere" her technique is directly inspired by the cinema. Yet overwhelmingly, and increasingly as years go by, her poems are not only related to, but directly dependent on music. *Gorgons,* for instance, is something of a calypsonian opera. In fact she is a composer as well, who has signed the music that accompanies *Gorgons* and *Rainbow Dragon Trilogy*. (Unfortunately, recordings are not yet available.) Her poetry is subtle in its rhythms and echoes. Yet it wields an immediate appeal, not only on readers, but also, and even more forcefully, on her live audiences.

—Christine Pagnoulle

JOHNSON, Jenny

Nationality: British. **Born:** Portsmouth, Hampshire, England, 2 November 1945. **Education:** Red Maids School, Bristol. **Family:** Married 2) Noel Harrower in 1990; one son. **Awards:** South West Arts awards. **Address:** Culthorpe, The Crescent, Woodthorpe, Nottingham.

PUBLICATIONS

Poetry

Going Home. Bath, England, Mammon Press, 1980.
Becoming and Other Poems. Bath, Mammon Press, 1983.
Poems 1983-6, with Frances Lovell. Bath, Mammon Press, 1987.
The Chromoscope. Bath, Mammon Press, 1991.
Towards Dawn. London, Diamond Press, 1991.
The Wisdom Tree (Poems 1975-1993). Salzburg, University of Salzburg Press, 1993.

Translator, *Five Poems from Sappho,* in *Poet's Voice Magazine,* New Series vol. 1, no. 2, December 1994.

*

Jenny Johnson comments:

Two themes to be found in my poetry are paradox, and the balancing of inner and outer experiences; much material is based on childhood and motherhood; and there are various influences on both form and content—Hebridean folk music, Emily Dickinson and Sylvia Plath, to name three....

*   *   *

Jenny Johnson wrote poetry from an early age, and was involved in both the Circle in the Square group in Bristol and the Nottingham Poetry Society in her twenties. It was only, however, when in 1977 she found herself a single parent in a flat of her own and with time on her hands, that her very individual style emerged. The sequence "A Year of Dreams" that followed is something quite unique in recent English poetry. There is a singing line that is irregular and rhythmic, and (though free verse) is in enormous contrast with the prose based cadences of her contemporaries. She herself would put this down to an interest in Hebridean folk song, but her early training in classics may well have played a part. The poems themselves are paradoxical and elusive, myths that flit by, usually without being fully formed. The influence of a Jungian friend seems to have been profound, but there are curious affinities with the French surrealists, which seem more likely to stem from an interest in modern painting than a knowledge of the poetry. All this apart there is an exuberance that remains powerful.

The wild freedom of "A Year of Dreams" was succeeded by a period of greater poetic discipline. The sequence *Becoming* was written during 1980. It lacks perhaps the sheer elation of *A Year of Dreams.* There is much more sense of pain, a feeling perhaps that the poet is emerging from a mystical experience into the real world; but most of the poems are ostensibly still the chart of an inner experience.

The group of short poems written after *Becoming* are perhaps Johnson's best work. They seem to operate at that point where the mind looks both inward towards dream, and outward towards the real world. The poems are often brief, yet belie that by their intensity. Such pieces as "The Contentious Wife," "Nonchalance," "The Dryad," or "William and Stella" have a charge that is unique to this poet. They are at once very controlled and disturbing. They are also as elusive as Johnson's Dryad: who, when an explorer's attendants "attempted to capture her ... [they] touched / nothing but the curious dust...."

After the publication of *Becoming and other poems* in 1983, Johnson, under considerable domestic pressures and also attempting to come to terms with her childhood, changed her style. She was undoubtedly influenced by Plath, and perhaps Lowell, but her work retains its considerable charge and originality. Of the poems about childhood Warden with its brilliant summary of what it is like to be a small shy child with intense, not altogether rational fears is especially fine. Arguably however the rhythms are less strong and instinctive.

Most important perhaps are a small group of poems that do not quite claim to rationality. "Ancient and Modern" is full of the over organization of childhood, but are these people school children, students, mental patients or all three? Is the cup in the last line some sort of grail? In "Catharsis" Penelope is Johnson perhaps as Jenny Johnson might have been in different circumstances. There is an eeriness that is peculiarly Johnson.

The work after 1987 includes some fine things, but there is repetition of previous themes, and a disturbing tendency to take the paraphernalia of the New Age rather too literally. Nevertheless Dawn and East particularly are very fine. Dawn with its hexameter like rhythm, and intricate fantasy is as good as anything Johnson has done.

The poet has not written to speak of since 1994, due to a serious illness. Just before this happened she produced a superb group of versions from Sappho, that are as much recompositions into Johnson's own idiom as translations, and show an unexpected gift for the dramatic.

—Fred Beake

JOHNSON, Judith (Emlyn)

Pseudonyms: Judith Johnson Sherwin. **Nationality:** American. **Born:** New York City, 3 October 1936. **Education:** The Dalton Schools, New York, 1954; Radcliffe College, Cambridge, Massachusetts, 1954-55; Barnard College, New York, B.A. (cum laude) 1958 (Phi Beta Kappa); Columbia University, New York (Woodrow Wilson fellow, 1958), 1958-59. **Family:** Married James T. Sherwin in 1955 (divorced); three children. **Career:** Promotion manager, Arrow Press, New York, 1961; instructor, Poetry Center, New York, 1976, 1978, 1981; poet-in-residence, Wake Forest University, Winston-Salem, North Carolina, 1980. Poet-in-residence, 1980-81, assistant professor of English, 1981-87, associate professor, 1988-91, since 1992 professor of English and women's studies, and chair of department of Women's Studies, 1995-96, State University of New York, Albany; president, 1975-78, and chairman of the Executive Committee, 1979-80, Poetry Society of America; member of Board of Directors, 1994-97, and president, 1995-96, Associated Writing Programs. **Awards:** Academy of American Poets prize, 1958; Yaddo fellowship, 1964; Poetry Society of America fellowship, 1964; Aspen Writers Workshop Rose fellowship, 1967; Yale Series of Younger Poets award, 1968; *St. Andrews Review* prize, 1975; *Playboy* award, for fiction, 1977; National Endowment for the Arts fellowship, 1981; Poetry Society of America Alice Fay Di Castagnola award, 1992; D. Litt Honoris Causa, St. Andrew's College, Laurinburg, N.C., 1992. **Address:** Department of English, State University of New York, Albany, New York 12222, U.S.A.

PUBLICATIONS

Poetry

Uranium Poems. New Haven, Connecticut, Yale University Press, 1969.
Impossible Buildings. New York, Doubleday, 1973.
Waste: The Town Scold, Transparencies, Dead's Good Company. Taftsville, Vermont, Countryman Press, 3 vols., 1977-79.
How the Dead Count. New York, Norton, 1978.
The Ice Lizard. New York, Sheep Meadow Press, 1992.

Plays

Belisa's Love (produced New York, 1959).
En Avant, Coco (produced New York, 1961).
[Two untitled multimedia works] (produced Brussels, 1971, 1972).
Waste (multimedia; produced London, 1972).

Short Stories

The Life of Riot. New York, Atheneum, 1970.

Other

Hungry for Light: The Journal of Ethel Schwabacher, edited by Judith E. Johnson and Brenda S. Webster, Baton Rouge, Indiana University Press, 1993.

*

Critical Studies: By Hayden Carruth, in *Harper's* (New York), June 1978, and *Nation* (New York), January 1979; *Choice* (Middletown, Connecticut), July-August and December 1978; Rochelle Ratner, in *Soho Weekly News* (New York), 7 September 1978; by Carol Saltus in *Women's Review of Books* (Massachusetts), December 1992; by Mimi Albert in *Poetry Flash* (San Francisco), November 1992; Leslie Ullman in *Kenyon Review* (Gambier, Ohio), summer 1993; by Dianne Blakely Shoaf in *American Book Review,* October-November 1993.

Judith Johnson comments:
My poetry comes across in readings as drama or music more than as text. I enjoy reading with cool jazz or with quiet electronic music which provides spaces in the sound and between the sounds. Much of my poetry is meant to be sung or chanted or belted out in the shower.

All my life I have refused to let myself be limited to any theory of what poetry should be, either in form or in content. I write traditional sonnet sequences and I write surreal poems and sound poems. Every form, every technique is of equal interest; I should feel dissatisfied with my mind if there were any approach to poetry that did not excite me to see if I could go out and do likewise.

My writing, poetry, fiction and drama, is both feminist and political, but it is neither didactic nor hortatory. I write about my life as a woman and as a political animal because that's where my life is, those are the questions I have to face. However, I don't know the answers; any answer I examine is hypothesis, not conclusion.

I try to make a rough music, a dance of the mind, a calculus of the emotions, a driving beat of praise out of the pain and mystery that surround me and become me. My poems are meant to make your mind get up and shout.

(1995) What I have been fashioning is a poetics of generosity to replace the poetics of parsimony that governs public life and art. Like many women writers, whatever I write has seemed to take its place in the mainstream poetic culture as "other" and as "excess." The critical reaction has often been some form of "You're something else!" or "You're too much!"—some uneasy blend of admiration and condemnation. To transform feminine excess and alterity from perceived weaknesses to strengths requires rethinking both literary norms and my location within or outside them. I have chosen to consider the energy in my work a form of generosity rather than a form of excess; to consider my poetics as normative rather than marginal; to imagine transformative poetics in metaphors other than the militaristic ones associated with terms like "avant-garde"; to phrase my changing locations within life and literature in terms of what they are rather than of what they are not; to enunciate plenitude rather than lack.

What I have been fashioning, like many contemporary poets whose theoretical vocabularies differ, is a poetics of transformation rather than a poetics of representation. Aristotelian poetics valued the memetic qualities of art: the imitation of an action rather than the action itself, holding the mirror up to nature rather than inventing and transforming and acting within nature. But just as contemporary scientific and mathematical theory seems to suggest the action of the observer within the experiment, so the poetics in which I participate stresses the poem as transformative act across a range of practices, varying from pure play, analogous to the sciences' pure research, to Marxist, feminist, or post-colonialist political activisms.

What I have been fashioning is a poetics of multiplicity, in which the capaciousness and porosity of meaning take on their own life within language. This requires a recasting of vocabulary: the idea of indeterminacy allows me to do some things, but multideterminacy or infinite determinacy allows me to do very different things. Uncertainty, in physics, allows us to recognize that we can know location or velocity but not both. But a point whose location we cannot determine may have multiple locations rather than no location, and this latter terminology with regard to how meaning moves, allows me to work more dynamically within the text. Zeno demonstrated the shortcomings of analytic processes when he used them to prove that the arrow did not move.

A magical or transformative poetics restores motion by accepting the principles of simultaneity and of multiple location.

* * *

Judith Emlyn Johnson, originally introduced to the poetry world as Judith Johnson Sherwin, is not only a poet but also a mixed-media artist, fiction writer, playwright, and critic. Her poems first appeared in the 1960s, introducing major themes which continue into her present work: technology and the devastating effects of modern politics, and the difficulty and necessity of loving in the modern world. Her poems both elucidate these problems and constitute a weapon to defy them. Her style is characterized by incantatory repetitions and a skewed, tense diction which strains the limits of conventional grammar and syntax, though she often incorporates these within classic forms, the sonnet and quatrain, updated with slant rhyme. Her similes and metaphors are extended and bizarre, drawn from the absurd artifacts of contemporary plastic culture but often also reminiscent of the 17th-century Metaphysical conceit. Yet her sensibility is ultramodern, influenced by and reflective of jazz music, radio ads, and technological innovations.

In her first book, *Uranium Poems,* words pile up and hammer on each other without breath break, reinforcing metaphor and message: uranium mining destroys the earth to procure ores to make bombs that destroy the world. This theme begets another: how consciousness of various deaths permeates our lives, especially the death that haunts love and the bitter political deaths of our time—the murders by Adolf Eichmann, Marilyn Monroe's suicide. In her second collection, *Impossible Buildings,* she is still hardheaded, but her language and forms are less rough-hewn. In "Materials," a sequence of ten sonnets, each poem focuses on a natural substance, such as ice, wood, or water, and each is made an elegant symbol for an aspect of sexual love. The prevailing theme is larger than love, however, as the title poem makes clear. "Impossible buildings," as in M.C. Escher's drawings, are built by the artist's mind at its creative work: "the construction is / the information."

The poems of her next book, *How the Dead Count,* while often elegiac in tone (as in the long title poem), are also often angry and satiric. The stock exchange mentality, Henry Kissinger, capitalist and technological abuses, all receive her contempt. Love comes back in this book too, as a freighted theme, a sometimes ebullient emotion, but frequently bereft and sad in severance from the loved one, as in the section titled "From Brussels." Her pain rises out of conflict with, and seems to be the price of, the poet's life as an independent woman and artist. This independence, however, is an elemental source of power, not destructive to that life or any other. In "Three Power Dances" she pits against technology the Native American mythic viewpoint, out of which she creates a totem of herself, "a great Female Bear / wide as a house sings / out of Her dark cave." The emphasis is on female being over male doing: "I hold back your day / your death dance, your night of war / This is My Power dance." This defiant yet compassionate sensibility profoundly animates the title poem, "How the Dead Count," an elegy for the young dead of the civil rights movement and the Vietnam War, which continues the theme of death intermingled with our lives. These dead "count"—they matter—because they bring creative richness to birth in us by the very extremity of their situation.

No creativity or contemporary emotion can disentangle itself from our technologized milieu, however, as is made clear in Johnson's book *Cities of Mathematics and Desire,* winner of the Poetry Society of America's Di Castagnola award. Here language experiments loop even higher in the imaginative air, yet they serve compassion, imitating speech impaired by stroke, collaging story, exclamation, rude fragments to convey a multilayered sense of deracinated yet exuberant modern urban life. The title poem is an epic taking off from William Carlos Williams's mythic theme of *Paterson*—a man is a city—to dramatize the interpenetration of impersonal forces, "mathematics," and personal passion, a condition which extends from the submicroscopic collision of particles to marriage to mysterious explosions in intergalactic space. It is an exalted theme orchestrated by Johnson's impressive gift for laser-sharp, bejeweled language. Her beautiful "machinery of connection" embraces the fallible and sublime human creature, offering meaning in the midst of chaos.

—Jane Augustine

JONES, Patricia Spears

Nationality: American. **Born:** Forest City, Arkansas, 11 February 1951. **Education:** Rhodes College, Memphis, B.A. 1973; Vermont College, Montpelier, M.F.A. in writing 1992. **Career:** Grants program director, Coordinating Council of Literary Magazines, New York, 1977-81; administrator, *Heresies Collective,* New York, 1982-83; program coordinator, Poetry Project at St. Mark's Church, New York, 1984-86; program specialist, New Works Program, Massachusetts Council on the Arts and Humanities, Boston, 1987-89; program director, Film News Now Foundation, New York, 1990-91; grant writer, 1991-94, director of planning and development, 1994-96, New Museum of Contemporary Art, New York; consultant, 1996—. Editor, *W.B. Magazine,* 1975. **Awards:** New York Foundation for the Arts award in poetry, 1986, fellowship, 1993; Goethe Institute travel grant, 1989; Divers Forms Artists Projects grant, 1991; National Endowment for the Arts Opera Music Theater Program award, 1993, fellowship, 1994; Bread Loaf Writers Conference fellowship, 1996; Foundation for Contemporary Performance Arts award, 1996. **Address:** 426 Sterling Place, Apt. 1C, Brooklyn, New York 11238, U.S.A.

PUBLICATIONS

Poetry

The Weather that Kills. Minneapolis, Coffee House Press, 1995.

Other

Editor, with others, *Ordinary Women: An Anthology of New York City Women Poets.* New York, n.p., 1978.

*

Patricia Jones comments:

I am one of those people whose love of words began quite early. I love to read just about anything. I started writing in early adolescence. It was a way of getting beyond the small town's social and cultural parameters. Growing up black in America in the 1950s and early 1960s was difficult, full of complex social obligations, negotiations, family secrets, and enormous social changes giving rise to the Civil Rights Movement. Plus there was soul music and rock and roll and jazz and film from places like Rome, Paris, and London, as well as Hollywood. From reading about the Living Theater to working with Mabou Mines; from listening to Jimmy Hendrix on the radio to hearing him live a few months before his death; from watching the Vietnam War on TV to protesting the war at college, I feel quite strongly the social dynamism of those early years tempered by my maturation as a person and a poet. I admire the willingness of my fellow artists to take risks, mess up, get up and try something else in an effort to communicate whatever it is that they (we) think is important. Words can kill or heal or merely disrupt the quotidian. I hope my work is in some way disruptive, delightful, different.

*   *   *

The 35 poems that make up Patricia Spears Jones first volume of poems *The Weather that Kills* can be grouped into poems concerned with the human condition, autobiography, love, music, and place. The poems are open in form and exhibit striking images which are potent with surprise and insight: businessmen are "podium-headed" and ""The oops of life like a stadium wave / wraps the planet" ("You Just Got the Call").

While the poems often announce their origins in specific circumstances, seldom do they remain within those confines, for Jones's method is to allow the poem to associatively and imaginatively expand into unusual and epiphanic intersections. Nowhere is this more so than in the poem "The Perfect Lipstick" in which "black men in sequined dresses" emerge from the historical process that begins with "Columbus in a toy ship. / Off to discover the perfect route— / the fastest way to China, the Indies, all that spice." Jones locates the poetic of the human condition in the risks that must be taken "in the new world where the most dangerous of dreams / come true" ("The Perfect Lipstick"), for we live in "an era of dangerous greed and too easily satisfied lust" ("You Just Got the Call"). Though there is a place for human action—morality, empathy, dissent—we are also made aware of the "weather," forces that are beyond human intervention: "We look across the lake. The mountains tremble / at an immeasurable speed. / And we have nothing to do with it" ("Measure"). Finally, there is nothing that outlasts the ravages of history but art: "And the print survives" ("Blumen"). The suite, "Halloween Weather" that concludes the volume is so various in what it touches and so rich in its collage of voice, image, and sound that the pulsations of global life are made tangible and cannot be refused: "we walk as if from one funeral to another ... happy for the privilege."

It is the everyday circumstances that we endure and do not comprehend that are the starting places of Jones's exploration of the human condition: "The Perfect Lipstick" is generated by a historical reenactment—"When the life-sized replicas of the Nina, / the Pina, and the Santa Maria / precariously sailed into New York harbor; "Measure" commences "In the traffic jam on the way to the picnic"; and "You Just Got the Call"—a poem on Keith Haring's death—opens with cartoonish intimacy as the artist dresses: "Swish, you put on your underwear."

Jones's handling of autobiography is informed by her awareness of the problems inherent in "mythic retelling": in "Glad All Over" she states that it is exactly the seductions of "Mythic retelling" that she rejects, and that is done so that she can confront a personalized history rather than expand her own life mythopoetically. Thus, though she refracts her own experience of the civil rights struggle through adolescent curiosity sparked by seeing Julian Bond at a 1965 SNCC rally, the poem's climax is reached at the text's halfway point, with her own mother's confrontation of police troopers, and from that vantage the poem expands to take in a score of "hard truths." Similarly, in "The Birth of Rhythm and Blues" her own birth is related to the traumatic, wild, and pleading music that her parents were surrounded by in the years of "global nightmare" after the Korean conflict, Billie Holiday, Big Boy Crudup, Little Richard, and Ruth Brown: "so they cut my mother's belly and drag me out / wailing too." The music is a necessity because song is "where the hurting stops and healing begins": but there is also a dialectic in music for it contains men "bleeding and bleeding into / music's deep well." Music also figures largely in "In My Father's House" as the poet tries to connect to a distant parent: "I'd listen to the albums' bright music / wishing the swirling strings, their incessant backbeat, / would make me love my father." Music also makes possible protest and social change in "Healing Sheath" ("Someone intones platitudes, / but the beat breaks another back.") and "Sly and the Family Stone Under the Big Tit" ("always loving the way we thought the world / should be").

Jones's handling of love is somewhat romantic. However, the love theme in *Weather* is marked by maturity, acceptance, and wisdom. "Encounter and Farewell" frames an erotic interlude in New Orleans that begins with the "foreplay" of a "walk / through the French Quarter exploring souvenir shops." The details of lovemaking are explicitly presented but they do not occupy the entirety of the world. There is a context of past and present and of other cities: "We are / making love as we did before in Austin and Manhattan." "5:25 A.M." is also rife with tender specifics ("The weight of you / is traced on my sheets"), but there is an ironic reciprocity formulated by life's contingencies—("That's why the stereo's too loud"), ("That's why the buses are late"). Love brings the world into focus, but it does not banish the irritations: the beautiful moments come out of "storms" and makes possible "a song so sweet it makes my teeth ache."

Jones's poems that address music and travel are never routine. Her sensibility is fresh, curious, and vital. San Francisco is plunged into the emergency of the AIDS epidemic: "Men here, lovers, friends, are / learning women's work." Likewise music is chiefly present as a means to increase our awareness of the presence of frustrating liabilities that refuse to be ameliorated; confronting Charlie Parker's death "of heartbreak," "Gossip" states that "What we love is the failing, the falling." Jones's implication is that because the masses of humans embrace destruction, it is the task of the poets to work towards the world's salvation, "It is what we do not speak of / when the radio plays / something memorable / and we lack the skill / to carry the tune."

—Jon Woodson

JORDAN, June

Nationality: American. **Born:** New York City, 9 July 1936. **Education:** Midwood High School, Brooklyn, New York; Northfield

School for Girls, Massachusetts, 1950-53; Barnard College, New York, 1953-55, 1956-57; University of Chicago, 1955-56. **Family:** Married Michael Meyer in 1955 (divorced 1966); one son. **Career:** Assistant to the producer of the film *The Cool World*, 1964; research associate, Mobilization for Youth Inc., New York, 1965-66; director, Voice of the Children, 1967-70; member of the English Department, City College, New York, 1967-70, 1972-75, and 1977-78, Connecticut College, New London, 1968, Sarah Lawrence College, Bronxville, New York, 1971-75, and Yale University, New Haven, Connecticut, 1974-75; associate professor, 1978-82, professor of English, 1982-89, and director of the Poetry Center and the Creative Writing Program, 1986-89, State University of New York, Stony Brook. Chancellor's Lecturer, 1986, and professor of African American studies and women's studies, 1989—, University of California at Berkeley. Poet-in-residence, Teachers and Writers Collaborative, New York, 1966-68, MacAlester College, St. Paul, Minnesota, 1980, Loft Mentor Series, Minneapolis, 1983, and Walt Whitman Birthplace, Huntington, New York, 1988; Reid Lecturer, Barnard College, 1976; playwright-in-residence, New Dramatists, New York, 1987-88; visiting professor, Department of Afro-American Studies, University of Wisconsin, Madison, Summer 1988. Political columnist, *The Progressive* magazine, 1989—, and *City Limits,* London, 1990—. **Awards:** Rockefeller grant, 1969; American Academy in Rome Environmental Design prize, 1970; New York Council of the Humanities award, 1977; Creative Artists Public Service grant, 1978; Yaddo fellowship, 1979, 1980; National Endowment for the Arts fellowship, 1982; National Association of Black Journalists award, 1984; New York Foundation for the Arts fellowship, 1985; Massachusetts Council on the Arts award, 1985; MacDowell Colony fellowship, 1987; Nora Astorga Leadership award, 1989. **Member:** Executive board, Teachers and Writers Collaborative, 1978—, PEN American Center, 1980-84, Poets and Writers Inc., 1979—, American Writers Congress, 1981—, Center for Constitutional Rights, 1984—, AuAuthors Guild, 1986—. **Address:** Department of Afro-American Studies, 3335 Dwinelle Hall, University of California, Berkeley, California 94720, U.S.A.

Publications

Poetry

Some Changes. New York, Dutton, 1971.
Poem: On Moral Leadership as a Political Dilemma (Watergate, 1973). Detroit, Broadside Press, 1973.
New Days: Poems of Exile and Return. New York, Emerson Hall, 1974.
Things That I Do in the Dark: Selected Poetry. New York, Random House, 1977; revised edition, Boston, Beacon Press, 1981.
Passion: New Poems 1977-80. Boston, Beacon Press, 1980.
Living Room: New Poems 1980-1984. New York, Thunder's Mouth Press, 1985.
Lyrical Campaigns: Selected Poems. London, Virago Press, 1989.
Naming Our Destiny: New and Selected Poems. New York, Thunder's Mouth Press, 1989.
The Haruko / Love Poetry of June Jordan. New York, Serpent's Tail / High Risk, 1994.
Kissing God Goodbye: New Poems. New York, Scribners, 1996.

Recordings: *Things That I Do in the Dark and Other Poems,* Spoken Arts, 1978; *For Somebody to Start Singing,* with Bernice Reagon, Black Box-Watershed, 1979.

Plays

Freedom Now Suite, music by Adrienne B. Torf (produced New York, 1984).
The Break, music by Adrienne B. Torf (produced New York, 1984).
The Music of Poetry and the Poetry of Music, music by Adrienne B. Torf (produced Washington, D.C., and New York, 1984).
Bang Bang Über Alles, music by Adrienne B. Torf, lyrics by Jordan (produced Atlanta, 1986).
I Was Looking at the Ceiling and Then I Saw the Sky (opera libretto), music by John Adams. New York, Scribner, 1995.

Other (for children)

Who Look at Me? New York, Crowell, 1969.
His Own Where—. New York, Crowell, 1971.
Dry Victories. New York, Holt Rinehart, 1972.
Fannie Lou Hamer (biography). New York, Crowell, 1972.
New Life, New Room. New York, Crowell, 1975.
Kimako's Story. Boston, Houghton Mifflin, 1981.

Other

Civil Wars: Selected Essays 1963-1980. Boston, Beacon Press, 1981; new edition, New York, Scribners, 1996.
On Call: New Political Essays 1981-1985. Boston, South End Press, 1985; London, Pluto Press, 1986.
Bobo Goetz a Gun. Willimantic, Connecticut, Curbstone Press, 1985.
Moving Towards Home: Political Essays. London, Virago Press, 1989.
Technical Difficulties, New Political Essays. New York, Pantheon, 1994.
June Jordan's Poetry for the People: A Revolutionary Blueprint. New York, Routledge, 1995.

Editor, with Terri Bush, *The Voice of the Children.* New York, Holt Rinehart, 1970.
Editor, *Soulscript: Afro-American Poetry.* New York, Doubleday, 1970.

Manuscript Collection: Radcliffe Schlesinger Archives, Harvard University, Cambridge, Massachusetts.

Critical Studies: "This Wheel's on Fire" by Sara Miles, in *Woman Poet: The East,* edited by Marilyn Hacker, Reno, Nevada, Women in Literature, 1982; "Black Poet Sees Politics as the Duty of an Artist" by Penelope Moffet, in Los Angeles *Times,* 3 September 1986; "The Love Poetry of June Jordan" by Peter Erickson, in *Callaloo* (Charlottesville, Virginia), vol. 9, no. 1, 1986; "The Craft that the Politics Requires" by Ellen Flanders, in *Fireweed,* no. 36, summer 1992; interview with Renee Oleander, *Associated Writing Programs Chronicle,* vol. 27, no. 4, February 1995; "Finding a Voice through Verse" by Peter Monaghan, in *Chronicle of Higher Education,* 23 February 1996.

*   *   *

Poet, essayist, and author of children's fiction, June Jordan is among the most varied and prolific of contemporary African American writers. Together her works chart the artistic concerns of a poet who successfully maintains a sense of spiritual wholeness and the vision of a shared humanity, while relentlessly engaging a brutal and often brutalizing reality. The resultant combination—of courage and vulnerability—is suggested by the poem "Things That I Do in the Dark," in which the poet describes herself as a "stranger / learning to worship the strangers / around me / whoever you are / whoever I may become."

Artistically, Jordan's work shows the influences of two radically different aesthetic criteria. She has clearly been influenced by the Black Arts movement, the cultural arm of the Black Power movement of the 1970s, whose tenets require the work of art to address itself to a black audience, explore the complexities of black life, and work towards the building of an autonomous, vital black culture. In subject matter, theme, and idiom, many of Jordan's poems evidence these tendencies. In others, however, she seems at one with trends in mainstream American poetry. These poems are intensely personal, syntactically experimental, thematically elusive.

The underlying unity of Jordan's work lies in its uncompromising humanism, eloquently expressed in the historically allusive chronicle *Who Look at Me?*, in which the speaker, sometimes a single black, sometimes blacks as a group, characterizes the search of African-Americans for visibility as "the search to find / a fatherhood a mothering of mind / a multimillion multi-colored mirror / of an honest humankind" and their militance as, ultimately, a rejection of "a carnival run by freaks / who take a life / and tie it terrible / behind my back." The poet's own militance does not end with the political and social struggles of blacks. She is keenly aware of the dehumanizing effects of economic exploitation ("Nowadays the Heroes" and "47,000 Windows"), as well as of the abuses of power too easily committed by government ("To My Sister Ethel Ennis" and "Poem Against the State [Of Things]").

Feminist concerns are poignantly expressed in the lyrical "Getting Down to Get Over," which celebrates the unique and often solitary role of the black woman, who is "A full / Black / glorious / a purple rose ... a shell with the moanin / of ages inside her / a hungry one feedin the folk / what they need." In the anguished "From an Uprooted Condition" the speaker, in quiet frenzy, ponders "the right way the womanly expression / of the infinitive that fights / infinity / *to abort*?" And, finally, the precarious position of all women—in a world dominated by men—is effectively portrayed in "On Declining Values."

Despite their profusion, there is an underlying pessimism to Jordan's love poems. The central problem is not the inherent transitoriness of romantic love, a fact which the poet quietly acknowledges in "On a New Year's Eve." Rather, she seems to suggest that love's true enemy is a harsh and merciless reality. Thus, in "The Wedding," "the early wed Tyrone / and his Dizzella" are doomed before their life together begins, for they are "brave enough / but only two." And in poems such as "Shortsong from My Heart," "West Coast Episode," and "On Your Love" relationships are deemed temporary havens, brief respites. Reality, in the form of an impersonal, troubling, often hostile world, always hovers in the background. It is that larger world which, inevitably, reclaims the individual, and perhaps this poet, as its own.

—Saundra Towns

JOSEPH, Jenny

Nationality: British. **Born:** Birmingham, Warwickshire, 7 May 1932. **Education:** St. Hilda's College, Oxford, 1950-53, B.A. (honors) in English 1953. **Career:** Reporter, Westminster Press Provincial Newspapers, mid-1950s; worked for Drum Publications in South Africa, 1957-59; pub landlady, London, 1969-72; language teacher, 1972-74; lecturer in English extramural and adult education departments. **Awards:** Eric Gregory award, 1961; Cholmondeley award, 1975; Arts Council grant, 1976; James Tait Black Memorial award for fiction, 1986; Society of Authors travelling scholarship, 1995; Forward Prize for best single poem, 1995; "Warning" chosen as public's favorite post-war poem, BBC, 1996. **Agent:** John Johnson, 45-47 Clerkenwell Green, London EC1R OHT, England. **Address:** 17 Windmill Road, Minchinhampton, Near Stroud, Gloucestershire GL6 9DX, England.

PUBLICATIONS

Poetry

The Unlooked-for Season. Northwood, Middlesex, Scorpion Press, 1960.
Rose in the Afternoon and Other Poems. London, Dent, 1974.
The Thinking Heart. London, Secker & Warburg, 1978.
Beyond Descartes. London, Secker & Warburg, 1983.
The Inland Sea. Watsonville, California, Papier-Maché Press, 1989.
Selected Poems. Newcastle upon Tyne, Bloodaxe, 1992.
Ghosts and Other Company. Newcastle upon Tyne, Bloodaxe, 1995.

Fiction

Excerpt from *Persephone.* Oxford, Argo Magazine, 1985.
Persephone. Newcastle upon Tyne, Bloodaxe, 1986.
Extended Similes. Newcastle upon Tyne, Bloodaxe, 1995.

Other

Nursery Series (Boots, Wheels, Water, Wind, Tea, Sunday; for children). London, Constable, 6 vols., 1966-68.
Beached Boats, photographs by Robert Mitchell. Petersfield, Hampshire, Enitharmon Press, 1991.

*

Jenny Joseph comments:

It is usually easier for a writer to talk about what he or she is interested in doing "now" or "next" than about what has been done. Work already published is there for all to see, and off the writer's hands. However there are things I can say have interested me in other writers—not that I would claim to be like them.

I am interested in the use of the speaking voice, not merely to provide a "realistic" character for dramatic monologues, but as material, recognizable straight away on one level to the reader, in the musical use of language, and I enjoy a singing quality in poetry. Poetry, it seems to me, is not a novel manqué or a play manqué or a piece of music manqué or a line of philosophic enquiry manqué, or political statement, but it should be able to deal with the material that goes into all these.

I think my poetry is fairly full of references to the surfaces of the world, but you could say that of anything that uses language; and it still contains a certain amount of enquiry into questions of "reality," i.e., how things work. "Art" and "artificial" are words which to me are closely allied. Art forms a separate world which to have any point must always feed through roots in non-art, just as language must depend on something that is not language for its life.

The fiction I wrote between 1972 and 1979 and which was published in 1986 *(Persephone)* uses prose and verse. My interest in the structure for this book came out of my attempt, in "The Life and Turgid Times of A. Citizen," a long poem in *The Thinking Heart,* to do a narrative poem where the thread was a consciousness rather than a conventional protagonist, the different verse forms representing different shifts of that consciousness. A work I have been writing during the 1980s—*Extended Similes*—which is also fiction, not discursive writing, is composed of short prose pieces. For these I wanted to use prose rhythms in service to poetic mode, metaphor and simile being at the heart of the poetic method to my mind, and my interest in this came about through attention to Johnson's prose style. My more recent verse, included in *Ghosts and Other Company,* includes "songs," tales, and longer pieces using perhaps rougher language rhythms, a mixture to be found in earlier volumes.

*   *   *

Jenny Joseph's poetry tends to be philosophical in tone; there is an air of detachment about her work. As she stated in *The Bloodaxe Book of Contemporary Women Poets,* through her writing she attempts to explore the outside world, not the labyrinth of her own mind; her ideal is to write something which becomes part of the currency of common language, like ballads or sayings. Her past as a scholar and a journalist are revealed in a meticulous attention to detail; she has a fine ear for dialogue and frequently incorporates direct speech into her poetry, and she also makes effective use of dramatic monologues.

The Unlooked-for Season, which won the 1961 Eric Gregory award, is rather hermetic; the poet is constantly testing the line between reality and imagination, between fiction and truth. Death and loss permeate the collection; winter prevails, and summer, "the unlooked-for season," is an "amnesty." Such poems as "Lazarus," "Danae," "Persephone Returns," and "Euridyce to Orpheus" suggest a preference for classical myth over contemporary life.

Joseph's second collection, *Rose in the Afternoon and Other Poems,* contains her best-loved and most often anthologized poem, "Warning," which begins,

When I am an old woman I shall wear purple
With a red hat which doesn't go, and doesn't suit me ...
I shall sit down on the pavement when I'm tired
And gobble up samples in shops and press alarm bells
And run my stick along the public railings
And make up for the sobriety of my youth ...

This delicious streak of rebellion reappears throughout the collection, as does the more relaxed, colloquial language of the poem. Her tone is still largely objective, but there is more warmth, more

empathy than in her earlier work; she is concerned with human characters rather than archetypes. The poems are full of striking images, as in "Women at Streatham Hill":

They stand like monuments or trees, not women ...
Nobody asks what they have done all day
For who asks trees or stones what they have done?
They root, they gather moss, they spread they are.
The busyness is in the birds about them ...

This collection contains some of Joseph's best dramatic monologues, such as "Old Man Going"; there is also an extremely effective long narrative poem, "Thoughts on Oxford Street from Provence and Elsewhere," which anticipates her fictional work, *Persephone,* in its interweaving of verse and prose. "Thoughts ..." assembles a vivid cast of outspoken characters, from the abusive old man who assaults the reader with such statements as "Don't waste my time thinking that I think / That you're of any interest— / Don't waste my time if you've fucking nothing for me ..." to the equivocal liberal who asks, "Can you accept the man who accepts you neither at your own estimate nor his?... Can you play a game if there not only are no rules but no one to play with?"

Joseph's third collection, *The Thinking Heart,* demonstrates a move toward lyricism and celebration in such poems as "Chorale" or "Not Able to Resist the Spring," which begins exuberantly, "There is too much stuff here: / Everything crowded, duplicated and far too many words...." The hint of subversiveness which revealed itself in the previous volume hovers just beneath the surface of many of these poems; when it breaks free, Joseph produces wonderful, witty pieces, and when it doesn't, there's a tenseness which is sometimes dramatic, though sometimes simply solemn. In this collection the poet frequently eschews dramatic monologue to address her reader directly. Though she doesn't deal overtly with women's issues, such poems as "Modern Witches" or "There Are More Accidents in the Home than on the Roads" reveal a delightful, sly streak of feminist indignation.

In *Beyond Descartes,* Joseph experiments with short, imagistic poems. There is an air of compression and mystery about these works, the poems like parables or icons. She also exhibits a new sense of social conscience, as though her earlier philosophical musings have been honed down and anchored to the real world. Her characteristic wryness and use of colloquial speech combine well in a poem like "Collection for Cripples," which ends with "Did the poor crippled lady ever get home, I wonder? / Sure, somebody better equipped than I will have helped her home."

The author of several books for children, Joseph would make her first venture into adult fiction with 1986's *Persephone.* As a tale of lost innocence, the book demonstrates a continuing concern for women's lives and gender politics, as the young Persephone loses her girlish illusions and gains the wisdom to tame the betrayer Hades. Joseph has said that *Persephone* is the work that has most satisfied her as a writer; with its integration of poetry, prose, parody, and myth, it combines the best of her narrative and poetic talents.

—Katie Campbell

K

KANTARIS, Sylvia

Nationality: British. **Born:** Sylvia Mosley, Grindleford, Derbyshire, 9 January 1936. **Education:** University of Bristol, 1954-58, B.A. (honors) 1957, Cert.Ed. 1958; Sorbonne, Paris, 1955, diploma in French studies 1955; University of Queensland, St. Lucia, 1964-71, M.A. 1967, Ph.D. 1972. **Family:** Married Emmanuel Kantaris in 1958; one son and one daughter. **Career:** English teacher, Withywood School, Bristol, 1958-59; English and French teacher, St. Paul's Way School, London, 1960-62; tutor in French, University of Queensland, 1963-66; Open University tutor, Southwest England, 1974-84; extramural lecturer, Exeter University, Devon, 1974-92; writer-in-the-community, Cornwall, 1986. **Awards:** *Poetry* Magazine award (Australia), 1969; Poetry Society Competition award, 1982; Major Arts Council Literature award, 1991; Society of Authors award, 1992. D.Litt.: University of Exeter, 1989. **Address:** 14 Osborne Parc, Helston, Cornwall TR13 8PB, England.

PUBLICATIONS

Poetry

Time and Motion. Sydney, Poetry Society of Australia, 1975; Helston, Cornwall, Menhir, 1986.
Stocking Up. Helston, Cornwall, Menhir, 1981.
The Tenth Muse. Liskeard, Cornwall, Peterloo Poets, 1983.
News from the Front, with D.M. Thomas. Todmorden, Yorkshire, Arc, 1983.
The Sea at the Door. London, Secker & Warburg, 1985.
The Air Mines of Mistila, with Philip Gross. Newcastle upon Tyne, Bloodaxe, 1988.
Dirty Washing: New and Selected Poems. Newcastle upon Tyne, Bloodaxe, 1989; Chester Springs, Pennsylvania, Dufour, 1990.
Lad's Love. Newcastle upon Tyne, Bloodaxe, 1993.

*

Critical Studies: In *Outposts Poetry Quarterly* (Sutton, Surrey), spring 1989; "Terpsichore and the Incredible Hulk: Sylvia Kantaris—An Accessible Contemporary" by David Wilkinson, in *In Black and Gold: Contiguous Traditions in Post-war British and Irish Poetry,* edited by C.C. Barfoot. Amsterdam and Atlanta, Georgia, DQR Studies in Literature 13, 1994.

Sylvia Kantaris comments:

With regard to form, I agree with Christina Rossetti, "In the poet, the ear dictates and the mouth listens." What fascinates me most is to discover the curious and humorous within the everyday—and I enjoy the sheer fun of mixing dictions outrageously.

(1995) I think the poet has one skin too few and that it *hurts.*

*　　*　　*

The publication of Sylvia Kantaris's *Dirty Washing,* which contains a substantial selection of her work together with a generous supplement of new poems, provides a fine opportunity to assess her achievement. It is a pleasant collection to read, mainly because of Kantaris's gentle conversational style, which relies on the subtle rhythms of the speaking voice. Because the style is difficult to maintain, it is not surprising that there are lapses into the prosaic from time to time. But at her best Kantaris is very good, her poems exerting a strong hold on the reader. When she starts a poem, as she often does, with a direct statement—

> It takes a certain savoir-faire to give a paper on
> some area of deconstructionism when
> I don't know what it means—

or

> I don't put the clock back. I just stop it
> for an hour and let time do the catching up

—then that hold is exerted straightaway. The extended metaphor in "Genesis" is a case in point:

> May I scream? I asked
> but they said no,
> so I held it between my teeth
> where it slowly spread.

Kantaris's style suits her brief narratives and certainly her probing reflections and descriptions. Her eye for detail often intrigues the reader:

> My grandmother's kitchen looks almost normal
> on the surface, though a bit too bare.
> Nobody really cooks there. The drawer
> contains two knives and forks which don't match;
> there are two pans in the cupboard and a few
> old mugs and plates. Nothing accumulates.

The poem gives not so much a picture of the kitchen as a character study of a grandmother. It is a characteristic of Kantaris's best poems that under the deceptively unassuming "ordinariness" of her vocabulary and syntax lie deep layers of metaphor and feeling.

Humor enlightens Kantaris's poetry too. "The Big One" and "O Little Star" are gems. While "Fairy Tales" is another example, here something deeper is revealed when Beauty

> Never stopped tormenting him
> until the beast emerged again
> from underneath the skin.

I am of two minds about the work Kantaris has written in collaboration with others. *The Air Mines of Mistila* with Philip Gross is successful enough, but in *News from the Front* with D.M. Thomas the two voices and stances are too disparate. Besides, Kantaris's own powers of expressing the emotional and the sensual are intense enough in themselves. "Parting," for example, with its extended symbolism of the railway, is beautifully done:

> So many partings glance away ahead of us
> to where the rain slants on an empty track.

Other examples are "Some Untidy Spot" and the gently (all the more powerful for that) impressive "An Innocent Adultery":

> ... the day before was just the kind
> of day for touching breasts, as he had said
> casually, as if words had no fingers.

—John Cotton

KAUFMAN, Shirley

Nationality: American. **Born:** Seattle, Washington, 5 June 1923. **Education:** University of California—Los Angeles, B.A. (cum laude) 1944; San Francisco State University, M.A. in English 1967. **Family:** Married 1) Bernard Kaufman, Jr. in 1946 (divorced 1974); three daughters; 2) Hillel Matthew Daleski in 1974. **Career:** Visiting lecturer, Tel Aviv University, Tel Aviv, 1971; University of Massachusetts, Amherst, 1974, University of Washington, Seattle, 1977, Hebrew University, Jerusalem, 1983-84; poet-in-residence, Oberlin College, 1979, 1989, 1994; teaching associate, School for Overseas Students, Hebrew University, 1980. **Awards:** International Poetry Forum United States award, 1969, for *The Floor Keeps Turning*. **Member:** Visiting Writers Series, American University, Washington, D.C., 1994. **Address:** 7 Rashba Street, 92264 Jerusalem, Israel.

PUBLICATIONS

Poetry

The Floor Keeps Turning. Pittsburgh, University of Pittsburgh Press, 1970.
Gold Country. Pittsburgh, University of Pittsburgh Press, 1970.
Looking at Henry Moore's Elephant Scull Etchings in Jerusalem during the War. N.p., Unicorn Press, 1977.
From One Life to Another. Pittsburgh, University of Pittsburgh Press, 1979.
Claims. New York, Sheep Meadow Press, 1984.
Rivers of Salt. Port Townsend, Washington, Copper Canyon Press, 1993.
Roots in the Air: New and Selected Poems. Port Townsend, Washington, Copper Canyon Press, 1996.

Other

Translator, *A Canopy in the Desert,* by Abba Kovner. Pittsburgh, University of Pittsburgh Press, 1973.
Translator, *Scrolls of Fire,* by Abba Kovner. Tel Aviv, Beth Hatefusoth, 1978.
Translator, *The Light of Lost Suns,* by Amir Bilboa. New York, Persea, 1979.

Translator, *My Little Sister* [and] *Selected Poems 1965-1985* by Abba Kovner. Oberlin, Ohio, Oberlin University Press, 1986.
Translator, with Judith Herzberg, *But What: Selected Poems,* by Herzberg. Oberlin, Ohio, Oberlin University Press, 1988.

*   *   *

"I've admired ... the surrealists, who take big leaps in their images," Shirley Kaufman once said in an interview, and surrealist technique is apparent in her first two books. Poems that begin in reality develop the logic of dreams, until they narrate memories and events with a ghostly determinism. There are several poems that maintain realistic, descriptive focus throughout, but more often a process of association leads to images that work allegorically, standing for a subject that must be decoded. In "Sorrow, Sorrow," fathers crying for deceased wives squeeze "their tears / in a salt shoe and throw it / back and forth across the net." This game represents the way emotions of mourning are played on in this family, but the exact terms of the analogy are obscure and demand exegesis.

Surrealism differs from allegory in that it doesn't refer to fixed systems of meaning, Surrealist art originates in the unconscious, a hidden source whose contents can only be inferred from the images it produces. Surreal meaning is formed by the "leaps" of association that Kaufman alludes to, and its meaning must be deduced by the same method. But these leaps aren't always into such estranged realms as that which provided the image of a tear-filled shoe. Kaufman also uses associative leaps to structure poems with common subjects. In such cases, the relationship between images gradually reveals an unsuspected network of meaning under the surface of daily life, in the manner of psychoanalysis.

This is noticeable in her second and third books. The poem "Looking at Henry Moore's Elephant Skull Etchings in Jerusalem during the War" first describes the etching, then gradually creates a series of images that evoke the skull: caverns she visits, it openings like a skull's: a ride through a fun-house tunnel that is like a trip into the skull of the elephant. By the end of the poem, she has become conscious of the relation these associations have in common with each other and the etching, and the hidden life they share takes on reality, as "The elephants come after us / in herds now / / they will roll over us / like tanks." The anxiety produced in a society at war was tapped into by the sight of the elephant's skull, which subsequently governed the poet's vision of reality, finding likenesses wherever she looks and finally taking on a life of its own, with a force equal to the horrors of battle.

Where Kaufman's first two books were more likely to dwell on personal losses, failures of intimacy and struggles with identity, her later books are more concerned with her relocation to Israel. These poems are less surreal, as they represent new realities she struggles to understand. The last poems in *From One Life to Another,* called "The Next Step," has no greater ambition than to tell "of the things around us / in the light / each morning." However modest this seems, it aims for meanings that dawn on the reader with the same revelatory force that we experience when a common metaphor, such as the one for understanding that this poem explores, is restored to its literal root: "dawn" is when light first appears. We forget this, but when we are led to see it again in a new light, it dawns on us with remarkable force. The sense of revelation doesn't stem from surrealist depth psychology, but from awareness of being itself.

"Claims" and "Rivers of Salt" contain "leaps" in their poems, but aren't concerned with surreal dislocations so much as bizarre contiguities that we take for granted: that consciousness can turn easily between the overwhelming threats like nuclear war, and the comfort in "small cups / of coffee," is more strange to consider than any dislocation dredged up by the surrealist imagination. *Claims*, a poem made of 62 lyrics, recalls Kaufman's grandmother's flight to Seattle from persecution in Czarist Russia, as it records the poet's transition to Israeli life. Like the Israeli poets she has translated from Hebrew, it also tries to measure the distance between present Israeli culture and its source in ancient times. Where Israeli poets rely on Biblical associations embedded in their living language, Kaufman uses her feel for minor incidents to dramatize this distance. "Promised Land" ends with the simple question "Now or then?" after someone has asked when a line on a map separating Arab from Jew was drawn. You can tell, through this casual exchange, how ancient past works into daily Israeli life as a presumption that the slightest gestures evoke.

—Will Broadus

KAY, Jackie

Nationality: Scottish. **Born:** Jacqueline Margaret Kay, Edinburgh, Scotland, 9 November 1961. **Education:** University of Stirling, 1979-83, B.A. (honors) in English 1983. **Family:** One son. **Career:** Writer-in-residence, Hammersmith, London, 1989-91. **Awards:** Eric Gregory award, 1991; Scottish Arts Council Book award, 1991, for *The Adoption Papers;* Saltire First Book of the Year award, 1991, for *The Adoption Papers;* Forward prize, 1992, for *The Adoption Papers;* Signal Poetry award, 1993, for *Two's Company;* Somerset Maugham award for *Other Lovers.* **Agent:** Pat Kavanagh, Peters Fraser & Dunlop, 503/4 The Chambers, Chelsea Harbour, London SW10 0XF, England. **Address:** 20 Townsend Road, London N15 4NT, England.

PUBLICATIONS

Poetry

The Adoption Papers. Newcastle upon Tyne, Bloodaxe, 1991.
That Distance Apart (chapbook). London, Turret, 1991.
Two's Company (for children). London, Puffin, 1992.
Three Has Gone (for children). London, Blackie Children's, 1994.
Other Lovers. Newcastle upon Tyne, Bloodaxe, 1993.

*   *   *

Jackie Kay can be classified as Scottish, since she was born in Edinburgh and took her degree at the University of Stirling. She can also be classified as being black since her membership of a Scottish family is by adoption, and indeed her first book was called, tellingly, *The Adoption Papers.*

Any sort of classification, however, will not do justice to a writer so vigorously individual. The sequence giving that first book its name is divided between three voices: those of a birth mother, of an adoptive mother, and of a daughter. They are characterized in part by different fonts of typeface. The sequence may owe something to a poem by Sylvia Plath, "Three Women," and certainly the mode is similarly dramatic. Like Plath, very often Kay seems to be writing for an ideal form of radio. We hear the voices quite distinctively. In a section called "Baby Lazarus"—a further allusion to Plath—spoken by the birth mother who has given away her baby, she says, "When I got home / I went out into the garden—the frost bit my old brown boots— / and dug a hole the size of my baby / and buried the clothes I'd bought anyway."

This plainness of diction, if it doesn't represent the entire adult situation, at least gives a sense of authenticity. It carries Kay through several poems that work by reason of interest in the experience retailed. "My Grandmother's Houses," as its title would suggest, creates the character of a grandmother in terms of the houses with which she is associated, including one that she is employed to clean. The author says, and we can be sure that it is the author speaking: "By the time I am seven we are almost the same height. / She still walks faster, rushing me down the High Street / till we get to her cleaning house. The hall is huge. / Rooms lead off like an octopus's arms." The eye is that of a child, and this child's-eye view is a strength in Kay's poetry, in that it makes for specificity. It is also a limitation.

Kay is able to get across what happens to a child with considerable atmosphere. In "Summer Storm, Capolona" she writes, "The poppies in the wheat have darkened to dried / blood; the air sharpens itself, a scythe, / you are giggling inside your window hook / when the first raindrops fall like cherries." It is not we who are giggling inside a window hood, but the poet; the poet, moreover, speaking as a child.

I Corinthians 13:11 tells us, "When I was a child, I spake as a child, I understood as a child, I thought as a child: but when I became a man, I put away childish things." Kay is not going to become a man, and it is certainly a fact that she has not put away childish things. In fact, her verse thrives upon them. The distracted mother in her science fiction poem, "I try my absolute best," is a child's idea of a mother. Her evocation of her enslaved ancestors, "Even the trees," has the vividness of retrospection, of atavism, "that is why we remember certain things and not others." The "we" stands for children; for children's beliefs, for children's memories.

The most ambitious poem of Kay's second collection, *Other Lovers,* is "The Year of the Letter." This would appear to be an adult subject: the survival and eventual destruction of a public library. Yet the experience of the library, rendered with characteristic delight, is that of a child preferring books to people. She takes out *Madame Bovary* when other children would prefer *Anne of Green Gables.* Her father catches her with a lesbian novel wrapped in the covers of *Bunty.* This is certainly one way of looking at a library; but there are other ways.

Whatever the misfortunes of her early life, Kay has turned them into account. It is like reading the opening chapters of a *David Copperfield* written by an author who never got beyond adolescence. There is no equivalent to a *Little Dorrit* in her output. The vocabulary is simple and vivid, but limited. The rhythms, irrespective of the author's true age, are those of a very young speaking voice.

At her best, she is superb at writing for children. Her strength is that she feels *with* them. A recent poem, as yet uncollected, "The School Hamster's Holiday"—and it is no deprecation to say this—would be ideal for class discussion:

I spent the rest of the weekend
tight-lipped and desperate
sponging that hamster with all my might ...

... I tried and tried to make Snowie white.
It was an impossible task.
Have you ever tried to shammy a hammy?

There is a Scottish accent here, and an allusion to the colour question. But is a child's accent and a child's view of colour.

It is true that her poems may very well awake the youth idea to poetry. The young idea, however, will presumably progress thenceforward; to Stevie Smith, to Blake, to Wordsworth. Whereas there is little indication, given the direction of her significant improvisatory talents, that Jackie Kay will ever enter the world of adults.

—Philip Hobsbaum

KAZANTZIS, Judith

Nationality: British. **Born:** Oxford, 14 August 1940. **Education:** Oxford University, Somerville College, B.A. in modern history 1961. **Family:** Married Alec Kazantzis in 1982; one daughter and one son. **Career:** Home tutor for the Inner London Education Authority during 1970s; poetry reviewer, *Spare Rib* magazine, six years; member of Women's Literature Collective, 1970s; committee member and panelist, South-East Arts, 1978-79. Poetry editor, *PEN Broadsheet.* Also artist: individual shows—Poetry Society Gallery, London, 1987; Combined Harvest Gallery, London, 1989. **Address:** 32 Ladbroke Grove, London W11 3BQ, England.

PUBLICATIONS

Poetry

Minefield. London, Sidgwick & Jackson, 1977.
The Wicked Queen. London, Sidgwick & Jackson, 1980.
Touch Papers, with Michèle Roberts and Michelene Wandor. London, Allison & Busby, 1982.
Let's Pretend. London, Virago, 1984.
A Poem for Guatemala. Leamington Spa, Yorkshire, Bedlam Press, 1986.
Judith Kazantzis. Leamington Spa, Leamington Poetry Society, 1987.
Flame Tree. London, Methuen, 1988.
The Florida Swamps. London, Oasis, 1990.
The Rabbit Magician Plate. London, Sinclair-Stevenson, 1992.
Selected Poems: 1977-1992. London, Sinclair-Stevenson, 1995.

Other

Editor, *The Gordon Riots: A Collection of Contemporary Documents.* London, Cape, 1966.
Editor, *Women in Revolt: The Fight for Emancipation: A Collection of Contemporary Documents.* London, Cape, 1968.

*

Judith Kazantzis comments:

I wrote poems all during my childhood and adolescence. Then there was a complete break until 1973 when reading Plath's *The Colossus* suddenly broke the resolution I'd made not to be a writer; she offered a language I could understand emotionally and as a poet technically. It was painting, psychoanalysis, and feminism that set off my poetry in the 1970s; but underneath all was the simple(?) experience of marrying and having two young children; so my first book makes reference to the claustrophobia and anger I was feeling then, and was consciously woman-centered; and my second book, more so, and it was wider in range, and more confident. I re-used Greek myth, and also fairytale. Contemporary issues were coming in more explicit forms. In 1982 I collaborated in a feminist trilogy, and my next publications have ranged from consideration of public issues (including a special interest in Latin America and U.S. relations with Latin America) to love poems and to considerations of mother-daughter, mother-son relationships. Exile and distance; my relationship to countryside and nature, and to city; time; all these were growing as themes. My *Selected Poems: 1977-1992* illustrates this wide-ranging kind of development over 15 years, influenced by much time spent in Key West and other parts of America, though my base is very definitely English.

*   *   *

Judith Kazantzis is a poet who speaks with an intensely personal, informal voice about matters of general public concern, and this ability to manage such a combination without the need to resort to full-blown rhetoric on the one hand or the confessional mode that seemed to proclaim itself as the quintessential voice of modern poetry in the late 1960s is remarkable.

Her first major collection, *The Wicked Queen,* was published in 1980, and the dominant characteristics of her work are already present in it in their full maturity—a wit that can be savage but that is deployed in the service of a quite justifiable rage at injustice; a feminism that may at times be strident, but with a stridency that is often necessary if one is to draw attention to what much of the world may choose to ignore. The themes range wide—from the stoning of an adulteress in Jeddah to a savage retelling of the tale of Little Red Riding Hood; from an imaginative reconstruction of the world of Queen Clytemnestra to the joyful, tender poem addressed to the poet's pregnant sister. There is a prickly restlessness about much of this writing, a willful, rebellious refusal to let go of a theme until all of its possibilities are exposed for all the world to see, appraise, or even jeer at if necessary. If the absurd posturings of men are often mocked, they are mocked deservedly, as in "Those Upright Men":

I heard of a tribe where the men
        held their erections all their lives,
like rhino horns: each
his own mascot before the main regiment of the body,
gorgeous trophies
        painful to bump ...

Her next major work was the long *A Poem for Guatemala.* Here poetry is deployed in the service of popular protest—a time-honored usage, of course. The poem itself is divided into such sections as "Duty," "The Morning Star," and "The Clinic," each chronicling particular instances of deprivation, injustice, cruelty. Its rhetorical flights are gently persuasive:

When will this land be free?
And the villages be uncovered from the tractor tread and
the flattened ranges of the loosened bull?
When will the Indians sow their seed corn
And the children grow tall in their parents' houses?

This poem represents a significant move forward for Kazantzis from the imaginative exploration of particular acts of injustice, whether they be offenses of one kind or another against her own sex, often seen through the medium of myth, historical example, or biblical precept, to a new, more extended mode of political realism, which in this instance includes a profound concern for the ramifications of American foreign policy in Central America. She explained, "This poem comes of a wish to honour the life-force and courage of Guatemalans living and dying in the current unnatural conditions. These conditions are not widely known. But among those of the Americas who live in exile either as refugees abroad or in their own land, the peoples of Guatemala, especially the indigenous peoples, figure in hundreds of thousands." Harold Pinter described it as "a major political poem ... beautifully wrought, concrete, passionate ... a most impressive achievement."

Her later collection, *Flame Tree,* is also firmly rooted in the political realities of these turbulent times. Themes of individual poems include the threat to the world's rain forests, criticism of the Thatcher government, the miners' strike of 1984, and the Falkland Islands War. "His Little Girl Feeds Daddy" deals with the government budget. It begins with

Here's
a sight of the boar
head in closeup, mounted
Stuffed on a wall, relaxed
before his tusking of
widows, disabled, geriatrics ...

The wit is savage, mordant, rollicking. The movement of the verse, as is the case with much of Kazantzis's poetry, depends upon the rhythms of the words chosen, and how these accumulate as they are spoken; the formal patterning depends upon the spoken impact of the piece. It is free verse of a kind, but discipline has been imposed from the start by the choice and disposition of the words themselves, which means that the poetry is never slack, never lacking in taut control. What is admirable about her use of language is the imaginative pressure behind the words, that sense of urgency that comes from having one's subject matter sharply, unflinchingly in focus:

Cop cars squeal, howl and gasp
Across the grid pattern. In my sleep
Huge worms fight at intersections,
Clapping and batting their brazen wings ...

Flame Tree swings from Europe to the Americas and back again, from childhood to maturity, from politics to the intensely personal concerns of friends and family, and all this is achieved without force, fuss, or gratuitous rhetorical flourish.

—Michael Glover

KEFALÁ, Antigone

Nationality: Australian. **Born:** Braila, Romania, 28 May 1935. **Education:** Attended secondary schools in Braila, Pireus and Lavrion, Greece, and New Zealand; Victoria University, Wellington, B.A. 1958, M.A. 1960. **Family:** Married 1) Robert Kerr in 1959 (divorced 1963); 2) Usher Weinrauch in 1964 (divorced 1976). **Career:** Teacher of English, New South Wales Department of Education, Sydney, 1961-68; administrative assistant, University of New South Wales, 1968-69; arts administrator, Australia Council for the Arts, Sydney, 1971-87. **Address:** 12 Rose Street, Annandale, New South Wales 2038, Australia.

Publications

Poetry

The Alien. Brisbane, Makar Press, 1973.
Thirsty Weather. Melbourne, Outback Press, 1978.
European Notebook. Sydney, Hale & Iremonger, 1988.
Absence: New and Selected Poems. Sydney, Hale & Iremonger, 1992.

Novels

The First Journey. Sydney, Wild & Woolley, 1975.
The Island. Sydney, Hale & Iremonger, 1984.

Other

Alexia: A Tale of Two Cultures, illustrated by Warwick Hatton (for children). Sydney, John Ferguson, 1984; Greek-English edition published as *Alexia: A Tale for Advanced Children,* illustrated by Nikos Kyprainos, Melbourne, Owl Publishing, 1995.

*

Bibliography: In *Bibliography of Australian Multicultural Writers* by Gunew and Mahyuddin, Melbourne, Deakin University, 1992.

Critical Studies: "Migrant Women Writers," in *Meanjin* (Melbourne), 1983, and *Framing Marginality,* Melbourne, Melbourne University Press, 1994, both by Sheja Gunew; "The Process of Becoming" by Judith Brett, in *Meanjin* (Melbourne), 1985; *Coming Out from Under* by Pam Gilbert, Sydney, Pandora Press, 1988; "The Politics of Nostalgia" by Efi Hatzimanolis, in *Hecate* (Brisbane), vol. 6, no. 1 / 2, 1990; *The Journeys Within—Striking Chords* by Nikos Papastergiadis, Sydney, Allen & Unwin, 1992; "Memory and Absence" by Michelle Tsokos, in *Westerly* (Perth), 1994.

*   *   *

In an interview published in *Poetry and Gender,* Antigone Kefalá refers to her childhood writing in Romania, her learning Greek (but not writing) in Greece, and her finally starting to write in English in her last year at an Australian university. She quotes Derek

Walcott, "To change your language you must change your life." Her initially musical concept of poetry has slowly "acquired more architectural form, became a tool through which some perceived truth could come alive."

Despite the success of the children of non-English-speaking migrants in school and their increasing success in business and science, writers for whom English was a second language rarely had serious books published in Australia in the mid-1970s. *The Alien* and then *Thirsty Weather* were pioneers, and readers found that they had to acquire a new taste. The bitterness was not hostile, but readers hesitated to call the mordant accuracy funny, even if it was sometimes about faceless migration authorities or New Zealanders. An example is "The Place":

> The ships, we had heard, had sunk
> weighted with the charity of the new world
> that kept on feeding us with toys ...

The same quality can be seen in "The Promised Land":

> I
> The roads were of candy
> the houses of ice cream
> the cattle of liquorice.
> Pretty, we said,
> drinking the green air,
> as in a fairy tale, we said,
> eating the green water, brackish,
> breathing the smoke that rose
> from the greenstone hills ...
>
> II
> The people carved in wood
> the mark of the knife still on them
> a nordic dream whittled to knick-knacks
> with glass beads in their sockets
> which they washed every night
> in detergents ...

Taking in images as light as skeletal leaves and yet invested with symbolic weight, readers in fact learn a new language for themselves and their places: "the girl with the cropped hair, / nervous lips, tortured fingers ..." ("The Lunch"); or "... soot raining on warehouses, railyards, the hotel / where we were waiting for the fixer ... / The gutters full of onions, / blue dusted porcelain the sky, / above the railway clock / the new translucent moon was flying" ("Ultimo Bridge").

Kefalá's *European Notebook* maintains her bleak and brooding outlook: "The hero came quite late / sniffing the air / his face like a skinned animal / eaten by maggots with ice heads / a musty smell about him / as he danced / his hollow eyes turned inward, / bleak tunnels with no end" ("The Party"). Greek tradition, local social occasions, memory, return—indeed the poet finds "fatality at the heart of each thing" ("The Wanderer"). "Suicide" is a poem of great beauty:

> This timelessness
> that rises out of the earth ...
> This silence,
> the ease that fills the trees,
> a promise of such bliss
> of self forgetfulness.

"The core of the experience I am trying to express," says Kefala, "is essentially a fatalistic one, my Greekness, I assume." This aspect shows in her scrupulous language and pacing and in a brevity that has nothing to do with "having nothing to say."

Kefalá writes sparingly, and selections of earlier work fill out later books. Her prose works also are slim, refined narratives, distillations of intense experience. In *Absence*—the title sequence of her 1992 volume of new and selected poems— "Growing Old" is "gathering this knowledge one / does not want, one can not use, / a useless knowledge that / repeats itself." Nights are menacing experiences of absence and degradation, spoken in a soft, even voice.

"What I am searching for now, is for a balance that will allow meaning and language to hold each other in a unity in which the weight of each is not visible." Kefalá's limpid language somehow carries nuanced meanings, but apathy and despair lurk behind the lines—even those positively titled "Freedom Fighter" and "Thanksgiving." No reader experiences Kefalá's poems as simple delight; equally, no reader can miss their stripped-back power.

—Judith Rodriguez

KEMP, Jan

Nationality: New Zealander. **Born:** Hamilton, New Zealand, 12 March 1949. **Education:** University of Auckland, B.A., 1970, M.A. (with honors) 1974; Auckland Teacher's College, teaching diploma, 1972. **Family:** Married 1) in 1969 (divorced, 1974); 2) Dieter Riemenschneider in 1997. **Career:** Teacher of English in schools in New Zealand, Malaysia, and Papua New Guinea, 1974-80; temporary lecturer, University of Papua New Guinea, 1981-82, University of Hong Kong, 1982-85, and University of East Asia, Macau, 1984-85; lecturer in English, National University of Singapore, 1985-94; currently Germanistik Magister Student, J.W. Goethe Universitaet, Frankfurt. **Awards:** New Zealand Literary Fund grant, 1976, and writer's bursary, 1979; Stout Centre fellowship, 1991. **Address:** Frankfurt, Germany.

PUBLICATIONS

Poetry

Against the Softness of Woman. Dunedin, New Zealand, Caveman Press, 1976.
Diamond and Gravel. Wellington, New Zealand, Hampson Hunt, 1979.
Ice-breaker Poems. Auckland, Coal-black Press, 1980.
Five Poems. Singapore, Arte and Materia Exhibition, 1988.
The Other Hemisphere. Washington, D.C., Three Continents Press; and Sydney, Butterfly Books, 1991.

Play

Radio Play: *Something Rich and Strange: A Look at the Nature of Poetry,* with Arthur Baysting, ABC Radio Melbourne, 1975.

*

Jan Kemp comments:

Reading performance of my poems—the public part, the presentation and the sharing of them—has been important to me from the start, when I wrote, published and read in the FREED group. We were "the young New Zealand poets" then, and we wanted to be heard.

I want the audience to hear the poem as I hear it when I write it, its cadence, intonation, patter, its run. With the first line that comes to me, the poem gives its own rhythm, word-field, tone. Writing it down, I am the poem, I become language at its most natural and instinctive, choosing its way for itself. It is a movement. It is a state of being very much alive. It is finding and being true to myself, to my voice. I also like the physical act of writing. I like calligraphy.

My relationship to language has changed over the years, but the impulse to write is the same, just as is the impulse to be silent.

*   *   *

A popular New Zealand poet, Jan Kemp made her name as a performance poet in the 1970s when she toured the country as one of the "Gang of Four" (with Sam Hunt, Hone TuWhare, and Alistair Campbell). Belonging to the radical sixties generation of David Mitchell, Ian Wedde, Alan Brunton, Russell Haley, and Murray Edmond, her work also demonstrates the experimental, open form verse techniques at a time when this was unusual for women writers (she was the only woman poet to be included in Arthur Baysting's 1973 anthology *The Young New Zealand Poets*). She has a natural flair for public delivery: even private subject matter is projected rhythmically, instantly accessible, as in "Poem" (*Against the Softness of Woman*):

A puriri moth's wing
lies light in my hand—

my breath can lift it

light on this torn wing
we lie on love's breath.

The very divergent themes of Kemp's work suggest contrasting attitudes to life: on one hand, especially in her early work, is heartfelt poetry about herself in love, full of wonder, yet vulnerable to disappointment; on the other is the external world, often surprising and dramatic, which she encounters with resilience and enjoyment. Her whole-hearted immersion in both spheres results in love poetry which is tremulous and vociferous, and more outgoing, lively poems which are teeming with life, charged by a sense of the exotic. In "Paperboygirl" different registers, voices, and discourses are signalled by italics, capitals, and extensive repetition, while staccato, onomatopoeic sound effects image the rapid, excited delivery of the morning's paper:

```
i run outside myself wet  slick
     flat              stick
        zip       zip
              trousers  flap
                    slap stick
     thonk thonk the papers are heavy

zap zap zap zap
this is what i bring BLANK NEWSPRINT....
```

THONK on yr doorstep
globe'n mayyyll
globe'n mayyyll

In fact these differences are really two sides of the same coin, because Kemp is essentially an extrovert with a tender heart. Even though she has written erotically yet despairingly about love, creating a personal drama of enchantment and disappointment, she is ultimately optimistic even about slippery emotions. The sense of being in love with life surfaces in her powerful rhythms, her humorous elaboration of social situations, her anecdotal, conversational style. These performance qualities make her poetry come theatrically to life before an audience; she can inflect her voice across a range of registers, and with an ear for mimicry echo snatches of other languages, the cacophony of street cries or animal sounds, and capture in surging, pulsating rhythm the melee of life rushing by as in "Hong Kong Headlong from a Motorbike" (*The Other Hemisphere*):

Free-running eleventh floor eye-level down Pokfulam viaduct
harbour views smack into the visor; three hundred
and fifty dizzy ships shoot out night stars
onto oiled blackness of the sea;

Other poems like "Father's Metamorphosis" (*The Other Hemisphere*), on her intimation of her father's death, combine a quieter mood with carefully judged images: "In the plane I knew, as the sun / blitzed the silver wing, that / he'd become the blinding light." More recently having moved from Singapore to Germany, Kemp's predisposition to lively anecdote has extended into extravagant, fanciful depictions: rhythmically powerful, as in "The Ballad of Donna Quixote," "I want to be / a Viennese lady / eating up Art in a cloche," these poems are inspired by the challenge of a new country and language. In "The Brink of Fluency":

Teetering on the brink of fluency
like someone on a uni-cycle
I fall
plötzlich
a mosquito
squashed again
by the allmächtige Hand
of German Grammar,
a black etching
on red smudge.

But they also veer into the surreal and fantastic, containing exotic images and describing fabulous encounters. Dietrich in "Professor Dietrich on the Dachstein" converses with the mysterious Prince Leopold, "interjecting between two mountaintops," "waving / his felt hat with the little feather / like a trig on a mountain / till the road went over the horizon"; "Wedding / Naming / Bells" playfully embellishes the merger of two names with Oriental and historical allusions, "Now I'll be madame Yu-hyphen-Mee / & you'll still be Sir Yu."

Kemp's poetry, grounded in the intonations of her speaking voice and emphatic rhythms, is preeminently suited to oral delivery, and is never purely cerebral; embracing the quotidian, inflected amusingly and lightheartedly, it ranges easily across many cultures and conveys richly diverse perspectives and voices.

—Janet Wilson

KENYON, Jane

Nationality: American. **Born:** Ann Arbor, Michigan, 23 May 1947. **Education:** University of Michigan, B.A. 1970, M.A. 1972. **Family:** Married the poet Donald Hall in 1972. **Career:** Poet. **Awards:** Hopwood award; National Endowment for the Arts fellow, 1981; New Hampshire Commission on the Arts fellow, 1984; Guggenheim Foundation fellow, 1992-93. **Address:** Eagle Pond Farm, Danbury, New Hampshire 03230, U.S.A. **Died:** 1995.

PUBLICATIONS

Poetry

From Room to Room. Cambridge, Massachusetts, Alice James Books, 1978.
The Boat of Quiet Hours. Saint Paul, Minnesota, Graywolf Press, 1986.
Let Evening Come. Saint Paul, Minnesota, Graywolf Press, 1990.
Constance. Saint Paul, Minnesota, Graywolf Press, 1993.
Otherwise: New and Selected Poems. Saint Paul, Minnesota, Graywolf Press, 1996.

Recording: *Jane Kenyon and Judith Moffett Reading Their Poems.* 1988.

Other

Translator, *Twenty Poems of Anna Akhmantova.* N.p., Eighties Press, 1985.

*   *   *

Jane Kenyon's poetry is acutely faithful to the familiarities and mysteries of home life, and it is distinguished by intense calmness in the face of routine disappointments and tragedies. Its passions are deftly represented with precise diction and without pretension. In the middle section of "American Triptych," a short sequence of prose poems from her first collection, Kenyon watches a children's baseball game, and her description of the flights of the baseball provides an apt metaphor for her poetry, "Sometimes it arcs higher than the house, sometimes it tunnels into tall grass at the edge of the hayfield."

Kenyon's poems are inevitably grounded by their respect for the limits of individual yearning. She is chastened but not mortified by the transience of "Things: simply lasting, then / failing to last," as she defines them in the tersely titled poem "Things." In this respect, Kenyon is a Keatsian poet; she wrote several poems about her Romantic predecessor, and like Keats, she attempts to redeem morbidity with a peculiar kind of gusto, one which seeks a quiet annihilation of self-identity through identification with benign things. "At the Spanish Steps in Rome," ends with an elegiac tribute to "the room where Keats died," in which "Everything that was not burned that day / in accordance with the law is there." Kenyon leaves her reader contemplating the ambiguously totemic significance of the dead poet's remaining possessions, now museum pieces for tourists. In other poems, Kenyon leaves us with a more consoling "look at" poetic objects. "Evening at a Country Inn" concludes, after three short stanzas of oblique references to

an unspecified problem, with a proposal for finding solace in absorbing observation:

> I know you are thinking of the accident—
> of picking the slivered glass from his hair.
> Just now a truck loaded with hay
> stopped at the village store to get gas.
> I wish you would look at the hay—
> the beautiful sane and solid bales of hay.

The final line of this poem is compelling because it distributes its aural effects such as alliteration and assonance across its grammatical structure, thereby contriving a temporary and reassuring linguistic orderliness opposed to the unpredictable trauma of the "accident."

Kenyon's desire for control does not discourage her from taking aesthetic chances. Her imagination often finds surprising combinations of words and images when it is startled by painful epiphanies. A humorous juxtaposition can speak volumes: "I am guest in this house. / On the bedside table *Good Housekeeping*, and / *A Nietzsche Reader....*" ("Ice Storm"). More frequently, Kenyon uses sudden disparity to display the darker side of her wit, as with the simile and slant rhyme in the last sentence of "Alone for a Week": "The bed on your side seemed / as wide and flat as Kansas; / your pillow plump, cool, / and allegoric...."

In the "Afterwork" to *Otherwise,* a posthumous collection of new and selected poems, Kenyon's husband, the poet Donald Hall, notes that the "beauty and resonance" of her poetry comes from her practice of "the art of the luminous particular." These particulars include the fragile, homely details of our creaturely existence among other living beings. Pet dogs, nesting rodents, everyday birds, stray insects, neglected peach trees, grasses mowed and unmowed, among many other country things, appear again and again in poems which contemplate our cultivation of a mundane moral order from an inhuman nature.

Kenyon was also devoted to representing in miniature the cycles of seasonal fruition and death, as can be seen in her several variations on Keats' famous ode "To Autumn," as well as her many poems on the other seasons. Kenyon's interest in such natural details was in part derived from her lifelong proximity to rural environments first during her childhood in Ann Arbor, Michigan, then during her adult life in Wilmont, New Hampshire. Her ongoing concentration on natural subjects ultimately enabled her to write, as it did Robert Frost and the English poet Edward Thomas, an impressive body of philosophically minded pastoral poetry that is honest about the pleasures and difficulties of country life while avoiding condescension, sentimentality, and unmerited irony.

In addition to the things of nature, Kenyon was particularly interested in human objects, especially the inglorious remnants of our lives: "yesterday's clothes cohere / humpbacked and headless on the chair" ("Waking in January Before Dawn"). These banal objects often imply stories about persons left out of a poem. For example, in "Litter," the "rattled" poet visits or returns to an unidentified home, and after noticing details such as coffee grounds, dry Cream of Wheat, and dry violets, focuses on "the blue plastic syringe / tips, strips of white tape, / and the backing from bandages / that the EMTs had dropped in haste." The power of this short passage comes from the contrast which its contents make with the preceding things in the poem, and the grim collective presence of the poem's still life in the absence of any direct reference to the suffering person who has been removed from the scene of an unnamed medical emergency.

Kenyon's tone ranges from stoic to melancholic. She may withhold affirmation because the poetic "moment passed, displaced / by others equally equivocal" (Main Street: Titon, New Hampshire"), or she may accept, when it is there, the consolation of "the delicate sadness of dusk" ("The Visit"). All of her poetry, however, is unified by its capable recreation of wonder at how the everyday world fills up and is emptied.

—Gary Roberts

KICKNOSWAY, Faye

Nationality: American. **Born:** Detroit, Michigan, 16 December 1936. **Education:** Wayne State University, B.A. 1967; San Francisco State College (now University), M.A. 1969. **Family:** Married Leonard Kicknosway in 1959 (divorced, 1968); one daughter, one son. **Career:** Instructor in English at Macomb Community College, Warren, Michigan, 1967-68, Michigan Lutheran College, Detroit, 1968, Wayne State University, Detroit, 1970-76, and John Woolman Quaker Boarding School, Nevada City, California, 1977-78; member of faculty of MFA Writing Program, Goddard College, Plainfield, Vermont, 1977, 1978-79; poet-in-residence, Oakland University, Rochester, Michigan, 1978-79, Interlochen, 1979, Auksburg College, 1980, University of Michigan, 1980, and University of Arizona, 1981; visiting professor, University of Hawaii, 1986. Has given poetry readings at high school and universities; artist, exhibiting artwork throughout the United States. **Awards:** Tompkins award, 1965-66; Miles Modern Poetry award, 1966, 1967; Woodrow Wilson fellowship, 1968-69; American Academy of Poets Prize, 1969; Michigan Arts Award, 1980; Michigan Artists grant, 1981; Annual Mid-Michigan Art Show awards, 1980, 1981; National Endowment for the Arts grant, 1985. **Address:** Honolulu, Hawaii, U.S.A.

Publications

Poetry

O. You Can Walk on the Sky? Good, illustrated by the author. Santa Barbara, Capra Press, 1972.
Poem Tree, illustrated by the author. N.p., Red Hanrahan Press, 1973.
A Man Is a Hook. Trouble: Poems, 1964-1973, illustrated by the author. Santa Barbara, Capra Press, 1974.
Second-Chance Man: The Cigarette Poems, illustrated by the author. Grindstone City, Michigan, Alternative Press, 1975.
Nothing Wakes Her, illustrated by the author. N.p., Oyster Press, 1978.
The Cat Approaches, illustrated by Brenda Goodman. Grindstone City, Michigan, Alternative Press, 1977
Bellfish, illustrated by the author. N.p., Oyster Press, 1977.

Asparagus, Asparagus, Ah Sweet Asparagus, illustrated by the author. West Branch, Iowa, Toothpaste Press, 1981.
She Wears Him Fancy in Her Night Braid, illustrated by the author. West Branch, Iowa, Toothpaste Press, 1983.
Who Shall Know Them, illustrated by the author. New York, Viking, 1985.
All These Voices: New and Selected Poems. Minneapolis, Coffee House Press, 1986.
The Violence of Potatoes. N.p., Ridgeway Press, 1990.

*   *   *

Faye Kicknosway approaches poetry as a shamanic process by which the poet can transform herself. She credits poetry with changing her own life. Employing techniques from the Beats and surrealists, her poems contain vivid imagery, earthy subject matter and metaphoric language. She has written in voices ranging from those of her American Indian forebears to those of sexually abused women.

Kicknosway came to poetry by accident. When a friend remarked that one of her letters reminded him of poetry, she decided to investigate what kind of poetry was being written. Inspired by what she read of contemporary verse, Kicknosway returned to school, earned college degrees in English, and began a teaching career.

Her early collections *O. You Can Walk on the Sky? Good* and *A Man Is a Hook. Trouble: Poems, 1964-1973,* focused on feminist themes. Kicknosway then published several signed, limited-edition chapbooks with Toothpaste Press and Alternative Press—both respected fine-edition presses. Representative of these chapbooks is *The Cat Approaches,* a gathering of related poems about felines as savage beast, aloof house pet, and wise mythological creature. The poems are a showcase for Kicknosway's trademark strong visual images: a cat displays "moon-shaped teeth"; a cat's paws are "pomegranates, its claws / tulips."

Kicknosway—a graphic artists who has illustrated many of her own collections and whose works have been exhibited in galleries nationwide—wrote poems based on the photographs of Walker Evans for the book *Who Shall Know Them.* Evans photographed Southern sharecroppers during the Great Depression of the 1930s, his images capturing the suffering his subjects were going through at the time. Kicknosway's poems go beyond mere descriptive reactions to the photographs in question to create surrealistic images inspired by the images. In this manner, she endows the original photographs with an added dimension, expanding the impact of the proud and struggling people they depict.

All These Voices: New and Selected Poems gathers poems from Kicknosway's earlier, limited-edition chapbooks. A large collection exhibiting both Kicknosway's strengths and weaknesses, *All These Voices* includes her early feminist poems, where she employs verse as a weapon against sexism, her surrealistic renderings of domestic situations, and prose poems about her family members.

Compared by some critics to the early works of poets Carolyn Forché and Marge Piercy, Kicknosway's poetry is more raw, less politically doctrinaire, filled with vivid imagery, and charged at its best with a surreal energy. Because so much of her work was printed in limited editions, Kicknosway is perhaps less well known than she deserves to be.

—Denise Wiloch

KILLINGLEY, Siew-Yue

Nationality: Chinese. **Born:** Kuala Lumpur, Malaysia, 17 December 1940; resident of Great Britain since 1968. **Education:** University of Malaya, Kuala Lumpur, B.A. in English (honors) 1963, M.A. in linguistics 1966; School of Oriental and African Studies, University of London, Ph.D. in linguistics 1972. **Family:** Married Dermot Hastings Killingley in 1963; one daughter. **Career:** School mistress at secondary schools in Malaysia, 1961-67; tutor, then visiting lecturer in English, University of Malaya, Kuala Lumpur, 1963-66; tutorial assistant in English, 1970-71, visiting lecturer in speech and professional studies, 1979-81, since 1987, tutor at Center for Continuing Education, University of Newcastle, Newcastle upon Tyne; lecturer, then senior lecturer in English, St. Mary's College of Education, Newcastle upon Tyne, 1972-80. Founding editor, Grevatt & Grevatt, Newcastle upon Tyne, beginning 1981; editor, *British Linguistic Newsletter* of the Linguistic Association of Great Britain, 1991-97. **Awards:** University of Malaya Departmental Book Prize, 1963; Federal Teaching Scholarship, 1961-63; University of London Forlong scholarship, 1968-70; Durham Cathedral Poetry Competition prize, 1982, for *In Sundry Places: Views of Durham Cathedral.* **Address:** Grevatt & Grevatt, 9 Rectory Drive, Newcastle upon Tyne NE3 IXT, England.

PUBLICATIONS

Poetry

Where No Poppies Blow: Poems of War and Conflict. Newcastle upon Tyne, Grevatt & Grevatt, 1983.
In Sundry Places: Views of Durham Cathedral. Newcastle upon Tyne, Grevatt & Grevatt, 1987.
Sound, Speech, and Silence: Selected Poems. Newcastle upon Tyne, Grevatt & Grevatt, 1995.

Other

Internal Structure of the Cantonese Word and General Problems of Word Analysis in Chinese. Kuala Lumpur, University of Malaya Press, 1979.
A Handbook of Hinduism for Teachers, with Dermot Killingley, Vivien Nowicki, Hari Shukla, and David Simmonds. Newcastle upon Tyne, Newcastle upon Tyne Educational Committee, 1980; 2nd ed., Grevatt & Grevatt, 1984.
The Pottery Ring: A Fairy Tale for the Young and Old. Newcastle upon Tyne Community Relations Council, 1981.
The Grammatical Hierarchy of Malayan Cantonese. Newcastle upon Tyne, S.Y. Killingley, 1982.
A Short Glossary of Cantonese Classifiers. Newcastle upon Tyne, Grevatt & Grevatt, 1982.
Hinduism Iconography Pack, with Dermot Killingley (children's textbook). Newcastle upon Tyne, Grevatt & Grevatt, 1984.
A New Look at Cantonese Tones: Five or Six? Newcastle upon Tyne, Grevatt & Grevatt, 1985.
Cantonese. München, LinCom Europa, 1993.
Sanskrit, with Dermot Killingley. München, LinCom Europa, 1995.

Learning to Read Pinyin Romanization and Its Equivalent in Wade Giles: A Practical Course. München, LinCom Europa, forthcoming.

Editor, with Dermot Killingley, *Farewell the Plumed Troop: A Memoir of the Indian Cavalry, 1919-1945,* by Dermot Killingley. Newcastle upon Tyne, Grevatt & Grevatt, 1990.

*

Manuscript Collection: University of Malay Library.

Critical Studies: "Peace Within: Individual Vigilance against Conflicts and Wars" by K.S. Maniam, in *Southeast Asian Review of English* (Kuala Lumpur), 1984; "The Question of Faith in *In Sundry Places: Views of Durham Cathedral*" by Susan Philip, in *Southeast Asian Review of English,* 1989.

Siew-Yue Killingley comments:

My work is drawn from all aspects of human and spiritual experience. I do not set out to write but jot things down fairly quickly if the urge appears, which it does from time to time. I then generally look it over at leisure to see if it is worth keeping and, if so, if it needs some revision. In much of my recent work, flute imagery and technique have become increasingly important.

A recurrent medium that I seem to have chosen is to write an extended cycle of poems, particularly Easter Cycles. Although these cycles contain references to the Nativity and Passion narratives, they are frequently also paradigms of actual human lives and conflicts not directly connected with the Christ story. Each cycle may be regarded as the end result of a set of observations and meditations on the nature of relationships in time, nature, religion, and between human beings. One example is *Song Pageant from Christmas to Easter, with Two Settings.* The two settings (by Percy Lovell) are for unaccompanied mixed voices and have been performed by various choirs in and around Newcastle. I have also give recitation from memory of this sequence. Other examples are *In Sundry Places: Views of Durham Cathedral,* the Easter Cycles contained in *Sound, Speech, and Silence: Selected Poems,* and several other unpublished Easter Cycles.

Early influences in childhood are hard to pin down as I was an eclectic reader, but perhaps Shakespeare, Wordsworth, and Tennyson were important influences as well as listening to Chinese flute music. In adulthood Shakespeare is still important, and among the many other writers I have greatly admired I must list Chaucer, Langland, Herbert, Hopkins, T.S. Eliot, and Norman Nicholson, a local poet.

*   *   *

Siew-Yue Killingley's poetry is at once traditional and innovative, pleasantly familiar and yet surprisingly fresh in both form and content. Much of her poetry draws from the great traditions of the English poetry and alludes to Christian biblical scripture. However, she brings something uniquely new to the poems. Her linguist's knowledge and awareness of language help her achieve a heightened sense of all aspects of language, and enable her to involve the reader in experiencing the power of language in a variety of ways. Her incorporation of childhood experience in Malaya and of her Chinese-Malaysian cultural heritage in her poems add new rhythms to the English language and offer different historical perspectives, thus broadening her range of technical versatility and scope of subject matter.

Some salient features of Killingley's poetry—religious themes, witty humor, penetrating intellect, ingenious turns of phrase, colloquial style, and conventional metric structure with rhymed couplet a dominant form—are reminiscent of the poems by John Donne and George Herbert among others. In her persistent search for meaning of human existence and for an understanding of the human condition through contemplation of Christianity, Killingley shares with Donne and T.S. Eliot a bold erudition and a metaphorical style.

Her employment of fluid and complex controlling images are similar to the functions of conceit in the poems of Donne and the extended analogies in Eliot's poems. Like Donne's conceit and Eliot's analogies which leap from the physical to the spiritual, from the personal to the cosmic and back again, Killingley's images bind the human to the divine, and the immediate to the beyond in many poems, especially those in *Song Pageant from Christmas to Easter, with Two Settings, In Sundry Places: Views of Durham Cathedral* and the three groups of Easter Cycles in *Sound, Speech, and Silence: Selected Poems.* Killingley, however, does not share Donne's kind of restless energy and religious doubt or Eliot's feelings of strain and anxiety. In her affirmation of religious faith, she is more like George Herbert, who expresses spiritual feelings with quiet subtlety and calm gentleness. Despite the overtone of Christianity in their titles, her cycles are not entirely devoted to religious themes. In fact, within her Easter cycles Killingley groups poems with references to biblical narratives together with poems of people's everyday "slices of life."

Her employment of the extended form of the cycle also departs from its traditional function of telling a story or unfolding an event. Rather, her cycles are like collages; they are juxtaposed observations of and meditations on the Nativity, the Passion, and Mary's Lamentation, and their significations in connection to human lives and relationships. The apparently disconnected poems within a cycle are actually linked together by a central theme. The result is a simultaneity of events accompanied by various states of emotions and feelings experienced by different people. The biblical figures and narratives are interwoven with real people and their lives and relationships. By allowing the images and events in the biblical text to mingle with those of the here and now, Killingley gives new life to the biblical figures and narratives while rendering them an intimate part of people's everyday experience.

In her representation of various relationships including those between mother and son, and husband and wife, Killingley often articulates emotions and thoughts from the women's perspectives. In her poems about love between mother and son such as those grouped under the title "Mother and Man," the mother's joy is accompanied by "inexpressible grief" because of her eventual loss of the son, not to death but to the son's sense of some elusive "manhood." In other poems she relates notions of manhood to the glorification of militarism, and eventually war and destruction. In "II. Drinks Party: In Absentia: Monday, 13th April," the poet exposes the illusion of permanence and the inequality between men and women signified by the grammatical paradigm of tense and voice of the English language: "John loves Mary; Mary is loved by John. / These are deceptive bits of the paradigm." Mary did not come to the party with her husband because "her still broken heart was raw / And bitter." The speaker comments: "Better so / Than forced to see herself / As deviant member / Of that two-term closed / Grammatical paradigm."

In other poems of the same cycle Killingley also makes deft use of English grammar to reveal the significations of Biblical images and events, including "Mary's partial view / of her son's last meal and testament, / Timelessly to be finished on the future cross— / And thus expressed in terms of tenselessness" ("Last Meal and Testament: Wednesday, 15th April"). While exploring the grammatical encoding of meanings, she achieves a compactness and conciseness which give depths to her deceptively simple poems and enhance the reader's aesthetic experience of recognition and revelation.

Killingley's bilingual and bicultural background also enriches her poetry. In the poems grouped under the general title "Fragments: Malaya 1942?-1945," she portrays Malaysians' lives under Japanese occupation from a child's perspective. By seeing the surrounding world through the eyes of a child, she subtly and poignantly reveals the brutality of the Japanese rule of terror, and relates its colonialism to the British colonialism in Malaysia with irony. She also employs devices found in Asian languages. In one of these poems, subtitled "Fragments," Killingley transforms and condenses the experience of living under colonization by a foreign power into the child's aural experience of the Japanese language, which Malaysian men were forced to learn. She connects the rhythmic chanting of the Japanese syllabary, "*ka, ki, ku, ke, ko, / sa, si, su, se, so,*" to the explosion of bombs—"those obtrusive / Japanese-British gifts"; the sounds of both are superseded by the "louder percussion" of a plate smashing on the floor, dropped by the "frightened" child. However, the child is not crushed by the power of these intruding and terrifying sounds: the poem ends in the initial five syllables of the Chinese language, asserting resistance in "the poetic cadence of non-speech" to the Japanese colonization.

Killingley is particularly interested in exploring the possibilities of "the poetic cadence of non-speech" in her poetry. In "CND March," she uses monotonously regular meters to enhance the mechanical march of the soldiers, and then deploys an irregular rhythm in the last line of each stanza in imitation of the rhythm of the way in which parading soldiers change step on the march—"one of the many cunningly executed displays," Killingley notes, "which compel our admiration." In accordance with the rhythmic irregularity, the statements of the last lines also subvert those in the proceeding lines.

Sounds and rhythms are not merely a technical aspect of Killingley's poems; they are also a recurring subject matter. In poems such as "Chromatic Notes at Dawn" and "Silence of Snowdrops," she contrasts and interweaves the sounds in nature with the sounds of cities and church bells, as she makes "colours run / Each into other" in poems such "Rose-hips in Allendale" and "Autumn Leaves (near Barnard Castle)." Sometimes, she interprets sounds and silence in spiritual terms as in "Mary (3): Words of Praise" and "Sound's Essence."

Her sensitivity to the variant musical tones and her capacity for achieving various rhythms in part result from her bicultural heritage. She delineates the contours and pauses of the Chinese flute music to illustrate the paradox of sound and silence: "At the end of a phrase the searching flute / Finds a breathing space, pure silence, / And waits. There the song considers / Its course in a pause, then pours out its essence" ("Sound's Essence"). In the eighth poem, "Flute and String: Easter Monday, 4th April" of "Sounds and Voices: Easter Cycle 1994," Killingley captures Christ's suffering on the cross by obliquely connecting the piercing and prolonged pain Christ endures to the "sound discords" from the strings of a musical instrument. In the opening poem "The Master Flautist (For Christinee Ring)" grouped under "Voices and Echoes," she describes with remarkable accuracy and masterful deftness the process and art of making music from a flute, which comes to life in the hands of a master flautist.

Killingley's experiment in new uses of language and new poetic rhythms achieves a simultaneity of multiple events, observations, feelings, and thoughts, embodied in images and sounds, each modifying and coloring the other in startling ways. The combination of the surprisingly colloquial and the strikingly unusual is an important feature of her poetry, which is intricately related to an underlying philosophy about the relationships between sensitivity and spirituality, between imagination and morality. This philosophy can also be found as a shaping force in the works of Herbert, Blake, Hopkins, Wordsworth, and T.S. Eliot, who have in one way or another influenced Killingley's poetry.

Despite its discernable connection to poetry of the past, Siew-Yue Killingley's verse is very much a poetry of her time and place. Perhaps more than any other contemporary poets, she renders Christianity an intimate part of people's lives, and intensifies people's spiritual, sensual, emotional, and moral awareness through the art of her poetry.

—Zhou Xiaojing

KIZER, Carolyn

Nationality: American. **Born:** Spokane, Washington, 10 December 1925. **Education:** Sarah Lawrence College, Bronxville, New York, B.A. 1945; Columbia University, New York, 1945-46; University of Washington, Seattle, 1946-47, 1953-54. **Family:** Married 1) Charles Stimson Bullitt in 1948 (divorced 1954), two daughters and one son; 2) John Marshall Woodbridge in 1975. **Career:** Founding editor, *Poetry Northwest,* Seattle, 1959-65; State Department specialist in Pakistan, 1964-65; director of literary programs, National Endowment for the Arts, 1966-70; lecturer or poet-in-residence, University of North Carolina, Chapel Hill, 1970-74, Washington University, St. Louis, 1971, Barnard College, New York, 1972, Ohio University, Athens, 1974, University of Iowa, Iowa City, 1975, Centre College, Danville, Kentucky, 1979, Eastern Washington University, Cheney, 1980, University of Cincinnati, Ohio, 1981, University of Louisville, Kentucky, 1982, State University of New York, Albany, 1982, Columbia School of Arts, New York, 1982, and Bucknell University, Lewisburg, Pennsylvania, 1983; acting director of graduate writing program, Columbia University, New York, 1972; professor, University of Maryland, College Park, 1976-77; professor of poetry, Stanford University, 1986; senior fellow in the humanities, Princeton University, 1986; professor, University of Arizona, Tucson, 1989, 1990. **Awards:** Masefield prize, 1983; American Academy award, 1985; Pulitzer Prize, 1985; Theodore Roethke prize; Poetry Society of America Frost Medal, 1988. Hon. Doc.: Whitman College, Walla Walla, Washington, 1986; Mills College, Oakland, California, 1989; St. Andrews College, Laurinberg, North Carolina; Washington State University, Pullman. **Address:** 19772 8th Street East, Sonoma, California 95476, U.S.A.

PUBLICATIONS

Poetry

Poems. Portland, Oregon, Portland Art Museum, 1959.
The Ungrateful Garden. Bloomington, Indiana University Press, 1961.
Five Poets of the Pacific Northwest, with others, edited by Robin Skelton. Seattle, University of Washington Press, 1964.
Knock upon Silence. New York, Doubleday, 1965.
Midnight Was My Cry: New and Selected Poems. New York, Doubleday, 1971.
Mermaids in the Basement: Poems for Women. Port Townsend, Washington, Copper Canyon Press, 1984.
Yin. Brockport, New York, Boa, 1984.
The Nearness of You: Poems for Men. Port Townsend, Washington, Copper Canyon Press, 1986.
Harping On: Poems 1985-1995. Port Townsend, Washington, Copper Canyon Press, 1996.

Recording: *An Ear to the Earth,* Watershed, 1977.

Other

Proses: Essays on Poets & Poetry. Port Townsend, Washington, Copper Canyon Press, 1994.
Picking and Chosing: Essays on Prose. Cheney, Washington, Eastern Washington State University, 1995.

Editor, with Elaine Dallman and Barbara Gelpi, *Woman Poet— The West.* Reno, Nevada, Women-in-Literature, 1980.
Editor, *The Essential John Clare.* Hopewell, New Jersey, Ecco Press, 1993.
Editor, *One Hundred Great Poems by Women.* Hopewell, New Jersey, Ecco Press, 1995.

Translator, *Carrying Over.* Port Townsend, Washington, Copper Canyon Press, 1988.

*

Manuscript Collection: Abbott Library, Buffalo, New York.

Critical Studies: *An Answering Music—On the Poetry of Carolyn Kizer,* edited by David Rigsbee, Boston, Ford Brown & Co., 1990.

*   *   *

Carolyn Kizer works in terms of the twinned tensions of life, those central paradoxes so directly felt by women. She poses the problem of the woman poet boldly in her remarkable "A Muse of Water":

We who must act as handmaidens
To our own goddess, turn too fast,
Trip on our hems, to glimpse the muse
Gliding below her lake or sea,
Are left, long-staring after her
Narcissists by necessity...

Mother and muse, Kizer can write tenderly of her own mother, who taught her to love nature even at its most loathsome, "a whole, wild, lost, betrayed and secret life / Among its dens and burrows." Although she has a poem on "Not Writing Poetry about Children," they are everywhere in her work. So are cats, symbols of the female condition, as in "A Widow in Wintertime":

> trying
> To live well enough alone, and not to dream
> Of grappling in the snow, claws plunged in fur,
>
> Or waken in a caterwaul of dying.

The daring and diffidence of womanhood are celebrated in poems of companionship like "For Jan, In Bar Maria." But Kizer's most constant, resonant theme is love and loss, analyzed in detail in the sequence "A Month in Summer." The work ends with a quotation from Basho, and it is in the fatalism of that civilization that Kizer finds a refuge and an artistic remedy for her womanly woes: "'O love long gone, it is raining in our room.' / So I memorize these lines, without salutation, without close." One of the best woman poets around, she is profoundly committed to the process of life, however painful.

The twinned tensions of male and female are explored systematically in later volumes, including *Mermaids in the Basement,* subtitled *Poems for Women,* and its complement, *The Nearness of You: Poems for Men.* Here old and new commingle, while between these works is *Yin,* which includes two wonderful autobiographical reveries, "Running away from Home" and "Exodus." In an era when a shrill feminism threatens to tilt the scales of past injustice, Kizer's view of the sexual universe contains polarity without hostility.

With like thrift Kizer has gathered her translations in *Carrying Over.* Urdu, Macedonian, and Yiddish testify to the diversity of her interests, but there also are translations from the great Tang poet Tu Fu, as well as of the passionate love poems of the Chinese woman poet Shu Ting, born in 1952. Old and young, past and present, yin and yang—Kizer has kept faith with her interests over several decades, and she can say with Chaucer's Criseyde that "I am my owne woman, wel at ese" in the dance of the dualities.

—John Montague

KLEPFISZ, Irena

Nationality: Polish. **Born:** Warsaw, Poland, in 1941; immigrated to Sweden, 1946, and to the United States, 1949. **Education:** City College of New York, B.A. and M.A.; University of Chicago, Ph.D. in English literature. **Career:** Translator-in-residence, Vivo Institute for Jewish Research, New York; teacher of creative writing and woman's studies, Vermont College; currently professor of women's studies and Jewish studies, Michigan State University, Lansing. Founding editor, *Conditions,* 1976-81; editorial consultant, *Bridges: A Journal for Jewish Feminists and Their Friends.* **Address:** c/o Women's Studies Department, Michigan State University, East Lansing, Michigan 48824, U.S.A.

PUBLICATIONS

Poetry

Periods of Stress. N.p., 1975.
Keeper of Accounts. Watertown, Massachusetts, Persephone Press, 1982.
Different Enclosures: The Poetry and Prose of Irena Klepfisz. London, Onlywomen Press, 1985.
A Few Words in the Mother Tongue: Poems Selected and New (1971-1990). Portland, Oregon, Eighth Mountain Press, 1990.

Recording: *Partisans of Vilna,* Chicago, Flying Fish, 1989.

Other

Why Children? N.p., 1980.
A Jewish Woman's Call for Peace: A Handbook for Jewish Women on the Israeli / Palestinian Conflict. N.p, n.d.
Dreams of an Insomniac: Jewish Feminist Essays, Speeches, and Diatribes. Portland, Oregon, Eighth Mountain Press, 1990.

Editor, with Melanie Kay-Kantrowitz, *The Tribe of Dina: A Jewish Woman's Anthology.* Boston, Beacon Press, 1989.

*

Critical Studies: "Stepmother Tongues," by Adrienne Rich, in *Tikkun,* vol. 5, no. 5, September / October 1990; "History Stops for No One," by Adrienne Rich, in *What Is Found There: Notebooks on Poetry and Politics,* New York, Norton, 1993.

* * *

Irena Klepfisz has long been an extremely important presence on the forefront of innovation of poetry in America and in multigenre critical writing of various kinds. Klepfisz's life work thus far has included searing essays probing issues of identity, memory and forgetting, history and cultural politics, as well as translations of Yiddish writers into English. Being that most of her poetry has been published by relatively small presses, the influence of her writing and scholarship has been, to some extent, overlooked by mainstream critics and, perhaps equally interestingly, by the more self-consciously avant-garde schools of writing. Her work does not assimilate itself neatly into any particular school of writing. Still, Klepfisz's poetry entails a poetics of teaching and translation, and of definition, stemming from a Jewish and lesbian-feminist consciousness that is, in her own words: "Alienated. Threatened. Individual. Defiant." Her poems defiantly challenge the enclosure of experience, the labor of writing, and memory and silence in the wake of Theodor Adorno's monumental statement that "after Auschwitz, to write a poem is barbaric."

While her most experimental poetry and essays have been combinations of Yiddish and English, she is, perhaps ironically, a quintessentially American writer in that her poetry project has been to address herself to the contradictions, intersections, and marginalizations of her identity as an American, as the daughter of working-class socialists, as an immigrant from Poland, as a secular Jew, as a Holocaust survivor, as a feminist, as a lesbian, as a childless woman, and as an activist on the left wing of American and international social critique.

Since, as Adrienne Rich has written in her essay "History Stops for No One," in *What Is Found There: Notebooks on Poetry and Politics,* "historical necessity has made [Klepfisz] the kind of poet she is," biographical details of the poet's life are important. Klepfisz's life, observes Rich, "began with almost total loss—of family, community, culture, country, language," her poetry is a "cultural re-creation" that comes out of the genocide of the Holocaust, known in Yiddish as *der khurbn,* a word that Klepfisz highlights as important because it "resonates with *yidishe geschikte*—Jewish history—linking the events of World War II with *der erste and tsveyster khurbn,* the First and Second Destruction (of the Temple)." Born in 1941 in Nazi-occupied Warsaw, Klepfisz's father and mother were secular Jews and members of the Jewish Bund, a socialist organization and resistance movement of the urban Jewish working class that was influential primarily in Eastern Europe and Russia. Her father, after being shot at and wounded but amazingly surviving a jump from the train transporting him from the Warsaw Ghetto to Treblinka, lived, only to be later killed in an air raid attack intended to annihilate Jews during the Warsaw Ghetto Uprising in 1943. Klepfisz was then only two years old. Her mother had blond hair and blue eyes and could "pass" as a gentile; because of this she was able to obtain Aryan identity papers and, with young Irena, escape to Warsaw, there to be hidden by Polish peasants. After the war, Klepfisz and her mother immigrated to Sweden and then to the United States, when Klepfisz was eight years old.

The languages of Klepfisz's cultural experience and the memories that those languages, those "mother tongue[s]," enclosed are subject to profound and fertile contradictions and reconstructions in her poetry. "I was taught that Yiddish is *mame-loshn,* mother tongue, the language of the Jews, the medium through which Jewish culture and politics are to be transmitted. *Mame-loshn* was the medium that gave all the tenets which I'd been taught form and substance. I internalized this and fought fiercely with anyone who disputed these facts" wrote Klepfisz in her 1989 essay "Secular Jewish Identity: *Yidishkayt* in America." But she goes on to observe "Yiddish was not my *mame-loshn.* Because I was born during the war and my mother and I were passing as Poles, Polish became my first language. I began writing in Polish. In 1946, my mother and I immigrated to Sweden, where we lived for the next three years. I attended school and learned to read, write and speak Swedish. At home I continued speaking Polish though I heard and understood the Yiddish of other DPs [Displaced Persons] living in our communal house. And then we came to America. I began speaking English and ever so slowly over the years, started to think, to dream in English. Eventually, English was the language I spoke with my mother."

Significantly, the Yiddish Klepfisz now uses in her poetic work and essays is "not the *mame-loshn* I would have used had I been born into a different Poland." Nor is it the "Anglicized Yiddish of American Jews." Instead, it is a "somewhat schooled, timid, sometimes fragmented Yiddish, insecure and embarrassed by its formality, its present starkness," as the poet notes in *The Tribe of Dina.* For Klepfisz, the question has always been, as she writes in her poem "*Di rayze aheym* / The Journey Home" (*A Few Words in the Mother Tongue, Poems Selected and New: [1971-1991]*): "*In der fremd* / Among stranger / *Vi azoy?* / how / she wonders / should I speak / *Velkhe verter* / which words / should I use / *in der fremd* / among strangers?"

For Klepfisz, language is indelibly encrusted in place and in a sense of mastery over circumstance. In her prose poem "*Bashert,*"

Yiddish for (pre)destined or fated, she approaches terrifying memories of her and her mother's isolation as refugees hiding in Poland during 1944, and then jumps to memories of her sense of isolation and remove from learned endeavors and scholarship as a student at the University of Chicago in 1964. She recounts her continued obsession with "another time, another place," and as she grapples with the suicide of a fellow survivor, long after the war, she asks, "Are there moments in history which cannot be transcended, but which act like time warps, permanently trapping all who are touched should have happened in 1944 in Poland and didn't, must it happen how? In 1964? In Chicago? Or can history be tricked and cheated?" She sees 1964 Chicago and "this alien country" of America not just as a geographical place but as an era in which she is rooted with great presence and with the privilege of perspective denied to the truly and indelibly displaced. Klepfisz records the "common rubble in the streets" of Chicago and directs her attention to "the American hollowness in which I walk calmly day and night as I continue my life." In "lines for food stamps, for jobs and a bed to sleep in" Klepfisz chronicles "A Holocaust without smoke."

Further into the poem, drawing on her experiences as a teacher of Black and Hispanic remedial English students in Brooklyn in 1971, Klepfisz continues her testimony in "*Bashert*" to interior and exterior "silent mass migration. Relocation." She layers onto her experience memories of another continent, the North American politics of race and class, and the embeddedness of these politics in teaching and learning of standard English:

> "They are here because they have not met the minimum standards of this college[...]Subject
> and verbal agreement. Sentence fragments. Pronoun reference. Vocabulary building.
> Paragraph organization. Topic sentence. Reading comprehension. Study skills.
> Discipline. All this to catch up, or as one student said to me, his eyes earnest: "I want to
> write so that when I go for a job they won't think I'm lazy."

What Klepfisz describes is a community of people displaced into a standard language that is at once a choice of survival and a coercion or "discipline" that becomes a means of earning distinctions between people and cultures. This is the "common rubble" of the destruction of cultures in Europe and America.

Over and above being a witness to history and her own "equidistan[ce] from two continents" Klepfisz records the epic scale of human struggle against predestined inequalities and erasures of what is alien, to dominate practices of understanding, social myths, historical records. As she writes in the final section of the serial poem "Cherry Plain: I have become a keeper of accounts." Klepfisz both resists and embraces the various stereotypes of the Jews, her "despised ancestors" as "inhuman usurers and dusty pawnbrokers," "keepers of accounts." She is "scrupulously accurate. I keep track of all distinctions. Between past and present. Pain and pleasure. Living and surviving. Resistance and capitulation. Will and circumstances. Between life and death."

In these poems, and in much of her other work, she probes beyond the suppression of female artistic talent in the feminized contexts of the domestic, clerical work, proofreading, copying, typing, correcting, recording, receptionist work. In "Work Sonnets with Notes and a Monologue about a Dialogue" (*A Few Words in* the *Mother Tongue)* she writes of a woman who "did not know how to use / the self erasing IBM not the special squeezer / to squeeze in the words she was the artist type," a poem about the gender narratives of droning female work appropriated by men, of type "some letters that had to get out and he said" while the artistic work of women is a "dream yearning / to form / through how much emptiness / must it speed / for how many centuries."

Hers is a poetry of precision, of great care to page space, punctuation, capitalization, translation, and length of line. This is a poetry, as Klepfisz writes in *Di Rayze aheym* / The Journey Home, where "All is present. / The shadows of the past / fall elsewhere." In her works incorporating Yiddish, she at once teaches and translates the language by spatial juxtapositions with the English and yet the "shadow" of the untranslatable in the past, and in mother tongues, persists in the "crowded darkness / *fur ir zikorn* / of her memory." This is a survivor poetry of life and death testimony, resistance and refusal to forget "distinctions" that memory, "aesthetic distance," and brute will and power can both retrieve and erase.

—Jenny Gough

KOGAWA, Joy

Nationality: Canadian. **Born:** Vancouver, British Columbia, 6 June 1935. **Family:** One son and one daughter. **Awards:** Books in Canada First Novel award, 1981, Canadian Authors Association Book of the Year award, Before Columbus Foundation American Book award, and American Library Association Notable Book designation, all 1982, all for *Obasan;* Periodical Distributors' Best Paperback Fiction award, 1983. D.L.: University of Lethbridge, 1991; Simon Frazer University, 1993. D. Litt.: University of Guelph, 1992. **Member:** Order of Canada, 1986. **Address:** 845 Semlin Dr., Vancouver, British Columbia V5L 4J6, Canada.

PUBLICATIONS

Poetry

The Splintered Moon. St. John, University of New Brunswick, 1967.
A Choice of Dreams. Toronto, McClelland & Stewart, 1977.
Jericho Road. Toronto, McClelland & Stewart, 1977.
Woman in the Woods. Oakville, Ontario, Mosaic Press, 1985.

Novels

Obasan. Toronto, Lester & Orphen Dennys, 1981; New York, Anchor, 1994.
Itsuka. Toronto, Viking Canada, 1992; revised edition, New York, Anchor, 1993.
The Rain Ascends. Toronto, Knopf, 1995.

For Children

Naomi's Road, illustrated by Matt Gould. Toronto, Oxford University Press, 1986.

*

Critical Studies: "Witnessing the Japanese Canadian Experience in World War II: Processual Structure, Symbolism, and Irony in Joy Kogawa's *Obasan*" by Cheng Lok Chua in *Reading the Literatures of Asian America,* edited by Amy Ling, and others, Philadelphia, Temple University Press, 1992; *Articulate Silences: Hisaye Yamamoto, Maxine Hong Kingston, Joy Kogawa* by King-Kok Cheung, Ithaca, Cornell University Press, 1993; interview with Janice Williamson in *Sounding Differences: Conversations with 17 Canadian Women Writers,* Toronto, University of Toronto Press, 1993; "Canadian Women of Color in the New World Order: Marlene Nourbese Philip, Joy Kogawa, and Beatrice Culleton Fight Their Way Home" by Heather Zwicker, in *Canadian Women Writing Fiction,* edited by Mickey Pearlman, Jackson, University Press of Mississippi, 1993; interview with Jeanne Delbaere in *Kunapipi,* vol. 16, no. 1, 1994; "Memory and the Matrix of History: Joy Kogawa's *Obasan* and Toni Morrison's *Beloved*" by Gurleen Grewal, in *Memory and Cultural Politics: New Essays in American Ethnic Literatures,* edited by Robert Hogan and others, Boston, North Eastern University Press, 1996.

*   *   *

Joy Kogawa is a Canadian writer of Japanese origin who is probably better known as the author of the novel *Obasan* than as a poet. Yet most of her verse has the hallmark of great poetry: it elicits a sense of wondering surprise at unexpected combinations of words or at clinching assonances that suggest emotions without spelling them out. Her poems manage to tell stories without ever slipping into the narrative mode. Even confronted by the most blatant injustices, she usually remains detached enough to instill humour in her indictment.

Too much direct exposure may in fact be the weakness of her second collection, *Jericho Road,* in which, in spite of distancing use of the third person and ample employment of metaphors, the feelings expressed are too raw. This is the case in "Blue Eels," which records a dream in which the rampant blue eels that "reared and / lurched like terrible horses" are equated with "our cold blue torrents of words / aggressive as metal." This stricture, however, does not apply equally to all poems in the collection. In "The Wedlocked," for instance, her bitterness towards marriage is couched in witty allusions "Jack and Mrs. Sprat / one lean one fat" and in images that are powerfully evocative of the presence of death in the rites of life, recalling Blake's famous line "and blights with plagues the Marriage hearse":

> they seeded their bed
> with promise and prayer
> the priest and kneeling congregation
> covered them with earth
> or
> with porcelain smiles with
> carved conversations they
> administered their marriage they
> executed their lives

In the last, longer poem, "Poem for Wednesday," the heart-rending dislocation of grief is reflected in the dislocation of syntax:

> but it's dark here Wednesday
> never comes my hands uprooted my
> hands crumbling I'll put down this

empty no longer with me river this
white breeze in a soundless
forest without trees.

This echoes, in the minor key of desolation, the rustling memories of past happiness, poured out in a flight of lyricism reminiscent of Dylan Thomas:

is it enough that we once
luminous yellow and green after rain
met secret elm, secret willow, each
tree breeze-shaped, our leaves
riotous with light . . .

Her writing is laced with the kind of biblical allusions that used to not require any particular gloss in countries with a Protestant background: Samson and the pillars to be pulled down, David and Bathsheba, Daniel in the fiery furnace, Abraham sacrificing Isaac, Jonah not warning Nineveh. She also plays upon nursery rhyme echoes, as in this poem in which she destroys a "strange green shoot" which was "leafing underground foliage" and is left with dull greyness:

Mistress Wary and contrary
how does these days
the garden grow?

With dust and ash
with ash and dust
and fine white fragile bones.

The Japanese influence is tenuous. I am not even sure that we can refer to her sense of concision and indirection as specifically oriental. Her poem "On Hearing Japanese Haiku" is delicately suggestive of a strand in her which belongs to that tradition, but no more:

Throat blossoms to sounds
Sama zama no mono
Stirrings in the sandy fibres of my flesh
And these ancient fingers
Gardening

The first half of her first collection, *A Choice of Dreams*, consists of poems reporting her impressions while she spent several months with relatives in Japan. It opens and closes with tributes. The first poem tells of her going back to the place where her ancestors are buried, "To the high hillside grave of my ancestors," where she perceives "the hiddenness [stretching] beyond my reach" and they greet each other through smiles and tears ("the pebbles that melt through my eyes"). The last poem, "Trunk in the Attic," takes her back to her own mother, absorbed "in some vaguely remembered girlhood / Of apple-shaped pears and sweet chestnuts / And utterly unabandoned babies," and thus providing a lasting living link with those islands "beyond seas beyond seas." Some of her impressions are humourously critical, as when she describes the effect of the Tokyo smog:

Jerky conversation, I cut the automatic
And turn to manual breathing, watch the
Red alert in my temple and
Try to adjust,

when she reflects in a chaotic language the confusion of the rush hour in Tokyo, when she points to the contrast between some elaborate rituals and harsh daily realities (in "Day of the Bride"), when she pictures the helpless attempts of Japanese girls to look like "Caucasian mannequins" ("Her thick black hair rustling / Under the peroxide rain"), or when she becomes entangled in the intricacies of the no-win game of "Gift Giving and Obligation" ("Walk away burdened with an obligation / To continue exchanging for eternity / Complete with rituals of accumulating thankfulness"). Sometimes the comic element is provided by outsiders—as in the case of the Australian at the Tourist Information centre who "bellows like a baby ox / Lost in a forest of fragility." At times strange habits such as the *ofuro* or public bath where "We merge as one warm vat / Of boiled jelly fish" have such overwhelmingly positive aspects that she wishes they could be exported. Other poems, however, are much too heavy to accommodate humour. "Hiroshima Exit" is trapped in the impossible task of assessing responsibilities

In round round rooms of our wanderings
Victims and victimizers in circular flight
Fact pursuing fact
Warning leaflets still drip down
On soil heavy with flames,
Black rain, footsteps, witnessings.

Her empathy with the animal world is evident in a number of pieces. In "The Chicken Killing" she becomes the chicken "dangling feet first from the sky," and she is the hooked fish at the "Jindaiji Temple Fishing Pond." Her love of cats leads to delightfully accurate, almost pornographic observation ("Tom Cat"):

He shakes down fresh alleys
To a new pet shop kitten
The dry water velvet cling
Pussy cat fur of her
Curling round his thirsty skin
Raised in an alley of alternatives

There are poems of great sensuality in the second section called "Forest Creatures," for instance, "Beach Poem" ("Walking in warm knee deep water / Watching tiny waves inside of waves") and "Waterfall" ("the pupils of your eyes / Were as large as Easter morning" with the amazed wonder of resurrection, which leads to the last lines: "we / Heard the sound of sunrise / The flesh sound of word").

The last section (titled "The Waiting Room") is heavy with the decision to have an abortion, yet still full of light tenderness, and of a passionate love for the unborn child couched in terms reminiscent of Elizabethan tragedies:

We are together in this deep soft trap
This well, this long falling I
Tripped the latch with my own hand
I have not stumbled I have rushed
Headlong towards the breakers
Carrying you tossing you from cliffs.

Woman in the Woods was published eleven years after *A Choice of Dreams.* In some regards it returns to motifs already present in *Jericho Road,* but most of the time they are refined away from

Jericho Road, but most of the time they are refined away from the nakedness of the 1977 collection. The image used for the cover has different connotations too. While the image on *Jericho Road* (probably some bird's light tripping on iced snow or sand) calls up the tired curves of an eroded rock, the Japanese woodcut of leaning trees on *Woman in the Woods* suggests interrelation and living abundance as well as the threatening shadows of complexities. In spite of recurrent concern with death and separation, the lighter tone is indicated in the repeated use of poems in the form of songs. The book begins with a "Bird Song" in which we are birds "weaned on the air" praying "to rise to sunlight" and reminded of our mortality by bleached bones that sing "inaudible songs." It ends with a "Water Song" in which fins turn into wings, fish turn into triumphantly flying birds. Close to these "songs" are a number of poems written in short tripping lines, which have the word "Poem" in their titles, as in a children's book. These include "Garden Poem" (very much about male dominance), "Ant and Bee Poem" (about the trickiness of words such as love), "Grief Poem" (pointing to the delicate beauty of an icicle shining in the sun in spite of utter desolation), "Wind Poem" (about the exhilaration of a high wind on a summer night), "Coaldale Poem" (about the Puritan reprobation of those who live in the bleak little town in Alberta where her mother settled), or "Fish Poem" (about little fish escaping hooks and nets, "safe and swift as prayer"). There is a sense in which the whole collection can be read as intended for children, in spite of the violence of the parting poems, such as "She has fled" (in which the man who remains alone looks at "two small kites" "seeking / strings"), "To Wash Away the Green" (with children painting grief away into warm colors), or "The Morning She Leaves" (which plays on the two images of dark blue pigeons and dead branches). Violence and grief are elements that have to be acknowledged. Just as children have to know about how Canadian citizens of Japanese descent were treated during World War II ("Road Building by Pick Axe").

Kogawa's art is eminently versatile. She is at her best when she trims her words and lights upon a short suggestive metaphor, as in these four lines about death:

One moment we attend
the brain's singing
then
we are the song.

—Christine Pagnoulle

KRAMER, Lotte (Karoline)

Nationality: British. **Born:** Lotte Karoline Wertheimer, in Mainz, Germany, 22 October 1923. **Family:** Married Frederic Kramer in 1943; one son. **Career:** Laundry hand, Berkhamsted, Hertfordshire, 1939-40, and Hampton, Middlesex, 1943-47; lady's companion, Oxford, 1940-43; dress shop assistant, Richmond, Surrey, 1953-57; voluntary worker, Peterborough Museum, 1977—. Also a painter: several individual exhibitions. **Member:** Writers in Schools, East Anglia, 1982—. **Address:** 4 Apsley Way, Longthorpe, Peterborough, Cambridgeshire PE3 9NE, England.

PUBLICATIONS

Poetry

Scrolls. Richmond, Surrey, Keepsake Press, 1979.
Ice-Break. Peterborough, Cambridgeshire, Annakinn, 1980.
Family Arrivals. Hatch End, Middlesex, Poet & Printer, 1981.
A Lifelong House. Frome, Somerset, Hippopotamus Press, 1983.
The Shoemaker's Wife and Other Poems. Frome, Somerset, Hippopotamus Press, 1987.
The Desecration of Trees. Frome, Somerset, Hippopotamus Press, 1994.
Earthquake and Other Poems. Ware, Hertfordshire, Rockingham Press, 1994.
Selected New Poems, 1980-1997. Ware, Hertfordshire, Rockingham Press, 1997.

*

Critical Studies: "The Poetry of Lotte Kramer" by Karin Andrews, in *Agenda* (London), vol. 22, no. 2, summer 1984, and *Outposts* (Frome, Somerset), no. 155, winter 1987; "Lotte Kramer" by George Szirtes, in *Eastword,* vol. 13, no. 4, April 1984; "The Dark Side of History" by Carol Rumens, in *Jewish Chronicle* (London), 14 September 1984; "Rallying Calls and Laments" by Ruth Fainlight, in *Jewish Quarterly* (London), vol. 34, no. 4, 1987; "Lotte Kramer" by Laurence Sail, in *Stand* (London), vol. 29, no. 2, spring 1988; "Heavy with Baggage from Home" by Gerda Cohen, in *Jewish Chronicle* (London), 12 March 1993; "Singer of Our Song" by Gerda Mayer, in *AJR* (London), February 1993; "Remember Us" by Stella Stoker, in *Orbis,* no. 94, autumn 1994; "How Shall We Sing the Lord's Song in a Strange Land" by Edward Storey, in *Month* (London), September / October 1994; "Lotte Kramer" by Wanda Barford, in *Jewish Chronicle* (London), 28 October 1994.

Lotte Kramer comments:

I began to write poetry rather late in life, facing up to traumatic childhood experiences in Nazi Germany after 35 years. Much of my work deals with that subject and its aftermath, with the dualism inevitably connected with it. But I also write about other subjects, with the world around me as immediate and in a wider sense. I also translate some German poetry, especially Rilke, some of which is published in my books.

*   *   *

I encountered Lotte Kramer's poetry in her collection, *Ice-Break,* in a batch of publications for review and remember how it shone out like a bright beacon among the others. *Ice-Break* contained some beautifully observed poems. There was "Sunday Morning," in which her painter's eye was exercised with telling effect. In other poems lines such as "the old town ached in buckled houses" and "Land falls from us / In long stiff tongues that grip the sky" were evidence of the same eye.

But Kramer's talent was not confined to the visual. In *Ice-Break* she captured mood and atmosphere just as acutely, as demonstrated in "Aspects of Home," where she writes of "This quietness that confiscates all else."

Since then Kramer has published additional collections in which she has consolidated her achievement. In *The Shoemaker's Wife* she demonstrates sharp perception and pursues her ability to produce meticulously crafted poems. In the poem "Pavement Cafe" we find her observing a couple: "She pours / The rhythm of her talk through wrists / and finger tips." Another poem conjures November with a fine choice of detail: "This auburn change of tired leaves / When light turns inward." A bag of cherries or the contents of an old shoe box may evoke memories.

Kramer's is a gentle talent that succeeds by its meticulousness in the choice and ordering of detail. At its best it can conjure a vignette in which the visual clarity is informed by mood and emotion, as, for example, in "Winter Appeasement," where

> She moves
> In her own rhythm, her doubt
> Bruising the silence,
>
> Rehearsing
> The ghosts of her winter
> Appeasement.

With Kramer, as with her contemporary Gerda Mayer (who also went to England as a child refugee in 1939), it is as if the passing years have gradually unlocked memories that had been quietly held in abeyance as too painful or too deep. Thus, in Kramer's collection *Family Arrivals* we find poems with titles such as "Invocation Of My Father," "The Red Cross Telegram," "Jewish Cemetery in Prague," and "Deportation" that convey powerful and remarkably disciplined expressions of deep-rooted memories and emotions:

> I want to lie with them in unknown graves
> And bury freedom of indulgent years.
> There is no judge
> To hear and end their cause.

It is as if Kramer had been waiting to perfect her art until she was able to cope with such profoundly disturbing subject matter. The beautifully controlled expression of these poems makes them the more potent.

—John Cotton

KUMIN, Maxine

Nationality: American. **Born:** Maxine Winokur, in Philadelphia, Pennsylvania, June 1925. **Education:** Radcliffe College, Cambridge, Massachusetts, A.B. 1946, M.A. 1948. **Family:** Married Victor M. Kumin in 1946; two daughters and one son. **Career:** Instructor, 1958-61, and lecturer in English, 1965-68, Tufts University, Medford, Massachusetts; lecturer, Newton College of the Sacred Heart, Massachusetts, 1971; visiting lecturer/professor/writer, University of Massachusetts, Amherst, 1972; Columbia University, New York, spring 1975; Brandeis University, Waltham, Massachusetts, fall 1975; Princeton University, New Jersey, spring 1977, 1979, 1982; Washington University, St. Louis, 1977; Randolph-Macon Women's College, Lynchburg, Virginia, 1978; Bucknell University, Lewisburg, Pennsylvania, 1983; Massachusetts Institute of Technology, Cambridge, 1984; Atlantic Center for the Arts, New Smyrna Beach, Florida, winter 1984; Univer-

sity of Miami (Florida), spring 1995; Pitzer College, Claremont, California, spring 1996. McGee Professor of Writing, Davidson College, Davidson, North Carolina, spring 1997. Poetry Consultant, Library of Congress, Washington, D.C., 1981-82. Woodrow Wilson visiting fellow, 1979—. Scholar, 1961-63, and officer, 1972—, Society of Fellows, Radcliffe Institute, Cambridge, Massachusetts. **Awards:** Lowell Mason Palmer award, 1960; National Endowment for the Arts grant, 1966; National Council on the Arts fellowship, 1967; William Marion Reedy award, 1968; Eunice Tietjens memorial prize (*Poetry,* Chicago), 1972; Pulitzer Prize, 1973; Radcliffe College award, 1978; American Academy award, 1980; Academy of American Poets fellowship, 1985; Levinson award, 1987; Sarah Joseph Hale award, 1992; Poets' Prize for *Looking for Luck,* 1994; Aiken Taylor Poetry Prize, 1995; Harvard Graduating School of Arts and Sciences Centennial Award, 1996. Honorary degrees: Centre College, Danville, Kentucky, 1976; Davis and Elkins College, Elkins, West Virginia, 1977; Regis College, Weston, Massachusetts, 1979; New England College, Henniker, New Hampshire, 1982; Claremont Graduate School, California, 1983; University of New Hampshire, Durham, 1984. **Member:** Bread Loaf Writers Conference staff, 1969-71, 1973, 1975, and 1977; Sewanee Writers' Conference staff, 1993, 1994. **Agent:** Curtis Brown, 10 Astor Place, New York, New York 10003. **Address:** 40 Hariman Lane, Warner, New Hampshire 03278, U.S.A.

PUBLICATIONS

Poetry

Halfway. New York, Holt Rinehart, 1961.
The Privilege. New York, Harper, 1965.
The Nightmare Factory. New York, Harper, 1970.
Up Country: Poems of New England, New and Selected. New York, Harper, 1972.
House, Bridge, Fountain, Gate. New York, Viking, 1975.
The Retrieval System. New York, Viking, 1978; London, Penguin, 1979.
Our Ground Time Here Will Be Brief. New York, Viking, 1982.
Closing the Ring. Lewisburg, Pennsylvania, Press of Appletree Alley, 1984.
The Long Approach. New York, Viking, 1985.
Nurture. New York, Viking, 1989.
Looking for Luck. New York, Norton, 1992.
Connecting the Dots. New York, Norton, 1996.
Selected Poems 1960-1990. New York, Norton, 1997.

Recording: *Progress Report,* Watershed, 1976.

Novels

Through Dooms of Love. New York, Harper, 1965; as *A Daughter and Her Loves,* London, Gollancz, 1965.
The Passions of Uxport. New York, Harper, 1968.
The Abduction. New York, Harper, 1971.
The Designated Heir. New York, Viking, 1974.

Short Stories

Why Can't We Live Together like Civilized Human Beings? New York, Viking Press, 1982.

Other

In Deep: Country Essays. New York, Viking, 1987.
To Make a Prairie: Essays on Poets, Poetry, and Country Living. Ann Arbor, University of Michigan Press, 1979.
Women, Animals, and Vegetables: Essays and Stories. New York, Norton, 1994.

Editor, *Rain,* by William Carpenter. Boston, Northeastern University Press, 1985.

Other (for children)

Sebastian and the Dragon. New York, Putnam, 1960.
Spring Things. New York, Putnam, 1961.
Summer Story. New York, Putnam, 1961.
Follow the Fall. New York, Putnam, 1961.
A Winter Friend. New York, Putnam, 1961.
Mittens in May. New York, Putnam, 1962.
No One Writes a Letter to the Snail. New York, Putnam, 1962.
Archibald the Traveling Poodle. New York, Putnam, 1963.
Eggs of Things, with Anne Sexton. New York, Putnam, 1963.
More Eggs of Things, with Anne Sexton. New York, Putnam, 1964.
Speedy Digs Downside Up. New York, Putnam, 1964.
The Beach before Breakfast. New York, Putnam, 1964.
Paul Bunyan. New York, Putnam, 1966.
Faraway Farm. New York, Norton, 1967.
The Wonderful Babies of 1809 and Other Years. New York, Putnam, 1968.
When Grandmother Was Young. New York, Putnam, 1969.
When Mother Was Young. New York Putnam, 1970.
When Great Grandmother Was Young. New York, Putnam, 1971.
Joey and the Birthday Present, with Anne Sexton. New York, McGraw Hill, 1971.
The Wizard's Tears, with Anne Sexton. New York, McGraw Hill, 1975.
What Color Is Caesar? New York, McGraw Hill, 1978.
The Microscope. New York, Harper, 1984.

*

Manuscript Collection: Bienecke Library, Yale University, New Haven, Connecticut.

Critical Studies: "The Art of Maxine Kumin" by John Ciardi, in *Saturday Review* (Washington, D.C.), 25 March 1972; *"Past Halfway: The Retrieval System* by Maxine Kumin" by Sybil Estess, in *Iowa Review* (Iowa City), vol. 10, no. 4, 1979; "Maxine Kumin's Survival" by Philip Booth, in *American Poetry Review* (Philadelphia), vol. 7, no. 6, November-December 1981; *Telling the Barn Swallow: Poets on the Poetry of Maxine Kumin* edited by Emily Grosholz, University Press of New England, 1997.

*   *   *

Maxine Kumin, who jokingly has referred to herself, the Earth Motherly nature poet, as "Roberta Frost," at first may seem to possess a very simple sense of the physical world. But she is a metaphysician too. Her best collection of poems, *The Retrieval System,* explores ideas which make the notion of death acceptable. Much has been made of her close friendship with Anne Sex-

ton, but its literary importance probably resides in forcing Kumin to leap out of her comfortable physical world of family and benevolent nature into a craggier world and personality, more like that of the curmudgeon Robert Frost.

Earth mythology is always about use and misuse. Thus the concerns of Kumin, as a person, become very central to the concerns of any twentieth-century citizen of the world—how can we survive the autumn, the "fall" of our misused earth? In "Grappling in the Central Blue," Kumin offers this ongoing theme in her poetry:

> Let us eat of the inland oyster.
> Let its fragrance intoxicate us
> into almost believing
> that staying on is possible
> again this year in
> benevolent blue October.

Over the years some of Kumin's best poems have concerned her children and her Demeter-like role, grieving the loss of them as they grow up, but what is most compelling is that she never accepts the impossibility of return, even if it be through magic or metaphysics. Body is as transformable as any other matter. She shows in "Seeing The Bones" her willingness to accept the pain of evolution,

> This year again the bruise-colored oak
> hangs on eating my heart out
> with its slow change,

but she insists on myth and magic, which make return / retrieval / reincarnation possible, as she concludes the poem with the ritual of reconstructing her lost daughter from old artifacts,

> I do the same things day by day.
> They steady me against the wrong turn,
> ...Working backward I reconstruct
> you.

The charm with which Kumin works out her belief in worldly return is captured in many poems, such as "The Retrieval System" ("It begins with my dog, now dead, who all his long life / carried about in his head the brown eyes of my father"). In a typical and lovely ("Soft as beetpulp, the cover / of this ancient Baedeker.") Kumin poem, "On Reading an Old Baedeker in Schloss Leopoldskron," she speaks of the ongoingness of the world, both people and "swans / in their ninetieth generation," returning often, as in "Primtivism Exhibit," to her "retrieval system" theme:

> Longest I look at the dread
> dog fetish, whose spiky back
> is built of rusty razorblades
> that World War II GI's let drop
> on atolls in the South Pacific
> they were securing from the Japs
> who did not shave, but only plucked
> stray hairs from chin and jaw.
> I like the way he makes a funk-
> y art out of cosmetic junk
> standing the cutting edge of old steel
> up straight to say, *World, get off my back.*

Kumin believes in the animal species and sees the human animal as having a chance for survival (from "In the Park"):

> You have forty-nine days between
> death and rebirth if you're a Buddhist.
> Even the smallest soul could swim
> the English Channel in that time

The best of Kumin's poems, like this one, always maintain a cool humor and charm. In addition to her rich and smooth wit, Kumin's greatest skill is to make images, wonderful images, that turn into big metaphors. Playing with dualities, and manipulating everyday language so that it works with complexity of idea and pattern, she is always invoking the irony which comes out of Dionysian tragedy. A few lines from "Marianne, My Mother, and Me" define Kumin's poetry and her life: "We / must be as clear as our natural reticence / will allow." The one thing that is clear throughout her substantial body of work is that she believes survival is possible, if only through the proper use of the imagination to retrieve those things which are loved well enough.

—Diane Wakoski

KYGER, Joanne

Nationality: American. **Born:** Vallejo, California, 19 November 1934. **Education:** Santa Barbara City College, California, 1952-56. **Family:** Married 1) Gary Snyder in 1960 (divorced 1965); 2) John Boyce in 1966 (died 1972). **Career:** Lived in Japan, 1960-64; performer and poet in experimental television project, 1967-68. **Awards:** National Endowment for the Arts grant, 1968. **Address:** c/o E.P. Dutton Inc., 375 Hudson Street, New York, New York 10014, U.S.A.

PUBLICATIONS

Poetry

The Tapestry and the Web. San Francisco, Four Seasons, 1965.
The Fool in April. San Francisco, Coyote, 1966.
Places to Go. Los Angeles, Black Sparrow Press, 1970.
Joanne. New York, Angel Hair, 1970.
Desecheo Notebook. Berkeley, California, Arif Press, 1971.
Trip Out and Fall Back. Berkeley, California, Arif Press, 1974.
All This Every Day. Bolinas, California, Big Sky, 1975.
Up My Coast / Sulla mia costa. Melano, Switzerland, Caos Press, 1978; Point Reyes, California, Floating Island, 1981.
The Wonderful Focus of You. Calais, Vermont, Z Press, 1980.
Mexico Blondé. Bolinas, California, Evergreen Press, 1981.
Going On: Selected Poems 1958-1980, edited by Robert Creeley. New York, Dutton, 1983.
Man: Two Poems (broadside). Pacifica, California, Big Bridge Press, 1988.
The Phone Is Constantly Busy to You (broadside). Lawrence, Kansas, Tansy Press, 1989.
Just Space: Poems 1979-1989. Santa Rosa, Black Sparrow Press, 1991.

Other

The Japan and India Journals 1960-1964. Bolinas, California, Tombouctou, 1981.
Phenomonological. Canton, New York, Glover Publishing, 1989.

*

Manuscript Collection: University of California, San Diego.

Joanne Kyger comments:

I myself am a West Coast poet, but I also feel an affinity for much of the work of the younger New York poets.

My vision of the poet changes so I can stay alive and the muse can stay alive. I report on my states of consciousness and the story I am telling.

*   *   *

Joanne Kyger is not the enchantress Circe, but she has admired her. Kyger's first book, *The Tapestry and the Web,* exhibits great mythic propensities. In it she reactivates the Odysseus myth, but unlike Pound and Joyce and Olson she enlarges the feminine aspect of the *Odyssey.* She is not Penelope, either, waiting on a man (or anyone else) for her fate. Her Penelope is not domesticated patience; rather, she is the mother of Pan. Kyger's destiny as poet is her own responsibility, and she has borne it as Pan, free-spirited and ranging. Her "Web" is metaphoric of the poem itself—patterned freely and self-supporting—the isolated narrative strands that, when bound together, capture the reader, bringing meaning.

Kyger's gifts as narrator are extraordinary. In fact, it is this technique that characterizes almost all her poems—a pattern marked by sudden cuts of consciousness, the narrative abruptly shifting in flight, not relying on startling imagery to signal changes of direction. A significant early poem is "The Maze," in which there are several entrances but only a single exit from bewilderment.

Overall, Kyger's early poems deliberately hold personality back. They are populated by disembodied presences—an unmoored "he" or "she," various "figures" engaged in vague but effective drama. Her "I" is a nonconfessional, impersonal, automatic speaker—Jack Spicer's influence, perhaps. In the later 1960s and 1970s she kept a greater account of herself, reporting directly in such books as *Joanne* and *All This Every Day* that it is "Joanne" who is interesting, wonderful to behold, making her sense out of the world. She has kept close to what she knows, absorbed by the day's contents and contentments while rejecting disposable, paper-plate America (as in "Don't Hope to Gain by What Has Preceded").

The turning point comes with "August 18" in *Places to Go,* where a new personality arises in phases like a moon over the mesa. By the time of *All This Every Day,* the "I" becomes more obviously the poet's own personality and steps out into quotidian daylight, where there are sharper outlines. Dates become titles—"October 29, Wednesday," "October 31"—and poems are entries in imagination's almanac, records of the day as lived a little closer to understanding, a catalogue of motives, concordances, accords. The daily brings with it a new ambition for *samadhi,* total consciousness, like Little Neural Annie attains in "Soon," with what has become characteristic humor for the poet:

> Little Neural Annie was fined $65 in the Oakland
> Traffic Court this season for "driving while in

a state of samadhi." California secular law requires
that all drivers of motor vehicles remain firmly seated
within their bodies while the vehicle is in motion.
This applies to both greater vehicles and lesser
vehicles.

Kyger puts the comic back in cosmic. Relationships, too, yield
attainment, as in these lovely lines: "She makes / herself, decorative, agreeable, for him. They nod / inside a flower, a wonderful
room." It is a leisurely, drifting poetry, stirring in the breeze, absorbing the occasional muffled chaos, a day's small panics. Only
in such a relaxed state do the lines work so effectively, without
the uneconomical expense of willful pressure.

Generally, Kyger's work is characterized by eagerness, even in
the face of a disaster such as the plundering of a camp cabin by a
bear. "Destruction" may well become her most famous poem—a
great chuckle of a poem, although a more formal analysis might
speak of its excellent dramatic device. The speaker follows the
bear's path of destruction, pad and pencil in hand, as if for a police report or insurance claim:

> He eats all the apples, limes, dates, bottled decaffeinated
> coffee, and 35 pounds of granola. The asparagus soup cans
> fall to the floor. Yum!... Rips open the water bed, eats
> the incense
> and

drinks the perfume ... Knocks *Shelter, Whole Earth Catalogue,*
Planet, Drum, Northern Mists, Truck Tracks, and
Women's Sports into the oozing water bed mess.
> He goes
down stairs and out the back wall. He keeps on going
for a long way and finds a good cave to sleep it all off.
Luckily he ate the whole medicine cabinet, including stash
of LSD, Peyote, Psilocybin, Amanita, Benzedrine, Valium
> and
aspirin.

Kyger's images are few; puns not essential; devices, tricks,
syncopations unintended; diction comfortable. Her lines are
biomorphic, ever-adjusting to what they seek to accomplish—
not to hold the world at bay or shore up ruined traditions but
extending out to join the oncoming freshened world. The value
of her work lies in its openness, its whimsy, the acceptance of
daily change. Her poems are attentive to a spirit's needs, a deep-
drawn aim within aimlessness. She has never been less than
autonomous and thus is beyond the futile eddies of taste. Always a free spirit, she has rarely spoken for any group larger
than her thoughts. It amounts to a style to which she has faithfully adhered.

—George F. Butterick

L

LAUTERBACH, Anne

Nationality: American. **Born:** New York, New York, 1942. **Education:** University of Wisconsin, Madison, B.A. 1964; Columbia University, 1966-67. **Career:** Editor and teacher at schools in London, England, 1967-73; art consultant to New York galleries, 1974-84; assistant director, Washburn Gallery, New York, 1984-86; visiting professor to various universities, 1985-90; member of M.F.A. writing faculty, Bard College, 1991—; professor of English for the Graduate Center, 1993, then Theodore Goodman Professor of Creative Writing, City College of the City University of New York. **Awards:** Woodrow Wilson Graduate fellowships, 1966-67; Creative Arts Public Service grant, 1978; Yaddo Residencies, 1980, 1982, 1984, 1994; Guggenheim fellowship, 1986; Ingram Merrill Foundation grant, 1988; New York State Council for the Arts grant, 1988; *American Poetry Review*'s Jerome J. Shestack prize, 1990; MacArthur fellowship, 1993. **Address:** c/o Graduate Center, City College of the City University of New York, 160 Convent Ave., New York, New York 10031, U.S.A.

PUBLICATIONS

Poetry

Vertical, Horizontal. Dublin, Seafront Press, 1971.
Book One. New York, Spring Street Press, 1975.
Many Times, But Then. Austin, Texas University Press, 1979.
Later That Evening. Brooklyn, Jordan Davies, 1981.
Closing Hours. New York, Red Osier Press, 1983.
Sacred Weather. New York, Grenfell Press, 1984.
Greeks, with Bruce Boice and Jan Groover. Baltimore, Hollow Press, 1984.
Before Recollection. Princeton, Princeton University Press, 1987.
How Things Bear Their Telling, with Lucio Pozzi. Colombes, Collectif Generation, 1990.
Clamor. New York, Viking, 1991.
And for Example. New York, Viking, 1994.
A Clown, Some Colors, A Doll, Her Stories, A Song, A Moonlit Cove, with Ellen Phelan. New York, Whitney Museum, 1996.
On a Stair. New York, Penguin, 1997.

*

Critical Studies: "The Poetry of David Shapiro and Ann Lauterbach: After Ashberry" by Thomas Fink, in *American Poetry Review,* 1988; interview with Molly Bendall in *American Poetry Review,* 1992; "Visions of Silence in Poems of Ann Lauterbach and Charles Bernstein" by Susan Schultz, in *Talisman,* Fall 1994; "Ann Lauterbach's 'Still' and Why Stevens Still Matters" by Charles Altieri, in *Wallace Stevens Journal,* Fall 1995.

*   *   *

In her essay "On Memory," Ann Lauterbach suggests, "it is not possible to write into the unknown, the future, without the known, the past. The past is always there, the setting, the stance; it constitutes us, and we are its constituents." Lauterbach's poetry troubles the relationship between past and future, known and unknown, absence and presence. "She could be seen undressing / That is, in the original version / She could be seen undressing," opens *Clamor*'s 1991 "Gesture and Flight," calling into question which "version" of the woman we are seeing as we read.

Lauterbach's poems investigate how what is said remakes what is seen, and how what is seen is an effect of what is said. Her rich imagery reflects her training as both a visual artist and a philosopher. She often lays out a scene in crisp, clear verse, only to call into question the terms by which it is summoned. In the first stanza of *Before Recollection*'s "An Aura of Abstraction Gives Way," each image glides and collides with the last, echoing and scraping against the sounds of prior words, adding up to a view that is both more and less than the sum of its parts: "Good rentals. Market for ice skates, skull caps, / Lake view flurries where dark / Takes up slack in winter, hit-or-miss splendor, / Flash lit. You could say 'christened rain,' / Pelt-on-a-roof absorbing touch, more-or-less skin deep / Snow down from the north to the mouth of a river." Each image is suggested by the prior one, yet it leads to an unsettling, incomplete scene in which it remains unclear what precisely is being observed, or who is the observer.

Lauterbach is often read as a directed descendant of Wallace Stevens and John Ashbery. Like these two American modernists, she is interested in philosophical questions concerning the relationship between the individual's perception of phenomena, her consciousness of self, and larger questions of time, memory, and language. Like Ashbery, Lauterbach uses form to indicate the limits of language to capture experience, while her work also suggest how experience may only be fully known through its expression in language. Her short lines seem both to interrupt and forge connections with one another, gesturing toward an impossible, perfect unity between an object and its representation. Yet whereas Ashberry and Stevens seem to distrust the personal and individual, Lauterbach continually returns to the lyric, individual voice.

In her recent work, Lauterbach's lush, personal voice has become even more prominent. *Clamor*'s "Gesture and Flight" moves from a scene of abstract observation of various versions of a woman undressing, to the more intimate, personal, apparently first-person account of this woman's inferiority, and back again to the original, exterior point-of-view:

> At first she had needed a coin,
> A shelter, marriage and these
> Led quickly to her doubt
>
> "feminine" "visceral"
> Quoted rudely
>
> Which then fell rudely
> Through a ring and into her chamber
> Where she could be seen undressing.

Rather than simply reflecting a feminine perspective, or expressing identifiably feminist themes and politics, Lauterbach's work explores, as she suggested in conversation with the author, "the ways in which formal considerations—as opposed to subject matters—might reflect a feminist perspective." Suturing together fragments of what might at first appear arbitrary, unrelated images and voices, Lauterbach examines how speech and identity are cobbled together through the gaps between language and self, objects and representations. By writing within these interstices, Lauterbach suggests a means of inscribing the voices of women, who are traditionally the visual objects rather than the speaking subjects of poetic discourse. In *And for Example*'s "Eclipse with Object," she stages this relationship between discourse's traditional subjects and its objects in intimate terms, mapping a historical "I" upon the gaze of a "You":

> There is a spectacle and something is added to history.
> It has as its object an indiscretion: old age, a
> gun, the prevention of sleep.
>
> I am placed in its stead
> and the requisite shadow is yours.
> It casts across me, a violent coat.

Lauterbach creates a powerful poetics in which the ontological question of writing and representation, memory and loss, absence and history, are infused with the personal, lyric voice occurring in the gaps between experience and its inscription.

—Jennifer Natalya Fink

LEGGOTT, Michele

Nationality: New Zealander. **Born:** 1956. **Education:** Attended schools in New Zealand and the United States. **Career:** Teacher of English, Auckland University. Poetry editor, *Landfall* and *Rambling Jack.* **Awards:** New Zealand Book Award for poetry, 1995, for *Dia.*

PUBLICATIONS

Poetry

Like This? New Zealand, n.p., 1988.
Swimmers, Dancers. Auckland, Auckland University Press, 1991.
Dia. Auckland, Auckland University Press, 1994.

Other

Reading Zukofsky's 80 Flowers. Baltimore, Johns Hopkins University Press, 1989.

Editor, with Mark Williams, *Opening the Book: New Essays on New Zealand Writing.* Auckland, Auckland University Press, 1995.

*   *   *

Michele Leggott's volumes have established her as a leading presence in New Zealand's school of post-modern writing. Influenced by the American poet Louis Zukofsky, on whose work she wrote a doctorate, subsequently published as *Reading Zukofsky's 80 Flowers*, her poetry smacks of American post-modernism in a local setting. She has also developed her stylistic trademarks and in *Dia* enriches her diction by borrowing from an earlier generation of women poets such as Ursula Bethell, Eileen Duggan, Robin Hyde. A feminist, Leggott pays homage to these literary forebears in order to look "for what

was lost when we asserted that good poetry in this country was shaped exclusively by British-derived Modernism of the 1930s and 1940s" and to "draw some of those shadowy figures back into the conversation about language and place":

> It is a kind of speaking together, problematic but full of possibilities. When I was then able to connect the language and preoccupations of these poets with a largely disappeared tradition of singing women that took me sometimes off the maps of literacy itself, I began to understand why their writing exerted such a hold once I knew how to listen.

Leggott's style ranges from minimalism to discursive, narrative poems like "Garbo in a Gown," or "Colloquy" (*Swimmers, Dancers*). Each of her collections contain sequences of linked poems through which she develops the dramatic and thematic potential of the genre. Characteristically she experiments with the formal elements of stanza and rhyme: shape and content are inseparable, sound and movement interact. In "The Rose Poems: 4" lark song is evoked in a series of dizzying euphonic variations.

> there's
> dwarf bramble
> all over
>   Alouette
> mountain
>   in August
>   *ah*
>   *gentle*
>   *gongle*
>   *air*
>   *for*
>   *jangles*
>   *raven*
>   *jokers*
>   *gentils*
>   *jongleurs*
> paired airs'
> zenith

Typographical poetry is also a favourite trope: "Micromelismata" (*Dia*) are two matching poems, both in the shape of lips. The wavy margins of "think this" (Like This?) image the movements of swimming or waves lapping.

>   think this
>   into abalone
>
>   nacre no body
>   embraces
>
>   acheless or
>   necklace
>
>   reckless
>   that kissed
>
>   detritus whist
>   forsake and
>
>   dance
>   unsounded

In the sequence "Tigers" (*Swimmers, Dancers*) she subverts stanzaic linearity and produces poems that are exact circles; the different "lines" and "stanzas" occupy corners and peripheries as well as the centre space so one can read both across and down:

> wavejumping
> down the coast   a
> eight months a year call up   step
> the weather office every morning   into
> second-guess the winds at the cape   heaven
> at Kina Rd   deliberate
> the swell   more coffee a look around the windows
> west sou'west getting up now   more avocado on toast

Leggott undercuts expectations of opening and closure by avoiding punctuation, and her poems seem to materialise onto and vanish off the page in a single, continuous undulating movement. In the superb sonnet sequence, "Blue Irises" (*Dia*), however, she hints at a syntactic structure by capitalising key initial words:

> I wanted to mouth you all over
> spring clouds spring rain spring
> tenderness of afternoons spent
> blazing trails to this
> place where breath roars through
> the famous architecture of a poet's ear
> Rose and peony buds and tongue
> ichthyous tumble honey and pearl—
> the runner's foot has touched and adored
> wisteria sprang after you, figs tipped
> green air astounded by your passage
> to the audient quays of the city
> Now it begins, another voyage after nemesis
> blue-eyed with the distance of it all

Entry into and exit from the poetic moment are signalled by the urgency of "I wanted ..." and the aphoristic final two lines.

The rapid, fluent pace of Leggott's verse often achieves a dancing effect, and reading it rhythmically while absorbing its dense, sensual surfaces—a mellifluous diction offset by startling images, unusual sound effects, neologisms ("ichthyous") or archaisms ("audient")—is a heightened poetic experience. The poetry of *Dia* is energetic in movement yet languorous in impact, contemporary in form yet dated in diction; fluid in syntactic transition yet linguistically opaque. A writer with a penchant for exotic evocations and intensely poetic language, Leggott's dynamic styles and linguistic performances convey unusual sensations and exalted, rhapsodic states.

—Janet Wilson

LEVERTOV, Denise

Nationality: American. **Born:** Ilford, Essex, England, 24 October 1923; emigrated to the United States, 1948; naturalized, 1955. **Education:** Private. **Military Service:** Nurse in World War II. **Family:** Married the writer Mitchell Goodman in 1947 (divorced 1975); one son. **Career:** Worked in an antique shop and book shop, London, 1946; nurse at British Hospital, Paris, spring 1947; taught at the YM-YWHA Poetry Center, New York, 1964, City College of New York, 1965, and Vassar College, Poughkeepsie, New York, 1966-67; visiting professor, Drew University, Madison, New Jersey, 1965, University of California, Berkeley, 1969, Massachusetts Institute of Technology, Cambridge, 1969-70, Kirkland College, Clinton, New York, 1970-71, University of Cincinnati, Spring 1973, and Tufts University, Medford, Massachusetts, 1973-79; Fannie Hurst Professor (poet-in-residence), Brandeis University, Waltham, Massachusetts, 1981-83; professor at large, Cornell University, Ithaca, New York, 1993—. Since 1981 Professor of English, then Emerita, Stanford University, California. Poetry editor, *The Nation,* New York, 1961, 1963-65, and *Mother Jones,* San Francisco, 1975-78. Honorary Scholar, Radcliffe Institute for Independent Study, Cambridge, Massachusetts, 1964-67. **Awards:** Bess Hokin prize, 1960, Harriet Monroe memorial prize, 1964, Inez Boulton prize, 1964, and Morton Dauwen Zabel prize, 1965 (*Poetry,* Chicago); Longview award, 1961; Guggenheim fellowship, 1962; American Academy grant, 1966, 1968; Lenore Marshall prize, 1976; Bobst award, 1983; Shelley memorial award, 1984; Robert Frost medal, 1990; National Endowment for the Arts Senior fellowship, 1991; Lannan award, 1992. D.Litt.: Colby College, Waterville, Maine, 1970; University of Cincinnati, 1973; Bates College, Lewiston, Maine, 1984; St. Lawrence University, Canton, New York, 1984; Allegheny College, Meadville, Pennsylvania, 1987; St. Michael's College, Burlington, Vermont, 1987; Massachusetts College of Art, Boston, 1989; University of Santa Clara, 1993; Seattle University, 1995. **Member:** American Academy, 1980; Corresponding Member, Mallarmé Academy, 1983. **Address:** c/o New Directions, 80 Eighth Avenue, New York, New York 10011, U.S.A.

PUBLICATIONS

Poetry

The Double Image. London, Cresset Press, 1946.
Here and Now. San Francisco, City Lights, 1956.
Overland to the Islands. Highlands, North Carolina, Jargon, 1958.
5 Poems. San Francisco, White Rabbit Press, 1958.
With Eyes at the Back of Our Heads. New York, New Directions, 1960.
The Jacob's Ladder. New York, New Directions, 1961; London, Cape, 1965.
O Taste and See: New Poems. New York, New Directions, 1964.
City Psalm. Berkeley, California, Oyez, 1964.
Psalm Concerning the Castle. Madison, Wisconsin, Perishable Press, 1966.
The Sorrow Dance. New York, New Directions, 1967; London, Cape, 1968.
Penguin Modern Poets 9, with Kenneth Rexroth and William Carlos Williams. London, Penguin, 1967.
A Tree Telling of Orpheus. Los Angeles, Black Sparrow Press, 1968.
A Marigold from North Viet Nam. New York, Albondocani Press-Ampersand, 1968.
Three Poems. Mount Horeb, Wisconsin, Perishable Press, 1968.
The Cold Spring and Other Poems. New York, New Directions, 1969.

Embroideries. Los Angeles, Black Sparrow Press, 1969.
Relearning the Alphabet. New York, New Directions, and London, Cape, 1970.
Summer Poems 1969. Berkeley, California, Oyez, 1970.
A New Year's Garland for My Students, MIT 1969-1970. Mount Horeb, Wisconsin, Perishable Press, 1970.
To Stay Alive. New York, New Directions, 1971.
Footprints. New York, New Directions, 1972.
The Freeing of the Dust. New York, New Directions, 1975.
Chekhov on the West Heath. Andes, New York, Woolmer Brotherston, 1977.
Modulations for Solo Voice. San Francisco, Five Trees Press, 1977.
Life in the Forest. New York, New Directions, 1978.
Collected Earlier Poems 1940-1960. New York, New Directions, 1979.
Pig Dreams: Scenes from the Life of Sylvia. Woodstock, Vermont, Countryman Press, 1981.
Wanderer's Daysong. Port Townsend, Washington, Copper Canyon Press, 1981.
Candles in Babylon. New York, New Directions, 1982.
Two Poems. Concord, New Hampshire, Ewert, 1983.
Poems 1960-1967. New York, New Directions, 1983.
El Salvador Requiem and Invocation. Boston, Back Bay Chorale, 1983.
Oblique Prayers: New Poems with 14 Translations from Jean Joubert. New York, New Directions, 1984; Newcastle upon Tyne, Bloodaxe, 1986.
The Menaced World. Concord, New Hampshire, Ewert, 1985.
Selected Poems. Newcastle upon Tyne, Bloodaxe, 1986.
Poems 1968-1972. New York, New Directions, 1987.
Breathing the Water. New York, New Directions, 1987; Newcastle upon Tyne, Bloodaxe, 1988.
A Door in the Hive. New York, New Directions, 1989.
Evening Train. New York, New Directions, 1992.
Sands of the Well. New York, New Directions, 1996.

Recordings: *Today's Poets 3,* with others, Folkways; *The Acolyte,* Watershed, 1985.

Short Story

In the Night. New York, Albondocani Press, 1968.

Other

The Poet in the World (essays). New York, New Directions, 1973.
Conversation in Moscow. Cambridge, Massachusetts, Hovey Street Press, 1973.
Denise Levertov: An Interview, with John K. Atchity. Dallas, New London Press, 1980.
Light Up the Cave (essays). New York, New Directions, 1981.
Seasons of Light, with Peter Brown. Houston, Rice University Press, 1988.
New and Selected Essays. New York, New Directions, 1992.
Tesserae. New York, New Directions, 1995.

Editor, *Out of the War Shadow: An Anthology of Current Poetry.* New York, War Resisters League, 1967.
Editor and Translator, with Edward C. Dimock Jr., *In Praise of Krishna: Songs from the Bengali.* New York, Doubleday, 1967; London, Cape, 1968.

Translator, *Selected Poems,* by Guillevic. New York, New Directions, 1969.
Translator, with Samuel Beckett, Edouard Roditi, and Alain Bosquet, *No Matter No Fact,* by Bosquet. New York, New Directions, 1988.
Translator, *Black Iris: Selected Poems, by Jean Joubert.* Port Townsend, Washington, Copper Canyon Press, 1989.

*

Bibliographies: *A Bibliography of Denise Levertov* by Robert A. Wilson, New York, Phoenix Book Shop, 1972; *Denise Levertov: An Annotated Primary and Secondary Bibliography* by Liana Sakelliou-Schulz, New York, Garland, 1989.

Manuscript Collections: Humanities Research Center, University of Texas, Austin; Washington University, St. Louis; Indiana University, Bloomington; Fales Library, New York University; Beinecke Library, Yale University, New Haven, Connecticut; Brown University, Providence, Rhode Island; University of Connecticut, Storrs; Columbia University, New York; State University of New York, Stony Brook.

Critical Studies: *Denise Levertov* by Linda W. Wagner, New York, Twayne, 1967; *Out of the Vietnam Vortex* by James Mersmann, Lawrence, University Press of Kansas, 1974; Hayden Carruth, in *Hudson Review* (New York), 1974; *The Imagination's Tongue: Denise Levertov's Poetic* by William Slaughter, Portree, Isle of Skye, Aquila, 1981; *From Modern to Contemporary American Poetry 1945-1965* by James E.B. Breslin, Chicago, University of Chicago Press, 1984; *Understanding Denise Levertov* by Harry Marten, edited by Matthew J. Bruccoli, Los Angeles, University of Southern California Press, 1989; *Twentieth Century Literature* by Ronald R. Janssen, Hempstead, New York, Hofstra University, 1992; *Under Discussion, Denise Levertov Selected Criticism* by Albert Gelpi, Ann Arbor, University of Michigan, 1993.

*   *   *

Although Denise Levertov was born and educated in England, not moving to the United States until the late 1940s, she has become a thoroughly American poet and literary figure. Many critics have called her a Black Mountain poet, in spite of the fact that it is not a term she feels comfortable with. However, her ideas about prosody, her association with the "breath line" of projective verse and her own co-option of the term "organic form," as well as her long publishing history with New Directions Press, which is most associated with the Pound / Williams aesthetic axis, give this identification some relevance.

American poetry, like American culture, has manifested from the beginning an unlikely combination of the material and the spiritual. The Whitman tradition clearly shows the mainstream poets reaching for a religious experience which is not doctrinally located. Levertov is no exception to this, and in her later work she can no longer conceal that she, who identified herself so fervently with political movements in the 1960s and 1970s, has always been a poet with spiritual longings, far more than worldly ones. Perhaps one of the reasons it has seemed unclear that Levertov has been writing religious poetry all these years, even though she often writes about God, is that her poems embody the physical, material world so well. Her poem "The Well" (*Breathing the Water*), for instance, is a kind of latter-day "Eve of St. Agnes":

> At sixteen, I believed the moonlight
> could change me if it would.
>   I moved my head
> on the pillow, even moved my bed
> as the moon slowly
> crossed the open lattice.

This "moonbathing" always resulted in lack of sleep and feeling ill, but she says that on the nights she permitted herself to sleep deeply, bathing in darkness allowed her to feel refreshed "and if not beautiful, / filled with some other power." In fact, this worldliness is the source of a belief in some primal, deep reality, or otherworldliness, underlying her materialism. In the poem "Death in Mexico" (*Life in the Forest*) she reveals her vision of a jungle world which is always out there, ready to reassert itself as soon as the ephemeral hand of civilization relaxes:

> Gardens vanish. She was an alien here,
> as am I...
>   Old gods
> took back their own.

In fact, Levertov sees all of civilization reverting to something which is more enduring than anything humanity has created. This vision of the inexorable Fall of man and banishment from the primal Garden cannot be touched by the poet's desire for human communication and peace, which is what has fueled her political poetry. Her work offers a paradox somewhat reminiscent of Robinson Jeffers's simultaneous belief that the human race is doomed but that we should still make political efforts to avert this. Levertov also believes art and concern, if not politics, can produce bits of light in doomed times.

While her politics have created a confusion of the lyric voice which has always pervaded her work, perhaps what critics have most misread is the poetry itself as political statement. Levertov has actually been writing a poetry of religious vision, one which comes out of American mysticism. It is a vision which allows Levertov to move beyond her politics, her Judeo-Christian morality, and most of all, her Romantic fear of the darkness, to a vision that portrays darkness as the other half of light.

In a lyric meditation from *A Door in the Hive* she makes clear how completely she believes that the spirit resides in the physical world.

> Is there someone,
>   an intruder,
> in my back yard? That slight
> scraping sound again—only a cat
> maybe?
>   —I look from the screendoor:
> Ah, it's you, dear leaves,
> only you, big wildly branching leaves
> of the philodendron,
> summering on the deck,
>   touching the floor of it, feeling
>   the chair,
>   exploring,
> As if you knew
>   the fall is coming.

In her more recent works, including *A Door in the Hive,* the highly spiritual, eight-part *Evening Train,* and *Sands of the Well,* Levertov's poetry continues to present a personal voice, eloquently vocative and American, about one's desires, needs, and wishes. Yet the myth she is working out in all the poems is that of the Garden. No personal wish or desire will be left when the man-made garden must finally revert to the primal forest which is greater than humanity, more savage and more powerful than anything we can create in art or life. Levertov accepts this, even offers a metaphor for the situation in her poem "The Blind Man's House at the Edge of the Cliff" from *A Door in the Hive:*

> he has chosen a life
> pitched at the brink ...
>
> He knows that if he could see
> he would be no wiser.
> High on the windy cliff he breathes
> face to face with desire.

> —Diane Wakoski

LEWIS, Gwyneth

Nationality: Welsh. **Born:** Cardiff, Wales, 4 November 1959. **Education:** Girton College, Cambridge, B.A. 1982; Harvard University, 1982-83, and Columbia University, 1983-84; Balliol College, Oxford, Ph.D. in English, 1989. **Family:** Married Leighton Denver Davies in 1993. **Career:** Welsh-language editor, *Poetry Wales,* 1980-82; poetry reader for *Partisan Review,* Boston, 1982-83; and *Paris Review,* New York, 1983-84; freelance book reviewer and news correspondent, 1983-88; researcher, scriptwriter, then assistant producer, Agenda, 1989-91; assistant producer of religious programs, 1992-93, then producer of factual programs, BBC Wales, 1993-95; guest lecturer, Columbia University writing program, 1995; chief assistant to controller, BBC Wales, 1997—. **Awards:** Urdd National Eisteddfod literature medals, 1976, 1977; Charity Reeves Prize, 1982; Gertrude Harley Prize for poetry, 1986-88; Major Eric Gregory award for young poets, 1988; BAFTA award for best feature programme, for "Close the Coalhouse Door," 1994; Oxford University Prize for English poem on a sacred subject, 1995; Aldeburgh Poetry Festival Prize, 1995, and Welsh Arts Council Book of the Year Prize, 1996, both for *Parables & Faxes.* **Member:** Welsh Academy. **Address:** 32 Waterloo Road, Penylan, Cardiff CF2 5DZ, Wales.

PUBLICATIONS

Poetry

Llwybrau Bywyd (pamphlet). Cardiff, Cwmni'r Urdd, 1977.
*Ar y Groesffordd (*pamphlet). Cardiff, Cwmni'r Urdd, 1978.
Sonedau Redsa. Cardiff, Gwasg Gomer, 1990.
Parables & Faxes. Newcastle upon Tyne, Bloodaxe Books, 1995.
Cyfrif Un ac Un yn Dri (title means "One and One Makes Three").
    Cardiff, Barddas, 1996.

*

Critical Studies: In *The Urgency of Identity,* edited by David T. Lloyd, Evanston, Illinois, Triquarterly Books, 1994; "Self-Mocking Landscapes" by Carol Rumens, in *Times Literary Supplement,* 7 July 1995.

*   *   *

The title *Parables & Faxes* perfectly sums up Gwyneth Lewis' first book of poems written in English. Both forms of communication, the riddling and the direct, are at work in every one of her lines, and her subject matter contrasts up-to-date, contemporary life with Biblical incidents and lessons. Christ's parables are distinguished by their comparison of something common, a grain of mustard seed, with the sublime Kingdom of Heaven, and to some extent Lewis has simply deepened that irony by updating her materials, substituting the common elements of our technological world for agrarian examples Christ drew from Galilee. The title of "A Golf-Course Resurrection" provides a characteristic example. This method of updating, mixing the "good news" of the gospel with the six o'clock news, often is the very point of her comparison, providing its conceptual occasion, and informing her style.

Lewis is a Christian poet, but the humorous image of golfers as "penitents" counting "the justices of handicap and par" guarantees her message won't be dreadfully earnest. She loads her lines with puns and word play that capture and embody her contrasts, and she relishes the inevitable ironies when the present and the distant past are interpreted through each other. The religious themes she is drawn to are the unsettling ones of apocalypse, last days and resurrection, where nothing is sitting ling enough to be reflected upon very subtly. These religious preoccupations are matched by her worldly concern for the threat of nuclear disaster. The violent release of time from the burden of history in Christian Eschatology is best imagined as like the unlocking of nuclear energy. "Something exploded / from inside a tomb" she writes in "Chernobyl Icon," using terms that could apply either to a reactor's meltdown or the tomb from which Christ was resurrected.

Whichever interpretation you emphasize, you cannot help but reach a point of decision, as Lewis' energetic prosody, with its heavy reliance on assonance, driving rhythm and punchy rhymes, drives her reader to the poem's message. Parables make a point, and Lewis ensures that you reach it. Critics have attributed her energetic, musical style to that of Dylan Thomas in particular, and to traditional Welsh verse forms generally, which make extensive use of these rich aural effects. Traditionally Welsh poetry is noted for intricate stanzaic patterns, which Lewis does not use, but she does strongly recall the *cynghanedd,* rules for the placement of consonants at fixed positions in a line. Gerard Manley Hopkins' sprung rhythm is partly the result of his studying Welsh *cynghanedd.* Perhaps more to the point, however, is that Lewis' awareness of the instability of language, of its being shaped by history and politics rather than given by nature or God, that makes her use of the medium as volatile as splitting an atom. Lewis has written poetry in Welsh that points up the colonial status of Wales, and she has also written in Welsh about other colonized cultures, most notably that of the Philippines. This historical and political awareness of the many human tongues complicates her concern for the one Word of God.

Lewis tries to back off from her volatile themes and methods in a sequence of 12 "Illinois Idylls," which offer the reader "snap-shots" of whip-poor-will's rather than wyverns from the Bayeux Tapestry. But despite the tradeoff of overdetermined, gothic images for casual impressions, the countryside at first seems anything but natural. Her initial images are of repressive, unnatural enclosures. She sees a correctional center, and that firms her resolve to bend all rules. Then, at the house, everything outside seems submerged in an aquarium "where it takes all our strength not to drown." It isn't entirely clear if she resents these prisons, or relies on them to protect her. When she does finally feel more at home, the poetic vision she is accustomed to, the parabolic comparison which relies on sharp, visible distinctions, is frustrated in its explorations of nature. Her inability to place things in the dark, to "pin it there" in a flashlight's beam, or to capture clearly the moment of transition at dusk when the house and farm reform "themselves to integrity," leaves her frustrated, resolved to try again, but sometimes resigned to taking her "fill / of the absent." Nature is a place where all contrasts dissolve except that between nature and her vision as a poet.

The book's final sequence of 25 poems has the same title as the book as a whole, and the poems are alternately labeled either "Parable" or "Fax." They actually seem barely distinguishable in their means or style, but undecidability is another of the lessons of a parable: a mustard seed is like the Kingdom of Heaven at the same time that it is also just a mustard seed. In a true parable, you wouldn't be able to tell the difference, but in our fallen world there can only be contrasts and comparisons in which now the message, now the physical body containing the message dominates. Indeed, "Parable" and "Fax" finally emerge in the last poem as characters, now elevated to the status of saints, each signifying a different religious tradition: Parable embodies the transcendent message of Western Christianity, while Fax represents the Eastern focus on the empirical and particular. They can only question each other about their different attitudes towards reality.

—Will Broaddus

LIFSHIN, Lyn

Nationality: American. **Born:** Lyn Diane Lipman, Burlington, Vermont, 12 July 1942. **Education:** Syracuse University, New York, B.A. 1961; University of Vermont, Burlington, M.A. 1963; Brandeis University, Waltham, Massachusetts; State University of New York, Albany, 1964-66; Bread Loaf School of English, Vermont. **Family:** Married Eric Lifshin in 1963 (divorced 1978). **Career:** Teaching fellow, State University of New York, Albany, 1964-66; educational television writer, Schenectady, New York, 1966; instructor, State University of New York, Cobleskill, 1968, 1970; writing consultant, Mental Health Department, 1970, and Empire State College, 1973, both Albany; poet-in-residence, Mansfield State College, Pennsylvania, 1974, University of Rochester, New York, 1986, Antioch Writers Conference, 1987, and Glenwood College, 1994, 1998; part-time instructor, Union College, 1980-85. **Awards:** Hart Crane award; Yaddo fellowship, 1970, 1971, 1975, 1979, 1980; MacDowell fellowship, 1973; Millay Colony fellowship, 1975, 1979; Creative Artists Public Service award, 1976; Cherry Valley Editions Jack Kerouac award, 1984, for *Kiss the Skin Off*; Madelin Sadin award, 1989. **Address:** 2142 Apple Tree Lane, Niskayuna, New York 12309-4714, U.S.A.

PUBLICATIONS

Poetry

Why Is the House Dissolving. San Francisco, Open Skull Press, 1968.

Femina 2. Oshkosh, Wisconsin, Abraxas Press, 1970.

Leaves and Night Things. West Lafayette, Indiana, Baby John Press, 1970.

Black Apples. Trumansburg, New York, Crossing Press, 1971; revised edition, 1973.

Tentacles, Leaves. Belmont, Massachusetts, Hellric Press, 1972.

Moving by Touch. Traverse City, Michigan, Cotyledon Press, 1972.

Lady Lyn. Milwaukee, Morgan Press, 1972.

Mercurochrome Sun Poems. Tacoma, Washington, Charis Press, 1972.

I'd Be Jeanne Moreau. Milwaukee, Morgan Press, 1972.

Love Poems. Durham, New Hampshire, Zahir Press, 1972.

Undressed. Traverse City, Michigan, Cotyledon Press, 1972.

Lyn Lifshin. Durham, New Hampshire, Zahir Press, 1972.

Poems by Suramm and Lyn Lifshin. Madison, Wisconsin, Union Literary Committee, 1972.

Forty Days, Apple Nights. Milwaukee, Morgan Press, 1973.

Audley End Poems. Long Beach, California, MAG Press, 1973.

The First Week Poems. Plum Island, Massachusetts, Zahir Press, 1973.

Museum. Albany, New York, Conspiracy Press, 1973.

All the Women Poets I Ever Liked Didn't Hate Their Fathers. St. Petersburg, Florida, Konglomerati, 1973.

The Old House on the Croton. San Lorenzo, California, Shameless Hussy Press, 1973.

Poems. Minneapolis, Northstone, 1974.

Selected Poems. Trumansburg, New York, Crossing Press, 1974.

Upstate Madonna: Poems 1970-1974. Trumansburg, New York, Crossing Press, 1974.

Shaker House. Tannersville, New York, Tideline Press, 1974.

Blue Fingers. Milwaukee, Shelter Press, 1974.

Plymouth Women. Milwaukee, Morgan Press, 1974.

Shaker House Poems. Chatham, New York, Sagarin Press, 1974.

Mountain Moving Day. Trumansburg, New York, Crossing Press, 1974.

Walking thru Audley End Mansion Late Afternoon and Drifting into Certain Faces. Long Beach, California, MAG Press, 1974.

Blue Madonna. Milwaukee, Shelter Press, 1974.

Poems. Gulfport, Florida, Konglomerati, 1974.

Green Bandages. Genesco, New York, Hidden Springs, 1975.

Old House Poems. Santa Barbara, California, Capra Press, 1975.

North Poems. Milwaukee, Morgan Press, 1976.

Naked Charm. N.p., Fireweed Press, 1976.

Paper Apples. Stockton, California, Wormwood, 1976.

Some Madonna Poems. Buffalo, White Pine Press, 1976.

More Waters. Cincinnati, Waters, 1977.

The January Poems. Cincinnati, More Waters, 1977.

Pantagonia. Stockton, California, Wormwood, 1977.

Mad Girl Poems. Wichita, Kansas, Caprice Out of Sight Press, 1977.

Lifshin & Richmond. Oakland, California, Bombay Duck, 1977.

Poems, with John Elsberg. Filey, Yorkshire, Fiasco, 1978.

Offered by Owner. Cambridge, New York, Natalie Slohm, 1978.

Leaning South. New York, Red Dust, 1978.

Glass. Milwaukee, Morgan Press, 1978.

Early Plymouth Women. Milwaukee, Morgan Press, 1978.

Crazy Arms. Chicago, Ommation Press, 1978.

Doctors. Santa Barbara, California, Mudborn, 1979.

35 Sundays. Chicago, Ommation Press, 1979.

Men and Cars. Ware, Massachusetts, Four Zoas Press, 1979.

More Naked Charm. Los Angeles, Illuminati Press, 1979.

Madonna. Stockton, California, Wormwood, 1980.

Lips on That Blue Rail. San Francisco, Lion's Breath, 1980.

Colors of Cooper Black. Milwaukee, Morgan Press, 1981.

Leaving the Bough. New York, New World Press, 1982.

Blue Dust, New Mexico. Fredonia, New York, Basilisk Press, 1982.

Finger Prints. Stockton, California, Wormwood, 1982.

In the Dark with Just One Star. Milwaukee, Morgan Press, 1982.

Want Ads. Milwaukee, Morgan Press, 1982.

Lobster and Oatmeal. Sacramento, California, Pinch Penny, 1982.

Reading Lips. Milwaukee, Morgan Press, 1982.

Hotel Lifshin. Eureka, California, Poetry Now, 1982.

Blue Horses Nuzzle Tuesday. Burlingame, California, Minotaur Press, 1983.

Madonna Who Shifts for Herself. Long Beach, California, Applezaba, 1983.

Naked Charm (collection). Los Angeles, Illuminati Press, 1984.

The Radio Psychic Is Shaving Her Legs. Detroit, Planet Detroit, 1984.

Matinee. Chicago, Ommation Press, 1984.

Kiss the Skin Off. Cherry Valley, New York, Cherry Valley Editions, 1985.

Remember the Ladies. East Lansing, Michigan, Ghost Dance Press, 1985.

Camping Madonna. Portlandville, New York, MAF Press, 1986.

Vergin' Mary and Madonna. El Paso, Texas, Vergin Press, 1986.

Raw Opals. Los Angeles, Illuminati Press, 1987.

The Daughter May Be Let Go. Harbor Beach, Florida, Clock Radio Press, 1987.

Red Hair and the Jesuit. Parkdale, Oregon, Trout Creek Press, 1988.

Many Madonnas, edited by Virginia I. Long. St. John, Kansas, Kindred Spirit Press, 1988.

Rubbed Silk. Los Angeles, Illuminati Press, 1988.

Dance Poems. Chicago, Ommation Press, 1988.

The Doctor. Los Angeles, Applezaba, 1990.

Blood Road. Los Angeles, Illuminati Press, 1989.

Reading Lips. Milwaukee, Morgan Press, 1989.

Skin Divers, with Belinda Subraman. Leeds, Yorkshire, Krax, 1989.

Under Velvet Pillows. Middletown Springs, Vermont, Four Zoas Press, 1989.

Not Made of Glass. Saratoga Springs, New York, Karista, 1990.

Sulphur River Lifshin Edition. N.p., Sulphur River, 1991.

Reading Lips. Milwaukee, Morgan Press, 1992.

Marilyn Monroe. Portland, Oregon, Quiet Lion, 1994.

Appleblossoms. East Lansing, Michigan, Ghostdance, 1994.

Parade. Stockton, California, Wormwood, 1994.

Shooting Kodachromes in the Dark. N.p., Penumbra Press, 1994.

Color and Light. N.p., Modest Proposal, 1995.

Blue Tatoo. Desert Hot Springs, California, Event Horizon Press, 1995.

Marilyn and Madonna. N.p., Taggerzine Press, 1996.

Cold Comfort: Selected Poems 1970-1996. Santa Barbara, Black Sparrow Press, 1997.

Caught in the Act. N.p., Atom Mind Press, 1997.

My Mother's Fire. N.p., Glass Cherry, 1997.

Recordings: *Lyn Lifshin Reads Her Poems,* Women's Audio Exchange, 1977; *Offered by Owner,* Slohm, 1978.

Play

Screenplay: *Not Made of Glass,* 1990.

Other

Editor, *Tangled Vines: A Collection of Mother and Daughter Poems.* Boston, Beacon Press, 1978, enlarged 2nd ed., 1992.
Editor, *Ariadne's Thread: A Collection of Contemporary Women's Journals.* New York, Harper, 1982.
Editor, *Lips Unsealed.* Santa Barbara, California, Capra Press, 1990.

*

Bibliography: By Marvin Malone, in *Wormwood Review* (Stockton, California), vol. 12, no. 3, 1971.

Manuscript Collection: University of Texas, Austin.

Critical Studies: By Bill Katz, in *Library Journal* (New York), June 1971, and December 1972; Carol Rainey, in *Road Apple Review* (Albuquerque, New Mexico), summer-fall 1971; Victor Contoski, in *Northeast* (La Crosse, Wisconsin), fall-winter 1971-72; James Naiden, in *Minneapolis Star,* 18 April 1972; Dave Etter, in *December* (West Springs, Illinois), 1972; "Lyn Lifshin" by Jim Evans in *Windless Orchard* (Fort Wayne, Indiana), summer 1972; Eric Mottram, in *Little Magazine* (New York), summer-fall 1972; *New York Times Book Review,* 18 December 1978; "Lyn Lifshin Issue" of *Poetry Now* (Eureka, California), 1980, and *Greenfield Review* (Greenfield Center, New York), 1983.

Lyn Lifshin comments:
I'm usually better at doing something than talking about how and why I do it. One time I spent days trying to say how I wanted the words to be connected to touch the reader's body. Somehow. Except that sounded strange and so I tore it up.... It seems to me that the poem has to be sensual (not necessarily sexual, tho that's ok too) before it can be anything else. So rhythm matters a lot to me, most, or at least first. Before images even. I want whoever looks at, whoever eats the poem to feel the way old ebony feels at 4 o'clock in a cold Van Cortlandt mansion, or the smell of lemons in a strange place, or skin.

Words that I like to hear other people say the poems are are: strong, tight, real, startling, tough, tender, sexy, physical, controlled—that they celebrate (Carol Rainey), reflect joy in every aspect of being a woman (James Naiden).

I always steal things I like from people: other poets, especially from blues, old black and country blues rhythms (after most readings, people come and ask how, where I started reading the way I do; another mystery, really). So I was glad to have Dave Etter say that *Black Apples* "comes on like a stack of Cannonball Adderley records, blowing cool, blowing hot, sometimes lyrical and sweet, sometimes hard bop, terse and tough."

*   *   *

Perhaps no other contemporary American poet has been as widely published as Lyn Lifshin, whose prolific production has sometimes overshadowed the true range and significance of her work. From her early poems (written soon after her departure from the academic milieu, to which she has but infrequently returned, unlike many other poets), in which she presents with painful accuracy the shallowness and insincerity of a world where one may "fail to understand the requirements," to her later work, in which she enters the lives of such diverse humans as women in early Plymouth and Indians on exhibit in museums, recounts the horrific events witnessed by onlookers and those persecuted during the Holocaust (*Blue Tattoo),* and deals straightforwardly with her own family (especially the relationship between mother and daughter), she has been a risk taker. That risk has been most obvious, perhaps, in her poems of sexuality, in which both the emotional and the physical relationships between men and women are laid bare. One would be hard-pressed to find another writer who has done as thorough a job of evoking the despair of a woman caught in the traps that social restrictions and marriage create for American women. However, she is far more than a poet with only one subject, even though her voice is one which is always recognizable.

Lifshin's poetry is characterized by a breathless quality, a voice reflected by the page of short lines, incomplete sentences, pauses, and sudden revelations. Her poems can be disarmingly simple—until that moment of explosion. At times, her candor—especially about sex—is as hard and cold as the sound of feet on the pavement of a red-light district late at night. Few have written more bitingly or more tenderly about modern sexual mores—especially as reflected in the lives of women. At other times, in her "Madonna poems," for example, she explores worlds where the line between physical experience and imagination blurs. Lifshin's many Madonnas are both modern and widely archetypal, as she presents us with a "Parachute Madonna," a "Shifting for Herself Madonna," and others both funny and sad.

Although her poems are the result of an almost religious devotion to her craft, she seems to reach many of the final versions of her poems not so much by rewriting and reworking a single poem as by producing series of poems which gradually—or even cumulatively—reach the desired effect. The result is a body of work which is impressive in its size, almost epic in proportion—an irony when one considers that few individual Lifshin poems are more than 30 lines in length. Her work might be seen, in fact, as a journey through her own life and through time, through the lives of other women (her work as an anthologist is an indication of her interest in the writing of women in general), creating what might be seen as a poetic collage of the latter part of the 20th century, its optimism and its depressions. In the midst of it all she has placed herself, continually searching for meaning and identity—as woman, as feminist, as poet, as one of Jewish heritage, as a threatened member of the human species in the confusing landscape of history, personal liberty, and social reality.

Where the writers of classical times wrote long, connected epics, Lifshin has ventured with her short lyrics. Her voice is that of a female Odysseus, sometimes confused, often innocent, but always tenacious, one whose journey takes us along and teaches us as we go.

—Joseph Bruchac

LIM, Shirley Geok-lin

Nationality: American. **Born**: Malacca, Malaysia, 27 December 1944; immigrated to the United States, 1969. **Education**: University of Malaya, Kuala Lumpur, B.A. in English literature (first class honors), 1967; Brandeis University, Waltham, Massachusetts, M.A. in English and American literature 1971, Ph.D. 1973. **Family**: Married Charles Bazerman in 1972; one son. **Career**: Lecturer and teaching assistant, University of Malaya, Kuala Lumpur, 1967-69; lecturer, Universiti Sains, Penang, Malaysia, summer 1974; visiting fellow, National University of Singapore, 1982; assistant professor, Hostos Community College, City University of New York, 1973-76; associate professor, Westchester College, State University of New York, 1976-90; professor of Asian American studies, 1990-93, professor of English and women's studies, 1993—, and Chair of Women's Studies, 1997—, University of California—Santa Barbara. Founding editor, *Asian America: Journal of Culture and the Arts,* 1992; National Endowment for the Humanities Academic Consultant for the Mercantile Library/New York Public Libraries, 1995. **Awards**: Fulbright scholar, 1969-72; National Endowment for the Humanities grants, 1978, 1987; Commonwealth Poetry Prize, 1980, for *Crossing the Peninsula;* Chancellor's Award for Excellence in Teaching, 1981; *Asia Week* short story prize, 1982; Poems on the Underground award (United Kingdom), 1989; American Book Award, 1990, for *The Forbidden Stitch*; Interdisciplinary Humanities Center Conference award, 1990-91, for "A Literature of One's Own: Asian American Transformations"; Senate Research Grants, 1990-91, 1991-92, 1993-94; Instructional Development award, 1991, for Asian American Gender Representations; United States Information Agency Academic Specialization grant, 1994; University of California Curriculum Integration grant, 1995; American Book Award, 1997, for *Among the White Moon Faces*; Fulbright Distinguished Lecturer, 1996. **Address**: 574 Calle Anzuelo, Santa Barbara, California 93111, U.S.A.

PUBLICATIONS

Poetry

Crossing the Peninsula and Other Poems. Kuala Lumpur, Heinemann Writing in Asia Series, 1980.
Modern Secrets: New and Selected Poems. Aarhus, Denmark, and London, Dangaroo Press, 1989.
No Man's Grove and Other Poems. Singapore, National University of Singapore English Department Press, 1985.
Monsoon History: Selected Poems, introduction by Laurel Means. London, Skoob Pacifica, 1994.
What the Fortunate Teller Did Not Say. N.p., 1997.

Fiction

Another Country and Other Stories, introduction by Laurel Means. Singapore, Times Books International, 1982.
Life's Mysteries: The Best of Shirley Lim, introduction by Laurel Means. Singapore, Times Books International 1995.
Two Dreams: New and Selected Stories, introduction by Zhou Xiaojing. New York, Feminist Press, 1997.

Other

Among the White Moon Faces: An Asian-American Memoir of Homelands. New York, Feminist Press, 1996.
Writing Southeast / Asia in English: Against the Grain. London, Skoob Pacifica, 1994.
Nationalism and Literature: Literature in English from the Philippines and Singapore. Quezon City, New Day Publishers, 1993.

Editor, *The Forbidden Stitch: An Asian American Women's Anthology.* Corvallis, Calyx, 1989.
Editor, *Approaches to Teaching Kingston's The Woman Warrior,* New York, MLA, 1991.
Editor, *Reading the Literatures of Asian America,* Philadelphia, Temple University Press, 1992.
Editor, *One World of Literature.* Boston, Houghton, 1993.

*

Critical Studies: "Speaking as Women: The Poetry of Shirley Lim and Lee Tzzu Pheng" by Lau Yoke Ching, in *Commentary,* vol. 7, no. 2-3, 1987; *The Cultural Politics of English as an International Language* by Alastair Pennycook, New York, Longman, 1994; "The Poetics of History: Three Women's Perspectives" by Leong Liew Geok, in *The Writers as Historical Witness*, edited Edwin Thimlsoo and Thim Kandiah, Singapore, University Press, 1995; "The 'Orient-ation' of Eden: Christian / Buddhist Dialogics in the Poetry of Shirley Geok-lin Lim, "*Christianity and Literature,* vol. 43, no. 2, winter 1994; with Nor Faridah Addul Manaf, in "More than Just a Woman," in *Tenggarra,* no. 34, 1995; "Shirley Lim—A Talent for Telling Tales," with Yeang Soo Ching, *New Straits Times* (Singapore), 8 August 1996; "Writer Lets Go of Her Past at Last," with Tan Gim Ean, *New Straits Times*, 4 September 1996.

*   *   *

Shirley Geok-lin Lim's poetry is characterized by border-crossings between nations, cultures, and traditions. Its multiple locations of geography reflect Asian diaspora and map out Lim's psychological and emotional traversing between worlds. Geographical locations in Lim's poetry are loaded with memories and cultural difference, including ethnic, racial, and gender conflicts. As the complexity of Lim's multicultural heritage provides her with rich sources for her creative energy, the layered internal and external conflicts produce dynamic tensions in her poetry. Her thematic concerns and technical strategies in general result from her conscious struggle to decolonize her colonial education and her subjectivity, to find her own voice and style, and to give voice to the silent and the silenced.

Lim has a passion for words, and for English, the only language she can write in. But the medium of her poetry has become problematic, being contested as the colonizer's tool and the burden of colonial inheritance. Moreover, English has also been used to mark racial boundaries and to exclude the "Other." As her speaker in "Lament" says: "I have been faithful / Only to you, / My language. I choose you / Before country, / ... They wink knowingly / At my stupidity— / I, stranger, foreigner, / Claiming rights to / What I have no right—." As a poet and woman of color, Lim faces the challenge of at once mastering and transforming the English idiom in her poems and resisting the pressure of nationalism and racism which questions her legitimacy in using English as the language of her art and all her writings.

In Lim's poems, materials from Anglophone culture, like those from Chinese, Malaysian, and American cultures, provide the topic, create the drama, and encode meanings in various ways. Sometimes a tired image or analogy in traditional English poetry comes to life and takes on startlingly new connotations in her work. In "Adam's Grief, Eve's Fall," for instance, Lim breaks away from traditional modes of lamenting the loss of Eden as a result of human frailty. The opening statement immediately suggests a departure: "Grieving no matter at how large a loss, / Is not enough." The speaker contends that the real challenge lies in "where to go from here, with only / Strange plants and rocks, creatures indifferently / Shy or ravenous," and how to live with the knowledge of good and evil but "With all voices withdrawn, excepting this: / Speech which is sufficient enterprise." Adam and Eve's loss of Eden, and their sense of alienation in a strange, indifferent world suggest a parallel to the experience of exile, which is a recurring theme in Lim's poems. But in this poem the more important concern is the power of speech / words in recreating a world and the self.

Lim further explores this theme in relation to imagination and formal structure in several poems such as "In Praise of a Master," "To What Ends?," "A Life of Imagination," "On Reading Coleridge's poem," "Imagine," "Thoughts on Cezanne Still-Life," and "To Marianne Moore," which are grouped in Section IV of *Monsoon History* as "A Life of Imagination." By exploring the creative power of imagination as a theme, Lim seems to be writing within the tradition of the English Romantic poetry. However, she departs from the Romantic mode in a voice and style uniquely her own. Unlike many Romantic poems, "No Alarms," a poem about the poet's creative process, neither celebrates the poet's visionary moment inspired by nature, nor laments the absence of imagination or exalted emotional state. It depicts a woman poet's urge to write poems late at night, "hoping for insight, / Image to make life certain," but poesie seems to have left her. "Drowned in this drowsiness I suffer / Nothing, see nothing waiting on the page, / No alarms, no passions, no order, no rage." As the title suggests, the poet's persona expresses no alarm, no anxiety or despair about not being able to enter the emotional state for writing poetry as the male Romantic poets' often do. Nevertheless, Lim involves the reader in a delightfully intimate experience of the poet's creative process through her vivid imagery, plain diction, and masterful manipulation of lines and metric structure.

Lim also seeks to find her own voice and establish a unique style by turning to her ethnic cultural heritage. She employs images from Asian history, culture, and the tropics in many of her poems to assert her ethnic and cultural identity, to articulate her immigrant's sense of exile and dislocation, and to protest against racial discrimination. In her dramatic monologue, "To Li Po," Lim evokes the Chinese poet of the Tang Dynasty (618-907), whose poetry she can only read in English translation. While articulating her kinship with Li Po, Lim emphasizes the absence of any sense of racial superiority in Li Po's attitude and therefore indirectly critiques racism. Lim's ethnic cultural identity in her poems is at once a subject matter and a site of social critique.

The sense of alienation in her chosen country, and her disconnection from her mother tongue and cultural origin are major themes in Lim's poems. However, her condition of living on the borders in-between worlds and cultures is not simply a historically and socially created situation; it is also a self-chosen position. As her speaker in "No Man's Grove" declares, "I choose to walk between water and land," Lim chooses the in-between space intersected by a hybrid cultural heritage to negotiate her identity. The speaker in "Modern Secrets" returns in a dream to a mother tongue she no longer speaks and her childhood in another country. But her estranged Chinese heritage, like her deprived childhood, is still with her. A similar feeling of at once belonging to and being disconnected from her ethnic and cultural heritage is also conveyed in "Visiting Malacca."

Lim's exploration of the in-between space of her ethnic and cultural identity generates a poetics of fragmentation and hybridity, which characterize the postcolonial literature of diaspora. Part of the cultural and psychological fragmentation results from the colonial history of Malaysia. Lim often deals with Malaysia's colonization with witty humour and cutting irony, as the speaker says "Simple natives believe in / Breastless women stuffed with God" ("Returning to the Missionary School"), and refers to her homesickness at Christmas as "second-hand nostalgia" ("Christmas in Exile").

Much of Lim's poetry is devoted to women's subjectivity and experience. Gender, intersected by race, ethnicity, and class, is a central concern in both her poetry and prose writings. Her poems about women speak in diverse voices of women as grandmother, mother, daughter, wife, poet, and prostitute. Lim's keen ear and versatile language skills enable her to portray women's lives with immediacy, and capture the distinct personalities of individual women. In "Dedicated to Confucius Plaza," she conveys an Asian American housewife's at-homeness in multiracial and multicultural America through a light, smooth rhythm and a repeated rhyme scheme. In "Birth, Sex, Death," she captures the speaker's personality and attitude though diction, syntax, and accent. Quite a number of Lim's poems about women concern a troubled and painful mother-daughter relationship, which can be better understood in the light of her autobiography, *Among the White Moon Faces*.

Lim's poetry resists being placed within any particular poetic school or tradition though some critics have identified it with the English Romantic tradition. Her poetry, written in apparently traditional form achieves a rare conciseness and precision. It disturbs, and challenges the reader to re-examine received notions about culture, language, and gender. It also offers pleasure and insights.

—Zhou Xiaojing

LOCHHEAD, Liz

Nationality: Scottish. **Born:** Lanarkshire, 1947. **Education:** Glasgow School of Art. **Address:** c/o Penguin Books, Ltd., 27 Wright's Lane, London W8 5TZ, England.

PUBLICATIONS

Poetry

Memo for Spring. Edinburgh, University of Edinburgh Press, 1972.
The Grimm Sisters. Edinburgh, n.p., 1981.
Dreaming Frankenstein and Collected Poems. Edinburgh, University of Edinburgh Press, 1984.

True Confessions and New Clichés. Edinburgh, University of
Edinburgh Press, 1985.
Bagpipe Muzak. London, Penguin, 1991.

Play

Mary Queen of Scots Got Her Head Chopped Off. Harmondsworth,
Penguin, 1989.

*   *   *

Scottish writer Liz Lochhead's 1972 verse collection *Memo for
Spring* made an immediate impact with its freshness and truth to
experience. The appeal was direct, and yet the writing used more
verbal devices than might appear at a glance or on a first hearing.
An ability to talk about very ordinary things—her young sister
trying on her shoes, a trip from Glasgow to Edinburgh, her grand-
mother knitting, the clang of steelworks, a child carrying a jug of
milk, the end of a love affair—is in a few poems flattened out
towards triviality or the prosaic, but for the most part the warmly
observing eye and ear are convincingly on target. The experience
has a Glasgow and Lanarkshire background, but one attractive
poem, "Letter from New England"—where elements of ironical
comment on small-town life are entertainingly presented through
the persona of a surprised visitor—shows an encouraging ability
to move into a wider world.

The author's subsequent books of poetry have confirmed her
promise and extended her range. *The Grimm Sisters* takes up
themes from ballad and fairy tale and retells the stories either from
a new angle or with a modern perspective. *Dreaming Franken-
stein,* a collection of her earlier volumes with a substantial and
impressive addition of new poems, shows both a development of
her storytelling gift and a deepening of her psychological probing
of human relationships, especially as seen from a woman's point
of view. The extension of Lochhead's work into the theater, with
plays on the Frankenstein and Dracula stories and an interest in
cabaret-type monologues, gives further evidence of a productive
and confident talent. Her dramatic monologues, songs, and per-
formance pieces were collected in 1985 in *True Confessions and
New Clichés,* a sparkling and witty book to read, even though its
contents are meant to be heard. Prose and verse, song and action,
come together in her extremely effective play, *Mary Queen of Scots
Got Her Head Chopped Off,* which takes a fresh and moving look
at Scottish history and the myths that run through it.

—Edwin Morgan

M

MACPHERSON, (Jean) Jay

Nationality: Canadian. **Born:** London, England, 13 June 1931. **Education:** Carleton University, Ottawa, B.A. 1951; University College, London, 1951-52; University of Toronto, M.A. 1955, Ph.D. 1964. **Career:** Member of the English department, Victoria College, University of Toronto, 1957-96. Publisher, Emblem Books, 1954-1972. **Awards:** *Contemporary Verse* prize, 1949; Levinson prize, *Poetry* magazine, Chicago, 1957; President's medal, University of Western Ontario, 1957; Governor-General's award for poetry, 1958. **Address:** 1 Guy Court, King St., Oxford OX2 6DB, England.

PUBLICATIONS

Poetry

19 Poems. Deyá, Mallorca, Seizin Press, 1952.
O Earth Return. Toronto, Emblem Books, 1954.
The Boatman. Toronto, Oxford University Press, 1957.
Welcoming Disaster: Poems 1970-1974. Toronto, Saannes, 1974.
Poems Twice Told. Toronto, Oxford University Press, 1981; New York, Oxford University Press, 1982.

Other

Four Ages of Man: The Classical Myths (textbook). Toronto, Macmillan, and New York, St. Martin's Press, 1962.
The Spirit of Solitude: Conventions and Continuities in Late Romance. New Haven, Connecticut, Yale University Press, 1982.

*

Critical Studies: By Kildare Dobbs, in *Canadian Forum* (Toronto), vol. 37, no. 438; "Poetry" by Northrop Frye, in "Letters in Canada. 1957," in *University of Toronto Quarterly,* no. 27; "The Third Eye" by James Reaney, in *Canadian Literature,* (Vancouver), no. 3; Milton Wilson, in *Fiddlehead* (Fredericton, New Brunswick), no. 34; Munro Beattie, in *Literary History of Canada* (Toronto), University of Toronto Press, 1965; "Poetry" by Michael Gnarowski, in "Letters in Canada: 1974," in *University of Toronto Quarterly,* no. 19, 1974; "In The Whale's Belly: Jay Macpherson's Poetry" by Suniti Namjoshi, in *Canadian Literature* (Vancouver), no. 79, 1978; "The 'Unicorn' Poems of Jay Macpherson" by Audrey Berner, in *Journal of Canadian Literature* (Ottawa), vol. 3, no. 1, Winter 1980; *Second Words: Selected Critical Prose* by Margaret Atwood, Toronto, Anansi, 1982, and Boston, Beacon Press, 1984; "Toward a Feminist Hermeneutics: Jay Macpherson's Welcoming Disaster" by Lorraine Weir, in *Gynocritics: Feminist Approaches to Canadian and Quebec Women's Writing,* Toronto, ECW, 1987; *Jay Macpherson and Her Works* by Lorraine Weir, Toronto, ECW Press, 1989.

* * *

Jay Macpherson's *The Boatman* has been accepted with enthusiasm by academic critics as well as the general public and has been reprinted many times since its first publication in 1957. The book is a subtly organized suite of lyrics—elegiac, pastoral, epigrammatic, and symbolist—that utilize the traditional forms of quatrain and couplet with great metrical virtuosity. It also shows a remarkable flair for the presentation of serious philosophical and, indeed, religious themes in verse that is sometimes beautifully lyrical and sometimes comic in the tradition of Lear or Gilbert or nursery rhymes—and sometimes both at once.

The Boatman has as its unifying theme the transmutation of time-bound physical reality into the eternal and the spiritual through the magical intermediary of man's imagination. Symbol and myth are the instruments, and the drama of man's Fall and Redemption is worked out in terms derived from the Bible, Milton, Blake, and such modern poets and scholars as Robert Graves and Northrop Frye. Among the protagonists whose fables supply the seeds of the mystical drama unifying the book are Noah, Leviathan, the Queen of Sheba, Mary of Egypt, Eurynome, Merlin, Helen, and such symbolic figures as the Plowman, the Fisherman, the Shepherd, and Angels. One of the reasons for the success of these poems is that they take the reader into the world of childhood faith through the unquestionable truth of fairy tale and legend. The elegance and grace of the writing and the authority with which wit and a sense of comedy are conveyed in verse that is both timeless and temporary also give the book an appeal to the most sophisticated of readers.

The Boatman and *Welcoming Disaster* complete Macpherson's poetical oeuvre. In 1981 the two books were published together, along with other poems, as *Poems Twice Told.* Macpherson is also the author of a scholarly study, *The Spirit of Solitude: Conventions and Continuities in Late Romance,* which includes a remarkable essay about the Canadian achievement in romance literature titled "This Swan Neck of the Woods." Here she explains that "Canadian literature is without strong individual characters on the whole, being much more forceful in its presentation of settings. Man appears rather generalized: what has character is the wilderness, the city, the snow, the sea."

Macpherson taught for many years at Victoria College in the University of Toronto, where, influenced by the literary critic Northrop Frye, she in turn influenced the poet and writer Margaret Atwood. For some years Macpherson was grouped with the poet and dramatist James Reaney and the poet Daryl Hine and was considered to be a leading member of a so-called mythopoeic school of writers led by Frye. The association did not win readers, but at least it drew attention to her work in respectable places. For instance, Macpherson and Hine are the only two Canadian poets listed by Harold Bloom in his influential *The Western Canon.*

—A.J.M. Smith and John Robert Colombo

MADGETT, Naomi Long

Nationality: American. **Born:** Naomi Cornelia Long, in Norfolk, Virginia, 5 July 1923. **Education:** Virginia State University, Petersburg, 1941-45, B.A. 1945; Wayne State University, Detroit, 1954-55, M.Ed. 1955; Greenwich University, Hilo, Hawaii, 1974-80, Ph.D. 1980. **Family:** Married 1) Julian F. Witherspoon in 1946 (divorced 1949), one daughter; 2) W. Harold Madgett in 1954 (divorced 1960); 3) Leonard P. Andrews in 1972 (died 1996). **Career:** Staff writer, *Michigan Chronicle,* Detroit, 1946-47; service representative, Michigan Bell Telephone, Detroit, 1948-54; teacher in Detroit Public Schools, 1955-65, 1966-68; associate professor, 1968-73, professor, 1973-84, Eastern Michigan University, Ypsilanti; research associate, Oakland University, Rochester, Michigan, 1965-66; lecturer, University of Michigan, Ann Arbor, 1970. Publisher and editor, Lotus Press, Inc., Detroit, 1974—; poetry editor, Michigan State University Press, East Lansing, 1993—. **Awards:** Wayne State University Arts Achievement award, 1985; Michigan Council for the Arts Creative Artist award, 1987, 1994; College Language Association Creative Achievement award, 1988, for *Octavia and Other Poems;* Arts Foundation of Michigan Literature award, 1990; Michigan Artist award, 1993; Michigan State University American Arts award, 1994; George Kent award, 1995; honorary degrees from Siena Heights College, 1991, Loyola University, 1993, and Michigan State University, 1994. **Address:** 18080 Santa Barbara Drive, Detroit, Michigan 48221, U.S.A.

PUBLICATIONS

Poetry

Songs to a Phantom Nightingale, as Naomi Cornelia Long. New York, Fortuny's, 1941.
One and the Many. New York, Exposition Press, 1956.
Star by Star. Detroit, Harlo Press, 1965.
Pink Ladies in the Afternoon. Detroit, Lotus Press, 1972.
Exits and Entrances, illustrated by Beverley Rose Enright. Detroit, Lotus Press, 1978.
Phantom Nightingale: Juvenilia. Detroit, Lotus Press, 1981.
Octavia and Other Poems. Chicago, Third World Press, 1988.
Remembrances of Spring: Collected Early Poems. East Lansing, Michigan State University Press, 1993.

Recordings: *Naomi Madgett Reading Her Poems,* 1978.

Other

Success in Language and Literature (textbook). Chicago, Follett, 1967.
A Student's Guide to Creative Writing (textbook). Detroit, Penway Books, 1980.

Editor, *A Milestone Sampler: 15th Anniversary Anthology.* Detroit, Lotus Press, 1988.
Editor, *Adam of Ifé: Black Women in Praise of Black Men.* Detroit, Lotus Press, 1992.

*

Manuscript Collections: Special Collections Library, Fisk University, Nashville, Tennessee.

Critical Studies: *Black Writers Past and Present* by Esther Spring Arata, New York, Morrow, 1975; *Drumvoices: The Mission of Afro-American Poetry* by Eugene B. Redmond, New York, Doubleday, 1976; essay by Robert P. Sedlack in *Dictionary of Literary Biography,* vol. 76: *Afro-American Writers, 1940-1955,* Detroit, Gale Research, 1988.

Naomi Long Madgett comments:

I consider myself a poet first. My involvement in teaching, editing and publishing grew from that. I write from experience—real, vicarious, or imagined—when I am emotionally involved in a situation, with a character or an idea. I have tried to find my own voice, have tried to be honest, and have not followed current trends. While my work begins on a personal level, it is my hope that the finished product will affect others and invite them to bring their own experience to the poem. My greatest hope is that even a small portion of my work will continue to have meaning to others after my voice is still.

I work at a poem until I feel that each word, each mark of punctuation, each distillation is as precise as I can possibly make it.

*   *   *

The daughter of a bookish Baptist minister who began writing poetry at an early age, Naomi Long Madgett's work divides into two concerns: expressions of personal emotion and issues of African American culture. Over the course of her long career, she moves from a youthful imitator of black and white romantic poets (Keats, Tennyson, Dunbar, Cullen, Anne Spencer, and Georgia Douglas Johnson) to modernist experiments in free verse, vernacular diction, and sequential form. Because the early publication of poems written between the seventh and tenth grades in *Songs to a Phantom Nightingale* place her in the beginning of an important 30-year period of poetry by African American women, critics have been interested in Madgett's early work; her response to this interest has been that she has brought out much of her juvenilia in two volumes, the most complete being *Remembrances of Spring.*

Though personally acquainted with Langston Hughes at the age of 14, Madgett's embrace of Romantic and Victorian English poets was a pervasive influence for many years; even in the free verse of her later volumes there is inverted syntax and stilted diction in poems as late as her collection that spans 1965-71. It is not until the love poem "Trinity: A Dream Sequence" in *Star by Star* that Madgett assumes a mode that is purged of imitation. "Trinity" is a blend of the elements that characterize Madgett's personal poetry: natural imagery, simplicity of theme, religious emotion, and the conventions of romantic poetry; here she has transcended the limitations of her early work and formed a modernist sequence of 19 short lyrics that are at once mystical, erotic, enigmatic, and piercing. The sequence concludes with a thrust into the unknown: "Then let them pray for us, / Pardoned but lost."

Though Madgett desired not to be an African American poet but a poet, it is clear that her concern with sociological issues gradually expanded. Of the 67 poems in *One and the Many,* nine are concerned with race, the rest largely with love. "Monkey Man" uses ridicule to protest antisocial behavior within the black community: "But Gin Stevens is coming to town, / So to hell with Sunday and God and rent / And educating the children and saving for a rainy day. / ... Grin you monkey, you!" More typical are poems directed to praising the strength and beauty that she sees in the black community and statements of social protest: in "Scorn Not My Station" she speaks of "A strength of which you cannot dream," and in "To My Country" asks "Then what will you say to the man who would not die / In spite of you?" Madgett's best known poem, "Midway," is included in the volume; the poem is a rhythmically stirring anthem of three stanzas that summarizes the course of the African American's response to adversities, resolving to the upbeat declaration that "Mighty mountains loom before me / and I won't stop now." In the poems that do not address racial themes Madgett demonstrates an increasing mastery of imagery and sound: particularly striking is the short lyric "Night Rider" with its rapturous romantic voice and stimulating visual effects: "Fling down the night's imperious delay, / Forestall the moth with star-singed wing."

With *Pink Ladies in the Afternoon* Madgett retreats from love poetry into a concern with domestic experiences; many of her poems in that collection and the ones that follow are concerned with her own past and there is uniformly present a nostalgic tone. In "Newblack" she strikes out at the new cultural style introduced by the militant nationalism of the period; the poem is a corrective that parodies the discourse of separatism. Poems in *Exits and Entrances* reach a new level of complexity of form and imagistic inventiveness in the monologue "Phillis": Speaking as Phillis Wheatley, the slave poet, the Africans are gathered in an "airless tomb," and the ship is a "helltrap of the dead and dying." The poem casts its light on both poet and subject in its forceful conclusion: "Lurking beneath the docile Christian lamb, / Unconquered lioness asserts: 'I am!'"

The poems in *Octavia and Other Poems* are often occasional and nostalgic, but they are neither sentimental nor obligatory. Particularly effective are the poems on her father, "He Lives in Me," and her poem for Langston Hughes, "Black Poet." The first is built up of Whitmanian catalogs that are rich in details and communicate an aura of earnest self knowledge. Allusions redolent of Old Testament imagery support the praise of Hughes in four free-verse stanzas: the compact poem moves from the "ripe fruit" of the poet's words to a consideration of the miracle of their origin: "Surely it is his / nimble fingers still / that teach us how / to harvest ripe figs / from thorn trees / that were supposed to die."

—Jon Woodson

MAGUIRE, Sarah

Nationality: British. **Born:** West London, England, 1957. **Education:** University of East Anglia, B.A. in English; studied at Cambridge University. **Career:** Writer, teacher, and broadcaster. Tutor, Arvon Foundation, 1990—; teacher of creative writing, London Lighthouse; writer-in-residence at an English prison, 1992-93; creative writing fellow, University of Leeds, 1996; represented British Council as poetry reader in Palestine, 1996. Contributor to periodicals and radio programs. **Address:** Notting Hill, London, England.

PUBLICATIONS

Poetry

Spilt Milk. London, Secker & Warburg, 1991.
The Invisible Mender. London, J. Cape, 1997.

*   *   *

The warm reception accorded to Sarah Maguire's first volume *Spilt Milk,* led to her inclusion in a promotion of 20 "New Generation Poets" sponsored by the British Arts Council in 1994. It was a well-deserved tribute to an interesting debut. *Spilt Milk* contains 33 poems, most of them fairly short, covering a wide range of themes delivered in a clean, uncluttered style. Maguire's tone, especially in her first collection, is inherently intimate and direct; the space between herself and the reader might be no more than that separating a couple of chairs. This immediacy is occasionally vitiated by a plethora of horticultural and botanical terms; Maguire trained as a gardener and evidently relishes displaying the knowledge she acquired in the process. A whole section in her second collection, *The Invisible Mender*, is devoted to poems on themes derived from her gardening years grouped under the heading of "Nursery Practices." But there is something engaging about finding a poet grounded in an essentially urban milieu who discovers rich sources of metaphor in plants and their propagation, and can tell her *Bellis perennis* from her *Festuca rubra commutata*.

It would be misleading, though, to suggest that horticulture forms more than a strand—if quite a broad one—in Maguire's creative make-up. She was born in London, and the phenomena of big city life, with its restlessness and latent sense of dislocation, occupy the foreground of much of her work. The poems of *Spilt Milk* deal with many issues and experiences in a variety of locations. The first poem addresses a friend in Warsaw at a time of the fall-out from Chernobyl, when television pictures were showing "gallons of contaminated Polish milk / swilled into sewers." Another evokes the pleasures of whiskey tasting allied to erotic enjoyment: "the hot sweet smoked malt / that I burned of and for you". Witty and sometimes almost surreal juxtapositions and connections enrich her verbal palette. In the title poem, for example, aspirins dissolving cloudily in a glass contrast with the milkiness of semen: sex as painkiller perhaps. And the last poem puns on a shark's organ of propulsion (fin) and other things joining it in coming to an end—a cigarette, maybe a relationship, and the collection itself.

The Invisible Mender, a more deliberately structured book than its predecessor, is divided into four sections on broadly thematic lines. There are numerous poems here of greater power and complexity than Maguire was able to achieve in *Spilt Milk*, although this enrichment has been won at the cost of a slight loss of immediacy, with even the poet's personality seeming more recessed. The six poems in the first section derived from experiences abroad and examine issues ranging from the reality of human progress to the nature of liberty—this in a powerfully moving poem which contemplates the Maryland State Penitentiary. A poem describing a visit to Jerusalem's Muslim quarter illustrates the vivid, almost filmic quality of Maguire's best writing and her robust choice of verbs:

> The Old City unspools behind me
> as I slip down the Suq Khan ez-Zeit
> close as a shadow to a hand.
>
> Sallow lamps pool on the ceiling
> threading me down
> to the bottom of light.

Another section, "Wires," consists—as Maguire puts it—of "a free adaption (or Lowellian imitation) of Marina Tsvetaeva's cycle of ten poems, 'Provoda,' inspired by Tsvetaeva's passionate epistolatory relationship with Boris Pasternak." This is a virtuoso rendering of intense emotions aroused by unconsummated erotic passion. Finally, after "Nursery Practices," there is a section of poems on more particularly personal and domestic themes. These are grouped under the name of the title poem "The Invisible Mender"—a touching mediation on the birth mother of Maguire, who was born to Irish parents, then adopted. This biographical fact may explain why her poetry can at times convey the impression of someone in a state of internal exile, whose core identity is something of a patchwork affair in need of occasional mending: "I read the signs but don't know where I am" ("Travelling Northwards"). In this light, stating the problem in a poem represents a means of self-location or—as Shakespeare has it—"by indirection find[ing] direction out." And it is on a positive note that the collection ends; with a poem which presents the reassembly of a dismantled saxophone as a metaphor for achieving wholeness: "and now you're making music, / Body and Soul."

—Rivers Carew

MAIDEN, Jennifer

Nationality: Australian. **Born:** Penrith, New South Wales, 7 April 1949. **Education:** Macquarie University, North Ryde, New South Wales, B.A. 1974. **Family:** Married David Toohey in 1984; one daughter. **Career:** Tutor in creative writing, Outreach, Evening College Movement, and Blacktown City Council, all New South Wales, and Fellowship of Australian Writers and University of Western Sydney, 1976-91. Writer-in-residence, Australian National University, Canberra, New South Wales, State Torture and Trauma Rehabilitation Unit, and University of Western Sydney, all 1989. **Awards:** Australia Council grant or fellowship, 1974, 1975, 1977, 1978, 1983, 1984, 1986; Harri Jones memorial prize; Butterly-Hooper award. **Address:** P.O. Box 4, Penrith, New South Wales 2750, Australia.

PUBLICATIONS

Poetry

Tactics. St. Lucia, University of Queensland Press, 1974.
The Occupying Forces. St. Lucia, Makar Press, 1975.
The Problem of Evil. Sydney, Poetry Society of Australia, 1975.
Birthstones. Sydney, Angus & Robertson, 1978.
The Border Loss. Sydney, Angus & Robertson, 1979.
For the Left Hand. Sydney, South Head Press, 1981.
The Trust. Wentworth Falls, New South Wales, Black Lightning Press, 1988.
The Winter Baby. Sydney, Angus & Robertson, 1990.
Bastille Day. Canberra, National Library of Australia, 1990.
Selected Poems of Jennifer Maiden. Ringwood, Victoria, and New York, Penguin, 1990.
Acoustic Shadow. Ringwood, Victoria, and New York, Penguin, 1993.

Novels

The Terms. Sydney, Hale & Iremonger, 1982.

Play with Knives. Sydney, Allen & Unwin, 1990.

Short Stories

Mortal Details. Melbourne, Rigmarole, 1977.

*

Critical Study: By Elizabeth Perkins, in *Linq* (Townsville, Queensland), vol. 16, no. 3, 1989.

*   *   *

"Ambivalent, ambidextrous, ambiguous, androgynous, amorous, ironic"—so Jennifer Maiden characterizes her poetry. "Teasing, intellectual irony, too, has always seemed to me a humane new channel toward pensive seduction for what otherwise, in more direct poetry, can be a jealous urge for power over the reader." Such poetic intent suggests demanding work, resistant to easy interpretation. It also promises, in its fruition, accomplished, complex poetry that is controlled, cerebral, and yet sensuous. Maiden's assured role as an Australian poet of significance attests that these promises have been kept.

The properties that Maiden lists (and to which might be added wit) are at work in her eight-part poem "The Trust." In a footnote she cautions that while the poem is "about" the reader-writer relationship, this is just one aspect of a work that "concentrates on all forms of intimacy." The first part begins in mid-conversation but soon warns the reader to maintain critical distance, while simultaneously beckoning us into the poem:

> ... Don't trust
> me yet: I don't know what I will still
> require of you, and you don't know
> as yet the depth and danger in your trust.
> There is no room here to run, and none
> in you that I can run from. Here she is!
>   ... We can wake her.
> When you do, you clasp her shoulders, fear
> that somehow your hands don't look right.

Three characters: a woman, a man, and an antelope (unicorn?) are brought to life within an enclosed garden. These resonant images undergo several transformations, with writer inviting reader into a series of carefully staged scenes: "just do / what you like to the oyster-woman, but / note that 'to' not 'with', / and save some fear for later"; "He's / alive and you are quite free to explore. Yes, / ignore that first ignoble moral scruple." The reader is cajoled into erotic experiences with the "characters," the writer standing guard and assuring privacy. In the fourth part the writer becomes actor:

> It isn't to escape that I have come, but
> your other's body's thin enough to hold,
> is artefactually fragile ...
> and every pulse is subtle, is a watch
> to tell me time and date and where and this,
> exclusive as a dream.

Within this enclosure the "others" change shape, die (the antelope as sacrifice), and are resurrected in different forms, while the garden freezes over and disappears.

The poem is, like the garden, enclosed. Its end is its beginning, for its last line is also the first ("here it is. As it is always said / we-begin-here-at-the-end and anything which comes / after that is what we will discuss"). Indeed, within this circularity there is "no room to run"; the transitional lines repeated to link sections of the poem often hinge on the impossibility of the escape routes of the real world: "If all things here were penetrably live, / you would trust in an escape by promises."

The poet's voice is sometimes hospitable: "flood the glass / and we will drink to you— / who'll never now be stranger to / our gates, which you must soon accept are gone"; "I have only / come to empty ashtrays, to clean / cages. Take your meal." Sometimes, however, it is admonitory: "and who and why / are these poor creatures married in our arms? / You have no right to pity. It is mine. / I own this army."

The true characters of "The Trust" are reader and writer; they manipulate the "others" like marionettes, an androgynous two in a collusion of mind, offering and enjoying bodies within the garden while dogs howl at the gates. The staged scenes increasingly reveal themselves as synonyms for intimate relationships in which roles are forever changing and that which is eaten later consumes. For instance, the sacrificed antelope becomes guest at a ceremonial meal: "The woman converts simply to a chair. / The man becomes a table, well. The small / antelope sits feeding now. / It is clovenly exquisite, / picking softly at smoked entrails." The ritual dance in the garden continues through sacrifice, death, resurrection, cyclic change (winter), impermanence within a cycle of renewal through change. "The Trust" is at once an exercise in the examination of the illusions of poetry ("The lyrical vulture / flexes his wings a little, on the ground / with her, you and no drama: and I wait") and in the exchanges of intimacy. The interplay of themes and adroit precision of language is illustrative of Maiden's work at its most accomplished.

Maiden's career has been extraordinarily prolific, and her collections are carefully shaped. *The Trust* and *The Problem of Evil* balance their complex long poems with shorter, lighter selections. "Falling to Prettiness," "Celebration," and "Language" ("I need to learn a language but not english / or at present any further maidenese. / I know some anglo-saxon but it is / a lonely language") contrast with "The Trust." "The Problem of Evil" is a poetic novella of guerrilla warfare that has received several interpretations (the incursion of poetry into the domain of prose; the war between the sexes). The poems that follow it ("Mobiles," "The Sponge") are set in recognizably domestic worlds. *For the Left Hand* is a volume on a single theme, a woman who has lived "thirty years in a house with the boxes, gentling." Longer poems "For the Left Hand" (1, 11, and 111) enclose a series of short "boxes," in each compartment a segment of her life.

Birthstones reaches beyond the jewels of each month. January has five lines on the garnet and "the myriad redness of birth" followed by "Truce," on the child within the womb: "You are as beautiful / as blood underwater ... Our shadows fuse & melt / & swim a dark survival / that panicked to be felt." "Seal Pup" twists these gentle images of birth and blood; a mother seal is killed by hunters, and her pup "suckles from the dead." The September sapphire, "One chill of mary-blue ... defying tenderness between / wearer & worn," precedes a brittle "Serenade" of "mutilated fondness" and "Mars & Venus," dominated by cool tones of blue and white, of "icy perfumes." One of the distinctive touches of "maidenese" is most surely felt in the imaginative pairings of Maiden's poetry.

—Nan Bowman Albinski

MARLATT, Daphne

Nationality: Canadian. **Born:** Daphne Buckle, in Melbourne, Victoria, 11 July 1942. **Education:** University of British Columbia, Vancouver, B.A. 1964; Indiana University, Bloomington, M.A. 1968. **Family:** Married Gordon Alan Marlatt (divorced, 1970); one son. **Career:** Instructor in English, Capilano College, North Vancouver, 1968, 1973-76; writer-in-residence, University of Manitoba, Winnipeg, 1982, University of Alberta, Edmonton, 1985-86, and University of Western Ontario, 1993; Ruth Wynn Woodward Professor of Women's Studies, Simon Fraser University, Burnaby, British Columbia, 1988-89; instructor in poetry, University of British Columbia, 1989-90. Poetry editor, *Capilano Review,* Vancouver, 1973-76; editor, with Paul de Barros, *Periodics,* Vancouver, 1977-81; associate editor, *Island,* 1980-83. **Awards:** Canada Council grant, 1969, 1973, 1985, 1987; honorary degree from University of Western Ontario, 1996. **Member:** Editorial collective, *Tessera,* 1983-91. **Address:** c/o Writers' Union of Canada, 24 Ryerson Avenue, Toronto, Ontario M5T 2P3, Canada.

PUBLICATIONS

Poetry

Frames of a Story. Toronto, Ryerson Press, 1968.
Leaf Leaf / s. Los Angeles, Black Sparrow Press, 1969.
(Poems). Kyoto, Origin, 1970.
Vancouver Poems. Toronto, Coach House Press, 1972.
Steveston. Vancouver, Talonbooks, 1974; revised edition, Edmonton, Alberta, Longspoon Press, 1984.
Our Lives. Carrboro, North Carolina, Truck Press, 1975; revised edition, Lantzville, British Columbia, Oolichan, 1979.
Solstice: Lunade. Buffalo, State University of New York, 1980.
Here and There. Lantzville, British Columbia, Island, 1981.
How Hug a Stone. Winnipeg, Turnstone Press, 1983.
Touch to My Tongue. Edmonton, Alberta, Longspoon Press, 1984.
Double Negative. Charlottetown, Prince Edward Island, Gynergy, 1988.
Salvage. Red Deer, Red Deer College Press, 1991.
Ghost Works. Edmonton, NeWest Press, 1993.
Two Women in a Birth, with Betsy Worland. Toronto and New York, Guernica, 1994.

Novels

Zócalo. Toronto, Coach House Press, 1977.
Ana Historic. Toronto, Coach House Press, 1988; London, Women's Press, 1990.
Taken. Toronto, Coach House Press, 1996.

Other

Rings (miscellany). Toronto, York Street Commune, 1971.
Selected Writing: Net Work, edited by Fred Wah. Vancouver, Talonbooks, 1980.
What Matters: Writing 1968-1970. Toronto, Coach House Press, 1980.
Mauve, text in French by Nichole Brossard. Montreal, nbj / writing, 1985.

Character, text in French by Nichole Brossard. Montreal, nbj / writing, 1986.

Editor, *Steveston Recollected: A Japanese-Canadian History.* Victoria, Provincial Archives of British Columbia, 1975.
Co-editor, *Opening Doors: Vancouver's East End.* Victoria, Provincial Archives of British Columbia, 1979.
Editor, *Lost Language,* by Maxine Gadd. Toronto, Coach House Press, 1982.
Editor, with others, *Telling It: Women and Language across Cultures.* Vancouver, Press Gang, 1990.

*

Critical Studies: Essay by L. Ricou, in *A Mazing Space: Writing Canadian Women Writing,* edited by Shirley Neuman and Smaro Kamboureli, Edmonton, Longspoon Press, 1986; *Line* (special Marlatt issue), no. 13, 1989; by Stan Drugland in his *The Bees of the Invisible: Essays in Contemporary English Canadian Writing,* 1991; in *Beyond Tish,* edited by Douglas Barbour, Edmonton, NeWest Press, 1991.

*   *   *

In "Musing with Mothertongue" (in *Tessera*) Daphne Marlatt notes that "language is first of all for us a body of sound." It is this sense of poetry (and, indeed, all language) as sound that gives Marlatt's work its characteristic rhythms and which explains, as well, the other quality which marks the writing: its meticulous attention to detail and form. The images that Marlatt selects are exact renderings of the environment she is describing, but their appropriateness extends beyond the mimetic; they fragment and rejoin to form impressions governed by the sounds they make in combination. These new relationships of word elements and phrases, sometimes created by spontaneous association and sometimes by carefully crafted quibbles, punctuation, or postmodern doubling—"this body my [d]welling place"—create in the poems, and even in the prose criticism, a series of new and deeper meanings as the writing progresses. It is as process, then, that the poems must be read and, in fact, that the whole of Marlatt's work should be seen. The later work interrogates the process even more strongly, questioning the relationship of female sexuality, mothering, and language within an *écriture féminine,* a concern for language as body. The novel *Ana Historic* overlays personal and social history onto the process of language, creating a biography as historiography. The later *Ghost Works* continues the layering of memory, autobiography, and narrative, though in a more straightforward diction with less conscious wordplay.

The early poems in *Frames of a Story* establish Marlatt's desire for an escape into a literary process which will free her two protagonists from the framing influence of their grandmother's strict past, even as it frees Marlatt from the framing structures of traditional literary expression. To some extent the dilemma is autobiographical in that Marlatt is the child of colonial British parents (a background she later explores in "In the month of hungry ghosts"). More important, the struggle of the two girls to see themselves and each other through new frames, to create a world out of their own perceptions, becomes the central aim of the poems. The two girls—each an extension of one aspect of Marlatt's own struggle toward commitment and self—do not succeed in finding freedom, nor does Marlatt find her independent voice.

In *Leaf Leaf / s,* however, Marlatt begins to assemble experience from the disparate images around her and to create poetry from the sounds these images evoke in words. The curious amalgam of visual and aural images that mark her writing from this point forms a series of complex photographs which simultaneously present a picture, its sounds, the effect of the image on the perceiver, and the resonance of that perception in the reader's ear. These four sets of stimuli for every impression, each one independent but all necessary for the total effect, force a process in reading which renders the poetry not only amazingly precise but also experiential. One does not observe the world Marlatt reports, but rather one enters it and, in fact, creates it with her.

Marlatt's vision has been called "phenomenological" by Douglas Barbour, Robert Lecker, and others, and certainly by the time she writes the *Steveston* poems it is clear that her universe has become one of sense perceptions. It is important, however, to observe the role of sound as one of these sensations, in itself a separate aspect of the world and an equal building block with other influences in which the poet finds herself immersed. This composite universe does not follow a sequential, conscious intellectual analysis in its groupings of phenomena, yet, in the relationship of sound to meaning and of personal experience to poetic moment, a strict relationship of cause and effect emerges. The layering of perception is perhaps most clearly seen in *Double Negative,* where a train trip across Australia links visual documents with memories of lovemaking between two women, with concepts of the desert, with the train as umbilical cord linking the earth as Mother to the "cyclical nature of female orgasm." Nowhere is Marlatt's a linear construct, however, not even aboard a train. She seeks in a central metaphor of birth for an explanation of the writing impulse and a feminine vision of causality. Indeed, in *Rings* the entrances of the husband into the private world of mother and child mark a shift from a soft and creative language to one of more complex, but less felt, ideas and of direct connections. The experiences that fill Marlatt's world become more and more fragments of feminine process: blood, water, a letting go, mouths as sucking. Again, in *Tessera* she suggests that "like the mother's body, language is larger than us and carries us along with it. It bears us, it births us, insofar as we bear with it."

The work since *How Hug a Stone* develops these concerns from a more overtly theoretical perspective. In retrospect, however, one can see in the earliest poems the clear roots of the poet's identification with language as an extension of the female body and the process of writing as linked to the processes of female sexuality, to menstrual blood, to flowing. The sounds become more gentle as they are freed of what Marlatt calls "terms for dominance tied up with male experience," such as those she employs in the angry sociological statements of *Steveston. Salvage* rewrites the experience of the *Steveston* poems and other early work, removing the discourse of dominance and bringing forward the feminist concerns which Marlatt feels were always in the background of the work. The pun of its title echoes the aim of *Double Negative* to "[im]print" the "negative term" *women* "in the positive." All the work retains astonishing clarity, and the precise patterns her work forms create the multiple and overlapping impressions which are the core of Marlatt's poetry.

—Reid Gilbert

MAYER, Bernadette

Nationality: American. **Born:** Brooklyn, New York, 12 May 1945. **Education:** New School for Social Research, 1965-66. **Family:** Three children. **Career:** Poet and educator; has taught poetry at numerous institutions, including at the St. Mark's Poetry Project, New York, and at the New School for Social Research. Lives in New York.

PUBLICATIONS

Poetry

Ceremony Latin. New York, Angel Hair, 1964.
Story. New York, 0 to 9 Books, 1968.
Moving. New York, Angel Hair, 1971.
The Basketball Article, with Anne Waldman. New York, Angel Hair, 1975.
Memory. Plainfield, Vermont, North Atlantic Books, 1975.
Studying Hunger. Berkeley, Serendipity Books, 1975.
Poetry. New York, Kulchur Foundation, 1976.
Eruditio ex Memoria. New York, Angel Hair, 1977.
The Golden Book of Words. Lenox, Massachusetts, Angel Hair, 1978.
Midwinter Day. Berkeley, Turtle Island Foundation, 1982.
Incidents Reports Sonnets. New York, Archipelago Books, 1984.
Utopia. New York, United Artists Books, 1984.
Mutual Aid. New York, Mademoiselle de la Mole Press, 1985.
Sonnets. New York, Tender Buttons, 1989.
The Formal Field of Kissing. New York, Catchword Papers, 1990.
A Bernadette Mayer Reader. New York, New Directions, 1992.
The Desire of Mothers to Please Others in Letters. Stockbridge, Massachusetts, Hard Press, 1994.

Other

The Art of Science Writing, with Dale Worsley. New York, Teachers & Writers Collaborative, 1989.
Proper Names and Other Stories. New York, New Directions, 1996.

*

Critical Studies: In *Obdurate Brilliance: Exteriority and the Modern Long Poem,* by Peter Baker, Gainsville, University of Florida Press, 1991; "The Colors of Consonance" (interview) by Ken Jordan, in *Poetry Project Newsletter,* no. 146, October / November 1992; interview with Michael Gizzi, in *Lingo,* no. 1, 1993; *Writing for Bernadette,* edited by William Corbett and Michael Gizzi, Great Barrington, Massachusetts, The Figures, 1995.

*   *   *

Bernadette Mayer writes an inclusive poetry that seeks to capture all the ephemeral phenomena that is normally experienced in everyday life. In all of her projects, Mayer has explained that she seeks to create the "unrepeatable work," a unique and honest expression of a particular experience. Her poetry combines memories, objects seen, dreams, and musings to create a landscape of consciousness on which the full interplay of the mind is given free rein. Her best known works are *Memory,* which began as a performance / installation piece, and *Midwinter Day,* a long poem chronicling the mental and physical events of a single day in the poet's life. Besides her own writing, Mayer has also taught poetry workshops for many years at the St. Mark's Poetry Project in New York City. Through her workshops in experimental poetry, she has taught a number of young poets who went on to form the Language school of poetry.

Mayer's first project to attract widespread critical attention was 1972's *Memory,* an installation of photographs and recorded spoken text set up at the 98 Greene Street Gallery in New York City. To create the exhibit, Mayer took some 1,200 color photographs—a roll of film every day during July of 1971—and recorded some seven hours worth of narration. The photos were arranged in rows along the gallery walls while Mayer's recorded voice commenting on the depicted scenes and digressing in creative ways from the thoughts the photos inspired was played over loudspeakers. An important early influence on the Performance Art movement, Mayer's *Memory* was partially published in book form in 1975. The printed text of the event resembles the barrage of words and images a resident might encounter and react to while walking through an urban setting.

A similar concern for the poet's social environment is found in Mayer's 1982 book *Midwinter Day,* in which the poet describes a day in her life in a single, multi-faceted 119-page poem. Alternating between verse to prose according to the poet's mood changes during the course of the poem, the book attempts to forge a larger spiritual or moral dimension from the seemingly-inconsequential events of an ordinary day. The poem includes sections of Mayer's dreams, descriptions of her surroundings, and familial memories. Her candid reporting of the actual conditions of a mind at work in the course of a day has drawn praise from critics who see her approach as being inherently beyond poetic theory of any kind and closer to an honest use of language as a means of expressing the reality of the human mind.

—Denise Wiloch

MAYER, Gerda (Kamilla)

Nationality: British. **Born:** Gerda Kamilla Stein, Karlsbad, Czechoslovakia, 9 June 1927; immigrated to Great Britain in 1939; became citizen in 1949. **Education:** Attended schools in Czechoslovakia and England, 1933-44; Bedford College, London, 1960-63, B.A. 1963. **Family:** Married Adolf Mayer in 1949. **Career:** Worked on farms in Worcestershire and Surrey, 1945-46; office worker in London, 1946-52. **Address:** 12 Margaret Avenue, London E4 7NP, England.

PUBLICATIONS

Poetry

Oddments. Privately printed, 1970.
Gerda Mayer's Library Folder. Kettering, Northamptonshire, All-In, 1972.

Treble Poets 2, with Florence Elon and Daniel Halpern. London, Chatto & Windus, 1975.
The Knockabout Show (for children). London, Chatto & Windus, 1978.
Monkey on the Analyst's Couch. Sunderland, Ceolfrith Press, 1980.
The Candy-Floss Tree (for children), with Norman Nicholson and Frank Flynn. Oxford, Oxford University Press, 1984.
March Postman. Berkhamsted, Hertfordshire, Priapus, 1985.
A Heartache of Grass. Calstock, Cornwall, Peterloo Poets, 1988.
Time Watching. London, Hearing Eye, 1995.

Other

Editor, *Poet Tree Centaur: A Walthamstow Group Anthology.* London, Oddments, 1973.

*

Gerda Mayer comments:

I have written square poems, pointed poems, my poems have been around.

*   *   *

Gerda Mayer's poems have that direct simplicity of approach that gives them an air of timelessness, something of the atmosphere of the folktales which will address God or the universe as if it were as casual as speaking over the fence to your next-door neighbor. I don't know if this has anything to do with Mayer's Czechoslovakian origins and memories, but I suspect it has; and the fact is there, her poems are like that. "Save the world God, save your creatures save us for a rainy day." Even when she is taking on current subjects and concerns such as the environment, the same approach comes to the fore and the "Consumer" assumes a fabulosity:

The Great Consumer
crops the ground bare
where are the flowers?
where the sweet parsnips?

It is the same quality which enables her to invest the everyday with the surreal clarity of dreams:

The waiter licks the tablecloth clean
he licks clean the plates the glasses the
flowers his tongue
moves between the prongs of the forks

It is a superb talent and it is Mayer's own, and it makes her a fine creator of poems for young people. Poems which, like all the best poems for young people, are not written down to them, but are a natural extension of the rest of her work, with the same sharp humor and directness of approach:

In childhood I took it for granted
that Adam and Eve were Jews:
though implied rather than stated
it was Good News.

Mayer's collection *Monkey on the Analyst's Couch* confirms her place alongside those other poets of a sharp-eyed sparkling wit

such as Stevie Smith. But at the back of Mayer's poetry is a depth of dark experience which makes her balanced and wry view of the world the more remarkable and worthy of our attention.

In *A Heartache of Grass* Mayer confronts that depth of dark experience more directly and has produced a moving and chastening collection of poems. The book is dedicated to Muriel and Trevor Chadwick, to whom, she says, "I owe my preservation." Behind the dedication is a story of physical and emotional survival, of heartrendings, and of the downright savagery of the Nazi regime. It is not that Mayer forgives, for who could forgive such mindless barbarity? It is not that she reconciles us to the horrors of that time; that would be asking the impossible. It is not that she lashes out in anger, which could be understood. What she does is to confront these outrages against common humanity with a human dignity and intelligence which is the opposite of what her enemies and her race's enemies stood for. That she can do this with humor is an even greater measure of her spirit. In this she is a model to those of us who strive toward Christian values and to many of her own coreligionists. The poem quoted above ends:

The swastikas of my childhood,
chalked up on the wall,
the rain and the years have washed away
And the Bible survives them all.

In *A Heartache of Grass* it is as if Mayer has been working toward this confrontation all the time. In her poem "Make Believe," addressed to her father Arnold Stein, who disappeared in the maelstrom that was Europe in 1940, she triumphantly and movingly succeeds:

That is why at sixty
when some publisher asks me
for biographical details,
I still carefully give
the year of my birth,
the name of my hometown:
GERDA MAYER born '27, in Karlsbad,
Czechoslovakia ... write to me, father.

A Heartache of Grass is a book to be read as a testament to the dignity of the human spirit and as a lesson in the use of poetry.

Eminently readable and deceptively simple, Mayer's poetry is penetrating stuff. It should be read with care, as readers can suddenly find themselves falling unexpectedly into great wells of meaning and emotion.

—John Cotton

McALPINE, Rachel

Nationality: New Zealander. **Born:** 1940. **Family:** Married; children. **Career:** High school teacher in New Zealand, 1960, 1979-83; consular clerk, British Consulate Genera, Geneva, 1961-63; writer-in-residence, Macquarie University, Sydney, 1982, and Canterbury University, 1986; freelance writer, 1984-92; lecturer, Doshisha Women's College, Kyoto, Japan, 1993—. **Address:** c/o Glenys Bean, 15 Elizabeth St., Freeman's Bay, Auckland, New Zealand.

PUBLICATIONS

Poetry

Lament for Ariadne. Dunedin, New Zealand, Caveman Press, 1975.
Stay at the Dinner Party. Dunedin, New Zealand, Caveman Press, 1977.
Fancy Dress. Auckland, Cicada, 1979.
House Poems. Wellington, New Zealand, Nutshell Books, 1980.
Recording Angel. Wellington, New Zealand, Mallinson Rendel, 1983.
Thirteen Waves. Feilding, New Zealand, Homeprint, 1986.
Selected Poems. Wellington, New Zealand, Mallinson Rendel, 1988.
Tourist in Kyoto. Wellington, New Zealand, Nutshell Books, 1993.

Plays

The Stationary Sixth Form Poetry Trip. Wellington, New Zealand, Playmarket, 1980.
Driftwood. Wellington, Victoria University Press, 1985.
Peace Offering. Auckland, Heinemann, 1988.
Power Play. Wellington, New Zealand, Playmarket, 1990.

Novels

The Limits of Green. Auckland, Viking, 1985.
Running away from Home. Auckland and New York, Penguin, 1987.
Farewell Speech. Auckland, Penguin, 1990.

Other

Song in the Satchel: Poetry in the High School. Wellington, New Zealand Council for Educational Research, 1980.
Real Writing. N.p., 1992.
Maria in the Middle (for children). Auckland, Viking, 1993.

*

Critical Studies: Interview with Michael Harlow, in *Landfall,* no. 145, 1983; interview with Harry Ricketts in his *Talking about Ourselves,* Wellington, Mallinson Rendel, 1986.

*   *   *

The author of seven volumes of poetry, Rachel McAlpine was inspired by the feminist movement to "stick her neck out" by altruistically writing for other women. Her first volume, *Lament for Ariadne,* coincided with International Women's Year in 1975, creating an association in readers' minds with her own liberation. Married and mother of four children when she began writing poetry in 1974, she later separated from her husband, but has subsequently written more verse, plays, and several novels. As an active feminist in the 1970s and 1980s, her originally personal and intimate poetry acquired more political overtones. Critics have acclaimed her vibrant voice and exuberant celebration of womanhood.

McAlpine's writing displays a natural affinity with her country's culture and landscape: her claim that she could be only a New Zealand writer is confirmed by an apt colloquial diction, as in two sequences of imagined dialogues: between "Sheila and the Honourable Member," and "A Chat with God the Mother." In five poems comprising "Katherine's Mansfield's Slippers" (*Fancy Dress*), intertextual allusions are the departure for literary impersonations. Writing on sexual politics, she declares with nonchalant sensuality ("A Good Day" from *Recording Angel*), "I've got the random hots / I like him and I've checked him out"; in "Darling" "the word I tried to swallow ... rises in my throat / like a softened Panadol." Despite a relatively spare, undecorated style, which can be provocative and hard-hitting, she makes her points suggestively, even tenderly: in "Ruaphehu" (*Fancy Dress*), the mother's breast is evoked as the mountain's snowy whiteness:

> a morning broods
> and breaks for you
> a mountain melts
> and makes
> milk and blood
> for you

She can also lightheartedly expand several themes from a single image: in *House Poems,* an illustrated collection of 15 poems concerning emotional security, marriage, and other illusions of domestic comfort, the house anthropomorphises in a symbiosis of self and dwelling realised through gritty and poignant images: in (i) it is a "one-legged peering monocled mad old hag"; in (xiv): "I fondle the house with my fur / my long golden country fur."

McAlpine's versatility lies in a chameleon-like shift of registers and approaches: domestic settings acquire the elemental powers of the animal world, just as landscapes image human dramas. She can inhabit a scene and, by making her observations bounce off an interior view, pinpoint a mood. Her most vivid poems concern women whose lives she imagines in terms of legend, parable, nursery rhyme, or fairy tale. But mocking scrutiny of her persona as poet is also a recurrent theme. A public voice despite her personal approach, she projects the private and familiar into the realm of the familiar and shared. "Zig-zag up a Thistle" (*Recording Angel*), a poem about separation, includes "small brave lives."

> A lark aspires to the orgasm
> of a Pegasus. A lady bird
> Uses cocksfoot
> for tightrope and trapeze

Many poems work lyrically through repetition, rhythm and refrain. In "Serenade for Sappho":

> wish I could sing you, lady
> sing you a soft black moth
> to ride in the blond night sky
> where the pale clouds are flowing

McAlpine does not experiment in any formal metrical sense, although she prefers the relaxed forms and minimal punctuation of open verse. Her techniques are intuitive and sustained by her subject matter rather than developed to investigate the world which she so emphatically celebrates. For that reason, the concrete, the colloquial, and the conversational outweigh the abstract, the speculative, and the idealistic. She has been drawn more to dramatic, narrative modes than into the realm of the long poem, and her departure from poetry after the mid-1980s into the genres of drama and fiction has been a logical one.

—Janet Wilson

McGUCKIAN, Medbh

Nationality: Irish. **Born:** Maeve McCaughan, Belfast, Northern Ireland, 12 August 1950. **Education:** Dominican Convent, Fortwilliam Park, Belfast, 1961-68; Queen's University, Belfast, 1968-74, B.A. 1972, M.A. in English and Dip.Ed. 1974. **Family:** Married John McGuckian in 1977; three sons and one daughter. **Career:** English teacher, St. Patrick's College, Knock, Belfast, 1975—. Writer-in-residence, Queen's University, 1986-88. Lives in Belfast. **Awards:** Eric Gregory award, 1980; Rooney prize, 1982; Arts Council award, 1982; Alice Hunt Bartlett award, 1983; Cheltenham prize, 1989. **Address:** c/o Gallery Press, Oldcastle, County Meath, Ireland.

PUBLICATIONS

Poetry

Single Ladies: 16 Poems. Budleigh Salterton, Devon, Interim Press, 1980.
Portrait of Joanna. Belfast, Honest Ulsterman Press, 1980.
Trio Poetry, with Damian Gorman and Douglas Marshall. Belfast, Blackstaff Press, 1981.
The Flower Master. Oxford and New York, Oxford University Press, 1982.
Venus and the Rain. Oxford and New York, Oxford University Press, 1984; revised edition, Oldcastle, Gallery Press, 1994.
On Ballycastle Beach. Oxford, Oxford University Press, and Winston-Salem, North Carolina, Wake Forest University Press, 1988.
Two Women, Two Shores, with Nuala Archer. Baltimore, New Poets, 1989.
Marconi's Cottage. Oldcastle, Gallery Press, 1991.
The Flower Master, and Other Poems. Oldcastle, Gallery Press, 1993.
Captain Lavender. Winston-Salem, North Carolina, Wake Forest University Press, 1994.

Other

Editor, *The Big Striped Golfing Umbrella: Poems by Young People from Northern Ireland.* Belfast, Arts Council of Northern Ireland, 1985.

*

Medbh McGuckian comments:

I don't really feel "established" enough to be of interest to the "general reader." My "work" is usually regarded as esoteric or exotic, but that is only because its territory is the feminine subconscious, or semi-conscious, which many men will or do not recognize and many women will or cannot admit. My poems do not

seek to chart "real" experience but to tap the sensual realms of dream or daydream for their spiritual value, which enhances and makes bearable the real. Through suffering, emotion, illness, people achieve order, art, strength. I believe wholly in the beauty and power of language, the music of words, the intensity of images to shadow-paint the inner life of the soul. I believe life is a journey upwards, beyond, inwards, a ripening process. As the body wearies the spirit is born. My themes are as old as the hills and out of date—love, nature, the seasons, children—but I hope what is new is the voice binding them all, sophisticating itself into something eventually simple.

*   *   *

It quickly became a commonplace to criticize Medbh McGuckian's poetry for obscurity, lack of focus, and a plethora of images. It was ever thus: the Irish, like the Scots and the Welsh, have long experienced and understood the tyranny of English lucidity, which seeks to control the very ways in which it is permissible to create meaning. McGuckian's poetry recognizes that one mode of resistance is obliquity, the refusal to be bullied into proprietorial, "acceptable" meaning. The same conflict lies behind such diverse works as Robert Graves's "Welsh Incident" and Seamus Heaney's *North.* Being Irish and female combine to place McGuckian at a double remove from the dominant powers. She responds with a power of her own, one born of awareness, for she has anticipated her (English) critics; in *Venus and the Rain* she declares that "This oblique trance is my natural / Way of speaking." She also can expose the connections between language and domination in lines like "my longer and longer sentences / Prove me wholly female," where what at first appears to be submissiveness and self-mockery turns out to subvert the reader's hasty assumptions.

McGuckian's poems revel in their imaginative and elaborate qualities. It is not just a matter of dense imagery and difficult metaphor. Meaning is constantly deferred; sometimes, by a careful twist, the meaning is placed out of reach *after* the reader thinks it has been grasped. Even her syntax questions the ways of dominance, for her long, accretive sentences deny us the easy passage which can come only when one clause is ruthlessly subordinated to another.

Yet all this is achieved with elegant wit, for the challenges to the unself-aware custodians of power and meaning are delivered implicitly, even in disguise. Sometimes the disguise is of a person innocent of most things beyond domesticity, certainly eschewing polemic or overtly political language, apparently engaged only in "a little ladylike sewing." But McGuckian's domestic subjects are saved from coziness by placing them near bold images of desire and sexuality. Woven like a sampler, *The Flower Master* is a deliberately florid book, structured with innumerable flower images. Likewise *Venus and the Rain* is conceived as a coherent whole, an attempt to map out a distinctively female mythology and eroticism. There are many other signs of McGuckian's talent, such as her ability to be extravagant and careful, modest and ambitious at the same time or the way in which the "I" enters and leaves even her earliest poems (in *Single Ladies*) with complete naturalness and assurance of tone.

These poems call forth from the reader a patient, slow approach, willingly given after one begins to understand McGuckian's aims. The contract between poem and reader is like that between lovers, with the poem rejecting whatever smacks of brusque violation. Secretive, these poems nevertheless yield up a charge of authentic emotion each time. Sexual approach or rejection, indeed, is their paradigm for the approach to meaning:

Yours is the readership
Of the rough places where I make
My sweet refusals of you, your
Natural violence.

There is, of course, a risk inherent in subversive obliquity. It is not the risk that a certain readership will be baffled but that the impulse to translate everything into something else can lead to involutions which divert one from one's own purposes, as McGuckian is aware when she writes of "my tenable / Emotions largely playing with themselves." Much of the language of *On Ballycastle Beach* remains figurative and interior to the point of difficulty ("lightning arranges the logarithms / Of ferns, equates the radius / Of the moon to the number of breaths / We draw in an hour"), but she has also always had another linguistic register of disarming simplicity:

As a child cries, all over, I kept insisting
On robin's egg blue tiles around the fireplace,
Which gives a room a kind of flying-heartedness.

The domestic, the unconscious, and the erotic are still predominant preoccupations, but the later part of the book suggests a widening of scope.

In its blending of the native and the exotic, and in its strivings with language, McGuckian's talent sometimes suggests the Yeats of "Crossways" and "The Rose." But her voice is quite distinctively her own. An almost feverish richness of vocabulary and image is set off against a calmness of tone which is generated by the meditative or descriptive statements and the leisurely syntax. At their best her poems leave the reader with the feeling that a new language, exhilarating and mysterious, is being found in which to treat of emotion.

—R.J.C. Watt

McHUGH, Heather

Nationality: American. **Born:** California, 20 August 1948. **Education:** Radcliffe College, Cambridge, Massachusetts, 1965-69, B.A. 1970; Denver University, M.A. 1972. **Family:** Married in 1968 (divorced); 2) married Niko Boris Nikolai Popov in 1987. **Career:** Visiting lecturer, Antioch College, Yellow Springs, Ohio, 1971-72; poet-in-residence, Stephens College, Columbia, Missouri, 1974-76; assistant, then associate professor of English, State University of New York, Binghamton, 1976-84; Milliman writer-in-residence, University of Washington, Seattle, 1984—. Visiting professor, Warren Wilson College, M.F.A. Program for Writers, Swannanoa, North Carolina, 1980—, Columbia University, New York, 1980 and 1981, and University of California, Irvine, 1982; Holloway Lecturer, University of California, Berkeley, 1987; Coal-Royalty Chair, University of Alabama, 1991; Elliston Poet, University of Cincinnati, 1992; visiting professor, University of California, Los Angeles, 1994, and University of Iowa, 1991, 1995.

Awards: Academy of American Poets prize, 1972; MacDowell Colony fellowship, 1973, 1974, 1976; National Endowment for the Arts grant, 1974, 1981; Houghton Mifflin New Poetry Series award, 1977; Creative Artists Public Service grant, 1980; Rockefeller Foundation Bellagio Residency, 1984; Guggenheim fellowship, 1989; National Book award finalist, 1994: Lila Wallace/ *Reader's Digest* Writers Award, 1996-97. **Member:** Board of Directors, Associated Writing Programs, 1981-83; Literature Panel, National Endowment for the Arts, 1983-86. **Address:** Department of English, University of Washington, Seattle, Washington 98195, U.S.A.

PUBLICATIONS

Poetry

Dangers. Boston, Houghton Mifflin, 1977.
A World of Difference. Boston, Houghton Mifflin, 1981.
To the Quick. Middletown, Connecticut, Wesleyan University Press, 1987.
Shades. Middletown, Connecticut, Wesleyan University Press, 1988.
Hinge & Sign: Poems 1968-1993. Middletown, Connecticut, Wesleyan University Press, 1994.

Other

Broken English: Poetry and Partiality. Middletown, Connecticut, Wesleyan University Press, 1993.

Translator, *D'après tout: Poems,* by Jean Follain. Princeton, New Jersey, Princeton University Press, 1981.
Translator, with Niko Boris, *Because the Sea Is Black: Poems of Blaga Dimitrova.* Middletown, Connecticut, Wesleyan University Press, 1989.

*

Critical Studies: By Mary Karr, in *Harvard Book Review* (Cambridge, Massachusetts), no. 5 / 6, Summer / Fall 1987; "Poetry Chronicle. Four Salvers Salvaging: New Work by Voigt, Olds, Dove, and McHugh" by Peter Harris, in *Virginia Quarterly Review* (Charlottesville), no. 64, Spring 1988; "Killing Joke" by Joshua Weiner, in *Threepenny Review* (Berkeley, California), Spring 1989; "COMMENT: No Perimeters" by Marianne Boruch, in *American Poetry Review* (Philadelphia), March / April 1989; by Joshua Clover in *Colorado Review* (Fort Collins), Spring 1994; "Among the Wordstruck: A Review of the Poems of John Ashberry and Heather McHugh" by Linda Gregorson, in *New York Times Book Review* (New York), 23 October 1994; by Marion K. Stocking, in *Beloit Review,* Fall 1994.

*   *   *

Heather McHugh took Browning's line "Our interest's on the dangerous edge of things" as the epigraph of *Dangers,* in which she contrives to "drive / together argument and matter till you know / not what the matter is but how it shouts." Even though she sounds solitary and defiant, choosing "the artifice of hate" through which "the face / refuses to shine," she seeks to know, and thus sustain, connections. For her "The sweetness / is of paradox." In the nine small dramas of singleness and interaction that comprise the book's middle, the characters are always endangered, always persistent. The coast, where water can threaten, is her favorite vehicle to show that, even though life comprises "little / gross and no net / worth," "you know you can't / live anywhere else."

McHugh's interest in *A World of Difference* is less social than spiritual. She assigns herself responsibility for comprehending. She repudiates confessionalism, caricaturing such writers as "gunning / their electrics, going / I I I I I," and insists that "vision isn't insight, / buried at last in the first / person's eye." She accepts a world in which "the form of life / is a motion" and "color is the frequency and not the object." In such a context, human importance is dubious. Take the lovers in "When the Future Is Black," who regard themselves as only a presence "designed to keep / / the past and future from forever / meeting." Although we like to insist that "we make / a world of difference," McHugh craves selfless transcendence. Unlike those who would name—i.e., possess—God and try to "read / themselves / into his will" (note the pun), she wants to forget "all names / / for worship" and "our history of longing" and be God's "great blue breath, / his ghost and only song."

A formidable task, presumptuous perhaps, even inviting madness—but McHugh maintains vigilance, scouring even her language for misleading and distracting meaning. "Always I have to resist / the language I have / to love," she says in "Like." But unlike the discursive, frequently rhymed, and metrical poems of *Dangers,* the spareness and eccentricity of *A World of Difference* produce remarkable clarity. "Language Lesson, 1976," for instance, after seeming to satirize sayings like "hold the relish" (meaning "forget it") and "love" (meaning, in tennis, "nothing"), becomes a powerful love lyric:

> I'm saying go so far
> the customs are untold,
>
> make nothing without words
> and let me be
> the one you never hold.

Personal crises enter the poems of McHugh's third and fourth books. "I / / have lost my certainty," she writes in *To the Quick,* "and spent my spirit in a waste / of one romance." Likewise, in *Shades* she rebounds from the death of a friend from AIDS—"Day and die are cast together"—yet she remains affirmative: "It's not / when, what or how we are / that makes one wonder / without end. It's *that.*"

The fundamental problem renews itself: "The ends / of life are rich, it's only / explanation that grows poor...." Poetry, McHugh declares in *Broken English,* "does not give itself as evidence, as inscription"; instead, "It *is* the place that suffers inscription. It bears the mark or scar of what was seen and what was grasped." A remarkable consistency of vision and language marks her entire work. Through language echoing Joyce, cummings, Berryman, and most of all Beckett, her tenacity of thought approaches radical watching.

The poems collected in *Hinge & Sign* contain riveting examples. In "Circus," "the elephant on pain / / of punishment, five times upon / the shovels of its toenails, kneels / for peanuts." By observing the pauses, construing phrases in each phase of their gathering, one finds the nuances of McHugh's vision. Paradoxically, while suggestions are multiple, the syntax plays with certainty. "Does darkness fall?" she asks in "Scenes from a Death"—"Or does the moviehouse of our mentality / just open...?" In declaratives such suggestions approach definition. In "Where" outdoors is "where nothing / is the whole idea" and "you're not / / as gone as in the house."

Point of view and persona have become fundamental in McHugh's later work. By proposing in "White Mind and Roses" that roses invent those who watch them, she recognizes humanity as the "animal / that sees the flowerer but not the flow." She also tries perspectives like a dog's and a seal's, as well as several human personae. Her 1990 work "32 Adults," inspired by collages of Tom Phillips, is a tour de force in point of view and character.

Among the credos that McHugh's epigrammatic style supplies, "to sort the never from the known" captures the essentiality of her endeavor. One limit becomes vivid as she tries futilely to see herself:

> ... someone who's always
> facing back, or inside-out, or rightside-down;
>
> someone who saw me first, and fixed herself;
> someone whose other faces I know nothing of.

Appropriately, this poem is named "Untitled."

—Jay S. Paul

McMASTER, Rhyll

Nationality: Australian. **Born:** Brisbane, Queensland, 13 August 1947. **Family:** Married Roger McDonald in 1967 (divorced, 1994); remarried 1995; three daughters. **Career:** Secretary, University of Queensland, Brisbane, 1966-71; nurse, Canberra Hospital, 1976-78; farmer, Braidwood, New South Wales, 1980-92; freelance editor, 1993-94. Poetry editor, *Canberra Times,* 1994; manuscripts assessor, National Book Council, 1994—. **Awards:** Harri Jones Memorial prize, 1971; Literature Board of the Australia Council fellowship, 1974, 1993; Victorian Premier's prize, 1986, for *Washing the Money;* Grace Leven prize, 1987, for *Washing the Money,* 1995, for *Flying the Coop;* Capital Arts Patron's Organization fellowship, 1997. **Agent:** Rose Creswell, Cameron's Management, Suite 5, Edgecliff Court, 2 New McLean Street, Edgecliff, New South Wales, 2027, Australia.

PUBLICATIONS

Poetry

The Brineshrimp. Brisbane, University of Queensland Press, 1972.
Washing the Money. Sydney, Angus & Robertson, 1986.
On My Empty Feet. Melbourne, Heinemann, 1993.
Flying the Coop (new and selected poems). Melbourne, Heinemann, 1994.
Chemical Bodies. N.p., 1997.

*

Manuscript Collection: National Library of Australia, Canberra.

*   *   *

Rhyll McMaster's first collection of poems, *The Brineshrimp,* was published in 1972. It immediately established her as a distinctive poet and was awarded the Harri Jones Memorial prize. Patrick White bought copies to give to his friends. David Malouf wrote of the collection, "Spare, tough, eloquent, these poems poke into corners of the ordinary and come up with discoveries that are sometimes scary, often hilarious, always enlarging of our sense of the pathos and mystery of things."

Malouf's assessment is well illustrated in "Discovering Parts of the Body":

Stepping out of the bath
my left heel from this angle looks very tender,
by which I mean inoffensive,
like an apple,
small, clean, thin-skinned, an nob of sweet Johnathan...
A dull strangeness
in looking at things closely;
I'll pretend I'm an Eastern lady
with heels like two ripe fruit.
The Hordes, when they catch me will want
to twist them off,
and eat them slice by slice.

It would be 14 years until McMaster's second collection, *Washing the Money,* appeared. A tiny volume of 40 pages, it is padded out with home photographs of characteristic acerbity and with an ultrasound of her third daughter, Stella, in utero at 15 weeks. A young woman's precise observations have been overtaken in this book by a meticulous, intense will to tease out both precision and resonance from tiny domestic moments from childhood, and the second half explores with characteristically quirky imagery the neighborhood world of contemporary living, as in "Clockface":

Night licks the backyard with its reptile tongue.
The baby gives her windy death's-head grin;
no comfort.
Who's awake? Is there anyone?
The illuminated clockface
tells the truth;
it shakes the future out with metal teeth.

On My Empty Feet is a more substantial volume that explores with chilling coolness and power the effects of a stroke suffered by McMaster's mother. The book also has a range of suburban voices in which the poet's ear for the rhythms of everyday speech are balanced by her always quirky and vivid sense of image. Only a year after this volume, McMaster published a book of selected poems that contained a substantial selection of new work. It is clear that, after the constraints of years of domestic priorities, a changed lifestyle has released a dramatic and sometimes terrifying new flow of creativity in "Handle with Care":

No-one will come alive to wisdom
in our own lifetime.
History will not teach us
a damned thing.

The infinite monster of sorrow
lurks under the lid.
Pushing up, he grins expansively.
He has always waited in the wings,
ready to twist me,
with my tight wishes,
like a soft tin can.

Of McMaster's *Chemical Bodies* one of Australia's senior literary figures, Geoffrey Dutton, has said, "Rhyll McMaster is one of the best poets writing in Australia today: in fact, in terms of consistent quality, I think she is the finest. She is at the peak of her powers and every poem gives evidence of deep thought, a wide range of intellectual curiosity, imagination and a technical control which has been refined to an extraordinary degree." This is surely in evidence in "Growing":

My hands are growing
old before my eyes;
shrivelling at the tips;
a receding grapevine....
I'm convinced my hands
are still interim;
older women wear challenging rings
to detract sight from knuckles and skin
that puckers and tightens
grim as a Final Notice.

On an incoming tide
they swim into sight,
resembling my mother's at forty-five.

—Thomas W. Shapcott

McNEIL, Florence

Nationality: Canadian. **Born:** Vancouver, British Columbia, 8 May 1940. **Education:** University of British Columbia, Vancouver, B.A. 1961, M.A. 1965. **Family:** Married David McNeil in 1973. **Career:** Instructor in English, Western Washington State College (now University), Bellingham, 1965-68; assistant professor, University of Calgary, Alberta, 1968-73, and University of British Columbia, 1973-76. Full-time writer, 1976—. **Awards:** Macmillan of Canada prize, 1965; Canada Council award, 1976, 1978, 1980, 1982; Canadian National Magazine award, 1979; Sheila Egoff prize, for children's literature, 1989. **Address:** 20 Georgia Wynd, Delta, British Columbia V4M 1A5, Canada.

PUBLICATIONS

Poetry

A Silent Green Sky. Vancouver, Klanak Press, 1967.
Walhachin. Fredericton, New Brunswick, Fiddlehead, 1972.

The Rim of the Park. Port Clements, British Columbia, Sono Nis
    Press, 1972.
Emily. Toronto, Clarke Irwin, 1975.
Ghost Towns. Toronto, McClelland & Stewart, 1975.
A Balancing Act. Toronto, McClelland & Stewart, 1979.
The Overlanders. Saskatoon, Saskatchewan, Thistledown Press,
    1982.
Barkerville. Saskatoon, Saskatchewan, Thistledown Press, 1984.
Swimming Out of History: Poems Selected and New. Parksville,
    British Columbia, Oolichan Press, 1991.

Plays

Barkerville (produced Vancouver, 1987).

Radio Play: *Barkerville: A Play for Voices,* 1980.

Other

*When Is a Poem: Creative Ideas for Teaching Poetry Collected
    from Canadian Poets.* Toronto, League of Canadian Poets, 1980.
Miss P and Me (for children). Toronto, Clarke Irwin, 1982; New
    York, Harper, 1984.
All Kinds of Magic (for children). Vancouver, Douglas & McIntyre,
    1984.
Catriona's Island (for children). Vancouver, Douglas & McIntyre,
    1988.
Breathing Each Other's Air. Vancouver, Polestar Press, 1994.

Editor, *Here Is a Poem.* Toronto, League of Canadian Poets, 1983.
Editor, *Do the Whales Jump at Night: An Anthology of Canadian
    Poetry for Children.* Vancouver, Douglas and McIntyre, 1990.

*

Critical Studies: In *Canadian Literature* (Vancouver), Autumn
1977; *CV 2* (Winnipeg), no. 4, Spring 1979 / Autumn 1982.

Florence McNeil comments:

I'm interested in visual imagery and contrasts. Therefore my
poetry is often about art and visual imagery, and my imagery is
mainly visual. I'm also intrigued by history and the passing of
time—how things remain the same and yet are different, how the
past not only informs but also judges us, and how we are haunted
by images of the past and the distant. I like to write about the
family, an important historical link or connection to me; I come
from Hebridean Scots, newly emigrated in the 1920s bringing with
them the Gaelic language and a romantic, ironic, self-effacing world
view. They have crept into much of my work—the sense of con-
tinuity with the past, with the ties of an extended family, and
with a culture in many ways at odds with the North American
culture provides much of my material.

I am also interested in linked, connected poems—*Emily,
Walhachin,* and *Barkerville* are all a series of connected poems.
The Overlanders is a long poem, based on an historical event. I
am interested in the narrative, perhaps because I heard so many
tales and legends as a child, but in transforming the narrative into
something that speaks to us today, creating a universal situation,
set of emotions. I use irony and wit in my writing—to underline
contrasts between reality and unreality. I've always been inter-
ested in the differences: representation of the thing and the thing

itself and the various shades of truth in what is perceived. Per-
haps it comes down to trying to untangle reality and illusion and
ponder the unanswerable question—is there any way to know. In
my poetry I try to go below the surface of things, if not to know,
at least to make peace with the entanglement of fact and fiction.
As I ventured into fiction, I found many of the same themes and
interests emerging: the visual imagery, the contrasts, the sense of
family, and of course the sense of story and narrative suggested
by my linked poems.

                    *   *   *

Although Florence McNeil cannot be identified with any spe-
cific group, she is, like many other Canadian poets, a graduate of
a university creative-writing program, and in dedicating *A Balanc-
ing Act* she thanks Earle Birney "for his help and encouragement
in the beginning." She also has a Canadian interest in the long docu-
mentary poem or linked series of poems based on historical mate-
rial about a person, tribe, place, or event. In *Walhachin,* she chose
a settler's "imagined monologue" to tell the story of Walhachin, a
town by the Thompson River in the British Columbian dry belt.
Despite initial prosperity the town returned to sagebrush and wil-
derness after World War I had killed many of its men and a disas-
trous rainstorm had destroyed irrigation flumes. (The fascination
with extinct communities is echoed in the title of another book,
Ghost Towns.) Monologue also unifies the poems in *Emily,* based
on the life and work of the great English-born West Coast painter
Emily Carr (1871-1945), who is able to "find a leaf large as the
coast."

In her book *Barkerville* McNeil draws on the gold rush days
of an 1860s boomtown in the Cariboo Mountains country of
northeastern British Columbia. Illustrated with period photo-
graphs, the book uses the metaphor of a stage set to exhibit a
frenetic cast of adventurers seeking riches. Reinforcing the the-
atrical motif are poems and prose poems about the Barkerville
Dramatic Society, Martin "the World-Renowned Wonder-Cre-
ating Magician," concerts and minstrel performances, and dance
hall girls. The effect is of a photograph album filled with vivid
snapshots, and the focal figure is Billy Barker, the hard-drink-
ing Cornish sailor who struck gold but died penniless in 1894:
"someone mentioned that he almost made it into the twentieth
century." Appropriately, *Barkerville* was produced as a stage
play in Vancouver in 1987.

The documentary impulse also extends to poems which il-
lustrate scenes from McNeil's own life, particularly in *The Rim
of the Park.* In her most substantial work, *Ghost Towns,* she
returns to her childhood, as well as to "Old Movies,"
"Montgolfier's Balloon," "Lilienthal's Glider," and the English
Channel crossing of Louis Blériot. Even when the personal "I"
intervenes, she is the onlooker. In "The Extra," perhaps her
best poem, she says, "I am half a Roman spectator / at the
cardboard coliseum," and she asks,

> is there a place (beyond the corner of the screen)
> to utilize
> my enduring inability
> to be completed?

Although sometimes at the expense of the imagistic incisive-
ness that marked poems like "At a Poetry Convention" ("The
moon shone with transparent purpose / cutting through the lean

quarrels of ice"), McNeil in later work has moved toward more fluid diction and increased openness of form. The sense of historical wonder remains, however. Her collection *Swimming Out of History* gathers poems from six previous books and adds new ones. In the title poem time and timelessness merge:

Only the clear wimple of water
radiating
my arms circling
like hands on a clock
that has no numerals
And time is now.

—Fraser Sutherland

McPHERSON, Sandra

Nationality: American. **Born:** San Jose, California, 2 August 1943. **Education:** Westmont College, Santa Barbara, California, 1961-63; San Jose State College, B.A. in English 1965; University of Washington, Seattle, 1965-66. **Family:** Married 1) Henry Carlile in 1966 (divorced 1985), one daughter; 2) Walter Pavlich in 1995. **Career:** Technical writer, Honeywell Inc., Seattle, 1966. Member of faculty, Writers Workshop, University of Iowa, Iowa City, 1974-76, 1978-80, and Pacific Northwest College of Art, Oregon Writers' Workshop, Portland, 1981-85; visiting faculty member, University of California, Berkeley, 1981; professor of English, University of California, Davis, 1985—. Poetry editor, *Antioch Review,* Yellow Springs, Ohio, 1979-81, and *California Quarterly,* 1985-88. **Awards:** Helen Bullis prize *(Poetry Northwest),* 1968; Bess Hokin prize, 1972, and Oscar Blumenthal prize, 1975 *(Poetry,* Chicago); Ingram Merrill grant, 1972, 1984; Poetry Society of America Emily Dickinson prize, 1973; National Endowment for the Arts grant, 1974, 1980, 1985; Guggenheim fellowship, 1976; American Academy and Institute of Arts and Letters award, 1987; Eunice Tietjens Memorial prize *(Poetry,* Chicago), 1991. **Address:** 2052 Calaveras Avenue, Davis, California 95616-3021, U.S.A.

PUBLICATIONS

Poetry

Elegies for the Hot Season. Bloomington, University of Indiana Press, 1970.
Radiation. New York, Ecco Press, 1973.
The Year of Our Birth. New York, Ecco Press, 1978.
Sensing. San Francisco, Meadow Press, 1980.
Patron Happiness. New York, Ecco Press, 1984.
Pheasant Flower. Missoula, Montana, Owl Creek Press, 1985.
Floralia. Portland, Oregon, Trace, 1985.
Responsibility for Blue. Denton, Texas, Trilobite Press, 1985.
At the Grave of Hazel Hall. Sweden, Maine, Ives Street Press, 1988.
Streamers. New York, Ecco Press, 1988.
Designating Duet. West Burke, Vermont, Janus Press, 1989.
The God of Indeterminacy. Urbana and Chicago, University of Illinois Press, 1993.

The Spaces between Birds: Mother / Daughter Poems, 1967-1995. Middletown, Connecticut, Wesleyan University Press / University Press of New England, 1996.
Edge Effect: Trails and Betrayals. Middletown, Connecticut, Wesleyan University Press / University Press of New England, 1996.
Beauty in Use. West Burke, Vermont, Janus Press, 1997.

Other

Editor, *Journey from Essex: Poems for John Clare.* Port Townsend, Washington, Graywolf Press, 1981.
Editor, with Bill Henderson and Laura Jensen, *The Pushcart Prize XIV: Best of the Small Presses, 1989-1990.* Wainscott, New York, Pushcart Press, 1989.

*   *   *

From her first book on, Sandra McPherson has demonstrated an unusual ability to organize diverse associations and experiences into rich, complex, and deeply satisfying poems. Hers is a world in which the presence of nature—she is unusually intimate with the natural world, even for a poet—calls for an imaginative response that looks to rival the curiosities, wonders, and coincidences of natural history and taxonomy. The human presence on the planet, complicating everything by its needs and appropriations, is never ignored, but the poet, while conscious of her own human fallibility, is able to bring a kind of objectivity to her scrutiny of life that keeps her clear of sentimentality or special pleading. The reader learns to trust her: the rigor of her designs, the scope of her sympathies, the shaping power of her imagination.

One can of course trace influences in McPherson's work, especially those of Sylvia Plath and Elizabeth Bishop, but she is very much her own person and voice from early on. A poem like "Resigning from a job in a Defense Industry," in her first collection, *Elegies for the Hot Season,* typifies her originality. It glances at the superficially exciting language of the technocratic world— "microhenries," "wee wee ductors," "blue beavers"—and then swerves to respond to the impoverished imaginations of fellow workers trying to preserve a sustaining relationship with the outside world; the speaker recalls the company talent show with its "oils and sentiment / Thick on still lifes and seacoasts, / The brush strokes tortured as a child's / First script." The level gaze hovers here between judgment and sympathy in a way that satisfies the poem's and reader's best instincts: "Someone / Had studied driftwood; another man, / The spray of a wave, the mania / Of waters above torpedoes." The poem captures a large segment of modern American life in a confident, unfussy way. It's clear even at this youthful stage that this poet can transcend her ordinary self and achieve, through apparently effortless language, a visionary outlook that never loses its rooting in ordinary experience.

Subsequent collections have deepened and widened this command, displaying a steady growth of mastery and a consistent development of style. One can follow details of the poet's life— marriage, motherhood, eventual divorce, mental illness in a daughter, remarriage, relations with adoptive parents, and a midlife reunion with birth parents—but their function is that more or less impersonal grounding in experience mentioned above. One can also monitor the sustaining presence of the natural world, as in this fifth section of a ten-part poem, "Studies in the Imaginary," from *The Year of Our Birth:*

A botany class comes close
where I am wandering the spongy ground around
a spring. How unlikely they will identify me,
stop and pronounce the existence of anyone
moving faster than locust or colt's foot.
But then, if I could even approach on foot

or with an extrovert word,
I wouldn't bow out to meditate, awkward
as that duck, green and bronze, strolling grass-spattered
through bamboo. Strangers
are so fast, no slowing you, no halting the wings
of the hummingbird.

Interesting things are being done with rhyme, sound, and form here, but it's the mystery of rhythm and encounter that is central both to the subject of the poem and the behavior of the language. The light touch and elusive control of statement might recall John Ashbery, but the expert handling of submerged drama and marshaled associations is clearly McPherson's own.

McPherson's structures can become so intricate and her associations so private that she occasionally loses her way or exhausts her reader's patience, but the time she takes with individual poems and with assembling her collections bespeaks a willingness to wait and work until she can "get it right." Emotional control, Bishop's way as against Plath's, a survivor's mode, seems more and more crucial to McPherson's success. The greater the possibilities for runaway feelings, the greater the need to rein them in through understatement and exceptionally careful orchestration of detail. A short poem from *Patron Happiness* helps make the point:

EARTHSTARS, BIRTHPARENTS' HOUSE

Geasters. She bent down
At the dappled base of the tree,
And among the brown leaves
Geasters stood up.

Oranges peel like these,
She said. Rinds bent back.

When it rains, their legs swell up
And walk.

    Stranger feet
Than mine
All those years
Outside your door.

The final stanza is charged with the emotion of a woman meeting her mother for the first time in middle age. It is powerful not only for its understatement but also for its objectified setting. Mother and daughter are not discussing their lives and feelings, but rather looking together at an unusual fungus. We sense that this is no dodge. The poet's "subjective" interest is as firmly fixed on the wonder of a name ("geaster" means "earthstar") and on the curious shape, texture, and behavior of a mushroom most people would pass without noticing as it is on her strange reunion. The poem's implicit claim is that there is finally no difference between fact and emotion, spirit and matter. It knits the world together again before our eyes. A reader who would fully understand the poem

must be willing to take the trouble to know what a geaster is—to look it up in a book or, better still, find one in the field. This poet will not encourage us to be lazy, unobservant, ignorant, or maunderingly subjective.

McPherson's interests also include the distinctively American arts of quilting and blues singing. She has typically informed herself exhaustively about these subjects before plunging into an imaginative relationship with them that, once again, has given rise to surprising, intricate, and moving poems. No one who reads one of her quilt poems, much less the series of them, is likely to look at a quilt with the same eyes again. Her sympathy with the unsung creators of her own culture has proved to be profound and revelatory, and she seems to be moving to the threshold of some of her strongest work. Her creative energies seem undiminished, and her teaching, at the University of California at Davis, has enhanced her contribution to American letters.

—David Young

McQUEEN, Cilla

Nationality: British and New Zealander. **Born:** Birmingham, England, 22 January 1949. **Education:** Columba College, Dunedin; Otago University, M.A. (honors) in French 1970. **Family:** Married Ralph Hotere in 1974; one daughter. **Career:** Teacher. Also artist: individual shows—Bosshard Galleries, Dunedin, 1982; Red Metro Gallery, Dunedin, 1983. **Awards:** New Zealand Book Award, 1983, 1989; P.E.N./Jessie Mackay award, 1983; Air New Zealand/P.E.N. travel award, 1984; Robert Burns fellowship, 1985, 1986; Fulbright Visiting Writer's fellowship, 1985; Inaugural Australian-New Zealand Writers' exchange fellowship, 1987; Goethe Institute scholarship, 1988; New Zealand Book award, 1991, for *Berlin Diary*. **Address:** 60 Liffey Street, Bluff, New Zealand.

PUBLICATIONS

Poetry

Homing In. Dunedin, McIndoe, 1982.
Anti Gravity. Dunedin, McIndoe, 1984.
Wild Sweets. Dunedin, McIndoe, 1986.
Benzina. Dunedin, McIndoe, 1988.
Berlin Diary. Dunedin, McIndoe, 1990.
Crikey (new and selected poems 1978-1994). Dunedin, McIndoe, 1994.

Recordings: *Bad Bananas,* Strawberry Sound, 1986-87; *Otherwise,* with Alistair Macdougall, 1989.

Plays

Harlequin and Columbine (produced Dunedin, 1987).
Red Rose Café (produced Dunedin, 1990).

Radio Play: *Spacy Calcutta's Travelling Truth Show,* 1986.

*

Critical Study: "Pilot Small's Transport across the Meniscus: The Poetry of Cilla McQueen" by Ian Wedde, in *Untold* (Christchurch), no. 3, Autumn 1985.

Cilla McQueen comments:

My work is concerned with duality, the theme of the meniscus, the borderline area between subjective and objective experience.

*   *   *

Stylistic changes have taken place in Cilla McQueen's poetry. The lyricism that tended to dominate the poems in her first volume yielded first to a pared-down, energetic, pop-inspired minimalism, then reemerged in *Benzina* with "beauty in spareness. / what is & what is not" ("Some Poets"). The distinctive aspects of her poetry remain: a painter's eye for detail and color, a sense of the dramatic, and a quirky sense of humor.

McQueen describes herself as "poet, composer and intermedia artist." This versatility has been combined with performance (as poet and musician with a rock group, for example); it also plays an important role in her writing through her fondness for visual patterns, references to pop culture, and synaesthetic imagery. In *Homing In* her "Words Fail Me" gaily knocks down artificial boundaries between the arts, as the poet's desire "to put into line what / the words are not fluid enough for" cause her to start

drafting lines on to graph paper
& pairing coordinates. I hope
that they can then be mass produced
in the form of sheet music which
can be sung anywhere.

The poem concludes with a visual pun on the inadequacies of language, paradoxical in its success:

Words
            fail me she says
& proceeds to fill several more lines
with scribbled black biro words fail me

Visual patterns, which should be seen on the page to gain their full effect—dropped lines, half lines—are important structural features of many other poems in *Homing In.* "Low Tide, Aramoana" and "Weekend Sonnets, Carey's Bay" share this mimetic approach to seascapes and emotions, as does "By the Water":

Dark glissades to meet the
light   on reefs of air: I find you
dismembered in the landscape
among indolent hills
                You disperse & are
gone again

The combination of sensual responses to landscape in "Words Fail Me" is the subject of "Synaesthesia," a much less visual poem in *Benzina.* Here, through the formality of rhymed iambic pentameter, the same boundaries are recrossed in a complex series of patterns and harmonies that are directed more toward the ear than the eye:

the eyes see patterns that the brain can sing
invisibly the music pictures sound
draws out the music inside everything
& sings the lines of light my hand has found

While experimenting with language and form, McQueen has also given her poetry satiric bite. "Living Here," one of her most frequently anthologized poems, pictures each New Zealander surrounded by a personal flock of sheep, "little human centres each within an outer / circle of sheep around us like a ring of / covered wagons." Gradually the human characters take on the characteristics of sheep, bleating "the safest place in the world to live," insulated but also isolated by their fleece:

We're calling fiercely to each other
through the muffled spaces   grateful for
any wrist-brush
                cut of mind or touch of music
lightning in the intimate weather of the soul.

The transition from whimsy is highly effective, its judgment softened just enough by the inclusive "we." "Living Here" also directs attention to the frequent images of electricity and lightning in the poems that succeed it, poems that deliberately try to leap the "muffled spaces" that inhibit communication.

Anti Gravity is a move in this direction, its title signifying McQueen's growing interest in the language of physics as well as her continuing attack on conformity. Gravity in one sense is successfully defied by the playfulness of her lines; gravity in its other sense can be less easy to defy. The stuntman in "That's Incredible" catches his falling parachute "with one second to spare" (a second in which the poet speculates "where the quasars drill out to infinite distance" and "while the time ripples past in numbers"). "Princess Alice the Incredible Lady Gymnast" meets a different end. Having "constructed a flying machine / of surpassing grace & lightness / out of shells & feathers & fishing-line," Princess Alice meets the fate of Icarus:

... a cloud of birds forced her down
in unfamiliar country
where a parliament of trees
condemned her for alienation from earth
& sentenced her forthwith
to dissolution
                (now you
                see her
                now you

Poetry also being, as it declares itself, "anti gravity," McQueen discusses its creation in terms of similar danger in "No Poem":

I like the relationship between thought & paper
to get faster ...
                the more you play around with words
the more they frighten you with the punch
they pack   like the images I cover my walls with
which ...
                have become unfixed scraps of reality
exploding on contact
                which is why we seem to be picking
our way through a minefield just a few of us anarchists
white flags & mortars both ways across no mans land

This sense of danger pervades the shorter, sharper poems of *Wild Sweets.* "Wild Sweets" alternates conventional images of romantic love with violence and danger: "what I mean by / love? a terrorist incident / a torn artery an electric arc a / touch without fear"; so, too, "A Lightning Tree": "I have made of words a lightning tree / to earth my dangerous love through poetry." These and other poems carry the electrical charge of "lightning in the intimate weather of the soul"; "Wink" and "Dreamscript 1" use cut-and-jump film techniques.

Benzina displays less of this kinetic energy. McQueen's voice here is generally quieter, more reflective, the lyricism that had been displaced returning with the brevity that had displaced it. *Wild Sweets* includes several poems of this kind ("Nuages," "Solstice"), *Benzina* far more. In "Under the Tree," "Silence," and "Rainlight" ("sun bows / mirrored colours / over / to join beneath us / to hold the water / calm in a bowl") their delicate stillness contrasts with a newer form of experiment, the prose poem ("Short Story, 1984") of short sentences and a dramatic use of punctuation.

But whether in pop or lyrical mode, McQueen could never be called a romantic. Even when grief and shock are her subjects, as in "Vegetable Garden Poem (1)," the emotions are buried in the middle of the poem ("a friend of ours shot himself / yesterday"), which ends with the poet "Trying to write. / Trying to disappear." In "Some Poets" she sets out quite clearly what her poetry is *not*—and, more importantly, what it *is,* for "Some poets,"

> they get
> shit on their shoes
> & trail it everywhere
>
> their
> ragged impossible
> tenderness
>
> ah so bloody romantic
> still I wish
>
> huh.
> fuck wishing.
>
> time for some
> naked light!
>
> beauty in spareness.
> what is & what is not.

—Nan Bowman Albinski

MEEHAN, Paula

Nationality: Irish. **Born:** Dublin, 25 June 1955. **Education:** Trinity College, Dublin, 1972-77, B.A. 1977; Eastern Washington University, Cheney, Washington, 1981-83, M.F.A. 1983. **Career:** Literacy organizer, South Inner City, Dublin, 1984-88. Conducts workshops in poetry for community groups, including North Cen-

tre City Community Action Project and the Fatima Mansions Development Group. Irish co-coordinator, poetry master classes, Summer Writing Workshop in Dublin, Eastern Washington University, 1985—. Teacher of writing workshops in prisons, Arts Council Writers in the Prison Scheme, 1986—. Poet-in-residence, The Frost Place, Franconia, New Hampshire, spring 1987; writer-in-residence, Trinity College, Dublin, 1992; writer by association, University College, Dublin, 1992; outreach residency with Verbal Arts Centre, Derry and Antrim counties, 1993; writer-in-residence, TEAM Theatre in Education Co., Dublin, 1994. **Awards:** Irish Arts Council bursary in literature, 1987, 1990. **Agent:** Peter Fallon, Loughcrew, Oldcastle, County Meath, Ireland.

PUBLICATIONS

Poetry

Return and No Blame. Dublin, Beaver Row Press, 1984.
Reading the Sky. Dublin, Beaver Row Press, 1986.
The Man Who Was Marked by Winter. Oldcastle, County Meath, Gallery Press, 1991; with foreword by Eavan Boland, Cheney, Washington, EWU Press, 1994.
Pillow Talk. Oldcastle, County Meath, Gallery Press, 1994.
Mysteries of the Home: A Selection of Poems. Newcastle upon Tyne, Bloodaxe, 1996.

Plays

Kirkle (produced Dublin 1995).
The Voyage (produced Dublin 1997).
Mrs Sweeney (produced Dublin 1997).

*   *   *

Paula Meehan's rise has been rapid since her first collection, *Return and No Blame,* appeared in 1984 and her second, *Reading the Sky,* in 1986. The poems are jaunty and warm, seeking a full, feminine voice. She looks back to tradition, assuming the voice of Liadain or rewriting one of the few human poems from the bardic tradition as if it were a woman speaking. She also uses North Dublin street talk; indeed, she seems more involved with the city than any Irish poet since Clarke and Kinsella.

Meehan's third book, *The Man Who Was Marked by Winter,* draws on the first two, but there is a new surety, as in "The Pattern," an expanded sequence for her mother. There is uneasiness as well, what Antoinette Quinn has called "a migrant restiveness," the poet as prowler, an uneasiness which also shows in the love poems. Meehan can be comic about male inefficiency, as in "My Love about His Business in the Barn," but "The Statue of the Virgin at Granard Speaks" is a poignant indictment of an Irish society that lets young women go to waste.

Athena, warrior and goddess of wisdom, is the image on the cover of *Pillow Talk,* and the complex nature of woman is a recurring theme. Traditional views are rejected in "Not Your Muse," but Meehan's father is transformed into Saint Francis in the opening poem, and there is a lovely lament for a broken marriage in "Not alone the rue in my herb garden ...":

> O my friend,
> do not turn on me in hatred,
> do not curse the day we met.

What is impressive about Meehan's later work is the increasing ease with which she deals with a variety of moods, from the gentle to the ferocious:

> From one breast
> flows the Milky Way, the starry path,
> a sluggish trickle of pus from the other.

She is one of the best younger poets around, and, as Eavan Boland says, her "themes are daring and open up new areas for her own work as well as for contemporary Irish poetry."

—John Montague

MINTY, Judith

Nationality: American. **Born:** Detroit, Michigan, 5 August 1937. **Family:** Married Edgar Minty in 1957; three children. **Education:** Michigan State University; Ithaca College, B.S., 1957; Western Michigan University, M.A., 1973. **Career:** Poet and freelance writer. Poet-in-residence, Central Michigan University, 1977-78, Syracuse University, 1979, Interlochen Center for the Arts, 1980; University of Oregon, 1983; and Humboldt State University, 1982—. **Awards:** International Poetry Forum award, 1973, for *Lake Songs and Other Fears;* Breadloaf Writer's Conference fellowship, 1974; *Poetry*'s Eunice Tietjens award, 1974; Yaddo fellowships, 1978, 1979, 1982; PEN Syndicated fiction award, 1985.

Publications

Poetry

Lake Songs and Other Fears. Pittsburgh, University of Pennyslvania Press, 1974.
Yellow Dog Journal. Los Angeles, Central Publications, 1979.
In the Presence of Mothers. Pittsburgh, University of Pennsylvania Press, 1981.
Counting the Losses. Aptos, California, Jazz Press, 1986.
Dancing the Fault. Orlando, University of Central Florida, 1991.

*   *   *

> I am mystic enough to believe that there is something of
> the past hidden deep within all of us.

The above quote, from the dust jacket of her first book of poems, *Lake Songs and Other Fears,* begins to say something of the interconnectedness of all things that Judith Minty's vision has explored over the course of her poetry career. It is this mystic, Whitmanian oneness, the merging of the self with the natural world and the merging of the public and the private that would pervade her work and provide poetic impetus.

Lake Songs won the 1973 United States Award of the International Poetry Forum and serves as a microcosm of the themes and directions Minty's work would develop over the course of the next 20 years. Reading her poems is sometimes like a walk in the woods with new and fresh eyes, escaping the tyranny of the domesticated word and its language while at the same time using that language to forge poetic description. Minty configures, to use the language of Annie Dillard (a writer with which Minty has much in common), "scrupulous" methods of description and seeing with "unscrupulous" ways of attempting to see the world more directly. Reading Minty's poems is to be constantly reminded of this fissure between the fleeting contemporary and the eternal and wild of the elemental. There is the constant struggle here to be the poet whose job is, in Wallace Stevens' words, to "become an ignorant man again / And see the sun again with an ignorant eye / And see it clearly in the idea of it."

Minty's revelations are those of someone who has walked the same path many times, seeing the same objects and landscapes. The same transformation reveals itself in her poem "November Morning," in *Lake Songs:*

> How many Novembers we walked this way
> never seeing until now
> blood creep outward on the snow
> like a Rorschach beetle,
> never hearing until now
> children who cry inside charred trees,
> never feeling until now
> the weight of clouds on our breath.

Transformation is always a key theme; whether it be the transformation that the natural world endures under human dominion, or the metaphorical transformation of people into landscape, of landscape into the human. Further, as is suggested by the above excerpt, these transformations between the human and the natural are seldom seen as idyllic or romantic. Minty is a poet who well understands not only the sublime beauty of nature, but also its terrifying power. Lake Michigan, for example, the watery landscape of "Lake Songs" and many other, later poems, is also a scene for many drownings; Minty's vision here is of grand beauty but also of a dark vastness which simultaneously provides and swallows life in all its forms.

In the foreword to *Yellow Dog Journal,* Deena Metzger aptly appropriates the activity of reading Minty's poems as a descent and return from nature, as the modern world has exiled itself from that community: "We descend, as Judith Minty [does], stripped by the four elements of earth, fire, wind and water in order to confront the bear, that fearsome dream animal ... that force of nature which we must nakedly pursue and escape." The bear, to Minty (as to Galway Kinnell, another writer who has much in common), is the symbol of the greatest force of the northern woods—mysterious, overpowering, and elementally with the natural world as a descent because we now come as novices, as suburbanites who are lost and challenged by the quiet fearfulness of this foreign landscape. When confronted, we stand, as Minty does, "in the chill, / the half-light, wondering what, / foolishness made me leave the familiar." There is, concurrently though, a great sense of Whitmanian renewal, a sense that the return will make us more complete.

There are finally, then, great political dichotomies and contradictions in Minty's poems. Her voice is that of a Detroiter amidst the forests *(Lake Songs, Yellow Dog Journal)*; a mother who finds herself without children ("Letters to My Daughters"); a woman attempting life in a world of men *(Counting the Losses)*. Her message is as spiritual as it is environmental, and is strengthened in her insistence that place matters. Minty's poems tell the tale of a tribe that has lost touch with its origins, with the very land that gave it life. A deeper understanding of the landscape and its origins is, then a deeper understanding of its relation to ourselves, our pasts and futures, our personal as well as our public lives. Through the forms of the lyrical, the narrative, the letter or the "confessive," Judith Minty's voice is one that quietly and assertively tells the reader to pay attention.

—Michael Rodriguez

MITCHELL, Elma

Nationality: Scottish. **Born:** Airdrie, Lanarkshire, Scotland, 19 November 1919. **Education:** Somerville College, Oxford, B.A. in English (first-class honors), 1941; University College, London, diploma in librarianship. **Career:** Librarian for BBC, London, 1941-43; librarian and information officer for various organizations, including British Employee's Confederation. **Address:** Tanlake Cottage, Buckland St. Mary, Chard, Somerset TA20 3QF, England.

PUBLICATIONS

Poetry

The Poor Man in the Flesh. Stockport, Cornwall, Peterloo Poets, 1976.
The Human Cage. Liskeard, Cornwall, Peterloo Poets, 1979.
Furnished Rooms. Liskeard, Cornwall, Peterloo Poets, 1983.
People Etcetera: Poems New and Selected. Liskeard, Cornwall, Peterloo Poets, 1987.

Recording: *U.A. Fanthorpe and Elma Mitchell,* Peterloo Poets, 1983.

*

Elma Mitchell comments:

My poetry was published in my middle or later years, thanks mainly to Harry Chambers, of Peterloo Poets, and to the great democratic revival of poetry after the Second World War. My published books are *The Poor Man in the Flesh* (1976), *The Human Cage* (1979), *Furnished Rooms* (1983), and *People Etcetera,* a new-and-selected collection published in 1987. Recently Penguin Modern Poets series have included a fair selection of my work in their "Penguin Modern Poets" paperback series.

I've enjoyed poetry from nursery rhymes onwards! and wrote it (badly, of course!) from an early age. School and university helped even more, and the post-war popularization of poetry still more. I still write for the joy of it, at the age of 78.

*   *   *

A quietly alert intelligence focused on the quotidian, the workday and working world is Elma Mitchell. She is part of a tradition very visible in contemporary poetry—Larkin or Brownjohn might well be cited as good representatives of it—and is singular for her lack of pose or pretension within it. Of this world, so imprisoning and which we know so well, she can write with a beautiful exactitude—that is, with an exactitude which evokes a kind of beauty:

A day of eight hours, in the clerkly concrete,
Has left me all unfit for the clouds' proportions
Over Blackheath, and the softly summoning blossoms.

She can make the ordinary radiant without giving it that artificial strandedness—that sense of the "aerial," to borrow a word of Duncan Bush's applied to Craig Raine's method of transforming things mundane. There is, of course, an especial art in dealing with the ordinary when it is also the contemporary; and a danger too. For the contemporary dates all to quickly and sometimes can become both obscure and lose linguistic force as in, for example, Mitchell's witty pun in "The Prophet" where she says, "I am Daniel, in the den of Lyon's": a great pun but one that is dead now that there are no more Lyon's coffee houses. As against that falling off through time of the too contemporary referent—even when, as in "The Prophet" it is juxtaposed with the timeless Biblical reference—a poem like "Odysseus Home" which fully uses myth yet, like Shakespeare in his *Troilus & Cressida,* recesses, as it were, the received view of Odysseus, Mitchell pulls off her mini-remake effortlessly and timelessly.

Like all the best poets, right from her first book, *The Poor Man in the Flesh,* Mitchell has had the gift for the memorable fine phrase or line, "I melt the clock and pour minutes out" and "I go a virgin to the bed of light." And, beyond that facility she can raise up feeling that gains in sincerity through being muted or understated, as in a poem like "Turning out the Mattresses" with its last line, "This bit of paper's your memorial"—so like the stain of dried tears.

Essential humanity is revealed through suffering or vulnerability. To pull this off in a poem without sentimentality requires more than an artless simplicity: it needs the firm restraint of the craftsman or, in Mitchell's case, the craftswoman. The lonely vulnerability of the woman whom one's love has once touched then, for some reason, passed by, is well brought out in her poem "Plain Jane":

One year on fire I had, and all the rest
Plain Jane,
Dust-pan and brush
The tinkle of keys
That lock my days.

Not a great poem, perhaps, but a moving one; and a perfect example of Emily Dickinson's categorical imperative to "tell it slant."

Sometimes, among a poet's works, one can encounter a poem that is the epitome of the poet's *credo* or, to borrow a phrase from Hamlet, is his or her "assay of bias." The excellent "Disabilities" from a later volume, *The Human Cage,* through which the persona ambles in full health:

I walk, normal
(For the moment at least) caged in my total armour
Of the right number of limbs, everything functioning

yet intensely aware that, "The sun brings out the colors and the cripples / Stumbling among each other in the shafts of dust." Clearly we are given to understand the poet is a quiet, unthrusting realist—with no illusions about the slow but certain attrition of time—possessed of a non-romantic outlook, who is always "wearing / Dark spectacles against a rose-colored sun." Of a romantic temperament himself, this critic can still admire the good sense of a different temperament when it leads to good poetry. For, in the end, it is not a matter of temperament when it leads to good poetry, but of imagination: "Piecing together ... / Complete, unwithering roses." Life is a catastrophe in many respects, of course, but, as Mitchell says in "Propitiation," it is—for the true poet—necessary to live "with this catastrophe / In imagination," in addition to living it in fact. What makes Mitchell more profound than many another realist poet (or pseudo-realist: for there are many such poets of that ilk about just now) is that she also knows that much which is true is "out of this world"; as she puts it:

I'm crying for the moon
That's what I'm crying for.

There is much more to say about this varied and relatively neglected British poet who writes always and ceaselessly at the emotional point where the conventional life of a woman (and most men for that matter) intersects with wilder existences. And that's a kind of theme she later develops through her Selected Poems *People Etcetera*, in poems like "It's the Sea I Want":

The whole boiling,
Destructive, disruptive, sterilising—
I think it's smashing

But, in the end, she remains only a "Tired Woman Sitting by the Sea," for "she will not run to the sea":

A topless, foam-born Venus
Summons, from under her cardigan,

yet "is patted back into place." At the deepest level, Elma Mitchell's poems are not just works in praise of the ordinary—as I set out to suggest—but are about the rigors and responsibilities of being civilized. And this, maybe, is their greatest achievement: a romantic gesture by the unromantic against barbarism.

—William Oxley

MITCHELL, Susan

Nationality: American. **Born:** New York City, 1944. **Education:** Wellesley College, Massachusetts. **Career:** Has held teaching positions at Middlebury College, Vermont, and Northeastern Illinois University. Holds the Mary Blossom Lee Endowed Chair in Creative Writing, Florida Atlantic University. **Awards:** National Endowment for the Arts fellowship; grants from the state arts councils of Massachusetts, Illinois, Vermont, and Florida; Claire Hagler fellow, Fine Arts Work Center, Provincetown; Hoyns fellow, University of Virginia; Guggenheim Foundation fellow, 1992; Lannan Foundation fellow, 1992; National Book Award finalist, 1992, for *Rapture;* Kingsley Tufts Poetry award, 1993. **Address:** c/o HarperCollins Publishers, 10 East 53rd Street, New York, New York 10022-5299, U.S.A.

PUBLICATIONS

Poetry

The Water inside the Water. Middletown, Connecticut, Wesleyan University Press, 1983.
Rapture. New York, HarperPerennial, 1992.

Other

Translator, "Canto 21" and "Canto 22," *Dante's Inferno,* in *Versions of the Inferno,* edited by Daniel Halpern. New York, Ecco Press, 1993.

*

Critical Study: "Possibilities of Paradise: Myth, Narrative and Lyric" by Bonnie Costello, in *Gettysburg Review,* Autumn 1992; "Underwater Pavilions" by Tam Lin Neville, in *American Poetry Review* (Philadelphia), no. 23, January / February 1994.

*   *   *

Susan Mitchell has published two volumes of poetry, *The Water inside the Water* and *Rapture.* Her poems, and the numerous honors they have garnered for their author, embody and reflect the world of mainstream American poetry. Winner of the first Kingsley-Tufts award, the recipient of fellowships from the National Endowment for the Arts, the Lannan Foundation, and the Guggenheim Foundation, as well as from the art councils of four states (Massachusetts, Illinois, Vermont, and Florida), twice a fellow at the Fine Arts Work Center in Provincetown, and a Hoynes Fellow at the University of Virginia, Mitchell holds the Mary Blossom Lee Endowed Chair in Creative Writing at Florida Atlantic University.

Mitchell's period style often begins with the pentameter line, which she expands or contracts from poem to poem, frequently transforming it into a unit that is closer to prose than to poetry. She is fond of repetition. She presents layers of detail yet leaves most connections *between* details largely up to the reader. On many occasions it appears that her poems have an almost aimless quality about them; they can seem laborious, elaborate, and self-conscious in expression: "... I'm devoted / to an enormous expanse of violet / which is how the Atlantic wants to be today." Time and again Mitchell burrows back to the familiar business of analyzing personal experience rather than allowing the artful presentation of experience itself to reveal the truth. What is most often lacking in this style is a fully formed individual point of view. Without one, writers who may feel deeply cannot sufficiently sort out their feelings to present them in the context that poetry requires. Thus, they have difficulty following where poetry would lead them.

In "The Child Bride," from *Rapture,* for example, Mitchell's release from a hospital occasions free association that brings up the woman that Poe almost married, Poe's wife, Dante's Beatrice, and Dante's intention in writing *The Divine Comedy* ("Paradise is what Dante did with loss")—and all of this comes in the first 12 lines. The method continues with a catalog of images found in the hospital and in those things in life that are a mystery to the author: pain, pleasure, water, Poe, and most important, the self. The poem's long middle offers extended clinical speculation on death and loss. Then, suddenly, poetry happens:

> ... Poe's child
> bride was singing when she had her first hemorrhage,
> as if music and blood flow from the same vein and the heart
> can pump only so much. The song split, traveling
> in two directions, and one was a foreign
> country always out of reach, a bird singing
>
> in a forest she could not enter, though Poe
> described it for her, a place where strange brilliant
> flowers, star-shaped, burst out upon the trees
> where no flowers had been known before.

For a shining moment the writer disappears in poetry itself, devoid of strategies and agendas. But the moment ends, followed by one more thick passage speculating on the nature and endurance of pain. This passage maneuvers the writer back to center stage, in control once more:

> ... I forget
> the name of my own country, forget
> which language is which.

Mitchell certainly is not alone in writing this period style, and on occasion there are indications that she is capable of greater artistry. "Bus Trip," also from *Rapture,* is one of her better poems:

> All across America children are learning to fly.
> On a bus leaving New Hampshire, on a bus
> leaving Colorado, I sat next to a child
>
> who had learned how to fly
> and she carried her flying clenched
> inside both fists. She carried her flying
>
> in a suitcase and in a stuffed dog
> made of dirt and the places where she had stood
> all night listening to the rain....

The simplicity here rings true. It is evocative and tender. It is enough.

—Robert McDowell

MOORE, Honor

Nationality: American. **Born:** New York, New York, 28 October 1945. **Education:** Radcliffe College, Harvard, B.A. 1967; Yale School of Drama, 1967-69. **Career:** Co-founder, Harvard Dramatic Club Summer Players, Cambridge, 1966; founder, Writers in Performance series, Manhattan Theater, 1971-74; visiting scholar, James Madison University, 1980; adjunct faculty, New York University, 1980-82; curator, Margarett Sargent Retrospective, Wellesley College, Wellesley, Massachusetts, 1993; visiting writer, University of Iowa, 1997. Contributor of poetry and essays to periodicals, including *American Poetry Review, Ploughshares, Nation, New York Times Magazine, New Yorker,* and *Ani.* **Awards:** Creative Artists Public Service grant in playwriting, 1976; National Endowment for the Arts creative writing fellowship, 1981; Connecticut Commission on the Arts grant, 1992; Lambda Literary award finalist, 1997, for *The White Blackbird.* **Agent:** Wylie Agency, 250 West 57th Street, #2114, New York, New York 10107, U.S.A.

PUBLICATIONS

Poetry

Leaving and Coming Back (chapbook). Emeryville, California, Effie's Press, 1981.
Memoir. Goshen, Connecticut, Chicory Blue Press, 1988.

Recording: *Take Hands: Singing and Speaking for Survival,* with others, Watershed, 1984.

Plays

Mourning Pictures (produced New York, 1974).
Years (produced American Place Theatre, 1978).
The Terry Project (produced New York, 1981).

Other

The White Blackbird: A Life of the Painter Margarett Sargent by Her Granddaughter. New York, Viking, 1996.

Editor, *The New Women's Theatre: Ten Plays by Contemporary American Women.* New York, Vintage, 1977.

*

Critical Studies: By Susan Braudy in *Ms.,* November 1974; interview in *BOMB,* Fall 1996.

*   *   *

Although Honor Moore's writing spans a number of genres, critics comment without fail on the "poetic" qualities of her language. Her poetry is synesthetic and formed, carefully constricted and yet spacious. Reviewers notice this and call on metaphors from other art forms to illuminate these aspects of her writing. Marilyn Hacker calls Moore's poetry painterly because she so capably transcribes the visual experience of an artifact or an event into an equally dazzling verbal experience. Her poems are full of color. In "Poem for the Beginning," from *Memoir,* the speaker recalls the previous night's phone conversation with an absent beloved:

> A six-pronged shell, gift from you, balances
> on its transparent stand, seems
> to float, image of heat, pink center of heat
> burning out, still and continuing, as if the hot
> color of a daylily opening were heat rather

than color. This cold between us is distance,
circumstance. Just how, I ask her, is separation good?
Going away, she says, coming back—almost
waving her hand as she speaks—
I like coming back, leaving and coming back. Coming back.

This poem typifies Moore's work in its thematic emphasis on absence and connection. The use of syllabic verse structure and the hourglass silhouette help to convey these themes. Notice, for example, how the indentations embody the notion of coming and going and mimic a conversational exchange. The patterns of repetition and variation as well as the careful punctuation of the lines, mask the formal structure of the poem as they do in many of the poems in this volume.

Moore is a master of technique. Her familiarity with English, French, and classical lyric traditions demonstrates an erudition that is rare among contemporary poets. *Memoir* is full of sestinas, villanelles, sonnets, sapphic and other classic lyrics, but one can hardly tell. Perhaps Moore's expertise is most evident in her deft and unobtrusive use of these forms. The repetition that is characteristic of sestinal, for instance, does not irritate; the shorter fourth lines of the sapphic stanzas in "Letter in Late July" do not seem forced:

> Dearest, I have resisted these, my first lines
> in more than a year, waiting for you to pass
> like a mood or a winter, but you persist—
> a landscape. It's green
>
> that limpid pre-dusk hesitation at the
> swell of New England summer, and I'm bereft.

Witness how memory is spatialized as landscape in the first stanza. It is no wonder that critics rely on metaphors borrowed from archaeology or architecture, to talk about Moore's work because it concerns the shapes that the past takes in the present. This is perhaps clearest in a piece that appeared in the *New York Times'* "Home Section" in which she connects the idiosyncratic shape of her family house with various of its eccentric residents.

Marilyn Hacker has said about Moore's poetry, that she "is redefining and examining what it means to be rooted in a family, a history, sometimes-contradictory traditions." Moore's non-fiction demonstrates this as well. *White Blackbird*, the biography of Moore's artist grandmother, Margarett Sargent, explores why she stopped painting in her 40s, despite critical success. Moore explains that she wrote the book to escape her grandmother's legacy; she needed to prove to herself that you could be a woman and an artist and not go mad. Those passages in which she describes Margarett Sargent's paintings verge on poetry. In the essay, "My Grandmother Who Painted," in *The Writer on Her Work*, which grew into the biography, Moore describe the painting *The Blue Girl*:

> A stranger, huge black hat's shadows smudge the white forehead, lips set, red, disturbed. Color, color. Light blue collars and pale neck, behind writhe thick green vines, exploding ultramarine blooms. Brown hair to the shoulder she sits, volcanic, holds the graceful white arm of an orange chair with both hands, as if to hold her to the canvas.

In a recent interview in *BOMB* magazine, Moore calls this language "phenomenological" and explains how it kept her writing.

The synesthetic atmosphere of Moore's writing can be traced to her early work in the theater. Her play, *Mourning Pictures*, began as a series of poems based on Moore's experience of her mother's death. The action centers on a mother's sick bed as her family contends with her six-month-long battle with cancer. It begins: "Ladies and gentleman, my mother is dying," and relentlessly circles around this fact, until the audience is compelled to listen. It is characterized by the same urgent, but controlled voice of the sestinas in *Memoir*. Susan Braudy speaks of the tears that theater producer, Mary Silverman, shed as Moore read the poems that were adapted into the play as a measure of Moore's talent. Her power to evoke suffering and joy, her insistence on connection, drives her work towards the intimate and the universal at once.

—Catherine D. Halley

MOSS, Thylias (Rebecca)

Nationality: American. **Born:** Thylias Rebecca Brasier, Cleveland, Ohio, 27 February 1954. **Education:** Syracuse University, New York, 1971-73; Oberlin College, Oberlin, Ohio, 1979-81, A.B. in creative writing 1981; University of New Hampshire, Durham, 1981-83, M.A. in English/Writing 1983. **Family:** Married John L. Moss in 1973; two sons. **Career:** Drama and Reading Rehabilitation Specialist, Bellevue Elementary School, Syracuse; order checker, 1973-74, junior executive auditor, 1975-79, data entry supervisor, 1974-75, The May Company, Cleveland; graduate assistant, 1981-83, lecturer, 1983-84, University of New Hampshire, Durham; instructor, Phillips Academy, Andover, Massachusetts, 1984-92; Fannie Hurst Poet, Brandeis University, Waltham, Massachusetts, 1992; visiting professor, University of New Hampshire, Durham, 1991-92; assistant professor, 1993-94, and associate professor, 1994—, University of Michigan, Ann Arbor. **Awards:** Cleveland Public Library Poetry Contest Winner, 1978, for "Coming of Age in Sandusky"; Dewar's Profiles Performance Artist award in poetry, 1991; American Academy and Institute of Arts and Letters Witter Bynner prize, 1991; Whiting Writer's award, 1991; Guggenheim fellowship, 1995; John D. and Catherine T. MacArthur Foundation fellow, 1996. **Member:** Academy of American Poets. **Agent:** Faith Hamlin, Sanford J. Greenburger Associates, 55 Fifth Avenue, New York, New York 10003. **Address:** P.O. Box 2686, Ann Arbor, Michigan 48106, U.S.A.

PUBLICATIONS

Poetry

Hosiery Seams on a Bowlegged Woman. Cleveland, Ohio, Cleveland State University Press, 1983.
Pyramid of Bone. Charlottesville, University of Virginia Press, 1989.
At Redbones. Cleveland, Ohio, Cleveland State University Press, 1990.
Rainbow Remnants in Rock Bottom Ghetto Sky. New York, Persea Press, 1991.

Small Congregations: New and Selected Poems. Hopewell, New Jersey, Ecco Press, 1993.
Last Chance for the Tarzan Holler. New York, Persea Press, 1997.

Plays

The Dolls in the Basement (produced New England Theater Conference, 1984).
Talking to Myself (produced Durham, New Hampshire, 1984).

Other

I Want to Be (for children). New York, Dial, 1993.
Tale of a Sky-Blue Dress (autobiography). New York, Avon, 1998.
Somewhere Else Right Now (for children). New York Dial, 1998.

*

Critical Studies: In *American Religion* by Harold Bloom, New York, Simon & Schuster, 1992.

Theatrical Activities:
Director and Actor: **Plays**—all her own plays; *Dolls in the Basement,* 1984; *Talking to Myself,* 1984. Actor: **Play**—Female lead in *Midnight Special* by Clifford Mason, 1973.

Thylias Moss comments:

The day, the hour, are lost to me, but one day I began to write when I was not quite seven years old. Since then, there has been no stopping. But the immediate provocation and necessity of that "then"; who knows? An odd compulsion, to begin this process of thoughts appearing from fingers as if the thoughts had been bled, but it began even as the universe began. First on heavy paper around which my mother's stockings came wrapped, stories and poems happened. She would discard the stiff paper and I saw it in the wastebasket, saw the mistake of the discarding, realized the possibilities had been trashed so I retrieved the paper and on it formed words for the first time. What was it that I should have been doing instead; what chore went neglected? It was silent, diligent enterprise, but I had seen the explosions on Sundays, the preacher's hands on a book, fingering words that inspired everything else that happened as the congregation huddled on its knees around the pulpit at altar call to be relieved of all human misery by a blues-dominated prayer and sermon that made the congregation swoon and that intoxicated them with the spirit of the Lord, wrenching out the misery in the healing rhythm, stripping them of everything but the Lord. Words made them shout, made them experience glory that perhaps was not actually there, their feelings providing glory with the only substance it had. How wondrous! I wanted to make such words. I wanted to make what the preacher called "text."

There was also the way my father could transform the world with just his words and voice, my father who established in the kitchen on Saturday nights while he drank whiskey, a school for his young brothers-in-law, a school to which I, at six by far the youngest pupil, was also invited. He lectured mostly on the dialectics of the soul, asking the forbidden questions, giving words power over any taboo, and thereby endowing them with an affirming ability that still delights the part of me that remembers his tale, at bedtime, of the girl that geese

surround, their feathers locked as tightly as a snow house. Around her they honk, their circle tightening, their feathers brushing against her, some of the feathers working their way into her skin until, when the circle widens, in the center is a goose princess whose new wings are a form of crown. Such words. Such influence.

* * *

Thylias Moss writes about American subjects: fathers and mothers, cooks, children, heroes, salvation, baseball. But her perspective may not be the anticipated one ("When I was 'bout ten we didn't play baseball"). Her themes are the strains in American culture: the split between sexual passion and love; alienation; salvation ("hear the stationmaster call: Cleveland, / Ottawa, Heaven— that's right, *Heaven;* not New Haven anymore!"); identity ("In me Choctaw and Cherokee mix / with unnamed African tribes"):

My ancestors weren't hippies, cotton
precluded a fascination with flowers.

Moss is in turn mocking, urbane, ironically self-deprecating, impassioned. She is concerned equally with morality and religion but focuses more on injustice than on politics. She yearns to heal, but she sees the rents in the social fabric too clearly to go much further without pointing. She is visionary in that she sees with ease the mythic connections between events. Thus, the potential extinction of species, including our own, becomes a tale of Little Red Riding Hood in which, if only it could end happily, the baboons and the mackerel and the egrets join "the grandmother / and Little Red Riding Hood / walking out of a wolf named Dachau" (from "There Will Be Animals").

Although Moss has great power and a gift for sudden deadly connections, there are weaknesses in her poetry. She can fall victim to the catalog ("child of the babushka, child of / the do-rag, child of the scarf, child of the veil, / child of the wig, child of the tortilla, child of / pita, child of hominy ..."). Her juxtapositions produce an arbitrary association that sometimes strains the poem, and the poems sometimes move too fast.

An example is "A Catcher for an Atomic Bouquet," which depends on the word "kiosk" to stand for Russia. The speaking persona for a time, however, becomes America, who goes to bed with Russia and loses her innocence, which produces Hiroshima. This is the "nuclear wedding" that the poet compares to her own wedding, her own human family, a devastating, gutsy self-appraisal. Nonetheless, the ending is puzzling:

Right now I've got my eye on the flamingo
withdrawing at least one leg he insists
won't be shit on.

To complete this surreal allegory, I think that we must know that the flamingo is native neither to North America nor Asia but rather to Africa. Thus, the theme of humanity's inhumanity returns to the poem's seminal beginning ("I have just watched 'Eyes on the Prize'"), but it twists again when we realize that within the poem one flamingo is already stuffed and hanging from the ceiling of a Chinese market in Hangzhou. At this point associations are linear: the poem's subject is extinction and war; the most egregious war in the former Hangchou was the people's rebellion of 1861, in which the

West, fearing to lose a lucrative market, switched sides, leaving the visionary Protestant-influenced rebel leader and his followers helpless before an army lead by a Britisher. The "Taiping" that the rebellion sought was, literally, "A Great Peace"—exactly what Moss's poems yearn for, a yearning restrained effectively by clear-eyed irony.

Moss is a spellbinding reader. One cannot take her voice lightly, for it is a preacher's voice, like amber honey on a straight razor. She sings what can only be called American jazz. Her best poems hold everything in suspension. "Small Congregations" does this, and so do "She Did My Hair Outside, the Wash a Tent around Us" and a dozen others. She builds entire poems from a chance rhyme ("Timex Remembered"). If she cannot save the world, she will at least sing: "Jazz is the consolation prize" ("Weighing the Sins of the World").

Moss's structures tend toward recursion. Emotion recycles within a poem, each cycle transforming the theme, as in this section from "One for All the Newborns," which begins with the joy of birth:

> ... Everything about it was wonderful, the method
> of conception, the gestation, the womb opening
> in perfect analogy to the mind's expansion.
> Then the dark succession of constricting years,
> mother competing with daughter for beauty and losing,
> varicose veins and hot-water bottles, joy boiled away,
> the arrival of knowledge that eyes are birds with clipped
> wings,
> the sun at a 30° angle and unable to go higher, parents
> who cannot push anymore, who stay by the window
> looking for signs of spring....

It is a surreal conceit—nativity stretches for a lifetime, bringing another birth, this time of an unwelcome, transforming awareness. Whereas they first looked for a child, parents now look for supernal help, but the sky is mathematical. We are left with the same image from which life began, only now it is the other side, the exhausted remainder. The poem addresses the situation again in its final lines:

> The miracle was not birth but that I lived despite my
> crimes.
> I treated God badly also; he is another parent
> watching his kids through a window, eager to be proud
> of his creation, looking for signs of spring.

Moss's poems are rooted in the fourth quarter of the 20th century, and all of the period's effects are here, its sounds, its materialism, its distrust of logic and government, its agonizing awareness of race, femininity, and sexuality. So too are its surreal devices, its loosely arranged line, casual enjambments in the service of the speaking voice, predilection for the startling and for speed and noise. Moss has a sense of humor that Horace could admire (and that in "Botanical Fanaticism" produces as outrageous and funny a pun as can be found anywhere). There is a fierceness in her, a prophet's compassion, and a vision that pierces anything fake. She betokens with one of the most interesting voices in American poetry today.

—Edward B. Germain

MOURÉ, Erin

Nationality: Canadian. **Born:** Calgary, Alberta, 17 April 1955. **Education:** University of Calgary, 1972-73; University of British Columbia, Vancouver, 1974-75. **Career:** VIA Rail Canada, Customer Service branch, Montreal, 1978—. Poetry teacher, Upper Canada Writers' Workshop, Summer 1984. **Awards:** National Magazine award (gold), 1983; Pat Lowther Memorial award, 1985; Governor General's award for poetry, 1988; National Magazine award (silver), 1994.

PUBLICATIONS

Poetry

Empire, York Street. Toronto, Anansi, 1979.
The Whisky Vigil. Madeira Park, British Columbia, Harbour, 1981.
Wanted Alive. Toronto, Anansi, 1983.
Domestic Fuel. Toronto, Anansi, 1985.
Furious. Toronto, Anansi, 1988.
WSW (West South West). Montreal, Véhicule Press, 1989.
Sheepish Beauty, Civilian Love. Montreal, Véhicule Press, 1992.
The Green Word: Selected Poems. Toronto, Oxford University Press, 1994.

*   *   *

Erin Mouré's poetics, strongly feminist and deconstructive, work to disrupt the status quo and dismantle systems that perpetuate stasis. Although this is evident in early collections, her later poetry goes further in its subversion of the normative structure of language. By so breaking up the "surface of sense," Mouré's poetry allows previously repressed voices to come through and speak against social strongholds of racism, sexism, and homophobia. Part of this process is syntactic, whereby she questions the validity of "correct" linguistic form by privileging a previously suppressed or submissive form. In *Furious,* Mouré exemplifies this by focusing on the preposition as a central figure of syntactic construction, for example in "Rolling Motion":

> Your face in my neck &
> arms dwelling upward face
> in my soft leg open
> lifted upward airborne soft
> face into under into rolling
> over every upward motion
> rolling open over your
> Face in my neck again over
> turning risen touch billows
> my mouth open enter
> dwelling upward face
> in your soft leg open
> lifted upward airborne soft
> face into under into motion
> over every upward open
> rolling open over your
> Face in my neck again
> & arms

To complement the poems in this collection, Mouré includes a final section entitled "The Acts," which serves partially to document the writing process of particular poems and describe her technique. On "Rolling Motion" she writes:

It is the force of the <u>preposition</u> that *alters* <u>place</u>! Can its displacement of the noun / verb displace also <u>naming</u>, displacing reality? Even momentarily. Make a fissure through which we can leak out from the "real" that is sewn into us, to utter what could not be uttered in the previous structure. Where we have not been represented, except through Dominant (in this case, patriarchal) speaking, which even we speak, even we women.

Mouré enunciates her feminist project by refusing to accept structures that either reinforce or, at least, do not question assumptions that privilege the belief system of the dominant order. Part of this process is the reflexive questioning of the poet that focuses not just on obvious power positions but on the reader's readily made assumptions of the act of interpretation. In *WSW (West South West)*, Mouré "responds" to the poem "Tucker Drugs" with a series of possible readings in "Naming a Poem Called Tucker Drugs," printed on the page facing the poem:

In which we don't know what weather is.
"A poem in which the weather is not mentioned."
"A poem with a dog, a car, a drug store, and a mother in
    it."
"A poem in which there is not much weather."
"A poem in which the possible weather is limited by the
    presence of a consumer object."
"A poem with a dog in it."
"Tucker Drugs."

People may make a mistake if you call it this. With
    representation &
naming being what they are, don't confuse people.

With such a tongue-in-cheek reference—the poet wants to, if not confuse, then seriously question the singularity of vision so often brought to a text—Mouré introduces a sense of plurality to the poem. The suggestion here is that under the surface are a surfeit of voices, despite the apparent rigidity of "representation & naming." This rigidity of discourse, and concomitant hegemonic values assumed by the dominant order, is further questioned in *Furious* in a pair of poems that play off each other. In the first poem, "Pure Reason: Science," the poet narrates the story of laboratory animals protesting their treatment:

The day the animals came on the radio, fed-up, the elec-
    trodes in their hands
beaming, small tubes leading into their brains where chem-
    icals enter,
& the bubbling light from that, the experiment
of science,
the washed fur on their faces & in their voice

The quick brown fox jumped over the lazy dog is a com-
    parison we reject,
they say.

Such already bleak, fantastic humor is effectively blackened, however, when Mouré turns her attention in "Pure Reason: Feminin-

ity" to the feminist project and the very real and utterly humorless situation of women in a male-dominated society:

The day the women came on the radio, fed-up, electrodes
    in their purses
beaming, small tubes leading into their brains where doctors
    enter,
the bubbling light from that, neuronic balance, the
    de/pression
of their inner houses,

washed skin on their faces & in their voice

*She belongs to a certain class of women whose
profession is to promote lust* is a comparison we reject,
they say to the judge.

While the humor of the first poem does not completely elide the danger inherent in oppressive power, its purpose here is to act as a palimpsest for the painful issue of patriarchal dominance and misreadings. Reading this latter poem, the reader is made deliberately aware of the former, and the insinuation is that control and domination is exercised by gender as well as species, perhaps in a far more insidious way.

Through her deconstructive verse, Mouré rigorously questions current and accepted political structures, taking them to task for their subjugating power. By playing with polyvocality in her poetics, she sets up a reflexive dialogue with herself and her reader. Mouré's rejection and deliberate complication of conventional narrative structures enable her to create a new vision that empowers those voices traditionally silenced. Hers is a poetics that rails against the dominant in order to effect change, to validate the subjugated, to dismantle and alter static, unreflexive, and oppressive systems.

—Ashok Mathur

MULFORD, Wendy

Nationality: Welsh. **Born:** Woking, England, 1941. **Education:** Cambridge University. **Family:** Married to Rev. Noel Bevan (second marriage); one daughter. **Career:** Publisher, Street Editions, Cambridge, 1972 (merged with Reality Street, 1993); senior lecturer, Thames Polytechnic, London, 1968-82; freelance writer and part-time lecturer in women's studies, creative writing, and religious studies; performer at poetry festivals. **Agent:** Curtis Brown Ltd., 162-168 Regent St., London Q1R 5TB, England. **Address:** 6, Benhall Green, Saxmundham, IP17 1HU, England.

PUBLICATIONS

Poetry

Bravo to Girls and Heroes. Cambridge, Street Editions, 1977.
No Fee: A Line or Two for Free, with Denise Riley. Cambridge, Street Editions, 1979.

Reaction to Sunsets. Lewes, Ferry Press, 1980.
The Light Sleepers: Poems 1980. Bath, Mammon Press, 1981.
Some Poems: 1968-1978, with Denise Riley. Cambridge, Street Editions, 1982.
River Whose Eyes. Saffron Walden, Avocado to Avocado, 1982.
The ABC of Writing and Other Poems. Southampton, Torque Press, 1985.
Late Spring Next Year: Poems 1979-1985. Bristol, Loxwood Stonleigh, 1987.
Lusus Naturae. London, Circle Press, 1990.
Nevrazumitelny: Poetical Histories, Cambridge, Street Editions, 1991.
The Bay of Naples (1986-88). London, Reality Street, 1992.
The East Anglian Sequence. Peterborough, Spectacular Diseases, forthcoming.
A Handful of Morning, Poems 1993-1997. Buckfast Leigh, Devon, Etruscan Books, forthcoming.

Other

This Narrow Place: Sylvia Townsend Warner and Valentine Ackland: Life, Letters, and Politics 1930-1951. London, Pandora, 1988.

Editor, with others, *The Virago Book of Love Poetry.* London, Virago, 1991; published as *Love Poems by Women.* New York, Fawcett Columbine, 1991.

*   *   *

Wendy Mulford first came in to prominence in the mid-1970s as a small press editor of considerable ability. Street Editions published a good deal of the work of that various group of poets, who are sometimes loosely called the Cambridge school, notable for Douglas Oliver's *In the Cave of Succession,* Veronica Forest Thompson's fine posthumous volume *On the Periphery,* and Alice Notley's *Poem for Frank O'Hara's Birthday.* Her own early work is very fresh, but contains something of the New York poets (Berrigan, O'Hara, Notley) and an occasional nod in the direction of her contemporaries in the Cambridge grouping.

In the late 1970s something much more individual emerged. Rhythms become extremely strong in a way that is most unusual in the poets of this period, and language is two and three edged, and almost abstract.

River Whose Eyes, in which this process becomes first apparent, is intriguing not least for sounding a little like Maggie O'Sullivan but before that poet emerged. It has both intense excitement and a certain darkness. *Reactions to Sunsets* is a series of interactions with contemporary music. Though lighter in tone, there is something of the same air of discovery in the dark that characterizes *River Whose Eyes.* "No way out underground / no astral relief behind narrow peaks / no perspex route through idiolect" to quote a moment of relative clarity.

The poems that were written in late 1980 and published as *The Light Sleepers* seem to mark both the completion of this phase, and the beginning of another. The short poems at the beginning of the book, while still surreally elusive, have much more of the outer world than those that came before. "Movement and Allegory" with its long swaying lines, and its sense of a contemporary woman talking in a dream, perhaps of a quest, but with utterly unexpected coherence, is perhaps Mulford's finest piece.

Late Spring Next Year is called "Poems 1979-1985," but in fact omits "Reactions to Sunsets" and "The Light Sleepers." It is nevertheless a full-sized volume, and a fine one. Despite an elusive poem to Helene Cixous, there is on the whole a new clarity, which is often bound up with the peace campaigns of the Eighties. This is not, however propaganda, but the private, often indeterminate musings of a politically involved person. "Setting Sail for the Falkland Islands: Fools Paradise" is one of the few good political poems of the period. It unites the unreality of the British task force sailing south, with a deep distrust of War, and even more nuclear War.

> The trap door opens only once, daffy duck
> when no words save us.

"Elegy for Male Lovers," written (perhaps significantly) in 1980, the same year as "Movement and Allegory," confronts the feminist view of man as inherently violent, not least to woman. However in the latter part of the poem the tenderness between man and woman in love seems to override the dialectic of the first part, at least for the time.

The 1986-88 meditations on paintings by Howard Hodgkin, *The Bay of Naples,* is in many ways the least satisfactory of Mulford's books. From her earliest work there has always been a tendency to bring in art and music in a way which is not integrated. In this case a whole volume suffers. The weakness of the book may however also reflect the beginnings of the sea change that has taken place in Mulford's poetry in the 1990s. This new period has seen the poet moving from Cambridge to rural East Anglia, remarrying, and addressing both rural and religious themes.

> At the dark waters' darkest edge
> solitaries
> keep appointment

A new dimension is added by an interest in the female saints of the Middle Ages, and their equality with their male equivalents, which was disrupted by the Protestant Reformation with its all male priesthood.

Her two new collections of poetry and her upcoming joint book with Sara Maitland on female sainthood should be significant events.

—Fred Beake

MURRAY, Rona

Nationality: Canadian. **Born:** London, England, 10 February 1924. **Education:** Queen Margaret's School, Duncan, British Columbia, 1933-41; Mills College, Oakland, California, 1941-44; Victoria College, British Columbia, 1960-61, B.A. 1961; University of British Columbia, Vancouver, 1963-65, M.A. 1965; University of Kent, Canterbury, Ph.D. 1972. **Family:** Married 1) Ernest Haddon in 1944, two sons and one daughter; 2) Walter Dexter in 1972. **Career:** Special instructor, University of Victoria, 1961-62; Head of English Department, Rockland School, Victoria, 1962-63; teaching assistant/lecturer, University of British Columbia, 1963-66; associate lecturer, Selkirk College, Castlegar, British Columbia, 1968-74; instructor, Douglas College, Surrey, British Columbia,

1974-76; visiting lecturer in creative writing, 1977-79, and in English, 1981-83, University of Victoria. **Awards:** British Columbia Centennial One-act Play award, 1958; Macmillan of Canada award, 1964; Norma Epstein award, 1965; Canadian Federation of University Women award, 1966; Canada Council grant, 1976, 1979; Pat Lowther award, 1982. **Address:** 3825 Duke Road, Victoria, British Columbia V9C 4B2, Canada.

PUBLICATIONS

Poetry

The Enchanted Adder. Vancouver, Klanak Press, 1965.
The Power of the Dog and Other Poems. Victoria, British Columbia, Morriss, 1968.
Ootischenie. Fredericton, New Brunswick, Fiddlehead, 1974.
Selected Poems. Delta, British Columbia, Sono Nis Press, 1974.
From an Autumn Journal. Toronto, League of Canadian Poets, 1980.
Journey. Victoria, British Columbia, Sono Nis Press, 1981.
Adam and Eve in Middle Age. Victoria, British Columbia, Sono Nis Press. 1984.
The Lost Garden. Victoria, British Columbia, Hawthorne Society, 1993.

Plays

My Love Is Dead (produced Victoria 1955).
Blue Ducks' Feather and Eagledown (produced Vancouver, 1958).
One, Two, Three Alary (produced Castlegar, British Columbia, 1970; produced Seattle, 1983).
Creatures (produced Seattle, 1980). Published in *Event 7* (New Westminister, British Columbia), no. 2, n.d.

Short Stories

The Indigo Dress and Other Stories. Victoria, British Columbia, Sono Nis Press, 1986.

Other

Journey Back to Peshawar (memoir). Victoria, British Columbia, Sono Nis Press, 1993.

Editor, with Walter Dexter, *The Art of Earth: An Anthology.* Victoria, British Columbia, Sono Nis Press, 1979.

*

Rona Murray comments:

In my poetry I attempt to record subjective, personal experience through concrete detail and, generally, through the manner in which the material is spaced on the page rather than through traditional forms, although recently I have been returning to the latter. There appear to be two distinct demands from which it grows: the first to form order, as I see it, out of chaos; the second to record certain ecstatic, usually numinous occurrences. The poems are literal rather than symbolic, and I have been astonished at critics who have ascribed symbolic meanings to my reality. *Adam and Eve in Middle Age* has a political, feminist basis, although I hope it moves beyond

this to a universal statement on the varying attitudes, in our culture, between the male and female. I consider poetry a "given" aesthetic form, realized in a state of excitement, with ease, and then subjected to the writer's critical judgment. Therefore, it appears to be most successful if the poet masters his techniques and then trusts to the mercy of inspiration. I believe that it originates in the subconscious, or in the right side of the brain, or in Yeats's *Spiritus Mundi,* and that all the scribe can do is to wait for its emergence when it chooses to manifest itself. Forced poetry appears to me to be inevitably boring ... one can be a professional fiction writer, but not a professional poet except in so far as one teaches, or writes about, the craft: not in its practice.

*   *   *

The work of Rona Murray is not well known across Canada, but it does have a devoted following on the West Coast, where she has lived since her eighth year, where she was educated, and where she has taught. Her work includes poems, plays, stories, and a travel memoir. She is a serious and thoughtful writer with a characteristic manner who deliberately calculates her effects and then makes the most of them. She is one of Robin Skelton's favorite poets.

It has been noted that the word "white" is a key word in Murray's work. The word may appear as a noun or as an adjective, but it is always used symbolically, conveying the twin notions of innocence and death. The double meaning is apparent in the following passages, taken from the first and the eighth poems in her *Selected Poems* (where the poems are numbered rather than titled):

I have been into the halls of the dead;
the old man said I wore white,
and white makes the woman invulnerable,
he said.

The whiteness   the birches
grasp me   closer
than   can
any lover or   friend.

The collection *Adam and Eve in Middle Age* counterpoints Murray's poems with reproductions of 11 paintings by the Victoria artist Phyllis Serota. The poems and paintings purport to deliver a message "to all the daughters of Eve." The message is meaningful in a postmodern fashion. Adam and Eve speak in turn, and as the reviewer Judith Fitzgerald has observed, "Here, in true anachronistic fashion, Eve writes poetry and Adam broods over the problems of state, taxes, the scarcity of jobs, and child abuse."

In an earlier collection, Murray noted, "I explore / five-finger exercises. / No more." But her poems, her probings, her attempts to find stasis in a changing world do more than that. They journey and return to discover the multiple significances of "white."

—John Robert Colombo

MUSGRAVE, Susan

Nationality: Canadian. **Born:** Santa Cruz, California, 12 March 1951. **Education:** Oak Bay High School. **Family:** Married Stephen

Douglas Reid in 1986; two daughters. **Career:** Instructor in English and creative writing, University of Waterloo, Ontario, 1983-85, Kootenay School of Writing, British Columbia, 1986, and Camosun College, Victoria, British Columbia, 1988—. Writer-in-residence, University of Waterloo, 1983-85, University of New Brunswick, Fredericton, 1985, Vancouver Public Library, 1986, Festival of the Written Arts, Pender Harbour, British Columbia, 1987, 1993, and 1994, Ganaraska Writer's Colony Fiction Workshop, 1988, Sidney Public Library, British Columbia, 1989, Ganges High School, 1989 and 1991, George P. Vanier Secondary School, 1991, Kaslo Summer School of the Arts, 1991, University of Western Ontario, 1992-93, Banff Center for the Arts, 1994; University of Toronto, 1995; Victoria School of Writing, 1996; writer-in-electronic-residence, York University, 1991-94. Columnist, Toronto *Star* and Vancouver *Sun.* Member, Stephen Leacock Poetry Awards advisory committee, and Writers in Electronic Residence advisory committee; member of poetry advisory committee, *In 2 Print* (magazine), 1995—. **Awards:** Canada Council grant, 1969, 1972, 1976, 1979, 1983, 1985, 1989, 1991, 1993, 1995; National Magazine award (silver), 1981; British Columbia Cultural Fund grant, 1991, 1994; b.p. nichol Poetry Chapbook first prize award, 1991; *Prairie Schooner* Reader's Choice award, winter 1993; CBC/*Saturday Night* Tilden award for poetry, 1996; Vicky Metcalf Short Story Editor's award, 1996. **Member:** Writers' Union of Canada (chair, 1997). **Agent:** Bukowski Agency, 182 Avenue Road, Toronto, Ontario M5R 2J1, Canada. **Address:** P.O. Box 2421, Station Main, Sidney, British Columbia V8L 3Y3, Canada. **E-Mail:** smusgrav@pinc.com.

Publications

Poetry

Songs of the Sea-Witch. Vancouver, Sono Nis Press, 1970.
Skuld (broadside). Frensham, Surrey, Sceptre Press, 1971.
Birthstone (broadside). Frensham, Surrey, Sceptre Press, 1972.
Entrance of the Celebrant. Toronto, Macmillan, and London, Fuller d'Arch Smith, 1972.
Equinox (broadside). Rushden, Northamptonshire, Sceptre Press, 1973.
Kung (broadside). Rushden, Northamptonshire, Sceptre Press, 1973.
Grave-Dirt and Selected Strawberries. Toronto, Macmillan, 1973.
Gullband (for children), illustrated by Rikki Dicornet. Vancouver, J.J. Douglas, 1974.
Against (broadside). Rushden, Northamptonshire, Sceptre Press, 1974.
Two Poems (broadside). Knotting, Bedfordshire, Sceptre Press, 1975.
The Impstone. Toronto, McClelland & Stewart, 1976; London, Omphalos Press, 1978.
Kiskatinaw Songs, with Séan Virgo. Victoria, Pharos Press, 1977.
Selected Strawberries and Other Poems. Victoria, Sono Nis Press, 1977.
For Charlie Beaulieu... (broadside). Knotting, Bedfordshire, Sceptre Press, 1977.
Two Poems for the Blue Moon (broadside). Knotting, Bedfordshire, Sceptre Press, 1977.
Becky Swan's Book. Erin, Ontario, Porcupine's Quill, 1978.
A Man to Marry, a Man to Bury. Toronto, McClelland & Stewart, 1979.

Conversation During the Omelette aux Fines Herbes (broadside). Knotting, Bedfordshire, Sceptre Press, 1979.
When My Boots Drive Off in a Cadillac. Toronto, League of Canadian Poets, 1980.
Taboo Man (broadside). N.p., Celia Duthie, 1981.
Tarts and Muggers: Poems New and Selected. Toronto, McClelland & Stewart, 1982.
The Plane Put Down in Sacramento (broadside). Vancouver, Hoffer, 1982.
I do not know if things that happen can be said to come to pass or only happen (broadside). Vancouver, Hoffer, 1982.
Cocktails at the Mausoleum. Toronto, McClelland & Stewart, 1985; revised edition, 1992.
Desireless: Tom York (1947-1988) (broadside). N.p., Celia Duthie, 1988.
Kestrel and Leonardo (for children), illustrated by Linda Rogers. N.p., Studio 123, 1990.
The Embalmer's Art: Poems New and Selected. N.p., Exile Editions, 1991.
In the Small Hours of the Rain. Victoria, British Columbia, n.p., 1991.
Forcing the Narcissus. Toronto, McClelland & Stewart, 1994.

Plays

Gullband (produced Toronto, 1976).
Valentine's Day in Jail (produced Vancouver, 1995).

Radio Play: *The Wages of Love,* 1987.

Novels

The Charcoal Burners. Toronto, McClelland & Stewart, 1980.
Hag Head (for children), illustrated by Carol Evans. Toronto, Clarke Irwin, 1980.
The Dancing Chicken. Toronto, Methuen, 1987.

Other

Great Musgrave. New York, Prentice-Hall, 1989.
Musgrave Landing: Musings on the Writing Life. Scarborough, Ontario, Prentice Hall, 1988.

Editor, *Clearcut Words: Writers for Clayoquot.* Victoria, British Columbia, Hawthorne Society for Reference West, 1993.
Editor, *Because You Loved Being a Stranger: 55 Poets Celebrate Patrick Lane.* N.p., Harbour Publishing, 1994.

*

Manuscript Collection: McMaster University, Hamilton, Ontario.

Critical Study: "The White Goddess: Poetry of Susan Musgrave" by Rosemary Sullivan, in *Contemporary Verse 2* (Winnipeg), 1975.

*   *   *

I happened to have an opportunity to speak with Susan Musgrave when I was trying to obtain her volume of poetry *Forcing the Narcissus.* Nervously identifying myself, I reminded her that I was the critic who on reading her early volumes had feared that she as well as her poetic persona might succumb to dark suicidal impulses. Her obsessive, poignant treatment of death, insanity, and blood reminded me of Sylvia Plath's poetry in *Ariel.* I later recanted this judgment, however, and although subsequent volumes continued to work in the starker vein of the early poetry, I knew better than quickly to confuse art with life. She laughed, saying that if I feared for her well-being then the fear would probably resurface when I read this volume. "It is dark," she said, or some words to that effect, but the darkness is largely a function of the publisher's will. Her editors removed the lighter verse, choosing to give the volume tonal unity, but in doing so they denied the reader the opportunity to hear a more carefree voice. The volume is full of images that strike with the force of a lash; they bring blood and pain, but they also bring beauty, forgiveness, and transcendence.

Looking back at Musgrave's works, I can see why the comparison to Plath's writings was almost unavoidable. The feminist stances of the two poets were similar; so were their attitudes toward men, lesbianism, and sex. Musgrave's imitation of Plath's "Daddy" and "Lady Lazarus" in her poem "Exposure" was unmistakable. She was the celebrant of death, "the spilled child," and all she looked at was transformed into death. In "The Opened Grave" she placed herself at the "edge of things." Her poems of witchcraft read like strange and deeply disturbing myths of blood rites and sexuality pervaded with violence. The inhabitants of her witch kingdoms resembled those in Gustave Doré's illustrations— beetles, white moths, and figures with bloated heads angling out of hunched shoulders and shriveled torsos, shaking their gnarled hands, leering at their prey. These lines from "Finding Love" are chilling:

> From my bed I could hear
> the ripe wound open, the thick sea
> pouring in. I told you, then,
> the first lie I had in my heart;
> the carcass of a dull animal
> slipped between our sights.

The poem "MacKenzie River, North" is another work imbued with terror.

What I failed to recognize was that although Musgrave's range was limited in her two collections, *Songs of the Sea-Witch* and *Entrance of the Celebrant,* and her themes were obsessive and derivative, her sense of the bizarre and her ability to evoke the mood of bewitched kingdoms could serve her well in an entirely different vein of poetry. In the earlier collections she used these gifts to evoke strange, disturbing worlds fraught with psychological significance. In the third section of *Grave-Dirt and Selected Strawberries* she transforms them to create a high-spirited, bawdy, and wonderfully affectionate pastiche of poems and prose in celebration of the strawberry. Musgrave gleefully parodies herself and writes in the best 18th-century traditions of comedy, bringing some of the writings of Erica Jong to mind. In her fanciful history the strawberry is her picaresque hero. His origins are traced, his baptism marked, and his emergence in the writings of others duly recorded, and all the facts about him that every strawberry lover would like to know are cataloged. Musgrave feigns an anthropological tone and hilariously records the harvest customs of the strawberry, its method of reproduction, its behavior in captivity, its sense of fellowship.

The collection is giddy, witty, and full of good fun. It could not be more unlike her other poetry.

Musgrave's writings from *Equinox* through *The Impstone* reflect continued growth in the kind of poetry that won her acclaim. "Memorial to a Lover" (*Two Poems*) imitates Plath. Others feature her interest in Indian lore and witchcraft. The moon poems, like the "Kiskatinaw Songs" (*Grave-Dirt and Selected Strawberries*) experiment with rhythms from songs, chants, and ballads. Poems like "The Firstborn" and *Equinox* represent Musgrave's best handling of the world of nightmare and demons, in which dark rituals are enacted between the self and its demon other.

The personal love poetry in *Cocktails at the Mausoleum* is softer and more mellow in its tone, some of it becoming much more loving. The shift in tone and Musgrave's widening of her range suggest that some critics were too quick to condemn her for the alleged anti-male stance they detected in some of the poems published in *A Man to Marry, a Man to Bury.* Many poems explore her private domain, her personal friends, and her journeys on the lecture circuit. These poems, such as "Black Morning," "We Come This Way But Once," and her Salmonberry Road poems, are reminiscent of the poetry of Frank O'Hara, in which personal material, friends, and particular geographical locations are cited to create the sense that direct personal experience is being recorded. These poems employ a colloquial idiom; they make references to private materials which mean something quite different to the poet than they can ever mean to the public; they depict a landscape of experience in which the city or creek or street is named simply because the very act of naming prevents the named thing from finally being appropriated.

Musgrave's Landing continues to combine an erotic poetry with the poetry of her dark imaginings, a poetry full of torture and dismemberment. Some of the poems are less controlled than usual, exploring almost wantonly the material of her dreams. Some of the dramatic monologues she has written recall the humor and wit displayed in her collection of poems about the strawberry. They are fanciful, brash, and bawdy. "My Boots Drive Off in a Cadillac" is told from the point of view of a prostitute. It and other poems in *Tarts and Muggers,* particularly "Boogeying with the Queen," show us a Musgrave writing a tough, cocky poetry.

Some of Musgrave's poetry is still written too much under the spell of the style as well as the subject matter of the confessional poets. Her poem about her trip to Plath's grave and another poem called "Salad Days" demonstrate that she can move beyond this mode, however. Her poem about her daddy, "You Didn't Fit," has a very original cast to it. Nonetheless, she remains very indebted to John Berryman, Theodore Roethke, Joyce Carol Oates, Robert Lowell, Ted Hughes, and even Jong. Her poems about environmental issues or the drug trade give voice to her social consciousness but remain too rhetorical and predictable. Only the "Requiem for Talunkwan Island," written from the point of view of a Haida ghost returning to the island, has a powerful and original voice, giving force to her complaint against the logging industry which has caused erosion of the land and made reforestation impossible.

Forcing the Narcissus is a heart-wrenching volume of poems. Many have appeared before, some are revised, and others are new. In "The Gift," the speaker foresees all the harrowing lessons from hell that an infant born of a drug-addicted mother will come to know: "After nine months of happiness / you're learning withdrawal, what it's like to be / fully human, how your mother only gives you / all she's got to give." The poems in the section "From the Wet Heart of the Wound" chart the raw emotions of a child brutalized by her father or a child reliving the loss of her father and the estrangement from her mother. "Family Plot" exudes the chill of the graveyard, calling forth painful memories and delving deeper into the storehouse of memory and the depths of graves. "The Spirituality of Cruelty" voices Musgrave's credo—art transfigures violence and pain. It is a restatement of Yeats's theme in "The Circus Animal's Desertion." All of the ladders start, all beauty comes from "the foul rag-and-bone shop of the heart." Musgrave's poetry is full of terror, and from it beauty is born.

—Carol Simpson Stern

MUSKE, Carol

Pseudonym: Carol Muske-Dukes. **Nationality:** American. **Born:** St. Paul, Minnesota, 17 December 1945. **Education:** Creighton University, Omaha, Nebraska, B.A. 1967; State University of California at San Francisco, M.A. in English and creative writing 1970. **Family:** Married 1) Edward B. Healton, M.D., in 1972 (divorced 1977); 2) David C. Dukes in 1983; one daughter. **Career:** Founder and director, Free Space creative writing program, Women's House of Detention, Riker's Island, New York, 1972-73; director, Art without Walls/Free space (writing program for women prisoners), New York, 1974-82; lecturer in creative writing, 1985-89, assistant professor, 1989-93, professor of English, 1993—, University of Southern California, Los Angeles. Instructor at New School for Social Research, New York University, Columbia University, University of Virginia, and University of Iowa. Jenny McKean Moore lecturer, George Washington University, 1980-81; visiting poet, University of California, Irvine, 1993. **Awards:** Dylan Thomas Poetry award, 1973, for "Swansong"; Pushcart Prize, 1978, 1988-89, 1992-93; Poetry Society Alice Fay Di Castagnola Award, 1979; Guggenheim Foundation fellowship, 1981; National Endowment for the Arts fellowship, 1984; Ingram-Merrill Foundation fellowship, 1988. **Member:** American Academy of Poets, Poets & Writers. **Agent:** Kim Witherspoon, Witherspoon Associates, 235 East 31st Street, New York, New York 10016, U.S.A.

PUBLICATIONS

Poetry

Camouflage. Pittsburgh, University of Pittsburgh Press, 1975.
Skylight. New York, Doubleday, 1981.
Wyndmere. Pittsburgh, University of Pittsburgh Press, 1985.
Applause. Pittsburgh, University of Pittsburgh Press, 1989.
Red Trousseau. New York, Penguin, 1993.
An Octave above Thunder: Selected and New Poems. New York, Viking Penguin, 1997.

Novels

Dear Digby (as Carol Muske-Dukes). New York, Viking, 1989.
Saving St. Germ (as Carol Muske-Dukes). New York, Viking, 1993.
Two Secrets (as Carol Muske-Dukes). Forthcoming.

Other

Women and Poetry. Ann Arbor, University of Michigan Press, 1997.

Translator, *Grey-Haired Ophelia: Selected Poems by Anna Swir.* Forthcoming.

*   *   *

Carol Muske's work, while well-anchored in daily life, moves far beyond to become a meditation on philosophical concerns like the nature of time and the value of life. This carefully achieved scope contributes much of what is powerful and persuasive in her work. Widely travelled, she is well read, has a strong fine arts background, and knows her science, especially biochemistry, which provides much of the focus for her second novel. However, her work avoids being pedantic. After a decade teaching creative writing to women prisoners in New York, she has considerable empathy for society's underdogs. In "Unsent Letter 2," the author tells of young, despondent pregnant woman:

> I want to take her in my arms, but
> I keep serving food, my hands in
> the clear plastic gloves ice-cold

This same poem shows how the author is able to move from the personal to the metaphysical. She muses about St. Augustine, who said our failure to understand the nature of time made us unable to truly comprehend miracles. In a sort of time-lapse photography, a bean pod held in the magus' hand becomes a blossoming plant. And, if the same thing could be done for this young woman:

> ... she'd have
> another human being in her arms, an infant
> —just like that—but she is homeless,
> nothing to hold her outside her self.
>
> ... we do not want
> to hurry it, the miracle. It's better that it be served
> in gradual sequence ... child, seducer, mother,
> father, child, seducer ... Faces: a food-line, a you
>
> one frozen location of mercy: a final divided portion
>   to set on each plate.

This compassion also allows Muske to look below the picturesque, as in "August 1974: A Tapestry," to the hidden suffering:

> Threading terror into the beautiful rugs,
> the skeletal little boys of Kashmir
> lifted fingers so sure of the whip
>
> they wove the whip deep into the warp—

The artist, seeing an ethical, as well as aesthetic, mission, become a witness, speaking for the oppressed:

the angry young woman, the foreman nodding
meekly, brandishing the whip,
split suddenly into myriad multicolored
threads as the shuttle is thrown
and the chanter chants the patterns

Muske's ability to empathize with people in a variety of times and places also allows her, in "Illness as Metaphor," to picture Keats' death in Italy, and bring him back at the same time,

alive and dying—gone forever
and just now climbing up the great
stairs, troubled and pale....

Or, in "Immunity," to find, reaching across time, an affinity with the poet Issa that allows her both to share his loss of a daughter, and rescue that lost daughter as she takes her own child into her arms:

I take her death into me
little by little—temple bells, grass—

happiness
when she smiles like this
when I see she'll live forever.

Muske is not the sort of poet well served by quoting a few pithy lines. She takes the time to spin out her poems; still, the effort of following the threads till they join together is worth the reader's time. The poems in each of these collections also fit into a larger tapestry as variations on each collection's central motif or theme. In the 1993 collection, *Red Trousseau,* "red" becomes a motif that carries a variety of associations: fire, alchemy, anger, desire, blood, and vitality. In "Red Trousseau," the Salem witch trials become a metaphor for sexual desire and sexual politics, one carried into other poems. "Prague: Two Journals" concerns Jan Palach, a Czech student whose 1968 self-immolation protested the Soviet invasion. The nine-part poem involves two visits in 1970 and 1990, the latter focussing on a talk with Palach's lover. At the conclusion, a stack of toothpicks the author's daughter has assembled in an astray collapses; but, though this makeshift pyre has collapsed, Palach "burns before us, he goes on burning." This poem, like many of Muske's, becomes a meditation on the nature of time, and a world caught up in time's illusions. In *Wyndmere,* she returns to her grandparents' and mother's past, catching glimpses of them in the places that mirror their lives. The world she sees, both firsthand and through these lives, is not a particularly nice one, but she sees it unflinchingly, as in "Wyndmere, Windemere," from this collection:

The world's wrong, mother,
Shelley said it when, at the end,
he got it right. And you, who knew
every word of his by heart, agreed.

—Duane Ackerson

N

NAMJOSHI, Suniti

Nationality: Indian. **Born:** Bombay, 20 April 1941. **Education:** University of Poona, B.A. 1961, M.A. 1963; University of Missouri, M.S. in business administration 1969; McGill University, Ph.D. in English literature 1972. **Family:** Companion of poet Gillian Hanscombe since 1984. **Career:** Lecturer in English literature, University of Poona, Fergusson College, Poona, India, 1963-64; officer, Government of India Administrative Service, New Delhi, 1964-69; lecturer, 1972-73, assistant professor, 1973-78, associate professor of English literature, 1978-89, Scarborough College, University of Toronto, Scarborough, Ontario. **Awards:** Ontario Arts Council award, 1976, 1977; Canada Council award, 1981; numerous Canada Council travel grants. **Member:** League of Canadian Poets. **Address:** Grindon Cottage, Combpyne Lane, Rousdon near Lyme Regis, DT7 3XW, England.

PUBLICATIONS

Poetry

Poems. Calcutta, Writers Workshop, 1967.
More Poems. Calcutta, Writers Workshop, 1971.
Cyclone in Pakistan. Calcutta, Writers Workshop, 1971.
The Jackass and the Lady. Calcutta, Writers Workshop, 1980.
The Authentic Lie. Fredericton, New Brunswick, Fiddlehead Poetry Books, 1982.
From the Bedside Book of Nightmares. Fredericton, New Brunswick, Fiddlehead Poetry Books, 1984.
Flesh and Paper, with Gillian Hanscombe. Seaton, Devon, Jezebel Tapes & Books, 1986.
Because of India: Selected Poems and Fables. London, Only Woman Press, 1989.

Short Stories

Feminist Fables. London, Sheba Feminist Press, 1981.
The Conversations of Cow. New Delhi, Rupa, and London, Women's Press, 1985.
The Blue Donkey Fables. London, Women's Press, 1988.
The Mothers of Maya Diip. London, Women's Press, 1989.
"Dusty Distance," in *The Inner Courtyard: Stories by Indian Women.* Calcutta, Rupa, 1991.
"Hey Diddle Diddle," with Gillian Hanscombe, in *By the Light of the Silvery Moon: Short Stories to Celebrate the 10th Birthday of Silver Moon Women's Bookshop.* London, Virago, 1994.
Saint Suniti and the Dragon and Other Fables. London, Virago, 1994.

Play

Circles of Paradise, with Gillian Hanscombe (produced London, 1994).

For Children

Adita and the One-Eyed Monkey. Boston, Beacon Press, 1986; London, Sheba Feminist Press, 1986.

Other

Ezra Pound and Reality: A Study of the Metaphysics of the Cantos (thesis). Toronto, McGill University, 1972.
Building Babel. Melbourne, Spinifex, 1996.

Recordings: In *Dykeproud, A Lesbian Poetry Reading from the Third International Feminist Bookfair* (recording), 1988; *Flesh and Blood* (video), with Gillian Hanscombe, 1990.

Translator, with mother, Sarojini Namjoshi, *Poems of Govindagraj,* by Ram Ganesh Gadkari. Calcutta, Writers Workshop, 1968.

*

Manuscript Collections: Harriet Irving Library, University of New Brunswick.

Critical Studies: "Suniti Namjoshi" by Monika Varma in *Facing Four,* Calcutta, Writers Workshop Publication, 1973; articles in *Canadian Woman Studies,* winter 1982, fall 1983; article by Mary Meigs in *Room of One's Own,* February 1984; "The New Poets I: Mamta Kalia, Suniti Namjoshi, Gauri Deshpande" by Sunanda Chavan in *The Fair Voice: A Study of Indian Women Poets in English,* New Delhi, Sterling Publishers, 1984; "Suniti Namjoshi—Art and Artifice in Her Work" by A.N. Dwivedi, in *Studies in Contemporary Indo-English Verse, Vol. I: A Collection of Critical Essays on Female Poets,* Bareilly, Prakash Book Depot, 1984; "Suniti Namjoshi: The Dual World of Her Early Poems" by Jasbir Jain, in *Problems of Postcolonial Literatures and Other Essays,* Jaipur, Printwell, 1991; essay by Diane McGifford in *Writers of the Indian Diaspora: A Bio-Bibliographical Critical Source,* Westport, Connecticut, Greenwood Press, 1993; "Literature of the Indian Diaspora in Canada" by Uma Parameshwa in *Commonwealth Literature: Themes and Techniques,* Delhi, Ajanta Publishers, 1993; "Sister Letters: Miranda's Tempest in Canada" by Diana Brydon, in *Cross-Cultural Performances: Differences in Women's Re-Visions of Shakespeare,* Urbana, University of Illinois Press, 1993; *Configurations of Exile: South Asian Writers and their Worlds* by Chelva Kanaganayakam, Toronto, TSAR, 1995; "'Cracking India': Minority Women Writers and the Contentious Margins of Indian Nationalist Discourse" by Harveen Sachdeva Mann, in *The Journal of Commonwealth Literature,* vol. 29, no. 2, 1994; *Configurations of Exile: South Asian Writers and Their World* by Chelva Kanaganayakam, Toronto, TSAR, 1995.

*   *   *

In *Flesh and Paper,* the persona of the poem, "There Is No Undiscovered Country" says,

'There is no undiscovered country,

...

There is only an ordinary planet,
where the shack falls down,
                              weather prevails,
and we must pay for safety
                         with a disguised
and difficult difference
                         and the habit of fear.
And there is only a man-made language
                         with its logic
of need and greed,
                         doom, dearth, despair.
But in spite of a hurtful history
shall we speak of a peopled place
  where women may walk freely
    in the still, breathable air?'

This poem captures some of the major themes of Suniti Namjoshi's poetry. Her poems are about her "hurtful history," about alienation and despair, about "disguised, difficult difference," that is, relationships which are forbidden by a patriarchal, heterosexual society, and about life's struggle and hopes. Her poems can be labeled as feminist, lesbian, expatriate Indian or Commonwealth, and arise out of her identity as a lesbian feminist Indian, Indo-Canadian woman. But her major concerns in her words remain "Aesthetic and Moral." She experiments with the poetic form and tries to understand life—her life and a woman's life. In her world of words, irony and revisions of fables become weapons to question and subvert the patriarchal structures and articulate a lesbian voice.

Her poetry shows a movement from apparently disguised neutral musings on the world to a lesbian woman musings about her world—from a "narrative distance" to a we / I who is a lesbian. Her first collection of poems, titled simply *Poems* and published in India, voices her various concerns: love, writing in English about India, and the "search for epithets of life." The issue of lesbian love is never directly addressed, yet poems like "Various Reasons." "Red Flower," and "Courtship" reveal a sense of unease, of walls which need to be broken down, of policeman symbolic of society's laws and the poets as in "Cain" is a schizophrenic, "Two souls lodged in one body, / ....Two worlds: unshared, unnatural." The world in which is part of patriarchal heterosexual society yet questions it and is a lesbian. This mode of disguise remains a strand in her other early poems like "Pinocchio." In "In English" she says, "Oriental Princess / How can I make these foreigners understand you are my / mother?" To talk about India, but not to exoticise it, to show a country of which you are part of to a Western audience is a issue she addresses in "was it quite like that?," "But you like what you see" and "I see what I can" in *Flesh and Paper.*

It is with her second and third volume of poetry that Namjoshi begins to voice social concerns also: unpleasant aspects of American life in "A Problem." the so-called sophistication of the westernized Indian society in poems like "Contemporary," and the ruthless utilitarian attitude towards cyclone, but they are not central to her concerns. Addressing poets in "For the Occasion," she says, "the death of the world / When it comes / we'll be ready, / singing a song, / proving nothing to no one at all, / but art was ever subjective."

Thus for art is subjective and her poetry published in later years become more personal. She uses mythologies, fables, fairy tales, literary personalities, and anecdotes and uses them to tell her story and also to highlight the patriarchal structures which underlie all these world of words by inverting, revisioning them. She quotes from Mary Shelley, "The fabrication of life is not a matter that may be undertaken lightly. It is an experiment fraught with peril." Her poems undertake this experiment with remarkable success. In *Authentic Lie* she talks about the pain of a child when her father dies—an exercise in grappling with her own grief and pain when her father died. She says, "Year after year / the corpse rots quietly.... The body is gone, / but the soul remains, / trailing terror.... Death is a skeleton, / his bones my own." The grief and pain is not resolved but the narrator decides to move on to talk about a more general anguish, the pain of living, of death, and of dreams and harsh reality.

In *From the Bedside Book of Nightmares,* Namjoshi explores her relationship with her mother, the tension because she is a lesbian, her relationship with her siblings, the pain of being the "bad daughter" and the pain of being "the creature." The pain of being outside the heterosexual society as well as the pain within it is revealed and reiterated again and again. She says, "We loved those kindly gentlemen, I mean, / your own father, and your daughter's father / But in our long ancestry / where are the women?" and 'There's something / obnoxious and cruel about me. / I don't shut up, / and I am not dead.' She rewrites Shakespeare's *The Tempest,* where the patriarchal Prospero is left out and Caliban—a female—and Miranda find love. Her later poems like "lost species" ("all right call them another species") are poems when the alibi, the fear and the distance has been shed and she is speaking to lesbians about lesbians.

Thus the shift is complete and though in some sense the universal tone of her poems are lost, they remain universal by virtue of their expressions of human emotions of love, hurt, pain, and hate. The poems cry out for understanding and her range of revisionary myths and fables questions, imperializing discourses, of gender and sexuality and race, and though not culturally or geographically specific are revealed in a personal context. The female is associated with nature and creativity and the clash between the natural and the artificial figure in her poems. Alice, Gulliver, Medusa, Circe, rose, sea, unicorn, all people her "world of words."

Structurally, her poems range from couplets to long poems. They are arranged as a prose or as lyric. They are epigrammatic, restrained commentaries or long poems. Namjoshi uses metaphors and similes, myths and fables, to suggest various layers of meanings on life. An innovative, creative poet, she captures universal, personal, and social experiences fabulistically.

—Angelina Paul

NICHOLS, Grace

Nationality: Guyanese. **Born:** 18 January 1950. Moved to England in 1977. **Education:** St. Stephen's Scots School, Georgetown; Progressive and Preparatory Institute, Georgetown; University of Guyana, Georgetown, diploma in communications. **Family:** Lives with the poet John Agard; two daughters (one from a previous marriage). **Career:** Teacher in Georgetown, 1967-70; reporter with national newspaper, Georgetown, 1972-73; information assistant, Government Information Services, 1973-76; freelance journalist in Guyana, 1977—. **Awards:** Commonwealth poetry prize, 1983; British Arts Council bursary, 1988; Guyana Prize for Poetry award, 1996, for *Sunris.* **Agent:** Anthea Morton-Saner, Curtis Brown, 162-68 Regent Street, London W1R STB, England.

PUBLICATIONS

Poetry

I Is a Long-Memoried Woman. London, Caribbean Cultural International, 1983.
The Fat Black Woman's Poems. London, Virago Press, 1984.
Come On into My Tropical Garden (for children). London, A. & C. Black, 1988.
Lazy Thoughts of a Lazy Woman, and Other Poems. London, Virago Press, 1989.
Sunrise. London, Virago Press, 1996.

Novel

Whole of a Morning Sky. London, Virago Press, 1989.

Other (for children)

Trust You, Wriggly. London, Hodder & Stoughton, 1980.
Baby Fish and Other Stories. Privately printed, 1983.
Leslyn in London. London, Hodder & Stoughton, 1984.
The Discovery. London, Macmillan, 1986.
No Hickory No Dickory No Dock (nursery rhyme), with John Agard. London, Viking, 1990.
Give Yourself a Hug (poems). London, A. & C. Black, 1994.
Asana and the Animals (poems). London, Walker, 1997.

Editor, *Black Poetry.* London, Blackie, 1988; as *Poetry Jump Up,* London, Penguin, 1989.
Editor, *Can I Buy a Slice of Sky?* London, Blackie, 1991.
Editor, with John Agard, *A Caribbean Dozen.* London, Walker, 1994.

*   *   *

Grace Nichols's career as a poet had a very distinguished start with the collection *I Is a Long-Memoried Woman,* which won the Commonwealth poetry prize in 1983. The collection charts the slave experience from the point of view of the black woman. It touches on the pain, fear, confusion, anger, and strength of slave women; the use of the first-person narrative gives the collection its intimate, lived-through, genuinely soul-searching tone, and yet Nichols is careful to point out that the "I" is every slave woman by giving her a "web of kin," a composite African ancestry, including most of the tribes who were enslaved. The collection is tightly organized, moving chronologically from "the beginning" through "the vicissitudes" of slave existence, "the sorcery" to cope with it, "the bloodling" which centers around the emotional agony of motherhood in slave conditions, and finally "the return," in which the slave finally rebels and is returned to herself. Cutting across this chronology is a consistent women's point of view and frame of reference. The African ancestral world is evoked in terms

of fertility goddesses, the power of traditional women, and their daily lives (cooking, farming, and child rearing), and the New World experience refers to the martyrdom of rebel women, heroines of the struggle, and to the hard labor and "namelessness" of the slave women.

The main strength of the collection lies in the courage with which Nichols searches out and discusses the most painful areas of the slave woman's condition: the fight to retain dignity and self-esteem in humiliating circumstances, the shame connected with the knowledge that there were black slave traders as well, and, most of all, the contradictions of motherhood, the pain which should have been joy and which led some slave women to kill their babies. Occasionally, the poet / persona gives in to depression and despair, as in the poem "Sunshine," which concludes with "the truth is / my life has slipped out / of my possession." The main cause for despair is not the harsh conditions but the severing of ties, the loss of tradition, roots, and rituals: "but I / armed only with / my mother's smile / must be forever gathering / my life together like scattered beads." The schizophrenic universe of this New World slave condition is convincingly and movingly described in poems like "Drum-Spell" and "Web of Kin." The latter poem also offers a possible, if hard, way out of the dilemma—"and my eyes everywhere reflecting / even in dreams I will submerge myself"—suggesting a slow gathering of strength through a period of watchfulness and suspended action.

The overall tone of the collection, however, is defiant, celebrating women's capacity for survival. Rebellion is traced in a hundred small ways. In poems like "Love Act," "Skin Teeth," and "Nanny" the traditional image of the smiling and happy female house slave is exploded, and "nanny / mistresswife" is seen to harbor self-awareness and controlled hatred until the moment is ripe and she gains her own freedom or—in the imagery of the book—she becomes "a woman / holding my beads in my hand." Form varies between free verse and ritualistic incantations and also relies on West Indian popular songs, some written in dialect, the rest in clearly marked West Indian English—styles that suit the subject perfectly.

The Fat Black Woman's Poems is a less unified collection, consisting of four unlinked sections. The first section, which gives the book its title, is a lighthearted, occasionally very funny exploration of the thoughts and problems of a fat, self-assured black woman. Seriousness lurks behind the fun, however, as in the poem "The Fat Black Woman Remembers," in which the poet / persona makes sure that her image does not coincide with the image of that other fat black woman, Jemima, "tossing pancakes / to heaven / in smokes of happy hearty / murderous blue laughter ... But this fat black woman ain't no Jemima / Sure thing Honey / Yeah." The following two sections, "In Spite of Ourselves" and "Back Home Contemplation," cover traditional themes in West Indian literature: the feeling of alienation from British society and thoughts about home and childhood, vacillating between nostalgia for the lost world of childhood and anger at present conditions of poverty and exploitation.

Lazy Thoughts of a Lazy Woman continues both the themes and the style of the previous collections. It starts off lightheartedly with poems about dust and grease and continues with a varied collection of thoughts and impressions about themes such as Eve, the Jamaican tourist industry, break dancing, and white male power. There is a greater emphasis on woman-centered or feminist themes in poems like "Ode to My Bleed" and "My Black Triangle." There is also a more extensive use of West Indian dialect. The tone is mostly light, offering sudden gifts of insight: "Even the undeserving / love floods / risking all." Despite this, Nichols's first collection remains among her most substantial, with the following two adding the dimension of humor.

—Kirsten Holst Petersen

NÍ CHUILLEANÁIN, Eiléan

Nationality: Irish. **Born:** Cork, 28 November 1942. **Education:** University College, Cork, B.A. in English and history 1962, M.A. in English 1964; Lady Margaret Hall, Oxford, 1964-66, B.Litt. in Elizabethan prose 1969. **Family:** Married Macdara Woods in 1978; one son. **Career:** Lecturer, 1966-85, senior lecturer, 1985—, Trinity College, Dublin; founder, with Pearse Hutchinson, Macdara Woods, and Leland Bardwell, *Cyphers* literary magazine, 1975. **Awards:** *Irish Times* prize, 1966; Patrick Kavanagh prize, 1973; O'Shaughnessy Prize, 1992. **Address:** Trinity College, University of Dublin, Dublin 2, Ireland.

PUBLICATIONS

Poetry

Acts and Monuments. Dublin, Gallery Press, 1972.
Site of Ambush. Dublin, Gallery Press, 1975.
The Second Voyage. Dublin, Gallery Press, and Winston-Salem, North Carolina, Wake Forest University Press, 1977; Newcastle upon Tyne, Bloodaxe, 1986.
The Rose-Geranium. Dublin, Gallery Press, 1981.
The Magdalene Sermon. Dublin, Gallery Press, 1989; as *The Magdalene Sermon and Earlier Poems,* Winston-Salem, North Carolina, Wake Forest University Press, 1991.
The Brazen Serpent. Dublin, Gallery Press, 1994; Winston-Salem, North Carolina, Wake Forest University Press, 1995.

Other

Editor, *Irish Women: Image and Achievement.* Dublin, Arlen House, 1985.
Editor, *Belinda* by Maria Edgeworth. London, J.M. Dent, 1993.
Editor, with J.D. Pheifer, *Noble and Joyous Histories: English Romances 1375-1650.* Dublin, Irish Academic Press, 1993.

*

Eiléan Ní Chuilleanáin comments:

My work issues from problems in everyday life but it does so obliquely, via myths, folklore, and history. It draws on visual description of rooms and landscapes, on childhood memories and literary allusions, and since these are sometimes enigmatic, my poems can be so too.

*   *   *

Since 1966, when she won the *Irish Times* prize for poetry, Eiléan Ní Chuilleanáin has written with a remarkable consistency of theme and method. Her subject matter is personal, but it is seen through a strange perspective. Although the "I" of the poems has always been the personal "I," it is revealed through odd angles and amazing connections between mythical moments and moments of skewed looking. She is a poet of empty kitchens, silent, well-lit places, well-scrubbed tables. She shares with Thomas Kinsella that peculiar ability to find genius in odd corners. The drama in her poems is a reductive one; a poem often begins with a moment of insight, an epiphany, and is then reduced to a series of physical descriptions. Her geography is askew because she is very sensitive to the play of light on objects. Her world is "ridged / Pocked and dented" with the decency of thought:

> And wake again in an afternoon bed
> Grey light sloping from window-ledge
> To straw-seated armchair. I get up,
> Walk down a silent corridor
> To the Kitchen. Twilight and a long scrubbed table....

In "The Ropesellers" she finds "a soft corner of sunlight," in "Atlantis" there is "Light wavering in water," while in "Chrissie," a poem from *The Magdalene Sermon,* "Light fills the growing cavity / That swells her, that ripens to her ending." Her ability to notice well-lit cavities and sunlit corners is symptomatic of solitary character or, at least, the flight toward solitude. But these solitudes are not aimless; they are loaded with adult perceptions and become energized with a deep unease:

> What man forgets, at home
> In the long noons of peace
> His own imprisonment or the day of his release?

It is in the sequence "Cork" that these images of well-lit places are fully orchestrated. The sequence originally accompanied drawings of Cork City by Brian Lalor and was subsequently republished in *The Rose-Geranium.* In "Cork" Ní Chuilleanáin tries to match Lalor's lines with her own; this time the well-lit corners are mainly exterior:

> The spiders are preparing for autumn.
> They weave throughout the city:
> Selecting the light for their traps,
> They swell with darkness.

Because of its peculiar geography—all "Insolent flights of steps," "gables and stacks," and "painted windowsills"—Cork City provides an ideal myth kitty for a poet with Ní Chuilleanáin's sensitivity. The success of the sequence lies in its perfect marriage of talent and material. "The Rose-Geranium" is a more sensual and human poem, with its touched textures, bodies folded, pillow, jam jar, and pear tree. The poet's presence is stronger and the descriptions more judgmental:

> I seek for depths as planets fly from the sun,
> What holds me in life is flowing from me and I flow
> Falling, *out of true.*

Despite these silent places there is a constant movement, both physical and spiritual, in Ní Chuilleanáin's poems. She has been a voyager through the physical world in ferryboats— "Shipbuilders all believe in fate; / The moral of the ship is death"—in airplanes—"We came down above the houses / In a stiff curve, and / At the edge of Paris airport / Saw an empty tunnel"—or through ferry and ferry road to "Dreaming in the Ksar Es Souk Motel." The places described are places of arrival, a half-carpeted room in Rome or a familiar bed in Oxford. In many of Ní Chuilleanáin's poems there is a displaced psyche, a much traveled and much disrupted point of view. The spirit seeks a resting place. The poet is never entirely unpacked before the psyche has to orientate itself again in "One more of your suddenly furnished houses." Her poems constantly say, "we live here now," with "now" the shifting sand upon which the poet builds a frantic, distracted foothold. Yet a foothold she does build, and the speed with which she builds has created a skeptical, edgy viewpoint. It is remarkably free from the many stultifying parishes of Irish poetry. Venturing forth, or voyaging, has provided Ní Chuilleanáin with her great intellectual context. Her world has remained passionately self-centered, but she is aware of the one voyaging pedigree:

> Turn west now, turn away to sleep
> And you are simultaneous with
> Maelduin setting sail ...
> With Odysseus crouching again
> Inside a fish-smelling sealskin,
> Or Anticlus ...

These mythical voyagers, Maelduin, Odysseus, and Anticlus, are the only pedigree Ní Chuilleanáin has acknowledged. She has chronicled the lives of various women from both a historical and personal viewpoint. In particular she has a strange empathy with Roman Catholic sisters, from convent life in "The Rose-Geranium"—"nothing is to be mine / Everything ours"—to convent life in Calais—"They handed her back her body, / its voices and its death." She has spoken of the used and subdued bodies of women and of the wife who collects the "rifled / Remains of her husband." But it is reticence rather than polemic that distinguishes her work. She is the least directly political of Irish poets, knowing that "In retrospect, it is all edge." Ní Chuilleanáin is one of the constant outsiders in Irish poetry, never staying in any one parish long enough to collect her polling card. She is free of prejudice and pretense. It is to the mythical voyagers that she owes allegiance. There is a whiff of much traveled intelligence from her work, as if she were up and going long before cow shit or bog water could cling to her boots.

—Thomas McCarthy

NÍ DHOMHNAILL, Nuala

Nationality: Irish. **Born:** St. Helens, Lancashire, 1952. **Education:** University College, Cork. **Family:** Married; four children. **Career:** Lived in Holland and Turkey, teaching English at Middle East Technical University; freelance writer and broadcaster on radio and television. Artist-in-residence, University College, Cork, 1991-92, and Portmarnock Community School, Dublin. **Awards:** Arts Council Bursary, 1979, 1981; Duais Sheáin Uí Ríordan, 1982,

1984, 1990; Gradam an Oireachtais, 1984; Duais na Comhairle Ealaíne um Fileochta, 1985, 1988; Irish American Foundation O'Shaughnessy award, 1988; American Ireland Fund Literature prize, 1991; Gulbenkian Foundation New Horizons bursary, 1995; honorary degree from Dublin City University, 1995.

PUBLICATIONS

Poetry

An Dealg Droighin. Dublin, n.p., 1981.
Féar Suaithinseach. Dublin, n.p., 1984.
Selected Poems / Rogha Dánta, with translations by Michael Hartnett. Dublin, Raven Arts Press, 1986.
Feis. Dublin, n.p., 1991.
Pharoah's Daughter, with translations. Oldcastle, County Meath, Gallery Press, 1990; Winston-Salem, North Carolina, Wake Forest University Press, 1993.
The Astrakhan Cloak, with translations by Paul Muldoon. Oldcastle, County Meath, Gallery Press, 1992; Winston-Salem, North Carolina, Wake Forest University Press, 1993.
Cead Aighnis. Dublin, n.p., 1998.

Plays

Jimín (for children). Dublin, Deilt Productions, 1985.
An Ollphiast Ghránna. Dublin, Deilt Productions, 1987.
Destination Demian. Paris, GES, 1993.

Screenplays: *An Gobán Saor,* 1993; *An T-aman Mothála / The Feeling Soul,* 1994.

Other

Editor, with Greg Delanty, *Jumping Off Shadows: Selected Contemporary Irish Poets.* Cork, Cork University Press, 1995.

*   *   *

Nuala Ní Dhomhnaill is one of the finest poets writing in the Irish language. The history, folklore, nationalism, religious, social, and gender politics that inform her writing also explain her decision not to write in English. Her poem "The Language Issue" begins: "I place my hope on the water / in this little boat / of the language" and concludes with a telling allusion to Moses:

> only to have it hither and thither,
> not knowing perhaps where it might end up;
> in the lap, perhaps,
> of some Pharoah's daughter.

Her reputation, established with her early work, has grown through translation into English by some of Ireland's leading poets including Medbh McGuckian, Seamus Heaney, Eilean Ní Chuilleanain, and Paul Muldoon.

Ní Dhomhnaill's themes are identifiably those of her country, most immediately her sense of locale. Characters, hills, towns and villages are all named, reflecting the pleasure of their being intimately known. Real individuals that have become local legends are used to tell universal stories, such as the rural spinster's fate: "She got an honours degree / in biology in Nineteen-four, / then went back to her homeland / at the butt of the hill, / its backside to the wind, / and stopped there all her days." ("In Memoriam Elly Ní Dhomhnaill").

There is a sense of discovery in these poems, a belief that, however familiar the subject, there is always more to find out:

> I've crossed the Conor Pass a thousand times
> if I've gone once, yet each time it unveils
> new stories, revelations clear to me
> as rocks along the road, as actual
> as words articulated

Ní Dhomhnaill shows here in "Driving West" a lack of ego or interference. Revelations, even the words that describe them, are not made but given, an impression borne out in the immediacy of her voice. She is a highly receptive poet, open to the mythical and the real, and skilled in eliding these two worlds.

A fine storyteller, Ní Dhomhnaill can weave together comedy and darkness, confrontation with casual chat. her poems can be reflective lyrics or sprawling narratives, incantatory or wisecracking. Her Ireland has music, priests, sea and weather but also power tools, pushchairs and television news. When she sees a spectacular sunset, it is in the rear-view mirror. In "First Communication," she fears "our latter-day foxes / and wolves—greed, drugs, cancer, skulduggery, the car-crash."

The joys of belonging somewhere are countered by the ominous shadows of small-town life: the public ownership of private pain; and what it is to be trapped by convention, expectation or your family. A broken doll dropped in a well becomes Ophelia. Conscious of what such a life does to women, Ní Dhomhnaill also displays a restless sensuality. She writes in celebration of a lover's body and aims to lose herself in consummation: "Look into my eyes, / look well. / I will not be there / when we are mouth to mouth." ("This Lonely Load").

Nuala Ní Dhomhnaill is wry and compassionate, but also rigorous. She neither flatters nor lulls her reader. It is up to cohere ourselves, to piece together our own significance, and do so modestly: "we must make do with today's / Happenings, and stoop and somehow glue together / The silly little shards of our lives, so that. / Our children can drink water from broken bowls" ("Aubade"). Above all, she values what we can do for one another: "for it's only the body heat / of our loved ones that keeps us alive" ("The Three Sneezes").

—Lavinia Greenlaw

NOTLEY, Alice

Nationality: American. **Born:** Bisbee, Arizona, 8 November 1945. **Education:** Barnard College, New York, B.A. 1967; University of Iowa, Iowa City, M.F.A. 1969. **Family:** Married the writer Ted Berrigan in 1972 (died 1983), two sons; 2) Douglas Oliver in 1988. **Awards:** National Endowment for the Arts grant, 1980; Poetry Center award, 1982; G.E. Foundation award, 1983, Fund for Poetry grant, 1987, 1989.

PUBLICATIONS

Poetry

165 Meeting House Lane. New York, "C" Press, 1971.
Phoebe Light. Bolinas, California, Big Sky, 1973.
Incidentals in the Day World. New York, Angel Hair, 1973.
For Frank O'Hara's Birthday. Cambridge, Street Editions, 1976.
Alice Ordered Me to Be Made: Poems 1975. Chicago, Yellow Press, 1976.
A Diamond Necklace. New York, Frontward, 1977.
Songs for the Unborn Second Baby. Lenox, Massachusetts, United Artists, 1979.
When I Was Alive. New York, Vehicle, 1980.
Waltzing Matilda. New York, Kulchur, 1981.
How Spring Comes. West Branch, Iowa, Toothpaste Press, 1981.
Three Zero, Turning 30, with Andrei Codrescu, edited by Keith and Jeff Wright. New York, Hard Press, 1982.
Sorrento. Los Angeles, Sherwood Press, 1984.
Margaret and Dusty. Minneapolis, Coffee House Press, 1985.
Parts of a Wedding. New York, Unimproved Editions Press, 1986.
At Night the States. Chicago, Yellow Press, 1988.
Selected Poems of Alice Notley. Hoboken, New Jersey, Talisman House, 1993.
The Descent of Alette. New York, Penguin, 1996.

Play

Anne's White Glove (produced New York, 1985). Published in *New American Writing,* 1, 1987.

Other

Doctor Williams' Heiresses: A Lecture. Berkeley, California, Tuumba Press, 1980.
Tell Me Again (autobiography). Santa Barbara, California, Am Here, 1981.
Homer's "Art". Canton, New York, Institute for Further Studies, 1990.
The Scarlet Cabinet: A Compendium of Books, with Douglas Oliver. New York, Scarlet Editions, 1992.

*   *   *

Alice Notley is an American poet whose expression has been shaped by a conscious indebtedness to the legacy of William Carlos Williams. Regarding herself as one of "Doctor Williams' Heiresses," Notley has realized that "you could use him to sound entirely new if you were a woman. It was all about this woman business. I thought we didn't need to read women—I mean find the hidden in the woodwork ones—so much as find the poems among whatever sex that made you feel free to say whatever you liked. Williams makes you feel that you can say anything, including your own anything."

In most of her published work "your own anything" for Notley centered around her life with her first husband, the poet Ted Berrigan, and their children in New York City's Lower East Side. Her poetry reflects her intelligence, humor, and commitment to her craft, and it is perhaps strongest when she is expressing her remarkable sensitivity to the nuances of human relationships. Rather than insist on her own emotional independence as an emancipated woman in the fashion of her New York contemporaries

Anne Waldman and Diane Wakoski, Notley stresses the bonds between people, savoring with great refinement the closeness and communication that result from shared feelings. With delicacy and simple wonder she describes the miracle of physical possession in "Song," from the collection *When I Was Alive*:

> Who shall have my fair lord
> Who but I who but I who but Alice
> By the black window
> Softly in November
> Who but I who but I who but Alice

In more complex poems like "Sonnet" (from *A Diamond Necklace*), Notley brilliantly explores the components of a long marriage between two famous people, the comedy team of George Burns and Gracie Allen:

> The late Gracie Allen was a very lucid comedienne,
> Especially in the way that lucid means shining and bright.
> What her husband George Burns called her illogical logic
> Made a halo around our syntax and ourselves as we
> laughed.
>
> George Burns most often was her artful inconspicuous
> straight-man.
> He could move people about stage, construct skits and
> scenes, write
> And gather jokes. They were married as long as ordinary
> magic
> Would allow, thirty-eight years, until Gracie Allen's death.
>
> In her fifties Gracie Allen developed a heart condition.
> She would call George Burns when her heart felt funny and
> fluttered.
> He'd give her a pill and they'd hold each other till the
> palpitation
> Stopped—just a few minutes, many times and pills. As magic
> fills
> Then fulfilled must leave a space, one day Gracie Allen's
> heart fluttered
> And hurt and stopped. George Burns said unbelievingly
> to the doctor,
> > "But I still have some of the pills."

Notley responds to a broad spectrum of U.S. culture, and her experiments with poetic forms and free verse owe as much to Gertrude Stein, Frank O'Hara, and Berrigan as they do to Williams. Like them, she believes that she is writing primarily to express her own personal tone of voice, which is her music and her breath. She understands Williams's concept of the variable foot to mean "the dominance of tone of voice over other considerations ... I break my lines where I do, as I'm being as various as my voice should be in our intimacy." She feels that her speech sounds as the voice of "the new wife, & the new mother" in her own time, but her intent is to make a poem rather than present a platform of social reform: "I'm not all that interested in being a woman, it's just a practical problem that you deal with when you write poems. You do have to deal with the problem of who you are so that you can be a person talking."

Describing herself as an "imperfect medium," Notley insists on her own limitations as a poet. She often deliberately deflates what she senses as her own pretensions, as in "The Prophet," a long poem from the collection *How Spring Comes*, which ends with the lines "You must never / Stop making jokes. You are not great you are life." When this tone of self-depreciation is absent, however, and she concentrates on presenting her keen perceptions of her subject, her work has considerably more substance. Despite her loyalty to Williams, it would appear from the evidence of her poetry that her reflections—like Emily Dickinson's—are as sharp as her observations. Notley should trust them more, along with her heart.

—Ann Charters

NYE, Naomi Shihab

Nationality: American. **Born:** Naomi Shihab, St. Louis, Missouri, 12 March 1952. **Education:** Trinity University, San Antonio, Texas, 1970-74, B.A. 1974. **Family:** Married Michael Nye in 1978; one son. **Career:** Visiting writer, University of Hawaii, fall 1991, University of Alaska, Fairbanks, spring 1994, Texas Center for Writers, Austin, 1995. Freelance visiting writer in schools around the country, 1974—. **Awards:** Texas Institute of Letters Poetry prize, 1980, 1982; National Poetry Series, 1982; Charity Randall prize, International Poetry Forum, 1989; I.B. Lavan award, Academy of American Poets, 1989; four Pushcart Prizes; Jane Addams Children's Book award, 1994. **Address:** 806 South Main Avenue, San Antonio, Texas 78204, U.S.A.

PUBLICATIONS

Poetry

Different Ways to Pray. Portland, Oregon, Breitenbush Books, 1980.
Hugging the Jukebox. New York, Dutton, 1982.
Yellow Glove. Portland, Oregon, Breitenbush Books, 1986.
Red Suitcase. New York, BOA Editions, 1994.
Words under the Words: Selected Poems. Portland, Oregon, Far Corner Books, Eighth Mountain Press, 1995.

Recording: *The Language of Life with Bill Moyers,* National Public Broadcasting, 1995.

Other

Sitti's Secrets (for children). New York, Four Winds Press, and London, Hamish Hamilton, 1994.
Benito's Dream Bottle (for children), illustrated by Yu Cha Pak. New York, Simon & Schuster, 1995.
Never in a Hurry (essays). Charleston, University of South Carolina Press, 1996.
Habibi (novel). New York, Simon & Schuster, 1997.
Lullaby Raft (for children). New York, Simon & Schuster, 1997.

Editor, *This Same Sky.* New York, Four Winds Press, 1992.

Editor, *The Tree Is Older Than You Are.* New York, Simon &
Schuster, 1995.

Editor, with Paul Janeczco, *I Feel a Little Jumpy around You.* New
York, Simon & Schuster, 1996.

*

Naomi Shihab Nye comments:

We go back and back, to where it all begins. The sources, the
mysterious wells. Each thing gives us something else.

It wasn't whether you were rich or poor, but if you had a big
life, that's what mattered. A big life could be either a wide one or
a deep one. It held countless possible corners and conversations.
A big life didn't stop at the alley or even the next street. It came
from somewhere and was going somewhere, but the word *better*
had no relation, really. A big life was interested and wore ques-
tions easily. A big life never for one second thought it was the
only life.

Something was in the closet, besides our clothes, which
might or might not be friendly. A branch scratched a curious
rhythm on the dark window. Our father came from Palestine, a
beloved land far across the sea. Some people called it the Holy
Land. Both my parents seemed holy to me. At night our father
sat by our beds, curling funny stories into the air. His musical
talking stitched us to places we hadn't been yet. And our
mother, who had grown up in St. Louis, where we were grow-
ing up, stood by our beds after our father's stories, floating
into sleep on a river of songs: "Now rest beneath night's
shadow." She had been to art school and knew how to paint
people the way they looked on the inside, not just the outside.
That's what I wanted to know about, too. What stories and
secrets did people carry with them? What songs did they hold
close in their ears?

Reading cracked the universe wide open—suddenly we had the
power to understand newspapers, menus, books. I loved old signs,
Margaret Wise Brown, Louisa May Alcott, Carl Sandburg, the
exuberant bounce of sentences across a page. I remember shaping
a single word—*city, head*—with enormous tenderness. In second
grade my class memorized William Blake's "Songs of Innocence."
Reading gave us voices of friends speaking from everywhere, so it
followed that one might write down messages, too. Already I wrote
to find out what I knew, and what connected. Sometimes writing
felt like a thank-you note, a response to what had already been
given.

My German-American grandmother gave me a powder puff,
which, when tapped 30 years later, still emits a small, mysterious
cloud.

My Palestinian grandmother gave me a laugh and a tilt of the
head.

My great-uncle Paul gave me a complete sewing kit a hundred
years old and one inch tall.

Whenever people have asked, "Where do you get ideas to write
about?" I wonder, "Where do you not?"

*   *   *

Poets have long observed that a persona is not merely the poet's
mask but also a version of the writer's self from some point in
the past where imagination is strongest. For many women poets
it is a childhood self, a lively, perhaps sexually neutral creature
free to explore the world as a self, not as a gendered person. Naomi

Nye is building a reputation in her prolific canon as the voice of
childhood in America, the voice of the girl at the age of daring
exploration. But more importantly she animates a sense of the
American girl as a mysterious priestess of nature, someone whose
eyes are full of animistic landscapes crammed with Mexican ghosts,
strange voices, paradox, and magic.

To make it all work Nye takes us into the ordinary world as if
we were accompanying her to the corner store for sugar or a bag
of flour. Instead, we are faced with a pixie with messages like this
one from "Eye-to-Eye" in *Difference Ways to Pray*:

> We will meet at the corner,
> you with your sack lunch,
> me with my guitar.
> We will be wearing our famous street faces,
> anonymous as trees.
> Suddenly you will see me,
> you will blink, hesitant,
> then realize I have not looked away.
> For one brave second
> we will stare
> openly
> from borderless skins.
> This is my salary.
> There are no days off.

Clear, limpid language is Nye's method of luring us away from
our notion of the world. We follow her out of conventional reality
into the dreamworld of a new, young Alice. She promises many
adventures, some of them quaint, Pollyannaish, and simple, a few
even pointless. But what she establishes poem by poem is a rare
voice of contentment, pure female happiness with the world as it
is. In a land of so much grim confessionalism, so much lyric anger
and disillusion, Nye has the field of optimism all to herself. An ex-
ample is found in "So Much Happiness" from *Hugging the Jukebox*:

> Since there is no place large enough
> to contain so much happiness,
> you shrug, you raise your hands, and it flows out of
>
>   you
> into everything you touch. You are not responsible.
> You take no credit, as the night sky takes no credit
> for the moon, but continues to hold it, and share it,
> and in that way, be known.

Nye seems to be rewriting Blake's *Book of Thel,* the voice of
innocence set down in the modern city. She does not avoid the
horrors of urban life, but she patches together the vision of simple
nature struggling up through the cracks of the city. In the title
poem from *Hugging the Jukebox,* she describes a small boy sing-
ing with a large voice in front of the jukebox in a Honduran bodega.
It may not seem like much to work with, but Nye makes it her
personal anthem. The boy is any child with a big voice singing to
the world:

> His voice carries out to the water where boats are tied
> and sings for all of them, *a wave.*
> For the hens, now roosting in trees,
> for the mute boy next door, his second-best friend.
> And for the hurricane, now brewing near Barbados....

The quiet, insistent argument of Nye's various books is that she can grasp the life of ethnic minorities in America (and elsewhere) by voicing a kind of unassuming gaiety about life. She reaches out in her poems to hug the marginalized and the denied, to put everyone on an equal footing with her. She declares her democratic passions in a trance of rapturous lyricism, the kind that only children know in their giddiest moments. It is an odd logic to spin out in a half dozen well-respected books, but this is Nye's strategy.

Nye later began moving toward an adult vision, but in fits and starts. In *Yellow Glove* even the title suggests something of her turn to womanly matters, and we also find the new tone in "When the Flag Is Raised":

> Today the vein of sadness pumps
> its blue wisdom through this room and
> you answer with curtains. A curtain lifts
> and holds itself aloft.
>
> Somewhere in Texas, a motel advertises
> rooms for "A Day, Week, Month, or Forever."
> The melancholia of this invitation
> dogs me for miles.

But in "Who's Who in 1941" a more familiar persona resumes:

> I'm being insulted in a library. The librarian thinks
>   I'm a high
> school student sneaking out of class. "Who do you think
>   you are?"
> she shouts. We are alone. I want to answer enigmatical-
>   ly. I am the
> ghost pressing against your window. I am the termite
>   feasting on the
> secret boards of your house. She stands, she glares
>   at me. She has a
> hairdo. The rest of the school is taking a test.

The same is found in "The Brick," which begins with

> Each morning in the gray margin
> between sleep and rising, I find myself
> on Pershing Avenue, St. Louis, examining bricks
> in buildings, looking for the one I brushed
> with my mitten in 1956.

As she tells us later in the poem, "the center of memory" is "the place where I get off and on."

Nye is important in other ways than as the voice of girlhood and optimism in contemporary life. She has emerged as the leading figure in Southwestern poetry and seems to articulate the female psyche of the region after a long, trying history of pioneering on the plains and prairies and having withstood the cramping stereotype of schoolmarm, rancher's wife, and silent guardian of household realms. Nye brings attention to the female as a humorous, wry creature with brisk, hard intelligence and a sense of personal freedom unheard of in the decades before.

In that sense Nye completes the work begun by her Texas forebears Lexie Dean Robertson and Vassar Miller, both of whom articulated the female imagination in highly disciplined lyrics. Nye goes beyond them in skill and pixieish intelligence, however. She continues to grow in her work and seems now to voice both sides of the female psyche, young and old, as in the moving lyric "New Year," also from *Yellow Glove*:

> Where a street might just as easily have been
> a hair ribbon in a girl's ponytail
> her first day of dance class, teacher in mauve leotard
> rising to say, We have much ahead of us,
> and the little girls following, kick, kick, kick,
> thinking what a proud sleek person she was,
> how they wanted to be like her someday,
> while she stared outside the window at the high wires
> strung with ice, the voices inside them opening out
> to every future which was not hers.

—Paul Christensen

O

OATES, Joyce Carol

Pseudonyms: Rosamond Smith; Fernandes/Oates. **Nationality:** American. **Born:** Millersport, New York, 16 June 1938. **Education:** Syracuse University, New York, 1956-60, B.A. in English 1960 (Phi Beta Kappa); University of Wisconsin, Madison, M.A. in English 1961; Rice University, Houston, 1961. **Family:** Married Raymond J. Smith in 1961. **Career:** Instructor, 1961-65, and assistant professor of English, 1965-67, University of Detroit; member of the department of English, University of Windsor, Ontario, 1967-78. Writer-in-residence, and currently Roger S. Berlind Distinguished Professor, Princeton University, New Jersey, 1978—. Publisher, with Raymond J. Smith, *Ontario Review,* Windsor, later Princeton, 1974—. **Awards:** National Endowment for the Arts grant, 1966, 1968; Guggenheim fellowship, 1967; O. Henry award, 1967, 1973, and Special Award for Continuing Achievement, 1970, 1986; Rosenthal award, 1968; National Book award, 1970; Rea award, for short story, 1990; Heideman award, for one-act plays, 1990; Bobst Lifetime Achievement award, 1990; Walt Whitman award, 1995; Pulitzer Prize finalist, 1995, for *What I Lived For;* Horror Writers of America Bram Stoker award, 1996, for *Zombie.* **Member:** American Academy, 1978. **Agent:** John Hawkins, 71 West 23rd Street, Suite 1600, New York, New York 10010. **Address:** 185 Nassau Street, Princeton, New Jersey 08540, U.S.A.

PUBLICATIONS

Poetry

Women in Love and Other Poems. New York, Albondocani Press, 1968.

Anonymous Sins and Other Poems. Baton Rouge, Louisiana State University Press, 1969.

Love and Its Derangements. Baton Rouge, Louisiana State University Press, 1970.

Wooded Forms. New York, Albondocani Press, 1972.

Angel Fire. Baton Rouge, Louisiana State University Press, 1973.

Dreaming America and Other Poems. New York, Aloe Editions, 1973.

The Fabulous Beasts. Baton Rouge, Louisiana State University Press, 1975

Seasons of Peril. Santa Barbara, California, Black Sparrow Press, 1977.

Women Whose Lives Are Food, Men Whose Lives Are Money. Baton Rouge, Louisiana State University Press, 1978.

Celestial Timepiece. Dallas, Pressworks, 1980.

Nightless Nights: Nine Poems. Concord, New Hampshire, Ewert, 1981.

Invisible Woman: New and Selected Poems 1970-1982. Princeton, New Jersey, Ontario Review Press, 1982.

Luxury of Sin. Northridge, California, Lord John Press, 1984.

The Time Traveller: Poems 1983-1989. New York, Dutton, 1989.

Plays

The Sweet Enemy (produced New York, 1965).

Sunday Dinner (produced New York, 1970).

Ontological Proof of My Existence, music by George Prideaux (produced New York, 1972). Included in *Three Plays,* 1980.

Miracle Play (produced New York, 1979). Los Angeles, Black Sparrow Press, 1974.

Daisy (produced New York, 1980).

Three Plays (includes *Ontological Proof of My Existence, Miracle Play, The Triumph of the Spider Monkey*). Windsor, Ontario Review Press, 1980.

The Triumph of the Spider Monkey, from her own story (produced Los Angeles, 1985). Included in *Three Plays,* 1980.

Presque Isle, music by Paul Shapiro (produced New York, 1982).

Lechery, in *Faustus in Hell* (produced Princeton, New Jersey, 1985).

In Darkest America (Tone Clusters and The Eclipse) (produced Louisville, Kentucky, 1990).

The Eclipse (produced New York, 1990).

American Holiday (produced Los Angeles, 1990).

Twelve Plays. New York, Dutton, 1991.

I Stand Before You Naked (produced New York, 1991).

How Do You Like Your Meat? (produced New Haven, Connecticut, 1991).

Black (produced Williamstown, Massachusetts, 1992).

Gulf War (produced New York, 1992).

The Secret Mirror (produced Philadelphia, 1992).

The Rehearsal (produced New York, 1993).

The Perfectionist (produced Princeton, New Jersey, 1993). Included in *The Perfectionist and Other Plays.* Hopewell, New Jersey, Ecco Press, 1995.

The Truth-Teller (produced New York, 1995).

Here She Is! (produced Philadelphia, 1995).

Novels

With Shuddering Fall. New York, Vanguard Press, 1964; London, Cape, 1965.

A Garden of Earthly Delights. New York, Vanguard Press, 1967; London, Gollancz, 1970.

Expensive People. New York, Vanguard Press, 1968; London, Gollancz, 1969.

Them. New York, Vanguard Press, 1969; London, Gollancz, 1971.

Wonderland. New York, Vanguard Press, 1971; London, Gollancz, 1972.

Do with Me What You Will. New York, Vanguard Press, 1973; London, Gollancz, 1974.

The Assassins: A Book of Hours. New York, Vanguard Press, 1975.

Childwold. New York, Vanguard Press, 1976; London, Gollancz, 1977.

Son of the Morning. New York, Vanguard Press, 1978; London, Gollancz, 1979.

Unholy Loves. New York, Vanguard Press, 1979; London, Gollancz, 1980.

Cybele. Santa Barbara, California, Black Sparrow Press, 1979.

Angel of Light. New York, Dutton, and London, Cape, 1981.

Bellefleur. New York, Dutton, 1980; London, Cape, 1981.

A Bloodsmoor Romance. New York, Dutton, 1982; London, Cape, 1983.

Mysteries of Winterthurn. New York, Dutton, and London, Cape, 1984.

Solstice. New York, Dutton, and London, Cape, 1985.

Marya: A Life. New York, Dutton, 1986; London, Cape, 1987.

You Must Remember This. New York, Dutton, 1987; London, Macmillan, 1988.

Lives of the Twins (as Rosamond Smith). New York, Simon & Schuster, 1987.

Soul-Mate (as Rosamond Smith). New York, Dutton, 1989.

American Appetites. New York, Dutton, and London, Macmillan, 1989.

Because It Is Bitter, and Because It Is My Heart. New York, Dutton, 1990.

Snake Eyes (as Rosamond Smith). New York, Dutton, 1992.

Black Water. New York, Dutton, 1992.

Foxfire. New York, Dutton, 1993.

What I Lived For. New York, Dutton, 1994.

Zombie. New York, Dutton, 1995.

You Can't Catch Me (as Rosamond Smith). New York, Dutton, 1995.

Tenderness. Ontario Review, 1996.

We Were the Mulvaneys. New York, Dutton, 1996.

Double Delight (as Rosamond Smith). New York, Dutton, 1997.

Man Crazy. New York, Dutton, 1997.

Short Stories

By the North Gate. New York, Vanguard Press, 1963.

Upon the Sweeping Flood and Other Stories. New York, Vanguard Press, 1966; London, Gollancz, 1973.

The Wheel of Love. New York, Vanguard Press, 1970; London, Gollancz, 1971.

Cupid and Psyche. New York, Albondocani Press, 1970.

Marriages and Infidelities. New York, Vanguard Press, 1972; London, Gollancz, 1974.

A Posthumous Sketch. Los Angeles, Black Sparrow Press, 1973.

The Girl. Cambridge, Massachusetts, Pomegranate Press, 1974.

Plagiarized Material (as Fernandes / Oates). Los Angeles, Black Sparrow Press, 1974.

The Goddess and Other Women. New York, Vanguard Press, 1974; London, Gollancz, 1975.

Where Are You Going, Where Have You Been? Stories of Young America. Greenwich, Connecticut, Fawcett, 1974.

The Hungry Ghosts: Seven Allusive Comedies. Los Angeles, Black Sparrow Press, 1974; Solihull, Warwickshire, Aquila, 1975.

The Seduction and Other Stories. Los Angeles, Black Sparrow Press, 1975.

The Poisoned Kiss and Other Stories from the Portuguese (as Fernandes / Oates). New York, Vanguard Press, 1975; London, Gollancz, 1976.

The Triumph of the Spider Monkey. Santa Barbara, California, Black Sparrow Press, 1976.

Crossing the Border. New York, Vanguard Press, 1976; London, Gollancz, 1978.

Night-Side. New York, Vanguard Press, 1977; London, Gollancz, 1979.

A Sentimental Education (single story). Los Angeles, Sylvester & Orphan Denys, 1978.

The Step-Father. Northridge, California, Lord John Press, 1978.

All the Good People I've Left Behind. Santa Barbara, California, Black Sparrow Press, 1979.

Queen of the Night. Northridge, California, Lord John Press, 1979.

The Lamb of Abyssalia. Cambridge, Massachusetts, Pomegranate Press, 1979.

A Middle-Class Education. New York, Albondocani Press, 1980.

A Sentimental Education (collection). New York, Dutton, 1980; London, Cape, 1981.

Last Day. New York, Dutton, 1984; London, Cape, 1985.

Wild Saturday and Other Stories. London, Dent, 1984.

Wild Nights. Athens, Ohio, Croissant, 1985.

Raven's Wing. New York, Dutton, 1986; London, Cape, 1987.

The Assignation. New York, Ecco Press, 1988.

Heat and Other Stories. New York, Dutton, 1991.

Where Is Here? Hopewell, New Jersey, Ecco Press, 1992.

Where Are Your Going, Where Have You Been? Princeton, New Jersey, Ontario Review Press, 1993.

Haunted: Tales of the Grotesque. New York, Dutton, 1994.

Will You Always Love Me? and Other Stories. New York, Dutton, 1995.

Other

The Edge of Impossibility: Tragic Forms in Literature. New York, Vanguard Press, 1972; London, Gollancz, 1976.

The Hostile Sun: The Poetry of D.H. Lawrence. Los Angeles, Black Sparrow Press, 1973; Solihull, Warwickshire, Aquila, 1975.

New Heaven, New Earth: The Visionary Experience in Literature. New York, Vanguard Press, 1974; London, Gollancz, 1976.

The Stone Orchard. Northridge, California, Lord John Press, 1980.

Contraries: Essays. New York, Oxford University Press, 1981.

The Profane Art: Essays and Reviews. New York, Dutton, 1983.

Funland. Concord, New Hampshire, Ewert, 1983.

On Boxing, photographs by John Ranard. New York, Doubleday, and London, Bloomsbury, 1987; expanded edition, Hopewell, New Jersey, Ecco Press, 1994.

(Woman) Writer: Occasions and Opportunities. New York, Dutton, 1988.

Editor, *Scenes from American Life: Contemporary Short Fiction.* New York, Vanguard Press, 1973.

Editor, with Shannon Ravenel, *The Best American Short Stories 1979.* Boston, Houghton Mifflin, 1979.

Editor, *Night Walks: A Bedside Companion.* Princeton, New Jersey, Ontario Review Press, 1982.

Editor, *First Person Singular: Writers on Their Craft.* Princeton, New Jersey, Ontario Review Press, 1983.

Editor, with Boyd Litzinger, *Story: Fictions Past and Present.* Lexington, Massachusetts, Heath, 1985.

Editor, with Daniel Halpern, *Reading the Fights* (on boxing). New York, Holt, 1988.

Editor, *The Best American Essays.* New York, Ticknor & Fields, 1991.

Editor, with Daniel Halpern, *The Sophisticated Cat: A Gathering of Stories, Poems, and Miscellaneous Writings about Cats.* New York, Dutton, 1992.

Editor, *The Oxford Book of American Short Stories.* New York, Oxford University Press, 1992.

Editor, *George Bellows: American Artist.* Hopewell, New Jersey, Ecco Press, 1995.

Editor, *The Essential Dickinson.* Hopewell, New Jersey, Ecco Press, 1996.

Editor, *American Gothic Tales.* New York, Plume, 1996.

Editor, *Story: The Art and the Craft of Narrative Fiction.* New York, Norton, 1997.

Editor, *The Best of H.P. Lovecraft.* Hopewell, New Jersey, Ecco Press, 1997.

*

Bibliography: *Joyce Carol Oates: An Annotated Bibliography* by Francine Lercangé, New York, Garland, 1986.

Manuscript Collection: Syracuse University, Syracuse, New York.

Critical Studies: *The Tragic Vision of Joyce Carol Oates* by Mary Kathryn Grant, Durham, North Carolina, Duke University Press, 1978; *Joyce Carol Oates* by Joanne V. Creighton, Boston, Twayne, 1979; *Critical Essays on Joyce Carol Oates* edited by Linda W. Wagner, Boston, Hall, 1979; *Dreaming America: Obsession and Transcendence in the Fiction of Joyce Carol Oates* by G.F. Waller, Baton Rouge, Louisiana State University Press, 1979; *Joyce Carol Oates* by Ellen G. Friedman, New York, Ungar, 1980; *Joyce Carol Oates's Short Stories: Between Tradition and Innovation* by Katherine Bastian, Bern, Switzerland, Lang, 1983; *Isolation and Contact: A Study of Character Relationships in Joyce Carol Oates's Short Stories 1963-1980* by Torborg Norman, Gothenburg, Studies in English, 1984; *Joyce Carol Oates: Artist in Residence* by Eileen Teper Bender, Bloomington, Indiana University Press, 1987; *Understanding Joyce Carol Oates* by Greg Johnson, Columbia, University of South Carolina Press, 1987; *Conversations with Joyce Carol Oates,* edited by Lee Milazzo, University, University Press of Mississippi, 1989.

*   *   *

Reviewers of Joyce Carol Oates's first poetry collection called her work apocalyptic and savage, adjectives that remain valid for her poetic canon. There are no lyric forms in Oates's work, and the poems do not tolerate surface readings or pregnant pauses. They evoke no tenderness or nostalgia. Each pierces the reader's sensibility, often with literal images of bodily penetration or destruction. Although these are intensely personal poems, many of which have furnished controlling metaphors or significant images in Oates's fiction, they stand independently, and the reader's struggle to understand them is like augury using one's own entrails. Almost always the persona is a victim—women, children, blue-collar males, semiliterate rural families—incapable of expressing the terrible intersection of personal and historic, public and private existence, and it is this which gives rise to the grief of the poem. There are silent voices too—for example, the autistic child and the mummified child bride in *Invisible Woman.*

Oates forges her disturbing visions through the sheer discipline of language and clarity of image, relying only on assonance and alliteration to heighten it. Even when a poem deliberately evokes the work of another poet, she shuns the poetic devices of the original and often inverts its vision—as demonstrated by the echoes of Emily Dickinson in "After Love a Formal Feeling Comes."

The isolated state of the individual is a given in Oates's poems, cutting across the thematic concerns. "Vanity," the nearly con-

ventional poem which closes *Anonymous Sins,* adumbrates this isolation; evoking the refrain of Ecclesiastes, the poem concludes: "The beloved is a cage / you cannot enter. Others can enter cheaply."

The vulnerability of children and the collusion of adults with the hostile forces which threaten them is a frequent theme. In *Anonymous Sins,* the cycle of songs "Three Dances of Death" echoes Blake's *Songs of Innocence and Experience.* In "American Morocco," an obese child, ridiculed by her parents' guests, accompanies them on a tour of the family's bomb shelter—a replica of El Morocco so secure that "Christ could not raise us / from our safe tinkly tomb." In "Happy Song: Not for Adults," a child trying frantically to please her parents becomes "... segments of bone / strained beyond your knowledge." "Back Country," in *Invisible Woman,* begins with a drunken father shooting his children's dog, which suffers, howls, bleeds, and is at last buried by neighbors. Fearful of the man, the neighbors rationalize his violence—both to the dog and to his own family—with "These things happen, / Dogs get in the way." The perceiving child understands that children do too.

The destructive quality of love between man and woman is a constant in Oates's poems. Rendered in images of fusion and decomposition, it is most frequently represented in *Love and Its Derangements,* where "Growing Together" uses a terrifying pun to present the progress of a sexual marathon which leaves the couple with hair grown into one another's bodies and toenails "... outlined in harmless old dirt; scrape against all our legs / for weeks." In "Giving Oneself a Form Again," a woman who has withdrawn from a period of intense sensuality seeks the Wordsworthian shape of a childhood soul, but she finds that after carnal knowledge "The child will not be touched"; she then retreats into autoeroticism, where, at orgasm, "like wasps the blood flares / and subsides" and the outline of her isolate body is "... iron spikes of fences / beside sidewalks of ice."

The narrative unity of *Angel Fire* compels the reader to recognize Oates's vision that all love is rooted in a desire for annihilation. "The Still Small Voice Behind the Great Romances" charts the persona's realization that her search for romantic love has been a desire "to see the sun slide over the edge / of the continent!—I always wanted that urgency / at the edge of satiation." In "How I Became Fiction," the female finds that even the stares of men, which once defined her, are gone—"... no darkness / would recover them, no alley make them male again—"and she becomes, as the males who once stared at her have become, only the character in a narration which is their hospital records. In "Prophecies," the long-awaited, lover is imagined as a devourer who cannot be tamed by physical beauty or by possessions and whose recognition as such lies just outside the consciousness, at the edge of the eye. The final poem of *Angel Fire,* which is used as an epigraph in the novel *Wonderland,* brings all of the buried knowledge into consciousness as the perceiver is forced to enter her own history and to turn "Iris into Eye."

The Fabulous Beasts experiments with the inclusion of two long prose pieces, but it is the shorter and more conventional Oates poems which contribute most to achieving the stated intention of revealing the relationship between the individual and an all-inclusive whole, the fabulous beast of history and nature. There is a fine poem to Sylvia Plath, "Mourning and Melancholia...." and another which honors Plath with a turn on her own lines; "Lies Lovingly Told" observes that "Every man adores / the woman who adores / the Fascist." The title poem is a vision of Yeats's rough beast, slouching toward the newsroom, indifferent to the historical location of the carnage in the grainy photographs which will be printed—they could be scenes from North Africa in 1939 or from Southeast Asia in 1968. This closing poem and two others, "In Case of Accidental Death" and "In the Air," suggest a transition to more public poems which appear in *Women Whose Lives Are Food, Men Whose Lives Are Money* and *Invisible Woman,* and they are among the finest works from Oates's hand. "In Case of Accidental Death" explores the insularity which sanctifies terrible events with the religious platitude that "it is somehow good" and because "being local is also a tradition / in this country." The resigned view of random violence in the poem echoes Auden's "Musée des Beaux Arts":

> But perhaps there will be ditchwater
> and spiky tart-smelling weeds
> and overhead a heavy airliner
> with passengers marveling
> at the landscape
> and an unswervable destination.

"In the Air" recounts the razing of an old house in images of atomic explosions, "The cellar rises / into daylight [revealing] the earth and its undigested things / we hoped no one outside the family / would ever see."

Women Whose Lives Are Food, Men Whose Lives Are Money continues familiar themes and techniques. Here again are the grim round of materialism and the violent embraces of lovers, devoid of any sign that they can be transcended. A number of the poems pivot on the tension between some concretely recalled event and the persona's struggle to extract meaning from it—for example, "After Sunset," "Guilt," "Skyscape," and "The Suicide"—but the tendency of the previous volume to explore public events expands. "Public Outcry" and "American Independence" present the media tendency to invite public statements from the uninformed on the insignificant and to consume in a manner that transforms everything "... to human heat, human flesh / human waste."

Invisible Woman includes an epilogue of fourteen poems previously collected but excludes any from *Anonymous Sins,* the first collection. Oates indicates here that she has chosen to reprint only those poems which best support the volume's theme of the invisibility of our deepest identity. The newly collected poems once again use familiar techniques to explore the constant themes, but there is a growth marked by the powerful distillation of the earlier treatments. The hand-to-mouth struggle and the outrageous expectations of American blue-collar life which required a dozen poems in *Women Whose Lives Are Food* are conveyed more powerfully by a single poem, "Jesus, Heal Me," a poem in which union meetings, layoffs, time clocks, and reusable brown lunch bags are juxtaposed with the redemption of a new covenant whose revelation is sought in the columns of lottery winners. The greater depth with which early themes are explored is evident in the four-line poem "A Miniature Passion," where the wasp sting-orgasm of "Giving Oneself a Form Again" has become "... so deep, / all my flesh was crater to it."

Finally, this excellent volume provides a vision of the male and female life, the private and the historically implicated life, in coexistence. "Celestial Timepiece," a quilt that provides an organizing metaphor in the novel *Bellefleur,* presents the history of quiltmaking as a woman's creating a map of her world. While men are off fighting on a map of death, homelessness, and hospitals, women produce "Here an entire world stitched to perfection," which can be hung on the wall like a conqueror's map and convey to those who touch it a history of frugal, fruitful domesticity, "Your fingers read it like Braille."

—Rose Marie Burwell

OLDS, Sharon

Nationality: American. **Born:** San Francisco, California, 19 November 1942. **Education:** Stanford University, California, B.A. (honors) 1964; Columbia University, New York, Ph.D. 1972. **Career:** Lecturer-in-residence on poetry, Theodor Herzl Institute, New York, 1976-80; visiting teacher of poetry, Manhattan Theatre Club, New York, 1982, Nathan Mayhew Seminars, Martha's Vineyard, Massachusetts, 1982, YMCA, New York, 1982, Poetry Society of America, 1983, Squaw Valley Writers' Conference, 1984-90, Sarah Lawrence College, Bronxville, New York, 1984, Goldwater Hospital, Roosevelt Island, New York, 1985—, Columbia University, New York, 1985-86, and State University of New York, Purchase, 1986-87; Fanny Hurst Chair in literature, Brandeis University, Waltham, Massachusetts, 1986-87; adjunct professor, 1983-90, director, 1988-91, and associate professor, 1990—, Graduate Program in Creative Writing, New York University. **Awards:** Creative Arts Public Service award, 1978; Madeline Sadin award, 1978; Guggenheim fellowship, 1981-82; National Endowment for the Arts fellowship, 1982-83; Lamont prize, 1984; National Book Critics Circle award, 1985; Lila Wallace/Reader's Digest fellowship grant, 1993-96. **Address:** Graduate Program in Creative Writing, Department of English, New York University, 19 University Place, Room 200, New York, New York 10003, U.S.A.

PUBLICATIONS

Poetry

Satan Says. Pittsburgh, Pennsylvania, University of Pittsburgh Press, and London, Feffer & Simons, 1980.
The Dead and the Living. New York, Knopf, 1984.
The Gold Cell. New York, Knopf, 1987.
The Matter of This World: New and Selected Poems. Nottingham, Slow Dancer Press, 1987.
The Sign of Saturn. London, Martin Secker & Warburg, 1991.
The Father. New York, Knopf, 1992; London, Martin Secker & Warburg, 1993.
The Wellspring. New York, Knopf, and London, J. Cape, 1996.

Recordings: *Coming Back to Life,* Watershed, 1984; *The Power of the Word* (with Bill Moyers), WNET, 1989; *Poetry in Person,* Modern Poetry Association, 1991.

*

Critical Studies: "Sharon Olds: Painful Insights and Small Beauties" by Jonah Bornstein, in *Literary Cavalcade* (New York), January 1989; "American Visionaries: Helen Keller and the Poets Muriel Rukeyser, Denise Levertov, and Sharon Olds," in *Women against the Iron Fist: Alternatives to Militarism 1900-1989,* by Sybil Oldfield, Cambridge, Massachusetts, Blackwell, 1989; "Talking to Our Father: The Political and Mythical Appropriations of Adrienne Rich and Sharon Olds" by Suzanne Matson, in *American Poetry Review* (Philadelphia), November / December 1989; "Sharon Olds Gathers Students into Poetry Family" by Rosemary Klein, in *Kimball Mountain Observer,* April 1992; "Olds Breaks New Poetic Ground" by Fran Fanshed in *Columbia Flier,* 5 November 1992.

Sharon Olds comments:

I began by working in close forms, and then more and more wanted a line-break and a poem-shape (the body of the poem on the page) which felt more alive to me.

Questions that interest me include: Is there anything that shouldn't or can't be written about in a poem? What has never been written about in a poem? What is the use, function, service of poetry in a society? For whom are you writing? (The dead, the unborn, the woman in front of you in the check-out line at Shop-Rite?)

I teach poetry workshops at New York University and at Goldwater Hospital (a New York City public hospital for the severely physically disabled). "If you do not bring forth that which is within you, that which is within you will destroy you. If you bring forth that which is within you, that which is within you will save you." (Heretical Gospel of Thomas)

Poets of the generation just ahead of mine whose work I've especially learned from and loved: Muriel Rukeyser, Galway Kinnell, Philip Levine, Ruth Stone.

*   *   *

Sharon Olds's poetry is intimate, personal, wrenched from her own life. Prosaic yet precise, it has a diamond-sharp clarity that makes it too hard to be confessional. It lacks the bitterness and anger so often found in contemporary women's poetry, as well as the wit and irony which tend to accompany that bitterness. Though not overtly spiritual, her work has an almost religious purity; it is cathartic. While some may find her grounding in domestic life too mundane, most readers are shocked and exhilarated by the extraordinary candor of her material and the lyricism with which she presents it. The work is strong, vibrant, celebratory—a far cry from the neurasthenic expositions of such predecessors as Emily Dickinson.

Her first collection, *Satan Says,* was described by Marilyn Hacker as "daring and elegant." It dealt with the experiences of adolescence and early motherhood. Whitmanesque in its celebration of the body and the self, it spoke with a confidence and eroticism rare in first collections. Poems like "The Sisters of Sexual Treasure" are remarkably frank: "As soon as my sisters and I got out of our / mother's house, all we wanted to / do was fuck, obliterate / her tiny sparrow body and narrow / grasshopper legs. The men's bodies / were like our father's body!... We could have him there, the steep forbidden / buttocks, backs of the knees, the cock / in our mouth, ah the cock in our mouth...." In a poem like "Prayer," which parallels the birth of a first child with a first sexual encounter, Olds contributes to that small but healthy branch of poetry which explores women's most intimate experiences. And in "The Language of the Brag," also about childbirth, she chal-

lenges the elders, placing her own work at the center of the American tradition:

> ... I have lain down and sweated and shaken
> and passed blood and feces and water and
> slowly alone in the centre of a circle I have
> passed the new person out
> and they have lifted the new person free of the act
> and wiped the new person free of that
> language of blood like praise all over the body.
>
> I have done what you wanted to do, Walt Whitman,
> Allen Ginsberg, I have done this thing,
> I and the other women this exceptional
> act with the exceptional heroic body,
> this giving birth, this glistening verb,
> and I am putting my proud American boast
> right here with the others.

Olds's second book, *The Dead and the Living,* won awards from both the American Academy of Poets and the National Book Critics. An exquisite collection, it displays a deepening and refining of her art. The first section, "Poems for the Dead," begins with poems honoring both public and anonymous figures—from Marilyn Monroe to the starving Armenians of 1921. The chilling "Aesthetics of the Shah" begins, "The first thing you notice / is the skill / used on the ropes, the narrow close-grained / hemp against that black cloth / the bodies are wrapped in...." "The Issue," about racial tension in Rhodesia, gives a detailed description of a bayoneted black baby, ending with the lines "Don't speak to me about / politics. I've got eyes, man." These poems, her most overtly political, move beyond the partisan to express a general compassion for humanity. Also in this section are poems for dead relatives, among which is "Miscarriage," with its stark realization that

> ... I never went back
> to mourn the one who came as far as the
> sill with its information: that we could
> botch something, you and I ...

The second section, "Poems for the Living," deals with childhood, love, marriage, children—"the tasting, and the / giving of life." Several of these poems, about a drunken, abusive father and a weak, abused mother, reveal extraordinary pain and potential hatred, but, as always in her work, the subjects are redeemed through confrontation and acceptance. As honest with herself as she is relentless with her subjects, the poet confesses in the magnificent "The Fear of Oneself" that "... you say you believe I would hold up under torture / for the sake of our children.... It is all I have wanted to do, / to stand between them and pain. But I come from a / long line / of women / who put themselves / first...."

Her third collection, *The Gold Cell,* concentrates on personal relationships with poems about motherhood, love, and lust, as in "Greed and Aggression," which begins, "Someone in the Quaker meeting talks about greed and aggression / and I think of the way I lay the massive / weight of my body down on you / like a tiger lying down in gluttony and pleasure on the / elegant heavy body of the eland it eats...." In this collection, as in her earlier ones, Olds celebrates the savage, fragile chaos of life with poems such as "Summer Solstice, New York City," which ends after a tense, dramatic description of a man trying to jump off a building:

> ... and they closed on him, I thought they were going to
> beat him up, as a mother whose child has been
> lost will scream at the child when it's found, they
> took him by the arms and held him up and
> leaned him against the wall of the chimney and the
> tall cop lit a cigarette
> in his mouth, and gave it to him, and
> then they all lit cigarettes, and the
> red, glowing ends burned like the
> tiny campfires we lit at night
> back at the beginning of the world.

—Katie Campbell

OLIVER, Mary

Nationality: American. **Born:** Maple Heights, Ohio, 10 September 1935. **Education:** Ohio State University, Columbus, 1955-56; Vassar College, Poughkeepsie, New York, 1956-57. **Career:** Chair of the Writing Department, 1972-73, and member of the writing committee, 1984, Fine Arts Work Center, Provincetown, Massachusetts; Mather Visiting Professor, Case Western Reserve University, Cleveland, 1980, 1982; poet-in-residence, Bucknell University, Lewisburg, Pennsylvania, 1986, and University of Cincinnati, Ohio, 1986; Banister Writer-in-Residence, Sweet Briar College, Sweet Briar, Virginia, 1991-95; William Blackburn Visiting Professor, Duke University, 1995; Catharine Osgood Foster Chair for Distinguished Teaching, Bennington College, Bennington, Vermont, 1996—. **Awards:** Poetry Society of American prize, 1962; Shelley memorial award, 1970; National Endowment for the Arts fellowship, 1972; Alice Fay di Castagnola award, 1973; Guggenheim fellowship, 1980; American Academy award, 1983; Pulitzer Prize, 1984; Christopher award for *House of Light,* 1991; L.L. Winship award for *House of Light,* 1991; National Book award for Poetry for *New and Selected Poems,* 1992. **Agent:** Molly Malone Cook Literary Agency, P.O. Box 338, Provincetown, Massachusetts 02657, U.S.A.

PUBLICATIONS

Poetry

No Voyage and Other Poems. London, Dent, 1963; revised edition, Boston, Houghton Mifflin, 1965.
The River Styx, Ohio, and Other Poems. New York, Harcourt Brace, 1972.
The Night Traveler. Cleveland, Bits Press, 1978.
Twelve Moons. Boston, Little Brown, 1979.
Sleeping in the Forest. Athens, Ohio Review Chapbook, 1979.
American Primitive. Boston, Little Brown, 1983.
Dream Work. Boston, Atlantic Monthly Press, 1986.
House of Light. Boston, Beacon Press, 1990.
New and Selected Poems. Boston, Beacon Press, 1992.
White Pine. New York, Harcourt Brace, 1994.

Blue Pastures. New York, Harcourt Brace, 1995.
West Wind. Boston, Houghton Mifflin, 1997.

Other

A Poetry Handbook. New York, Harcourt Brace, 1994.

* * *

> life's winners are not the rapacious but the patient:
> what triumphs and takes new territory
>
> has learned to lie for centuries in the shadows
> like the shadows of the rocks.

Mary Oliver did not lie in the shadows for centuries before receiving her Pulitzer Prize for poetry in 1984. She has been a very quiet, modest poet, however, whose work reflects a pastoral life lived (first in Ohio, then in Provincetown) with plants and animals far more than with human beings. Her early work was reviewed by both Philip Booth and Joyce Carol Oates as being influenced by Robert Frost, and, like Frost, her first book, *No Voyage and Other Poems,* was published in England.

Like Frost, she also has migrated to a home in New England, whose landscape dominates the poetry in both *Twelve Moons* and *American Primitive.* She is also like her mentor in being anything but the "primitive" that her work guilefully suggests. In fact, if one thinks of a tradition in American letters created by Thoreau—the man who talked about the value of independence, self-subsistence, and a life connected with the land while in fact, as Leon Edel points out, living in a cabin close enough to his mother's house to enable him to go there every day for home-baked cookies and other things he didn't care to provide for himself—then we can see Oliver as part of that tradition. Her poems enrich the fantasy life of Americans who read the L.L. Bean catalogues and dress for hunting, hiking, and the outdoor life, while in fact not ever facing the hardships which are part of that life.

Reading Oliver's poetry gives that same wonderful vicarious satisfaction. Her knowledge of plants and animals is so rich that no one could question its authenticity. But it is presented, not in realistic, but beautiful images; (speaking of raccoons) "walking, / silvery, slumberous, / each a sharp set of teeth, / each a grey dreamer"; (speaking of hibernating snakes) "and their eyes are like jewels— / and asleep, though they cannot close. / And in each mouth the forked tongue, / sensitive as an angel's ear"; (about being in a swamp) "I feel / not so much wet as / painted and glittered / with the fat grassy / mires, the rich / and succulent marrows / of earth"; (about egrets)

> Even half-asleep they had
>   such faith in the world
> that had made them—
>   tilting through the water,
>   unruffled, sure,
>   by the laws
> of their faith not logic,
>   they opened their wings
>   softly and stepped
>   over every dark thing

so that one never experiences fear, pain, frustration, being out of control, all the miseries that we urbanized creatures usually feel in the wilderness. Oliver's poetry gives each reader the illusion that the natural world is graspable, controllable, beautiful. In addition, the reader feels that she *is* facing truth, reality, all the struggles that she knows are out there.

This vision of gentleness and possibility, that the natural world *is* obtainable and belongs to anyone who simply opens his or her eyes, comes from Thoreau, through Frost, and is one which not a lot of other contemporary poets have really grappled with. (Perhaps Maxine Kumin would be another example of a poet who works in this mode.) However, Oliver's poems have been compared by Robert DeMott to Roethke and Galway Kinnell, saying that all three poets are "sensitive to visitations by the 'dark things' of the wood." But if Oliver writes of "dark things," they are friendly, benevolent dark things. Even her vision of death is gentle, pastoral, and haunting, rather than fearful and violent. What all the critics seem to be pointing out is that there is alive today in American poetry a strain of writing which glorifies man's natural relationship to animals, plants, and the nonhuman world. It seems to be a necessary vision, one where beauty and simplicity, achieved through a nonviolent portrait of nature's ecosystems, could replace nuclear holocaust. Oliver writes this vision clearly, persuasively, and with natural elegance.

—Diane Wakoski

OSTRIKER, Alicia

Nationality: American. **Born:** Brooklyn, New York, 11 November 1937. **Education:** Brandeis University, B.A., 1959; University of Wisconsin, M.A. 1961, Ph.D. 1964. **Family:** Married Jeremiah P. Ostriker in 1958; two daughters and one son. **Career:** Assistant professor, 1965-68, associate professor, 1968-72, then professor of English and Creative Writing, 1972—, Rutgers University, New Brunswick, New Jersey; member of editorial board, *Feminist Studies;* poetry editor, *Lilith.* **Awards:** Poetry Society of America's William Carlos Williams award, 1986, for *The Imaginary Lover;* National Book Award in Poetry finalist, 1996, for *The Crack in Everything;* awards from the New Jersey Arts Council, the National Endowment for the Arts, the Rockefeller Foundation, and the Guggenheim Foundation. **Address:** 33 Philip Drive, Princeton, NJ 08540, U.S.A.

PUBLICATIONS

Poetry

Songs: A Book of Poems. New York, Holt, 1969.
Once More Out of Darkness and Other Poems, Berkeley, Berkeley Poets' Press, 1974.
A Dream of Springtime: Poems, 1970-78. New York, Smith / Horizon Press, 1979.
The Mother / Child Papers. Los Angeles, Momentum Press, 1980.
A Woman under the Surface. Princeton, New Jersey, Princeton University Press, 1982.

The Imaginary Lover. Pittsburgh, University of Pittsburgh Press, 1986.
Green Age. Pittsburgh, University of Pittsburgh Press, 1989.
The Nakedness of the Fathers: Biblical Visions and Revisions (includes prose). New Brunswick, New Jersey, Rutgers University Press, 1994.
The Crack in Everything. Pittsburgh, University of Pittsburgh Press, 1996.

Other

Vision and Verse in William Blake. Madison, University of Wisconsin Press, 1965.
Writing Like a Woman ("Poets on Poetry" series). Ann Arbor, University of Michigan Press, 1983.
Stealing the Language: The Emergence of Women's Poetry in America. Boston, Beacon Press, 1986.
Feminist Revision and the Bible: The Bucknell Lectures on Literary Theory. Cambridge, Blackwell, 1993.

Editor, *William Blake: The Complete Poems.* New York, Penguin, 1977.

*

Critical Studies: "An Interview with Alicia Ostriker" by Katharyn Machan Aal, in *Poets & Writers*, November / December 1989; "Exploring the Depths of Relationships in Alicia Ostriker's Poetry" by Janet Ruth Heller, in *Literature and Psychology*, vol. 38, no. 1-2, 1992; "Secrets and Manifestos: Alicia Ostriker's Poetry and Politics" by Pamela Cook, in *Borderlands: Texas Poetry Review*, no. 2, Spring 1993.

Alicia Ostriker comments:

My earliest influences as a poet were the formal poets I learned in school. Between the ages of 15 and 21 I tried as well as I could to be some sort of compound of Keats, Hopkins, and W.H. Auden. Somewhere during graduate school I began writing in open forms, which took root for me during the years of the Vietnam War: improvisational form was somehow a corollary for the hope that we were not fully determined by our history, that the future—our next move, and the one after that—was in some sense a thing we might invent. I saw myself in these years especially as belonging to the American tradition of Whitman, William Carlos Williams, and Allen Ginsberg; I dedicated one chapbook to Whitman as "the grandmother of American poetry" and still consider myself Whitmanic: I believe, that is, that the best thing American poetry can do for the world is practice inclusiveness: to include every sort of experience, every level of language. Everything is grist for the mill of the poet; nothing is "unpoetic." In part that meant I could, and must, write from the life of a woman's body joined to a woman's mind.

In the mid-1970s I began voraciously reading postwar poetry by American women, and wrote two critical books exploring the significance of women's poetry. It would be impossible to list all the women poets who have influenced me and given me courage, but they include H.D., Anne Sexton, Adrienne Rich, Maxine Kumin, Sharon Olds, Ntozake Shange, June Jordan, and Lucille Clifton. And always, among my greatest heroes, is William Blake, whose heterodox vision continues to inspire whatever idealism I possess. For the last ten years I have been obsessed with the Bible;

The Nakedness of the Fathers is my version of Blake's revisionist impulse with sacred texts.

*   *   *

Throughout her career, poet-critic Alicia Ostriker has resisted the pressures which privilege one creative identity over the other, poet before the critic or critic before the poet. Her life's writing—five scholarly books, eight books of poetry and a ninth book (*The Nakedness of the Fathers: Biblical Visions and Revisions*, 1994) which marvelously blends both prose and poetry—steadfastly refuses the prevalent cultural rift between poets and scholars. In a beautifully crafted autobiographical essay, "Five Uneasy Pieces" (1997), she writes: "I have tried to make my criticism and poetry feed each other. To write intelligent poems and passionate criticism." Reviewing her critical and poetic accomplishments, one cannot help but conclude that she has succeeded.

Her critical-scholarly career began with the publication of *Vision and Verse in William Blake* (1965), a meticulous analysis of Blake's prosody which still serves as an invaluable resource in the study of Blake's technique. Ostriker's choice of Blake as a poetic mentor reveals much about her early (and enduring) poetic tastes. In "The Road of Excess: My William Blake," Ostriker traces the history of her "romance with Blake":

What did I like? First of all, Blake had the reputation of being 'mad.' I liked that. He wrote as an outsider; I liked that because I was one myself. His white-hot intellectual energy excited me, along with his flashing wit and irony, his capacity for joy and delight.

She continues to detail her recognition of Blake's own masculinist biases which propelled her towards a search for the women poets who could articulate what Blake could not. Reflecting on her successful search, she recounts, "I found a radical collective voice and vision equivalent to Blake's—equivalently outrageous, critical of our mind-forged manacles, determined to explore and rethink everything, and inventing poetic forms to embody new visions." Ostriker has gone on from this epiphany to write two significant books which detail her growing passion for the works of women poets: *Writing Like a Woman* (1983) and *Stealing the Language: The Emergence of Women's Poetry in America* (1986). The latter is particularly noteworthy in its ambitious mapping of an identifiable tradition of women's poetry in America, beginning with Anne Bradstreet and continuing to the 1980s. According to James E.B. Breslin, *"Stealing the Language* is literary history as it should be written—based on an extraordinary range of reading, written with passionate involvement, grounded in acute readings of particular poems and filled with provocative general statement."

Critical responses to Ostriker's poetry are quick to remark on what feminist scholar Elaine Showalter calls her "unwavering intelligence" as well as her "compassionate and ironic" voice. In terms of focus and thematic concerns, her books of poetry vary widely. While her work is grounded in her identity as both woman and feminist, her poems are not restricted to the recording of female experiences or consciousness. As a *Publisher's Weekly* reviewer comments, "Hers is a poetry of commitment, not so much to womankind as to humankind." Diana Hume George notes that Ostriker's "prophetic" vision "makes her return endlessly to the

ordinary, phenomenal world, inhabited by women and men like herself, where the real work must be done."

In "Five Uneasy Pieces," Ostriker describes the affirmative, life-embracing vision undergirding her poetry:

... there was always a part of me for which everything—everything, the brick building of public housing, cracked sidewalks, delivery trucks, subways, luminous sky of clouds, wicked people—was spectacle. Glorious theater. The vitality of those hard streets, poverty and ignorance bawling through our lives, was a sight to behold. The swing and punch of the bad language I was told not to imitate was live music to my ears, far more interesting than proper English. Literature—any art—exists to embody such perception. Exists to praise what is. For nothing.

Thus, we find in one of her earliest books, "Sonnet. To Tell the Truth," an ironic poem about the "brick Housing Authority buildings" of her childhood in Brooklyn, New York, "For whose loveliness no soul had planned"; or alternately, her meditation on "the kindliness of old men ... something incommunicably vast," as she remembers the lost grandfathers and older male friends who nurtured the young girl-child, "Petted me, taught me checkers patiently." She concludes, "It seems to me then God's a grandfather; / Infinite tenderness, infinite distance— / I don't a minute mean that I believe this! / It's but a way to talk about old men" ("Old Men").

Ostriker writes poems about marriage, struggles for intimacy, childbirth, the necessary, painful separations between parent and child, teaching, art, aging, losses, desire, and more. Throughout, her love of the world is unabated. In "Hating the World," she tells a former student, "Do you know, to hate the world / Makes you my enemy?," while in "The Death Ghazals," we read: "Where there's life there's hope. We bequeath this hope / To our children, along with our warm tears." Ostriker's persistent poetic faith in the face of hard truths culminates in her 1996 collection, *The Crack in Everything*, where among other poems of beauty and survival she includes "The Mastectomy Poems," created from her own experience with breast cancer. "You never think it will happen to you, / What happens every day to other women," she begins. In them, Ostriker fulfills her own poetic mandate: "to press the spirit forth / Unrepentant, struggling to praise / Our hopeless bodies, our hopeless world" ("The Book of Life").

Most recently, Ostriker's poetry and criticism have focused on her identity as both woman and Jew. She states in *People of the Book: Thirty Scholars Reflect on Their Jewish Identity* that she feels "a preoccupation amounting to obsession with Judaism, the Bible, God." In "Five Uneasy Pieces," Ostriker places her current work "in the tradition of midrash," retelling the Biblical narratives in search of a spiritual home within Judaism. *The Nakedness of the Fathers* (1994) is a remarkable testament to the passion and intelligence of Ostriker's career, ample evidence of the poetic and critical distances she has traveled and a clue to where she may be heading. Refuting accusations of blasphemy, witchery, ignorance or insanity, Ostriker writes:

I remember things, and sometimes I remember
My time when I was powerful, bringing birth
My time when I was just, composing law
My time playing before the throne
When my name was woman of valor

When my name was wisdom
And what if I say the Torah is
My well of living waters
Mine

—Anne F. Herzog

O'SULLIVAN, Maggie

Nationality: British. **Born:** 1951. **Family:** Married; children.
Career: Production assistant and researcher, BBC-TV, 1973-88;
founder, Magenta Press, London, c. 1984; freelance writer and lecturer, 1988—. **Awards:** State University of New York fellowship,
1993; Six Towns Poetry Festival commission, 1996, for *Winter
Ceremony*. **Address:** Middle Fold Farm, Colden, Hebden Bridge,
West Yorkshire HX7 7PG, England.

PUBLICATIONS

Poetry

Concerning Spheres. Bristol, Broken Ground, 1982.
An Incomplete Natural History. London, Writers Forum, 1984.
A Natural History in Three Incomplete Parts. London, Magenta,
    1985.
Un-assuming Personas. London, Writers Forum, 1985.
Divisions of Labour. Newcastle upon Tyne, Galloping Dog, 1986.
From the Handbook of That and Furriery. London, Writers Forum, 1986.
States of Emergency. Oxford, ICPA, 1987.
Unofficial Word. Newcastle upon Tyne, Galloping Dog, 1988.
EXCLA, with Bruce Andrews. London, Writers Forum, 1993.
In the House of the Shaman. London, Reality Street, 1993.
Ellen's Lament. Toronto, Pushy Broadsheets, 1993.
That Bread Should Be. London, Read Write Create, 1996.
Palace of Reptiles. Los Angeles, Sun & Moon, 1997.

Other

Editor, *Out of Everywhere: Linguistically Innovative Poetry by
    Women in North America and the UK.* London, Reality Street
    Editions, 1996.

*

Critical Studies: *Responses* (Maggie O'Sullivan issue), no. 6,
1992; Interview with Adrian Clarke, in *Angel Exhaust,* no. 6, Winter
1996; *Pages* (Maggie O'Sullivan issue), 1997.

*   *   *

Drawing on a cross-section of linguistically based poetic theory
and practice as well as various performative traditions, Maggie
O'Sullivan's poetry is both lyrical and exploratory. O'Sullivan's
work follows the associative and allusive properties of sounds to
push meaning forward and to, as she says, "celebrate" the pleasure and possibilities of poetic language.

In common with lyrical traditions of poetry, her work makes
use of traditions that include music or song such as the lament, a
genre she employs in her poem, "Hannah's Lament" and in her
book *Ellen's Lament.* The lament is a rich and systematically
marginalized genre in Britain, especially in Ireland where the lament, called *caoineadh,* is paralleled by *waulking* in Scotland and
in English translated as *keening.* It is primarily a women's tradition, a performative genre whereby the responsibility of reacting
to death of a community member and / or loved one falls on the
lament poet who acts out grief and its accompanying disorder,
often while simultaneously using her lament as an occasion to
posthumously challenge the actions in life of the dead, or to challenge state and church authorities or the social authority of men
and family. More than a memorial, lamenting has been historically
an act of social resistance itself, since its history in Ireland has
been one which brought women into direct conflict with Catholic
clergy. Church pronouncements issued between 1631 and 1800
forbade priests to take part in funerals where a lamenter was
present, and threatened the female keeners with excommunication.
The lament is a genre entrenched in centuries of attempted coercive containment of female speech to which the "odds of harm"
are pronounced. O'Sullivan writes in her poem "Hannah's Lament": "Hannah's lament / As opposed to scape, No A Haunt /
No, a Hurt / Nor Odds of Harm / Reading."

What she has written of other "linguistically innovative" writers in *Out of Everywhere: Linguistically Innovative Poetry by
Women in North America and the U.K.,* is also true of her. Her
writing aligns itself with a tradition of poetry that explicitly of
implicitly offers a critique of what O'Sullivan calls "the agenda-based and cliché-ridden rallying positions of mainstream poetry."
Like others in this tradition, O'Sullivan is critical of the idea that
poems much be "about" something a notion which arguably has
parallels with Archibald MacLeish's modern(ist) dictum that "a
poem should not mean but be." The belief that language offers a
transparent window on the world is dismissed by the many who
calls themselves avant garde, experimental poets and innovators,
inadequate terms of convenience for poetry that foregrounds language as a changeable social formation, capable of changing the
methods of thought and common sense as ruling cultures know it.
As part of this critical tradition, O'Sullivan poetry rallies to its
own (counter) position and foregrounds the non-transparency and
endless allusiveness of the English language in order to call into
question its syntactical and lexical linguistic constructions that have
by and large been dominated, weakened or extinguished by the
social and political power of the imperial English, nation and language alike. Her work imagines "unknown tongues," sounds as
yet unrealized, possible poetic language forms that have been
muffled by normalizing traditions that have standardized the reception of poetry in English and rendered normative certain experience and in the ways it is represented. In the place of more transparent meaning, her poetry occupies the space of the liminal, as a
site of heightened consciousness of sensory perception.

It is due to the liminal quality to her work that O'Sullivan's
poetry resembles the poetry of English Romantic tradition and
its modernist extensions, defined its emotional and sensual qualities and conveying what theorist of the lyric Herbert Read defined as "not just emotion, but the imaginative prehension of emotional states." A mood of burgeoning disquiet is evoked by such
poems as "Hill Figure" which, instead of deploying more traditional and explicitly rhetorical commonplaces of argument, employs tongue twisting and tactile words, some nonce words cre-

ated for the occasion of the poem, unusual syntax and visually free use of page space to conjure the mood of a pastoral environment, albeit one that is threatened with destruction or imminent demise. "Hill Figures, anthologized in *Out of Everywhere,* begins "nailed eagles beryl alter vanish / Owls, blood bed / Birdgear turbulent / Ruled / it, / Raven" as O'Sullivan seems to scan the images of a natural landscape to reap a seemingly archetypal or symbolic meaning from birds—ravens, owls, crows, predatory birds—as the harbingers of loss and death. She combines imagery culled from pastoral and pastorale genres with vocabulary suggesting decay and the attenuation of language at the edges of meaning and its loss. These elements of O'Sullivan's poems coalesce into an emblematic enactment of the obsolescence of descriptors of decay. Words stop as if limits and as if they are in a constant process of palimpseset (that is, overwriting) or atrophy themselves. For example, in "Hill Figures" O'Sullivan writes "tinning lengths / fin / bred- / Brinks." This musical poetry exists at the "brinks" of language and its performative soundings.

O'Sullivan seems to use vocabulary to suggest genres that can all be thrown in the mix of a poem, even while some these genres have not traditionally been "assembled" together in poetry. Verbs in "Hill Figures" include "Ruled, acquiescing, resist, skinning, tinning, herding, bucklin" and throughout the poem O'Sullivan weaves words culled from abnormal psychology and from biological and environmental sciences, for example, words like "autistic, invert, DOSAGES, skull, chema, nexions: poisons" with ballad-like words that suggest song, "Twisted / merry go / supperates / congregates / rolled-a-run / lettering" to "figure" the possibilities of mixing other genres with the ballad genre, a genre that usually, by definition, tells it tales without psychological or scientific explanations for the events that unfold in them. In "narcotic properties," another poem anthologized in *Out of Everywhere,* O'Sullivan similarly deploys the vocabulary of the natural world and of song to suggest the pastoral and ballad and combines these with the genre of pseudo / science and instruction, "LISTEN AS THE SKEWERED TRAMPLING OF THE DOOMED ANIMALS ear into nethery Singes." The result is a poem with language "singed," at once rendered melic and "singed" as one might "singe" or burn the carcass of a dead animal or bird to remove its feathers.

O'Sullivan uses half / part words, words with elided consonants and vowels, the blank page space and the hyphen to suggest words not on the page but haunting the poem. In "Garb" the word garbage and garble, as shadow or subtextual words, lurk outside of the space of the poem with other obsolete and rare meanings of the word "Garb" which could mean a bundle, a method or custom or a sheaf of grain. Associative references to cultural customs appear alongside the poem's "scholia" or marginal commentary on, of all things, tabloids, as in "major misses tabloid ballast." O'Sullivan uses the formal techniques of, for example, Paul Bunyan's *Pilgrim's Progress* or Samuel Taylor Coleridge's *The Rime of the Ancient Mariner* to do this, which not incidentally are two poems about spiritual quest and liminal experience. While it is a popular and mainstream informational medium, people have often imagined the crafted language of poetry to be the opposite of the language of the tabloid and thus the tabloid, that most classed, and perhaps feminized, genre, has been through marginal to poetry. O'Sullivan stands this idea on its head. Her own habitual and painterly vocabulary of images and descriptions from the nature and musical borrowings from song here "headline," in tabloid-like capital letters, on the side of poem stanzas, alongside words from popular media with all its pumped-up drama of mis-

fortune, tragedy, the banal and the unbelievable. Here an "anorexia pressed Topt Tusser" lurks with the carnivalesque "headless legless peepshow bleeding" of O'Sullivan's imagination to create the effect of a carnivalesque enactment and implicit commentary on the ability or disability, of language to be meaningful despite the constant and pressurized banalities of its everyday use in hyperbolic and sing-song mainstream media presentations.

—Jenny Gough

OSWALD, Alice

Nationality: British. **Born:** 1966. **Education:** University of Oxford, B.A. in classics; trained in horticulture at Wisley. **Family:** Married the playwright Peter Oswald; one child. **Career:** Poet and gardener, working at Tapley Park, Devon, and the Chelsea Physic Garden. **Awards:** Gregory Award, 1994.

PUBLICATIONS

Poetry

The Thing in the Gap-Stone Style. Oxford and New York, Oxford University Press, 1996.

*   *   *

Alice Oswald's poems have a quirky individuality that beguiles even as it risks mannerism. She is, to date, the author of a single full-length collection *The Thing in the Gap-Stone Style,* a title which suggests that whimsy, playfulness and imaginative chanciness will be high on the author's agenda. Such a suggestion is confirmed by pieces such as "My Neighbour, Mrs Kersey," a sonnet in off-rhymed couplets that turns the poet's neighbour into "a dream-self on the other side" and half-grieves for "a loss / of difference." The poem senses delicately the existence of gaps and links.

Elsewhere in the collection Oswald writes love poems that celebrate both separateness (as in "Woman in a Mustard Field") and intimacy (as in "Wedding"). "Woman in a Mustard Field" is a short, semi-surreal ballad descriptive of the poet's awakening "From love to light." It manages adroitly to move from the coyly psychedelic ("and whoops I found a mustard field / exploding into flowers") to the quieter revelation of the conclusion's "living world / that grows without your love." This poem suggests that to be bound up in another person is to lose a sense of the infinite variety of life; a reward of Oswald's poetry is the way it comes at familiar topics in surprising and unfamiliar ways. But sometimes the emphasis on novelty can draw attention to itself without yielding deeper intimations. "Wedding" is an ingenious sonnet, in which each line builds incrementally on the previous line rather like a nursery rhyme. Yet the last two lines are breezy rather than precise: "and when the luck begins, it's like a wedding, / which is like love, which is like everything."

Here as elsewhere the blurb's description of Oswald as "Influenced by the rhythms of Hopkins" misfires since her rhythms and diction have little of the earlier poet's fidelity to the physical. One does not find in Oswald, as Geoffrey Hartman finds in Hopkins, "an unwillingness to release [the] mind from the physical contact of words." In fact, Oswald's better poems are concerned with release and its twinned consequences: reduction and transformation. "The Moon Addresses Her Reflection" works with a tough knowledge of "each other's nothingness." The monologuing moon and reflection can either settle for "the weights and disciplines of love" or the reflection can leave the moon so that the moon reverts (rather as in a poem by Wallace Stevens) to being merely what it is. Here the final note is one of reduction. In the first of three poems titled "Sea Sonnet," outlines vanish in a mode that miniaturizes Romantic or Transcendental gestures towards infinity: "and when it rains, the very integer / and shape of water disappears in water." The third "Sea Sonnet" depicts a more alienated awareness in which the only contact between people and things is virtual, and awareness capped by the concluding off-rhyme between the incidental nature of any love the poet may feel and the presence on the sand of "one blue towel, one white towel." More comical in its treatment of apartness, "The Melon Grower" uses its tercets to describe a turbulent relationship between a melon grower and his wife.

Fantastical, artfully artless, at times a touch self-regarding, Oswald's poetry requires its reader to be attuned to its wish to catch the world off-guard. Two poems which successfully realize this wish are the "The Thing in the Gap-Stone Stile" and the long piece, "The Three Wise Men of Gotham Who Set Out to Catch the Moon in a Net." The first of these poems can be read as Oswald's poetic apologia, not quite taking responsibility for effects by which she is, nevertheless, delighted. This is a sharp, humorous, and self-aware piece, able to poke fun at her "pose" while defending it; able, too, to suggest how she wants her reader to respond, "almost / abstracted on a gap-stone between fields." Oswald's poems are themselves "almost abstracted" in the double sense of withdrawing themselves from the real and of turning the real into signs out of which the "almost abstractions" that are poems can be made. Everything depends for her, as for certain kinds of structuralist and post-structuralist thinkers, on the "gap" "between fields." "The Three Wise Men of Gotham," about the attempt to catch the moon by the men of Gotham, enters explicitly a world that has lurked in the wings of the collection: the world of Nonsense, the madcap, lunatic sphere of Edward Lear and Lewis Carroll. What is effective about the poem is the way its regular pentameters suggest that the road (or waterway) of folly may indeed lead to the palace of an existential visionary wisdom. That wisdom consists in acceptance of "the journey" and pleasure in the scraps of beauty (like bits of the moon floating on the water) to be found in the midst of the danger and adventure of living.

—Michael O'Neill

OWEN, Jan

Nationality: Australian. **Born:** Adelaide, South Australia, 18 August 1940. **Education:** University of Adelaide, 1958-62, 1974, B.A. 1963. **Family:** Married 1) Balazs Bajka in 1964 (divorced 1972), one son and one daughter; 2) Anthony Brown in 1972 (separated 1995), one son. **Career:** Laboratory assistant, Waite Institute, Adelaide, 1957-60; library assistant, 1961, librarian, 1962-64, 1966, Barr Smith Library, Adelaide; librarian, South Australian Institute of Technology Library, 1969-71, Salisbury College of Advanced Education Library, 1971-75, and Technical and Further Education College, Gillies Plains, 1981-84. Creative writing teacher in schools, colleges, and universities throughout Australia, 1985—. **Awards:** Ian Mudie award, 1982; Jessie Litchfield prize, 1984, for *Boy with a Telescope;* Grenfell Henry Lawson prize, 1985; Harri Jones Memorial prize, 1986, for *Boy with a Telescope;* Anne Elder award, 1986, for *Boy with a Telescope;* Mary Gilmore prize, 1987, for *Boy with a Telescope;* Wesley Michel Wright Poetry prize, 1992. **Agent:** Margaret Connolly, 17 Ormond Street, Paddington, New South Wales, Australia. **Address:** 14 Fern Road, Crafers, South Australia 5152, Australia.

PUBLICATIONS

Poetry

Boy with a Telescope. Sydney, Angus & Robertson, 1986.
Fingerprints on Light. Sydney, Angus & Robertson, 1990.
Blackberry Season. Canberra, Molonglo Press, 1993.
Night Rainbows. Melbourne, Heinemann, 1994.

*

Manuscript Collection: Australian Defence Force Academy (University of New South Wales), Canberra.

Critical Study: "Being Observant, Keeping Faith" by Alan Gould, in *Quadrant* (Sydney), April 1995.

Jan Owen comments:

My poetry is lyrical for the most part but often with an ironical or humorous edge. Common themes are transience and loss, contradiction, the hidden or other; I'm drawn to difference, to otherness, and to the implicit rather than the explicit, what is hidden within (not beneath) appearances. I would like to be able to say, "Nothing alien is alien to me." So I write about the tiny and the faraway, stars and insects, other times and places. My subject matter is fairly wide and includes modern physics, math, and grammar, as well as exploration, war, art, trees, gemstones, domesticity, relationships, childhood.... Imagination and perception come before introspection for me, and other people are perhaps the most common subject of all; the human psyche seems to infiltrate even poems on carnations, tektites, zippers, etc.

My early work has been called exuberant, philosophical, funny, but more recent work is darker in tone and subject matter, though humor is still evident.

I write in traditional rhymed forms—a lot of sonnets—as well as free verse. Sound is very important to me and I think Plath, Roethke, Judith Wright were influences here, as well as the rhymes taught me as a child, the early Australian ballads, and poems such as Coleridge's "Ancient Mariner" read and learned at an early age. I admire the Australian poets Gwen Harwood and Les Murray, the Americans Galway Kinnell, Randall Jarrell, Frost, Ammons, and Sharon Olds, and the Eastern European poets Zbigniew Herbert, Miroslav Holub, and Wislawa Szymborska. Yehuda Amichai is also certainly a poet I hope to learn from.

It has been said that I write poems that deliberate, that I attempt to reconcile a thing's meaning with its being. According to

Alan Gould I share with Plath and Hughes "the notion that a pe-
culiarly rich ground for poetry is that which falls between the
eye's capacity for precision and focus, and the intellect's knowl-
edge that all significances, no matter how glittering, are unstable."

*   *   *

Jan Owen made an immediate impact on many of her fellow
poets and contemporaries with her first collection, *Boy with a Tele-
scope,* published in 1986. It received two of the important hon-
ors reserved for new poets in Australia—the Anne Elder prize
and the Mary Gilmore award. Even before her first book, how-
ever, she had been noticed, and during the early 1980s she won
several prizes for individual poems and was published regularly
in journals and, later, anthologies. Many critics felt that her work,
after the larrikin decade of the 1970s, represented a return to stan-
dards of craft and poise and a concern for subtlety and nuance. In
the sometimes abrasive Australian poetry scene of the 1980s her
work was hailed by Chris Wallace-Crabbe and others as evidence
of a new generation of poets reaching maturity and writing with-
out ostentation or gimmickry, something always regarded as dan-
gerous in the local cultural environment, where laconism is more
highly regarded than bravado.

Owen's second collection, *Fingerprints on Light* (1990), main-
tains the sensitivity to detail and concreteness of image that can
resonate beyond itself. These qualities can be seen, for example,
in "Digging Potatoes":

> My grandfather turned the earth
> all morning long in the skittery autumn sun
> on the weedy patch by the stable wall,
> stacking unsteady pyramids
> of dirty dimpled knees in the bonfire air
> while the tame-tease willy wagtail
> skimmed the flung-up clods
> and thought me a rival for witchetty grubs.

The ten-page sequence "Write to Me at Rochefort" displays
Owen's ambition and willingness to work on a larger canvas. It is
within a tradition well established in Australia, what is known as
the voyager poem. Early navigators and Pacific explorers have in-
spired many poets since Kenneth Slessor's landmark "Five Vi-
sions of Captain Cook" (1931). Owen's poem is based on early
French voyagers, and although it uses the devices of diary entries,
letters, and impressionistic notes, it maintains her characteristic
lyric tautness and concludes with a reference to the Aborigines
and their encounter with change. The use of Aboriginal words in
the last section carries allusions to the earlier Jindyworobak move-
ment of determined Australianism, as well as to the later, envi-
ronmentally inspired attempt to reclaim a wider Australian heri-
tage. The following lines are from "Eora Tribe":

> Shaking their wings like this like this
> like the clan of *Gareway* shaking their wings
> over the place of Sting-rays shaking their feathers
> those people pale as the moon *Yenadah*
> folding their wings to the place of Sitting-Down
> those people pale as bone
> making the horns of *Yettadah* on their boughs
> following running water looking for food
> calling the earth *boodjeri*

> calling the fire *boodjeri*
> resting by *Jujabala*
> resting in the place of Making Canoes.

The influence of Les Murray's "The Buledelah-Taree Holiday
Song Cycle" (1976) is also evident here. (Murray's bucolic con-
cerns may be thought to be evident in other of Owen's poems as
well, though her own impeccable lyricism and sharpness identify
her work more tellingly.)

Blackberry Season (1993), which offers a greater refinement in
these qualities, was quickly followed by *Night Rainbows* (1994).
The latter is a rich and varied collection that can move from the
eight-poem sequence "Describing Words" (more frolicsome and
virtuoso than Judith Wright's earlier sequence "Some Words") to
a Christian nativity sequence ("This Marriage") and a skillfully
wicked set of parodies on fellow Australian poets, "Imperson-
ations." The impression in this book is of energy, flow, release,
and an increasingly flexible and vigorous craftsmanship. Owen al-
ready has an impressive corpus of work, and she shows every
sign of increasing mastery and outreach.

—Thomas W. Shapcott

OWENS, Rochelle

Nationality: American. **Born:** Brooklyn, New York, 2 April 1936.
Education: Lafayette High School, Brooklyn, graduated 1953; at-
tended Alliance Francaise, Paris, Laval University, Quebec, and
University of Montreal. **Family:** Married George Economou in
1962. **Career:** Worked as a clerk, typist, telephone operator;
founding member, New York Theatre Strategy; visiting lecturer,
University of California, San Diego, 1982; adjunct professor, and
host of radio program *The Writer's Mind,* University of Oklahoma,
Norman, 1984; Distinguished Writer-in-Residence, Brown Univer-
sity, Providence, Rhode Island. **Awards:** Ford Foundation grant,
1965; Rockefeller Foundation grant, 1965, 1975; Creative Artists
Public Service grant, 1966, 1973; Yale University School of Drama
fellowship, 1968; Obie award, 1968, 1971, 1982; Guggenheim fel-
lowship, 1971; National Endowment for the Arts grant, 1974; Vil-
lager award, 1982; New York Drama Critics Circle award, 1983;
Rockefeller Foundation Bellagio Stucy Center fellowship (Italy).
Agent: Dramatists Guild, 1501 Broadway, Suite 701, New York,
New York 10036. **Address:** 1401 Magnolia, Norman, Oklahoma
73072, U.S.A.

PUBLICATIONS

Poetry

Not Be Essence That Cannot Be. New York, Trobar Press, 1961.
Four Young Lady Poets, with others, edited by LeRoi Jones. New
    York, Totem-Corinth, 1962.
Salt and Core. Los Angeles, Black Sparrow Press, 1968.
I Am the Babe of Joseph Stalin's Daughter. New York, Kulchur,
    1972.
Poems from Joe's Garage. Providence, Rhode Island, Burning
    Deck, 1973.

The Joe 82 Creation Poems. Los Angeles, Black Sparrow Press, 1974.

The Joe Chronicles Part 2. Santa Barbara, California, Black Sparrow Press, 1979.

Shemuel. St. Paul, Minnesota, New Rivers Press, 1979.

French Light. Norman, Oklahoma Press with the Flexible Voice, 1984.

Constructs. Norman, Oklahoma, Poetry Around, 1985.

Anthropologists at a Dinner Party. Tucson, Arizona, Chax Press, 1985.

W.C. Fields in French Light. New York, Contact II, 1986.

How Much Paint Does the Painting Need? New York, Kulchur, 1988.

Black Chalk. Norman, Oklahoma, Texture Press, 1992.

Rubbed Stones: Poems from 1960-1992. Norman, Oklahoma, Texture Press, 1994.

New and Selected Poems, 1961-1996. San Diego, California, Junction Press, 1997.

Recordings: *A Reading of Primitive and Archaic Poetry,* with others, Broadside; *From a Shaman's Notebook,* with others, Broadside; *The Karl Marx Play,* Kilmarnock, 1975; *Totally Corrupt,* Giorno, 1976; *Black Box 17,* Watershed Foundation, 1979; *The Wild River: Rochelle Owens Reading Rubbed Stones,* 1995.

Plays

Futz (produced Minneapolis, 1965; New York, Edinburgh, and London, 1967). New York, Hawk's Well Press, 1961; revised version in *Futz and What Came After,* 1968, in *New Short Plays 2,* London, Methuen, 1969.

The String Game (produced New York, 1965). In *Futz and What Came After,* 1968.

Istanbul (produced New York, 1965; London, 1982). In *Futz and What Came After,* 1968.

Homo (produced Stockholm and New York, 1966; London, 1969). In *Futz and What Came After,* 1968.

Beclch (produced Philadelphia and New York, 1968). In *Futz and What Came After,* 1968.

Futz and What Came After. New York, Random House, 1968.

The Karl Marx Play, music by Galt MacDermot, lyrics by Owens (produced New York, 1973). Included in *The Karl Marx Play and Others,* 1974.

The Karl Marx Play and Others (includes *Kontraption, He Wants Shih!, Farmer's Almanac, Coconut Folksinger, O.K. Certaldo*). New York, Dutton, 1974.

He Wants Shih! (produced New York, 1975). In *The Karl Marx Play and Others,* 1974.

Coconut Folksinger (broadcast 1976). In *The Karl Marx Play and Others,* 1974.

Kontraption (produced New York, 1978). In *The Karl Marx Play and Others,* 1974.

Emma Instigated Me, published in *Performing Arts Journal I* (New York), spring 1976.

The Widow, and The Colonel, in *The Best Short Plays 1977,* edited by Stanley Richards. Radnor, Pennsylvania, Chilton, 1977.

Mountain Rites, in *The Best Short Plays 1978,* edited by Stanley Richards. Radnor, Pennsylvania, Chilton, 1978.

Chucky's Hunch (produced New York, 1981). In *Wordplays 2,* New York, Performing Arts Journal Publications, 1982.

Who Do You Want, Peire Vidal? (produced New York, 1982). With *Futz,* New York, Broadway Play Publishing, 1986.

Three-Front (produced Omaha, Nebraska, 1989; as *Guerre à trois,* produced Radio France, 1991). In *Europe Plurlingue,* Paris, n.d.

Screenplay: *Futz* (additional dialogue), 1969.

Radio Plays: *Coconut Folksinger,* 1976 (Germany); *Sweet Potatoes,* 1977.

Television Play: (video): *Oklahoma Too: Rabbits and Nuggets,* 1987; *How Much Paint Does the Painting Need?,* 1992; *Black Chalk,* 1994.

Short Stories

The Girl on the Garage Wall. Mexico City, El Corno Emplumado, 1962.

The Obscenities of Reva Cigarnik. Mexico City, El Corno Emplumado, 1963.

Other

Editor, *Spontaneous Combustion: Eight New American Plays.* New York, Winter House, 1972.

Translator, *The Passersby,* by Liliane Atlan. New York, Holt, 1993.

*

Manuscript Collections: Mugar Memorial Library, Boston University; University of California, Davis; University of Oklahoma, Norman; Lincoln Center Library of the Performing Arts, New York; Smith College, Northampton, Massachusetts; New York Public Library, Billy Rose Theatre Collection.

Critical Studies: In *World* (New York), no. 29, April 1974; "Rochelle Owens Symposium," in *Margins* (Milwaukee), no. 24-26, 1975; *Contemporary Authors Autobiography Series,* Detroit, Gale Research, 1985; in *Parnassus* (New York), vol. 12, no. 2, 1985; in *Modern American Drama, 1945-1990* by C.W.E. Bigsby, New York, Cambridge University Press, 1992; by Susan Smith Nash in *Talisman* (Hoboken, New Jersey), no. 12, Spring 1994.

Theatrical Activities:
Director and actress: **Television**—*Oklahoma Too: Rabbits and Nuggets,* 1987.

Rochelle Owens comments:

I know that the only tradition that interests me as a writer is the tradition of breaking away from the fixed and familiar patterns to living new structures and the creation of new forms, with all its risks and manifold facets.

For over 30 years I've been a poet as well as a playwright, sometimes writing literary criticism. As a young woman, I was part of the experimental theater community in New York City. Writing poetry is compelling, complex work and is always marked with sensory surprises. My stylistic mode, insistencies, and power are to synthesize experience with refrains of sound, sonority, and echoes with striking language patterns that form inner worlds. I have an elusive relationship with the natural world I suppose, and subjective reflection, transcendence, draws from various archetypal motifs. I would like the reader to linger over the beautiful constructs that access and process the mind of the poet. All of my poetry can be listened to, the syntactical and lexical components concord with the invisibility of space and time represented by the whiteness of the page; I want the poetry to paint dimensions that offer up astonishing riddles that challenge the reader so that she or he can perceive new boundaries. Conventional interpretations leave a gap between the reader and sea of poetics and life, where symbol, image, and paradox create new terminologies.

My commitment has been to take American poetry to extended domains. It is for the reader who seeks a new poetic idiom. I want a poetry of respiration and architectural music; a reinvented narrative that is itself a shining structure. Every presence of image, immense or unseen, space, and time tells tales, and the sensory and metaphysical twists of consciousness and the radical engagement of language and silence are the poem as creation, whose realism cannot be denied. It is my own passionate memoir, a model of my mind shaping itself, of matter and psyche where intuition and reason reveal waving immediacy. The poems burn strange messages into our consciousness. We recognize the fact that poetry can be the essential document to the condition of our time.

*   *   *

Rochelle Owens is better known as a playwright than as a poet, but her poems enact her theatrical imagination and provide an essential stimulus to it. In poetry (as distinct from drama) she can concentrate exclusively on verbal invention, coining words and splashing them disjunctively on the page, disrupting grammar, and free-associating with maximum tonal contrast:

O IF I FORGET THEE O ZION
LET AMERICA'S BALLS RUST

Of Jewish background and married to a Greek, Owens relishes the interplay of deviant personae and images stolen from both "high" and "low" culture that serve as metaphors for polar conflicts—Jew versus Christian, Turk versus Greek, white versus black, male versus female, the sacred versus the secular, the powerful versus the helpless. In *The Joe 82 Creation Poems,* through the voices of the primal couple Wild-Man and Wild-Woman, Owens redesigns the myths of creation to reflect both the internal artistic energy of every mind and the external feminist struggle of women to escape the prevalent male-dominant ideas which have led to an insane and polluted world. Wild-Woman, Lilith-like and joyous, expresses the disordering which is needed to re-create a new order on the planet, "mother" earth. Wild-Woman's energy is

defeated, however, in morally bankrupt American society, as the poet dolefully makes clear in a tone of protest and deep hopelessness through the acid portraits of "Anthropologists at a Dinner Party." This double-column diatribe, to be read "across and down and up," describes a racist, sexist "round-haunched anthropologist / of Pict descent" (the Picts being a mix of Scottish aborigines and Aryan invaders) who studies Native American Indians and is "worried that people of mixed / races were opportunists."

Owens presents an antidote to this male hegemony in *W.C. Fields in French Light,* poems meditating on the Cathedral of Sacré Coeur in Paris in "the voice of W.C. Fields" and expressing a humorous, androgynous, multinational vision. The woman artist becomes the conduit of the universal unconscious as her subjective journey to the "sacred heart" of all things has her walk "up the hill to Sacré Coeur." There, holding nothing back, "I hurl the javelin to the top." The poem ends without a period, leaving the poet in continuous upward trajectory.

French culture also influences *How Much Paint Does the Painting Need,* another formally innovative book in which color forms from Cubist and modernist paintings are "translated" onto the page in rectangular blocks as if framed on canvas, thus equating poetry and painting. As in abstract expressionism, these forms are seen "tearing into the yellow rhythms into the emergency / of blue between the bubbles ... the pigment forged / into the base of the skull the territory breaking / out of the paint between the spaces tearing through."

The paradoxes of "tearing through"—the acts of violence which create culture—are explored in Owens's series poem *LUCA: Discourse on Life and Death* and in her selected *Rubbed Stones: Poems from 1960-1992.* Here three major themes intertwine, represented by three characters: the artist, represented by Leonardo da Vinci (Lenny) and his anatomy notebooks—"we murder to dissect"; the artist's object, *Mona Lisa* (Mona), who is also the female model anatomized; and Freud (Sigmund, Siggy), the analyst of the psyche, or soul. The overall premise is that the analytic Western mode of rational thought destroys, whereas unconscious thought creates, symbolized here by the Ur-mind of pre-Columbian cultures whose dug up remains are not understood by "the anthropologists at the dinner party." These men also destroy the living culture, so that the poem ends with the grim image of a crucified Osage woman. The poet has no answers, only complex free associations thrust up from the unconscious to mix with conscious thought on human suffering, mortality, and uncontrollable social forces. They signal Owens' accomplishment: she continues by means of unique and far-reaching inventiveness in language to tear through destruction itself, bursting boundaries to make it postmodernly new.

—Jane Augustine

P

PASTAN, Linda

Nationality: American. **Born:** Linda Olenik, New York City, 27 May 1932. **Education:** Fieldston School, New York; Radcliffe College, Cambridge, Massachusetts, B.A. 1954; Simmons College, Boston, M.L.S. 1955; Brandeis University, Waltham, Massachusetts, M.A. 1957. **Family:** Married Ira Pastan in 1953; two sons and one daughter. **Awards:** Dylan Thomas award, 1955; Swallow Press New Poetry Series award, 1972; National Endowment for the Arts grant, 1972; Bread Loaf Writers Conference John Atherton fellowship, 1974; Alice Fay di Castagnola award, 1977; Maryland Arts Council grant, 1978; Bess Hokin prize (*Poetry,* Chicago), 1985; Maurice English award, 1986; poet laureate of Maryland, 1991-94; International Poetry Forum Charity Randall citation, 1995. **Agent:** Jean V. Naggar Literary Agency, 336 East 73rd Street, New York, New York 10021. **Address:** 11710 Beall Mountain Road, Potomac, Maryland 20854, U.S.A.

PUBLICATIONS

Poetry

A Perfect Circle of Sun. Chicago, Swallow Press, 1971.
On the Way to the Zoo. Washington, D.C., Dryad Press, 1975.
Aspects of Eve. New York, Liveright, 1975.
The Five Stages of Grief. New York, Norton, 1978.
Selected Poems. London, Murray, 1979.
Setting the Table. Washington, D.C., Dryad Press, 1980.
Waiting for My Life. New York, Norton, 1981.
PM / AM: New and Selected Poems. New York, Norton, 1982.
A Fraction of Darkness. New York, Norton, 1985.
The Imperfect Paradise. New York, Norton, 1988.
Heroes in Disguise. New York, Norton, 1991.
An Early Afterlife. New York, Norton, 1995.
Carnival Evening: New and Selected Poems. New York, Norton, 1998.

Recording: *Mosaic,* Watershed, 1988.

*   *   *

Linda Pastan has long seen herself as Eve—one of the fallen, not the temptress. The bathers in "At Woods Hole" "learn nothing, lying / on sand hot and pliant as each other's flesh." Trapped in sensuality, they may appreciate beauty, but that is part of the cosmic deception: "waves seem to bring the water in forever / even as the tide moves surely out." Like Poe, Pastan has been conscious of the limits of the mind and the impossibility of exceeding them. In "The Last Train" she imagines one boy fascinated with disappearing buffalo and another with the vanishing long-distance passenger train, and she concludes that we all "follow sleep as well as we are able / along disintegrating paths of vapor, / high above the dreamlike shapes of clouds."

But Pastan seems more willing to abide by the limits of consciousness than does Poe. Her effort has been to clarify this hu-

manness. In "At the Gynecologist's," her "body so carefully / contrived for pain" "gallop[s] towards death / with flowers of ether in my hair." Acutely aware of her mortality, she does *try* to escape it. She senses "what wildness / is left" in "Bicentennial Winter," and though she is tempted to skate the frozen Potomac, she does not partake of that "dangerous / freedom." She finds violence instead of beauty in "Evening at Bird Island," "under my rocking floor / fish swallow other fish, / feeding / like bad dreams / under the surfaces of sleep." The problem is that the human necessarily pervades everything, "There is a figure in every landscape."

While Pastan's vision has been consistent throughout her books, *The Five Stages of Grief* most effectively arrays responses. There is *denial,* when life is made up largely of the familiar and even deaths "wait like domestic animals," "patient and loving" ("After"). In *anger* she would just as soon "everything happen / off-stage" and let her stay "with the scenery" ("Exeunt Omnes"). The stage of *bargaining* produces minimal consolations, as set forth in "Ice Age":

> We must learn
> the cold lessons
> the dinosaurs learned:
> to freeze magnified
> in someone else's history;
> to leave our bones behind.

In *depression* even the sun seems like a "huge stone / rolled against the door of death / to hold it shut" ("It Is Still Winter Here"). Finally, there is *acceptance,* when the sun is "warm amnesia" and a woman and her griefs sing back and forth ("Old Woman"). But acceptance, though "its name is in lights," seems unattainable; as the title poem says, "Grief is a circular staircase."

In the 1980s Pastan's vulnerability intensified. "At all / the outposts of my body," she writes in "Low Tide," "the driftwood fires / burn down, / and a stranger stands / shooting a perfect / arc of urine / into the ashes." Aging, her children's leaving, and especially her parents' deaths bring disequilibrium, "There is nobody / left standing between you / and the world, to take / the first blows / on their shoulders."

But *The Imperfect Paradise,* which concludes with new poems of Eden, approaches reconciliation. Instead of denying grief, Pastan locates it against the possibility of the benign, as in "The Imperfect Paradise":

> If landscape were the genius of creation
> And neither man nor serpent played a role ...
>
> Would [God] have rested on his bank of cloud
> With nothing in the universe to lose,
> Or would he hunger for the human crowd?

One can know the miracle of renewal. In "Grudnow" Pastan depicts her immigrant grandfather as having willed such optimism: just as "He always / sipped his tea through a cube of sugar / clenched in his teeth," "he sipped his life here, noisily, / through all he remembered / that might be sweet in Grudnow." This renewal manifests itself in the wit and extravagance of "In the Rear-view Mirror," "The Safecracker," and "The Ordinary Weather of Summer," as well as in Pastan's success with uncharacteristically formal verse in "Turnabout" and the six-sonnet title poem. To speak in her terms, she has permitted two opposing forces—the Edenic, often humanized in her gardener husband, and the evil of death—to find equilibrium.

Heroes in Disguise is Pastan's most affirmative book. She makes emphatic use of "relax" and "forgive" and speaks often of happiness. Images of gardens—particularly planting—abound, and she declares allegiance to the mysteries of nature. Pastan celebrates "that old song" desire as well. In short, she attests to her acceptance of earth and self despite their imperfections. During a plane flight ("In Midair"), as she looks out over "a kind of blueprint of earth," she sees humanity "suspended / / by an act of faith, part way / to what we think of as heaven, / and somehow alive."

—Jay S. Paul

PEACOCK, Molly

Nationality: American. **Born:** Buffalo, New York, 30 June 1947. **Education:** State University of New York, Binghamton, B.A. (magna cum laude) 1969; Johns Hopkins University, Baltimore, Maryland, (Danforth Fellow), M.A. (honors) 1976. **Career:** Director of academic advising, 1970-73, and coordinator of innovational projects, 1973-75, State University of New York, Binghamton; poet-in-residence, Delaware State Arts Council, Wilmington, 1978-81, and Buckness University, 1993; writer-in-residence, University of Western Ontario, 1995-96. Artist-in-residence, MacDowell Colony, 1975, 1976, 1979, 1982, 1985, 1989, and Yaddo Colony, 1980, 1982. Visiting lecturer, YMCA, New York, 1986—, Hofstra University, Hempstead, Long Island, New York, 1986, 1988, Columbia University, New York, 1987, Barnard College, 1989, 1990, and New York University, 1989. Learning specialist, Friends Seminary, New York, 1981-92. **Awards:** Creative Arts Public Service award, 1977; Ingram Merrill Foundation award, 1978, 1988; New York Foundation for the Arts award, 1985, 1990; National Endowment for the Arts fellowship, 1991; Woodrow Wilson Foundation fellowship, 1994, 1995, 1996. **Member:** Poetry Society of America (president, 1989-94). **Address:** 505 East 14th Street, #3G, New York, New York 10009, U.S.A; "Villanelle," 229 Emery Street East, London, Ontario N6C 2E3, Canada.

PUBLICATIONS

Poetry

And Live Apart. Columbia, University of Missouri Press, 1980.
Raw Heaven. New York, Random House, 1984.
Take Heart. New York, Random House, 1989.
Original Love: Poems. New York, Norton, 1995.

Other

Editor, *Poetry in Motion: 101 Poems from the Subways and Buses,* with others. New York, Norton, 1996.

*

Critical Studies: "A Venusian Sends a Postcard Home" by Christopher Benfey, in *Parnassus* (New York), vol. 12, no. 2, 1985; "Traditional Form and the Living, Breathing American Poet" by Fred Muratori, in *New England Review / Breadloaf Quarterly* (Boston), vol. 9, no. 2, Winter 1986; "Four from Prospero" by David Wojahn, in *Georgia Review* (Athens), vol. 43, no. 3, fall 1989.

Molly Peacock comments:

Subjects that are often explosive in nature and verse that often experiments with traditional form are some characteristics of my poetry. The main theme that has concerned me is love, in all its manifestations: family love, eroticism, love of self, altruism, religious love, and hatred, of course, too. I favor honesty that sometimes shocks, and temper this with the traditional music of rhyme; therefore even the most painful subjects are examined with lush language and a sense of play. The poems in *Raw Heaven* spin off from the traditional sonnet, with highly sensual points of view. In *Take Heart* I use greater dramatic tension, writing about an alcoholic father, abortion, religious faith, and nuclear war. I hope that hallmarks of my work are humor, daring, and resilient lyric structures.

*   *   *

Molly Peacock is part of that generation of American poets who came of age during the Vietnam War, the largest single such generation in U.S. history, a group that cut its aesthetic teeth on Dadaism, surrealism, and the "logic of classical consummations" which modernism, perhaps erroneously, presupposed to be its inheritance and trial. Peacock's generation, much influenced by feminism, is primarily revisionary, formed by electronic American life and propelled by the apocalyptic psychoanalytical and political imperatives of a relentless questioning of what is conscious and what is unconscious, what is private and what is public, what is spirit and exactly where spirit becomes entangled with the body of matter as matters move their way. This generation has entered literature somewhat as a hand-held cannon enters a push-button war, and the Freudian undergarments of such imagery are something Peacock's poetry has much explored.

Peacock's body of work—*And Live Apart, Raw Heaven, Take Heart,* and *Original Love*—is rightly identified as being an important part of the resurgence of inherited forms that took place in the poetry of the United States in the 1980s. Her contribution, distinguished by its metaphysical idiom and approach, is marked by idiosyncrasies which call to mind Marianne Moore's work, while it was Elizabeth Bishop's poetry which released Peacock into the colloquial eloquence she has made purely—with imperfection as part of her aesthetic—her own. Peacock has found her freedom in being bound, and her signature use of rhyme has been particularly inventive, amusing, skilled, and put to dramatic use. In "She Lays" (from *Raw Heaven*), one of Peacock's hallmark poems, a scene of masturbation is a poignant occasion both linguistically, sexually, and socially: "... revelation without astonishment, / understanding what is meant. / This is world-love. This is lost I'm."

A reader moves through Peacock's obsessive rhyme schemes, sometimes further conceptualized by use of an anagram or some other *a priori* warp, with both ease and inevitability. It is not so much end rhyme that gives her work such a formal poise—though there is, characteristically, incessant end rhyme—but more to the point is the deployment of endless sound chambers in her poems which render the very movement of words inherently formal, artful, and self-conscious but awash in the bravura of the meaning the words go after, come after. Her meters often form into free verse (her work has mistakenly been reviewed in America as iambic, perhaps presumed because of her use of rhyme), but the most important formal device of her poetry is the underlying dramatic form which is always driving the machine, bending the meanings in their propulsion toward closure, sculpting a lineation wherein each line is both an action, a recovery, and a horizon. Her use of rhyme is akin to the uses to which James Cummins put the sestina form in his book of poems *The Whole Truth*—ebullient, exacting, rending thought and heart in a narrative of movements which are absolutely integral and inevitable to the subject matter at hand.

Peacock's work stands out among many in her generation by its shameless use of abstract idiom and imagery, turning, in effect, an ongoing revision of William Carlos Williams' "No ideas but in things" on its imagistic head. Williams' dictum somehow remains at the center of American phenomenology, and the concreteness it has inspired in North American poetry has made for both high moments of objectivist epiphanies and low instances of materialistic listings and descriptions. In terms of rhetorical effusion Peacock's work harks back more to a Yeats and in terms of theme and tone more to the moral metaphysics we might associate with a Donne or a Landor.

In contemporary terms Peacock's work is also remarkably close in spirit and execution to W.D. Snodgrass and particularly the Snodgrass of *Heart's Needle*. Autobiographical somewhere to the side of Ginsberg's mad mouthings, Plath's spells, and Lowell's historical self-absorptions, Peacock's work advances the terrain of *Heart's Needle* both in its ingenious (and unobtrusive) use of rhyme and in its ruminations upon psychological and social states and circumstances. Her work makes much of sexuality, abortion, life in cities, life spent close to or distant from others, and life spent in response to the unaffording costs and persistently available revenues and expenses of our childhoods. Peacock has found the means to present psychological material in a context which is not solipsistic, while she delineates social states mercifully devoid of politically correct cant.

—Liam Rector

PHILIP, Marlene Nourbese

Nationality: Caribbean. **Born:** Moriah, Tobago, 1947. **Education:** University of the West Indies, B.A. in economics 1938; University of Western Ontario, M.A. in political science 1970, LL.D. 1973. **Family:** Married to Paul Chamberlain; three children. **Career:** Practiced immigration and family law, 1975-82; freelance writer, 1982—; teacher of creating writing and women's literature at schools, including York University, University of Toronto, and Ontario College of Art. **Awards:** Casa de la Americas prize, 1988; Canadian Children's Book Centre Choice award, 1989; Guggenheim fellowship, 1990; Macdowell fellowship. **Address:**c/o Mercury Press, 137 Birmingham St., Stratford, Ontario N5A 2T1, Canada.

PUBLICATIONS

Poetry

Thorns. Toronto, Williams-Wallace, 1980.
Salmon Courage. Toronto, Williams-Wallace, 1983.

She Tries Her Tongue, Her Silence Softly Breaks. Charlottetown, Ragweed, 1989.

Novels

Harriet's Daughter. London, Heinemann, 1988.
Looking for Livingstone: An Odyssey of Silence. Stratford, Ontario, Mercury Press, 1991.

Other

Frontiers: Essays and Writings on Racism and Culture. Stratford, Mercury Press, 1992.
Showing Grit: Showboating North of the 44th Parallel. Toronto, Poui Publications, 1993.

*

Critical Studies: "After Modernism: Alternative Voices in the Writings of Dionne Brand, Claire Harris, and Marlene Philip" by Lynette Hunter, in *University of Toronto Quarterly,* vol. 62, no. 2, 1992 / 1993; "Canadian Women of Color in the New World Order: Marlene Nourbese Philip, Joy Kogawa, and Beatrice Culleton Fight Their Way Home" by Heather Zwicker, in *Canadian Women Writing Fiction,* edited by Mickey Pearlman, Jackson, University Press of Mississippi, 1993; "To 'Heal the Word Wounded': Agency and the Materiality of Language and Form in Marlene Nourbese Philip's *She Tries Her Tongue, Her Silence Softly Breaks*" by Brenda Carr, in *Studies in Canadian Literature,* vol. 19, no. 1, 1994; "Marlene Nourbese Philip and the Poetics / Politics of Silence" by Cristanne Miller, in *The Semantics of Silences in Linguistics and Literature,* edited by Gudrun Grabher and Ulrike Jessner, Heidelberg, Universitaetsverlag C. Winter, 1996; "Dream of the Mother Language: Myth and History in *She Tries Her Tongue, Her Silence Softly Breaks*" by Naomi Guttman, in *MELUS,* vol. 21, no. 3, fall 1996; "Mixing It Up in Marlene Nourbese Philip's Poetic Recipes" by Cristanne Miller, in *Women Poets of the Americas,* edited by Jacque Brogan, University of Notre Dame Press, 1997.

*   *   *

For the 1997 *Who's Who of Canadian Women,* Marlene Nourbese Philip stated: "I am a poet and writer who lives in the City of Toronto with my husband and children. My supreme endeavor is to contribute to a more just and equitable society whenever I can. My achievement is to continue to have faith that this is possible and to face obstructions to that goal with some equanimity and dignity."

As one can gather from the above statement, Philip's writing is informed by her political commitment to justice, an end to institutionalized racism and equal recognition of people of color in Canadian society. Receiving critical acclaim for her third book of poetry, *She Tries Her Tongue, Her Silence Softly Breaks,* which won the Casa de las Americas prize in 1988 while still in manuscript, Philip has still had difficulty publishing her work. Her juvenile novel, *Harriet's Daughter,* was rejected by many Canadian presses because its protagonist and most of the novel's characters are black Canadians. The novel was finally published in England by Heinemann and later by the Women's Press in Canada and has been extremely successful in Great Britain, Canada, and the Caribbean.

Difficult to pigeon-hole as a writer because of her experimentation with form, Philip's oeuvre maintains certain thematic consistencies: the search for an identity and a language in which to express the losses of culture, myth, and history which resulted from African slavery and its legacy in the Caribbean; the challenges of split identity for African-Caribbean peoples growing up in a British-colonial culture; the problems for members of the African-Caribbean diaspora as they move to the United States, Canada, England, and elsewhere for economic and educational opportunities; and the significance of language and silence, especially for women, people of color, the displaced, and the colonized.

Writing in many identifiable genres: poem, novel, and essay, Philip often deliberately blurs traditional generic boundaries by including, for example, a long introductory essay in her book of poems, *She Tries Her Tongue,* and weaving poetry into her essay, "Dis Place the Space Between." As the title of that essay makes clear, Philip's goal is to work "the space between" the traditional genres in order to challenge her readers on several levels—the level of form or genre, the level of language, and the level of subject—so that what we take away from her work is a new understanding not simply of *her* work but of the ways in which we are trained to "read" prose and poetry in our culture. Philip questions the value of the traditional boundaries between forms because she questions all tradition and is interested in having audience question their assumptions about the boundaries between "fact" and "fiction."

Philip is particularly interested in the predicament of language for the African-Caribbean community who, as a result of the European slave-trade and racism, were denied the right to speak their original African languages in the New World. Lamenting the great losses of identity and culture this denial has wrought, some Caribbean writers promote the reproduction of Caribbean vernacular speech in their work to the exclusion of standard English. Philip herself, however, works in a variety of English dialects, believing that to write only in Caribbean English would restrict her artistic options as well as the truth. As she writes in the introductory essay to *She Tries Her Tongue,* "It is *in the continuum of expression* from standard to Caribbean English that the veracity of experience lies." "Discourse on the Logic of Language," a poem made up of several texts displayed on the page in a non-traditional manner, stresses this double-blind of language for the Caribbean writer, for, as Philip writes, "English / is my mother tongue," but it is also a "father tongue," and thus "a foreign language," or "a foreign anguish."

Playing with and in the dialects of this "continuum" is one of Philip's many strengths as a poet as are her consistent puns, repetitions, internal rhymes and non-traditional uses of the page. The poem, "Questions! Questions!" from *She Tries Her Tongue,* begins with the lines "Where she, where she / be, where she gone? / Where high and low meet I search / find can't, way down the island's way." This is part of a series of poems which reenact the mythical search for the "mother tongue" or the original language that has been lost because of displacement to the New World.

Coming out of her examination of the experience of language for Caribbean English speakers in *She Tries Her Tongue,* the book *Looking for Livingstone: An Odyssey of Silence,* explores the possibilities of silence as a means of communication and resistance. Described by some critics as a postmodern novel, the book charts "the traveler's" journey "to the interior" in search of Livingstone, the 19th-century English "discoverer" of central Africa. Taking place in a world whose space and time referents are unfamiliar to us (a journal entry might begin: "THE HUNDREDTH DAY OF THE HUNDREDTH MONTH IN THE SEVEN BILLIONTH YEAR OF OUR WORLD"), Philip has her "Traveler" meet several tribes whose names are all anagrams of the word silence. During each of these encounters she learns something about the significance of her search, though often it is unclear what she is learning. For example, during her visit to the NEECLIS, the Traveler is locked up in a room with yarns and a loom and asked to "Piece together the words of your silence" "Or weave a tapestry." Ultimately the Traveler "discovers" silence itself, and how it can be used for power as well as for oppression. As Philip states in interview with Janice Williamson: "I was trying to grapple with whether silence comes before the word, or whether silence has any validity. I think to be silenced is a bad thing; I'm not sure that silence is necessarily a bad thing, particularly is you impose it on yourself for your own reasons."

—Naomi Guttman

PIERCY, Marge

Nationality: American. **Born:** Detroit, Michigan, 31 March 1936. **Education:** University of Michigan, Ann Arbor (Hopwood award, 1956, 1957), A.B. 1957; Northwestern University, Evanston, Illinois, M.A. 1958. **Family:** Married Ira Wood (third marriage) in 1982. **Career:** Instructor, Indiana University, Gary, 1960-62; poet-in-residence, University of Kansas, Lawrence, 1971; visiting lecturer, Thomas Jefferson College, Grand Valley State College, Allendale, Michigan, 1975; visiting faculty, Women's Writers' Conference, Cazenovia College, New York, 1976, 1978, 1980; staff member, Fine Arts Work Center, Provincetown, Massachusetts, 1976-77; writer-in-residence, College of the Holy Cross, Worcester, Massachusetts, 1976; Butler Professor of Letters, State University of New York, Buffalo, 1977; Elliston Professor of Poetry, University of Cincinnati, 1986; DeRoy Distinguished Visiting Professor, University of Michigan, 1992. **Awards:** Borestone Mountain award, 1968, 1974; National Endowment for the Arts grant, 1978; Rhode Island School of Design Faculty Association Medal, 1985; Carolyn Kizer prize, 1986, 1990; Sheaffer Eaton-P.E.N. New England award, 1989; Golden Rose Poetry prize, New England Poetry Club, 1991; May Sarton award, New England Poetry Club, 1991; Brit ha-Dorot award, Shalom Center, 1992; Barbara Bradley award, New England Poetry Club, 1992; Arthur C. Clarke award, 1993. **Member:** Massachusetts Cultural Council (member, board of directors, 1982-85), Massachusetts Council on the Arts and Humanities. **Agent:** Lois Wallace, Wallace Literary Agency, 177 East 70th Street, New York, New York 10021; and Sara Fisher, A.M. Heath, 79 St. Martin's Lane, London WC2N 4AA, England. **Address:** Box 1473, Wellfleet, Massachusetts 02667, U.S.A.

PUBLICATIONS

Poetry

Breaking Camp. Middletown, Connecticut, Wesleyan University Press, 1968.

Hard Loving. Middletown, Connecticut, Wesleyan University Press, 1969.

A Work of Artifice (broadside). Detroit, Red Hanrahan Press, 1970.

4-Telling, with others. Trumansburg, New York, Crossing Press, 1971.

When the Drought Broke (broadside). Santa Barbara, California, Unicorn Press, 1971.

To Be of Use. New York, Doubleday, 1973.

Living in the Open. New York, Knopf, 1976.

The 12-Spoked Wheel Flashing. New York, Knopf, 1978.

The Moon Is Always Female. New York, Knopf, 1980.

Circles on the Water: Selected Poems. New York, Knopf, 1982.

Stone, Paper, Knife. New York, Knopf, and London, Pandora Press, 1983.

My Mother's Body. New York, Knopf, and London, Pandora Press, 1985.

Available Light. New York, Knopf, and London, Pandora Press, 1988.

Mars and Her Children. New York, Knopf, 1992.

Eight Chambers of the Heart, Selected Poems. London, Penguin, 1995.

What Are Big Girls Made Of? New York, Knopf, 1997.

Recordings: *Laying Down the Tower,* Black Box, 1973; *Reclaiming Ourselves,* Radio Free People, 1973; *Reading and Thoughts,* Everett Edwards, 1976; *At the Core,* Watershed, 1976; *New Letters on the Air,* University of Missouri—Kansas City, 1989; *be careful, there's a baby in the house,* Green Linnet Records, Inc., 1991.

Play

The Last White Class: A Play about Neighborhood Terror, with Ira Wood (produced Northampton, Massachusetts, 1978). Trumansburg, New York, Crossing Press, 1980.

Novels

Going Down Fast. New York, Simon & Schuster, 1969.

Dance the Eagle to Sleep. New York, Doubleday, 1970; London, W.H. Allen, 1971.

Small Changes. New York, Doubleday, 1973.

Woman on the Edge of Time. New York, Knopf, 1976; London, Women's Press, 1979.

The High Cost of Living. New York, Harper, 1978; London, Women's Press, 1979.

Vida. New York, Summit, and London, Women's Press, 1980.

Braided Lives. New York, Summit, and London, Allen Lane, 1982.

Fly Away Home. New York, Summit, and London, Chatto & Windus, 1984.

Gone to Soldiers. New York, Summit, and London, M. Joseph, 1987.

Summer People. New York, Summit, and London, M. Joseph, 1989.

He, She and It. New York, Knopf, 1991; as *Body of Glass.* London, M. Joseph, 1992.

The Longings of Women. New York, Fawcett, and London, M. Joseph, 1994.

City of Darkness, City of Light. New York, Fawcett, 1996.

Other

The Grand Coolie Damn. Boston, New England Free Press, 1970.

Parti-Colored Blocks for a Quilt. Ann Arbor, University of Michigan Press, 1982.

Editor, *Early Ripening: American Women's Poetry Now.* London and New York, Pandora Press, 1987.

*

Bibliography: In *Contemporary American Women Writers: Narrative Strategies* edited by Catherine Rainwater and William J. Scheick, Lexington, University Press of Kentucky, 1985; *Marge Piercy: An Annotated Bibliography* by Patrick Doherty, 1995.

Manuscript Collection: Harlan Hatcher Graduate Library, University of Michigan, Ann Arbor.

Critical Studies: "A Black Poet Speaks of Poetry" by June Jordan, *American Poetry Review,* July / August 1974; "Marge Piercy: A Collage" by Nancy Scholar Zee, *Oyez Review* (Berkeley, California), vol. 9, no. 1, 1975; *Ways of Knowing: Critical Essays on Marge Piercy* edited by Sue Walker and Eugenie Hamner, Mobile, Alabama, Negative Capability Press, 1986; "You Are Your Own Magician: A Vision of Integrity in the Poetry of Marge Piercy" by Jean Rosenbaum, and "Marge Piercy: A Vision of the Peaceable Kingdom" by Victor Contoski, both *Modern Poetry Studies,* no. 8, 1977; "Excellence in Poetry" by Hayden Carruth, *Harper's Magazine* (New York), November 1978; "'Grabbing the Gusto' Marge Piercy's Poetry by Jerome Judson, *Writer's Digest* (Cincinnati, Ohio), no. 61, 1981; "Imagery of Association in the Poetry of Marge Piercy" by Edith Wynne, *Publications of the Missouri Philological Association,* 1985; "Amber Mayflies of the Moment: A Brief Introduction to Marge Piercy and Her Poems," *Outlet,* Dubuque, Iowa, 1993; *An Alchemy of Genres: Cross-Genre Writing by American Women* by Diane P. Freedman, University Press of Virginia, 1994.

Marge Piercy comments:

I have always worked to try to make my poems accessible and meaningful to an audience. That does not mean that the poem is necessarily simple; it is as complicated as it needs to be. A poem can speak through rich and complex imagery as long as it is emotionally coherent. I also write a type of poem with little or no ornament, just as I also work in long line, short lines, and lines that hover around iambic tetrameter or pentameter. In making the arrangement of sounds and silences that the notation of a poem on the page is supposed to create in the air or in the reader's mind, I am working in measures drawn from American speech and American prosody. However, my influences are various, ancient as well as modern, and international.

I imagine that I speak for a constituency, living and dead, and that I give utterance to energy, experience, insight, words flowing from many lives as well as my own. In truth I don't make much distinction between the sources inside and outside. What I mean by being of use is not that the poems function as agitprop or that they are didactic, although some of them are. I have no more hesitation than Pope or Hesiod did to write in that mode as well as many others. What I mean is simply that readers will find poems that speak to and for them, take those poems into their lives and say them to each other and put them up on the kitchen or bathroom or bedroom wall and remember bits of them in stressful or quiet times. That the poems may give voice to something in the experience of our lives has been my intention. For women especially to find ourselves spoken for in art gives dignity to our pain, our anger, our lust, our losses. We can hear what we hope for and what we fear, in the small release of cadenced utterance.

*   *   *

Marge Piercy is one of the most prolific poets; she has a large international following, and her work has been translated into a number of languages. Her poetry is informal, often prosy, and based on the rhythms of American speech. In her introduction to *Circles on the Water* she explains, "once in a great while I do work in rhyme ... mostly in the center of lines rather than on the end where to my ear it sticks out and chimes." Although Piercy strives to be "accessible and meaningful," her poems are studded with classical references and she aligns herself with Pope and Hesiod in the didacticism of some of her work.

Coming to maturity in the 1960s, she began writing as a political poet, drawing inspiration from her roots as an American, working-class, Jewish woman. Her first two volumes, *Breaking Camp* and *Hard Loving,* reveal her preoccupation with the civil rights, peace, and women's movements.

In the mid-1970s her poetry took on a rural focus when she moved from New York to a farmhouse on Cape Cod. The rhythms of rural life inspire many of her later poems, particularly in the volumes *Living in the Open* and *The 12-Spoked Wheel Flashing.* Moving from nature to Mother Earth in *The Moon Is Always Female,* Piercy channels her earlier feminism into an exploration of femininity. Fascinated with pagan relics and lunar myths, the poet relates the cycles of her own life to the cycles of the seasons. Love, lust, and personal commitment are prevailing concerns, and Piercy begins to confront her background in a theme which comes to fruition in her later volume *My Mother's Body.* Though written in memory of her mother, this book is really a tribute to all unacknowledged women:

I am pregnant with certain deaths
of women who choked before they
could speak their names
could know their names
before they had names to know.
("They Inhabit Me")

In the title poem, Piercy tackles her mother's death: "My father heard the crash but paid / no mind, napping after lunch, / yet fifteen hundred miles north / I heard and dropped a dish. / Your pain sunk talons in my skull / and crouched there cawing." Eventually the poet reconciles herself to her lost mother: "This body is your body, ashes now / and roses, but alive in my eyes, my breasts, / my throat, my thighs. You run in me / a tang of salt in the creek waters of my blood, / you sing in my mind like wine. What you / did not dare in your life you dare in mine."

In the second section life is reaffirmed through marriage, though Piercy resists any easy homilies. "Witnessing a Wedding" warns, "It is not strangeness in the mate / you must fear, and not the fear / that loosens us so we lean back ... but familiarity we must mistrust, / the word based on the family / that fogs the sight and plugs the nose." The final two sections concentrate on the mundane rituals of daily living with some delightfully sensual, original poems like "Six Underrated Pleasures," which praises folding sheets, picking beans, taking hot baths, planting bulbs, canning, and sleeping with cats:

They are curled into flowers
of fur, they are coiled

hot seashells of flesh in my armpits, around my head
a dark sighing halo.
They are plastered to my side,
a poultice fixing sore muscles
better than a heating pad.
They snuggle up to my sex
purring. They embrace my feet

Piercy's collection *Available Light* continues to honor vegetable love in such poems as "Morning Love Song," which begins: "I am filled with love like a melon / with seeds, I am ripe and dripping sweet juices. / If you knock gently on my belly / it will thrum ripe, ripe." Strongly autobiographical, the collection displays a wry sense of humor; for example, "Something to Look Forward To" is a mischievous exposé of menopause:

How often halfway up the side of a mountain,
during a demonstration with the tactical police
force drawn up in tanks between me and a toilet;
during an endless wind machine panel with four males
I the token woman and they with iron bladders,

I have felt that wetness and wanted to strangle
my womb like a mouse.

One of the most moving poems in the collection, "Joy Road and Livernois," illustrates Piercy's ability to rail against injustice without ever losing sense of the individuals behind the politics; after charting a group of childhood friends through prostitution, addiction, suicide, and madness, the poet confesses that

I got out of those Detroit blocks where the air
eats stone and melts flesh, where jobs
dangle and you jump and jump, where there are
more drugs than books, more ways to die
than ways to live, because I ran fast
ran hard, and never stopped looking back.
It is not looking back that turned me
to salt, no, I taste my salt from the mines
under Detroit, the salt of our common juices.
Girls who lacked everything except trouble,
contempt and rough times, girls
used like urinals, you are the salt
keeps me from rotting as the years swell.
I am the fast train you are travelling in
to a world of a different color, and the love
we cupped so clumsily in our hands to catch
rages and drives onward, an engine of light.

Beneath the politics, behind the feminist, the nature seeker, or the amused, amazed, or enraged lover, there is always a sense of reverence, an irrepressible celebration of life.

—Katie Campbell

PITT-KETHLEY, (Helen) Fiona

Nationality: British. **Born:** Edgware, Middlesex, 21 November 1954. **Education:** Haberdashers' Aske's Girls' School, 1960-71;

Chelsea School of Art, London, 1972-76, B.A. (honors). **Agent:** Giles Gordon, Anthony Sheil Associates, 43 Doughty Street, London WC1N 2LF. **Address:** 7 Ebenezer Road, Hastings, East Sussex TN34 3BS, England.

PUBLICATIONS

Poetry

London. Privately printed, 1984.
Rome. Bath, Mammon Press, 1985.
The Tower of Glass. Glasgow, Mariscat Press, 1985.
Sky Ray Lolly. London, Chatto & Windus, 1986.
Gesta. London, Turret, 1986.
Private Parts. London, Chatto & Windus, 1987.
The Perfect Man. London, Abacus, 1989.
Dogs. London, Sinclair-Stevenson, 1993.

Novels

The Misfortunes of Nigel. London, Peter Owen, 1991.
The Maiden's Progress. London, Turret, 1992.

Other

Journeys to the Underworld. London, Chatto & Windus, 1988.
Too Hot to Handle. London, Peter Owen, 1992.
The Pan Principle. London, Sinclair-Stevenson, 1994.

Editor, *The Literary Companion to Sex.* London, Sinclair-Stevenson, 1992; New York, Random House, 1994.

*

Fiona Pitt-Kethley comments:

I am a satirist. My satire is aimed chiefly at contemporary hypocrisies. A lot of these are centered around sexuality. I think my work differs from all past satire in one respect. In order not to seem self-righteous I satirize myself at the same time as criticizing others, using incidents from my own life to illustrate the points I am making.

(1995) I am one of the most versatile and hard-working authors on the poetic scene. Apart from poetry, my main vocation, I have produced travel books, novels, anthologies, and a massive amount of journalism. I am currently a critic for the London *Times* and have worked for most of the quality newspapers. I have also traveled extensively as I am writing a book of essays on the world's red-light districts. I have performed my poems around the country and for radio and TV. I have, to date, been considered too controversial for any major grants or awards but hope that this situation will change.

*   *   *

Readers of the *London Review of Books* have come to half expect, when scanning the classifieds, to light upon the statement that FIONA PITT-KETHLEY IS AVAILABLE. The demands of publicity are disconcerted by such compliance: whosoever compelleth her to go a mile, she goeth with him twain—even the innuendo is astringently straightforward. She is available to give readings from her own poetry, whose effect is doubtless doubled,

but perhaps also skewed, by the memorable name thus promoted, with its suggestion that The Roedean Rake is Coming Clean.

For actually—an important distinction—it was the Chelsea School of Art. She has a good poem, "The Hidden Persuaders," which shows her ignoring a sixth-form book list for the Oxbridge-bound ("all modern, serious but popular"):

> I gave the lot up and went in for Art.
> I'll wash my own brains, thank you very much.

Fair enough, but in the poems she brings to market, she washes other peoples' dirty linen and comments with the traditional freedom of washerwomen. The subject of her satire is often that heavy inheritance of nervous hypocrisy, incompetence, and miscalculation that thwarts and inflames appetite in the Sons of Adam. The pitiful instances are real, and the voice that speaks the poems, being unambiguously her own, seems in turn wide-eyed, explosively amusing, and more than a touch caddish.

Occasionally, for instance, we get a whiff of *l'esprit* (or *la revanche*) *d'escalier.* She will placard her victim by name:

> *Ken Roberts*
>
> Ken Roberts rings me up to ask if I
> like going to the cinema alone—
> and, like a fool, I stop to talk to him.
>
> He says he bets that he could turn me on.
> (I bet he can't.) I say this, but it's hard
> to put his kind of bubbly pervert down.

Hard? Maybe—but that last phrase does it. The Voice of Female Experience has him formulated, sprawling on a pin, and it is memorably funny. Sometimes, though, her tactics are really deplorable. An earlier version of one of her better poems included a name whose owner begged her to remove it. She could have justifiably refused, but complied—only to spell out the whole story in a footnote that effectively revealed her correspondent's identity and left the sour taste of spite mixed in with the clean one of indignation.

She can write marvelously without either:

> We smelt the baby oil from the back row.
> The "Senior Mr. Hastings" was judged first.
> The oldest held a world above his head
> (invisible) to music of the spheres.

These almost Dickensian escapes from the predictable are accomplished with such ease that one puzzles at her relapses. Of these, the most important occur in the 70-line poem, central to her work as a whole, called "Prostitution." It is one of those poems ("Gents Only," the splendid "Phone Call," and, of course, her *L.R.B.* small ad are others) where the exploitative hypocrisies of sex are linked to those of the book trade. Some lines can take your head off:

> Chatto's my pimp. My cut is five percent
> (well in arrears)

or, more winsomely:

> What should I do, what chances do I have?
> Arvon—the poet's pools? (Yes we all try.)

Surely, here, she has found her major subject? And what possibilities! The ghosts of Pope and Gissing, of Pound and Aphra Behn hover near the midnight belfry. Will the iron tongue of Satire sound again? Or will we hear naught but Obsession, beating its leathery wings?

> The under-thirties Gregory Awards?
> (Twenty to women out of 144.)
> I was turned down for one of those six times.
> Anthony Thwaite seems guilty on that score.

What a disappointment! What thin and bitter gruel!

> Of course, the Arts Council does grants...just three.
> But '87 was Caribbean Year,
> so every applicant *had to be* black.

The Female Casanova is changing before our eyes into The Mad Victim. The bloody buggers in suits are going to get off. Again.

The truth is that, as with most of us, Pitt-Kethley's sense of justice is too self-centered to appeal convincingly to others. Her anecdotes, therefore (and her poems are nearly always anecdotal), do not always escape the monotonies of parti pris, and, as a result, their principled hedonism and frankness seem weirdly ungenerous. She is at her best when a burst of verbal inventiveness and humor wins us into complicity. And that happens either at her most delicate ("Mr. Hastings") or at her most indelicate:

> Large cocks are good for narcissism, not sex.
> Their owners have this tendency to stand
> as if they're waiting for a prize at Cruft's.
> 'What a big boy! Aren't I the lucky girl?'
> we're meant to say. They're Ozymandias-like
> about their things.

—Hugh Buckingham

PRATT, Minnie Bruce

Nationality: American. **Born:** Selma, Alabama, 12 September 1946. **Education:** University of Alabama, B.A. (with honors) 1968; University of North Carolina at Chapel Hill, Ph.D. in Renaissance English literature 1979. **Family:** Married Marvin E. Weaver in 1966 (divorced 1976); two sons; companion of Leslie Feinberg since 1992. **Career:** Instructor, Fayetteville State University, Fayetteville, North Carolina, 1975-80; assistant professor of English, Shaw University, Raleigh, North Carolina, 1980-82; member of graduate faculty of women's studies program, George Washington University, Washington, D.C. 1984-88; faculty member of women's studies program, University of Maryland, College Park, 1984-91; writer-in-residence, Community Writer's Project, Syracuse, New York, 1988; member of graduate faculty, Union Institute, Cincinnati, Ohio, 1990—. Member of editorial collective, *Feminary: A Feminist Journal for the South, Emphasizing Lesbian Visions,* 1978-83. **Awards:** Woodrow Wilson fellowship, 1968; Fulbright fellowship, 1968; National Endowment of the Arts fellowship, 1968, creative writing fellowship, 1990; Academy of American Poets Lamont Poetry Selection,

1989, for *Crime against Nature; American Voice* Harriet Simpson Arnow Prize, 1990, for "I Am Ready to Tell All I Know"; American Library Association Gay/Lesbian Book Award, 1991, for *Crime against Nature;* Fund for Free Expression Lillian Hellman/Dashiell Hammett award, 1991; Gustavus Myers Center Outstanding Book Award, 1992, for *Rebellion: Essays 1980-1991.* **Agent:** Charlotte Sheedy, 65 Bleecker St., 12th Floor, New York, New York 10012, U.S.A. **Address:** P.O. Box 8212, Jersey City, New Jersey 07308, U.S.A.

PUBLICATIONS

Poetry

The Sound of One Fork (chapbook). Durham, North Carolina, Night Heron Press, 1981.
We Say We Love Each Other. San Francisco, Spinsters Ink, 1985; Ithaca, New York, Firebrand Books, 1992.
Crime against Nature. Ithaca, New York, Firebrand Books, 1990.
Walking Back Up Depot Street. Ithaca, New York, Firebrand Books, forthcoming.

Other

Yours in Struggle: Three Feminist Perspectives on Anti-Semitism and Racism, with Elly Bulkin and Barbara Smith. N.p., Long Haul Press, 1984.
Rebellion: Essays 1980-1991. Ithaca, New York, Firebrand Books, 1991.
S / HE (short stories). Ithaca, New York, Firebrand Books, 1995.

*

Critical Studies: "Poets Live the Questions: Jewelle Gomez and Minnie Bruce Pratt Discuss Politics and Imagination" in *Out / Look,* spring 1992; interview with Elaine Auerbach, in *Belles Lettres,* vol. 8, no. 1, Fall 1992.

Minnie Bruce Pratt comments:

I grow up and read Shelley who says of another nightsinging bird: "A poet is a nightingale, who sits in darkness and sings to cheer its own solitude with sweet sounds."

But I ask myself, "What if the singer—the poet, the writer, the person who moves through the world—has been taught to fear the darkness? How do I sing in a language imbued with the most grotesque images of darkness? A language in which solitude exists only in relation to a damaged damned other?

In the place I grew up, my saw-mill county-seat town in Alabama, the people who ran its economic / sexual system, the racist state, were determined to regulate mind, body, and imagination.

But there was always the danger that folks might decide to go back to raw data, to our sensual and sensory experiences, to the immediate history and shared memory of our lives. We might begin to make our own comparisons, draw our own conclusions, act individually and collectively, write poems and stories about what was not allowed.

So judgements were erected as partitions between us. And the authorities put up signs, everywhere. These were the public words, relentless repetitive reminders. Words that were an attempt to convince us of the inevitability of white racial superiority, of the impossibility of escape from the fact that some were bosses and others servants, of the immovability of a whole system of category and metaphor.

Of course, almost every Southern child, white or black, stopped at least once at water labeled Black or White, and sneaked a sip. We said "This is just like *my* water. What's the difference between us?"

But this was a hidden, secret making of a bond between us. This was a private unspoken metaphor. Any public speech or action that crossed the arbitrary divisions of "race" was discouraged by the authorities, to say the least. To say the most, people often died when, with their lives, they sought to imagine, and then make, a way out of the categories that had been imposed on them.

Public transgression was violently punished, while those who made the laws did their best to control what Trotsky has called "the physical power of thought"—the way an account of the ideas and deeds arising from one struggle for freedom might fire the imagination, and then the actions, of people in other circumstances. For instance, at one time the state I lived in had a "literature ordinance." This law made it a crime to possess one or more pieces of "radical" literature—defined as anti-fascist or labor publications, and as liberal magazines like *The Nation* and *The New Republic.*

For anything might happen if we began to question the words *Black* and *White.* What if we began to question the weight those words carried? If we saw the way some folks' backs bent under the weight, and other folks walked free, and that the reasons given in the words *Black* and *White* made no sense.

Anything might happen if we went underneath the words, back to our bodies, and asked them to speak. Anything might happen if we listened to the other one speaking of her and his life. Our pleasure and pain might not seem so different. Things that we'd been taught were opposite might seem to agree. We'd been kept apart by a rule called "law," called "right reason." Together, we might become creators of a new humanity, a new commonality.

Anything might happen if we took the horrors and wonders of our lives, and claimed ourselves with words that refused to abide in the opposition, the ranking of white and black, or, for that matter, male and female, normal and queer.

Queerness was not marked officially with any sign. But anyone who crossed White and Black was assumed to be queer. Any lover across guarded borders, and challenger to the necessity of rich and poor, any one who brought together contradictions that had been separated into good and evil—that person was called *queer.*

Art was queer, and so were artists. And so was the innate human ability to create—the ability from which language itself arises. The power to see correspondences between two things and make a word from that. The power to make metaphor, to lead people with words to a new connection between disparate realities. The power to find similarities between dissimilars and create language for what is shared.

The gift of carrying life back and forth, back and forth, the work like breath between two distinctly different others. That gift was the queerest act of all.

*   *   *

On the dustjacket of her most recent volume of poetry, *Crime against Nature,* Minnie Bruce Pratt is described as a "lesbian poet, essayist, and teacher." But Pratt's work seems to transcend such categories. She combines her work as a poet, an essayist, and a

teacher with her work as a grass-roots activist. That is not to say that her poetry is didactic. Far from it, she puts the aesthetic to work in the service of the political without surrendering her sense of beauty or compromising her vision of human equality.

Pratt's career as a poet began with the publication of her chapbook, *The Sound of One Fork,* which deals directly with the poet's process of coming to know and understand herself as a lesbian and as a white woman. These themes are developed in her first volume of poems, *We Say We Love Each Other,* in which a community of women emerges as a vital force in the poet's journey towards self-discovery.

The second book of poetry, *Crime against Nature,* is dedicated to Pratt's two sons, Ranson and Ben, who were taken from her when her ex-husband discovered she was a lesbian. In "Poem for My Sons," Pratt prays for her sons to remember her "as a woman making slowly toward / an unknown place." She asks her children's forgiveness for having let their father take them, but she also asks for justice. In "No Place," we are privy to the thoughts of a woman who feels alienated, even among women:

> Groups of women pass by, talking, as if we are not
> there. Who can I ask for help? I am awkward,
> at a loss. We are together, we have come across.
> We have no place to go.

The book registers the anguish and uncertainty of a mother who is ready to give up her shame. Indeed, the self-doubt of the early poems gives way to a righteous anger in the six-part, title poem at the end of the book. In "Crime against Nature" Pratt points to the irony of a system that regards her love for women as a "crime against nature" but refuses to see the concept of child "custody" as the "prison term" it seems to be.

Pratt makes particularly interesting use of punctuation in these poems; they are full of caesuras, pregnant pauses, that refuse to let the reader hurry through. In an interview with Elaine Auerbach Pratt explains that *Crime against Nature* "is in fact a long poem, but I didn't think of having to make a very coherent narrative out of it." The pieces of the book are designed to allow the reader "to pace themselves through this very difficult material."

Pratt is not, if she ever was, simply a lesbian's poet. She identifies as a lesbian, but in *S / HE* her 1995 book of stories, she interrogates those categories of identity such as gender, sex, race, sexuality, and class, that have been assigned to her by other people. In the autobiographical essay called "Gender Quiz," that begins the book, she explains:

> I have lived my life at the intersection of great waves of social change in the United States in the twentieth century: the Black civil rights and liberation movements, the women's liberation movement, the lesbian / gay / bisexual liberation movement, the transgender liberation movement. The theory developed by each has complicated our questions about the categories of race, sex, gender, sexuality, and class. And these theories have advanced our ability to struggle against oppressions that are imposed and justified using these categories.

According to Pratt, questions such as "male or female?" or "white, black, other?" which are ubiquitous and seemingly innocuous, need to be rephrased in order to include those who fall between such categories. Pratt wants us to ask ourselves, "how many ways are there to have the *sex* of girl, boy, man, woman?" and to ask each other, "What is your dream of who you want to be?"

Written in the first person, these episodic stories are autobiographical and speak of both sexual passion and harassment in a language that is refined enough to be called poetry. One paragraph-long story, "Ashes," could easily be a prose poem. Note the extensive use of rhyme and assonance in the following passage: "you told me you began to cry when you read the work *ashes* in one of my poems, you didn't know why." Like the poems in her earlier volumes, these stories are infused with a revolutionary spirit, even at the level of language. The pieces are narrative, yet Pratt suggests that they "give theory flesh and breath."

While it is generically innovative, Pratt's work is thematically coherent. In her 1984 essay, "Identity: Skin Blood Heart," reprinted in *Rebellion,* she makes clear that identity can be based on notions of skin and blood that divide people; she implies that it takes heart to overcome our cultural differences. Since her early work has been reprinted by Firebrand Books, it reaches an ever widening audience and in its wake, forms the community that Pratt finds a continuing source of inspiration.

—Catherine D. Halley

PUGH, Sheenagh

Nationality: British. **Born:** Birmingham, England, 20 December 1950. **Education:** Mundella Grammar School, Nottingham; University of Bristol, 1968-71, B.A. (honors) in German and Russian 1971. **Family:** Married Michael J.H. Burns in 1977; one son and one daughter. **Career:** Higher executive officer, Welsh Office, Cardiff, 1971-79; branch secretary, Society of Civil Servants, Cardiff, 1974-79. Tutor in creative writing, Glamorgan University, 1993—. **Awards:** Babel translation prize, 1984; British Comparative Literature Association translation prize, 1985; Cardiff International Literature Festival prize, 1988, 1994. **Address:** 4C Romilly Road, Canton, Cardiff CF5 1FH, Wales.

PUBLICATIONS

Poetry

Crowded by Shadows. Bridgend, Glamorgan, Poetry Wales Press, 1977.
What a Place to Grow Flowers. Swansea, Triskele, 1979.
Earth Studies and Other Voyages. Bridgend, Glamorgan, Poetry Wales Press, 1982.
Beware Falling Tortoises. Bridgend, Glamorgan, Poetry Wales Press, 1987.
Selected Poems. Bridgend, Glamorgan, Seren Books, 1990.
Sing for the Taxman. Bridgend, Glamorgan, Seren Books, 1993.
Id's Hospit. Bridgend, Glamorgan, Seren Books, 1997.

Other

Translator, *Prisoners of Transience.* Bridgend, Glamorgan, Poetry Wales Press, 1985.

*

Critical Studies: "The Poetry of Sheenagh Pugh" by John Whitehead, in *Babel* (Munich), no. 4, 1984; "Sheenagh Pugh: Interview with Richard Poole," in *Poetry Wales,* January 1995.

Sheenagh Pugh comments:

I write because I like to play with words, to record what interests me and to sound off about what annoys—same as anyone else does. Themes I have kept going back to include death, loneliness, snooker, political tyranny, and fellow-feeling. I wrote some "green" poems early in the 1980s, before anyone else was doing it, but not a lot of people noticed—getting on a bandwagon too early is as bad as too late.

The poets I like best, and have tried to learn from, are Sorley MacLean, Andreas Gryphius, Hans-Ulrich Treichel, and above all Robert Henryson. I like poems to be crafted and literate and not written in chopped-up prose, but not written either in a language which defies the understanding of reasonably intelligent persons. And I like them to be about something that matters; not silly verbal games for bored academics. I hate being called a "woman poet" and have no time for anyone who thinks gender matters outside a bedroom. For actual enjoyment, I prefer translating, especially German poetry of the Thirty Years War period.

*   *   *

Sheenagh Pugh, though born in Birmingham, established her reputation in Wales, where she has lived for a number of years. She is regarded as one of the strongest and most original voices in poetry in Wales, which is, no doubt, due to the freshness and unconventionality of her approach. Her family roots include a Welsh grandmother, but her roots in writing are as cosmopolitan as any poet in Britain. She read Russian and German at Bristol University, and her collection of translations, *Prisoners of Transience,* which won the Babel translation prize in 1984, is perhaps her most notable achievement.

Pugh's first book, *Crowded by Shadows,* drew praise from several reviewers, most notably D.M. Thomas, who called it "The most promising first collection I have read for years.... Her poetry does not, refreshingly, try to put the world to rights, nor finger the abscess of private emotion; instead, it lays itself open to the world of others." Her second collection, *Earth Studies and Other Voyages,* builds on that principle as its title sequence explores the feelings of space travelers who have escaped an earth which seems no longer worth inhabiting and who now live on *Terra 2.* Under titles such as "Geography 1 & 2," "History 1 & 2 & 3," and "Biology 1 & 2 & 3," Pugh allows herself the detachment to sum up ironically the character and failings of the planet as we have used and abused it. One of the astronauts remembers returning from a trip to Iceland:

> When I got back
> to Heathrow, and walked out into Reading.

> I damn near choked on this warm gritty stuff
> I called air; also on the conjecture
> that we'd all settle for second best
> once we'd forgotten there was something more.

This represents a fall from grace in that, when asked about "heaven," one of the older travelers says,

> If you really want to know
> what I think about heaven, the truth is
> I think I lived there.

The 19 poems which constitute the *Earth Studies and Other Studies* sequence may well be one of the earliest examples of a consciously green poetry in Britain.

The other poems in Pugh's second collection, the "Other Voyages" of the title, deal with sailors and conventional sea journeys but also with "Old Widowers" and "The T.V. Hero":

> the likeness of a make-believe man
> fills our space more harmlessly than most.

It is not a feminist point that Pugh is making here; women appear off-center in the bulk of her poetry, like the females in "St. Cuthbert and the Women" who "move, / far off, in their brave colours, bright / as illuminated manuscript initials" and who water the island "with their laughter, their chat about / some small happiness." It is the male personal pronoun which predominates in her writing, which can be off-putting. She has written in *Planet* magazine and elsewhere about her stance on issues of gender in writing. She wants there to be no difference, no significance, a position that has failed to satisfy other women writers who see things in more confrontational terms. She chooses only two women poets in her selection of translations in *Prisoners of Transience,* though that is surely more indicative of the history of women's writing in Europe than any sinister predilection on the part of the poet.

These translations, from two French poets and 13 from the German, range from the twelfth century to Stefan George, who died in the year that Hitler became chancellor of Germany. Pugh's versions respect the rhyme schemes of the originals, though she wisely recognizes that half rhymes are just as acceptable to modern readers. She employs these rhymes and the basis of the iambic pentameter to good effect, and I wonder if her third collection of original poetry, *Beware Falling Tortoises,* published two years later, suffers from the experience. Too often in this collection the poetry lacks tautness and satisfactory resolution; the writing, I feel, could have benefited from the sort of prosodic discipline of which *Prisoners of Transience* proved Pugh most capable. Poems such as "I Am Roerek," "Pharisees," and "He Was a Man of His Word" are thus less accomplished than "She Was 19 and She Was Bored," "A Short History of Cocaine Abuse," and "Memoirs of a Dutch Tulip Merchant." This last is evidence that Pugh can fashion a dramatic monologue—

> I remember I sold
> a single *Semper Augustus*—in '31,
> I think it was, the year the Austrians
> burned Magdeburg—for thousands: everyone
> wanted *Augustus.* It had a white ground
> striped with crimson and iron; the more broken

the colours were, the more it was worth.

This is much more effective than "Crusaders," the poem which follows it. In "Crusaders" the modern voice projects unconvincingly from the character of a medieval knight. Again, in the three-poem sequence "Dieppe" Pugh's attempts to capture the soldiers' voices too often slacken the lines so that the poetry is lost. These attempts to enter fully into character do work, however, to complement the dominant mode of her poetry, which is that of the author's dispassionate gaze and the wry comment. It might be assumed that Pugh's models are Philip Larkin and the Movement rather than Anne Sexton and Sylvia Plath; she maintains, however, "I was, until recently, incredibly ignorant of *all* English verse; all my models, if I had any, were mediaeval, Henryson, mainly." Certainly she is closer to Fleur Adcock than Wendy Cope, and, no matter how strongly one feels that she may be tempted by the neat rhyme and the obvious barb, she generally is in control of her verse. The problem with the poet assuming the role of wry commentator is that the reader may grow to dislike the persona and suspect smugness. Larkin is saved from this fate by his increasingly frequent revelations of his own vulnerability; he is deliberately transparent in the way that his frailty shows beneath the commentary. Pugh rarely offers the reader a glimpse of her deepest feelings. We encounter her brain but not so obviously her heart. These lines from "Cameraman" seem apposite:

> Do not be tempted
> to turn the camera inward:
> your stricken looks are no concern
> of the public's. They need the word
>
> on what you saw, not how
> you felt. It is they who must feel
> they saw it; they were there; so
> involved, they condemn somewhat
> the remote like of you.

Time and the vagaries of life may well pull Pugh more centrally into her own poetry. With the appearance in 1990 of her *Selected Poems* and the culling of weaker work, Pugh would seem to have reached the middle point of her achievement as a poet. If she can successfully build on her strengths as a translator and deploy further the prosodic skills she has exhibited there in the service of her often unnerving eye, then she should establish herself as one of the more notable contemporary voices.

—Tony Curtis

R

REPLANSKY, Naomi

Nationality: American. **Born:** Bronx, New York, 23 May 1918. **Education:** Hunter College, New York, 1935-38; University of California, Los Angeles, B.A. 1956. **Family:** Companion of Eva Kollisch since 1986. **Career:** Worked variously as a lathe operator, stewardess aboard an ocean liner, assembly worker, draftswoman, medical editor, bibliographic coder, and computer programmer. Teacher of English, Gardiner's Ecole de Langues, Paris, 1949-50; poet-in-residence, Pitzer College, Claremont, California, 1981; teacher of writing workshops at Henry St. Settlement and Educational Alliance, New York, 1982-94. Translator from the German of poems by Hofmannsthal, Claudius, and Brecht for anthologies and periodicals. **Awards:** National Book Award nomination, 1952, for *Ring Song*. **Address:** 711 Amsterdam Ave., #8E, New York, New York 10025, U.S.A.

PUBLICATIONS

Poetry

Ring Song. New York, Scribner, 1952.
Twenty-one Poems, Old and New (chapbook). New York, Ginko, 1988.
The Dangerous World: New and Selected Poems, 1934-1994. Chicago, Another Chicago Press, 1994.

Play

Adaptor, *St. Joan of the Stockyards* by Bertold Brecht, produced New York, 1978.

*

Manuscript Collection: Berg Collection, New York Public Library.

Critical Studies: "On Naomi Replansky's Poems" by Patricia Hample, in *Lamp in the Spine* (St. Paul, Minnesota), 1973-74; "Fragile Strengths, Complex Simplicities" by Florence Howe, in *Women's Review of Books,* December 1995; "Justice, Poverty and Gender: Social Themes in the Poetry of Naomi Replansky" (thesis) by Ashley Ray, City University of New York, 1996.

Naomi Replansky comments:

My chief poetic influences have been: William Blake, folk songs, Shakespeare, George Herbert, Emily Dickinson, and Japanese poetry.

*   *   *

Naomi Replansky's poetic output consists of two collections widely spaced in time: 1952's *Ring Song* and 1994's *The Dangerous World: New and Selected Poems, 1934-1994.* The critical response to her first collection drove Replansky into a self-imposed silence from which it took some 40 years to recover.

Ring Song was written when Replansky was between the ages of 15 and 19, although it was published when she was in her early thirties. Nominated for a National Book Award at the time of its publication in 1952, *Ring Song* contains poems that M.L. Rosenthal in *New Republic* believed were "alive and bright with color and feeling" and which Shirley Barker of *Library Journal* noted were "of high artistic merit." The product of a self-taught, working-class woman who learned the craft of poetry while working in factories and stores, the collection features Replansky's rhymed couplets focusing on the joy of surviving adversity. The title poem, for example, ends with the couplet "When the cold does not destroy / I leap from ambush on my joy." Other poems touch on political issues of the time, focus on everyday life among factory workers, or speak of failed love.

Although some critics gave Replansky's *Ring Song* good notices, there were others who pointed out the inevitable flaws in poems written by someone so young. Lawrence Ferling in the *San Francisco Chronicle* found "some very uneven writing" and opined that "in a few years she may be writing some very wonderful things." A.M. Sullivan in *Saturday Review* praised Replansky's "vitality" and "freshness," but found "too much cynicism" in evidence. Rosenthal claimed that some of the poems were "highstrung, even shrill at times" and showed evidence of being "set down with not quite enough revision."

Such criticism silenced Replansky and she published no new poetry for many years, although still writing. Feminist critics credit the male literary establishment for driving Replansky to silence, although the criticism she received for a first collection does not, in retrospect, seem particularly harsh. Nonetheless, it was not until 1995 that a second collection of her work appeared. *The Dangerous World: New and Selected Poems, 1934-1994* gathers 25 poems from the first volume (some of them revised) and 42 poems written in the intervening years. The new collection includes many love poems, including "The Oasis" in which Replansky celebrates her lesbian lover: "I thought the desert ended, and I felt / The fountains leap. / Then gratitude could answer gratitude / Till sleep entwined with sleep." In the collection's title poem she worries of her lover that "You hold me as a glass holds water. / You can be shattered like a glass." *The Dangerous World* offers readers a more self-assured version of the poet than that found in *Ring Song,* one who is secure and happy, one suspects, because of the love she has found late in her life. It also exhibits Replansky's gift for writing delicate lyrics that celebrate in simple, sculpted language the joys and beauties of her life.

—Denise Wiloch

RETALLACK, Joan

Nationality: American. **Career:** Poet and theorist. Currently teaches in interdisciplinary honors program, University of Maryland. Visiting Butler Chair Professor of English, State University of New York, 1998-94; poet-in-residence at numerous institutions, including Brown University, Stanford University, University of

Maine, University of California, San Diego, and Mills College. Associate, Bard College Institute for Writing and Thinking. **Awards:** Columbia Book Award, 1994, for *Errata 5uite;* Gertrude Stein award for Innovative American Poetry; National Endowment for the Arts grant for *WESTORN CIV CONT'D, An Open Book.*

PUBLICATIONS

Poetry

Circumstantial Evidence. Washington, D.C., Sultan of Swat Books, 1985.
How to Do Things with Words. College Park, Maryland, Sun & Moon Press, n.d.
Errata 5uite. Washington, D.C., Edge Books, 1993.
AFTERRIMAGES. Middletown, Connecticut, Wesleyan University Press, 1995.

Performance Pieces

WESTERN CIV. N.p, n.d.
WESTORN CIV CONT'D, An Open Book. N.p., n.d.
And That's It, music by Andrew Culver, produced 1998.

Other

":RE:THINKING:LITERARY:FEMINISM: (three essays onto shaky grounds)," in *Feminist Measures: Soundings in Poetry and Theory,* edited by Lynn Keller and Christanne Miller. Ann Arbor, University of Michigan Press, 1994.
MUSICAGE: Cage Muses on Words*Art*Music: John Cage in Conversation with Joan Retallack. Middletown, Connecticut, Wesleyan University Press, 1996.

*

Critical Studies: Article by A.L. Nielsen, in *Washington Review,* vol. 11, no. 5, 1995; "Women Writers and the Restive Text: Feminism, Experimental Writing and Hypertext" by Barbara Page, in *Postmodern Culture,* vol. 6, no. 2, January 1996.

*   *   *

In her poetry and criticism, Joan Retallack explores the spaces beyond what she sees as a male hierarchical poetics. Utilizing self-imposed structural limitations which create a literary space in which her poems can operate, Retallack sets up a tension between the structure of her poem and the uncontrolled, chance occurrences of language which are contained within the structure.

In *Errata 5uite* Retallack creates a collection of poems structured around the five lines of a musical staff and the errata slip found in published works when a mistake has been discovered after printing. Using these two restrictions as the framework for her book, Retallack constructs five-line poems that create a matrix where the reader may explore the nature of reading within a text series in which errors have been deliberately added and preserved within the poems. The corrections are also incorporated into the text, so that a self-revising language is presented which hybridizes itself while being read. The authority of the errata slip—and its inherent power to direct the reader's attention into a specific meaning-pattern—is subverted by Retallack's refusal to

correct grammatical and other errors but rather present them in process, allowing such mistakes to divert the meanings of the poems into uncontrolled directions. Thus, her highly structured poems contain within themselves a language of untamed meanings.

Retallack also builds her poems from the writings of others, using fragments of their works as the building blocks of her poems in a manner reminiscent of the visual collage. By playing swatches of quotation against one another, Retallack sets up reverberations of meaning in a multi-voiced chorus of narratives. Writing in the *Washington Review,* A.L. Nielsen finds that Retallack's poems are structured linguistic situations in which chance events occur, "There is an artistry in knowing how to place oneself in the way of an accident, and an even greater artistry in knowing how to set forth a form into which something of interest might chance to fall."

In her critical writing, Retallack argues for a non- or multi-linear poetry which goes beyond what she characterizes as the controlled, hierarchical and logical writing of traditional, male-oriented poetry. In the essay ":RE:THINKING:LITERARY:FEMINISM," she states that a female-oriented poetics "may well be more relevant to the complex reality we are coming to see as our world than the narrowly hierarchical logics that produced the rationalist dreamwork of civilization and its misogynist discontents."

—Denise Wiloch

RICH, Adrienne (Cecile)

Nationality: American. **Born:** Baltimore, Maryland, 16 May 1929. **Education:** Roland Park Country School, Baltimore, 1938-47; Radcliffe College, Cambridge, Massachusetts, A.B. (cum laude) 1951 (Phi Beta Kappa). **Family:** Married Alfred H. Conrad in 1953 (died 1970); three sons. **Career:** Lived in the Netherlands, 1961-62; taught at YM-YWHA Poetry Center Workshop, New York, 1966-67; visiting poet, Swarthmore College, Pennsylvania, 1966-68; adjunct professor, Graduate Writing Division, Columbia University, New York, 1967-69; lecturer, 1968-70, instructor, 1970-71, assistant professor of English, 1971-72, and professor, 1974-75, City College of New York; Fannie Hurst Visiting Professor, Brandeis University, Waltham, Massachusetts, 1972-73; professor of English, Douglass College, New Brunswick, New Jersey, 1976-78; A.D. White Professor-at-Large, Cornell University, Ithaca, New York, 1981-85; visiting professor, San José State University, California, 1985-86; professor of English and feminist studies, Stanford University, California, 1986—. Clark Lecturer and distinguished visiting professor, Scripps College, Claremont, California, 1983; Burgess Lecturer, Pacific Oaks College, Pasadena, California, 1986. Columnist, *American Poetry Review,* Philadelphia, 1972-73; co-editor, *Sinister Wisdom,* 1980-84. **Awards:** Yale Series of Younger Poets award, 1951; Guggenheim fellowship, 1952, 1961; Ridgely Torrence memorial award, 1955; American Academy award, 1961; Amy Lowell traveling scholarship, 1962; Bollingen Foundation grant, for translation, 1962; Bess Hokin prize, 1963, and Eunice Tietjens memorial prize, 1968 (*Poetry,* Chicago); National Translation Center grant, 1968; National Endowment for the Arts grant, 1970; Shelley memorial award, 1971; Ingram Merrill Foundation grant, 1973; National Book award, 1974; Donnelly fellowship, Bryn Mawr College, Pennsylvania,

1975; Fund for Human Dignity award, 1981; Ruth Lilly prize, 1986; Brandeis University Creative Arts Medal, 1987; Elmer Holmes Bobst award, 1989; Commonwealth award in literature, 1991; Frost Silver medal of the Poetry Society of America, 1992; *Los Angeles Times* Book award in poetry, 1992; Lenore Marshall/*Nation* award, 1992; William Whitehead award, 1992; Lambda Book award, 1992; The Poets' prize, 1993; Fred Cody award, 1994; Harriet Monroe prize, 1994; Academy of American Poets fellowship, 1992; MacArthur fellowship, 1994. D.Litt.: Wheaton College, Norton, Massachusetts, 1967; Smith College, Northampton, Massachusetts, 1979; Brandeis University, 1987; City College of New York, 1990; Harvard University, 1990. **Member:** Editorial collective, *Bridges: A Journal for Jewish Feminists and Our Friends*, 1989-93. **Address:** c/o W.W. Norton, 500 Fifth Avenue, New York, New York 10110, U.S.A.

PUBLICATIONS

Poetry

A Change of World. New Haven, Connecticut, Yale University Press, 1951.
(Poems). Oxford, Fantasy Press, 1952.
The Diamond Cutters and Other Poems. New York, Harper, 1955.
Snapshots of a Daughter-in-Law: Poems 1954-1962. New York, Harper, 1963; London, Chatto & Windus, 1970.
Necessities of Life: Poems 1962-1965. New York, Norton, 1966.
Selected Poems. London, Chatto & Windus, 1967.
Leaflets: Poems 1965-1968. New York, Norton, 1969; London, Chatto & Windus, 1972.
The Will to Change: Poems 1968-1970. New York, Norton, 1971; London, Chatto & Windus, 1973.
Diving into the Wreck: Poems 1971-1972. New York, Norton, 1973.
Poems Selected and New 1950-1974. New York, Norton, 1975.
Twenty-One Love Poems. Emeryville, California, Effie's Press, 1976.
The Dream of a Common Language: Poems 1974-1977. New York, Norton, 1978.
A Wild Patience Has Taken Me This Far: Poems 1978-1981. New York, Norton, 1981.
Sources. Woodside, California, Heyeck Press, 1983.
The Fact of a Doorframe: Poems Selected and New 1950-1984. New York, Norton, 1984.
Your Native Land, Your Life. New York, Norton, 1986.
Time's Power: Poems 1985-1988. New York, Norton, 1989.
An Atlas of the Difficult World: Poems 1988-91. New York, Norton, 1991.
Collected Early Poems, 1950-1970. New York, Norton, 1993.
Selected Poems, 1950-1995. Knockeven, Ireland, Salmon Publishers, 1996.

Recordings: *Today's Poets 4,* with others, Folkways; *Adrienne Rich Reading at Stanford,* Stanford, 1973; *A Sign I Was Not Alone,* with others, Out & Out, 1978; *Planetarium: A Retrospective,* Watershed, 1986; *Tracking the Contradictions: Poems 1981-1985,* Watershed, 1987.

Plays

Ariadne. Privately printed, 1939.
Not I, But Death. Privately printed, 1941.

Other

Of Woman Born: Motherhood as Experience and Institution. New York, Norton, 1976; London, Virago, 1977.
Women and Honor: Some Notes on Lying. Pittsburgh, Motheroot, 1977; London, Onlywomen Press, 1979.
On Lies, Secrets, and Silence: Selected Prose 1966-1978. New York Norton, 1979; London, Virago, 1980.
Compulsory Heterosexuality and Lesbian Existence. Denver, Antelope Press, 1980; London, Onlywomen Press, 1981.
Blood, Bread, and Poetry: Selected Prose 1979-1985. New York, Norton, 1986; London, Virago, 1987.
What Is Found There: Notebooks on Poetry and Politics. New York, Norton, 1993.

Translator, with William Stafford and Aijaz Ahmad, *Poems by Ghalib.* New York, Hudson Review, 1969.
Translator, *Reflections* by Mark Insingel. New York, Red Dust, 1973.

*

Manuscript Collection: Schlesinger Library, Radcliffe College, Cambridge, Massachusetts.

Critical Studies: *Adrienne Rich's Poetry* edited by Barbara Charlesworth Gelpi and Albert Gelpi, New York, Norton, 1975, revised edition, 1993; *American Triptych: Anne Bradstreet, Emily Dickinson, Adrienne Rich* by Wendy Martin, Chapel Hill, University of North Carolina Press, 1984; *The Transforming Power of Language: The Poetry of Adrienne Rich* by Myriam Díaz-Diocaretz, Utrecht, HES, 1984; *Reading Adrienne Rich: Reviews and Re-visions 1951-1981* edited by Jane Roberta Cooper, Ann Arbor, University of Michigan Press, 1984; *Translating Poetic Discourse: Questions on Feminist Strategies in Adrienne Rich* by Díaz-Diocaretz, Amsterdam, Benjamins, 1985; *A New Tradition? The Poetry of Sylvia Plath, Anne Sexton, and Adrienne Rich* by Janice Markey, Frankfurt, P. Lang, 1985; *The Aesthetics of Power: The Poetry of Adrienne Rich* by Claire Keyes, Athens, University of Georgia Press, 1986; "Adrienne Rich: North America East," in *Praises and Dispraises,* by Terrence DesPres, New York, Viking, 1988; "'Driving to the Limits of the City of Words': The Poetry of Adrienne Rich," in *The Didactic Muse,* by Willard Spiegelman, Princeton. New Jersey, Princeton University Press, 1989; *Skirting the Subject: Pursuing Language in the Works of Adrienne Rich, Susan Griffin, and Beverly Dahlen* by Alan Shima, Uppsala, Uppsala University Press, 1993; *The Dream and the Dialogue: Adrienne Rich's Feminist Poetics* by Alice Templeton, Knoxville, University of Tennessee Press, 1994.

*   *   *

Adrienne Rich's earliest volume, *A Change of World,* introduces two themes that have persisted throughout her career: the pyrrhic victories of human accomplishment in the battle against time and the plight of being a woman. Many poems describe the patience and accommodation every woman must learn if she is to remain in a relationship with a man, who by nature is distant and detached, in an "estranged intensity / Where his mind forages alone" ("An Unsaid Word"). *The Diamond Cutters and Other Poems* reiterates how patience, resignation, and isolation are a woman's fate:

"We had to take the world as it was given," she writes, for "[we] live in other people's houses" ("The Middle-Aged"). The title poem in *Snapshots of a Daughter-in-Law* treats the woman's "blight" in a mythic, historical, and literary context. In fact, Rich insists, the traditional and proper roles of good wife and house-keeper are a woman's funeral preparations: "Soon we'll be off. I'll pack us into parcels / stuff us in barrels, shroud us in news-papers" ("Passing On"). The perverse dependency upon men for sustenance, and the isolation from other women which accompanies this, lead women to self-hatred. The only real alternatives are depression or suicide: "A thinking woman sleeps with monsters / The beak that grabs her, she becomes."

Necessities of Life concentrates primarily upon erotic experience. The poet is in search of both a comfortable relationship with her own body and a relationship with a woman that will give her the childlike (and even womblike) security she has lost. To her lover she says, "Sometimes at night / you are my mother / ... and I crawl against you, fighting / for shelter, making you / my cave" ("Like This Together"). In *Leaflets,* her political rage surfaces. As poet and woman, she calls for sisterhood, a new politics, and a new language. Her resistance is active, "I'd rather / taste blood, yours or mine, flowing / from a sudden slash, than cut all day / with blunt scissors on dotted lines / like the teacher told." *The Will to Change* deals with the problems of retaining the "oppressor's language" ("The Burning of Paper Instead of Children"). It is essential to return to feeling, she argues, and she connects erotic sexuality, poetry, and political action: "When will we lie clear headed in our flesh again?" she asks, for whenever "a feeling enters the body / [it] is political." Finally, admitting that "we have come to an edge of history when men ... have become dangerous to children and other living things, themselves included," she commits herself to total sexual-political warfare.

Diving into the Wreck admits her total antipathy toward men: "I hate you," she says to her male adversary, and continues, "The only real love I have ever felt / was for children and other women." "Phenomenology of Anger" is a militantly feminist poem that rages against repressed human energy, which men handle in war and murder, but which women escape only in "Madness, Suicide, Death." "The Stranger" goes beyond sexual warfare as Rich, the poet who is a prisoner of language, becomes androgynous; perhaps love and nurturing will be restorative, "I am the androgyne / I am the living mind you fail to describe / in your dead language," she writes, and as "mermaid" and "merman," she concludes, "We circle silently / about the wreck / we dive into the hold."

In *Your Native Land, Your Life,* Rich raises a confident and elegant political voice. She accepts her "verbal privilege" as a poet to incite her audience to action against the injustices endured by every minority—from American Indian and black to Jew and lesbian. As the title suggests, she reflects on her own experiences in order to raise larger moral issues. Many poems are intimate revelations of her experiences as a Jew, woman, and daughter ("the eldest daughter raised as a son, taught to study but not to pray"). "Sources" raises key questions about identity, choices, and helplessness: "*With whom do you believe your lot is cast? / From where does your strength come? /* I think somehow, somewhere / every poem of mine must raise those questions / ... There is a *whom,* a *where* / that is not chosen that is given and sometimes falsely given / in the beginning we grasp whatever we can to survive." At times she worries that she is becoming self-consciously political and wonders if "Everything we write / will be used against us / or

against those we love." Ultimately, however, through the common pain of human relationships and survival in time, there may be a transcendent "purification." She would connect herself with the world's pain, even though "the body's pain and the pain on the streets / are not the same but you can learn / from the edges that blur / you who love clear edges / more than anything watch the edges that blur."

In *Time's Power* Rich again recalls her childhood loneliness and a life mixed "with laughter / raucousing the grief" and suggests that in the end "all we read is life. Death is invisible / ... Only the living decide death's color" ("Living Memory"). She has been like a visitor to a foreign land, in an alien universe: "So why am I out here, trying / to read your name in the illegible air? / —vowel washed from a stone, / solitude of no absence, / forbidden face-to-face / ... / trying to hang these wraiths / of syllables, breath / without echo, why?" Other poems recall the wounds of a painful mother-daughter relationship and Rich's special sensitivity to women's, especially lesbians,' experiences—as victims of a hostile, punitive culture. Several historical poems are particularly interesting, including "Letters in the Family" and "Harper's Ferry."

Rich shoulders the burdens of the world in *An Atlas of the Difficult World.* In many poems she clearly transcends the role of feminist poet, now deeply concerned with how, in any number of disenfranchised groups, various elements—history, culture, and individuals—create and impose evil upon the innocent. Her subjects range from the victims of the concentration camp to a woman beaten by her husband in a trailer to two lesbians brutally attacked while vacationing. Gays and lesbians become emblematic of the many in society scarred by injustice and indignity.

The title poem, in 13 parts, is a devastating image of the individual lost in the American "Sea of Indifference, glazed with salt." She says of this society, "I don't want to know / wreckage, dreck and waste," but as she admits, "these are the materials" of "our fissured, cracked terrain." America is "a cemetery of the poor / who died for democracy." Among her heroes—always the more modest members of society—are Leo Frank, hung in 1915 solely because he was a Jew; the father of Anne Sullivan (Helen Keller's teacher), forced to come to America during the Irish potato famine; Latino migrant workers in California; the imprisoned George Jackson.

The volume also returns to familiar themes of feminist rage: "You were a woman walked on a leash. / And they dropped you in the end" ("Olivia"); the difficulties of childhood ("That Mouth"); age ("She"); Jewish female identity ("Eastern War Time"); and death ("Final Notations"). Some of her descriptive passages, particularly of nature, are unusually beautiful. She writes of the black-eyed Susan, that flower which, during "Late summers, early autumns / ... binds / the map of this country together," that here is "the girasol, orange gold- / petalled / with her black eye / [which] laces the / roadsides from Vermont to / California / ... her tubers the / jerusalem artichoke / that has fed the Indians, fed the hobos, could feed us all." The poet asks, "Is there anything in the soil ... that makes for / a plant so generous?" It is what is called "humanity"—politically, socially, and ecologically—which is responsible for natural and individual "waste": "The watcher's eye put out, hands of the / builder severed, brain of the maker starved / those who could bind, join, reweave, cohere, replenish / now at risk in this segregate republic." The concept of "waste" haunts the volume.

—Lois Gordon

RIDDELL, Elizabeth (Richmond)

Nationality: Australian. **Born:** Napier, New Zealand, 21 March 1907. **Family:** Married Edward Neville Greatorex in 1935 (died 1964). **Awards:** Walkley award; Emeritus Fellow, Australia Council, 1984; New South Wales Poet of the Year, 1983; New South Wales Best Book of the Year, 1983. **Address:** 91 York Road, Queens Park, New South Wales 2022, Australia.

PUBLICATIONS

Poetry

Forbears. Sydney, Angus & Robertson, 1961.
Poems. Sydney, Ure Smith, n.d.
Occasions of Birds. Canberra, Officina Brindabella, 1987.
From the Midnight Courtyard. Sydney, Angus & Robertson, 1989.
Selected Poems. Sydney, Angus & Robertson, 1992.
The Difficult Island. Canberra, Molonglo Press, 1994.

*

Manuscript Collection: Australian National Library, Canberra.

Elizabeth Riddell comments:

I was recruited into journalism in Sydney, New South Wales, Australia, straight from boarding school in New Zealand and launched on to a career in news reviews, features, etc. Worked two years in Britain, part of the time on the *Daily Express,* returned to Sydney journalism, and in 1942 opened an office in New York for my paper. I transferred to London and in September 1943 transferred to Paris as a war correspondent where my base was the Hotel Scribe. Back to Australia, where I continued in feature journalism until I retired. Have been interviewed at boring length on radio and TV, have now decided not to talk any more for publication. Writers should write. I have refused politely all British or Australian honors as irrelevant.

Three of my books—*Poems* published by Ure Smith, *Occasions of Birds* and *The Difficult Island*—were limited editions. All have disappeared into collectors' hands.

*   *   *

Elizabeth Riddell first gained widespread interest as a poet in Australia with her second collection, *Forebears,* published in 1961. Her first book, *The Untrammelled* (1940), is not represented in her *Selected Poems* of 1992, a collection that won the Book of the Year award in New South Wales and the gold medal of the Australian Literature Society.

Forebears collected together work from the World War II era to the emerging technological age. Its concluding poem is "After Lunik Two." Although its most famous individual poem is about the wartime separation of lovers ("The Letter"), the overriding characteristic of the work in this volume is that of a wry but often passionate observer, the journalist becomes accessible to vulnerability as well as to wit and irony.

It was 26 years before Riddell published further poetry, and the later works, collected in the limited-edition *Occasions of Birds* (1987) and then in *From the Midnight Courtyard* (1989) and in

Selected Poems, were all written when she was in her seventies and older. Riddell was in her eighties when *The Difficult Island* appeared in 1994. Although death is a real presence in these poems, what is vital—and what has given them such a wide readership—is a communication of urbane sophistication, gaiety, and a hard-hitting intolerance of falsity. As the author herself once said in an interview, "When I was younger I was very addicted to the beautiful phrase. Now I'm ruthless with it."

In her late work Riddell can range from poems about her favorite cats to sardonic portraits of friends. Her cadence sometimes plays surprising games, with echoes of the nursery and of the cut and thrust of newspaper talk. The writing is not so much ruthless as rueful, though the wink is not unintentional and the elegy can be undercut by a determined snort.

—Thomas W. Shapcott

RILEY, Denise

Nationality: English. **Born:** 1948. **Education:** Sussex University, Ph.D. in philosophy. **Career:** Poet. Has worked as a translator.

PUBLICATIONS

Poetry

Marxism for Infants. Cambridge, Street Editions, 1977.
No Fee: A Line or Two for Free, with Wendy Mulford. Cambridge, Street Editions, 1979.
Some Poems: 1968-1978, with Wendy Mulford. Cambridge, Street Editions, 1982.
Dry Air. London, Virago, 1985.
Mop Mop Georgette: New and Selected Poems. London, Reality Street Editions, 1993.

Other

War in the Nursery: Theories of the Child and Mother (history). London, Virago, 1983.
"Am I That Name?": Feminism and the Category of "Women" in History. Basingstoke, Macmillan, and Minneapolis, University of Minneapolis Press, 1988.

Editor, *Poets on Writing: Britain, 1970-1991.* Basingstoke, Macmillan, 1992.

*   *   *

Because most of us are trained to read lineally, with expectations of receiving consecutive flow, we may initially find Denise Riley's poetry strange; although it is not syntax she fractures but rather registers of both meaning and voice. And by means of this fracturing she creates surprise and tension. Several "voices" may be identified: the lyric (surprisingly), the self-deprecating, the self-conscious, the panic-stricken, and the sensuous. Not all will occur in any one poem, but a number may, as in 1963's "Lure":

I roamed around around around around acidic yellow, globe oranges burning, slashed cream, huge scarlet flowing anemones, barbaric pink singing, radiant weeping When will I be loved?

Or consider the sudden wit, founded in reasonableness in "A Misremembered Lyric":

Do shrimps make good mothers? Yes they do.
There is no beauty out of loss; can't do it—

This centripetal bringing of disparate elements to a locus, a point of intersection, is key in that we are asked to read these voices in concert, and at the same time to see them as playing individually upon each other. We shan't get a proper sense of the achievement unless we manage to relate to this individualized collectiveness.

Are some of the voices in her work of greater significance than others? Probably not. In a 1995 letter to the editor, Riley characterized as "slight" the poem "Castalian Spring" which *Stand Magazine* subsequently published:

A gush of water, welling from some cave, which slopped down to a stone trough squatting stout and chalky as a morning sky

Perhaps she wished to deny the lyric voice so evident in the poem, yet the adjectives "stout and chalky" offer a surprising aspect of the object's existence; and this joyous energy of the poem extends from the physical sensation, "The heat of the day peeled off" to the witty but not unserious if tentative offering of "I ... rhymed / *Sieg* with *Krieg,* so explaining our century; I was hooked / on my theory of militarism as stemming from lyricism."

In a sense, that "theory of militarism" obliquely "explains" why many voices in her work lock into, or even interrupt, each other; for the predominance of a single voice, but especially perhaps the lyric voice, would appear to offer a supremacist vision with which she would be unhappy.

This multifarious mode, of modes made of monads, offers a self—it need not be explicitly autobiographical—that is, by the nature of what is being operated, a vulnerable one. It is a tough, yet fragile consciousness that frequently emerges *in the professions themselves*; thus the poet: "If, if only / I need not have a physical experience! To be sheer air, and mousseline." ("Dark Looks"). Oh to be sure delicate material! Of course, the poet is in part teasing us, but later, in a mode that is self-conscious yet one that almost directly addresses the reader, we get, "So take me or leave me. No, wait, I didn't mean leave / me, wait...."

Consciousness of self we now know interlocks with conscience, but conscience has had a few falls over the century, especially where it operates not out of those acts which one has committed, but, on the contrary, on behalf of others whose predicament one does not share, yet with whom one empathizes. So to express empathy yet not seem proprietorial with one's conscience requires a complex set of registers. Yet not so complex as to obliterate the sympathy. Yet not so strong as to erase the victim. Thus the mode of what I take to be self-address in "Laibach Lyrik: Slovenia, 1991": "Cut the slavonics now. Cut the slavonics." The bold long lines, instigating the voice of the dispossessed, comprise one aspect of a complex unselfish poetry that looks to answer the poetry of the uni-

fied dominating voice. Denise Riley's poetry permits us to hear a moving, alternative mode to such domination.

—Jon Silkin

RODGERS, Carolyn M(arie)

Nationality: American. **Born:** Chicago, Illinois, 14 December 1945. **Education:** University of Illinois, Navy Pier, 1960-61; Roosevelt University, Chicago, 1961-65, B.A. in English 1981; Chicago State University, 1982; University of Chicago, M.A. in English 1984. **Career:** Y.M.C.A. social worker, Chicago, 1963-68; instructor in Afro-American literature, Columbia College, Chicago, 1969, and University of Washington, Seattle, 1970; writer-in-residence, Albany State College, Georgia, 1971, Malcolm X College, Chicago, 1971-72, and Roosevelt University, 1983; visiting professor of Afro-American literature, Indiana University, Bloomington, 1973; English remediation tutor, Chicago State University, 1981. Currently teaches at Columbia College. Columnist, Milwaukee *Courier.* Formerly Midwest editor, *Black Dialogue,* New York. **Awards:** Conrad Kent Rivers award, 1968; National Endowment for the Arts grant, 1969; Gwendolyn Brooks fellowship. **Address:** 12750 South Sangamon, Chicago, Illinois 60643, U.S.A.

PUBLICATIONS

Poetry

Paper Soul. Chicago, Third World Press, 1968.
Two Love Raps. Chicago, Third World Press, 1969.
Songs of a Blackbird. Chicago, Third World Press, 1969.
Now Ain't That Love. Detroit, Broadside Press, 1969.
For H.W. Fuller. Detroit, Broadside Press, 1970.
Long Rap / Commonly Known as a Poetic Essay. Detroit, Broadside Press, 1971.
How I Got Ovah: New and Selected Poems. New York, Doubleday, 1975.
The Heart as Ever Green. New York, Doubleday, 1978.
Translation. Chicago, Eden Press, 1980.
Eden and Other Poems. Chicago, Eden Press, 1983.
Morning Glory. Chicago, Eden Press, 1989.
We're Only Human. Chicago, Eden Press, 1994.
A Train Called Judah. Chicago, Eden Press, 1996.
The Girl with Blue Hair. Chicago, Eden Press, 1996.

Novel

A Little Lower than the Angels. Chicago, Eden Press, 1984.

*

Carolyn M. Rodgers comments:

I write because I love to and I don't know anything better to do except, perhaps, compose music and songs. I hope I leave a rich legacy of Afro-American literature behind, like many of my favorite Afro-American writers did.

*   *   *

Carolyn M. Rodgers's poetry is a poetry of naming. What is to be named is how the personal and the political are interwoven in our behavior, in our dreams, in our daily ideologies. The difficulty for the namer, Rodgers would have us see, is in showing how the strands come together—in making one voice represent the many threads that compose the single psyche within culture: "I've had tangled feelings lately ... / there are several of me and / all of us fight to show up at the same time" ("Breakthrough"). In the course of her work Rodgers speaks as a militant for black unity, as a lover, as a daughter, as a devout Christian, as a self-conscious artist. These personae, both complementary and contradictory, constitute a powerful image of black womanhood fighting to define itself against the power and privilege of the white world.

Given the dynamics of racial oppression, the plurality of Rodgers's voice is perhaps less remarkable than the fact of the voice per se. In "The Quality of Change" the poet refers to a muted past that reaches into the present:

> we have spent the years
> talking in profuse & varied
> silences to people
> who have erected walls for themselves
> to hear through.

Her poems, especially the early works, are efforts to break the silences, to break down the walls. The reader must hear the harshness of life in the streets of Chicago ("U Name This One"):

> where pee wee cut lonnell fuh fuckin wid
> his sistuh and blood baptized the street
> at least twice ev'ry week and judy got
> kicked outa grammar school fuh bein pregnant
> and died tryin to ungrow the seed

Those things that have been hidden, hushed, or repressed in African American culture must be recognized and understood, as are the forms of "high" white culture ("To the White Critics"):

> my baby's tears are a three-act play, a sonnet, a novel,
> a volume of poems.
> my baby's laugh is the point and view,
> a philosophical expression of
> oppression and survival

The self that challenges the oppressor also challenges itself, and Rodgers's work makes clear the complications that arise from trying to be free of damaging constraints. Many of her most personal poems address the problem that what is wrong usually comes packaged with what is right—a slavish sexuality may be the most honest ("Now Ain't That Love?"); the least visible revolutionary strategy may be the most effective ("For H.W. Fuller"); material possessions may provide an intensely necessary pleasure ("Things"). The poems about her mother, for example, "It Is Deep," illustrate the contradictions of maternal gifts; this woman who

> thinks that I am under the influence of
>   **communists**
> when I talk about Black as anything
> other than something ugly

is also

> very obviously,
> a sturdy Black bridge that I
> crossed over, on

In Rodgers's aesthetic the challenge to the poet is to give form to the "consistent incongruity" ("Breakthrough") that characterizes her life. The measure of her success is our understanding that the incongruity is ours.

—Janis Butler Holm

RODRIGUEZ, Judith

Nationality: Australian. **Born:** Judith Green, Perth, Western Australia, 13 February 1936. **Education:** Brisbane Girls' Grammar School, 1950-53; University of Queensland, St. Lucia, 1954-57, B.A. (honors) 1957; Girton College, Cambridge, 1960-62, M.A. 1965; University of London, Cert. Ed. 1968. **Family:** Married 1) Fabio Rodriguez in 1964, (divorced 1981), three daughters and one son; 2) Thomas W. Shapcott in 1982. **Career:** Resident teacher, Fairholme Presbyterian Girls' College, Toowoomba, 1958; lecturer, University of Queensland Department of External Studies, 1959-60; lecturer in English, Philippa Fawcett College of Education, London, 1962-63, and University of the West Indies, Kingston, Jamaica, 1963-65; lecturer, St. Giles School of English, London, 1965-66, and St. Mary's College of Education, Twickenham, Middlesex, 1966-68; lecturer, 1969-76, senior lecturer, 1977-85, La Trobe University, Melbourne; writer-in-residence, University of Western Australia, Nedlands, 1978, and Rollins College, Winter Park, Florida, 1986; lecturer on Australian literature, Macquarie University, North Ryde, New South Wales, 1985; visiting fellow, Western Australian Institute of Technology, South Bentley, 1986; lecturer in English, Macarthur Institute of Higher Education, Milperra, Sydney, 1987; lecturer in writing and writer-in-residence, Royal Melbourne Institute of Technology, 1988-89; writer-in-residence, Ormond College University of Melbourne, 1988-89; lecturer in writing, Victoria College, 1989—; senior lecturer, Deakin University, 1993. Poetry editor, *Meanjin,* Melbourne, 1979-82; poetry columnist, Sydney *Morning Herald,* 1984-86. Poetry consultant, Penguin Books Australia, 1989—. Also artist and illustrator: individual shows in Melbourne, Brisbane, Adelaide, and Paris. **Awards:** Australia Council fellowship, 1974, 1978, 1983; South Australian Government prize, 1978; Artlook Victorian prize, 1979; P.E.N. Stuyvesant prize, 1981; Feminist Fortnight Favourite, 1989, for *New and Selected Poems.* AM (Member of the Order of Australia), 1994; Christopher Brennan award, 1994. **Address:** P.O. Box 231, Mont Albert, Victoria 3127, Australia.

PUBLICATIONS

Poetry

Four Poets (as Judith Green), with others. Melbourne, Cheshire, 1962.
Nu-Plastik Fanfare Red and Other Poems. St. Lucia, University of Queensland Press, 1973.

Broadsheet Number 23. Canberra, Open Door Press, 1976.
Water Life. St. Lucia, University of Queensland Press, 1976.
Shadow on Glass. Canberra, Open Door Press, 1978.
Three Poems. Melbourne, Old Metropolitan Meat Market, 1979.
Angels. Melbourne, Old Metropolitan Meat Market, 1979.
Arapede. Melbourne, Old Metropolitan Meat Market, 1979.
Mudcrab at Gambaro's. St. Lucia, University of Queensland Press, 1980.
Witch Heart. Melbourne, Sisters, 1982.
Mrs. Noah and the Minoan Queen, with others, edited by Rodriguez. Melbourne, Sisters, 1983.
Floridian Poems. Winter Park, Florida, Rollins College, 1986.
New and Selected Poems. St. Lucia, University of Queensland Press, 1988.
The Cold. Canberra, National Library of Australia (Pamphlets Poets), 1992.

Plays

Poor Johanna (produced Adelaide, 1994). In *Heroines,* edited by Dale Spender. Melbourne, Penguin, 1991.
Lindy, with Robyn Archer (opera libretto). Music by Moya Henderson. N.d.

Other

Noela Hjorth, with Vicki Pauli. Clarendon, South Australia, Granrott Press, 1984.

Editor, *Mrs. Noah and the Minoan Queen.* Melbourne, Sisters, 1983.
Editor, with Andrew Taylor, *Poems from the Australian's 20th Anniversary Competition.* Sydney, Angus & Robinson, 1985.
Editor, *I sogni cantano l'alba: poesia contemporeana,* translated by G. Englaro. Milan, Lanfranchi, 1988.
Editor, *The Collected Poems of Jennifer Rankin.* St. Lucia, University of Queensland Press. 1990.

Translator, *Your Good Colombian Friend,* by Jairo Vanegas. Upper Ferntree Gully, Papyrus Press, 1995.

*

Manuscript Collection: Fryer Research Library, University of Queensland, Brisbane.

Critical Studies: Interviews in the Australian National Archive, 1976, *Women and Writing: Into the Eighties,* Clayton, Victoria, Monash University, 1980, *Uomini e Libri 97* (Milan), January/February 1984, *Bagdala* (Novi Sad, Yugoslavia), 1984, and *A Woman's Voice: Conversations with Women Poets* by Jennifer Digby, University of Queensland Press, 1996; Sydney *Bulletin,* 1985, *The Age* (Melbourne), 3 January 1987, and *Linq* (Townsville, Queensland), 1987; "More Wow than Flutter" by Les A. Murray, in *Quadrant* (Sydney), October 1976; "Bolder Vision than Superintrospection" by P. Neilsen, in *The Age* (Melbourne), 12 March 1977; "Sea Change" by C. Treloar, in *Twenty-Four Hours* (Sydney), August 1977; "Restless, domestic ..." by Chris Wallace-Crabbe, in *Australian Book Review* (Melbourne), December 1980; "A Positive Poetic" by Jennifer Strauss, in *Australian Book Review* (Melbourne), April 1983; "The White Witch and the Red

Witch: The Poetry of Judith Rodriguez" by Delys Bird, in *Poetry and Gender: Statements and Essays in Australian Women's Poetics,* St. Lucia, University of Queensland Press, 1989; "A Lifetime Devoted to Literature: A Tribute to Judith Rodriguez" by Jennifer Strauss, in *Southerly* (Sydney), 1992; "Judith Rodriguez," in *Dialogues with Australian Poets* by R.P. Rama, Calcutta, Writers Workshop Press, 1993; "An Interview with Judith Rodriguez" by Peter Haddow, in *Famous Reporter* (Kingston, Tasmania), 1993.

Judith Rodriguez comments:

I write poetry to live more fully. I dare to hope that poetry strengthens the best we can think and do. There's a delightful self-indulgence in this dialogue with readers, and with those who have lived and will live.

My first close critic was the poet John Manifold.

Writing for stage and collaborating with a composer have been exciting, loosening up, new-way adventures for me.

Establishing a poetry list for Penguin Books Australia has been a marvelous experience.

* * *

Judith Rodriguez first attracted attention (under her maiden name Judith Green) in 1962 as one of the contributors to *Four Poets,* a volume that presented the early work of four young writers with Brisbane affiliations and, in effect, announced the emergence of a new force in Australian poetry. More than a decade later this force came to be tagged "the Queensland Octopus" to indicate a sort of energy that was less regional than adaptive. Although each of the original four (Rodriguez, David Malouf, Rodney Hall, and Don Maynard) came to occupy important editorial positions, they did so in states other than Queensland, which is often regarded as the Deep South of Australian culture.

In her first poems Rodriguez displayed a vigorous manipulation of language (barely kept in check by the formal lyricism of the time) to serve the ends of immediacy and directness of expression. There is the sense of a new writer still seeking a style and a voice, though the uneven "Essay on M.K." comes closest to pushing the author into genuine self-exploration. It was not until a long period in Europe and Jamaica and an uneventful return to Australia that her second volume, *Nu-Plastik Fanfare Red,* was published. The increase in command and in certainty of direction is immediately clear in poems such as "Sojourners at Phoenix":

> They are here, Svetlana, as they were there.
> Men. Difficult to love. Difficult not to.
>
> Slavers strung out in harness, iron-galled;
> smiths of ideals, lining up at the anvil for thrashing.
>
> Stalin, that fathered five-year plans and prisons.
> And an architect of together. You can't say fairer.
>
> And when you left, Svetlana, and when you left
> with nothing ahead but maybe
>
> glimmer in the jaws of the escape hatch
> you could not perhaps slip through whole ...

Her poetry had become imbued with a warm female sharpness—precisely observed moments and objects and responses, place rather than time, people through things, humanity through attitudes. Her tone had become clipped, never sloppy, and her poems were as tightly packed as a larder full of preserves. She had found a way with language to contain her wide experience and range of interests.

Rodriguez's next book, *Water Life,* was illustrated (or, rather, complemented) with the author's own vigorous and sensuous linocuts, and it received a major literary award. Her femininity is never embittered, though the exploration of her womanness has been increasingly fruitful for her writing and her development and has led to moments of painful honesty. *Water Life* summed up not only stages in the poet's own intellectual and emotional development but also that of a generation of women, and in ways it was directed to growth and celebratory instincts rather than rejection and self-immolation. The later small collection, *Shadow on Glass,* refines the characteristic Rodriguez energy to an almost clenched lyricism. It could be said that the lyrical mode has always exercised this poet's mind, but only in her late work has the combination of song-flow and mind-stress fully cohered, and even then, fitfully. She is in many ways the most exciting and explorative of the so-called Queensland Octopus generation, her work providing the sense of an intellect—and a female strength—in the course of liberation and growth. In any terms her achievement and challenging way with language are apparent.

Publication of *New and Selected Poems,* nearly half of which is new work, reinforces the idea of water as a strong underlying principle used often with quite unconventional modes of approach to the idea of feminine fluidity and suppleness. What is more immediately apparent, though, in this impressive volume is the unique personal voice, quirky yet touching universal recognitions, direct and anecdotal without losing (or underlying too vehemently) the poet's apprehension of the numinous. At the first Feminist Book Fair in Melbourne in 1989 the work was regarded by many as one of the outstanding books presented.

Since 1988 Rodriguez has published only one poetry booklet, *The Cold* (1992). The publication is dominated by a long poem addressed to the older poet Barbara Giles. The poem indicates a development toward the longer, retrospective viewpoint in Rodriguez's work, something reinforced by other poems in the publication. Rodriquez's presence during this period also has been evident as both a translator of Jairo Vanega's novel *Your Good Colombian Friend* and through her position as poetry adviser to Penguin Australia, where she has invigorated the publisher's list and brought new vigor to the marketing of Australian poetry.

—Thomas W. Shapcott

ROSE, Wendy

Pseudonym: Chiron Khanshendel. **Nationality:** American, of Hopi-Miwok and Scots descent. **Born:** Bronwen (Wendy) Elizabeth Edwards, in Oakland, California, 7 May 1948. **Education:** Cabrillo College and Contra Costa College; University of California, Berkeley, M.A. in anthropology 1978. **Family:** Married Arthur Murata in 1976 (marriage ended, 1976). **Career:** Instructor in Native American studies at University of California, Irvine, 1974; lecturer in Native American studies and manager of Lowie Museum of Anthropology bookstore, University of California, Berkeley, 1979-83; lecturer in Native American studies at Mills College, Oakland, California, and Contra Costa College, San Pablo, both 1983, California State University, Fresno, 1983-84, University of Minnesota, Duluth, 1992, and University of Minneapolis, Minneapolis, 1993; instructor at Fresno City College, Fresno, 1984—. Editor, *American Indian Quarterly,* 1982-83; member of editorial board, *American Indian Culture and Research Journal,* 1983-88, *Puerto del Sol,* beginning 1986, and *Sacred Worlds: Journal of Native American Traditions,* beginning 1992. Professional artist, exhibiting around the United States. **Awards:** Elliston Poetry Award finalist, 1980; Pulitzer Prize nomination, 1980, for *Lost Copper,* and 1985; National Endowment for the Arts fellowship, 1981-82; numerous nominations for Pushcart Prize. **Member:** Editorial board, *American Indian Culture and Research Journal,* 1983-88, *Puerto del Sol,* 1986—, and *Sacred Worlds: Journal of Native American Traditions,* 1992—. **Address:** American Indian Studies Program, Fresno City College, 1101 East University Avenue, Fresno, California 93741, U.S.A.

PUBLICATIONS

Poetry

Hopi Roadrunner Dancing, illustrated by the author. Greenfield Center, New York, Greenfield Review Press, 1973.

Taos Poems, illustrated by Duane Niatum. Greenfield Center, New York, Greenfield Review Press, 1974.

Long Division: A Tribal History. New York, Strawberry Press, 1976.

Academic Squaw: Reports to the World from the Ivory Tower. Marvin, South Dakota, Blue Cloud Press, 1977.

Builder Kachina: A Home-going Cycle. Marvin, South Dakota, Blue Cloud Press, 1979.

Lost Copper, illustrated by the author, introduction by N. Scott Momaday. Banning, California, Malki Museum Press, 1980.

What Happened When the Hopi Hit New York. New York, Contact II, 1982.

The Halfbreed Chronicles and Other Poems, illustrated by the author. Los Angeles, West End Press, 1985.

Going to War with All My Relations. Flagstaff, Arizona, Northland, 1994.

Now Poof She Is Gone. Ithaca, New York, Firebrand Books, 1994.

Bone Dance: New and Selected Poems, 1965-1993. Tucson, University of Arizona Press, 1994.

What the Mohawk Made the Hopi Say, with Maurice Kenny. Saranac Lake, New York, Strawberry Press, 1995.

Other

Aboriginal Tattooing in California. Berkeley, University of California, Archaeological Research Facility, 1979.

*

Critical Studies: "Finding the Loss" by Kenneth Lincoln, in *Parnassus: Poetry in Review,* vol. 10, no. 1, 1982; "Blue Stones, Bones and Troubled Silver: The Poetic Craft of Wendy Rose" by Andrew Wiget, in *Studies in American Indian Literatures,* vol. 7, no. 2, spring 1983; interview with Carol Hunter in *Coyote Was Here: Essays on Contemporary Native American Literary and Political Mobilization,* Aarhus, Denmark, University of Aarhus Press, 1984; "The Bones Are Alive: An Interview with Wendy Rose" by Joseph Bruchac, in *Survival This Way: Interviews with Ameri-*

can *Indian Poets,* Tucson, University of Arizona Press, 1987; "Wendy Rose: Searching through Shards, Creating Life" by James R. Saucerman, in *Wicazo SA Review,* vol. 5, no. 2, fall 1989; "Anthropological Roles: The Self and Others in T.S. Eliot, William Carlos Williams, and Wendy Rose" by C. Irmscher, in *Soundings,* vol. 75, no. 4, winter 1992; "The Nether World of Neither World: Hybridization in the Literature of Wendy Rose" by Karen Tongson-McCall, in *American Indian Culture & Research Journal,* vol. 20, no. 4, 1996.

*   *   *

Wendy Rose has, for the past quarter century, been one of the leading voices of a resurgent Native American poetry. A writer who is also a professional artist, a "spy" in the camp of the anthropologists, and a chronicler of the sufferings of displaced peoples and biracial outcasts worldwide, she lives in many worlds at once. Included in virtually every major anthology of Indian writers, and many contemporary poetry anthologies and journals, her poems are scars that talk and songs that heal.

Rose has been called "an alchemical Indian poet [who] has incarnated her words with native integrity" by Kenneth Lincoln in *Parnassus.* Yet her creativity finds expression in the visual arts, as well. She notes the "tremendous number" of Indian writers who also illustrate books, and links this to Native American rejection of rigid categories. Her pen & ink drawings and watercolors grace a number of her books, as well as those of other writers. In a powerfully evocative, spare style, she depicts Indian women merging with mountains, growing from rocks, emerging from earth. These are the *kachinas,* spirits of nature, and the ancestors that feature so prominently in Hopi mythology. These are also the phantoms that haunt her poetry: the dishonored corpses of Wounded Knee, the singing bones of numberless victims of conquistadors and missionaries, cavalrymen and cowboys, anthropologists and bureaucrats.

"The bones are alive," she said in an interview with Joseph Bruchac, and she sees in her task as "storykeeper" and healer the necessity of invoking ghosts so as to give them voice, to invite them to "live in my tongue / and forget / your hunger," as she wrote in *Hopi Roadrunner Dancing.* Her role as anthropologist is to be what critic Karen Tongson-McCall labels, the "invisible insider." As Rose confessed to Bruchac: "I'm not in the Ivory Tower. I'm a spy." Forced into an anthropology career by the refusal in the early 1970s of the English and comparative literature departments at the University of California—Berkeley to place value on American Indian literature, Rose in 1978 satirized the university in *Academic Squaw: Reports to the World from the Ivory Tower.* Since earning a graduate degree in 1978, she has become a prominent figure among those attempting to reconfigure the field of Native American anthropology. Her poems often recall the appalling history of "bones auctioned," sacred objects sold, and bodies stuffed, all for museum display. In one poem, "The Three Thousand Dollar Death Song," she imagines using her insider status to liberate Indian artifacts, "Watch them touch each other, measure reality, / march out the museum door."

If Rose's work is rooted in ethnography and in the living myths of Indian peoples, it is also largely based on her own experience. She has said, "Everything I write is fundamentally autobiographical, no matter what the style or topic." Born a "half breed," she was rejected by both societies, doubly so because having a white mother meant she could not claim membership in the matrilineal

Hopi tribe. Estranged from both parents for much of her life, she endured a wretched adolescence involving drug abuse, street life, a brief but violent marriage, and, at age 18, shock treatments and institutionalization. In her autobiographical essay "Neon Scars," she cautions us not to dismiss her work as purely metaphorical, "When I speak of the bruises that rise on my flesh like blue marbles, do you understand that these are real bruises that have appeared on my flesh?" It is one of the tasks of her poetry to expose such bruises to the healing air, yet unlike many white "confessional poets," her work transcends self-analysis to focus on others who, like herself, were born, "between the eyes of two worlds that / never match." So she recounts stories of victims of colonialism, the Holocaust, and the atom bomb. She tells the stories of people degraded while alive and exhibited in museums or sideshows after death: Truganniny, the last of the native Tasmanians, and Julia Pastrana, a Mexican Indian.

Since Rose grew up apart from tribal lands, she realizes, "my community is urban Indian and pan tribal." So she draws on numerous Indian societies, and cultures as remote as Tasmania, for historical and mythological sources. Her influences are diverse as well, from Robinson Jeffers to N. Scott Momaday. Her poetry, she says, owes much to European writing traditions, yet observers, from Momaday to Andrew Wiget, have seen the imprint of native storytelling traditions as well. Wiget, for instance, makes a convincing case that the "continual revision" of her poems as they appear in subsequent editions reveals a desire to "reaffirm the poetic self" in a manner consistent with oral culture as against the "death" of the poem once it achieves final closure in print. Yet, even there, her poems, like the bones, speak. As the Hopi taunt their white conquerors in one of her songs, "See Pahana [whiteman], / how we nest / in your ruins," she writes in "Naayawva Taawi."

—John Roche

ROSSELLI, Amelia

Nationality: Italian. **Born:** Paris, 1930; daughter of anti-fascist martyr Carlo Rosselli. **Education:** Educated in France, England, and the United States. **Career:** Translator, Comunità (publishing house), Rome, c. 1948; began writing poems in the early 1960s, encouraged by Pier Paolo Pasolini; has also worked as a journalist, editor, and musician. **Awards:** Pasolini Prize, 1981, for body of work; Knight Officer of the Order of Merit of the Italian Republic, 1986; Libero De Libero, 1988, for *Antologia poetica.* **Died:** Diagnosed with Parkinson's disease in 1969; committed suicide in Rome, 11 February 1996.

PUBLICATIONS

Poetry

24 poesie. Turin, Einaudi, 1963.
Variazioni belliche. Milan, Garzanti, 1964; translated by Lucia Re and Paul Vangelisti as *War Variations,* Los Angeles, Sun & Moon Press, 1997.
Serie ospedaliera. Milan, Saggiatore, 1969.

Documento, 1966-1973. Milan, Garzanti, 1976.

Primi scritti, 1952-1963. Milan, Guanda, 1980.

Impromptu. Genoa, San Marco dei Giustiniani, 1981.

Contributor, *The New Italian Poetry: 1945 to the Present,* edited and translated by Lawrence Smith. Berkeley, University of California Press, 1981.

Appunti sparsi e persi. Reggio Emilia, Aelia Laelia, 1983.

La Libellula. Genoa, SE, 1985.

Contributor, *The Defiant Muse: Italian Feminist Poems from the Middle Ages to the Present,* edited and translated by Beverly Allen, Muriel Kittel, and Keala Jane Jewell. New York, Feminist Press, 1986.

Antologia poetica, edited by Giacinto Spagnoletti. Milan, Garzanti, 1987.

Sonno-Sleep (1953-1968). Rome, Rossi e Spera, 1989.

Sleep: poesie in inglese. Milan, Garzanti, 1992.

Other

Diario ottuso (1954-1968) (prose). Rome, IBN, 1990.

Editor, *Epistolario familiare* by Carlos and Nello Rosselli. Milan, Sugarco, 1979.

*

Critical Studies: "Amelia Rosselli" by Rebecca West, in *An Encyclopedia of Continental Women Writers,* New York, Garland, 1991; "At the Margins of Dominion: The Poetry of Amelia Rosselli" by Nelson Moe, in *Italica* (Madison, Wisconsin), no. 62, 1992; "Poetry and Madness" by Lucia Re, in *Forum Italicum* (Tallahassee, Florida), 1992; "Amelia Rosselli" by Pietro Frassica, in *Dictionary of Literary Biography,* vol. 128: *20th-Century Italian Poets,* Detroit, Gale Research, 1993; "Amelia Rosselli" by Cristina Della Coletta, in *Italian Women Writers: A Bio-Bibliographical Sourcebook,* Westport, Connecticut, Greenwood Press, 1994.

*   *   *

Confessional, cryptic, confident, crooked: Amelia Rosselli toggles the mind while ringing in a new ear (two lapses in cliché she might appreciate). This Italian poet's ever-difficult poems sprint the fine line between musical pleasure and mental pain, creating a beautiful tangle of literature, linguistics, mathematics, music, philosophy, and religion.

And while she is obviously no stranger to erudition, here is a poet who also never loses sight of the basics: passion, faith, strife, death. Rosselli speaks of the body in love and anguish, the mind at war and play, and readers expecting tidy narratives and rapturous closure will be puzzled (if not disappointed) by her complex and distorted work. In what could almost be an *ars poetica* from her book *Variazioni belliche* (*War Variations,* as translated by Lucia Re and Paul Vangelisti), Rosselli's speaker "arrange[s] absurd prayers" while "the whole world [is] collapsing." The "wishing net" is to blame for allowing the possibility of "get[ting] damaged" to arise, but by the poem's end, it is still "not clear why the bomb falls."

"I Hate Peace," Rosselli writes in a section of her *Primi scritti, 1952-1963,* a collected volume of diary fragments, poems, and prose in her three primary languages (Italian, English, and French). While this particular phrase might be the scribble of a woeful 25 year old, it is certainly a sentiment that haunts her entire body of work. Rosselli's poems, while residing in the somewhat detached public space of language, also affirm language's power to express the personal, unutterable closeness of violence and grief. At times, she seems to want to do away with writing altogether, perhaps wishing that a poem could somehow be inhaled back to its origins in the body and mind. Witness this short poem from her English-language volume, *Sleep*:

> a soft sonnet is all the strength i have to create,
> full easy life have i ever and ever
> again and again destroyed, but it was god crying
> within me turn out all
> lights! No love be granted to he who
> hates all love save life
> writ on paper there goes my
> seed wild into
> death.

While the gift is most blatant (and least successful) in her clever, yet often overbearing "October Elizabethans," Rosselli, like all great poets, has the ability to don many literary hats and, in turn, make them entirely her own. It is not known how familiar she may have been with their work, but one will find the wry, mind-plumbing feminism of Emily Dickinson and the hilarious terror of John Berryman lurking in many of her poems. Traces of many European writers, most notably the small—"s" surrealism of Paul Celan, the quizzicality of Italo Calvino, and the paranoiac prose of Franz Kafka, are of course present as well.

Despite their pessimistic and often brutal tones, Rosselli's poems are wonderfully dense linguistic symphonies, and it is hardly surprising that film scores and musicals also appear on her long list of artistic accomplishments. Her use of poetic devices ranges from conventional rhyme, anaphora, enjambment, alliteration, and repetend to more complex innovations such as "absolute space" (Rosselli's own audio-visual gridding design in which each line of verse has the same fixed length, thus fastening her pliable and often distorted language into a sturdy word-cube), and careful, yet seemingly effortless, use of *lapsus* (grammatical and / or linguistic "error") which can be found in these lines from another untitled poem in English:

> Would you have me fry in my soup? Or
> be the everlasting damsel in her skirts?
> Or shove mysteries unto your gaping nostrils
> till they were aflame?

The first line of "Snow," as translated by Lawrence R. Smith in *The New Italian Poetry: 1945 to the Present,* reads, "They seem to be tiny insects celebrating." By the third line of the poem, we come to find that the snowflakes are celebrating "pain split into difficult attentions / and a gathering of daring action." If we take "celebration" to mean a deviation from routine, then the word serves as a fair and accurate description of what Rosselli's fresh language does. Like the snow in the poem, her words are beautifully futile, equal parts obscurity and enlightenment. Hers is a poetry of the ephemeral human state: a constant shuttling between inevitable pain and wishful wholeness. It is, like all of us, armed and dismantled, able and away.

—Graham Foust

301

RUMENS, Carol (-Ann)

Nationality: British. **Born:** Carol-Ann Lumley, London, 10 December 1944. **Education:** St. Winifred's Convent School, London; Coloma Convent Grammar School, Croydon, Surrey, 1955-63; Bedford College, University of London, 1964-66. **Family:** Married David Rumens in 1965; two daughters. **Career:** Publicity assistant, 1974-77, and advertising copywriter, 1977-81, London; poetry editor, *Quarto,* London, 1981-82, *Literary Review,* London, 1982—. Creative writing fellow, Kent University, Canterbury, 1983-85; Northern Arts writing fellow, Newcastle University, 1988-90; writer-in-residence, Queens' University, Belfast, 1991-94. Currently, instructor in creative writing, Queens' University, Belfast. Regular book reviewer, *Observer,* London. **Awards:** Alice Hunt Bartlett award, 1982; Arts Council award, 1982; Cholmondeley award, 1984. Fellow, Royal Society of Literature, 1984. **Address:** c/o Chatto & Windus, 20 Vauxhall Bridge Road, London SWIV 2SA, England.

PUBLICATIONS

Poetry

Strange Girl in Bright Colours. London, Quartet, 1973.
A Necklace of Mirrors. Belfast, Ulsterman, 1978.
Unplayed Music. London, Secker & Warburg, 1981.
Scenes from the Gingerbread House. Newcastle upon Tyne, Bloodaxe, 1982.
Star Whisper. London, Secker & Warburg, 1983.
Direct Dialing. London, Chatto & Windus, 1985.
Selected Poems. London, Chatto & Windus, 1987.
The Greening of the Snow Beach. Newcastle upon Tyne, Bloodaxe, 1988.
From Berlin to Heaven. London, Chatto & Windus. 1989.
The Greening of the Snow Beach. Newcastle upon Tyne, Bloodaxe, 1988.
Thinking of Skins: New & Selected Poems. Newcastle upon Tyne, Bloodaxe, 1993.
Best China Sky. Newcastle upon Tyne, Bloodaxe, 1995.

Play

Nearly Siberia (produced Newcastle upon Tyne and London, 1989).

Novel

Plato Park. London, Chatto & Windus, 1987.

Other

Editor, *Making for the Open: The Chatto Book of Post-Feminist Poetry 1964-1984.* London, Chatto & Windus, 1985.
Editor, *Slipping Glimpses: Winter Poetry Supplement.* London, Poetry Book Society, 1985.
Editor, *New Women Poets.* Newcastle upon Tyne, Bloodaxe, 1990.
Editor, *Brangle Poets.* Belfast, Brangle Publications, n.d.

*   *   *

Carol Rumens wrote in a Poetry Book Society bulletin on the occasion of the publication of her collection, *Unplayed Music,* "Experiencing things imaginatively as an alternative for dealing with 'real' occurrences is, I suppose, an activity especially familiar to anyone who writes." Because "real" is in quotation marks, we can assume a particular meaning, which I take to be "directly experienced." It is possible (indeed it is the strength of Rumens' poetry that she does this so well) to experience imaginatively occurrences which, while not direct to the poet, were direct occurrences to others. These occurrences, while not unreal, have to be apprehended by the poet imaginatively. She goes on to say in another bulletin that "I do not belong to that school of thought which says in the face of extreme horror, suffered by others, one should be silent. On the contrary I believe that all the forces of imagination should be employed to speak of their suffering."

I labor this point because some of the most telling of Rumens' later poems have been concerned with the sufferings, horrors, persecutions, and exiles during and deriving from the history of Europe in the first half of the twentieth century, subjects which many of those who lived through that period have deliberately avoided as being too immediate in their enormity and their emotional charge for what they felt would be an adequate response. That Rumens' distance from these events allows her to experience them imaginatively, and that her use of this particular aspect of the intelligence is such that the empathy she achieves in a poem such as "Outside Osweicin" is stunning, is a source of the power of her work. In the early 1980s Rumens' interest in Eastern Europe and Russia began to predominate, and it was then that she began to dare to take on subjects of such overwhelming impact.

Most of the poems in Rumens' first collection and in *Star Whisper* that followed display an acute observation and an ability to touch the nerves underlying the domestic and the personal. This is especially true of her love poems, where her technical accomplishment makes no small contribution to their quality and effectiveness. This quality is best illustrated by quoting what is as near a perfect poem as I have encountered in recent years, "The Last Day of March":

> The elms are darkened by rain
> On the small, park sized hills
> Sigh the ruined daffodils
> As if they shared my refrain
> —that when I leave here, I lose
> All reason to see you again.
>
> What's finishing was so small,
> I never mentioned it.
> My time, like yours, was full,
> And I would have blushed to admit
> How shallow the rest could seem;
> How so little could be all.

Rumens' group of love poems shares this ability to give depth of meaning and emotional truth to what are common experiences. The simply named "Love Poem" is another example of this, while "The Ballad of the Morning After" makes the connection explicit:

> And that's the story of our lives,
> The whole damned human race

Rumens' collection *From Berlin to Heaven* is of a piece with her work as a whole. As the title conveys, the poems are related to her travels but move from the basically descriptive to the metaphysical.

—John Cotton

RYAN, Gig (Elizabeth)

Nationality: Australian and British. **Born:** Leicester, England, 5 November 1956. **Education:** LaTrobe University, Melbourne, 1974; Sydney University, 1983-87; University of Melbourne, 1991-93, degree in Latin and Ancient Greek 1993. **Career:** Also works as songwriter and musician. **Awards:** Australia Council Literature Board Writers grant, 1979, 1982, 1988, 1997; co-winner, Anne Elder award, 1988. **Address:** 1189 Burke Road, Kew, Melbourne 3101, Australia.

PUBLICATIONS

Poetry

The Division of Anger. Sydney, Transit Press, 1981.
Manners of an Astronaut. Sydney, Hale & Iremonger, 1984.
The Last Interior. Melbourne, Scripsi, 1986.
Excavation. Sydney, Picador, 1990.
Pure and Applied. Sydney, Paper Back Press, 1997.

Recording: *Six Goodbyes,* Big Home Productions, 1988; *Prosperity,* Broken Windmill Records, 1997.

*   *   *

The publication of Gig Ryan's *The Division of Anger* in 1981 announced, with a certain *frisson* among audiences at readings in Sydney and Melbourne, the presence of a new *enfant terrible.* Ryan's harsh delivery, each phrase chopped down at the end, emphasized her preoccupation with people moving among drugs, disgust, venality, and a jeering despair.

Backed by the resolutely urban poet John Tranter, the publisher and editor of *Transit Poetry,* Ryan has continued to carry out his agenda for a realism under fluorescent light that favors the explicit argot of urban disillusionment. The realism is trenchant and unrelenting enough at times to get in the way of an appreciation of Ryan's brilliant ways of unsettling the reader, her constantly resourceful subjective notation, her montage technique, her deliberate banality and bad taste and pasted-on similes, her occasional sentimentality, and, finally, her ability to be very funny. The following is from "Getting it":

> He kisses, his pale guilt blowing
> like a flower. You're luxurious, unsure.
> Your eyes opening like telescopes
> on a clean brain.
> You're so silly in the kitchen, like a new
>   appliance ...

> Will you buy me a dark salmon citroen
> please, with all your brilliant money,
> how it smells like a bank-clerk.

The same qualities are seen in "Dying for it"—

> He copes with the table.
> I would kill a thousand crocodiles for you.
> His sincerity clacking like chain-mail,

> death-hot, and your dead throat moves
> one dream down

—and in "In the lovely crowd":

> You want a man to apologise to,
> He avoids the place now like Queensland,
> as his radical politics fatten ...

Manners of an Astronaut is described in the blurb as a "deeply coherent 'discontinuous narrative,'" though the narrative probably matters little to Ryan's fans enjoying the authentic mix in each poem. There is no obvious buildup of characters and situations among the monologues. *The Last Interior* continues the vein of anger and disgust, with the incitement of "bad-behaviour" opening lines, as in "Four":

> Now that my obsession's had it, I'm bored.
> You waver before me like bad television.
> and
> Getting drunk, I insult everybody.
> and
> They shoot up in the kitchen.
> and
> We lay on the floor, getting speed
> and your face like an airport
> and
> In love again like plaster ...

Those who had been waiting for development in Ryan's art probably felt that the moment had come when *Excavation* was published. Here are poems about the media, politics ("The mind's shacks are stranded and overpopulated, South Africa," "On first looking into Fairfax's Herald"), and social problems ("Living in a vacant lot"). Sharp-edged phrases still overlap everywhere; epigrams are up and non sequiturs down. This is clearly a controlled and varied menu and, even when cynically dismissive, near enough to good-humored, as in "Gone too":

> He says I'm a liar
> I shelve death back into my head
> The sick cells, the murder
> I figured it was a goer,
> new, and all
> Why are you so weak?
> I like him like air.
> He tells me to fuck off: what's new?
> A great girl friend vacuums and builds a temple
> Not me
> I turn the heart into a quiver,
> shoot and forget.

No one, even those such as Alan Wearne and John Forbes among the near contemporaries who support her most strongly, writes like Ryan. Her hand is immediately recognizable within a few lines. She is one of the ablest younger "established" poets in Australia, though the question stands as to a perceived sameness in her work. Her development, particularly if she continues to broaden the interests she deals with, will be interesting to watch.

—Judith Rodriguez

S

SALTER, Mary Jo

Nationality: American. **Born:** Grand Rapids, Michigan, 15 August 1954. **Education:** Harvard University, Cambridge, Massachusetts, B.A. (cum laude) 1976; New Hall, Cambridge, M.A. (with first class honors) 1978. **Family:** Married Brad Leithauser in 1980; two daughters. **Career:** Instructor, Harvard University, Cambridge, Massachusetts, 1978-79; staff editor, *Atlantic Monthly,* Boston, 1978-80; instructor in English conversation at various institutions in Japan, 1980-83; lecturer, Mount Holyoke College, South Hadley, Massachusetts, 1984—. Poet-in-residence, Robert Frost Place, 1981. **Awards:** Discovery prize (*Nation*), 1983; National Endowment for the Arts fellow, 1983-84; Academy of American Poets Lamont Poetry prize, 1988, for *Unfinished Painting;* Ingram-Merrill Foundation fellowship, 1989; American Academy and Institute of Arts and Letters Witter Bynner Foundation Poetry prize, 1989; Academy of American Poets Lavan award, 1990; Guggenheim fellowship, 1993; Amy Lowell Poetry Travelling Scholar, 1995-96. **Address:** c/o Alfred A. Knopf, 201 East 50th Street, New York, New York 10022, U.S.A.

PUBLICATIONS

Poetry

Henry Purcell in Japan. New York, Knopf, 1985.
Unfinished Painting. New York, Knopf, 1989.
Sunday Skaters. New York, Knopf, 1994.

Other

The Moon Comes Home (for children). New York, Knopf, 1989.

*   *   *

Mary Jo Salter is one of the best of the younger poets now writing in traditional forms. Her work has variety, grace, humor, and depth. Her first book, *Henry Purcell in Japan* (1985), opens with a poem that introduces many of the themes that inform much of her subsequent work. "For an Italian Cousin" recounts the speaker's reaction as her cousin shows her the Roman Catholic church she attends and describes the local observance of Good Friday. The speaker is shocked by the waxen image of Christ on the chapel's crucifix and by her cousin's naïveté:

> Tempted to joke, I'm silenced by
> the trusting expression on her face,
> flushed with the light of this stained glass
> where Christ is always about to die.

Yet, the speaker thinks of another church, San Marco in Venice, where images have shown her "a world I've pieced / together with a kind of faith, at least"; the mosaics there seem less stone than flesh:

> A puzzle of figures floats on the walls
> and in golden domes, and you have the feeling

> this heavenly gold is not a ceiling—
> but space itself, from which no one falls.

The voice here, as in most of Salter's poems, is controlled and plausibly conversational; the speaker's mind makes rapid connections and associations, many of them metaphorical; and the speaker brings an American sensibility self-consciously to bear upon remote surroundings. Salter and her family have spent significant stretches of time abroad, in Japan, Paris, and Iceland, and these places have provided settings for many of her poems.

Salter received the Lamont award of the Academy of American Poets for her second collection, *Unfinished Painting* (1989). Reflecting a few more years of practice, the poems are more fully achieved technically, and the balance between the attractive ingenuity of slighter poems and the depth of feeling in more solemn ones is more assured. There is the wit that rhymes "umbrage" and "Cambridge" and sees in the face of Big Ben "a daily mirror of the Times," and there is the heart for elegies to the poet's mother and for Etsuko, a Japanese friend. The title poem, about a painting reproduced on the book's jacket, again confronts the tension between time's passage and those objects that evoke single moments. The painting is by the poet's mother and portrays the poet's brother as a child.

Sunday Skaters (1994), Salter's third collection, begins with several poems evoking the joys and the trials of love and of parenthood, both experienced and observed. Here is "Lullaby for a Daughter," the shortest but not the least of these:

> Someday, when the sands of time
> invert, may you find perfect rest
> as a newborn nurses from
> the hourglass of your breast.

In these poems close but apparently effortless observation is backed by a deep moral sense that greatly enriches Salter's work, though it never makes it too solemn to be believed. Solemnity, in fact, is scarce here, even when the poems are at their most serious, for Salter is constantly alert for the small jokes the language plays upon itself.

The book ends with two longer poems of notable ambition. "Two American Lives" evokes crucial moments in the lives of Thomas Jefferson and Robert Frost and, according to notes at the back of the book, required considerable research. The poems live, however, on their own terms and bring great moments to life, free of the sound of index cards.

In the space of little over a decade Salter's collections have established her as one of the most important and engaging of American poets born since 1950.

—Henry Taylor

SANCHEZ, Sonia

Nationality: American. **Born:** Birmingham, Alabama, 9 September 1934. **Education:** Hunter College, New York, B.A. in political science 1955; New York University, 1959-60; Wilberforce University, Ohio, Ph.D. in fine arts, 1972. **Family:** Married Etheridge Knight (divorced); one daughter and two sons. **Career:** Staff member, Downtown Community School, 1965-67, and Mission Rebels in Action, 1968-69, San Francisco; instructor, San Francisco State College, 1967-69; lecturer in black literature, University of Pittsburgh, 1969-70, Rutgers University, New Brunswick, New Jersey, 1970-71, Manhattan Community College, New York, 1971-73, and City University of New York, 1972; associate professor, Amherst College, Massachusetts, 1972-73, and University of Pennsylvania, Philadelphia, 1976-77; associate professor of English, 1977-79, professor of English, 1979—, Faculty Fellow, Provost's Office, 1986-87, Presidential Fellow, 1987-88, and Laura Carnell Chair in English, Temple University, Philadelphia. Columnist, *American Poetry Review,* 1977-78, and Philadelphia *Daily News,* 1982-83. **Awards:** P.E.N. award, 1969; American Academy grant, 1970; National Endowment for the Arts award, 1978; Smith College Tribute to Black Women award, 1982; Lucretia Mott award, 1984; Before Columbus Foundation award, 1985; PEW fellow, 1993. **Address:** Department of English, Temple University, Broad and Montgomery, Philadelphia, Pennsylvania 19041, U.S.A.

PUBLICATIONS

Poetry

Homecoming. Detroit, Broadside Press, 1969.
WE a BaddDDD People. Detroit, Broadside Press, 1970.
Liberation Poem. Detroit, Broadside Press, 1970.
It's a New Day: Poems for Young Brothas and Sistuhs. Detroit, Broadside Press, 1971.
Ima Talken bout The Nation of Islam. Astoria, New York, Truth Del., c.1971.
Love Poems. New York, Third Press, 1973.
A Blues Book for Blue Black Magical Women. Detroit, Broadside Press, 1974.
I've Been a Woman: New and Selected Poems. Sausalito, California, Black Scholar Press, 1978; revised edition, Chicago, Third World Press, 1985.
Homegirls and Handgrenades. New York, Thunder's Mouth Press, 1984.
Under a Soprano Sky. Trenton, New Jersey, Africa World Press, 1987.
Wounded in the House of a Friend. Boston, Beacon Press, 1995.
Does Your House Have Lions? Boston, Beacon Press, 1997.

Recordings: *Homecoming,* Broadside Voices, 1969; *We a BaddDDD People,* Broadside Voices, 1969; *A Sun Woman for All Seasons,* Folkways, 1971; *Sonia Sanchez and Robert Bly,* Black Box, 1971; *Sonia Sanchez: Selected Poems, 1974,* Watershed, 1975; *IDKT: Captivating Facts about the Heritage of Black Americans,* Ujima, 1982.

Plays

The Bronx Is Next (produced New York, 1970). Published in *Drama Review* (New York), Summer 1968.
Sister Son/ji (produced Evanston, Illinois, 1971; New York, 1972). Published in *New Plays from the Black Theatre,* edited by Ed Bullins, New York, Bantam, 1969.

Dirty Hearts '72, in *Break Out! In Search of New Theatrical Environments,* edited by James Schevill. Chicago, Swallow Press, 1973.
Uh, Uh: But How Do It Free Us? (produced Evanston, Illinois, 1975). Published in *New Lafayette Theatre Presents,* edited by Ed Bullins, New York, Doubleday, 1974.
Malcolm Man/Don't Live Here No Mo,' produced Philadelphia, 1979.
I'm Black When I'm Singing, I'm Blue When I Ain't, produced Atlanta, 1982.

Short Stories

A Sound Investment. Chicago, Third World Press, 1980.

Other

The Adventures of Fathead, Smallhead, and Squarehead (for children). New York, Third Press, 1973.
Crisis in Culture. Black Librarian Press, 1983.

Editor, *Three Hundred Sixty Degrees of Blackness Comin' at You.* New York, 5X, 1972.
Editor, *We Be Word Sorcerers: 25 Stories by Black Americans.* New York, Bantam. 1973.

*

Critical Studies: "Sonia Sanchez and Her Work" by S. Clarke, in *Black World* (Chicago), June 1971; "The Poetry of Three Revolutionists: Don L. Lee, Sonia Sanchez, and Nikki Giovanni" by R. Roderick Palmer, in *CLA Journal* (Baltimore), September 1971; "Sonia Sanchez Creates Poetry for the Stage" by Barbara Walker, in *Black Creation* (New York), Fall 1973; "Notes on the 1974 Black Literary Scene" by George Kent, in *Phylon* (Atlanta), June 1974; *Black Women Writers at Work* edited by Claudia Tate, New York, Continuum, 1983; *Black Women Writers (1950-1980)* edited by Mari Evans, New York, Doubleday, 1984.

*   *   *

As a mature poet Sonia Sanchez continues to write for political, economic, and social purposes, seeing no necessary dichotomy between cause-oriented, utilitarian writing and art. Earlier, as a leading poet of the Black Arts movement and believing that African Americans were expressing thoughts that previous generations had been afraid to utter, she saw the times as propitious and urgent for black artistic militancy. "I write because I must," she once declared, and "if you write from a black experience, you're writing from a universal experience as well."

In an early poem Sanchez writes, "white people / ain't rt bout nothing," and she chastises blacks who adopt white values and lifestyles. To blacks who "have come to / believe that we are / not" she gives the prescription "inhale the ancient black breath." Thus, she teaches that African Americans must know their enemies, accept themselves, demonstrate ethnic pride and unity, be moral, act communally, and go about the serious business of intelligent and courageous self-direction. In delivering such messages, then and now, much of her poetry is direct, uncompromising, demanding, militant, even abrasive. Yet, it is not without tenderness, a quality openly evident in her poems for children and in her love poems—notably those dealing with love among African Americans and between man and woman.

As her collected works show, Sanchez's poetry has not been static in substance and technique. *Homecoming* is a young poet's grappling with conceptions of self, others, and the world. *We a BaddDDD People* stresses black strength and self-love, identification of the human and institutional enemies of black people, "we"-ness in place of the personal and subjective "I." *It's a New Day,* "poems for young brothas and sistuhs," warns of dangers and points out the necessity for unity, wholeness of spirit, and clearness of purpose and actions. Having by this time joined the Nation of Islam, in *Love Poems* Sanchez tones down her language as she explores the dynamics of healthy and healthful relationships among black people. The poet's still-evolving technical style is apparent in *A Blues Book for Blue Black Magical Women,* an autobiographical, perhaps confessional, volume. Addressed to "Queens of the Universe" and divided into the sections "Past," "Present," "Rebirth," and "Future," it is not an anthology or collection but rather a thematically united poetry that ironically and satirically echoes T.S. Eliot's *The Waste Land.* While Eliot is pessimistic, however, Sanchez is determinedly optimistic.

I've Been a Woman is a gathering of new and selected poems. In the evolving of her poetry Sanchez has tended not to move from exhorter to persuader, but she is always the teacher. "C'mon yall," she encourages, "on a safari / into our plantation jungle / minds / and let us catch the nigger / roamen inside of us," and she invites, "Come into Black geography / you, seated like Manzu's cardinal, / come up through tongues / multiplying memories." *Under a Soprano Sky* continues her technical and thematic predilections. The volume especially continues the topicality and real-person subjects in her poems and demonstrates well her use of the specific in the conveying of broader philosophical positions.

In *Wounded in the House of a Friend* Sanchez's volition for entering the pain-filled corridor of human life is apparent. She supports her own contention that "this is not a small voice / you hear," as she nimbly and powerfully speaks in the multiple voices of the hopeless and the hope-filled. She broadens her political, social, and cultural landscape of racism and sexism to include a heightened awareness of the daily and personal traumas of infidelity, drug addiction, abuse, and rape that afflict a global humanity. Sanchez stages the title poem, "Wounded in the House of a Friend," as an absurdist drama in which the loss of shared values destroys a marriage. The male and female speakers trudge through the emotional sludge of suspicion and hurt and of recognition and resolution, finally to understand that the husband's "wolfdreams" of adulterous relationships and his aspirations for a spiraling corporate career are opposed to the wife's penchant for down-to-earth activism.

Sanchez's voice resonates with the clarity of a seasoned eavesdropper as she shares the narratives of human pain. Drug abuse is the dominant theme in "Love Song No. 3," where an 18-year-old drug addict hammers her grandmother to death to gain access to insurance money, and in "Poem for Some Women," where a drug-addicted mother temporarily trades the "prettiest little girl," her seven-year-old daughter, to satisfy her "jones jones jones / habit habit habit" for drugs. In "Eyewitness: / Case No. 3456" the female speaker "nicks" the reader with the wrenching agony of the knife she endures at the hands of a rapist. Sanchez's ability to gaze at life with an unflinching stare and to capture and manipulate the screaming and moaning voices that enter her cultural, political, and social domain is evident in both the physical and emo-

tional scars of the victims and the psychological wounds of the perpetrators.

Sanchez seeks balance in the work by ending with a signature series of haiku and tanka that breathlessly alter the terrain with fragments of memory: "if i had known then / what i know now, i would have / picked my own cotton." But it is through her tributes that Sanchez's persistent and resilient spirit soars. She weaves the trials of the past with the hopes of the future as she pays homage to *Essence* magazine, Spelman College, Bill Cosby, James Baldwin, and the singing group Sweet Honey and the Rock.

Over the years Sanchez has tended to depend less on poetic statement and more on indirection, thereby asking more of the reader. In her figurative language she favors the imagistic, metaphorical, and ironical. Many of her allusive constructs depend upon emotive and, increasingly in her later works, intellectual recognition by African Americans, a recognition often reliant on what critic Stephen Henderson would call the reader's and hearer's ethnic "saturation." For example, in an ironic image reversal she writes about patriarchal poet Sterling A. Brown as "griot of the wind / glorifying red gums smiling tom-tom teeth," and in a poem about singer Billie Holiday she says, "speak yo / strange / fruit amid these / stones."

As to structure, Sanchez usually fits form to substance. Her poems are modern in their nontraditional spatial configurations, unconventional syntax and mechanics, portmanteau terms, and improvisational quality. Occasionally she uses the sonnet form. She composes haiku and tanka, and although they follow line and syllabic conventions, they tend in substance to be statements rather than suggestive evocations of fleeting experiences. Overall, while her poetry has become less literal and more subtle and cerebral, it is still characteristically pointed.

Much of Sanchez's poetry is principally addressed to African Americans, among whom she is popular. She also, however, has a sizable white following, especially among those whom she characterizes as "progressive" whites. Critics' assessments of Sanchez's poetry vary. It is not unusual for academic and establishment critics and anthologists, who rely upon traditional, received criteria and canons, to pay only passing attention to her earlier work. Women critics tend to regard her poetry very favorably and in fact began paying serious attention to her work well before her rediscovery by African American critics. African American critics and literary academicians generally consider Sanchez to be an unusually talented and significant poet.

—Theodore R. Hudson and B. J. Bolden

SATYAMURTI, Carole

Nationality: British. **Born:** Farnborough, Kent, 13 August 1939. **Education:** University of London, 1957-60, 1972-79, B.A. 1960, Ph.D. 1979; University of Illinois, Champaign, 1960-61, M.A. 1967; University of Birmingham, England, 1964-65, postgraduate diploma in social work 1965. **Family:** Married T. V. Sathyamurthy in 1963 (divorced 1986); one daughter. **Career:** Lecturer, University of Singapore, 1963-64; social worker, Save the Children Fund, Kampala, Uganda, 1965-67; social worker, Ealing Child Guidance Clinic, London, 1967-68. Since 1968 lecturer, senior lecturer, then principal lecturer, University of East London. Writer-in-residence,

University of Sussex, 1997. **Awards:** National Poetry Competition First prize, 1986; Arts Council (UK) Writers' award, 1988. **Address:** 15 Gladwell Road, London N8 9AA, England.

PUBLICATIONS

Poetry

Broken Moon. Oxford University Press, 1987.
Changing the Subject. Oxford University Press, 1990.
Striking Distance. Oxford University Press, 1994.

Other

Occupational Survival. Oxford, Basil Blackwell, 1981.

Editor, with Noel Parry and Michael Rustin, *Social Work, Welfare & the State.* London, Edward Arnold, 1979.

*

Carole Satyamurti comments:

Many of the poems I write are concerned, from different points of view, with the way in which one life touches on another. By this I mean not just the influence that people have on each other but, more specifically, the *otherness* of others, and the way we imagine them—or fail to. The "other" life in question may be that of a stranger, or someone we think we know well; or it may be our own other lives—past, future or potential.

The epigraph for *Striking Distance* is Elizabeth Bishop's startling question, "Why should I be my aunt / or me, or anyone?" ("In the Waiting Room") and many of the poems are an exploration of different dimensions of that existential shock. It does seem to me very strange and arbitrary that I inhabit one skin rather than another, and I often have the vertiginous illusion that, by really attending to another state of being, one might enter into that other person, that other life. There's a tension between the connectedness and separateness of lives, between sameness and difference, that several of the poems try to capture. The distance between people can seem striking.

Someone accused me once of writing as if I wished that language wasn't necessary. I do mind absolutely about language, but I want it to act as a window rather than a mirror—framing, letting light in, allowing as clear a view as possible of what lies beyond it. This is not to imply some simple equivalence between language and what it denotes—Derrida is right. Nor do I think that what the language refers to is itself straightforward. But, primarily, I search for a precision, a "rightness" of language, rather than an exciting inventiveness.

We go through our lives, if we're lucky, with something that feels like a self. But there are times when we don't "feel ourselves," or when we feel we'll never be the same again. Many of my poems are about turning points, real or imagined, moments that mark a shift between one way of being and another.

The voice varies. To write in a different persona, for instance, is itself an imperfectly achieved act of imagining the other, and always in the recognition that one can hardly ever get within striking distance of it.

*   *   *

The hallmark of Carole Satyamurti's poetry at its best is the clarity and precision of its language, the sharpness of its visual imagery, and its concerns. She seeks, she tells us in an article for the Poetry Book Society, "a rightness of language rather than an exciting inventiveness." She goes for substance rather than style. Nevertheless, her first collection, *Broken Moon,* displays a proper poetic concern for language and its place in our identities. The first impressive and substantial poem in the book, "Between the Lines," treats of a childhood where "words are dust-sheets, blinds," and where "adults buried questions under bushes." It is a place where the developing child is "striving for language that would let me out" and "where people were difficult to read." A later poem, "Erdywurble," pursues the matter of language further, to the point where a flawed child invents his own language until "his words trickled, stopped." The language and the child die together.

This concern continues in Satyamurti's later collections of poems. In *Changing the Subject* the poem "Birth Rite" explores experience beyond words to a deeper language:

> To be reborn with you
> I shed responsibility,
> my social face,
> speech, consciousness.
> I reach back to the dark.

Then there are those everyday encounters with ambivalence and ambiguity in "How Are You?" or with the hierarchy of nomenclature in "Knowing Our Place."

There are, of course, other concerns in Satyamurti's poetry. It is a humane poetry in which, she tells us, she is concerned with "the otherness of others." A direct confrontation with this comes in the acceptance of the fact that her daughter has grown up and has assumed her own individuality. This is movingly expressed in the poem "Pulling Away."

There can be sharpness as well as insight in Satyamurti's observations along with a waspish sense of humor. "Singapore 1963," a poem that is close to being perfect, illustrates not only her skill in conjuring visual imagery but also her mastery of a fierce irony. The street market is presented vividly in admirably economic images both visual and aural: its "naptha glare," the paucity of the listed offerings displayed on the spread mat, and the "cat-cries aimed at those almost as ragged as herself." The self-important commentary of the poet's companion, "rehearsing your lecture as we walked," is a counterpoint that is juxtaposed with savage irony but that also underlines the concern of the poem itself.

Another special personal quality in Satyamurti's poetry is that of sympathetic courage, which is to be found in her longish sequence of poems "Changing the Subject." As the title indicates, these poems return to the matter of language.

The evasion of the subject of cancer and even the word itself is the starting point. They move on to a deeper consideration, rooted firmly in the life and routines of hospital life and with a deeply sympathetic concern for the other patients, which underlines her own courageous stance. If this sounds daunting, it is redeemed by Satyamurti's sureness of touch and poetic sensibility.

—John Cotton

SCALAPINO, Leslie

Nationality: American. **Born:** Santa Barbara, California, 25 July 1947. **Education:** Reed College, B.A.; University of California, Berkeley, M.A. **Family:** Married 1) Wesley St. John in 1969 (divorced 1973); 2) Tom White in 1987. **Career:** Member of English faculty, College of Marin, Kentfield, California, New College of California, San Francisco, 1982, 1983-84, San Francisco State University, 1984, University of California, San Diego, 1990, Bard College, summers 1992-97, San Francisco Art Institute, fall, 1995, 1996, 1997, and Mills College, 1996-97. Co-editor, *Foot,* 1979. Publisher, O Books, 1986—. **Awards:** Woodrow Wilson fellowship; National Endowment for the Arts fellowship, 1976, 1986; Before Columbus Foundation award, 1988; San Francisco State University Poetry Center award, 1988; Lawrence Lipton award, 1988. **Address:** 5729 Clover Drive, Oakland, California 94618, U.S.A.

PUBLICATIONS

Poetry

O and Other Poems. Berkeley, California, Sandollar Press, 1976.
The Woman Who Could Read the Minds of Dogs. Berkeley, California, Sandollar Press, 1976.
Instead of an Animal. Berkeley, California, Poltroon Press, 1977.
This Eating and Walking at the Same Time Is Associated Alright. Bolinas, California, Tombouctou, 1979.
Considering How Exaggerated Music Is. Berkeley, California North Point Press, 1982.
That They Were at the Beach. Berkeley, California, North Point Press, 1985.
Way. Berkeley, California, North Point Press, 1988.
Crowd and not evening or light. Oakland, California, and Paris, France, O Books, 1990.
Green and Black: Selected Writings. Hoboken, New Jersey, Talisman, 1996.

Plays

The Present (produced San Francisco, 1993).
The Weatherman Turns Himself In (produced San Francisco, 1993).
Goya's L.A., a play (produced San Francisco, 1995). Elmwood, Connecticut, Potes & Poets Press, 1994.

Novels

The Return of Painting, The Pearl, and Orion / A Trilogy. Berkeley, California, North Point Press, 1991; second edition, Hoboken, New Jersey, Talisman, 1997.
Defoe. Los Angles, Sun & Moon Press, 1994.
The Front Matter, Dead Souls. Middletown, Connecticut, Wesleyan University Press, 1996.

Other

How Phenomena Appear to Unfold (essays and plays). Elmwood, Connecticut, Potes & Poets Press, 1990.

Objects in the Terrifying Tense / Longing from Taking Place (essay). New York, Roof Books, 1994.

*

Critical Study: The Leslie Scalapino issue of *Talisman* (Hoboken, New Jersey), no. 8, 1992.

Leslie Scalapino comments:

I write using numerous forms, wanting to track continual change. If there were one sentence written on my work, I would like it to be, "Leslie Scalapino has made lots of changes and does not avoid reality."

*   *   *

Leslie Scalapino is a situational poet. Like the language poets with whom she is associated, Scalapino focuses less on isolated events and heightened responses (including her own) than on the cultural matrices which produce them. To know why something happened, or why she (re)acted the way she did, Scalapino looks not for the personal, mythical, symbolic, or historical "point of origin" but for patterned webs of circumstance. She writes series of poems or stanzas, for instance, rather than individual lyrics. Her work is elliptical like Emily Dickinson's, repetitive like Gertrude Stein's, minimally narrative like Ernest Hemingway's, and spatially exploratory like H.D.'s and Robert Duncan's. But Scalapino finds her own way to patch together her stories.

Consider these stanzas from Scalapino's prose piece "that they were at the beach—aelotropic series":

It'd have to be some time ago—I got cake on me, handed to me by my mother, we're in a taxi. Men in another car— beside me, I'm somewhat immature in age—whistled and called to me customary stemming from seeing me eating the cake

(so I'm embarrassed)

Scalapino's congested narrative spurts are more customary in a Hemingway or Raymond Carver story than in a prose poem. The past is made present not by ignoring the frame—the narrative commentary—but by foregrounding it. Stein's "continuous present" is the time of narration. Comparing one of her works to a comic book, Scalapino explains that "the writing does not have actual pictures. It 'functions' as does a comic book—in being read. And read aloud to someone the picture has to be described or seen and then what the figure it says read." The situation here is complex and unusual: the mother and child, eating in lurches, are not at home; the men whistling are not neighbors. The embarrassment (both past and retroactive) is equally situational: to the men the child is a "piece of cake" along with her mother, who cannot protect the child from seeing herself in their eyes. The "customary" origin both of the men's and of her "reaction" is given in a series of participles and gerunds. These relational words and syntactical networks are privileged in Scalapino's work over isolated verbs or nouns. "That" in "That they were at the beach," like "Considering" in "Considering how exaggerated music is," constructs the societal loom of what is taken for granted for anything to happen.

In the series "walking by," which opens her looming book-length poem *Way,* Scalapino plays her oral history off disjunctive, reflective Dickinsonian verse. The poem and book begin with a syntactical strand:

to have
seem-
ed still—
though not
wanting to
be serene
—their—

I was in school; the bus driver seeing a girl crossing the
street hadn't stopped—she'd been hit—so the other
students—the boys—would hit the side of the bus everyday

when we went around that corner—our understanding the
driver—and clairvoyant

their—to
simply
make
that—
having
occur-
red to me

Again, we're thrown into a situation, and a syntax, that is bigger than we are, even with Scalapino's advantage of hindsight. The pattern is an intricate weave of seeing and being seen (compare "serene"), homicide and prank, man and boys and girls, and pluperfect with past perfect and present infinitive. The girl is as mute and "still" (silent, continuous) as the victim she witnesses; the accident has "occurred" and is still "occurring" ("run in the way," "happen," "think of") to her. The muted framing verses, which afford less perspective than the grim little story itself, mark an interior style in which the basic participants and grammatical elements are sorted out. These halting verses have displaced Scalapino's concluding parentheses—"(so I'm embarrassed)"—as hesitant conclusions to the "accident" and its aftermath.

Scalapino's fragmented webs of consciousness are quilts of social conscience. In "bum series," also from *Way,* Scalapino patches together the "bums" (to use their situational, political name) who have died from exposure on the docks, the "new wave" person in imported "bum-wear," popular (along with homelessness) during the Reagan years, and the unloading freighters, adding to the trade imbalance that produces more bums:

to their
social struggle in their
whole setting, which is
abroad and its
relation to the freighter

to the person of
new wave attire—that
person's relation to
the freighter

when the bums are not
alive—at this time—though

were here, not abroad—and
not aware in being so of a
social struggle

These nonsequential, floating stanzas mime their apparently isolated incidents and individuals. But the syntactical loom, which would subordinate clauses, promote its "main" subject and predicate, and reveal deviations from proper word order, never surfaces. The class-bound global sentence remains a piece of resistance. The drama in Scalapino's vast, minimal poetry is its setting, and her settings are among the most engaging in contemporary poetry.

—John Shoptaw

SCHNACKENBERG, Gjertrud

Nationality: American. **Born:** Tacoma, Washington, 27 August 1953. **Education:** Mount Holyoke College, South Hadley, Massachusetts, B.A. (summa cum laude) 1975. **Family:** Married Robert Nozick in 1987. **Awards:** Radcliffe College Bunting Institute fellowship, 1979-80; Lavan award, 1983; American Academy-Institute of Arts and Letters Rome fellowship, 1983; National Endowment for the Arts fellowship, 1986; Guggenheim fellowship, 1987. H.D.L.: Mount Holyoke College, 1985. **Address:** c/o Farrar Straus & Giroux Inc., 19 Union Square West, New York, New York 10003, U.S.A.

PUBLICATIONS

Poetry

Portraits and Elegies. Boston, Godine, 1982; revised edition, New
   York, Farrar Straus, 1986; London, Century Hutchinson, 1987.
The Lamplit Answer. New York, Farrar Straus, 1985; London, Century Hutchinson, 1986.
A Gilded Lapse of Time. New York, Farrar Straus, 1992; London,
   Harville, 1995.

*   *   *

In the mid-1980s a new American formalism was signaled and discussed. By 1987 Alan Shapiro in *Critical Inquiry* was able to declare, "Open the pages of almost any national journal or magazine, and where, ten years ago, one found only one or another kind of free verse lyric one now finds well-rhymed quatrains, sestinas, villanelles, sonnets and blank verse dramatic monologues or meditations." Perhaps this New Formalism had something to do not only with a dialectical reaction to dominant modes of American poetry but also to the proliferating creative writing programs in universities. In any event, the American renaissance in formal strategies led to poems being published that were neither better nor worse than most verse available at any time. For most poetry published is, alas, tedious and unlit.

But some of the poets associated with the New Formalism demand serious attention, not least Gjertrud Schnackenberg, who has used meter and rhyme without subduing emotional currents in each of her three collections—*Portraits and Elegies, The Lamplit Answer,* and *A Gilded Lapse of Time.* She has—to adapt a phrase of Richard Wilbur—employed her cadences and rhyme not as ornament but as emphasis.

Her first book, *Portraits and Elegies*—well named, for that is what the poems in it exactly are—was published in 1982. Her elegies, though corseted, are full of feeling. They conjure up, through the telling of anecdotes, a once-loving father-daughter relationship. These touching memories of her father are a form of celebration as well as being a requiem. In 12 separate poems she celebrates her father's piano playing; his ability to extract a significant lesson from some mundane incident—such as a bird dropping excreta on his head; his courteous behavior during a brush with a bow-tied English cyclist at Cambridge; father-and-daughter trips that involve night fishing and visits as tourists to Norway, Rome, and Germany.

The total effect of these dozen beautifully composed elegies is to hear the speaking voice of a young woman in controlled mourning, rather than one displaying a "grief approaching lunacy."

There is a second notable sequence, in this first book, of 16 poems called "19 Hadley Street." These prove to be snapshots of the denizens of an affluent house over two centuries. The album's initial pages reveal a married couple in 1960, the husband fatally ill with cancer. We turn the pages and return to voices of the past, first to the wife as a child in 1905, then to earlier generations who have lived in that same house on Hadley Street. These sepia poems of domesticity, happy or tragic, are set against the appropriate historical background until we are led to the root, to the engendering guilt that is intrinsic to American history:

> ... Your mother lost her wits
> When news came that a squaw was torn to bits
> By village dogs in Hockanum ...

After that dazzling debut, we were not disappointed by the poems in Schnackenberg's second volume, *The Lamplit Answer,* though here some of the narratives and portraits seem overlong and labored. Apart from empathetic glimpses of Chopin, Simone Weil, and Darwin, we are surprised by such grim, Grimm-like, fairy-tale variants as "Two Tales of Clumsy" which feature death's representative, a certain "No-No." (This poem, by the way, contains, surprisingly, an occasional aural error, as in the fourth line below.)

> To Mrs Clumsy since that happy time
> She summoned Clumsy with her dinner chime.
> And there is Clumsy's darling lying dead.
> How like a rubber ball bounces her head
> As No-No drags her feet-first from this life.
> Then No-No dresses up as Clumsy's wife...

The humorous tone of this macabre fairy story is extended to a sequence of love poems. These, addressed to a lover who has abandoned her, though ostentatiously witty and clever, cannot be current of feeling that motors them, and thus the sequence is saved from frivolity. Moreover, Schnackenberg has the knack of being able to lift the conclusion of her poems with a striking image or simile—"window squares like Bibles closed forever, squares of black"—or with sheer eloquence, as in her first book in the ending to the elegy called "Bavaria," where she recalls how she stood outside Neuschwanstein castle, accompanied by her father, a professor of history:

> We linger, for a moment, at the gates:
> Here Ludwig, in his grisly innocence,

Plucked water lilies planted an hour since
By silent gardeners, hurled his dinner plates
At statue niches peopled with assassins,
And wept that Nietzsche called his love a Jew.
It is November 1962,
A siren from the village rises, spins
Itself into a planet of alarm
That hangs a moment in the wilderness,
And dusk comes through the forest with Venus,
Star of emergency, upon its arm.

The poet is at her best when her historical perspectives are personalized in this way and when emotion is recollected in tranquility. Those suspicious of the possibilities of the New Formalism should turn, for instance, to "Supernatural Love," the final impressive poem in *The Lamplit Answer.* Here the poet reinhabits a scene from childhood where, once again, the dramatis personae are father and daughter. The poem resonates in the mind long after the book is closed because of its rhymes and meter, because of theme, feeling, and telling image, because of the evidence of an intricately organizing mind that skillfully stitches all these together.

—Dannie Abse

SEGUN, Mabel

Pseudonyms: Mabel Imoukhuede; Mabel Jolaoso; Dorothy Okanima. **Nationality:** Nigerian. **Born:** Mabel Aig-Imoukhuede, in Ondo, Ondo State, 18 February 1930. **Education:** University College, Ibadan, Nigeria, B.A. (second-class honors) in English literature, Latin, and history 1953. **Family:** Married 1) Olujimi Jolaoso in 1952 (divorced 1957); 2) Oludotun Segun in 1960 (divorced 1975), two sons and one daughter. **Career:** Hansard editor for Nigerian legislature, 1958-61; information officer in charge of overseas publicity, Western Nigeria Information Service, Ibadan, 1961-63; editor, *Modern Woman,* 1964-67; head of broadcasting unit, Federal Department of Education, 1968-70; teacher at various schools in Ibadan, Lagos, and Benein City, 1970—; principal education officer, 1971-73, acting vice-principal, 1978-79, then chief education officer and head of department of English and social studies, 1977-79, National Technical Teachers' College, Yaba, 1971-73; deputy permanent delegate to UNESCO, Paris, 1979-81; chief federal inspector of education, Lagos, Nigeria, 1981-82; senior research fellow, Institute of African Studies, University of Ibadan, 1982-89; currently director, Children's Literature Documentation and Research Centre, Ibadan. Short stories, articles, book reviews, and poetry published in numerous anthologies and periodicals; freelance broadcaster for "Voice of Nigeria," Lagos, 1964-70, WNTV Schools Program, Ibadan, British Broadcasting Corporation, NBC Television, and Nigerian Television. **Awards:** Nigerian National Festival of the Arts Literature Prize, 1954, for short fiction "The Surrender"; Radio Nigeria Artiste-of-the-Year, 1977; International Youth Library fellowship (Munich, Germany), 1993; numerous awards for table tennis competitions, including National Sports Commission award, 1988. **Address:** 18A Solel Boneh Way, New Bodija, U.I.P.O. Box 20744, Ibadan, Nigeria.

PUBLICATIONS

Poetry

Under the Mango Tree, with Nevill Grant (for children). London, Longman, 1980.
Conflicts and Other Poems. Ibadan, New Horn Press, 1986.

For Children

Youth Day Parade. Ibadan, Daystar Press, 1984.
Olu and the Broken Statute. Ibadan, New Horn Press, 1985.
The First Corn. Lagos, Longman Nigeria, 1989.
The Twins and the Tree Spirits. Ibadan, Children's Literature Documentation and Research Centre, 1991.
ABC Song. Lagos, Malthouse Press, forthcoming.

Other

My Father's Daughter (autobiography). Lagos, African Universities Press, 1965.
Friends, Nigerians, Countrymen. Ibadan, Oxford University Press, 1977; as *Sorry No Vacancy,* Ibadan, University Press, 1985.
My Mother's Daughter (autobiography). Ibadan, African Universities Press, 1987.
Ping Pong: 25 Years of Table Tennis (memoirs). Ibadan, Daystar Press, 1989.
The Surrender and Other Stories. London, Longman, 1995.

Editor and contributor, *Illustrating for Children.* Ibadan, Children's Literature Association of Nigeria, 1988.

Translator, *Olowolayemo* by Femi Jeboda. Ibadan, Longman Nigeria, forthcoming.

*

Critical Studies: *African Authors: A Companion to Black African Writing* edited by Donald E. Herdeck, Washington, D.C., n.p., 1974; in *Daughters of Africa* edited by Margaret Busby, New York, Pantheon, 1992.

*   *   *

Mabel Jolaoso Segun (nee Imoukhuede) has had a varied literary career, including publishing in the genres of poetry, non-fiction, and books for young people. In addition to her collection *Conflict and Other Poems* (1987), her poetry has been published in Swiss and German journals, as well as journals like *Black Orpheus* and *Odu,* both published in Ibadan, Nigeria, and in the anthology *Schwarzer Orpheus.*

In the often anthologized poem, "The Pigeon-Hole," Segun explores the themes of self-knowledge and self-trust:

How I wish I could pigeon-hole myself
and neatly fix a label on!
But self-knowledge comes too late
and by the time I've known myself
I am no longer what I was.

I knew a woman once
who had a delinquent child.

she never had a moments peace of mind
waiting in constant fear,
listening for the dreaded knock
and the cold tones of policeman:
"Madam, you're wanted at the station."
I don't know if the knock ever came
but she feared on right till
we moved away from the street.
She used to say,
"It's the uncertainty that worries me—
if only I new for certain..."

If only I knew for certain
what my delinquent self would do...
But I never know
until the deed is done
and I live on fearing,
wondering which part of me will be supreme—
the old and tested one, the present
or the future unknown.
Sometimes all three have equal power
and then
how I long for a pigeon-hole.

Segun's use of free-verse contrasts sharply with the highly structured, three-part poem, which illuminates the speaker's three-part personality. In part one, the speaker's desire for a definitive sense of self is neatly compressed into a five-line stanza that acknowledges the self-growth that accompanies maturity. Part two of the poem expands the speaker's sense of anxiety by offering an anecdotal model of a woman whose life is plagued by a similar sense of "uncertainty." Finally, in part three of the poem, the speaker addresses the "delinquent" part of herself, which she fears may disrupt the comfort zone of her "old and tested" personality. In search of psychological and emotional safety, the speaker longs to trade the "future unknown" for a trustworthy pigeon-holed personality of certainty and consistency.

Segun expresses a similar dilemma in the poem "Conflict," where the speaker seeks both cultural and individual escape:

Here we stand
infants overblown,
poised between two civilisations,
finding the balance irksome,
itching for something to happen,
to tip us one way or the other,
groping in the dark for a helping hand
and finding none.
I'm tired, O my God, I'm tired,
I'm tired of hanging in the middle way—
but where can I go?

Though the speaker begins with a tone of cultural inclusiveness in the opening lines, "Here we stand.... two civilisations," by the final three lines of the poem, it is clear that the speaker is also groping for individual guidance. The mournful line, "I'm so tired, O my God," establishes a stark contrast between the "we" and "us" of the collective community and the speaker's own personal anguish. A sense of cultural and personal entrapment permeates the poem by the visible enclosure of the opening line, "Here we stand," and the closing line, "but where can I go?"

Segun's writings subtly comment on the tensions that abound in her country and how they impact the individual. In her essay, "Polygamy—Ancient and Modern" (from *Friends, Nigerians, Countrymen,* 1965; published as *Sorry, No Vacancy,* 1985), she employs both prose and poetry to explore what Margaret Busby calls the "inescapable fact of polygamy" in African society.

—B.J. Bolden

SENIOR, Olive (Marjorie)

Nationality: Jamaican (immigrated to Canada in 1991). **Born:** Jamaica, 23 December 1941. **Education:** Carleton University, Ottawa, 1963-67, B.S. 1967. **Career:** Reporter and sub-editor, *Daily Gleaner* newspaper, Jamaica; information officer, Jamaica Information Service, 1967-69; public relations officer, Jamaica Chamber of Commerce and editor, *JCC Journal,* 1969-71; publications editor, Institute of Social and Economic Research, University of the West Indies, Jamaica, and editor, *Social and Economic Studies,* 1972-77; freelance writer and researcher, part-time teacher in communications, publishing consultant, and speech writer, Jamaica, 1977-82; managing editor, Institute of Jamaica Publications, and editor, *Jamaica Journal,* 1982-89; freelance teacher, writer, lecturer, internationally, 1989-94; visiting lecturer/writer-in-residence, University of the West Indies, Cave Hill, Barbados, 1990. Director of fiction workshop, Caribbean Writers Summer Institute, University of Miami, Florida, 1994, 1995. Dana Visiting Professor of creative writing, St. Lawrence University, Canton, New York, 1994-95. **Awards:** Commonwealth Writers' prize, 1967; Gold, Silver, and Bronze medals for poetry and fiction, Jamaica Festival Literary Competitions, 1968-70; winner in two categories, Longman International Year of the Child Short Story Competition, 1978; Institute of Jamaica Centenary medal for creative writing, 1979; UNESCO award for study in the Philippines, 1987; Jamaica Press Association award for editorial excellence, 1987; United States Information Service, International Visitor award, 1988; Institute of Jamaica, Silver Musgrave medal for literature, 1989; F.G. Bressani Literary prize for poetry, 1994, for *Gardening in the Tropics.* Hawthornden fellow, Scotland, 1990; International Writer-in-Residence, Arts Council of England, 1991. **Agent:** Nicole Aragi, Watkins/Loomis Agency, 133 East 35th Street, Suite 1, New York, New York 10016, U.S.A.

PUBLICATIONS

Poetry

Talking of Trees. Kingston, Calabash, 1986.
Gardening in the Tropics. Toronto, McClelland & Stewart, 1994.

Short Stories

Summer Lightning. London, Longmans, 1987.
Arrival of the Snake-Woman. London, Longmans, 1989.
Quartet, with others. London, Longmans, 1994.
Discerner of Hearts. Toronto, McClelland & Stewart, 1995.

Other

The Message Is Change. Kingston, Jamaica, Kingston Publishers, 1972.
Pop Story Gi Mi (four booklets on Jamaican heritage for schools). Kingston, Ministry of Education, 1973.
A-Z of Jamaican Heritage. Kingston, Heinemann & Gleaner Company Ltd., 1984.
Working Miracles: Women's Lives in the English-Speaking Caribbean. London, James Currey, and Bloomington, Indiana University Press, 1991.

*

Critical Studies: Olive Senior issue of *Callaloo* (Baltimore), vol. 11, no. 3, Summer 1988; in *Critical Strategies* by Malcolm Kinnery and Michael Rose, Boston, Bedford Books / St. Martin's Press, 1989; in *Out of the Kumbla: Caribbean Women and Literature,* edited by Carole Boyce Davies and Elaine Savory Fido, New York, Africa World Press, 1990; in *Caribbean Women Writers,* edited by Selwyn Cudje, Wellesley, Massachusetts, Calaloux Publications, 1990; in *Motherlands. Black Women's Writing from Africa, the Caribbean and South Asia,* edited by Susheila Nasta, London, Women's Press, 1991; in *Come Back to Me My Language: Poetry and the West Indies* by J.E. Chamberlin, Champaign, University of Illinois Press, 1993; in *Woman Version: Theoretical Approaches to West Indian Fiction by Women* by Evelyn O'Callaghan, London, Macmillan, 1993; "The Fiction of Olive Senior" by Richard F. Patteson, in *Ariel, A Review of International English Literature* (Calgary, Alberta), vol. 24, no. 1, January 1993.

*   *   *

In a headnote to the last section of her first book, *Talking of Trees* (1985), Olive Senior quotes Bertolt Brecht: "What kind of period is it when to talk of trees is almost a crime because it implies silence about so many horrors?" Senior, as if to answer Brecht, writes serious and noisy poems about the natural world while little ignoring the horrors of Jamaica's colonial history. In the long title poem she writes,

> Our roots tied up the harbour
> Mangroves of resistance.

In this and other poems Senior locates Jamaica's political history in its botanical one, drawing from the historical fact that Jamaica was colonized and peopled with slaves because of its agricultural importance:

> Cane trash mi life
> Cane break mi spirit
> Cane sweeten mi bizzie
> Banana rotten mi clothes

Senior's second book, *Gardening in the Tropics* (1994), contains a sequence of 12 poems that begin with the title phrase. But the most powerful poem of the collection may be her "Meditation on Yellow," which examines the meaning of the color in both its aesthetic and political senses. The poem is addressed to (one assumes white) tourists, served by black waiters, who take tea at three in the afternoon. It begins with an apology of sorts for the blackness of the toast and the waiter's skin but then becomes a litany of angry explanation:

> but I've been travelling long
> cross the sea in the sun-hot
> I've been slaving in the cane rows
> for your sugar
> I've been ripening coffee beans
> for your morning break

The list goes on to include bananas, oranges, ginger, cocoa, and aluminum, all of which the speaker has been growing or mining from the land.

Senior recognizes that the system of colonization she so aptly describes is not limited to physical labor but also manifests itself in the educational system and in the English language itself. She addresses the problem of language in "Pineapple":

> With yayama
> fruit of the Antilles,
> we welcomed you
> to our shores,
> not knowing in
> your language
> "house warming"
> meant "to take
> possession of" and "host"
> could so easily turn hostage.

The educational system refuses to recognize the landscape in which it operates. In "Colonial Girls School" Senior writes about the "Borrowed images" that "willed our skins pale" and "yoked our minds to declensions in Latin / and the language of Shakespeare." This system "Told us nothing about ourselves... / There was nothing of our landscape there / Nothing about us at all." Like fellow Caribbean poet Derek Walcott, however, Senior writes mostly in the Standard English of her education, even as she makes her central subject the landscape and her gardening and writing (which she obviously intends to link metaphorically).

Senior also explores the ways in which the assumptions enforced by the educational system are internalized by the family. (It is hard to label any of her poems autobiographical, since her strongest form is dramatic monologue and she is often obviously not writing as herself.) In "Cockpit Country Dreams" the speaker quotes her mother, who had forced her to choose only one of the family's histories as her own:

> Listen child, said my mother
> whose hands plundered photo albums
> of all black ancestors: Herein
> your ancestry, your imagery, your pride.
> Choose this river, this rhythm, this road.
> Walk good in the footsteps of these fathers.

It is interesting that the last line here contains a grammatical flaw assigned to the mother; it's as if her origins (likely in patois) cannot be hidden, even as she tries hard not to reveal them. At her best Senior turns this contrast on its head, exploring the strengths of her place and her writing of it. In "Gardening on the Run" she again conflates the acts of writing and gardening:

> We are always there
> like some dark stain in your
> diaries and notebooks, your
> letters, your court records,
> your law books—as if we had
> ambushed your pen. Now I have
> time to read (and garden), I who
> spent so many years in disquiet,
> living in fear of discovering,
> am amazed to discover, Colonist,
> it was you who feared me.

The poet's act of discovering her origins in the natural and historical worlds thus reverses that of Columbus discovering the New World. It proves liberating to Senior, however, as a gardener and, more importantly, as a poet.

—Susan M. Schultz

SHANGE, Ntozake

Nationality: American. **Born:** Paulette Williams, Trenton, New Jersey, 18 October 1948; took name Ntozake Shange in 1971. **Education:** Schools in St. Louis and New Jersey; Barnard College, New York, 1966-70, B.A. (cum laude) in American studies 1970; University of Southern California, Los Angeles, 1971-73, M.A. in American studies 1973. **Family:** Married David Murray in 1977 (2nd marriage; divorced); one daughter. **Career:** Faculty member, Sonoma State College, Rohnert Park, California, 1973-75, Mills College, Oakland, California, 1975, City College, New York, 1975, and Douglass College, New Brunswick, New Jersey, 1978; associate professor of drama, University of Houston, 1983—. Artist-in-residence, Equinox Theater, Houston, 1981—, and New Jersey State Council on the Arts. **Awards:** New York Drama Critics Circle award, 1977; Obie award, 1977, 1980; Columbia University Medal of Excellence, 1981; Los Angeles *Times* award, 1981; Guggenheim fellowship, 1981. **Address:** c/o St. Martin's Press, 175 Fifth Avenue, New York, New York 10010, U.S.A.

PUBLICATIONS

Poetry

Melissa and Smith. St. Paul, Bookslinger, 1976.
Natural Disasters and Other Festive Occasions. San Francisco, Heirs, 1977.
Nappy Edges. New York, St. Martin's Press, 1978; London, Methuen, 1987.
Some Men. Privately printed, 1981.
A Daughter's Geography. New York, St. Martin's Press, 1983; London, Methuen, 1985.
From Okra to Greens. St. Paul, Coffee House Press, 1984.
Ridin' the Moon in Texas: Word Paintings. New York, St. Martin's Press, 1988.
The Love Space Demands: A Continuing Saga. New York, St. Martin's Press, 1992.

Recording: *I Live in Music,* Watershed, 1984; *Beneath the Necessity of Talking: Performance Piece,* American Audio Prose Library, 1989.

Plays

for colored girls who have considered suicide when the rainbow is enuf (produced New York, 1975; London, 1980). San Lorenzo, California, Shameless Hussy Press, 1976; revised version, New York, Macmillan, 1977; London, Eyre Methuen, 1978.
A Photograph: Lovers-in-Motion (as *A Photograph: A Still Life with Shadows, A Photograph: A Study of Cruelty* produced New York, 1977; revised version, as *A Photograph: Lovers-in-Motion,* also director: produced Houston, 1979). New York, S. French, 1981.
Where the Mississippi Meets the Amazon, with Thulani Nkabinda and Jessica Hagedorn (produced New York, 1977).
Spell #7 (produced New York, 1979; London, 1985). Included in *Three Pieces,* 1981; published separately, London, Methuen, 1985.
Black and White Two-Dimensional Planes (produced New York, 1979).
Boogie Woogie Landscapes (produced on tour, 1980). Included in *Three Pieces,* 1981.
Mother Courage and Her Children, adaptation of a play by Brecht (produced New York, 1980).
From Okra to Greens: A Different Kinda Love Story (as *Mouths* produced New York, 1981; as *From Okra to Greens* in *Three for a Full Moon,* produced Los Angeles, 1982). New York and London, S. French, 1983.
Three Pieces: Spell #7, A Photograph: Lovers-in-Motion, Boogie Woogie Landscape. New York, St. Martin's Press, 1981.
Three for a Full Moon, and Bocas (produced Los Angeles, 1982).
Educating Rita, adaptation of the play by Willy Russell (produced Atlanta, 1983).
Three Views of Mt. Fuji (produced New York, 1987).

Novels

Sassafrass: A Novella. San Lorenzo, California, Shameless Hussy Press, 1977.
Sassafrass, Cypress and Indigo. New York, St. Martin's Press, 1982; London, Methuen, 1983.
Betsey Brown. New York, St. Martin's Press, and London, Methuen. 1985.
Liliane: Resurrection of the Daughter. London, Methuen, 1995.

Other

See No Evil: Prefaces, Essays, and Accounts 1976-1983. San Francisco, Momo's Press, 1984.
Whitewash (for children), illustrated by Michael Sporn. New York, Walker, 1997.

*

Theatrical Activities:
Director: **Plays**—*The Mighty Gents* by Richard Wesley, New York, 1979; *A Photograph: Lovers-in-Motion,* Houston, 1979.
Actress: **Plays**—The Lady in Orange in *for colored girls who have considered suicide when the rainbow is enuf,* New York, 1976; in

Where the Mississippi Meets the Amazon, New York, 1977; in *Mouths.* New York. 1981.

Critical Sources: *Diving Deep and Surfacing: Women Writers on Spiritual Quest* by Carol P. Christ, Boston, Beacon Press, 1980; *Scars of Conquest / Masks of Resistance: The Invention of Cultural Identities in African, African-American, and Caribbean Drama* by Tejumola Olaniyan, New York, Oxford University Press, 1995.

*   *   *

Ntozake Shange is a contemporary black poet, playwright, and novelist. Like many postcolonial writers, Shange attempts to forge a place within the literary tradition for forms, styles, and subject matter that have been excluded from it. That tradition has largely been determined by white males, and Shange's verse draws attention to the cultural and gender specificity of their concerns. Whereas the white male tradition has foregrounded sameness and universality, traditions that politically serve to support its own value systems and ideology, Shange's poetry foregrounds difference and demands that difference be allowed to make itself felt. In poems like "2 march 1984 (cowry shells & heart)," from *Ridin' the Moon in Texas,* Shange voices black culture's rejection of the value system that has been imposed upon it:

> our rhythms   our guitar pulses
> are prohibited on the subway / considered déclassé
> north of 57th street / south of gramercy park
> our hearts don't beat
> they sweep us off our feet
> block the chaos & tumult the white people
> call civilization / ...

As Shange asserts in this passage, different cultures move to different rhythms, and the attempt to homogenize those differences inevitably leads to their repression by the dominant culture. Shange focuses on the oppression of white male culture and its literary dictates and draws attention to the fecundity of those voices it has ignored and silenced. Stylistically, her poetry is also different and signifies her rejection of white male literary forms. The lack of punctuation in Shange's writings reflects the idea that punctuation has been used to control and restrict the natural flow of language. In turn, the dialect in which she writes works in opposition to a white, "educated" discourse and reflects the cadence and rhythm of black speech. Poems like "A Celebration of Black Survival" display their roots in the black oral tradition and effect the lyrical movement of songs:

> what does it mean that blk folks cd sing n dance?
> why do we say that so much / we don't know what we mean /
> i saw what that means / good god / did i see / like i cda
> waked on the water myself / i cda clothed the naked &
> fed
> the hungry / with what dance i saw tonight / ...

While Shange's poetry attempts to forge a place for African Americans, as well as the oppressed people of the Third World, it is also committed to forging a place for women. In works like "Some Men" Shange concentrates on the plight of women, emphasizing the effects of men's efforts to make women conform to male standards:

> he kept the space empty. so no one wd ever imagine
> that a woman lived there / which is what he wanted
> for no one to know.
> if she lived empty & angular as he did, she'd become
> less a woman & part of the design / where anything he
> wanted to happen / happened.

As this poem suggests, for a woman to conform to male expectations of her is to lose her feminine self, a self that differs from male conceptions of what it should be. Shange's verse rejoices in femininity and in the differences she draws between female and male. It also highlights the gifts womanhood offers, and in poems like "torso" Shange tries to combat the ways in which femininity has been trivialized and marginalized in patriarchal discourse:

> ... a petal
> of a woman not knowing
> her fragrance enchanted
> men who could not bring themselves
> to call her name
> all they could do was turn away
> their eyes shut tightly
> refusing to lose the vision, the scent
> of the petal of a woman
> the flower meandering
> by the hummingbirds

Shange's prioritization of feminine traits is mirrored in the form of her poetry, which is fluid and circular rather than pointed and direct. Her verse is oriented toward the body and in particular highlights the nonrestrictive impetus of black feminine culture. The imagery of gestation and birth that she frequently employs emphasizes the connection between femininity and creative fecundity. Just as her celebratory poems about black culture often resemble song, so the verse she writes in support of femininity relies on dance. Dance becomes Shange's means of drawing attention to the natural movements of the female body. In poems like "i'm a poet who," from her play *for colored girls who have considered suicide when the rainbow is enuf,* she equates dance with femininity, since dance, she suggests, provides a vehicle for the expression of feminine experience:

> hold yr head like it was ruby sapphire
> i'm a poet
> who writes in english
> come to share the worlds witchu...
> come to share our worlds witchu
> we come here to be dancin
> to be dancin
> to be dancin
> baya

Shange's efforts to combine poetry and dance constitute further subversion of traditional forms. She dubs *for colored girls* a "choreopoem," thus signaling its blend of poem, play, and dance. Similarly, *Ridin' the Moon in Texas* is a combination of poetry and visual art. By mingling artistic forms Shange's poetry attempts to subvert the traditional boundaries that have been erected between genres, styles, forms, and experiences. In so doing, she promises to be an important figure in forging a place for minority writings which refuse to conform to traditional white male literary expectations.

—Priscilla L. Walton

SHAPCOTT, Jo

Nationality: British. **Born:** London, 24 March 1953. **Education:** Trinity College, Dublin, B.A. (first-class honors), 1976; Dublin College of Music, 1974-76; St. Hilda's College, Oxford, B.A. 1978; Harvard University, 1978-80; University of Bristol, diploma (with distinction) in adult and community education 1984. **Career:** Lecturer in English, Rolle College, Exmouth, 1981-84; education officer, 1984-86, acting senior education officer, 1986, Arts Council, London; education officer, South Bank Centre, London, 1986-91; Judith E. Wilson Senior Visiting Fellow in creative writing, Cambridge University, Pembroke College, 1991. Lyricist and librettist. **Awards:** Harvard University Harkness fellowship, 1978-80; South West Arts Literature award, 1982; Poetry Society National Poetry prizes, 1985, 1993; Commonwealth Prize, 1989, for *Electroplating the Baby; New Statesman* Prudence Farmer award, 1989. **Address:** London, England.

PUBLICATIONS

Poetry

Electroplating the Baby. Newcastle upon Tyne, Bloodaxe Books, and Chester Springs, Pennsylvania, Dufour, 1988.
Phrase Book. Oxford and New York, Oxford University Press, 1992.
Motherland. Gwaithel & Wilwern, 1996.

Editor, *Emergency Kit: Poems for Strange Times,* with Matthew Sweeny. London, Faber, 1996.

*   *   *

The only poet to have won the British Poetry Society's National Poetry Competition twice should be a sufficient accolade. But what is the special quality of Jo Shapcott's poetry?

The word most often used of her poetry is "surrealistic." Not a description of which Shapcott herself is very fond. It is a term too restrictive for labelling or pigeon-holing her work, but her prize winning poem "The Surrealists' Summer Convention Came to Our City" probably prompted it:

> We were as limp as the guide book
> to the city

This recalls Salvador Dali's limp watches melting in the desert sun. And here I think is a clue. What is called Shapcott's surrealism grows out of her poetic observation of her experiences, such as where Dali imposes his images on his pictures with the result that they are often rootless and sometimes superficial with the shelf-life joke. I suspect this popular surrealism is at the bottom of Shapcott's rejection of this label. Her "surrealism" (if we must call it such) is organic, while that of Dali and his followers is synthetic.

"Electroplating the Baby" (the title poem of her first major collection) is an idea that would appear to have all the trappings of surrealism about it. Yet it derives from something that people actually believed and acted upon however mistakenly. So—

It would be impossible to say.
It is infinitely possible.

If I were to look for a single word to describe Shapcott's poetry it would be "protean." The subject of many of her poems are just that. "Superman," Tom of "Tom and Jerry Visit England" change shapes and natures,

I banged full face into a query—
and ended up with my front shaped
like a question mark for hours.

And even Shapcott's sheep transform themselves. It is an important aspect of the art of poetry to transform the way we look at things. Shapcott's poetry does just that.

Then there is her more recent and superb poem "Thetis." Thetis was the sea goddess with the faculty for infinitely changing her form. Here is found the most important aspect of Shapcott's poetry, the quality of its language. In "Thetis" the sensual power of her language is such that you can enjoy the sensation with the Goddess as she slips into her shapes.

as I stretch
my limbs for the transformation I'm laughing
to feel the surge of other shapes beneath my skin.

I think
my soul has slithered into this

Low tremendous purrs start at the pit
of my stomach, I'm curving through long grass,
all sinew, in a body where tension
is the special joy—

The skillful use of assonance and alliteration makes this poem a *tour de force* of voluptuous imagery in which the reader shares the physical joy of changing shape. What is found is a poet's vision beautifully expressed.

The theme of shape changing is pursued in such poems as "Today I Am a Vogue Model" and "Elephant," as in the pursuit of appropriately sensual language in which to express them. And it is the language of Shapcott's poems that is the key to their excellence. A single word will reverberate in a poem, such as "distant" in her poem "Motherland":

Distance. The word is ingrained like pain.
So much for England and so much
for my future to walk into the horizon
carrying distance in a broken suitcase.

—John Cotton

SHUTTLE, Penelope (Diane)

Nationality: British. **Born:** Staines, Middlesex, 12 May 1947. **Education:** Staines Grammar School, 1952-59; Matthew Arnold County Secondary School, 1959-65. **Family:** Married Peter Redgrove in 1980; one daughter. **Career:** Part-time shorthand typist, 1965-69. **Awards:** Arts Council grant, 1969, 1972, 1985; Greenwood poetry prize, 1972; Eric Gregory award, 1974. **Address:** Falmouth, Cornwall. **Agent:** David Higham Associates Ltd., 5-8 Lower John Street, London WlR 4HA, England.

PUBLICATIONS

Poetry

Nostalgia Neurosis. Aylesford, Kent, St. Albert's Press, 1968.
Branch. Rushden, Northamptonshire, Sceptre Press, 1971.
Midwinter Mandala. New Malden, Surrey, Headland, 1973.
The Hermaphrodite Album, with Peter Redgrove. London, Fuller D'Arch Smith, 1973.
Moon Meal. Rushden, Northamptonshire, Sceptre Press, 1973.
Autumn Piano and Other Poems. Liverpool, Rondo, 1974.
Photographs of Persephone. Feltham, Middlesex, Quarto Press, 1974.
The Songbook of the Snow and Other Poems. Ilkley, Yorkshire, Janus Press, 1974.
The Dream. Knotting, Bedfordshire, Sceptre Press, 1975.
Webs on Fire. London, Gallery Press, 1975.
Period. London, Words, 1976.
Four American Sketches. Knotting, Bedfordshire, Sceptre Press, 1976.
The Orchard Upstairs. Oxford, Oxford University Press, 1980; New York, Oxford University Press, 1981.
The Child-Stealer. Oxford, Oxford University Press, 1983.
The Lion from Rio. Oxford, Oxford University Press, 1986.
Adventures with My Horse. Oxford, Oxford University Press, 1988.
Taxing the Rain. Oxford, Oxford University Press, 1994.
Building a City for Jamie. Oxford, Oxford University Press, 1996.

Plays

Radio Plays: *The Girl Who Lost Her Glove,* 1975; *The Dauntless Girl,* 1978.

Novels

An Excusable Vengeance, in *New Writers 6.* London, Calder & Boyars, 1967.
All the Usual Hours of Sleeping. London, Calder & Boyars, 1969.
Wailing Monkey Embracing a Tree. London, Calder & and Boyars, 1974.
The Terrors of Dr. Treviles, with Peter Redgrove. London, Routledge, 1974.
The Glass Cottage: A Nautical Romance, with Peter Redgrove. London, Routledge, 1976.
Jesusa. Falmouth, Cornwall, Granite Press, 1976.
Rainsplitter in the Zodiac Garden. London, Calder & Boyars, 1977; Nantucket, Longship Press, 1978.
The Mirror of the Giant. London, Calder & Boyars, 1980.

Short Story

Prognostica. Knotting, Bedfordshire, Martin Booth, 1980.

Other

The Wise Wound: Menstruation and Every Woman, with Peter Redgrove. London, Gollancz, 1978; as *The Wise Wound: Eve's Curse and Everywoman,* New York, Marek, 1979; revised edition, London, Paladin, 1986; as *The Wise Wound: Myths, Realities, and the Meaning of Menstruation,* New York, Bantam, 1990.

*

Penelope Shuttle comments:

What do we desire? We desire to know our human feeling more fully. What is this human feeling of ours? What happens when our feeling meets another's human feeling? What is our human feeling about being in the world? Is society human or inhuman? What powers are in the world, beyond human feeling? Are there any?

Poetry is a way of thinking about all these things.

We live, it is evident, in an over-visual and de-natured culture, where our deepest and most natural human feelings and experiences, be they sensual or cerebral or of our dream life, are under constant threat. In a corrupted culture, the concerns of poetry (our human feelings) are resented and repressed. They get in the way of business. Where's the profit margin in such feelings?

Poetry is the means of holding to these human feelings of ours. It is how to keep them alive, despite the many weapons set against them. Poems remind us of the transformative possibilities of our lives. Poems give us the chance to be more and more human.

I believe poetry is non-nihilist, non-sadistic, non-disposable. It is where the word testifies to everything we are when we are most alive and experiencing our feeling of being human.

In the poem's magical space is reminder, rescue, and challenge. Pain is also there, and pain's healing, a way through.

Who and what and how we are struggles to find meaning all through our lives; poetry witnesses and fuels and conserves that meaning.

We desire to know our human feeling more fully, we desire belief in the validity of our human feeling. Poetry shows us just how much human feeling matters, and that poetry will come with us all the way to where real life is lived.

*   *   *

Although Penelope Shuttle is the author of some extraordinary novels, she is by nature a poet. For a long time her gift manifested itself surrealistically in works of intense emotional oppression. Like her coauthor and husband, Peter Redgrove, Shuttle dared, very young, to open her imagination to the teachings of the unconscious. In all her writings she remains passionately committed to exploring hidden regions of (primarily) the woman's psyche in a dream imagery wholly her own.

Shuttle's early, disturbing writing can now be seen in relation to her mature development. Four collections of poetry appeared after 1980, and all were remarkable achievements, both in matter and style. In *The Orchard Upstairs,* the prevalent symbols are directly related to the poet's sensual experience of pregnancy and childbearing. These delicate poems tell the truth "but tell it slant"—especially in the title poem, which sets up a dichotomy

between outside and inside, destruction and creation, male and female, while all the time recognizing their vital interconnectedness:

> Outside, the wind and the rain,
> a darkness lurching against the threadbare house:
> inside, the orchard upstairs

The orchard, the womb, the bearer of "fruits," sacrifices itself in the act of giving birth to the child. The woman suffers, in so doing, not only physically but also through loss of innocence—and indeed, loss of her pregnant self:

> A small speck or stain
> on my heart.
> It is my sadness for the lost room,
> the pillaged house.

The loss finds compensation in the gain of a child, the daughter whose presence haunts the poems of *The Child-Stealer.* Here childbearing is still the theme, but it alternates with a second theme, that of childhood—the poet's own and her daughter's. The child stealer is the witch of menstruation who carries away the unborn, the figure of Lilith in a myth of life and death in which death is not evil but a necessary, wise opposite. Childhood is understood in a Blakean light, but Shuttle's taut language intercepts sentimentality:

> In the boundless afternoon
> the children are walking
> with their gentle grammar on their lips
>
> from door to door
> the little ones go, brightly tranquil,
> repenting nothing.
>
> How safe their journey,
> their placid marching,
> famous and simple voyage.

The reader is persuaded that these impossible children, these stolen ones who will never be, are indeed, in the poet's imagination, real enough to undertake the crusade they are seen to embody. It is as if, by writing the poem, Shuttle had created children in her mind that she could not create in her body.

The Lion from Rio pursues the theme of wife, mother, husband, and child in poems more explicitly sexual, in some cases charmingly anecdotal. At her best, though, Shuttle is a symbolist of female experience. Her mental landscape peacefully assimilates house, garden, and "flaxen river" through which cavort her emblems of physical energy: horse, snake (plus, occasionally, hedgehog), and the lion of life itself.

The poem "Horse of the Month" in her third collection suggested that the title of her fourth collection, *Adventures with My Horse,* would center on the theme of menstruation. Actually, the collection is full of animals, real and symbolic, described with wit and a refreshing zest for language. Like Redgrove, Shuttle subscribes to some innocent Romantic inversions: serpent and pregnant sow are saviours in an Eden presided over by Selena the moon rather than the sun god Apollo. That there is scarcely room for evil in this imaginary womb-enclosed world is something to be pondered. But Shuttle triumphs in poems like "Dressing the Child," in which a river becomes the knitted sleeve of a continuously re-born and conscientiously mothered child-earth:

> Wide spindling river,
> out-of-fashion green and cream
> woollen river cast on huge brown needles,
> bare tree-trunks garter-stitching
> the currents, purling the banks,
> armholing the bridges, casting-off barges.
> The winter river is a long coarse sleeve
> of flecked and brindled wool
> into which I shove your thundery arm, the cuff
> of ribbed bushes scratchy-tight on your wrist.

—Anne Stevenson

SILKO, Leslie Marmon

Nationality: American. **Born:** 1948. **Education:** Attended Board of Indian Affairs schools, Laguna, New Mexico, and a Catholic school in Albuquerque; University of New Mexico, Albuquerque, B.A. (summa cum laude) in English 1969; studied law briefly. **Family:** Has two sons. **Career:** Taught for two years at Navajo Community College, Tsaile, Arizona; lived in Ketchikan, Alaska, for two years; taught at University of New Mexico; professor of English, University of Arizona, Tucson, 1978—. **Awards:** National Endowment for the Arts award, 1974; *Chicago Review* award, 1974; Pushcart prize, 1977; MacArthur Foundation grant, 1983. **Address:** Department of English, University of Arizona, Tucson, Arizona 85721, U.S.A.

PUBLICATIONS

Poetry

Laguna Woman. Greenfield Center, New York, Greenfield Review Press, 1974.
Storyteller (includes short stories). New York, Seaver, 1981.

Play

Lullaby, with Frank Chin, adaptation of the story by Silko (produced San Francisco, 1976).

Novel

Ceremony. New York, Viking Press, 1977.
Almanac of the Dead. New York, Simon & Schuster, 1991.
Yellow Woman. New Brunswick, New Jersey, Rutgers University Press, 1993.

Other

The Delicacy and Strength of Lace: Letters between Leslie Marmon Silko and James A. Wright, edited by Anne Wright. St. Paul, Minnesota, Graywolf Press, 1986.
Sacred Water: Narratives and Pictures. Tucson, Flood Plain, 1993.

Yellow Woman and a Beauty of the Spirit: Essays on Native American Life Today. New York, Simon & Schuster, 1996.

*

Manuscript Collection: University of Arizona, Tucson.

Critical Studies: *Leslie Marmon Silko* by Per Seyersted, Boise, Idaho, Boise State University, 1980; *Four American Indian Literary Masters* by Alan R. Velie, Norman, University of Oklahoma Press, 1982; *Place and Vision: The Function of Landscape in Native American Fiction* by Robert M. Nelson. New York, P. Lang, 1993.

*   *   *

Leslie Marmon Silko's reputation rests upon her ability as a storyteller, and her output of poems has been relatively small. Her poems are a central part of her work as a writer, however, and she often uses the forms of poetry even in the middle of such works of prose fiction as *Ceremony.* She makes little use of simile and metaphor in her verse, with image and narration being the key elements. Her autobiographical book *Storyteller* is an interesting combination of old photographs, conventional short stories, and story poems. Silko herself denies that some of her poems are poems, seeing them instead as stories placed on the page with line breaks which help to replicate more clearly the motion of a storytelling voice.

The world of Silko's poetry is very much shaped by a Native American consciousness. Born in Albuquerque, New Mexico, she was brought up at Laguna Pueblo among relatives whose roots went back many generations in traditional ways. Though regarded as one of the most acculturated of the pueblos, Laguna still possesses a strong sense of history and continuity. On the other hand, because Laguna adopted many European ways (and a number of whites who married into the pueblo, Silko's "great-grandpa Marmon" among them), it is not surprising that it has produced not only Silko but also several other significant writers whose concerns are those of the "half-breed," the person of mixed blood. Rather than viewing this heritage as a curse, Silko has used European literary forms to move toward the strength of the Laguna earth and the stories of her family. These stories are both personal reminiscences and very old myths, and at times the two blend. The boundary lines between the real world and the world of legends and between the modern and the ancient, though continuing past are very thin in all of her work. Indeed, her sense of time is not at all a European one. The reader feels that in her poems all things are very much interconnected. Her world is a world of both tremendous changes brought by Western civilization and a lastingly strong natural environment (of which the Native American is part) in which everything is possessed of the power to be and become.

Changing is an important theme in Silko's work. "Bear Story" tells of how the bears can call people to them and make them become bears themselves. There are characters in Laguna and other Southwestern Indian stories (the stories which she grew up with and which she always returns to) who are changers, who make others change, and who can change themselves. The coyote is a prime example. The earthy, ironic humor in the poem "Toe'osh: A Laguna Coyote Story" has made it one of her most often-quoted poems.

Silko is also a writer who celebrates the strength of women, and the title of her first book, *Laguna Woman,* underscores her identification with her own sex. Whether it is Silko herself, the mythic Yellow Woman, or her own grandmother, Marie Anaya Marmon, the women in Silko's poems are strong, independent, even wildly indomitable.

In such poems as "Where Mountain Lion Lay Down with Deer" we see Silko's non-Western sense of time. Things from past and present coexist and change each other:

> I smell the wind for my ancestors
> pale blue leaves
> crushes wild mountain smell.
> Returning
> up the gray stone cliff
> where I descended
> a thousand years ago
> Returning to faded black stone
> where mountain lion lay down with deer.

The image of the mountain lion and the deer may remind one of the biblical lion and lamb, but the animals have different roles in this place, are charged with a different mythic power. Silko says later in the same poem that

> The old ones who remember me are gone
> the old songs are all forgotten
> and the story of my birth.
> How I danced in snow-frost moonlight
> distant stars to the end of the Earth...

Her words are not a lament, however. They do not convey a sense of loss but rather a deep continuity which goes beyond conventional ideas of individual reality. Although she is a child of more than one culture, her voice clearly speaks for the Native American way—not a way which is gone, but one which continues beyond time, changing and unchanged.

—Joseph Bruchac

SMITHER, Elizabeth (Edwina)

Nationality: New Zealander. **Born:** Elizabeth Edwina Harrington, New Plymouth, 15 September 1941. **Education:** New Plymouth Girls' High School, 1955-59; extra-mural studies at Victoria University, Wellington, and Massey University, Palmerston North, 1959-60; New Zealand Library School, Wellington, 1962. **Family:** Married Michael Duncan Smither in 1963 (divorced 1984); one daughter and two sons. **Career:** Library assistant, 1959-62, cataloguer, 1962-63, children's librarian, 1963-64, and fiction librarian, New Plymouth Public Library, 1979—. **Awards:** New Zealand Literary Fund bursary, 1977, 1988, and traveling bursary, 1984; Freda Buckland award, 1983; University of Auckland literary fellowship, 1984; Scholarship in Letters, 1987, 1992; New Zealand Book award for poetry, 1990. **Address:** 19-A Mount View Place, New Plymouth, New Zealand.

PUBLICATIONS

Poetry

Here Come the Clouds. Martinborough, Taylor, 1975.
You're Very Seductive, William Carlos Williams. Dunedin, McIndoe, 1978.

Little Poems. New Plymouth, T. J. Mutch, 1979.
The Sarah Train (for children). Eastbourne, Hawk Press, 1980.
Casanova's Ankle. Auckland, Oxford University Press, 1981.
The Legend of Marcello Mastroianni's Wife. Auckland, Auckland University Press-Oxford University Press, 1981.
Shakespeare Virgins. Auckland, Auckland University Press, 1985.
Professor Musgrove's Canary. Auckland, Oxford University Press, 1986.
Gorilla, Guerilla. Auckland, Earl of Seacliff Art Workshop, 1986.
Animaux. Wellington, Modern House, 1988.
A Pattern of Marching. Auckland, Auckland University Press, 1989.
A Cortège of Daughters. Newcastle upon Tyne, Cloud Press, 1993.
The Tudor Style: Poems New & Selected. Auckland, Auckland University Press, 1993.

Stories

Nights at the Embassy. Auckland, Auckland University Press, 1990.
Mr. Fish and Other Stories. Dunedin, McIndoe, 1994.
The Mathematics of Jane Austin. Auckland, Godwit, 1997.

Novels

First Blood. London, Hodder & Stoughton, 1983.
Brother-Love, Sister-Love. Auckland, Hodder & Stoughton, 1986.

Other

Tug Brothers (for children). Auckland, Oxford University Press, 1983.
Taranaki, with David Hill, photographs by Jane Dove. Auckland, Hodder & Stoughton, 1987.
The Journal Box (journal). Auckland, Auckland University Press, 1996.

Editor, with David Hill, *The Seventies Connection.* Dunedin, McIndoe, 1980.
Editor, with C.K. Stead and Kendrick Smithyman, *The New Gramophone Room: Poetry and Fiction.* Auckland, University of Auckland, 1985.

*

Manuscript Collection: Hocken Library, University of Otago, Dunedin.

Critical Studies: "A Way of Understanding Ourselves" by Elizabeth Caffin, in *Landfall* (Christchurch), no. 118, 1976; "Maurice Shadbolt Talks to Elizabeth Smither," in *Pilgrims* (Christchurch), no. 5-6, 1978; "*The Legend of Marcello Mastroianni's Wife,* and *Casanova's Ankle,* Elizabeth Smither" by Shawna Macivor, in *Landfall* (Christchurch), no. 141, 1982; "Elizabeth Smither Interview by the Editor" by David Dowling, in *Landfall* (Christchurch), no. 151, 1984; "Smithereens" by Bill Manhire, in *Listener* no. 127, 4 June 1990.

Elizabeth Smither comments:
My view of poetry changes with each poem. Poetry itself remains the most exciting form, the most compressed and vital; formal or informal it perpetually re-creates itself to new demands.

Other mediums have evasive techniques but poetry is direct, forcing a confrontation between the world and the self. For me there is no forward planning or even knowledge of the subject: technique is created at the moment of writing: I write to find out everything. The best poems are both intensely personal and impersonal, teaching something about the true nature of personality. I see poetry always expanding, in advance of theory, like the universe itself, and if few poets write the poems they want, the chase is the greatest pleasure.

*   *   *

Elizabeth Smither began writing effectively when she was about 30 and fairly quickly found her voice (and a reputation), so that she is substantially a poet without any juvenilia. She has done some traveling beyond New Zealand, where her home is not in one of the larger cities but in a provincial port, where a sleepy hollow is backed by a lush pastoral scene dominated by a spectacularly dead volcano, grounded in a long-term history of Maori settlement and a short-term history of European settlement but one with a notable passage to it of nineteenth-century colonial warfare. There is little recourse to that local history in Smither's poems, although she has explored something of it in her prose, and scarcely more to do with either landscape or seascape, or evident awareness of the transforming of the sleepy hollow as the oil rigs on- and offshore work away at their surroundings, the natural gas enterprises breed, the petrochemical plants riot over the paddocks. In neither earlier nor later books occurs much that may be confidently thought to come from family or immediate social experience. Some from family; some from friendships; much from responding to literature, responding imaginatively. "Imagine this, now..." and she does. It is impressively a poetry of imagination. Where the poetry is of experience, it is likely to have some qualifying or mediating effect again from literature, or from a quiet Roman Catholicism.

The poems are rarely long-lined, customarily shortish-lined pieces which probably will not reach halfway down the page. They have a peculiarity in punctuation, of a kind which M. K. Joseph, another Catholic poet, used at one stage in his career. Syntax is disrupted in a modestly venturesome way which one may judge is aimed at evoking an illusion of immediacy, as of a slightly breathless utterance, whether the poet is assumed to be speaking in her own person or whether it is one or another of her personae, male or female, or a speaker whose sex is in neither way assertive. The voice of the later poems (including the poems of *Casanova's Ankle*) is more likely to be a woman's and so too the viewpoint.

Sympathetic, empathetic, able to command that quick, shrewd comment which delights the reader simply because it *is* so aptly shrewd or provocative, Smither's poems are not poems of wit in any usual sense any more than they are in a usual sense self-centered. She may be in them, but also distant from them. She may advertize that she attaches herself to modernist modes, as of Williams, Lowell, or Kinnell, but she is also distanced from those modes, not fully committed to them. To be more venturesome would become her.

She is a conservative modernist. If you look at her evidenced Catholicism, you see the Catholicism of family custom, plus an awareness of tradition—Saint Teresa, Saint Ignatius, Saint Paul—and something latter-day, Teilhard de Chardin, but not as late as Hans Küng. The poems of faith are poems of rapprochement, of subjective-objective or attachment-detachment, records of an impulse to reconcile at least two modes of tradition. She effects a reconciliation which complements by way of one particular universe of discourse the compromises apparent in her favored strategies as a "maker."

The matter of playing off traditions is one thing. Recurring to compressed statement is another, in which calculated quizzical relating of tenor and vehicle in metaphor continues to result not so much in conveying a metaphoric statement as in exciting a sense of incongruity without (as one might expect) a likely consequent nuance of comedy, yet increasingly more likely to dispose toward irony. Prosy reality reimagined is heightened, disturbingly heightened even if Smither has from the start pinned and still usually pins her poetics on and over a firm basis of sentences. It is only when the sentences cumulate that the exposition becomes something other, a deceptive something other.

The heavy haulers pull their sometimes fantastically sculpted pieces of machinery to the industrial sites. Lights blaze from gantry and rig between sea and mountain. As Wallace Stevens did in Hartford, Smither sits to work with her back to the window.

—Kendrick Smithyman

SOLT, Mary Ellen

Nationality: American. **Born:** Gilmore City, Iowa, 8 July 1920. **Education:** Iowa State Teachers College, B.A. 1941; University of Iowa, M.A. 1948; Indiana University School of Letters, 1957-58. **Family:** Married Leo Frank Solt in 1946 (deceased); two daughters. **Career:** Teacher of English at high schools in Iowa and New York City, 1941-52; assistant professor, 1970-73, associate professor, 1973-80, then professor emeritus of comparative literature and director, Polish Studies Center, 1980-91, Indiana University, Bloomington. Contributor of poetry to periodicals, including *Poetry* and *Chicago Review.* Poetry has been included in several multimedia presentations and in exhibitions, including at Galaria "X"ZPAP, Wroclaw, Poland, 1979, Coffman Gallery, University of Minnesota, 1983, Galleria e Libreria il Segno, Turin, Italy, 1985, and Fruit Market Gallery, Edinburgh, Scotland, 1990. **Awards:** Folio award, 1960, for article "William Carlos Williams: Poems in the American Idiom"; several design awards, 1969, for *Concrete Poetry: A World View;* Indiana University travel grant, 1970, creative activity grant, 1979-82, research grant, 1986-88; Polish Council of State Gold Badge of Order, 1981, for efforts on behalf of cultural exchange between the United States and Poland; National Endowment for the Humanities travel grant, 1986, fellowship, 1987-88. **Address:** 25520 Wilde Avenue, Stevenson Ranch, California 91381, U.S.A.

PUBLICATIONS

Poetry

Flowers in Concrete. Bloomington, Indiana University Press, 1966.
A Trilogy of Rain. Urbana, Illinois, Finial Press, 1970.
The Peoplemover 1968: A Demonstration Poem (chapbook). Reno, West Coast Poetry Review, 1978.
Marriage: A Code Poem. Champaign, Illinois, Finial Press, 1976.

Other

Editor, with Willis Barnstone, *Concrete Poetry: A World View.* Bloomington, Indiana University Press, 1968.

Editor, *Dear Ez: Letters from William Carlos Williams to Ezra Pound.* Bloomington, Indiana, privately printed, 1985.

*

Media Adaptations: *The White Flower* (film), 1975.

Critical Studies: "Concretist Poets and Poetry" by David Rosenthal, in *Poetry,* no. 112, 1968; "Recent Combings from the Concrete Fringe," in *Times Literary Supplement,* vol. 12, no. 2, 1970; "Poem Objects" by Alicia Ostriker, in *Partisan Review,* no. 40, 1973.

*   *   *

The concrete poems of Mary Ellen Solt collected in *Flowers in Concrete* (1966) are among the most distinctive and witty examples of this form, which came into its own in the 1960s. Concrete poetry, also sometimes referred to a "visual poetry," owes partial homage to the "emblematic" poems of 17th-century English metaphysical poets such as George Herbert, who constructed shaped poems like "The Altar" in visual designs that underscored the poem's title and / or theme. More recently, just prior to the work of Solt and other concrete poets, some Beat poets such as Gregory Corso, in poems like the mushroom-cloud shaped "Bomb," had also explored the poem's visual potential on the page. And, of course, the very act of breaking poetry into lines not only underscores the auditory pleasures of words and the places a poet pauses for breath, but can also enhance the poem's charms on the page. However, such quibbles about antecedents aside, poets like Solt were able to suggest new possibilities for interaction between the written word and words as design.

The editor of Solt's collection, George Sadek, has this to say in his introduction:

> When publishing concrete poetry, it is sometimes difficult to draw the line between the contributions, as well as the final responsibilities, of the poet and the typographer. The literary and visual meaning of concrete poetry as conceived by the poet and interpreted by the typographer is somewhat analogous to a stage production of a play.

The comparison with theater here is an interesting one. Playwrights of the 1960s often lumped together as practicing "theater of the absurd" sometimes considered the published words of their scripts as being merely the melodies that actors, like jazz artists, could improvise upon. The Beat poets and their immediate successors in the same period also tended to approach their printed words, with similar flexibility, as notes on a page, the springboard for a performance. However, concrete poetry, unlike the work of the absurdist playwrights or Beat poets, pushed experimentation in an opposite direction; instead of freeing words from the page, language becomes more closely wedded to paper and print. These are not poems to be performed by the poet; instead, the book itself is a series of stages on which the poems perform.

Sadek also mentions that at least one of these works, the calligraphic poem sequence "Dogwood: Three Movements," was "selected by the editor on purely visual merits." This statement might lead the reader to infer that this is the sort of poetry that takes the visual appearance of words, or lines, on a page, to a logical extreme, where "lines" of poetry and drawn lines become all-but-interchangeable. However, as one of the better-known of Solt's concrete "flowers," "Forsythia," illustrates, the evocative power of words has not been jettisoned—instead, it's enhanced in a way to which the reader may not be accustomed. This particular poem, like some of the others in the collection, is also an anagram poem. Perhaps the anagram itself could be considered an early example of visual poetry—the effect of starting each line with a letter that, combined, spell out the title word, is likely to be lost on a mere listener. This anagram poem, in less adroit hands, might have appeared on the page this way:

> FORSYTHIA
> OUT
> RACE
> SPRING'S
> YELLOW
> TELEGRAM
> HOPE
> INSISTS
> ACTIONS

But, even in this variant form, in addition to the visual imagery's own appeal ("Forsythia out race spring's yellow telegram"), there is the wit inherent in the anagram, which adds another layer of visual appeal. However, Solt doesn't stop there; she positions the letters of FORSYTHIA horizontally, so lines of verse can grow upward, forming the plant. Finally, the letters of the title word are also repeated, growing outward from the lines of the anagram to suggest the branches of the plant. "FORSYTHIA" is both constructed upon as the basis of an anagram poem and deconstructed into its component letters, which choose to mimic the organic form of the plant. If compression is the soul of poetry, this poem has a lot of soul. Other poems, like "Zinnia," display the almost dizzying potential of a single word, repeated, to turn design, becoming the very thing it designates. This kind of poetry is a sort of minimalist composition, practicing on the page what composers like Philip Glass do with sound. And, whether in music or poetry, compelling work can be constructed around a handful of notes or words.

—Duane Ackerson

SONG, Cathy

Nationality: American. **Born:** Honolulu, Hawaii, 1955. **Education:** Wellesley College, B.A. 1977; Boston University, M.F.A. 1981. **Family:** Married Douglas Davenport, three children. **Career:** Teaches creative writing at various universities. Contributor to periodicals, including *Asian-Pacific Literature, Hawai'i Review, Poetry,* and *Seneca Review.* **Awards:** Yale Younger Poets Award, 1982, for *Picture Bride;* Poetry Society of America Shelley Memorial Award; Hawaii Award for Literature; National Endowment for the Arts fellowship. **Address:** Honolulu, Hawaii.

PUBLICATIONS

Poetry

Picture Bride. New Haven and London, Yale University Press, 1983.
Frameless Windows, Squares of Light. New York and London, Norton, 1988.
School Pictures. London and Pittsburgh, University of Pittsburgh Press, 1994.

Other

Editor, with Juliet S. Kono, *Sister Stew: Fiction and Poetry by Women.* Honolulu, Bamboo Ridge Press, 1991.

*

Critical Studies: "Cathy Song: 'I'm a Poet Who Happens to Be Asian American'" by Debbie Murakami Nomaguchi, in *International Examiner* (Seattle, Washington), vol. 2, no. 11, 2 May 1984; "'Third World' as Place and Paradigm in Cathy Song's *Picture Bride*" by Gayle K. Fujita-Sato, in *MELUS,* vol. 15, no. 1, 1988; "Women Disclosed: Cathy Song's Poetry and Kitagawa Ukiyoe" by Masami Usui, in *Studies in Culture and the Humanities,* 1995; *And the View from the Shore: Literary Traditions of Hawaii* by Stephen Sumida, Seattle, University of Washington Press, 1991; "Divided Loyalties: Literal and Literary in the Poetry of Lorna Dee Cervantes, Cathy Song and Rita Dove" by Patricia Wallace, in *MELUS,* vol. 18, no. 3, 1993; "Cathy Song" by Susan M. Schultz, in *Dictionary of Literary Biography,* vol. 196, Detroit, Gale Research, 1996.

*   *   *

The work of Cathy Song entered the American consciousness in 1983, when her first collection, *Picture Bride,* was selected for publication by the Yale Series of Younger Poets. Since that time and the publication of two additional collections, critical estimation of her poetry has continued to grow.

In the foreword to *Picture Bride,* editor Richard Hugo asserts that "in Cathy Song's quietude is a function of the precision and control she brings to her work." Her poems are highly crafted, skillfully wrought and, as several critics have identified, extremely visual in composition. In *Picture Bride,* Song pays explicit homage to two visual artists: Japanese printmaker Kitagawa Utamaro and American painter Georgia O'Keeffe. She divides this collection into five sections named for O'Keeffe's sensual flower studies (Black Iris, Sunflower, Orchids, Red Poppy, and The White Trumpet Flower) and imagines O'Keeffe confronting her desert vista in "From the White Place": "So dry, there are no flowers / to paint, / but this pelvic mountain / thrusting toward light and heat." Writing for Utamaro in "Beauty and Sadness," Song says that the artist's models:

> ...arranged themselves
> before the quick, nimble man
> whose invisible presence
> one feels in the prints
> is as delicate
> as the skinlike paper

he used to transfer
and retain their fleeting loveliness.

Song herself is often a similar invisible presence in her poetry, radiating a potent strength and clarity of voice from within her beautiful and many times (as the above example demonstrates) spare arrangements of language.

Song is best known for her articulate negotiations of the multiple pulls of identity. The American-born daughter of a Chinese mother and Korean father, coming to adulthood in the fertile landscape of a former plantation town in Hawaii, Song demonstrates her struggle with the seductions and despairs of assimilation—as well as a continuity located in an attention to the past and to ancestry. She says in "Lost Sister" (*Picture Bride*): "You find you need China: / your one fragile identification, / a jade link / handcuffed to your wrist."

In the title of her second collection, *Frameless Windows, Squares of Light,* Song alludes to the "framed" moments of the present that act as catalysts to carry us into other realms of experience. Often Song makes use of these frames to explore an imagined past in the countries that have been left behind, but never lost. In the poem "Points of Reference" from her third book, *School Figures,* the poet speaks of such a moment: "It was like falling through a mirror / into someone else's story, / the years when the children were small. / Your mother's story perhaps." Here, as in so many other of Song's pieces, the other's point of reference becomes her own—at least for a short while.

In her imaginative reflections on the China and Korea of her parents' past, Song finds her own pathways back, as well as forward, into the current realities of her life as poet, woman, wife, mother, and Asian-American. In "Heaven" (*Frameless Windows*), she offers a moment with her son, who imagines China as a heaven to which they'll go after death. She infers here the spaces across which one must reach out, spatially and temporally, to make connections with that past: "China, that blue flower on the map, / bluer than the sea / his hand must span like a bridge / to reach it."

Some critics have felt that Song's skill moves at times toward an excess of control—too careful a hand in the precise ordering of image and phrase. Like Ikebana, the Japanese art of floral arrangement of which she writes in the poem of the same name (*Picture Bride*), Song's work in certain moments can lean toward too naked an exposure of the art of arranging language. Yet in this poem, Song makes it clear that even in its precision and beauty her work does not lack teeth. She speaks in the final stanza of the flower "which, just this morning, / you so skillfully wired into place." "How poised it is!" she goes on to say, "the stem snipped and wedged / into the metal base— / to appear like a spontaneous accident." The juxtaposition that Song makes in this poem is between the careful arrangement of the traditional Japanese woman's body ("lacquered hair"; skin a "bruised white / like the skin of lilies") and the flower "wedge" firmly into place. "Hold the arrangement" she says to the woman of her prepared body—"If your spine slacks / and you feel faint, / remember the hand-picked flower / set in the front alcove." In moments such as these, Song's passionate struggles with an American present and an Asian cultural past—and the problematic nature of her relationship with the possibilities for identity offered by each—speak with a powerful voice.

At its best, Song's work evokes in the reader a sense of that profound and "spontaneous accident," capturing in its phrases all of the potentialities of both past and present. From her multiple positions within American culture, she claims a certain freedom in movement and sight that seeks to reflect the spontaneity of the instant. And in experiencing the poet's distinct view of those instants of time, be they from present life or a real / imagined past, the reader experiences one of the greatest joys of Song's work.

—Anne-Elizabeth Green

SPIRES, Elizabeth (Kay)

Nationality: American. **Born:** Lancaster, Ohio, 28 May 1952. **Education:** Vassar College, Poughkeepsie, New York, 1970-74, B.A. 1974; Johns Hopkins University, Baltimore, Maryland, 1978-79, M.A. 1979. **Family:** Married the novelist Madison Smartt Bell in 1985; one daughter. **Career:** Visiting assistant professor, Washington College, Chestertown, Maryland, 1981; freelance writer, Columbus, Ohio, and Baltimore, Maryland, 1977-80; writer-in-residence, Loyola College, Baltimore, Maryland, 1981-82, and Goucher College, Towson, Maryland, 1982—; visiting associate professor, Johns Hopkins University, Baltimore, 1984-96. Distinguished Chair for Achievement, Goucher College, 1996—. **Awards:** National Endowment for the Arts fellowship, 1981, 1992; Amy Lowell traveling scholarship, 1986; Sara Teasdale Poetry award, 1990; Guggenheim fellowship, 1992; Whiting award, 1996. **Member:** Academy of American Poets. **Agent:** Jane Gelfman, Gelfman Schneider Literary Agents, Inc., 250 West 57th Street, New York, New York 10107, U.S.A. **Address:** 6208 Pinehurst Road, Baltimore, Maryland 21212, U.S.A.

PUBLICATIONS

Poetry

Globe. Middletown, Connecticut, Wesleyan University Press, 1981.
Swan's Island. New York, Holt, 1985.
Annonciade. New York, Viking, 1989.
Worldling. New York, Norton, 1995.

Other

With One White Wing. (for children). New York, Margaret K. McElderry Books / Simon & Schuster, 1995.
The Mouse of Amherst (for children). New York, Farrar Strauss, 1998.

Editor, *The Instant of Knowing: The Occasional Prose of Josephine Jacobsen.* Ann Arbor, University of Michigan Press, 1997.

*

Critical Study: "Post-American Style" by Tony Whedon, in *Iowa Review* (Iowa City), vol. 23, no. 1, 1993.

*   *   *

Supple free verse shapes Elizabeth Spires's quietly remarkable poetry, on occasion its lines judiciously tapped into place by

rhyme and meter. There are several directions in the movement of her work. In one, life for the poet comes to position itself more and more consciously within "the shaded porch of generation, / big enough for everyone," as her account of identity cycles from childhood to parenthood and gains a broader and historically colored perspective. In another lost love bends in transit from bitterness and pain into knowledge and from there into a conjugal haven; the painful loss of a lover and separation from a son through divorce balance thematically in poems about consolidation with a new partner, aided by the birth of a daughter. Finally, the poetry juggles the tension between the longing for heaven and the longing to reconcile with death, as only a lapsed Roman Catholic appears to know the ineradicable stir of these longings. All three strands can be seen in early to late work as Spires pulls the fabric of her poetry firmly and authoritatively beyond the prosaic and into the true territory of the lyric, into myth and fable.

Consciously or unconsciously, this ambitious and comprehensive design plays out within a consistently developing imagery. The mirrors and lights of a boardwalk, a fun house show, and the prostitutes of the photographer Bellocq's Storyville all learn to coexist with the mirrors, bells, and monasteries of a later preoccupation, as the colorful objects of public spectacle, a pervasive interest, turn increasingly inward and, one might say, upward. Choice, or rather choosing as a consequence of what the self sees imaginatively, makes an early appearance, as in the concluding lines from "Mirrors"; even in the heat of love the representations that we make to others are always, perhaps only, representations that we make to ourselves:

> When you bend over me, asking
> why I cried out, I see
> my face in your eyes, the jetty's
> yellow beacon flashing
> a warning on the walls around us.
> Any promises we make
> will be promises to ourselves.

In later poems the mirroring of self and other becomes increasingly complex. While the poem just quoted points to the ways in which even loving selves remain isolated, later poems affirm and fissure that loving dialectic as both expansion and suffocation. In other exercises of reflection and split consciousness there are poems that explore mirroring indirectly through the device of the dramatic monologue. In "The Comb and the Mirror" the mermaid speaker reports on love's spell in which "self gives back the self / in love's unreflecting mirror," but the angle of her attraction is a fatal embrace. In other mirrors women, like those in "Storyville Portraits," helplessly see themselves contracting:

> *... Who reflects who?*
> thinks the woman in the mirror,
> her life narrowing before her,
> a series of identical rooms,
> each smaller than the one before,
> so that she grows smaller and more terrified

In still other poems implied mirrors are ubiquitous—the shield of children's bodies reflecting the sun, the poet's face swimming in the tea plate she holds, and so on. Mirrors in lakes and seas also bind us to a material nature reflecting back a material selfhood, while other mirrors refract family likeness, sister to sister, or an older self—one's own or one's daughter's—back to a younger self.

In "The Travellers" and in poems like "Waving Goodbye" and "Stonington Self-Portrait" the doubled and dissolving self of the mirror watcher extends to other connecting meditations, in which the pairing is not only that of self and watcher but also Spires's characterization of time and in which the present reflects back past or future. A "now" peels back to a "then," and a long ago shades a present which is relentlessly other, often some inexplicable relative of the dead but changeless.

Mysteriously, what the gaze dwells on frequently becomes something else, an interior image, an alter ego like the heron / angel in "Two Watchers," who echoes the mysterious heron self seen in the earlier "Patchy Fog," who with "hungering heron eye" waits

> until the morning's
> curtain parts and shafts of sunlight make
> the heron cry, cry out, to see itself defined,
> bright burning outline in sky's water, and beat
> its wings and fly, smoke into smoke, toward heaven,
> mind that masterminds the pond's closed circle.

What has been a basic figure, reflection, from *Annonciade* onward moves to become transformation.

This does not happen with anything approaching an angelic certainty, however, as the heaven toward which the heron directs his flight clouds over intermittently. In *Annonciade* Spires mixes prose and poetry in a piece called "Falling Away," naming the experience of lapsed religious belief. The work returns in memory to a classroom in which "the crucifix above the front blackboard [hangs] in a face-off with the big round clock on the back wall." At 11 years of age the speaker's task is to imagine heaven and hell and to measure eternity. In the clock of her own time, in recurring nightmare, the speaker returns "in my adult mind and body among children" still trying to master the earlier lesson: "Standing in the dark hallway, I'm thinking how I'll finally see through the keyhole into that polarized world of good and evil, guilt and absolution, that even a fallen-away Catholic can't escape. After all I have all time. Have all eternity."

True to this project, sensing the presence of the transcendent and faithful to its definitions, her poems attempt to see behind the mirror into the object's real weightiness, beneath its skin, and over the horizon into those other layers of being, whether the layers are celestial or simply other—not a question that can be safely answered. But a generous risk taking is in this poet's nature. The final poem of her book *Worldling* does not hesitate for a moment to invoke a larger, more visionary economy. Reading a parable about human mutability to her daughter at night, she says,

> Our only paradise is here,
> and we are rich as misers, rich in change!
> We hold in our empty hands a currency of days
> that we must spend down to the very last,
> no holding back allowed. But sleep now.
> And I'll sleep, too, to wake with you,
> wake to the everlasting present of our life.

—Lorrie Goldensohn

STAINER, Pauline

Nationality: British. **Born:** Burslem, 5 March 1941. **Education:** St. Anne's College, Oxford, 1960-63, B.A. 1963; Southampton University, M.Phil. 1967. **Awards:** Hawthornden fellowship, 1987; Skoob Index on Censorship Competition award, 1992; National Poetry Competition prize, 1992. **Address:** Cruannie, Sourin, Ronsay, Orkney, Northern Isles KW17 2PR, England.

PUBLICATIONS

Poetry

The Honeycomb. Newcastle upon Tyne, Bloodaxe, 1989.
Little Egypt. The Brotherhood of Ruralists, 1991.
Sighting the Slave-Ship. Newcastle upon Tyne, Bloodaxe, 1992.
The Ice-Pilot Speaks. Newcastle upon Tyne, Bloodaxe, 1994.
The Wound-Dresser's Dream. Newcastle upon Tyne, Bloodaxe, 1996.

Recording: *Words from Jerusalem* (videotape), British Broadcasting Corporation, 1995.

Other

Translator, with Ase-Marie Nesse, *The No-Man's Tree.* Guildford, Surrey, Making Waves, n.d.

*   *   *

I first encountered the poetry of Pauline Stainer at the adjudication of the Stroud International Poetry Competition in 1981. Her poem "The Honeycomb" was awarded second prize, and it was obvious that she had been robbed. "The Honeycomb" was quite the most outstanding poem on offer that day, and so I found deep pleasure when some years later her first collection was published with the title *The Honeycomb.* Why did it take so long? It is a story of poetic injustice, although Stroud did make amends in 1984 when it awarded her first prize.

As an example of the extended use of an image, "The Honeycomb" is a small masterpiece. It begins

> They had made love early in the high bed,
> Not knowing the honeycomb stretched
> Between lathe and plaster of the outer wall.

The poem then continues to throb with the activity of the bees in their comb: "their vibration swelled the room." This, together with the voluptuous sweetness of the honey "in the virgin wax," parallels the lovemaking in the room, leading to a beautifully apt conclusion:

> Now winters later, burning the beeswax candle,
> Could he forget his tremulous first loving
> In the humming dawn.

As an introduction to the writing skills and the sensuous use of language in Stainer's poetry, "The Honeycomb" sets the tone.

Since then, however, this direct style has developed into a more oblique one. In "The Ice Pilot Speaks" we find an extended presentation of a series of coded messages lit with brilliant flashes of vivid imagery—

> The bisque-doll
> on the seabed
> mouthing the Titanic

—or, in a scene of a visceral hell—

> Loki is bound
> with his own entrails
> but who will wear
> this smoking scarlet?

From this the reader is expected to construct a cumulative vision and sense. The method works beautifully in such poems as "Leper at Dunwich" and "Kinga Chapel" and works superbly in "War Requiem," where the effect is electric:

> against the flicker
> of the crematorium
>
> the orchestra
> disrobing in the shower room

But in the longer "The Ice Pilot Speaks" I feel that Stainer demands too much of her readers. The clues are too teasing and demand too esoteric a knowledge. It is as if the reader is witnessing the flickerings, however brilliant, on the walls of a Platonic cave of the mind, offering a glimpse of a higher reality.

Stainer's strength is in her powerful visual imagery. It is not surprising that it often expresses itself in poems about painters and paintings. In her "Turner Is Lashed to the Mast" she catches the very essence of his art:

> how water
> makes the wind visible,
> how the sea strikes
> like a steel gauntlet.

She does the same for Stanley Spencer in her "The Infinite Act":

> the disciples shoal
> along the malthouse wall,
> principalities and powers
> smoke their bayonets

—John Cotton

STEVENSON, Anne (Katherine)

Nationality: British. **Born:** Cambridge, England, 3 January 1933. **Education:** University High School, Ann Arbor, Michigan, 1947-50; University of Michigan, Ann Arbor (Hopwood award, 1951, 1952, 1954), B.A. 1954 (Phi Beta Kappa), M.A. 1962; Radcliffe Institute, Cambridge, Massachusetts, 1970-71. **Family:** Married 1) R. L. Hitchcock in 1955 (divorced), one daughter; 2) Mark Elvin in 1962 (divorced), two sons; 3) Michael Farley (divorced); 4) Peter Lucas in

1987. **Career:** School teacher, Lillesden School, Hawkhurst, Kent, 1955-56, Westminster School, Georgia, 1959-60, and Cambridge School, Weston, Massachusetts, 1961-62; advertising manager, A & C Black publishers, London, 1956-57; tutor, Extra-Mural Studies, University of Glasgow, 1970-73; counselor, Open University, Paisley, Renfrew, 1972-73; writing fellow, University of Dundee, 1973-75; fellow, Lady Margaret Hall, Oxford, 1975-77; writer-in-residence, Bulmershe College, Reading, Berkshire, 1977-78, and University of Edinburgh, 1987-89. Co-founder, with Michael Farley and Alan Halsey, Poetry Bookshop, Hay-on-Wye, Powys, 1979. Northern Arts Literary Fellow, Newcastle and Durham, 1981-82 and 1984-85. Founding co-editor, *Other Poetry,* Leicester, 1978-83, Mid-Day Publications, Oxford, and Other Poetry Editions. Member of literature panel, Arts Council, 1983-85; board member, Poetry Book Society, London, 1986-88. **Awards:** Scottish Arts Council award, 1973; Southern Arts bursary, 1978; Welsh Arts Council bursary, 1981; Athena Award, University of Michigan, 1990. Fellow, Royal Society of Literature, 1978; fellow, University of Michigan Institute for the Humanities, 1993. **Address:** 9 Coton Road, Grantchester, Cambridgeshire CB3 9NH, England.

PUBLICATIONS

Poetry

Living in America. Ann Arbor, Michigan, Generation Press, 1965.
Reversals. Middletown, Connecticut, Wesleyan University Press, 1969.
Correspondences: A Family History in Letters. Middletown, Connecticut, Wesleyan University Press, and London, Oxford University Press, 1974.
Travelling behind Glass: Selected Poems 1963-1973. London, Oxford University Press, 1974.
A Morden Tower Reading 3. Newcastle upon Tyne, Morden Tower, 1977.
Cliff Walk. Richmond, Surrey, Keepsake Press, 1977.
Enough of Green. London, Oxford University Press, 1977.
Sonnets for Five Seasons. Hereford, Five Seasons Press, 1979.
Minute by Glass Minute. Oxford, Oxford University Press, 1982.
Green Mountain, Black Mountain. Boston, Rowan Tree Press, 1982.
Making Poetry. Oxford, Pisces Press, 1983.
A Legacy. Durham, Taxus Press, 1983.
Black Grate Poems. Oxford, Inky Parrot Press, 1984.
The Fiction-Makers. Oxford, Oxford University Press, 1985.
Winter Time. Ashington, Northumberland, MidNAG, 1986.
Selected Poems, 1956-1986. Oxford and New York, Oxford University Press, 1987.
The Other House. Oxford, Oxford University Press, 1990.
Four and a Half Dancing Men. Oxford and New York, Oxford University Press, 1993.
The Collected Poems. Oxford, Oxford University Press, 1996.

Plays

Radio Plays: *Correspondences,* 1975; *Child of Adam,* 1976.

Other

Elizabeth Bishop. New York, Twayne, 1966; London, Collins, 1967.

Bitter Fame: A Life of Sylvia Plath. Boston, Houghton Mifflin, and London, Viking, 1989.

Editor, *Selected Poems,* by Frances Bellerby. London, Enitharmon Press, 1986.
Editor, *The Poetry Book Society.* London, Hutchinson, 1991.
Editor, *The Gregory Anthology,* with Dannie Abse. London, Hutchinson, 1995.

*

Critical Studies: By Dorothy Donnelly, in *Michigan Quarterly Review* (Ann Arbor), Fall 1966 and April 1971; Jay Parini, in *Lines Review* (Edinburgh), no. 50, September 1974, and in *Ploughshares* (Cambridge), Autumn 1978; "The Transitory Walker: Feeling for Continuities in the Poetry" by Dewi Stephen Jones, in *New Welsh Review* (Lampeter), Autumn 1989.

Anne Stevenson comments:

Each of my collections, I suspect, represents a chapter in a quest for a poetry both personal and responsible, at once truthful, passionate, and carefully crafted. In the 1960s I was questioning the assumptions I'd grown up with: what was good, what was evil, what was love, what was responsibility, by what freedom of will could I choose my life? *In Correspondences* I set forth the drama of my own (and some of America's) internal contradictions. I emerged into the near nihilism of *Enough of Green* when I was living in Oxford, and then rejected academia for the visionary release of *Minute by Glass Minute* in the Welsh border country. For a time I considered myself to be a "religious poet," but ultimately I decided the attractions of absolute belief were a delusion. *The Fiction-Makers* is a set of variations on a theme by Shakespeare-cum-Bentham: all the world's a stage, and all we can truly believe—even, perhaps, in mathematics and the natural sciences—are our own ideas. Writing a biography of Sylvia Plath convinced me that poetry today is at a turning point. Nostalgic wistfulness, individual self-pity, political idealism, angst, fury, vindictiveness, all the emotional magnets of the Romantics, are, in the last analysis, fictions. They have been replaced in poetry, in the 20th century, chiefly by abstract experiment with language, which, of course, is starvation fare for poets. *The Other House* is an attempt at a new departure; it's a slender book of poems, but I like to think it makes its peace with language, and that it finally turns away from the mirrors of self-interest and begins to look out the window.

*   *   *

"We were the very landscape / We walked through," Anne Stevenson wrote in her first volume, *Living in America.* The correspondence of physical and moral landscapes has recurred throughout her work, whether the "Landscape without regrets" of the Sierra Nevada (*Reversals*), the modest frugality of Cambridge and the Fens, or the isolation and asperity of the northeast coast of Scotland, which is the setting for most of the poems in *Enough of Green.* "Living in America" describes a continent that threatens its residents, its two shores "hurrying towards each other" while "Desperately the inhabitants hoped to be saved in the middle, / Pray to the mountains and deserts to keep them apart." "The Suburb" gives human face to this fear—a sullen and domesticated defeatism that says, "Better / to lie still and let the babies run through me"—while "The Women" quietly records a similar suppression in its picture of "Women, waiting, waiting for their husbands, / sit[ting] among dahlias all the afternoons, / while quiet processional seasons drift and subside at their doors like dunes."

But much of Stevenson's poetry has been a revolt against this tyranny of environment over self. *Correspondences,* a "Family History in Letters," traces 150 years in the life of the Chandler family on both sides of the Atlantic. In the last letter of the volume the fictitious poetess Kay Boyd writes to her father from London of her flight from the United States: "'Nowhere is safe.' / It is a poem I can't continue. / It is America I can't contain." Flight here involves refusing "the tug back" of "allegiance to innocence which is not there," deliberately leaving it unclear whether it is innocence or allegiance which is lacking. The "correspondences" of the title are in one sense those between the unsustainable poetic project and the unimaginable magnitude of America. But in the letters themselves new correspondences emerge as successive generations live through corresponding dilemmas, flights, and returns, sometimes unwittingly using the same language to describe their plights. Thus Kay's sister, Eden, writes to her of a recurring nightmare after their mother's death, asking her to come home in words which echo their ancestor Reuben Chandler, a prodigal son writing to his father, a Vermont minister, in 1832 of his own wish to return. Kay's desire to "make amends for what was not said," not just in her own relationship with her parents but also through all the fraught generations of her family, to "Do justice to the living, to the dead," likewise recalls that earlier father writing to his errant daughter in Yorkshire, mourning a husband lost at sea. Preferring, in her father's words, "the precarious apartments of the world / to the safer premises of the spirit," his daughter nevertheless chooses a fall from grace that brings a profounder suffering than he, in his naive self-righteousness, can ever know. Kay Boyd, having the last word in the book, makes it clear that this is a price worth paying.

Travelling behind Glass attempts to justify this peripatetic living as a conscious moral choice. The title poem toys with residence, imagining "A heart at grass" among the "predictable greens" of an accepted landscape but opts instead for "the paranoid howl of the / highway," where the "carapace" of the car becomes a symbol of the freewheeling will that prefers even the risk of madness to domesticity. The theme of renunciation is reiterated in *Enough of Green.* This volume makes it clear that it is precisely the green world of the senses ("love grown rank as seeding grass") which has to be renounced in favor of the steely, ascetic discipline of an art which has replaced the Christian God as taskmaster. There is in all Stevenson's poetry an extremist's desire for the sterility and outrage of the puritan's scalpel. What makes the Scottish landscape so attractive is its sense of life as stress and erosion, an attrition which uncovers the essential contours of a mind and a place.

There is a certain relentlessness of imagination, a dogged, insistent quality, to Stevenson's poetry, but it is protected from the stridency of those "intense shrill / ladies and gaunt, fanatical burnt out old women," whose fate she clearly fears in "Coming Back to Cambridge" and elsewhere, by both an elegiac sadness and a sly, wicked wit. The former is revealed in those poems which speak of love as the "remorseless joy of dereliction" ("Ragwort"), a song made out of deprivation and loss; the latter appears in a poem such as "Theme with Variations," with its cool worldliness.

Minute by Glass Minute uses landscape as the embodiment of contrary impulses. The sequence at its heart, "Green Mountain, Black Mountain" contrasts the cold, green mountains of Vermont, where she spent her childhood, with the "lusher Black Mountains of South Wales (rich in history and myth, but new to me)" of later residence. In part an elegy for her American parents, it speculates on the dialectical tension of Old and New Worlds, puritan and hedonistic impulses, a landscape threaded with history compared with one still apparently inviolate. "Threads," as a trope which links meaning, handwriting, stitching, and affiliation, threads through the sequence, raising questions about that larger impulse to establish connections, stitch together significances, which pervades the volume. The landscapes of this volume are damp, bedrizzled, and misted, and even summer is "steamy" with wet. Weather gets in the way of an eye that wants simplicity and transparency of meanings. In one poem she charges Blake with romantic obfuscation: "How dare you inflict imagination on us! / What halo does the world deserve?" But she also recognizes her own incompetence before a world that refuses meanings, where "Even my cat knows more about death than I do." She is driven to quiet fury by the inadequacy of words, unable to paint "the mudness of mud" or the "cloudness of clouds." But this poem, "If I Could Paint Essences," sums up the antitheses of her vision, admitting that just as she arrives at the "true sightness of seeing" she unexpectedly wants to play on "cellos of metaphor," "And in such imaginings I lose sight of sight." Whatever else might be said, it is certainly true that Stevenson does not, in *Minute by Glass Minute,* lose sight either of words or things.

—Stan Smith

STEWART, Susan

Nationality: American. **Born:** York, Pennsylvania, 15 March 1952. **Education:** Dickinson College, B.A. in English 1973; Johns Hopkins University, M.A. in poetry 1975; University of Pennsylvania, Ph.D. in folklore 1978. **Career:** Poet-in-the-schools, Pennsylvania Council on the Arts, 1978-82; assistant professor, 1978-81, associate professor, 1981-85, director, M.A. program in creative writing, 1984-85, professor of English 1978—, Temple University, Philadelphia. **Awards:** National Endowment for the Arts grant in poetry, 1981-82, 1984, 1988; Pennsylvania Council on the Arts grant in poetry, 1984, 1988, 1989-90; Guggenheim Foundation fellowship, 1986-87; Georgia Press "Second Book" award, 1987, for *The Hive;* Temple University Creative Achievement award, 1991; Getty Center for the History of Art and the Humanities senior scholar, 1995; Lila Wallace/*Reader's Digest* Writer's Award for poetry, 1995; Pew fellowship in the arts, 1995. **Address:** Department of English, Temple University, Philadelphia, Pennsylvania 19122, U.S.A.

PUBLICATIONS

Poetry

Yellow Stars and Ice. Princeton, Princeton University Press, 1981.

The Hive. Athens, Georgia, and London, University of Georgia Press, 1987.
The Forest. Chicago, University of Chicago Press, 1995.

Other

Crimes of Writing: Problems in the Containment of Representation. New York, Oxford University Press, 1991.
On Longing: Narratives of the Miniature, the Gigantic, the Souvenir, the Collection. Baltimore, Johns Hopkins University Press, 1984.
Nonsense: Aspects of Intertextuality in Folklore and Literature. Baltimore, Johns Hopkins University Press, 1979.

*   *   *

In her three volumes of poetry, Susan Stewart uses deceptively unadorned images to examine how the act of remembering objects may entice, threaten, violate, and enchant the rememberer. Stewart is not only a masterful poet, but a well-respected cultural theorist. Whether she is examining the art of collecting or writing poems about forests. Stewart's work confronts the relationship between narrative, desire, memory, and objects.

Her first volume, *Yellow Starts and Ice* (1981), most explicitly stages the tension between recollection and presence. In "Letter Full of Blue Dresses," Stewart opens by envisioning a pastoral, prototypically American scene in which "Two Amish girls are running / on the far side of the meadow." The poem then shifts to a disconcerting image of the speaker's body being penetrated by the objects of her gaze: "to step / off the end of a plank like this / is to walk into another life, / where the first snow could enter / my skin..." Like many of Stewart's early poems, "Letter" evokes the 19th-century gothic sensibility of Edgar Allen Poe, with its obsessive focus on the force of objects to animate and destroy the observer. Stewart revises the tropes of English romantic poetry, with its emphasis on the spiritual power of poetry to capture and transform experience, recasting romanticism in an American, postmodern light. Using short, declarative lines, her poems explore how language itself may be a ceremonial, spiritual act, capable of summoning both the sacred and the profane.

In *The Hive* (1987), her focus oscillates between the private and a more public voice. In "Blue Willow," the poem's narrator connects the remembered objects of her childhood to the violence and passion of an Oedipal family drama where "A woman grows up / in her father's house while / everything else stays the same." Her memory charges the ordinary objects found within the house with an erotic, violent power: "The heavy doors / are locked into place, / one after the other; the sky / behind the grate, an appalling / ceramic blue." The narrator moves in the next stanza from the private drama within the Oedipal house to a general statement regarding the nature of love: "It's true that the idea / of pure love depends / on the cruelty of the father." She then returns to her highly personal tone: "Last night I dreamed of a paradise where the fences / were shuffled by the wind / and I gave each tree its / proper name..." By injecting a voice of public proclamation into her interior reveries, Stewart infuses her poems with a subtle feminist critique of the terms by which memory and desire are produced.

This meshing of the personal with the social is further intensified in her 1995 collection, *The Forest.* Divided into two sections,

"Phantom" and "Cinder," these poems feature stanzas of longer, densely clustered lines which themselves resemble thickly grown forests. The forest is posed as a multivalent symbol in these poems: it is an ecologically threatened natural body; a site of political violence; an allegory for the process of memory; and a sign of human community under threat of erasure by postmodern, technologized culture. As Robert Pogue Harrison suggests, "In this book a forest of memories gives way to a memory of forests." Memories and forests are both poised on the verge of extinction, endangered, perhaps already vanished.

In the opening poem, "The Forest," the speaker delivers a direct, apostrophic address to the reader: "You should lie down now and remember the forest, / for it is disappearing— / no, the truth is it is gone now / and so what details you can bring back / might have a kind of life." The final stanza, rather than resolving the relationship between forests and people, instead suggests, "Once we were lost in the forest, *so strangely alike and yet singular, too,* / but the truth is, it is, lost to us now." Stewart is not only exploring the interpenetration between subjects and objects, but also their estrangement, their ineluctable difference from one another. This powerful collection both intensifies and extends the concerns of Stewart's earlier work, creating a haunting, evocative forest of poems.

—Jennifer Natalya Fink

STRAUSS, Jennifer

Nationality: Australian. **Born:** Jennifer Wallace, Heywood, Victoria, 30 January 1933. **Education:** University of Melbourne, 1951-54, B.A. (honors) 1954; University of Glasgow, 1957-58; Monash University, Ph.D. 1991. **Family:** Married Werner Strauss in 1958; three sons. **Career:** Lecturer, University of Melbourne, 1961-63; lecturer, 1964-71, senior lecturer, 1971-91, and associate professor, 1991—, Monash University, Melbourne. Visiting scholar, University of North Carolina, Chapel Hill, 1974, and Australian National University, Canberra, 1988; visiting professor, Centre for Medieval Studies, University of Toronto, Ontario, 1982. Member of literature committee, Ministry for the Arts, Victoria, 1983-85; chair, Premier's Literary Awards Committee, 1989-91, member, 1996. **Awards:** *Westerly* Sesquicentenary prize, 1979. **Address:** 2/12 Tollington Avenue, East Malvern, Victoria 3145, Australia.

PUBLICATIONS

Poetry

Children and Other Strangers. Melbourne, Nelson, 1975.
Winter Driving. Melbourne, Sisters, 1981.
Labour Ward. Melbourne Pariah Press, 1988.

Other

"Stop Laughing! I'm Being Serious:" Studies in Seriousness and Wit in Contemporary Australian Literature. Townsville, Foundation for the Study of Australian Literature, 1990.

Boundary Conditions: The Poetry of Gwen Harwood. St. Lucia, University of Queensland Press, 1992; second edition, 1996.
Judith Wright. Melbourne, Oxford University Press, 1996.

Editor, with Bruce Moore and Jan Noble, *Middle English Verse: An Anthology.* Melbourne, Monash University, 1976; revised edition, with Charles A. Stevenson, 1985.
Editor, *The Oxford Book of Australian Love Poems.* Melbourne, Oxford University Press, 1993.

*

Manuscript Collection: Australian Defence Force Academy, Canberra.

Critical Studies: "Pensive Seductions: New Collections by Four Women Poets" by Yvonne Rousseau, in *Age Monthly Review* (Melbourne), February 1989; "What the Witness Spoke: Jennifer Strauss, Labour Ward" by Noel Rowe, in *Southerly,* vol. 52, no. 1, 1992.

Jennifer Strauss comments:

People—their psychological states and social conditions—interest me more than landscape, and the direction of that interest has been influenced by feminist thought. If all my poems are personal, very few are unequivocally autobiographical. Mostly I write because things disturb rather than distress. I want to make something out of that disturbance, which isn't necessarily caused by obvious disorder—the wrong kind of order can be the most disturbing of all. And the poem does not exorcise the original feeling; poems are neither problem solvers nor dissolvers.

I have never been able to produce a finished poem by making up my mind to write a (=any) poem at a particular time, much less by making up my mind to write in a particular form. I can only write when a particular poetic idea germinates in the kinds of experiences in which there are intersections of thought and feeling, past and present, particular and type. The "idea" of a poem is not an idea at all in a philosophical or even discursive sense. It's a dimly perceived shape, and the defining of that shape is a process of discovering as much as of "making." My output is small. I write the kind of poems I can: I admire a great many other kinds.

*   *   *

A phrase she uses in "The Pain of Others," "a little winter sun," could be used as a definitive image of Jennifer Strauss's poetic world. Though she is eloquent in her exploration of private and public worlds, rarely in her poetry does the intimate world of a loving family escape the shadow of wider realities. Into a peaceful kitchen, for example, "The morning paper / Spills its daily due / Of blood and bastardry," and refuge is only sought, not found, in a child's sunlit nursery, for "Dark in the quiet pulsing of your blood / I hear the jackboots thud the wild world over" ("For Nicholas, One Year Old"). In a later poem, "Models," a children's game and reflections on history coalesce in a tellingly ironic comment on human nature:

Makers of cities
Makers of wars
The boys are playing.

They are painting the tanks.
For more than an hour now
They have not quarrelled.

In "Collage: The Personal Is Political" the connections between domestic and political violence are relentlessly probed through the fate of children at the hands of abusing parents and warring governments. The demand "LET THERE BE JUSTICE" raises the question of degrees of guilt and degrees of punishment:

Let there be trials
the parents will go to jail
and so they should
and so they should
the pilots may have nightmares
and so they should
but the torturers
will draw their pay
the generals wear their medals

The combination of sensibility and hard logic, of a refined and taut poetics, has always been a mark of Strauss's work. While her development has increasingly been toward a wry disengagement from the often close personal voice of the earlier poetry, awareness of the frailty of love and of institutionalized violence remains a strong current in her work. One process of this disengagement has been the increasing use in her second and third volumes of dramatic monologues of characters from literature, history, or myth ("Guinevere Dying," Jezebel's maid in "A Just Cause," "Wife to Horatio," the "Bluebeard Rescripted" poems). The sun in their often bleak landscapes derives from individual courage, stoicism, self-awareness, as in "Labour Ward," where the brevity of a journey combines birth, rebirth, and death:

In grief,
Joy's a foreign country.
It's there, but you need a visa.
No-one will issue it;
You must bear it yourself.

"Epitaphs for Casualties," a section heading from her first volume, could serve as cover title for many of her poems, in which defiance and a grim humor often serve as saving graces. "Pinecones and My Grandmother" praises the "sharp-tongued" woman who "Taught to a timid child / Something of fortitude, / Not to flinch / At barbs on the wire fence. / 'If the head gets through, / The rest,' she said / 'Will follow.'" The adult voice applies that wisdom differently, escaping conventions that her grandmother accepted and requiring the head to take second place: her heart "has made up its mind / To get through the fence." With similar defiance the speaker in the monologue "Wife to Horatio," explaining a successful retreat from the dark intricacies of life in Elsinore, has acted to safeguard the future. Her daughter Ophelia is "playing by the river," but

There'll be no drowning here.
I've seen to it that she knows how to swim.

There is no such comfort in action for the persona of the moving, biting "Guenevere Dying." Measured, ironic, uncompromising, this is one of Strauss's most striking poems. Wild Cornish

Gwen, first caught in "the sweet cage" of love, is saved from death only to be caged again in a convent. Merlin, Arthur, Lancelot all betray her; the priest permits her to see the sky from her cell "'Not ... to pleasure the rotting flesh / But to nourish the labouring soul.'" A pear tree, her wedding gift, is the symbol for her life; although it is beautiful, it is barren, and Arthur condemns it as lacking in utility: "We owe the land / Good husbandry!" When it is burned, its ashes blow "through the casement onto my marriage bed." In Gwen's rescue from the fires of martyrdom woman and nature are joined ("'A brand plucked from the burning,'" admonishes the priest; "'I am bruised all over on men's imperatives,'" Gwen reflects):

Men slaughter men with sword and lance
'Honourably': trees and women they burn—
Always afraid of female blood.
Barren, barren...
          Burning, burning...

A casualty of "Crown, Honour, Chivalry," Gwen speaks her own bitter epitaph. Throughout the poem the association of women with the natural world resonates against the imperatives of the masculine world, where Gwen's "Honest desire ... starved in that garden of cultivated souls." Imagery, logic, and language speak for the higher culture of the natural order denied in "good husbandry," the barbarism and cruelty of court and church.

Another deathbed monologue, this by a casualty of similar orthodoxies, is that of a nineteenth-century Viennese physician, "Ignaz Semmelweis." A pioneer in the treatment of puerperal fever, Semmelweis also dies incarcerated (in an insane asylum), his death proof of his theory of sepsis. The evil against which he fights is the belief that childbirth is "accursed ... from Eve downwards," that women midwives, uncontaminated by work in the dissection rooms, must go:

They don't punish enough. Better believe
God vindictive
Than a doctor dirty.

Here and in "The Anabaptist Cages, Munster," *Labour Ward* juxtaposes images of the cruelty and ignorance of the past with those of the present ("The Snapshot Album of the Innocent Tourist"). A series of love lyrics are not exempt from a form of irony. In these, disruptions of an established mood come from the speaker, varying from the darkness of "Search and Destroy" ("was it the language / of love or of war?") to "Aubade," a gentle morning song which ends with the poet's "faithless fingers" itching to transcribe experience.

—Nan Bowman Albinski

SZUMIGALSKI, Anne

Nationality: Canadian. **Born:** London, England, 3 January 1922. **Education:** Privately educated. **Family:** Married Jan Szumigalski in 1945; two daughters and two sons. **Military Service:** Civilian relief worker, British Red Cross and Friends Ambulance Unit, 1943-46. **Career:** Teacher of creative writing in poetry in Saskatoon, Saskatchewan, elementary and secondary schools and instructor of poetry at Saskatchewan Summer School of the Arts, 1971—. Founder and coordinator of Saskatoon Poets. **Awards:** Canada Council grant, 1976, and Senior grant, 1990; Saskatchewan Poetry prize, 1977-78; Writer's Choice award, 1986, 1987; Silver Magazine award, 1987, 1991; Saskatchewan Order of Merit, 1989; Woman of the Year, YWCA, 1989; Arts Board award for lifetime excellence in the arts, 1990; Governor General's Award for poetry, 1996. **Address:** 9 Connaught Place, Saskatoon, Saskatchewan S7L 1C7, Canada.

PUBLICATIONS

Poetry

Woman Reading in Bath. Toronto, Doubleday, 1974.
A Game of Angels. Winnipeg, Turnstone Press, 1980.
Risks: A Poem. Red Deer, Alberta, Red Deer College Press, 1983.
Doctrine of Signatures. Saskatoon, Saskatchewan, Fifth House, 1983.
Instar: Poems and Stories. Red Deer, Alberta, Red Deer College Press, 1985.
Dogstones: Selected and New Poems. Saskatoon, Saskatchewan, Fifth House, 1986.
Journey, with Terrence Heath. Red Deer, Alberta, Red Deer College Press, 1988.
Rapture of the Deep. Regina, Saskatchewan, Coteau Books, 1991.
Voice. Regina, Saskatchewan, Coteau Books, 1995.

Plays

Z: A Meditation on Oppression, Desire and Freedom. Regina, Saskatchewan, Coteau Books, 1995.

Radio Plays: *The Eyes of the Fishes,* with Terrence Heath, Canadian Broadcasting Corporation, 1973; *The Exile's Catalogue,* with Heath, Canadian Broadcasting Corporation, 1977; *The Chrome Paps,* with Heath, Canadian Broadcasting Corporation, 1978; *Wild Man's Butte,* with Heath, Canadian Broadcasting Corporation, 1979.

Other

The Word, the Voice, the Text: The Life of a Writer. Saskatoon, Fifth House, 1990.

*

Critical Studies: "Nightmare Vision: Anne Szumigalski" by Kathleen Geminder, in *Essays on Canadian Writing* (Downsview, Ontario), no. 18-19, 1980; *Heading Out: The New Saskatchewan Poets,* edited by Don Kerr and Anne Szumigalski, Regina, Saskatchewan, Coteau Books, 1986.

*   *   *

With great success, Anne Szumigalski has put into practice the conception of poetry outlined in *The Word, the Voice, the Text,* her book of reflections on the writer's life and art. Emphasizing that poetry "is power, is energy" rather than being a containable intellectual pursuit, she affirms her belief in "the poet as iconoclast" and proclaims that it is the poet's duty to cast down idols and "start, even at the age of 60, even at the age of 90, new phases and new forms."

Szumigalski herself did not start publishing until relatively late in life—her first collection appeared when she was 52—but in the two succeeding decades she has produced an oeuvre remarkable for its imaginative energy and experiential range. "Victim," from *Woman Reading in Bath,* points toward some of the hallmarks of her later achievement: finely realized and surrealistically juxtaposed details, irregular verse paragraphs that relate to each other more suggestively than sequentially, and a strong fictional impulse that uses narrative situation concisely in the service of subtle lyrical implication. The poem moves from an unnamed "cliff edge—where so many murders are done" and where a movie is being filmed—to a reminiscence of someone walking with "my darling Mr. B," to the revelation that the narrator was murdered "last Thursday" and is now being carried by Mr. B "in a seashell / In his trousers pocket among / The sticks of Dentyne gum and the spent flashbulbs." The shift to a Lilliputian perspective conveys perfectly the essential helplessness of the victim, her sense of being literally in someone else's pocket. Other poems in her first collection are less successful, constrained by the smaller compass and shorter lines of their more conventional free-verse structures and unduly limited in their experiences by the "I" and "you" they focus on. A notable exception is the "Stefan Sequence," where the spatial and chronological breadth gives more room to Szumigalski's particular talents.

Those talents found a much more promising ground in *Wild Man's Butte,* a "stereophonic" poem sequence written for radio and coauthored with Terrence Heath. The sequence centers on the experiences of a surveyor lost in the Saskatchewan badlands in 1910, and it ranges among his thoughts, the reports of his superiors as they attempt to find him, his love for a blind Indian woman, and an Assiniboian creation myth that parallels and frames the central story. The structure provides a sufficiently broad outlet for Szumigalski's narrative energy, and its opposition of surveyor and Indian woman draws on an antithesis that the poet, with her love of Blakean contraries, frequently finds inspiration in: measured Apollo versus liberated Dionysus—the grandfather's methodical gardening versus the child's imaginative descent "down the cellar steps into the darkness and damp" in "Story" (*Instar*); Da, who was "not the kissing kind" and who wanted his daughter to be "a serious person," versus tippling, singing, laughing Gran in "You" (*Rapture of the Deep*); Angle, "that indwelling cousin" who takes years to build his house "so carefully," while "the Celt within" sings "ecstatic and undulating songs" in "A House with a Tower" (*A Game of Angels*).

It is plain that Szumigalski's sympathies lie with Dionysus and the Celt, and, especially in the poems written for and after *Doctrine of Signatures,* she has found the formal means to translate those sympathies into wonderfully strong and memorable writing. Such poems as "The Arrangement," "Heroines," and "Morning" use fragmentary narrative as a means of generating rippling pools of implication in frequently unpunctuated verse paragraphs that are set as prose except for word-sized white spaces between the syntactical groups within them. They allow the reader to participate in the sense of the world's ultimate mystery that can be generated by surrealism at its best. "Mates," like John Ashbery's more extensive but less subtle "The Instruction Manual," invites us to experience a process in which the world of thought and the "real" world mutually create and question each other's reality. Yet, the imaginative amplitude of the poems has not been purchased at the cost of precise attention to detail. The finely controlled imagery of these lines from "A Pineal Casement" gives a concise embodiment to the poem's speculations about the affinities of mental and physical experience, and the lack of punctuation conveys the deftness of the "fit" that is alluded to: "in the same way that the cotter fits neatly through any of the latcheyes the nub of the mind may slip through any of several ideas."

In volume after volume Szumigalski has continually broadened the effectiveness and range of her unique voice. Her collection *Rapture of the Deep* takes us effortlessly from life as lived by an elderly woman in a provincial city ("Grey") to the life of "The Elect," a mysterious group that rises up from "holy depths of earth" and whose members cannot remember their names until the poem ends in this act of christening: "At last a child in blue cotton leans down to us. 'Daffs,' she says, and, taking each of us by the neck, yanks for the love of God." The child's creator once described the poet's work as "the business of children," and Szumigalski continues to thrive in her business of appropriating the world and naming it into consciousness of itself.

—Julia Reibetanz

SZYMBORSKA, Wislawa

Nationality: Polish. **Born:** Bnin, Poland, 2 July 1923. **Education:** Jagiellonian University, Cracow, 1945-48. **Family:** Widowed. **Career:** Member of editorial staff, *Zycie Literackie,* Cracow, 1952-81. **Awards:** Cracow Literary prize, 1954; Gold Cross of Merit, 1955; Minister of Culture prize, 1963; Knight's Cross, Order of Polonia Resituta, 1974; Goethe award, 1991; Nobel Prize for Literature, 1996. **Address:** ul. 18 Stycnia 82/89, 30-079 Cracow, Poland.

PUBLICATIONS

Poetry

Dlatego zyjemy ("That's What We Live For"). Warsaw, n.p., 1952.
Pytania zadawane sobie ("Questions Put to Myself"). Warsaw, n.p., 1954.
Wolanie do Yeti ("Calling Out to Yeti"). Warsaw, n.p., 1957.
Sól ("Salt"). Warsaw, Panstowowy Instytut Wydawniczy, 1962.
Sto pociech ("No End of Fun"). Warsaw, Panstowowy Instytut Wydawniczy, 1967.
Poezje wybrans ("Selected Poems"). Warsaw, Ludowa Spóldzielnia Wydawnicza, 1967.
Poezje. Warsaw, Przedmowa Jerzego Kwiatkowskiego, 1970.
Wybór poezji. Warsaw, Czytelnik, 1970.
Wszelki wypadek ("Could Have"). Warsaw, Czytelnik, 1972.
Wybór wierszy ("Selected Poems"). Warsaw, Panstowowy Instytut Wydawniczy, 1973.
Wilka liczba ("A Large Number"). Warsaw, Czytelnik, 1976.
Sounds, Feelings, Thoughts: 70 Poems, translated by Magnus J. Krynski and Robert A. Maguire. Princeton, Princeton University Press, 1981.

Poezju wybrane (II) ("Selected Poems II"). Warsaw, Ludowa Spóldzielnia Wydawnicza, 1983.
Ludzie na moscie. Warsaw, Czytelnik, 1986; translated by Adam Czeniawski as *People on a Bridge,* London, Forest, 1990.
Poezji = Poems (bilingual edition), translated by Magnus J. Krynski and Robert A. Maguire. Crackow, Wydawnictwo Literackie, 1989.
Wieczor autorski: wiersze ("Author's Evening: Poems"). Warsaw, Anagram, 1992.
Koniec i poczatek ("The End and the Beginning"). Warsaw, Wydawnictwo Literackie, 1993.
View with a Grain of Sand: Selected Poems, translated by Stanislaw Baranczak and Clare Cavanagh, New York, Harcourt, 1996.

*

Critical Studies: *Contemporary Polish Poetry: 1925-1975* by Madeline Levine, Boston, Twayne, 1981; *Breathing under Water and Other East European Essays* by Stanislaw Baranczak, Cambridge, Harvard University Press, 1990; "Subversive Activities" by Edward Hirsch, in *New York Review of Books,* 18 April 1996; interview with Dean E. Murphy in *Los Angeles Times,* 13 October 1996; "Wislawa Szymborska and the Importance of the Unimportant" by Bogdana Carpenter, in *World Literature Today,* Winter 1997.

*   *   *

Winner of the 1996 Nobel Prize for Literature, Polish poet Wislawa Szymborska writes a modest, restrained and thoughtful poetry which paradoxically asks large questions and subtly criticizes pretension. Her poem "No Title Required," for example—the title is typical of her self-effacing approach—ends with the lines: "I'm no longer sure / that what's important / is more important than what's not." This humble uncertainty defines Szymborska's poetic manner.

In a country whose recent history is one of oppression and rebellion, Szymborska has chosen not to write of politics. Unlike fellow Polish Nobel Prize-winner Czeslaw Milosz, who has used his poetry to confront Poland's occupation by the Nazi and Soviet regimes, she has stayed away from writing of her nation's troubles. But not writing about politics does not mean that Szymborska has been aloof from politics. During the early 1950s she wrote for a time in the style of Socialist Realism in poems that glorified the virtues of communism; by the late 1950s she had renounced this work. In the 1980s, during the period of martial law imposed by the Polish communist government in response to the Solidarity union movement, Szymborska was publishing poems under pseudonyms in underground dissident journals.

But Szymborska's own involvement in Poland's turbulent political history has not extended to her poetry. She often characterizes history itself as a malevolent force in human affairs, one that is forced upon humankind as a justification for further destruction. Instead, Szymborska ruminates on the details of daily life and personal relations, aspects of existence she believes have always remained essentially the same and which are, truly, the only subjects of lasting value. Death, loneliness, love, faith and other universal themes are constants in her poetry.

Szymborska uses simple, direct language to express her thoughts. The Swedish Academy noted the "finely chiseled diction" of her poems. But the seemingly casual musings she captures in her poems are deceptive and full of irony. Her work reverberates long after it is read. Critics have pointed to her assumed naivety from which she examines the pretensions and tragedies of ordinary life. Her poem "Nothing Twice" speaks of a relationship in simple words and with a delightful irony: "With smiles and kisses, we prefer / to seek accord beneath our star, / although we're different (we concur) / just as two drops of water are."

Although she is apolitical, Szymborska writes in the poem "Children of the Age" that "Apolitical poems are political too." That is, her wry examination of the world as it exists must necessarily be a political statement of sorts, albeit a statement based on the personal rather than the ideological. She writes in "A Great Number" that there are "Four billion people on this earth of ours, / but my imagination is unchanged. / It does not do well with great numbers. / It is still moved by what is individual." Speaking to Dean E. Murphy in the *Los Angeles Times,* Szymborska explained:

"There are some poets who write for people assembled in big rooms, so they can live through something collectively. I prefer my reader to take my poem and have a one-on-one relationship with it."

Popular since the late 1950s in her native Poland, Szymborska was little known elsewhere until the Nobel Prize announcement. Her quiet, personal poems—when compared to the political rebellion of many other poets from Eastern Europe—seemed out of step with the times. Never a prolific writer—she has published some 200 poems in a career spanning 40 years—Szymborska has not created the body of work normally associated with a Nobel Prize-winner. But, as Bogdana Carpenter remarked in *World Literature Today,* each of her poems "is a masterpiece."

—Denise Wiloch

T

TAFDRUP, Pia

Nationality: Danish. **Born:** Copenhagen, Denmark, 29 May 1952. **Education:** Copenhagen University, B.A. 1977. **Awards:** Danish State Art Foundation scholarships, 1984; Holger Drachmann grant, 1986; Henri Nathansen Birthday grant, 1987; Otto Rung grant, 1987; Tagea Brandt grant, 1989; Edith Rode grant, 1991; Einar Hansen grant, 1991; N. Bang grant 1992; Anckerske grant 1994; *Weekend Avisen* literature prize, 1995; Morten Nielsen grant, 1995; Emil Aarestrup Medal, 1996. **Member:** Danish Academy, Danish PEN Centre, Danish Language Council. **Address:** Rosenvængets Sideallé 3. 2.th, 2100 Copenhagen Ø, Denmark.

PUBLICATIONS

Poetry

Når der går hul på en engel ("When an Angel's Been Grazed"). N.p., 1981.
Intetfang ("Nohold"). N.p., 1982.
The Innermost Zone. N.p., 1983.
Springflod. N.p., 1985; translated by Anne Born as *Spring Tide,* London, Forest Books, 1989.
Hvid Feber ("White Fever"). N.p., 1986.
Sekundernes Bro ("The Bridge of Moments"). N.p., 1988.
Krystalskoven ("The Crystal Forest"). N.p., 1992.
Territorialsang, en Jerusalemkomposition ("Territorial Song: A Jerusalem Cycle"). N.p., 1994.

Plays

Døden i Bjergerne ("Death in the Mountains"), produced 1988.
Jorden er blå ("The Earth Is Blue"), produced 1991.

Other

Over vandet går jeg, Skitse til en Poetik ("Walking over the Water: Outline of a Poetics"). N.p., 1991.

*

Critical Studies: "Lysets Engel, en Tafdrupkomposition" by Marianne Barlyng, in *Nordica Bergensia 12,* 1996; "Digtet i dialog med verden og historien, en samtale med Pia Tafdrup" (interview) by Mai Misfeldt, in *Spring, Tidsskrift for moderne dansk litteratur,* no. 9, 1995.

* * *

Pia Tafdrup is the leading Danish woman poet of the 1980s and 1990s. Her published oeuvre forms a remarkably consistent development and expansion of a talent both intellectually formidable and spiritually beautiful. She speaks in a late 20th-century voice that echoes the European tradition of writers such as Rainer Maria Rilke and Marcel Duchamp, and is in sympathy with Swed-

ish modernists like Göran Sonnevi, Lars Norén, Gunnar Björling, and Werner Aspenström.

Tafdrup's style is entirely her own. In her intensely serious work with language and meaning she constantly breaks boundaries, not by constructing new words but in wrestling to extract and clarify ideas that occupy her creating intellect and feeling heart. Lines can be short or long according to the nature of the material; indentation is used in an almost physical way, and needs to be carefully followed by her translators. The poem on the page strives to achieve a balance between the physical and the intellectual, not least through musicality.

In a study of Tafdrup's work, "The Angel of Light," the Danish critic Marianne Barlyng identifies an immanent logical development from collection to collection, the books relating to each other as thesis, antithesis and synthesis. This is seen in the first three books, *When An Angel's Been Grazed, Nohold,* and *The Innermost Zone.* Tafdrup's first collection appeared when she was 31, at a point when life and education had matured her so that her published work was perfected from the start and thus presents a full-grown body in style and form. Her mind and spirit can express wide-ranging subjects in a consistently meticulous and elegant manner. These three books reflect the concerns and problems of a youthful, always sensitive and passionate woman.

The titles, *Spring Tide, White Fever,* and *The Bridge of Moments* similarly form a trilogy. *Spring Tide* follows the course of a passionate love relationship; unusually, the poems tell of the woman's emotions in a strongly erotic, organic style. She is the protagonist in each poem's description, without excluding the "you," the other, the man who is her lover, or her own femininity. While physical description is strong in these poems, the physical moves outward to encompass universality: "I have made my heart big / and await you / between walls, between floor and ceiling / in a circle of light / in an ecstasy / of golden drops / the body waits / in my body." Towards the end of *Spring Tide* passion is burning itself out. In the next collection, *White Fever,* the pain of a broken relationship is sometimes expressed in images of death in the form of a hare, at first alive, then shot, strung up, skinned, cut open and bleeding. Tafdrup creates many startling images and metaphors: a farewell touch is "stone flaked by stone," "after a seizure of furious metals / berries melt black / on the tongue," all nature changes into horror. But in *The Bridge of Moments,* reconciliations occur within poems on various subjects. In a feature article in *Politiken* newspaper (24 September 1988), the poet comments: "So much in our time is concerned with breaking all bridges, with severance and parting, but the theme of *The Bridge of Moments* is the longing for those moments when communication succeeds or another connection is made. The book is about building bridges over distances, about crossing accepted boundaries. About seconds between heart and heart."

In *The Crystal Forest* aspects of stillness are a central theme, expressed in images of the natural world, which occur in more detail than in the other books. Tafdrup never anthropomorphizes nature but uses its variety for the purpose of contemplating language. "This metaphorics of the elements—water, air, earth—describes both the world and the poem, or perhaps rather the world in the poem, points ahead to the following collection, like a kind of echo room for both preceding and forthcoming work," according to Barlyng.

> My direction is along all roads
> that are only the same road onward
> the years' geometric network
> ignited by a coursing fire in the blood
> that road which gives me myself / back to myself.

Territorial Song is another brilliant step forward. Given Tafdrup's origins, her cast of mind and spirit, and her previous experience and achievement, it seems an inevitable development. The book's subtitle is *A Jerusalem Cycle;* its contents chart the poet's visit to Jerusalem during which she composes poems about this city she has in a sense come home to. Tafdrup is Jewish although brought up in a Danish cultural setting, and not in the orthodox faith. *Territorial Song* refers to birds' way of staking claim to their living space. In a metaphoric sense this is what Tafdrup's poems do, through them she comes home to her mythical, historical city of poetry and life. By so doing she brings together the various strands of her own experience. "A city built of light / a lake of fire for the soul / a clarity sweeps through us / / Jerusalem, the mother / who alternately blesses and tortures her children / in the name of love."

—Anne Born

TEMPLETON, Fiona

Nationality: Scottish. **Career:** Poet and performance artist. Founding member, Theatre of Mistakes, London. Artist-in-residence, Capp. St. Project, San Francisco, 1992; Senior Judith E. Wilson Visiting fellow, Cambridge University, c. 1996. Lives in New York City. **Awards:** National Endowment for the Arts grant, 1986.

PUBLICATIONS

Poetry

London. College Park, Sun & Moon Press, 1984.
Realities (excerpts) (chapbook). England, Sound & Language, 1995.
Hi Cowboy. England, Pointing Device, 1997.
ssh off (from Siobhan's drawings) (chapbook). Cambridge, Rempress, 1997.

Plays

YOU—The City (produced New York 1988; produced London 1989). New York, Roof Books, 1990.
Delirium of Interpretations (produced 1991). Los Angeles, Sun & Moon Press, 1996.

Performance Pieces

Cells of Release. N.p., n.d.
Going. N.p., 1977.
Thought/Death. N.p., 1980.

The Seven Deadly Jealousies (with Julian Maynard-Smith). N.p., 1982.
Experiments in the Destruction of Time. N.p., 1983.

Other

Cells of Release (installation text). New York, Roof Books, 1997.

Compiler, with Anthony Howell, *Elements of Performance Art.* London, Theatre of Mistakes/Ting Books, 1976.

*   *   *

Since the mid-1970s, Fiona Templeton has earned recognition as a prominent experimental poet, playwright, and performance artist. Her first book of poetry, *London* (published in 1984 but begun as early as 1977), offers a new perspective on the formal and ideological possibilities of the prose poem. The collection consists of a series of unpunctuated prose paragraphs grouped in sections of more or less equal length. Far from subscribing to the epiphanic "pedestrianism" one usually expects from a conventional city poem, each paragraph reads like a concatenation of visual and verbal icons whose internal logic is highly difficult to apprehend.

Another important consequence of the experimental structure and lack of syntactic coherence of Templeton's *London* is the absence of a coherent pattern by which to identify the central consciousness of the poem. The marks of individual subjectivity remain all the more indeterminate as the speaking or writing "I" often seems to be fumbling for a means of affirming her existence as a mere sign invested with different meanings and use-values by its immediate physical and societal surroundings. While her hopes, moods, and desires remain largely unstated, her very sense of identity seems complicated by the legal, political, technical, or commercial imperatives of the age:

> I'll do advisory moment serve queen or foster data processing man and pray off
> and find us at old underground station bucking lace on a data processing age
> well do I pal do an advertising vision great queen's earl's class if I can continue
> a half on art men in yellow age rough sin per cent of new sins rail vice now
> what can we do for you for full details of art men in yellow age's ring

If the exact significance of such associational wanderings often remain inscrutable, recognizable icons of British culture (here, the underground station and Britain's monarchic and aristocratic sub-text) nonetheless emerge from the recesses of the poem's many-layered discourse. Despite its asyntactic dynamics, Templeton's prose therefore does not fall into the abstract or "areferential" category, as each of the sections of the collection points not only to easily recognizable elements of the urban landscape but also to a number of social and cultural phenomena, including family values, the relationship between art and capital, religion, unemployment, class consciousness, the mass media, as well as various forms of domestic, racial, and sexual politics.

In more general terms, *London* delineates the variable trajectories of a self's consciousness revealed primarily through its interaction with (and subjection to) specific cultural codes and institutions. One of the main strengths of the collection indeed lies in Templeton's skillful juxtaposition of details of the urban landscape with idiosyncrasies of the "speaker"'s mental wanderings, tensions and cultural habits. Templeton's vision of the city as a geographical and linguistic maze without a center discloses the poem itself as a set of fragmented cultural idioms that jam the codes of sense-making and frequently sap the self's attempts at self-expression. Ultimately, the unlikely combination of rambling, thinking, observing, and talking that makes up the body of *London* points to a collective voice subsuming, at least in part, the variety of individual utterances and linguistic registers contained in the collection. This concern with the interplay of the personal and the social is also apparent in *You—The City,* "an intimate Manhattanwide play for an audience of one" in which Templeton's exploration of the collective consciousness of the city builds to an interactive performance-meditation on the paradoxical dialectics of relationship and privacy.

The structural cohesiveness of Templeton's collection is achieved not just by the poem's overall dedication to the city of London but also by the repetition of key words placed in different contexts and therefore subject to successive interpretations. The effect of this "repetition with variation" technique—which is reinforced by Templeton's constant use of puns and alliterative effects—is to focus the reader's attention on how changes in the sequential arrangement of words on the page constantly recontextualize their meaning and create new possibilities for intermingling (and often contradictory) reading patterns and semantic metamorphoses.

Hi Cowboy, Templeton's more recent printed collection, is a much more discursive and argumentative work in which the prose paragraph becomes an exploration site for a consciousness struggling to understand human relationships in terms of complex economic, intellectual, and libidinal transactions:

> The case against love steals its redness, says it was a loan.
>   Realized because the
> names we gave curved arms shut. Conversation between
>   disheveled and local,
> tampax and our languid tribute, licence and vanity, the bull-
>   calf and the heifer,
> first of a series, dying, should thrill through stew? Curt
>   and equal, name no
> hour, neglect alleged illicit groan.

Perhaps Templeton's most impressive achievement is to write a kind of prose poetry which, even though it reflects the poet's awareness of the discrepancy between language and meaning, can nonetheless attend to its own operations as both the vector of individual experience and the promise of an ever-changing relation between self and world. By subordinating the poet's perception of self to the creation of a hybrid medium that combines the conversational and the analytical, the lyrical and the critical, Templeton's writing holds out the possibility for new directions for a poetic idiom that seeks to captures the difficulties and conflicts that inhabit the social practice we call language.

—Michel Delville

THESEN, Sharon

Nationality: Canadian. **Born:** Tisdale, Saskatchewan, 1 October 1946. **Education:** Simon Fraser University, Burnaby, British Columbia, B.A. 1970, M.A. 1974. **Family:** Married 1) Brian Fawcett in 1966, one son; 2) Peter Thompson. **Career:** Has worked as a dental assistant, cab driver, and record librarian. Currently English teacher, Capilano College, Vancouver, British Columbia. Poetry editor, *Capilano Review,* 1978-89.

PUBLICATIONS

Poetry

Artemis Hates Romance. Toronto, Coach House Press, 1980.
Radio New France Radio. Vancouver, Slug Press, 1982.
Holding the Pose. Toronto, Coach House Press, 1983.
Confabulations: Poems for Malcolm Lowry. Lantzville, British Columbia, Oolichan, 1984.
The Beginning of the Long Dash. Toronto, Coach House Press, 1987.
The Pangs of Sunday. Toronto, McClelland & Stewart, 1990.
Aurora. Toronto, Coach House Press, 1995.

Other

Editor, *Selected Poems: The Vision Tree* by Phyllis Webb. Vancouver, Talonbooks, 1982.
Editor, *The New Long Poem Anthology.* Toronto, Coach House Press, 1991.

*

Manuscript Collection: McGill University, Montreal.

Critical Studies: "Knots of Energy: The Contest of Discourses in Sharon Thesen's Poetry" by Rob Dunham, and "The Barren Reach of Modern Desire: Intertextuality in Sharon Thesen's 'The Beginning of the Long Dash'" by Steven Scobie, both in *Sagetrieb* (Orono, Maine), vol. 7, no. 1, Spring 1988.

*   *   *

In her first book, *Artemis Hates Romance,* Sharon Thesen warns that "the defoliated / imagination is the end / of all lyric" ("Day Dream"). The flowering of Thesen's writing, witnessed in the volumes of poetry published beginning in 1980, is a clear indication that her own imagination is in full bloom. Thesen's lyricism, however, is not unremittingly bright and fragrant, for it lives in and grows out of a world marked by limitation and loss.

Thesen's early volumes in particular are characterized by fairly grim explorations of the limits of love, loneliness, anger, and despair. In a 1988 interview in the *Malahat Review* she calls these works her "mad," "sad," and "bad" books, respectively. In *Artemis Hates Romance* Thesen vents her rage and sorrow at the failures of romantic relationships, stating that "there is no / metaphor for love that is not / redness & pain" ("Wilkinson Road Poems") and that the appearance of love "brings dread to the heart, / knowledge / unasked for" ("The Argument Begins with a"). In a poem called "Dedication" Thesen's anger is specifically targeted at "'honeybunch,'" otherwise addressed as "you stupid fucker" and "you slimy hogstool," for his part in arresting her career as a poet: "you never thought I'd do / it did ya ... / it's no goddamn thanks to you, hiding my / typewriter and always wanting fancy dinners all the time."

Holding the Pose is a quieter work, inhabited by cheating hearts and icy hearts, brokenhearted skies and rain, dim places and painful yellow tulips. Early in the volume, in a poem entitled "Discourse," Thesen concludes with irony that "finally there's not / all that much / you can say," and yet she continues to write, "another word written, and another" in "the daily effort to solve / the puzzled heart" ("Hello Goodbye"). Declaring that "it is my own pain / I write" ("X"), Thesen in this book sifts through her memories in order to heal herself, her imagination. Her meditations on the painful past are not maudlin or self-pitying, however, for in "Praxis" she firmly tells herself (and the reader) to "imagine a future better / than now" and to "stop crying. Get up. Go out. Leap / the mossy garden wall / the steel fence or whatever / the case may be."

Confabulations, is a series of poems for and about deceased poet Malcolm Lowry. In the *Malahat Review* interview Thesen explains that the work is "a confabulation with a kind of suffering that I identified with and understood deeply" and that Lowry provided "a persona through which I could speak that material without having to write confessional autobiographical poetry." These poems are a powerful evocation of Lowry's struggles with both alcohol and language and of Thesen's struggles with the darkness of her own world (which is also ours). "*This world* / scissored your mind," she writes, "bone-dry shreds of ecstacy / & terror igniting / your fragile nests." In his own voice, Thesen's Lowry declares, "I wake up / weeping the whole grief of the world / strangling my vocabulary." The volume's most haunting phrase, "where I am it is dark," speaks not only of Lowry's nightmare world but also of the one we all live in and share.

The Beginning of the Long Dash marks the beginning of a change of tone in Thesen's work; she herself has called it her "glad" book. This change is particularly evident in "The Landlord's Flower Beds," where the roses are "white, / yellow, red, pink, all colors / of the rainbow" and where they "almost / pull you out of bed at night." Flowers also perform a vital function in "The Occasions"; here the "pale pink roses / are the tenderest things," and "sitting with them you understand / the perfection of all things," though that understanding proves in the end to be transitory.

This volume also contains a number of poem sequences, a tangible indication of Thesen's expanding vision as she moves from a personal into a larger cultural milieu. The title poem, for example, is a philosophical meditation on the state of the world (social, moral, political) as the twentieth century draws to a close, framed as a contemplation on the Christmas and New Year's season. In Thesen's fin de siècle world "the five most compelling words / are *sex, free, cure, money,* and *baldness,* / a chain of conditions ranging from heaven to hell," and "there's nothing to eat / but images to hunger for." The poem's title refers to the National Research Council Official Time Signal indicating 10:00 Pacific Standard Time, and as Thesen explains in the *Malahat Review* interview, it has a double meaning. On the one hand it signals that "there's lots of time," but on the other hand it can be read metaphorically: "it's a long dash all right, but toward what are we headed?"

If the poems in Thesen's volume *The Pangs of Sunday* are any indication, the poet herself has headed in different directions.

Alongside typically wry lyrics like "The Scalpel," "Elegy, The Fertility Specialist," and "Emergency," where Thesen declares succinctly that "human love / is not so easy as speech / will allow," there are poems at once surreal and ordinary. Animals accompany the poet to corner letter boxes and the grocery store, and "when I put on / a fancy dinner, a few animals / are under the table staring at the guests." Empty pineapple shells "attract the wrong sort of chicken / who wear black thongs and carry a knife," the "crawfish garnish / outmanoeuvre[s]" Napoleon, and "adjacent recipes / clash by night" in the surreal kitchen where Thesen cooks up "Chicken in a Pensive Shell." Finally, as the volume closes, the poet rides her "lovely horse / into the perfume department / at Eaton's," declaring, "We tried not to break anything / but also we were not abstract." In this new material and throughout her previous work Thesen moves through all our ordinary days, making unusual, even startling connections. Hers is a poetry of careful observation, of precise statement; it challenges the way we see ourselves and see the world and ourselves in the world.

—Susan Schenk

TWICHELL, (Penelope) Chase

Nationality: American. **Born:** New Haven, Connecticut, 20 August 1950. **Education:** Trinity College, Hartford, Connecticut, 1970-73, B.A. 1973; University of Iowa, Iowa City, 1974-76, M.F.A. 1976. **Family:** Married Russell Banks in 1989. **Career:** Editor, Pennyroyal Press, West Hatfield, Massachusetts, 1976-85; visiting assistant professor, Hampshire College, Amherst, Massachusetts, 1983-85; associate professor, University of Alabama, Tuscaloosa, 1985-88; lecturer Princeton University, New Jersey, 1989—. **Awards:** National Endowment for the Arts fellowship, 1987, 1993; Guggenheim fellowship, 1990; Literature award, American Academy of Arts and Letters, 1994. **Member:** Academy of American Poets. **Agent:** Ellen Levine, Suite 1801, 15 East 26th Street, New York, New York 10010, U.S.A.

PUBLICATIONS

Poetry

Northern Spy. Pittsburgh, University of Pittsburgh Press, 1981.
The Odds. Pittsburgh, University of Pittsburgh Press, 1986.
Perdido. New York, Farrar Straus, 1991; London, Faber, 1992.
The Ghost of Eden. Princeton, New Jersey, Ontario Review Press, and London, Faber, 1995

Other

Editor, with Robin Behn, *The Practice of Poetry: Writing Exercises from Poets Who Teach.* New York, HarperCollins, 1992.

*   *   *

Chase Twichell's poems move through the natural world much as a biologist moves over the landscape collecting and cataloging specimens. Their chronicle of personal experience is similarly meticulous and edgy with the tone of the tough, unsentimental conclusions for which the author is noted.

In *The Odds* (1986) Twichell embellishes the crisp style of her debut volume, *Northern Spy* (1981), by opening herself to the first-person narrative. Central to the collection are two longer poems, "My Ruby of Lasting Sadness," which looks back on youthful romance, and "A Suckling Pig," a relentless depiction of psychological and physical excesses among a privileged set of New England friends. "Her agony," Gerald Stern has said, "is the certain delicate moment where the mind realizes its isolation, its loneliness and its longing."

Twichell's most intense encounters with her agony may be found in the poems of her third volume, *Perdido*. Much of this book dwells on the subject of love, springing from love's occasions to full awareness of that "certain delicate moment." Sex is an especially vibrant bridge from the mundane to revelation. In "Remember Death," for example, the narrator looks past the shoulder of her lover "up into the high vaults / of the Church of the Falling Leaf." She notes but chooses to endure the sticks hurting her back and the wasps departing and returning to their nest above. She observes and does her best to give in to the conflicting energies of the moment and let life happen.

In "The Condom Tree" this impulse triggers a reevaluation of a childhood memory. Again, the door opens on the occasion of sex. During lovemaking the narrator closes her eyes and travels back to her tenth year, when, one day by the river, she came on a young maple tree which the older children of the neighborhood had adorned with condoms: "was it beautiful," the poet asks, "caught in that dirty floral light, / or was it an ugly thing?" Such basic questions of value and certainty always emerge from the core of this poet's explorations. "Her poems," C.K. Williams has written, "manifest a sharp ironic awareness of what's expected of a woman's sensitivity, and a gratifying willingness to play off these expectations in illuminating ways." This observation seems accurate. In "The Condom Tree" the poet recalls that the tree was "Beautiful first, and ugly afterward":

That must be right,
though in the remembering
its value has been changed again,
and now that flowering
dapples the two of us
with its tendered shadows,
dapples the rumpled bed as it slips
out of the damp present
into our separate pasts.

In memory and experience value is always changing. Twichell's clearest message is to accept responsibility and to remain open to—and aware of—the world's ever changing pulse.

—Robert McDowell

U-V

URDANG, Constance (Henriette)

Nationality: American. **Born:** New York City, 26 December 1922. **Education:** Fieldston School; Smith College, Northampton, Massachusetts, A.B. 1943; University of Iowa, Iowa City, M.F.A. 1956. **Military Service:** Military intelligence analyst, United States Department of the Army, Washington, D.C., 1944-46. **Family:** Married Donald Finkel in 1956; two daughters and one son. **Career:** Copy editor, Bellas Hess Inc. publishers, New York, 1947-51; editor, P.F. Collier & Son publishers, New York, 1952-54; coordinator, Writers Program, Washington University, St. Louis, 1977-84; visiting lecturer, Princeton University, New Jersey, 1985. **Awards:** *Carleton Miscellany* Centennial award, 1967; National Endowment for the Arts grant, 1976; Delmore Schwartz memorial award, 1981. **Address:** 2051 Park Avenue, Apartment D, St. Louis, Missouri, 63104, U.S.A.

Publications

Poetry

Charades and Celebrations. New York, October House, 1965.
The Picnic in the Cemetery. New York, Braziller, 1975.
The Lone Woman and Others. Pittsburgh, University of Pittsburgh Press, 1980.
Only the World. Pittsburgh, University of Pittsburgh Press, 1983.
Alternative Lives. Pittsburgh, University of Pittsburgh Press, 1990.

Novels

Natural History. New York, Harper, 1969.
Lucha (novella). Minneapolis, Coffee House Press, 1986.
American Earthquakes: A Novel. Minneapolis, Coffee House Press, 1988.
The Woman Who Reads Novels and *Peacetime* (novellas). Minneapolis, Coffee House Press, 1990.

Other

Editor, with Paul Engle, *Prize Stories '57.* New York, Doubleday, 1957.
Editor, with Paul Engle and Curtis Harnack, *Prize Stories '59.* New York, Doubleday, 1959.
Editor, *Random House Vest Pocket Dictionary of Famous People.* New York, Random House, 1962.

*

Manuscript Collection: Washington University, St. Louis.

*   *   *

Constance Urdang's first volume of poems, *Charades and Celebrations,* revealed a poet fully in command of poetic craft and concerned with exploring two major themes: what it means to be a woman, expressed through myths and metaphors of the moon, and what the arbitrary accidents of life altogether might mean, expressed through a collage technique of free-associative juxtapositions. In the introduction to her next volume of poems, *The Picnic in the Cemetery,* Richard Howard said, "It is still a celebration, the new Constance Urdang poem—the picnic in the cemetery is a feast aware of the dead...." Her themes deepen: pain, loneliness, betrayal, old age, sickness, and death are the human condition seen through the particulars of the lives of women.

Death takes many forms, especially for women—in "The Girl" and "Becoming a Woman" the deaths of childishness and conventionality come with taking on the difficulties of adulthood. Alienation of love means death in the three "Adultery" poems; "Childless Woman" and "Abortion" deal with painful experiences unique to women, ambiguously linking death and birth. In "Walking Around" the bag woman evidently finds means to resist death, but only true mystics, like "The Woman with Three Eyes," can see beyond death by transcending the injury, loneliness, and fear that are the lot of the world's elderly and poor. Implicit in these poems is the landscape of unfeeling, unseeing America, as in "The Players and the Game." Life in America, life altogether, is a game of Monopoly in which both capitalism and hope are failing, and those who lose out tend to be women.

The first section of Urdang's 1980 volume, *The Lone Woman and Others,* celebrates the *femme sole* and other unpopular, unenticing types of women—witch, menopausal woman, old maid, runaway girl—without pitying or romanticizing them. The poems in the second section create objective correlatives from domestic existence, the house itself and objects—umbrellas, kites—which show the roots of cosmic events in the unremarkably mundane: assassinations begin in "the assassination-kitchen." The last section opens onto larger landscapes, providing a segue into Urdang's 1983 collection, *Only the World,* whose title comes from the epigraph by Martin Buber: "There is no world of appearances, there is only the world." Thus, landscapes—Mexico, Chicago, Brazil, the Ozarks, suburbs, indoors, outdoors—are real and simply themselves, and exploratory travel among them is the fundamental activity of the human body and mind. Going out and returning are seen as contradictory yet primal impulses in "Coming Home," "Ways of Returning," "Aesthetics of Escape," and "The Wish to Settle Down," which concludes that the only resting place is "the final one." Language is the one transcendent element in this landscape; the ability to name creates life: "And I understand why / The Mexicans have a dozen words for *brick*"; thus "the world is full of poets" because words, which belong to everyone, are the building blocks—the bricks—of the world.

In the 1980s Urdang turned more definitively to prose, with several fine novellas, but she did not forsake poetry. *Alternative Lives* shows her generous gaze and modest, precise diction again playing over the landscape of Mexico, friends, writers and writing, travel, returning to the "Port of Authority" in New York where she grew up. These days the world is disjunct and cacophonous, not so good for literature or for the living. She concludes, "Silent, solitary in the starless night / I am besieged by invisible regiments, / The clamorous armies of the have-nothings. / Where are the nine proud walkers / Who might have smoothed this discord into song?"

We need those "nine proud walkers," the nine muses of classical civilization, but Urdang must be accounted their agent. Poetry, said the classically minded T.S. Eliot, should not be "poetic"; it should try to point beyond itself. Urdang's excellent poems point beyond themselves to a powerful and kindly vision of the real, language's utmost accomplishment.

—Jane Augustine

VALENTINE, Jean

Nationality: American. **Born:** Chicago, Illinois, 27 April 1934. **Education:** Milton Academy, 1949-52; Radcliffe College, Cambridge Massachusetts, 1952-56, B.A. (cum laude) 1956. **Family:** Married James Chace in 1957 (divorced, 1968); two daughters. **Career:** Poetry workshop teacher, Swarthmore College, Pennsylvania, 1968-70, Barnard College, New York, 1968, 1970, Yale University, New Haven, Connecticut, 1970, 1973-74, Hunter College, New York, 1970-75; member of the faculty, Sarah Lawrence College, Bronxville, New York, 1974—. **Awards:** Yale Series of Younger Poets award, 1965; National Endowment for the Arts grant, 1972; Guggenheim fellowship, 1976. **Address:** 527 West 110th Street, New York, New York 10025, U.S.A.

Publications

Poetry

Dream Barker and Other Poems. New Haven, Connecticut, Yale University Press, 1965.
Pilgrims. New York, Farrar Straus, 1969.
Ordinary Things. New York, Farrar Straus, 1974.
Turn. Oberlin, Ohio, Pocket Pal Press, 1977.
The Messenger. New York, Farrar Straus, 1979.
Home, Deep, Blue: New and Selected Poems. Cambridge, Massachusetts, Alice James, 1988.
Night Lake. Lewisburg, Pennsylvania, The Press of Appletree Alley, 1992.
The River at Wolf. Cambridge, Massachusetts, Alice James Books, 1992.
Night Porch. Falmouth, Massachusetts, Harlequin Ink, 1994.
The Under Voice: Selected Poems. Dublin, Ireland, Salmon / Poolbeg, 1995.
Growing Darkness, Growing Light. Pittsburgh, Carnegie Mellon University Press, 1997.

Recording: *The Resurrected,* Watershed, 1989; *The River at Wolf,* Alice James Books, 1992.

*

Manuscript Collection: Lamont Library, Harvard University, Cambridge, Massachusetts.

*   *   *

In Jean Valentine's first book, *Dream Barker,* her poems transform dreams into living experience by means of luminous language which echoes the unconscious mind's revelations. In the later volumes *Ordinary Things* and *The Messenger* she almost reverses this process to show life as veiled and inconclusive, suggestive rather than definitive, dreamlike. The elliptical yet lucid craft of these poems presents experience as only imperfectly graspable. The poems ride lightly on the waves of thought, more textures than statements. While in *Dream Barker* she refers openly to events such as first love, wedding, childbirth, parenthood, by the 1970s her poems had become mistier and more private in their references. No premature conclusion mars the sense of emotional atmosphere as more important than external incident. She does not try to evade the pain of existence; her sensitivity to it perhaps necessitates the oblique approach. She writes of the loss of love, separations, a child's death, or war without raising her voice, always without bitterness or self-aggrandizement.

Valentine's reluctance in her early work to refer overtly to her personal life evidently led to her interest in translation, a way of speaking through another poet's voice but leaving the reader to decide the extent of affinity between the two writers. In *Ordinary Things* she included a translation of the Dutch poet Huub Oosterhuis's "Twenty Days' Journey," a moving meditation on the death of someone the poet has deeply loved. She seems attracted to this poem's dream-nightmare quality of grief which completely consumes yet is delicately expressed: "my body turns to mist but still stays alive, / an eye that will not close."

The sense of love enduring beyond personal absence or presence also marks Valentine's own long poem "Fidelities," in which she is reading a letter from a lover. As she reads, her room becomes his; the park is both present and remembered, becoming another field in which both are walking. Her world is softened and subdued, bounded by solitude, memories, and letters, peaceful days providing perspective on her life. Friendship is a major motif of *The Messenger;* she befriends in memory her parents and old acquaintances and cradles and resolves her feelings for them. The poems are sometimes titled merely with a date, and they often quote the words of others in gently free-associative style, usually fragmented in structure, which is faithful to flickering thought.

But thought no longer flickers in the new poems which accompany Valentine's selected work in the 1988 volume *Home, Deep, Blue.* Here a decided change is revealed, a remission of the subdued, near-hesitant mood. More confidence and bravery, less fear of stepping out into experience, result in bolder syntax and images stronger in outline and in bright colors—with brown, blue, and white gold in just the first two poems of the volume. Dream and memory remain prime motivators, but a new earthiness invigorates her reflections. The title "Awake, This Summer" encapsulates the poet's rejuvenation; she has awakened from, it seems, circumstances which quelled her spirit and enchained her words. The season is summer; it is ripeness and love—new, blest, thoroughly enjoyed.

This alteration of the poetic voice becomes even clearer in Valentine's 1992 collection, *The River at Wolf.* Many poems in this volume are set in the American West, some having been written at Ucross, a writers' retreat near Sterling, Wyoming. All of them, even those on her mother's death, exude a sunlit physicality which strengthens her perennially tender thoughtfulness and sensitivity. Dreams themselves enact more vivid dramas, inviting freer interpretations. "Barrie's Dream, the Wild Geese" begins "I dreamed about Elizabeth Bishop and Robert Lowell" and continues with

> he was talking, and talking to us
> he was saying, 'She is the best—'
> Then the geese flew over,
> and he stopped talking. Everyone stopped talking,
> because of the geese.

It is true that Lowell thought that Bishop was "the best," but here one sees that Valentine is the best, not only to the lover-dreamer. Her diction ever tactful, her perfect landings after a free-associative swing, "consciousness of this big form," all enable the release of unconscious mind out of its hiding place into conscious light:

> The sound of their wings!
> Oars rowing laborious, wood against wood: it was
> a continuing thought, no, it was a labor,
> how to accept your lover's love. Who could do it alone?
> Under our radiant sleep they were bearing us all night long.

The wild goose is the Chinese poet's symbol for freedom.

While Valentine's expressive powers were always rare and great, in *Night Porch* and *Growing Darkness, Growing Light,* she has continued to add to them exuberance and the creative freedom to fly even higher.

—Jane Augustine

VAN DUYN, Mona (Jane)

Nationality: American. **Born:** Waterloo, Iowa, 9 May 1921. **Education:** University of Northern Iowa, Cedar Falls, B.A. 1942; University of Iowa, Iowa City, M.A. 1943. **Family:** Married Jarvis Thurston in 1943. **Career:** Instructor in English, University of Iowa, 1944-46, and University of Louisville, Kentucky, 1946-50; lecturer in English, 1950-67, adjunct professor of poetry workshops, 1983, and Visiting Hurst Professor, 1987, Washington University, St. Louis; lecturer, Salzburg Seminar in American Studies, 1973. Poetry consultant, Olin Library Modern Literature Collection, Washington University. Editor, with Jarvis Thurston, *Perspective: A Quarterly of Literature,* St. Louis, 1947-67. **Awards:** Eunice Tietjens memorial prize, 1956, and Harriet Monroe memorial prize, 1968 (*Poetry,* Chicago); Helen Bullis prize *(Poetry Northwest),* 1964; National Endowment for the Arts grant, 1985; National Council for the Arts grant, 1967; Borestone Mountain poetry prize, 1968; Hart Crane memorial award, 1968; Bollingen prize, 1971; National Book award, 1971; Guggenheim fellowship, 1972; Loines award, 1976; Academy of American Poets fellowship, 1981; Cornell College Sandburg prize, 1982; Shelley memorial prize, 1987; Pulitzer prize, 1991; U.S. Poet Laureate, 1992-93. D.Litt.: Washington University, 1971; Cornell College, Mt. Vernon, Iowa, 1972; University of Northern Iowa, 1991; University of the South, 1993; George Washington University, 1993; Georgetown University, 1993. Chancellor, Academy of American Poets, 1985. **Member:** National Academy of Arts and Letters, National Academy of Arts and Sciences. **Address:** 7505 Teasdale Avenue, St. Louis, Missouri 63130, U.S.A.

PUBLICATIONS

Poetry

Valentines to the Wide World. Iowa City, Cummington Press, 1959.
A Time of Bees. Chapel Hill, University of North Carolina Press, 1964.
To See, To Take. New York, Atheneum, 1970.
Bedtime Stories. Champaign, Illinois, Ceres Press, 1972.
Merciful Disguises: Published and Unpublished Poems. New York, Atheneum, 1973.
Letters from a Father and Other Poems. New York, Atheneum, 1983.
Near Changes. New York, Knopf, 1990.
If It Be Not I: Collected Poems, 1959-1982. New York, Knopf, 1993.
Firefall: Poems. New York, Knopf, 1993.

Recordings: *Mona Van Duyn and Elliott Coleman Reading Their Poems in the Coolidge Auditorium,* Gertrude Clarke Whittall Poetry and Literature Fund, 1971; *Mona Van Duyn Reading Her Poems,* Gertrude Clarke Whittall Poetry and Literature Fund, Library of Congress, 1990; *The World as It Is,* Watershed, 1990; *Mona Van Duyn,* Academy of American Poets Archives, 1991.

Other

Matters of Poetry. Washington D.C., Library of Congress, 1993.

*

Manuscript Collection: Olin Library, Washington University, St. Louis.

*   *   *

The awarding of the Bollingen prize in 1971 to Mona Van Duyn and her receipt of the National Book award in poetry that same year brought long overdue general recognition to this fine poet, whose insight, humor, and technical skill had seemed for a long time to be appreciated largely only in her native Midwest. Many national awards followed, and in June of 1992 she was appointed poet laureate and consultant in poetry at the Library of Congress.

The appeal of her poems comes from the double sense of their adherence to the formal tradition of poetry while at the same time they get "down to the bone" of human experience. "The wintry work of living, our flawed art" is a basic theme. Her poetic craft emanates from, in fact is identical with, the conscious intelligence which everyone has and uses to shape everyday happenstance into meaningful experience: "The world blooms and we all bend and bring / from ground and sea and mind its handsome harvests." Poetry making thus becomes a metaphor for activities of living minds. "Join us with charity," she says in "To My Godson, On His Christening," "whose deeds, like the little poet's metaphors, / are good only in brave approximations, / who design, in walled-up workrooms, beautiful doors." In "Three Valentines to the Wide World" she calls the beauty of the world "merciless and intemperate" and suggests that against "that rage" we must "pit love and art, which are compassionate." The tension in Van Duyn's poems rises from two dualisms: the world seen as cruel but lovely, a "brilliant wasting"; and the tension between strict forms (often long-lined, slant-rhymed quatrains) and prose-like statements varying from Yeatsian elegance to Midwestern colloquialism.

Love and art pitted against the merciless world is a theme which enables Van Duyn to range wide and deep. She can be philosophical, ironic, elegiac, or penetratingly personal as she explores the tensions in this intermingling, which appear notably in poems on marriage. In one section of "Toward a Definition of Marriage" the marital relationship is described in literary terms:

It is closest to picaresque, but essentially artless ...
How could its structure be more than improvising,
when it never ends, but line after line plod on ...
But it's known by heart now; it rounded the steeliest shape to
shapelessness, it was so loving an exercise.

The expanded parallelism between life and poetry is brilliantly developed in "An Essay on Criticism," in which the poet adapts Pope's eighteenth-century title and heroic couplet form to meditate philosophically while opening a package of dried onion soup in her kitchen. No tears fall from chopping real onions, and poetic words, abstract on the page, can wait for centuries till water is added from a later reader's tears to enliven them. But the poet's tears fall now, caused by life—a friend's confession of a secret love—not by poetry, and these tears, reminders of mortality, command her to command us that "we must care right away!"

Caring deeply for her own childhood pain and for that of her ill and dying parents, she records family history in the persona poems of *Bedtime Stories* and in the elegies of *Letters from a Father,* of which "The Stream," on her mother's death, poignantly expresses primal loss. In this volume concentration on family life is counterbalanced, as all along in her work, by poems based on travel, rendering a sense of wide-ranging life through observations of Spain, France, the Missouri Ozarks, and Maine, where she and her husband spent many summers. In the collection *Firefall* the elegiac mode predominates as friends die and old age comes on. But sure of her always supple craft, she also enjoys playing with poetic tradition by creating "minimalist sonnets" of 14 very short lines broken into quatrains with a final two- or six-line stanza. These are terse, sometimes witty, sometimes reminiscent of Emily Dickinson.

The final elegiac poems are the strongest among the strong poems here. In "The Delivery" a cruel incident of childhood is seen as delivering her own self to her, a kind of birth. "Falls" invokes memories of the firefall in Yosemite Park and at Niagara Falls, with both fire and water symbolizing her own creative livingness even as it implicitly falls toward death. The poem ends with lovely lines epitomizing her poetic triumph yet in depth of spirit almost suggesting an epitaph: "May one who comes upon a final book / and hunts in husks for kernel hints of me / find Niagara's roar still sacred to dim ears, / Firefall still blazing bright in memory." Let it be so.

—Jane Augustine

VOIGT, Ellen Bryant

Nationality: American. **Born:** Danville, Virginia, 9 May 1943. **Education:** Converse College, Spartanburg, South Carolina, B.A.

1964; University of Iowa, Iowa City, M.F.A. 1966. **Family:** Married Francis George Wilhelm Voigt in 1965; one daughter and one son. **Career:** Technical writer, College Pharmacy, University of Iowa, 1965-66; teacher of literature and writing, Goddard 1970-79, and director of writing program, 1976-79, Goddard College, Plainfield, Vermont; associate professor of creative writing, Massachusetts Institute of Technology, Cambridge, 1979-82. Visiting faculty member, graduate program for writers, Warren Wilson College, Swannanoa, North Carolina, 1981—. Lila Wallace/Woodrow Wilson Visiting Writer; Faculty member, Aspen Writers' Conference, Breadloaf Writers' Conference, Indiana Writers' Conference, Napa Valley Writers' Conference, and Ropewalk Writers' Conference. Advisory editor, *Arion's Dolphin,* 1971-75. Also professional pianist. **Awards:** Vermont Council on the Arts grant, 1974-75; National Endowment for the Arts grant, 1976-77; Guggenheim fellowship, 1978-79. **Address:** P.O. Box 16, Marshfield, Vermont 05658, U.S.A.

Publications

Poetry

Claiming Kin. Middletown, Connecticut, Wesleyan University Press, 1976.
The Forces of Plenty. New York, Norton, 1983.
The Lotus Flowers. New York, Norton, 1987.
Two Trees. New York, Norton, 1992.
Kyrie. New York, Norton, 1995.

*   *   *

Ellen Bryant Voigt's poems concern themselves with separation and connection. She is a careful observer of both nature and human behavior, and her vision is clear and compassionate at the same time.

Her first book, *Claiming Kin,* seeks parallels everywhere between human life and nature. It is nature, for example, that gives us a model for hope. Perhaps we, like the snake, may "rise up in new skins / a full confusion of green"("Snakeskin"). On the other hand, nature's more ominous lessons are acknowledged as well. The black widow spider, for example, ties sensuality and fertility to death. Voigt's nature poems complement the poems in which she attempts to claim and come to terms with her human kin. Many of her poems concern the family, which she characterizes as "the circle of fire." In the long poem "Sister," the speaker returns to her family to deal with her mother's illness and finds herself reexamining the tangle of feelings that comprise her relationship with her sister:

When we were little
I used to wish you dead;
then hold my breath and sweat
to hear yours
release, intake, relax into sleep.

In *The Forces of Plenty,* her second volume, Voigt examines many of the same themes, but whereas her writing has become more confident, her stance has, perhaps wisely, become less so. She moves away from the exuberant lushness of *Claiming Kin,* with its "thick pythons, / slack and drowsy, who droop down / like untied sashes / from the trees" ("Tropics") and its emphasis on what joins, to look more closely at what separates. Ironically, as the speaker remarks in "January," it is our very ability to reflect on nature that separates us from it:

> If I think I am apart from this, I am a fool.
> And if I think the black engine of the stove
> can raise in me the same luminous waking,
> I am still a fool,
> since I am the one who keeps the fire.

A sense of mortality pervades this book, which includes several elegies, making life and happiness more precious and more fragile. In "Year's End" two parents' relief at their own child's recovery from illness is tempered by the knowledge that a friend's child has just died, and they listen to their own child's breath "like refugees who listen to the sea, / unable to fully rejoice, or fully grieve."

The Lotus Flowers incorporates and finds salvation in some of the hard truths first observed in *The Forces of Plenty.* In "The Farmer," for example, a man stung by a swarm of bees is saved by "the years of smaller doses— / like minor disappointments, / instructive poison, something he could use." These poems, however, are even more deeply rooted in personal experience and in her rural Southern background. There is a tinge of melancholy in her poems about the past, a lament for the loss of innocence, as in "Nightshade," in which the daughter cannot forgive her father for accidentally poisoning the dog and says that "without pure evil in the world, / there was no east or west, no polestar / and no ratifying dove." In its concern with place and pattern, the title poem is a culmination of this book's themes. The shape made by the girls on their pallets—"spokes in a wheel"—echoes the shapes of the constellations they study, and the stars in these constella-

tions mirror the lotus flowers, now "folded / into candles," through which the girls had earlier rowed. In this poem the opposition between nature and humanity, innocence and knowledge, individual and community seems temporarily resolved.

This resolution shifts, however, in *Two Trees,* the most austere and foreboding of her books. Although, like her previous volumes, it contains poems of family and nature, it is most concerned with the spiritual aspects of these subjects, and music and myth provide its major subjects and metaphors. The emphasis here is on what separates—the music that "keeps the girl apart / as she prefers ..." ("Variations: At the Piano") or "beauty that divides us" ("First Song")—and on the loss of innocence. The title poem, retells the expulsion from paradise and the eternal longing that results: "while the mind cried out / for that addictive tree it had tasted, / and for that other crown still visible over the wall." A sense of resignation pervades the book. What makes us human is not an ability to control our fate but our need to struggle and reach out to one another: "The one who can sings to the one who can't / who waits in the pit, like Procne among the slaves, / as the gods decide how all such stories end" ("Song and Story"). Her innovative adaptation of musical variations, in which three sets of poems called "variations" expand aspects of a titled poem, skillfully merges theme and technique and makes of this collection a haunting whole.

Voigt's style has grown more flexible with each book in order to accommodate her increasingly complex vision. Her subjects range from the intimacies of daily life to the exploration of our place in the universe. We can only look forward to more work from a poet who dares to say that "Nothing is learned / by turning away" ("Talking the Fire Out" from *The Forces of Plenty*).

—Kathleen Aguero

W-Z

WAKOSKI, Diane

Nationality: American. **Born:** Whittier, California, 3 August 1937. **Education:** University of California, Berkeley, B.A. in English 1960. **Family:** Married 1) S. Shepard Sherbell in 1965 (divorced 1967); 2) Michael Watterlond in 1973 (divorced 1975); 3) Robert J. Turney in 1982. **Career:** Clerk, British Book Centre, New York, 1960-63; English teacher, Junior High School 22, New York, 1963-66; lecturer, New School for Social Research, New York, 1969. Poet-in-residence, California Institute of Technology, Pasadena, spring 1972; University of Virginia, Charlottesville, autumn 1972-73; Willamette University, Salem, Oregon, spring 1974; University of California, Irvine, fall 1974; Hollins College, Virginia, 1974; Lake Forest College, Illinois, 1974; Colorado College, Colorado Springs, 1974; Macalester College, St. Paul, 1975; Michigan State University, East Lansing, spring 1975; University of Wisconsin, Madison, fall 1975; Whitman College, Walla Walla, Washington, fall 1976; University of Washington, Seattle, spring-summer 1977; University of Hawaii, Honolulu, fall 1978; and Emory University, Atlanta, 1980-81. United States Information Agency lecturer, Romania, Hungary, and Yugoslavia, 1976. Writer-in-residence, Michigan State University, 1976—. **Awards:** Bread Loaf Writers Conference Robert Frost fellowship, 1966; Cassandra Foundation award, 1970; New York State Council on the Arts grant, 1971; Guggenheim grant, 1972; National Endowment for the Arts grant, 1973; Fulbright fellowship, 1984; Michigan Arts Council grant, 1988; Michigan Arts Foundation award, 1989; William Carlos Williams prize, 1989; University Distinguished Professorship, 1990. **Address:** 607 Division, East Lansing, Michigan 48823, U.S.A.

PUBLICATIONS

Poetry

Coins and Coffins. New York, Hawk's Well Press, 1962.
Four Young Lady Poets, with others, edited by LeRoi Jones. New York, Totem-Corinth, 1962.
Dream Sheet. New York, Software Press, 1965.
Discrepancies and Apparitions. New York, Doubleday, 1966.
The George Washington Poems. New York, Riverrun Press, 1967.
Greed Parts One and Two. Los Angeles, Black Sparrow Press, 1968.
The Diamond Merchant. Cambridge, Massachusetts, Sans Souci Press, 1968.
Inside the Blood Factory. New York, Doubleday, 1968.
A Play and Two Poems, with Robert Kelly and Ron Loewinsohn. Los Angeles, Black Sparrow Press, 1968.
Thanking My Mother for Piano Lessons. Mount Horeb, Wisconsin, Perishable Press, 1969.
Greed Parts 3 and 4. Los Angeles, Black Sparrow Press, 1969.
The Moon Has a Complicated Geography. Palo Alto, California, Odda Tala Press, 1969.
The Magellanic Clouds. Los Angeles, Black Sparrow Press, 1970.
Greed Parts 5-7. Los Angeles, Black Sparrow Press, 1970.

The Lament of the Lady Bank Dick. Cambridge, Massachusetts, Sans Souci Press, 1970.
Love, You Big Fat Snail. San Francisco, Tenth Muse, 1970.
Black Dream Ditty for Billy "The Kid" Seen in Dr. Generosity's Bar Recruiting for Hell's Angels and Black Mafia. Los Angeles, Black Sparrow Press, 1970.
The Wise Men Drawn to Kneel in Wonder at the Fact So of Itself. Los Angeles, Black Sparrow Press, 1970.
Exorcism. Boston, My Dukes, 1971.
This Water Baby: For Tony. Santa Barbara, California, Unicorn Press, 1971.
On Barbara's Shore. Los Angeles, Black Sparrow Press, 1971.
The Motorcycle Betrayal Poems. New York, Simon & Schuster, 1971.
The Pumpkin Pie, Or Reassurances Are Always False, Tho We Love Them, Only Physics Counts. Los Angeles, Black Sparrow Press, 1972.
The Purple Finch Song. Mount Horeb, Wisconsin, Perishable Press, 1972.
Sometimes a Poet Will Hijack the Moon. Providence, Rhode Island, Burning Deck, 1972.
Smudging. Los Angeles, Black Sparrow Press, 1972.
The Owl and the Snake: A Fable. Mount Horeb, Wisconsin, Perishable Press, 1973.
Greed Parts 8, 9, 11. Los Angeles, Black Sparrow Press, 1973.
Dancing on the Grave of a Son of a Bitch. Los Angeles, Black Sparrow Press, 1973.
Stilllife: Michael, Silver, Flute, and Violets. Storrs, University of Connecticut, 1973.
Winter Sequences. Los Angeles, Black Sparrow Press, 1973.
Trilogy: Coins and Coffins, Discrepancies and Apparitions, The George Washington Poems. New York, Doubleday, 1974.
Looking for the King of Spain. Los Angeles, Black Sparrow Press, 1974.
The Wandering Tattler. Mount Horeb, Wisconsin, Perishable Press, 1974.
Abalone. Los Angeles, Black Sparrow Press, 1974.
Virtuoso Literature for Two and Four Hands. New York, Doubleday, 1975.
The Fable of the Lion and the Scorpion. Milwaukee, Pentagram Press, 1975.
Waiting for the King of Spain. Santa Barbara, California, Black Sparrow Press, 1976.
The Laguna Contract of Diane Wakoski. Madison, Wisconsin, Crepuscular Press, 1976.
George Washington's Camp Cups. Madison, Wisconsin, Red Ozier Press, 1976.
The Last Poem, with *Tough Company,* by Charles Bukowski. Santa Barbara, California, Black Sparrow Press, 1976.
The Ring. Santa Barbara, California, Black Sparrow Press, 1977.
Overnight Projects with Wood. Madison, Wisconsin, Red Ozier Press, 1977.
Spending Christmas with the Man from Receiving at Sears. Santa Barbara, California, Black Sparrow Press, 1977.
The Man Who Shook Hands. New York, Doubleday, 1978.
Pachelbel's Canon. Santa Barbara, California, Black Sparrow Press, 1978.

Trophies. Santa Barbara, California, Black Sparrow, Press, 1979.

Cap of Darkness, Including Looking for the King of Spain and Pachelbel's Canon. Santa Barbara, California, Black Sparrow Press, 1980.

Making a Sacher Torte: Nine Poems, Twelve Illustrations, with Ellen Lanyon. Mount Horeb, Wisconsin, Perishable Press, 1981.

Saturn's Rings. New York, Targ, 1982.

The Lady Who Drove Me to the Airport. Worcester, Massachusetts, Metacom Press, 1982.

Divers. N.p., Barbarian Press, 1982.

The Magician's Feastletters. Santa Barbara, California, Black Sparrow Press, 1982.

Looking for Beethoven in Las Vegas. New York, Red Ozier Press, 1983.

The Collected Greed: Parts 1-13. Santa Barbara, California, Black Sparrow Press, 1984.

The Managed World. New York, Red Ozier Press, 1985.

Why My Mother Likes Liberace. Tucson, Arizona, Sun / Gemini Press, 1985.

The Rings of Saturn. Santa Barbara, California, Black Sparrow Press, 1986.

Emerald Ice: Selected Poems 1962-1987. Santa Rosa, California, Black Sparrow Press, 1988.

The Archaeology of Movies and Books:

   Medea the Sorceress. Santa Rosa, California, Black Sparrow Press. 1991.

   Jason the Sailor. Santa Rosa, California, Black Sparrow Press, 1993.

   The Emerald City of Las Vegas. Santa Rosa, California, Black Sparrow Press, 1995.

   The Ice Queen. Tuscaloosa, Alabama, Parallel Editions, 1994.

Other

Form Is an Extension of Content. Los Angeles, Black Sparrow Press, 1972.

Creating a Personal Mythology. Los Angeles, Black Sparrow Press, 1975.

Variations on a Theme. Santa Barbara, California, Black Sparrow Press, 1976.

Toward a New Poetry. Ann Arbor, University of Michigan Press, 1980.

Unveilings, photographs by Lynn Stern. New York, Hudson Hill Press, 1989.

*

Manuscript Collection: University of Arizona Library, Tucson.

Critical Studies: "A Terrible War: A Conversation with Diane Wakoski" by Philip Gerber and Robert Gemmett, in *Far Point 4* (Winnipeg), Spring-Summer 1970; "Symposium on Diane Wakoski," in *Margins* (Milwaukee), January / February / March 1976; "Diane Wakoski's Personal Mythology: Dionysian Music, Created Presence" by Taffy Wynne Martin, in *Boundary 2* (Binghamton, New York), vol. 10, no. 3, Spring 1982; "Diane Wakoski: Disentangling the Woman from the Moon," in *Women as Mythmakers: Poetry and Visual Art by Twentieth-Century Women,* by Estella Lauter, Bloomington, Indiana University Press, 1984; "Wakoski's Poems: Moving Past Confession" by Linda W. Wagner, in *Still the Frame Holds,* edited by Sheila Roberts, San Bernadino, Borgo Press, 1993.

Diane Wakoski comments:

I think of myself as a narrative poet, a poet creating both a personal narrative and a personal mythology. I write long poems, and emotional ones. My themes are loss, imprecise perception, justice, truth, the duality of the world, and the possibilities of magic, transformation, and the creation of beauty out of ugliness. My language is dramatic, oral, and as American as I can make it, with the appropriate plain surfaces and rich vocabulary. I am impatient with stupidity, bureaucracy, and organizations. Poetry, for me, is the supreme art of the individual using a huge magnificent range of language to show how special, different, and wonderful his perceptions are. With verve and finesse. With discursive precision. And with utter contempt for pettiness of imagination or spirit.

*   *   *

One of the most important and controversial poets in the United States, Diane Wakoski is also one of the most prolific. Early appraisals of her work as a product of her association with the Deep Imagists of New York and later efforts to discount it as "confessional," angry, and self-pitying have all proved inadequate or unjust. Like Whitman she uses the autobiographical self to create an American voice, but like Wallace Stevens she has made the human imagination the real subject of her work. In her efforts to show how the mind may work to acknowledge or create beauty in virtually any situation, she has found the storyteller's narration as useful as the image and the actor's use of masks and roles more telling than the *cri de coeur.* The self in her body of work has become an instrument to awaken the imaginative consciousness of others. Paradoxically, this intellectual poet, who makes no secret of her love for classical music or her wide-ranging interests in science and mythology, is warmly received by large audiences not because she "spills her guts" (to use Anne Sexton's famous phrase) but because her digressive style allows so many points of entry into the webs of thought and feeling she creates.

Wakoski has devised an idiosyncratic form of the long poem that allows her to be discursive or imagistic, factual or mythical, mundane or visionary, and to shift from one of these levels to another without losing her audience by relying primarily on common language and ordinary rhythms of speech. Varying line lengths are used to make melody, determine tempo, and draw attention to each word. In her series designated The Archaeology of Movies and Books, which uses the Greek tales of Medea and Jason and the city of Las Vegas as focal points, she includes not only her trademark poems but also intersperses excerpts from books on quantum physics and gambling in Las Vegas, along with prose letters to presumably fictional men, Jonathan and Craig, wherein "Diane," as Postmistress, Moon Woman, Lady of the Light, can discuss anything that she considers relevant to the poems or the quoted passages. The books are Foucaultian not only in their digging for the personal and cultural elements (both classical and popular) that have shaped Diane's consciousness as an American but also in laying bare the "discipline of self" she pursues so actively and self-consciously on our behalf.

Wakoski has been interested in mythology—as a source of identity, as a target for critique, and as an ongoing creative enterprise—from the beginning. Her best works have always engaged the most enduring problems of the relationship between ourselves and other human beings, nature, or the cultural ideas (such as justice, power, or beauty) that order human lives. One of her most ambitious books, *The Collected Greed,* containing poems that appeared in chapbooks from 1968 to 1984, shows both the continuity of her poetic interests and the seriousness of her effort to develop a distinctive aesthetic stance (analogous to Baudelaire's *aesthetique du mal)* capable of treating the less attractive sides of human lives. Her poems confronting "the man's world" in the historical figure of George Washington and her singular creation of a fantasy figure called the "King of Spain" are only the most obvious manifestations of a pervasive tendency to filter ordinary experience through the perspective of mythic characters. Although her late poems continued to be filled with real and imagined people, Wakoski takes increasing pleasure in the phenomena of nature, for example, in the lady slipper, which she loves "more than jewels or gold or men," or in the mushroom's inky "cap of darkness" (a phrase she has also used to refer to her invisible Athena-like helmet for combating the ghost of greed, which she defines as the inability to choose). The title poem of *Emerald Ice* presents a jewel the color of fresh basil with the "liquid hardness" of ice to epitomize her poetry of the previous thirty years.

Perhaps Wakoski's most impressive achievement has been to imagine a female self who is painfully aware of imperfections—her own as well as her culture's—but who can nonetheless celebrate the adequacy of the poet's imagination and also dream of a poetic "territory" that is "inexorably" her own. Her talent, courage, conscience, breadth of vision, and insight into human weakness seem likely to make this remarkably coherent oeuvre one of the hallmarks of our time.

—Estella Lauter

WALDMAN, Anne (Lesley)

Nationality: American. **Born:** Millville, New Jersey, 2 April 1945. **Education:** Bennington College, Vermont, B.A. in English 1966. **Family:** Married Reed Eyre Bye in 1980 (divorced); one son. **Career:** Assistant director, 1966-68, and director, 1968-78, St. Mark's Church-in-the-Bowery Poetry Project, New York; founding co-director, with Allen Ginsberg, Jack Kerouac School of Disembodied Poetics, Naropa Institute, Boulder, Colorado, 1974—. Associated with Stevens Institute of Technology, Hoboken, New Jersey, 1981-82, New College of California, San Francisco, 1982, York University, Toronto, 1984, Institute of American Indian Arts, Santa Fe, New Mexico, 1985, University of Maine, Portland, summer 1986, and Naropa Institute of Halifax, Nova Scotia, summers 1986, 1987. **Awards:** Dylan Thomas award, 1967; Cultural Artists grant, 1976; National Endowment for the Arts grant, 1980; Shelley Memorial Award, 1996. **Member:** Board of Directors, Giorno Poetry Systems Institute, New York; Eye and Ear Theatre, New York. **Address:** Naropa Institute, 2130 Arapahoe Avenue, Boulder, Colorado 80302, U.S.A.

PUBLICATIONS

Poetry

On the Wing. New York, Boke, 1967.
Giant Night. New York, Angel Hair, 1968.

O My Life! New York, Angel Hair, 1969.
Baby Breakdown. Indianapolis, Bobbs Merrill, 1970.
Up Through the Years. New York, Angel Hair, 1970.
Giant Night: Selected Poems. New York, Corinth, 1970.
Icy Rose. New York, Angel Hair, 1971.
No Hassles. New York, Kulchur, 1971.
Memorial Day, with Ted Berrigan. New York, Poetry Project, 1971.
Holy City. Privately printed, 1971.
Goodies from Anne Waldman. London, Strange Faeces Press, 1971.
Light and Shadow. Privately printed, 1972.
The West Indies Poems. New York, Boke, 1972.
Spin Off. Bolinas, California, Big Sky, 1972.
Self Portrait, with Joe Brainard. New York, Siamese Banana Press, 1973.
Life Notes: Selected Poems. Indianapolis, Bobbs Merrill, 1973.
The Contemplative Life. Detroit, Alternative Press, n.d.
Fast Speaking Woman. Detroit, Red Hanrahan Press, 1974; 20th anniversary edition, San Francisco, City Lights, 1996.
Fast Speaking Woman and Other Chants. San Francisco, City Lights, 1975; revised edition, 1978.
Sun the Blond Out. Berkeley, California, Arif, 1975.
Journals and Dreams. New York, Stonehill, 1976.
Shaman. Boston, Munich, 1977.
4 Travels, with Reed Bye. New York, Sayonara, 1978.
To a Young Poet. Boston, White Raven, 1979.
Countries. West Branch, Iowa, Toothpaste Press, 1980.
Cabin. Calais, Vermont, Z Press, 1982.
First Baby Poems. Boulder, Colorado, Rocky Ledge, 1982; augmented edition, New York, Hyacinth Girls, 1983.
Make-Up on Empty Space. West Branch, Iowa, Toothpaste Press, 1984.
Skin Meat Bones. Minneapolis, Coffee House Press, 1985.
Invention. New York, Kulchur, 1985.
The Romance Thing. Flint, Michigan, Bamberger, 1987.
Blue Mosque. New York, United Artists, 1987.
Helping the Dreamer: Selected Poems 1966-1988. Minneapolis, Coffee House Press, 1989.
Not a Male Pseudonym. New York, Tender Buttons, 1990.
Lokapala. New York, Rocky Ledge, 1991.
Fait Accompli. Boulder, Last Generation, 1992.
Iovis: All is Full of Jove. Minneapolis, Coffee House Press, 1993
Troubairitz. N.p., Fifth Planet Press, 1993.
Kill or Cure. New York, Penguin Poets, 1994.
Iovis II. Minneapolis, Coffee House Press, 1997.

Recordings: *John Giorno and Anne Waldman,* Giorno, 1978; *Fast Speaking Woman,* S Press Tapes, n.d.; *Uh-Oh Plutonium!,* Hyacinth Girls, 1982; *Crack in the World,* Sounds True, 1986; *Made Up in Texas,* Paris, 1986; *Anne Waldman* (video), Lannan, 1991.

Other

Editor, *The World Anthology: Poems from the St. Mark's Poetry Project,* and *Another World.* Indianapolis, Bobbs Merrill, 1969-71.
Editor, with Marilyn Webb, *Talking Poetics from Naropa Institute.* Boulder, Colorado, Shambala, 2 vols., 1978-79.
Editor, *Nice to See You: Homage to Ted Berrigan.* Minneapolis, Coffee House Press, 1988.
Editor, *Out of This World: Anthology from the St. Mark's Poetry Project.* New York, Crown, 1991.

Editor, with Andrew Schelling, *Disembodied Poetics: Annals of the Jack Kerouac School.* Albuquerque, University of New Mexico Press, 1994.

Editor, *The Beat Book.* Boston, Shambhala, 1996.

Translator, with Andrew Schnelling, *Songs of the Sons and Daughters of Buddha.* Boston, Shambhala, 1996.

*

Critical Studies: By Alicia Ostriker, in *Partisan Review* (New Brunswick, New Jersey), Spring-Summer 1971, and *Parnassus* (New York), Fall-Winter, 1974; Gerard Malanga, in *Poetry* (Chicago), January 1974; Richard Morris, in *Margins* (Milwaukee, Wisconsin), October-November 1974; Aram Saroyan, in *New York Times Book Review,* April 1976; *The Beats: Literary Bohemians in Postwar America,* edited by Ann Charters, Detroit, Gale Research, 2 vols., 1983.

*   *   *

"Poetry should be a joy ... a pleasure ... The whole thing of the suffering poet ... it's so unnecessary. You can get so intense that you can't produce. There's work to be done." Whatever else it may or may not do, Anne Waldman's poetry keeps this promise. Most often her poems find their inspiration and shape in an implicitly celebratory display of the diverse pleasures of things—life in New York, world travel, sex and friendships, even her own fantasies and dreams. The high-spiritedness, rich humor, and eager openness that sustain her work derive less from the idealism than from the affluence of the 1960s. But then, she can't help it if she's lucky. What matters is that she improves upon her luck, for the imaginative persuasiveness of her best poems recalls Whitman's insight that "the most affluent man is he that confronts all the shows he sees by equivalents out of the stronger wealth of himself." Poetry, for Waldman, justifies itself as the show of life, and the pleasures it offers are inherent in the process whereby the impulses of life are released into living forms.

If she dismisses the "suffering poet," it is almost always in the spirit of one for whom suffering can properly show itself only indirectly, as the elusive and finally unappeasable passion that both nourishes and chastens the poet's creative play: "There is work to be done." Nowhere is this element in her work more crucial than in her best-known poem, "Fast Speaking Woman," which goes like this, with very little variation of pattern, for nearly 600 lines:

> I'm a witch woman
> I'm a beggar woman
> I'm a shade woman
> I'm a shadow woman
> I'm a leaf woman
> I'm a leaping woman

This remarkable piece could never hold our attention for six lines, let alone 600, were it not for its creative recklessness, at once desperate and playful. This is a matter, chiefly, of Waldman's splendidly uninhibited aesthetic opportunism, so that each line seems generated by some underplayed excess of the matter and movement of preceding ones. The imaginative power of the poem inheres in the immediacy of its language yet remains apart, its freshness not just unharmed but actually enriched by any show it has made.

"Fast Speaking Woman" is something of a tour de force, but even in its extremity it is characteristic of the aims and methods of Waldman's work. She is committed to the classic American mode of "open-form" or "projective" verse, though, despite the idiomatic pungency and speed of her language, the music of her poetry is closer to that of song than of speech. This is especially true of the "chants" in the collection *Fast Speaking Woman,* but even her less regular pieces, the best of which, I think, are in *Baby Breakdown* ("I Am Not a Woman" and "Conversational Poem") and, especially, *Journals and Dreams* ("Blues Cadet," "Mirror Meditation," "My Lady," and "When the World Was Steady"), strike the ear not as speech but as snatches of song stitched into even more various musical patterns—a variousness in music which answers to and resolves a rich contradictoriness of feeling and perception.

From its beginnings the open-form tradition has rested on some form of belief in the correspondence between inner and outer worlds, but one must go back to Whitman to find precedent for Waldman's astonishingly unstudied practical faith that discoveries of self are revelations of a world and vice versa. The epigraph to "Fast Speaking Woman" is "I is other," and what counts in her work is less the tenacity than the nonchalance of her exploration of the truth of this. She neither apologizes for her egotism nor worries about her otherness. Coming from any poet this is exhilarating, but coming from a woman it is truly revolutionary. The word "woman" appears in nearly every line of "Fast Speaking Woman," yet it receives little rhythmic or semantic stress; it is treated simply as the natural point of departure and return for each excursus of self, as if nothing better could or need be imagined than to create a world in terms of a woman's acts of self-realization. The form of this poem gives the game away more unmistakably than others, but it is far from the only one to play that game with extraordinary inventiveness and grace.

—John Hinchey

WALDROP, Rosmarie

Pseudonym: Rosmarie Keith. **Nationality:** American. **Born:** Kitzingen/Main, Germany, 24 August 1935. **Education:** Universität Würzburg, 1954-56; Université d'Aix-Marseilles, 1956-57; Universität Freiburg, 1957-58; University of Michigan, 1959-66, M.A. 1960, Ph.D. 1966. **Family:** Married Keith Waldrop in 1959. **Career:** Assistant professor, Wesleyan University, Middletown, Connecticut, 1964-70; poet-in-the-schools, Rhode Island, 1971-72; visiting poet, Southeastern Massachusetts University, 1977; visiting lecturer, 1977-78, and visiting associate professor, 1983, 1990-91, 1993, 1997, Brown University, Providence, Rhode Island; visiting lecturer, Tufts University, Medford, Massachusetts, 1979-81. Co-editor and publisher, Burning Deck Press, 1968—. Co-founder, playwright, and director, Wastepaper Theater, Providence, 1973-83. **Awards:** Hopwood award, 1963; Humboldt award, 1970-71, 1975; Howard award, 1974-75; Translation Center award, 1978; National Endowment for the Arts fellowship, 1980, 1994; Rhode Island Governor's Arts award, 1988; Fund for Poetry, 1990; PEN Book-of-the-Month-Club Citation in Translation, 1991; DAAD Berlin Artists Program, 1993; Landon Translation award, 1994. **Address:** 71 Elmgrove Avenue, Providence, Rhode Island 02906, U.S.A.

PUBLICATIONS

Poetry

The Aggressive Ways of the Casual Stranger. New York, Random House, 1972.
The Road Is Everywhere or Stop This Body. Columbia, Missouri, Open Places, 1978.
When They Have Senses. Providence, Burning Deck, 1980.
Nothing Has Changed. Windsor, Vermont, Awede Press, 1981.
Differences for Four Hands. Philadelphia, Singing Horse Press, 1984.
Streets Enough to Welcome Snow. Barrytown, New York, Station Hill, 1986.
The Reproduction of Profiles. New York, New Directions, 1987.
Peculiar Motions. Berkeley, California, Kelsey Street Press, 1990.
Lawn of Excluded Middle. New York, Tender Buttons, 1993.
A Key into the Language of America. New York, New Directions, 1994.

Novels

The Hanky of Pippin's Daughter. Barrytown, New York, Station Hill, 1986.
A Form / of Taking / It All. Barrytown, New York, Station Hill, 1990.

Other

Against Language? The Hague, Netherlands, Mouton, 1971.

Editor, with Keith Waldrop, *A Century in Two Decades.* Providence, Burning Deck, 1982.

Translator, *Bodies and Shadows* by Peter Weiss. New York, Delacorte, 1969.
Translator, *Elya* by Edmond Jabès. Bolinas, California, Tree Books, 1973.
Translator, *The Book of Questions* by Edmond Jabès. Middletown, Connecticut, Wesleyan University Press, 1976.
Translator, *The Book of Yukel / Return to the Book* (volumes II and III of *The Book of Questions)* by Edmond Jabès. Middletown, Connecticut, Wesleyan University Press, 1977.
Translator, *Yaël / Elya / Aely* (volumes IV, V, and VI of *The Book of Questions)* by Edmond Jabès. Middletown, Connecticut, Wesleyan University Press, 1983.
Translator, with Harriett Watts, *The Vienna Group: Six Major Austrian Poets.* Barrytown, New York, Station Hill Press, 1985.
Translator, *Paul Celan, Collected Prose.* Manchester, Carcanet, and New York, Sheep Meadow, 1986.
Translator, with Tod Kabza, *Archeology of the Mother: A Selection of Poems by Alain Veinstein.* Peterborough, Cambridgeshire, Spectacular Diseases, 1986.
Translator, *The Book of Dialogue* by Edmond Jabès. Middletown, Connecticut, Wesleyan University Press, 1987.

Translator, with Connel McGrath, *Late Additions: Selected Poems by Emmanuel Hocquard.* Peterborough, Cambridgeshire, Spectacular Diseases, 1988.
Translator, *The Book of Shares* by Edmond Jabès. Chicago, University of Chicago Press, 1989.
Translator, *Some Thing Black* by Jacques Roubaud. Elmwood Park, Illinois, Dalkey Archive Press, 1990.
Translator, *The Book of Resemblances* by Edmond Jabès. Middletown, Connecticut, Wesleyan University Press, 1990.
Translator, *Intimations The Desert* (volume II of *The Book of Resemblances)* by Edmond Jabès. Middletown, Connecticut, Wesleyan University Press, 1991.
Translator, *From the Book to the Book* by Edmond Jabès. Middletown, Connecticut, Wesleyan University Press, 1991.
Translator, *Rimbaud in Abyssinia* by Alain Borer. New York, William Morrow, 1991.
Translator, *Dawn* by Joseph Guglielmi. Peterborough, Cambridgeshire, Spectacular Diseases, 1991.
Translator, *The Ineffaceable The Unperceived* (volume III of *The Book of Resemblances)* by Edmond Jabès. Middletown, Connecticut, Wesleyan University Press, 1992.
Translator, *The Book of Margins* by Edmond Jabès. Chicago, University of Chicago Press, 1993.
Translator, *A Foreigner Carrying in the Crook of His Arm a Tiny Book* by Edmond Jabès. Middletown, Connecticut, Wesleyan University Press, 1993.
Translator, *Heiligenanstalt* by Friederike Mayröcker. Providence, Burning Deck, 1994.
Translator, *The Plurality of Worlds of Lewis* by Jacques Roubaud. Normal, Illinois, Dalkey Archive Press, 1995.
Translator, *Mountains in Berlin: Selected Poems by Elke Erb.* Providence, Burning Deck, 1995.
Translator, *The Little Book of Unsuspected Subversion* by Edmond Jabès. Stanford, California, Stanford University Press, 1996.

*

Critical Studies: "The Ambition of Senses" by Craig Watson, in *Montemora #8* (New York), 1981; "Non-Euclidean Narrative Combustion" by Joan Retallack, in *Parnassus* (New York), Summer 1988.

*   *   *

Rosmarie Waldrop began her writing life with a little book of prose called *Against Language?* This was her manifesto to the world that language, such as we use every day and pour into our daily newspapers and novels and poems, was exhausted. When the fund of words and expressions is exhausted, the mind itself goes brittle, social vision shrinks, and life is more or less imprisoned in the triteness of a used-up consciousness. It is the duty of writers, she tells us in this manifesto, to go to the edges of language, to work out what is for now the unsayable, the unknowable, and to revive speech. Here is how she puts her argument in the conclusion:

> The poets who are seriously dissatisfied with our conventions of language (and do not just take this attitude as an excuse or because it is fashionable) are working at the borders of the unsayable and unknowable. They are trying to explore the areas bordering pure spirit or the

void, unformed matter or energy, and their realm of 'things' considered as having a self-sufficient being alien to man. And since our language is our world, changing the language seems a possibility of changing our ways of seeing and thus to some extent changing what is seeable and knowable.

This attractive program was set forth some few years before the public became aware of language poetry, the school of American poets who studied Wittgenstein and Derrida and pursued the notion that language is a finite realm within a broader human consciousness. It could be said that they wanted to explore the rest of consciousness beyond "the city of words." The theory goes that if the speaker deranges syntax (Rimbaud's suggestion) and explodes grammatical structure—where sexism, white bias, imperialist master-class illusions, and subject-object dichotomies (Cartesian thinking) are concealed—it is possible to liberate the tongue so as to enter the hinterlands of knowledge obscured by the walls of conventional language.

These absolutes are not new to poetry. Emerson spoke of an attitude to nature that would free the voices within and restore wholeness of vision. Pound's notion of the image as a glimpse at the gods in nature and Olson's "human universe" prepared the way for Waldrop's pronouncements. She tells us that poetry has always borrowed from the arts and music, but she adds that it must also borrow from autism and mathematics so as to gain the ground which consciousness otherwise excludes. Autism gives us a window into daydreams, and mathematics is "pure relation."

The result is an eerie mode of lyric, in prose poem format, in which subtleties are uncovered, as in Waldrop's squibs in *The Reproduction of Profiles*:

> You told me, if something is not used it is
> meaningless, and took my temperature which I
> had thought to save for a more difficult day.
> In the mirror, every night, the same face, a
> bit more threadbare, a dress worn too long.
> The moon was out in the cold, along with the
> restless, dissatisfied wind that seemed to
> change the location of the sycamores. I ex-
> pected reproaches because I had mentioned the
> word love, but you only accused me of steal-
> ing your pencil, and sadness disappeared with
> sense. You made a ceremony out of holding
> your head in your hands because, you said, it
> could not be contained in itself.

Implicit here and elsewhere in Waldrop's poetry is the principle that things are alive in their own dynamics and that they make relations and forms from an imagination in nature. The poet is witness, an imitator of natural creativity, not a copyist. By subduing some of the instrumental logic of the self, nature regains its original autonomy and instructs the human soul.

Beneath Waldrop and her language peers is a steadily building faith in nature religion. The codes in which they write this new logic of expression, with its strange Piranesi staircases going nowhere, rising and falling in goalless antiprogress, suggest a new, secular Latin prayer book, a priesthood of nature mystics in America. The more we hear of "reenchantment" in contemporary discourse, the easier it is to believe that language mysticism is the means by which the old spells, visions, and reverence for otherness are returning to mind.

Consider the following passage in "Overshadowed," from *The Aggressive Ways of the Casual Stranger*:

> Spidery running
> a phantom child
> all the dead are eager
> to be remembered
> the concave world where
> souls smelled
> and pleasure came in a net full of fish
> glassy
> desolate

This is a lyric at the edge, but it is also about something, Waldrop's childhood years growing up in Germany. We get glimpses here and there of cold, removed parents, the German rituals that are now tainted in retrospect by visions of the Holocaust. Waldrop does not write the equivalent of Sylvia Plath's "Daddy," which draws its fire from conventional logic. Instead, she writes from several ongoing conscious tracks of thought, picking a few details from one, merging them with a few from another. The style is similar to the recollective mode of Lyn Hejinian and to Leslie Scalopino, Susan Howe, and other language masters.

Here is another sample of the mode from "Menstruation," also in *The Aggressive Ways of the Casual Stranger*:

> My appetite's for waking
> chill crystals in the clouds
> pebble seeds
> Flaubert devoted years to
> accumulation of details
> worthless
> next to a bare wall
> I insist on living
> with words
> vicarious birth vicarious existence
> each month my womb cries
> its mouth swollen

What one often hears in Waldrop's poetry are the words "sleep," "waiting," "mist," "grey," and "solitude" and mathematical terms like "equation" and "correspondence." But she also has a fine, inventive ear for new phrases, like these from "Kind Regards," included in *Streets Enough to Welcome Snow*:

> Your air of kind regards
> kind randomness
> of a museum
> canvas sneakers
> along with raspberry lips
>
>   *
>
> lately you say I've had an awkward
> pull
> toward the past tense
> my remarks renovate
> details in oil

If there is a plot, it is the regaining of Waldrop's own autonomy in a marriage, the working up of a separate consciousness with its own vision of the world. She writes often about an Amerindian woman named Saltwoman, her alter ego. The surprising function of this figure is that Waldrop makes her from the kind of sleep talk she writes, and it holds our attention. It works, perhaps more deeply and strongly than conventional taste will sometimes want to admit.

—Paul Christensen

WEBB, Phyllis

Nationality: Canadian. **Born:** Victoria, British Columbia, 8 April 1927. **Education:** University of British Columbia, Vancouver, B.A. in English and philosophy 1949; McGill University, Montreal, 1953. **Career:** Secretary, Montreal, 1956; teaching assistant, English Department, University of British Columbia, Vancouver, 1960-64; program organizer, 1964-67, and executive producer, 1967-69, Canadian Broadcasting Corporation, Toronto; guest lecturer, University of British Columbia, 1976-77, Banff Centre, Alberta, 1981; writer-in-residence, University of Alberta, 1980-81; adjunct professor, Creative Writing Department, University of Victoria, British Columbia, 1989-93. **Awards:** Canadian Government Overseas award, 1957; Canada Council bursary, 1963, and award, 1969, 1981, 1987; Governor-General's award, 1982; Officer of the Order of Canada, 1992. **Address:** 128 Menhinick Drive, Salt Spring Island, British Columbia V8K 1W7, Canada.

PUBLICATIONS

Poetry

Trio, with Gael Turnbull and Eli Mandel. Toronto, Contact Press, 1954.
Even Your Right Eye. Toronto, McClelland & Stewart, 1956.
The Sea Is Also a Garden. Toronto, Ryerson Press, 1962.
Naked Poems. Vancouver, Periwinkle Press, 1965.
Selected Poems 1954-1965, edited by John Hulcoop. Vancouver, Talonbooks, 1971.
Wilson's Bowl. Toronto, Coach House Press, 1980.
Sunday Water: 13 Anti Ghazals. Lantzville, British Columbia, Island, 1982.
The Vision Tree: Selected Poems, edited by Sharon Thesen. Vancouver, Talonbooks, 1982.
Water and Light: Ghazals and Anti Ghazals. Toronto, Coach House Press. 1984.
Hanging Fire. Toronto, Coach House, 1990.

Other

Talking. Montreal, Quadrant, 1982.
Nothing but Brush Strokes: Selected Prose. Edmonton, NeWest, 1995.

*

Bibliography: By Cecelia Frey, in *The Annotated Bibliography of Canada's Major Authors,* vol. 6, edited by Robert Lecker and Jack David, Toronto, ECW Press, 1985.

Manuscript Collections: National Library of Canada, Ottawa; Talonbooks Archives, Vancouver; Simon Fraser University Library, Burnaby, British Columbia.

Critical Studies: "The Structure of Loss" by Helen Sonthoff, in *Canadian Literature* (Vancouver), Summer 1961; "Phyllis Webb and the Priestess of Motion" in *Canadian Literature* (Vancouver), Spring 1967, and introduction to *Selected Poems 1954-1965,* 1971, both by John Hulcoop; introduction by Sharon Thesen to *The Vision Tree,* 1982; "I and I: Phyllis Webb's 'I Daniel,'" in *Open Letter* (Toronto), no. 2-3, Summer-Fall 1985, and "Surviving the Paraph-Raise," in *Signature, Event, Cantext,* Edmonton, Alberta, NeWest Press, 1989, both by Stephen Scobie; "Proceeding before the Amorous Invisible: Phyllis Webb and the Ghazal" by Susan Glickman, in *Canadian Literature* (Vancouver), Winter 1987; "Phyllis Webb as a Post-Duncan Poet" in *Sagetrieh* (Orono, Maine), vol. 7, no. 1, 1988, and "You Devise. We Devise," in *West Coast Line,* both by Pauline Butling, no. 6, Winter 1991-92; *Phyllis Webb and Her Works* by John F. Hulcoop, Toronto, ECW Press, 1991.

*   *   *

Phyllis Webb is a poet of austere dedication whose relatively small number of finely crafted poems have slowly attracted the attention of readers. Her work also has influenced other poets and helped to change the course of poetry in Canada during the years in which she has been steadily honing her craft.

Webb's first poems appeared at the beginning of the 1950s in *Contemporary Verse,* Alan Crawley's historic little magazine. Since then she has published only sparsely. She always seems reluctant to release a poem into print or speech, and her works, when they do appear, have been honed to an extraordinary intellectual spareness. Yet her image as a diffident and reclusive poet is not entirely justified. She has at times been politically active on the left, as when at the age of 22 she stood unsuccessfully as a social democratic candidate in the British Columbia provincial elections. In the mid-1960s, working for the Canadian Broadcasting Corporation, she devised and was the first producer of the highly regarded program *Ideas.* The venerable program has continued to flourish long after Webb retired from the world of public action to her retreat on Salt Spring Island, a place of relative seclusion in the channel between Vancouver Island and mainland British Columbia.

Webb shared her first volume, *Trio,* with two poets remarkably unlike herself, Gael Turnbull and Eli Mandel. Her first individual volume, *Even Your Right Eye,* appeared in 1956, and while *The Sea Is Also a Garden* and the sparse *Naked Poems* were issued together in the early 1960s, her *Selected Poems* of 1971 included nothing published after 1965. There was a long gap before her next collection, *Wilson's Bowl,* appeared in 1980. This was followed in 1982 by *The Vision Tree: Selected Poems* and *Sunday Water: 13 Anti Ghazals* and in 1984 by *Water and Light: Ghazals and Anti Ghazals. The Vision Tree,* the book nearest to a volume of collected poems, represents the work of more than 30 years in a mere 154 pages.

Webb's later books have finally established her among Canada's leading poets, although her influence on younger poets had been evident long before. Northrop Frye described *Wilson's Bowl* as "a landmark in Canadian poetry," and *The Vision Tree* won her the establishment recognition of a Governor-General's award. She continues to write in seclusion, to polish, and, very often, to discard.

For Webb, in fact, growing in maturity as a poet has meant withdrawal for long periods, a narrowing of the circle of the creative self in keeping with the solipsistic character of much of her verse. More than 25 years ago she said that "The public and the person are inevitably / one and the same self." But while this may have been true of the Webb who campaigned as a socialist candidate, it has not been true for many years of the poet who has become concerned with personal emotions, the loneliness of living, the knife edge paths on which we painfully dance our way to death. She no longer sees art as a "remedy," as a "patched, matched protection for Because."

The result is perhaps foreshadowed in the early poem "Is Our Distress":

> This our inheritance
> is our distress
> born of the weight of eons
> it skeletons our flesh,
> bearing us on
> we wear it
> though it bears us.

The philosophic pessimism—in unguarded moments breaking down into self-pity—which these lines suggest has tended to control the development of thought in Webb's poems. It has led her to move from the elaborate and the assured toward the simplified view of anarchists like Kropotkin, the view that the less one demands of existence, the less one has to defend. One of "Some Final Questions," a section of *Naked Poems,* reads

> Now, you are sitting doubled up in pain.
> *What's that for?*
>
> doubled up I feel
> small like these poems
> the area of attack
> is diminished

The Naked Poems are indeed reductive in terms of verse as well as life. They were prepared for by a work in *The Sea Is Also a Garden,* "Poetics against an Angel of Death," in which Webb says,

> Last night I thought I would not wake again
> but now with this June morning I run ragged to elude
> The Great Iambic Pentameter
> who is the Hound of Heaven in our stress
> because I want to die
> writing Haiku
> or, better,
> long lines, clean and syllabic as knotted bamboo. Yes!

Indeed, Webb's poems at this point became quasi-haiku, small, simple, as packed with meaning as stone artifacts, and punctuated by periods of stubborn silence. These "naked poems," austerely beautiful as weathered bones, are crucial to her career. In the later poems of *Wilson's Bowl* and in their successors Webb emerged into what is in fact a structure of "long lines, clean and syllabic as knotted bamboo." The poems of this last period are no longer minimalist. They expand not only formally into complex patterns of sound but also in thought, in what Webb herself has called "the dance of the intellect in the syllables," and there is

a return on an apolitical level to the humane considerations of her earliest phase, as she weaves the problems of self and other into pieces like her "Kropotkin Poems":

> *The Memoirs of a Revolutionist* before me, things fall
> together now. Pine needles, arbutus bark, the tide
> comes in, path to the beach lights with sun-fall.
> Highest joys? The simple profundity of a deadman works at
> my style. I am impoverished. He the White Christ.
> Not a case of identification. Easier to see myself
> in the white cat asleep on the bed. Exile. I live
> alone. I have a phone. I shall go to Russia. One
> more day run round and the 'good masterpiece of work'
> does not come. I scribble. I approach some distant dream.
> I wait for moonlight reflecting on the night sea. I can
> wait. We shall see.

Webb, more than most other poets, has forced herself to know the limitations of her talent, and in this way she has learned its full powers. The stark, elliptical beauty of the collection *Hanging Fire* places her, with Douglas Barbour and Fred Wah, in the forefront of the Canadian language poets. Some titles of the poems she calls "?" are used as triggers for meditations, which are sometimes on the sound of the words themselves. Wit, insight, and musical instinct combine to penetrate and then illuminate what was unknown before.

—George Woodcock and Patience Wheatley

WICKS, Susan

Nationality: British. **Born:** Tumbridge Wells, Kent, 24 October 1947. **Education:** University of Hull, B.A. (1st class honors) in French 1971; University of Sussex, Ph.D. 1975. **Family:** Married John Collins in 1974, two daughters. **Career:** Lecturer, then maître assistante associée in English, Université de Dijon, Dijon, France, 1974-76; assistant lecturer in French, University College, Dublin, 1976-77; part-time tutor and instructor, University of Kent, 1983—; teacher of residential weekend course in poetry, University of Oxford, 1997. **Awards:** Hedgebrook residency, 1991; Aldeburgh Poetry Festival prize, 1992, for *Singing Underwater;* Southeast Arts Writer's bursary, 1993-94; MacDowell Colony residency, 1996; Poetry Book Society Choice, and T.S. Eliot prize shortlist, both 1996, both for *The Key.* **Agent:** Jane Turnbull, 13 Wendell Road, London W12 9RS, England. **Address:** c/o Faber & Faber, 3 Queen Square, London WC1N 3AU, England.

PUBLICATIONS

Poetry

Singing Underwater. Boston and London, Faber, 1992.
Open Diagnosis. Boston and London, Faber, 1994.
The Clever Daughter. London, Faber, 1996.

Novel

The Key. London, Faber, 1997.

Other

Driving My Father (memoir). New York, Basis Books and London, Faber, 1995.

*   *   *

Susan Wick's poetry is remarkable for the intensity with which it grasps the here-and-now. At times the attempt to register "the momentousness of ordinary, intimate experience," as the blurb on her first collection *Singing Underwater* has it, can be unpersuasive: "Swing-bin" fails to lift into significance a list of bin-contents despite the poem's final "subterranean / tremor" (caused by thrown-away spaghetti). More often, Wick's short lines, active diction, and sharp enjambments give life to her writing. The title poem of her first collection depicts the poet's daughter singing "Happy Birthday" below water, "You tug on me and gesture, / mouth opening and closing, / wrapping me in water." There, the last line has the effect, for the poet, of a re-birthing presided over by her child. "Rings" makes witty use of its opening comparison, "Let me die like an onion." Other poems from *Singing Underwater* show a capacity for the spookily reworked nursery rhyme (as in "Ha Ha Bonk") which can bring Stevie Smith to mind. The collection reveals, too, an unglamorizing fascination with the physical as the ground of existence (several poems, such as "On Turning Away" and "Post Partum," are concerned with birth and new life). And there is a pervasive awareness of the topsy-turvy, unstable nature of day-to-day living, best captured in "Hall of Mirrors," in which the poet sees her face bizarrely distorted in a kettle.

Throughout *Singing Underwater,* edgy constraint wars with a feeling for all that challenges constraint, whether in a disturbing or a luminous way. Lyrical impulses seethe rawly, sliding away from easy harmonies and fluencies. Wick's second collection *Open Diagnosis* is more overtly confessional, though in poems such as "You Hate Me" the voice confessing is as much a dream self as a waking ego. The second of the book's three sections includes poems about the poet's own illness: in "Caul" the poet writes of her father that "Now his only daughter / has M.S."; "Germinal" opens "This is my disaster"; and "Coming Out" "comes out" exuberantly about loss of health. In these poems there is a bracing absence of self-pity. So in "Coming Out" Wicks revels in the saying of what she was always going to be; any sense of the predestined is trumped by the poet's freedom to imagine.

Adversity prompts celebration in other poems in the collection; the resulting blend of attitudes is the subject of "Glad Game" that takes as its epigraph the following; "('... *euphoria, which has been said to go with having M.S...*')." In this poem Wicks offers a wry defense of her poetry's relish for iridescent, oddly unalluring detail when she writes, "my head is all flecked with coral, magenta, / indigo, such gorgeous dandruff." Briefly, she sounds like Medbh McGuckian, but Wicks is, mercifully, less opaque than the Irish poet. That's not to deny her imagination's ability to surprise, as in, say, "The Ark Speaks." In this risk-taking, bravura piece the poet imagines herself as an ark occupied by creatures from bulls to roaches; the poem concludes with a buoyantly imagined moment of release as, "keel nested in branches," "A door creaked, a hand opened."

Wick's most recent collection *The Clever Daughter* followed hard in the heels of her sharp, unsentimental prose work, *Driving My Father,* in which she describes taking care of her elderly father. It's typical of Wicks that she brings into the domain of language an experience that, though familiar to many people, especially women, is rarely the stuff of literature. Incidents in this prose work reappear in *The Clever Daughter,* as "My Father's Handkerchiefs" illustrates; in both prose and poem Wick's imagination dwells on the mucus-stiffened state of the handkerchiefs (the poet washes and irons them for the father "to snort his thick grief into," in the poem's words). But, as the handkerchiefs are likened in the poem to "my daughter's / origami monsters," the down-to-earth is connected to the strangely transformative in a way that characterizes Wick's finest work. Similarly, from its opening words "The evening my mother died we first saw / its face," "Fox" suggests obscure links between awareness of obstinate mystery. Reviewing Gerald Stern's *Odd Mercy* in *Poetry Review* (vol. 86, no. 1, 1996), Wicks remarks that his world "is double. Everywhere there is a preoccupation with opposites," and the same holds true of her most intriguing poems in *The Clever Daughter.* The volume's emotional subtlety goes hand in hand with increased technical skill, evident not only in the reworking of the sonnet form in a number of pieces but also in the sustaining of long sentences and patterns of sound. Sometimes merely odd, more often oddly good, Susan Wick's work freshly illuminates the fact that poetry is, above all, an act of close verbal attention.

—Michael O'Neill

WILLARD, Nancy

Nationality: American. **Born:** Ann Arbor, Michigan, 26 June 1936. **Education**: University of Michigan, B.A. 1958; Stanford University, M.A. 1960; University of Michigan, Ph.D. 1963. **Family:** Married Eric Lindbloom in 1964, one son. **Career:** Lecturer in English, Vassar College, Poughkeepsie, New York, 1965—; instructor, Bread Loaf Writer's Conference, 1975. **Awards:** University of Michigan Hopwood Award, 1958; Woodrow Wilson fellowship, 1960; Devins Memorial Award, 1967, for *Skin of Grace*; O. Henry Award, 1970; Lewis Carroll Shelf Award, 1974, for *Sailing to Cythera and Other Anatole Stories*, and 1979, for *Island of the Grass King: The Further Adventures of Anatole*; National Endowment for the Arts grant, 1976; Society of Children's Book Writers Special Honor Book Plaque, 1981; John Newbery Medal, Caldecott Honor Book Award, and American Book Award nomination, all 1982, all for *A Visit to William Blake's Inn: Poems for Innocent and Experienced Travelers*; Creative Artist Service Award; National Endowment for the Arts fellowship (fiction), 1987-88; National Book Critics Circle award nomination, 1990, for *Water Walker*; Michigan Library Association Michigan Author award, 1994. **Address**: Poughkeepsie, New York, U.S.A.

PUBLICATIONS

Poetry

In His Country: Poems. Ann Arbor, Michigan, Generation, 1966.

Skin of Grace. Columbia, University of Missouri Press, 1967.

A New Herball: Poems. Baltimore, Ferdinand-Roter Gallerias, 1968.

Nineteen Masks for the Naked Poet: Poems. Santa Cruz, Kayak, 1971.
Carpenter of the Sun: Poems. New York, Liveright, 1974.
Household Tales of Moon and Water. San Diego, Harcourt, 1982.
The Ballad of Biddy Early. New York, Knopf, 1987.
Water Walker. New York, Knopf, 1990.
Poem Made of Water. San Diego, Brighton Press, 1992.
A Nancy Willard Reader: Selected Poetry and Prose. Hanover, New Hampshire, University Press of New England, 1993.
Selected Poems. N.p., McKay, 1996.
Swimming Lessons: New and Selected Poems. New York, Knopf, 1996.

For Children

Sailing to Cythera and Other Anatole Stories. New York, Harcourt, 1974.
All on a May Morning. New York, Putnam, 1975.
The Merry History of a Christmas Pie: With a Delicious Description of a Christmas Soup. New York, Putnam, 1975.
The Snow Rabbit. New York, Putnam, 1975.
Shoes without Leather. New York, Putnam, 1976.
The Well-mannered Balloon. New York, Harcourt, 1976.
Simple Pictures Are Best. New York, Harcourt, 1977.
Strangers' Bread. New York, Harcourt, 1977.
The Highest Hit. New York, Harcourt, 1978.
Island of the Grass King: The Further Adventures of Anatole. New York, Harcourt, 1979.
Papa's Panda. New York, Harcourt, 1979.
A Visit to William Blake's Inn: Poems for Innocent and Experienced Travelers. New York, Harcourt, 1981.
The Marzipan Moon. New York, Harcourt, 1981.
Uncle Terrible: More Adventures of Anatole. New York, Harcourt, 1982.
The Nightgown of the Sullen Moon. New York, Harcourt, 1983.
Night Story. New York, Harcourt, 1986.
The Mountains of Quilt. New York, Harcourt, 1987.
Firebrat. New York, Random House, 1988.
The High Rise Glorious Skittle Skat Roarious Sky Pie Angel Food Cake. New York, Harcourt, 1990.
Pish, Posh, Said Hieronymous Bosch, with Leo D. Dillon. New York, Harcourt, 1991.
Beauty and the Beast. New York, Harcourt, 1992.
Sorcerer's Apprentice. New York, Scholastic, 1993.
A Starlit Somersault Downhill. Boston, Little Brown, 1993.
The Alphabet of Angels. New York, Scholastic, 1994.
The Voyage of Ludgate Hill: Travels with Robert Louis Stevensen. New York, Harcourt, 1994.
Gutenberg's Gift: A Book Lover's Pop-Up Book. New York, Harcourt, 1995.
Among Angels, with Jane Yolen. New York, Harcourt, 1995.
Cracked Corn and Snow Ice Cream: A Family Almanac. New York, Harcourt, 1996.
The Good-Night Blessing Book. New York, Scholastic, 1996.
The Tortilla Cat. New York, Harcourt, 1997.

Other

The Lively Anatomy of God (short stories). New York, Eakins, 1968.

Testimony of the Invisible Man: William Carlos Williams, Francis Ponge, Rainer Maria Rilke, Pablo Neruda. Columbia, University of Missouri Press, 1970.
Childhood of the Magician (short stories). New York, Liveright, 1973.
Angel in the Parlor: Five Stories and Eight Essays. New York, Harcourt, 1983.
Things Invisible to See (novel). New York, Knopf, 1984.
East of the Sun and West of the Moon (play). New York, Harcourt, 1989.
Telling Time: Angels, Ancestors, and Stories. New York, Harcourt, 1993.
Sister Water. New York, Knopf, 1993.

Recordings: *Things Invisible to See,* 1991; *Island of the Grass King,* 1992; *Sailing to Cythera,* 1992; *Uncle Terrible,* 1992; *Sister Water,* 1993.

*

Media Adaptations: *A Visit to William Blake's Inn: Poems for Innocent and Experienced Travelers* (videorecording), Random House, 1986.

Critical Studies: In *Western Humanities Review,* autumn 1975; *Open Places,* fall / winter 1975-76; *Michigan Quarterly Review,* winter 1975; *Prairie Schooner,* Summer 1976; "'From the Odd Corner of the Imagination': A Conversation with Nancy Willard" by Stan Sanvel Rubin, in *The Post-Confessionals: Conversations with American Poets of the Eighties,* Rutherford, New Jersey, Farleigh Dickinson Press, 1989; in *English Journal,* April 1990.

*   *   *

To consume the entire body of Nancy Willard's poetry at a gulp would be to forfeit savoring the soothe and snap of American poetry in its dynamic stages over the last three decades. Aside from scanning Willard's 1996 collection, *Swimming Lessons,* most readers will not do so. Yet the sea change in the genre is recorded here, beginning with the Beat influence, Theodore Roethke, and James Wright (see Willard's "Swimming" in *Skin of Grace*) and on through the move away from formalism to free verse and thought, as well as a surrealism reminiscent of John Ashberry in Willard's "The Church": all are evident in Willard's development as a poet.

When *Skin of Grace* won the Devins Memorial Award and publication by the University of Missouri Press in 1967, Willard had already found a voice of fond reverence for the holiness of common things: apple, bread, forest, parent and grandparent, flower, string, stone, water, etc. After this firm handshake of hers with the world and with formalist style, each piece transforms its known image into some greater miracle. After

> eons of chitin and shale[,] drummers
> under the earth, the cicadas
>   have waited for seventeen summers
> to break their shell,
>   shape of your oldest fear
> of a first world
>   of monsters. We are not here.

We are instantly drawn into the poem and shuttled back into subliminal fear, the lurking, real hunger of evil. With the magic of the word (as Robert Bly notes, a poem can and should leap), we are luckily elsewhere. Much of the book is sweeter than this, and the groundwork for Willard's forthcoming novels have been outlined in several of these poems. Also, her love of language and story is already apparent. Even so, the book's faults are many. For example, in the title poem's line, "where deer drinking conquer the armed men," readers require a historicist's keen ear of opposition to the Vietnam War for the Munchian scream of horror that carries the image, whereas a young audience may wonder, "What is this?" Yet the miracles are many, as in "Swimming":

> I tried to walk on water as a child
> and plunged into a valley sunk so blue
> my eyes smarted with rainbows in the dark.

That these older poems stand meaningfully proud for 30 years, and more, later is a testament to Willard's craft and vision. They also stand boldly in comparison to poems from *In His Country* (1966), in which "kings ... lay withered in sleep with costly things," eggs are "a jury noncommittal / as the bald heads of / a dozen uncles," and the negative is "the inner garment of time / which reverses our knowledge." Always, the creatures and objects of nature are meant to hold our reverence, with human machinations drawn silly by comparison and the reader distanced by revulsion to them.

Even in her early work, themes of nature in motion and personified are evident, for example, in *A New Herball* (1968) with the "rocks coming alive underfoot" and the moon that "hangs her thin wire around his [the poet's] ankle, / hangs her tiny hook into the gills of his heart." However, this book yields to the surreal much more than its predecessors do: "I am a song. / Someone is writing me down. / I am disappearing into the ear of a rose, ..." or "At last, I saw a green lion / eating a hole in the sun, ..." Moreover, we are given conundrums to mull and puzzle out—"day in night, night in hand / hand in pocket, pocket in poem, / poem in bone, bone in flesh, / flesh in flight." The poem itself withdraws from the world of meaning into one of rapid evolution. As Willard says at the beginning of *Testimony of the Invisible Man* (1970), "The *Ding*-poets (literally "Thing," meaning image-poets) want to remake your world by destroying the stereotyped modes of thinking and seeing that prevent you from knowing it." Clearly, this early lesson impressed her and influenced her work.

By comparison, the poems in *Carpenter of the Sun* (1974) are less formal and more humorous: "Train tracks shook our flesh from our bones / Lying on the back seat of a nervous Chevy," and "If they don't take animals, / I cannot possibly stay at the Hilton." At the same time, a new element works its way into the context: "you" as the unborn child, and "how beautifully the child I carry on my back / teaches me to become a horse." The transformations of these bones is more subtle but equally satisfying.

In *Household Tales of Moon and Water* (1982), Willard abandons her former surrealism and poetic devices for a childlike playfulness: "Can I eat a star? / Yes, with the mouth of time / that enjoys everything." Here begins a lasting immersion in Zen-like composure: "somebody small and glad, / the Finder, the Shining One," and "Water gave me this book. / It was not written for me. / It is written for birds, / / snakes, fishes." Simultaneously, the adult voice wrenches truths from simple observations, "Whatever I try to hold perishes." Here, Willard shows an increasing need to let go: "I remember the mad preacher of Indiana / who chose for the site of his kingdom / the footprint of an angel and named the place / New Harmony. Nothing of it survives." This more mature voice also shows greater conscious attention to first lines, "Mercy is whiter than laundry" and "An egg is grand thing for a journey." Perhaps it is from understanding more of death that these poems' beginnings are given closer attention by this "I."

That voice develops simpler language and contexts into even more complex themes in *A Nancy Willard Reader* (1993). There is a growing sense of loss in "When There were Trees": "Already the trees are a myth, / half gods, half giants in whom nobody believes." Likewise, in "The Poet's Wife Watches Him Enter the Eye of the Snow," "She knew he was writing a poem / because everything in the room / was slowly sifting away, ..." Given the great caring in the poems, we too are meant to care, to suffer the pain of living that all things must endure although we are but observers.

By contrast, Willard's "New Poems" from *Swimming Lessons* speak predominantly in apostrophe: "you" as the beloved, the father, the hat, the fire-starter, the fruit bat, the jellyfish, and so on. Much of the imagery is likewise personified: the disobedient fence "lies down," the geese "want to invent the snow," trees are soldierly, bathtubs noble, barns have gender, puffballs modesty. Conversely, the live thing, the alligator's belly, is "tiled / like the floor of the shower / in some dinghy." This is a floor no one would dare touch with a naked foot, echoing Willard's early treatment of evil.

What consistently happens in her poetry is that which should happen naturally in all verse: detail, movement and instantaneous transformation. The reader is lifted, even propelled, into new remembrances of simple objects and circumstances in our common experience. There is nothing that we did not know, only that which we are amazed to remember. These poems are visionary images of how things at once could be, have been and are. Nancy Willard reminds us most powerfully that, more than acting as servants or descriptive devices in the world, words create worlds.

—Maril Nowak

WRIGHT, C(arolyn) D.

Nationality: American. **Born:** Mountain Home, Arkansas, 6 January 1949. **Education:** Memphis State University, Memphis, Tennessee, 1969-71, B.A. 1971; University of Arkansas, Fayetteville, 1973-76, M.F.A. 1976. **Family:** Married Forrest Gander in 1982; one son. **Career:** Graduate teaching assistant, University of Arkansas, Fayetteville, 1973-76; poet-in-the-schools, Office of Arkansas Arts and Humanities, 1976-78; office manager, The Poetry Center, San Francisco State University, 1980-82; visiting professor, Iowa Writer's Workshop, 1996; professor, Brown University, Providence, Rhode Island, 1983—. Co-editor, Lost Roads Publishers, Providence, Rhode Island. **Awards:** National Endowment for the Arts fellowship, 1982, 1988; Witter Bynner Poetry prize, 1986; Guggenheim fellowship, 1987; Bunting Institute fellowship, 1987; General Electric award for younger writers, 1988; Whiting Foundation award, 1989; Rhode Island Governor's award for the Arts, 1990; Poetry Center Book award, 1992; Lila Wallace Writers' award, 1992; State Poet of Rhode Island, 1994. **Address:**

English Department, x1852, Brown University, Providence, Rhode Island 02912, U.S.A.

PUBLICATIONS

Poetry

Alla Breve Loving. Spokane, Washington, Mill Mountain Press, 1976.
Room Rented by a Single Woman. Fayetteville, Arkansas, Lost Roads Publishers, 1977.
Terrorism. Fayetteville, Arkansas, Lost Roads Publishers, 1978.
Translation of the Gospel Back into Tongues. Albany, State University of New York Press, 1981.
Further Adventures with You. Pittsburgh, Carnegie-Mellon Press, 1986.
String Light. Athens, University of Georgia Press, 1992.
Just Whistle. Berkeley, California, Kelsey Street Press, 1993.
Tremble. New York, Ecco Press, 1996.

Recording: *C.D. Wright* (videotape), The Poetry Center at San Francisco State University, 1992.

Other

The Reader's Map of Arkansas. Fayetteville, University of Arkansas Press, 1995.

Editor, *The Lost Roads Project: A Walk-in Book of Arkansas.* Fayetteville, University of Arkansas Press, 1995.

*

Critical Studies: "Politics and the Personal Lyric in the Poetry of Joy Harjo and C.D. Wright" by Jenny Goodman, in *Melus: Theory, Culture, and Criticism,* vol. 19, no. 2, summer 1994.

C.D. Wright comments:

Poetry is my central station. All that can converge in a given individual intersects there for me, under the big clock. Many of my influences are extra-literary—friends, trees. Others answer to other arts—music, photography. Other disciplines—folklore, recent history. Still others, to temperament—leftist. And of course, a lifetime of reading helter skelter through the layers of time and translation only gaining consistency and some pattern, from rural to urban, with contemporary American poetry. I still try to sustain a certain tolerance toward the whole field even as my own writing seems to be shifting allegiances. I try not to forfeit what can never be recovered—my hardheaded, idiomatic bedrock. I try not to remain ignorant of the ever-changing present tense of poetry. Some say the genre is anachronistic. I say, these people, their lives have become too prosaic.

*   *   *

In the prose text "hills," which introduces her 1986 collection *Further Adventures with You,* C.D. Wright explains that her poems "are about desire, conflict, the dearth of justice for all. About persons of small means. They are succinct but otherwise orthodox novels in which the necessary characters are brought out, made intimate ..., engage in dramatic action and leave the scene forever

with or without a resolution in hand or sight. Each on the space of a page or less." This statement captures several qualities common to all the work of this Arkansas-born poet, whose earliest writing was dialect based and regional in focus: its storytelling impulse, its focus on everyday things and events, its backdrop of melancholia and brooding violence, its necessarily elliptical brevity. Yet, in a crucial respect Wright's later work has superseded the *ars poetica* she offers in "hills," for the relation between poetry and prose in her writing has become more complex and her lineated stories veer demonstratively towards less orthodox forms.

Typical of Wright's earlier "orthodox novels" is the poem "Vanish," from *Translations of the Gospels Back into Tongues* (1981). This is a poem of memory, loss, and desire—all states of absence that Wright's poem comes to occupy, offering its lineaments of story to mark the place which the vanishing experience had occupied and now leaves bare. The poem offers fragmentary recollections of an encounter between a girl and a sailor, perhaps before the funeral of the girl's brother. The encounter ended long ago without issue, and the sailor and girl have separated. The poem's first-person voice shifts over the course of the poem's 31 lines from the aged sailor to the now mature girl. "Vanish" begins

> Because I did not die
> I sit in the captain's chair
> Going deaf in one ear, blind in the other.
> I live because the sea does.

By the end, however, the girl's fading memories swallow up the sailor's voice, consigning it to the near oblivion of the sea swell:

> Because I did not marry
> I wash by the light of the body.
> Soap floats out of my mind.
> I have almost forgotten
> The sailor whose name I did not catch,
> His salty tongue on my ear,
> A wave on a shell.

Only between these two drifting buoys of consciousness may the broken pieces of their common story surface, traces of the shipwrecked possibilities of love.

Wright's stories are often mediated through a wounded interiority or a dreaming mind, as in the title poem of her 1986 book, "Further Adventures with You":

> We are on a primeval river in a reptilian den.
>
> There are birds you don't want to tangle with, trees
>   you cannot identify ...
>
> Somehow we spend the evening with Mingus
> in a White Castle. Or somewhere. Nearly drunk. He says
>   he would like to play for the gang.

The dream, with its expression of unspoken wishes, its mobilization of childhood memories and ephemera of the day, its enigmatic yoking of distant scenes, serves as an apt model for the lyric consciousness implicit in Wright's poetry generally and not only in her "dream poems." For dreams, despite their apparent incoherence, are ways of revisiting what in our waking lives is irrecoverable, whether because of passing time or by our failure to attend to it as it was lived. Poetry, too, may be such a mode of dreamlike remembrance. As Wright suggests in "The box this comes in," an allegorical "deviation on poetry," a meditation on poetry via the image of an antique box, "Within the limits of this diminutive wooden world, I have made do with the cracks of light and tokens of loss and recovery that came my way."

Both *Further Adventures with You* and *String Light,* however, exhibit Wright's discovery of nonverse forms, which in turn seem to shift the center of gravity of her poetry from states of desire towards the experiential richness of language forms as such. Thus, in her sequence "The Ozark Odes" the section titled "Arkansas Towns" is dedicated purely to the delightful and strange place-names of Wright's home state—

Acorn
Back Gate
Bald Knob
Ben Hur
Biggers
Blue Ball

—all the way up to "Whisp," "Yellville," and "Zent."

Similarly, the prose poems subjoined to "What No One Could Have Told Them" isolate a single detail (a toddler urinating, the child yawning) and repeat it in new word contexts until the detail takes on luminosity as language, independent of its humble content. Wright's numerous prose poems, and above all the Kerouac-like "sketching" of "The Night I Met Little Floyd" and "The Next Time I Crossed the Line into Oklahoma" (both in *String Light*), bear out the distinction she drew in "hills"—whereas her poems are based on narrative, she says, her prose "is about language if it is about any one thing."

—Tyrus Miller

WRIGHT, Judith (Arundell)

Nationality: Australian. **Born:** Armidale, New South Wales, 31 May 1915. **Education:** Blackfriar Correspondence School, New South Wales; New England Girls School, Armidale; University of Sydney. **Family:** Married J.P. McKinncy (died 1966); one daughter. **Career:** Secretary and clerk, 1938-42; clerk, Universities Commission, 1943-44; university statistician, University of Queensland, St. Lucia, 1945-48. Commonwealth Literary Fund Lecturer, Australia, 1949, 1962; honors tutor in English, University of Queensland, 1967. **Awards:** Grace Leven prize, 1950, 1972; Commonwealth Literary Fund fellowship, 1964; Australia Britannica award, 1964; Australian Academy of the Humanities fellowship, 1970; Australian National University Creative Arts fellowship, 1974; Senior Writers fellowship, 1977; Fellowship of Australian Writers Robert Frost memorial award, 1977; Asan World prize, 1984; Premier's prize, New South Wales, 1987; The Queen's Prize for Poetry, 1992; Human Rights for Poetry award, 1995. D.Litt.: University of Queensland, 1962; University of New England, Armidale, 1963; Sydney University, 1977; Monash University, Clayton, Victoria, 1977; Australian National University, Canberra, 1981; Griffith University, Nathan, Queensland, 1988; University of Melbourne, 1988. **Member:** Australia Council, 1973-74. **Address:** c/o Post Office, Braidwood, New South Wales 2622, Australia.

PUBLICATIONS

Poetry

The Moving Image. Melbourne, Meanjin Press, 1946.
Woman to Man. Sydney, Angus & Robertson, 1949.
The Galeway. Sydney, Angus & Robertson, 1953.
The Two Fires. Sydney, Angus & Robertson, 1955.
Australian Bird Poems. Adelaide, Australian Letters, 1961.
Birds. Sydney, Angus & Robertson, 1962.
(*Poems*), selected and introduced by the author. Sydney, Angus & Robertson, 1963.
Five Senses: Selected Poems. Sydney, Angus & Robertson, 1963.
City Sunrise. Brisbane, Shapcott Press, 1964.
The Other Half. Sydney, Angus & Robertson, 1966.
Poetry from Australia: Pergamon Poets 6, with Randolph Stow and William Hart-Smith, edited by Howard Sergeant. Oxford, Pergamon Press, 1969.
Collected Poems 1942-1970. Sydney, Angus & Robertson, 1971.
Alive: Poems 1971-72. Sydney, Angus & Robertson, 1973.
Fourth Quarter and Other Poems. Sydney, Angus & Robertson, 1976; London, Angus & Robertson, 1977.
The Double Tree: Selected Poems 1942-1976. Boston, Houghton Mifflin, 1978.
Journeys, with others, edited by Fay Zwicky. Melbourne, Sisters, 1982.
Phantom Dwelling. Sydney, Angus & Robertson, 1985; London, Virago Press, 1986.
A Human Pattern (selected poems). Sydney, Angus & Robertson, 1990; Manchester, Carcanet, 1992.
Collected Poems. Sydney, Angus & Robertson, and Manchester, Carcanet, 1994.

Recording: *Judith Wright Reads from Her Own Work,* University of Queensland Press, 1973.

Short Stories

The Nature of Love. Melbourne, Sun, 1966; revised, Sydney, ETF Publishing, 1997.

Other

Australian Poetry (lecture). Armidale, New South Wales, University of New England, ca. 1955.
King of the Dingoes (for children). Melbourne, Oxford University Press, 1958; London, Angus & Robertson, 1959.
The Generations of Men. Melbourne, Oxford University Press, 1959.
The Day the Mountains Played (for children). Brisbane, Jacaranda Press, 1960; London, Angus & Robertson, 1963.
Range the Mountains High (for children). Melbourne, Lansdowne Press, and London, Angus & Robertson, 1962; revised edition, Lansdowne Press, 1971.
Country Towns (for children). Melbourne, Oxford University Press, 1963; London, Oxford University Press, 1964.
Charles Harpur. Melbourne, Lansdowne Press, 1963; revised edition, Melbourne and London, Oxford University Press, 1977.
Shaw Neilson (biography and selected verse). Sydney, Angus & Robertson, 1963.

359

Preoccupations in Australian Poetry. Melbourne and London, Oxford University Press, 1965.

The River and the Road (for children). Melbourne, Lansdowne Press, 1966; London, Angus & Robertson, 1967; revised edition, Lansdowne Press, 1971.

Henry Lawson. Melbourne, London, and New York, Oxford University Press, 1967.

Conservation as an Emerging Concept. Sydney, Australian Conservation Foundation, 1970.

Because I Was Invited (essays). Melbourne, Oxford University Press, 1975; London, Oxford University Press, 1976.

The Coral Battleground. Melbourne, Nelson, 1977.

The Cry for the Dead. Melbourne, Oxford, and New York, Oxford University Press, 1981.

We Call for a Treaty. Sydney, Collins / Fontana, 1985.

Born of the Conquerors (essays). Canberra, Aboriginal Studies Press, 1991.

Going on Talking (essays). Springwood, New South Wales, Butterfly Books, 1992.

Editor, *Australian Poetry 1948.* Sydney, Angus & Robertson, 1949.

Editor, *A Book of Australian Verse.* Melbourne and London, Oxford University Press, 1956; revised edition, 1968.

Editor, *New Land, New Language: An Anthology of Australian Verse.* Melbourne and London, Oxford University Press, 1957.

Editor, with A.K. Thomson, *The Poet's Pen.* Brisbane, Jacaranda Press, 1965.

Editor, with Val Vallis, *Witnesses of Spring: Unpublished Poems,* by Shaw Neilson. Sydney, Angus & Robertson, 1970.

Editor, with others, *Report of the National Estate.* Canberra, Government Publishing Service, 1974.

Editor, with others, *Reef, Rainforest, Mangroves, Man.* Cairns, Wildlife Preservation Society of Queensland, 1980.

*

Bibliography: *Judith Wright: A Bibliography,* Adelaide, Libraries Board of South Australia, 1968; *Judith Wright* by Shirley Walker, Melbourne, Oxford University Press, 1981.

Critical Studies: *Focus on Judith Wright* by W.N. Scott, Brisbane, University of Queensland Press, 1967; *Critical Essays on Judith Wright* edited by A.K. Thomson, Brisbane, Jacaranda Press, 1968; *Judith Wright* by A.D. Hope, Melbourne, Oxford University Press, 1975; *Judith Wright: An Appreciation* edited by N. Simms, Hamilton, New Zealand, Outrigger Press, 1976; *The Poetry of Judith Wright: A Search for Unity* by Shirley Walker, Melbourne, Arnold, 1980; *Judith Wright* by Jennifer Strauss, Melbourne, Oxford University Press, 1995.

Judith Wright comments:

The background of my work lies in my main life concerns, as an Australian whose family on both sides were early comers to a country which was one of the last to be settled by the whites, and were from the beginning farmers and pastoralists. Brought up in a landscape once of extraordinary beauty, but despised by its settlers because of its unfamiliarity, I have, I suppose, been trying to expiate a deep sense of guilt over what we have done to the country, to its first inhabitants of all kinds, and are still and increasingly doing. This is one aspect of the sources of my work. I have never for long been an urban-dweller, and the images I use

and also my methods no doubt reflect my ties to the landscape I live in. I tend to use "traditional"—i.e., biological—rhythms more than free or new forms, which I see as better adapted to urban living and urban tensions and problems.

Another strong influence on my work has been my relationship with my husband whose philosophical investigation of the sources and development of Western thought I shared in till his death. As a woman poet, the biological aspect of feminine experience has naturally been of importance in my work also. I expect my poetry is of a kind which no urban technological society will produce again, but I have tried to remain faithful to my own experience and outlook rather than engage in experimental verse for which it does not fit me.

Over the years since 1970 I have been increasingly concerned with questions of conservation and the situation of Australian Aborigines, and my participation in active organizations on both issues is reflected in my work during this time.

*   *   *

Judith Wright, one of Australia's most distinguished and best-loved poets and an ardent conservationist, unites in her poetry a vision of wholeness, a synthesis of body, mind, and spirit that stands counter to the alienation of modern life. Ever aware of the "link between the decline of our inner and of our outer worlds," she continually seeks to forge this lost unity against "our decaying capacities for imagination, vision and creation," our separation from the natural world. In poems on untouched nature she pursues this quest to "name and know / beyond the flowers I gather / the one that does not wither— / the truth from which they grow," ("The Forest," *Five Senses*). Wright evokes the spontaneity of nature in the personification of "The Wattle-Tree," which breaks "into the truth I had no voice to speak: / into a million images of the Sun, my God" (*The Two Fires*). This spontaneity she also credits to an earlier Australian poet, seeking like him to "live ... fed on by unseen poetry ... [and] give these heavy words away" ("For John Shaw Neilson," *The Other Half*). This search for the essence of a reality implicit in the everyday reaches an epiphany of loving communion with the landscape and its "ravelled shore" and "contours of dunes" when, in "Jet Flight over Derby,"

I lost my foreign words
and spoke in tongues like birds.

This desire to go beyond language resulted in a new form of expression in *Phantom Dwelling.* In "Brevity" Wright heralds a change to pared-down forms in the two concluding sections of the volume, confiding that "these days I don't draw / very deep breaths":

I used to love Keats, Blake.
Now I try haiku
for its honed brevities,
its inclusive silences.

Issa. Shiki. Buson. Basho.
Few words and with no rhetoric.
Enclosed by silence
as is the thrush's call.

In the minimalist poems that follow Wright achieves her contact with that "unseen poetry," as in "Caddis-fly" ("Small twilight helicopter") or "Fox" ("Fox, fox! / Behind him follows the crackle of his name").

But while nature and, in particular, the landscape of the Australian bush are the loved and constant subjects of Wright's poetry, so too are human feelings and actions. Though rarely particularizing its subjects, her poems of human love can capture tenderness and wonder in its universal aspects, as in one of her best-known poems, "Woman to Man," a moving meditation on an unborn child:

> This is our hunter and our chase,
> the third who lay in our embrace.
> This is the strength that your arm knows,
> the arc of flesh that is my breast,
> the precise crystals of our eyes.

The poetic control and precision of language in this and its companion poems counterpoise the two acts of creation, producing some of Wright's most successful work.

In "Bullocky" and "Brother and Sisters" Wright captures the world of the pioneers; in others, among them the early "Nigger's Leap, New England" and "The Bora Ring," the spirits of the Aborigines haunt their land and its settlers, "the tribal story / lost in an alien tale." The living "Dark Ones" haunt also:

> On the other side of the road
> the dark ones stand.
> Something leaks in our blood
> like the ooze from a wound.

These "night ghosts of a land / only by day possessed," silently watching as "faces of pale stone" turn aside, and the association of the Aborigines with the land describe one of the other symptoms of alienation that Wright often confronts. In her poetry, as in her prose, she reminds white Australians that their refusal to acknowledge the Aborigines' spiritual rights to land lies at the heart of their own loss of contact with the natural world. Her own love of the "unseen poetry" of nature, and its significance as a creative, spiritual force, gives her particular respect for those who sustained and nurtured it as a spiritual force of their own.

It is appropriate that "Patterns," the final poem of *Phantom Dwelling*—last of a sequence titled "The Shadow of Fire (Ghazals)"—should bring together in a series of couplets the renewing and destructive forms of fire, Wright's recurrent image of the spirit. While the dual aspects have been opposed in earlier poems, here the emphasis is on reconciling these opposites. Even the "thousand suns" of nuclear explosion is contained in the Heraclitean philosophy of flux, itself not a stranger in her work:

> All's fire, said Heraclitus; measures of it
> kindle as others fade. All changes yet all's one.
>
> We are born of ethereal fire and we return there.
> Understand the Logos; reconcile opposing principles ...
>
> 'Twisted are the hearts of men—dark powers possess them.
> Burn the distant evildoer, the unseen sinner.'
>
> That prayer to Agni, fire-god, cannot be prayed.
> We are all of us born of fire, possessed by darkness.

Here the word (Logos) has been absorbed into the principle of reconciliation, as the poem balances light and dark, destruction and salvation, evil and good; fire is the "ethereal" source of life as well as apocalypse. "Patterns" includes and transcends all the earlier images of fire, that of the wattle tree, of the creative fire that derives from homely images ("Cleaning Day"), of the napalm of Vietnam, of "the contained argument of the bomb" ("The Precipice"). It is entirely consistent that Wright should forge the broken links of outer and inner worlds by combining these oppositions in a poem of Christian symbolism, classical philosophy, modern science ("Strontium in the bones ... is said to be 'a good conductor of electricity'") and in a form that is based on a Persian verse form (the ghazal). From a poet whose life work has been the definition of light and darkness, the fusion of the broken, this is a poem that brings the universe itself into an embracing and forgiving whole.

—Nan Bowman Albinski

ZWICKY, (Julia) Fay

Nationality: Australian. **Born:** Julia Fay Rosefield, Melbourne, Australia, 4 July 1933. **Education:** University of Melbourne, 1950-54, B.A. (honors). **Family:** Married 1) Karl Zwicky in 1957, one son and one daughter; 2) James Mackie in 1990. **Career:** Concert pianist, 1950-65; senior lecturer in English, University of Western Australia, Perth, 1972-87. Member of literature board, Australia Council, Sydney, 1978-81; poetry editor, *Westerly,* Perth, and *Patterns,* Fremantle, 1974-83; associate editor, *Overland,* Melbourne, 1988—, and *Southerly,* Sydney, 1989—. **Awards:** New South Wales Premier's award, 1982; Western Australian Literary award, for non-fiction, 1987; Western Australian Premier's award for poetry, 1991. **Agent:** Australian Literary Management, 2A Armstrong Street, Middle Park, Victoria 3206. **Address:** 30 Goldsmith Road, Claremont, Western Australia 6010, Australia.

PUBLICATIONS

Poetry

Isaac Babel's Fiddle. Adelaide, Maximus, 1975.
Kaddish and Other Poems. St. Lucia, University of Queensland Press, 1982.
Ask Me. St. Lucia, University of Queensland Press, 1990.
A Touch of Ginger, with Dennis Haskell. Applecross, Folio, 1991.
Poems 1970-1992. St. Lucia, University of Queensland Press, 1993.

Short Stories

Hostages. Fremantle, Western Australia, Fremantle Arts Centre Press, 1983.

Other

The Lyre in the Pawnshop: Essays on Literature and Survival 1974-1984. Nedlands, University of Western Australia Press, 1986.

Editor, *Quarry: A Selection of Western Australian Poetry.* Fremantle, Western Australia, Fremantle Arts Centre Press, 1981.

Editor, *Journeys: Judith Wright, Rosemary Dobson, Gwen Harwood, Dorothy Hewett.* Melbourne, Sisters, 1982.

Editor, *Procession: Youngstreet Poets 3.* Sydney, Hale & Iremonger, 1987.

*

Critical Studies: "Finding a Voice in 'This Fiercely Fathered and Unmothered World': The Poetry of Fay Zwicky" by Joan Kirkby, in *Poetry and Gender,* edited by David Brooks and Brenda Walker, St. Lucia, University of Queensland Press, 1989; "Fay Zwicky: The Poet as Moralist" by Ivor Indyk, and "On the Shifting Sands of Our Experience: Fay Zwicky's Poetry" by Elsa Linguanti, both in *Southerly* (Sydney), vol. 54, no. 3, September 1994.

Fay Zwicky comments:

Certain themes run with obdurate consistency through the three collections spanning a period of 20 years or so. Chief among these is probably an affirmation of the human speaking voice, often discerned in opposition to the oppressive silence of an inarticulate culture.

Some poems in the first book, *Isaac Babel's Fiddle,* weave a densely-textured mythic structure around the settlement in Australia of my Jewish ancestors in the middle of the nineteenth century. The sense of exile implicit in the migrant assimilation process is linked with an awareness of being bound to a diminishing past while remaining ambiguously ironic about the preservation of constraining traditions. Under masks and a variety of voices, the poems explore the lot of the traditionally silent female who is also a member of an ethnic minority group and thus doubly sentenced.

Finding a voice also informs the looser lines of poems in *Kaddish and Other Poems.* These have more breathing space, take more risks with form, and, as in the title poem with its four distinctively symphonic movements, take their shape from musical models. Several poems set up an argument either as internal monologue or as exploration of traditional mythological characters. In the "Ark Voices" sequence, a capricious God is questioned about survival, its penalties and obligations. Other poems are concerned with identity in a contemporary context, and the artist's ambiguous role in keeping faith with the history of human suffering in a heedless society.

The third collection, *Ask Me,* ranges further afield with poems written after visits to China, India, and America. Several deal with experiences as a hospice worker and two long elegies provide a climax to the growing sense of life's fragility. The speaking voice has become less urgent, the irony less lacerating. Although there are fewer masks and "literary" allusions, a more colloquial emphasis, these poems continue to articulate the dimensions of a vision apparent in earlier work questioning the limits of speech and silence.

*   *   *

Fay Zwicky's poetry might well take as its epigraph Gwen Harwood's line "a fire-talented tongue will choose its truth." It will also choose its mode of telling, and Zwicky's often fierce truths are diversely told—confrontationally, obliquely, passion-

ately, intellectually, astringently, compassionately. There is something characteristic about the title *Ask Me* (1990). Challenging the dismissively antonymic "Don't ask *me,*" it declares allegiance to involvement and to that seriousness of mind which Zwicky defends so purposefully as literary critic. It is seriousness rather than solemnity, and its enunciation, always compatible with wit and colloquialism, has shifted over time, as "In Memory of Vincent Buckley," toward celebrating

> those blessed moments of the ordinary,
> rarer than ornaments of beaten gold and twice as rare
> to those intransigent for truth amid imposture.

More directly, *Ask Me* indicates preparedness to answer. Zwicky has a humanist commitment to communication: "language is the product of a deep-rooted web of potential for empathy between people, a shared structure" ("Influence and Independence," *Overland* 1978). Disintegration of language and the social fabric go together, leaving those unable or unwilling to resist with "the despair and frustration of being unable to communicate or to love, the impotence of refusing responsibility for the word." Since writers must "put in a word for life"—"Lot's Wife (Take 18)"— Zwicky questions positive cultural evaluations of silence. In the 1983 *Quadrant* essay "Speeches and Silences" she argues that the transcendental concept of "reaching beyond words" for an "ineffable purity of vision ... may appear as condescending and aggressive withdrawal to those ... who are prepared to lay themselves on the line in the only mode of communication available."

The idea that to fail to speak is to fail love informs the volume *Kaddish.* This opens with a ritual prayer for her dead father in which Zwicky finally voices and memorializes a contentious love; it closes with a ritualized plea to be forgiven the poems that have died "under each inert hour of my silence":

> the many I have frozen with irony
> the many I have trampled with anger
> the many I have rejected in self-defence
> the many I have ignored in fear

The negativity toward irony is symptomatic of Zwicky's preparedness to question received wisdom. Much of her work can be seen as challenging assumptions prevalent in discursive constructions of Australian identity and of female identity. In questioning the valorization of silence, she argues specifically that Australian exaltation of strong, silent stoicism may lead to a spiritual desert, so that to be "An Australian" is to be "Wordless / In a dumb landscape." This is, she argues, especially oppressive for women, because stoic silence is construed as masculine virtue, "leaving the female to flounder without the longed-for verbal signposts needed for the articulation of feeling."

Nonetheless, Zwicky gets in her word, engaging argumentatively with her personal and cultural heritage, with the love she can deny neither her Jewish father nor the patriarchs of Western thought and literature. Refusing either silence or relegation to the trivial, and always aware of the dangers of becoming "a sullen parody of independence" ("Father in a Mirror"), she combines passion and the gothic with a robust and acerbic deflation. The effects can be unsettling: psychologically, as in "Cleft," a powerful evocation of dissociated (and dismembered) female sexuality; or aesthetically, as in "The Name of the Game," where she matches kitchen intimations of death against "the fine literary stance" of Donne or Hemingway.

Like many contemporary women poets, Zwicky raids the world of patriarchal myth in order to provide a voice for the silent or question the distribution of power. Probably her greatest achievement in the mythic mode lies in the wonderfully sensuous, pragmatic, exuberant pathos of the voices with which Mrs. Noah and the animals address God in "Ark Voices." In her articulation of what it is to be "speechless and unspoken to," her refusal to reciprocate the language of tyranny, and her insistence on compassion, Mrs. Noah remains a speaking presence capable of being translated into the joyful enumerator of names in "Southern Spell." If the ego demands speech, the communicative life demands that we be able to listen, and, having listened, the poet commemorates. *Ask Me* concludes with the elegy "For Jim," in which the dying man's "Remember" is answered by the poem's enactment of the poet's promise, "I will. / I do." The elegiac note, frequent in *Ask Me* and dominant in the collection *Poems 1970-1992,* achieves an Orphic plangency in the poems remembering not only the lost lover who was her first husband but also the lost self, the lost time and (Indonesian) place of that love's beginning. The sequence may end in grief for the poet—"Ashamed of outliving you" and "a long way from that house, that window"—but the poetry evokes as richly present a life spoken for even in the words that speak its loss.

—Jennifer Strauss

NATIONALITY INDEX

American

Diane Ackerman
Ai
Paula Gunn Allen
Maya Angelou
Gloria Anzaldúa
Rae Armantrout
Robin Becker
Sujata Bhatt
Chana Bloch
Roo Borson
Lucie Brock-Broido
Gwendolyn Brooks
Ana Castillo
Lorna Dee Cervantes
Diane Chang
Maxine Chernoff
Marilyn Chin
Sandra Cisneros
Lucille Clifton
Jane Cooper
Lucha Corpi
Jayne Cortez
Beverly Dahlen
Tina Darragh
Toi Derricotte
Diane di Prima
Sharon Doubiago
Rita Dove
Barbara Drake
Rachel Blau DuPlessis
Louise Erdrich
Ruth Fainlight
Carolyn Forché
Kathleen Fraser
Alice Fulton
Erica Funkhouser
Tess Gallagher
Sandra M. Gilbert
Nikki Giovanni
Louise Glück
Patricia Goedicke
Jorie Graham
Judy Grahn
Susan Griffin
Barbara Guest
Marilyn Hacker
Rachel Hadas
Jessica T. Hagedorn
Joy Harjo
Lyn Hejinian
Jane Hirshfield
Linda Hogan
Fanny Howe
Susan Howe
Lisa Jarnot
Paulette Jiles
Judith Johnson
Patricia Spears Jones
June Jordan
Shirley Kaufman

Jane Kenyon
Faye Kicknosway
Carolyn Kizer
Maxine Kumin
Joanne Kyger
Anne Lauterbach
Denise Levertov
Lyn Lifshin
Shirley Geok-lin Lim
Naomi Long Madgett
Bernadette Mayer
Heather McHugh
Sandra McPherson
Judith Minty
Susan Mitchell
Honor Moore
Thylias Moss
Carol Muske
Alice Notley
Naomi Shihab Nye
Joyce Carol Oates
Sharon Olds
Mary Oliver
Alicia Ostriker
Rochelle Owens
Linda Pastan
Molly Peacock
Marge Piercy
Minnie Bruce Pratt
Naomi Replansky
Joan Retallack
Adrienne Rich
Carolyn M. Rodgers
Wendy Rose
Mary Jo Salter
Sonia Sanchez
Leslie Scalapino
Gjertrud Schnackenberg
Ntozake Shange
Leslie Marmon Silko
Mary Ellen Solt
Cathy Song
Elizabeth Spires
Susan Stewart
Chase Twichell
Constance Urdang
Jean Valentine
Mona Van Duyn
Ellen Bryant Voigt
Diane Wakoski
Anne Waldman
Rosmarie Waldrop
Nancy Willard
C. D. Wright

Australian

Caroline Caddy
Lee Cataldi
Rosemary Dobson
J. S. Harry
Dorothy Hewett

Antigone Kefalá
Jennifer Maiden
Rhyll McMaster
Jan Owen
Elizabeth Riddell
Judith Rodriguez
Gig Ryan
Jennifer Strauss
Ania Walwicz
Judith Wright
Fay Zwicky

British
Fleur Adcock
Moniza Alvi
Elizabeth Bartlett
Patricia Beer
Anne Beresford
Alison Brackenbury
Heather Buck
Kate Clanchy
Wendy Cope
Julia Copus
Carol Ann Duffy
Maureen Duffy
Helen Dunmore
Jane Duran
U. A. Fanthorpe
Vicki Feaver
Elaine Feinstein
Elizabeth Garrett
Lavinia Greenlaw
Sophie Hannah
Selima Hill
Elizabeth Jennings
Amryl Johnson
Jenny Johnson
Jenny Joseph
Sylvia Kantaris
Judith Kazantzis
Lotte Kramer
Sarah Maguire
Gerda Mayer
Cilla McQueen
Maggie O'Sullivan
Alice Oswald
Fiona Pitt-Kethley
Sheenagh Pugh
Denise Riley
Carol Rumens
Gig Ryan
Carole Satyamurti
Jo Shapcott
Penelope Shuttle
Pauline Stainer
Anne Stevenson
Susan Wicks

Canadian
Margaret Atwood
Roo Borson

Marilyn Bowering
Dionne Brand
Di Brandt
Elizabeth Brewster
Nicole Brossard
Norma Cole
Jeni Couzyn
Lorna Crozier
Mary di Michele
Joan Finnigan
Kristjana Gunnars
Claire Harris
Anne Hebert
Paulette Jiles
Joy Kogawa
Jay Macpherson
Daphne Marlatt
Florence McNeil
Erin Mouré
Rona Murray
Susan Musgrave
Anne Szumigalski
Sharon Thesen
Phyllis Webb

Caribbean
Marlene Nourbese Philip

Chilean
Marjorie Agosín

Chinese
Siew-Yue Killingley

Danish
Pia Tafdrup

Dutch
Judith Herzberg

French
Anne-Marie Albiach
Caroline Bergvall

Ghanaian
Ama Ata Aidoo

Greek
Olga Broumas

Guyanese
Grace Nichols

Indian
Meena Alexander
Kamala Das
Eunice de Souza
Suniti Namjoshi

Irish
Sara Berkeley

TITLE INDEX

The following list includes the titles of all books listed in the Poetry section of the entries in the book. The name in parenthesis is meant to direct the reader to the appropriate entry where full publication information is given.

Messenger (Valentine), 1979
Metamorphopsia (Cole), 1988
Metel: stixi (Akhmadulina), 1977
Mexico Blondé (Kyger), 1981
Mezza Voce (Albiach), 1984
Midnight Was My Cry (Kizer), 1971
Midwinter Day (Mayer), 1982
Midwinter Mandala (Shuttle), 1973
Mimosa (di Michele), 1981
Mind Has Mountains (Jennings), 1966
Minefield (Kazantzis), 1977
Minute by Glass Minute (Stevenson), 1982
Mirrors of Astonishment (Hadas), 1993
Mrs. Noah and the Minoan Queen (Rodriguez), 1983
Modern Fairy Tale (Beresford), 1972
Modern Secrets (Lim), 1989
Modulations for Solo Voice (Levertov), 1977
MOIRA (Cole), 1995
Moments of Grace (Jennings), 1979
Monkey on the Analyst's Couch (Mayer), 1980
Monkey Shadows (Bhatt), 1991
Monkeys' Wedding (Couzyn), 1972
Monsoon History (Lim), 1994
Monster (di Prima), 1961
Moon Crossing Bridge (Gallagher), 1992
Moon Has a Complicated Geography (Wakoski), 1969
Moon Is Always Female (Piercy), 1980
Moon Meal (Shuttle), 1973
Moonshots (Adnan), 1966
Mop Mop Georgette (Riley), 1993
Morden Tower Reading 3 (Stevenson), 1977
Mordre en sa chair (Brossard), 1966
More Naked Charm (Lifshin), 1979
More Waters (Lifshin), 1977
Morning Glory (Rodgers), 1989
Morning in the Burned House (Atwood), 1995
Mortal Light (Garrett), 1990
Moscow Mansions (Guest), 1973
Mother/Child Papers (Ostriker), 1980
Mother Love (Dove), 1995
mother, not mother (Brandt), 1992
Motherland (Shapcott), 1996
Motorcycle Betrayal Poems (Wakoski), 1971
Mountain Moving Day (Lifshin), 1974
Mouth on Paper (Cortez), 1977
Moving (Mayer), 1971
Moving by Touch (Lifshin), 1972
Moving House (Bornholdt), 1989
Moving Image (Wright), 1946
Mudcrab at Gambaro's (Rodriguez), 1980
Mujeres de humo (Agosín), 1987
Museum (Dove), 1983
Museum (Lifshin), 1973
Musicality (Guest), 1988
Mutual Aid (Mayer), 1985
My Bird Book (Cole), 1991
My Black Horse (Gallagher), 1995
My Darling Camel (Hill), 1988
My Father Was a Toltec (Castillo), 1988
My First Play (Darragh), 1974
my hands to myself (Darragh), 1975

My House (Giovanni), 1972
My Mother's Body (Piercy), 1985
My Mother's Fire (Lifshin), 1997
My Wicked, Wicked Ways (Cisneros), 1987
Mysteries of the Home (Meehan), 1996

Naked Charm (Lifshin), 1976
Naked Poems (Webb), 1965
Nakedness of the Fathers (Ostriker), 1994
Naming Our Destiny (Jordan), 1989
Nancy Willard Reader (Willard), 1993
Nappy Edges (Shange), 1978
Når der går hul på en engel (Tafdrup), 1981
Narcissa Notebook (Drake), 1973
Natural Affinities (Funkhouser), 1983
Natural Birth (Derricotte), 1983
Natural Disasters and Other Festive Occasions (Shange), 1977
Natural History in Three Incomplete Parts (O'Sullivan), 1985
Near Changes (Van Duyn), 1990
Near-Johannesburg Boy (Brooks), 1986
Nearness of You (Kizer), 1986
Necessary Sugar (di Michele), 1983
Necessities of Life (Rich), 1966
Neck Verse (Fanthorpe), 1992
Necklace of Mirrors (Rumens), 1978
Necromance (Armantrout), 1991
Nevrazumitelny (Mulford), 1991
New As.... (di Prima), 1969
New Days (Jordan), 1974
New Faces of 1952 (Chernoff), 1985
New Handbook of Heaven (di Prima), 1963
New Herball (Willard), 1968
New Italian Poetry (Rosselli), 1981
New Mexico Poem, June-July 1967 (di Prima), 1968
New Shoes (Fraser), 1978
New Territory (Boland), 1967
New Year's Garland for My Students (Levertov), 1970
News from the Front (Kantaris), 1983
Next (Clifton), 1987
Night Feed (Boland), 1982
Night Lake (Valentine), 1992
Night Photograph (Greenlaw), 1993
Night Porch (Valentine), 1994
Night Rainbows (Owen), 1994
Night-Scene, the Garden (Alexander), 1992
Night Traveler (Oliver), 1978
Night Walk (Borson), 1981
Night Workers of Ragnarok (Gunnars), 1985
Nightless Nights (Oates), 1981
Nightmare Factory (Kumin), 1970
Nineteen Masks for the Naked Poet (Willard), 1971
No Fee: A Line or Two for Free (Mulford, Riley), 1979
No Hassles (Waldman), 1971
No Language Is Neutral (Brand), 1990
No Longer Two People (Crozier, as Lorna Uher), 1979
No Man's Grove (Lim), 1985
No Voyage (Oliver), 1963
Noche estrellada (Agosín), 1996
Nodes (Cluysenaar), 1969
Nonconformist's Memorial (Howe), 1993
North Poems (Lifshin), 1976

Sun the Blond Out (Waldman), 1975
Sunday before Winter (Bowering), 1984
Sunday Skaters (Salter), 1994
Sunday Water: 13 Anti Ghazals (Webb), 1982
Sundial (Clarke), 1978
Sunrise (Nichols), 1996
Sunrise North (Brewster), 1972
Sure Shot (Funkhouser), 1992
Survivors (Beer), 1963
Swan's Island (Spires), 1985
Swimmers, Dancers (Leggott), 1991
Swimming Lessons (Willard), 1996
Swimming Out of History (McNeil), 1991

Taboo Man (Musgrave), 1981
Tabula Rosa (DuPlessis), 1987
Tactics (Maiden), 1974
Taina: novye stikhi (Akhmadulina), 1983
Take Heart (Peacock), 1989
Taking Notice (Hacker), 1980
Talismans for Children (Atwood), 1965
Talking of Trees (Senior), 1986
Tamarind Season (Goodison), 1980
Taos Poems (Rose), 1974
Tapestry and the Web (Kyger), 1965
Tarts and Muggers (Musgrave), 1982
Taxing the Rain (Shuttle), 1994
Ten Oxherding Pictures (Clifton), 1989
Tender (Derricotte), 1997
Tentacles, Leaves (Lifshin), 1972
Tenth Muse (Kantaris), 1983
Terrible Children (Hacker), 1967
Terrible Stories (Clifton), 1996
Territorialsang, en Jerusalemkomposition (Tafdrup), 1994
Terrorism (Wright), 1978
Thanking My Mother for Piano Lessons (Wakoski), 1969
That Bread Should Be (O'Sullivan), 1996
That Distance Apart (Kay), 1991
That They Were at the Beach (Scalapino), 1985
There (Adnan), 1996
There: In the Light of the Darkness of the Self and of the Other (Adnan), 1997
There's Sky above My Sky (di Michele), 19??
Thing in the Gap-Stone Style (Oswald), 1996
Things That I Do in the Dark (Jordan), 1977
Thinking Heart (Joseph), 1978
Thinking of Skins (Rumens), 1993
Third Child; Zian (Bowering), 1978
Thirsty Weather (Kefalá), 1978
Thirteen Waves (McAlpine), 1986
This Big Face (D⸱   ⸱t), 1988
This Eati⸱₋ ⸱⸱d W⸱ ⸱ing at the Same Time Is Associated Alright (Scalapino), 1979
This Kind of Bird Flies Backward (di Prima), 1958
This Series Has Been Discontinued (Finnigan), 1981
This Time of Year (Fainlight), 1994
This Water Baby (Wakoski), 1971
This Way Daybreak Comes (Anzaldúa), 1986
Thomas and Beulah (Dove), 1986
Thorns (Philip), 1980
Those Who Ride the Night Winds (Giovanni), 1983

Thought Is the Bride of What Thinking (Hejinian), 1976
Threads: Rosa Luxemburg from Prison (Cooper), 1979
Three Fates (Dobson), 1984
Three Has Gone (Kay), 1994
Three Zero, Turning 30 (Notley), 1982
Through the Glass, Darkly (Finnigan), 1963
Thrown Voices (Duffy, C.), 1986
Tigers (Adcock), 1967
Time and Motion (Kantaris), 1975
Time of Bees (Van Duyn), 1964
Time-Slips (Cluysenaar), forthcoming
Time Traveller (Oates), 1989
Time Watching (Mayer), 1995
Time-Zones (Adcock), 1991
Times and Seasons (Jennings), 1992
Time's Power (Rich), 1989
Tinerete (Cassian), 1953
To a Young Poet (Waldman), 1979
To Be of Use (Piercy), 1973
To Disembark (Brooks), 1981
To See the Matter Clearly (Fainlight), 1968
To See, To Take (Van Duyn), 1970
To Stay Alive (Levertov), 1971
To the Quick (McHugh), 1987
To Us All Flowers Are Roses (Goodison), 1990
Tomb of the Kings (Hebert), 1967
Tombeau des rois (Hebert), 1953
Tongues We Speak (Goedicke), 1989
Tonight This Savage Rite (Das), 1979
Touch of Ginger (Zwicky), 1991
Touch Papers (Kazantzis), 1982
Touch to My Tongue (Marlatt), 1984
Tough Company (Wakoski), 1976
Tourist in Kyoto (McAlpine), 1993
tout regard (Brossard), 1989
Toward the Splendid City (Agosín), 1994
Towards Dawn (Johnson, Jenny), 1991
Tower of Glass (Pitt-Kethley), 1985
Trail That Turns on Itself (Goedicke), 1978
Train Called Judah (Rodgers), 1996
Translation (Rodgers), 1980
Translation into Fiction (Harris), 1984
Translation of the Gospel Back into Tongues (Wright), 1981
Transparence of November Snow (Borson), 1985
Transparency of Grief (Crozier), 1996
Travel/Writing (Walwicz), 1989
Travelling behind Glass (Stevenson), 1974
Travelling to Find a Remedy (Harris), 1986
Tread Carefully in Paradise (Johnson, A.), 1991
Treble Poets 2 (Mayer), 1975
Tree Telling of Orpheus (Levertov), 1968
Trees of August (di Michele), 1978
Tremble (Wright), 1996
Trembling Hearts in the Bodies of Dogs (Hill), 1994
Tremendous World in Her Head: Selected Poems (Hewett), 1989
Tributes (Jennings), 1989
Trilogy of Rain (Solt), 1970
Trio (Webb), 1954
Trio Poetry (McGuckian), 1981
Trip Out and Fall Back (Kyger), 1974
Triumph of Achilles (Glück), 1985

NOTES ON
ADVISERS AND CONTRIBUTORS

ABSE, Dannie. Poet, playwright, and novelist. Author of poetry collections *Tenants of the House,* 1959, *Way Out in the Centre,* 1981, and *On the Evening Road,* 1994; also author of novels, including *Some Corner of an English Field,* 1956, and *There Was a Young Man from Cardiff,* 1994. **Essay:** Gjertrude Schnackenberg.

ACKERSON, Duane. Employment economist, State of Oregon Employment Department, Salem, Oregon. Former director of creative writing, Idaho State University, Pocatello, Idaho. Author of *The Bird at the End of the Universe,* 1997, *The Eggplant and Other Absurdities,* 1977, and articles in *Contemporary Poets.* Editor, *A Prose Poem Anthology,* 1970, and *"But Is It Poetry?": An Anthology of One Line Poems,* 1972; editor and co-contributor, *Works: Edson Benedikt Ackerson,* 1972; co-editor, *54 Prose Poems,* 1974. Publisher/editor of poetry magazine *The Dragonfly* and Dragonfly Press, 1969-77. Co-translator, *The Great Mystical Circus* (Brazilian poet Jorge de Lima), 1978. **Essays:** Ai; Barbara Drake; Sandra Gilbert; Carol Muske; Mary Ellen Solt.

AGUERO, Kathleen. Assistant professor, Pine Manor College, Chestnut Hill, Massachusetts. Author of *Thirsty Day,* 1977, and *The Real Weather,* 1987. Editor of *A Gift of Tongues: Critical Challenges in Contemporary American Poetry,* 1987, *An Ear to the Ground: An Anthology of American Poetry,* 1989, and *Daily Fare: Essays from the Multiculture Experience,* 1993. **Essays:** Robin Becker; Ellen Bryant Voigt.

ALBINSKI, Nan Bowman. Senior research associate, A-NZ Studies Center, Pennsylvania State University, University Park. Author of *Women's Utopias in British and American Fiction,* 1988, and numerous articles on utopian, Australian, and New Zealand fiction. **Essays:** Dorothy Hewett; Jennifer Maiden; Cilla McQueen; Jennifer Strauss; Judith Wright.

ANDRE, Michael. Executive director, Unmuzzled Ox Books and Magazine, New York. Author of the poetry books *Get Serious, My Regrets, Studying the Ground for Holes, Letters Home, Jabbing the Ass Hole Is High Comedy,* and *It As It.* Also author of *The Poets' Encyclopedia;* contributor of articles to *Art News* and *Village Voice.* **Essay:** Maxine Chernoff.

ARCHAMBEAU, Robert. Assistant professor of English, Lake Forest College, Lake Forest, Illinois. Author of articles about contemporary poetry and postcolonialism in various journals. Editor, *The Poetry of John Matthias,* forthcoming from Ohio University Press. **Essay:** Di Brandt.

AUGUSTINE, Jane. Associate professor of English, Pratt Institute, Brooklyn, New York. Author of *Lit by the Earth's Dark Blood,* 1977, and *Journeys,* 1985; contributor of fiction to *Images of Women in Literature,* 4th edition, 1986, and poetry to literary magazines. **Essays:** Marilyn Hacker; Judith Johnson; Rochelle Owens; Constance Urdang; Jean Valentine; Mona Van Duyn.

BEAKE, Fred. Co-editor of the *Poet's Voice;* editor of Mammon Press. Poetry reviewer for *Stand* and *Acumen.* Contributor of poems, translations, and some criticism to various British magazines. Author of works of poetry, including *The Fisher Queen,* 1988, *The Whiteness of Her Becoming,* 1992, *The Imaginations of Mr. Shelley,* 1993, and *Towards the West,* 1995. Currently at work on a book on H.D. and a translation of Aristophanes. **Essays:** Wendy Mulford; Jenny Johnson.

BIRKETT, Jennifer. Professor of French studies, University of Birmingham. Author of *The Sins of the Fathers: Decadence in France and Europe, 1870-1914,* 1986. Editor and translator of *The Body and the Dream: French Erotic Fiction 1846-1900,* 1983, and editor of *Determined Women: The Construction of the Female Subject, 1900-1990* (with Elizabeth Harvey), 1990. **Essays:** Anne Cluysenaar; Elaine Feinstein.

BOLDEN, B.J. Assistant professor of English, Chicago State University, Chicago, Illinois. Former visiting associate professor of African-American studies, University of Illinois at Urbana-Champaign. Managing editor, *Warpland: A Journal of Black Literature and Ideas,* published by the Gwendolyn Brooks Center at Chicago State University. Author of *Urban Rage in Bronzeville: Social Commentary in the Poetry of Gwendolyn Brooks, 1945-1960,* 1997. **Essays:** Ama Ata Aidoo; Diana Chang; Lucille Clifton; Sonia Sanchez; Mabel Segun.

BORN, Anne. Freelance poet, critic, and translator. Tutor of poetry at Exeter & Devon UK Arts Centre. Formerly tutor of Danish at Cambridge University, and English literature at Oxford University. Author of nine poetry collections, including *Seeing Through,* 1994, and *Slant as an Open Door,* 1995. Contributor of articles to *PN Review, Industrial Archaeology Review, Transactions of the Devonshire Association,* and other periodicals. Many published translations, including Isak Dinesen's *Letters from Africa,* novels by Henrik Stangerup, and poetry by Pia Tafdrup, Agneta Pleijel (Swedish), Bo Carpelan, and Solveig von Schoultz (Finland-Swedish). **Essay:** Pia Tafdrup.

BROADDUS, Will. Graduate, Yale University, 1982; winner of Albert Stanborough Cook Prize for poetry. Editorial posts include Charles Scribner's Sons Publishers, and associate editorships at Atheneum, and Chelsea House Publishers. Associate editor and contributing writer, *Foundation News Magazine;* author of poetry reviews to *Boston Book Review.* **Essays:** Jessica Hagedorn; Shirley Kaufman; Gwyneth Lewis.

BRUCHAC, Joseph. Editor, *Greenfield Review,* Greenfield Center, New York. Author of numerous collections of poetry, including *Near the Mountains,* 1987, and *Langes Gedachtins/Long Memory,* 1989, as well as novels, collections of traditional Native American stories, and a book of interviews with Native American poets. Editor of *Songs from This Earth on Turtle's Back,* 1983, *New Voices from the Longhouse,* 1989, and many other books. **Essays:** Lyn Lifshin; Leslie Marmon Silko.

BUCKINGHAM, Hugh. Senior lecturer in English, Richmond College, Surrey. **Essay:** Fiona Pitt-Kethley.

BURWELL, Rose Marie. Professor of English, Northern Illinois University, DeKalb. Author of *A Chronological Catalogue of the Reading of D.H. Lawrence,* 1970 (addenda in *D.H. Lawrence Review,* 1973), and several articles on Joyce Carol Oates. Contributor to *A D.H. Lawrence Handbook,* 1982. **Essay:** Joyce Carol Oates.

BUTTERICK, George F. Former curator of literary archives and lecturer in English, University of Connecticut, Storrs. Author of *A Guide to the Maximus Poems of Charles Olson,* 1978, *Editing the Maximus Poems: Supplementary Notes,* 1983, and several books of poetry, including *The Collected Poems,* edited by Richard Blevius, 1988. Editor of *The Postmoderns: The New American Poetry Revised,* 1982, and works by Vincent Ferrini and by Charles Olson. Died 1988. **Essay:** Joanne Kyger.

CAMPBELL, Katie. Writer and freelance journalist, London. Author of *What He Really Wants Is a Dog* (short stories), 1989, and *Let Us Leave Them Believing* (poetry), 1991. **Essays:** Fleur Adcock; Gillian Clarke; Lorna Goodison; Jenny Joseph; Sharon Olds; Marge Piercy.

CAREW, Rivers. Former chief sub-editor, BBC World Service, London. Joint editor, *The Dubliner/Dublin Magazine,* 1964-69. Co-author, *Figures out of Mist* (poems), 1966. Contributor to *The Concise Encyclopedia of English and American Poets and Poetry* (Hutchinson). Contributor of article on T.S. Eliot and Georges Rouault, *The Hibbert Journal.* **Essays:** Heather Buck; Helen Dunmore; Alison Fell; Sarah Maguire.

CATON, James. Former lecturer, Buffalo State College, New York. **Essay:** Beverly Dahlen.

CHARTERS, Ann. Professor of English, University of Connecticut, Storrs. Author of *Nobody: The Story of Bert Williams,* 1970, *Kerouac: A Biography,* 1973, *I Love: The Story of Vladimir Mayakovsky and Lili Brik* (with Samuel Charters), 1979, and a study of ragtime. Editor of *The Beats: Literary Bohemians in Postwar America,* 2 vols., 1983, *The Story and Its Writer,* 1990, *The Portable Beat Reader,* 1992, *The Kerouac Reader,* 1995, and *Selected Kerouac Letters,* 1995. **Essay:** Alice Notley.

CHRISTENSEN, Paul. Professor of modern literature, Texas A&M University, College Station. Author of several books of poetry, as well as *Charles Olson: Call Him Ishmael,* 1979. Editor of *In Love, In Sorrow: The Complete Correspondence of Charles Olson and Edward Dahlverg,* 1990, and *Minding the Underworld: Clayton Eshleman and Late Postmodernism,* 1991. **Essays:** Lyn Hejinian; Naomi Shihab Nye; Rosmarie Waldrop.

COLOMBO, John Robert. Poet and editor; columns have appeared in *Toronto Star* and other periodicals. Author of books, including *Abracadabra,* 1967, *Proverbial Play,* 1975, and *Off Earth,* 1987. Editor of numerous poetry anthologies; translator. **Essays:** Elizabeth Brewster; Kristjana Gunnars; Jay Macpherson.

COOKSON, William. Editor, *Agenda* magazine, London. Author of books of poetry *Dream Traces,* 1975, *Spell,* 1986, and *Vestiges (1955-1995),* 1995, as well as *A Guide to the Cantos of Ezra Pound,* 1984. Editor of *Ezra Pound: Selected Prose, 1909-1965,* 1973, and *Agenda—An Anthology 1959-1993,* 1994. **Essay:** Anne Beresford.

COTTON, John. Chairman of The Poetry Society, 1972-74 and 1977, treasurer, 1986-89. Author of *Old Movies and Other Poems, Kilroy Was Here* (both Chatto & Windus), *The Storyville Portraits,* and *Here's Looking At You Kid* (both Headland Publications). Contributor to numerous magazines including *Ambit, Times Literary Supplement, Acumen,* and *Poetry* (Chicago). Advisory editor, *Contemporary Poets,* St. James Press. **Essays:** Moniza Alvi; Elizabeth Bartlett; Wendy Cope; Sophie Hannah; Sylvia Kantaris; Lotte Kramer; Gerda Mayer; Carol Rumens; Carole Satyamurti; Jo Shapcott; Pauline Stainer.

CURTIS, Tony. Senior lecturer in English, Polytechnic of Wales, Pontypridd. Author of poetry collections, including *The Deerslayers,* 1978, and *Taken for Pearls,* 1993. **Essay:** Sheenagh Pugh.

DAVIDSON, Cynthia. Ph.D. in English, University of Illinois, Chicago. Editor of *Rio, an Online Journal of the Arts.* Author of *Athena's Mother* (poems); also author of "Riviera's Golem, Haraway's Cyborg," an article about the relationship of Baudrillard's simulation of crisis to events in William Gibson's *Neuromancer,* published in *Science-Fiction Studies,* no. 69, 1996. Contributor of poems to *ACM, Private, Wire,* and other journals. **Essays:** Chana Bloch; Nina Cassian; Judith Herzberg.

DELVILLE, Michel. F.N.R.S. Senior research assistant, University of Liège, Belgium. Author of *J.G. Ballard* (forthcoming); contributor of articles on William Faulkner, Margaret Atwood, James Joyce, Gertrude Stein, Charles Tomlinson, and Michael Moorcock to various periodicals. **Essays:** Anne-Marie Albiach; Fiona Templeton.

DILLARD, R.H.W. Professor of English, Hollins College, Virginia. Editor-in-chief, *Children's Literature;* vice-president, *Film Journal.* Author of collections, including *The Greeting: New and Selected Poems,* 1981, and *Just Here, Just Now,* 1994. **Essay:** Carol Ann Duffy.

DORSINVILLE, Max. Professor of English, McGill University, Montreal. Author of *Caliban without Prospero: An Essay on Quebec and Black Literature,* 1974, *Le Pays Natal: Essais sur les Litteratures Du Tiers-Monde et du Quebec,* 1983, and *Solidarites: Tiens-Monde et Litterature Comparee,* 1988. Contributor of articles to *PMLA, Canadian Literature,* and *Livres et Auturs Quebecois.* **Essay:** Joan Finnigan.

DOVE, Rita. See her own entry. Advisor, *Contemporary Women Poets.*

DOWLING, David. Senior lecturer in English, Massey University, Palmerston North, New Zealand. Author of *Introducing Bruce Mason,* 1983, *Bloomsbury Aesthetics and the Novels of Forster and Woolf,* 1984, *Fictions of Nuclear Disaster,* 1986, *William Faulkner,* 1989, and *Mrs. Dalloway,* 1990. Editor of *Novelists on Novelists,* 1983, *Every Kind of Weather: Bruce Mason,* 1986, and *Katherine Mansfield: Dramatic Sketches,* 1988. **Essay:** Lauris Edmond.

ELLEDGE, Jim. Professor of English, Department of English, Illinois State University. Poet, fiction writer, scholar, editor. Author of four books of poetry, including *Into the Arms of the Universe* which won the Stonewall Series award; also author of six scholarly books. Contributed to numerous journals, including *Paris Review, Chicago Review, Fiction International,* and *Crazyhorse.* Publisher and editor of Thorngate Road, a press. **Essays:** Paula Gunn Allen; Judy Grahn; Susan Griffin.

ETTER, Carrie. M.F.A., University of California, Irvine. Author of poetry published in periodicals, including *Ascent, Cimarron Review, Literary Review, Poet & Critic, Poet Lore, Poetry Wales, Seneca Review,* and numerous other journals, as well as anthologies. Author of book reviews. Former Southern California editor, *Po-*

etry Flash: A Literary Review and Calendar for the West. **Essay:** Sharon Doubiago.

FINK, Jennifer. Ph.D., New York University, 1997. Has written widely on contemporary women poets. Editor, currently completing a book on Evelyn Lau and Meena Alexander to be published by University of Minnesota Press. **Essays:** Anne Lauterbach; Susan Stewart.

FOUST, Graham. Former editor of *Phoebe: A Journal of Literary Arts.* Poems appear in various journals, including *Lingo, Painted Bride Quarterly, no roses review,* and *Volt.* **Essays:** Norma Cole; Amelia Rosselli.

FRASER, Kathleen. See her own entry. **Essay:** Lisa Jarnot.

GERMAIN, Edward B. Instructor in English, Phillips Academy, Andover, Massachusetts. Editor of *Flag of Ecstasy: Selected Poems of Charles Henri Ford,* 1972, *Shadows of the Sun: The Diaries of Harry Crosby,* 1977, and *English and American Surrealist Poetry,* 1977. **Essay:** Thylias Moss.

GILBERT, Reid. Professor of English and drama, Capilano College, Vancouver; member of editorial board, *Canadian Theatre Review* and *Theatre Research in Canada.* Author of play *A Glass Darkly,* 1972; contributor of articles in *Theatre Journal, Theatre Research International,* and other journals. **Essay:** Daphne Marlatt.

GIUNTA, Edvige. Assistant professor of English, Jersey City State College. Former visiting assistant professor of English at Union College, New York. Author of articles in various journals; contributor to *Feminist Writers,* 1996. **Essay:** Ana Castillo.

GLOVER, Michael. Freelance writer and editor. Reviewer for *Books and Bookmen, British Book News, PN Review, Melbourne Age, Observer,* and *School Librarian.* **Essay:** Judith Kazantzis.

GOLDENSOHN, Lorrie. Teacher of poetry and fiction writing, Vassar College, Poughkeepsie, New York. Author of *The Tether* (poems), 1984, and *Elizabeth Bishop: The Biography of a Poetry,* 1992. **Essays:** Olga Broumas; Jane Cooper; Elizabeth Spires.

GORDON, Lois. Professor of English and comparative literature, Fairleigh Dickinson University, Teaneck, New Jersey. Author of *Stratagems to Uncover Nakedness: The Dramas of Harold Pinter,* 1969, *Donald Barthelme,* 1981, *Robert Coover: The Universal Fictionmaking Process,* 1983, *American Chronicle: Six Decades in American Life 1920-1980,* 1987, *American Chronicle, Seven Decades in American Life, 1920-1989,* 1990, and numerous articles on contemporary authors and American culture. **Essay:** Adrienne Rich.

GOUGH, Jenny. Poet; 1992 graduate of Temple University's M.A. program in creative writing. Contributor of poetry to *6ix, TO:, CHAIN* and *The Gertrude Stein Awards for Innovative American Poetry,* 1994-95; also contributor of articles on art to the *Washington Review.* **Essays:** Rachel Blau DuPlessis; Irena Klepfisz; Maggie O'Sullivan.

GREEN, Anne-Elizabeth. Doctoral candidate, New York University, New York. Assistant in the undergraduate program in women's studies, New York University. Editorial director of *revolution/evolution,* graduate and undergraduate journal of contemporary gender issues at New York University. **Essays:** Marilyn Chin; Cathy Song.

GREENLAW, Lavinia. Poet, freelance writer, teacher, and reviewer. Has held several writers residencies, including one at the Science Museum, London. British Council fellow in writing, Amherst College, Amherst, Massachusetts, 1995. Author of collections, including *Night Photograph,* 1993, and *A World Where News Travelled Slowly,* 1997. See her own entry. **Essays:** Vicki Feaver; Elizabeth Garrett; Nuala Ní Dhomhnaill.

GUTTMAN, Naomi. Assistant professor of English, Hamilton College, Clinton, New York. Her book of poems, *Reasons for Winter,* 1991, won the A. M. Klein Award for poetry in 1992. Her article "Dream of the Mother Language: Myth and History in *She Tries Her Tongue, Her Silence Softly Breaks*" on the work of M. Nourbese Philip is forthcoming in *MELUS.* Contributor of poetry and fiction to numerous journals. **Essay:** M. Nourbese Philip.

HALLEY, Cathy. Instructor, University of Iowa, Iowa City. Author of articles about lesbian humorists and poets to various journals. **Essays:** Honor Moore; Minnie Bruce Pratt.

HERZOG, Anne. Assistant professor of English, West Chester University, West Chester, Pennsylvania. Currently researching the intersection of politics and poetry among U.S. women poets. Also co-editor of critical collection *"How Shall We Tell Each Other of the Poet": The Life and Writings of Muriel Rukeyser.* **Essay:** Alicia Ostriker.

HINCHEY, John. Member, Department of English, Swarthmore College, Pennsylvania. **Essay:** Anne Waldman.

HOBSBAUM, Philip Dennis. Titular Professor in English Literature, Glasgow University. Chairman of writers' groups in London, Belfast, and Glasgow. Author of books, including *Coming Out Fighting,* 1969; *Ten Elizabethan Poets* (editor), 1969; *A Reader's Guide to Charles Dickens,* 1972; *Women and Animals,* 1972; *Tradition and Experiment in English Poetry,* 1979; *A Reader's Guide to Robert Lowell,* 1988; *Wordsworth: Selected Poetry and Prose* (editor), 1989; *Metre, Rhythm and Verse Form,* 1995, and *Keats: Bicentenary Readings,* 1997. **Essays:** Kate Clanchy; Jackie Kay.

HOEY, Allen. Professor and writing coordinator, Division of Language and Literature, Bucks City Community College, King of Prussia, Pennsylvania. Author of the poetry books *A Fire in the Cold House of Being,* 1987, and *What Persists,* 1992, as well as poems in many journals, including *Georgia Review, Hudson Review Poetry,* and *Southern Review.* Contributor since 1991 to *Contemporary Literary Criticism.* **Essay:** Jane Hirshfield.

HOLM, Janis Butler. Associate professor of English, Ohio University, Athens, and associate editor, *Wide Angle: A Quarterly Journal of Film History, Theory, Criticism, and Practice.* Author of articles on cultural perceptions of gender. Editor of *The Mirror of Modestie.* **Essay:** Carolyn M. Rodgers.

HUDSON, Theodore R. Editorial consultant and former graduate professor of English, Howard University, Washington, D.C.

Author of *From LeRoi Jones to Amiri Baraka: The Literary Works,* 1973, and numerous articles. **Essays:** Lucille Clifton; Sonia Sanchez.

HUK, Ramona. Associate professor of English, University of New Hampshire, Durham. Author of *Stevie Smith* (forthcoming). Contributor of articles about contemporary poets and poet-dramatists to numerous books and journals. Editor, contributor to, and introducer of *Contemporary British Poetry: Essays in Theory and Criticism,* 1996. **Essay:** Caroline Bergvall.

JAMES, Charles L. Professor of English, Swathmore College, Pennsylvania. Author of *The Black Writer in America* (bibliography), 1969. Editor of *From the Roots: Short Stories by Black Americans,* 1970. **Essay:** Gwendolyn Brooks.

KOHLI, Devindra. Professor of English, University of Kashmir, Srinagar; editor, *The Indian Literary Review.* Author of *Virgin Whiteness,* 1968, and *Kamala Das,* 1975. Co-editor of *Heritage of English,* 1980. **Essay:** Kamala Das.

LAUTER, Estella. Chair, English Department, University of Wisconsin, Oshkosh. Author of *Women as Mythmakers: Poetry and Art by 20th-Century Women,* 1984. **Essay:** Diane Wakoski.

LUCAS, Rose. Lecturer in literature, Monash University, Caulfield East, Victoria, Australia. **Essay:** J.S. Harry.

MACGREGOR, Lynne. Freelance writer; essays on Sappho and other women writers published in *Feminist Writers,* 1996. **Essay:** Lorna Dee Cervantes.

MAGEE, Wes. Freelance writer. **Essay:** Patricia Beer.

MATHUR, Ashok. Co-Publisher, *disOrientation chapbooks* (an alternative-format poetry series), and member of the editorial collective, *absinthe* (a literary journal). Author of a book of poems, *Loveruage,* 1994. **Essay:** Erin Mouré.

MATTHEWS, William. Professor of English, City College of the City University of New York. Former associate professor and director of creative writing, University of Washington, Seattle. Author of *Ruining the New Road,* 1970, and *Time & Money: New Poems,* 1995, among others. **Essay:** Jorie Graham.

MAXWELL, Glyn. Freelance writer. **Essay:** Selima Hill.

McCARTHY, Thomas. Librarian, Cork Corporation; poetry editor, *Stet* magazine, Cork. Author of many books of poetry, including *Seven Winters in Paris,* 1989, and the novel *Without Power,* 1991. **Essay:** Eilean Ní Chuilleanain.

McDOWELL, Robert. Publisher and editor, Story Line Press, Brownsville, Oregon. Author of *Quiet Money* (poetry), 1987, *The Diviners* (poetry), 1995, and *Sound and Form in Modern Poetry* (with Harvey Gross), 1995. Editor of *Poetry after Modernism,* 1990. **Essays:** Lucie Brock-Broido; Chase Twichell.

MELTZER, David. Chair, undergraduate writing and literature program, New College of California, San Francisco. Author of poetry volumes, including *The Dark Continent,* 1967, *32 Beams of Light,*

1970, and *The Name: Selected Poetry, 1973-1983.* **Essays:** Diane Di Prima; Susan Howe.

MEYER, Bruce. Member, Department of English, University of Windsor, Ontario. Author of *In Their Words: Interviews with 14 Canadian Writers.* Editor of *Arrivals: Canadian Poetry in the Eighties, The Selected Poems of Frank Prewett,* and *Separate Islands: Contemporary British and Irish Poetry.* **Essay:** Lorna Crozier.

MILLER, Julie. Former member of the Department of English, Ohio University, Athens. **Essays:** Rita Dove; Alice Fulton.

MILLER, Tyrus. Assistant professor, Department of Comparative Literature and English, Yale University, New Haven, Connecticut. Author of *Earthworks* (poems); articles in *Textual Practice, Hambone,* and *Paideuma;* and essays on Mina Loy, C. Day Lewis, and Walter Benjamin in edited volumes. **Essays:** Barbara Guest; C.D. Wright.

MILLS, Elizabeth M. Associate professor of English, Davidson College, Davidson, North Carolina, where she has been teaching literature by women, surveys, and seminars in poetry and prose to undergraduates since 1985. Mary Lynch Johnson Lecturer, Meredith College, Raleigh, 1996. Contributor of numerous articles to various periodicals, including *Contemporary Southern Writers,* 1994, and *Oxford Companion to Women's Writing in the United States,* 1995; also contributor of reviews in journals, including *Carolina Quarterly, Pembroke Magazine,* and *South Atlantic Review.* Author of guest forword, *Contemporary Women Poets.*

MONTAGUE, John. Teacher and poet. Former Paris correspondent for the *Irish Times.* Author of books, including *A Chosen Light,* 1967, *The Cave of Night,* 1974, and *Time in Armagh,* 1993. **Essays:** Carolyn Kizer; Paula Meehan.

MORGAN, Edwin. Emeritus professor, Glasgow University. Author of books, including *Emergent Poems,* 1967, *Sonnets from Scotland,* 1984, and *Sweeping Out the Dark,* 1994. **Essay:** Liz Lochhead.

NICHOLOSON, Colin. Senior lecturer in English, University of Edinburgh. Editor of *Alexander Pope: Essays for the Tercentenary,* 1988, and *Margaret Laurence: Critical Essays on the Fiction,* 1990. **Essay:** Eunice De Souza.

NOWAK, Maril. Affiliated with Department of English, Rochester Institute of Technology, Rochester, New York. Contributor of essays to *Contemporary Writers,* 1996, *Exploring Novels,* 1997, and *Contemporary Popular Writers,* 1996. **Essay:** Nancy Willard.

O'BRIEN, Sean. Poet and founding editor, *Printer's Devil,* Brighton, East Sussex. Collections include *The Indoor Park,* 1983, *Boundary Beach,* 1989, and *Ghost Train,* 1995. **Essay:** Kathleen Jamie.

O'NEIL, Michael. Professor of English, University of Durham, U.K. Author of *The Muman Mind's Imaginings: Conflict and Achievement in Shelley's Poetry,* 1989, *Percy Bysshe Shelley: A Literary Life,* 1989, *The Stripped Bed* (poems), 1990, and *Auden, MacNeice, Spender: The Thirties Poetry* (with Gareth Reeves),

1992. Editor of *Shelley*, 1993, *Fair Copies of Shelley's Poems in European and American Libraries*, 1997, and *Keats: Bicentenary Readings*, 1997. **Essays:** Sara Berkeley; Alice Oswald; Susan Wicks.

OXLEY, William. Poet and philosopher; has also worked as accountant, part-time gardener, and actor. Contributor of poetry to magazines and journals as diverse as *Sparrown* and *The Formalist* (USA), *The Scotsman, New Statesman, Agenda, Stand, The Independent, The Spectator,* and *The Observer.* He has also read his work in UK and European radio. Most recent books of poetry include *In The Drift of Words*, 1992, *Cardboard Troy*, 1993, and *Collected Longer Poems*, 1994. Translator of the poetry of L.S. Senghor *(Poems of a Black Orpheus*, 1981); former member of the general council of the Poetry Society and ex-assistant editor of *Acumen;* editor of anthology *Completing the Picture*, 1995. **Essays:** Elma Mitchell; Jane Duran.

PAGNOULLE, Christine. Senior lecturer in English-French translation and in English literatures, University of Liège, Belgium, specializing in 20th-century poetry. Author of *Malcolm Lowry: voyage au fond de nos abîmes*, 1977, and *David Jones: A Commentary on Some Poetic Fragments*, 1987, and of numerous articles on Caribbean, African, and Canadian writers as well as on literary translations. Editor of three books, two collections of essays on translation, *Les gens du passage*, 1993, *Cross-Words* (in collaboration with Ian Mason), 1995, and *Writing on Short Stories: A Tribute to Paulette Michel-Michot*, 1997. Translator of contemporary poetry, both for anthologies and for periodicals. **Essays:** Amryl Johnson; Joy Kogawa.

PAUL, Angelina. Fulbright visiting scholar, University of Pennsylvania, Philadelphia. Doctoral candidate in English literature at the University of Hyderabad, India. Currently doing research in American fiction about India. Interested in American fiction, Indian writing in English, and Native American Literature. **Essay:** Suniti Namjoshi.

PAUL, Jay S. Professor and chair of English, Christopher Newport University, Newport News, Virginia. Author of poetry, fiction, essays, and reviews in periodicals. **Essays:** Nikki Giovanni; Heather McHugh; Linda Pastan.

PERLOFF, Marjorie. Professor of English and comparative literature, Stanford University, California. Author of *Rhyme and Meaning in the Poetry of Yeats*, 1970, *The Poetic Art of Robert Lowell*, 1973, *Frank O'Hara: Poet among Painters*, 1977, *The Other Tradition: Towards a Postmodern Poetry*, 1980, *George Oppen, Man and Poet*, 1981, *The Poetics of Indeterminacy*, 1982, *The Dance of the Intellect: Studies in the Poetry of the Pound Tradition*, 1985, *The Futurist Moment*, 1986, *Poetic License: Essays in Modern and Postmodern Poetics*, 1989, and *Radical Artifice: Writing Poetry in the Age of Media*, 1991. Editor of *Postmodern Genres*, 1989, and *John Cage: Composed in America* (with Charles Junkerman), 1994. Advisor, *Contemporary Women Poets.* **Essay:** Kathleen Fraser.

PETERSEN, Kristen Holst. Member of the Commonwealth Literature Division, University of Aarhus, Denmark; reviewer for *Danida.* Author of *A Critical View of John Pepper Clark's Selected Poems*, 1981. Editor of *Enigma of Values* (with Anna Ru-

therford), 1975, *Cowries and Kobos: The West African Oral Tale and Short Story* (with Rutherford), 1981, and *Displaced Persons* (with Rutherford), 1988. **Essay:** Grace Nichols.

POTOK, Rena. Lecturer, University of Pennsylvania, Philadelphia. Associate editor, *Jewish Quarterly Review.* Author, *Occupied Territories: Bodies and Borders in Modern Irish and Israeli Fiction* (in progress); contributor of articles about Palestinian Israeli and Jewish American literature to *Borders, Exiles, Diasporas*, 1998, and *Jewish American Women Writers*, 1994. Translator of poems by Anton Shammas, published in *International Quarterly.* **Essay:** Etel Adnan.

PURSGLOVE, Glyn. Lecturer in English, University College, Swansea. Author of *Francis Warner and Tradition: An Introduction to the Plays*, 1981, and *Francis Warner's Poetry*, 1988. Editor of *Distinguishing Poetry: Writings on Poetry by William Oxley*, 1989, and *Tasso's "Aminta" and Other Poems by Henery Reynolds.* **Essay:** Alison Brackenbury.

RAY, David. Professor emeritus, University of Missouri, Kansas City. Published works include *The Farm in Calabria and Other Poems*, 1980, and *Wool Highways*, 1993. Editor of numerous anthologies. **Essay:** Patricia Goedicke.

RECTOR, Liam. Author of *The Sorrow of Architecture* (poetry), 1984, *American Prodigy* (poetry), 1994. Contributor of poems, essays, and reviews in many journals. Editor of *The Day I Was Older: On the Poetry of Donald Hall*, 1989. **Essay:** Molly Peacock.

REIBETANZ, Julia M. Department of English, University of Toronto. Author of several articles and book on T.S. Eliot, *A Reading of Four Quartets*, Ann Arbor, 1983; forthcoming article on "Reflexivity in the Poetry of Richard Wilbur," *University of Toronto Quarterly.* **Essays:** Mary di Michele; Anne Szumigalski.

ROBERTS, Gary. Ph.D. candidate in English and American literature, Brandeis University. Contributor of articles, book reviews, and interviews to *Chicago Literary Review.* **Essay:** Jane Kenyon.

ROBINSON, James K. Professor of English, University of Cincinnati. Editor of *The Mayor of Casterbridge* by Hardy and of several anthologies. **Essays:** Tess Gallagher; Louise Glück.

ROCHE, John. Lecturer, State University of New York at Geneseo. Formerly taught at Michigan State University, Emory University, and Buffalo State College. Former coordinator of Archives Book Shop Poetry and Prose Reading Series, East Lansing, Michigan, and organizer of poetry events at Michigan State. Contributor of essays in *The Walt Whitman Quarterly Review, Educational Theory, Interdisciplinary Humanities, 19th-Century Transcendental Quarterly,* and *Feminist Writers*, 1996; also contributor of numerous book reviews to *Choice.* **Essays:** Bella Akhmadulina; Jayne Cortez; Wendy Rose.

RODDICK, Alan. Public health dentist, Christchurch, New Zealand. Author of *The Eye Corrects: Poems 1955-1965*, and *Allen Curnow*, 1980. Editor of two books of poetry by Charles Brasch. **Essay:** Jenny Bornholdt.

RODRIGUEZ, Judith. See her own entry. Advisor, *Contemporary Women Poets.* **Essays:** Caroline Caddy; Lee Cataldi; Antigone Kefala; Gig Ryan.

RODRIGUEZ, Michael. Lecturer at University of Illinois, Chicago; assistant editor of fiction journal, *Other Voices.* **Essay:** Judith Minty.

SADLER, Geoff. Freelance writer of western novels as Jeff Sadler and Wes Calhoun, and of a trilogy of plantation novels, as Geoffery Sadler. Author of a five-volume history of Chesterfield librarians and of *Journey to Freedom,* 1990, *Shirebrook in Old Picture Postcards,* 1993, and *Shirebrook,* 1994. Editor of *Write First Time: An Anthology of Work by the Shirebrook and District Writers' Group,* 1992. **Essays:** Maureen Duffy; Ruth Fainlight.

SCHENK, Susan. Assistant professor of English, University of Western Ontario, London, and editor, Brick Books. **Essay:** Sharon Thesen.

SCHULTZ, Susan M. Assistant professor of English, University of Hawaii, Honolulu. Author of *Another Childhood* (poetry chapbook), 1993; contributor of articles on modern and contemporary poetry to *Arizona Quarterly, Raritan, Sagetrieb, Talisman,* and other journals; also contributor of reviews to *Postmodern Culture* and *American Book Review.* Editor of *The Tribe of John: Ashbery and Contemporary Poetry,* 1995. **Essay:** Olive Senior.

SEDGWICK, Fred. Freelance writer and lecturer based in Ipswich, UK. Author and sometimes co-author (with wife Dawn) of seven books on education, including *Personal, Social, Moral Education,* 1994, and *Read My Mind: Young Children, Poetry and Learning,* 1997. Also author of poetry, both for adults and children (most recently *Pizza, Curry, Fish and Chips,* 1994. He is currently writing books on language and young children, and Shakespeare in the primary school. **Essay:** Julia Copus.

SHAPCOTT, Thomas W. Executive director, National Book Council of Australia; Former partner in Shapcott and Shapcott, Accountant. Author of poetry collections including *Begin with Walking,* 1972, *Turning Full Circle,* 1979, and *The City of Home,* 1995. **Essays:** Rosemary Dobson; Rhyll McMaster; Jan Owen; Elizabeth Riddell; Judith Rodriguez.

SHOPTAW, John. Member, Department of English, Princeton University, New Jersey. **Essay:** Leslie Scalapino.

SILKIN, Jon. Former professor of English and American literature, Tsukuha University, Japan, 1991-94. Author of ten collections of poetry and two critical studies; editor of several anthologies. **Essay:** Denise Riley.

SINGH, Minnie. Assistant professor of English, Loyola College, Baltimore. **Essays:** Sujata Bhatt; Imtiaz Dharker.

SMITH, A.J.M. Former professor of English, Michigan State University, East Lansing. Author of six books of poetry, including *The Classic Shade: Selected Poems,* 1978, as well as books on Robert Bridges, E.J. Pratt, and Canadian literature. Editor of many general collections of poetry and specialized collections of Canadian writing. Died 1980. **Essay:** Jay Macpherson.

SMITH, Anna. Lecturer, Department of English, University of Canterbury, Christchurch, New Zealand. Author of *Julia Kristeva: Readings in Exile and Estrangement;* contributor of essay on Keri Hulme to *Opening the Book: New Essays on New Zealand Literature,* edited by Michele Leggot and Mark Williams, 1995. **Essays:** Anne French; Keri Hulme.

SMITH, Laurel. Professor of English, Vincennes University, Vincennes, Indiana. Associate editor, *Tecumseh Review.* Contributor of articles about modern and contemporary writers in various journals; also contributor of poems to various little magazines. **Essay:** Linda Hogan.

SMITH, Stan. Professor of English, University of Dundee; director, with R.J.C. Watt, Auden Concordance Project; and general editor, Longman Critical Reader Series and *Longman Studies in 20th-Century Literature* Series. Author of *A Sadly Contracted Hero: The Comic Self in Post-War American Fiction,* 1981, *Invisible Voice: History and 20th-Century Poetry,* 1982, *W.H. Auden,* 1985, *Edward Thomas,* 1986, *W.B. Yeats: A Critical Introduction,* 1990, and *The Origins of Modernism: Eliot, Pound, Yeats and the Rhetorics of Renewal,* 1994. **Essay:** Anne Stevenson.

SMITHYMAN, Kendrick. Teacher and poet; author of collections including *The Blind Mountain and Other Poems,* 1950, *Dwarf with a Billiard Cue,* 1978, and *Auto/Biographies,* 1992. **Essay:** Elizabeth Smither.

SOJKA, Eugenia. Ph.D. in contemporary Canadian women's writing; literature instructor, Department of English, Memorial University of Newfoundland, St. John's. Contributor of articles include "Margaret Laurence and Her Existentialist Vision of Life," in *Symposium on Contemporary Literatures and Cultures of the United States of America and Canada,* 1988; "Can(n)on Firing: 'Fiction Theory' and the Texts of English Canadian and Anglo-Québec Women Writers," *Critical Mass,* summer 1992; and "Framing the Frame: A Suggestion about Critical Discourse for the Analysis of Canadian Feminist Language Oriented Writing," *Free Exchange 1993, Appropriate Discourse, Conference Proceedings.* Author of numerous reviews, including "Claire Harris's *Dipped in Shadow,*" forthcoming in *Canadian Book Review Annual 1996.* **Essay:** Claire Harris.

SRIVASTAVA, Aruna. Assistant professor of English, University of Calgary, Alberta. **Essay:** Meena Alexander.

STERN, Carol Simpson. Dean of the graduate school and professor, Department of Performance Studies, Northwestern University, Evanston, Illinois. Author of *Performance: Texts and Contexts* (with Bruce Henderson), 1993. **Essay:** Susan Musgrave.

STEVENSON, Anne. See her own entry. **Essay:** Penelope Shuttle.

STOCKS, Anthony G. Freelance writer. **Essay:** Margaret Atwood.

STRAUSS, Jennifer. See her own entry. **Essay:** Fay Zwicky.

SUTHERLAND, Fraser. Journalist and freelance editor; contributor of numerous articles and poetry reviews to periodicals, including *Toronto Daily Star, Globe and Mail,* and others. Author of poetry collections, including *In the Wake of,* 1974, and *White-faces,* 1986. **Essays:** Marilyn Bowering; Florence McNeil.

SYLVESTER, William. Professor of English and comparative literature, State University of New York, Buffalo. Author of *Honky in the Woodpile,* 1982, *Dig the Flower Children,* 1983, *Listen to the Ice,* 1984; contributor of poetry and criticism to various journals. **Essay:** Maya Angelou.

TAYLOR, Henry. Professor, American University, Washington, D.C. Author of poetry collections including the Pulitzer Award-winning *The Flying Change,* 1985. **Essay:** Mary Jo Salter.

THOMAS, Carol. Instructor in English, Bowie State University. Former instructor at University of Connecticut—Avery Point in departments of English and women's studies. Author of articles on women's issues and frequent lecturer. **Essay:** Sandra Cisneros.

THWAITE, Anthony. Poet and educator; editorial consultant, Andre Deutsch Publishers, London. Author of poetry collections including *The Owl in the Tree,* 1963, *New Confessions,* 1974, *Telling Tales,* 1983, and *The Dust of the World,* 1994; also author of critical works including *Twentieth-Century English Poetry,* 1978, and *Poetry Today: A Critical Survey of British Poetry, 1960-1995* (third edition), 1996, as well as numerous editorships of anthologies. Advisor, *Contemporary Women Poets.*

TOWNS, Saundra. Lecturer in English, Bernard Baruch College, City University of New York. Author of *Lillian Hellman,* 1989; contributor of essays and reviews to *The Nation, Black Books Bulletin, Black World, Black Position,* and other periodicals. **Essay:** June Jordan.

TRUE, Michael. Professor of English, Assumption College, Worcester, Massachusetts. Author of *Homemade Social Justice,* 1982, *Justice-Seekers, Peacemakers: 32 Portraits in Courage,* 1985, *Worcester Area Writers, 1680-1980,* 1987, *To Construct Peace: 30 More Justice Seekers,* 1991, *Ordinary People: Family Life and Global Values,* 1992, and *An Energy Field More Intense Than War: The Nonviolent Tradition and American Literature,* 1995. Contributor of articles to *Commonweal, America, The Progressive, New Republic, Boston Globe, Harvard Divinity Bulletin, American Writers,* and *Contemporary Literary Criticism.* Editor of *Daniel Berrigan: Poetry, Drama, Prose,* 1988. **Essay:** Joy Harjo.

WAGNER-MARTIN, Linda W. Hanes Professor of English, University of North Carolina, Chapel Hill. Author of *The Poems of William Carlos Williams,* 1964, *Denise Levertov,* 1967, *The Prose of William Carlos Williams,* 1970, *Hemingway and Faulkner: Inventors, Masters,* 1975, *Introducing Poems,* 1976, *John Dos Passos,* 1979, *Ellen Glasgow: Beyond Convention,* 1982, *Sylvia Plath: A Biography,* 1987, and *The Modern American Novel 1914-1945,* 1989. Editor of *Critical Essays on Sylvia Plath,* 1984, *Sylvia Plath: The Critical Heritage,* 1988, *Critical Essays on Anne Sexton,* 1989, and (with others) *Oxford Companion to Woman's Writing in the United States,* 1995. **Essay:** Carolyn Forché.

WAKOSKI, Diane. See her own entry. Advisor and co-author of introduction, *Contemporary Women Poets.* **Essays:** Maxine Kumin; Denise Levertov; Mary Oliver.

WALTON, Priscilla L. Assistant professor, University of Lethbridge, Alberta. Author of critical essays in various journals, including *North Dakota Quarterly, Ariel, Scripta Mediterranea,* and *Comparative Literature in Canada.* **Essay:** Ntozake Shange.

WATT, R.J.C. Lecturer in English and dean of students, Faculty of Arts and Social Sciences, University of Dundee. Author of an introductory study of Hopkins; contributor of articles on modern poetry, textual problems in Shakespeare, and literary computing. **Essay:** Medbh McGuckian.

WERNER, Theresa. Editor and freelance writer, London. **Essay:** Lauris Edmond.

WHEATELY, Patience. Coordinator of the Living Archives series published by the League of Canadian poets. Former chair of the Feminist Caucus of the League of Canadian Poets. Taught creative writing at the Thomas More Institute for Adult Education in Montreal. Author of two books of poetry, including *A Hinge of Spring,* 1986, and *Good-Bye to the Sugar Refinery,* 1989. Contributor to numerous literary magazines including *Descant Book, Space, Canadian Woman Studies; Wascana Review;* Canadian Women Writers issue of *Prairie Schooner; Amethyst Review; Prairie Journal;* work also appears in anthologies: *Voice of War,* 1995; *Vintage 94,* 1995, *bite to eat place,* 1995, and *Close to the Heart,* 1996. **Essays:** Roo Borson; Paulette Jiles; Ann Hebert; Phyllis Webb.

WILLY, Margaret. Lecturer, British Council and Morley College, London. Author of poetry books *The Invisible Sun,* 1946, and *Every Star a Tongue,* 1951, as well as critical studies of Chaucer, Traherne, Fielding, Browning, Crashaw, Vaughan, Emily Bronte, and English diarists. Editor of two anthologies and of plays by Goldsmith. **Essay:** Elizabeth Jennings.

WILOCH, Denise. Freelance writer and editor of reference book materials. **Essays:** Marjorie Agosin; Gloria Anzaldua; Dionne Brand; Nichole Brossard; Lucha Corpi; Tina Darragh; Erica Funkhouser; Fay Kicknosway; Bernadette Mayer; Naomi Replansky; Joan Retallack; Wislawa Szymborska.

WILSON, Janet. Senior lecturer, Department of English, University of Otago, Dunedin, New Zealand. Co-director of Research Centre for New Zealand Studies; editor, *Journal of New Zealand Literature;* author and editor, *Roger Edgeworth's Sermons: Preaching in the Reformation from c.1535 to c.1553,* 1993; also contributor of various articles on Middle English literature, and New Zealand literature and post-colonialism. **Essays:** Janet Frame; Jan Kemp; Michele Leggott; Rachel McAlpine.

WOODCOCK, George. Former associate professor of English, University of British Columbia, Vancouver, and contributing editor, *Dissent,* New York. Author of numerous poetry collections, including *Tolstoy at Yasnaya Polyana and Other Poems,* 1991, and *The Cherry Tree on Cherry Street and Other Poems,* 1994, as well as plays and other books. Died 1995. **Essay:** Phyllis Webb.

WOODSON, Jon. Associate professor of English at Howard University; previously taught at Towson State University; contributor to *African American Review, The Oxford Companion to Women's Literature, Furious Flower: Conversations and Essays*

ISBN 1-55862-356-6

90000